MARRIAGES
and FAMILIES

Mary Ann SCHWARTZ
Northeastern Illinois University

BarBara Marliene SCOTT
Northeastern Illinois University

Upper Saddle River, New Jersey 07458

Library of Congress Cataloging-in-Publication Data

SCHWARTZ, MARY ANN.
Marriages and families: diversity and change / Mary Ann Schwartz, BarBara Marliene Scott. — 4th ed.
p. cm.
Includes bibliographical references and index.
ISBN 0-13-097956-2 (pbk.)
1. Marriage—United States. 2. Family—United States. I. Title: Marriages and families. II. Scott, BarBara Marliene. III. Title.

HQ536.S39 2003
306.8'0973—dc21 2002070362

AVP, Pubisher, Nancy Roberts
Senior Acquisitions Editor: Chris DeJohn
Managing Editor: Sharon Chambliss
AVP, Director of Manufacturing and Production: Barbara Kittle
Project Manager: Joan Stone
Copy Editor: Mary Louise Byrd
Prepress and Manufacturing Manager: Nick Sklitsis
Prepress and Manufacturing Buyer: Mary Ann Gloriande
Creative Design Director: Leslie Osher
Art Director: Kathryn Foot
Cover Photo: Jose Ortega/Stock Illustration Source, Inc.
Director, Image Resource Center: Melinda Reo
Manager, Rights and Permissions: Zina Arabia
Interior Image Specialist: Beth Boyd-Brenzel
Photo Researcher: Melinda Alexander
Line Art Manager: Guy Ruggiero
Electronic Art Creation: Mirella Signoretto
Senior Marketing Manager: Amy Speckman

This book was set in 11/12 Janson Text by Lithokraft II
and was printed and bound by Webcrafters, Inc.
The cover was printed by Phoenix Color Corp.

Printed in the United States of America

10 9 8 7 6 5 4 3 2 1

ISBN: 0-13-097956-2

PEARSON EDUCATION LTD., LONDON
PEARSON EDUCATION AUSTRALIA PTY, LIMITED, SYDNEY
PEARSON EDUCATION SINGAPORE, PTE. LTD
PEARSON EDUCATION NORTH ASIA LTD, HONG KONG
PEARSON EDUCATION CANADA, LTD., TORONTO
PEARSON EDUCACIÓN DE MEXICO, S.A. DE C.V.
PEARSON EDUCATION—JAPAN, TOKYO
PEARSON EDUCATION MALAYSIA, PTE. LTD
PEARSON EDUCATION, UPPER SADDLE RIVER, NEW JERSEY

The twenty-first century began in the midst
of much violence—ethnic and religious conflicts,
terrorist attacks, and ongoing civil wars.
Today, millions of families continue to suffer
the loss of loved ones, destruction of
their homes, and unimaginable deprivations.
We respectfully dedicate this fourth edition
to these families and to their
courageous struggles to rebuild their lives.

Brief Contents

Chapter 1	Marriages and Families over Time	1
Chapter 2	Ways of Studying and Explaining Marriages and Families	30
Chapter 3	Understanding Gender: Its Influence in Intimate Relationships	59
Chapter 4	The Many Faces of Love	86
Chapter 5	Dating, Coupling, and Mate Selection	117
Chapter 6	Sexuality and Intimate Relationships	153
Chapter 7	Nonmarital Lifestyles	200
Chapter 8	The Marriage Experience	226
Chapter 9	Reproduction and Parenting	262
Chapter 10	Evolving Work and Family Structures	306
Chapter 11	Violence and Abuse	336
Chapter 12	The Process of Uncoupling: Divorce in the United States	375
Chapter 13	Remarriage and Remarried Families	404
Chapter 14	Marriages and Families in Later Life	427
Chapter 15	Marriages and Families in the Twenty-First Century: U.S. and World Trends	455
	Appendixes	500

Contents

Boxes xvi

Preface xviii

About the Authors xxiv

Chapter 1

MARRIAGES AND FAMILIES OVER TIME 1

Contemporary Definitions of Marriages and Families 2
What Is Marriage? 2 What Is a Family? 3 Race, Class, and Gender, 4

Family Functions and the Debate over Family Values 4
Social Functions of Families, 5 Contrasting Views of Families, 6

Debunking Myths about Marriages and Families 8
Myth 1: The Universal Nuclear Family, 9 Myth 2: The Self-Reliant Traditional Family, 9 Myth 3: The Naturalness of Different Spheres for Wives and Husbands, 11 Myth 4: The Unstable African American Family, 11 Myth 5: The Idealized Nuclear Family of the 1950s, 12

Families in Early America 13
Colonial Families, 13 African American Families under Slavery, 15 Free African American Families, 17 Slavery's Hidden Legacy: Racial Mixing, 17 Native American Families, 18

Families in the Nineteenth Century 19
Emergence of the Good Provider Role, 19 The Cult of Domesticity, 19 Changing Views of Childhood, 19 The Impact of Class and Ethnicity, 19 Immigration and Family Life, 20 The Economic Roles of Women and Children, 20 Ethnic and Racial Family Patterns, 20 Mexican American Families, 21

Families in the Early Twentieth Century 22
The Emergence of the Companionate Family, 22 The Great Depression, 22 World War II and Its Aftermath, 22 Changing Patterns of Immigration, 23 Lessons from History, 24

Contemporary Patterns in Marriages and Families 24

Looking Ahead: Marriages and Families in the Future 25

The Sociological Imagination 25

Writing Your Own Script 26

Summary 27

Key Terms 28

Questions for Study and Reflection 28

Additional Resources 28

Chapter 2

WAYS OF STUDYING AND EXPLAINING MARRIAGES AND FAMILIES 30

The Sociology of Marriages and Families 32

Studying Marriages and Families: The Link between Research and Theory 32

Methodological Techniques in the Study of Marriages and Families 34
Surveys, 35 Observation, 36 Case Studies, 36 Ethnography, 37 Scientific Methodologies Used by Feminist Researchers, 38

A Critical Look at Traditional Research on Marriages and Families 38
A More Inclusive Sociology, 39 Contemporary Marriage and Family Scholarship, 41

Theoretical Perspectives 42
Structural Functionalism, 43 Conflict Theory, 46 Symbolic Interactionism, 47 Social Constructionism, 48 Social-Exchange Theory, 49 The Developmental Family Life Cycle Model, 50 Feminist Theories and Perspectives, 51

Men's Studies and Marriage and Family Research 54
Men in Families, 54

Summary 56

Key Terms 57

Questions for Study and Reflection 57

Additional Resources 57

Chapter 3

UNDERSTANDING GENDER: ITS INFLUENCE IN INTIMATE RELATIONSHIPS 59

Distinguishing Sex and Gender Roles 61

The Process of Sex Differentiation, 61 Gender Differences: The Nature–Nurture Debate, 61

Traditional Meanings of Femininity and Masculinity 64
Traditional Gender Roles: Female and Male, 64 Gender Variations: Race, Class, and Culture, 65

Gender Roles in Transition 65

Theories of Gender Role Socialization 67
Psychoanalytic/Identification Theory, 68 Social-Learning Theory, 69 Cognitive-Development Theory, 70 Enculturated-Lens Theory, 70

Agents of Socialization 71
Parents, 71 Language, 72 Peers, 72 Play and Organized Sports, 73 Teachers, 73 The Mass Media, 74

Consequences of Gender Stereotyping 77
Lifestyle Choices, 77 Self-Esteem, 77 Self-Confidence, 79 Mental Health, 80 Women, Men, and Friends, 81 Patterns of Communication, 82

Changing Realities, Changing Roles 83

Summary 83

Key Terms 84

Questions for Study and Reflection 84

Additional Resources 85

Chapter 4

THE MANY FACES OF LOVE 86

What Is This Thing Called Love? 87
Love as a Social Construction, 88 How Does Romantic Love Develop in Contemporary Society? 89 Love in Western Society: A Historical Perspective, 89 The Importance of Love, 92

How Do People Express Love? 94
Lee's Six Styles of Loving, 95

Love versus Friendship, Infatuation, and Liking 96
Close Friendship versus Love, 96 Infatuation versus Love, 99 Liking versus Love, 99

Some Theories of Love 99
The Wheel Theory of Love, 100

The Theory of Love as a Story 101
Love Stories, 101 Love as a Social Exchange, 103 Love as Limerence, 103

Love Across Gender, Sexuality, and Race 104
Gender Differences in Love Relationships, 104 Lesbian and Gay Love Relationships, 107 Female-Male Relationships among African Americans, 108

Obstacles to Love and Loving Relationships 109
Traditional Gender Role Socialization, 109 Patriarchy as an Obstacle to Lesbian Love, 109 Lack of Trust, 110 Jealousy and Envy, 110

Romantic Love Today 113

Summary 114

Key Terms 115

Questions for Study and Reflection 115

Additional Resources 116

Chapter 5

DATING, COUPLING, AND MATE SELECTION 117

Mate Selection in Cross-Cultural and Historical Perspective 119
Mate Selection Cross-Culturally, 119 Mate Selection in the United States: A Historical Perspective, 121 Functions of Dating: Past and Present, 125

The Intersections of Race, Gender, Class, and Sexual Orientation 126
Dating Patterns among African Americans, 127 The Impact of Gender, 128 The Impact of Social Class on the Dating Process, 128 Lesbian and Gay Dating, 130

Theories of Mate Selection 131
Exchange Theories, 131 Filter Theories, 133

Mate Selection: Finding and Meeting Partners 133
The Marriage Market and the Pool of Eligibles, 133 Freedom versus Constraint in Mate Selection, 134 Other Factors That Affect Mate Selection, 138 Personal Qualities and Mate Selection, 139 The Life Cycle and Mate Selection, 140

Meeting Partners: Where and How 140
School, Church, and Work, 141 Singles' Bars and Gay Bars, 141 Self-Advertising: Personal Ads, 141 Dating Clubs and Dating Services, 142 Computer Dating and the Internet, 143 Dating in Cyberspace, 143

The Future of Dating 146

Violence in Dating and Intimate Relationships 146
Physical Abuse, 146 Date and Acquaintance Rape, 148

Breaking Up 149

Summary 151
Key Terms 151
Questions for Study and Reflection 151
Additional Resources 152

Chapter 6

SEXUALITY AND INTIMATE RELATIONSHIPS 153

Human Sexuality: Past and Present 155
Jewish Traditions and Human Sexuality, 156 Christian Traditions and Human Sexuality, 157 Sexuality in the United States: An Overview, 157 Sexual Attitudes and Behavior in the Twentieth Century and Beyond, 158

Sexuality as Social Learning 165
Sources of Sexual Learning, 165

Sexual Orientations 171
Heterosexuality, 171 Homosexuality, 171 Bisexuality, 175

The Physiology of Sexuality 175
The Sexual Response Cycle, 175

Human Sexual Expression 176
Autoeroticism, 176 Interpersonal Sexual Behavior, 179 Sexual Expression among Lesbians and Gays, 180

Sexuality Across the Life Cycle 180
Nonmarried Sexuality and Pregnancy, 180 Marital Sexuality: Does Good Sex Make Good Marriages? 185 Extramarital Sexuality, 185 Postmarital Sexuality, 186 Sexuality and Aging, 186 Women, Aging, and Sexuality, 187

Sexual Dysfunctions 188

Sexual Responsibility: Protecting Yourself from AIDS and Other STDs 189
AIDS, 189

Summary 197
Key Terms 198
Questions for Study and Reflection 198
Additional Resources 199

Chapter 7

NONMARITAL LIFESTYLES 200

Historical Perspectives 201
Singlehood in Early America, 202 Singlehood in the Nineteenth and Early Twentieth Centuries, 202 Singlehood Today: Current Demographic Trends, 203

Demystifying Singlehood 204
Individual Decision Making, 204 The Influence of Social and Economic Forces, 204 Types of Singles, 205 Advantages and Disadvantages of Singlehood, 206

Single Lifestyles 207
Income, 208 Support Networks, 209 Life Satisfaction, 209 The Never-Married in Later Life, 210

Heterosexual Cohabitation 211
Historical Perspectives, 211 The Meaning of Cohabitation Today, 211 Reasons for Cohabitation, 213 Advantages and Disadvantages of Cohabitation, 215 Cohabitation and the Division of Labor, 215 Cohabitation and Marital Stability, 215 Cohabitation: International Perspectives, 216 Cohabitation and the Law, 217

Lesbian and Gay Relationships 218
Methodological Issues, 218 Demystifying Lesbian and Gay Relationships, 219 Living Together: Domestic Tasks, Finances, and Decision Making, 219 The Social and Legal Context of Lesbian and Gay Relationships, 219 Life Satisfaction: Elderly Lesbians and Gays, 221

Communal Living and Group Marriage 222
Advantages and Disadvantages of the Communal Lifestyle, 222 Communes, Shared Housing, and the Future, 222 Group Marriages, 223

Summary 224
Key Terms 224
Questions for Study and Reflection 224
Additional Resources 225

Chapter 8

THE MARRIAGE EXPERIENCE 226

Why Do People Marry? 228
Sociological Perspective, 230

The Meaning of Marriage 230
Marriage as a Commitment, 230 Marriage as a Sacrament, 231 Marriage as a Legal Contract, 231 Some Legal Aspects of the Marriage Contract, 232

Change and Continuity in the Meaning of Marriage 236
Provisions of the Modern Marriage Contract, 236 The Marriage Contract Today, 237 Marriage Traditions in the United States, 240 The Wedding, 242

Marriage and Gender 244
"Her" Marriage, 245 "His" Marriage, 245

Transitions and Adjustments to Marriages 245
A Typology of Marital Relationships, 246

Heterogamous Marriages 247
Interracial Marriages, 247 Interethnic Marriages, 251 Interfaith Marriages, 252

Marital Satisfaction, Communication, and Conflict Resolution 253

Summary 259

Key Terms 260

Questions for Study and Reflection 260

Additional Resources 260

Chapter 9

REPRODUCTION AND PARENTING 262

Historical Overview: Fertility Trends in the United States 263
Current Fertility Patterns, 264

To Parent or Not? 265
The Costs of Parenthood, 265 The Benefits of Parenthood, 266 The Social Pressures to Procreate, 266 The Child-Free Option, 266 Delayed Parenting, 267

Controlling Fertility 268
Reasons for Not Using Contraceptives, 269

Abortion 269
Historical Perspectives, 270 Race, Class, and Age, 270 Public Attitudes toward Abortion, 271

Infertility 271
Causes of Infertility, 272 Consequences of Infertility, 272

Reproduction without Sex: The New Technologies 272

The Choice to Parent 274

Conception 275
Multiple Conception and Births, 275 Sex Preference and Selection, 276

Pregnancy 277
Prenatal Development and Care, 277 Prenatal Problems and Defects, 278

Expectant Fathers 281
The Cultural Double Bind, 281

Parental Adjustments, Adaptations, and Patterns of Child Rearing 283
Parental Roles, 284 Gender Differences in the Experience of Parenthood, 287 Styles of Parenting, 289 Race and Class, 291 Lesbian and Gay Parents, 298 Single Parents, 299 Teenaged Parents, 301

Summary 303

Key Terms 304

Questions for Study and Reflection 304

Additional Resources 305

Chapter 10

EVOLVING WORK AND FAMILY STRUCTURES 306

The Transformation of Work and Family Roles 308
Reasons Women Work, 309

Work and Family Structures 310
Traditional Nuclear Families, 310 The Two-Person Career, 311 Dual-Earner Families, 311 Commuter Marriages, 312

The Impact of Work on Family Relationships 312
Marital Power and Decision Making, 313 Marital Happiness, 313 Husbands and the Division of Household Labor, 314 Child Care, 316

Integrating Work and Family Life: Resolving Role Conflict 318
Strategies for Conflict Resolution, 318

Inequities in the Workplace: Consequences for Families 318
Occupational Distribution, 319 The Race–Gender Gap in Earnings: Good News and Bad News, 320 Sexual Harassment, 321

The Economic Well-Being of Families 322
An Uncertain Future: The Widening Income Gap, 323 Who Are the Poor? 324 Unemployment and Underemployment, 324 Homelessness, 327 The Welfare Debate, 329

Restructuring the Workplace 330
Workplace Changes, 331 Family Leave, 331

Summary 333

Key Terms 334

Questions for Study and Reflection 334

Additional Resources 335

Chapter 11

VIOLENCE AND ABUSE 336

The Roots of Family Violence: A Historical Context 338
Violence against Women, 338 Violence against Children, 339 Violence against the Elderly, 339 Violence against Siblings, 340

Family Violence and U.S. Culture 340
The Media, 341

Myths about Violence and Abuse 343

Physical Assault: The Case of Battered Women 346
What Is Woman Battering? 347 How Prevalent Is Woman Battering? 347 Theories of Spousal or Partner Abuse, 349 Why Do Women Remain in Abusive Relationships? 350 Confronting Intimate Violence, 352

The Sexual Assault of Women 352
Rape Myths, 354 Marital Rape, 354

The Criminal Justice Response to Woman Assault 355
Attitudes and Behaviors, 357 Have We Made Progress? 358

The Effects of Physical and Sexual Assault on Women 358

Coping and Survival Strategies 358

A Comparative Look at Battered Men 360

Child Assault and Abuse 362
The Physical Assault of Children, 363 The Sexual Assault of Children, 366

Elder Abuse in the United States 369
What Is Elder Abuse? 369 Who Are the Abused and the Abusers? 370

Sibling Abuse 370

Summary 372

Key Terms 373

Questions for Study and Reflection 373

Additional Resources 373

Chapter 12

THE PROCESS OF UNCOUPLING: DIVORCE IN THE UNITED STATES 375

Historical Perspectives 377
Divorce in Early America, 377 Divorce in Nineteenth-Century America, 377 Twentieth-Century America: Efforts at Reform, 379
Race, Ethnicity, and Divorce, 379

Who Gets Divorced, and Why? 381
Factors Affecting Marital Stability, 381

The Process of Divorce 384
Stages in the Divorce Process, 384 The Six Stations of Divorce, 384

The Causes of Divorce 385
Societal Factors, 385 From the Perspective of Divorced People, 386 From the Perspective of Family Therapists, 387

The Impact of Divorce on Spouses 387
Common Consequences of Divorce, 387 Gender Differences in Divorce, 389 Recovering from Divorce, 393

The Impact of Divorce on Children 393
Short-Term versus Long-Term Effects, 394
Children and Divorce in Other Countries, 395
Changing Patterns in Child Custody, 395

Reaching Accord: Counseling, Collaborative Law, and Mediation 398

Attempts at Reform: Covenant Marriage 399

Other Forms of Marital Disruption 400

Summary 401

Key Terms 402

Questions for Study and Reflection 402

Additional Resources 403

Chapter 13

REMARRIAGE AND REMARRIED FAMILIES 404

Historical Perspective 406

Cultural Images of Stepfamilies 407

The Process of Remarriage 407
Dating and Courtship Patterns, 407 The Decision to Remarry, 408 Patterns of Remarriage, 409
The Stations of Remarriage, 410

Stages in the Development of Remarried Families 412

Remarried Families: Roles, Interactions, and Reactions 412

Children and the Remarriage Service, 412 Children in Remarried Families, 412 Stepmothers: A Bad Rap? 417 Stepfathers: Polite Strangers? 418 Lesbian and Gay Stepfamilies, 419 Ex-Spouses: Do They Fade Away? 419

The Strengths and Benefits of Remarried Families 419

The Quality of the Remarital Relationship 420
Stability in Remarriage, 421

Recommendations for Social Policy 424
Clarification of Legal Norms, 424 Modification of the Tax Code, 424 Education, 424

Summary 425
Key Terms 425
Questions for Study and Reflection 426
Additional Resources 426

Chapter 14

MARRIAGES AND FAMILIES IN LATER LIFE 427

Characteristics of Later-Life Families 428
The Sandwich Generation, 429 Diversity in the Family Life Cycle, 430 Changing Age Norms, 431

The Demographics of Aging: Defining "Old" 431
Age Categories of the Elderly, 431 Gender and Marital Status, 432 Race, Ethnicity, and Class, 433 Poverty among the Elderly, 434

Living Arrangements 434
Housing Patterns, 435

Marriages in Later Life 436
Marital Quality and Satisfaction, 437 Adjustment to Retirement, 437

Intergenerational Relationships 439
Quality of Relationships, 440 Patterns of Support, 440

Evolving Patterns of Kinship: Grandparenthood 442
Styles of Grandparenting, 442 Benefits and Conflicts, 443 Great-Grandparenthood, 444

The Child-Free Elderly 445

Sibling Relationships 445

Health and Illness 446

Family Caregiving 446
The Spouse as Caregiver, 447 Adult Children as Caregivers, 447

The Experience of Widowhood 448
Stages of Widowhood, 448 Gender Differences in Widowhood, 450 Beyond Widowhood, 451 Lesbian and Gay Elderly, 451

Implications for Social Policy 452

Summary 453
Key Terms 453
Questions for Study and Reflection 453
Additional Resources 454

Chapter 15

MARRIAGES AND FAMILIES IN THE TWENTY-FIRST CENTURY: U.S. AND WORLD TRENDS 455

Challenges of a World Economy 457

Inequities in Income and Wealth 458

Health and Health Care 459
Trends in Drug Use and Associated Health Problems, 465 Alcohol, 466 Addiction and the Family, 467

Meeting the Needs of Children: Foster Care and Adoption 468
Problems within the Child Welfare System, 468 Characteristics of Adoptive Parents, 469 International Adoptions, 470 Transracial (Interracial) Adoptions, 471

The Challenge of Racism and Ethnic and Religious Discrimination in Family Life 472
Racism in the United States, 473 Racism in a Global Context, 476

Safety and Security: Gangs, Street Violence, and Violence in America's Schools 477

Terrorism and War 483
Terrorism in the United States, 484 War, 485 A World of Refugees, 489

Families Coping with Loss: Dying and Death 491
The Process of Dying, 491 The Needs and Tasks of the Dying, 491 National Mourning, 492 The Right-to-Die Movement, 494

Strengthening Marriages and Families: The Ongoing Challenges of Living in a Global World 496

Summary 497
Key Terms 498
Questions for Study and Reflection 498
Additional Resources 499

Appendix A

Sexual Dysfunctions and Sexually Transmitted Diseases 500

Appendix B

Human Anatomy and Reproduction 504

Appendix C

Methods of Abortion 507

Appendix D

Methods of Birth Control 508

Glossary 512
References 519
Photo Credits 558
Name Index 559
Subject Index 568

Boxes

STRENGTHENING MARRIAGES AND FAMILIES

Introducing Family Therapy 10

Resolving Gender Issues 68

Talking Frankly about Our Sexual Needs 190

Communication, Conflict Resolution, and Problem Solving in Marriages and Intimate Relationships 255

Resolving Problems 388

Coping with the Caregiving Role 449

Talking about Terrorism and War 488

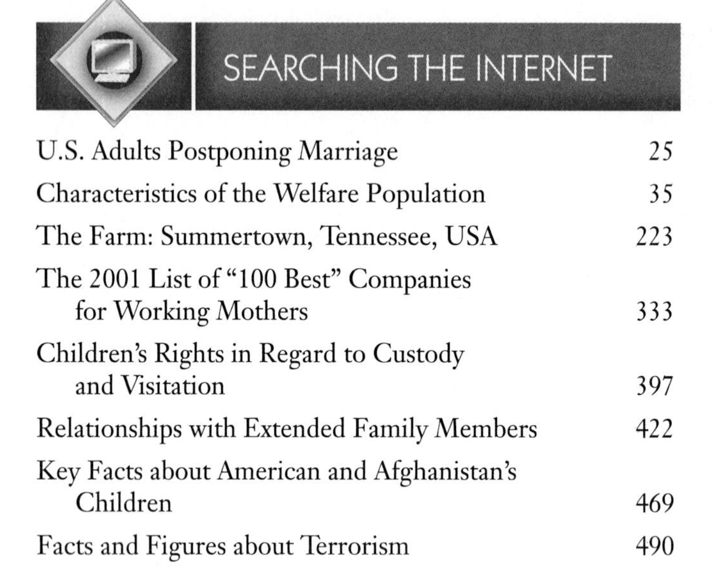

SEARCHING THE INTERNET

U.S. Adults Postponing Marriage 25

Characteristics of the Welfare Population 35

The Farm: Summertown, Tennessee, USA 223

The 2001 List of "100 Best" Companies for Working Mothers 333

Children's Rights in Regard to Custody and Visitation 397

Relationships with Extended Family Members 422

Key Facts about American and Afghanistan's Children 469

Facts and Figures about Terrorism 490

IN OTHER PLACES

Child and Teenage Marriages in India and Western Kenya 7

Marriage and Family Patterns in Kenya 42

Gender Equality in Vanatinai and Backlash in Bangladesh and Afghanistan 66

The Meaning of Love across Cultures 93

Interracial Dating in South Africa 144

Sex Work and the Transmission of AIDS in Ladysmith, South Africa 196

Certification of Single Women 207

Marriage Traditions and Rituals in the United States and around the World 238

Shared Paternity 289

Global Responses to Violence and Sexual Assault against Women 356

Cross-Cultural Patterns in Divorce 378

The Role and Status of the Elderly: Varied and Changing 441

SOCIAL POLICY ISSUES

Boys and Men Are Gendered, Too 78
Coming Out 221
Protecting Fetal Rights 280
Is Welfare Reform Working? 330
Who Receives Child Support? 391
The Debate over Physician-Assisted Suicide 495

WRITING YOUR OWN SCRIPT

Define It, and Knowledge Follows 26
The Family Life Cycle: Locating Your Family 56
Reflections on Gender 83
A Social Construction of Love 114
Personal Biography and Social Structure: Selecting a Mate 150
Identifying Sexual Values 197
The Marital Decision 224
Preparing Your Relationship Contract 256
To Parent or Not? 302
Work/Family Decisions 332
Recognizing Abusive Behavior 371
Evaluating Relationships 400
Thinking about Remarriage 424
Thinking about Later Life 452
Thinking Globally 496

APPLYING THE SOCIOLOGICAL IMAGINATION

Doing Sociology: Linking Theory and Research Methods 55
Gendered Communication 82
Is There a Love Story for You? 104
How Do the Media Portray Love? 106
Choosing a Mate: A Content Analysis of Personal Ads 143
Human Sexuality in the Mass Media, Past and Present 169
What Went Wrong? 216
Are You at Risk? 383
What's in a Card? 423
Is Ageism Dead? 430

FAMILY PROFILE

Vicki, Alex, and Kate Byard 212
Laural and Ralph Kemp 250
The Tyrpak Family 284
Laura Anderson 360
The Maring Family 421
The Gottlieb Family 438

Preface

In this fourth edition of *Marriages and Families: Diversity and Change*, there is a conscious effort to present a continuity of major issues, concerns, and themes on contemporary marriages, families, and intimate relationships. Our initial resolve when writing the first edition of this textbook has not changed, and it informs this fourth edition as well. The subtitle of this book, *Diversity and Change*, continues to be the major thematic framework that runs through all 15 chapters and is informed by the scholarship of a wide variety of scholars, most notably scholars of color and feminist scholars in sociology and from across a number of other academic disciplines. The emphasis on diversity helps students to understand that there are many different forms of intimate relationships beyond the traditional heterosexual, two-parent, white, middle-class family and the legally sanctioned heterosexual marriage. As we show throughout this textbook, marriages and families more generally include single-parent families, headed by women or men; lesbian or gay families with or without children and with or without a live-in partner; adoptive and foster families; biracial and multiracial families; cohabiting couples involving heterosexual or homosexual partners; and blended families that emerge following divorce, remarriage, or simply when people bring to a new relationship children from a previous intimate relationship. In this context, we treat marriages and families as social constructs whose meanings have changed over time and from place to place.

Consistent with this position, we continue to give high priority to framing our discussions of marriages and families in historical context. Most, if not all, aspects of our lives, are shaped by larger historical circumstances. To be born during a particular historical period is to experience intimacy, marriage, family life, childbearing and child rearing, family decision making, household labor, and marital and family satisfaction (to name a few) in particular ways that are germane to the time, place, and social structure within which we find ourselves. For example, the economic growth and prosperity of the 1950s, a period during which the nuclear family was idealized, encouraged or made possible this particular family structure. During this period both women and men married at early ages, had children within a relatively short interval from the wedding, and generally stayed married until the death of one spouse. For many families, a husband's income was sufficient to support the family. Thus, wives and mothers typically remained at home fulfilling domestic and child-care roles. Although economic conditions have changed, now often requiring multiple wage earners, this 1950s "idealized" image continues to dominate popular discourse on marriages and families. In the 1990s, however, most children were growing up either in single-parent families or in families where both parents worked outside the home. Framing our discussion of marriages and families in historical context not only provides students with knowledge about marriages and families in earlier periods of U.S. history but also enables them to understand and interpret the changes that are occurring around them in marriages and families today.

Our objectives in this fourth edition are simple yet significant:

- to help students recognize and understand the dynamic nature of marriages, families, and intimate relationships;
- to enable students to recognize, confront, and dispel prominent myths about marriages, families, and intimate relationships;
- to help students see the interactive relationships of race, class, gender, and sexual orientation;
- to encourage an informed openness in student attitudes that will empower them to make informed choices and decisions in their own marriage, family, and intimate relationships;
- to enable students to see how marriages, families, and intimate relationships around the world are increasingly affected by global events, particularly trade imbalances, armed conflicts, and acts of terrorism; and
- to provide students with a comprehensive introduction to a number of key issues facing marriages and families in the twenty-first century.

In this age of rapid communication and technological changes, not only does the evening news bring into our homes stories about marriages and families in distant places, but more importantly the news also calls attention to how political and economic decisions, both national and international, affect families in the United States as well as those in other countries of the world. For example, decisions of multinational corporations to relocate from one country to another in pursuit of lower labor costs and less regulation impact families in both countries. On the one hand, family budgets and patterns of living are often seriously disrupted when a family member loses a job because of a plant relocation. On the other hand, family patterns are also affected when members must work for subsistence level wages, often in an unhealthy environment. In this example, the experiences of these families are globally interdependent.

In addition, issues of violence and the massive abuse of human beings both nationally and internationally crowd our psyches. On the one hand, in the United States, racism, hate crimes, street violence, the escalation of violence in schools, and terrorist attacks are indeed very troubling issues faced by all families. On the other hand, the violence and atrocities related to political, cultural, and ethnic wars such as in Afghanistan, Kosovo, Bosnia, Rwanda, and Burundi have had devastating consequences for millions of families. These global incidents are not unrelated to life in the United States as many of the survivors of these atrocities seek refuge in the United States. In turn, both human and financial resources must be reallocated from domestic agendas to help meet humanitarian commitments around the world. By examining the process of globalization and its consequences or, as C. Wright Mills (1959) suggested, by grasping history and biography and the connections between the two, students should be better able to understand their personal life experiences and prepare themselves for meeting the challenges of living in a global society.

Rapid changes in the racial and ethnic composition of the U.S. population, due to immigration and differential fertility rates, have focused our nation's attention on diversity. Although some dimensions of this issue are new, a historical review quickly shows that throughout U.S. history marriages and families have taken many diverse forms. A focus on structured relationships such as race, class, and gender allows us to see how marriages and families are experienced differently by different categories of people. In this fourth edition, we continue to make a special effort to treat this diversity in an integrative manner. Thus, we have no separate chapters on class or families of color. Instead, when marriage and family experiences are differentiated by race, class, or gender, these differences are integrated into the discussion of specific experiences. Two examples will illustrate this point. First, although the vast majority of all Americans will eventually marry, the marriage rate is lower for some groups than others. White females are more likely to marry than African American females, who are confronted with an increasing shortage of African American males of comparable age and education. Second, although both women and men suffer from the dissolution of their marriages through divorce or death, gender also differentiates those experiences in important ways. The most striking difference is an economic one: the standard of living declines for women but improves for men.

It is not always easy to discuss diversity, partly because our thinking about diversity is itself diverse. One of the first issues we face in discussing diversity is language—what are the appropriate designations to use to refer to different groups at this point in time? Names are often controversial and reflect a power struggle over who has the right or authority to name. Not surprisingly, those in positions of power historically have assumed that right and authority. As the "named" groups themselves become more powerful and vocal, however, they often challenge the naming process and insist on designations they believe more clearly express their sense of their own identity. For example, as a result of pressure from people with mixed ancestry, the U.S. Census Bureau gave official recognition to a biracial or multiracial category on its year 2000 census forms. However, even this is not without problems. The multiracial category has yielded significant changes in the number of reported members in various racial and ethnic groups of color. This fact has political and economic significance in terms of the distribution of governmental resources and services.

Although there is no unanimity on these matters even among members of the same group, some terms have emerged as preferred terms. Thus, for example, Latina/o is preferred to Hispanic, Native American is preferred to American Indian, lesbian and gay are preferred to homosexual, and African American is preferred to black. Throughout this text we try to be consistent in using the preferred terms. When we make specific comparisons by race, however, we use the terms *black* and *white* for ease of presentation. In addition, we have consciously avoided using the term *minority group* to refer to racial and ethnic groups in our society. Instead, we use the term *people of color*. Although this term is not problem-free, it avoids an implicit assumption in the term *minority* that groups so designated are not part of the dominant culture in terms of shared values and aspirations.

NEW AND EXPANDED FEATURES

Marriages and Families: Diversity and Change continues to be distinguished from other textbooks in a number of important ways including the new and expanded features of the fourth edition.

In the News

Each chapter begins with an "In the News" feature. These are true stories of people caught up in the web of marriage and family relationships. Following each "In the News" feature is a series of questions under the heading "What would you do?" This feature helps students to see the relevance of many political, economic, and cultural issues to ordinary people's lives and invites them to reflect on the topics to be covered in that chapter in light of their own value expectations and experiences.

Strengthening Marriages and Families Box

This box appears in several key chapters and utilizes a question-and-answer format with family therapist Joan Zientek. The purpose of this box is to introduce students to the concept of family therapy and show them how such therapy can help family members confront some of the many problems that today's families might encounter. For example, in Chapter 8 Joan Zientek describes how couples can improve communication and resolve conflicts, and in Chapter 15 she provides guidance to parents on how to talk to their children about terrorism.

Searching the Internet Box

These boxes present up-to-date data on relevant topics discussed in the chapter and provide students with the Internet Websites where they can go to do further research on their own. For example, in Chapter 1 students can learn at a glance statistics that reveal the current patterns of marriages and living arrangements. In Chapter 15 students can compare the status of children in the United States with that of children in Afghanistan. In addition, at the end of some of these chapters students are provided with thought-provoking questions that test their ability to use the sociological imagination while utilizing resources found via the Internet.

Family Profiles Box

This popular feature from the second edition has been expanded to include profiles of a single parent of adopted children, a survivor of domestic violence, and a couple who is raising four children. These photos and profiles of real people, including what they see as the major challenges in their current stage of their family life cycle and the philosophy that guides their behavior in their relationships, serve as a good basis for students to examine their own attitudes and values regarding where they are in their family's life cycle.

In Other Places Box

This box will continue to offer insights into the diverse structures and functions of marriages and families, both global and local. For example, in Chapter 5 students can read about interracial dating in South Africa. Each "In Other Places" box includes a series of questions under the heading "What do you think?" These questions require students to reflect on cultural similarities and differences. It also helps students understand that culture is relative.

Social Policy Issues Box

This box not only extends coverage of complex and unresolved social issues but also discusses policy initiatives in these areas. For example, in Chapter 9 students are asked to reflect on issues concerning fetal rights and the rights of pregnant women, particularly if the woman abuses alcohol or other drugs; and students can explore controversial policies related to the emerging trend of defining a "viable fetus" as a child covered by child abuse laws. Thus, pregnant women are increasingly being prosecuted for behaviors such as smoking, drinking, and abusing drugs (see Chapter 11).

Writing Your Own Script Box

These exercises again can be found at the end of each chapter. Students and instructors have told us that this focused approach makes it easy for students to reflect on their own life choices and in writing their own marital or relationship scripts. In this way, students are encouraged to think sociologically about their personal decision making in light of the relevant research presented in that chapter.

Applying the Sociological Imagination Box

The content of these boxes challenges students to use a sociological perspective in analyzing aspects of marriages and families. It requires students to see the relationship between personal behavior and how society is organized and structured. For example, in Chapter 4 students are asked to read some examples of Robert Strenberg's theory of love as a story and then reflect on and identify their own personal story of love. Other boxes in this category examine contemporary marriage and family situations.

New and Expanded Themes

In addition to these special features, we have enriched each chapter by incorporating hundreds of new research studies. We have also included new photos, examples, tables, and figures to illustrate contemporary marriage and family concepts, events, trends, and themes.

- Changing immigration patterns have resulted in greater racial, ethnic, and racial diversity among families in the United States and throughout the world (Chapters 1 and 15).
- Just as families are changing, so, too, is the discipline of sociology. Although in the past, women and people of color were involved in research and theorizing about marriages and families, their contributions were largely ignored. Today, however, women and people of color are gaining much deserved recognition as researchers and theorists (Chapter 2).
- Generally, when we think of changes in gender roles, we think of change in a linear pattern moving toward greater equality. However, the experiences of Afghan women show that this pattern does not apply everywhere. For example, the Taliban regime reversed many of the rights of Afghan women when they took control of Afghanistan in late 1996 (Chapter 3).
- Love takes many different forms (Chapter 4).
- Contemporary dating and mate selection take a number of new forms, including cyberdating (Chapter 5).
- For most American teens oral sex is not "really" sex; real sex is vaginal intercourse. This perspective puts young people in jeopardy of contracting sexually transmitted diseases, including HIV/AIDS. The incidence of AIDS is increasing dramatically around the globe (Chapter 6).
- Despite great controversy, Vermont became the first and, to date, only state granting legal recognition to same-sex unions. The lifestyles of the unmarried population continue to take many diverse forms (Chapter 7).
- Although some people think of premarital agreements as cold, unromantic, and businesslike, an increasing number of couples are making them part of their marriage preparation. Additionally, because conflict is now being recognized as a normal part of intimate relationships, many couples are participating in marriage preparation classes that teach conflict resolution skills (Chapter 8).
- Polls show that an increasing number of fathers desire to spend more time and develop a closer relationship with their children. New research documents the importance of fathers in the lives of children, indicating that when fathers provide strong emotional, financial, and other support, their children are likely to be healthier physically and psychologically (Chapter 9).
- Despite the economic prosperity of the 1990s, the income gap between wealthy and poor families widened considerably. Research shows that America's working families lose a

staggering $200 billion in income annually because of the gender wage gap, an average of $4000 a family. The September 11 terrorist attacks led to a sharp increase in unemployment, particularly among families whose wage earners worked in jobs that service the middle and upper classes such as child-care workers, bellhops, waiters, and cab drivers (Chapter 10).

- Violence within families continues to be a major problem in the United States and in many other countries. The most vulnerable family members are children 3 years and younger and the elderly. Contemporary judicial and legislative approaches to domestic violence are sometimes more punitive toward the victim than the perpetrator (Chapter 11).
- Although the overall divorce rate has decreased slightly over the past several years, the rate remains high and varies among different groups and in different geographic regions. For example, recent statistics show that people living in the "Bible Belt" states such as Tennessee, Arkansas, Alabama, and Oklahoma have higher rates of divorce than people living in socially more liberal states like New York, Connecticut, and Massachusetts (Chapter 12).
- Estimates are that 30 percent of all U.S. children are living in stepfamilies. Although no precise figures exist on the number of children being raised in lesbian and gay stepfamilies, the increasing use of reproductive technology (Chapter 9) and changes in adoption laws (Chapter 15) suggest that more children will live in lesbian and gay stepfamilies in the future (Chapter 13).
- People are living longer. There now are more than 60,000 centenarians in the United States. Contrary to popular stereotypes, the vast majority of older people maintain their independence and enjoy an active social life. An emerging trend among the elderly is unplanned parenthood. That is, an increasing number of grandparents are assuming primary parenting responsibility for their grandchildren. Over 4.5 million children now live in 2.4 million grandparent-headed households (Chapter 14).
- As globalization expands, so, too, does the inequality that accompanies it, leaving many individuals and families behind. Rising inequality can result in an increase in racial bias, xenophobia, isolationist tendencies, and religious intolerance. In this process, individuals and societies who are among the most disadvantaged sometimes respond with violence and acts of terrorism (Chapter 15).

PEDAGOGY: READER INVOLVEMENT

Marriages and Families: Diversity and Change is intended as a text that challenges students to become involved in a direct way in examining their personal belief systems as well as societal views of the many forms that marriages and families have taken in the past and are taking in the present. Based on over 40 years of combined teaching experiences, we have found that a course on the sociology of marriages and families almost always invokes concern and interest among students regarding how the general principles and descriptions of marriages and families in a given textbook apply to and are similar to or different from their own personal experiences. Thus, throughout the process of revising this book, we continued to utilize an innovative, sensitive, and inclusive approach to writing about marriages and families. We use a sociological and feminist/womanist perspective, encouraging the application of the sociological imagination to everyday life. In this context, we focus on the link between social structure and our personal experiences of marriages, families, and intimate relationships. That is, we examine how cultural values, historical context, economic and political changes, and structured relationships of race, class, gender, sexual orientation, and age interact and affect individuals and groups as they create, sustain, and change their various intimate relationships. There are many benefits to using a sociological approach to study marriages and families. Most importantly, such an approach enables us to understand the constraints and opportunities that affect our lives and those of other people, thereby positioning us to make more discriminating and successful decisions and exercise greater control over our lives.

The positive response of students as well as instructors to the pedagogical strategies included in the first three editions encouraged us to continue them in this edition. It has been gratifying to hear how these strategies have facilitated students' involvement in understanding marriages and families and empowered them to make more informed lifestyle decisions.

Key Terms

The important terms and concepts that help us to understand and analyze marriages and families are boldfaced and defined in the text. The key terms are also listed at the end of each chapter and defined in the glossary at the end of the book as a way of facilitating the study and review process.

Chapter Questions

Throughout this edition, students will find a shaded question mark that asks them to apply the material in the chapter to their own experiences and to critically evaluate aspects of interpersonal relationships.

End-of-Chapter Study Aids

At the end of each chapter, students will find a summary of the chapter's main points, a list of key terms, a set of questions for study and discussion, and suggestions for additional resources. These resources include traditional sociological materials. New to this edition are suggested relevant literary works pertaining to a topic or general theme of the chapter. The use of literature is intended to enrich the study of sociology and provide yet another springboard from which students can develop a more in-depth understanding of various sociological concepts. In addition, we introduce students to a number of Internet sites whereby they can explore and do independent research on marriage and family issues. The chapter summary and key terms are designed to facilitate a quick review of the material in the text. The study questions and suggested readings are to help students stretch their understanding of marriages and families beyond the contents of this textbook. Among some of the questions for study and discussion are some which ask students to use the Internet to access and evaluate information on a variety of topics, for example, demographic patterns, support groups, work and family issues, and wedding rituals and costs. Given the fluidity of many Websites, we have listed only those that have proven to be relatively stable over time, that are well documented, and that are updated as needed.

Appendixes

The appendixes included at the back of the book supplement the text's sociological discussion of key aspects of relationships by providing technical information on sexual dysfunctions and sexually transmitted diseases (Appendix A), human anatomy and reproduction (Appendix B), abortion techniques (Appendix C), and methods of birth control (Appendix D).

SUPPLEMENTS

Instructors and students who use our textbook have access to a number of materials specially designed to complement the classroom lectures and activities and enhance the students' learning experiences.

For the Instructor

Instructor's Resource Manual This essential instructor's tool includes detailed chapter outlines, learning objectives, teaching suggestions, discussion questions, and class exercises. Also included is a test bank that contains over 1600 questions in multiple-choice, true/false, and essay formats. All multiple-choice and true/false questions are page referenced to the text.

WIN/MAC Prentice Hall Test Manager This computerized software allows instructors to create their own personalized exams, to edit any or all test questions, and to add new questions. Other special features of this program, which is available for Windows and Macintosh, include random generation of an item set, creation of alternate versions of the same test, scrambling question sequence, and test preview before printing.

ABCNEWS ***ABC News/Prentice Hall Video Library for Marriages and the Family*** Selected video segments from award-winning ABC News programs such as *Nightline*, *ABC World News Tonight*, and *20/20* accompany topics featured in the text. An Instructor's Guide is also available. Please contact your Prentice Hall representative for more details.

Prentice Hall Marriage and Family PowerPoint™ Transparencies This set of 200 PowerPoint slides combines graphics and text in a colorful format to help you convey sociological principles in a new and exciting way. For easy download, please visit our Website at http://www.prenhall.com/sociology_central.

Distance Learning Solutions Prentice Hall is committed to providing our leading content to the growing number of courses being delivered over the Internet by developing relationships with the leading course management platforms. Please visit our technology solutions Website at http://www.prenhall.com/demo for more information or contact your local Prentice Hall representative.

For the Student

Study Guide Created for the students, this manual offers chapter-by-chapter outlines, learning objectives, and a chapter review that includes key points and self-test questions keyed to the text.

Companion Website™ In tandem with the text, students can now take full advantage of the World Wide Web to enrich their study of material found in the text. This resource correlates the text with related material available on the Internet. Features of the Website include chapter objectives, study questions, Census updates, as well as links to interesting material and information from other sites on the Web that can reinforce and enhance the content of each chapter. Address: **www.prenhall.com/schwartz**

A Prentice Hall Guide to Evaluating Online Resources, Sociology, 2003 This guide provides a brief introduction to navigating the Internet, along with references related specifically to the discipline of sociology. Also included with the guide is access to **ContentSelect.** Developed by Prentice Hall and EBSCO, the world leader in online journal subscription management, ContentSelect is a customized research database for students of sociology. Free to students when packaged with this text.

ACKNOWLEDGMENTS

Although we continue to refer to this book as ours, we recognize that such an endeavor can never singularly be attributed to the authors. As with any such project, its success required the assistance of many people from many different parts of our lives. Our interaction with students both within and outside the classroom continues to have a significant impact on our thinking and writing about marriages and families and that impact is quite visible in this fourth edition. Our decisions to retain, and, in some cases, update, certain pedagogical aids, such as the boxed features and the examples used in the text, were made in response to student questions, reactions, and discussions in our classrooms. Student feedback was also instrumental in the development of the applied exercises, which we have found to be most effective in teaching about marriage and family issues and concerns.

We would especially like to thank the skilled librarians at Northeastern Illinois University, particularly Richard Higginbotham and Patrice Stearley, for their invaluable assistance in helping us to track down the latest data on marriages and families. We also wish to acknowledge the skilled professionals at Prentice Hall—the editors, artists, designers, and researchers who saw this edition through the process, from its inception through the many stages of development and production. We owe a particular debt of gratitude to Sharon Chambliss, Managing Editor, Sociology/Anthropology, whose support, patience, and perseverance was a major factor in our completing this project. We are grateful to our production editor, Joan Stone, who once again provided valuable suggestions and assistance throughout the revision process. Joan's professional yet friendly e-mails gently moved us to our final goal. Along the way she was always responsive to our questions and supportive of our efforts. We are also indebted to our photo researcher, Melinda Alexander, who found the appropriate shots to illustrate key concepts and issues discussed in the text. Our thanks also to copy editors and permission editors whose tasks were so essential to the production of this book.

The timely, thoughtful, and extensive reactions, suggestions, and critical reviews of the previous editions of this textbook were greatly appreciated and, in each case, they have helped us avoid major mistakes and weaknesses while enhancing our ability to draw upon the strengths of the book. We are also grateful to the reviewers of this edition: Robert F. Corwyn, University of Arkansas at Little Rock; Keith F. Durkin, Ohio Northern University; and Robin Jarrett, University of Illinois–Urbana.

We are especially appreciative of the strong support we received from our colleagues in the Sociology Department at Northeastern Illinois University. In this regard, we especially thank the Sociology Department administrative assistant, Arlene Benzinger, whose diligent efforts assisted us in numerous ways.

We again wish to acknowledge and thank our marriages and families (nuclear, extended, blended, and fictive) for continuing to love, understand, and support us as we undertook, for yet another time, the demands and responsibilities involved in researching, writing, and revising this fourth edition. As in the past, when our time, attention, and behavior were dedicated to this endeavor, often at the expense of our time, attention, and activities with them, they remained steadfast in their support and encouragement. Now that we have finished this edition, they are as proud as we are and rightfully so, for this book, too, is as much theirs as ours. Its completion is due in large part to their understanding and the sacrifices they made in order to facilitate our ability to revise this book. We thank our parents, Helen and Charles Schwartz and Lillian Johnson, for their love and continuing support throughout our lives. As always, our partners, Richard and Roger, gave us their unconditional support and contributed to partnerships that were significantly critical to our meeting the various demands and deadlines that revising this book engendered. In addition, we continue to acknowledge our children, Jason, Roger Jr., and Dionne, and granddaughters Courtney and Mariah for their unwavering love, patience, and understanding when our work forced us to miss family gatherings. We thank them all, especially for providing us with continuing opportunities for the exploration and understanding of marriage and family life.

Last, but certainly not least, we wish to acknowledge and thank each other. As with the previous editions, this book has been a joint effort in every sense of the word. We continue to value each other's skills, perspective, humor, and experiences and this collaborative effort has deepened our appreciation and respect for one another. We continue to learn from one another about diversity and the differential impact of race on various intimate relationships. In the process, we continue to learn more about a particular type of intimate relationship, one based upon love, respect, commitment, understanding, tolerance, and compassion: namely, friendship.

Keeping In Touch

Just as we appreciate all of the comments, suggestions, and ideas that we received on the first three editions of this textbook, we would like to hear your reactions, suggestions, questions, and comments on this new edition. We invite you to share your reactions and constructive advice with us. You can contact us at: m-schwartz@neiu.edu or b-scott1@neiu.edu.

Mary Ann Schwartz
BarBara Marliene Scott

About the Authors

Dr. Mary Ann Schwartz has been married over 25 years. She earned her Bachelor of Arts Degree in Sociology and History from Alverno College in Milwaukee, Wisconsin, her Master's Degree in Sociology from the Illinois Institute of Technology in Chicago, and her Doctorate in Sociology from Northwestern University in Evanston, Illinois. She is Professor Emeritus of Sociology and Women's Studies and former Chair of the Sociology Department at Northeastern Illinois University, where she co-founded and was actively involved in the Women's Studies Program. She also served as a faculty consultant to the Network for the Dissemination of Curriculum Infusion, an organization that presents workshops nationally on how to integrate substance abuse prevention strategies into the college curriculum.

Throughout her educational experiences, Professor Schwartz has been concerned with improving the academic climate for women, improving student access to higher education, and improving the quality of undergraduate education. As a union activist, Professor Schwartz worked to win collective bargaining for higher education faculty in Illinois. She served as union president at Northeastern and spent over eight years as the Legislative Director for the University Professionals of Illinois where she lobbied for bills of interest to higher education faculty and students. She edited the union's newsletter, *Universities 21*, that is devoted to sharing ideas on academic issues.

Professor Schwartz's research continues to focus on marriages and families, socialization, nonmarital lifestyles, work, aging, and the structured relationships of race, class, and gender. Although she found teaching all courses thought-provoking and enjoyable, her favorites were Marriages and Families; Women, Men, and Social Change; and Introductory Sociology. In her teaching she employed interactive learning strategies and encouraged students to apply sociological insights in their everyday lives. Seeing students make connections between their individual lives and the larger social forces that influence them remains one of the most rewarding and exciting aspects of her teaching career.

Dr. BarBara M. Scott has been married over 37 years and is the proud mother of two sons and two granddaughters. As a wife and mother of two small children, she returned to school, earning a Bachelor of Arts Degree in Sociology and two different Master's Degrees. a Master of Arts Degree in Sociology and a Master of Philosophy from Roosevelt University in Chicago, and later a Doctorate in Sociology from Northwestern University in Evanston, Illinois. Dr. Scott is a Professor of Sociology and Women's Studies and former Chair of the Criminal Justice, Social Work, Sociology, and Women's Studies Department at Northeastern Illinois University. She is a strong advocate for curriculum transformation and the integration of race, class, gender, and sexual orientation into the college curriculum, as well as a social activist who has been in the forefront of organizing among national and international women of color, both within and outside academia.

Professor Scott has received meritorious recognition for her work and has served over 27 years as an educational and human resource consultant. She has coordinated the Women's Studies Program, is a founding member of the university's Black Women's Caucus, and is the faculty sponsor for the undergraduate chapter of Alpha Kappa Alpha Sorority on her campus. Her research and teaching interests include marriages and families, particularly African American families; the structured relationships of race, class, and gender; institutionalized racism and inequality; cultural images and the social construction of knowledge in the mass media; and Africana Women's Studies. She finds teaching challenging and invigorating, and among her favorite courses are Marriages and Families, Sociology of Black Women, and Introductory Sociology. She is an enthusiastic advocate of *applying sociology* to the everyday worlds in which we live and routinely engages her students in field research in the communities in which they live and work. After years of teaching, she still gets excited about the varied insights that sociology offers into both the most simple and the most complex questions and issues of human social life.

Chapter 1

Marriages and Families over Time

IN THE NEWS: **KARACHI, PAKISTAN**

On February 19, 1998, Kanwar Ahson was arrested and taken to Karachi District Court to face charges of having sex outside of marriage. What made his story newsworthy was that Riffat Afridie, the woman he had sex with, was his lawful wife. Riffat, a member of the minority Pathan ethnic group, had married Kanwar, a member of the dominant Mohajir ethnic group, over her father's objection. The news of their marriage set off ethnic rioting in Karachi, which left two people dead and eight others seriously injured. A council of tribal elders subsequently declared that Pathan "honor" had been violated when Riffat married outside her tribe; they threatened further violence unless Riffat, who went into hiding, was found and arrested. A month after his release from prison, Kanwar Ahson was severely wounded. Riffat's father and brother are suspects in the shooting. At last report, Riffat and Kanwar, who is still recovering from his wounds, live in hiding, moving frequently to avoid detection. (Associated Press, 1998)

WHAT WOULD YOU DO? Imagine that your family forbids you to marry someone you love. Would you marry anyway, knowing that both of your lives might be in danger? What causes some groups to feel so strongly about who their children marry?

Author's Update: Kanwar and Riffat's story is not an isolated event. On April 6, 1999, in Lahore, Pakistan, Samia Sarwar, a 29-year-old mother of two sons, was killed in her lawyer's office. Her family had threatened to kill her when she told them she was seeking a divorce (Patel, 2000). In yet another incident, a 23-year-old Jordanian, Rania Arafat, was shot by her younger brother for refusing to marry the cousin to whom she'd been promised by her family (Perkins, 2000). According to the Human Rights Commission of Pakistan, more than 1100 women are deliberately killed each year for "violating cultural traditions." Many experts believe that the reported number of such "honor killings" is only a fraction of the actual killings that take place. Although both political and religious leaders have spoken out against this practice, it remains rampant in a number of Middle Eastern communities where the perpetrators, mostly male family members, generally go unpunished. Opponents of attempts to outlaw "honor killings" argue that without such controls on women, families would disintegrate.

The family, and marriage as a process that can generate it, exists in some form in all societies. Families are created by human beings in an attempt to meet certain basic individual and social needs, such as survival and growth. Marriage and family are among the oldest human social institutions. An **institution** consists of patterns of ideas, beliefs, values, and behavior that are built around the basic needs of individuals and society and that tend to persist over time. Institutions represent the organized aspects of human social existence that are established and reinforced over time by the various norms and values of a particular group or society. The family as an institution organizes, directs, and executes the essential tasks of living for its members.

Families, however, encompass cultural patterns as well as social structure. For example, as the case of Kanwar Ahson illustrates, the cultural recognition of mating is intimately bound up with family norms and customs about who are appropriate mates. As we discuss in detail in Chapter 5, two of the most common ways in which families regulate who their members can mate with is through rules of *exogamy* (the requirement that marriage must occur outside a group) and *endogamy* (the requirement that marriage occur within a group). Clearly, among the various ethnic groups in Karachi, marital endogamy is so important that an infraction of the rule is not only considered a violation of tribal customs but also cause for violent retribution. Although, historically, marriage and family have been considered the most important institutions in human society, humans have created many other important institutions—for example, education, government, the economy, religion, and law.

CONTEMPORARY DEFINITIONS OF MARRIAGES AND FAMILIES

Because all of us belong to some sort of family and have observed marriages (including our parents' and maybe our own), we probably think we know exactly what the terms *marriage* and *family* mean. Although marriage and family go hand in hand, they are not one and the same. You might ask, then, exactly what are they? Take a few minutes to jot down your perceptions, definitions, and ideas about each of these institutions. How did you define them? Not surprisingly, many of your definitions and images of marriages and families are probably still tied to the myth of the white middle-class family of husband, wife, and 2.2 children, an image that is relentlessly portrayed in reruns of 1950s and 1960s family sitcoms. This pattern is far from typical today, however. More accurate definitions of marriages and families must take into account the many different forms of marriages and families that have existed historically and still exist today, both in the United States and in other countries and cultures.

What Is Marriage?

Marriage has been defined in the United States as a legal contract between a woman and a man who are at or above a specified age and who are not already legally married to someone else. Although some people still regard this definition as adequate, increasing numbers of scholars and laypersons alike consider it too narrow. By focusing on the legal aspect of marriage alone it excludes a variety of relationships, such as some heterosexual and homosexual cohabitive relationships that function in much the same way as legally sanctioned marriages, albeit without the same legal protection. Thus, in this book we utilize a more encompassing and reality-based definition of **marriage** as a union between people (whether widely or legally recognized or not) that unites partners sexually, socially, and economically; that is relatively consistent over time; and that accords each member certain agreed-upon rights.

Types of Marriages Marriages across cultures generally have been either monogamous or polygamous. **Monogamy** involves one person married to a person of the other sex. Although, legally, monogamy refers to heterosexual relationships, any couple can be monogamous if they are committed exclusively to each other sexually and otherwise during the course of the relationship. Monogamy is the legally recognized marriage structure in the United States. However, approximately one-half of all marriages in this country end in divorce, and the vast majority of divorced people remarry. Thus, the U.S. marriage pattern is more accurately classified as **serial monogamy.** Individuals may marry as many times as they like as long as each prior marriage was ended by death or divorce.

In some societies, polygamy is the accepted marriage structure. **Polygamy** is a broad category that generally refers to one person of one sex married to several people of the other sex. It can take one of two forms: **polygyny,** in which one male has two or more wives; and **polyandry,** in which one female has two or more husbands. Although both forms of polygamy are illegal in the United States, some religious groups here routinely practice polygyny. For example, despite the illegality of polygamy, it thrives in Utah, where an estimated 50,000 residents are part of families with more than one wife. One man in Salt Lake City is believed to have fathered as many as 200 children by several wives. Although the Church of Jesus Christ of Latter-day Saints renounced polygamy over 100 years ago and excommunicates its practitioners, Mormons participating in plural marriages defend polygamy as a fulfillment of their religion as prescribed by their ancestors (Janofsky, 2001).

A third form of marriage is **cenogamy,** or **group marriage,** in which all of the women and men in a group are simultaneously married to one another. Like polygamy, this form of marriage is also illegal in the United States. In the mid-1800s, however, the Oneida Community, a communal group living in New York, practiced cenogamy until they were forced to disband.

What Is a Family?

What is a family? is not a question to be taken lightly. Clearly, over the last decade questions and issues relating to family, marriage, and intimacy have become highly publicized, causing many of us to question what family, family values, marriage, and intimacy are and how these terms relate to our lives. Social definitions of what constitutes a family vary. In addition, as the stories of Kanwar and Riffat and of "honor killings" suggest, social definitions of families raise important public policy issues. These issues are related to issues of power and control and the ability of individuals and institutions to exert their will over others. An important question in this regard is: Who defines or who has the right to define *family?* Power gives one the leverage not only to define but also to set public policy based on a particular set of beliefs, in turn impacting the ways in which various individuals are treated. One thing that seems clear from the vignette is that static images and definitions of families from the past do not provide us with an accurate picture of families today.

Like marriage, family has been defined historically in rigid and restrictive language. For example, the U.S. Census Bureau defines a family as two or more persons living together and related by blood, marriage, or adoption. As with the popular definition of marriage, this definition of family is limiting in that it does not take into consideration the considerable diversity found in families. Thus, we define **family** as any relatively stable group of people who are related to one another through blood, marriage, or adoption, or who simply live together, and who provide one another with economic and emotional support. In addition, a family can be a group of people who simply define themselves as family based on feelings of love, respect, commitment, and responsibility to and identification with one another. This concept of family has a subjective element in that it takes into account people's feelings of belonging to a particular group. Thus, communes as well as cohabiting individuals either of the same or other sex, who identify themselves as a family, meet these criteria and can be considered families.

Most Americans, it seems, agree with this broader definition. For example, only 22 percent of those polled in 1989 defined a family exclusively in terms of blood, marriage, or adoption. The overwhelming majority, 74 percent, defined a family as any group of people who love and care for one another (Coontz, 1992).

Types of Families As with marriages, several types of families are worth noting. The **family of orientation** is the family into which a person is born and raised. This includes, for example, you, your parents, and your siblings, if any. In contrast, when we marry or have an intimate relationship with someone or have children, we create what sociologists call the **family of procreation.** Some of us were born into a **nuclear family,** consisting of a mother, father, and siblings. Others were born into an **extended,** or **multigenerational, family,** consisting of one or both of our parents, our siblings, if any, and other relatives, including grandparents. In both urban and rural areas of the United States, a form of the traditional extended family is often evident. That is, in many neighborhoods, especially those with ethnic or poor and working-class groups, a variety of relatives live, not necessarily in the same household but in very close proximity to one another (upstairs, next-door, down the block, around the corner), interact on a frequent basis, and provide emotional and economic support for one another. Some sociologists have labeled this family form the **modified extended family.**

As you read this book, you will discover that the family mosaic in the United States is not limited to nuclear and extended families. As our definition implies, there is a wide variety of families and, thus, a wide variety of terms to identify them. For example, *voluntarily child-free families* consist of couples who make a conscious decision not to have children. *Single-parent families* (resulting either from divorce, unmarried parenthood, or death of a parent) consist of one parent and her or his children. Sometimes these families are specifically described as female- or male-headed families. In either case, legal marriage is not a criterion for family status, as the parent may or may not have been legally married. *Reconstituted, blended,* or *stepfamilies* are formed when a widowed or divorced person remarries, creating a new family that includes the children of one or both spouses. Over the past 29 years, an increasing number of Americans live in *racially and ethnically mixed families.* There are now more than 1.3 million interracial couples in the United States and 1.6 million Latinas/os married to non-Latinas/os. In addition, there are more than 2 million children of mixed races. In fact, mixed-race births are now the third largest category of births (U.S. Census Bureau, 2000; "Some Statistics on Bi-Racial Families," 1999). *Lesbian* and *gay families* are composed of individuals of the same sex who live together and identify themselves as a family; these relationships may or may not include natural-born or adopted children.

An increasing number of people living in the United States, especially children, live in foster families. A *foster family* consists of one or two parents and one or more children who have been taken away from their biological families and become wards of the state. Foster parents typically raise these children as their own. Other contemporary forms of the family include two families living in the same household, and what some social scientists call the "*surrogate*, or *chosen, family*"—a set of "roommates" or group of people either of different or the same sex who choose to share the same household and who define themselves as a family.

Traditionally, families in the United States have had a patriarchal structure. A **patriarchal family** is a family in which the male (husband or father) is the head of the family and exercises authority and decision-making power over his wife and children.

Race, Class, and Gender

Race, class, and gender are three of the most important social categories of experience for individuals and families in the United States, primarily because these categories also represent significant, comprehensive, and structured systems of oppression for some individuals and groups and privilege for others. Historically, some families in the United States have experienced social, political, and economic inequalities vis-à-vis other families, principally as a consequence of their race, ethnicity, ancestry, social class, sex or gender, or other characteristics defined as inferior.

At a very elementary level, we can say that family experiences are shaped by the choices that individual members make. However, the options that families have available to them and, thus, the choices they make are either limited or expanded by the ways in which race, class, and gender are organized. To fully understand families and how they function, then, we must examine the influence of race, class, and gender on family resources and processes and explore how these factors have shaped and continue to shape the experiences of families throughout the United States.

Race, class, and gender are interrelated or interactive categories of social experience that affect all aspects of human life, shaping all social institutions and systems of meaning, including the institutions of marriage and family, as well as family values. By "interrelated," we mean that there are complex interconnections among race, class, and gender such that families are not separately affected because of the racial composition of their members, to which is added the influence of their economic situation, after which comes the impact of the gender of their members. In other words, race, class, and gender are not independent variables that can be tacked onto each other or separated at will. They are concrete social relations that are interconnected with one another, and their various intersections produce specific effects. Thus, any concrete analysis of marriages and families must take this into account. As sociologists Margaret Andersen and Patricia Hill Collins (1992) have observed, race, class, and gender are part of the total fabric of experience for *all* families. Although these categories are different aspects of social structure, individual families experience them simultaneously. The meaning of the concepts of race, class, and gender as interrelated or interactive categories of experience refers not only to the simultaneity of oppression or privilege but also to the multiplicative relationships among these experiences (for example, see King, 1990).

Understanding race, class, and gender in this way also allows us to see the interrelationship of other important categories of social experiences, such as ethnicity, sexual orientation, age, religion, geographic location, historical context, and physical and mental abilities. Later in this chapter we will see that many of these categories of experience have been interwoven in family form and functioning throughout U.S. history.

FAMILY FUNCTIONS AND THE DEBATE OVER FAMILY VALUES

Historians and the lay public alike have often discussed families in terms of the vital social functions they serve for individuals and the society at large. These functions have included regulation of sexual behavior, reproduction, social placement, socialization, economic cooperation, and the provision of care, protection, and intimacy for family members.

The growing visibility of multiracial families calls attention to the diversity of American families. It also makes it even more critical that policies relating to marriages and families address the intersections of race, class, and gender on family functioning.

Social Functions of Families

Regulation of Sexual Behavior Every society is concerned about the sexual behavior of its members. In most societies sexual behavior is regulated and enforced within the context of families. Although the **norms**—cultural guidelines or rules of conduct that direct people to behave in particular ways—governing sexual behavior vary among societies, no known society allows its members to have sexual relations with whomever they please. For example, all societies prohibit sexual relations between blood or close relatives; this is known as the *incest taboo.* Forcing people to have sexual relations outside the family unit promotes alliances between families, reinforces their social independence, and prevents or minimizes sexual jealousies and conflicts within families. The set of relatives subject to the taboo varies across societies, however. Whereas in most societies parents and siblings are subject to the incest taboo, in ancient Egyptian and Hawaiian societies, siblings in the royal families were permitted to mate with and marry one another; in some cases, father–daughter marriages were also permitted. This system preserved the purity of royalty and enabled the royal family to maintain its power and property and prevented the splintering of its estate through inheritance.

Moreover, in most contemporary societies sexual relations are linked with marriage. Even in those societies where it is not, their members' sexual behavior is nonetheless regulated so that it reinforces the social order. For example, among the Masai (a polygynous pastoral group in Africa), where men dominate in the family, young wives of older men are allowed discreetly to take lovers from the unmarried warrior class. If the wife becomes pregnant from such a relationship, family stability is not disrupted. The children from these unions simply belong to the husband and further increase his wealth and prestige.

Reproduction To perpetuate itself, a society must produce new members to replace those who die or move away. In most societies, families are given the primary responsibility for reproducing the species. The reproductive function of families is considered to be so important that many societies employ a variety of practices to motivate married couples to have children. For example, in the United States, couples typically receive tax exemptions and other tax breaks for each child they produce. Couples who cannot or consciously choose not to have children are penalized by tax laws and are sometimes stigmatized by society's members. In addition, sexual intercourse that occurs outside of marriage or that will not produce children, such as lesbian or gay sexual relations, is highly stigmatized and discouraged.

In contrast, in certain societies concern with reproduction translates primarily into a concern with population control. Families are motivated to keep society manageable through population control. For example, in China, material incentives, such as work bonuses, free medical care, and other privileges for the child, are given to married couples who agree to limit their reproduction to one child.

Social Placement When new members are born into society, they must be placed within the social structure with a minimum of confusion and in a way that preserves order and stability. The **social structure** of society refers to the recurrent, patterned ways that people relate to one another. It consists of an intricate web of social **statuses,** a position in a group or society, and **roles,** a set of behaviors associated with a particular status. Members of society must be placed within these statuses and motivated to play the appropriate roles. One of the ways in which families function is to assign social status to individuals on the basis of their membership within that particular family. The status placement function of families occurs at a number of levels. On one level, families confer statuses that orient members to a variety of interpersonal relationships involving parents, siblings, and a variety of relatives. In addition, simply by being born into or raised in a particular family we automatically inherit membership in, and the status of, certain basic groups, including racial, ethnic, religious, class, and national. Social status influences almost every aspect of our lives. It influences the way we see the world as well as how the world sees us. Much of what we think of as our unique values and preferences are really the results of our assignment to certain statuses through our families. Some societies still arrange marriages of young children to perpetuate the social structure (see the "In Other Places" box).

SOCIALIZATION Human babies are born with no knowledge of the norms, values, and role expectations of their society. However, they soon learn what their society considers to be appropriate ways of acting, thinking, and feeling. Children's social development, as well as the continuation of society, depends on the **socialization** process, a lifetime of social interaction through which people learn those elements of culture that are essential for effective participation in social life. Today, as in the past, families are the primary transmitters of culture to each new generation of the young. Many people in our society believe that because parents are more likely than others to be deeply committed to their own offspring, they are thus the best or most appropriate socializing agents. Compulsory education, however, has placed a significant amount of the socialization function in the hands of the state and schools. In addition, the increasing need for mothers to work outside the home has placed part of this function in the hands of child-care workers; and the mass media, especially television, have become important agents of socialization.

ECONOMIC COOPERATION Children have physical and economic needs as well as social needs. They must be fed, clothed, and sheltered. Providing for these needs is the basis of the economic function of families. Families are responsible for the physical and economic well-being not only of their children but of all members of their family. In the past, families consumed primarily goods that they produced. Although this is no longer true, families are still productive economic units; however, the value of what they produce is less recognized today. The goods and services produced by families today are delivered primarily by women (for example, child care and housework). Because men have moved outside the home to work and receive wages and women's work inside families is unpaid, the productive and essential nature of families achieved through the work that women (and some stay-at-home husbands) do has been overlooked, downplayed, and often trivialized. Nevertheless, families continue to divide essential tasks among their members and cooperate economically to meet each one's physical, social, and economic needs. Each member's economic fate is tied to that of the family as a whole.

CARE, PROTECTION, AND INTIMACY A large amount of sociological and psychological research indicates that, in addition to the necessities of life, human infants also need warmth and affection. In addition, during infancy and early childhood humans cannot take care of themselves and thus are totally dependent on their caretakers. Furthermore, even as adults humans need intimacy and often need other human beings for care and protection during periods of illness, disability, or other dependencies. Ideally, families function to provide an intimate atmosphere and an economic unit in which these needs can be met. As the center of emotional life, families can provide love, caring, and emotional support that cannot easily be obtained outside the family context. For many of us, throughout our lives our families will be our most important source of comfort and emotional support.

Any given family may or may not perform any or all of these functions. The family as an institution is so diverse that not all families fulfill all of these functions, and those who do do not always fulfill them well. That we live in a time of transition and change is unquestionable. Thus, many of the activities previously identified by social scientists as family functions have been taken over by or are shared with other societal institutions, such as schools, religious organizations, mass media, and government agencies. The socialization of children and stabilization for adult family members, however, remain one of the primary functions of families.

Contrasting Views of Families

Some people see the loss of family function as a contributing factor to a variety of social ills that beset modern families. A proponent of this point of view, social scientist Christopher Lasch (1977, 1978) contends that the encroachment of outside institutions, especially the state, has left modern families with too few functions to perform. Even the socialization function, which had been a primary function of families, has been largely taken over by an educational system that increasingly communicates a set of values and behaviors that may conflict with the realities of some families. Thus, the function of modern families has been reduced to a small number of specialized functions, such as affection and companionship. Lasch, along with a number of other people, including a long line of politicians, believes that families are in grave danger today, perhaps even in a state of crisis and moral decay. Many of these people consider the family to be seriously flawed and its breakdown the major source of most societal ills (illegitimacy, divorce, declining educational standards, drug addiction, delinquency, violence, HIV/AIDS). Others view the family as the foundation of society. While some people view the family with nostalgia and confusion, others see it as foundational but undergoing massive changes that are connected to other transformations that society is living through.

These contrasting views of the family, and many gradations of them, are as prevalent today as they were in the 1990s when sparked by the so-called conservative revolution. In this first decade of the twenty-first century, marriages and families continue to be in a state of transformation and to be political issues. Some political conservatives, for example, want to put fathers back at the head of families as the breadwinners and protectors of women and children. Some liberals (among them feminists), on the other hand, have long argued that the patriarchal family is the major source of women's oppression and inequality.

IN OTHER PLACES

CHILD AND TEENAGE MARRIAGES IN INDIA AND WESTERN KENYA

On the festival of Akha Teej, many villages and towns in India's northern states of Rajasthan, Madhya Pradesh, Uttar Pradesh, Bihar, and West Bengal, where about 40 percent of the total Indian population lives (approximately 420 million Indians), take on a holiday atmosphere. Open-sided wedding tents in brightly patterned fabrics, known as pandals, dot the area. In one elaborate joint ceremony that recently took place in the village of Madhogarh, six sisters were married to boys from other villages. The youngest bride, Hansa, was 4 and her groom, Sitaram, was 12. After spending her wedding night at home, Hansa traveled to her in-laws' village to stay for a few days. Although tradition demands that girl brides return to live with their families until the onset of puberty, many find themselves working as servants in their in-laws' households. Despite the Child Marriage Restraint Act passed in 1971, and another law that prescribes 18 as the minimum age for a woman to marry and 21 for a man, child marriages remain popular. A 1993 government survey of more than 5000 women living in Rajasthan found that 56 percent had married before they were 15. Of those women, 14 percent married before they were 10, and 3 percent married before they were 5 (Burns, 1998).

A 2-year-old bride drinks from her mother's breast during her wedding ceremony in a small village in Rajasthan, India. Her 8-year-old groom sits nearby.

Marriage of adolescent girls is also commonplace in India. In Kuria, a cattle-keeping community in western Kenya, girls as young as 12 are often forced by their parents to marry. In Nepal, 40 percent of the girls are married by age 15. In Afghanistan and Bangladesh, over 50 percent of girls are married by age 18. Sub-Saharan Africa follows close behind; there, over 40 percent of girls have been married before the age of 18 ("Child Marriages," 2001).

The reasons for these early marriages are steeped in tradition and economics. Many parents believe that early marriage protects their daughters from sexual depredations. Perhaps even more important is the fact that many of these families are poor, often having annual incomes of $500 or less. Thus, securing an early marriage for daughters can relieve parents of the need to support daughters in the future.

Women's rights activists, social workers, and government officials are concerned about the long-term consequences of child marriages, including soaring birth rates, grinding poverty, high illiteracy and infant mortality rates, and shortened life expectancy, especially among rural women. Pregnancy-related deaths are the leading cause of mortality for girls aged 15 to 19 worldwide. Domestic violence rates are also high. Those trying to end the practice of early marriage concede that the practice is unlikely to disappear until people's economic lives show significant improvement.

What do you think? *What are the costs and benefits of child marriage for both the individual and the larger society? Should governments ban the practice of child marriages? What do you think is the appropriate age for people to marry? Explain.*

Some people have seen evidence of the decline and moral decay of families in terms of a number of contemporary patterns of marriage and family life today: the transformation of women's roles both inside the home and in the world at large, the increasing number of children and families that are beset by serious stresses and troubles, the high divorce rates, lower marriage and birth rates, the increase in single-parent families, the high rate of welfare dependency, sexual permissiveness, the increasing number of public disclosures of incest and sexual and mental abuse of children, the increasing number of unmarried couples living together openly, unmarried mothers keeping their babies, and the legalization of abortion. In addition, a number of individual events that occurred during the closing decade of the twentieth century gave credence to those who view the traditional family as under siege or in decline. For example, survey data during the 1990s indicated that one in four sixth graders in New Haven, Connecticut, was sexually active; a Virginia woman made national news after castrating her husband, who she claimed had repeatedly raped and abused her over the course of their married life (that same year close to 4 million women were battered by a husband or lover); several cities passed domestic partnership laws giving lesbian and gay cohabiting couples some of the same legal rights previously reserved for married couples; and scientists at George Washington University successfully cloned human embryos, raising the possibility that in the near future, couples can have identical twins of different ages (Newman, 1995).

Given events like these, many people, from social scientists to public officials to ordinary people, feel that the tradition of human family life is being replaced by an alien and destructive set of relationships that is tearing at the very heart of U.S. society. Critics of the modern family, such as political conservatives and other "traditionalists," attribute this family breakdown to a general decline in family values, which, in turn, is often associated with feminism, the sexual revolution, lesbian and gay liberation, generous welfare policies, and the increasing demands for social and political rights (Stacey, 1996). Indeed, the decade of the 1990s witnessed protracted public discourse about family values that turned into a polarized, often angry political and scholarly debate and included a media blitz on profamily-values stories in magazines and newspapers, on radio and television talk shows, and in scholarly journals where a variety of people, including some sociologists, lamented the loss of an idealized family past. While staunch political and religious conservatives carried the profamily campaign in the 1980s, academicians, most of them also political conservatives, became the chief profamily spokespersons in the 1990s. Grounding their claims in social science, they declared that the primary source of family decline over the past three decades has been cultural, and they called for a restoration of the supremacy of the nuclear family. One thread of this debate resulted in a scathing critique, by sociologist Norvell Glenn (1997a), of marriage and family textbook authors who take a feminist approach to the study of marriages and families and/or who stress the diversity of marriage and family life, suggesting that they do not focus enough on the positive aspects of traditional (two-parent) marriage and family life.

On the other side of these debates are those who are equally concerned about the problems of modern families but who view current events and trends in marriage and family life as indicative of the redefinition of marriages and families in the context of the massive transformation that took place worldwide over the last several decades. They concede that marriages and families may perform fewer direct functions for individual members than they did in the past and that there are serious problems associated with marriage and family life today. They argue, however, that marriage and family life are still extremely important to most people in the United States. They cite census data that indicate that the United States has perhaps the highest marriage rate in the industrial world. For example, in 2000, slightly over 96 percent of women and slightly under 96 percent of men aged 65 and older were currently or had been married (Fields and Casper, 2001). Although people may delay marriage, almost everyone (90 percent) marries—at least once—and almost all who do marry either have or want to have children. And although the United States has one of the highest divorce rates in the world, the overwhelming majority of divorced people remarry. This point of view suggests that marriage and family life in the United States today is a complex mixture of both continuity and change (see, for example, Skolnick and Skolnick, 1999).

Furthermore, those who take this point of view cite survey results that report that most people in the United States hold the family in high regard and report high levels of satisfaction with their own family life. They refute the idealized version of families of the past and give us instead a picture of a traditional family that was often rigid and oppressive. They remind us that members of traditional families were often expected to fit into roles that were based on a clear division of labor along age and gender lines. Frequently, this resulted in a very restrictive life, especially for women and children. They also question the premise that family values and traditional family structure are one and the same and that both are synonymous with stability. What, they ask, are family values? What have they been historically? Are they fundamentally different today than in the past? Who is to say which family values are correct?

How does the polarization of the discourse on family values to a two-sides approach affect our understanding of what is happening to families today? Is there only one accurate image of the family? Were families of yesterday really the way we perceived them to be? Were the "good old days" really that good for all marriages and families? Why is valuing families, regardless of the form they take, considered to be antifamily by some groups? Explain.

DEBUNKING MYTHS ABOUT MARRIAGES AND FAMILIES

Take another few minutes to think about the "traditional family." Again, if you are like most people, your vision of the traditional family is similar to or the same as your more general view of families. Therefore, you probably described the traditional family in terms of some combination of the following traits:

- Members loved and respected one another and worked together for the good of the family.
- Grandparents were an integral and respected part of the family.

- Mothers stayed home and were happy, nurturant, and always available to their children.
- Fathers worked and brought home the paycheck.
- Children were seen and not heard, mischievous but not "bad," and were responsible and learned a work ethic.

These images of past family life are still widely held and have a powerful influence on people's perceptions and evaluations of today's families. The problem, however, is that these are mostly mythical images of the past based on many different kinds of marriages and families that never coexisted in the same time and place. A leading authority on U.S. family history, Stephanie Coontz (1992), argues in her book *The Way We Never Were* that much of today's political and social debate about family values and the "real" family is based on an idealized vision of a past that never actually existed.[1] Coontz further argues that this idealized and selective set of remembrances of families of yesteryear in turn determines much of our contemporary view of traditional family life. A look at some statistics and facts from our historical past supports her argument.

- We bemoan the increasingly violent nature of families (and rightfully so). As you will see in Chapter 11, however, the United States has a long and brutal history of child and woman abuse. Therefore, we cannot blame domestic violence on recent changes in family life or on the disappearance of family values and morals.
- We think that contemporary high school dropout rates are shockingly high. As late as the 1940s, however, less than one-half of all young people entering high school managed to finish, producing a dropout rate that was much higher than today's.
- Violence in all aspects of society is high today, but before the Civil War, New York City was already considered the most dangerous place in the world to live. As a matter of fact, the United States has had the highest homicide rates in the industrial world for almost 150 years. And among all the relationships between murderers and their victims, the family relationship is most common.
- Although alcohol and drug abuse are at alarmingly high rates today, they were widespread well before modern rearrangements of gender roles and family life. In 1820, for example, alcohol consumption was three times higher than today. There was also a major epidemic of opium and cocaine addiction in the late nineteenth century. Over time, these and other problems led to the emergence of a new field called family therapy that is designed to help families cope with and resolve problems (see the "Strengthening Marriages and Families" box).

[1]The rest of our discussion concerning the myths and realities of family life, past and present, owes much to the work of Coontz. She has written profusely on the social origins and history of U.S. families from the 1600s forward. She has also lectured extensively in Europe and the United States on family history and sociology. She places contemporary family crises in the context of history and exposes many of the myths that surround and cloud contemporary discussions and debates about family values and the way U.S. families actually were.

As these facts show, our memory of past family life is often clouded by myths. A **myth** is a false, fictitious, imaginary, or exaggerated belief about someone or something. Myths are generally assumed to be true and often provide the justification or rationale for social behaviors, beliefs, and institutions. And, in fact, most myths do contain some elements of truth. As we will see, however, different myths contain different degrees of truth.

Some family myths have a positive effect in the sense that they often bond individual family members together in familial solidarity. When they create unrealistic expectations about what families can or should be and do, however, myths can be dangerous. Many of the myths that most Americans hold today about traditional families or families of the past are white middle-class myths. This is true because the mass media, controlled primarily by white middle-class men, tend to project a primarily white middle-class experience as a universal trend or fact. Such myths, then, distort the diverse experiences of other familial groups in this country, both presently and in the past, and they do not even describe most white middle-class families accurately. We now take a closer look at five of the most popular myths and stereotypes about the family that are directly applicable to current debates about family life and gender roles: (1) the universal nuclear family, (2) the self-reliant traditional family, (3) the naturalness of different spheres for wives and husbands, (4) the unstable African American family, and (5) the idealized nuclear family of the 1950s.

Myth 1: The Universal Nuclear Family

While some form of marriage and family is found in all human societies, the idea that there is a universal, or single, marriage and family pattern blinds us to the historical reality and legitimacy of diverse marriage and family arrangements. The reality is that marriages and families vary in organization, membership, life cycles, emotional environments, ideologies, social and kinship networks, and economic and other functions. Although it is certainly true that a woman and man (egg and sperm) must unite to produce a child, social kinship ties or living arrangements, however, do not automatically flow from such biological unions. For example, although some cultures have weddings and cultural notions about monogamy and permanence, other cultures lack one or more of these characteristics. In some cultures, mating and childbirth occur outside of legal marriage and sometimes without couples living together. In other cultures, wives, husbands, and children live in separate residences.

Myth 2: The Self-Reliant Traditional Family

The myth of the self-reliant family assumes that, in the past, families were held together by hard work, family loyalty, and a fierce determination not to be beholden to anyone, especially the state. It is popularly believed that such families never asked for handouts; rather, they stood on their own feet even in times of crisis. Unlike some families today, who

STRENGTHENING MARRIAGES AND FAMILIES

Talks with Family Therapist Joan Zientek

Joan Zientek

INTRODUCING FAMILY THERAPY

In various chapters throughout this textbook we will call on Joan Zientek, a marital and family therapist, to answer questions about how families cope with major problems and what they can do to strengthen family relationships. Ms. Zientek is a graduate of the Family Institute, Institute of Psychiatry of Northwestern Memorial Hospital Medical School. She has been in private practice for over 16 years. In addition, she presents seminars on various family and human relations topics to school faculties, parent groups, and service organizations, as well as serving as a consultant to many school districts. Ms. Zientek developed and conducts a program entitled *FOCUS ON E.Q.: A Social Skills Training Program for Kids* and is the author of *Mrs. Ruby's Life Lessons for Kids*, a storybook and workbook on emotional intelligence.

What Is Family Therapy?

Family therapy is a systems approach to helping families function more effectively. It views the family as a web of interlocking relationships within which every member is intimately linked in a powerful way with every other person in the family. Family therapy starts with the assumption that an individual's problems are an overt manifestation of a larger, less obvious family systems problem. Thus, its focus is not primarily the individual family member, but the system of relationships that exists. The expectation is that changes in the system will illicit changes in individual members, and vice versa, and changes in the individual will effect system changes as well. Thus, at times, when for a variety of reasons all family members cannot be present for therapy, positive changes in the family system can be effected by working with just an individual or with several family members.

Who Can Benefit from Family Therapy?

All individuals and families experience problems from time to time, and, for the most part, many of these can be resolved without therapy. However, when a couple marries, the intensity of that bond, its reminiscent impact, along with the demands of negotiating life as a dyad, often cause latent unresolved issues from childhood to emerge. These get acted out in the marriage relationship and can be disruptive and confusing to the couple. Also, as families move from one life stage to another, from the birth of children to the retirement years, some individuals and families may need special support to make the required adaptations in family patterns and relationships. At other times, situational difficulties may be due to divorce, remarriage, illness, death, unemployment, or relocation. Individual family members may have problems that stem from emotional and biochemical issues, such as depression, attention deficit disorder, obsessive-compulsive disorder, or the addictions of alcohol, drugs, or gambling. Although some problems are more deep-seated than others, anyone who is willing to work on resolving them is likely to benefit from family therapy.

Do Myths about Family Life Have Any Relationship to How Families Function?

They can. Family relationships are often portrayed in the media and in the love songs that have endured over time as smooth, effortless, and a haven of emotional support. In the heart of many of us is the deep desire to believe that the fairy tale of family life truly does exist. Often what we find, however, is that meeting the challenges of day-to-day living, against a backdrop of different genetic makeup and temperament of individuals, different family of origin experiences, as well as the dictates of cultural expectations, often results in an interesting mix that does not always work smoothly or equally to the benefit of all family members. The tension between the idealized expectations of family life and the problems that emerge from the complex family dynamic can place a family in jeopardy and, therefore, in need of help.

watch the mail for their government checks, families of yesteryear did not accept or expect "charity." Any help they may have received came from other family members.

This tendency to overestimate the self-reliance of earlier families ignores the fact that external support for families has been the rule, and not the exception, in U.S. family history. Although public assistance has become less local and more impersonal over the past two centuries, U.S. families have always depended to some degree on other institutions. For example, colonial families made extensive use of the collective work of others, such as African American slaves and Native Americans, whose husbandry and collective land use provided for the abundant game and plant life colonial families consumed to survive. Early families were also dependent on a large network of neighbors, churches, courts, government officials, and legislative bodies for their sustenance. For example, the elderly, ill, and orphaned dependents were often taken care of by people who were not family members, and public officials often gave money to facilitate such care. Immigrant, African American, and native-born white workers could not have survived in the past without sharing and receiving assistance beyond family networks. Moreover, middle-class as well as working-class families were dependent on fraternal and mutual aid organizations to assist them in times of need.

Myth 3: The Naturalness of Different Spheres for Wives and Husbands

This myth dates to the mid-nineteenth century, when economic changes led to the development of separate spheres for women and men. Prior to this, men shared in child rearing. They were expected to be at least as involved in child rearing as mothers. Fatherhood meant much more than simply inseminating. It was understood as a well-defined set of domestic skills, including provisioning, hospitality, and child rearing (Gillis, 1999). With industrialization, wives and mothers became the caregivers and moral guardians of the family, while husbands and fathers provided economic support and protection and represented their families to the outside world. Thereafter, this arrangement was viewed as natural, and alternative forms were believed to be destructive to family harmony. Thus, today's family problems are seen as stemming from a self-defeating attempt to equalize women's and men's roles in the family. It is assumed that the move away from a traditional gendered division of labor to a more egalitarian ideal denies women's and men's differing needs and abilities and thus destabilizes family relations. Those who hold to this myth advocate a return to traditional gender roles in the family and a clear and firm boundary between the family and the outside world. As we shall see later on, however, the notions of separate spheres and ideal family form are far from natural and have not always existed.

Myth 4: The Unstable African American Family

Although many critics of today's families believe that the collapse of the family affects all racial and ethnic groups, they frequently single out African American families as the least stable and functional. According to sociologist Ronald Taylor (1998), myths and misconceptions about the nature and quality of African American family life are pervasive and deeply entrenched in American popular thought. Although there are far fewer systematic studies of black families than of white families, African American families have been the subject of far more sweeping generalizations and myths. The most pervasive myth, the myth of the collapse of the African American family, is fueled by racist stereotypes and media exaggerations and distortions that overlook the diversity of African American family life. No more is there one black family type than there is one white family type.

Nonetheless, this myth draws on some very real trends that affect a segment of the African American community. In the 1960s, social historian Andrew Billingsley (1968) called attention to the division of the African American community along class lines and demonstrated the importance of social class in any analysis of African American families. According to Billingsley, three distinct classes were visible in the African American community: (1) a small upper class that stresses family and is politically conservative; (2) a middle class concerned with family, respectability, and individual and family achievement; and (3) a lower class made up of stable working-class families and both stable and multiproblem poor families. It is generally from the multiproblem poor families within the lower class (which some contemporary sociologists refer to as an "underclass") that stereotypes and generalizations are made about all African American families.

This segment of African American families experiences a pattern of chronic and persistent poverty. Some of the most visible manifestations of this pattern are high levels of unemployment, welfare dependency, low marriage rates, high rates of teenage pregnancy, mother-focused families composed of a mother and her dependent children, an increasing number of crack-addicted babies, and an escalating level of violence. For example, although nonmarital childbearing is no longer unusual among most groups in the United States, for African Americans in general it has become majority behavior. At the close of the twentieth century, 69 percent of African American babies were born to unmarried mothers (U.S. Census Bureau, 2000), a trend especially evident among lower-income and less educated African Americans. In addition, there has been a major increase in the number of African American one-parent families. Although these trends have occurred among white families as well, their impact on black families has been much more substantial, resulting in increasingly different marital and family experiences for these two groups (Taylor, 1998).

Based on middle-class standards, these trends seem to support the myth of an unstable, disorganized family structure in part of the African American community. And, indeed, among some individuals and families, long-term and concentrated poverty and despair, racism, social contempt, police brutality, and political and governmental neglect have taken their toll and are often manifested in the behaviors just described. To generalize these behaviors to the entire African American community, however, is inaccurate and misleading. Moreover, to attribute these behaviors, when they do occur, to a deteriorating, immoral family lifestyle and a lack of middle-class family values ignores historical, social, and political factors, such as a history of servitude, legal discrimination, enforced segregation and exclusion, **institutional racism**—the systematic discrimination against a racial group by the institutions within society—and structural shifts in the economy and related trends that have created new and deeper disparities in the structure and quality of family life between blacks and whites in this society. In addition, such claims serve to perpetuate the myth that one particular family arrangement is a workable model for all families in modern society.

As it happens, most of the common knowledge whites and others have about the nature of African American families is not true. Many of the current "facts" they cite are half-truths that seriously impede responsible discussion of the dilemmas facing African American families today. Without much doubt, not only the black underclass but also many black families across class differ from the white middle-class ideal primarily because their circumstances are and have been different. Nevertheless, these differences have often been exaggerated, and where they occur among African American families they frequently have been sources of strength rather than weakness. According to Coontz, many of the variations found in African American families have produced healthy individuals with a strong group consciousness that has helped them cope with widespread racism, violence, and poverty and often to rise above these limitations. (These variations are examined in later chapters of this text.) This view is supported, in part, by statistics that show that an increasing number of African Americans are graduating from high school, attending college, and experiencing some advances in economic and material well-being. Many sociologists today take the position that there is no one family type; African American families, like other families, should be viewed as unique and essential subcultural family forms and not simply as deviant departures from white middle-class family forms.

Myth 5: The Idealized Nuclear Family of the 1950s

During the 1950s, millions of Americans came to accept an image of the family as a middle-class institution consisting of a wise father who worked outside the home; a mother whose major responsibility was to take care of her husband, children, and home; and children who were well behaved and obedient. This image, depicted in a number of 1950s family sitcoms, such as "Leave It to Beaver," "Father Knows Best," "The Donna Reed Show," and "The Adventures of Ozzie and Harriet," is said to represent the epitome of traditional family structure and values. Many critics today see the movement away from this model as evidence of the decline in the viability of the family, as well as a source of many family problems.

It is true that, compared with today, the 1950s were characterized by younger ages at marriage, higher birth rates, and lower divorce and premarital pregnancy rates. To present the 1950s as representing "typical" or "normal" family patterns, however, is misleading. Indeed, the divorce rates have increased since the 1950s, but this trend started in the nineteenth century, with more marital breakups in each succeeding generation. Today's trends of low marriage, high divorce, and low fertility are actually consistent with long-term historical trends in marriage and family life. Recent changes in marriage and family life are considered deviant only because the marriage rates for the postwar generation represented an all-time high for the United States. This generation married young, moved to the suburbs, and had three or more children. The fact is that this pattern was deviant in that it departed significantly from earlier twentieth-century trends in marriage and family life. According to some, if the 1940s and 1950s had not happened, marriage and family life today would appear normal (Skolnick and Skolnick, 1999). Although some people worry that young people today are delaying marriage to unusually late ages, Figure 1.1 shows that the median age at first marriage in 2000, 25.1 for women and 26.8 for men, the highest levels since these data were first recorded in 1890, more closely approximates the 1890 average than it does the 1950s' average of 20.3 for women and 22.8 for men. The earlier age at marriage in the 1950s was a reaction to the hardships and sacrifices brought about by the depression and World War II. Thus, marriage and family life became synonymous with the "good life." Furthermore, images of the good life were now broadcast into living rooms across the country via the powerful new medium of television. Even then, however, there were signs that all was not well. Public opinion polls taken during the 1950s suggested that approximately 20 percent of all couples considered themselves unhappy in marriage, and another 20 percent reported only "medium happiness" (quoted in Mintz and Kellogg, 1988:194).

Connected to the myth of the idealized nuclear family is the myth that families have been essentially the same over the centuries, until recently when they began to disintegrate. The fact is that families have never been static, they have always changed: When the world around them changes, families change in response. The idea of the traditional family of old is itself relative. According to John Gillis (1999), we are in the

Figure 1.1

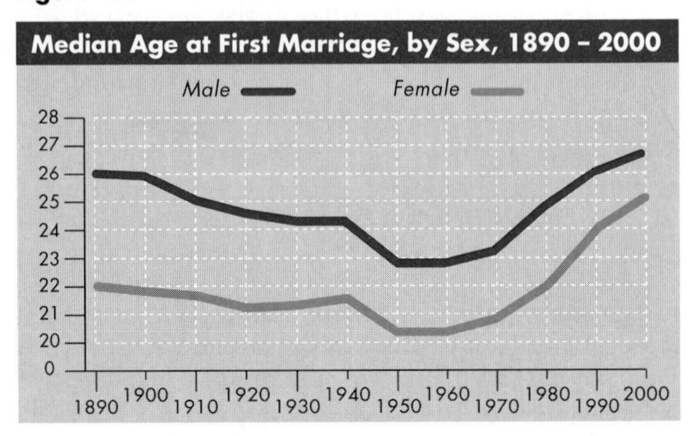

Source: Adapted from Arlene F. Saluter, 1995, "Marital Status and Living Arrangements: March 1994," U.S. Census Bureau, *Current Population Reports*, Series P-20-484 (Washington, DC: U.S. Government Printing Office): A3, Table A-2; and J. Fields and L. M. Casper, 2001, "America's Families and Living Arrangements: March 2000," U.S. Census Bureau, *Current Population Reports*, Series P-20-537 (Washington, DC: U.S. Government Printing Office): 9.

Television portrayals of nuclear families have changed dramatically from the idealized 1950s images of *Father Knows Best* and *Ozzie and Harriet* to the more outrageous behaviors of the members of the Simpson family and the trials and tribulations of the Sopranos, headed by mob boss Tony Soprano.

habit of updating our notion of the traditional family so that the location of the golden age of the family constantly changes. For example, for the Victorians, the traditional family was rooted in a time period prior to industrialization and urbanization; for those who came of age during World War I, the traditional family was associated with the Victorians themselves. Although there is growing acceptance of diverse family forms, many people today still think of the 1950s and 1960s as the epitome of traditional marriage and family life.

This discussion of mythical versus real families underscores the fact that not all families are the same; there is not now and never has been a single model of the family. Families and their experiences are indeed different; however, difference does not connote better or worse. The experiences of a poor family are certainly not the same as those of a rich family; the experiences of a young family with young children are little like those of either a child-free family or an older family whose children have "left the nest." Even within families the experiences of older members are different from those of younger members, and the experiences of females and males are different. Certainly the experiences of Latina/o, Native American, Asian American, and black families are not the same as those of white families, regardless of class. Nor are lesbian and gay family experiences the same as heterosexual family experiences. Families are products of their historical context, and at any given historical period families occupy different territories and have varied experiences, given the differential influence of the society's race, class, and gender systems.

FAMILIES IN EARLY AMERICA

When the first English and Dutch settlers arrived on the eastern seaboard of North America in the early seventeenth century, there were already between 1 and 2 million people living here, composing more than 240 distinct groups, each with its own history, culture, family, and patterns of **kinship**—people who are related by blood, marriage, or adoption, or who consider one another family (Mintz and Kellogg, 1988). By the end of that century, a variety of immigrants, primarily from Scotland, Ireland, Germany, and France, had arrived in North America. In addition, large numbers of Africans were forcibly brought to the colonies and sold into slavery. Thus, from the very beginning, the United States was economically, racially, ethnically, religiously, and familially diverse. Consequently, any attempt to describe families of the past must take this diversity into account. One chapter in a textbook cannot possibly convey how all these different groups struggled to adapt to a new and often hostile environment and at the same time to create and maintain a stable family structure. Thus, our depiction of family life in the seventeenth and eighteenth centuries is limited to three groups: white colonial families, African American families, and Native American families. A great deal of African American family history was connected with slavery. Because slavery ended only after the Civil War, our discussion of African American families contains references to the nineteenth century as well.

Colonial Families

Our knowledge of family life among the first immigrants to this country comes primarily from three sources: (1) surviving physical objects, such as furniture, tools, and utensils; (2) personal diaries, letters, sermons, literary works, and wills, which contain references to the relationships that existed among different family and community members; and (3) census data and other public records. Given that these materials represent only fragmentary remains of that period, our understanding of family life in colonial America is somewhat impressionistic. We do know, however, that there was considerable variation in family organization among the colonists, reflecting the differences in cultural backgrounds that they brought with them, as well as differences in the local conditions they encountered in the areas in which they settled. Limitations of space prevent a full discussion of this diversity; hence, our discussion focuses primarily on family life in the northern colonies and incorporates some examples from the other colonies.

HOUSEHOLD COMPOSITION A popular belief about colonial America is that most people lived in extended families. Research, however, shows that the opposite was true. Early colonial families, with few exceptions, were nuclear families, consisting of wife, husband, and children (Greven, 1970; Laslett, 1971). Immediately after marriage, the couple was expected to establish their own household. About the only exception to this pattern was when elderly parents were unable to care for themselves and, out of necessity, had to live with their adult children. Nevertheless, colonial families differed in at least three major respects from the modern nuclear family. First, non-kin, such as orphans, apprentices, hired laborers, unmarried individuals, and children from other families, could and often did join colonial households. These "servants," as they were referred to, lived and worked as regular members of the household. Additionally, at times local authorities would place criminals and poor people with families. These people were to provide service to the household in return for care and rehabilitation.

Second, the family formed the basic economic unit of colonial society. Women, men, and children combined their labor to meet the subsistence needs of the family. Until approximately the middle of the eighteenth century, relatively little was produced to sell. Calling this pattern the "family-based economy," social historians Louise Tilly and Joan Scott (1978:12) observed, "Production and family life were inseparably intertwined, and the household was the center around which resources, labor, and consumption were balanced."[2] Hence, as the basic economic unit of life, the family was synonymous with whoever lived and worked within the household, rather than being strictly defined by blood and marital ties.

Finally, unlike today, the functions of the colonial family and the larger community were deeply intertwined. In his book *A Little Commonwealth*, historian John Demos (1970:183–84) describes how the family in Plymouth colony functioned as a business, a school, a vocational institute, a church, a house of corrections, and at times a hospital, an orphanage, and a poorhouse. Although the family was involved in these tasks, public authorities determined how the tasks were to be met. Social life was highly regulated. Individuals were told where to live, how to dress, what strangers to take in and for how long. Unlike today, there was little privacy within or among households. Sexual matters, for example, were discussed openly. Because much of daily living took place in common rooms, children were not sheltered from knowledge of sexual matters. Public documents from that period show that neighbors often reported violations of sexual norms and that punishment for such violations was carried out in public. For example, a woman could be flogged if she refused to name the father of a child born out of wedlock. If marriage followed a premarital pregnancy, however, little concern was expressed. This was not uncommon, as is evidenced by the fact that in seventeenth-century Maryland, one-third of the immigrant women whose marriages are recorded were pregnant before the ceremonies (cited in Coontz, 1988:89).

MARITAL ROLES The colonial family was a patriarchy. Fathers were regarded as the head of the family, and they exercised authority over wives, children, and servants. Men represented their households in the public sphere and held positions of leadership in the community. However, not all fathers were in this position. Those without property themselves came under the rule of the propertied class. The ownership of property gave men considerable power in their families, and their decisions to distribute property to their offspring had a profound effect on their children's choice of careers and on when and whom their children married. This practice often kept children economically dependent on their parents for much of their adult lives.

Legally, a father had the right to determine who could court his daughters, and it was up to him to give or withhold consent from a child's marriage. His decision was based largely on whether the marriage would maintain or enhance the economic and political status of the family. Although romantic love may have existed between courting couples, marriage was viewed first and foremost as an economic arrangement, with the assumption that affection would develop after marriage (Mintz and Kellogg, 1988). Evidence of this attitude and its subsequent change comes from an examination of divorce records. It was only after 1770 that divorce records named loss of affection as a reason for terminating the marriage.

Under these patriarchal arrangements, wives were expected to be submissive and obedient to their husbands. Although unmarried women had the right to own property, enter into contracts, and represent themselves in court, after marriage the English concept of *coverture* was evoked, whereby the wife's legal identity was subsumed in that of her husband, giving him the authority to make decisions for her. This doctrine was often ignored in practice, however. Records show that some colonial women, especially widows, entered into contracts and operated stores; ran taverns; and worked as millers, tanners, blacksmiths, silversmiths, shoemakers, and printers—occupations usually held by men.

Although both wives and husbands contributed their skills and resources to the household, the actual division of labor was based on sex. For the most part husbands did the planting, harvesting, bookkeeping, and supervisory tasks. Wives

[2]This pattern was not unique to Europe and colonial America. The family-based economy can still be found in rural areas around the world, especially in developing countries.

were responsible for cooking, sewing, milking, cleaning, and gardening. In addition, they produced many products for home consumption and traded surplus goods with other families. A wife sometimes served as a "deputy husband," assuming her husband's responsibilities when he was away on business or military duty. Thus, women often performed traditional male tasks. Men, however, only infrequently reciprocated by performing women's domestic chores (Riley, 1987:13). Today, our culture views child rearing as predominantly women's work. Yet, according to historian Carl Degler (1980), child rearing in the colonial period was mainly the task of fathers, who were responsible for transmitting religious values and for instilling discipline in their offspring. As we shall see, economic changes in the nineteenth century caused a major shift in family roles.

CHILDHOOD The social experiences of colonial children differed in several major ways from those of children today. First, survival to adulthood was less likely. Death rates among children were higher than among other age groups. In the more prosperous and healthier communities in seventeenth-century New England, one out of ten children died in infancy; in other communities, the rate was one out of three (Mintz and Kellogg, 1988:14). Initial interpretations of these high death rates suggested that parents protected themselves emotionally by developing an indifference toward young children. Historical documents belie this viewpoint, however, revealing the immense sorrow parents experienced at the death of a child.

Second, child rearing did not occupy the same place it does today. For example, well-to-do families often employed wet nurses to breast-feed and care for infants so that mothers could concentrate their attention on household duties. Children were not viewed as "innocent beings"; rather, they were seen as possessing original sin and stubborn willfulness. Thus, child-rearing practices were designed to break down a child's willful nature. Religious instruction, threats, and even physical beatings were frequently used to discipline wayward children. There were even "stubborn child" laws in early New England that prescribed the death penalty for persistent disobedience to parents. Although there is no record that such sanctions were ever invoked, their very existence symbolized society's concern for domestic tranquility (Powers, 1966).

Third, childhood itself was quite short. Around the age of 6 or 7, both girls and boys assumed productive roles. Girls were taught domestic skills, such as sewing, spinning, and caring for domestic animals. Like their mothers, they also assisted their fathers in the fields or in the shops. Young boys worked small looms, weeded fields, and were taught a craft. Finally, around the age of 14, many colonial children from all social classes were "put out" to other families to learn a trade, to work as servants, or to receive the proper discipline their natural parents could not be expected to deliver (Mintz and Kellogg, 1988).

There was, however, at least one aspect of colonial childhood that is similar to today. Many children in colonial families spent part of their life in a single-parent family. For example, parental death rates in late–seventeenth-century Virginia were so high that most children were reared by just one parent, and more than one-third lost both parents (Darrett and Rutman, 1979:153). Thus, many colonial children, like millions of children today, lived part of their lives in stepfamilies, a topic we discuss in detail in Chapter 13.

Thus far, the family patterns we have been discussing applied primarily to the white settlers. People of color had very different experiences. In the process of adapting to their environment, they created some distinct patterns of family life.

African American Families under Slavery

Andrew Billingsley (1968) points out three important elements that distinguish the experience of African Americans from that of other groups in the United States.

1. Unlike most of their colonial contemporaries, African Americans came to America from Africa and not from Europe.
2. They were uprooted from their cultural and family moorings and brought to the United States as slaves.
3. From the beginning and continuing even today, they were systematically excluded from participation in the major institutions of U.S. society.

Numerous writings have traced the problems of modern African American families to the experience of slavery. Clearly, slavery had a devastating effect on families. The day-to-day stresses of living as a slave and many specific practices of slaveholders undermined the authority and stability of many of these families. Slaveholders often prohibited legal marriages among slaves, sold family members away from one another, and sexually exploited African American women. Nonetheless, a growing body of research shows that many slaves established strong marital and family arrangements that endured for long periods of time, even under conditions of separation. Family arrangements followed fairly distinct patterns, beginning with courtship and often marriage, followed by childbearing and child rearing.

SLAVE MARRIAGES Although southern laws prohibited slaves from contracting legal marriages, some slaveholders granted permission for their slaves to marry, and a few even provided separate living quarters or household goods for the new couple. For many slaves the solemnity of the occasion was marked by a religious ceremony at which either a black or white minister officiated. Between 1841 and 1860, half of the marriages in South Carolina's Episcopal churches were between slaves (Blassingame, 1979:166). Other marriage rituals were used as well, the most common of which involved the couple's jumping over a broomstick. A former Alabama slave, Penny Anderson, described the ceremony this way: "After supper dey puts de broom on de floor and de couple takes de hands and steps over de broom, den dey am out to

Descendants of third president Thomas Jefferson and descendants of his slave, Sally Hemings, pose for a group shot at his plantation in 1999 for the first time in 170 years during the Monticello Association's annual meeting in Charlottesville, VA.

bed" (quoted in Gutman, 1976:275). These rituals, however, did not guarantee that a couple could live together. Slave spouses often had different owners and lived on different plantations; thus, they could see each other only when their masters permitted visits or when, risking severe punishment, they went off on their own.

Although many slave marriages were stable, slave couples lived under the constant fear of forced separation. The reality of these fears was expressed in some of the vows these couples took, "Until death or distance do you part" (quoted in Finkelman, 1989:xii). This fear became a reality for many slave couples, as evidenced by numerous accounts of ex-slaves who referred to earlier marriages terminated by sale to new owners. Some slaves, however, fought back against this separation. Historian Eugene Genovese (1974) found considerable evidence that when couples were separated by their masters, they often ran away in an attempt to be together. Furthermore, one of the first things African Americans did after the Civil War was to seek out lost relatives on other plantations and to legalize marriages made unofficially under slavery.

According to Genovese, slave communities exhibited a high degree of sexual equality. This pattern has been linked to the slaves' African heritage and to the similar work roles they had on the plantations, where women worked alongside men in the fields and in the master's house. Although slave parents did not have legal authority over their own children, there is considerable evidence to show that both women and men had ongoing involvement with their families and that both sexes participated in child rearing.

Childhood Despite the abuses of slavery, African Americans succeeded in forming and maintaining families. Nineteenth-century census data show that both before and after slavery, most African Americans lived in two-parent households. According to plantation records examined by social historian Herbert Gutman (1976), slave women frequently bore their first child in their late teens. Because of harsh living conditions, more than one-third of the babies born to slave women died before the age of 10, a rate double that for white infants (Mintz and Kellogg, 1988:72, 73). As soon as they were able, slave children worked in the barnyards or in the master's house and soon followed their parents into the fields. Between the ages of 7 and 10, children had to leave their parents' cabin and move into quarters occupied by other unmarried youth.

Slave parents had to overcome many obstacles to hold their families together. Many succeeded in asserting some small measure of independence by securing additional food for their families by hunting small game and cultivating small gardens. Like other parents, they instructed their children in religious and cultural beliefs and trained them in various crafts. They also developed networks of extended kin that helped family members survive the material privations and harsh treatment under slavery and the chaotic economic conditions that followed them into freedom after the Civil War.

Extended Kinship Patterns According to Gutman (1976), strong kinship feelings among slaves are evident from the naming practices of slave families. Table 1.1 shows that slave parents frequently named their children after fathers, grandparents, recently deceased relatives, and other kin. Gutman believed that this kin network was especially important in helping slaves adapt to family breakup. When children were sold to neighboring plantations, any blood relative living there took over parental functions. In the absence of such relatives, strangers assumed these responsibilities. Slave children were taught to call all adult slaves "aunt" and "uncle" and younger slaves "sister" and "brother," practices that created a sense of mutual obligation and responsibility among the broader slave population. Later, these naming practices enabled scholars to trace descendants of slave families.

Free African American Families

Prior to the Civil War, there were approximately 250,000 free African Americans in the United States. About 150,000 lived in the South, and the remaining 100,000 lived in the North (Mintz and Kellogg, 1988). Many slaves freed themselves by running away; others were freed by slaveholders after the American Revolution. A few managed to buy their own freedom. Freedom, however, did not mean full integration into the larger society. In many communities, both in the North and South, free African Americans were not allowed to vote, hold public meetings, purchase liquor, marry whites, or attend white churches and schools. Although some men were able to earn a livelihood as carpenters, shoemakers, tailors, and millwrights, most lived in conditions of extreme poverty (Berlin, 1974).

Most free African American families were structured around two-parent households. Nevertheless, as today, inadequate family income, high levels of unemployment, illness, and early death put considerable strain on these families. One study found, for example, that in Philadelphia during the nineteenth century, between one-fourth and one-third of the city's African Americans lived in female-headed households, a figure two to three times higher than that for other groups in the city. This differential is explained by two factors. First, slaveholders tended to free women rather than men. Employment opportunities were better for women than men in urban areas, as whites sought black women to be domestic servants, cooks, nurses, and seamstresses. Many fathers remained slaves and could not migrate with their families. Consequently, free African American women outnumbered men in urban areas. Second, then as now, life expectancy was lower for African Americans, especially for men, leaving many women widowed by their 40s. When property holdings are held constant, however, the higher incidence of one-parent families among African Americans largely disappears, revealing the significant impact of economic factors on family stability (Mintz and Kellogg, 1988:78–79).

Table 1.1

Naming Practices among the Stirling Plantation Slaves, West Feliciana Parish, Louisiana, 1808–1865

Date of Birth	Name of Newborn	Name of Parents	Relation of Newborn to Person with Same Name
1808	Leven	Big Judy–Leven	Father
1833	Julius	Dolly–Sidney	Father's father
1836	Ginny	Clarice–John	Mother's mother
1837	Hannah	Liddy–Luke	Mother's sister
1839	Barika	Nelly	Mother's husband (stepfather)
1846	Antoinette	Henrietta	Mother's sister's son (dead)
1846	Hester	Harriet–Sam	Father's sister
1853	Monday	Sophy–Sampson	Father's brother
1865	Duncan	Antoinette–Primus	Dead sibling

Source: Adapted from Herbert G. Gutman, 1976, *The Black Family in Slavery and Freedom, 1750–1925* (New York: Vintage Books): 119–21.

Slavery's Hidden Legacy: Racial Mixing

Rumors about a sexual liaison between Thomas Jefferson, the third president of the United States, and his young slave, Sally Hemings, circulated during his lifetime but were not responded to by Jefferson. Hemings, who was born in 1772 or 1773, was the illegitimate half-sister of Jefferson's wife Martha—the offspring of a relationship between Martha's father, John Wayles, and a slave, Elizabeth Hemings. For almost two centuries, most white historians debunked the notion of Jefferson's fathering a child with a slave, citing his negative views on racial mixing and his moral stature. As a result of their own cultural biases, some of these historians ignored corroborating evidence and discredited the strong oral tradition attesting to the relationship that was passed down through Hemings's descendants. However, recent DNA tests performed on the descendants of the families of Thomas Jefferson and Sally Hemings have illuminated a hidden legacy of slavery—the common biological heritage of many whites and African Americans. These test results, reported in the prestigious journal *Nature* (1998), offer compelling new evidence that Jefferson fathered at least one of Hemings's children, her last son, known as Eston Hemings Jefferson. Eston, who was said to have borne a striking resemblance to Thomas Jefferson, was freed by Jefferson in his will and moved first to Ohio, where he worked as a professional musician, and then to Madison, Wisconsin, where he lived his life as a member of the white community. Three other surviving Hemings children were allowed to leave the plantation, and at least two of them, like Eston, are believed to have blended into white society, leaving behind numerous descendants who even today are unlikely to suspect that their ancestry is either African or presidential (Murray and Duffy, 1998).

However, as more historians trace African American and white families across time, the more likely are we to discover common biological roots. For example, Edward Ball (1998/1999), a white man remembering the childhood stories his father told him of his rice planter ancestors in South Carolina, set out in search of his family history. Through his painstaking research of family and community records across the country, he was able to track down many descendants of Ball slaves and coax them into telling the oral traditions of their families, which revealed much about the lives of blacks and whites of earlier generations. After the publication of his *Slaves in the Family*, he was contacted by other Ball slave descendants and discovered that he, too, shared common ancestry with them.

What the DNA tests can't answer, and what is frequently missing from narratives of biological mixing, is the nature of the intimate relationship between the races. It was certainly true that slaveholders legally could, and frequently did, sexually assault and rape their slaves. However, evidence in the Jefferson–Hemings case points more in the direction of a caring and loving relationship than an openly abusive or exploitive one. That members of different racial and ethnic groups can and do have happy and successful marital relationships can be seen by examining current interracial marriages, a subject we will discuss in more detail in Chapter 8.

Although education and economic development have provided a middle-class lifestyle for some Native Americans, many others continue to experience high levels of poverty and unemployment.

Native American Families

A review of the literature on family life among early Native American peoples reveals that no one description adequately covers all Native American families. Prior to European settlement of North America, Native American peoples were widely dispersed geographically. As a result, each group developed an economic system, a style of housing, and a kinship system that fit the demands of its particular environment. Even those groups living in the same region of the country were likely to develop different organizational patterns (Mintz and Kellogg, 1988). For example, there were two basic language groups among the Woodland groups living in the Northeast: the Algonquin and the Iroquois. The social and economic unit of the Algonquins was a dome-shaped structure called a *wigwam*, usually occupied by one or two families. In contrast, the basic social unit of the Iroquois was the *longhouse*, a large, rectangular structure containing about ten families.

Among groups living in the Southeast, social life centered around the extended family. After marriage, the new husband went to live in his wife's family's household. For many tribes living in what is now California, however, that pattern was reversed, and the wife moved in with her husband's family after marriage. The basic economic unit for the Eskimos who inhabited the Arctic regions was either a family composed simply of wife, husband, and children or a household containing two such families.

Rules of Marriage and Descent Native American women married early, many between the ages of 12 and 15. Men were usually several years older than women when they married. There was considerable variation in mate selection among different groups. Some permitted free choice, whereas others practiced arranged marriages. The rules of marriage also varied from one group to another. Although most Native American peoples practiced monogamy, some were polygamous. Unhappy marriages were easily dissolved in some groups, with either spouse able to divorce the other. Among some peoples, special practices governed widowhood. In the *sororate*, a widower married a sister of his deceased wife; in the *levirate*, a widow married one of her dead husband's brothers.

Rules of descent also varied among Native American societies. Some societies, like that of the Cheyenne, were **patrilineal,** whereby kinship or family lineage (descent) and inheritance come through the father and his blood relatives. Others, like that of the Pueblos, were **matrilineal,** whereby kinship or family lineage (descent) and inheritance come through the mother and her blood relatives. Historical records indicate that Native American families were generally small. Infant and child mortality were high. Additionally, mothers nursed their children for two or more years and refrained from sexual intercourse until the child was weaned. In contrast to early European families, Native American parents rarely used physical punishment to discipline their children. Instead, they relied on praise, ridicule, and public rewards to instill desired behavior. Among some groups, child care was in the hands of mothers; among others, fathers and maternal uncles played a more significant role. From early on, children worked alongside their parents and other adults to learn the skills that would be required of them as adults.

Consequences of European Contact One of the first consequences of contact with Europeans was a sharp increase in mortality rates. Native Americans lacked immunity to the diseases carried by white settlers. Consequently, thousands died from influenza, measles, smallpox, and typhoid fever. And although some of the early contact between the two groups was friendly and characterized by mutual exchanges of goods and services, the clash of cultural differences soon dominated intergroup contacts. Europeans found it difficult to understand and even harder to appreciate the diverse patterns of family life that existed among Native Americans. Ethnocentrism, the belief that one's culture is superior to others, led the Europeans to denigrate the lifestyles of Native Americans and to treat them as subhuman. This inability and unwillingness to accept Native American culture as valid, combined with the introduction of firearms and alcohol and the ever-increasing competition for land, led to violent clashes between the two groups. In the end, many Native Americans were displaced from their homelands and forced onto reservations, where many of their cultural values and practices were systematically undermined. Other Native Americans "disappeared" into the larger population, publicly not acknowledging their ancestry. This changed somewhat in 1990, when large numbers of young adult Native Americans living in large cities suddenly appeared in the census count. This development has been attributed to the popularity of movies like *Dances with Wolves* that portrayed Native Americans in a positive light, as well as the ongoing struggle of many tribes to revitalize their culture and build a strong economic base for their members.

FAMILIES IN THE NINETEENTH CENTURY

Major changes occurred in the United States at the beginning of the nineteenth century, radically transforming family life. New technology brought about the creation of the factory system, which required a concentrated supply of labor away from the home. Wage labor took the place of working private family farms or shops as the main means of earning a living. The patriarchal preindustrial household no longer functioned as a unit of economic production. Consequently, it grew smaller in size as apprentices and other live-in laborers gradually left to find work in the new factories. Over time the nuclear family of only parents and children became the new family form, a form that has lasted well into the twentieth century. Work and family became separated, leading to the development of a division of family labor that divided the sexes and the generations from each other in new and far-reaching ways. These changes did not affect all families in the same way, however. There were significant variations across race and class.

Emergence of the Good Provider Role

In the opening stages of industrialization, women and children worked in the factories. After that period, however, men became the predominant workers in the factories, mines, and businesses of the nation. According to sociologist Jessie Bernard (1984), a specialized male role known as the *good provider* role emerged around 1830. The essence of this role was that a man's major contribution to his family is economic, that is, as primary (and often sole) wage earner. Masculinity became identified with being a successful breadwinner (Demos, 1974). To be a success in the breadwinning role men had to concentrate their energies on work, and other roles, such as husband, father, and community member, became less important. Consequently, husbands and fathers were often emotionally as well as physically distant from their families. More and more, a man's status and, therefore, that of his family depended on his occupation. A man's success was measured by whether he could afford to keep his wife and children out of the labor force.

The Cult of Domesticity

The movement of production out of the household affected the roles of women, too. Although from the beginning of U.S. history women were encouraged to think of themselves primarily in a domestic role, as industrialization advanced this ideology became even more prevalent. Now women were expected to stay at home, have children, and be the moral guardians of the family. This *cult of domesticity*, or as historian Barbara Welter (1978) called it, the "cult of true womanhood," was the counterpart to the good provider role. If men were to spend long hours working away from home, then women would offer men emotional support, provide for their daily needs, raise the children, and, in short, create for men a "haven in a heartless world" (Lasch, 1977). Aspects of this domestic role were oppressive and limiting for women, who by and large were excluded from most institutional life outside the family.

Changing Views of Childhood

The economic transformation that took place in the early nineteenth century altered not only marital roles but also children's roles. Childhood came to be seen as a distinct period, a time of innocence and play without much responsibility. Children no longer had to begin productive work at an early age. Instead, they became economic dependents. During this time, children's birthdays became occasions to celebrate, and the first specialty toy stores for children were opened. For the first time, books written especially for children were published, and other books were targeted for mothers to give them guidance about child rearing.

The Impact of Class and Ethnicity

The family lifestyle just described applied primarily to white middle- and upper-class families, in which the father made a "family wage" that enabled him to support his entire family. In contrast, large numbers of African American, immigrant, and native-born white working-class men found it impossible to support their families on their income alone. Thus, the working-class family did not embrace the ideal of privacy and separate spheres of a nuclear unit to the same degree that the middle class did. Working-class family boundaries were more fluid. Between 1850 and 1880, the number of extended families among the urban, industrial, immigrant working class increased (Coontz, 1988:306).

Additionally, working-class family life, both for blacks and whites, did not develop in isolation from the community. Alleys, stoops, gangways, and streets functioned as common areas where adults could socialize, exchange information, and observe their children at play. Contrary to many stereotypes of working-class families, there was no simple or rigid gender differentiation in these activities. In fact, "in the 1880s, when the first modern investigations of working-class family life were undertaken by the Massachusetts Bureau of Labor Statistics, one of the findings that most shocked and dismayed the middle-class male investigators was that working-class men would cook, clean, and care for the children while their wives were at work and they were not" (quoted in Coontz, 1988:306).

Immigration and Family Life

Many working-class families in the nineteenth century were immigrants. Between 1830 and 1930, over 30 million immigrants left their homes to come to the United States. The first wave of immigrants was predominantly from Northern and Western Europe—England, Germany, Ireland, and Scandinavia. Beginning in the early 1880s, immigration patterns shifted to Southern and Eastern Europe—Italy, Greece, Austria, Hungary, and Russia. Historians refer to the Slavs, Italians, Greeks, and Eastern European Jews who came to the United States at this time as the "new" immigrants. Frequently, the decision to emigrate followed economic or political upheavals. At the same time, immigrants were attracted to the United States by the promise of land and jobs.

The manner of emigration varied. Some immigrants, especially the Italians, Poles, and Slavs, came without families, planning to return home after making their fortunes. A Polish folk song conveys the enormity of disruption such families experienced when the father returned after several years: "There my wife was waiting for me. And my children did not know me. For they fled from me, a stranger. My dear children I'm your papa; three long years I have not seen you" (quoted in Daniels, 1990:219). Other unaccompanied immigrants hoped to earn enough to send for their families. Still others came with their families and planned to settle permanently in the United States. To help ease their problems of adjustment, these new arrivals, whether alone or with families, sought out family, friends, or neighbors from their native country who were already settled here.

All immigrant groups faced a common set of problems: language barriers, periodic unemployment, difficulties in finding housing, inadequate income, and often hostility from native-born workers, who feared the immigrants would take their jobs and lower the overall wage scale. Each group of immigrants developed distinct family and work patterns in response to these problems. At the same time, immigrants shared many common experiences with native-born members of the working class. Among the most serious of these was the need to have more than one breadwinner so that they could make ends meet.

The Economic Roles of Women and Children

Women and children in the working class contributed to the material support of the family in a variety of ways. Overall, a working-class wife did not work outside the home unless her spouse lost his job or was unable to work because of illness or injury. Maintaining a household was a full-time job. Working-class wives grew some of their own food, baked bread, carried water and wood for cooking and heating, managed the family finances, and coordinated the schedules of working members. Additionally, wives often supplemented family income by taking in boarders or by doing laundry or sewing in their homes. Working outside the home was more common among first-generation immigrant women whose husbands earned less than their native-born counterparts. The choice of occupation varied among ethnic groups. For example, Polish women chose domestic work over factory work, whereas the opposite pattern was true for Jewish women (Coontz, 1988).

Working-class children did not experience the luxury of a playful childhood. Children were employed in factories by the age of 8. Even though children and women worked as hard and as long as men, often in unhealthful and unsafe environments, they were paid considerably lower wages than men. "Until the end of the nineteenth century, women customarily received about one-third to one-half of the prevailing male wage, a sum seldom sufficient even for a single woman to support herself" (Kessler-Harris, 1981:62).

Ethnic and Racial Family Patterns

Racism and discrimination also made a profound difference in how work and family roles were constructed. For example, although immigrant Chinese males were recruited to build the railroads of America, they were not allowed to build families. The Chinese Exclusion Act of 1882 restricted Chinese immigration and thus restricted Chinese women from joining the men already here. "From 1860 to 1890 the sex ratio fluctuated from 1284 to 2679 Chinese men per 100 Chinese women" (Wong, 1988:235). Faced with this unbalanced sex ratio and prevented by law from marrying whites, single Chinese laborers were destined to remain bachelors if they stayed in the United States. Married Chinese laborers, who were required to leave their families behind, could play the good provider role only minimally by sending money home to China. Sociologist Evelyn Nakano Glenn (1983) called this pattern of maintenance the "split-household family system."

With the end of slavery, black men, like white men, preferred that their wives remain at home. African American men had difficulties finding jobs, however, and the jobs

Sojourner Truth, born a slave in Ulster County, New York, was sold four times before she was 30 years old. She obtained her freedom in 1827. An electrifying public speaker, she became a forceful advocate for human rights for all people.

they did find tended to pay very poorly. Thus, these men could not afford to keep their wives and daughters from working. "In 1900 approximately 41 percent of black women were in the labor force, compared with 16 percent of white women" (quoted in Staples, 1988:307). Sojourner Truth, a former slave, speaking as far back as 1851 at a women's rights convention in Akron, Ohio, eloquently addressed the exclusion of African American women from the "cult of true womanhood."

> That man over there says that women need to be helped into carriages, and lifted over ditches, and to have the best place everywhere. Nobody ever helps me into carriages, or over mud puddles, or gives me any best place! And ain't I a woman? Look at me! Look at my arm! I have ploughed and planted, and gathered into barns and no man could head me! And ain't I a woman? I could work as much as a man—when I could get it—and bear the lash as well! And ain't I a woman? I have borne thirteen children, and seen them most all sold off to slavery, and when I cried out with my mother's grief, none but Jesus hear me! And ain't I a woman? (Quoted in Schneir, 1972:94–95)

Mexican American Families

Similarly, Chicanos (Mexican Americans) were rarely able to exercise the good provider or domestic roles exclusively either. After the Mexican–American War in 1848, the United States annexed a considerable amount of Mexico's territory, an area that encompasses present-day Texas, New Mexico, Arizona, and California. The Mexicans who lived within this new region were granted U.S. citizenship and the right to retain ownership of their land by the Treaty of Guadalupe Hidalgo. Through the unscrupulous practices of some Anglos, however, many of the original Chicano landowners soon lost their land. The erosion of the Chicano agrarian economic base had a profound impact on Mexican American family life.

Family and Kinship One of the most distinctive features of the Chicano family was its emphasis on familism, "a constellation of values which give overriding importance to the family and the needs of the collective as opposed to individual and personal needs" (Bean, Curtis, and Marcum, 1977:760). Although the primary family unit was nuclear and patriarchal in form, there was heavy reliance on extended kinship networks for emotional and economic support. Another centuries-old source of support was the ritual kinship of *compadrazgo*, which linked two families together. Within this system, *madrinas*, or godmothers, and *padrinos*, or godfathers, were carefully chosen from outside the kinship circle to become members of the extended family, participating in all the major events of their godchildren's lives. In effect, they assumed the role of *compadres*, or coparents, providing discipline, companionship for both parents and godchildren, emotional support, and, when needed, financial aid (Griswold del Castillo, 1984).

Marital Roles Chicano households tended to be large. In part this was due to a high fertility rate, but households also expanded in response to economic privation as kin and unrelated individuals, especially children, were taken in by other families. Households practiced a fairly rigid division of labor based on gender. Wives were expected to stay home and take responsibility for domestic chores and child rearing. They were also expected to be the carriers of cultural traditions and to organize celebrations of important rituals, such as baptisms, weddings, saints' days, and funerals.

In contrast, men were expected to protect and control their families and to perform productive work outside the household. This traditional male role is sometimes referred to as *machismo*. Although some writers have called attention to the negative aspects of this role, such as male infidelity and oppression of women (Madsen, 1964), most contemporary social scientists believe that these aspects have been exaggerated. More recent research tends to focus on what has been called a "genuine machismo," characterized by bravery, courage, and generosity (Mirande, 1985).

Signs of Change White settlers bought up large tracts of land in the Southwest and instituted commercial agricultural production. The displaced Chicanos became a source of cheap labor. Much of this work was seasonal, and men experienced periodic unemployment. At times, men migrated in search of jobs in the mines or on the railroads. As a result, their wives became heads of families, sometimes on a permanent basis as a result of prolonged separation, divorce, or, more frequently, desertion. Even when men worked full-time, their wages were often insufficient to support their families. Consequently, wives and mothers were drawn into the labor force, most frequently in low-paying domestic or agriculture-related work, such as canning and packing-house work. Kinship structures were weakened as entire families left the area to find work. With the entrance of wives into the labor force and the frequent migration of families outside their familiar cultural area, the foundation of the patriarchal family structure began to erode. Working wives demanded more power in decision making, and by the twenty-first century a new balance in gender relations was already being observed. Like other families before them, the Chicano family was realigning itself.

FAMILIES IN THE TWENTIETH CENTURY

Although applicable only to certain groups, these idealized images of men as providers and women as homemakers continued to influence popular thought about the family well into the twentieth century. However, economic and political changes were already at work to undermine these roles. Technological innovations led to the mass production of goods and to the development of large-scale corporations. These developments affected almost every aspect of social relationships.

In this new work environment, the demand for child labor declined, and schools assumed more of the responsibility for the socialization of children. Young working-class women increasingly left domestic service for better opportunities in industry and in the expanding clerical fields. As a result, social contacts increasingly took place outside the family as women and men worked in proximity to each other. New products, such as movies, amusement parks, and the automobile, changed family recreation patterns. Young adults dated without chaperons and placed more emphasis on personal and sexual attractiveness. Women, dissatisfied with the restrictions of their domestic role, became activists for women's rights, particularly the right to vote.

The Emergence of the Companionate Family

These changes gradually led to a shift away from the nineteenth-century ideal of the family. In its place emerged the idea of a more personal and companionate model for heterosexual relationships, based on mutual affection, sexual fulfillment, and sharing of domestic tasks and child rearing. Personal happiness came to be viewed as the primary goal of marriage. New symbols, for example, the observance of Mother's Day, were created to celebrate family life. Although economic and social inequalities persisted across groups, this new model of the family took hold, and many of the distinct cultural differences among families began to disappear.

Other changes were helping reshape families. Medical advances reduced the rate of infant mortality so that couples felt less pressure to have large families to ensure the survival of some children. Life expectancy had increased. Thus, families were less likely to be disrupted by the premature death of spouses. In the short span of 40 years, from 1900 to 1940, the chances of a marriage lasting 40 or more years increased from one in three to one in two (Mintz and Kellogg, 1988:131).

There was another side to these changes in family life, however. As more people came to expect companionship and emotional fulfillment in marriage, they also became more willing to terminate an unhappy relationship. In a manner reminiscent of today's controversy over "family values," people in the 1920s and 1930s disagreed over the significance of these changes. Some saw the increase in the divorce rate, the decline in the birth rate, the increase in the number of married-women workers, and the change in sexual behavior as a sign of family disintegration and a breakdown of moral values. Others, however, interpreted these same patterns as signs of greater freedom of choice and as a continuing response to changing economic and social conditions in the larger society.

The Great Depression

In the 1930s, families were rocked by an economic crisis of staggering proportions. Millions of workers throughout the country were unemployed for periods of one to three years or longer. The consequences of joblessness were enormous. Some families became homeless and wandered from city to city in hopes of finding food and shelter; other families were forced to share living quarters. Young adults delayed marriage, couples postponed having children, and the number of desertions increased. The depression affected all members of the family, but in particular it undermined the male breadwinner role. This inability to support their families eroded the self-esteem of many fathers. Growing numbers of women became the major source of family income. Although all groups suffered economic hardships during the depression, the elderly, the poor, and those in low-paying, unskilled jobs—predominantly people of color—were hardest hit. Family stability was often a casualty of economic instability.

The severe problems confronting millions of families led to a shift in thinking about the family. No longer could the myth of the self-reliant family be sustained. Clearly, outside support was necessary if families were to weather the economic upheavals. The government responded to the depression by creating a series of social programs, known collectively as the New Deal, to aid distressed workers and their families.

World War II and Its Aftermath

No sooner was the depression over than another major upheaval confronted families. World War II brought about numerous changes, primary among them being the dramatic increase in the marriage rate. Between 1940 and 1946, it is estimated that 3 million more Americans married than would have been expected had rates remained at prewar levels (Bailey, 1978:51). There were many reasons for this upsurge. Some couples had postponed marriage because of the depression and were now financially able to marry. Others feared that if they didn't marry now, it might prove to be too late later on. Some servicemen, fearing death in battle, asked women to marry them "to give them some happiness before going off to fight." Similarly, there was a dramatic increase in the birth rate as many couples decided to have a child right away.

Millions of families were disrupted by wartime migration to find work and by long-term separations for military service. These disruptions resulted in changes in family roles and functioning. With husbands and fathers off to war, wives, mothers, and teenagers went to work in war-related industries. During the war years, 250,000 women worked in plants manufacturing electrical equipment; 100,000 worked in ammunition plants; 300,000 built airplanes; and 150,000 worked as riveters, welders, and crane operators in the nation's shipyards (cited in Mintz and Kellogg, 1988:161). "Rosie the Riveter" became a popular image of the woman factory worker. These changes made conditions difficult for families. Although some preschool children were cared for in government-sponsored day-care centers, many mothers had to find child care on their own. As raw materials were diverted to support the war effort, many families faced shortages in housing and other consumer goods.

Although the majority of families experienced some dislocation during the war years, this experience was most intense for Japanese Americans on the West Coast, who were forcibly relocated from their homes to detention centers in isolated regions of several western states. This massive relocation was inspired by fear, prejudice, and economic jealousy and resulted in depression, deprivation, and often family conflicts among the detainees.

Problems did not end with the cessation of hostilities. Families that had been separated for several years had enormous adjustments to make. Many reunited couples were like strangers to each other. Spouses had grown in different ways. Wives who had assumed both the financial and the economic responsibilities for their families had experienced a sense of independence, self-confidence, and self-sufficiency that was often at odds with their husbands' desire to return to a traditional family arrangement. Postwar housing shortages contributed to family strain as newly reunited couples found themselves living with other relatives in overcrowded conditions. Children who spent some of the war years as "latchkey" kids, taking care of themselves while their mothers worked, resented the new imposition of parental discipline. Many families were unable to survive the tensions and hardships created by the war and its aftermath. Divorce rates soared. In 1940, one marriage in six had ended in divorce; by 1946 the figure stood at one in four (cited in Mintz and Kellogg, 1988:171).

During World War II the image of Rosie the Riveter became popular. However, the ideology of women as men's helpmates had not changed, as evidenced in the language of this poster.

Changing Patterns of Immigration

After World War II, political and economic turmoil around the world led many other groups to leave their homelands in search of a better life. For example, the number of foreign-born people in the United States jumped from 10.3 million in 1950 to 19.7 million in 1990, increasing from nearly 7 percent of the population to about 8 percent. From 1990 to 1999, additional immigration brought the total to 26.4 million, approximately 10 percent of the population (U.S. Census Bureau, 2000). Although historically most immigrants to the United States came from Europe, by 1999 there had been a dramatic shift in the countries of origin of immigrants living in the United States. Now more than half (51 percent) come from Latin America, 27 percent from Asia, but only 16 percent from Europe. This change has resulted in greater racial and ethnic diversity. Each group of immigrants arrived under different social and economic conditions, and each group brought some distinct family and kinship patterns. The frequent discrimination experienced by these newcomers forced many of them to adopt new survival strategies, often necessitating changes in their traditional patterns of family life. Current trends in immigration and differential patterns of fertility continue to change the composition of our population, adding to the rich diversity of family life in the United States.

Lessons from History

What lessons can we draw from this historical review? Five points seem relevant:

1. Although families have changed continuously over time, this change has not been in any single direction.

2. We cannot say with any certainty which changes have been good or bad. Rather, each change brings with it gains and losses. For example, the creation of childhood as a separate and distinct period created many opportunities for children's growth and development, but it also kept children dependent on parents for longer periods of time.

3. Throughout history there has never been a perfect family form that has protected its members from poverty or social disruption, nor has any one structure provided a workable model for how all families might organize their relations in the modern world.

4. Understanding the source of our idealized view of the "traditional" family can lead us to develop a more realistic sense of families, both in the past and in the present. Studying families in the past can help us see how they endured and adapted to historical changes. It also helps us realize that many of the changes we observe in contemporary families and that cause us concern, such as the increasing number of children living in poverty and unstable families, are not a result of changing family values, per se. Rather, they are more frequently reactions to rapid economic and social transformations taking place on an unprecedented scale. To take one example, within our lifetime we have witnessed the rise of a global economy, which has meant greater competition for the United States. Thus, today's families and the communities in which they live confront powerful forces that are redesigning and redistributing jobs, increasing inequality, and shifting population in and out of cities and regions across the country.

5. Given the past, it is likely that additional changes in family life will continue to occur as families continue to adapt to changing economic, social, and political forces. The more we understand these changes and their impact on families, the more likely that we can develop social policies to assist families in adapting to these changes. We will explore these themes throughout the remainder of the text.

CONTEMPORARY PATTERNS IN MARRIAGES AND FAMILIES

Given this review of the history of families in the United States, today's patterns may seem more a continuation of trends rather than a startling new phenomenon. For example, over the last hundred years there has been a steady increase in the number of mothers of small children who are in the labor force (see Chapter 10) and in the percentage of couples who divorce before their children reach adulthood.

In tracking these changes, the U.S. Census Bureau distinguishes between households and families. **Households** are defined as all persons who occupy a housing unit, such as a house, apartment, single room, or other space intended to be living quarters (Ahlburg and DeVita, 1992:5). Figure 1.2 reveals some of the changes in U.S. households between 1970 and 2000. One of the most significant changes is the increase in nonfamily households, which grew from 19 percent of all households in 1970 to 31 percent in 2000. According to the Census Bureau, nonfamily households are made up of individuals living alone; people of the same sex who share living quarters, often for financial reasons; cohabiting couples; adults who delay or forgo marriage; or those who are "between marriages."

Figure 1.2

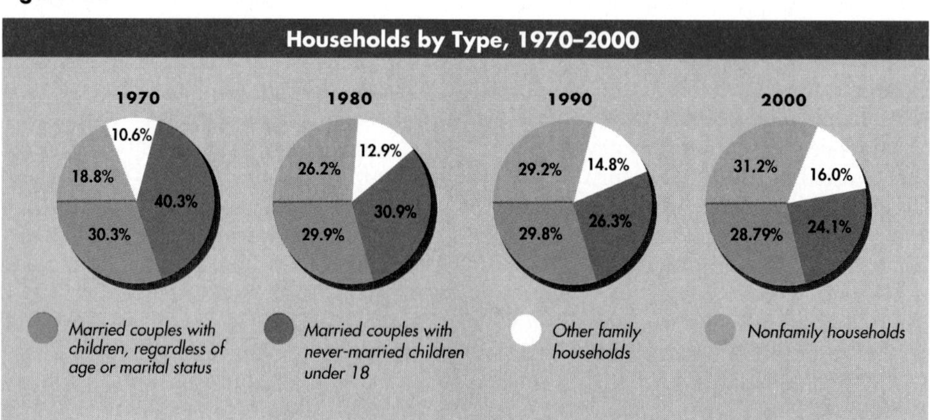

Source: Adapted from J. Fields and L. M. Casper, 2001, "America's Families and Living Arrangements: March 2000," U.S. Census Bureau, *Current Population Reports*, Series P-20-537 (Washington, DC: U.S. Government Printing Office): 3, Figure 1.

Additional information on households and other marriage and family patterns can easily be accessed by visiting the U.S. Census Bureau Web site. As the "Searching the Internet" box shows, households are getting smaller and the proportion of households consisting of one person living alone is increasing. Individuals are delaying marriage for longer periods of time. Twenty-two percent of women aged 30 to 34 have never married, up from 6 percent in 1970. In addition, the number of single parents has increased dramatically. The number of single mothers rose from 3 million to 10 million over the past 30 years, and the number of single fathers climbed from 393,000 to 2 million. Each of these patterns will be examined in detail in subsequent chapters.

LOOKING AHEAD: MARRIAGES AND FAMILIES IN THE FUTURE

As we discussed earlier, during the latter part of the twentieth century many changes occurred in the composition of families. For example, between 1970 and 1990, traditional families—married couples with children—declined from 50 percent to 37 percent of all families, and single-parent families doubled from 6 percent to 12 percent. Family composition began to stabilize by 2000, with traditional families declining only 2 percent (to 35 percent) and single-parent families increasing only 1 percent (to 13 percent). Nevertheless, the concerns that many people raised about the viability and future of families remain on the public agenda. Much of the debate centers on questions regarding the form families should take, the degree to which divorce harms children, and the degree to which same-sex marriages would undermine the meaning of families when the real challenge ahead is how to help all people construct and maintain marriages and families that provide personal satisfaction and that contribute to the general welfare of society. Meeting this challenge requires solving several structural problems: insufficient well-paying jobs; lack of health insurance; inadequate educational opportunities; poor health care; inadequate and costly day care for working parents; lack of resources to care for elderly relatives; inadequate housing; discrimination; and unrealistic expectations about marriages and families. Additionally, millions of families throughout the world have and are experiencing enormous suffering, loss, and deprivations because of terrorist acts and racial, ethnic, and religious conflicts. We will discuss how these structural factors and widespread violence both on local and international levels impact marriages and families throughout the remainder of this textbook.

THE SOCIOLOGICAL IMAGINATION

This brief review of the history of the family in the United States reveals an ongoing pattern of diversity and change. Sociologist C. Wright Mills (1959) observed that in an age of rapid change, ordinary people often feel overwhelmed by the events confronting them, feeling that their private lives are a series of traps over which they have little control. They feel that cherished values are being replaced with ambiguity and uncertainty. Mills argued that people can counter this sense of frustration and powerlessness and come to understand their own experiences by locating themselves within their

SEARCHING THE INTERNET

U.S. ADULTS POSTPONING MARRIAGE

- In the past three decades, the proportion of those who had never married doubled for women aged 20 to 24, from 36 percent to 73 percent, and more than tripled for women aged 30 to 34, from 6 percent to 22 percent.
- In the 30 years from 1970 to 2000, the average size of the nation's households decreased from 3.14 to 2.62 persons.
- The proportion of households consisting of one person living alone increased from 17 percent in 1970 to 26 percent in 2000.
- The number of single mothers increased between 1970 and 2000, from 3 million to 10 million; over the same time frame, the number of single fathers increased also, from 393,000 to 2 million.

http://www.census.gov/Press-Release/www/2001/cb01-113.html

historical period. By this he meant that we can understand our own life chances by becoming aware of those of all individuals in our same circumstances. Thus, Mills called on us to develop a **sociological imagination** to grasp history and biography and the relations between the two within our society. To do this requires asking three questions: (1) What is the structure of a particular society, and how does it differ from other varieties of social order? (2) Where does this society stand in human history, and what are its essential features? and (3) What varieties of women and men live in this society and in this period, and what is happening to them?

The sociological imagination allows us to distinguish between what Mills called "personal troubles of milieu" and the "public issues of social structure." A "trouble" is a private matter, occurring within the character of the individual and within the range of her or his immediate relationship with others. An "issue," however, is a public matter that transcends the local environment of the individual. For example, any couple may experience personal troubles in their marriage, but the fact that approximately 1 million divorces occurred in 1998 is an indication of a structural issue having to do with the institution of marriage and the family and with the other societal institutions that affect them. Mills argued that many of the events we experience are caused by structural changes. Thus, to understand the changes that affect our personal lives, we must look beyond our private experiences to examine the larger political, social, and economic issues that affect our lives and the lives of others in our society.

Although applying the sociological perspective offers many benefits, four general ones stand out: (1) It allows us to take a new and critical look at what we have always taken for granted or assumed to be true; (2) it allows us to see the vast range of human diversity; (3) it allows us to understand the constraints and opportunities that affect our lives and those of other people; and (4) it enables us to participate more actively in society (Macionis, 1991). Throughout the remainder of this textbook, we will stress the application of the sociological imagination in everyday life, focusing on social structure: How cultural values, historical context, economic and political changes, and various social-structural variables and social systems, such as race, class, gender, sexual orientation, and age, interact and affect the personal experiences of individuals and groups as they create, sustain, and change their marriages and families.

WRITING YOUR OWN SCRIPT

A course on the sociology of marriages and families usually invokes concern and interest among students about how the general principles and descriptions in the textbook apply to their own lives. As you have seen in the discussion of the sociological imagination, a guiding theme in the discipline of sociology is that individual lives are influenced, patterned, and shaped by large and powerful social forces that are beyond the control of any one individual. At the same time, individuals are not passive in this process. Individuals act in ways that influence these larger social forces. Therefore, there is a connection between our own personal and private experiences and the culture, society, groups, marriages, and families to which we belong. In this textbook, we stress the application of the sociological imagination in everyday life.

WRITING YOUR OWN SCRIPT

DEFINE IT, AND KNOWLEDGE FOLLOWS*

As you have seen in this chapter, the structure and lifestyles of marriages and families are diverse. However, for many people in the United States today, family is still defined in very narrow terms. According to Joan Ferrante (1995), narrow social definitions enable narrow legal definitions to persist, and both such definitions can cause pain and deprivation, or simply discomfort, for individuals. Thinking about popular cultural definitions of the family, as well as narrow legal definitions, where do you and your family fit?

Write a brief sociological description of your family. Some questions or issues to pay particular attention to are How do you define family? Think about your own family and the individual members. What or who constitutes family for you? Does your idea of family include distant cousins (third and beyond) and great-great-aunts and uncles? Does it include people who are not related to you by blood, adoption, or ancestry? Is your definition of family consistent with that of other family members? If not, how does it differ? Do you make a distinction between the notion of "family" and that of "kinship"? If yes, how so? What is the structure of your family? What are the typical marriage types in your family? Marriage eligibility customs? Residential patterns? Family power patterns? You might want to make a family tree, starting with yourself and going back as far as you can.

*The title of this box is borrowed from the ideas of Joan Ferrante (1992) concerning the power to define.

That is, we stress the personal relevance of the topics, issues, and concerns addressed in this book with the goal of helping you, the reader, fully appreciate the connection between yourself (the individual) and society. In this context, in each chapter we present a box entitled "Writing Your Own Script" to reinforce your knowledge of and ability to apply the sociological imagination.

"Writing Your Own Script" is simply an exercise that utilizes an everyday life approach to the study of marriages and families. It encourages you to become directly involved in the learning process by using your own personal experiences (and those of others you know) as a way of understanding and critically examining or evaluating both the commonly shared elements as well as the uniqueness of your own personal life. Throughout our lives, all of us are confronted with life events, living arrangements, and other activities about which we must make decisions. Some of the most important of these decisions are those concerning marriage and family living. One way of doing this is to keep a personal journal of your thoughts and reactions to the material presented in the text.

In the "Writing Your Own Script" exercises you are provided with a more formalized process for reflecting on and planning your own life script. As you complete each chapter of the book, you are in a good position to reflect, examine, and evaluate your feelings and desires regarding the life choices you have made or will be making over the course of your lifetime. You can select only those exercises or marriage and family issues that are of immediate concern to you, or you can reflect and write in every exercise presented. The exercises correspond to key topics discussed in each chapter; therefore, it is important that you understand and refer back to the chapter, if necessary, as you think about your own life. Even if you have already made some decisions, such as getting married and having children, these exercises can give you added or new insight into how well your decision making worked and can perhaps suggest other areas where improvements can be made. The exercises can also simply help you understand your life experiences and those of others within the sociohistorical and political contexts in which they occur.

To be sure, what you do now (how you write your own script) is not written in stone. The "Writing Your Own Script" exercises are simply one method among many that allow you to understand your life and begin making informed choices by applying the sociological imagination. Some of these choices, like becoming a parent, are permanent, whereas others, such as entering into or dissolving a relationship, can be altered. In addition, we should realize that the choices we make at various stages of our lives may affect later options. For example, a decision to delay marriage or childbearing into our 30s or 40s may result in fewer, if any, options to engage in these behaviors at a later date.

To best utilize the "Writing Your Own Script" exercises, consider the following: (1) the factual information presented in each chapter; (2) the key life events and activities around which the "Writing Your Own Script" exercises are built; (3) the options available to you in each area of decision making; (4) the larger social forces that may affect the range of options available to you; (5) the possible positive and negative consequences (advantages or disadvantages) of each option; and (6) how social forces and your own personal values may interact to influence your choices and those of others.

SUMMARY

Marriage and family are among the oldest human social institutions. Each society develops its own patterns of marriage and family life, and these patterns vary considerably across and within cultures. In recent years, family values have become a topic for debate in the United States. Such debates are often clouded by mythology about the way families used to be. Myths are false, fictitious, imaginary, or exaggerated beliefs that can create unrealistic expectations about what families can or should be. Five of the most popular myths and stereotypes directly applicable to current debates about family life and gender roles are (1) the universal nuclear family; (2) the self-reliant traditional family; (3) the naturalness of the separate spheres of wives and husbands; (4) the unstable African American family, and (5) the idealized nuclear family of the 1950s.

The discussion of mythical versus real families underscores the fact that not all families are the same; there is not now and never has been a single model of the family. Families are a product of their historical context, and at any given historical period families occupy different territories and have varied experiences. Race, class, and gender are three interlocking categories of social experience that affect all aspects of human life; they shape all social institutions and systems of meaning, including the institutions of marriage and family, and the discussion of family values.

From the very beginning, the United States was economically, racially, religiously, and familially diverse. Native Americans, white ethnic settlers, Africans forcibly brought to this country as slaves, and Chicanos whose land was annexed by the United States all struggled to create and maintain a stable family structure in a new and often hostile environment. Over time these and other immigrant groups confronted powerful economic and political forces, such as industrialization, depressions, and wars, which led to major transformations in family life.

A course on the sociology of marriages and families can help us develop a sociological imagination and facilitate our understanding of how many, if not all, of the concepts and issues pertaining to marriage and family lifestyles apply in our own lives, and at the same time are linked to social structure and historical circumstance. One way to appreciate fully the connection between our own personal and private experiences and the culture, society, groups, marriages, and families to which we belong is to engage in "writing your own script"—a process for utilizing the sociological imagination to reflect on and plan your own life script.

KEY TERMS

institution
marriage
monogamy
serial monogamy
polygamy
polygyny
polyandry
cenogamy (group marriage)
family
family of orientation
family of procreation
nuclear family
extended (multigenerational) family
modified extended family
patriarchal family
norms
social structure
status
role
socialization
myth
institutional racism
kinship
patrilineal
matrilineal
households
sociological imagination

QUESTIONS FOR STUDY AND REFLECTION

1. In this chapter we have described some of the major functions of families, historically and presently. Do any or all of these functions apply to your family experiences? Describe how you have experienced these functions within your family. Be specific. What other social institutions (e.g. schools, government, religion) have served as vital social functions for you or your family members? What, if any, conflicts have arisen as a result of your or your family's participation in these social institutions?
2. What is meant by the idea that race, class, and gender are interactive systems rather than individual variables? Think about your own family of orientation, and take one particular aspect of your family life as an example. Discuss briefly how race, class, and gender act simultaneously to shape that aspect of your family life.
3. Given the tremendous number of immigrants this country has had, it is likely that you, a relative, classmate, neighbor, or someone else you know has migrated to the United States. Interview that person, focusing on the reasons for coming and the ways in which that experience has affected her or his life. To what extent, if any, have that person's family patterns and structures been changed as she or he adjusted to life in the United States.
4. Most people agree that marriages and families underwent major changes during the last half of the twentieth century; however, few people link these changes to larger societal changes that have taken place. Identify some of the major social changes that have taken place during the past 50 years (for example, the development of the Internet, cloning, dismantling of welfare) and discuss their impact on contemporary marriages and families. Reflect on your own family and consider how one such change has affected your family and/or families like yours.

ADDITIONAL RESOURCES

SOCIOLOGICAL

COONTZ, STEPHANIE, MAYA PARSON, AND GABRIELLE RALEY, EDS. 1999. *American Families: A Multicultural Reader.* Boston: Routledge. This anthology consists of a variety of articles that illustrate the diversity of American family life. It underscores the point that there is no singular model of marriage and/or family.

FONER, NANCY, RUBEN G. RUMBAUT, AND STEVEN J. GOLD. 2000. *Immigration Research for a New Century: Multidisciplinary Perspectives.* New York: Russell Sage Foundation. This collection of essays explores the rich variety of the immigrant experience, ranging from itinerant farm workers to Silicon Valley engineers. It also provides the fresh insights of a new generation of immigration researchers.

GORDON, MICHAEL, ED. 1983. *The American Family in Social-Historical Perspective,* 3d ed. New York: St. Martin's Press. A rich source of articles on family life in the seventeenth, eighteenth, and nineteenth centuries.

GORDON-REED, ANNETTE, 1997. *Thomas Jefferson and Sally Hemings: An American Controversy.* Charlottesville: University Press of Virginia. This compelling work provides a meticulous review of the evidence surrounding the Jefferson–Hemings relationship.

LITERARY

HURSTON, ZORA NEALE. 1978. *Their Eyes Were Watching God.* Urbana: University of Illinois Press. This novel chronicles a proud independent African American woman's quest for identity, through three marriages, on a journey back to her roots. It is an excellent demonstration of the intersections of race, class, gender, and culture and its impact on identity/self-concept and intimate relationships. (Originally pubished 1937.)

TARKINGTON, BOOTH. 1989. *The Magnificent Ambersons.* Bloomington: Indiana University Press. A historical novel portraying the changing fortunes of three generations of an American dynasty and at the same time illuminating the changing social fabric of the United States.

INTERNET

www.asanet.org/Sections/Family/family.htm Maintained by the American Sociological Association Section on Families, this site is devoted to topics concerning families.

http://www.cdc.gov/nchswww/nchsshome.htm The National Center for Health Statistics provides data on births, marriages, divorces, and deaths in the United States.

Ways of Studying and Explaining Marriages and Families

IN THE NEWS: MINNEAPOLIS, MINNESOTA

Do day-care centers breed bullies? According to researchers from the National Institute of Child Health and Human Development (NICHD), there is a direct correlation between aggressiveness in children and the amount of time children spend in child care. At a meeting of the Society for Research on Child Development in Minneapolis, in April 2001, researchers formally presented this and other findings from a major, long-term NICHD–funded study of children in non-maternal care. The NICHD early child care study, purported to be the largest and most authoritative study of its kind, found that the more hours that toddlers spend in child care, the more likely they are to be aggressive, disobedient, and defiant by the time they are in kindergarten, much more so than those who stay at home with their mothers. Moreover, these children are also more likely to bully, fight with, or act mean toward other children. The researchers said that this correlation held true regardless of the quality of care; whether the children came from rich or poor homes; whether they were looked after by a relative, a nanny, or at a center; whether the mothers themselves provided sensitive care; and whether they were girls or boys. On the other hand, there were also quite convincing findings from the study that the quality of child care has a positive association with a range of social and academic skills. That is, children in day care show better language skills and short-term memory by the age of 4 than other children the same age.

This finding notwithstanding, it was the link between aggressiveness and day care that got the most media attention, with screaming headlines such as "Day care turns out bullies." Not surprisingly, the negative findings set off explosive debates around the country. According to E. J. Dionne of the *Washington Post,* "When researchers offer new findings or some incident sparks a new discussion, we quickly polarize and, verbally at least, start shooting at each other. . . . The culture-war style of public debates in the U.S. makes it inevitable that one side or the other will feel under assault" (2001:1). This is exactly what happened when the NICHD study findings were reported. Mothers who hold jobs outside the home were cast as the enemies of mothers who, at some point or another, chose to stay at home with their children. Many working mothers saw the study findings as one more attack against them, and some stay-at-home mothers said that the study confirmed what they had always thought. Adding to the furor over the study's findings is the fact that one of the study's 13 lead researchers has been accused by his colleagues of grabbing the spotlight, making pronouncements about the study that were not based on conclusive data, and generally creating a panic (Sweeney, 2001).

Given that this was a very large study that looked at many factors about the experience of children in day care, does the aggression finding really mean anything? Are the study's findings really that polar? Do they really sound a death knell for day care? Clearly, the experts, including the team of researchers who conducted the study, are not in agreement over what the findings really mean. Although they agree that the study was scientific and extremely rigorous, they also believe that it raises as many questions as it answers. For example, the study looked only at time children spent away from their mothers, not their fathers. And although it found that 17 percent of children in long-term child care experienced behavioral problems later on, an overwhelming majority (83 percent) of children did just fine. Complicating things further is the study's finding that quality day care is associated with increased skills in intellectual ability, such as language and memory.

These points were lost in the sound-bite debate that the findings generated. According to Christopher Forrest, associate professor of pediatrics and health policy at Johns Hopkins University, "The public reads the bottom line. They act on that without putting the study into context. In politics, there is always a context. The same is true for science, but it doesn't get reported that way" (quoted in Stolberg, 2001). The bottom line: What remains unclear is whether child care actually causes the problem or whether children likely to become aggressive happen to be those who spend more hours in child care. It is also unclear whether reducing the amount of time in child care will reduce the risk that a child will turn into a mean-spirited bully (Vedantam, 2001).

WHAT DO YOU THINK? Albeit based on a minimum number of facts, what kind of theory can you put forth to explain both sets of findings reported here? Why did these findings engender such controversy? What are the policy implications of studies such as this? Is science ever truly neutral or objective?

THE SOCIOLOGY OF MARRIAGES AND FAMILIES

Some of you might think that because you are already a member of a family, you know all there is to know about marriages and families. If this is the case, you might be asking what sociology can add to what you already know. The answer is that sociologists go beyond our individual experiences to study marriages and families in social, historical, political, and cross-cultural contexts. They have conducted thousands of studies on a wide range of marital and family behaviors, relationships, characteristics, and problems, ranging from the sexual behavior of members of marriages, families, and other intimate relationships to fathers' involvement in child rearing and child care to the long-term effects of television viewing on the behavior of children. These studies have yielded a tremendous amount of data that have contributed significantly to what we thought we knew about marriages and families. For example, research by sociologists and other social scientists on the role of television in the parenting of American children has shed light not only on the influence of television (both positive and negative) on children's behavior but on children's cognitive development as well. For instance, similar research has found a strong correlation between frequent physical aggression and frequent viewing of all but educational children's programs. Educational children's programs, on the other hand, like quality day care, have been found to be related to prosocial behavior and to the use of mature language in school (Wiggins, 1994).

Furthermore, from their research, sociologists have generated a number of theories that help explain issues like why and how marriages and families emerged, how they are sustained over time, how people involved in these relationships interact with and relate to each other, the effect children have on marriages, what significance marriages and families have for U.S. society, and how and why marriages and families change over time. In this chapter we examine the ways in which sociologists discover facts—do research—about marriage and family behaviors and devise theories or explanations of these behaviors. We begin with a consideration of the link between research and theory.

STUDYING MARRIAGES AND FAMILIES: THE LINK BETWEEN RESEARCH AND THEORY

Sociology involves observing human behavior and society and then making sense out of what we observe. Thus, both research and theory are involved. However, as the controversy and debate surrounding both the announced results of the NICHD early child care study and the alleged aggressive and defiant behavior of one of the study's many investigators indicate, neither research nor theory is developed in a cultural or political vacuum. As we will see, the social and political climate, as well as the ideological viewpoint of the researcher, has an impact on what is researched, how it is interpreted, and whether or not it is widely shared—or for that matter, how it is shared—with the public (for example, which findings are stressed and which are omitted or downplayed). Politics aside, the link between research and theory is obvious: For example, research about marriages and families provides us with important observations about these intimate relationships. Various marriage and family theories and perspectives provide us with basic points of view or frameworks that help us analyze and understand these observations.

What exactly is a theory? A **theory** is an explanation of some phenomenon. Theories relate ideas and observations to each other as well as help explain them. They contain certain assumptions about the world and about the nature of society and human behavior. Different assumptions lead to different problems and questions and, potentially, to different answers or explanations about society and human behavior. In addition, most theories include stated or unstated value judgments concerning the topic or issues related to the topic. For example, if we use a theory that assumes that the family is a system held together through a basic harmony of values and interests and that consensus and stability are desirable in the family (a value judgment) because they facilitate this cooperation, then we are most likely to ask questions concerned with order, stability, and balance, such as how do families function in an orderly and consensual way to maintain or preserve their families over time? And we are less likely to raise questions pertaining to disorder, disagreement, and open hostility in families.

Actually, if you think about it, no theory or perspective on human society and behavior is unbiased or completely value-free. Because they contain assumptions about the nature of human beings and their societies, all such theories implicitly or explicitly suggest that certain arrangements are desirable, good, or better than others. All social theories include these kinds of value judgments.

How do we know, then, if a particular theoretical perspective provides a viable explanation of its subject matter? The answer to this question lies in an understanding of the relationship between theory and scientific research. Theories are important sources of ideas for researchers to test. **Scientific research** provides us with empirical evidence as a basis for knowledge or theories. By **empirical evidence** we mean data or evidence that can be confirmed by the use of one or more of the human senses. Scientific research also allows us to test **hypotheses,** statements of relationships between two or more **variables**—factors that can have two or more values—to determine what is as opposed to what we think should be. As used in scientific research, the term *independent variable* is used to identify a cause—it is a variable that causes change in or affects another variable. The term *dependent variable* refers to the consequence of some cause—it is a variable that is changed or affected by some other variable.

All scientific research is guided by the **scientific method,** a set of procedures intended to ensure accuracy and honesty throughout the research process. An aim of the scientific method is to prevent our personal biases from distorting our research. The scientific method involves making systematic and objective observations (collecting information), making precise measurements, and reporting the research techniques and results to other interested parties. If followed, these procedures generally lead researchers to the facts of a situation or event, regardless of what we might hope or believe to be the facts. These procedures also permit others to repeat research studies to validate or invalidate previous findings, thereby allowing us to expose researcher biases where they might appear. For example, in the case of the NICHD early child care study (discussed at the beginning of this chapter), the researchers followed the procedures of scientific research. Thus, any concerns about researcher bias can be addressed through a replication and validation of the study's findings.

Generally speaking, the scientific method refers to the procedures that science uses to (1) select or formulate research questions and operationalize (state in concrete terms)

Day-care centers like the one pictured here have become topics of controversy in the social science field. However, there is general agreement that children in day care develop cognitive skills at a faster rate than other children the same age.

concepts; (2) select an appropriate research design; (3) collect data; (4) analyze the data; and (5) draw conclusions and report the findings. How these steps are actually carried out is dictated by a number of issues, including the particular research question under study and the researcher's conceptual scheme. Research is also sometimes influenced by practical matters, such as the availability of funding, who funds the research (and publishes it), access to subjects, and time constraints. Research is also sometimes influenced by politics. Consequently, biases, compromises, selectivity, and other nonscientific issues often creep into the scientific research process and can have an effect from the beginning to the end of the process. For example, you might recall the 1999 firing of the editor of the prestigious *Journal of the American Medical Association* (*JAMA*) for publishing a Kinsey Institute sex study that showed that most college students did not consider oral sex as "having sex." This finding could have supported then-President Bill Clinton's definition of sex in the Republican-led impeachment process that centered largely around the president's intimate relationship with White House intern Monica Lewinsky. In the firing of the *JAMA* editor, political partisan issues surrounding the sexual conduct of a sitting president could well have played a role in the editor's firing, but more importantly, the firing could have influenced how the public viewed the Kinsey Institute's research.

How exactly are theory and research related? Theory provides insights, often in the form of abstract ideas, into the nature of individuals and society, and research provides the objective observations upon which theories are verified. It is a reciprocal, or back-and-forth, relationship. For example, theories that cannot be confirmed by evidence gathered through scientific research mean nothing. Similarly, facts have meaning only when we interpret them and give them meaning based on some theoretical perspective. Contrary to popular belief, facts do not speak for themselves.

METHODOLOGICAL TECHNIQUES IN THE STUDY OF MARRIAGES AND FAMILIES

People today are bombarded with information about marriages and families. We hear, for example, that old-fashioned family moral values have disappeared, that children are having babies, that family and intimate violence are increasing, and that entire families are living on the streets. To ascertain what is really happening with marriages and families, we must therefore learn how to separate what is factual from what is not. As previously explained, scientific research enables us to see what is, as opposed to what might be or what we hoped would be. Most research, like theory, begins with the questions why and how. A goal of research is to provide specific answers to these questions by gathering empirical evidence. Ultimately, the answers form explanations or theories about some aspect of human behavior and human society.

A potential problem for all scientific research is objectivity. Researchers constantly have to be aware of how their personal attitudes, expectations, and values might affect their research. It is not possible, even when using the scientific method, to measure or observe social phenomena without committing ourselves to some theoretical perspective. Theory is always implicated in the research process, although it is most often implicit—hidden from view. Therefore, we should be aware that researchers bring theoretical biases to the research process: the problems selected for study, the methods chosen to study those problems, the unique and individual observations made, and general assumptions about the world and about human behavior. The methodological procedures followed have a great effect on the interpretation of the data (Smith, 1981). Although the scientific method minimizes research bias to a great degree, no one has found a way to eliminate it totally. Therefore, as consumers of massive amounts of research information, we must carefully examine the information we receive and be prepared for the possibility that what is presented as reality is not impartial. A good example in this regard is the controversy surrounding how one of the lead investigators of the NICHD early child care study reported the findings. Some of his fellow investigators have accused him of monopolizing the press and making dire pronouncements about child care that are not based on "conclusive data." Others say that the investigator has an agenda that he has been pushing for some time; for years he has emphasized the negative aspects of child care to the exclusion of the positive aspects, which suggests that he may not have been completely impartial in how he presented the study's findings.

As pointed out earlier, because the study of marriages and families deals with everyday life, we often think we already know all there is to know about these issues. Most people, for example, probably believe that they know all there is to know about welfare and welfare recipients. Popular views of welfare include the notion that women who receive welfare have baby after baby as a way to collect higher payments. The findings of scientific research, however, tell a very different story. For example, a recent profile of the welfare population shows that the fertility behavior of women on welfare does not differ from that of women in the general population. The majority of welfare recipients (74 percent) have only one or two children. And, like the general population, the average number of children in a welfare family is less than two (Report from the Urban Institute, 1999). Past research has shown that the longer a woman receives welfare, the less likely she is to have additional children (Rank, 1989).

Much of the research on welfare families to date reflects a white middle-class bias. Based on a mythical model of white middle-class families as a measuring rod, welfare families (often regardless of the empirical evidence) generally have been described as pathological, disorganized, lacking a work ethic, and locked into a way of life that perpetuates an endless cycle of so-called illegitimate births.

Before we accept such viewpoints as factual, we must carefully analyze the evidence presented to support the conclusions. This process includes asking questions such as: Are the conclusions actually supported by the empirical evidence?

Are the findings presented in such a way that they can be tested by others? What are the biases of the research, and does the researcher state them up front? Take a look at the Searching the Internet box, for example. Do the facts shown on the screen match the myths or popular notions about welfare recipients?

Basically, we should assess research in terms of its reliability and validity. **Reliability** is the degree to which the research yields the same results when repeated by the same researcher or other researchers. **Validity** is the degree to which the study measures exactly what it claims to be measuring. We should also keep in mind that conclusions are not final but are always open to question and reinvestigation.

In the remainder of this section we examine some of the primary methods used in marriage and family research: surveys, observation, case studies, and ethnographies. We also address who and what does and does not get studied by researchers, and why. In this regard, we pay close attention to issues of ethics and conscious and unconscious biases in the conduct of research on marriages and families.

Surveys

One of the quickest ways to find out what we want to know about people is to ask them. **Surveys** do just that: They enable us to gather information by asking people questions. Surveys are particularly useful when what we want to know about people is not easily observable, such as the private lives of married or cohabiting couples. The two basic methods by which researchers ask their questions and receive answers are interviews and questionnaires. The **interview** usually involves one person, the interviewer, asking another person questions, with the interviewer recording the answers. The **questionnaire,** in contrast, usually provides autonomy to the person answering the questions. It is typically a set of printed questions that people read on their own and then record their answers. The survey is the most widely used method of studying marriages and families. It is likely that you or someone you know has participated in a survey regarding some marriage and family issue. You may even have conducted your own survey for a class assignment or some other project. For example, in marriage and family classes students are often asked to survey their parents or grandparents concerning the dating patterns of their youth.

A good example of the use of the survey in marriage and family research is Phillip Blumstein and Pepper Schwartz's (1983) now-classic study of U.S. couples. This large-scale survey provided important insights into how couples make decisions, what importance sex has in their lives, and how factors such as jobs and money shape their relationships. In terms of sexuality, for example, Blumstein and Schwartz found that, in general, the longer people were together, the greater their chance of having an outside sexual relationship, a phenomenon that Blumstein and Schwartz termed "nonmonogamy." In their sample, nonmonogamy varied according to the type of relationship a couple shared. For example, married couples were much less likely to be nonmonogamous than were heterosexual cohabiting couples. Lesbians were slightly less likely than cohabiting heterosexual couples to be nonmonogamous, whereas gay couples were the most likely of all to be nonmonogamous.

SEARCHING THE INTERNET

CHARACTERISTICS OF THE WELFARE POPULATION

- Ten percent of welfare adults are married; 36 percent are separated, divorced, or widowed and the remaining 54 percent have never married.
- Eighty-one percent of welfare mothers are in their 20s and 30s;
6 percent are under the age of 20 and 13 percent are 40 or older.
- Welfare mothers are fairly evenly distributed across racial and ethnic groups: 37 percent are white, 36 percent are African American, and 20 percent are Latina.
- Fifty-eight percent of all welfare recipients have at least a high school education, including some who have attended college.
- Seventy-four percent of welfare recipients have only one or two children. Consistent with the fertility patterns of the general public, the average welfare family has fewer than two children.
- Over two-thirds of women who are on welfare had some recent work experience before applying for public assistance.

http://www.doleta.gov/ohrw2w/recruit/urban.html

One of the major advantages of interviews and questionnaires is that they allow researchers to gather large amounts of information at a relatively low cost. On the negative side, the questionnaire method imposes the researcher's point of view on the people being studied by forcing them to respond to questions in terms of preestablished categories of answers. For example, a couple might be given a choice of four categories to describe their relationship when none of these categories is truly appropriate. Another disadvantage is that survey methods must rely on people's ability and willingness to give accurate information, especially when the survey involves information about behavior that is typically considered private, such as sexual relationships or family violence. Thus, survey results are sometimes distorted because the respondents say what they think the researcher wants to hear.

Observation

Surveys are good for telling us what people say they do. What people say they do and what they actually do are not always the same, however. An alternative to asking people questions is to observe their behavior systematically. Observational studies are useful when researchers have only a vague idea of the behavior they want to study, when they want to study people or situations that are not accessible to the general public, or when there is no other way to get the information. Researchers may observe behavior in a manner that does not intrude on the situation under study, or they may participate in or become a part of the interaction they are studying. This latter approach is referred to as participant observation. Regardless of the approach, observational studies require the researcher to develop a specific set of questions in advance of the study as a way to guide the collection of data.

An interesting example of an observational study that is relevant to the study of marriages and families is one conducted by researchers Pandora Pound, Caroline Sabin, and Shah Ebrahim (1999) in order to identify aspects of the process of care that might explain improved outcomes for patients on stroke units. The researchers knew from previous research that patients on stroke units have improved outcomes compared with those on general wards; that stroke units were associated with long-term reduction of death, dependency, and institutionalization, with benefits being independent of age, sex, or stroke severity. Based on their observation of 12 patients at each of 3 locations—a stroke unit, an elderly care unit, and a general medical ward—the researchers found that stroke-unit patients spent more time out of bed and out of their room and had more opportunities for independence than patients on the medical ward. There were more observed attempts in the stroke unit than on the general medical ward to interact with drowsy, cognitively or speech-impaired patients. Stroke-unit patients also spent more time with visitors. Similar aspects of care were also observed in the elderly care unit, where patients also spent less time sleeping or disengaged and more time interacting with nurses, and were given appropriate help more often than patients elsewhere. The researchers concluded that these aspects of patient care might help explain the improved outcomes on stroke units.

A major advantage of observation is that it is by far the best method for collecting data on nonverbal behavior. In addition, it not only allows researchers like Pound, Sabin, and Ebrahim to observe "process," but it also allows them to examine behavior or "process" in its natural environment (for example, a stroke unit, an elderly care unit, and a general medical ward). Although observation is less restrictive or artificial than some other data collection methods, the presence of the observer makes bias a real possibility. When people are aware that they are being observed, they frequently modify their behavior, either deliberately or subconsciously. This phenomenon, referred to by social scientists as the **Hawthorne effect,** can sometimes be a serious drawback of observational studies. Other problems with observational studies include the following:

- They usually take a long time and thus can be expensive.
- They generally involve only a limited number of subjects.
- They offer the researcher little control over the research situation.

However, the depth of understanding gained through observation research compensates for the disadvantages and has greatly added to our knowledge about marriages and families.

Case Studies

Sociologists who study a particular category of people or a particular situation typically do so as a **case study.** The case study is a detailed, in-depth examination of a single unit. Case studies use newly collected and preexisting data, such as those from interviews, participant observation, or existing records, for in-depth examination of a particular individual, group, or organization. Used in research on issues pertaining to marriages and families, case studies can provide a comprehensive and holistic understanding of behaviors within a single setting. Researcher John Bartkowski's 1999 study of how gender, domestic labor (that is, the allocation of financial provision, household tasks, and child care responsibilities), and family power operate as processes within three white, relatively privileged, conservative Evangelical households is an example of the case study method applied to marriage and family issues. Bartkowski used the case study approach to trace how domestic labor issues emerged, were negotiated, and (at times) resolved through gender strategies employed by these couples. He found that contrary to the stereotypical view of conservative Evangelicals as rigid conformers to a traditional division of labor by gender, these couples exhibited both traditional and progressive gender practices.

Although the couples embraced the Evangelical ideology of wife–husband roles in the family (the dominant family discourse within contemporary Evangelicalism champions husband providership and wifely domesticity), they sometimes reconfigured or reversed their beliefs about gender, if only temporarily. For example, one husband whose wife worked outside the home indicated that he greatly appreciated the support that his wife provided both financially and emotionally, yet he also clearly believed that the financial provision for his family was his primary responsibility. Equality, per se, was not the guiding principle in the decision for his wife to work. Rather, in this husband's estimation, he should provide his wife with the "choice" to work or not, whereas he felt that he didn't have a choice in the matter; it was his obligation.

According to Bartkowski, employed Evangelical wives and mothers may find themselves doubly burdened from shouldering both their traditional homemaking responsibilities—the dominant ideology of femininity within Evangelicalism—and their newly found co-provider role. For example, despite her best efforts, one wife in the study was unable to parlay her extensive labor force commitments into a lightened domestic workload in the home. The study found that, in dealing with their deviation from the prevailing definitions of Evangelical wifehood/motherhood, the women used a "both/and gender strategy" that entailed working two full-time jobs, as both co-provider and homemaker, during the family workday. This gender strategy seemed to be religiously motivated because it enabled these women to retain for themselves the "homemaker" label, which remains closely linked with femininity in their conservative Protestant circle despite its broader cultural devaluation. Bartkowski's findings underscore the importance of viewing gender and domestic labor as a product of interpersonal negotiation, while at the same time they highlight how gender relations are mediated by cultural forces such as conservative religious ideologies.

One of the advantages of a study like Bartkowski's is that it provides a great deal of detail about the research subject. In addition, the case study approach offers long-term, in-depth analysis of various aspects of the phenomenon being studied. A disadvantage is that each case study focuses on a very specific case and thus cannot be generalized to the larger population. For example, the Bartkowski findings apply to the specific conservative Evangelical families that he studied and not to all conservative Evangelical families. Furthermore, as with observation, the presence of the researcher may change how people act or interact. Overall, however, case studies have provided some significant insights into marriage and family processes. They have helped researchers understand and explain how families create roles, patterns, and rules that various family members follow, very often without even being aware of them.

Ethnography

In general, **ethnography** is a research technique for describing a social group from the group's point of view. Ethnography is not about pursuing or uncovering an objective reality (which is typically the focus of quantitative analyses). Rather, it is a technique for examining the many different versions of reality from the point of view, or through the eyes, of the researched. Therefore, by necessity, ethnographers use **qualitative methods,** methods designed to study conditions or processes that are hard to measure numerically, rather than **quantitative methods,** which are designed to study variables that can be measured numerically, to collect their data. In essence, the ethnographer attempts to gain cultural knowledge from the people she or he is studying. Ethnographic research is particularly useful and relevant in areas of study where researchers have historically studied and measured other groups from the perspective of their own cultural, racial, or class biases. In this context, ethnography has special relevance as a technique for studying marriages and families that heretofore have been studied primarily from the cultural perspective of white middle-class male researchers.

An interesting example of ethnographic research in this regard is a study undertaken by Robin Jarrett in 1992 of low-income African American family life. Specifically, Jarrett explored hypotheses advanced by quantitative sociologists concerning the African American underclass, especially those put forth by William J. Wilson in his 1987 work titled *The Truly Disadvantaged.* Using aggregate data and statistical analyses of African American family structure and dynamics, these researchers had put forth a generalized profile of these families as dysfunctional. In contrast, utilizing ethnographic techniques, Jarrett found that inner-city African American family life is far more complex and heterogeneous than such a one-dimensional profile suggests. Jarrett utilized a two-step qualitative study that began with focus group interviews and moved to in-depth case studies based on participant observation and in-depth interviews of multiple family members. Her case study report of one of these families provides evidence that is consistent with other ethnographies of African American family life, which describe well-functioning families within impoverished neighborhoods. Jarrett's ethnographic research moves us beyond a one-dimensional view of inner-city African American families and documents the presence of various individual and family lifestyles within African American neighborhoods. She found that in response to neighborhood conditions, well-functioning African American families continue to live in and coexist with street-oriented lifestyles in impoverished areas despite the tremendous odds that Wilson and other quantitative researchers articulate so well.

An advantage of ethnographic studies such as Jarrett's is that they provide firsthand accounts of those whose lives we are studying. Ethnographic research specifically and qualitative methods more generally provide an avenue for the voices of those we study—voices that are silenced by quantitative methodologies. Critics, on the other hand, contend that methodological biases limit the reliability and validity of qualitative data. They suggest, for example, that retrospective interviews can elicit idealized accounts of behavior or that the data may be compromised by memory lapses or the respondent's need to present a particular picture of self or the situation. The fact is, however, that all research methods are inherently limited. Therefore, to circumvent some of these biases, researchers should use a variety of strategies (such as in the case of the Jarrett study) to act as checks on potential threats to reliability and validity and to reduce some of the sources of researcher bias (Jarrett, 1992).

Scientific Methodologies Used by Feminist Researchers

Feminist scholars are concerned with whom researchers study and how they study them, how conclusions are drawn, and what evidence those conclusions are based on. They are particularly concerned with how women have either been omitted from scientific research or have been studied according to male models of attitudes and behavior. Much of their work is a corrective to these problems.

You are probably wondering what is distinctive about the methods that feminists use. Are their methods fundamentally different from the scientific methods that other researchers use? In fact, no method of research is of itself a feminist method. According to feminist sociologist and researcher Marjorie DeVault (1990), what distinguishes feminist methods is what feminist researchers do—how they use the methodologies available to them. For example, feminist researchers generally avoid using the more abstract, impersonal methods that characterize quantitative methods. Rather, they rely heavily on qualitative methods. A person using quantitative methods to study rape might measure the rate of rape among various groups of women. On the other hand, one using qualitative methods might measure the reaction to rape or coping strategies devised by rape victims as recounted by the victims themselves. In particular, feminist researchers often utilize field methods such as the in-depth, face-to-face interview; participant observation; and ethnography. Although other researchers also use these methods, feminist researchers differ in how they define their research goals and how they view their own role as researcher.

A basic goal of feminist research is to present information that had been previously ignored or suppressed, and thus to make visible both the experiences of the people they study (particularly women) in all their diversity and the **ideologies,** or systems of beliefs, that have kept these experiences invisible. In this respect, gender is at the forefront of the analysis, with special attention paid to how race, class, and gender interact and affect the lives of women and men. A major advantage of how feminists do their research is the way they define their role as researcher. As researchers they are conscious of the need to be respectful of the people they are studying, to be personal, collaborative, inclusive, and empowering.

These qualities characterize feminist methods because researchers consciously use techniques of data gathering that allow them to utilize the perspectives of their subjects. Instead of imposing their personal interpretations on the experiences of the people they study, feminist researchers develop theories and explanations that reflect the real-life experiences of their subjects, as reported by the subjects themselves. Ideally, feminist research is inclusive of the experiences of all women, not just a few, and it is empowering to the extent that it seeks to avoid defining women solely as victims. For example, as we will see in Chapter 11, although women are often victims of violence and abuse, they are also survivors. So feminist researchers view women as actively involved in the world in which they live.

An example of the feminist methodology applied to the people that researchers study can be found in the research on upwardly mobile African American women conducted by one of this text's authors, BarBara Scott. Scott (1988) used the life history method of collecting data about the experiences of these women. Her research showed that race and gender are important factors in upward mobility as well as family socialization. These women's self-reports of the process of mobility as they experienced it have greatly added to our knowledge about mobility, an area of research from which women and people of color were previously almost totally excluded.

The choice of the life history method reflects a central assumption of the feminist researcher that behavior can best be understood from the perspective of the persons involved. Scott assumed that her subjects understood their experiences better than other people did, and she respected their way of reporting and interpreting these experiences. Using this method, Scott avoided substituting her own interpretations for those of the women she studied. Her methodology was at once personal and collaborative. Scott was both the researcher and the researched in the sense that she, being an upwardly mobile African American woman, shared many of the experiences of her respondents.

The very features that feminist researchers consider advantageous and confirming have been singled out by critics as an important limitation of this research. Because this research is intentionally personal and collaborative, for example, critics immediately raise the question of objectivity. Many feminist researchers agree that their work is subjective in that it is research on people like themselves—other women. But, they argue, it is also objective in that women's experiences are explained in terms of the forces that shape their lives. Thus, like most research, which to date has been male-centered, feminist research clearly has a point of view and views social change as an important goal. Sociologist Howard Becker (1977) has addressed the role of values in sociological research and why researchers are sometimes accused of bias in their work. According to Becker, we can never avoid taking sides, but we can use research methodologies impartially enough so that the beliefs that we hold can be proved or disproved.

A CRITICAL LOOK AT TRADITIONAL RESEARCH ON MARRIAGES AND FAMILIES

Historically, sociology as a discipline has claimed as one of its major goals the improvement of social life. Today, most sociologists operate from this premise and believe that the purpose of their research is to affect social policy and provide the impetus for social change. Some critics, such as feminist scholars, have argued that in practice sociology has not lived up to this goal. Until the upsurge of feminist research and scholarship, women, their experiences, and their consciousness were largely absent from traditional sociological research and the theoretical paradigms that guide sociological thinking (Andersen, 1988). The same can be said for people of color. In addition, sociological researchers historically have failed to recognize groups other than the white middle class. That is, white middle-class marriages and families have been used as the norm against which other families are measured. When lower-class and working-class families differ from the white middle-class model, they are defined as deviant. At the other end of the class continuum, the upper classes have been the subject of little scientific research. Thus, much of what we know is based on a model of the family that represents only a small proportion of today's marriages and families.

A More Inclusive Sociology

Social science research often mirrors current issues and trends of society. In this context, scholars across academic disciplines are wrestling with new sensitivities and concerns with gender as a social construction and with issues pertaining to cultural diversity. Today, researchers are more cognizant of the intersections of social constructions such as race, class, gender, and sexual orientation and are moving beyond conventional topics and traditional research methods to develop a more inclusive base of knowledge about marriages and families. Although traditional sociological research has provided important insights into marriages and families, there are important limitations. Whether intended or not, much of this research presents a skewed picture of marriages and families, one rooted primarily in white middle-class and/or male experiences that have rendered women and various groups of color and their experiences invisible, as if they did not exist. And when they were studied, it was often within a social pathology or sociology of deviance framework. Because of the tremendous impact of this research for our ongoing understanding of marriage and family life, it is worth noting some of these past limitations. One way of exploring the limitations of traditional sociological research on marriages and families is to examine who does (did) and does not (did not) get studied.

Conventional topics studied by sociologists lead us to ignore issues that would illuminate women's lives. When women have been studied in traditional marriage and family research, for example, it has usually been in terms of a one-dimensional stereotypical model of women as nurturant caregivers and caretakers confined to the home. Most of this research has been conducted by men who use themselves as the standard. Gender is seldom considered to be a significant factor that influences behavior. Evidence of this trend recurs in study after study that draws conclusions about marriage and family life based on investigations in which all the research subjects are male. This approach is particularly evident in research concerning issues of individual and family mobility.

The large-scale study of the U.S. occupational structure conducted by noted social scientists Peter Blau and Otis Duncan (1967), for example, was, until recently, the definitive statement in the mobility literature. Blau and Duncan concluded that social mobility was simply a function of education and social origins and that no other conditions affect chances for mobility in the United States. Clearly, this set of conclusions ignores the reality of gender and its differing impact for women and men. In fact, Blau and Duncan's research study was based on a national sample of 20,000 men. No women participated.

Following this pattern, subsequent mobility research was primarily male-specific, measuring mobility strictly by comparing men occupationally with their fathers. When women's mobility was addressed, it was primarily that of white women, and it was measured by comparing the husband's occupational standing with that of the woman's father. In general, women's mobility was seen as a function of male status, that of either a father or a husband. This model of social mobility is particularly problematic for some women, including a large percentage of African American women, who historically have been required to work outside the home to help support their families. The percentage of women in the work force, across race, has risen dramatically over the last several decades, yet women's pay continues to lag behind that of their male counterparts. To be sure, this phenomenon has significant implications for current and future mobility studies.

Like feminist scholars, African American and other scholars of color have long criticized social science research for the negative and stereotypical ways in which African Americans, various people of color, women, and poor and working-class families have been portrayed. African American women scholars have been particularly vocal in their critiques concerning many myths and half-truths about African American women and their role in their families.

The longest lasting of these seems to be the myth of the "black matriarchy." One of the most widely publicized documents on African American family life, sociologist and government researcher Daniel Moynihan's 1965 study titled "The Negro Family: The Case for National Action," illustrates dramatically the use of social science methodology to promote ideas that are based on questionable data and oversimplification. Based on U.S. census data, Moynihan found that almost 25 percent of African American families were female-headed, a statistic he cited as evidence of a "matriarchy." Moynihan then explained the problems in the African American community in terms of this alleged structural feature of African American families. Although Moynihan recognized the historical fact of slavery and its impact on African American family life, he essentially placed the burden of an alleged family pathology squarely on the shoulders of African American women. In addition, even if one accepts his notion of a black matriarchy, he failed to

While we are sometimes afforded a glimpse into the social world of the wealthy through the mass media, there is little systematic research on the daily lives of upper-class families, particularly if they are not white Anglo-Saxon protestant.

explain what is innately problematic or detrimental about matriarchies. Although the Moynihan Report, as it is often called, has been widely criticized in the social science literature, some contemporary sociologists argue that although the methodology was flawed and he overgeneralized his findings vis-à-vis African American families, Moynihan nonetheless identified important trends. These trends, as we have found today, characterized not only the African American families he described but also white and various other racial and ethnic families as well.

In addition to women and African Americans, various groups of color are often overrepresented, misrepresented, or not represented at all in marriage and family research. For example, compared with research about other groups in U.S. society, very little research has been done on Native American families; thus, little is known about these families. Because Native Americans are small in number and often live in remote areas of the country, they are, perhaps, the most invisible group of color. When they are studied, it is often either within erroneous or outdated models of family life that are generalized to a very diverse group of people or within a pathology/deviance model. Currently, about 2 million Native Americans live in the United States. These diverse peoples include Cherokee, Sioux, Chippewa, Navajo, Seminole, Lakota, and more than 500 other nations representing over 150 languages. Yet, traditional research continues to refer to Native Americans as if they were a homogeneous group. Traditional research on Native American families seldom presents family members as having agency, that is, initiating actions based on their own values and judgments rather than simply reacting to outside forces such as government pressure, exploitation, and oppression. Therefore, although we know much about the rates of alcoholism and suicide (alleged pathologies in response to oppression) in some of these families (though we are not exactly sure which families since these data too are often generalized), we know very little about their family relations or process. Furthermore, regional, cultural, and tribal differences are not distinguished when researchers have reported about Native Americans in generalized language. For example, some Native American families live in cities, others on reservations or in rural areas; some Native Americans have assimilated, some have not. These distinctions alone make for vast differences among and across Native American families.

On the other hand, while there is increasing attention to and research on Latinas/os (as one of the fastest-growing groups of color currently in the United States), the family patterns of these groups are often misunderstood or misrepresented. A major problem in this regard is that popular images of and myths about Latina/o families sometimes merge with scientific research on such families. Moreover, according to Maxine Baca Zinn (1994), very often Latina/o groups are lumped together under the hybrid label *Hispanic*, which has the effect of obscuring important differences among various Latina/o groups. Although most Latinas/os share a common language and cultural ancestry, the diversity among Latinas/os makes generalizations about their family lifestyles exceedingly difficult.

Like other groups of color, Asian Americans are a diverse group with diverse family lifestyles. Yet researchers, especially since the 1970s, have focused almost entirely on the economic and educational achievements of some Asian American families, with the result being a rather widespread depiction or generalization of "success"—strong family ties, strong work ethic, academic excellence, self-sufficiency, and a low level of welfare dependency—to all Asian American families. This is not to say that such characterizations do not describe the realities of some Asian American families; however, the tendency, both in American popular culture and in scholarly research, is to put forth the notion of a monolithic "model minority" model of Asian American families. If nothing else, such a lumping of all Asian American families together obscures the legacy of racism and the difficulties associated with acculturation these families have experienced, with the result that not all Asian American families have been successful.

While perhaps the most frequently researched of all families of color, much of the research on African American families focuses primarily on lower- and working-class families. As critics have pointed out, not only are most of the subjects of marriage and family research on African American families from the lower class, but they are frequently from the most deprived segment of the lower class. Little systematic research exists focusing on middle-class families of color, especially the upper middle class.

Even less is known about wealthy families across race. Thus, like gender and race, class is an important factor in who gets studied and how they are studied and in who does not get studied. Across race and gender little research is carried out on upper-class families. Power is an issue here. Because women, people of color, and the lower classes generally lack power, they are either largely ignored by researchers or they are easily accessible to researchers, some of whom allow their race, sex, and class biases to affect their research. Those individuals and families with considerable wealth and power can control researchers' access to them and thus researchers' ability to use them as subjects. Because there is so little information on the marriage and family lifestyles of the upper classes, Americans, hungry for a glimpse of such lifestyles, are fascinated with media portrayals of how such families live. Whether these portrayals reflect the real world of upper-class marriages and families is not readily known because there is so little scientific information against which to compare.

Estimates vary, but somewhere between 2 percent and 10 percent of the U.S. population is homosexual. Despite popular stereotypes and the increasing visibility of lesbians and gays, we are only just beginning to learn about some aspects of their family lifestyles, such as their reproductive choices and ways of parenting. Traditionally, if lesbians and gay couples were referred to at all in research or textbooks, they were treated at best as an aberration of the "real" family and at worst denied family status overall.

While lesbians and gays are similar in their behavior, they are not a monolithic group. They vary across race, class, age, and other important social characteristics. Yet the lesbians and gays that are studied are most often young, white, and middle class. Few studies focus on lesbians and gays of color or older lesbians and gays across race and class. Indeed, over the past decade, as we (the authors of this textbook) conducted research for each of the previous editions of this book, a major obstacle in our quest to be inclusive was the lack of research on diverse family groupings such as lesbian and gay families. When we did find research on lesbians and gays, for example, much of the traditional research was narrowly focused or concerned with their sexual behavior. Like others in the population, lesbians and gays are ongoing, active members of marriages, families, and intimate relationships. Thus, such narrowly focused research perpetuates many popular myths about homosexuality and is misrepresentative of the diversity of family lifestyles in the United States. Fortunately, this situation is changing as more researchers are broadening their focus to study diverse populations and a wide range of marriage and family structures and lifestyles.

Contemporary Marriage and Family Scholarship

Although sociology as a discipline has not always made good on its claim to give accurate accounts of the social world and its social problems, a growing number of sociologists and interdisciplinary scholars are using the perspectives that the discipline offers, including a feminist perspective, to develop and transmit more complete and accurate understandings of marriages, families, and intimate relationships.

Unfortunately, shoddy research methodologies, faulty generalizations, and researcher biases, myths, stereotypes, oversimplifications, and misrepresentations continue to affect some research on marriages and families. Much of this research continues to be heterosexist as well as sex-, race-, and class-specific, even though it is generalized as applicable to the largest possible population. Social scientist Marianne Ferber's observation on this subject seems appropriate here: "It is interesting to note . . . one significant difference between studies concerned with only men as opposed to those investigating women. The latter tend to be unmistakably labeled, while the former have titles which give no hint that they are restricted to men" (1982:293).

Scientific research on marriages and families does not exist in a vacuum. Its theory and practice reflect the structure and values of U.S. society. In a society where massive inequalities in power, wealth, and prestige exist among classes and racial groups, as well as between women and men, scientific research, its methods, content, and conclusions, reflect these inequalities. Given this reality, social research must be evaluated by who is or is not the researcher, who does and does not get studied, which theoretical paradigms and underlying assumptions are accepted, which methods are used and how, and what the research actually says and does not say about the subjects.

To their credit, contemporary family researchers exhibit a growing recognition of race, class, gender, and sexual diversity in marriage and family lifestyles. Although no research techniques are specific to people of color, women, poor and working-class people, or lesbians and gays, some existing methods seem more productive than others. For example, as we have already pointed out, various field methods, such as face-to-face interviews, participant observation, and case studies, enable the research subjects to tell their stories from their own point of view. In this context, contemporary scholarship has opened up a new and healthy discourse in the area of marriage and family research. This continuing discourse has greatly enhanced our knowledge of marriages and families. In addition, any attempt to understand marriage, family, and intimate relationships within U.S. society must necessarily be informed by the implications of the globalization of the world's societies. Thus, a new and increasing emphasis on cross-cultural and global research has increased our awareness of how global connections profoundly impact our lives and has provided further insights about marriages and families in the multicultural worlds in which humans live. In the "In Other Places" box in this chapter, we take a look, for example, at a Kenyan-born sociologist, Wamucii Njogu, and her marriage and family research conducted in her native Kenya.

Now let us turn our attention to the other half of the scientific enterprise, namely, theories pertaining to marriages and families.

IN OTHER PLACES

MARRIAGE AND FAMILY PATTERNS IN KENYA

As family sociologists, one of our continuing messages is that there are diverse ways in which marriages and families are structured. Cross-cultural research is important in that it allows us to learn and understand cultures different from our own while at the same time appreciate how much all humans have in common. Learning about diverse cultural structures and lifestyles helps to deepen our understanding of sociological concepts. Comparisons and contrasts of diverse marriage and family lifestyles allow us to apply concepts and theories that broaden our understanding of their meaning. They also challenge ideas of a single model of marriage and family life and highlight the flexibility of humans in creating diverse cultures.

It is often said that social research interests are sparked by personal biography. Wamucii Njogu is a classic example. An assistant professor of sociology at Northeastern Illinois University in Chicago, Dr. Njogu is an internationally known scholar and

Dr. Wamucii Njogu

a member of the Union for African Population Studies, the International Union for the Scientific Study of Population, and the Population Association of America. Born and raised in Kenya, she speaks three languages fluently, and received her Ph.D. at the University of Wisconsin at Madison. As a bilingual bicultural sociologist, she has been able to move back and forth between her native country and the United States and examine both cultures as an "outsider from within." Sociologically, this has had important implications for her research interests, the kinds of questions she asks, the issues that she finds problematic, and the nature of her analyses and contributions to marriage and family theory and research. Some examples from her biography reflect this connection.

Dr. Njogu was first attracted to the study of sociology when, as an undergraduate student at the University of Nairobi, she was assigned to write a sociological research paper. Coming from a background in which her parents owned a large farm and employed a large number of poor rural workers, Dr. Njogu decided to focus on poverty among these workers and the question of how these people came to be where they were in the stratification structure. Her findings, namely, that these workers typically came from generations of such workers, that within these families some members (primarily women) were worse off than others, and that these families generally had a large number of children whom they could not adequately support economically, led her to her long-standing interests in stratification, gender inequality, fertility, family

THEORETICAL PERSPECTIVES

Try as we may we cannot separate theory from real life. The way we look at and understand society and human behavior depends on our theoretical perspective. In sociology, there is no single theory of marriages and families. Many different perspectives exist. By *perspective* we simply mean a broad explanation of social reality from a particular point of view. These perspectives provide us with a basic image of society and human behavior. They define what we should study, what questions we should ask, how we should ask them, what methods we should use to gather information, and how we should interpret the answers or information we obtain. In addition, theoretical perspectives often generate subtheories or theory models. Social scientist David Cheal (1989) describes a **theory model** as a minitheory, a set of propositions intended to account for a limited set of facts.

To understand properly the sociology of contemporary marriages and families, we should know something about the different views that are part of the discipline of marriage and family study. It is therefore worthwhile not only to describe the different theoretical perspectives but also to look at them with a critical eye to weigh their relative advantages and disadvantages as explanation systems.

In the remainder of this chapter we examine and critique some of the major theoretical approaches and perspectives used in the field of sociology. As you study these different approaches, pay particular attention to how the choice of a theoretical perspective will influence not only the way data are interpreted but also the very nature of the questions asked. Consider how a different theoretical perspective would lead to a different set of questions and conclusions about marriages and families.

Sociologists approach the study of human behavior and society with a particular set of theoretical assumptions. As in other disciplines, sociology contains not just one but a number of theoretical perspectives. Although there is some debate over how many sociological perspectives exist, there is formation, and child fostering/informal adoption.

Her interest in gender inequality is also tied to the fact that she comes from a long line of female-headed households (which defies tradition in the patriarchal society into which she was born), including a paternal grandmother who, after the death of her husband, defied cultural tradition by refusing to marry her dead husband's brother. Remaining single, this woman raised her children alone and instilled in them egalitarian values. Consequently, Dr. Njogu's father raised her and her male siblings as equals. Her research on female law students' participation in the classroom was shaped by her own experiences as a female student in high school and college in Kenya. Because of the preference for males in her culture, monies for school go first and foremost for boys' education. Dr. Njogu, thus, was one of a small percentage of Kenyan women who attended high school and of an even smaller percentage attending college. She was an extremely bright student, which "was not the thing to do" in Kenya, she says. As a result, the boys called her names, such as "girl/boy," because only boys were supposed to be in school and to be smart. This helped her understand, not just in abstract terms, but because of her personal experiences, what sexism and gender inequality meant.

Most recently, Dr. Njogu has conducted research and written a series of papers on HIV/AIDS in Kenya. For example, using data collected in Kenya in 1998, Dr. Njogu studied the relationship between HIV/AIDS knowledge and risk prevention or safe sexual behavior. Although HIV/AIDS has killed individual family members and, sometimes, whole families, this deadly reality has not translated into safe sexual behavior, particularly for young women. In a report of her findings at the International Union for the Scientific Study of Population in Salvador, Brazil, Dr. Njogu indicated that the gender gap is one of the greatest barriers to sexual behavior change in Kenya. For example, young Kenyan women are less likely than their male counterparts to know that AIDS can be transmitted through sexual intercourse or that condoms can protect them against infection. The difficulty experienced by women in implementing prevention strategies is another reason why AIDS knowledge may not necessarily lead to behavior change. Young women in Kenya consider their risk of contracting HIV/AIDS to be high, not because of their own behavior but because of their partners' past and current sexual behavior. This knowledge notwithstanding, unequal gender relations and other cultural traditions prevent women from protecting themselves against HIV infection.

According to Dr. Njogu, cross-cultural research not only fosters a better understanding and appreciation for cultural diversity but also often serves to debunk some of the myths created by research that uses Western culture as the model of marriage and family life.

What do you think? *Is there a similar gender gap in HIV/AIDS knowledge in the United States? What role does gender play in risk prevention behavior among young American adults? What can we learn from cross-cultural research about the differential impact on family members of diseases such as HIV/AIDS?*

general agreement that three basic perspectives form the backbone of what has been called mainstream sociology: structural functionalism, conflict theory, and symbolic interaction. In addition, we examine the social-constructionist, social-exchange, developmental family life cycle, and feminist theoretical perspectives. Although most of these theories are broad, applying not only to marriages and families, we examine them as they have been used to explain marriage and family life generally, or some specific aspect of marriage and family life in the United States.

Structural Functionalism

In the history of the sociology of marriages and families, structural functionalism has been one of the leading theoretical perspectives used to explain how families work and how they relate to the larger society. Basically, **structural functionalism** views society as an organized and stable system, analogous to the human system, that is made up of a variety of interrelated parts or structures. Each structure performs one or several functions or meets vital social needs. These structures, sometimes called subsystems, are the major social institutions in society and include the family, economy, government, and religion. Each of these structures has a function for maintaining society. The family, for example, through reproduction, provides society with new members, which ensures that society is ongoing. At least in theory, all institutions in society work in harmony for the good of society and themselves. Thus, a functional analysis examines the ways in which each part of a system (society or any one of its parts) contributes to the functioning of society as a whole. In this analysis, the terms *system* and *structure* refer to the interrelatedness or interaction of the parts. *Function* refers to the consequence or impact of something for itself and other parts of the system as well as the system as a whole.

Many Americans believe in a singular model of the family to which all families must conform. Those families that do not conform are seen as problematic. People who believe that families must be structured in a certain way (for example, two parents) to fulfill important family tasks and who see single-parent or female-headed families, stepfamilies, and the changing role of women in marriages and families as threats to marriage and family life or as indicative of the demise of the family share a common view with structural functionalists. Are you a structural functionalist? Do you share these views?

The Family from a Functionalist Perspective In analyzing the family, a person using the functionalist perspective would ask general questions, such as: What do families contribute to the maintenance of society? How does the structure of society affect families? How do families mesh with other institutions in society? Not only does this perspective view society as a system, but it regards families themselves as systems. Therefore, a functional analysis would examine such issues as how families organize themselves for survival and what functions families perform for society and for their individual members. Take, for example, the question of teenage suicide. A person using a functionalist perspective might ask questions about how the family functions vis-à-vis individual family members who contemplate suicide.

According to functionalists, family functions historically have been divided along gender and age lines. Women and men must perform different tasks, as must younger and older people. Particularly since the Industrial Revolution, an important family task has been to provide economic support for family members. If the family is to survive, someone has to earn money by working for wages outside the home. At the same time, someone must work inside the home to maintain it for the wage earner as well as for other family members. This division of labor along gender lines is said to make women and men interdependent.

Functionalists are interested not only in the intended, overt, or **manifest functions** of social institutions such as the family but in the unintended, unrecognized, or **latent functions** as well. Thus, a manifest function of having children might be to continue the family lineage or to add to marital satisfaction. Because children can add stress to a relationship, however, the introduction of children in the early years of family life often has the latent function of decreasing marital satisfaction. In addition, not all features of a social system are **functional**—performing a positive service by helping to maintain the system in a balanced state or promoting the achievement of group goals. Some features of the system might actually hamper the achievement of group goals and disrupt the system's balance. Such features are said to be **dysfunctional.** A single feature can be functional and dysfunctional at the same time. For example, the movement of married women into the labor force might be defined as functional in that their salaries contribute to the family income but defined as dysfunctional in that their time with their families is limited. A classic example of the use of the structural-functional perspective to explain how marriages and families work is embedded in the "nuclear family model" popularized in the mid 1950s by the late sociologist Talcott Parsons.

The Nuclear Family Model Recall from Chapter 1 that as Western societies became industrialized and urbanized in the late nineteenth and early twentieth centuries, the nuclear family emerged as the dominant family type to meet the needs of an industrial economy. Talcott Parsons (1955, 1964) agreed with the structural-functional assumption that the family is an adaptive system that performs essential functions for its individual members as well as for society as a whole. He argued, however, that in modern society the functional importance of the nuclear family has declined as many of its functions have been taken over and performed by other social institutions. This is particularly true in terms of the family's economic function. The modern nuclear family is no longer an economic unit. (This issue is often debated in the literature and will be discussed in more detail in Chapter 10.) According to Parsons, the two major functions of the modern family are now socialization of the young and personality stabilization of adults. Personality stabilization is the process whereby individuals internalize society's values and expectations concerning gender-appropriate behavior to the point where these values and cultural expectations become a consistent part of the individual's identity throughout her or his lifetime.

The nuclear family model places great emphasis on the isolation of the nuclear family from the extended family. It also emphasizes that a differentiation of gender roles within the family is a functional necessity for the solidarity of the marriage relationship. Parsons described the male role in this regard as instrumental and the female role as expressive. The personality traits needed to carry out these roles are quite different. **Instrumental traits** encourage self-confidence, rationality, competition, and coolness—qualities that facilitate male success in the world of work. In contrast, **expressive traits** encourage nurturance, emotionality, sensitivity, and warmth—qualities that help women succeed in caring for a husband, children, and a home.

Critique Probably no other sociological perspective has been the center of as much attention, controversy, and criticism as structural functionalism. Parsons's nuclear family model has often been at the center of some of this controversy. Some of the major criticisms of this model are the same as those directed against functionalism generally: The model is specific to a particular time and place, does not utilize a historical context, and does not deal with the diversity of experiences that has always characterized U.S. families. What seemed true about marriages and families in the 1950s is less true today. The latest census data confirm that fewer and fewer families fit the Parsonian nuclear family model.

In addition, married-couple families often exhibit a diversity of structures and roles that the Parsonian model does not account for. Using this model, for example, how can we explain the growing number of men today who are openly nurturant, caring, and sensitive—traits that Parsons describes as exclusively expressive and female? The nuclear family model is especially criticized for its rigid, exaggerated, and oversimplified view of marital interaction generally and of women's experiences specifically (Cheal, 1989).

Karl Marx

Max Weber

Emile Durkheim

Jane Addams

W. E. B. Dubois

Harriet Martineau

Patricia Hill Collins

Randall Collins

Arlie Hochschild

Although women and African Americans were involved in the early development of sociology, their contributions went largely unrecognized until the last two decades, when a movement for a more inclusive scholarship took hold.

For example, how does the nuclear family model apply to African American families under slavery, where legal marriage was prohibited and women's and men's roles were interchanged? Similarly, can it explain the diversity in Native American families, particularly those in which women exercised economic power in subsistence residential units that were the basis of their tribal economy?

Although functionalism has provided important insights, such as how marriages and families work and presumably why they exist, several important criticisms have been raised about this perspective generally. For example, although functionalism may be a useful framework for identifying a society's structural parts and the alleged functions of these parts, what function a particular structure serves, and why, are not always clear. What, for example, is the function of the division of labor in the family along gender lines? Is it efficiency and survival, as the functionalists maintain, or is it the perpetuation of the social dominance of certain categories of people, namely, men and the subordination of others, namely, women? Another important criticism is the conservative bias of functional analysis. Critics argue that by assuming that consensus lies at the basis of any social order, functionalists tend to promote and rationalize the status quo and to understate disharmony and conflict. Thus, they do not consider that something might be wrong with the system itself.

Although structural functionalism was the dominant theory in the field for over 30 years, the changing political consciousness of the 1960s brought about increasing criticism of this perspective. Today there is widespread recognition that structural functionalism generally and the nuclear family model specifically are limiting when used to analyze families in the United States and are therefore no longer representative of "mainstream" sociological thought on families. Consequently, functionalism has greatly declined in importance as a viable frame of reference for understanding society, its institutions, and its members. In fact, some of its strongest supporters during its peak now declare that it is "embarrassing" (Moore, 1978) and "dead," and that it should be abandoned and replaced by more enlightened perspectives (Turner and Maryanski, 1979). However, its impact, especially on the public, can still be detected. Today, when people talk about the family, they often have in mind the functionalist model of the nuclear family. For many people the nuclear family remains the ideal form, even though such families are less prevalent today than they were in the past.

Conflict Theory

Since the 1960s, the conflict perspective has become increasingly popular and important in modern sociology and in the works of feminist scholars across academic disciplines. There are several different approaches to conflict theory; however, all of them have their roots in the nineteenth-century pioneering writings of Karl Marx. Thus, our discussion here is of a very general nature and combines various strands of thought on conflict theory today. First, however, we take a brief look at Marxian theory.

Karl Marx Karl Marx (1818–1883) was an economist, political agitator, and social theorist who did much to revolutionize social and philosophical thinking about human society. Appalled by the brutal treatment of workers and their families during the nineteenth-century Industrial Revolution in Europe, Marx sought to understand the causes of this condition, in hopes of changing it. Basically, he believed that the problem lay in the social organization of industrial societies. Such societies were capitalistic: The means of production were privately owned and were used to maximize profits.

For Marx, every aspect of social life is based on economic relationships. For example, he believed that all industrialized societies are characterized by competition and conflict between two main groups: the capitalists (owners of the land and factories) and the proletariat (workers). These two groups have fundamentally opposing interests, as well as unequal power. Conflict arises because the capitalists can maximize their profit only by exploiting the proletariat. At the same time, it is in the interest of the proletariat to revolt and overthrow the capitalist system and to establish a classless society in which wealth and power would be distributed evenly. Thus, meaningful social change comes about only as a result of the struggle between competing groups. In essence, for Marx, economic power explains the structure of societies and social relationships. Order and balance are always tenuous in capitalist societies. Such societies are held together by the power of capitalists to dominate the workers.

Relative to the fundamental sociological question, What is the relationship between the individual and society? Marxian theory addresses both structure and action. It deals with structural factors in that it stresses that the historical circumstances of capitalism limit most of the choices open to people. At the same time, it stresses the action element in that it recognizes the capacity of workers to join together as a class-conscious group to collectively change existing economic and social conditions (Light, Keller, and Calhoun, 1989).

Themes of Conflict Theory Like functionalism, **conflict theory** focuses on social structures and institutions in society. The basic assumption of the conflict perspective, and perhaps the one that most sets it apart from functionalism, however, is the notion that conflict is natural and inevitable in all human interaction, including family systems. Therefore, a complete understanding of society is possible only through a critical examination of competition, coercion, and conflict in society, especially those processes that lead some people to have great power and control and others to have little or no power and control. Thus, of major concern are the inequalities that are built into social structures or systems. Rather than focusing on interdependence, unity, and consensus, conflict theorists focus on society as an arena in which individuals and groups compete over limited resources and fight for power and control. A key assumption here is that certain groups and individuals have much greater power and access to key resources than others do.

From this perspective, disorder, disagreement, and open hostility among individuals and groups are viewed as normal, and stability is the condition that requires explanation.

For the purposes of our discussion, we can reduce conflict theory to three central themes: (1) Humans have basic interests or things they want and attempt to acquire; (2) power is at the base of all social relationships, and it is always scarce, unequally distributed, and coercive; and (3) values and ideas are weapons used by different groups to advance their own ends rather than to define society's identity and goals (Wallace and Wolf, 1991). Given these assumptions, the conflict perspective leads us to ask questions about the sources of tension among individuals and groups with different amounts of power, the techniques of conflict control in society, and the ways in which those with power perpetuate, maintain, and extend that power. In short, a major underlying question of conflict analysis is, Who benefits from and who is systematically deprived by any given social arrangement?

The Family from a Conflict Perspective Whereas functionalists focus on the tasks that serve the interests of the family as a whole, conflict theorists see families, like all societal institutions, as a set of social relationships that benefit some members more than others. Thus, a conflict theorist might ask general questions, such as: How is social inequality built into the structure of marriages and families? What is the role of a marital partner or family member in promoting family disintegration or change? When conflict occurs in the family, who wins? Who loses? How are racial, ethnic, gender, class, and other inequalities perpetuated through the operation of the family?

From this perspective, marriages and families can be viewed as smaller versions of the larger class system, where the well-being of one class (men) is the result of the exploitation and oppression of another class (women). The family exploits women specifically by encouraging them to perform unpaid housework and child care so that men can devote their time to capitalist endeavors. Historically, those men who had the power to do so defined marriages and families in such a way that women were the sexual property of men. In consequence, marriage became a legally and socially enforced contract of sexual property. Although women in the United States are no longer legally defined as the property of men, other examples of male domination of women abound. For example, women continue to have major responsibility for and perform the major portion of housework and child rearing, even though most women are now in the paid labor force (Hochschild, 1997; U.S. Census Bureau, 2000).

In essence, then, the basic source of male dominance and women's subordination is the home and family. Although functionalists may view the family as a refuge, for the conflict theorist the question is, What kind of refuge is it, and whom does it benefit? The link between the traditional family and social inequality involves a number of conflicts that are discussed in some detail in later chapters of this book, including violence against women, children, and the elderly; divorce; female-headed families; and the feminization of poverty.

Critique For many people, especially those who experience oppression, the conflict perspective offers a concrete set of propositions that explain unequal access to resources in terms of institutional structure rather than personal deficiencies. A major strength of this perspective is the way in which it relates social and organizational structure to group interests and the distribution of resources. Furthermore, it provides a historical framework within which to identify social change: the major shifts in the distribution of societal resources and social and political power. By tracing social behavior back to individuals' interests and the purposeful way they pursue them, it suggests a model to explain social and political change. And finally, unlike functionalism, the conflict perspective does not treat norms, values, and ideas as external to, and constraints on, individual behavior. Rather, the conflict perspective views human beings as very much involved in using the system of norms, values, and ideas as much as being used by it. Those who have the power use these systems to further their individual or group interests.

Conflict theory is not without its criticisms. One major criticism is that the underlying assumptions that power is people's main objective and conflict is the major feature of social life are too narrow. Some critics argue, for example, that within the family, societal norms encourage certain behaviors that either prevent conflict or keep it under control. Thus, for example, disagreements among family members usually can be resolved without the use of physical force.

In addition, the conflict perspective is often criticized for explicitly advocating social change, thereby giving up some of its claim to scientific objectivity. Furthermore, conflict theory, like functionalism, raises the issue of value neutrality. Whereas structural functionalists evaluate social patterns in a system in terms of whether they are positive or negative, conflict theorists are purposely critical of society. Both of these positions pose a dilemma for value-free sociology. Most conflict theorists try to separate their value judgments from their analysis of society. However, when they focus on inequalities in society and claim, for example, that a more equitable distribution of tasks and resources between the sexes is desirable, the inherent value judgment is quite clear. These problems notwithstanding, the conflict perspective is a useful framework for analyzing how factors such as race, class, gender, age, and ethnicity are linked to the unequal distribution of valuable resources in marriages and families, including power, property, money, prestige, and education.

Symbolic Interactionism

Functionalism and the conflict perspective both concern themselves with macropatterns (large-scale patterns) that characterize society or groups like families as a whole. In contrast, the **symbolic-interaction** perspective focuses on micropatterns (small-scale patterns) of face-to-face interaction among people in specific settings, such as within marriages and families. This perspective is based on the notion that society is made up of interacting individuals who communicate primarily through the use of shared **symbols**—objects, words, sounds, and events that are given meaning by members of a culture—and construct reality as they go about the business of their daily lives. The most important set of symbols that humans use is language. People interact with one another based on their understandings of the meanings of words and social situations as well as their perceptions of what others expect of them within those situations. Thus, a major emphasis is on individuals and their social relationships, the subjective meanings of human behavior, and the various processes through which people come to construct and agree on various definitions of reality.

THE FAMILY FROM A SYMBOLIC-INTERACTION PERSPECTIVE

When using the symbolic-interaction perspective as a frame of reference for analyzing marriages and families, one might ask questions such as: How are marriages and families experienced? How do individual family members interact to create, sustain, and change marriages and families? How do family members attempt to shape the reality perceived by other family members? How do the behaviors of family members change from one situation to another?

According to the late sociologist Ernest Burgess (1926), the family represents a unified set of interacting individuals. That is, unity in family life comes about as a result of interactions among various family members. In this sense, the concern is with marriages and families as social processes rather than with their structure. Thus, a symbolic interactionist would argue that the reality of marriage and family life is not fixed but is *socially constructed* and is constructed differently by various family members with different roles, privileges, and responsibilities. The **social construction of reality** is the process whereby people assign meanings to social phenomena—objects, events, and characteristics—that almost always cause those who draw upon these meanings to emphasize some aspect of a phenomenon and to ignore others. These assigned meanings have tremendous consequences for the individuals involved, depending on how they interact with each other, what decisions they make, and what actions they take (Ferrante, 1992).

Taking this perspective, sociologist Jessie Bernard (1982) has argued, for example, that women and men are likely to view and experience their marriages differently. Referring to this phenomenon as "her" and "his" marriages, Bernard contends that due to traditionally different sex role socialization and expectations, women have less power than men in marriages and families. Married women, therefore, must make certain accommodations, some of which may have negative effects on their mental health. In this respect, the psychological costs of marriage are much greater for wives than for husbands, and the benefits are far less.

Social Constructionism

As the limitations of an objectivist explanation of social life have become more and more evident in postmodern society, many social scientists and other scholars (not only sociologists but also social workers, political scientists, lawyers, and historians) increasingly have sought to explain social life in terms of a subjectivist approach. These scholars use what is referred to as a *social-constructionist perspective.* **Social constructionism** is an extension of symbolic-interaction theory, in which the analysis is framed entirely in terms of a conceptualization of the social construction of reality. A guiding principle is that human experience is not uniform and cannot be generalized to all people. The important facts of human social life are not inherent in human biology but are developed through a complex process of human interaction in which we learn both the attitudes and the behaviors appropriate to our culture and attempt to modify these scripted behaviors and attitudes in order to make them more palatable. Those using a social-constructionist perspective argue that the meaning of social reality is neither transhistorical nor culturally universal, but rather varies from culture to culture and within any culture over time. Some fundamental assumptions of this perspective and symbolic interactionism generally are

- Reality is invented, constructed largely out of the meanings and values of the observer.
- Language is a mediating influence on all constructions; we bring forth realities through our interactions with other human beings.
- We cannot know an objective reality apart from our subjective views of it.
- Culture, history, politics, and economic conditions all influence individual experiences of social reality.

SOCIAL CONSTRUCTIONISM AND THE FAMILY Almost any subject related to marriage and family life can be analyzed within the context of the social-constructionist paradigm. One example of the application of the constructivist perspective that is especially relevant to the sociology of marriages and families can be seen in terms of the concept of gender. Gender is a socially constructed system for classifying people as girl or boy, woman or man, feminine or masculine (Chapter 3 is devoted to an in-depth discussion of gender within a broad context of social constructionism). Take masculinity, for example: Men are not born to follow a predetermined biological imperative encoded somewhere in their physical makeup. Rather, to be a man is to participate in the social life of a culture as it defines manhood and masculinity. Thus, it is to participate in society as a gendered being. In this sense, men are not born but made by culture. Men also make themselves, actively constructing their masculinities within a social and historical context. Therefore, the reality of being a male in twenty-first-century U.S. society and its impact on marriage, family, and intimate relationships is quite different from that experienced by individual men, marriages, and families one hundred years ago. It is also very different from being a male in South Africa, Sri Lanka, Southeast Asia, Bosnia, Kosovo, Albania, Israel, or the former Soviet Union. In this same context, the roles of males as husband, father, brother, lover, worker, and so on, are all shaped by our cultural constructions and agreements about gender. The social construction of masculinity in the United States defines men's roles in the family as economic provider and protector of women and children. In New Guinea, among the Tchambuli, however, men are expected to be submissive, emotional, delicate, and dependent.

The social-constructionist perspective is both historical and comparative. In the case of marriages, families, and intimate relationships, such a perspective allows us to explore the ways in which the meanings of social reality, of social experiences vary across marriages, families, and cultures, as well as how they change over historical time. This perspective enables us to better understand gender and its relationship in marriages and families. Thus, how culture and individual men construct masculinity has a very real impact on how men relate to women and children in marriages, families, and intimate relationships. The implication here is that all such relationships are social productions and have no intrinsic meaning. That is, they have no meaning outside that which is understood by the actors. As you continue to read this textbook, you will find that we apply the social-constructionist perspective wherever relevant. Thus, you will find a range of topics, including violence, intimacy, gender, parenting, motherhood, fatherhood, and sexuality, discussed within the framework of constructionism.

Critique The symbolic-interaction perspective brings people back into our analyses. Rather than seeing humans as passive beings who simply respond to society's rules, interactionists give us a view of humans as actively involved in constructing, shaping, sustaining, and changing the social world. It is a useful framework for examining the complexities of relationships and the daily workings of marriages and families, complexities that functionalism and the conflict perspective miss. One of the major advantages of this perspective is that it helps us understand how the roles we play are so important in our social constructions of reality.

Likewise, social constructionism is a useful approach to studying human social life and offers a viable alternative to traditional static, ahistoric, and deterministic theoretical perspectives. According to some scholars (for example, Rosenblum and Travis, 1996), an important advantage of a constructionist approach is that it enables us to understand that certain categories of human experience, such as race, sex, sexual orientation, and class, have social significance; that is, these categories are socially created and arbitrary. Instead of viewing people as essentially different by virtue of these labels, social constructionism leads us to question not the *essential* difference between categories, but rather the origin and consequence of the labeling or categorization system itself. Thus, as we will see throughout this textbook, categories such as race are not clear-cut; racial categories do not exist apart from the social and cultural milieux in which they operate.

Neither symbolic interactionism nor social constructionism are without limitations or critics. In focusing attention on the subjective aspects of human experiences and the situations in which they occur, both perspectives ignore the objective realities of inequality, racism, sexism, and the differential distribution of wealth, status, and power among various groups; they also minimize the impact of these phenomena on individuals and families. Criticisms directed specifically at social constructionism include the claim that it is inherently inconsistent, that its theoretical assumptions are contradictory. Some critics argue that there is not a clear agreement about what constitutes constructionism. Most often those who criticize constructionism are objectivists who argue that (1) social constructionism springs from a particular set of moral and political values or biases, and (2) social constructionism is simply an exercise in *debunking* previously held truths (Best, 1995). These criticisms notwithstanding, a social constructionist perspective provides a framework by which to make sense of what categories such as marriage, family, race, ethnicity, class, and sexual orientation mean in both historical and contemporary context; and it heightens our awareness of the socially constructed nature of everyday life.

Social-Exchange Theory

Probably the theoretical perspective most often used in the discipline to study marriages and families is **social-exchange theory.** This theory adopts an economic model of human behavior based on costs, benefits, and the expectation of reciprocity; for this reason it is sometimes referred to as the rational-choice perspective. It tends to be very close to the way that many of us see and explain behavior in our everyday lives.

Have you ever wondered why some person you know or heard about remained in an unhappy relationship? Did you try to analyze this behavior by asking what the person might be getting out of the relationship versus whatever makes her or him unhappy (in other words, the pluses, or benefits, and minuses, or costs, of the relationship)? Did the person eventually leave the relationship? Did you wonder what finally made her or him end it? Was your answer that the costs finally became too great or outweighed the benefits? If you have ever engaged in this type of cost–benefit analysis to explain your own or other people's actions and relationships, you were using a basic social-exchange perspective.

Social-exchange theory shares many of the assumptions of symbolic-interaction theory and thus, in broad terms, is another extension of interaction theory. Social-exchange theory is so named because its underlying premise is that social exchange forms the basis of all social interaction. Exchange theorists view social interaction as an exchange of tangible or intangible goods and services, ranging from money or physical labor to social recognition, love, and respect. Humans are thought to be rational beings who, in making decisions, weigh the profits to be gained from a particular action against the costs it will incur. Only when people feel that the gains of their interactions outweigh the costs do they adopt the behavior. People, then, engage in those actions that bring them the greatest benefits at the least cost. They will continue to engage in these actions as long as they perceive them to be profitable.

The two best-known proponents of social-exchange theory are George Homans and Peter Blau. Homans (1961) focused on actual behavior that is rewarded or punished by the behavior of others. According to Homans, humans react to stimuli based on need, reward, and reinforcement. Thus, in the various exchange relationships in which humans engage, the rewards will usually be proportional to the costs. Blau (1964), on the other hand, was more concerned with explaining large-scale social structures. According to Blau, not all exchange can be explained in terms of actual behavior. Rather, exchange, like other interactions, is a subjective and interpretative process. Blau agrees with Homans that humans want rewards, and in exchange interactions each person receives something perceived as equivalent to that which is given. Blau refers to this as "fair exchange." He contends, however, that our relationship choices and decisions are not made purely on the basis of the perceived rewards but are affected by various social influences, such as family and friends.

A good example of this can be seen in terms of various interracial relationships. An interracial couple might find their relationship mutually beneficial and satisfying, with the benefits far outweighing the costs. Social approval of the relationship may be very important to the couple, however. Thus, if family and friends strongly disapprove, the couple might decide to terminate the relationship.

The Family from a Social-Exchange Perspective Marriage and family literature is filled with examples of social exchange. Most experts agree that marriage and family life are characterized by an exchange of goods and services. Thus, most exchange analyses of marriage and family behavior focus on relations between couples. Typically, a person using an exchange perspective is concerned with questions like those previously asked of you. In the language of exchange theory, for example, we might explain the observation that when women work they gain power in the family (see Chapter 10) with the reasoning that in exchange for their economic contribution, working women share more equitably in decision making.

Family sociologists, particularly those concerned with dating, mating, and marital behavior, have long used exchange theory to explain this behavior. As we will see in Chapter 5, many sociologists use exchange theory to explain how people in the United States choose whom to date and marry. They contend that Americans search for the best possible mate (product) given their own resources (physical attractiveness, intelligence, youth, status, money). People in this situation weigh a range of costs and benefits before choosing a mate. As you read this textbook, think about the value of different types of resources and the exchange processes at work in understanding a variety of marriage and family behaviors and relationships.

Critique Exchange theory assumes that humans are rational, calculating beings who consciously weigh the costs versus the benefits of their relationships. A major problem with this notion of human behavior is that it cannot be disproved. Almost any behavior can be explained simply by saying that it must have had some value to the person involved, whether or not this is really the case. Furthermore, the notion of rational choice is limiting in that humans do not always act rationally, nor do we always agree on what rational behavior is. We do not always choose relationships or interactions simply because the rewards outweigh the costs. In fact, sometimes the reverse is true. One way of analyzing the "battered-woman syndrome" (discussed in Chapter 11) is to assume that women stay in abusive relationships not because the rewards outweigh the costs but because other factors, such as fear of physical violence if they leave, override all other considerations.

These criticisms notwithstanding, an exchange perspective provides us with a unique framework for explaining many face-to-face relationships. It provides insight into people's values, goals, and perceptions of reality. Exchange theory is probably most valuable for explaining people's actions when we want to know and understand the details of individual behavior.

The Developmental Family Life Cycle Model

Developmental family life cycle theory pays close attention to changes in families over time and attempts to explain family life in terms of a process that unfolds over the life course of families. Sociologist Paul Glick (Glick and Parke, 1965) was the first to analyze families in terms of a life cycle. According to Glick, families pass through a series of stages: (1) family formation (first marriage); (2) start of childbearing (birth of first child); (3) end of childbearing (birth of last child); (4) "empty nest" (when the last child leaves home); and (5) "family dissolution" (death of one spouse). Other life cycle theories identify somewhat similar stages.

According to such developmental theories, families change over time in terms of both the people who are members of the family and the roles they play. At various stages in the family life cycle, the family has different developmental tasks to perform. Each new stage in the family life cycle is brought on by a change in the composition of the family. These changes, in turn, affect various aspects of the family's well-being, including its economic viability. At each stage of development, the family is confronted with a distinct set of tasks whose completion is considered to be essential both for individual development and success at the next stage. One of the most widely used developmental theories in family sociology is an eight-stage model developed by Evelyn Duvall (1977).

As you study this model of family development, think about your own family and other families you know. How do these families fit into such a model? How do they differ? If they differ, does this mean that these families are abnormal or dysfunctional? (To pursue this activity, see the "Writing Your Own Script" box at the end of this chapter.)

Stage 1: Beginning families. At this first stage of development, the married couple does not have children and is just beginning married life and adjusting to it.

Stage 2: Childbearing families. The family is still forming in this stage. The first child is born, and women are deeply involved in childbearing and child rearing.

Stage 3: Families with preschool children. The family's oldest child is somewhere between 2 1/2 and 6 years of age. The mother is still deeply involved in child rearing. This stage lasts about 3 to 4 years.

Stage 4: Families with schoolchildren. The oldest child (or children) in the family is school-aged. With children in school, the mother is free to pursue other options, such as work outside the home.

Stage 5: Families with teenagers. In this stage, the oldest child is between 13 and 20 years old. The family must adjust to having adolescents in the home and adapt to their growing independence. This stage may last up to 7 years.

Stage 6: Families as launching centers. At this stage, the oldest child has been launched into adulthood. Families must develop adult relationships with grown children as they adjust to children leaving the family "nest." This stage lasts until the last child leaves home, usually a period of about 8 years.

Stage 7: Families in the middle years. This stage is sometimes called the "empty-nest" stage. It is a distinct new stage in the developmental cycle of the family and spans the time from when the last child leaves home to retirement or old age.

Stage 8: Aging families. Members of the family who work outside the home have retired at this stage. In this stage families must cope with events related to aging, such as chronic illnesses and the eventual death of one of the spouses. The remaining spouse must then deal with the factors and experiences associated with widowhood.

CRITIQUE Although developmental family life cycle theory generally calls attention to the changing nature of family relationships over time, distinguishing a "typical" family life cycle is difficult, if not impossible. As family norms change, the stages of family development also vary. In fact, some scholars believe that the stages of the family life cycle have become increasingly useful as indicators of change rather than as stages that all or even most families can be expected to experience. Although life cycle theories give us important insights into the complexities of family life, a shortcoming is that they assume that most families are nuclear families with children. Thus, such theories present a "typical" family life cycle descriptive of the "conventional" family. As with structural functionalism, for example, family life cycle theories do not incorporate the diversity of family lifestyles prevalent in U.S. society. Where, for example, do families without children, single-parent families, and remarried families fit in these models?

Moreover, families within various racial and ethnic groups develop through stages that are not recognized in these models. For example, due in part to their general disadvantaged economic position, many families of color and poor families across race take in relatives at some time in the family life cycle. In addition, a growing number of families in all classes are taking in and caring for aging parents. What does a developmental family life cycle model tell us about these families? Not only does such a theory omit these arrangements, but it generally implies a linear, or straight-line, progression in family life that few families actually experience. Families, for example, may progress through several of the early stages only to go back and repeat earlier stages, particularly if children are involved.

Furthermore, developmental theories such as Duvall's generally assume that developmental tasks, particularly those in the early stages, are gender-specific. Consider, for example, Duvall's first four stages. Each stage is defined entirely in terms of the presence of children and the role of women as caretakers and caregivers. Men and their parenting roles are totally omitted.

Feminist Theories and Perspectives

Feminist theory is not a single unified view; there is no single feminist theory. Rather, there are many types of feminist theory, just as there are many types of sociological theory. Nonetheless, this single label is often used to represent a diversity of feminist perspectives that contain certain common characteristics or principles. In this regard, feminist theory presents a generalized set of ideas about the basic features of society and human experience from a woman-centered perspective. It is woman-centered in three ways: (1) The starting point of all its investigations is the situations and experiences of women; (2) it treats women as the main subjects in the research process, that is, it attempts to view the world from the distinctive vantage points of women; and (3) it is critical and activist on behalf of women (Lengermann and Brantley, 1988).

A word of caution: Not all theories that deal with women or gender issues are feminist theories. To be considered feminist, a theory must reflect a feminist consciousness—an awareness rooted in a commitment to activist goals. In addition, it should adopt three basic philosophical approaches: (1) Gender is the central focus; (2) status quo gender relations are viewed as problematic in that women are defined as subordinate to men; and (3) gender relations are viewed as the result of social, not natural, factors (Chafetz, 1988).

Basically, all feminist theory attempts to answer two fundamental questions. The first is, Where are women? The second is, Why is this situation as it is? In addressing these questions, feminist theory typically focuses on the ways in which specific definitions of gender affect the organization of social institutions and patterns of gender inequality. Feminists have encouraged us to make the personal political.

This helps us understand that individual behavior and experiences within marriages, families, and intimate relationships are part of and impacted by larger societal institutions and other social, political, and historical factors. Finally, a major objective of feminist theory is social change. Perhaps more than most theories, feminist theories are explicitly and self-consciously political in their advocacy of social change.

In general, feminist theories and perspectives demonstrate how traditional ideas and theories have been derived from the particular experiences of some men and then have been used as universal standards against which all others have been viewed and judged. Asking sociological questions and studying marriages and families from a feminist perspective transforms traditional models of inquiry. No matter the discipline, however, when men's experiences are the standard, women and other subordinated groups (including many men) appear incomplete, inadequate, or invisible. On the other hand, when women's experiences are taken seriously, new methods and theoretical perspectives must be established (Andersen, 2000). For example, feminist theory and scholarship make central considerations of the ways that race, ethnicity, sexuality, and class influence our marriage and family experiences. Feminist scholars, for instance, have revised our thinking about motherhood as a static universal category of experience. Scholarship such as Denise Segura's study (1994) of how heterosexual Chicana and Mexicana immigrant women balance work and family roles shows not only how the meaning and practice of motherhood are culturally constructed, and thus vary among different groups of women, but also that a white middle-class model of motherhood has been taken by some scholars to be a universal standard by which all other mothers are evaluated.

Although feminist theory is interdisciplinary, it is especially compatible with the sociological imagination because it links individual experience to social organization. Like other major sociological categories such as race and class, gender also influences the distribution of wealth, power, and privilege; how much we will learn and earn; how long we and our children will live; and how we are defined by others. As we have stated, there are many types of feminist theory and, as their various names imply, not all of them adopt the same focus. Listed below are brief descriptions of several prominent feminist theoretical perspectives. As you will find, we cannot always easily distinguish one from another.

- ***Liberal feminist theory*** assumes that at the basis of women's inequality is **sexism,** a set of beliefs about the superiority of men and inferiority of women that justifies prejudice and discrimination against women. Thus, the focus of this perspective is almost entirely on issues of equal opportunity and individual choice to the neglect of questions about how gender inequality emerged or the effects of race and class inequality in women's experiences. Its analysis for change, therefore, is limited to issues of reform relative to equal opportunity and individual choice.
- ***Socialist feminist theory*** rejects the reform orientation of liberal feminist theory. Rooted in classical Marxism, this perspective maintains that the sexual division of labor is the first form of class conflict. Thus, class and gender hierarchies become the base from which socialist feminist theorists explain systems of oppression such as capitalism, patriarchy, and domination. Of particular concern here are issues of production, reproduction, socialization, and sexuality and how they exhibit and maintain inequalities.
- ***Marxist feminist theory*** combines the classic Marxian class analysis and the feminist principle of social protest. This perspective begins with the premise that gender oppression is a reflection, first and foremost, of people's class position and only secondarily a reflection of gender itself. In general, women's inequality is explained in terms of class oppression and property inequality, exploited labor, and alienation. Marxist feminists advocate the abolition of capitalism (and thus class and class oppression) through revolutionary action as the solution to gender inequality.
- ***Radical feminist theory*** contends that oppression is pervasive throughout society. Most radical feminist theories see patriarchy as the basic cause of women's oppression, and in the process they downplay the impact of race and class oppression in women's experiences. A key point in these analyses is the description of patriarchy as physical and psychological violence practiced by men and male-dominated institutions against women.
- ***Lesbian feminist theory*** maintains that oppression of lesbians, like racial, class, and sexual oppression, is important in determining women's inequality. Lesbian feminists focus on the reasons for the dominance of heterosexuality. Adrienne Rich (1980), for example, argues that heterosexuality is political in nature in that it is "compulsory" in patriarchal societies and that lesbianism represents resistance and a threat to patriarchy. Some lesbian theorists have been among the first to explore how some women, themselves oppressed, actively participate in the oppression of other women; for example, white women oppressing women of color, heterosexual women oppressing lesbians. Thus, much of their writing calls for the eradication of prejudice and discrimination within the community of women itself. In addition, some lesbian feminists (as well as some nonlesbian feminists) advocate "separatism"—both the sexual separation of women from men and the wider separation of women from male culture and institutions—as a strategy of liberation. There is no common consensus, however, about how much separatism is necessary or how it will function.
- ***Women-of-color feminist theory,*** like other feminist perspectives, is an umbrella term for a wide range of viewpoints. Taking as a starting point that women of color have typically been omitted from all analyses, including feminist analyses, women-of-color feminists begin their analyses by bringing women of color from the margins to the center of analysis (see, for example, bell hooks, 1984). A basic premise is that there is no common unified female experience. Rather, each individual woman is shaped not only by her experiences of gender and sexuality but also by her particular experiences of the intersection of race, class, and culture. Thus, a major emphasis is on forms of racism, sexism, and classism and how these factors are interrelated and affect the lives of all women.
- ***Black feminist thought*** has at its roots the goal of making African American women's standpoint visible. One of the more popular articulations of this theoretical perspective is

Patricia Hill Collins's work, *Social Construction of Black Feminist Thought* (1989). Collins takes as a starting point that African American women's political and economic experiences have allowed them to develop a particular analysis of racism and sexism in the United States, as well as specific strategies of resistance. This perspective challenges the idea that oppressed groups are not conscious of their oppression and are somehow less capable than their oppressors of understanding the relations of ruling. More importantly, it goes far in challenging the notion that there can be and is one feminist theory or feminist perspective because people's positions in the social structure give rise to distinct standpoints or perspectives on the world. Thus, an inclusive feminist perspective takes into account the many distinct standpoints and diversity among women and men.

THE FAMILY FROM A FEMINIST PERSPECTIVE A feminist investigation of marriages and families asks both macro- and microlevel questions. Macrolevel questions include, What are the causes of women's inequality in marriages and families? How does the structure of marriages and families maintain gender inequality? How can change toward greater equality in marriages and families be brought about? Microlevel questions include, What social and interpersonal processes occur in families to generate gender differences and inequality? What roles do various family members play in perpetuating gender inequality? What kind of power structures exist within marriages and families, and how do they affect the distribution of tasks and resources in marriages and families?

Taking the position that women's subordination is based in the social relationships within marriages and families, the objective of an analysis of marriages and families is to explain the ways in which gender inequality is reinforced and maintained in these relationships. On a macrolevel, for example, a vast Marxist feminist literature asserts that women's oppression is built into and sustained by the patriarchal family structure. On a microlevel, a body of feminist theory exists that, by focusing on what these theorists refer to as the "reproduction of gender" in families, explains how gender inequality and oppression are reinforced and maintained (Chodorow, 1978). These theories suggest that gender identity and gender-specific behaviors are produced and reproduced through the socialization process as women expose their offspring to a variety of gender-specific learning experiences during the childrearing process.

CRITIQUE There are many critiques of feminist theory. That feminist theory is woman-centered is the most frequent criticism, especially from mainstream sociologists. Basically, the criticism is that feminist theory is biased and excludes male experiences and perspectives. Feminist theorists respond to this criticism by asserting that the partiality to women in their work is necessary given the history of devaluation or exclusion of female experiences and perspectives in traditional social theories. They argue that the inclusion of female experiences and perspectives does not exclude men and male perspectives.

Chilean activist Isabel Allende captures the feminist principle that "the personal is political." Here, she testifies as a witness in a 1997 court case in Madrid concerning Spanish persons who "disappeared" during the dictatorship of Chilean General Augusto Pinochet, whose military junta ousted her father, President Salvador Allende, from office.

In addition, some critiques have come from feminist scholars themselves, who differ in their conceptualizations of the causes of women's oppression and the goals of feminist theory. For example, radical feminists criticize the liberal feminist notion that the major political goal for feminists should be equal opportunity for women and men. Critics contend that because this approach does not address such structural issues as class and race inequality, it would help only some women but would not help many others, particularly poor women and women of color. Marxist feminist theory is often criticized for its focus on women's oppression as a reflection of the more fundamental class oppression in society. This single focus on economic production largely ignores the importance of social and cultural factors.

One very important criticism of most feminist theories is that they are biased toward the experiences of white, middle-class, heterosexual women. In particular, feminist theory is criticized for not including an adequate analysis of race. Even when such theories deal with issues of race, class, and heterosexuality, they often focus primarily on the life experiences of the poor or working class, women of color, or lesbians. Such analyses cloud the fact that all women experience race, class, gender, and sexual orientation, albeit in different ways. In some cases, for example, women are economically disadvantaged and denied access to power and privilege because of their skin color, sexual orientation, or social class. In other cases, these same factors can enhance access to social and economic resources. For example, women with white skin or a heterosexual orientation might enjoy certain privileges, whereas women with black skin or a homosexual orientation can suffer discrimination and be denied basic opportunities. In the final section of this chapter we briefly examine some of the contemporary literature on men and their roles in marriages and families.

MEN'S STUDIES AND MARRIAGE AND FAMILY RESEARCH

As we have seen throughout this chapter, there are many critical social and political issues related to explanations of marriage and family life in the United States. Whether or not we accept the feminist claim that their theories and research do not exclude the experiences or perspectives of men, since the 1980s a parallel movement has developed among some male activists and scholars who call for a larger, visible place in feminist analyses, one that pays attention to the oppression that males experience as a result of social conditioning and learning. They argue that the same values that have restricted women have also restricted men to their roles as aggressors. Not surprisingly, the ongoing inclusive work on women has given rise to men's studies, the academic arm of this movement. That this new field has gained momentum in recent years is evidenced in the fact that at least 500 colleges now offer courses on men and masculinity (Zernike, 1998). Although there is no specific masculinist theory, it is worthwhile to note the general viewpoint or perspective in this newest academic discipline, particularly as it relates to marriage, family, and intimacy.

One might say that we have always had "men's studies," since, historically, men have been at the center of most scientific analyses of human behavior and human societies. However, men's studies is not just about men and centering men in research and theory. Rather, it specifically challenges the patriarchal male bias in traditional scholarship, the existing sexist norms in society, and, like women's studies, it combines theory and practice to create a more just society. The line between men's studies and the men's rights movement is often blurred. However, men's studies looks primarily at the question long asked in feminist analysis: Why are men the way they are? Recognizing that gender and sexism impact men's as well as women's lives, men's studies encompasses a critical examination of the functional and dysfunctional aspects of the traditional male gender role for men, women, children, and society at large. It begins with the basic premise that there is no hierarchy of oppression. Men, like women, are oppressed by a social conditioning that makes them incapable of developing and expressing a wide range of personality traits or skills and limits their experiences (Franklin, 1988; Zernike, 1998).

As with feminist theory, the network of men's studies consists of not one but several diverse perspectives. In fact, the theories and perspectives of much of men's studies parallel feminist theories and perspectives, so much so that some feminist scholars have declared that men's studies is explicitly feminist (see, for example, Andersen, 2000). Thus, like feminist perspectives, perspectives in men's studies consider gender to be a central feature of social life—one of the chief organizing principles around which our lives revolve—examining how gender shapes men's ideas, opportunities, and experiences. Too often, there is the tendency for the public and in some academic settings to assume that only women are gendered beings, as if men had no gender. We know, however, from women's and men's studies that this is not the case. Rather, gender affects the experiences of both women and men, albeit in different ways. Thus, like feminist theories and perspectives, the perspectives of men's studies frame their analyses within the context of the diversity among men, recognizing, on the one hand, that not all men are sexist in their attitudes, beliefs, and behaviors and yet, on the other hand, that as a group, men benefit from gender privilege but this privilege varies according to race, class, and sexual orientation. Finally, as do feminist theories, men's studies view sexuality as an important component of the race-gender-class matrix of domination. Thus, feminist and men's studies scholars alike analyze social, political, and cultural structures in societies that privilege heterosexuality and oppress lesbians and gays simply because of their sexual orientation (Andersen, 2000; Kimmel and Messner, 2001).

Men in Families

As we have indicated, a new politics of masculinity has emerged that claims that men's oppression is often overlooked in theoretical analyses of marriages and families. Although many impressive analyses have documented the exploitation of women, little if any attention has been given to the massive disruption and destruction that contemporary economic and political institutions have wreaked on men or the kinds of constraints and inequities that society's gender stereotypes impose on men. Indicative of this growing movement to explore men's concerns is the emergence of the American Men's Studies Association (AMSA) founded in 1991 and of scientific journals, such as *The Journal of Men's Studies*, which premiered in 1992 and is devoted to research and theory on men's lives and issues. Likewise, in the 1990s popular culture, a number of men's journals debuted with a purpose of exploring the contemporary masculine psyche and issues. In the movies, actor Arnold Schwarzenegger played a pregnant man in the movie *Junior*. And at the end of the decade five TV sitcoms featured single dads. The 1990s also witnessed an explosion of scholarship on men, as well as the ways in which cultures shape or construct definitions and ideas about masculinity and how individual men embody it.

What does it really mean, for example, to be a man, a father, a friend, a lover in contemporary U.S. society? Scholarship in men's studies has increasingly delved into such questions. Relative to marriages and families, this scholarship examines how men actively construct masculinity within a social and historical context and explores their experiences—in marriage, fatherhood, and their emotional and sexual relationships with women and with other men. One of the most important issues for U.S. marriages and families over the past decade has been that of fatherhood. Debates centered around questions such as: Are men becoming more nurturing and caring fathers and developing parenting skills such as those we routinely expect from women? Men's studies scholarship on this issue has caused us to broaden our perspective about fatherhood, recognizing that the diversity of fatherhood is evidenced by different groups of men, such as gay fathers, Chicano and African American fathers, and poor and working-class fathers.

In his study of the lifestyles of gay husbands and fathers, Brian Miller (2001) reported among his findings that although these husbands and fathers perceived their gayness as incompatible with traditional marriage, they perceived their gayness as compatible with fathering. Gays in heterosexual marriages who leave their spouses and enter the gay world report that gay relationships are more harmonious than heterosexual marital relationships. They also report that fathering is more salient once they have left their heterosexual marriages. As more alternatives for fathering have become available within the gay community, fewer gays have become involved in heterosexual marriages and divorce. Adoption, surrogate parenting, and alternative fertilization are some of the methods that have expanded the opportunities for fatherhood regardless of sexual orientation.

On some levels, a "new father" has emerged. An increasing number of young husbands have joined their wives in birthing courses, have donned empathy bellies, and have taken part in the actual delivery of their children. There is little evidence, however, that these experiences by themselves produce a strong father–child (or wife–husband) bond or lead to greater participation by fathers with their children. As we shall see in Chapters 9 and 10, few new fathers assume a major role in child care and child rearing. According to the politics-of-masculinity perspective, for most men, no matter how much they would like to be more active in parenting, the demands of outside employment and the continuing definition of men and masculinity in terms of "work" and "family provider" preclude such participation.

Critique A major criticism of the new politics of masculinity concerns those perspectives that view men as primary victims. Some feminist critics, for example, claim that the politics of masculinity is reactionary and sexist, depicting men as innocent victims of conniving and selfish women or of social structures and institutions that in fact they control. Another criticism is that although many of these analyses focus on the structural and institutional nature of men's exploitation and oppression, they have not clearly identified the alleged oppression or oppressors in society. Some feminist scholars argue that these perspectives as well as the men's rights movement generally are simply strategies for reaffirming men's authority in the face of the challenge presented by feminism (Carrigan, Connell, and Lee, 1987). Another criticism is that the new politics of masculinity is far more therapeutic (healing of men's egos) than political or activist.

Although recognizing the pervasive victimization of women, many proponents of masculinity theory nonetheless caution against the view of some feminists that being a male in and of itself and not the systems of social control and production is responsible for the exploitation of women. Although this point is well taken, according to critics it neglects to emphasize that the systems of social control and production in the United States are owned and controlled by men (albeit, white middle- and upper-class men). Thus, the issues of gender and the exercise of power cannot be separated.

In conclusion, we have seen that sociology offers a variety of theories and perspectives. Although each framework is somewhat distinct, the various frameworks are not completely incompatible with each other. Rather, they can and often do offer complementary insights. Before moving on to the next chapter, take a moment to reflect about theory and theorizing. Having studied the various theories in this chapter, try to apply the sociological imagination by constructing your own "minitheory," as described in the "Applying the Sociological Imagination" box.

APPLYING THE SOCIOLOGICAL IMAGINATION

DOING SOCIOLOGY: LINKING THEORY AND RESEARCH METHODS

Virtually every practical decision you make and every practical opinion you hold has some theory behind it. Consider any marriage and family behavior or event of interest to you. Develop a "minitheory" to explain the behavior or event. What are some of the major assumptions you make about human beings, society, marriages, families, women, and men? Is your theory a micro- or macrolevel explanation? Which one of the theoretical perspectives or theory models does your theory most resemble? After you have developed your minitheory, consider that you or some researcher wants to test it. What kinds of questions might you ask? Which research methodology would be most appropriate to test your theory? Why?

WRITING YOUR OWN SCRIPT

THE FAMILY LIFE CYCLE: LOCATING YOUR FAMILY

Think about the developmental family life cycle theory model discussed in this chapter. Develop a life cycle model of your own family. Which stages of the model discussed in the chapter are applicable to your immediate family? Has it progressed directly through these stages? Have some stages been revisited? Which stages are not covered by the model? Why not? Describe some of the major roles, responsibilities, and adjustments that have been necessary at each stage of your family's life cycle.

SUMMARY

Sociology involves observing human behavior and then making sense out of what we observe. Therefore, both research and theory are involved. Theory is an explanation of some phenomenon, and scientific research includes a set of methods that allow us to collect data to test hypotheses and develop theories. The two are linked in that theory provides insights into the nature of human behavior and society, and research provides the empirical observations from which the theories are verified. Sociologists studying marriages and families have used a variety of research methodologies: surveys, observation, case studies, and ethnographies. Each of these methods has both advantages and limitations.

Although sociology as a discipline claims that the improvement of social life is a major goal, some feminist scholars have argued that in practice sociology has not lived up to this goal. A telling sign is who gets studied and how, and who is left out and why. Until recent times, conventional topics studied by sociologists and their theoretical perspectives had either ignored issues relevant to the lives of women, poor people, lesbians, gays, and people of color or studied them within white and male middle-class models. Given this history, there is a need for a new scholarship on marriages and families that recognizes race, class, and gender diversity in marriages and families.

Just as there is no single method for studying marriages and families, there is no single theory to explain these institutions. There are four mainstream theoretical perspectives that, while not specifically family theories, can be utilized to explain marriages and families. Structural functionalism and conflict theory provide frameworks for analyzing the determinants of large-scale social structure. Symbolic-interaction theory allows us to focus on individuals within marriages and families and the interaction between couples or among family members. Social-exchange theory is guided by the assumption that people are rational and logical, and that they base their actions on what they think is the most effective way to meet their goals.

Moreover, a number of sociological theories designed specially to address issues concerning marriage and family life are also being utilized. The most common are the nuclear family and the developmental family life cycle theories. Each is an extension of the larger, more encompassing functional perspective and thus provides both the advantages and limitations of a functional analysis. The nuclear family theory, popularized by Talcott Parsons, suggests that the family is an adaptive system that performs essential functions for its individual members as well as for society as a whole. In contrast, the developmental life cycle theoretical perspective focuses on changes in families over time and offers an explanation of family life in terms of a process that unfolds over the life course of marriages and families. Other theories that have important theoretical implications for studying marriages and families include social constructionism and feminist theories. Social constructionists speak of reality as invented or constructed out of the interactions between individuals in face-to-face interactions. It suggests that gender relationships within marriages, families, and intimate relationships are not uniform and universally generalizable to all people. Rather, they are social productions that have no meaning outside that which is understood and agreed upon by the actors. On the other hand, feminist theory is not a single unified view; rather, there are many types of feminist theory. A basic premise of all feminist theories is that women are oppressed and their lives are shaped by a number of important experiences, such as race, class, gender, and culture. However, different theories pay primary attention to different sets of women's experiences as causing or contributing to their inequality and oppression.

Finally, in recent years, we have witnessed a growing number of male voices advocating a larger and more visible place in feminist analyses, one that pays attention to the oppression that men experience as a result of gender role socialization. To date, however, very little effort has been made to extend these ideas into a practical agenda for social and political change.

KEY TERMS

theory
scientific research
empirical evidence
hypothesis
variables
scientific method
reliability
validity
survey
interview
questionnaire
Hawthorne effect
case study
ethnography
qualitative methods
quantitative methods
ideologies
theory model
structural functionalism
manifest functions
latent functions
functional
dysfunctional
instrumental traits
expressive traits
conflict theory
symbolic interactionism
symbols
social construction of reality
social constructionism
social-exchange theory
developmental family life cycle theory
sexism

QUESTIONS FOR STUDY AND REFLECTION

1. Why do sociologists need different theoretical perspectives to explain marriage and family behavior? Why isn't one perspective sufficient?
2. Search the Internet using the keyword *men's studies.* Try to find articles about the latest scholarship in men's studies as well as articles that discuss the actions of men's studies activists and what they are doing to change men. What can we learn from this scholarship and activism?
3. An implication of the social-constructionist perspective is that social relationships are symbolic productions and have no intrinsic meaning. Do you agree with this point of view? Why or why not? Can you think of some aspect of marriage, family, or intimate relationships that is not a social construction?
4. Identify a family from a culture other than the United States. Interview family members in terms of a range of issues including family values, norms, customs and rituals relative to marriage, childbearing, and child rearing. Compare your findings to families born and raised in the United States. How does your research help you to understand these sociological concepts and what does it tell us about the diversity of marriages and families?

ADDITIONAL RESOURCES

SOCIOLOGICAL

ALTMAN, I., AND J. GINAT. 1996. *Polygamous Families in Contemporary Society.* New York: Cambridge University Press. An interesting research study of the family relationships of fundamentalist Mormons in the United States who continue to practice polygamy in accordance with their religious beliefs.

KIMMEL, MICHAEL, AND MICHAEL MESSNER, EDS. 2001. *Men's Lives.* New York: Macmillan. An anthology organized around specific themes that define masculinity and the issues that men confront over the life course. The authors incorporate a social-constructionist perspective that examines how men actively construct their masculinity within a social and historical context. Related to this construction and integrated throughout the book are the variations that exist among men across race, class, and sexual orientation.

MARSHALL, CATHERINE, AND GRETCHEN B. ROSSMAN. 1995. *Designing Qualitative Research,* 2d ed. Thousand Oaks, CA: Sage. An excellent user-friendly guide for qualitative researchers that includes a number of vignettes from the educational fields studied by the authors as well as other researchers.

LADNER, JOYCE A., ED. 1973. *The Death of White Sociology.* New York: Vintage Books. Now a classic, this anthology presents the works of a group of African American writers and scholars who critique mainstream sociology for accepting white bourgeois standards as the norm and consistently treating all other social patterns—especially those found in African American cultures—as "deviant."

LITERARY

GERRITSEN, TESS. 1996. *Harvest.* New York: Simon and Schuster. An interesting novel about an "organs for cash" ring, run by an elite cardiac transplant team of doctors operating out of a prestigious New England hospital. Although this novel does not pertain to sociological research specifically, it does raise a number of important ethical issues that researchers and other professionals responsible for the well-being of human research subjects must consider.

DJERASSI, CARL. 1991. *Cantor's Dilemma.* New York: Penguin. This novel describes the fierce competition that drives scientific superstars as they strive to receive coveted recognition for their work. Of particular relevance are the ethical issues of scientific research.

INTERNET

www.census.gov U.S. Census Bureau. An excellent resource for the latest statistical data on marriages and families. Pick a letter of the alphabet for a topic of interest to you (for example, fatherhood, motherhood, or parenting) and find the latest statistics on the topic.

www.NCFR.com National Council on Family Relations. The NCFR is the major scientific organization devoted to the study of marriages, families, intimate relationships, and children.

Chapter 3

Understanding Gender: Its Influence in Intimate Relationships

IN THE NEWS: **BALTIMORE, MARYLAND**

On February 2, 1999, a jury awarded Kevin Knussman, a helicopter paramedic, $375,000 in the first sex discrimination case brought under the Federal Family and Medical Leave Act. The Maryland state trooper testified that when he requested an extended leave from his job to care for his newborn daughter, he was refused because he is male. Knussman said he was told by a personnel manager that "God made women to have babies and unless you can have babies, you can not be a primary caregiver" and that "unless your wife is in a coma or dead, you can't be the primary care provider."

The Federal Family and Medical Leave Act requires employers with 50 or more employees to grant up to 12 weeks of unpaid family leave to care for a new baby or a family member who is ill. Under the law, workers with accrued vacation, personal, or sick leave can use it to receive paid time. Because Knussman, a trooper for 20 years, had accumulated more than 1,200 hours of sick leave and 250 hours of annual and personal leave, he requested four to eight weeks of paid family leave in October 1994, two months before the baby's due date. His request was denied. In late November, his wife was hospitalized after experiencing difficulties with the pregnancy. On December 2, a personnel manager informed Knussman of a new Maryland law that allowed state employees with primary responsibility for newborns to use up to 30 days of their sick leave to care for a baby.

However, when Knussman requested a leave under the Maryland law, the personnel manager told him that he could not have 30 days because only women can breast-feed and, therefore, only women could be primary providers. He said that, as a secondary provider, Knussman could use up to 10 days, which is what he ended up taking. His daughter was born prematurely and Knussman made repeated requests to have his leave extended because his wife was having medical difficulties. His supervisors denied these requests again, repeating that mothers were primary providers and fathers were secondary. Knussman returned to work on December 29, 1994, after being warned that he would be considered AWOL if he did not return. He filed his discrimination suit the following April.

Attorney Betty Sconion who represents the state police in this case said she would file a motion to overturn the verdict. Changes in the Maryland law removed the distinction between primary and secondary providers, and it now allows all employees to take 30 days leave to care for a newborn. When his second daughter was born two years later, Knussman requested and was granted the full 12 weeks paternity leave (Lewin, 1999).

WHAT WOULD YOU DO? If your wife was expecting a baby, would you request a parental leave? (If you were expecting a baby, would you want your husband to request a parental leave?) Explain. Given the clear language of the federal law, why do you think Trooper Knussman's supervisors denied his request? How would you have voted if you were a member of that jury? Explain.

What are little girls made of?
Sugar and spice
And all that's nice,
That's what little girls are made of.
What are little boys made of?
Snaps and snails
And puppy dogs' tails,
That's what little boys are made of.

—Anonymous nursery rhyme

Who hasn't, at one time or another, smiled on hearing this nursery rhyme? On one level we don't take it seriously, believing it just a cute and harmless caricature of girls and boys. Yet on another level it suggests that there are differences between females and males and that both sexes must, therefore, be treated differently. On the basis of this belief system, society constructs an elaborate sex–gender system that has serious ramifications for every facet of our lives, as the experience of Trooper Knussman so clearly revealed. This chapter explores the meaning of sex and gender, the process by which we acquire gender identity, and the role gender plays in marital and family relationships.

(2000) chronicled th
Made Him, other in
forward to tell their
satisfaction with the
John, rejected theirs
ing number of scie
practice of infant se
tors above medical o
of sex and gender as
as do many other so
gery following the b
favor treatments cen
(Dreger, 1998; Faust

*If you wer
what trea
What do y
of infant
advantages and disad
should make the decis
ents, or the persons the*

Another variation
case of **transsexual**
born with the body c
not accept their assig
with their biological
surgery and take hor
is congruent with th
such cases received a
and writer James M
the story of his tr
Conundrum (1974),
McCloskey (now De
theorist at the Univ
Recently, two school
ters to parents info

People often exp
Source: © Tribune

DISTINGUISHING SEX AND GENDER ROLES

If you were asked, Who are you? chances are you would reply by saying: I am a male, female, Latina/o, African American, Asian American, Native American; or a student, parent, daughter, son, wife, husband, mother, father, friend. Such responses reflect the statuses we have and the roles we play in the social order. Sociologists use the term *role* to refer to a set of expected behaviors associated with a specific status, the position we hold in society. These positions, by and large, determine how we are defined and treated by others and also provide us with an organizing framework for how we should relate to others. We are born into some of these statuses—for example, female, male, daughter, son, white, black—and therefore have little control over them. These are called **ascribed statuses.** Others are **achieved statuses,** acquired by virtue of our own efforts. These include spouse, parent, employee, student, teacher. Every status, whether ascribed or achieved, carries with it a set of role expectations for how we are to behave.

Role expectations are defined and structured around the privileges and obligations the status is believed to possess. For example, our society has traditionally expected males, especially fathers, to be strong, independent, and good providers. In return, they expect to be admired, respected, and obeyed. Females, especially mothers, are expected to be nurturing, caring, and self-sacrificing. In return, they expect to be loved and provided for. Such shared role expectations serve an important function in society. By making our behavior fairly predictable, they make social order possible.

Role expectations can be dysfunctional as well, however. They can be defined so rigidly that behavior and expression are seriously curtailed, to the detriment of the individual and the society at large. For example, because society fails to encourage or support fathers as primary care providers for their offspring, many father–child relationships remain emotionally distant. Rigid role definitions often lead to the development of stereotypes, in which certain qualities are assigned to an individual solely on the basis of her or his social category. **Gender role stereotypes** refer to the oversimplified expectations of what it means to be a woman or a man. Stereotyping is used to justify unequal treatment of members of a specific group. For example, until recently, women serving in the military were believed to be unfit for combat and, thus, were denied the opportunity for career mobility associated with combat experience. Although many stereotyped ideas such as these have been discarded as invalid, some individuals and groups still believe that women and men are inherently unsuited for certain roles, a point we will return to later in this chapter.

The status of being female or male in our society affects all aspects of our lives; thus, sociologists regard it as a **master,** or **key, status**. For this reason it is important to understand the dynamics associated with gender status and to distinguish between the concepts of sex and gender.

Sex refers to the biological aspects of a person—the physiological characteristics that differentiate females from males. These include external genitalia (vulva and penis), gonads (ovaries and testes), sex chromosomes, and hormones. These characteristics are the source of sex role differences—women menstruate, get pregnant, and lactate; men have erections and ejaculate seminal fluid. In contrast, **gender** refers to the socially learned behaviors, attitudes, and expectations that are associated with being female or male, what we call *femininity* and *masculinity*. Whereas a person's sex is biologically determined, gender behaviors and expectations are culturally constructed categories and, as such, change over time. Thus, gender is learned; we acquire gender through interacting with others and the social world (Wood, 1996). **Gender identity** is a person's awareness of being female or male. It sounds simple, doesn't it? We are either female/feminine or male/masculine, are we not? In fact, as we shall see, human development is not as simple as it first appears.

The Process of Sex Differentiation

Our biological sex is established at the moment of conception, when each genetic parent contributes 23 chromosomes to the fertilized egg for a total of 46 chromosomes (23 chromosomal pairs). One pair of chromosomes, the sex chromosomes, determines whether a fertilized egg will develop into a female (XX) or male (XY) fetus. Contrary to past belief, the father's genetic contribution determines the child's sex, in that he provides either an X or a Y chromosome, whereas the mother always provides an X chromosome. The process of sex differentiation does not begin until approximately the sixth week of embryonic development, however. Prior to that time, the XX and XY embryos are anatomically identical, each possessing a set of female ducts and a set of male ducts.

The process of sex differentiation is as yet not completely understood. Genetic researchers have identified a sex-determining gene on the Y chromosome that appears to set in motion a chemical chain of events that leads to the development of testes, a prostate gland, and other distinctive male characteristics (Hoyenga and Hoyenga, 1993). Until recently, scientists were less clear about female development and assumed that the lack of the Y or male chromosome resulted in female development by default. Then, in 1994, molecular biologists at Italy's Padua University and at Baylor University in Houston, Texas, isolated a gene on the X chromosome called "dosage sexual sex reversal" (DSS), which sets in motion the development of ovaries and other distinct female characteristics. These researchers also discovered that the ovary gene, if present in excessive amounts, can override genes that ordinarily would produce males (Gura, 1994a).

Gender Differences: The Nature–Nurture Debate

Because chromosomes and hormones play a critical role in sex differentiation, it is logical to ask whether they also play a role in the physical, behavioral, and personality differences

In any given historical period, some people are likely to reject their society's definitions of appropriate gender role behavior. During the Civil War, a number of women, eager to fight for a cause they believed in, disguised themselves as men in order to enlist in the Union and Confederate armies. One such soldier was Frances Clalin, pictured here in nineteenth-century female attire and in her cavalry uniform.

Although the nature–nurture debate has been framed as an either–or proposition, these data suggest that differences between females and males develop out of a complex interaction of biological and cultural factors. Before examining **gender role socialization**, a process by which people acquire the gender roles that their culture defines as appropriate for them, let us look at the content of these gender roles.

TRADITIONAL MEANINGS OF FEMININITY AND MASCULINITY

In Chapter 2 we discussed the theory of structural functionalism and the Parsonian dichotomy of expressive (female) and instrumental (male) roles. The assignment of these roles is based on the assumption that females and males are fundamentally different from each other and that the content of these roles reflects the biological differences between the sexes. Beginning in the 1960s and continuing to the present day, a number of studies have found a broad consensus among different groups of people regarding the existence of different personality traits associated with each sex. For example, a Gallup poll in which adults were read a list of ten personality traits and asked which were generally more true of women or men found that women were most often described as emotional, talkative, affectionate, patient, and creative. In contrast, aggressive, courageous, ambitious, and easygoing led the list of traits attributed to men (Newport, 2001). Women and men were in general agreement about the assignment of these traits but, with the exception of only one trait, aggressive, women were more likely than men to say that all the traits apply to their gender. In all cases only a minority of respondents said that the traits described both genders equally. However, 40 percent of the women and 40 percent of the men said that one trait, intelligent, described both genders equally. The traits used to describe each sex are fairly consistent across cultures. A cross-cultural study of 25 countries found that in every country sampled, women were thought to be "sentimental" and "submissive," whereas traits such as "adventurous" and "forceful" were associated with men (Williams and Best, 1990).

Keep in mind that this type of research describes only the extent to which people possess an awareness of female and male stereotypes; it does not indicate whether or not they accept them as true or, for that matter, whether or not the stereotypes are actually true. Other research, utilizing a methodology that allowed respondents to rate the degree to which traits characterize both the typical woman and the typical man, found several interesting patterns. Two sets of adjectives became evident: First, there were those that represented prototypical traits (the clearest examples of each category—for women it was a niceness/nurturance dimension, whereas for men it was a potency/power dimension), and second, there were more peripheral traits, those less strongly associated with each category. Considerable overlapping occurred, with the core adjectives for one gender tending to fall in the periphery for the other gender (DeLisi and Soundranayagam, 1990).

Traditional Gender Roles: Female and Male

Historically, the female gender role clustered around family relationships and was patterned after the belief that a woman's place is in the home. Based on this belief, women are expected to marry; have children; and be nurturing, emotional, caring, and attractive. They should not be aggressive, loud, competitive, or independent; rather, they

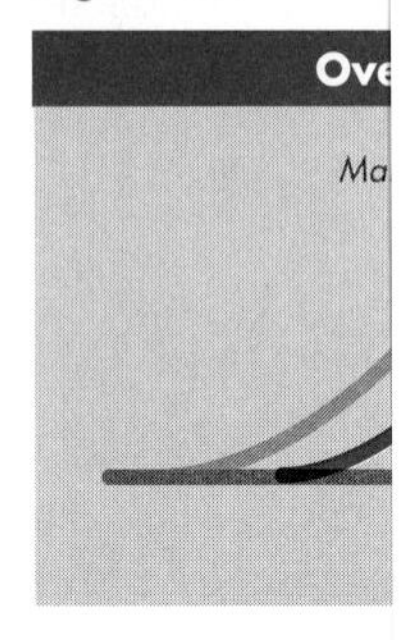

should be passive, submissive, and dependent on their husbands. If women are employed, their work must not interfere with family obligations. To ensure that women can be homemakers, men are to be providers and protectors. Thus, they are expected to be achievement-oriented, competitive, strong, aggressive, logical, and independent. They should not be emotional, expressive, or weak, and must be in control at all times.

Now that you have thought about masculinity and femininity in general terms, close your eyes and think of Latino/a, African American, Native American, and Asian American women and men. Do you visualize the same characteristics, or do you see some differences?

Gender Variations: Race, Class, and Culture

Gender stereotypes—the overgeneralized beliefs about the characteristics associated with being female or male—are widely shared within a society. Nevertheless, as we can see in the "In Other Places" box, they do vary somewhat from one society to another. In the United States, traditional gender roles have routinely been associated with white middle-class heterosexuals. Although only a limited amount of research on gender beliefs across race and class lines is available, from this research it does appear that people perceive different stereotypical traits in other groups. For example, one study asked college students to use a list of 23 adjectives to describe the characteristics of black and white middle-class women and black and white working-class women. The results revealed that race and class affect people's perceptions of gender roles. Although all four groups were depicted in ways consistent with the feminine stereotype, the ways in which white women and middle-class women in general were described were most like the traditional views of women. Black women were viewed as less passive, dependent, status-conscious, emotional, and concerned about their appearance than white women (Landrine, 1985).

These findings are consistent with other research that showed that as a group, African American women are perceived as being less deferential than white women (Halberstadt and Saitta, 1987). Relatively little information is available on gender stereotypes of other racial or ethnic groups. One study, however, suggests that Latinas generally tend to be viewed as more submissive and dependent, hence more feminine, than white women (Vazquez-Nuttall, Romero-Garcia, and DeLeon, 1987). Similarly, Asian American women have been described as very feminine and as making desirable brides because "they are cute (as in doll-like), quiet rather than militant, and unassuming rather than assertive. In a word, non-threatening" (Lai, 1992:168).

Anthropologist Margaret Mead (1935) was among the first to explore how concepts of masculinity and femininity vary across cultures. In studying three tribal groups, she found that both Mundugumor women and men behaved ruthlessly and aggressively, behaviors usually identified as "masculine." Among the Tchambuli, women were dominant and impersonal, whereas the men were more emotionally dependent, just the reverse of the patterns typically found in our culture. Arapesh women and men usually exhibited traits often described as "feminine"—caring, cooperative, and nonaggressive.

Similarly, other anthropologists have observed societies in which gender relations are not rigidly defined. For example, in Nepal, both women and men are expected to be nurturing, and both sexes provide care for children and the elderly (Wood, 1996). Shared child care is also characteristic of the Mbuti Pygmies of Zaire, a society in which both women and men hunt cooperatively. Among the Agta of the Philippines, both women and men hunt, fish, and gather vegetation (Estioko-Griffin, 1986). Tahitian women and men of the South Pacific are expected to be passive and cooperative (Gilmore, 1990). What are we to make of these findings? As Susan Basow points out:

> Gender is not the only variable by which people are stereotyped. Each one of us is situated in sociological space at the intersection of numerous categories—for example, gender, race or ethnicity, class, sexual orientation, and able-bodiedness. These social categories interact with each other in complex ways. A woman who is white, working-class, lesbian, and differently abled will be viewed very differently from a black, middle-class, heterosexual, able-bodied woman. (1992:4–5)

In sum, humankind is not composed of two homogeneous groupings—one feminine and one masculine. Rather, there is a rich diversity within each gender. To encompass this diversity, Harry Brod (1987), a pioneer in the field of men's studies, has suggested substituting the term *masculinities* for *masculinity*. The same argument could be made regarding the diverse forms of femininity. Although research has shown that Americans tend to adhere to a fairly consistent grouping of gender stereotypes, increasing evidence shows that some people are challenging these stereotypes and creating more flexible gender roles for themselves.

GENDER ROLES IN TRANSITION

Perhaps you find it difficult to identify with the traditional gender roles described in the previous section. Given the many changes that have occurred during your lifetime, that would not be surprising. Of special significance are certain demographic changes: patterns of continuing education for both women and men, the movement of married women into the labor force, delayed marriage and childbearing, high divorce rates, and increased life expectancy, especially for women. These changes, along with the liberation movements of the 1960s and 1970s, have challenged traditional gender roles. Thus, as we shall see throughout this book, there has been a definite shift from traditional to more egalitarian gender roles, at least ideologically if not always behaviorally.

IN OTHER PLACES

GENDER EQUALITY IN VANATINAI . . .

From 1977 to 1979 and again for short periods in 1981 and 1987, anthropologist Maria Lepowsky (1993) lived with and recorded the customs and rituals of the people of Vanatinai, a remote island of 2300 inhabitants off the coast of Papua New Guinea. Lepowsky points out that the women and men of Vanatinai socialize, work, and raise children side by side in an almost equal manner. In contrast to other Pacific island cultures, she found no evidence of male cult activities or separate men's meeting houses nor did she find a concept of male superiority. Instead, she found that both women and men participate in community decision making and the island's economy. Both women and men share access to social and economic power and prestige by participating in ceremonial exchanges of valuables, such as greenstone ax blades and coconut-leaf baskets, and by playing host to highly valued mortuary rituals. Older siblings, both female and male, learn to share in caring for younger siblings. Although there is significant overlap between women's and men's roles, there are some distinctions. Activities, such as spear-throwing and sorcery, are restricted to men. The reason for this, however, is not due to any perception of male superiority, but rather it is because women are valued as the life-givers whereas men are valued as life-takers. Her findings are documented in her book, *Fruit of the Motherland: Gender in an Egalitarian Society.*

. . . AND BACKLASH IN BANGLADESH AND AFGHANISTAN

Two decades ago Muhammad Yunus and his Grameen Bank began a program of microcredits, small-scale loans to poor women living in Bangladesh, an impoverished Asian country where half the people live below the poverty line and two-thirds of the population generally and 80 percent of all women are illiterate. Under the program, women receive loans of $25 to $75 to help them launch a small cottage industry. To get the loan, the women must pledge to practice family planning and to repay the loan and interest on a weekly basis. Since the inception of the program, Bangladesh's birth rate has been cut in half, and women have begun to assert their rights (Schmetzer, 1999b). With their new-found economic independence, women can now reject marriage proposals that in this traditional society often amounted to being passed from father to husband as serfs. From its inception, the program was violently opposed by Muslim extremists, who saw it as "un-Islamic" and a threat to male-dominated family life. In the beginning, opposition was directed at Yunus and his bank—branch banks were burned, and his staff and female clients were beaten. Then, in the 1990s, rejected suitors and their accomplices began throwing sulfuric acid into the faces of women who represented this new independence. Many women are afraid to report such incidents to the authorities who keep no official statistics and attribute the problem to "ignorant men in backward parts of the country." The media in Bangladesh report a yearly rate of over 200 acid mutilations that have left thousands of women blinded, scarred for life, and dependent on street begging for their own and their children's survival (Schmetzer, 1999a).

Another form of gender discrimination has arisen in Afghanistan. Until recently, thousands of Afghan women studied at the University of Kabul; thousands more worked as teachers, doctors, and in other professional capacities. Then, in late 1996, Islamic Taliban militia captured the Afghan capital of Kabul and quickly imposed control over two-thirds of the country. Taliban's religious leaders barred girls from school and women from work. Since the vast majority of teachers were women, many boys' schools were forced to close as well. Afghan women had to wear a *burqa* (a head-to-toe covering) whenever they appeared in public. Violations brought swift and severe punishment. With the defeat of the Taliban, there is hope women's status will improve.

What do you think? *How do these three different societies inform the nature–nurture argument regarding gender roles and gender relationships? Can traditional gender roles be changed without causing a serious backlash? Explain. What do the experiences in Bangladesh and Afghanistan suggest about the permanency of gender roles?*

A recent national survey found that a majority of women and men believe there still are more advantages to being a man rather than a woman, that women should have equal work opportunities, that increased gender equity has enriched both sexes, and that there should be gender equality in the home. At the same time, however, a majority of women and men believe that social and economic changes that altered traditional gender roles have made building successful marriages, raising children, and leading satisfying lives more difficult than in the past. They also continue to hold some traditional views about childrearing. For example, 69 percent of the men and 68 percent of the women agreed that it would be better if women could stay home and just take care of the house and children. Attitudes differed markedly by age, however; people under 50 were far more likely than older people to reject traditional beliefs about gender roles (Morin and Rosenfeld, 1998).

Ex-police officer Tom Ashton, in his uniform and later as Claire Ashton, leaves a Shrewsbury courthouse where she claimed that she was unfairly dismissed from the police force because of her sex change.

Women today have considerably more options in the workplace, and they are exercising more control over their private lives as well. Men, too, are questioning their roles. For many men this means de-emphasizing their work role and emphasizing their family role. Both women and men feel freer to express a much wider range of personality traits than the traditional gender roles would allow. Because changes in women's roles have been more open to public view than those in men's roles, we are more likely to be aware of assertive and strong women than of gentle and nurturing men. Research commissioned by the American Association of Retired Persons, however, revealed that men spend just as much time as women do at listening, hand-holding, and expressing concern in familial caregiving situations (Behrens, 1990).

Nevertheless, considerable controversy about these changes remains. Not all people are happy with their direction. Some find them confusing, and others prefer a return to a more traditional world. A 24-year-old truckdriver complained, "My girlfriend drives me crazy at times. She wants to be paid the same as a man and to have every opportunity a man does. But she still wants to be treated like a woman. She doesn't believe women should be drafted, and if I don't open the door for her or help her with her coat, she gets upset." A 24-year-old medical student finds that some men feel threatened by changes in gender roles. "Jim and I dated in college. I thought he was a liberated male, but I found out differently when he took me to meet some of his friends. On the way he told me not to tell them I was going to be a doctor. He said he didn't want them to think his girlfriend was smarter than he was."

Other people support the movement toward gender equality in theory but have trouble implementing the ideas in their everyday lives. Several factors combine to make change difficult. First, people who hold privileged positions have a vested interest in keeping them. Thus, some men may resist sharing power and authority with women at work and at home, whereas some women may resist sharing with men the aspects they most enjoy about the traditional role, such as nurturing children. Second, existing social arrangements tend to reinforce traditional gender roles. To take just one example, on the average, women are still paid less than men. Thus, even if a couple should prefer an arrangement in which the husband is the primary parent and the wife the primary breadwinner, simple household economics might make this impossible. Third, as we will see in the next section, gender identities develop early in life, and much of what we learn from parents and other role models is still based on traditional gender norms. Although many women and men manage to challenge these norms successfully, gender socialization remains a powerful force in shaping gender identity. As family therapist Joan Zientek points out in the "Strengthening Marriages and Families" box, gender issues are often deeply embedded in the problems that families experience. When this occurs, family members must recognize and resolve those gender issues if the family is to function effectively.

THEORIES OF GENDER ROLE SOCIALIZATION

Although socialization is a lifelong process, it is especially significant in our formative years. Psychologists and sociologists have developed several theories to explain the

STRENGTHENING MARRIAGES AND FAMILIES

Talks with Family Therapist Joan Zientek

RESOLVING GENDER ISSUES

Do Gender Issues Affect Family Functioning?

Indeed, they do. Despite efforts to achieve equality between women and men, gender differences continue to exist and get played out in the family circle, often creating tension in relationships among various family members. Household chores can become a battleground. Today, the majority of women work outside the home, yet the tasks of running the household, managing the details of the children's lives, as well as keeping the family connected to the extended family and the community, still fall primarily on the woman's shoulders. Even in families where the mom stays at home, at the end of the day, when dad returns tired from the stress of the workday and mother is exhausted from the endless demands of clinging toddlers, tensions over household chores and child care can be intense.

One of the most salient gender issues occurs around the expression of affect in the relationship. The work of psychologist William Pollack suggests that by the age of 5, boys, unlike their female counterparts, have learned to mask their feelings and have come to view feelings as internal states rather than as a dynamic that exists between people. Later in life, this pattern sets up a dynamic game of pursuit and withdrawal between a couple. In a stereotypical fashion, the woman pursues the man and demands that he speak and reveal his inner life. The man, who many times does not have a clue as to how he should respond, withdraws and the game is set in motion, leaving both parties feeling isolated and dissatisfied.

Further, parents may become concerned about their son's behavior if the exhibited behavior tends to fall on what society considers to be the feminine side of the behavior continuum. Similarly, if daughters act too "tomboyish" or too "sexy," anxiety and arguments between parents about how the child should be raised can ensue. Even if parents are not in conflict over these issues, pressures and interference from the extended family can negatively impact the family dynamic.

How Can Family Therapy Help People in Such Situations?

Some issues can be resolved merely through an educational process. Assuring parents that their son's and daughter's behavior fits into the normal range and that their children should be supported and not pushed into or away from certain interests and activities may be all that is needed to begin a healing process between parents and offspring. At times, work has to be done to help the couple create appropriate boundaries between the generations without alienating extended family members. Other issues may necessitate changing expectations, setting priorities, and/or negotiating commitments regarding the household division of labor. The more difficult dynamic to change is the one in which couples are polarized relative to an issue. In this case, each party needs to identify their part in keeping the polarization alive and make the needed changes in their behavior instead of waiting for the other to change.

socialization process with respect to the acquisition of gender roles.

Psychoanalytic/Identification Theory

One prominent theory, known as **psychoanalytic/identification theory**, originated with Sigmund Freud (1856–1939), the founder of modern psychoanalysis. Freud believed that children learn gender-appropriate behaviors by unconsciously identifying with their same-sex parent and that they pass through a series of stages in their development. During the first two stages, the oral and the anal stages, the experiences and behaviors of girls and boys are similar. Both identify with the mother, who is their primary caretaker. However, in the third stage, the phallic stage, which occurs around the age of 3 or 4, the development of girls and boys proceeds in different directions. By this age children not only are aware of their own genitals but also of the fact that their genitals differ from those of the other sex. According to Freud, it is in this third stage that identification occurs. Children begin learning how to behave in gender-appropriate ways as they unconsciously model their behavior after that of their same-sex parent. Freud called the boy's development the Oedipus complex, based on the mythical Greek character who unknowingly killed his father and married his mother. According to Freud, the young boy experiences sexual feelings for his mother and sees his father as a rival for her affections. Hence, he wants to get rid of his father. At the same time, however, he becomes aware that he has a penis and that his mother does not. Unconsciously, he fears that if his father were to learn of his feelings for his mother, the father would castrate him. Thus, he resolves the Oedipus complex by identifying with his father (becoming like him) and giving up his desire for his mother. Thus, the boy acquires the appropriate gender role.

The path to feminine identification takes a different turn for girls. Freud called this development the Electra complex, after a mythical Greek woman who urged her brother to slay their mother, who had killed their father. According to Freud, a girl realizes that boys have something she doesn't—a penis. Because she is missing this organ, she develops a sense of inferiority and jealousy and blames her mother for this deformity, a condition Freud refers to as penis envy. At first she takes her love away from her mother, focusing on her father as her love object. Gradually, however, she realizes she can't have her father, and she reestablishes her identification with her mother, with the goal of one day becoming a mother herself.

What are we to make of Freud's theory? Like Greek mythology, it makes fascinating reading, but because it maintains that the process of identification is unconscious, verifying it empirically is impossible. Other than psychoanalytical reports, which are subject to observer bias, there is little if any scientific evidence of either castration anxiety in boys or penis envy in girls. Furthermore, whether children that age understand the relationships between gender and genitalia is questionable. Finally, Freud's view of women as inadequate or incomplete contains an antifemale bias that later identification theorists sought to modify.

Karen Horney (1967) challenged the notion that women view their bodies as inferior and argued that a girl's psychosexual development centers around her own body rather than that of the male. She also argued that what women envy is not the male penis, per se, but what it symbolizes—men's higher status, freedom, and power. Erik Erikson (1968) suggested that male dominance is, in part, related to womb envy, the jealousy men have for women because of their unique ability to bear children.

Nancy Chodorow (1978, 1990), whose concept of "gender reproduction" was discussed in Chapter 1, sees gender identity as emerging from the social organization of parenting roles. Women mother; men do not. She sees this "asymmetrical organization of parenting" as the basis for gender inequality and the source of identification problems for boys. Boys must psychologically separate from their mothers and pattern themselves after a parent who is frequently absent. As a result, they form personalities that are more detached from others and in which emotional needs are repressed. Girls, on the other hand, continue their relationship with their mothers and, through this ongoing interaction, acquire the capabilities for mothering and emotional attachment behaviors. Implicit in Chodorow's work is the belief that shared parenting between women and men would be beneficial to society. As with Freud's theory, the results of these theory modifications have yet to be tested and verified. In particular, research is needed to discover whether or not similar patterns exist across racial, ethnic, and social class groupings here in the United States. For example, Denise Segura and Jennifer Pierce (1993) question whether Chodorow's theory adequately accounts for patterns observed in Mexican American families, where child-rearing practices include multiple mothering figures, such as grandmothers, godmothers, and aunts. Finally, as we saw earlier, in some other non-Western societies both women and men participate in child care. Thus, while Chodorow's developmental pattern provides insights into some Western families, it cannot be applied universally to all families.

Social-Learning Theory

The perspective known as social-learning theory has its roots in behaviorism, the theory that human behavior is the result of a reaction to objective stimuli or situations. **Social-learning theory** asserts that gender roles and gender identity are learned directly through a system of positive reinforcement (rewards) and negative reinforcement (punishments) and indirectly through observation and **modeling,** learning through imitation. In direct learning, for example, parents reward their daughters with encouragement and approval for engaging in gender-appropriate behavior, such as playing with dolls and dressing up in mother's jewelry and high heels. If boys engage in this same behavior, however, they are punished and told, "Boys don't act that way." Research indicates that at younger ages girls enjoy greater flexibility in engaging in cross-gender behavior than do boys (Lynn, 1966; Martin, 1990). This finding is not unique to U.S. culture. Finnish parents also are more accepting of cross-gender behavior for girls than for boys (Sandnabba and Ahlberg, 1999). A girl can be a "tomboy," but a boy who engages in cross-gender behavior risks being labeled a "sissy." Sociologist David Lynn suggests that this harsher treatment of boys for acting "girllike" leads boys to develop a dislike and contempt for females and femininity, which may explain their later hostility toward females (see Chapter 11).

Social-learning theory maintains that behavior that is regularly followed by a reward is more likely to be repeated, whereas behavior that brings forth punishment is more likely to be discontinued. Thus, children quickly develop an awareness that females and males are different and that separate gender roles are appropriate for each sex.

Children also learn which behaviors are appropriate for their gender by observing and imitating their parents and other adults, their peers, and media personalities. Social-learning theorists believe that children initially model themselves after those who are readily available and perceived as powerful (who control rewards and punishment), warm and friendly (nurturing), and similar to the self (same sex). This modeling view of the same sex is similar to those of psychoanalytic/identification theorists. However, social-learning theorists do not accept the notion that behavior is fixed according to early learning patterns. Rather, they believe that behavior and attitudes change as situations and expectations in the social environment change. As children grow older, the range of role models expands, and the work of crafting a gender identity continues.

A considerable amount of research supports social-learning theory. Nevertheless, social-learning theory alone cannot fully explain gender role acquisition. For one, modeling is more complex than the theory suggests. Children do not always model themselves after same-sex individuals. In addition, subcultural differences as well as differences in family structures may affect the variety and choice of available role models. Moreover, learning theory treats children as passive learners. In reality, parent–child interaction is two-directional, in that a child's behavior may have a significant influence on parental behavior as well.

Cognitive-Development Theory

Fundamental to **cognitive-development theory** is the belief that the child's mind matures through interaction with the surrounding environment. In contrast to social-learning theory, cognitive-development theory asserts that children take an active role in organizing their world. They manage this by creating schemas, or mental categories, that emerge through interaction with their social environment. Subsequently, as new information is encountered, it is processed and assimilated into these categories, or the categories are adjusted to fit the new information. Psychologist Lawrence Kohlberg (1966) adapted cognitive-development theory to explain the emergence of children's gender identities. Early on (about age 2 to 3) children become aware that two sexes exist; they can identify and label themselves and others as girls or boys. This labeling process, however, is based not on anatomical differences but on superficial characteristics such as clothes—girls wear dresses and pastel colors, whereas boys wear pants and bold colors. According to Kohlberg, at this stage children have not yet developed gender identity. This doesn't develop until children are 6 or 7 years old and have the mental ability to grasp the concept of constancy or permanency. Prior to this time they are too young to realize that all people can be so classified and that sex is a permanent characteristic that cannot be changed simply by changing clothes or hairstyles.

One of the ways children learn what is expected of them as they grow up is through imitating adults, as this 5-year-old is doing by dressing up in his father's clothes.

Cognitive-development theory maintains that once gender identity is developed, children are able to organize their behavior around it. That is, they strive to behave in a way that is consistent with their own sex, and they attach value to their behavior. Children come to view gender-appropriate behavior in a positive manner and gender-inappropriate behavior as negative behavior that should be avoided.

A considerable body of research gives support to cognitive-development theory. For example, researchers found evidence that children become more accurate at gender differentiation and labeling as they get older (Coker, 1984). In addition, cognitive-development theory helps explain children's, especially boys', strong preferences for sex-typed toys and for playing with same-sex peers (Zuckerman and Sayre, 1982).

Other researchers have criticized some aspects of cognitive-development theory. John Money and Anke Ehrhardt (1972) question the timing of gender identity. Their research implies that an important aspect of gender identity is present at as early as 2 years of age; changing a child's sex after that age proves difficult. In a similar vein, other researchers have found that a great deal of sex typing—the degree to which men and women identify with societal definitions of masculinity and femininity (Basow, 1992)—and preference for sex-typed toys occurs before the age attributed to gender permanency (Downs, 1983; Bussey and Bandura, 1984). This apparent discrepancy may simply represent two different phases of gender development. The earlier sex typing may be due to differential reinforcement and imitation, whereas the sex typing that occurs later, after the development of the idea of gender permanency, may be a result of cognitive development (Basow, 1986).

The most serious criticism of cognitive-development theory is that it overemphasizes gender learning as something children do themselves and minimizes the role culture plays in gender socialization. Hence, as psychologist Sandra Bem (1983:609) writes, "The typical American child cannot help observing, for example, that what parents, teachers, and peers consider to be appropriate behavior varies as a function of sex; that toys, clothing, occupations, hobbies, the domestic division of labor—even pronouns—all vary as a function of sex." In a later work, Bem (1993) criticizes cognitive-development theory for minimizing the role of culture in gender role socialization and offers an alternative theory, the enculturated-lens theory, to explain gender role acquisition.

Enculturated-Lens Theory

In her **enculturated-lens theory** of gender role acquisition, Bem argues that hidden cultural assumptions about how societal members should look, behave, and feel are so deeply embedded in social institutions and cultural discourse and, hence, individual psyches that these behaviors and ways of thinking are systematically reproduced from one generation to the next. Although every culture contains a wide array of such assumptions, or *lenses*, as Bem calls them, her analysis focuses on three gender lenses: (1) gender polarization, whereby females and males are perceived as fundamentally different from each other—these differences, in turn, constitute a central organizing principle for social interaction; (2) androcentrism, which encompasses the beliefs that males are superior to females and that males and male experiences are the normative standard against which women should be judged; and (3) biological essentialism, which views the first two as natural and inevitable results of the inherent biological differences between females and males.

Bem argues that gender acquisition is a special case of socialization, or what she calls *enculturation*. Accordingly, individuals are constantly receiving *metamessages*, lessons about what is valued and important in their culture. For example, a metamessage about gender is being sent when children observe only mothers doing household tasks. As we will see in the next section, from birth on children quickly learn these social constructions and come to see them as natural, being unaware that other constructions are possible. However, Bem does not consider individuals passive in this process. Rather, she sees them as active, pattern-seeking individuals who evaluate themselves in response to these patterns and decide whether or not to conform to them.

Although Bem acknowledges that all societies must enculturate new members, she believes that the lenses of gender polarization and androcentrism must be altered. She proposes that parents begin this process by providing their children with an alternative lens for organizing and making sense out of the world, for example, an "individual differences" lens that would highlight the "remarkable variability of individuals within groups" (1983:613).

Empirical testing is required to determine how valid Bem's theory is. Nevertheless, an examination of the various **agents of socialization**—individuals, groups, and organizations that help form an individual's attitudes, behaviors, and self-concept—does provide us with insight into the content of gender messages and how they are communicated in our society.

AGENTS OF SOCIALIZATION

Gender role socialization begins at birth and continues throughout an individual's lifetime. In our interaction with parents, teachers, and peers, and through books, television, and movies, we are constantly taught values, attitudes, and behaviors that our culture sees as appropriate for each sex.

Parents

Parents provide children with their first exposure to gender learning and play a key role in helping children develop a sense of themselves as females and males. An extensive body of research indicates that parents think of and treat their daughters and sons differently, even though they frequently are not aware of doing so. This process begins early. Researchers found that many expectant parents relate to their fetus on the basis of whether they believe it to be a girl or a boy. Perceived female fetuses were thought of as "graceful and gentle," whereas the movements of perceived male fetuses were described as "strong" (Stainton, 1985). When asked by researchers to describe their newborns, parents described daughters as delicate, soft, and tiny and sons as strong, big, athletic, and well-coordinated, even though the infants did not differ significantly by sex on measures of weight, length, muscle tone, heartbeat, or reflexes (Rubin et al., 1974; Reid, 1994).

Consistent with these findings, other researchers have found that parents, especially fathers, tend to engage in more rough-and-tumble play with infant and young sons than they do with daughters (MacDonald and Parke, 1986). Studies of father–child interaction show that fathers play more interactive games with young sons, promoting visual, fine-motor, and locomotor exploration with them, whereas they have more verbal interaction with daughters and appear to encourage closer physical proximity with them. The consequence of this differential play activity may be that boys learn to be more independent and aggressive than girls do (Bronstein, 1988). In fact, traits of dependence and helplessness may be encouraged in girls as a result of parents acting on the belief that daughters need more help than sons (Burns, Mitchell, and Obradovich, 1989).

Not only do parents play differently with their children, they also communicate differently with them. Stories told to daughters tend to contain more emotion words than do stories told to sons. By the time they are age 6, girls typically use more specialized emotion words than boys do (Adams et al., 1995; Kuebli et al., 1995). In contrast, other researchers have found that mothers tend to speak to sons more explicitly, ask them more questions, and use more action verbs in conversing with them. Thus, sons seem to receive more of the kind of verbal stimulation that is associated with reasoning skills (Weitzman, Birns, and Friend, 1985), whereas the interactions with daughters encourage the development of emotional sensitivity to people's feelings and expressions (Goleman, 1996).

Clothing Parents also dress their children differently, initially perhaps to give clues to others so that they can be assured of responding appropriately on the basis of sex. The type of clothing children wear serves other functions as well, however. Frilly dresses are not conducive to rough-and-tumble play. Boys' clothing, by and large, is less restrictive than is girls' clothing. Therefore, boys are encouraged to be more active and aggressive in their play than girls are.

Toys and Games Studies of children's rooms revealed another way in which parents affect the gender identities of their children. The decor frequently reflected traditional gender stereotypes—florals and pastels for girls, animals and bold colors for boys (Rheingold and Cook, 1975; Stoneman et al., 1986). More important, however, the rooms contained a marked difference in toys. Boys had a wide range of toys (educational, sports, tools, objects, large and small vehicles), many of which promote outdoor play, whereas girls' toys were less varied in type (dolls, housekeeping objects, and crafts) and promote mainly indoor activities (Rheingold and Cook, 1975; Pomerleau et al., 1990). In her research on children's toys, sociologist Marsha Liss (1992) found that parents are much more likely to give their children requested gender-typical toys than they are to give gender-atypical ones.

These findings take on greater significance when we consider the way toys function in the learning process. Toys for boys tend to promote exploration, manipulation, construction, invention, and competition. Girls' toys typically encourage creativity, nurturance, and attractiveness (Lott, 1994). Thus, girls and boys may develop different cognitive and social skills based on play activities, which in turn may lead to very different opportunities as adults.

CHORES A distinction between inside and outside activities is also apparent in the chores assigned to children. Girls are expected to do inside work (wash dishes and clean the house), whereas boys are given activities outside the home (yard work and emptying the trash). Because girls' chores are daily ones whereas a great deal of what boys do is sporadic, girls spend more time doing chores than boys do. A study by researchers Teresa Mauldin and Carol Meeks (1990) of sex differences in children's time use found that boys spend more time in leisure activities and less time in household and personal care than do girls. There are some variations, however. Middle- and upper-income parents are less likely to assign gender-linked chores than are parents from lower-income backgrounds. The assignment of gender-linked chores occurs less frequently in African American homes, where both daughters and sons often are socialized toward independent and nurturing behaviors (Hale-Benson, 1986; P. H. Collins, 1991; Lips, 1993). From early on, then, patterns for a division of labor based on sex are formed and will likely carry over into adult marital roles. As we will see in Chapter l0, even when women work full-time, they still do the bulk of the housework.

Language

One of the first tasks facing a developing child is the mastery of language skills. There is growing agreement among social scientists that children's acquisition of gender identity and their perception of gender roles are strongly influenced by language. Research shows that the English language contains a number of gender biases. For example, the words *man* and *he* can be used to exclude females—"It's a man's world," "The best man for the job"—or they can be used generically to refer to both women and men—mankind. In fact, the use of male terms frequently serves to exclude females. Think of the words *policeman*, *fireman*, *postman*, *chairman*, *spokesman*, *congressman*, *workman*. Whom do you visualize in these roles? Researchers have found that most people visualize men when such terms are used (Wilson and Ng, 1988). Other studies show that elementary school children give male-biased responses to story cues that contain the pronoun *he* (Hyde, 1984). When the masculine pronoun is used, as it frequently is in textbooks to refer to doctors, lawyers, and public officials, children tend to associate those roles with males. Thus, many children may limit their aspirations to what appear to be gender-appropriate occupations. To counter this restrictive influence, many publishers have moved to a more gender-neutral language, using *they*, *he or she*, *police officer*, *firefighter*, and *mail carrier*.

Peers

The games children play and the people with whom they play them also influence the acquisition of gender identity. At about the age of 3 a process of sex segregation begins. This process accelerates during the school years. Researchers have found that girls and boys both prefer same-sex groups. Psychologists Eleanor Maccoby and Carol Jacklin (1987) explain girls' same-sex preference as stemming from unrewarding mixed-sex play activities. Since boys play more roughly than girls and use physical assertion to resolve differences, they tend to dominate and bully girls in mixed-sex play groups. In contrast, girls enjoy more cooperation and mutuality in same-sex groups.

Boys also prefer same-sex groups, but their motivation is different. Aware of men's higher status, boys attempt to dissociate themselves from girls and anything that suggests femininity (Whiting and Edwards, 1988). Thus, girls and boys grow up in different peer subcultures that reinforce both real and perceived gender differences. Because opportunities for cross-sex interactions are so limited, most gender stereotypes go largely unchallenged. That such behavior exists and is reinforced by social approval is substantiated by a large body of research that shows that from preschool to high school, children who engage in traditional gender role behavior are more socially acceptable to their peers than are children who engage in nontraditional roles (Martin, 1990). Peers may play an even more significant role in the lives of African American males. Distinct bodily movements, athletic prowess, sexual competence, and street smarts, including how to fight and defend oneself, are lessons learned in the context of the male African American peer group (Hale-Benson, 1986). According to Richard Majors:

> Black people in general, and the black man in particular, look out on a world that does not positively reflect their image. Black men learned long ago that the classic American virtues of hard work would not give us the tangible rewards that accrue to most members of the dominant society. We learned early that we would not be Captains of Industry or builders of engineering wonders. Instead, we channeled our creative energies into construction of a symbolic universe. Therefore, we adopted unique poses and postures to offset

the externally imposed "zero" image. Because black men were denied access to the dominant culture's acceptable avenues of expression, we created a form of self-expression—the "Cool Pose." (1995:82)

Play and Organized Sports

Sociologist Janet Lever (1978) observed and interviewed fifth graders about their activities and found many differences between girls' and boys' activities. She believes boys' activities better prepare them to succeed in modern industrial societies. Girls' games have only a few rules and frequently involve only a minimum of roles (for example, jumping rope or tag), whereas boys' play groups are larger, have complex rules, and involve a variety of roles. Girls' activities require more cooperation, whereas boys' games are organized around competition. Hence, boys' games provide more training for leadership and complex organizational roles than do girls' games.

Rarely has anyone questioned the physical, psychological, and social benefits that active play and organized sports contribute to boys' and men's lives. Only recently, however, have researchers documented the enormous benefits of sport participation for girls and women: physical (lower risks of obesity, heart disease, and osteoporosis), psychological (higher self-esteem, better body image, enhanced sense of competence and control, reduced stress and depression), and academic (better grades, higher standardized test scores, and lower risk of dropping out) (Pipher, 1994; President's Council on Physical Fitness and Sports, 1997; Zimmerman and Reavill, 1998). Since the passage of the Education Amendment Act of 1972 and its Title IX provision, more money went into athletic programs for girls and women. The results of this investment are readily seen in the growing number of professional women athletes like Serena and Venus Williams (tennis), Laila Ali (boxing), Annika Sorenstan (golf), Lisa Leslie (basketball), Jackie Joyner-Kersee (track and field), Zoe Cadman (jockey), and the numerous athletes in the Olympic Games. However, gender stereotypes and limited socialization experiences prevent many girls and women from engaging in sport activities, even at a recreational level. According to the Women's Sports Foundation (1998), girls who have not participated in sports by age 10 have only a 10 percent chance of participating at age 25.

Recent research found that playing with "masculine" (rather than "feminine") toys and games, playing in predominantly male or mixed-gender groups, and being considered a tomboy distinguished between women who later became college athletes and those who did not (Giuliano and Popp, 2000). In a similar vein, earlier research found that women in nontraditional occupations (for example, lawyers and physicians) were, as children, more likely to have played with boys and to have engaged in more competitive male activities than were women in more traditional occupations (for example, teachers and librarians) (Coats and Overman, 1992). Thus, breaking down gender-prescribed play in early childhood would most likely lead to more widespread female participation in sport and physical activity, providing them not only myriad physical and psychological benefits but wider career choices as well.

Teachers

Teachers also play a major role in the socialization of children. If you were to ask elementary school teachers whether they treat girls and boys differently, most would probably say no, even though a wide range of research studies reveals differential patterns of interaction between teachers and female and male students.

Tennis is no longer a white-male dominated sport. Today women and people of color, like sisters Serena and Venus Williams, are among the top winners in the game.

Think back to your elementary and high school days. Were girls and boys in your classes treated in the same way? Who were the class officers? How was playground space allocated? How were sports organized? Did girls and boys do the same classroom chores? Did you have other-sex friends (nondating relationships) in grammar school? In high school? In college? In marriage?

When teachers structure classroom activities along sex-separated lines, it encourages competition between the sexes—for example, girls against the boys in math or spelling contests. Often, playground space is allocated in a gender-specific manner, with boys occupying the large fixed spaces for team sports and the girls having a more limited space for their activities, usually closer to the school building and with adult supervision. This use of space conveys subtle messages, that girls need more protection than boys and that boys are entitled to more space.

Teacher behavior can send other gender messages to students as well. Studies at all educational levels show that teachers provide more assistance to and challenges for boys than for girls (Sadker and Sadker, 1994). Other studies show that boys receive more praise for creative behavior, whereas girls receive more praise for conforming behavior (Grossman and Grossman, 1994).

Gender is not the only variable affecting student–teacher interaction. The race of the student may trigger different behaviors on the part of teachers. Overall, Asian American students are often perceived as the best students and treated accordingly (Basow, 1992). African American girls, compared with white girls, receive less in the way of teacher feedback and academic encouragement, and African American boys receive the most frequent teacher referrals to special education programs (U.S. Department of Education, 1997).

Messages like these are often reinforced by the curricular materials used in the classroom. Researchers Piper Purcell and Lara Stewart (1990), for example, found many examples of gender stereotyping in children's readers. Although both sexes are depicted in a wider range of activities than had previously been the case, certain basic trends remain. Boys and men are featured more often than girls and women, and they tend to be portrayed in more active and powerful positions (Orenstein, 1994; Sapiro, 1999). And, despite new guidelines for publishers, males are still primarily portrayed in stereotyped ways—that is, as competitive, aggressive, and argumentative (Evans, 2000).

Even at the college level researchers have observed differential treatment of females and males. For example, in many classes professors call on male students more often than on female students, they interrupt female students more than they do male students, and they are more likely to refer to female students as "girls" or "gals" while referring to male students as "men." Female students are not always taken as seriously as male students, particularly in fields traditionally dominated by males, such as math and science (Hall and Sandler, 1985; Myers and Dugan, 1996). A 22-year-old female student complained of discriminatory treatment by a math professor: "There were only two other women in the advanced calculus class I was taking. The professor didn't want us there. He made jokes about women not being able to balance their checking accounts, and he always seemed surprised when one of us solved his math challenges. I was going to drop his course because he made me feel like a freak for liking math, but my advisor encouraged me to stay with it."

The Mass Media

That the mass media play an important part in shaping the values, beliefs, and behaviors of modern societies is difficult to dispute. Let us take television as an example. More than 98 percent of U.S. households have at least one television set, almost 85 percent have videocassette recorders and 67 percent subscribe to cable television; 42 percent of households have computers and 26 percent have Internet access (U.S. Census Bureau, 2000). In the average home the television set is on 6 or more hours per day. The average school-aged child watches approximately 27 hours of television every week. By the age of 18, the average U.S. child has spent twice as much time (22,000 hours) watching television as attending school (11,000 hours) and has seen 350,000 commercials (Staples and Jones, 1985; Tracy, 1990). Black children and adolescents watch more television than do their white peers, and children from blue-collar families spend more time in front of the television set than do children from middle-class families.

What gender messages do these children (and adults) get when they watch television? To answer this question researchers employ a technique called **content analysis**, whereby they examine the actual content of programs. They do this by counting particular items within specific categories, for example, the number of males and females featured in the program. As we shall see, most programming, from children's shows to prime time, casts its major characters in traditional roles.

Children's Shows Content analysis reveals that children's shows are predominantly white-male-oriented, featuring more than twice as many male as female roles. This discrepancy implies that boys are more significant than girls, an image that is reinforced by the way in which female and male characters are portrayed. In a major study of commercial children's television programs, researcher Earle Barcus (1983) found that the sexes are presented in a biased and somewhat unrealistic way. Females are more likely to be found in minor roles with little responsibility for the outcome of the story and are rarely shown working outside the home. In contrast, male characters are depicted in a variety of occupations to which many boys realistically can aspire.

Little has changed since that study. According to one report, television executives decided to feature only males as dominant characters, with females playing peripheral roles, if any, during fall 1991 Saturday morning programs. This decision was based on a finding that boys will watch only shows with male leads but that girls will watch shows with either female or male leads (Carter, 1991). Even in the popular and highly acclaimed "Sesame Street," the major characters often portray a restricted view of female and male behavior.

Children, especially girls, are aware of the narrowness of television's portrayal of girls' lives. A 1995 Harris survey of 2000 girls and boys in grades 3 through 12 found that females are likely to feel that their age and gender are underrepresented on TV. Between 43 percent and 55 percent of girls and young women say there are too few programs about females their age, about girls engaged in interesting adventures, and about women in challenging careers. Furthermore, twice as many girls as boys complained that TV displays too much sex (45 percent to 22 percent) and too much violence (37 percent to 19 percent) (Moore, 1995).

Table 3.1

Children's Attitudes toward Weight Gain

Survey Question	"Yes" Response		
	Totals	Females	Males
Do you want to lose weight now?	42.0%	55.0%	28.5%
Have you ever thought you looked fat to other people?	41.4	54.4	27.8
Have you ever been afraid to eat because you thought you would gain weight?	23.0	32.5	13.0
Have you ever tried to lose weight by dieting?	31.4	42.6	19.7

Source: Ann C. Childress, Timothy D. Brewerton, Elizabeth L. Hodges, and Mark P. Jarrell, 1993, "The Kids' Eating Disorders Survey (KEDS): A Study of Middle School Students," *Journal of American Academy of Child and Adolescent Psychiatry* 32:843–850.

Prime-Time Television The situation is not much different on prime-time television. Although there has been an increase in the number of female roles, as well as more programming that deals with issues of gender equality (Dow, 1996), much of prime-time television still adheres to gender stereotypes (Signorielli, 1999). Besides appearing more frequently and having the majority of major roles, male characters are older, more mature, and more authoritative than female characters. Besides being younger, female characters are typically thin, physically attractive, and scantily attired. For example, one study found that 46 percent of the female characters were thin or very thin compared with just 16 percent of male characters (Signorielli, 1997). Such findings may help explain reports of eating disorders in girls as young as 9. Timothy Brewerton of the Medical University of South Carolina surveyed 3100 fifth- to eighth-grade students. As Table 3.1 shows, although 41.4 percent felt they were too fat, girls were twice as likely to feel that way as boys (54.4 percent to 27.8 percent). More significantly, 42.6 percent of the girls but only 19.7 percent of the boys said they had tried to lose weight by dieting. Furthermore, 32.5 percent of the girls and 13.0 percent of the boys indicated that they had at some time felt afraid to eat because they worried about gaining weight. A recent survey of 6728 adolescents in grades 5 to 12 revealed a similar pattern. Almost half (45 percent) the girls and 20 percent of the boys reported that they had dieted at some point. Additionally, 13 percent of the girls and 7 percent of the boys reported disordered eating behaviors (Neumark-Sztainer and Hannan, 2000). This gender differential reflects patterns observed in adults as well. For women in particular, weight is perceived as a crucial indicator of their social acceptability. Although this perception seems to

For Better or For Worse® **by Lynn Johnston**

By the time children are in their teens, they have internalized images of the ideal body form for their sex.
Source: © Lynn Johnston Productions, Inc./Dist. by Universal Press Syndicate, Inc.

hold across all racial and ethnic groups, social classes, and sexual orientations (Thompson, 1994; Wood, 1994) African American women appear to be less obsessed than white women about how much they weigh and about dieting (Nielsen, 2000). A likely explanation for this difference is that, in general, African Americans have less restrictive definitions of female beauty, including how much a woman weighs. Thus, it is not surprising to find that of the 8 million people in the United States estimated to have eating disorders, the vast majority are white women (National Association of Anorexia Nervosa and Associated Disorders, 2001). Among the most common eating disorders are anorexia nervosa and bulimia. A person suffering from anorexia nervosa refuses to eat enough to maintain normal weight for her/his weight and height and has an intense fear of gaining weight. A person suffering from bulimia engages in binge eating and then to prevent weight gain induces vomiting or uses laxatives, diuretics, enemas, or other medications. Both disorders can be life threatening.

According to George Hsu, director of the Eating Disorders Program at Tufts University School of Medicine, there is a close parallel between the rates of eating disorders and dieting. In his research he found that the increase in eating disorders is directly proportional to the number of people going on diets. In countries like Taiwan, Singapore, and China, where dieting is becoming fashionable, eating disorders, largely unknown in the past, are becoming more common (Goleman, 1995).

Although the dominant image of women in television continues to conform to an idealized female body image, some exceptions like the character Eleanor in "The Practice," played by Camryn Manheim, are beginning to appear.

Although we cannot assume a direct cause-and-effect relationship between television images and behavior such as eating disorders, there is mounting evidence to suggest that such a relationship does exist. For example, in the Harris poll referred to earlier, 15 percent of the girls and 8 percent of the boys reported that they had dieted or exercised to look like a TV character (Moore, 1995). More recent studies of adolescent girls found that they frequently compare themselves to the thin-ideal images routinely provided in television and the print media. Many respondents in these studies reported that these comparisons led them to feel dissatisfied with their bodies, increased their desire to be thin, and, in some cases, motivated them to engage in eating disordered behaviors (Botta, 1999; Field et al., 1999). Further, an analysis of commercials aimed at children found that the overwhelming majority (86 percent) of commercials advertising products to enhance personal appearance were aimed at girls (Ogletree et al., 1990). Similarly, a review and comparison of 14 studies of television advertising from 5 different continents over a 25-year period also found that women were far more likely than men to be shown with body products (Furnham, 1999). This early and ongoing emphasis on the importance of appearance for females likely plays a role in the higher incidence of eating disorders experienced by females.

Gender role stereotyping is also evident in the content of the programs and their television characters. Although there are some notable exceptions ("ER," "Family Law," and "The Practice"), the vast majority of programs depict women in a limited range of roles; mostly in home or family situations, regardless of whether they are employed. When women characters are employed, their occupations are generally high-status ones, for example, lawyers, doctors, or business executives, a pattern not typical of the majority of working women. Thus, television distorts the reality of the working lives of most women and perhaps gives viewers an erroneous notion that gender barriers have disappeared.

In contrast, male characters are shown as powerful individuals, interacting in a wide variety of settings. Just as in children's readers, males are depicted as the problem solvers, whereas females generally are characterized as needing male help in solving their problems. There is one notable case in which women outperform men, however: They are seven times more likely to use sex or romantic charm to get their way (Condry, 1989). And there is one way in which male portrayals do not fare so well: Male characters are much more likely than female characters to use force or violence to get what they want and to commit crimes (Signorielli, 1997). Studies in other countries reveal similar patterns. For example, research examining samples of televised sports in Sweden found gender differences regarding both quantity and type of coverage. Less than 10 percent of the total examined sports news time covered female athletes, and less than 2 percent of the time was used to cover women athletes in sports categorized as masculine (Koivula, 1999).

Stereotyping in the mass media is not limited to gender. Although racial and ethnic groups are more visible in programming today than in the past, they continue to be underrepresented both on and off camera. This is especially true for Asian Americans, Latinas/os, and Native Americans (Coltrane and Messineo, 2000).

In sum, gender stereotypes are presented in various degrees by all the agents of socialization. Even when parents make efforts to treat their daughters and sons equally, other socializing forces may undermine those efforts. As we have seen, rarely are either women or men portrayed in terms of the rich diversity and complexity that constitutes the human condition. Thus, it is not surprising that many children develop a stereotypic gender schema in the process of acquiring their gender identity. However, the socialization process itself does not tell us why one gender role is more highly valued than another. Although a discussion of the causes of gender inequality is outside the scope of this text, the theories discussed in the previous chapter, particularly structural functionalism and conflict theory, give some insight into how existing social arrangements define and support gender inequality. For now let us turn our attention to the many ways in which our lives are affected by the cultural constructions of gender.

CONSEQUENCES OF GENDER STEREOTYPING

Imagine for a moment that you had to spend the next year of your life as a member of the other sex. How would your life be different? What advantages and disadvantages would you experience as a female? As a male?

Studies show that each gender role has its advantages. Women live longer, can express their emotions more easily, and have closer interpersonal relationships than men do. Men have more power, both economically and socially, and greater freedom, and they experience less sexual discrimination or harassment than women do. However, as the "Social Policy Issues" box on page 78 makes clear, this does not mean that all men enjoy these privileges or that men, as a group, escape any negative effect of gender socialization. Nevertheless, both women and men perceive the female role as having more disadvantages than the male role. A Gallup poll survey found that 62 percent of all the adults surveyed believe men in the United States have a better life than women do. In that same survey, 71 percent of the women and 52 percent of the men believe that society favors men over women (Newport, 1993). A cross-cultural study of 22 countries found similar results with respondents in 15 countries agreeing that society favors men over women (Gallup Poll, 1996). Indeed, the fact that women and men are socialized differently has major consequences for individuals, families, and society at large. This is particularly true when existing social arrangements reinforce these differences, for example, institutionalized patterns of inequities in pay and job opportunities that disregard individual abilities. The scope of this book allows us to consider only a few of these consequences, so we will focus on lifestyle choices, self-esteem, self-confidence, mental illness, female–male friendships, and patterns of communication.

Lifestyle Choices

Although women have made major advances in a wide range of fields, from construction work to executive business positions, this progress is still more the exception than the norm. Current gender expectations continue to limit women's lifestyle choices. For example, the choice of a single lifestyle by a growing number of women is still viewed as second best. Women who wish to combine career and family often must do so without much societal support. High-profile women who challenge the status quo are often suspected of undermining "family values." In 2001, when acting Governor Jane Swift of Massachusetts gave birth to twin girls, she was immediately criticized for putting her political ambitions ahead of her family.

Men, too, have found their lifestyle choices limited by traditional gender expectations. Not all men can or want to achieve "success" as defined by having a meaningful career or a high-paying job. Yet they are pressured to assume the role of the major breadwinner in the family. As a result, they may experience a serious conflict between their work and family roles. In addition, if they are not considered financially successful, they may be viewed as unsuitable marriage prospects.

Self-Esteem

Given that society values traits identified as masculine more highly than those identified as feminine, we might well expect to find gender differences in **self-esteem,** the overall feelings—positive or negative—that a person has about her- or himself (Alpert-Gillis and Connell, 1989). The research literature generally bears this out. As a category, females have lower self-images than males do. This does not mean, however, that all females have lower self-esteem than all males. At least two factors seem to play a crucial role in the relationship between gender and self-esteem: age and the degree of individual sex typing.

AGE A major study by the American Association of University Women (AAUW) of a national sample of more than 3000 students in grades 4 through 10 found that not only did boys have higher self-esteem in elementary school than girls did but that the gap between them widened in high school. In elementary school, 60 percent of the girls and 69 percent of the boys agreed with the statement, I'm happy the way I am. By high school, only 29 percent of the girls and 46 percent of the boys felt that way. There were

SOCIAL POLICY ISSUES

BOYS AND MEN ARE GENDERED, TOO

The past three decades of research on the ways girls are treated and the overall status of women in the United States led to some significant improvements in women's personal and professional lives. For example, women now receive over half of all bachelor's and master's degrees; although still trailing men, women now earn 74 cents for every dollar men make, up from 59 cents in the early 1970s; today, women have more options in both family and career matters than they did in the 1950s; and, over the past 30 years, women have increased their presence at every level of government. These achievements have inspired some researchers to ask how boys and men are faring today. Their preliminary answers suggest that many are in serious trouble starting from birth. For example, males are more likely than females to die in infancy, to be diagnosed with learning problems, to be given Ritalin for hyperactivity or attention deficit disorder, to drop out of school, to be incarcerated, to be both the perpetrators and victims of violence, to remain unmarried, and if married, to abandon their families (Renzetti and Curran, 1999).

Researchers studying boys believe these problems arise out of a combination of factors—inadequate socialization, biology, and the content of cultural messages. Barney Brawer, director of the boys segment of the Harvard Project on Women's Psychology, Boys' Development, and the Culture of Manhood, believes that a crisis in masculinity is occurring because, while society has become clear about what it wants for girls, it has not for boys (Rosenfeld, 1998). Geoffrey Canada (1998) agrees, arguing that existing cultural images of men often give boys mixed messages. For example, strength is confused with violence; virility is confused with promiscuity; adventure is confused with recklessness; and intelligence is confused with arrogance, racism, and sexism. In a similar vein, teacher-researcher Barb Wilder-Smith recounts how a bike-shopping expedition with her 5-year-old son led her to see that boys, like girls, are victims of gender stereotyping. Her son's favorite color was pink, so he asked for a pink bike, but the salesman told him he couldn't have a pink bike, that pink was for girls and he had to have a red or blue bike. Her son told the salesman, "That's ridiculous, colors aren't boys or girls, and pink is my favorite color." He got his pink bike but he also got teased so much that he put a sign on his bicycle basket that read, "I like pink. I am still a boy. I have a penis" (quoted in Rosenfeld, 1998:A1). These researchers believe that now that girls are growing up with more options and opportunities than in the past, boys are experiencing more limited expectations and that familial, educational, and economic institutions are not preparing boys to survive in a world in which traditional masculine strategies that rely on physical strength and dominance are becoming outmoded.

Views such as these have received mixed reactions. Feminists, both females and males, fear that the hard-won gains for girls will be short circuited in a rush to meet the newly defined needs of boys or that a new version of "anatomy is destiny" will rear its head. Those researching boys' experiences are fearful of being misinterpreted as antiwomen. Consequently, social programs and policies regarding ways to improve the lives of both genders are mired in controversy. For example, the popular "Take Our Daughters to Work Day" led to criticisms about the exclusion of sons, and proposals to have all-male elementary schools led parents to ask, "What about our daughters?"

What do you think? Is there a crisis of masculinity in the United States as these researchers believe? Explain. Can we develop programs that meet the needs of boys and men without jeopardizing the gains that girls and women have made? Explain.

some interesting differences by race and ethnicity, however. Among elementary school girls, 55 percent of white girls, 65 percent of black girls, and 68 percent of Latinas reported being "happy as I am." By high school, only 22 percent of white girls, 58 percent of black girls, and 30 percent of Latinas agreed with that statement. The reason that black girls avoid such a drastic erosion in self-esteem compared with other girls is not entirely clear but may have to do with parental socialization that emphasizes strength and independence for their daughters (cited in the AAUW Report, 1995:19, 21). This finding, documented in other studies as well, is attributed to the conflicting expectations girls encounter when they reach puberty. Girls who were energetic, self-confident, and independent now experience pressure to behave in ways that will make them attractive to and popular with boys, even though this behavior might conflict with their own desires and abilities (Gilligan, 1990).

Early adolescence is a significant transition period for both sexes, but research reveals it to be a particularly difficult time for girls. Girls are growing up sooner than they did in the past. The age of a girl's first period, called *menarche*, has been falling for decades. Many of today's 10- and 11-year-old girls are at the same biological point that 16-year-olds were in 1800. In 1900, the average age for menarche

The United States has one of the highest incarceration rates in the world. Many experts believe that the large number of male prisoners today is a result of a national crisis in masculinity whereby boys and men receive mixed messages about what it means to be a man.

was 14; by 1988, the average age had dropped to 12.5, and experts believe it will slip even lower (Creager, 1995). Researchers believe there is a correlation between how physically mature a girl looks and how people treat her. As girls reach puberty they are pressured to conform to gender roles more than they were before. The transition of little girl to young woman involves meeting unique demands in a culture that both idealizes and exploits the sexuality of young women. Thus, adolescent girls experience a conflict between their autonomous selves and their need to be feminine. Under these conditions, it is not surprising that many young women experience an erosion in self-esteem.

Sex Typing The second factor that helps explain the observed gender differences in self-esteem is sex typing. Over the last several decades, social scientists have asked people to describe themselves using a list of personality traits thought to be characteristic of women and men. Scores are tallied and individuals are then categorized as masculine (high on instrumental traits, such as independence, strength, aggressiveness), feminine (high on expressive traits, such as understanding, emotion, dependence), or androgynous (having both instrumental and expressive traits). Researchers reported that the highest levels of self-esteem are found among both females and males who are high in masculine traits or who are androgynous (the latter's high self-esteem is attributed to the presence of instrumental traits). Conversely, feminine sex-typed individuals have considerably lower levels of self-esteem.

Self-Confidence

As with self-esteem, girls and boys differ in levels of self-confidence, and the gap widens with age. In response to the statement "I am good at a lot of things," 45 percent of elementary school females agreed, compared with 55 percent of their male counterparts. In high school, however, only 23 percent of the girls agreed, compared with 42 percent of the boys (AAUW, 1991). At least two patterns are associated with these perceptions. First, females tend to underestimate their abilities, whereas males overestimate theirs. In a small but insightful study, Edward Kain (1990:113) asked his students to grade their own papers. He found an almost perfect correlation between sex and grade estimation: The females gave themselves significantly lower grades, whereas the males gave themselves significantly higher grades. Kain concluded, "By the time students have reached college age, the cultural lessons about gender appear to be strongly internalized."

Second, some activities may be avoided if they are seen as inappropriate for one's sex, regardless of ability. For example, females often consider themselves less competent in fields that have been traditionally defined as masculine, such as math and science, than males who have the same grades. Viewed in this light it is not surprising that, as one researcher discovered, "Preschool boys handle more tools, throw more balls, construct more Lego bridges, build more block towers, and tinker more with simple mechanical objects than do girls" (Kahle, 1990). In a similar vein, another study found that by third grade, only 37 percent of the girls, but over half of the boys (51 percent), had used microscopes, while by eleventh grade 17 percent of females compared with 49 percent of males had used an electricity meter (Mullis and Jenkins, 1988).

These play activities are not unimportant. They teach important mental and motor skills, and because girls are not encouraged—indeed, they may even be discouraged—from pursuing such activities, they are at a disadvantage as they grow older. These findings are significant, not only for their implications regarding self-confidence, but also for their economic implications. Society may be losing potential mathematicians and scientists simply because of narrowly defined gender roles. Similarly, society loses out when qualified men avoid entering fields deemed "woman's work" (see Chapter 10).

Mental Health

Gender differences in mental health have long been observed. To take just one example, studies of both clinical populations and the general public consistently find that adolescent girls and women have higher rates of depression than adolescent boys and men do, a ratio of about two to one (Cyranowski et al., 2000). As many as one out of every four women experiences clinical depression sometime during her life (McGrath et al., 1990). There is considerable evidence that gender stereotypes play a pivotal role in these rates (Landrine and Klonoff, 1997). The higher rates of depression found among women may be a result of the fact that women are more likely than men to seek help for their problems (Klerman and Weissman, 1980). This behavior is consistent with traditional gender roles. The traditional feminine role grants women permission to seek help from others, whereas the traditional masculine role requires men to be strong and to "ride out" their problems (Real, 1997).

The attitudes and behaviors of mental health professionals are also important in understanding gender differences in mental illness. Historically, the mental health field has frequently reflected gender-related stereotypes. In one study, for example, researchers asked a number of clinicians to define a healthy woman, a healthy man, and a healthy, mature adult of no specified sex. Clinicians described a healthy woman as more emotional, more submissive, less independent, less aggressive and competitive, more easily excitable, more easily hurt, and more concerned with her appearance than a healthy male. Significantly, when describing a healthy adult of no specified sex, clinicians listed a number of traits traditionally associated with the male stereotype, such as independence and assertiveness. Thus, women were viewed as possessing characteristics that are less positive and less healthy than those of a typical healthy adult (Broverman et al., 1970). Such an association implies that women who conform to the traditional feminine role don't measure up to the mental health standards of the general adult population.

Clinicians today are more sensitive to gender bias and are unlikely to list different characteristics for healthy adult females and healthy adult males. Nevertheless, some clinicians still hold an adjustment standard of mental health. Thus, women and men who conform to traditional gender roles are likely to be seen as healthier than those who deviate from these roles. Assertive and independent women and gentle and nurturing men may therefore be viewed as maladjusted (Robertson and Fitzgerald, 1990; Gilbert and Scher, 1999).

Marital status and level of marital power are also related to feelings of depression. Wives who share decision making with their husbands report lower levels of depression than those in unequal relationships (Whisman and Jacobson, 1988). As Susan Basow (1992) observes, women's lives themselves may add to their risk of being depressed. Women are more likely to be unemployed, poor, or in a low-status job. As wives, they feel pressured to make sure that the household runs smoothly and the needs of all family members are satisfied, even when this means that their own needs go unmet.

Blue-collar trades such as automobile mechanics are increasingly opening their doors to women. Here a Latina repairs the engine on a customer's car.

Although, overall, men fare better on measures of mental health than women do, some aspects of the traditional masculine role can easily become detrimental. When taken to extremes, dominance and aggression can lead to psychologically and physically destructive behavior. Furthermore, the cultural connection between work and male identity can create considerable psychological stress for unemployed men. Lack of education, inadequate job skills, and discriminatory practices make this particularly problematic for poor men and men of color. Additionally, men's emotional lives are often deficient because of their inability to verbalize their love or show affection. Thus, rigid adherence to traditional gender norms may interfere with the development of good mental health for both women and men. This latter point raises an interesting question. Can both women and men benefit from becoming androgynous, that is, sharing masculine and feminine traits?

Research shows that masculine-oriented individuals (high on instrumental traits), both female and male, experience less anxiety, strain, depression, neuroticism, work impairment, achievement conflicts, and dissatisfaction in their lives than do feminine-oriented individuals (Nezu and Nezu, 1987; Long, 1989; Basow, 1992). Similarly, traits traditionally defined as feminine can be beneficial to women and men. The ability to express feelings and show sensitivity to those around one enhances interpersonal adjustment and the ability to form intimate relationships. For example, researchers Lawrence Ganong and Marilyn Coleman (1987) found that androgynous individuals are more expressive in their feelings of love, better able to self-disclose, and more tolerant of faults in their loved ones than are more traditionally oriented people. With this in mind, let's examine the meaning that friendship has in the lives of women and men.

As more women and men pursue similar occupations and work together, the possibilities for development of cross-sex friendships increase.

Women, Men, and Friends

According to Lillian Rubin (1985:59), throughout most of the history of Western civilization, "men's friendships have been taken to be the model of what friendship is and how it ought to be. . . . Women's friendships didn't count, indeed were not even noticed." As recently as 1969, anthropologist Lionel Tiger hypothesized that men have a genetically based tendency to form nonerotic bonds with other males, and that these male bonds are stronger and more stable than those formed between women. An impressive array of research studies over the past 25 years, focusing on the similarities and differences between female and male friendship patterns, has not substantiated Tiger's hypothesis. Conversely, much of this research is consistent with Rubin's assessment.

> The results of my own research are unequivocal: At every life stage between twenty-five and fifty-five, women have more friendships, as distinct from collegial relationships or workmates, than men, and the differences in the content and quality of their friendships are marked and unmistakable. (1985:60–61)

Overall, women's friendships tend to be characterized by intimacy, self-disclosure, nurturance, and emotional support. Conversation is a central part of women's friendships (Walker, 1994; Johnson, 1996). Men's friendships, in contrast, focus more on shared activities such as sports, politics, and business and tend to be less intimate than women's friendships (Inman, 1996). While definitive reasons for these gender differences have not yet been substantiated, several explanations appear plausible. In contrast to men, women are more likely to be socialized to be more relationship-oriented. The emphasis on male competitiveness may make it difficult for men to self-disclose to one another, thereby making men feel vulnerable. Finally, the fear of being labeled homosexual may prevent men from developing emotional attachments to other men.

Despite these differences, both females and males report about the same level of satisfaction with their friendship activities (Mazur, 1989). Thus, although they may connect with others in different ways, both women and men share a common need for meaningful relationships with others of their sex. Although difficult to achieve, this need for connectedness sometimes manifests itself in cross-sex friendships.

Cross-Sex Friendships A single parent who lives with her mother and her 9-year-old daughter told this story.

> Recently Jane had a male school chum over to the house. The grandmother was home and the mother was at work. The two children went up to Jane's room to play computer games. Upon realizing they went upstairs, the grandmother became excited and sent the boy home, telling her granddaughter that it was inappropriate for him to be there.

What do you think motivated the grandmother's behavior? No doubt you have observed mixed-sex groups of preschool children at play. However, this pattern begins to change in elementary school. Like this grandmother, adults become fearful that cross-sex friendships can become sexual. Thus, whether consciously or not, from early on society erects barriers to cross-sex friendships. Some of these barriers are reflected in the organization of elementary schools, with their frequent gender-segregated activities; others are embedded in the belief that women and men have opposite characteristics. As noted earlier, however, as children age, they exhibit more gender flexibility. One consequence of this is the tendency for cross-sex friendships to increase during adolescence and early adulthood. A study by Ruth Anne Clark (1994) of 10- to 16-year-olds found that as age increased so did the tendency to choose other-sex peers for interaction. In all grades, boys, but not girls, showed a slight preference for the other sex. The nature of the interaction, however, influenced the gender preference—both girls and boys preferred a male as a conversational partner for telling stories and joking, whereas girls were chosen as a preferred partner for cheering, advice, or suggestions on how to explain a complicated idea. These patterns continue in adulthood, when men more frequently choose women for conversational partners than women choose men (Reisman, 1990). College students have the highest incidence of cross-sex friendships (Werking, 1994). However, heterosexual marriage or a serious involvement frequently acts against maintaining cross-sex friendships. Lillian Rubin (1985) sees this response as keeping with the cultural expectation that romantic commitment and commitment to family must come before friendships. The fact that our culture provides few models of enduring cross-sex friendships contributes to the difficulty in forming and maintaining such relationships (Rawlins, 1993). Gendered patterns of communication can also exaggerate both the perceived and the real differences between women and men and thus hinder the formation of cross-sex friendships.

Patterns of Communication

Linguistic scholars from Robin Lakoff (1975) to Deborah Tannen (1990, 1994) report that women and men often speak essentially different languages and have different communication goals, which leads to miscommunication between them. According to Tannen, women speak and hear a language of intimacy and connectedness, whereas men speak and hear a language of status and independence. She calls women's conversational style "rapport talk," the goal of which is to signal support, to confirm solidarity, or to indicate they are following the conversation. In contrast, Tannen sees men's conversational style as "report talk," intended to preserve independence and to negotiate and maintain status in a hierarchical order. These contrasting styles can be problematic in intimate relationships, especially in the realm of self-disclosure. As we will see in other sections of this text, men often find self-disclosure difficult, even to their wives.

APPLYING THE SOCIOLOGICAL IMAGINATION

GENDERED COMMUNICATION

Have you ever noticed that when speaking women tend to

- say "we"?
- listen while making eye contact, often nodding or smiling to indicate agreement or understanding?
- be indirect? "The bookkeeper needs help. What would you think of helping her out?" The male listener interprets "thinking" as an option.
- ask for opinions before giving their views, to make others feel involved?
- anticipate a problem and head it off with the result that nobody gets credit because nobody knew there was a problem?
- use disclaimers? "This may seem foolish, but . . ."

Have you ever noticed that when speaking men tend to

- say "I"?
- listen, revealing little information?
- be direct? "The bookkeeper needs help. Take care of it."
- state views upfront, confronting any challengers?
- permit a problem to unfold, solve it, and take the credit for the solution?
- be assertive? "It is clear that . . ."

According to sociolinguist Deborah Tannen (1994), author of *Talking from 9 to 5. Women and Men in the Workplace: Language, Sex and Power,* gender differences in speaking styles can affect workplace behavior, including who gets heard, who gets credit, and how work gets done. Tannen believes that, although there are individual differences, overall women and men have characteristic ways of speaking. She believes that both styles make sense and are equally valid in themselves, but that the differences in style may cause trouble in social interaction.

Design an observational study of female–male conversations at your place of employment. Record how many times the participants spoke, the number of interruptions that took place (and by whom), the conversational styles that were used, and the facial expressions and listening styles that were employed. To what extent do they reflect the patterns observed by Tannen? Do you think that the conversational styles you observed contribute to any problems in the workplace?

WRITING YOUR OWN SCRIPT

REFLECTIONS ON GENDER

As this chapter illustrates, gender is a significant factor in our lives. Social expectations about gender are so deeply woven into the fabric of our society that they often seem natural. Even when we are unhappy about some aspect of our lives, we often fail to see the connections between existing cultural assumptions and social arrangements and our own experiences. Take time to reflect on the role of gender in your experiences.

Questions to Consider

1. How has being a male or a female affected your life to this point? Do you feel you missed out on anything because of your gender? What, if anything, would you change about being a woman or a man in today's society?
2. How satisfied are you with your physical appearance? If you could change any aspect of your appearance, what would it be? Why?
3. What are your friendship patterns like? Are you satisfied with the number of cross-sex friendships you have? What are some of the social barriers to developing and maintaining cross-sex friendships? What might you do to increase the likelihood of having more cross-sex friendships?

Another linguist, Jennifer Coates (1986), concluded that women normally use conversation as an opportunity to discuss problems, share experiences, and offer reassurance and advice. Men, however, do not see the discussion of personal issues as a normal component of conversation. If someone discloses to them, they are likely to assume the role of expert and offer advice. Thus, in couple relationships women often complain that men don't express their feelings, and men say they feel burdened by such complaints. Such gender differences may result in stress and conflict in marriage.

CHANGING REALITIES, CHANGING ROLES

Whether we like it or not, the world we inhabit today is quite different from that of our parents and grandparents. Consider two examples that will be discussed in detail in later chapters: (1) More married mothers are working than ever before, many of them in sexually integrated work settings; and (2) increasing numbers of women (and some men) are finding themselves solely responsible for their family's economic and social welfare. Yet, as we have seen throughout this chapter, some of the agents of socialization continue to perpetuate traditional views of white middle-class femininity and masculinity, often in ways that have negative consequences for women's and men's development and self-esteem. Many of these patterns of socialization are not sufficient to provide solutions to the psychological and economic strains experienced by many people today. Thus, it is necessary to seek new ways to socialize children, to enable them to make satisfying personal choices and to live full and satisfying human lives.

Psychologist Sandra Bem (1983:613) offers two strategies to meet this goal. First, she encourages parents to teach their children that the only definitive gender differences are anatomical and reproductive. Second, she suggests that parents help children substitute an "individual differences" schema that emphasizes the "remarkable variability of individuals within groups" for the gender schema they currently use for organizing and processing information. Sociologist Hilary Lips (1993:397) sums up the possible benefits of such an approach: "As a society, we may finally come to the realization that the function and qualities stereotypically associated with each gender are valuable and necessary—and much more interchangeable and shareable than we used to think."

SUMMARY

Each of us occupies a number of statuses that carry with them expectations for behavior. Some of these are ascribed statuses, such as sex and race. Others are achieved by our own efforts, for example, becoming a parent or a teacher. Role expectations serve an important function in society in that they make behavior predictable. However, expectations can be defined so rigidly that they become dysfunctional for individuals and for society as a whole.

The status of being female or male in our society affects all aspects of our life. Thus, it is important to distinguish between the concepts of sex (being female or male) and gender (the socially learned behaviors, attitudes and the expectations associated with being female or male). From early on, we are taught to behave in gender-appropriate ways by parents, peers, teachers, and the mass media.

Psychoanalytic/identification theory, social-learning theory, cognitive-development theory, and enculturated-lens theory have been advanced by social scientists to explain how we acquire our gender identity. Although there is some empirical support for these theories, they do not explain why women and men are treated unequally. For this answer we must examine existing social arrangements.

The traditional notions of femininity and masculinity are based on white middle-class definitions, and they do not accurately reflect the race and class variations in gender role perceptions. Traditional gender roles limit the lifestyle options of both females and males.

Gender roles are in transition as a result of new demographic and social patterns. Increasing numbers of individuals can be identified as androgynous, having characteristics of both genders. Research shows that both females and males who are high in instrumental (masculine) traits tend to have higher self-esteem and better mental health than those high on expressive (feminine) traits. Researchers have found that androgynous individuals are more expressive in their feelings of love, better able to self-disclose, and more tolerant of faults in their loved ones than more traditionally oriented individuals are.

Although they connect with others in different ways, both females and males have a common need for meaningful relationships with others of the same sex. Women's friendships are characterized by intimacy and self-disclosure, whereas men's friendships focus more on shared activities. Gendered patterns of communication exaggerate both the perceived and real differences between women and men and hinder the formation of cross-sex friendships.

KEY TERMS

ascribed status
achieved status
gender role stereotypes
master (key) status
sex
gender
gender identity
intersexuality
transsexuals
gender role socialization
psychoanalytic/identification theory
social-learning theory
modeling
cognitive-development theory
enculturated-lens theory
agents of socialization
content analysis
self-esteem

QUESTIONS FOR STUDY AND REFLECTION

1. Distinguish between sex and gender. Why is it important to make this distinction? Many scientists today argue that sex and gender are fluid rather than dichotomous. What do they mean by this? What evidence is there to support this position?
2. Think back to your childhood as far as you can go. When is the first time that you can recall that you were aware of being a girl or a boy? (*Hint:* Sometimes these are painful events, for example, when we asked for a toy and were told it wasn't appropriate for our gender or when we were criticized "for behaving like a member of the other gender.") How did you feel at the time? How would your life be different today if you were the other gender? Compare and contrast the theories advanced by social scientists to explain the process of gender acquisition. Using yourself as an example, which theory do you think explains how you acquired your gender identity? Is any one of these theories, or are all of them combined, sufficient to explain the content of gender roles in our society? Explain your position.
3. Assume that you are entertaining visitors from another culture who are unfamiliar with the patterns of female–male relationships in the United States today and who do not want to make any major mistakes in their interactions during their visit. What would you tell them? What problems might they run into without this knowledge?
4. Consider the following proposition: Young girls and boys should be raised alike, with similar toys, play activities, and with the same expectations regarding their education and future careers. Do you agree or disagree with this proposition? Explain and provide evidence to support your position.

ADDITIONAL RESOURCES

SOCIOLOGICAL

FAUSTO-STERLING, ANNE. 2000. *Sexing the Body: Gender Politics and the Construction of Sexuality.* New York: Basic Books. Drawing on astonishing real-life cases, the author argues that individuals born as mixtures of male and female should not be forced to change their bodies to fit a flawed societal definition of normality.

PIPHER, MARY. 1994. *Reviving Ophelia: Saving the Selves of Adolescent Girls.* New York: Ballantine Books. A critical examination of the dangers of being a young female, with suggestions for how adults can help young women.

POLLACK, WILLIAM S. 1998. *Real Boys: Rescuing Our Sons from the Myths of Boyhood.* New York: Random House. The author argues that many of the problems that boys have stem from their early socialization experiences.

TAVRIS, CAROL. 1992. *The Mismeasure of Women.* New York: Simon and Schuster. A critical look at the problems involved when female behavior is measured against standards based on male behavior.

ZINN, MAXINE BACA, AND BONNIE THORNTON DILL, EDS. 1991. *Women of Color in American Society.* Philadelphia: Temple University Press. Articles that examine the lives of African American, Latina, Native American, and Asian American women.

LITERARY

DIAMANT, ANITA. 1997. *The Red Tent.* New York: Picador. Told in the voice of the Biblical Dinah, this novel reveals the traditions and turmoils of ancient womanhood.

GRAHAM, KATHARINE. 1997. *Personal History.* New York: Vintage. This memoir reads like a novel, telling the true story of a woman socialized to the traditional role of wife and mother who, after her husband's death, takes over the *Washington Post* and becomes one of the most powerful women in the world.

INTERNET

http://www.now.org The National Organization for Women (NOW) is a grassroots political action organization.

http://web.indstate.edu/spsmm The Society for the Psychological Study of Men and Masculinity is a good place to get information on men's lives.

Chapter 4

The Many Faces of Love

IN THE NEWS: **ROME, ITALY**

The Korean wife of a Roman Catholic archbishop accepted his decision to dissolve their marriage and return to the church. Archbishop Emmanuel Milingo (head of the Zambian diocese in Lusaka) and Maria Sung were married in a ceremony organized by the Reverend Sun Myung Moon, head of the Unification Church movement. Not surprisingly, the marriage caused outrage in the Catholic church, and Milingo was threatened with excommunication unless he chose the church ahead of his wife. After meeting with Pope John Paul II and then his wife, Milingo disappeared to consider his position. Later, Milingo, who once said that celibacy was poisoning the priesthood, announced in a public interview that he had left his wife and had embraced the pope's appeal for him to return to the church and keep his vow of priestly celibacy. Then, accompanied by a host of Vatican officials, the archbishop met his wife in a Rome hotel and gave her a letter that explained his reasons for dissolving the marriage. In part, the letter said: "My commitments in the life of the church with celibacy, don't allow me to be married. . . . The call from my church to my commitment is just." After the meeting, Sung declared that "for the great love for my husband, I'll respect his decision to leave me. But that does not change the feeling I have for him in my heart." She vowed that she would never be with another man and would try to support the archbishop in his work throughout her life, saying that she hoped they would be reunited "in the after life." According to Sung, Milingo gave her a rosary as a parting gift and "expressed love for her as a brother to a sister." A spokesman for Sung described the meeting as "wonderful" and reported that "both of them expressed a lot of love for each other." (CNN.com, August 30, 2001)

WHAT WOULD YOU DO? If you "fell in love" with a person (religious figure or not) who had taken a vow of celibacy, would you marry that person? If yes, if the person later indicated that her/his love for you was like that felt for a sibling, would you try to preserve the marriage? If yes, why? Could you live a satisfying married life without romantic love? If no, why not? Is such love in contradiction to Western notions about love and marriage? How does this incidence demonstrate the intersections of politics, religion, and meanings of love?

"Love is blind." "Love makes the world go 'round." "Love is a many splendored thing." "True love never dies." "Love at first sight." "Love conquers all." How many sayings like these can you think of? In Western societies, probably more than in any others, love is a central feature of life. It is such a major part of our lives today that most of us cannot imagine life and relationships without love. Most Westerners believe that love gives life meaning, that it is essential to a healthy and satisfying life. In the United States, people of all ages devote considerable time and effort to and thinking about love and intimate relationships. Love is referred to or appears as a central theme throughout American popular culture, in the lyrics of all types of music, poems, sonnets, short stories, novels, films, plays, television, and art. The love affairs and love scandals of movie stars and other well-known people are mainstays in popular media, and we hunger for more and more of this "love" news. The advice columns of daily newspapers, daytime television talk shows, and soap operas, as well as a popular literature and even academic courses on how to attract, impress, satisfy, keep, and even dump the lover of our choice, all exemplify the extent to which love and intimacy occupy our thoughts and actions. Almost everyone at one time or another has been or will be in love. Yet, few of us can say exactly what love is.

As the "In the News" article demonstrates, humans express many kinds of love, probably as many as there are types of people who love and are loved. Love encompasses a wide variety of feelings and behaviors, ranging from those we feel for our parents, friends, siblings, and children to those we feel for our spouses or partners. However, the type of love that is dominant in most of our lives, at one time or another, is romantic love. Although a common thread of caring is woven through all love relationships, the major difference between these feelings of love and romantic love is the element of *eroticism*—concerning or intending to arouse sexual desire. Although all types of love are important and merit discussion, our primary concern in this chapter is with romantic or erotic love.

WHAT IS THIS THING CALLED LOVE?

How would you respond to the question, What is love? If we asked 100 people to define love, we would probably get 100 different responses. Love, it seems, is an elusive emotion. Most of us insist that we experience it at some time in our lives, but we have extreme difficulty explaining it in words. Love is surrounded by myths and metaphors; we dream and hope of finding the love of a lifetime who will love us no matter what and who will transform an otherwise ordinary life into one of bliss. People have been known to do all sorts of things in the name of love: wage wars, forsake family and friends, sign away fortunes, or give up royal standing. We claim that love is blind, and so, blindly, we subject ourselves to a wide range of emotions from ecstasy to torment, and all in the name of love.

Because each of us expresses and experiences love differently, there are a variety of definitions and types of love. Some writers, for example, view love as an emotion that causes us to act irrationally. Other writers believe it to be an emotion that is much more centered on self than on another person; or a giving of the heart and soul, the giving of a person's total self; or an ideology that narrows people's perception of the world; or an innate undeniable aspect of what makes us human. Still other writers have defined love as a contrivance, a fantasy concocted by human beings over the centuries, a cultural delusion that originated in the twelfth century with wandering troubadours and knights in shining armor (Marriott, 2001). Some writers have even argued that love is a male invention used to exploit women. Definitions of love describe it in terms of any one or several of the following characteristics: deep emotional attachment, openness, self-disclosure, physical attraction, and personal growth. Although many social scientists steer clear of singular definitions of love because, in their view, love varies in degree, intensity, over time, and across social contexts, William Goode's definition of love is still perhaps the most widely cited in the scientific literature: "A strong emotional attachment, a cathexis, between adolescents or adults of opposite sexes, with at least the components of sex, desire, and tenderness" (1959:49). Although we agree that love defies a single definition, in order to facilitate a broader understanding of the concept, we will, nonetheless, use a more general and inclusive definition than that of Goode. In this context, we use the term **romantic love** to refer to, very generally, the intense feelings, emotions, and thoughts coupled with sexual passion and erotic expression that a person directs toward another, as well as the *ideology*—the set of beliefs—that upholds it.

Although romantic love is often considered to be unique to Western and modern cultures, anthropologists have found that it does exist in some "traditional" societies. For example, anthropologists William Jankowiak and Edward Fischer (1992) examined 166 traditional cultures and found evidence of romantic love in 88 percent of them. Individuals within these cultures sang love songs and even eloped; the folklore of many of these societies portrayed various types of romantic entanglements. Jankowiak and Fischer suggested that the reason that romantic love has not been found in most traditional societies is because social scientists have either simply overlooked this aspect of traditional culture or they have not had sufficient access to these cultures in order to study love. Thus, they concluded that romantic love, which they equate with passionate love, constitutes a human universal, or, at the least, a "near-universal."

Think about how you define love. Is your definition consistent with that of others around you? How do you know when you are in love?

Love as a Social Construction

People tend to think of love as an individual choice fired by our biological engines. Although research from the biological sciences shows that biochemistry underlies our emotional behavior throughout every stage of human love, of interest to sociologists is how love is conditioned by the cultural context, historical period, and institutional structures in which it occurs. In this context, while love emerges out of the unique context in which individuals encounter one another, the feelings that develop between people are love only when they define it as such. And the criteria that people use to arrive at the conclusion that they are in love are social in origin.

Culture plays an essential role in this process, particularly in terms of whom we choose to love. In early childhood, we develop specific likes and dislikes in response to family, peers, experiences, cultural prescriptions, and definitions of love, of beauty, and worthiness, so that by the time we are teenagers we have developed a mental picture of whom we will find attractive and fall in love with. Anthropologist Helen Fisher (1999) refers to this mental image that we carry around as an unconscious mental template, or **love map**—a group of physical, psychological, and behavioral traits that one finds attractive in a mate. Culture not only plays a critical role in whom we will find attractive but also in when we begin to court, where and how we court, and how we pursue a potential mate.

According to a social-constructionist point of view, love can only be understood as symbolic or a social construction that by itself has no intrinsic meaning. While feelings of romantic love and passion have a physiological component, neither is based solely on our body reactions. Rather, they are also based upon the way in which we interpret and label our feelings and reactions. Take the classic example: You walk into a crowded room; your eyes lock on those of a stranger across the room; after a brief moment of staring you smile at each other; a short time later you find a reason to approach each other, and as you do so your heart begins to beat rapidly, you experience a shortness of breath, and you feel the blood rush to your face. What do these physiological responses signify? How do you interpret them? Do you have the flu? Have you had much too much to drink? Or is the room's thermostat simply out of control?

If you have grown up in the United States, you have learned from family, peers, and the mass media that what you are feeling can be interpreted in terms of love. These feelings do not have to be interpreted in terms of love, however. It is the context in which they occur (in a room where we have just locked eyes with a stranger) that leads us to that interpretation. The point here is that our emotional states are symbolic states and as such require interpretation and naming to give them meaning (Karp and Yoels, 1993). That is, the meanings of objects, emotions, and situations reside in our responses to and interpretations of them. In this sense, definitions of love vary because love is a social construction with no fixed meaning. What we define as love is rooted in both societal and cultural values as well as the values of the groups to which we belong.

While no one has quite figured out why we fall in love, over half (52 percent) of American adults believe that it can happen at first sight. Perhaps you are among this 52 percent; maybe you have experienced love at first sight. A recent Gallup poll asked about people's past romantic behavior and found that four in ten Americans say that they have actually fallen in love at first sight, with men being slightly more likely than women to say they have fallen in love at first sight. Moreover, three-fourths of those polled believe that there is "one true love out there"; that there is "only one person that they are destined to fall in love with" (Carlson, 2001). In the harsh cold light of reality, however, sociological research shows that our "destiny" is tempered by formal and informal cultural norms and values concerning partner eligibility that filter out millions of potential lovers, one of whom just might have been "our destiny" or "one true love." This research helps us understand and supports the constructionist point of view of love as a social construction. As we will see in Chapter 5, social factors such as race, class, age, sexual orientation, religion, and geographic location eliminate thousands, if not millions, of potential mates.

How Does Romantic Love Develop in Contemporary Society?

In the United States, love develops within the context of a popular culture that inundates us with messages about love: whom we should love, how, when, under what conditions, and how we should behave when we're in love. Based on an accumulation of research over the years, the typical developmental sequence of heterosexual love in the twenty-first century, particularly over the last 50 years, seemed to be: Girl meets boy; they interact; they discover that they have common interests, values, and backgrounds; they find that they like each other; they begin to date; they are physically attracted to each other. Because they like and are physically attracted to each other, they date more frequently and grow more fond of each other. As the relationship continues and deepens, the couple typically progresses through stages of initiating, intensifying (falling in love), working out problems and making adjustments, and finally making a commitment to one another (Wood, 1994). At some point, they define their feelings as love. Feeling love for one another, they become engaged and plan to marry. The relationship may or may not include sexual activity, but if it does, sex is probably defined in terms of the couple's love for each other. This sequence is discussed in greater detail in Chapter 5. The development of lesbian and gay love relationships parallels that of heterosexuals, with stages of initiation, more frequent contact, intense infatuation, working out problems, and a maturing commitment (Wood, 1994).

Not all love relationships, of course, develop along this sequence. For some people, love happens slowly over time; they seem to slide gently into love as they progress through these various stages. For other people, it's love at first sight; lightning strikes, and the heart palpitates. Thus, sometimes the stages are reversed; at other times some of them are omitted. Sometimes, for example, the sequence begins with sexual attraction. In addition, not all love relationships culminate in sex or marriage. In fact, in recent years, several of these stages may not apply to some couples who engage in a series of "involvements" that may or may not lead to marriage. And given that love is now advertised as something that can be taught in a classroom, a new developmental sequence may be emerging that begins with people taking a class in flirting or the art of falling in love. In any event, several social scientists have attempted to explain some of these newer modifications to the traditional developmental course of love. Later in this chapter we examine some of these theories. First, however, we must understand the history of love and its development in Western society.

Love in Western Society: A Historical Perspective

Romantic love has been portrayed in a variety of ways in Western cultures for centuries. Many of today's myths and legends about romantic love come from antiquity (Fisher, 1999). The love story of Isis and Osiris was recorded in Egypt more than 3000 years ago. Ovid composed poems to romantic love in the first century B.C. in ancient Rome. And the *Kuma Sutra* (Hindu words for "love" and for "pleasure and sensual gratification," respectively), a Hindu treatise on the art of love, including explicit sexual instructions, was composed sometime between the first and fourth centuries A.D.

As we have discussed, today romantic love is almost always linked to sex and marriage. The moment we think of any one of these concepts, the other two come to mind. For example, we refer to sexual intercourse as "making love" (some people refer to it as "the marriage act"), we marry because we are "in love," marriage is viewed as a "love relationship," and sex is said to be a "natural expression of love." And when we are no longer in love, we separate, divorce, or break up. We tend to think that one naturally follows another.

It has not always been this way, however. For much of human history, although marriage and sex were related, there was no conception of love as a necessary part of either. In most societies throughout history, and in many societies in the world today, people marry not out of romantic love but out of obligation to parents and family. In the typical case, a strong sense of family duty and obligation to parents is symbolically transferred on marriage to a spouse who is chosen by one's parent or grandparents (Coltrane, 1998). The linking of love with sex and marriage is a unique feature of romantic love, a type of love that is relatively new in human social history. It slowly developed in Western societies over many centuries, and its roots can be traced to ancient Greece and Rome.

LOVE IN ANCIENT GREECE Most writers trace contemporary notions of romantic love to Greek society of the fifth century B.C. and the writings of the philosopher Plato. Plato defined love as the highest expression of human virtue because of its ability to inspire people to be kind, honorable, and wise. Plato distinguished several types of love: *Agape* is a selfless love; it is spontaneous and altruistic and requires nothing in return. *Eros* is a selfish love, with an emphasis on physical pleasure. It is based on sexual attraction and can be either homosexual or heterosexual. *Philos* is a deep friendship or brotherly love and includes a love for humanity.

Romantic love can be both exhilarating and practical. It often begins with love at first sight, passion, and exclusive attention to one another. However, over time, the practicality of long-term love sets in as couples must meet the requirements of everyday living.

Source: Reprinted with special permission of King Features Syndicate.

The erotic love that Plato and other Greek philosophers idealized was a combination of the purely physical and the extremely spiritual. Although sex and beauty were its goals, it was not, however, focused on one's marriage partner. Marriages were arranged by families, and men married primarily to reproduce a line of male heirs. The primary role of women was to bear and care for children. Greek men often kept their wives locked up in their homes while entertaining themselves with cultivated prostitutes (Pomeroy, 1975). Women were considered to be inferior to men and thus were generally uneducated and accorded low social status. Because the ancient Greeks believed that high status made people attractive, and given that the emphasis of love was on mind and heart, women were considered unattractive and thus unfit for *agape*. As a result, ancient Greeks downplayed the significance of heterosexual love. Because only males were considered attractive and good or worthy companions, the highest form of love in ancient Greece typically involved an older man's infatuation with a beautiful adolescent boy (Dover, 1978). Male homosexual love was considered to be as natural as heterosexual love. Contributing to the prevalence of homosexual love relationships was the fact that men who showed a love for or sexual interest in women were considered to be womanlike or effeminate (Murstein, 1974).

The Greek influence on modern ideas and practices of love can be found throughout our society. For example, we often hear people refer to relationships as "platonic." The idea of platonic love is rooted in the Greek emphasis that love is of mind and heart, and even today the term continues to mean essentially love without sex. The idea of platonic love is most often attributed to Plato; thus, it bears his name. Some contemporary researchers (for example, Solomon, 1981), however, have claimed that this attribution is misleading, as some of Plato's writings indicate that he recognized a connection between love and sex.

Love in Ancient Rome Female and male relationships in ancient Rome were considerably different from those in ancient Greece. They therefore gave rise to a very different form of love from that described by Plato. Upper-class Roman women were more educated and worldly, and more socially and intellectually equal to Roman men than were their counterparts in Greek society. Thus, in contrast to ancient Greece, love in Roman society was oriented primarily toward heterosexual love. Love still was not connected to marriage, however. Marriages continued to be arranged by families and took place for the economic, social, and political advantages they accorded.

Love most often occurred in secret, outside these arranged marriages. It consisted primarily of meaningless flirtation and brief encounters between couples. The most important part of a love relationship was the seduction of a desirable person. To be desirable, potential lovers, especially women, had to be physically attractive. Love in this context had to be secretive: If exposed, men could be severely fined by the offended husband; women, however, could lose their lives. The severer punishments for women reflected a general sexual double standard that is still evidenced today by the fact that we define love relationships differently for each gender, as we will see later in this chapter.

The Early Christian Idea of Love The arrival of Christianity promoted the idea of the love of God, a spiritual love that was different from Plato's ideal forms of love. The Christian church considered the overt sexuality and eroticism of the Greeks, Romans, and pagans as an immoral abomination. The early Christian idea of love was one of a nonsexual, nonerotic relationship, and the ideal person was expected to deny all desires of the flesh to attain holiness. If people could not control their desires of the flesh (that is, remain celibate) they could marry, but even between married couples, sexual desire and attraction were frowned upon. Noteworthy in this context are the Penitentials of Theodore, seventh-century Archbishop of Canterbury, which contained a list of punishments for those who could not abstain. For example, a man who had intercourse with his wife had to take a bath before entering the church, and newly married people or women who had given birth were likewise barred from the church for a period of time followed by a set penance (Queen, Habenstein, and Quadagno, 1985; Williams, 1993). As Christianity spread throughout the Western world, so too did the ideals of celibacy and virginity. From the Christian ideas about love and sexuality grew the notion that priests and nuns should live a celibate life, an ideal that is still part of the Roman Catholic faith but one that often has been challenged in recent times as evidenced in the "In the News" article opening this chapter.

Although not the same, the Christian idea of love emphasized aspects of *agape*, especially the idea of honor and devotion to be directed to the spiritual community rather than to individuals. At the very least, the downplaying of eroticism in Christian love weakened the relationship between married couples, making it relatively easy for people to forsake personal relationships and devote themselves instead to the Christian community (Albas and Albas, 1989a).

Courtly Love Not everyone accepted the Christian definition of love. In particular, many among the powerful nobility challenged the Christian notion and espoused a new idea of love—referred to as *courtly love*—that combined two basic ideas of the time period: male chivalry and the idealization of women. Courtly love, which emerged sometime between A.D. 1000 and 1300, involved flirtatious and romantic overtones that marked the beginning of chivalry and was the precursor to our modern version of romance—aptly called *court*ship (Collins, 1986; Coltrane, 1998).

The ideas and messages of courtly love were first heard during this period in the love songs and romantic poetry of French troubadours, a unique class of minstrel knights who traveled from one manor to another singing and reciting poetry and sonnets in exchange for food and shelter. Their songs and poetry were directed toward aristocratic noblewomen whom they idealized in their lyrics and tales about beautiful and superior ladies who were inaccessible to their suitors. Courtly love was a break from earlier idealizations of love because in courtly love noblewomen were exalted, albeit in a spiritual sense. Their beauty and remoteness were worshiped as never before. As it is commonly referred to today, they were placed on a pedestal. One could flirt with a noblewoman and even have sex with her, but she remained unattainable as a permanent love object. Adultery, however, was common. Because noblewomen and their lords had not usually married out of love or developed a close personal relationship, erotic courtly romances frequently developed between ladies and visiting knights (or troubadours). The elaborate and mischievous seduction games of courtly love among the wealthy classes continued into the eighteenth century (Coltrane, 1998).

Although this form of chivalrous love was confined to a small segment of the population and was not associated with marriage, the courtly love rituals of the nobility laid the groundwork for more popular ideas about love and romance among the general population. As in the past, marriages were arranged. Love and romance were not considered essential elements of marriage and thus were most often found outside of marital relationships. In its popular manifestation, courtly love was basically nonsexual. Sex was considered to be animalistic, dishonorable, and degrading, so courtly love required that there be no sexual relations between lovers. Couples could, however, and sometimes did, lie nude in bed together and caress each other, but they could not have intercourse (Bell, 1971). Sex was primarily for reproduction and thus was generally reserved for marital relationships.

According to Morton Hunt (1959), the emergence and development of romantic love was greatly influenced by a number of features of heterosexual relations during this period, most notably the idea that love should be reciprocal or mutual. With the emergence of courtly love, for the first time, women were considered to be an important part of the love relationship, worthy of the love and passion of men. Most researchers of the subject contend that a major contribution of courtly love was to raise women's status from that of a despised person to one worthy of being worshiped and loved. Many women today, however, insist that setting women apart to be worshiped and protected by men keeps women dependent on men for definitions of self and love and for care and protection. Thus, they criticize the concept and practice of courtly love because it ignores the needs of women, limits women's expression and behavior, and impedes their progress toward gender equality (Cancian, 1991).

Whatever we might think of courtly love, its impact on Western thought and romantic behavior cannot be overstated. In fact, a number of the romantic ideas of courtly love are still apparent in contemporary notions of love. For example, the ideas today that you can't love two people at the same time, that love makes your heart beat wildly, and that love can occur at first sight emerged from the period of courtly love. From these beginnings, romantic love became an institutionalized component of upper-class and then middle-class marriage and family life. Eventually, as Western societies became industrialized and urbanized, romantic love became institutionalized among the lower and working classes as well.

The Institutionalization of Love in Marriage As the market economy developed and capitalism spread, the roles and functions of individuals and societal institutions changed, and the ideal of the family as a separate domestic sphere began to develop. For example, work became institutionalized outside the family, and separate institutions to educate the young and to provide religious training emerged. As the family lost or passed on to other institutions many of its old functions, industrialism created new demands, roles, and responsibilities for families and their members. The most relevant of these new responsibilities for the continued development and spread of romantic love was the responsibility of the family to provide emotional strength and support to its members.

Changing patterns of production and consumption encouraged within the family the development of both economic cooperation and marital love between wives and husbands. Although strongly influenced by the upper- (or noble) class notion of courtly love, the emerging industrial middle class rejected the central idea that love is to be found outside of marriage. Rather, love began to be viewed as a mutual caring that should occur *before* and continue to develop throughout the course of a marriage; it was supposed to last a lifetime. In many respects, love became a kind of emotional insurance that kept wives and husbands tied together "until death do us part." For this to work effectively, however, it was necessary to develop a new cultural attitude toward sex, one that connected it to love and kept it confined to marriage (Coltrane, 1998).

By the late nineteenth century in the United States, as the middle classes enjoyed more leisure time, courtship came to be extended over a longer period, and the idea of love and romance in such relationships had become widespread among all classes. By the early twentieth century, this concept of love was an essential part of the courtship process (see Chapter 5). Although love was now blended with marriage, it was not yet blended with sex. Romantic love and sex were considered almost polar opposites. For example, romantic love was thought of as tender, warm, and caring, whereas sex was thought of as crude and vulgar. The blending of love and sex ultimately grew out of the sexual revolution of the 1920s, an era that witnessed a marked increase in premarital sexual behavior. In addition, attitudes about sex changed noticeably as people began to tie it to love, intimacy, and marriage.

Today, romance, love, and sex are inseparably intertwined, and some people believe that the intimacy generated by one may actually enhance the others. Whether or not this is true, today it is believed that romantic love without sex is incomplete and sex without love is emotionally shallow and exploitative (Seidman, 1992). However, although most Americans believe that love is an important basis for beginning and maintaining a marriage, and that sex should be a part of a loving relationship, recent national polls indicate that they do not believe that sex should be necessarily reserved for marriage. Thus, they do not see premarital sex as wrong, but do see extramarital and casual sex as wrong. On the other hand, roughly about one-fourth of Americans find sexual activity recreational and do not need love or commitment as a prerequisite (Sprecher, 1989; Saad, 2001). Such attitudes highlight the degree to which our ideas about love, marriage, and sex have changed over time. They also alert us to the fact that the Western sequence of "love, marriage, and then comes the baby carriage" reflects several culturally based assumptions about the nature of intimate heterosexual relationships. These assumptions are by no means universally shared, particularly in non-Western cultures; even in Western societies, this sequence of love, intimacy, and marriage has not always prevailed. This point is certainly illustrated in the "In the News" article opening this chapter and, as the discussion in the "In Other Places" box demonstrates, it is important to take into account the cultural context and cultural factors that contribute to the development of love and intimacy in a particular society.

The Importance of Love

Researchers have found that in U.S. society, love is extremely important both in terms of our physical as well as our emotional health and well-being. Numerous studies demonstrate that love improves our health, that being in love romantically and/or being loved are positively related to good physical and emotional health. According to one medical expert, Joseph Nowinski (1980), a satisfying love affair is one of the best medicines for fighting off physical diseases. His claim is based on what he says are two well-known facts: (1) How we feel emotionally affects our health, and (2) being in love can create a natural emotional high. Nowinski says that a variety of studies show that married couples or those in a satisfying relationship have fewer psychological problems; single women, on the other hand, have the most. Moreover, other experts in the field contend as well that long-term love relationships (even if no longer passionate) appear to have a positive effect on the health of those involved (Pert, 1997; Ornish, 1998; Lacey, 1999). New research confirms the health-improving and life-affirming effects of love on the human body. For example, by studying the heart's rhythms, researchers have discovered that when we feel love, or any positive emotion such as compassion, caring, or gratitude, the heart sends messages to the brain and secretes hormones that positively affect our health. Love and intimacy also may help protect against infectious diseases. When we feel loved, nurtured, cared for, supported, and intimate, we are much more likely to be happier and healthier. We have a much lower risk of getting sick and, if we do, a much greater chance of surviving (Ornish, 1998). Conversely, being unloved has been shown to be related to heart disease and early death among unmarried people. Not being loved or the loss of love also has been linked to depression and can even lead some people to commit suicide (Tennov, 1979; Davis, 1985). While feeling loved appears to benefit our health, giving love seems to do the same for our aging process. The results of a study of more than 700 elderly adults showed that the effects of aging were influenced more by what the participants contributed to their social support network than what they received from it. In other words, the more love and support they gave, the more they benefited (Lacey, 1999). According to Susan and Clyde Hendrick (1992), love may not be essential to life, but it certainly seems essential to joy. They contend that romantic love compensates for the drudgery and illness in our lives. By loving and being loved, we are *more* intelligent, attractive, and even saintly.

IN OTHER PLACES

THE MEANING OF LOVE ACROSS CULTURES

Although romance and romantic love are not new to the world, their value among all classes of people (not just the elite) and their connection to marriage are a modern phenomenon, arising in industrial society (Luhman, 1996). In earlier times, both in Western and non-Western societies, because people's personal identities were not highly differentiated from the collective identity of their group, the social context did not provide the conditions under which romantic love could develop. However, as societies became industrialized, *collectivism*—the emphasis on the superiority of the group—gave way to *individualism*, an emphasis on promoting one's self-interest, personal autonomy, self-realization, individual initiative, and decision making. Some researchers have suggested that romantic love is most likely to emerge under these conditions of individualism (see, for example, Dion and Dion, 1998).

In any event, because romantic love figures so importantly in the culture and lives of people in many Western societies today, we tend to think of it as the only proper basis for forming intimate relationships. However, the concept of romantic love is not found in all cultures and when it is, it is not necessarily the basis for establishing intimate relationships. Studies across cultures reveal very different attitudes toward romantic love and the ways in which it is channeled into long-term relationships.

Among the !Kung of southern Africa, love is an important commodity for women, and it is intimately connected to their sexuality. A !Kung woman's sexuality is her primary means for negotiating the conditions of her relationships with men, and it is also believed to be an important source for the mental well-being of women. According to the !Kung, if a girl grows up not learning to enjoy sex, her mind will not develop normally and, once she is an adult, if she doesn't have sex her thoughts are ruined, and she is forever angry. In terms of loving relationships, a woman's sexuality attracts lovers and a loving relationship and maximizes her independence. By taking lovers, a !Kung woman proclaims her control over her social life, because in !Kung culture, women's sexuality is believed to be a major source of vitality and life for men; without it, they would die (Robbins, 1993).

In contrast, in traditional Chinese culture, romantic love and sexuality are far less important than other factors as a basis for intimate relations between women and men. Whereas !Kung women use their sexuality to attract lovers, the sexuality of Chinese women figures very little in their relationships with men, both before and after marriage. Unions between Chinese women and men are arranged by the heads of their families, and female virginity is both valued and necessary for a successful match. A Chinese woman's sexuality is not negotiable; rather her value is in her potential to become a mother of a male child. In fact, becoming a mother cements her relationship with her husband (Robbins, 1993). The concept of romantic love does not fit very well in traditional Chinese society, where the individual is expected to take into account the wishes of others and the primary ties of love and intimacy are linked to family relationships—with parents, siblings, other relatives, and one's children. Romantic love, however, is not a totally foreign concept to the Chinese. In ancient feudal China, falling in love before marriage was not unusual, although parental consent was necessary before the marriage could occur. However, over the 2000-year period in which the traditional Chinese family flourished, romantic love was considered to be dangerous and harmful to the development of a "good" marriage, in which women and men took on the proper roles of subservient daughter-in-law and respectful son (Queen, Habenstein, and Quadagno, 1985).

It is interesting to note that among recent cohorts of young adults in China and other Asian countries, there are signs of change toward greater valuing of love as a basis for marriage. For example, in Japan, the number of "love marriages" has increased significantly over the past four decades. Although the older generation of Japanese still hold onto traditional values, survey data indicate a strong desire among young Japanese women for "love" or "love-based" marriage. A similar trend is emerging in China as Chinese women's roles are changing from passive compliance and obedience to their husbands and in-laws to a more active role in family and intimate relationships (De Mente, 1989; Dion and Dion, 1998).

What do you think? *How might intimate relationships be different if the U.S. view of love was similar to the !Kung? To the traditional Chinese? Explain. Which of the two views of love and intimacy presented here comes closer to approximating your personal viewpoint? Explain.*

The importance of love in general can also be viewed within the larger context of human social development. Love is essential to the survival of human infants and the social, psychological, and emotional well-being of adults. Various sociological and psychological theorists have argued, for example, that from infancy through adulthood, humans have a need for love and attachment with other human beings. Sociological studies of children who have experienced extended isolation from other humans have found that the lack of bonding, attachment, and love with at least one other human being has a detrimental effect on the physical, psychological, and emotional development of the child (Davis, 1940, 1947). Later in their life cycle, these children are often unable to develop intimate love relationships because they did not experience such relationships when they were young. For adults, the experience of extended isolation often causes deep feelings of depression, anxiety, and nervousness (Middlebrook, 1974). Other research (Hazan and Shaver, 1987; Shaver and Hazan, 1988; Shaver, Hazan, and Bradshaw, 1988) supports this conclusion, noting that the type of attachment pattern learned as an infant serves as a blueprint for later adult relationships, especially romantic love relationships. This research suggests that a person's attachment style is related to aspects of her or his childhood and remembered relationships with parents or other caregivers.

The experience of self-love or what some social scientists refer to as *self-esteem*, the personal judgments individuals make regarding their own self-worth, seems to be an important prerequisite for loving others. It has been suggested repeatedly in the literature that the ability to feel love, to express it, and to accept it from others is a learned behavior, acquired through our early experiences in infancy and childhood. Infants must be loved so that they can learn how to love. Like romantic love, self-love is tied to an individual's social situation. For example, several studies show that one's self-esteem is directly linked to the love expressed toward that individual by her or his significant others. When significant others give positive feedback, self-esteem increases and, conversely, when feedback is consistently negative from significant others it lowers self-esteem. Thus, infants who are held, touched, caressed, and otherwise shown love develop a self-love; that is, they come to see themselves as important and worthy of love. In adulthood, the people most likely to succeed in their intimate relationships are those who have been socialized in childhood to develop their potential to love.

Love not only dominates our everyday consciousness, it is also a yardstick against which we evaluate the quality of our everyday lives (Karp and Yoels, 1993). The level of love we perceive as existing in our intimate relationships affects how we feel about ourselves and others. It seems, then, that those of us who are most happy with our lives define that happiness in terms of a loving relationship (Swanbrow, 1989). We typically define a satisfying relationship as one in which there is an intense commitment to love (Hendrick, Hendrick, and Adler, 1988). Attachment theory is an important framework for a sociological understanding of love because it reminds us that love is a learned emotion. It reminds us that we learn how to love not only from our culture but also from individuals, particularly those with whom we form our first love relationships (Wood, 1996).

HOW DO PEOPLE EXPRESS LOVE?

People express romantic love in a variety of ways. Some focus on commitment; some on passion; and others on caring, respect, or intimacy. Some people focus on a combination of these and other factors associated with love. This diversity in love and loving has inspired some social scientists to attempt to classify love in terms of its component parts or in terms of various types and styles of loving.

In his now classic book *The Art of Loving* (1956), psychoanalyst Erich Fromm popularized the notion that there are

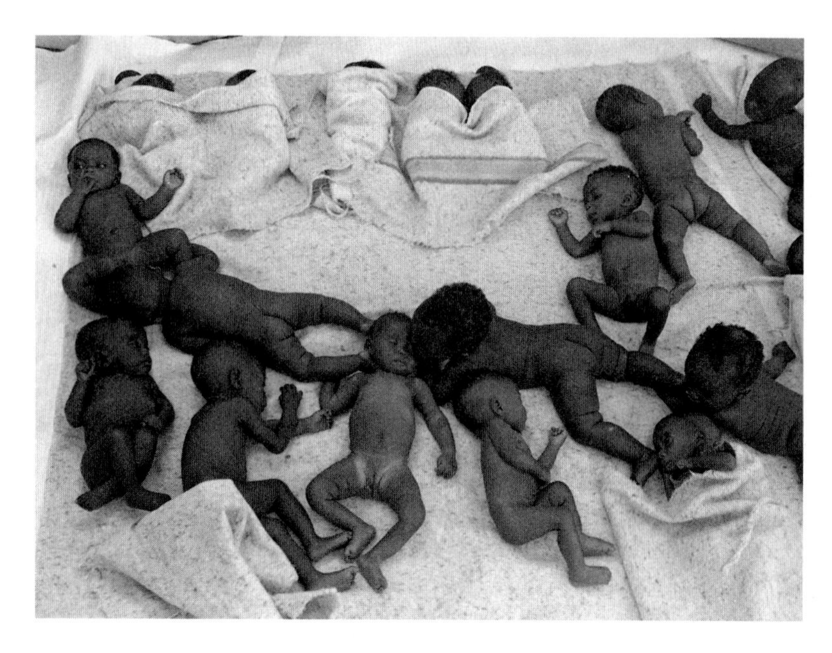

Babies lay on the floor of a makeshift orphanage near Goma, Zaire as a result of the ethnic conflict in Rwanda. Sociologists have suggested that the physical needs of children to be held, touched, and caressed are often not addressed in institutions such as this one. This lack of nurturing can lead to problems in the development of children's positive self-concept and, later, their ability to express and accept love as adults.

many different kinds of love, only one of which is erotic or romantic love. Other kinds of love Fromm identified include brotherly, maternal, paternal, infantile, immature, and mature love. According to Fromm, love has four essential components: (1) care (we want the best for the people we love), (2) responsibility (we are willingly sensitive and responsive to their needs), (3) respect (we accept them for what they are), and (4) knowledge (we have an awareness of their needs, values, goals, and feelings). When people share these components, they then become a couple or a pair. Fromm cautioned, however, that contrary to popular belief, love is not a simple process. Finding the *right* person is difficult and requires a lot of work and practice. Fromm suggested that *falling in love* is very different from *being in love*, which involves facing the realities of living together. He further suggested that being a loving person is the best way to be loved.

Consider the following discussion of styles of loving and think about your own style of loving. Where does your definition of love and style of loving fit, if at all, in Lee's typology of styles of loving?

Throughout human history love has been expressed in a variety of ways. However, the type of love that is dominant in most of our lives, at one time or another, is romantic love.

Lee's Six Styles of Loving

Whenever the subject of styles of loving comes up in the scientific literature, it is the research of Canadian sociologist John Alan Lee that is most often referred to. Using data from over 4000 published accounts of love in conjunction with 112 personal interviews, Lee (1974) concluded that there are many types of love relationships. Half of Lee's respondents were females and half were males. All were white, heterosexual, and under the age of 35. Based on findings from this group, Lee proposed six basic styles of loving. Using an analogy of a color wheel, he identified three primary styles of love relationships (analogous to the three primary colors of red, yellow, and blue): eros, ludus, and storge. In the same way that all other colors are a mixture or combination of the three primary colors, Lee contends that all other styles of love represent a combination of these three primary styles. The three most important compounds or mixtures of the three primary styles of love are mania, pragma, and agape. The six styles of loving are described here.

Primary Styles of Love **Eros** is characterized by an immediate, powerful attraction to the physical appearance of another ("love at first sight"). Erotic lovers are often preoccupied with pleasing their lover, and sexual intimacy is strongly desired. In fact, they often engage in sexual relations soon after they meet a partner. This is the type of love that is presented to us, for example, day after day in soap operas, where the lovers eye each other, hear romantic music, glide toward one another, hearts pounding, collapse in each other's arms, and become sexually intimate. Nothing is more problematic for an eros lover than to have a partner who lacks her or his sexual enthusiasm. If the partner is not openly erotic, the relationship will usually be of short duration.

In contrast to eros, **ludus** is playful, nonpossessive, and challenging love, without a deep commitment or lasting emotional involvement. Ludus love is carefree and casual; it turns love into a series of challenges and puzzles to be solved. A ludus lover often has several partners simultaneously or encourages her or his partner to have other relationships to prevent the partner from becoming too attached. Unlike with eros, sex is not an integral part of the love relationship. The ludus lover engages in sex simply for the fun of it and not as a means to a deep emotional relationship. Thus, this style of loving seldom leads to a long-term relationship or marriage.

Storge (pronounced "stor´gay") describes a style of loving that is said to be unexciting and uneventful. An affectionate style of love with an emphasis on companionship, it usually develops slowly, beginning as a friendship and gradually developing into love. It is typical of people who grew up together in the same neighborhood. Storge is long-lasting, but it is not passionate. Sexual intimacy occurs late in the relationship and often results in marriage or cohabitation. Even if the relationship ends, storgic lovers often remain good friends.

Derived Styles of Love Derived loves combine two or more of the primary styles. For example, **mania** combines eros and ludus. Manic love is characterized by obsession and possessiveness. It is a jealous and stressful love that demands constant displays of attention, caring, and affection from the partner. According to Lee, this type of love seldom, if ever, develops into a long-lasting, committed relationship. Marcia Lasswell and Norman Lobsenz (1981) have suggested that this style of loving might be associated with low self-esteem and a poor self-concept.

In contrast, **pragma,** which combines ludus and storge, is logical, sensible, and practical. A pragmatic lover rationally chooses a partner who shares her or his background, interests, concerns, and values. Compatibility is a must. Not surprisingly, computer dating and matching services are based on a pragmatic viewpoint.

Finally, **agape** (pronounced "ah´GAH pay"), a style of love that combines eros and storge, is selfless and giving, expecting nothing in return. It represents the classical Christian idea of love as altruistic, undemanding, and chaste. Agape lovers tend to advocate and adhere to sexual abstinence. It is a kind of love that is characteristic of saints. Lee reports that he did not find a single agape lover in his study. Can we safely assume that Archbishop Emmanuel Milingo (see "In the News" at the beginning of this chapter) was not in Lee's samples?

According to Lee, although people generally prefer one particular style of loving, they often express more than one style. This can be true over many different relationships or within one particular relationship. For example, a relationship might begin with an erotic style of loving, but as the relationship matures, it might change to a friendship or companionate (storge) style. Lee also observed that the compatibility of styles of loving between two people is important to the success of a love relationship. That is, we have to find a partner who shares the same definition and style of loving as we do if we expect to have a mutually happy and satisfying relationship. The greater the differences between a couple in their style of loving, the harder it is for them to relate to each other.

Interestingly, in their extensive research on romantic love, social scientists Susan and Clyde Hendrick found a number of gender differences in styles of loving. According to the Hendricks (1983, 1987, 1995, 1996), while women and men do not differ significantly on eros or agape, gender differences on other love attitudes or styles consistently show up. For example, their research repeatedly shows that men are more ludic in orientation than women, and women are typically more storgic and pragmatic than men. In addition, women report a more manic orientation than men. Working with Nancy Adler (Adler, Hendrick, and Hendrick, 1987), the Hendricks found very few differences between male heterosexuals and male homosexuals in their love attitudes. They thus concluded that gay and straight men are similar in love styles. On the other hand, the Hendricks have found that women and men are similar in rating the typical features of love, and they are similarly passionate and altruistic in their love styles. In fact, although gender differences were apparent, the genders were more similar than different. Only more research in this area will enable us to determine if these differences are changing or shifting as the culture and society changes (Hendrick and Hendrick, 1996).

Moreover, Hendrick and Hendrick (1993) have also found that among many contemporary college students, lovers are also best friends. In written accounts of their love as well as their ratings on the Love Attitude Scale, research respondents described their relationship most often in terms of storge, or friendship, love. In one study, almost one-half of the respondents identified their romantic partner as their closest friend. These results certainly indicate the importance of storge or friendship in ongoing, contemporary heterosexual romantic relationships. In an investigation of the differences between people who are falling in love versus those who are not in love, the Hendricks found that people who were in love were more erotic, more agapic, and less ludic than people who were not in love.

Although Lee's typology is ideal (in the real world, no one's love style matches any of Lee's styles perfectly) and based on a sample of white heterosexuals under the age of 35, were you able to identify your style of loving in one of Lee's six styles? How close or how different are you and your partner's style of loving? Are you more similar than different or more different than similar?

A philosopher once said that we know the taste of love but few of us can distinguish the many flavors of love. Given the various types and styles of love it is possible to experience, how do we distinguish what we feel from true love, puppy love, friendship, liking, or infatuation? Perhaps the next section will help you answer this question.

LOVE VERSUS FRIENDSHIP, INFATUATION, AND LIKING

How do we know when we're in love? Will we hear bells? Will our heart skip a beat? Will it last, or is it just a passing emotion? Are we old enough to know if it's love? When we were young we were told our feelings of love were not really true love, that they were either "puppy love" or infatuation. Furthermore, we were told not to fret, because we would know when it was true love. Such responses imply that there is a "fake love" or that some other emotion can very easily be confused with love, but that love is some special feeling that we will recognize the minute we experience it. If this is the case, how do we tell the difference? How do we know if what we feel is not simply friendship, infatuation, or liking? And what happens to let us know when the feeling is love?

Close Friendship versus Love

Over the last several decades, a number of researchers have attempted to distinguish love from liking, friendship, and infatuation. In one study, researchers Keith Davis and Michael Todd (1985) compared close friendship and love and found that while the two are alike in many ways, there are crucial differences between them that make love relationships both more rewarding and, at the same time, more volatile. Davis and Todd's prototype of friendship includes the following eight characteristics:

- ***Enjoyment:*** For the most part, close friends enjoy being in each other's company.
- ***Acceptance:*** They accept each other for what they are; they don't try to change each other.
- ***Trust:*** They share the feeling that the other will act in her or his best interest.
- ***Respect:*** Each assumes that the other exercises good judgment in making life choices.
- ***Mutual assistance:*** They are willing to aid and support each other; they can count on each other when needed.
- ***Confiding:*** They share feelings and experiences with each other.
- ***Understanding:*** Each has a sense of what is important to the other and why the other behaves in the manner that she or he does.
- ***Spontaneity:*** Both feel free to be themselves rather than pretend to be something that they're not.

Love, in contrast, is friendship and more: It is passion and caring. But it is also instability and mutual criticism. Some social scientists (Tennov, 1979; Solomon, 1981; Davis and Todd, 1985) have described romantic love as unstable in that it involves an almost endless series of emotional highs (joys or positive emotions) and lows (despair or negative emotions). It includes all the characteristics of friendship as well as two broad clusters of characteristics not found in friendship: a passion cluster and a caring cluster. The *passion cluster* includes *fascination*, preoccupation with each other and desire to be together all of the time; *exclusiveness*, with top priority given to the love relationship, making another such relationship with someone new unthinkable; and *sexual desire*, the desire to be physically intimate with each other. The *caring cluster* consists of *giving the utmost*, caring so much for each other that each gives her or his all to the relationship; and being a *champion* or *advocate*, helping and supporting each other in all types of situations. Figure 4.1 illustrates the similarities and differences between friendship and loving.

Social scientists have suggested that, like romantic love, friendship is important to our emotional and even physical well-being. It helps us maintain a sense of social reality and staves off feelings of isolation in a largely anonymous world. According to psychotherapist James Grotstein, "Friendship governs all intimate relationships and it is more profound than sex and love" (quoted in Sheehy, 2000). Like romantic love, the development and expression of platonic love or friendship is also heavily influenced by social factors. Research shows that friendship formation is largely a product of our daily interaction patterns rather than of chance or "good chemistry." Friendships tend to develop with the people we see most often—those with whom we work, go to school, are enrolled in the same class, or members of our church or synagogue, health club, and so on. Similarly, friendships tend to form among those who are in close geographic proximity. Like romantic love, friendship grows best out of similarity. We tend to build the strongest friendships with those who

Figure 4.1

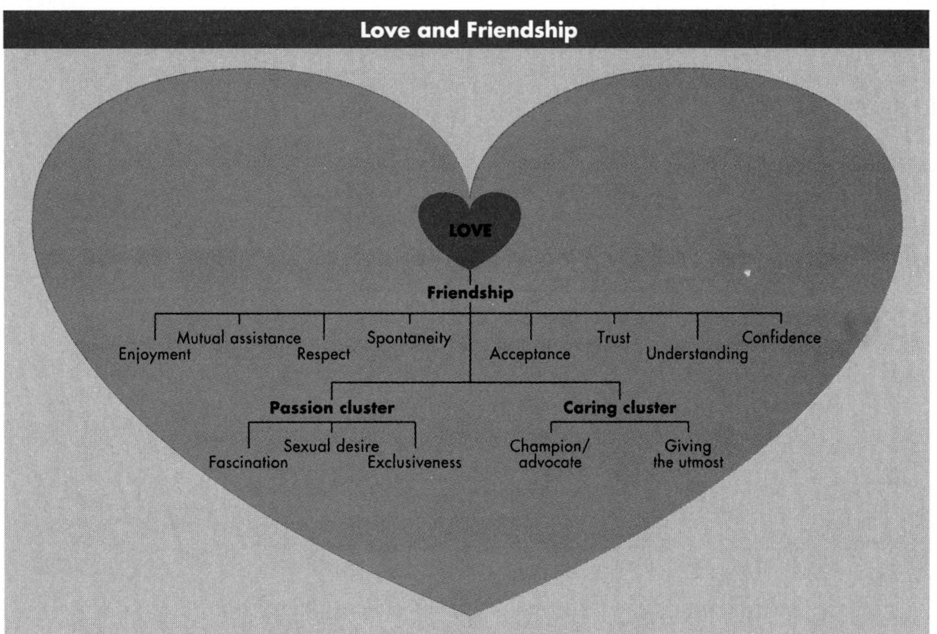

Source: Adapted from Keith Davis, 1985, "Near and Dear: Friendship and Love Compared," *Psychology Today* (February): 24. Reprinted with permission from *Psychology Today* Magazine. Copyright © 1985 by Sussex Publishers, Inc.

It is not always easy to distinguish love from close friendship because they share so many of the same characteristics. Couples in love, as well as close friends, often enjoy just being in each other's company.

hold attitudes similar to our own. We also tend to connect with those who share our physical and social characteristics—appearance, income, educational level, race, and so on.

On the level of experience, various research studies show that the way in which we define and express friendship differs in terms of important social characteristics, such as race, gender, sexual orientation, and social class. For example, some research indicates that the number of close friends that men have increases from adolescence until around age 30, falling off thereafter. In contrast, the research for women is mixed. Some research shows that for women, the number of important friendships rises gradually over the life span, whereas other research suggests that there is a slump in early adulthood followed by an increase beginning somewhere between the late 30s and 40s. In general, however, from middle to late life, a man is less likely to have a close friend the older he gets, whereas a woman's chance of having at least one such friendship doesn't change with age. Although there are documented gender differences in friendship development and patterns, recent research indicates that women and men share many patterns and styles of friendship. For example, like women, men rely on their male friends for emotional support and intimacy. In addition, many friendship activities such as seeing friends for dinner, sharing ritual events, and visiting are things that both women and men friends do (Walker, 1994, 2001). In fact, according to Barry Wellman (1992), there has been a widespread *domestication* of male friendship, with men seeing friends in their home in much the same way that women do (quoted in Walker, 2001).

In the past, most of the research on friendship has been conducted using white middle-class heterosexual females and males (usually college students). However, recent researchers have noted that women and men who are other than white, middle class, and heterosexual may have different types of friendships from that cited in much of the friendship literature (Franklin, 1992; Hansen, 1992). For example, recent research indicates that for people of color, particularly women, *ethnic empathy* is a key factor in choosing friends. Although they often have cross-race friendships, their shared experiences with friends of their own race or ethnicity allow them to do what they feel they cannot do with friends of a different race, namely, share the experience of dealing with racism and the impact that it has on their daily lives (Sheehy, 2000). According to Gail Sheehy (2000), this issue of ethnic empathy is compounded for people whose backgrounds are racially mixed. Similar to people of color, an important dimension of lesbian and gay friendships is a sense of shared history, a sense of sister/brotherhood, and a sense of shared marginal identity. And, like for many people of color, forming friendships with people with whom they can be themselves is important to lesbians and gays, given a cultural context that typically does not approve of that "self." Many lesbians and gays indicate a need to develop friendships with others like themselves who are in dissent and out of the cultural mainstream (Rubin, 1986; Nardi, 2001).

Friendship studies focusing on social class show that working-class Americans conceive of friendship as an exchange of goods and services; gifts and favors indicate the strength of a friendship bond. In contrast, this kind of material exchange is not part of the middle-class definition of friendship. Middle-class individuals tend to view friendship as an emotional or intellectual exchange; they also frequently conceive of friendship simply as the sharing of leisure activities. Who our friends are also varies by class. Friends among the working classes are highly likely to be relatives—siblings, cousins, parents—whereas friends among the middle classes are typically nonblood relations. Further, among working-class individuals, friendships are overwhelmingly same sex, most often local, and friends have known each other for much longer periods of time than is typical of middle-class friends. Interaction among working-class friends is said to be more frequent than among middle-class friends, with some researchers suggesting that working-class friends interact, on average, once a week or more. In contrast, members of the middle classes are more open to cross-gender friendships and, because middle-class lifestyles often involve a high degree of geographic mobility, middle-class friendships are as often long-distance as they are local. Not only are middle-class friendships often maintained after individuals move out of the immediate geographic area but also, because of geographic mobility, friendships among middle-class individuals often develop when people meet as they travel to different locales. As a result of this distance factor, middle-class friends typically report less frequent contact than do their working-class counterparts (Allan, 1989; Blieszner and Adams, 1992; Elles,

1993; Walker, 1995; Ruane and Cerulo, 1997). Research findings such as these support our contention that even the most personal of experiences such as love and close friendship are greatly influenced by the social worlds in which we live.

Infatuation versus Love

That warm and wonderful feeling that we are experiencing, is it love or merely infatuation? How do we begin to know and tell the difference? All too often we confuse these two emotions. **Infatuation** involves a strong attraction to another person based on an idealized picture of that person (Bessell, 1984). It usually focuses on a specific characteristic of the person and has a strong physical (sexual) element. Some social scientists have defined infatuation as passion without commitment. In contrast to love, infatuation is generally superficial and of short duration. It can, however, develop into love. The differences between infatuation and love are outlined in Table 4.1.

What do you think of the assessment of love and infatuation presented in Table 4.1? The author implies that love is a mature emotion whereas infatuation is a very immature emotion. Do you agree or disagree? Does it seem to you to be an overly biased conception of love? How would you define the difference between love and infatuation? Is there really a difference?

Table 4.1

Differences between Love and Infatuation

- ***Infatuation*** leaps into your blood.
- ***Love*** usually takes root slowly and grows with time.
- ***Infatuation*** is accompanied by a sense of uncertainty. You are stimulated and thrilled but not really happy. You are miserable when she or he is absent. You can't wait until you see her or him again.
- ***Love*** begins with a feeling of security. You are warm with a sense of her or his nearness, even when she or he is away. Miles do not separate you. You want her or him near, but near or far, you know she or he is yours and you can wait.
- ***Infatuation*** says, "We must get married, right away. I can't risk losing her or him."
- ***Love*** says, "Don't rush into anything. You are sure of one another. You can plan your future with confidence."
- ***Infatuation*** has an element of sexual excitement. If you are honest, you will discover that it is difficult to enjoy one another unless you know it will end in intimacy.
- ***Love*** is the maturation of friendship. You must be friends before you can be lovers.
- ***Infatuation*** lacks confidence. When she or he is away, you wonder if she or he is with another woman or man. Sometimes you even check to make sure.
- ***Love*** means trust. You may fall into infatuation, but you never fall in love.
- ***Infatuation*** might lead you to do things for which you might be sorry, but love never will.
- ***Love*** leads you up. It makes you look up. It makes you think up. It makes you a better person than you were before.

Source: "How to Decide Whether It's Love or Infatuation." *Chicago Sun-Times* (1980):2. Weekender section.

Liking versus Love

Liking has been described by some writers as friendship in its most simple form. Liking is generally distinguished from loving as the more logical and rational and the less emotional and possessive of the two emotions. It is believed that liking is the foundation for love. Although liking is closely related to love, several researchers have identified some differences.

The most frequently cited research distinguishing liking from loving was conducted in the 1970s by social scientist Zick Rubin (1973, 1974). According to Rubin, both liking and love consist of the same basic elements: care, respect, tolerance, need, trust, affection, and attraction. What sets the two apart is their differential emphasis on these components. For example, when we love someone the emphasis is on care, trust, need, and tolerance. In contrast, when we like someone the emphasis is on affection, attraction, and respect. The degree of emphasis we place on the various components of like and love is not absolute. Rather, it will vary in terms of intensity from one time to another, from one relationship to another, and sometimes even within a relationship over time.

Several other researchers have produced findings that are generally consistent with Rubin's conclusions (Dermer and Pyszczynski, 1978; Steck et al., 1982). However, the difficulty in distinguishing between liking and loving is expressed by researchers Elaine Hatfield and William Walster (1978), who contend that the only real difference between like and love has to do with the depth of our feelings and the degree to which we are involved with the other person.

As this discussion of love, friendship, liking, and infatuation reveal, much of the literature and research in this area of intimacy is somewhat dated. Not much research in this area has been conducted since the 1980s. Does this mean that Americans are less concerned with love and intimacy today than in the past and thus researchers no longer find it a hot topic for their research? What do you think? Regardless of how we answer this question, a number of theoretical explanations (now considered classics) of why and how people fall in love are worth noting. In the next section we will explore a select sample of such theories.

SOME THEORIES OF LOVE

In recent decades, the works of several social scientists and researchers have provided us with significant insights into the nature of love. These works have laid the groundwork and become the benchmark for our current theoretical understanding of the topic. Some of the more insightful theories or explanations of love today include the wheel theory of love, love as a story, love as a social exchange, and limerence theory.

The Wheel Theory of Love

Generally, when we think about love we think about something unpredictable, sudden, and uncontrollable; something that happens somewhat haphazardly and out of the blue. For most of us, this is not how love happens. Rather, according to sociologist Ira Reiss (1960, 1971), love emerges and develops over time as we interact with the other person. Although there are more recent theories of love, Reiss's theory of love as a developmental process remains a classic. Stressing our need for intimacy, Reiss focuses on what he sees as the circular progression of love as a couple interacts over time. Describing this progression in terms of a wheel—the **wheel theory of love**—Reiss proposes that love involves four major interpersonal processes: rapport, self-revelation, mutual dependence, and need fulfillment. Each of these processes can be thought of as individual spokes on a wheel (see Figure 4.2).

RAPPORT Love can develop only between people who relate to each other. Lovers must develop a sense of *rapport*—feeling at ease or relaxed with one another. A key factor here is social background. In general, we are more at ease and communicate better with people with whom we share a common background and lifestyle. Furthermore, we seem to feel rapport with people with whom we share ideas about social roles. Thus, two people who believe that women's and men's roles are flexible and can thus be interchanged are far more likely to feel rapport than a couple in which only one of the partners feels this way.

Although similarity is important in the development of love, two people who are different are not necessarily precluded from developing a love relationship. Family sociologist Robert Winch and his colleagues (1954), for example, have suggested that people who have different, but complementary, personality characteristics are attracted to each other—the notion that "opposites attract" (see Chapter 5). In addition, love relationships develop between people from different racial, ethnic, religious, and age groups. This fact notwithstanding, some researchers believe that a love relationship can develop only when both partners share certain fundamental values (Murstein, 1971). It seems that if a couple share basic social values, then other differences are not as difficult to overcome.

Figure 4.2

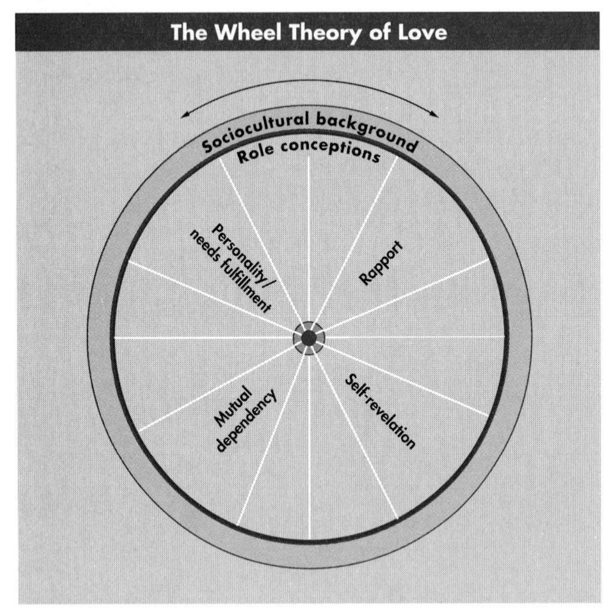

Source: Adapted from Ira Reiss, 1971, "Toward a Sociology of the Heterosexual Love Relationship," *Marriage and Family Living* 22 (May): 139-45. Reprinted with permission of Abbey Press, St. Meinrad, Indiana.

SELF-REVELATION Ease of communication leads to *self-revelation;* the disclosure of intimate and personal feelings. People who feel at ease are more likely to open up and reveal things about themselves than they otherwise would. A couple who feel comfortable with each other want to know more about each other than the kind of superficial information we usually learn about people when we first meet. For example, they want to know what similarities and differences exist between them; how great or how small these similarities and differences are; and how, if at all, they will affect the relationship. As with the development of rapport, a person's background is critical to self-revelation, determining in large part what and how much she or he will reveal about her- or himself. Often, factors like race, ethnicity, social class, gender, and age are important determinants of how willing people are to disclose personal feelings. We often distrust people different from ourselves. Because of this attitude, factors such as race often present initial barriers to the development of trust. Unlike in fairy tales such as *Cinderella,* vast differences in two people's background and other social and cultural characteristics generally prevent the development of a successful love relationship. These characteristics act as filters when two people first come into contact. People tend to make snap judgments about another person's potential as a lover on the basis of them (Newman, 1995:237). If a relationship endures beyond rapport and self-revelation, the participants tend to grow closer and begin to think about the longevity of their relationship and making a commitment to one another.

MUTUAL DEPENDENCE As two people develop a sense of rapport and feel comfortable enough with each other to self-disclose, they develop what Reiss describes as a *mutual* *dependence*—a reliance on each other for fulfillment. At this stage two people become a couple. They come to need and depend on each other to share their lives, their happiness, their fears, their hopes and dreams, and their sexual intimacies. They develop interdependent habit systems; ways of acting, thinking, and feeling that are no longer fun or fulfilling when done alone. For example, eating dinner without the other partner may become a lonely experience in that the pleasure of the meal now depends not only on the preparation and taste of the food but on the presence of the other person. The social and cultural background of the couple continues to play an important role in this stage of love. For example, the forms of dependent behaviors that develop between a couple depend on the kinds of behaviors they mutually agree on as acceptable, which in turn are influenced by their backgrounds and value systems. Mutual dependence leads to the fourth and final stage in Reiss's wheel theory: the fulfillment of personality needs.

Fulfillment of Personality Needs Reiss defines the fulfillment of personality needs as the ability of each partner to satisfy the needs of the other. Reiss describes this stage in terms of a consistent pattern of needs exchange and mutual dependence that develops within a relationship. For example, as the couple satisfies each other's basic needs, their sense of rapport increases, which leads to greater self-disclosure and more mutually dependent behaviors, which in turn lead to still greater needs fulfillment.

In his wheel analogy, Reiss captures this circular process of the development of love. All four processes are interdependent. Thus, a reduction in any one of them affects the development or continuation of a love relationship. As long as the wheel moves forward (the processes flow into each other), love develops and increases. However, when the wheel turns in the reverse direction—when there is a reduction in one of the processes—love may not develop, or if it has already developed, it may diminish. For example, if a couple are forced to spend less time with each other and they eventually develop divergent interests, their mutual dependence could weaken, which in turn could lower self-disclosure, which could lead to a reduced sense of rapport.

Reiss's pioneering theory of love as a process has sparked other researchers to extend or modify his theory using other metaphors besides the wheel. For example, social scientist Delores M. Borland (1975) uses the analogy of a clock spring to explain how love develops in a series of windings and unwindings as love intensifies and ebbs. These windings and unwindings occur as each new event takes place in the couple's relationship and can lead toward a closer, more intimate and mutually understanding relationship, or they may cause tensions that weaken the relationship. Essentially, such theories share with the Reiss model the notions that social background plays an important role in how and if love relationships will develop and that love is basically a matter of social as well as personal definition. Critics of these theories (for example, Albas and Albas, 1987) note that one of their shortcomings is that they ignore the variation in intensity among the different stages of a love relationship.

THE THEORY OF LOVE AS A STORY[1]

Love is often as unpredictable as the climax of a suspense novel. We might wonder from time to time why we or someone we know seem destined to make the same mistakes in love over and over, as if the fate of our intimate relationships was a written script. According to social scientist Robert J. Sternberg, in essence it is a script. As much as social scientists have attempted to explain the mysteries of love through their theories and scientific laws, Sternberg suggests that the best explanations of romantic love just may be *Wuthering Heights*, *Casablanca*, or the soap opera "General Hospital." Sternberg believes that love between two people follows a story. Thus, if we are to understand romantic love, we have to understand the stories that dictate our beliefs and expectations of love. We begin writing these stories as children, and they predict the patterns of our later romantic experiences.

Sternberg is not new to the field of "love theories." His initial work on love, *The Triangular Theory of Love* (1986, 1988), which continues to be cited in most textbooks on marriage and family, suggested that love is composed of three interlocking components in a triangle-like relationship: intimacy, passion, and commitment (each component can be represented as one point on a triangle), with different loving relationships having different combinations of these elements. *Intimacy*, which rests at the top of the triangle, refers to the bonding and emotional closeness or connectedness that a couple feels for each other. *Passion* refers to the romantic feelings, desires, and arousal that partners feel for each other. And *commitment* refers to a person's attachment to another person. It develops over time and represents a couple's desire to be faithful to one another and to stay together. Love is not static, however. All love relationships undergo some change over time; thus, each vertex of the love triangle will not be equal. If, however, vertexes are very unequal—there is too much mismatch among the components—the relationship will fail. When gender role socialization is added to the mix, there is increased difficulty in maintaining equal vertexes (Lindsey, 1994). For example, according to this theory, women attach greater importance to the commitment vertex, and men attach greater importance to the passion vertex. Complete love requires all three components. The absence of all three components represents *nonlove*.

Although interesting, Sternberg's triangular theory of love has some limitations. Indeed, in recent years, Sternberg himself has indicated some dissatisfaction with this theory. For example, he now believes that his theory

[1]This description of Robert J. Sternberg's "love story theory" draws heavily from Sternberg's latest work (1998, 2001).

leaves important questions about love unanswered such as: What makes people the kind of lovers they are? And what attracts us to other lovers? Based on research he conducted over the past decade with hundreds of couples in Connecticut, as well as ongoing research on the subject, Sternberg says that he found answers to these and other questions about romantic love in stories. He found that people describe love in many ways but their descriptions reveal their *love story.*

Love Stories

Sternberg identified 25 love stories that people tell: the sacrifice, police, travel, pornography, horror, recovery, gardening, business, fantasy, war, humor, and collection stories, for example (for the other story types, see Sternberg, 1998). Sternberg and one of his students developed this love story classification scheme after analyzing their research subjects' ratings on a scale of 1 to 7 of the extent to which a group of statements characterized their intimate relationships. Their highest-ranked statements indicated their personal love story. For example, a person who strongly agrees with the statement "I believe close relationships are like good partnerships" tells a *business love story*, whereas a person who says that they "typically end up with partners who scare them"—or that they "like to intimidate their partner"—tells a *horror love story.* According to Sternberg, the most common love stories people tell are the *travel love story* ("I believe that beginning a relationship is like starting a new journey that promises to be both exciting and challenging"), the *gardening love story* ("I believe any relationship that is left unattended will not survive"), and the *humor love story* ("I think taking a relationship too seriously can spoil it"). The least popular or common love stories include the *horror* ("I find it exciting when I feel that my partner is somewhat frightened of me"), *collectibles* ("I like dating different partners simultaneously"), and *autocratic government* ("I think it is more efficient if one person takes control of the important decisions in a relationship") stories.

In essence, Sternberg's love story theory suggests that our love stories begin soon after birth as we start to form our ideas about love based on our individual personality, our early socialization experiences, our observations of our parents' relationships, as well as popular culture descriptions of love and romance in the mass media. We eventually seek to live out these notions of love in our personal lives. Sternberg posits that the course of love typically begins with a physical attraction and similar interests and values. Eventually, however, the couple may notice that something is missing in the relationship. Usually, the missing something is story compatibility. If a couple's stories don't match, there is an underlying lack of coordination to their interaction and their love relationship may not go very far. In contrast, when two people's love stories match this is what keeps their love alive; it is the key to compatibility with a romantic partner.

Although no one story guarantees a successful love relationship, some stories do seem to predict failure more than others (for example, the business, collectibles, government, horror, mystery, police, recovery, science fiction, and theater stories).[2] The key to a happy healthy love relationship is that both partners have compatible love stories—that is, compatible relationship expectations. According to Sternberg, his ongoing collaborative research on the subject of love supports the idea that the more similar their love stories, the happier couples are together. Stories are compatible if they include complementary roles in a single story, such as audience-comedian in the humor love story, or if the stories are similar enough so that they can be merged into a new, unified story. According to Sternberg, we end up with the same kind of bad partners in love relationships not because of bad luck but because we subconsciously find people to play out our love stories or we force our stories on the people we meet. Love story compatibility, however, isn't the only thing needed in a successful romantic relationship. Once we understand the ideas and beliefs behind our love stories we must analyze our stories: Decide which romantic tale we really want to tell and whether or not it has the potential to lead to a successful relationship, and, if not, determine what about it we like and don't like and what appears to not work for us and then set about changing our story for success. See if you can identify your love story in the box "Is There a Love Story for You?".

Love as a Social Exchange

Whatever our love story, it seems that it can be described in the language of social-exchange theory (recall the discussion of social-exchange theory in Chapter 2). While Reiss's theory identifies the stages in the process of love and relationship development and Sternberg suggests that our love stories determine the patterns of our romantic experiences, family sociologist John Scanzoni (1980) uses some basic principles of economics to explain *why* we are attracted to and fall in love with some people and not with others and *why* we pursue and remain in some relationships and avoid or break off others.

Basically, Scanzoni argues that love, like any other commodity, involves an exchange of rewards between two interested parties. The process of rewarding each other and gratifying each other's needs is continuous and forms the basis on which the relationship rests. Some of the more obvious rewards of intimate relationships include love, caring, sensitivity, sexual gratification, companionship, liking, friendship, warmth, protection, and emotional and financial support. Some costs might be jealousy and conflict, the time and effort required to keep the other partner satisfied, and

[2] Police ("I believe it is necessary to watch your partner's every move"), recovery ("I often find myself helping people get their life back in order"), science fiction ("I often find myself attracted to individuals wo have unusual and strange characteristics"), theater ("I think my relationships are like plays").

undesirable personal or social characteristics. Although these types of exchanges are not always acknowledged and usually do not seem as cold and calculating as the market metaphor makes them sound, according to social-exchange theory, virtually every romantic encounter involves an implicit, if not explicit, exchange of sexual and emotional goods. As long as the love relationship is mutually rewarding it will continue, but when it ceases to be rewarding it will end. Thus, although people in love clearly care about each other, love is not totally altruistic. Research (for example, Rusbult, 1983) indicates that people who are happiest in their intimate relationships are typically couples who provide one another with far more rewarding experiences than costly ones.

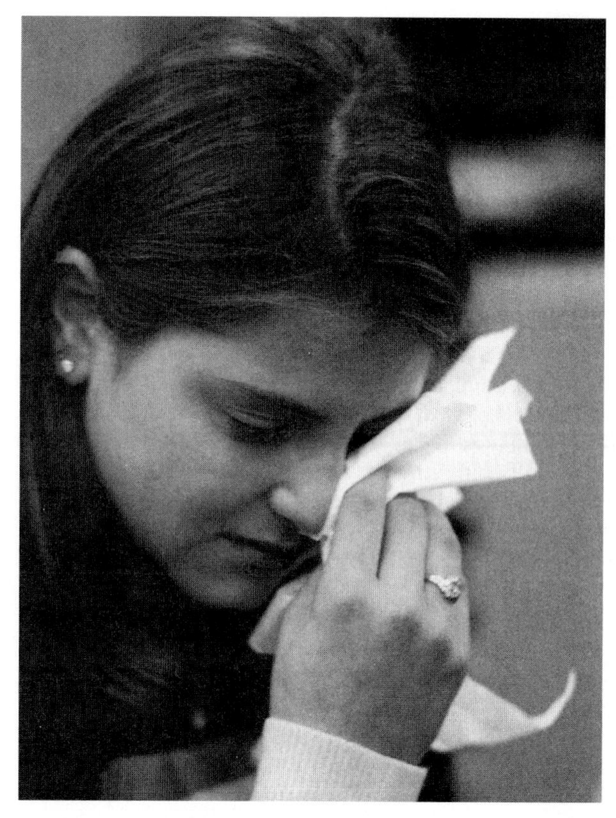

Olympic gymnast Dominique Moceanu, 17, wipes a tear during a court hearing in which she sought a permanent protective order from her father whom she claimed stalked her and tried to hire someone to kill two of her friends.

Love as Limerence

Another pioneering theory of love comes to us from the discipline of psychology. Limerence theory, advanced by psychologist Dorothy Tennov (1979), provides important insights into the distinction between being in love and other types of loving. Tennov uses the term **limerence** to refer to a style of love characterized by an extreme attraction, a complete absorption or obsessive preoccupation of one person with another. She defines this emotion as being "in love" as opposed to "love," which she defines as caring and concern for another person.

Based on the findings from her study of the love experiences of over 500 people, Tennov concluded that limerence is a state of mind; that its most important features lie in the fantasies and ideas that one person has about another. Thus, the focus of limerence theory is on the experience of falling or being in love rather than on the relationship itself. Although some people never experience limerence, Tennov suggests that the majority do.

Limerence theory underscores the high level of intensity associated with romantic love; it describes and explains the extreme highs and lows that many people experience in their love relationships. Positive limerence can bring an elated feeling, whereas negative limerence can bring feelings of despondency, despair, pain, and depression. Limerence can be characterized by (1) its speed of occurrence at the onset, (2) its intensity, (3) whether or not the feeling is reciprocated, and (4) the length of time it lasts. As these characteristics show, there is no typical limerent experience. Tennov's description of limerent feelings encompasses a wide spectrum including incessant or continuous thoughts about the lover, mood swings depending on the lover's actions, being completely closed to the possibility of someone else as a lover, a fear of rejection, a preoccupation or obsession with the lover to the neglect of other interests and concerns, and idealizing the lover.

Tennov's concept of limerence is very similar to that of infatuation. Both stress emotional intensity in romantic relationships, especially in the early stages and particularly for some people. In addition, Tennov's discussion of limerence shares many similarities with Davis and Todd's findings concerning romantic love. In fact, many of the features she identifies with limerence parallel those identified by Davis and Todd as characteristic of the passion cluster.

Do any of these attributes apply to a current or past love relationship in which you have been involved? Most of us can probably identify with one or more of these attributes, especially in the beginning of our romantic love relationships. At that point we won't believe anything negative about our lover; we can't eat, sleep, or enjoy ourselves when we are away from our lover; we daydream about her or him; we feel hurt and dismayed at the thought that she or he may not return our feelings. Does this sound familiar?

Tennov's discussion of limerence calls to mind what could happen when limerence is taken to an unhealthy extreme. The almost obsessive compulsion with another person could develop into a full-fledged obsession that has been immortalized in films, novels, and other aspects of popular culture as a "fatal attraction" and that is all too often a reality. Such full-fledged obsessions in the real world have had fatal consequences not only for the parties involved but often for intimates involved with the couple as

APPLYING THE SOCIOLOGICAL IMAGINATION

IS THERE A LOVE STORY FOR YOU?

Can you find your love story among the four stories here, taken from Robert J. Sternberg's book *Love Is a Story*. Consult his book for a full discussion of all his love story types.

Rate each statement on a scale from 1 to 9, 1 meaning that it doesn't characterize your romantic relationships at all, and 9 meaning that it describes them extremely well. Then average your scores for each story. In general, averaged scores of 7 to 9 are high, indicating a strong attraction to a story, and 1 to 3 are low, indicating little or no interest in the story. Moderate scores of 4 to 6 indicate some interest, but probably not enough to generate or keep a romantic interest. Next, evaluate your own love story. There are only four listed here; see Sternberg's book for more.

Story #1

1. I enjoy making sacrifices for the sake of my partner.
2. I believe sacrifice is a key part of true love.
3. I often compromise my own comfort to satisfy my partner's needs.

SCORE ________

The **sacrifice story** can lead to happy relationships when both partners are content in the roles they are playing, particularly when they both make sacrifices. It is likely to cause friction when partners feel compelled to make sacrifices. Research suggests that relationships of all kinds are happiest when they are roughly equitable. The greatest risk in a sacrifice story is that the give-and-take will become too out of balance, with one partner always being the giver or receiver.

Story #2
Object

1. The truth is that I don't mind being treated as a sex toy by my partner.
2. It is very important to me to gratify my partner's sexual desires and whims, even if people might view them as debasing.
3. I like it when my partner wants me to try new and unusual, and even painful, sexual techniques.

SCORE ________

Subject

1. The most important thing to me in my relationship is for my partner to be an excellent sex toy, doing anything I desire.
2. I can never be happy with a partner who is not very adventurous in sex.
3. The truth is that I like a partner who feels like a sex object.

SCORE ________

There are obvious advantages to the **pornography story.** The disadvantages are also quite clear. First, the excitement people attain is through degradation of themselves and others. Second, the need to debase and be debased is likely to keep escalating. Third, once one adopts the story, it may be difficult to adopt another story. Fourth, the story can become physically as well as psychologically dangerous. And, finally, no matter

well. Most people's limerence, however, does not go to this extreme. In fact, according to Tennov, if limerence is mutual it can lead to a love affair, a commitment, and ultimately to marriage.

LOVE ACROSS GENDER, SEXUALITY, AND RACE

Romantic love is often considered to be a universal feeling. As we have noted, however, not everyone experiences romantic love. Furthermore, when we do experience such love, a number of other important life experiences come into play, making love different for each of us. Probably the most powerful individual differences that affect how we experience love are gender, sexual orientation, and race. For example, do women and men experience romantic love similarly or differently? Do lesbians, gays, and heterosexuals experience romantic love similarly or differently? And, how, if at all, does race impact the experience of love?

Gender Differences in Love Relationships

Although both women and men experience love and consider it to be an important experience and relationship, a considerable body of research shows, as we have already seen with styles of love, that females and males construct their realities of love generally in very different terms (Brehm, 1992). We should bear in mind, however, that, like friendship research, much of this research is also based on survey responses of white, middle-class, heterosexual couples.

Contrary to American cultural stereotypes that women are more sentimental than men, more likely to fall in love at first sight, and more likely to stick by their partners no how one tries, it is difficult to turn the story into one that's good for psychological or physical well-being.

Story #3

Terrorizer

1. I often make sure that my partner knows that I am in charge, even if it makes her or him scared of me.
2. I actually find it exciting when I feel my partner is somewhat frightened of me.
3. I sometimes do things that scare my partner, because I think it is actually good for a relationship to have one partner slightly frightened of the other.

SCORE ________

Victim

1. I believe it is somewhat exciting to be slightly scared of your partner.
2. I find it arousing when my partner creates a sense of fear in me.
3. I tend to end up with people who sometimes frighten me.

SCORE ________

The **horror story** is the least advantageous of the stories. To some, it may be exciting. But the forms of terror needed to sustain the excitement tend to get out of control and to put their participants, and even sometimes those around them, at both psychological and physical risk. Those who discover that they have this story or are in a relationship that is enacting it would be well-advised to seek counseling and, perhaps, even police protection.

Story #4

1. I think fairy tales about relationships can come true.
2. I do believe that there is someone out there for me who is my perfect match.
3. I like my relationships to be ones in which I view my partner as something like a prince or princess in days of yore.

SCORE ________

The **fantasy story** can be a powerful one. The individual may feel swept up in the emotion of the search for the perfect partner or of developing the perfect relationship with an existing partner. It is probably no coincidence that in literature most fantasy stories take place before or outside of marriage. Fantasies are hard to maintain when one has to pay the bills, pack the children off to school, and resolve marital fights. To maintain the happy feeling of the fantasy, therefore, one has to ignore, to some extent, the mundane aspects of life. The greatest disadvantage of fantasy relationships is the possibility for disillusionment when one partner discovers that no one could fulfill the fantastic expectations that have been created. This can lead partners to feel dissatisfied with relationships that most others would view as quite successful. If a couple can create a fantasy story based on realistic rather than idealistic ideals, they have the potential for success; if they want to be characters in a myth, chances are that's exactly what they'll get: a myth.

Source: Adapted from Robert J. Sternberg, *Love Is a Story: A New Theory of Relationships* (New York: Oxford University Press, 1998).

matter what and that men are hard-hearted, rational, in control of their emotions, and able to fall out of love quickly, research on love and intimacy shows us that not only are these stereotypes wrong, but the opposite is actually true. Men are more romantic and give greater importance than do women to the desire to fall in love. Women, on the other hand, tend to initiate a breakup more often than men, and they seem better able than men to put aside feelings of rejection and to redefine their relationship as friendship (Peplau, 1994).

In studying the difference between liking and loving, Zick Rubin (1973) found that females distinguish much more sharply between liking and loving than males do. Rubin suggested that this is true because women are much more in tune with their feelings than men are. Given that men are socialized to be task-oriented as opposed to social–emotional, they are often unable to make the fine distinctions in their feelings that women are. Yet some researchers (Hatfield, 1983) have found that when men are in love, they tend to describe their love in slightly more passionate terms than do women.

In contrast to the popular view of women chasing reluctant men and coyly maneuvering them into an unwanted relationship (the notion of love as a feminine pursuit), it seems that men tend to start a relationship with a much more romantic perspective than females do (Sprecher and Metts, 1989). Although both women and men seem to enjoy the chase and are often stimulated by someone they find somewhat mysterious (Fisher, 1999), men tend to fall in love more quickly and earlier in their relationships, stay in love longer, have crushes, and fall in love with someone who doesn't love them in return more often than do women (Rubin, 1973; Hill, Rubin, and Peplau, 1976; Brehm, 1992). On the other hand, women are more likely than men to emphasize relationships and intimacy, but they are less impulsive than men about falling in love. Thus, women's love is more likely than men's to develop incrementally or practically (Hendrick and Hendrick, 1989; Wood, 1994). Once a relationship develops, women tend to form a more intense and lasting love bond (Walsh, 1991; Knox et al., 1999, 2000) and are willing to sacrifice more for love than men are (Hatfield, 1983). Women also tend to be more expressive than men, fall in love harder (Murstein, 1986), more intense and more likely to idealize the love object (Kanin, Davidson, and Scheck, 1970), and they tend to prefer emotional closeness, whereas men prefer giving instrumental help and sex. For example, women, express love by talking about and acknowledging their feelings for the other person, whereas men express their love through action—doing things for the other person (Tavris, 2000).

In terms of intimacy, women generally regard intimacy, self-growth, self-understanding, and positive self-esteem as important benefits of romantic love, and loss of identity and innocence about relationships as important costs. Men, on the other hand, regard sexual satisfaction as an important benefit, and monetary losses from dates as an important cost. Furthermore, women tend to spend more time trying to cultivate and maintain love relationships than do men. However, as we have indicated, women are also the ones more likely to decide when to break off a relationship. Men are more resistant to breaking up and have a harder time recovering after a breakup. For example, once a relationship is over, men, more often than women, tend to feel sad, lonely, depressed, and unwilling to give up on the relationship. Men are also more violent and possessive when romantic relationships end (Herman, 1989; Hill, 1989).

These findings seem consistent with female and male socialization in U.S. society. Females are taught almost from birth to be loving, caring, and nurturant. Men, in contrast, are taught to be detached, independent, and unemotional. Obviously, these basic differences do not hold for every woman or man. Rather, they are general tendencies that are subject to change and have sometimes changed over time. The gender gap in the ways that women and men approach romantic love relationships, for example, seems to be closing as women's and men's lives become more similar. For example, studies during the late 1960s and early 1970s (see, for example, Kephart, 1967) showed that women and men differed fairly significantly in terms of exercising control over their romantic feelings. For instance, when a sample of college students was asked: "If someone had all the qualities you desired, would you marry them if you were not in love with them?" only 1 in 4 women said no, while 2 out of 3 men said no. This led the researchers to conclude that women exercise more control over their feelings and are more careful about falling in love than are men. However, as attitudes and behaviors have changed over time—as gender-specific socialization has loosened somewhat—responses to this same question in the 1990s (see, for example, Allgeier and Wiederman, 1991) indicated that women and men were equally committed to the idea that love is a prerequisite for marriage (9 out of 10 women as well as 9 out of 10 men said that being in love is essential to marrying). Finally, there is some evidence that women's seeming superiority in love is not really as strong as it first seems. Many studies show small or guarded differences between women and men and, according to Francesca Cancian (1993), these studies are often biased against men and focus on verbal self-disclosure, a quality that is stereotypically feminine.

The Feminization of Love Discussions and investigations of gender differences in love relationships have led some sociologists, such as Francesca Cancian (1993), to call attention to how heavily gendered our ways of thinking about love are. According to Cancian, part of the reason that men seem so much less loving than women is because men's love behavior is measured with a feminine ruler. She describes the social organization of love in the United States in terms of the concept of the "*feminization of love*"—love as a central aspect of the female domain and experience and defined purely

APPLYING THE SOCIOLOGICAL IMAGINATION

HOW DO THE MEDIA PORTRAY LOVE?

It is always interesting to examine a culture through the images and messages transmitted by its media. Do a content analysis of U.S. film over the last decade, or compare films made before and after the 1970s, tracing the changes, if any, in the definition of love and the portrayal of love for women and men. If films are not accessible, you might find a content analysis of another form of media, such as books, television shows, or popular music, equally interesting and revealing.

What types of changes in the portrayal of love did you find? How does the information in this chapter help you account for such changes? Was love portrayed the same way for all groups, or did it vary according to race, class, gender, age, and sexual orientation? Try to categorize the styles of loving presented in the media in terms of either the Lee or Cancian models. Is lesbian or gay love portrayed? If so, how? Does it fit any of the models that have been discussed in this chapter?

in female terms. Cancian's research demonstrates that social scientists generally use a "feminized definition of love" in their research. That is, only women's style of loving is recognized as love. At least since the nineteenth century, love has been defined primarily in terms of characteristics that women are thought to be particularly skilled in, such as emotional expression, self-disclosure, and affection. Such a definition typically ignores aspects of love that men prefer, such as providing instrumental help or sharing physical activities. It also presumes that men lack feelings and emotional depth and that relationships and feelings are unimportant in men's lives. Men are thought of as incompetent at loving because the common view of romantic love overlooks the instrumental, pragmatic aspect of loving and stresses primarily the expressive aspect. And based on the myth that women both need love more than men do and are more skilled at loving than men are, love has become a preoccupation with women.

One of several problems with this incomplete and overly feminized view of love, says Cancian, is that it contributes to male dominance of women because it leads women to focus on interpersonal relationships while encouraging men to achieve independence from women and to specialize in the occupational activities that are more highly regarded in this society. She argues that ideally love should be **androgynous;** that is, it should include a wide range of attitudes and behaviors with no gender role differentiation. An androgynous view of love validates both feminine and masculine styles of loving and considers both to be necessary parts of a good love relationship.

?

What do you think? Do you agree with Cancian, or do you think that differentiation along gender lines in terms of love has disappeared? What evidence can you give to support your position? Try applying a sociological analysis to this issue (see the "Applying the Sociological Imagination" box). How close are your findings to what you already knew or have experienced?

Lesbian and Gay Love Relationships

Love is experienced not only by heterosexual couples but also by lesbian and gay couples. However, just as there is no distinct heterosexual style of loving, there is also no distinct homosexual value orientation toward love relationships. Instead, what appears to be more important than sexual orientation is one's sex—being female or male—and one's background. Women's goals in intimate partnerships are similar whether the partner is male or female. The same is true of men (Peplau, 1986). Regardless of the sexual orientation of the two partners, research indicates that most partners want to love and be loved, want to be emotionally close, expect fidelity in the relationship, and expect the relationship to be long-term. In general, patterns of lesbian and gay love are very similar to heterosexual love. Unlike heterosexual couples, however, lesbian and gay couples often feel compelled to hide their feelings of love because many people do not approve of such relationships. Although Americans tend to prize romantic love, they are generally hostile to love and intimacy between people of the same sex. Because of societal disapproval, gay lovers frequently look to each other to satisfy all their needs. Thus, gay love is often intense and sometimes possessive. In this sense, it is often both highly emotional and highly physical.

Social science research has traditionally been heterosexist and homophobic (Renzetti and Curran, 1999). Much of what was written about lesbians and gays before the 1960s was written by heterosexuals and discussed from a psychoanalytic and/or pathology perspective, which until recently focused almost exclusively on lesbian and gay sexual behavior. Although specific information and research on love among lesbians and gays continue to be limited, an emerging literature on lesbian and gay relationships across a wider span of social behavior is now being conducted by lesbian and gay social scientists, and their findings refute many of the common myths about lesbian and gay intimacy.

For example, one of the most long-standing stereotypes of lesbian and gay relationships is that they are fleeting, uncommitted, and primarily sexual. However, although gays do have more partners on average than heterosexual men, most establish enduring intimate relationships. And research indicates that lesbian couples generally have more stable and longer-lasting love relationships than either heterosexual couples or gay male couples. In the few studies that have included older lesbians and gays, researchers have found that relationships lasting 20 years or more are not uncommon. The long-term nature of these relationships often persists even after the couple is no longer "in love." For instance, research shows that when lesbian and gay partners break up, they frequently maintain a close relationship with one another by making a transition from being lovers to being friends (Blumstein and Schwartz, 1983; Loewenstein, 1985; Weston, 1991; Kelly, 1995).

Another popular myth about lesbian and gay relationships is that they are unhappy, abnormal, and dysfunctional. However, a study of matched sets of lesbians, gays, and heterosexual women and men involved in a current romantic/sexual relationship found no significant differences among the three sets of couples in terms of love and relationship satisfaction. Like the heterosexual couples, lesbians and gays reported very positive feelings for their partners and generally reported that their relationships were highly satisfying and very close (Peplau and Cochran, 1980). Findings such as these negate the persistent negative cultural images of lesbians and gays as unhappy individuals who are unsuccessful in developing enduring relationships, who drift from one sexual partner to another, and end up old and alone. This is not to imply, however, that all lesbian and gay couples are euphorically happy and problem-free. Rather, the point is that lesbian and gay couples are no more unhappy, abnormal, or dysfunctional than are heterosexual couples.

As you have probably noted already, there are more differences between women and men in the expression and experience of love than there are differences between same sex and heterosexual love. According to researchers Michelle Huston and Pepper Schwartz (1996), gender affects, and is affected by, the organization of lesbian and gay love. Gender identity and gender roles impact the dating process for lesbians and gays, the maintenance of romantic relationships, the ways in which lesbian and gay partners communicate with one another, as well as the organization of power and the division of labor within these relationships. In this regard, gay couple relationships, but even more so in lesbian relationships, equality between partners is highly valued, and couples work hard to maintain an egalitarian relationship. Because many lesbians and gays do not allow themselves to be constrained by many of the conventional ways of organizing romantic relationships, they have created egalitarian schemes for dividing up responsibilities and rights within their relationships.

Huston and Schwartz suggest that heterosexual couples can learn much from the egalitarian models developed by lesbians and gays, which demonstrate that equality in a romantic relationship is not only rewarding but also quite possible. However, over and above the lessons we learn about equality in relationships, the study of lesbian and gay love relationships also gives us key insights into the contextual nature of gender. Although each of us is an individual, we are all part of a culture that holds very traditional and often rigid and stereotypical notions about what it means to be women and men. Sometimes these rigid gender roles are practiced in lesbian and gay relationships, but research indicates that most often they are not. Huston and Schwartz suggest that many lesbians and gays have overcome much of this socialization to become more androgynous, a lesson that heterosexuals can learn if they wish to change the current power imbalances prevalent in many of their relationships.

It is important to keep in mind that lesbian and gay relationships are not monolithic; there is no typical lesbian or gay couple or relationship. Rather, as with heterosexual couples, there is enormous variation among lesbian and gay couples. The emerging scholarship on lesbian and gay couples emphasizes this diversity. It also expands our existing knowledge base about love and intimate relationships by increasing the diversity of types of relationships studied to include same-sex partnerships and close relations.

Female–Male Relationships among African Americans

As with research on lesbians and gays, there is little systematic data on love and the organization of romantic relationships across race. To the extent that the American public is informed about such relationships among various racial and ethnic groups often we have had to rely on a popular literature that may or may not accurately capture the essence of these relationships, given that their bottom line is the selling of their product and profit. For example, over the past several decades, this popular literature has repeatedly reported a crisis in African American female–male love relationships. According to several popular and scholarly writers on the subject, African American women and men have experienced some difficulty in developing and maintaining meaningful love relationships. This is said to be due, in part, to the suspicions and mistrust generated by years of racism and exploitation, and the pitting of one sex against the other by forces outside their control. The African American struggle, along with other struggles such as the women's movement, has increased the levels of education and occupational mobility for African American women (and men) and has added to what some people describe as the aggressive, assertive, and self-sufficient nature of African American women.

In turn, some African American women argue that it is difficult for them to develop a committed relationship based on equity because although the roles of women in society have changed, the attitudes of some African American men have not kept pace. Because racism has made achievement of a position of power in the larger society difficult if not impossible for many African American men, many of these men continue to hold on to the one venue where they have been able to exert power: their intimate relationships with African American women.

Contrary to this talk of a crisis, however, African American romantic relationships are no more or no less characterized by crisis than are such relationships for other racial and ethnic groups, and African American females and males tend to fall in love as often and confront the same kinds of obstacles to their relationships as do individuals in other racial and ethnic groups. For example, like women in other racial and ethnic groups, African American women perceive a lack of male commitment as a key obstacle to love and romance. In a recent poll conducted by *Ebony* magazine (cited in Hughes, 2001), these women reported that what they want in an intimate relationship is a supportive, romantic man who openly expresses his deepest love and feelings and listens attentively to theirs. Above all, they said, they want a lover who is not afraid of commitment. Some experts on African American love and intimate relationships refute the stereotype of African American men as noncommittal, nonpassionate, and afraid of responsibility. Instead, they argue that when they are in love, African American men are committed to the relationship and passionate about pleasing the woman they love. On the other hand, they find that for African American men, like other men, romance is a term that they hardly think about and they sometimes get it mixed up with "sex" (Hughes, 2001).

Although little scientific research has been conducted on differences in styles of loving across race in the United States, evidence suggests that there is a difference in the way blacks and whites view love. Research indicates, for example, that blacks tend to have a more romantic view of love (Mirchandi, 1973). In any case, continuing racism and discrimination in U.S. society, coupled with the changing social roles of women and men, will no doubt continue to exert pressure on the development and maintenance of love relationships between African American women and men. As for other groups of color, scientific research on love and

Mass media portrayals of African Americans, such as the recent television program, *My Wife and Kids,* serve a useful purpose by counteracting popular stereotypes about African American families and female/male relationships.

intimacy is even more scarce than that for African Americans. Indeed, this is an area of research that is sorely in need of the skills and insights of scholars across academic disciplines.

OBSTACLES TO LOVE AND LOVING RELATIONSHIPS

Few people thrive in an environment of social isolation, so we desire and pursue meaningful love relationships. Unfortunately, a number of individual and cultural factors serve as obstacles to the development and maintenance of love. Some of the most troublesome of these factors are traditional gender role socialization, patriarchy, lack of trust, and jealousy.

Traditional Gender Role Socialization

As the discussions in Chapter 3 and throughout this chapter reveal, differential gender role socialization often creates very different attitudes and behaviors in females and males. Nowhere is this more evident than in the ways in which the two genders view love relationships. Research has shown that women and men seem to have different priorities when it comes to love relationships. Several researchers have found considerable evidence of an emotional division of labor within heterosexual love relationships, with one partner (usually the woman) more oriented toward the relationship than the other is. That is, the relationship and what it should consist of is more familiar to and central in the life and behavior of one partner than it is in that of the other. Likewise, homosexual couples tend to consist of one partner who is more oriented toward the relationship than the other is (Blumstein and Schwartz, 1983).

Researcher Robert Karen (1987) discussed this differential relationship orientation between women and men in terms of who gives and who gets. According to Karen, men get much more out of love relationships than they give. Women, because of the way they have been socialized, are able to be compassionate, to give support, and generally to be there for their partners. Men in contrast require emotional understanding and tenderness but have not been taught to give it. Thus, they often have less access to their feelings than women do. Consequently, it is often the woman who reaches out and makes emotional contact. Feeling this emotional inequality, some women console themselves with the belief that they can rely on their inner strength to make up for what they do not get from their partners. This emotional imbalance between women and men can be an obstacle to either the development or the maintenance of a loving relationship.

Patriarchy as an Obstacle to Lesbian Love

A number of scholars have identified the patriarchal structure of Western society as an obstacle to same-sex love. Focusing on lesbian love, some of these scholars contend that romantic love between women is outlawed and repressed because it is viewed by men as a threat to the patriarchal structure of intimate relationships and to heterosexuality generally. To these scholars, heterosexuality includes not only sex between women and men but also patriarchal culture, male dominance, and female subordination, all of which benefit men (Faderman, 1989). The centrality of patriarchy in mate selection is evidenced in the concept of heterosexuality and the notion that women are dependent on men for emotional as well as social and economic well-being. Some of the more common assumptions of patriarchy and heterosexualism are that women's primary love and sexual orientation are naturally directed toward men and that heterosexuality is ordained by nature. Thus, heterosexuals have seldom questioned these assumptions, even though there is ample evidence that lesbian love has existed throughout history and has been accepted at different times by various societies.

From a lesbian perspective, such assumptions not only legitimate heterosexuality as the norm but also denigrate women's romantic relationships with other women, defining these relationships as deviant or pathological. We need only to look at the social sanctions brought against women who love women (as well as men who love men) to understand how, through social control, heterosexuality is maintained as the norm and homosexuality is defined as deviant. For example, society subverts any public expression of homosexual consciousness or behavior, defining it with terms such as evil, sick, sinful, a crime against nature (Andersen, 1993). Such ideas and attitudes are detrimental both to lesbians' sense of self-worth and their ability to establish romantic relationships with other women.

Until women's and men's sexuality is freed from the constraints of patriarchy and heterosexism and society recognizes that there is no one right way to express love, women and men who choose to love people of the same sex will continue to face a wide range of obstacles to the development of romantic love relationships. In the meantime, however, a growing number of lesbians today openly choose other women as love objects even though the patriarchal system continues to define their behavior as deviant and severely restrict their ability to love other women. For many of these women, their selection of a partner is not just a personal choice but rather is a political choice as well.

Lack of Trust

Do you trust your partner? Does your partner trust you? Is it important to your relationship that each of you trusts the other? Why?

Trust is probably important to your relationship because with it you and your partner can relax; you can feel secure about the relationship and not worry about whether it will continue. Social researchers John Rempel and John Holmes (1986) designed a trust inventory scale to address these questions. According to Rempel and Holmes, **trust**—the degree of confidence a person feels when he or she thinks about a relationship—is one of the most important and necessary aspects of any close or intimate relationship. Because trust can mean something different depending on what aspect of the relationship we are focusing on, Rempel and Holmes identified three basic elements of trust: predictability, dependability, and faith.

Predictability is the ability to foretell our partner's behavior, the knowledge that she or he will consistently act in our best interests. For confidence to grow and trust to develop, it is not enough simply to know in advance how our partner will behave. A sense of predictability must be based on the knowledge that our partner will act in positive ways. As the relationship progresses, however, we begin to focus more on our partner's specific qualities, such as dependability and trustworthiness, and less in terms of predictable behavior. This leads to the second element of trust, dependability. Dependability can be defined as the knowledge that our partner can be relied on when we need her or him. Both predictability and dependability are based on the assumption that people will behave in a fairly consistent manner (the same in the present as they did in the past). But because human behavior is changing, there is no guarantee that this will be so. Therefore, we often remain committed to a relationship based on sheer faith. Faith allows people to go beyond previous observed behaviors to feel assured that the partner will continue to be loving and caring. Faith is rooted in predictability and dependability, but it goes beyond what has actually happened in the past. Each of these components helps form the basis for a trusting relationship; none by itself is sufficient. Rather, the extent to which we trust our partner depends on the degree to which each component is interwoven with the others.

Jealousy and Envy

Although love can provide us with wonderful feelings and experiences, it often has a dark side as well: jealousy. Most of us have experienced jealousy at one time or another. Some of the most important relationships have been destroyed by it. So what is this powerful emotion, what causes it, who is most likely to exhibit it, and what consequences does it have for our relationships?

As is the case with love, there are perhaps as many definitions of jealousy as there are people who experience it. It has been defined somewhat tongue in cheek as "a cry of pain," "the fear of annihilation," and "the shadow of love" (Adams, 1982:39). On a more serious side, however, most researchers on the subject define **jealousy** as the thoughts and feelings that emerge when an actual or desired relationship is believed to be threatened. It is the fear of losing someone whom you love or who is very important to you. To precipitate feelings of jealousy, the perceived threat of loss does not have to be real; instead, it can be potential or even completely imaginary. The key is that we *believe* that the relationship is threatened.

In response to such a perceived threat, jealous people try to protect themselves and/or their love relationship by thoughts, feelings, or actions. Researchers have also found that jealousy involves not one but a number of interrelated emotions including anger, anxiety, uncertainty, fear of loss, vulnerability, hatred, shame, sorrow, humiliation, abandonment, betrayal, loneliness, hopelessness, suspicion, and pain. According to researcher Gordon Clanton (Clanton and Smith, 1986), while jealousy often brings about damage (psychological or physical), it is seldom the case that jealous persons actually mean to do harm. Rather, they usually are simply reacting to one or more of the emotions associated with jealousy, believing that they are protecting either their relationship and/or the "ego of the threatened partner."

There are probably as many definitions of jealousy as there are people who experience this emotion. As with love, women and men differ in terms of how they view and experience jealousy.

Source: Reprinted with special permission of King Features Syndicate.

Jealousy is sometimes confused with or considered to be the same as envy. The two are, however, different emotions. **Envy** refers to unhappiness or discontent with ourselves that arises from the belief that something about ourselves (our personality, achievements, possessions) does not measure up to someone else's level. Envy involves feelings of inferiority, coveting what someone else has, rather than the fear of losing someone (Parrot and Smith, 1987).

A great deal of the research on the topic of jealousy has been conducted by psychologists and social psychologists and thus reflects their concern with the effects of interpersonal attributes on attitudes and behavior. In contrast, a sociological analysis of love and jealousy would focus far more on social-structural and cultural properties, such as norms or collective agreements of a particular society or of particular groups within the society, that govern whom and how we should love and under what circumstances we feel jealous. In this context, jealousy, like love, can be thought of as a social construction, an emotion that is shaped by a person's culture. It is not biologically determined. Thus, what makes people feel jealous will vary from one culture to another and change over time even within a culture.

The Nature and Pattern of Jealousy The causes of jealousy vary from externally to internally induced factors. External factors include behaviors such as flirting or spending excessive amounts of time with someone other than the partner. Studies such as those by social psychologists Ayala Pines and Elliot Aronson (1983) report that most episodes of jealousy arise from external factors. Some cases, however, stem from internal factors that reside in the individual personality and can include feelings of insecurity and distrust learned from previous experiences. Some studies have found, for example, that jealousy is closely associated with low self-esteem and a high level of dependence on one's partner. One study, for example, found that among married couples the individuals who tended most often to be jealous were those who felt insecure about themselves and believed that they would not be successful in getting someone else if their partner left them (Hansen, 1985).

The experience of jealousy varies greatly from relationship to relationship and from individual to individual. Researchers have found, however, that those who are most likely to be jealous are women, people in open or multiple relationships, people who are unhappy with their lives overall or with their love relationship, less educated people, younger people, and people who are unfaithful themselves (Pines and Aronson, 1983; Salovey and Rodin, 1989). Jealousy also varies from one historical period to another and from culture to culture. Examining research studies and records spanning a 200-year period, social psychologist Ralph Hupka (1981, 1985) found consistent differences across cultures in both the degree to which jealousy is present in a society and the ways in which it is expressed. This finding led him to classify societies as either high-jealousy or low-jealousy cultures.

Highly stratified societies and those in which heavy emphasis is placed on sexual exclusiveness, such as in the United States, exhibit a high level of jealousy whereas societies with little or no stratification, where individual property rights are discouraged and sexual gratification and companionship are easily accessible to all people, exhibit a low level of jealousy. A Native American group, the Apaches of North America, are an example of a high-jealousy culture. Among the Apaches, great emphasis is placed on female virginity and on male sexual gratification. Male sexual pleasure must be earned after a prolonged period of deprivation, and it must be judiciously protected from all intruders. Apache wives and children are so important to the status of Apache men that when the men are away from their families, they engage close relatives to watch their wives secretly and report their wives' behavior to them when they return home. In contrast, the Toda of southern India are an example of a low-jealousy culture. Jealousy in this culture is rare because there is little of which to be jealous. The Todas take a sharing attitude toward people and things; neither are defined as personal property. In addition, the Todas place few restrictions on sexual pleasure, and neither marriage nor heirs are prerequisites for social honor and prestige.

Based on his findings of high- and low-jealousy cultures, Hupka concluded that jealousy is not biologically determined; rather it is a learned emotion. We learn what our particular culture defines as valuable and in need of protection. Hupka's findings are consistent with sociological research that suggests that jealousy is a social emotion learned through the socialization process. The existence and expression of jealousy depend very much on how love and love relationships are defined; which people, things, and relationships are valued in a particular society. In other words, jealousy is rooted in the social structure of a society insofar as cultural norms provide the cues that will or will not trigger it. For example, sociologist Kingsley Davis (1977) argued that jealousy is the product of the practice of monogamy. If you are socialized in a society that practices monogamy, cultural norms require you to think of your partner in exclusive terms. Thus, adultery or nonexclusivity is resented and causes jealousy. An interesting example of the influence of socialization and cultural definitions of intimate relationships (that is, monogamy versus nonexclusivity) and the incongruence that sometimes occurs between ideological viewpoints and personal feelings about a valued relationship is provided in Candace Falk's (1984) examination of the life and ideology of Emma Goldman. Goldman, an early feminist (from the early twentieth century), known for her so-called radical political and social views, espoused among other things, the notion of free love and freedom from sexual jealousy. Nonetheless, Falk reports that although Goldman spoke and wrote extensively about the perils and negative impact of jealousy, and the pettiness and small-mindedness of jealous people, Goldman herself was beset by jealousy of her lover, who, although he professed his love for Goldman, had a number of sexual liaisons with other women.

On the other hand, if you were born and raised in a culture such as ancient Japan, where extramarital sexual relationships (or nonexclusivity) was the norm for both women and men and acknowledged publicly, such relationships would not provoke sexual jealousy from either gender (Cherry, 1987). According to Cherry, over time, however, cultural norms surrounding marriage and intimate relationships in Japan changed such that women were gradually prohibited from having extra lovers (extramarital sexual relationships), while men continued to engage in extramarital sexual liaisons with concubines. With this change in cultural norms and expectations, Japanese men could now express jealousy of their wives; however, wives were culturally prohibited from feeling jealousy of their husbands.

Even today in contemporary Japan, while extramarital sexual liaisons are prohibited for both women and men, nonetheless Japanese men (especially businessmen) often seek out and utilize the services of prostitutes. According to Cherry, Japanese wives seldom if ever react to this behavior with jealousy. Rather, they tend to define such behavior as harmless because it does not involve love. In essence, Japanese women have learned within the cultural framework and constructs of their society that they should not be jealous of their husband's indiscretions with prostitutes because such sex is "casual" and is not a threat to their marriage. On the other hand, if the husband has a mistress, Japanese wives become extremely jealous. In this cultural context, a mistress is viewed as very threatening to a marriage in that Japanese men who have mistresses also often have a second set of children as well.

In summary, the cultural basis of jealousy is well illustrated in the facts that (1) the basis for jealousy and the types of behavior appropriate to the expression of jealousy can and often do change over time, (2) the same behavior can provoke different feelings and actions in different cultures (for example, in the United States, given the cultural norm of exclusivity in marriage and intimate relationships, women and men alike are likely to feel and/or express jealousy if their partner has a sexual liaison with another person or persons, regardless of whether or not it is defined as "casual" or "nonthreatening sex"), and (3) within the same culture, the same behavior (for example, the extramarital sexual behavior of husbands) stimulates feelings and expressions of jealousy under one set of circumstances and does not under another set of circumstances.

Gender Differences in Jealousy The literature on jealousy indicates that women and men may experience this emotion differently. Some of the more prevalent findings concerning the differences between women and men in the United States in terms of the ways that they feel and act when they are jealous are

- Women feel jealousy more intensely than men do.
- Jealousy causes women greater suffering and distress than it does men.
- Men are less likely than women to stay in a relationship that makes them jealous (Pines and Aronson, 1983).
- Women are more likely than men to fight to win back a lost lover rather than give up the relationship (Reik, 1946). When men feel jealous they try to repair their self-esteem, whereas women try to repair the relationship (make themselves and the relationship better so that he won't desire another partner) (Shettel-Neuber, Bryson, and Young, 1978).
- Women's feelings of personal inadequacy lead to jealousy, whereas men feel jealousy first, which then leads to feelings of inadequacy, that something is wrong with them.
- Men are more likely than women to express their jealousy in the form of violence. They are also more likely to shift the blame for both their jealousy and their violent response from themselves to a third party (Hoff, 1990).
- Women more often consciously attempt to make their partner jealous as a way of testing the relationship (see if he still cares), of increasing rewards (get their partner to give them more attention or spend more time with them), of bolstering their self-esteem, of getting revenge, or of punishing their partner for some perceived transgression (White, 1980a).

Are any of these gendered patterns of jealousy familiar to you? Are they consistent with your personal experiences with love and jealousy? If not, how do you account for any differences?

DESTRUCTIVE JEALOUSY Although in the past jealousy was considered to be an indication or natural proof of love, today it is increasingly seen as destructive and as a sign of some deficiency in the individual or the relationship. Jealousy can be destructive in terms of the toll it takes on the individual psyche, in the form of deep depression, fear, anxiety, self-doubt, and low self-esteem. It can also be physically damaging and life-threatening when it is expressed in terms of anger, violence, and the desire for revenge.

Some researchers (Smith and Clanton, 1977; Clanton and Smith, 1986) have found that jealousy has some legitimate functions, such as to alert us to threats to our personal security and to our important relationships. Just as physical pain alerts us to threats to our physical well-being, the psychological pain of jealousy alerts us to threats to the security of our love relationships. Jealousy can also be a way of releasing pent-up anxieties and emotions that otherwise could lead to violence. More often than not, however, jealousy is destructive to our relationships.

Managing Destructive Jealousy If jealousy is such a damaging emotion, what can we do either to prevent it or to deal with it in a constructive manner? Social researchers Lynn Smith and Gordon Clanton (1977) suggest four options for dealing with jealousy: (1) Get out of the relationship, (2) ignore or tolerate those behaviors that make you jealous, (3) attempt to change your partner's behavior, and (4) work on your own jealousy. How we manage jealousy depends on the type of jealousy we feel and our commitment to the relationship. If we are interested in maintaining our relationship, we must bring jealousy out in the open. This process involves self-examination: How does jealousy make me feel? How would I prefer to feel? Which actions cause me to feel jealous? Which behaviors or thoughts can I modify to reduce or eliminate my feelings of jealousy?

As we answer these questions, we must look beyond the specific incidents that disturb us to the underlying causes of our jealousy. For example, Is my jealousy caused by my partner's behavior, or is it rooted in my own feelings of inadequacy and low self-esteem? If the latter, perhaps I should try to discover ways to bolster my self-concept and develop self-confidence. We must also evaluate our situation realistically. For example, Is this situation the best for me? Does my partner return my love? If I decide the relationship is worth saving, perhaps I could move beyond my self-analysis of jealousy and share my feelings with my partner. We can share our goals for our relationship and reiterate or redefine what we expect from each other—the kinds of behaviors that are and are not acceptable. In this way, we can work together to change some of the behaviors and attitudes that spark jealous episodes. If these actions fail, both partners might consider counseling or therapy.

Moreover, if we understand the cultural basis of love and jealousy, we can also question the extent to which our personal feelings are rooted in cultural constructions and expectations about intimate relationships in the United States and, thus, the extent to which they are changeable. Whatever course is taken, it should be a collaborative effort. Both parties must agree on how they see the relationship and what they want for the future.

ROMANTIC LOVE TODAY

Heterosexual love and romance in the early years of the twenty-first century reflect the changes that have been evident in the roles of women and men since the emergence of the contemporary women's movement. In the past, female and male roles in love and romance were clearly, if not rigidly, defined, usually as a power relationship characterized by male dominance and female submission. Today, however, dramatic changes have taken place in the relationships between heterosexual lovers, especially among the middle classes. At the same time, however, many traditional aspects of love, dating, intimacy, and mate selection remain firmly entrenched in U.S. society. The result is a great deal of anxiety and uncertainty as couples try to balance traditional norms with current developments in the absence of clear-cut rules and guidelines.

The contemporary women's movement and the subsequent rise in the level of education and employment opportunities for women, in combination with the sexual revolution, have affected the ways in which women and men relate to one another in their intimate relationships. Women have become more independent and more vocal about their desire to control their own destinies. Unlike their foremothers, many women today no longer define themselves in terms of a man or the lack of one.

The changing nature of female and male roles in intimate relationships has left some couples confused about how to relate to each other and has presented a number of problems that hamper the development or maintenance of love relationships. For other lovers or potential lovers, the challenge to traditional male-dominated intimate relations has set the stage for the development of a new, more equitable type of relationship. Many women and men are confronting the conflicts generated by changing gender roles by changing themselves. In general, women and men have accelerated the trend identified by social researchers in the 1980s and 1990s dealing with each other in a new way, "not as one-dimensional entities who fit into narrow and rigid roles but as whole and complete human beings" (Simmons, 1988:139). If this trend continues, as we progress through the twenty-first century, love relationships might be closer to the androgynous love ideal, and lovers may overcome many of the barriers that are currently caused by gender role stereotypes.

WRITING YOUR OWN SCRIPT

A SOCIAL CONSTRUCTION OF LOVE

This chapter has examined the concept of love in Western society, paying particular attention to love as a social construction and the differential experiences of love and the organization of love relationships based on sex or gender, race, and sexual orientation. As the context of this chapter suggests, love is a complex phenomenon, as is our socialization into "love-appropriate" behavior.

Consider how you learned about romantic love and how you learned to behave in culturally appropriate ways within romantic love relationships. Think back to your earliest memories of cultural influences on your views. What did you learn about romantic love from your family? From popular culture? If you have siblings of a different sex, were they given the same messages about romantic love and the appropriate organization of such relationships in your family? In the larger culture? How does your economic class, race, sex/gender, sexual orientation, age, and historical location affect your attitude about and experience of romantic love? Do you agree that romantic love is a meaningless construct outside of a cultural context? If not, why not? Write a brief analysis of a specific romantic love relationship you are currently in (if you are not presently in one, consider a previous relationship or that of someone you know) and critically reflect on it, using the following questions as a guide:

How would you describe each partner in the relationship in terms of gender role ideology: feminine, masculine, androgynous?

What, if any, impact does the organization of gender have on the way in which you and your partner relate to and love each other? Contribute to the success of the relationship?

Are there conflicts regarding intimacy (for example, over sharing intimacy)? Is one partner more self-disclosing than the other? Can this be related in any way to gender/gender role socialization? If so, how?

Think of, at minimum, two factors that contribute to one partner having more power in the relationship than the other.

If you are part of a same-sex romantic love relationship, relate two examples of how myths about same-sex love relationships impact your specific relationship. What effects does homophobia have on your relationship?

Is jealousy present in the relationship? If so, identify and evaluate the source of the jealousy.

Is the jealousy destructive to the relationship? What steps have you taken (or will you take) to change the situation?

Think of, at minimum, two ways in which androgyny or egalitarian gender roles might result in increased intimacy and mutual satisfaction in the relationship.

SUMMARY

Love is a central feature of life in Western societies. References to love can be found throughout popular culture. Because each of us expresses and experiences love differently, there are a variety of definitions of love and many different kinds of love. However, romantic love can be distinguished from other kinds by its erotic component. It can be defined as the intense feelings, emotions, and thoughts coupled with sexual passion and erotic expression that one person directs toward another, as well as the ideology that upholds it. According to a social-constructionist perspective, love can be understood only as symbolic or as a social construction of a particular historical time, location, culture, and people, having by itself no intrinsic meaning. Romantic love is relatively new in human social history. Its developmental roots in Western societies can be traced to ancient Greek and Roman cultures.

Researchers have found that love is extremely important to our physical and emotional health and well-being. Studies of children and adults who have suffered extended isolation from other humans indicate the learned nature of love and our dependence on other people to provide us with the experiences of love. There is great diversity in the ways in which people express romantic love. Some researchers have attempted to define love by isolating its various components, whereas others have defined it in terms of several styles of loving. Still other researchers have distinguished love from friendship, infatuation, and liking.

Ira Reiss uses a wheel analogy to explain love as a developmental process, whereas Robert Sternberg theorizes that love is a story that dictates our beliefs and expectations of love. A popular sociological framework for examining love is social-exchange theory. Using basic economic concepts such as reward, costs, and profits, social-exchange theory explains why people are attracted to and fall in love with one another. Psychologist Dorothy Tennov uses the concept of limerence to refer to a style of love that is characterized by extreme attraction, complete absorption, or obsessive preoccupation of one person with another. Researchers have noted a variety of ways in which women and men differ in terms of how they feel and express love. For example, men fall in love more quickly than women and remain in love longer.

Love is experienced by lesbian and gay couples as well as by heterosexuals. In gay couple relationships, but even more so in lesbian relationships, equality between partners is highly valued, and couples work hard to maintain an egalitarian relationship. Because many lesbians and gays do not allow themselves to be constrained by many of the conventional ways of organizing romantic relationships, they have created egalitarian schemes for dividing up responsibilities and rights within their relationships. Regarding race, little research has been conducted that focuses exclusively on love and the organization of romantic relationships across race. According to that research which exists on African Americans' love relationships, African American women, like most other women, want a lover who is supportive, romantic, openly expressive of his deepest love and feelings, listens attentively to theirs, and above all, is not afraid of commitment. On the other hand, contrary to popular male myths about love, when they are in love, African American men are committed to the relationship and passionate about pleasing the woman they love.

A number of social and political obstacles hamper the development or maintenance of a loving relationship. These include traditional gender role socialization, patriarchy, the lack of trust, and jealousy. Jealousy is the dark side of love and can be detrimental to the development or maintenance of a long-term love relationship. As with love, jealousy can best be understood as a social construction, that is, as an emotion that is largely shaped by a given culture. In addition, as with love, there are gender differences in the expression of jealousy. We can manage or eliminate jealousy by looking inward and working out the problems that make us susceptible to jealousy, or we can talk to our partner. We can also share with her or him our feelings and expectations for the future of the relationship while coming to an agreement about what behaviors are and are not acceptable within the relationship.

Heterosexual romance today reflects the changes that have been evident in the roles of women and men since the contemporary women's movement. In general, women and men in the 1990s accelerated earlier trends toward dealing with each other on a more equitable basis. If this trend continues as we progress through the twenty-first century, romantic love relationships might be increasingly androgynous or egalitarian in nature.

KEY TERMS

romantic love
love map
eros
ludus
storge
mania
pragma
agape
infatuation
liking
wheel theory of love
limerence
androgynous
trust
jealousy
envy

QUESTIONS FOR STUDY AND REFLECTION

1. What does being in love mean to you? Are love and romance necessary for a satisfying intimate relationship? Explain. What is the difference between liking, loving, and infatuation? Have you ever loved someone without liking her or him? Is it important to like the person you love? To be her or his friend? Can a relationship last without these elements? Explain.
2. Using Ira Reiss's wheel theory of love, consider your own love relationships. How do they fit into this model of love as a developing process? Does your love relationship deviate from the Reiss model? How would you explain this? Are all of his stages healthy for a love relationship?
3. Research indicates that our ability to establish and maintain love relationships is profoundly impacted by our childhood experiences and the development of self-love. In some families, children are given positive feedback and are often told verbally that they are important and that they are loved, while in others the expression of love is more subtle, or absent altogether. When you were growing up, did you receive positive feedback? Were you verbally told that you were loved? How were you shown that you were loved? Do you think these early childhood experiences have had an impact on your self-esteem? On how you show love today? Explain.
4. What do sociologists mean when they say that love, romance, and jealousy are socially constructed? What evidence do you see of this process in popular culture, particularly the media that you watch, hear, or read? If love is a social construction, what can heterosexual couples learn from lesbian and gay couples' organization of love relationships? Explain.

ADDITIONAL RESOURCES

SOCIOLOGICAL

ABRAHAM, LAURIE, L. GREEN, J. MAGDA KRANCE, J. ROSENBERG, AND C. STONER, EDS. 1993. *Reinventing Love: Six Women Talk about Lust, Sex, and Romance.* New York: Plume. An interesting personal account of six women's experiences of love, including first love, sex, romance, love partners, and problems in love relationships.

CLARK, DON. 1987. *The New Loving Someone Gay.* Millbrae, CA: Celestial Arts. A very good examination and discussion of lesbian and gay relationships.

HENDRICK, SUSAN, AND CLYDE HENDRICK. 1992. *Liking, Loving, and Relating.* Belmont, CA: Wadsworth. An up-to-date, comprehensive overview of personal relationships with discussions on attraction, love, and sexuality. It includes recent research data and case studies.

NARDI, PETER M., ED. 1992. *Men's Friendships.* Newbury Park, CA: Sage. An excellent collection of articles and research pertaining to men's friendships, intimacy, sexual boundaries, and gender roles.

LITERARY

SEGAL, ERICH. 1988. *Love Story.* New York: Bantam Books (c. 1970). A wonderful heartfelt classic love story about a rich Harvard jock and a wisecracking Radcliffe music major who have nothing in common but love and everything to share but a lifetime. It is often described as not just a love story but an experience and one that all college students should have. This novel was made into a film that might seem dated today, but the words of the author remain contemporary. An excellent way to provoke class discussion about love, death, and dying and how Americans deal with each.

WALLER, ROBERT JAMES. 1997. *The Bridges of Madison County.* New York: Warner Books. A legendary love story about a 52-year-old *National Geographic* photographer and free spirit who comes to Madison County on assignment and a 45-year-old farm wife and mother of two children waiting for the fulfillment of a girlhood dream. This book raises a number of sociological issues, including extramarital love/love affairs, love and the intersections of age and gender, and forbidden love.

INTERNET

http://www.lovingyou.com This site provides a library of love stories, poetry, cards, and dedications. It also includes chat groups, relationship advice, and a variety of links to other romantic-oriented sites.

www.studentadvantage.com/dating This site provides dating and relationship information.

Chapter 5

Dating, Coupling, and Mate Selection

IN THE NEWS: **ARLINGTON, VIRGINIA**

College women looking for Mr. Right might be looking in the wrong place if they expect to find him on campus, so says a recent study titled "Hooking Up, Hanging Out, and Hoping for Mr. Right: College Women on Dating and Mating Today." The 18-month study of the attitudes and values of today's college women regarding sexuality, dating, courtship, and marriage was commissioned by the Independent Women's Forum and conducted by the Institute for American Values' 16-member Courtship Research Team, led by sociologist Norval Glenn and an institute affiliate, Elizabeth Marquardt. The study was based on telephone interviews with a nationally representative sample of 1000 college women and interviews with 62 women on 11 college campuses.

According to the research report, college women are confused about the dating-mating game on campus, protesting that they basically have two options: "hooking up" briefly with a guy for casual sex or being joined at the hip and virtually living together. They feel that they either have too little or too much commitment, neither of which contributes much to finding a husband while in college, a goal 63 percent of the women studied at least partly embrace. This doesn't mean they want to get married on graduation day, says Marquardt. But many of these women see the college campus as their last great chance to meet the opposite sex.

The researchers found that "hookups" are common and the major reason for the lack of clarity about relationships. About 40 percent of the women said they had experienced a hookup and 10 percent reported having done so more than six times. Although the women's definition of a hookup varied, 75 percent agreed that it was when a woman and a man get together for a physical encounter and don't necessarily expect anything further. According to these women, a "physical encounter" can mean anything from kissing to having sex, both without emotional involvement. Typically, "hookup" partners are almost strangers and have been drinking or are drunk. Most women are ambivalent about hookups and report a range of feelings about the practice from feeling desirable to feeling awkward if they had hoped for some grander relationship. Some women reported feeling strong, desirable, and sexy.

The flip side of this dating coin is what the researchers call the "joined at the hip" relationship that develops quickly, is very intense and exclusive, and involves sharing everything. At the same time, dating is also synonymous with "hanging out," in which women and men spend loosely organized, undefined time together, without making their interest in one another explicit, unless they hook up, at which point dating and hooking up become one and the same. It seems that women and men on college campuses no longer "date" in the old-fashioned sense. For example, only about 50 percent of college women seniors reported having been asked out on six or more dates by men since coming to college, and a third of the women surveyed said they had been asked out on only two dates or fewer. Moreover, many of the old rituals of dating are gone. Today, men rarely acknowledge being part of a couple, and the only ritual that researchers found was "The Talk," in which women ask, "Are we committed or not?" When she asks, he decides ("Hooking Up, Hanging Out," 2001; Peterson, 2001).

WHAT WOULD YOU DO? If you are single and open to dating, would you "hook up"? If you are married, would you have engaged in this form of dating when you were single? As a parent, would you encourage or discourage your offspring from engaging in such dating practices? Explain.

Dating, coupling, and mating—these concepts call up a variety of images. Close your eyes. What images come to mind when you think about dating in U.S. society today? Do you think of youth, "swinging," sex, "singles," fun, marriage, or love? Do you think of college campuses where hundreds of young women and men rub elbows and do you think of couples "hooking up" and "hanging out"? Many of these are familiar images associated with dating and mate selection in the United States, images that are relentlessly transmitted through the media. Do these images match the reality of your life? Do they match the reality of the lives of most unmarried people? Do they match the reality of mate selection for your parents? Your grandparents?

As this mental exercise might have illustrated, for many people the idea of dating and mate selection brings to mind love, marriage, and family. Traditionally, we have assumed that attraction leads to dating, dating to love, and love to marriage. Indeed, we have assumed that the major function of dating is to teach people to form intimate heterosexual relationships and to prepare people for marriage. As the "In the News" discussion of dating suggests, this sequence of attraction, dating, love, marriage, and family is still espoused and held onto by many, particularly college women. And the researchers who conducted the study reported in the "In the News" story that opened this chapter obviously fall into this camp as well, given that in the study's recommendations the authors stress that young people must be guided with sensitivity and support toward marriage. They posit that socially defined dating and courtship is an important pathway to more successful marriages. However, this is frequently not the viewpoint for many others. An increasing number of people are either delaying marriage or not marrying at all. Some are pursuing alternatives to marriage (see Chapter 7). Still others, as the research indicates, simply "hook up" and/or "hang out" with little hope that it will lead to marriage, if that is the goal. In addition, not all dating is heterosexual. As we discuss more fully later in this chapter, like heterosexual couples, lesbian and gay couples date for recreational and entertainment purposes, but the development of love and long-term relationships are most often the goal. And finally, many dating relationships are based solely on material or sexual interests, not on notions of romantic love.

So what does this mean for current relationships among both heterosexual and homosexual couples? Is today's pattern of mate selection a continuation of trends of the past? Are dating relationships and mate selection really that different today than they were 50 years ago? A century ago? Are they the same around the world?

Specific courtship procedures, like mate selection generally, have varied considerably from one culture to another and from one historical period to another. In the next section we explore some of the historical and cross-cultural trends in courtship, dating, and mate selection.

MATE SELECTION IN CROSS-CULTURAL AND HISTORICAL PERSPECTIVE

Did you know that dating is not a common practice in most countries? In general, when we speak of **dating** we are referring to a process of pairing off that involves the open choice of mates and engagement in activities that allow people to get to know each other and progress toward coupling and mate selection. In places such as China, India, South America, and most countries in Africa, dating is very rare. In addition, it is forbidden in most Muslim countries, including Iraq, Egypt, Iran, and Saudi Arabia. Only in Western countries such as the United States, Great Britain, Australia, and Canada is dating a common form of mate selection. In these countries, dating is perhaps the single most important method by which people get acquainted with each other, learn to interact heterosexually, and select a mate.

Sociologists use the term **mate selection**[1] to refer loosely to the wide range of behaviors and social relationships individuals engage in prior to marriage and that lead to long- or short-term pairing or coupling. An essential element in mate selection is **courtship,** a process of selecting a mate and developing an intimate relationship. Dating is simply one stage in the courtship process, a process that involves an increasing level of commitment that might culminate with the ultimate commitment, marriage. Whatever its end, mate selection is an institutionalized feature of social life. According to family sociologist Ira Reiss (1980), all known societies exhibit some form of courtship, marriage, and family that ensures the production and nurturing of young people. The process of mate selection ranges from agreements and arrangements among religious or community leaders or the families of prospective partners to choices made by the partners themselves with only limited consultation with parents or other relatives.

Mate Selection Cross-Culturally

How do people around the world select a marriage or life partner? As we have indicated, in Western societies some form of courtship and dating is the major process used to select a mate. However, most of the world's societies do not have the "open" courtship and dating system common in the United States and other Western nations. Rather, mate selection varies across a continuum of practices around the world. These customs range from arranged matches by village shamans who match mates according to astrological signs; to contractual arrangements between families (usually fathers), in which a mate may be required to serve as an indentured servant to the bride's parents; to the outright purchase of a mate; to the seemingly free choice of individuals based on criteria ranging from notions of love to physical attractiveness to economic considerations. In some cultures, mate selection begins as early as infancy, in others the process begins at 8 or 9 years of age, and in still others it begins in late adulthood.

Much of the literature on mate selection cross-culturally differentiates methods of mate selection according to a traditional/nontraditional or industrialized/nonindustrialized dichotomy. In most traditional (nonindustrialized) societies, for example, family and/or religious groups try to preserve cultural consistency, family unity, friendship, and religious ties through arranged marriages. For instance, among the Hopi, ancient Chinese, Hebrews, and Romans,

[1]The term *mate selection* is used consistently in marriage and family literature in descriptions of the process of dating and marriage. However, we thought it was worth noting an interesting and somewhat humorous request from a reviewer of this textbook, who asked if we could change our language from *mate selection* to *partner selection* because the term *mate selection* sounds rather like "two lions looking for each other out in the Kalahari desert." What do you think?

Dating and mate selection rituals vary across cultures. Some practices, like those of the Wodaabe of Niger, Africa, where men dress as females to attract brides, may seem strange to North Americans. However, the liberal, unchaperoned dating and mating practices of North Americans appear strange to those whose customs include arranged marriages and the absence of courting.

mating was arranged by the head of the kinship group, who continued to exercise some degree of control over young people even after they married. These practices continue in many traditional cultures today. For example, in India, arranged marriages, complete with ostentatious receptions and large dowries provided by the bride's family, continue to dominate the mate selection process. In order to preserve family loyalty, marriages continue to be carefully arranged, with brides and grooms rarely choosing their own mate. Arranged marriage stems from a cultural concern with family unity and family cooperation. Thus, the background of a potential bride or groom is just as important as individual personality traits when two families join through marriage. Moreover, since most Indians look on marriage as a lifelong commitment and view divorce as a shameful tragedy, it is customary to call on the wisdom of family elders and ask them to search out and investigate potential mates (Lessinger, 2002). Many young people not only expect their elders to choose a mate for them, but prefer that they do so.

In this mate selection process, there is little or no opportunity for the couple to interact with one another, get to know one another before the matching, or freely decide to be a couple, remain a couple, or to marry. The goal is marriage, and potential mates do not typically meet until the day of the wedding and, most often, have not even seen pictures of one another (Ramu, 1989). Families negotiate issues of money, status, health, and even physical appearance so as to make the best or most profitable match. Arranged marriages serve important social functions. For example, they serve to extend existing family units and they reinforce ties with other families in the community, thereby strengthening the social order and organization of the community (Lee and Stone, 1980).

The advantages of arranged marriages have been pointed out both by researchers as well as by various individuals who participate in this cultural pattern. According to researchers on the subject, arranged marriages tend to be very stable. Divorce is almost unheard of, except in cases where one of the persons is infertile. In addition, although romantic love is not a consideration in these matches, love grows between the couple over the years; the relationships are generally very harmonious; and because there is no courtship period, premarital sexual intimacy and pregnancy are minimal to nonexistent. Many people who participate in a system of arranged mate selection, particularly those who immigrate to Western societies, find it preferable to "free-choice" mate selection. Women in particular say that arranged mate selection spares them the "hassle" or "silliness" of dating such as spending an inordinate amount of time trying to attract, snare, and keep a man; worrying whether you are attractive enough or whether you are too fat; wondering whether the man will discard you without any concern for your self-respect. Unlike in American dating, for example, in arranged systems of mate selection there is very little risk of being rejected (Temple, 1998).

Not all traditional societies subscribe to a pattern of arranged mate selection. For example, G. N. Ramu (1989) describes a traditional society in Mexico, the Tepoztlan, in which individuals (especially men), not parents, take the initiative in mate selection. In this culture young men initiate mate selection by writing a love letter to a young woman whom he is interested in marrying. If the young woman responds favorably to the letter, then a meeting between the two is arranged. If she does not respond, then the young man must start the process all over again with someone else.

Political, social, and/or economic change, especially industrialization, in cultures around the world has brought about some significant changes in mate selection customs cross-culturally. For example, in some cities in India today, mate selection combines the traditional aspects of arranged marriages with various nontraditional methods. Among the middle classes, traditional matchmakers or marriage brokers are often replaced by advertisements in newspapers and the use of computer dating services to find a mate. This modern method of arranged marriages is not confined to India. Immigration has added a number of features that are not part of the traditional institution of arranged marriages. In the United States, for example, advertisements in immigrant newspapers like *India Abroad* give an indication of how the institution of arranged marriages is changing and adapting to Western (American) culture. Researcher Johanna Lessinger (2002) points out how, within the framework of arranged marriages, these ads show a noticeable decline in the importance placed on caste, language group, and even religion in mate selection if people are otherwise compatible in terms of education and profession. In addition, increasing attention is paid to individual and personal qualities such as a sense of humor or weight and beauty.

Moreover, "semiarranged" marriage has become a feature of upper-middle-class mate selection in both India and the United States. This process involves parents introducing suitable, prescreened potential mates to their offspring, who are then allowed a courtship period during which to decide if they like each other well enough to marry. This process allows parents to retain some control in the mate selection process while accommodating their children's desires for a "love relationship," fueled by both the Indian and American media (Lessinger, 2002).

In some societies, a shortage of marriageable women has significantly changed traditional patterns of mate selection. For example, while mate selection customs in traditional Chinese society consisted of parent-arranged marriages in which the bride's parents received a "bride price," the mating process changed considerably during the 1990s, when there was a dramatic decrease in the number of marriageable women. According to Chinese census data, the ratio of single men to women was about three to one. Although in the past the majority of Chinese adults were married by age 30, in the mid-1990s more than 8 million Chinese in their 30s had not yet married, and the ratio of men to women in this age group was a staggering ten to one.

A leading explanation for the scarcity of adult females centers on the desire of many Chinese couples to have a boy rather than a girl. This preference for male babies has resulted in a high percentage of Chinese girls dying before adulthood due to poor nutrition, inadequate medical care, desertion, and even infanticide, or murder, at the hands of their parents. After generations of tampering with nature, it appears that millions of Chinese men today will live out their lives as bachelors because there are simply not enough women available.

Among other factors, this shortage of women in the pool of potential mates has led to a shift from traditional means of mate selection to new and unconventional means (by Chinese standards) of finding a mate. For example, Chinese women and men increasingly use computer dating services to help them find a mate. The first computer dating service opened in Beijing in 1989, and even the government has gotten into the mate selection process with several government-sponsored computer dating and matchmaking services.

Seventy percent of those using computer dating services are males. The scarcity of Chinese women has given them a newly found edge in a mate selection process that historically treated them as chattel. The down side of Chinese women's leverage in mate selection, and a jolting reminder of their continued oppression, can be seen in an observation made by Chinese sociologists and journalists: "With men unable to find wives as sexual partners there could be an increase in prostitution, rape, and among men, suicide" (Shenon, 1994:5). In addition, as a result of the shortage of Chinese women, there has been a significant rise in the numbers of bounty hunters, who kidnap city women and deliver them to rural farmers desperate for brides.

A transformation of the mate selection process as a result of the glut of single men is occurring in other nations as well. Often this transformation combines modern contemporary demands and traditional customs. For example, based on figures put out by the United Nations, India, with nearly 900 million people, has a sex ratio among the single population of 133 men to every 100 women. As in China, Indian custom values males (Shenon, 1994).

In nonindustrialized nations and often in rural areas within industrialized nations, mate selection continues to be predominantly arranged. For example, in Turkey (a predominantly rural country), three-fourths of all marriages are arranged (Fox, 1980). On the other hand, in Japan, a highly industrialized society today, traditional arranged coupling and mate selection has given way to matches and relationships based on love. However, as in China, there is a shortage of eligible women for mate selection. The scarcity of available Japanese women is the result of a number of social factors, including higher levels of education among women, more women entering the labor force, and an increasing number of women delaying marriage to a later age or opting to remain single. This has left a high percentage of Japanese men without mates. While matchmakers still operate in the mate selection arena in Japan, their roles have changed significantly to include teaching Japanese men how to court and select a wife (Thornton, 1994).

Mate Selection in the United States: A Historical Perspective

Historically, mate selection in the United States has been based on notions of romantic love, a sentiment shared by both women and men. For most contemporary Americans, choosing a mate is the culmination of the process of dating, although not necessarily its goal. Although dating, by definition, is supposed to be separate from selecting a marriage partner, many Americans nonetheless expect that dating will provide them with valuable experience that will help them make an informed choice of a marriage partner ("Hooking Up, Hanging Out," 2001; Whyte, 2001). However, courtship and dating are about much more than simply leading one to a marital partner. They are also about economic relationships, family control (or the lack thereof), power dynamics, competition, popularity, having sex, recreation, and consumption patterns (Ferguson, 2001). Dating has been described by some social commentators (for example, Waller, 1937) as a "courtship game" that has its own set of rules, strategies, and goals. Over time, changing gender norms and power dynamics have contributed to adjustments, adaptations, and/or modifications in the rules and expectations of mate selection, culminating in the process we recognize today. Thus, contemporary patterns of mate selection are linked to our past.

EARLY U.S. COURTSHIP AND THE DEVELOPMENT OF DATING As in many societies around the world, mate selection in the United States has always centered on heterosexual pairing or coupling. Since the process was meant to lead to legal marriage, historical descriptions and early mate selection research focused only on heterosexual couples. Thus, the discussion that follows is based on historical and research data for heterosexual mate selection.

In the early history of the United States mate selection was characterized by community/family/parental control over the process. For example, it included an array of activities, almost all of which involved couples keeping company under family or community supervision. In colonial times marriage was considered to be of utmost importance in bringing order and stability to daily family living. Thus, there was a stress on coupling and mate selection. During this period couples came together through a variety of means, including matrimonial advertisements and third-party go-betweens. Demographic considerations as well as very precise cultural norms often dictated the ways in which couples came together (Ramu, 1989). For example, due to a severe shortage of women in the American colonies, different patterns of mate selection evolved. Some men cohabited with Native American women; others imported brides from across the Atlantic. Moreover, the requirement of parental approval of a mate, especially among the prosperous classes, put further constraints on the mate selection process for young people. For example, throughout this period, young people tended to marry in birth order, and marriage to cousins was not uncommon (Ferguson, 2001).

As the eighteenth century progressed, explicit rules continued to govern the courting process. Although parents could not legally choose a partner for their offspring, they continued to exercise considerable power over mate selection. Daughters, in particular, were strictly supervised. If a young man wanted to court a young woman, he had to meet her family, get their permission to court her, and be formally introduced to her. In fact, colonial law required a man to secure the permission of a woman's father before he could court her. Even after a man gained permission to court a particular woman and the two people were formally introduced, they were often chaperoned (especially upper-class women) at social events.

This process of mate selection eventually assumed a formal pattern referred to as "calling." In this form of mate selection, the initiative and control were in the hands of women. For example, a male suitor would be invited to call upon a female at her home. He was expected to come "calling" only if he was invited to do so. The invitation usually came from the mother of the woman, but eventually the woman herself extended the invitation. If a woman had several suitors at one time, a man might be told that the woman was not at home to receive him. In this instance, he was expected to leave his calling card. If this happened many times, it was meant to give the man the message that the woman was no longer interested in him (Whyte, 2001).

If a serious relationship developed between a couple, they advanced from calling to "keeping company." Keeping company was a very formal and upright relationship that developed only after people had become attracted to or felt romantic about each other. According to Martin Whyte (2001), keeping company was a precursor of the twentieth-century custom of "going steady." Unlike in calling, couples who kept company were expected to be monogamous; that is, a woman was expected to keep company with only one man.

Keeping company involved a variety of activities, and couples kept company in some unique and interesting ways. For example, in colonial New England, unmarried couples practiced bundling, in which they spent the night in bed together, wrapped in bundling blankets or separated only by a long wooden bundling board down the middle of the bed. Only the outer garments could be removed, and the woman sometimes was placed in a sack sealed at the neck. This arrangement evolved in response to harsh winters and the difficulty of traveling, both of which made it difficult for a young man to return home after an evening of courting. Although such a practice would seem to discourage sexual contact, it apparently did not. Researchers Daniel Smith and Michael Hindus (1975) have estimated that approximately one-third of all eighteenth-century brides were pregnant at the time of their wedding.

Significant for the evolving pattern of dating in the United States were industrialization; the rise of free, public, coeducational, and mandatory schooling; and the mass movement of women (predominantly working-class women) into the mills and factories, allowing them increased contact with men. These events helped loosen parents' hold on their children. However, the mass production of the automobile probably had the most profound impact on the course of mate selection in North America. The automobile increased the mobility of young people and made a number of activities and places accessible to them. It also gave young people a new and private place for **getting together,** a pattern of dating that involves women and men meeting in groups, playing similar roles in initiating dates, and sharing equally in the cost of activities. Initiative and control in the mate selection process shifted from women to men. Men now asked women out, instead of waiting to be invited to call upon women. And courting moved from the parlor to the front seats and backseats of cars, resulting in the emergence and institutionalization of dating. Some social scientists have gone so far as to suggest that the automobile became, in some sense, a "bundling bed on wheels."

Dating in the United States: The 1920s through the 1990s By the 1920s, amid the increased affluence and leisure of the white middle classes, dating became the major method of mate selection in this country. The affluence and leisure of the white middle class gave rise to a youth culture whose members were relatively free to pursue their personal interests and social life. The rigid Victorian sex ethic (see Chapter 6) of the past was replaced with a new sexual intimacy as part of the courtship process. Couples took the initiative to get to know each other; they dated for fun, pleasure, relaxation, and recreation rather than with marriage as the primary goal. This new method of mate selection moved from one controlled by parents to one based on the open and mutual choice of peers. The initiative, and much of the control that females once had in mate selection, now shifted to the male as men asked women out rather than waiting for her invitation to "call."

The term *dating* originally referred to a specific date, time, and place of meeting. Thus, to speak of dating simply meant that two people of the opposite sex met at a mutually agreed-upon place and time and engaged in conversation. Dating has not remained constant over the decades. A variety of sociopolitical and historical factors such as the Great Depression of the 1930s, World War II, and the middle-class prosperity of the 1950s helped to shape dating as we know it today.

During the 1920s and 1930s dating was especially visible on college campuses. Although college students represented only a small and select portion of America's youth—primarily white and middle class—their activities and behavior became the model for other youth. In a pioneering study of college dating patterns, sociologist Willard Waller (1937) described dating on college campuses in the 1920s and 1930s as a competitive system that involved rating prospective partners based on clear standards of popularity. Material signs included owning an automobile, possessing the right clothing, belonging to the right fraternity or sorority, and, of course, having money. By the 1930s, **going steady**—an exclusive relationship with one person—was a clear and entrenched part of the mate selection process. It was an intermediate stage between casual dating and engagement. With the stock market crash of the late 1920s, the prohibition of liquor, and the depression of the 1930s, the national mood changed dramatically. However, the changes that occurred in popular culture, and their impact on mate selection and dating, continued to be visible in later decades.

During the 1940s and 1950s, dating spread from college campuses to most cultural groups in the United States. During this period, dating became essentially a filtering process in the sense that a person dated many people before settling down with one person. Only then did serious dating or courtship begin, with the ultimate goal being marriage (Ramu, 1989). Acceptance of the idea that dating should culminate in marriage seems to be reflected in the fact that the 1950s had the highest percentage of married adults on record (Cherlin, 1981).

Researcher Ersel LeMasters (1957) described going steady as an important dating pattern of the 1940s and 1950s. According to LeMasters, dating involved six stages of progressively deeper commitment from the first date in the junior high school years to marriage in the late teens or early 20s. Going steady, the third stage, occurred somewhere in the late high school years and involved a transition from the first two stages, the noncommitment of casual dating in junior high school and the random dating in the early high school years. The fourth stage occurred in college, when the couple entered into an informal agreement to date each other exclusively. The final two stages were engagement and marriage. This sequential model of dating tended to be more common among the middle classes than among other classes. According to researchers, lower-income and working-class youth tended to speed up the process, generally marrying at an earlier age.

Like other cultural patterns, dating patterns incorporate many of the values of the larger society. Thus, dating in the 1940s and 1950s clearly revealed U.S. society's emphasis on traditional gender roles, marriage, and the sexual double standard, with the male being the aggressor and the female playing a submissive role. For example, it was up to the male to initiate the date, and the female, in a dependent mode, had to wait to be picked or asked out. The male then was expected to pick up the female at her home, take her to a place of his choosing, pay for all expenses, and return her to her home at a respectable hour. The sexual double standard was also evident in the desired outcomes of dating. For males a primary expected outcome of dating was sex, whereas for females it was commitment and marriage. Although women exercised some degree of control through their ability to give or withhold their affection and their bodies, the absence of parental control and pressure to respond to a man's initiatives put women in a weaker position than they had been under the earlier system of "calling."

During the 1960s and 1970s, changing sexual norms, the increasing availability of contraceptives, a decline in parental authority, and the increasing activism of young people helped reverse the conservative dating trends of the 1940s and 1950s. Dating was transformed into a casual and spontaneous form of courtship. Greatly influenced by the women's movement, women no longer waited to be asked out but instead began to initiate dates and intimate relationships. There was an increasing emphasis on each person paying her or his own way. This was particularly common among middle-class youth, who were financially more independent than poor and working-class youths (Ramu, 1989). Paying one's own way was seen as a way of reducing the exploitation of young women by males who, in the past, expected sexual favors in return for the money spent on dating.

By the late 1960s people were delaying marriage to a later age. Sexual intimacy, which had traditionally been closely confined to marriage or the courtship period that led directly to marriage, became a common part of dating. The increasing separation of sex from marriage during the 1960s and 1970s was probably most evident in the rising number of couples living together outside legal marriage. During the 1970s, *cohabitation*—living together without being legally married—became a common extension of the traditional dating continuum, especially on college campuses among urban middle-class whites, and served as either an alternative or adjunct to steady dating and engagement (Gwartney-Gibbs, 1986). Cohabitation is discussed in detail in Chapter 7.

In the 1980s and 1990s, dating started at an earlier age and lasted longer than it had in previous generations. Adolescents as young as 13 years of age participated in some form of dating or pairing off, a decrease in age of 3 years since World War I. If we consider the fact that the average age at first marriage in the 1980s was somewhere around 25, then the average person in the United States was dating and courting for over 10 years before getting married. As the age at first marriage continued to increase slightly in the 1990s, more people were spending more time in a number of dating relationships with a variety of people before marrying, if they married at all.

The longer period of dating for most people also contributed to a change in the ways dating in the last two decades of the twentieth century was structured and perceived. There is some consensus among sociologists that although most Americans continued to find mates through dating of some sort in the 1990s, dating was no longer what it was prior to the mid 1960s. Not only had the structure and content of dating changed, but so had the terminology. The terms *dating* and *going steady* became passé, replaced with terms such as *seeing*, *being with*, *going with someone*, *hooking up*, and *hanging out*. Although some people continued to date in the traditional pattern, in which each person has specific roles to play, most people preferred to say they were "going out" with someone. According to some researchers, not only did the terminology of mate selection change, but dating itself became passé. These researchers argue that dating was replaced by informal pairing off in larger groups, often without the prearrangement of asking someone out (Whyte, 2001).

Contemporary Trends in Dating Although the term *dating* was less commonly used in the 1980s and 1990s, the practice nonetheless continues, albeit in different forms. Today, dating is based far more on mutuality and sharing than on traditional gender roles. The 1990s trend of dating as recreation and entertainment, with an emphasis on sociability, continues to cause a change in the pattern or progression of intimacy and commitment from initial meeting to marriage. Describing contemporary mate selection in the United States, a colleague of ours commented, with some degree of frustration: "People don't date anymore: they just get together; they just have sex, live together, and then go their separate ways." While this was a nonscientific observation, it is nonetheless fairly consistent with scientific research that reports that contemporary dating patterns include considerably more casual sexual involvements and fewer committed relationships than in the past.

Dating is no longer necessarily the means to the end of marriage. Getting together, hanging out, or generally sharing fun activities on a date is now an end in itself.

Recall, for example, the research reported on at the beginning of this chapter. Looking specifically at dating among college women, the researchers found that women and men on college campuses may "hang out," spending time together, but they do not "date" in the old-fashioned sense. According to the researchers, dating carries multiple meanings for college women today. Although they found evidence of four widely used and different meanings for the term, the two most common were "hooking up" and "joined at the hip." On the one hand, the dating pattern might be a "hookup," wherein two people get together briefly for casual sex without any emotional commitment. On the other hand, a college couple who is "dating" is sometimes in a fast-moving, highly committed relationship that includes sexual activity, sleeping at one another's dorm most nights, studying together, sharing meals, and more. Rarely, though, does it involve going out on "dates" ("Hooking Up, Hanging Out," 2001).

This dating pattern on college campuses notwithstanding, in general young adults believe that current patterns of dating are more natural and healthier than they were in the past. Although, as in every generation, some couples still follow a traditional pattern, for many couples dating, sexual intimacy, living together, becoming engaged, and sometimes having a child have become a common part of heterosexual relationships that may or may not culminate in marriage.

Moreover, today people are ever more aware that mate selection is not just a heterosexual phenomenon, nor is dating just for the young at heart. Dating (or whatever term we choose to use) involves lesbians and gays, the very young as well as an increasing number of older people who either have never married or are divorced or widowed. Although dating among older adults differs somewhat from dating among high school and college students, many similarities exist. This is especially the case in terms of dating as recreation and entertainment.

Dating among the general population, like on college campuses, has become very time-contained, sometimes existing only for the moment for sexual or recreational purposes, with no pretense that it is a prelude to courtship or marriage. New trends in dating in the twenty-first century have led some observers to suggest that dating is no longer the self-evident activity that it was in the past. That is, what constitutes dating today has become so ambiguous that many singles, after "getting together" with someone they like, find themselves wondering afterward if it was a date or not. For example, a special contributor to the *Chicago*

Dating in the twenty-first century takes many forms. Today it is not unusual to see homosexuals as well as heterosexuals enjoying each other's company. Some individuals prefer to share fun activities within a group setting.

Tribune recently wrote that he and an old work acquaintance had gotten together over beers a couple of times, and everything seemed to be going well until he called to invite her to a concert whereupon she asked: "Are these things dates? Because I enjoy talking with you, but I don't think I want to date" (McKeough, 2001:2). Similarly, a 32-year-old Chicago woman indicated that she had had a million dates where she thinks: "I don't know, maybe he just wants to be friends. If I think of [him] as a friend, I won't be hurt if [he] is not into me" (quoted in McKeough, 2001:2). According to Jeff Wise, a self-defined "media coordinator" for the American Dating Association, based in Los Angeles, there is such a thing today as a *non-date date*. When two people go out, if one person is not aware of the romantic intentions of the other then it's a non-date date. Risk avoidance is at the base of this kind of getting together—avoiding getting hurt if the person you're getting together with ultimately rejects you (McKeough, 2001).

Although much of the discussion of contemporary dating patterns is descriptive of the white middle class, with some limitations it can be generalized to other groups. Later in this chapter we pay particular attention to the intersection of race, class, gender, and sexual orientation in patterns of dating.

Functions of Dating: Past and Present

As we have seen, dating no longer implies that marriage is inevitable, or even desirable. Of all the stages in the mate selection process, dating is the one that carries the least commitment to continuing the relationship. So why do people date? The reasons are many and varied; however, researchers have identified some specific functions dating fulfills for the individual and, ultimately, for society's continuity. The meaning and functions of dating, of course, depend in large part on the person's age and sex and the particular stage in the dating process. One researcher, G. N. Ramu (1989), summarizes the functions of dating in terms of socialization, recreation, status grading and achievement, and mate selection leading to marriage. As you consider these functions of dating, bear in mind that they have been formulated primarily with young heterosexual couples in mind.

Socialization The socialization function usually occurs in the early stages of dating. Through dating, people learn the norms, roles, and values that govern heterosexual relationships. One impact of the women's movement has been to change the ways in which some women and men define their roles in intimate relationships. Thus, for example, if a man finds he cannot accept an aggressive, self-confident, and self-reliant partner, or a woman finds that she will not accept a passive role, dating helps them to discover this and to realize what kind of roles they are willing to play in an intimate relationship. Dating is a competitive situation in which an individual can test and refine a number of interactive skills with respect to the opposite sex. For young people, dating also provides an opportunity for sexual experimentation and growth. Obviously, the socialization function of dating is not limited to heterosexual or young couples. Socialization does not end in our youth, and it therefore continues to be an important function of dating even as we grow older.

In addition, the socialization function of dating can serve to enhance the ego or sense of self. According to anthropologist Margaret Mead (1935), a major way that we develop a personality and gain a sense of self is through our relationships with other people. If a positive self-concept is attributable in part to successful experiences with others, then an important stage in an individual's personality development can occur during successful dating experiences. If the dating experience goes well it can have the impact of enhancing our self-confidence and self-esteem.

Recreation For most people, regardless of age, dating provides an opportunity to relax, have fun, and enjoy themselves in the company of someone they like. Ramu (1989) and other social scientists distinguish between adolescent and adult patterns when discussing the recreational function of dating. The assumption is that dating in adolescence serves a recreational function (the seeking of fun and thrills): It is often an end in itself. In contrast, in adulthood it involves courtship, often directed toward finding a marriage partner.

Status Grading and Achievement Most Americans view dating in positive terms. Thus, the more one dates, the more likely one's status and popularity will increase. Status grading and achievement in dating is a process whereby women and men are classified according to their desirability as dating partners. For example, very often on college campuses, people try to date those people who are rated as the most desirable on campus, for example, females seeking to date the most popular athletes on campus and males seeking to date the most attractive females, to boost their own status and prestige.

According to Ramu (1989), although this principle may have been operable in the 1930s, the changing values governing sex roles today and the importance attached to qualities other than beauty and athletic prowess have reduced the importance of status seeking among contemporary dating couples. Do you agree? Has status grading and achievement decreased in dating today? On college campuses in particular? Do college women still attempt to date the most popular athletes or other high-status men on campus? Do college men still try to date the most popular or most attractive women? Does status play a role in your dating behavior?

Mate Selection Although mate selection is no longer the primary objective of dating, as we have said, it continues to be the primary strategy for mate selection in the United States. The increasing divorce rates notwithstanding, Americans are still highly committed to marriage. Thus, although dating initially simply brings people together for recreational and romantic purposes, over time it can become a means of socialization for marriage. An accumulation of dating experiences helps those who want to marry in their efforts to find a marriage partner. Given the longer dating period today, dating continues to fulfill the function that researchers S. A. Lloyd and R. M. Cote (1984) described as **anticipatory socialization**—socialization that is directed toward learning future roles, in this case marriage roles.

Not only does dating perform different functions, but these functions can vary according to an individual's reasons for dating. A person's primary reason for dating will influence that person's behavior in the dating relationship. The general change in the reasons that Americans date accounts for the significant changes we see in contemporary patterns of dating. One study, conducted by researchers James Skipper and Gilbert Nass (1966), suggested that a person's motivation for dating can be placed on a continuum ranging from completely expressive (dating as an end in itself) to completely instrumental (dating as a means to some larger goal). Skipper and Nass further suggested that a person's emotional involvement in the dating experience may also be placed on a continuum ranging from no emotional involvement to complete emotional involvement.

A person's place on these two continua is determined by her or his motive. For example, if the primary motive is mate selection, the person will probably have strong instrumental orientation (dating should lead to marriage) and strong emotional involvement. If, in contrast, the motivation is either recreation or status achievement, the individual is likely to have both low instrumental orientation and low emotional involvement. Skipper and Nass suggest that dating couples will seek to continue their relationship if either the emotional involvement or the instrumental orientation is high.

Think for a minute about your most recent dating relationship. Would you categorize your attitude as more expressive or instrumental? What about your degree of emotional commitment? How would you rate your partner on these criteria?

THE INTERSECTIONS OF RACE, GENDER, CLASS, AND SEXUAL ORIENTATION

Dating, like all other social behaviors, is rooted in social as well as historical conditions of life. People's experiences (including their dating experiences) emerge from the social, political, and economic structure of a society. As we discussed in Chapter 1, race, class, gender, and sexual orientation are basic and central categories of experience that set particular limits on behavior and engender specific kinds of experiences. If we are to move away from an analysis that stems only from the experience of the white middle and upper classes, we must consider how race, class, gender, and sexual orientation influence dating and mate selection patterns.

Although we cannot provide a comprehensive picture of dating and mate selection for all groups, we can provide some insight into these processes for some groups. Unfortunately, the literature in this area continues to be highly limited. The most extensive literature on dating among groups of color deals with African Americans. Little work has been done on courtship among Native Americans, Asian Americans, and Latinos. For example, although we know that family networks continue to make up the fabric of contemporary Native American social organization and are central to the day-to-day functioning of Native Americans, we do not know how these families are formed vis-à-vis courtship and mate selection. Nor do we know whether Native Americans have been affected by the larger cultural patterns of dating and courtship. And, despite the existence of a growing body of data on lesbian and gay relationships, most studies focus specifically on sexual behavior rather than more generally on the whole process of mate selection.

Dating Patterns among African Americans

The practice of dating among African Americans varies by region, historical period, social class, and age. According to Robert Staples (1991), a sociologist who has written widely on African American singles and mate selection, in the past, when African Americans lived in small, cohesive communities in the rural and urban South, what might be called dating behavior centered on the neighborhood, church, and school. Generally, dating was a casual process in which women and men met, formed emotional bonds, and eventually married. Individuals generally were encouraged to date people whose reputation was generally known to members of the community. As African Americans began to move to urban areas outside the South, however, the greater anonymity associated with urban life modified their dating patterns. The school and house party became major centers for heterosexual fraternizing, particularly among the lower class. Dating patterns among the middle class did not differ significantly from those of the larger society and included activities like movies, dances, and bowling.

According to most research, traditional dating patterns among blacks, as among whites and other groups, is more prevalent among the middle and upper class than the lower class. For the African American middle class, dating is typically sequential, occurring over the course of several stages: getting together in the teen years; keeping company on the porch and, eventually, in the house, under family supervision; group dating; and, finally, individual one-on-one dating, engagement, and, most often, marriage (Scott, 1988). Research comparing black and white dating attitudes and expectations indicates that blacks are less flexible and more traditional than whites in several aspects of dating-related attitudes and expectations. For example, whites typically endorse more flexible role patterns in dating and seem less concerned with a traditional dating protocol (such as the expectation that males will bear the costs of dating) than do blacks (Ross and Davis, 1996). This fact notwithstanding, since the 1970s, blacks, like whites and several other groups, have been delaying marriage until later ages, which means they are dating, or getting together, for longer periods of time than in the past.

According to Staples (1991), the historically low **sex ratio**—the number of men to every 100 women—in the African American community has traditionally limited the dating and mate selection options of African American women. Some researchers have suggested that numerical scarcity inflates male value, giving them a decided advantage in the dating/mating game (see, for example, Tucker and Mitchell-Kernan, 1999). Thus, African American men, whose marriage market value has been enhanced by their scarcity, apparently believe that they can be "choosier" in terms of mate selection. The consequence is that many African American women who want to date may find themselves either left out of the game completely or having to settle for far less than their ideal. Moreover, compounded by the fear of sexually transmitted diseases, particularly AIDS, mating and dating is taking on new forms to facilitate the meeting of compatible members of the opposite sex. Although Staples offers no figures or statistics to support his position, he suggests that these factors have led some African American women to date and have sexual liaisons with married men. Other researchers (for example, J. Scott, 1980) have suggested the same. According to Staples, these women claim that they feel safer with married men because generally the only other person these men are sexually involved with is their wife, and these women believe that most wives are not "fooling around." Whatever the case, these factors appear to have contributed to a proliferation, in the 1980s and 1990s, of singles clubs and dating services aimed at African American urban professionals.

Over these same decades, African Americans seeking a dating partner or eventual marital partner relied increasingly on the use of personal ads in African American and general singles magazines. Another place to meet a potential mate became the "happy hour" at popular bars frequented by African American professionals at the end of the workday. This activity continues to be a favorite among many of today's urban African American professionals. Furthermore, the black church continues to be a place to meet a dating partner. It seems that a large number of African American professionals are coming back to the black church and, according to Staples, these "buppy" (the acronym for "black urban professional") churches tend to sponsor special events that bring single people together for fun and relaxation. Some churches have even organized a singles auxiliary and publish a singles newsletter. Today, almost nowhere is off-limits for meeting a potential partner. As with other groups, middle-class African Americans meet at places such as launderettes, health clubs, tennis courts, and jogging tracks (we will discuss these again later in this chapter).

Age is an obvious factor in dating. As African American women age, the already small pool of eligible males available to date shrinks even further. According to one 42-year-old African American woman, few women her age actively date because there are so few single men their age to date. The perception is that those single men who are out there are either dating younger women or dating white women. At the other end of the age continuum, research has found that African American high school students who date place more emphasis on materialistic factors than personality factors when choosing a partner, whereas white students rank personality traits more highly. However, at the college level, there does not appear to be a specific pattern of traits that African American students look for in a dating partner (Smith, 1996).

A notable characteristic of contemporary African American dating patterns is the significant increase in interracial dating, especially on college campuses. This pattern is attributed, in part, to the fact that many middle-class and high-status African Americans live and/or work in worlds that tend to be racially mixed or where there are few other African Americans. This has important implications for who they meet and socialize with, which, in turn, is an important factor in the formation of dating and intimate relationships. It is also attributed to the desegregation of many of the nation's public school systems, workplaces, and other social settings. It is probably also due to the liberation of many white youth from parental control and the rejection of racist values conveyed throughout society. In the case of African American women, dating across race is also due, in some part, to the low sex ratio. In general, both within and outside the African American community, interracial relationships are viewed as a positive step toward smoother race relations by some, and as "sellout" behavior and denial of racial heritage by others. In any event, rates of interracial marriage continue to be a very low percent of all marriages—further evidence that dating does not necessarily lead to marriage.

The Impact of Gender

Perhaps more than most relationships, dating is affected by gender roles and stereotypes. Society traditionally has conveyed certain messages concerning dating: We should mate with the opposite sex; women are supposed to want a masculine man; men are supposed to want a feminine woman; men should initiate the relationship and sexual behavior, although women may guide them by flirting; men should be dominant and women submissive; and sexuality is supposed to be more important to men, and love or commitment to women. As we shall see later in this chapter, although these messages are still widespread, they frequently do not reflect the realities of contemporary relationships.

Discussing gender differences in dating in the context of social-learning theory, social scientist Susan Basow (1992) contends that men's dating scripts focus on planning and paying for the date as well as initiating sexual behavior, whereas women's scripts focus on enhancing their appearance, making conversation, and controlling sexual behavior. Many of us apparently have learned these sexual scripts well. For example, as you read in Chapter 4, researchers have documented that women and men have different orientations to romantic love and that this difference continues when they consider a prospective mate (Dion and Dion, 1998). Women and men have traditionally differed in terms of the characteristics they look for in a mate. Women, on the one hand, prefer men who are well educated and have financial stability (Melton and Lindsey, 1987). They place greater value on qualities of a prospective mate such as working, saving, and paying bills. Men, on the other hand, especially upwardly mobile men, emphasize physical and sexual attractiveness (Fischer and Heesacker, 1995).

Other gender differences in dating and courtship behavior include differences in how women/girls and men/boys signal their interest in each other. A study by researchers Carolina de Weerth and Akko Kalma (1995) confirms the findings of earlier studies, which found that the genders differ in various tactics used to initiate courtship behavior. For example, although eye contact was the most frequently used initiation tactic for both genders, women used indirect tactics more often than men, while men engaged in direct verbal tactics more often than women. Interestingly, when presenting themselves, men stressed personal characteristics that are traditionally interpreted as female-valued (such as tenderness) more often than women did, whereas women stressed characteristics that are traditionally interpreted as male-valued (such as being prestigiously occupied) more than men did. This apparent reversal in gender roles in dating can be linked to the changing function of courtship behavior generally and various societal developments relative to women and men's roles in the larger culture.

Americans aren't the only people who display gender differences in dating and courtship attitudes and behavior. According to a University of Michigan study, of 37 cultures in 33 countries, regardless of the culture, most men want intellectually smart, good-looking, young wives. Women, too, want husbands who are intellectually smart, but they also want them to be a bit older, ambitious, and have bright financial prospects (United Press International, 1990). One implication of studies such as this is that the social construction of a dating reality, like other traditional realities, exaggerates differences between the sexes and constrains behaviors within the sexes.

The Impact of Social Class on the Dating Process

Although dating as a method of mate selection is a universal practice in the United States, social class, like race and gender, profoundly impacts whom we meet, whom we are attracted to, and who is available to date. As with race, there is a scarcity of research specifically focused on dating practices across class. The research that does exist is generally dated and focuses almost entirely on the "premarital" sexual behavior of lower-class youth. One comes away from this research with the sense that dating is essentially a middle- and upper-class phenomenon, and that mate selection is somehow problematic among the lower classes, especially among people of color in this class; but with little or no data or understanding of the *process of dating* for the two classes at each end of the class continuum: lower and upper classes. One thing we do know is that although social classes are not sharply delineated in the United States, people's location in the class structure vis-à-vis factors such as race, education, income, and occupational status is related to differences in attitudes, values, approach to life, behavior, and access to the means necessary to realize one's goals in life. So, how does social class affect dating and mating behavior? Individuals from similar social class backgrounds share similar interests and goals, which are the bases for dating and mate selection choices. Thus, most people in the United States date and marry within their social class.

Upper Class Dating within the upper strata of U.S. society tends to be far more regulated than it is for other classes. According to the literature (for example, Whyte, 1990), children in upper- and middle-class families are more likely than children from working-class and poor families to be socialized to delay gratification and focus on education and career preparation rather than romance and sex. Thus, upper- and middle-class women and men tend to start dating later, delay intimacy, and marry later. This appears to be true across race. For example, data from a study of upwardly mobile African American women reveal that these women, more often than not, were consciously socialized to delay dating and serious relationships until after they had completed a college education (Scott, 1988).

Moreover, social class is related to dating and mate selection in a number of other ways. For example, individuals from the middle and upper classes are generally viewed as more attractive dating partners and potential marital partners than those from the lower classes. Furthermore, upper-class families still exert considerable influence over mate selection. They tend to use their considerable resources to influence their offspring to either delay dating and marriage or to marry whom they consider to be a suitable mate and match for the family. For example, the 1990s on-again, off-again romance between the late John F. Kennedy Jr. (son of the late president John F. Kennedy and the late Jacqueline Kennedy Onassis) and Daryl Hannah (a movie actress) for many years was reported to have been greatly influenced by Jacqueline Kennedy Onassis, who allegedly did not think that Hannah was right for her son. Thus, although the highly publicized couple romanced together over a number of years and Hannah allegedly pushed for a wedding, the couple never made it to the altar. John Jr. subsequently married the late Carolyn Bessette, an affluent and brainy suburbanite whose extraordinary looks, sophistication, and ambition, according to insiders, were strikingly similar to those of the late Jacqueline Kennedy Onassis (Bumiller, 1996). Many observers of the "rich and famous" claim that it was Jacqueline Kennedy Onassis's disapproval of Hannah and her quiet influence over her son that prevented the two from marrying.

In any event, many of the activities of young people in this class are closely supervised by parents or other adults who chaperon the young people's activities. Dates are sometimes arranged by parents, and dating partners are almost always selected from within their own ranks. Seldom do upper-class members date someone from the middle or lower classes, and dating a number of partners is the norm. Adults also exercise more control over the sexuality of young people than is true of other classes. When upper-class women reach 18, they are formally presented to society. After this "coming out" they engage in a number of activities, during which they encounter a number of eligible men. If the couple become engaged, the man presents the woman with an expensive ring, and the engagement is announced in the society pages of the print media. The wedding, which is generally a very formal and often very lavish affair, is attended by the rich and famous, and is usually announced in the newspapers and the electronic media. For example, the 1999 wedding of Melissa Rivers, which is said to have cost her mother, comedienne Joan Rivers, over one million dollars, was attended by a long list of the "Who's Who" among this country's elite and celebrities.

Middle Class Dating behaviors among middle-class youths, at least traditionally, are fundamentally no different from those of the upper classes. Middle-class dating behaviors are likewise generally supervised by adults, although not to the same degree as are those of their wealthier counterparts. Dating activities among middle-class couples include going to sports events and engaging in sporting activities such as ice-skating and tennis, going to the beach, going out to dinner, and entertaining at home. On the one hand, going steady remains common among some segments of the middle classes and usually leads to an engagement. Engagements of middle-class couples, like those of wealthy couples, are usually announced in the print media. Weddings are fairly elaborate and expensive and are often performed in a church or synagogue. On the other hand, contemporary dating and mate selection patterns among middle-class youth include increasing freedom from parents' watchful eyes and supervision. For example, proms and homecoming parties often include a continuation of the celebration in rented hotel rooms and suites, where both same-sex groups as well as mixed-sex groups spend the rest of the night together, presumably under the watchful eyes of adults, although very often they are unsupervised. In addition, in some middle-class communities, **cruising**—where a group of teenagers (usually males) pack into a car and drive around the neighborhood looking for females to pick up—is a popular pattern in the mate selection process. Both these patterns of contemporary dating have caused parents and other community members some degree of alarm. In both cases, the youth involved are often accused of engaging in drinking alcoholic beverages, public littering and loitering, and loud and sometimes rude behavior.

Although the term *mixer*—an informal school dance designed to bring together people of both sexes so they can get acquainted with one another—may seem outdated to some (it was a method of mate selection common in the 1960s and 1970s), it is still a method used in heterosexual mate selection (Holland and Eisenhart, 1990) by both the middle and working classes.

Lower Class Most research on dating suggests that lower-class families tend to exercise the least control over mate selection. Dating among this group is most often very informal and often includes simply "hanging out"—getting out of often small and cramped living quarters in favor of such places as bowling alleys and local bars. Serious, unsupervised dating usually begins in the mid teens and is often exclusive or monogamous. Lower-class couples often skip the engagement phase and progress directly to marriage. When engagements occur, they are not usually announced in the press, and weddings are often small, inexpensive, and informal. Sometimes they are conducted in the home of one of the partners.

It should be noted that just as the lines separating various social classes are often blurred, so too are methods of dating and mate selection across class. Thus, methods of dating and mate selection are similar and sometimes overlap across social classes. For example, formal rites of passage such as coming-out parties can be found among the middle as well as the upper classes. Many middle-class groups present their daughters to the community and society by means of coming-out parties to signal the daughters' readiness to date and assume other adult responsibilities. In some middle-class African American communities, for example, this coming-out party is often in the form of a cotillion. The cotillion is a fairly elaborate formal affair and a very significant event in the life of a young middle-class African American female. Such an event involves family and friends and can cost parents several thousand dollars as their daughters make this very public and symbolic transition to adulthood. Likewise, in some Latino communities, the *quinceañera* represents a social and religious coming-out celebration for Latinas. It includes a religious mass followed by a reception for the young woman, who may begin dating after her *quinceañera.* Traditionally, these rites of passage activities have focused exclusively on females. However, recently, among some middle-class African Americans, the *botillion* has emerged as a rite of passage for African American males. As with the cotillion, parents present their offspring—in this case, their sons—to the community and society to signal their readiness to date and assume more adult responsibilities. Moreover, other methods such as cruising, school and church mixers, and hanging out are methods found among the lower and working classes as well as the middle classes, albeit sometimes in modified forms.

Lesbian and Gay Dating

We know very little about the dating and mating behavior of lesbians and gays because relatively little research has been done specifically in this area. Moreover, the research that exists deals primarily with sexual behavior and lifestyles. Because society continues to stigmatize homosexual behavior, much mate selection behavior is carried out in the privacy of homes and recreational establishments frequented only by lesbians and gays. Like heterosexual couples, most lesbians and gays date for recreational and entertainment purposes, but the development of love relationships is also an important goal. In this regard, the function of dating for some lesbian and gay couples is to find a mate with whom they can share love, psychological and economic support, and perhaps children (Parrot and Ellis, 1985). Because lesbians and gays are legally prohibited from marrying, for some lesbians and gays the ultimate goal of mate selection is a type of symbolic marriage, such as a domestic partnership, in which cohabiting lesbians and gays officially register as a couple. (Chapter 7 contains more detailed discussion of these topics.)

Finding a permanent partner is not always easy for lesbians and gays. For example, according to Michelle Huston and Pepper Schwartz (1996), in isolated, rural, and some urban areas, lesbian and gay meeting places are nonexistent. Thus, traditional places for meeting potential partners are closed off to them. Furthermore, because many lesbians and gays are closeted (especially in isolated areas), they often do not know who is a potential mate. Even in urban areas where there are large homosexual populations, meeting a potential partner is not always easy. A large number of lesbians and gays remain "closeted"; thus, finding potential partners in gay bars and other gay-oriented meeting places limits the field of eligibles and potential partners to those lesbians and gays who feel comfortable in such settings.

As with heterosexuals, there appear to be some fundamental gender differences in the dating and mate selection behaviors of lesbians and gays. For example, lesbian bars are not nearly as common as gay bars; therefore, women cannot always count on them as a place to meet potential partners. In addition, lesbian bars serve primarily as a social gathering place for already-established lesbian couples, and the behavioral norms at these bars prescribe behavior that consists of couples socializing rather than individuals cruising and looking for a pickup. Because these bars tend to be frequented by couples, it is unlikely that one will meet an unattached person in these bars. Therefore, lesbians tend to meet their partners through lesbian friendship networks, mutual acquaintances, and through participation in various lesbian and women's political and activist groups (Huston and Schwartz, 1996), with the period of courtship lasting on average two to three years (Harry, 1983). Their partners tend to be women they have known for a while and with whom they have had no prior sexual relationship. Lesbians tend to practice a kind of serial monogamy in that they may have several partners over the course of their lifetime but are involved in only one intimate relationship at a time. In contrast, as we noted in Chapter 4, the courtship period for gays—as for heterosexual men—is often relatively short and is most often preceded by sexual relations.

While the subculture of gay bars has been a prime place for gays to meet potential sexual partners it has also acted to inhibit long-term partnerships. For example, research indicates that a major characteristic that gays look for in a potential partner is physical attractiveness; they prefer a partner who is very handsome—a trait that does not ensure a long-lasting relationship. Until recent times, the subculture of gay bars did not encourage gay men to form long-term relationships. In many places, singlehood rather than couplehood is still the norm (Huston and Schwartz, 1996).

In general, dating and mating patterns among lesbians and gays do not appear to be significantly different from those found among heterosexual women and men. Thus, these patterns seem much more reflective of female and male socialization patterns than of patterns specific to lesbians and gays (Harry, 1983; Huston and Schwartz, 1996).

African American Lesbian and Gay Dating Research pertaining to lesbian and gay mate selection across race is especially scarce. One study by Vickie Mays and Susan Cochran (1991) of 530 middle-class African American lesbians provides some insights into mate selection among this group. The study does not convey a comprehensive picture of the dating process, but it does provide some important data. For example, although two-thirds of the subjects were in a serious relationship, only one-third lived with their partner. The average age at which the women reported first being attracted to a woman was about 16. Their first lesbian experience did not occur until approximately age 19, however. Prior to their current relationship, almost all the women had been involved in a sexual relationship with another African American woman. In addition, two-thirds had at least one such relationship with an Anglo woman, and 39 percent reported a lesbian relationship with some other woman of color. The median number of sexual partners was nine, which is similar to that reported by research on white lesbians.

Regarding African American gays, according to Cochran and Mays (1991), dating and mate selection may be influenced by sociocultural factors such as the unavailability of same-race, same-sex partners; residential immobility; fewer social and financial resources than whites generally and white gays specifically; and a general lack of employment opportunities. Thus, African American gays, like many African American heterosexual women, often have difficulty finding a potential partner. The traditional networks where mate selection takes place in the white gay subculture, such as gay bars, baths, and other public gathering places, are not always accessible to black gays due to actual or perceived racism. Thus, courtship among African American gays is more likely to center around home entertainment.

An interesting finding about African American gay sexuality comes from a 1978 study comparing the sexual behavior of black and white gays. In this study, Alan Bell and Martin Weinberg reported that black gays tend to be more bisexual in their behaviors than white gays. This finding implied that African American gays were dating both women and men either concurrently or alternately over some specified period of time. Today, such behavior is no longer implied but, rather, a documented reality. With the alarming increase in HIV/AIDS cases among African American women who have had unprotected sex with men, health experts estimate that as much as 60 percent of African American gays infected with the HIV/AIDS virus are bisexual or living an alternative secret sexual life referred to as "down low." African American men living on the down low date and/or have sex with other men and also date and/or have sex with women, but they do not identify themselves as gay or bisexual. Such behavior is attributed to the intense homophobia alleged to exist within African American communities (we present a more detailed discussion of this behavior in Chapter 6).

Other comparisons generated by the Bell and Weinberg study of black and white gays include the following: Black and white gays reported equivalent numbers of sexual partners, both lifetime and over a 12-month period; black gays were significantly less likely than white gays to engage in brief relationships with anonymous partners; over two-thirds of the blacks reported that more than half of their partners were white men. This last finding is in stark contrast to white gays in the same study, none of whom reported that more than half of their partners were black. Thus, it seems that as in heterosexual dating and mate selection, a shortage of eligible potential mates may encourage coupling with people of other races and ethnicities.

THEORIES OF MATE SELECTION

Thus far we have discussed mate selection cross-culturally, historically, and within the context of U.S. society. We have also paid particular attention to issues of race, class, gender, and sexual orientation in dating behavior. A complete understanding of mate selection in these contexts requires a theoretical framework that shows how these and other social, economic, and political factors are variously related and influence mate selection. Obviously no one theory can accomplish this. In the next section, we present some of the most frequently used theoretical explanations of mate selection: exchange theories, which include stimulus–value–role theory and equity theory, and filter theory.

Exchange Theories

Within the discipline of sociology, exchange theories are perhaps the most often used explanations of interpersonal attraction and mate selection. Although these theories were not developed specifically to explain mate selection, they provide some interesting insights into the process. You might recall from Chapter 2 that traditional exchange theory revolves around the notion that individuals attempt to maximize their rewards and minimize their costs to achieve the most favorable outcome possible. Applied specifically to mate selection, various exchange theories hold that people looking for mates try to maximize their chances for a rewarding relationship. In other words, we enter into and remain in an intimate relationship as long as we perceive that the rewards outweigh the costs. When our relationships are no longer rewarding we discontinue them (Surra, 1991). If each person maximizes outcomes, then stable relationships will develop between people who have very similar levels of resources, because they will exchange comparable resources.

Social scientist John Edwards (1969) refers to this principle as the *exchange theory of homogamous mating*. According to Edwards, within any pool of eligibles, a person looking to get married will seek out a person who she or he thinks will maximize her or his rewards. We therefore enter or do not enter into a romantic relationship depending on whether the other person possesses both tangible resources, such as money, and intangible resources, such as physical appearance. People with equivalent resources are most likely to maximize each other's rewards. Because couples with equivalent resources are most likely to have homogamous characteristics, mate selection is homogamous with respect to a given set of characteristics. As the relationship progresses, a couple engage in many other exchanges, including those involving power. Seldom are both parties equally interested in continuing the relationship. Thus, the one who is least interested has an advantage and is in a position to dominate. Some researchers have described this as the *principle of least interest*, whereby, in essence, the person with the least interest trades her or his company for the other person's acquiescence to her or his wishes (Waller and Hill, 1951).

In traditional mate selection, men maximized their rewards because they generally had a range of rewards to offer, such as social status, economic support, power, and protection. In contrast, women generally had a limited set of resources, primarily involving their physical appearance and their ability to bear and care for children. Today, however, women have more rewards to offer and thus can be more selective in choosing a mate. Instead of the traditional male tradeoff of economic security, many women today are looking for men who are expressive, sensitive, and caring, and who are willing to share housework and child-rearing responsibilities. Men who do not possess these characteristics are finding themselves less desirable and sought-out as a potential mate. Along the same lines, instead of the traditional female tradeoff of physical attractiveness and nurturance, many men today are looking for women who are assertive, creative, and self-confident, and who can contribute to the economic support of a family. So exchange theories help us understand how people develop a close relationship through an exchange of rewards. But why is it that some people develop an intimate relationship while others do not?

Stimulus–Value–Role Theory A popular variation of the general exchange theory of mate selection is Bernard Murstein's (1980, 1987) *stimulus–value–role theory* of interpersonal attraction. According to Murstein, in a situation of relatively free choice, attraction and interaction depend on the exchange value of the assets and liabilities that each person brings to the situation. In the mate selection process couples move through three stages: stimulus, value, and role. They are first attracted to each other by an initial stimulus, and then they test their suitability for establishing a permanent relationship with each other by comparing their value orientations and agreement on roles. Responding to critiques of his theory by his colleagues, Murstein updated his theory such that the three stages are not mutually exclusive but rather work together to move a couple toward a committed relationship (Surra, 1991).

In the *stimulus stage*, two people are attracted to each other by some stimulus, such as good looks, the way one walks, or notoriety. Whatever the stimulus, it draws the two people together initially and tends to energize the relationship past the boundaries of simple friendship. If both partners feel the situation is equal concerning the exchange of resources, they will likely proceed to the value stage. In the *value stage*, the compatibility of the couple is tested with regard to a variety of mutually held beliefs and values, including religion, politics, marital and family expectations, attitudes about money and work, and lifestyle preferences. The more similar the two people's values, the stronger their attraction becomes and the more likely they will progress toward a long-lasting relationship. Couples with similar values may move on to the *role stage*. This stage provides each partner with the opportunity to see how the other acts out her or his roles in real-life situations. If mutual benefits at this stage are positive and fairly equal, the couple may choose to get married. That is, if the couple's roles are complementary; if their feelings and behavior about issues such as power and authority in the relationship, the division of labor, and other expectations that they have for each other are the same or similar, then the couple might proceed to marriage. The key here is that these three stages act as filtering devices for evaluating a dating relationship to determine if it will continue or end.

Equity Theory Yet another variation of exchange theory that is used to explain mate selection is *equity theory*. When used in this sense, the term *equity* signifies "fairness." Equity theory proposes that a person is attracted to another by a fair deal rather than by a profitable exchange (Walster, Walster, and Traupmann, 1978). It argues that most people believe that they should benefit from a relationship in proportion to what they give to the relationship. People are attracted to those from whom they get as much as they give. Two people do not usually seek the exact same things in a relationship; however, they are attracted by a deal that is fair to them. Values involved in judging equity range from physical attractiveness to family background to anything that a given person might value. If the relationship is inequitable people will try to move the relationship to an equitable level. The greater the inequity, the harder it will be to move the relationship to an equitable level, however.

Filter Theories

As our discussion thus far indicates, mate selection involves a complex process of making choices within the context of a range of factors that can restrict or enhance our ability to choose. David Klimek (1979) describes this process in terms of a series of filterings. As Figure 5.1 suggests, individuals use a series of filters to sort through a large number of potential mates to arrive at the final choice. Each filter, in descending order, reduces the pool of eligible mates until relatively few eligibles are left. We then choose a mate from among this group. *Filter theories*, or *process theories* as they are sometimes called, suggest that many factors are involved in the marital choice. In the next section we discuss some of the most prevalent of these factors, including the marriage squeeze and gradient, race, class, age, religion, sex/gender, propinquity, and family and peer pressure. After reading this section you should be more conscious of the fact that even Americans do not have complete freedom of choice in mate selection.

MATE SELECTION: FINDING AND MEETING PARTNERS

"There's supposed to be more women than men, so where are they?" "I know there are a lot of good men out there—you just have to know where to find them." Do these comments sound familiar to you? Increasingly over the last decade single women and men looking for "Ms. Right" or "Mr. Right" have lamented the mounting problem of finding someone to date or marry. And, once they meet, how does each one know that the other is the right person? What attracts them to each other? What do they do once attracted to one another? How people meet and where, how or why they are attracted to each other and not someone else, are some of the most basic questions surrounding mate selection. As you will see in the following discussion, finding a mate has become almost a national pastime in the United States. Some people go to great lengths to meet a potential mate, as revealed later in the chapter in the discussion of where and how people meet potential partners.

Figure 5.1

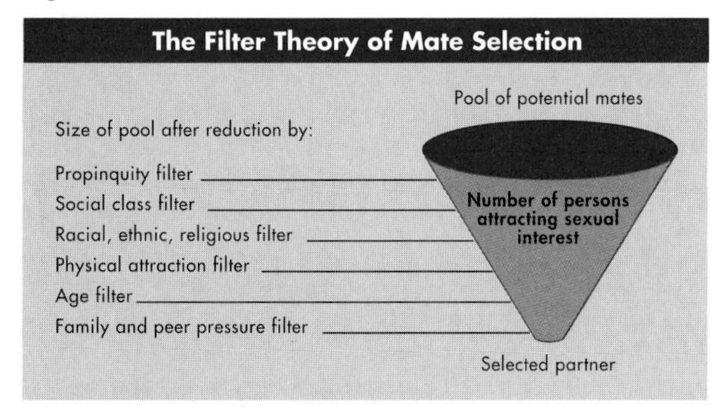

Source: Adapted from David Klimek, 1979, *Beneath Mate Selection and Marriage: The Unconscious Motives in Human Pairing* (New York: Van Nostrand Reinhold): 13.

Do you know how your parents met? Was it love at first sight? How alike are they? What about you? Are you looking for a mate or partner? What characteristics do you look for in a mate? Character? Social conscience? A strong religious conviction? Money? Is it difficult to find someone who meets your standards? Think about your own dating and mate selection experiences and priorities as you continue reading this chapter. At the end of this chapter you may find that your thinking has shifted, or perhaps you have become aware of priorities and feelings that you never realized you had.

The Marriage Market and the Pool of Eligibles

Throughout our history, various romantic theories of love and mate selection have suggested that when the time is right we will meet a "fair maiden" or "Prince Charming" without much effort on our part. Most such notions imply that mate selection is a rather unsystematic and random event determined by the "luck of the draw" or by a power higher than ourselves.

In reality, meeting prospective mates, choosing partners, developing a dating relationship, and falling in love are not random activities but are all predictable and are structured by a number of social and demographic factors. For example, if you are a female college student in a dating relationship, without meeting you or your partner we could predict fairly accurately many things about your partner. For example, he is probably a college student like you (or he has already completed college or attended college at some prior time), he is probably of the same racial or ethnic background and social class as you, he is probably a little taller than you, a few years older, and as religious or spiritual as you are. We might even predict that you both are similarly attractive. (And if he isn't you probably will not have a lasting relationship. Research shows that we are attracted to and tend to marry people who have a similar level of physical attractiveness.) Most likely the two of you are similarly intelligent. Likewise, if you are a male student in a dating relationship the same predictions apply, with a few differences: Your partner is probably your age or 1 to 5 years younger, and she is probably your height or shorter. Although we may not be 100 percent correct, for many of you we are probably very close.

The point here is that we have not randomly guessed about the characteristics of people who date and marry. Rather, we have used the knowledge that sociologists have provided us about the principles of homogamy, endogamy, and exogamy in mate selection. In the following discussion we define these principles and describe how they apply to mate selection in the United States.

Marriage Market Historically, sociologists have described mate selection in terms of a **marriage market.** That is, they use the analogy of the commercial marketplace to explain how we choose the people we date, mate, live with, and marry. The marriage market concept implies that we enter the mate selection process with certain resources and we trade these resources for the best offer we can get. In this sense, the marriage market is not a real place but a process.

Regardless of how we choose mates, as exchange theory suggests, some sort of bargaining and exchange probably takes place. For example, in societies and subcultural groups where marriages are arranged by someone other than the couple, the parent or matchmaker carefully tries to strike the best possible bargain. Large **dowries**—sums of money or property brought to the marriage by the female—are often exchanged for valued characteristics in a male, such as high status. Indeed, valued resources like dowries can also act to make up for a person's supposed deficiencies. Thus, if a woman is considered unattractive but has a large dowry, she might be able to exchange the dowry for a highly prized mate. Although the idea of swapping or exchanging resources in mate selection may seem distant and applicable only to those cultures in which marriages are arranged, this process is very much a part of mate selection in the United States.

Although the nature of the marital exchange has changed, the market has not been eliminated. Despite some improvements in their bargaining position, women remain at a disadvantage vis-à-vis men in the mate selection marketplace. Although women have entered the labor force in record numbers and have become increasingly independent, their actual earnings are far below those of their male counterparts, as is their ability to earn. Furthermore, many of the traditional resources that women could offer, such as child care, housework, and sexuality, can be obtained by men outside marriage and thus have less value in the marriage market. Women are further disadvantaged by the sexual double standard attached to aging: As women age they are considered to be unattractive and undesirable by men.

Does this description of the marital marketplace sound cold, calculating, and unromantic? Even if we are uncomfortable with the idea, most of us engage in the exchange of various personality and social characteristics in our quest for a mate.

Pool of Eligibles Theoretically, every unmarried person in the United States is a potential eligible mate for every other unmarried person. Realistically, however, not every unmarried person is equally available or accessible to every other unmarried person. The people whom our society has defined as acceptable marriage partners for us form what sociologists call a **pool of eligibles.** For almost all of us, the pool of eligibles consists of people of the same race, class, and educational level as ourselves. With amazing consistency, we are very much like the people we meet, date, fall in love with, and marry—far more so than can be attributed simply to chance. Sociologists refer to this phenomenon as **homogamy:** the tendency to meet, date, and marry someone very similar to ourselves in terms of important or desirable characteristics.

As we learned in Chapter 1, two of the most common sets of social rules governing mate selection and the pool of eligibles are exogamy and endogamy (see Figure 5.2). **Exogamy** refers to marriage outside a particular group. So, our pool of eligibles is first narrowed by society's exogamous norms. The most common exogamous norms in the United States are those that prohibit us from dating or marrying someone who is a family member or who is of the same sex. As you know from Chapter 1, the incest taboo is a universal norm that narrows our pool of eligibles by eliminating close blood relatives. Regarding same-sex partners, people of the same sex are considered to be socially unacceptable mates and are also excluded, at least theoretically.

The opposite of exogamy is **endogamy,** marriage within a particular group. Endogamous norms can be formal, such as the laws in many U.S. states prior to 1967 that prohibited interracial marriage. Most, however, are informal. For example, social convention dictates that we marry someone near our own age.

Freedom versus Constraint in Mate Selection

Although we have increasing freedom and expanded options in choosing dating and life partners today than in the past, our freedom to choose a mate continues to be constrained by cultural norms that sort people according to race, ethnicity, religion, social class, residence, and related factors. The romantic belief that mate selection is based on love and our expanded mate selection options notwithstanding, these factors best predict who meets, dates, falls in love with, and marries whom. Let's look at how our pool of eligibles is loosely or closely organized around these factors. Although all of these factors are interrelated, we will examine each one separately. Two of the most important factors are the marriage squeeze and the marriage gradient.

The Marriage Squeeze Why do you think some people who want a mate and are actively looking cannot connect? Why do women complain more often than men about having difficulty finding a mate? Is there someone out there for all of us, no matter what resources we have to offer? Or will some of us not find a mate no matter how hard we look? In reality there is not someone out there for everyone. If those people being advised to "sit tight and wait" are women born after World War II, they may be waiting for a very long time. Demographic data reveal that at any given time in the United States since World War II, there has been a greater number of women than men who are eligible for marriage and looking for a partner. Sociologists have defined this imbalance in the ratio of marriage-aged men to marriage-aged women as a **marriage squeeze,** whereby one sex has a more limited pool of eligibles than the other does.

Demographic data indicate that the marriage squeeze reversed itself in the 1990s such that by the year 2000,

Figure 5.2

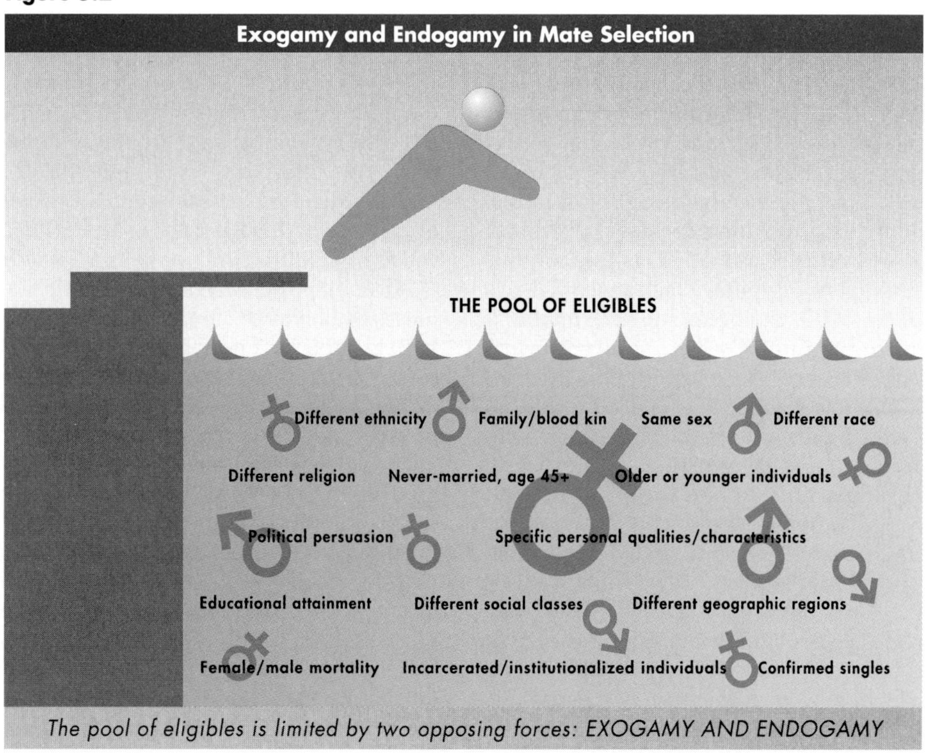

Source: Adapted from a drawing by John Chauncey Byrd, Chicago, 1993.

never-married men outnumbered never-married women, 31 percent to 25 percent. More important, when we consider the total population of unmarried adults (never-married, separated, divorced, and widowed), 15 years of age and older in 2000, as Table 5.1 shows, a greater percentage of unmarried men than unmarried women can be found in each of the three age categories: 25 to 29, 30 to 34, and 35 to 39 (the ages family sociologists have designated as the marriageable years). This reversal of the marriage squeeze seems to be the case for blacks, whites, and Latinos. However, these percentages alone do not tell the whole story. Many women continue to find their options for dating and mate selection limited even though theoretically there are more eligible men than women. This might be accounted for, in part, by the fact that women tend to date and marry men who are three to five years older than themselves. Given this, when we look at the data in Table 5.1 we can see, for example, that although unmarried men outnumber unmarried women within their respective age categories, when we look at the percentage of unmarried women in a particular age category and compare it with the next highest age category of unmarried men, there is a noticeable decrease in the pool of eligibles for women. Although the causes are different, as we noted earlier, countries like India, China, and Japan are experiencing a similar marriage squeeze with high percentages of single men and a scarcity of single women.

Moreover, African American women, it seems, continue to be vulnerable to the marriage squeeze. In our earlier discussion of dating patterns among African Americans, we mentioned the historically low sex ratio in the African American

Table 5.1

Percentage of Unmarried Women and Men by Selected Age Categories, 2000

	Females	Males
Never-married 15 years and older	25.1%	31.3%
Unmarried (overall)* for selected ages		
25–29	48.3	57.5
30–34	35.1	39.8
35–39	32.2	33.5

*Includes all categories of singles: never-married, separated, divorced, and widow/widower.

Source: U.S. Census Bureau, Statistical Abstract of the United States, Current Population Report: *America's Families and Living Arrangements, 2000* (Washington, DC: U.S. Government Printing Office): 11, Table 5.

community. In 2000, the sex ratio of African American men to every 100 African American women was about 89. According to some observers, the low sex ratio will continue to deny large numbers of African American women a comparable mate well into the future. Perhaps more important than the sex ratio itself is a consideration of structural and attitudinal factors that work to limit the real (versus ideal) pool of eligibles for African American women. For example, if we take into account the lower life expectancy for black men (lower than for white males and all females), coupled with the increasing numbers of young black men who are victims of homicides (in 1997, the homicide rate for black males was 47.1 compared to 6.7 for white males and when we look only at black males in the marriageable years of 25–34, the homicide rate was a staggering 71.1 compared to 8.5 for white males) and the disproportionate numbers who are incarcerated (one-quarter of African American males 20 to 29 years of age are either in prison, on parole, or on probation), the pool of eligible men—those who are desirable dating partners and mates—is drastically decreased (Lindsey, 1990; Amott, 1993; Anders, 1994; U.S. Census Bureau, 1998, 2000).

Women in Australia faced a similar marriage squeeze in the 1980s and 1990s when there were 97 men for every 100 women; the excess of single women is expected to continue for some time. Researcher Bettina Arndt (1985) attributed part of this problem to older women outliving their partners. Australian women tend to favor older men, a preference that perpetuates the shortage of available partners. Researchers speculate that women over the age of 35 today will be most affected, since there were only 65 available men for every 100 of these women in the 1990s. Researchers also suggest that this trend could be reversed if Australian women would begin marrying men who are younger than themselves.

The Marriage Gradient Another factor that affects the availability of eligible mates in the marriage market is the marriage gradient. In most cultures, including that of the United States, informal norms encourage women to marry men of equal or higher social status. Numerous studies of U.S. mate selection and marriage bear out this pattern. For example, only about 33 percent of women with four or more years of college marry men with less education, whereas 50 percent of men with four or more years of college marry less educated women (Westoff and Goldman, 1988). In general, when men marry outside their social class level, they more often marry downward than upward. Furthermore, the higher a man's occupational level, the more likely he will marry downward. Conversely, when women marry outside their social class, they most often marry upward. The tendency to marry upward in social status is referred to as **hypergamy;** marriage downward is known as **hypogamy**. Thus, in most cultures, women practice hypergamy, and men practice hypogamy.

This pattern of marriage gives rise to a phenomenon we call the **marriage gradient.** Because women marry upward and men marry downward, men at the top have a much larger field of eligibles than do men at the bottom. The reverse is true for women: Those at the top have a very small pool of eligibles, whereas those on the bottom have a much wider range of men to choose from. This pattern therefore works to keep some of the highest-status women and lowest-status men from marrying. Although the description here is of marital patterns, the same general trend has been found to operate prior to marriage as well. This tendency has been called by some a *dating* or *mating gradient.*

Although the marriage gradient traditionally provided most women with upward mobility, this is not necessarily the case today. The increasing economic independence of some women has made marriage less of a mobility mechanism. Because of the shortage of eligible men (real or perceived), many women are dating and marrying downward instead of upward. For example, a woman with a college degree was heard to say: "If I could find a kind plumber with a sense of humor, I'd marry him."

As with the marriage squeeze, the marriage gradient is very prominent for African American women. One study (Staples, 1981b) found that as income level rises, so do the number of men who are married and living with their wives. In contrast, African American women who have a college degree are the least likely of all African Americans to have married by the age of 30. And African American men least likely to marry or remarry are those with less than a high school education. A fundamental problem for middle-class or high-status African American women is that men who have a similar status are either already married or are seeking a younger mate. In an article on black–white interracial dating, Lynn Norment (1994) notes social psychologist Julia Hare's observations and perspective relative to the paucity of eligible African American men available for African American women (especially educated African American women) to date. According to Hare, the more education and income an African American woman has, the fewer suitable African American men there are on her level. According to some estimates, there are between 35 and 45 single African American men who are in college or have jobs for every 100 African American women. When these men date or marry white women, the pool shrinks even further. Thus, the largest number of African American men in educated African American women's pool of eligibles are those with a lower status. Therefore, educated African American women who are interested in a mate often must date or marry down. Some of these women, while interested in dating and/or marriage, are not willing to settle for less than their ideal, so they neither date nor marry.

Race Some of the most important norms in mate selection in the United States revolve around race and ethnicity. Dating, mate selection, and marriage are probably most endogamous and homogamous in terms of race. We currently have little reliable data on the number of contemporary couples who date interracially. We do know that about 98 percent of marriages in this country occur within the same racial group (U.S. Census Bureau, 2000). Although marriage is not an exact barometer of who dates whom, because all dating does not result in marriage, it can give us some indication of who chooses whom as a mate. We discuss interracial marriage in detail in Chapter 8.

Many of us would like to think of the United States as having made significant gains in terms of race relations over the years. According to recent survey data, attitudes concerning interracial intimacy, dating, and marriage are changing. For example, in a study of racial attitudes in America, researchers Howard Schuman and Charlotte Steeh (1992) report that in 1991, 44 percent of white Americans approved of interracial marriage, up considerably from 4 percent in 1958. A 1995 survey ("New Survey Shows," 1995) found that half of *all* Americans report that they would be willing to date someone of another race if they were single. Overall, men and blacks are more open to dating and marrying someone of a different race than are women and whites. The poll's finding that approval of interracial relationships is increasing particularly among younger Americans is supported by a 1997 *USA Today*/Gallup poll, which found that 57 percent of teens who date said that they have dated someone of another race or ethnic group (white, black, Latina/o, or Asian), and another 30 percent said they would have no objection to doing so. These findings were strongly supported by anecdotal data from dozens of interviews with teachers, school counselors, principals, parents, and students from across the country. These data contrast that of two decades ago when, in a 1980 Gallup poll, only 17 percent of teens said they had dated interracially, although Latinas/os were not specifically included in that count.

Interesting, and perhaps an important factor here, is parental and school acceptance of interracial dating. Most of the teens polled (66 percent black; 74 percent Latina/o; 75 percent white) said that interracial dating is "no big deal" at their schools, and in most cases parents aren't a major obstacle. Sixty-four percent of teens said their parents either didn't mind that they date interracially or wouldn't mind if they did. Almost all teens (97 percent) said they or other teens date interracially because they find the person attractive and because they "care about the person they're dating" (91 percent). Most of the teens insist that interracial dating is no different than any other kind and, in their opinion, it is here to stay. Several sociological factors can help explain this rising trend in interracial dating among young people:

- a heavy immigration of Latinas/os and Asians has increased the chances of meeting people of a different racial/ethnic background;
- the enrollment of students of color in public schools nationally has increased to a record high of 35 percent; and
- the increasing acceptance of interracial marriage.

According to Karen S. Peterson (1997), as "Americans struggle with racially charged issues from affirmative action to record-breaking immigration" this emerging dating pattern among high school students could signal a shift in the way the nation will come to look at race. However, although attitudes are changing and interracial dating is more common than ever before, some racial barriers remain, particularly between black and white teens. Interracial dating is still not accepted everywhere, and it continues to be controversial in many areas of the country. While dating outside of one's race may be less taboo today than it was 30 or 50 years ago, it still raises eyebrows and closes minds. Interracial couples still upset families, inspire stares and comments, and are often targets of hostility and violence. Although nearly two-thirds of whites say they approve of interracial marriage, such attitudes do not always translate into behavior (Nelson, 1992; Tyson, 1997). Interracial couples are having a particularly hard time in the midst of rising racial and ethnic tensions in this country today. Since the 1980s, race relations have been particularly strained. Racial slurs, race riots, bigotry, the dramatic increase in the number of reported hate crimes during the 1990s, and the continued racially motivated violence, including widely publicized cases of black men being killed or beaten for associating with white women, have given many observers cause for translating the *USA Today*/Gallup poll survey data with extreme caution.

Not only do individual attitudes and behavior impact interracial dating but various American institutions have also played a key role in manipulating who dates whom relative to race and ethnicity. For example, Bob Jones, a fundamentalist school in North Carolina, at one time in its recent history refused to admit African Americans but later admitted them under a restriction that there was to be no interracial dating or marriage (Arkes, 1991). However, in March 2000, in the wake of the controversy stirred by President George W. Bush's visit to the fundamentalist Christian school a month earlier, the school's president, Bob Jones III, announced that he had met with school administrators and decided to end the ban on interracial dating (CNN, 2000). In a similar vein, in Minnesota, the Department of Human Rights investigated the interracial dating policy at Pillsbury Baptist Bible College after it was brought out that the school's policy has discouraged dating between the races since its founding in the 1950s ("Probe Interracial Dating Policy," 1987).

Think about your own dating history and that of people you know such as family members. You can use the exercise in the box titled "Writing Your Own Script" to analyze some of your own attitudes and those of people you know concerning the issue of race and intimate relationships.

Social Class Sociologists typically measure class using a composite scale consisting of level of educational attainment, occupation, and level of income. As we have seen, much of our behavior is affected by our location in the status hierarchy. People who share a similar social class background tend to share common interests, goals, lifestyles, and general behavior. These kinds of compatibility of interest and general homogamy are the bases of intimate relationships. As with race, Americans mate with people from their own socioeconomic class with far greater frequency than could be expected simply by chance. As you learned earlier, this is especially true among the upper classes of all races. It has often been observed that the upper classes expend more efforts to control the mate selection of their offspring than do other classes because they have much more to lose if their children marry outside their social class (Ramu, 1989). Even on those occasions when a person marries someone of a different race, ethnicity, religion, or age group, the couple will most likely be from the same social class.

Because social researchers disagree on the nature and number of social classes in U.S. society, it is difficult to determine accurate statistics on class endogamy. We know, however, that courtships and marriages tend to be highly endogamous for such class-related factors as education and occupation. Educational homogamy is most observable for women with four or more years of college, who tend to marry men with comparable or higher levels of education, and for men who have never attended college (Bulcroft and Bulcroft, 1993).

Age Are you involved in a relationship with a person who is much older or younger than you? Do you know others who are? What about your parents? Is your mother older or younger than your father? When you see a much younger woman with an older man do you think: Gee, she must be looking for a father figure, or My God, he's robbing the cradle? Age norms represent yet another important constraint on our freedom to choose a mate. Although no laws require us to date, live with, or marry people within our age group, informal norms and pressures operate to keep mate selection fairly homogamous in terms of age. Most Americans mate with people from a closely related age group. For most of us this means that we date and marry people roughly within two to five years of our own age. Although the sanctions for dating or marrying someone very much older or younger (within the law) than oneself are mild, most people adhere to the age custom in selecting a mate. When they deviate, it usually goes unnoticed for the most part, unless, of course, the principals are wealthy or high-profile celebrities. The case of former Playboy Playmate Anna Nicole Smith is a case in point. Still in her 20s, Smith met and married billionaire oil tycoon J. Howard Marshall, who was more than 60 years her senior. The match caused raised eyebrows and charges that she was a "gold digger." Despite her protests to the contrary, most Americans do not believe that people extremely older or younger than their partner can be seriously in love. The marriage is still newsworthy, as Smith is suing her stepson for a portion of her now-deceased husband's fortune. In later marriages or remarriages, age differences are likely to be a little wider, although they continue to follow the general pattern of age homogamy.

Religion How important is religion in your choice of a partner? Historically, in the United States religion has played a significant role in mate selection. Several studies conducted over the years have found that as many as 90 percent of people who marry select partners who are religiously similar to themselves (see, for example, Kerckhoff, 1976; Murstein, 1986; Shehan, Bock, and Lee, 1990). Most of this research indicates that Jews in this country have been most homogamous in terms of dating and marriage than any other religious group. However, since the 1960s, the proportion of Jews marrying non-Jews (or gentiles) has risen steadily, from 11 percent of those who married prior to 1965 to 57 percent in the late 1980s. According to Joe Feagin and Clairece Feagin (1996), this trend toward interfaith marriages among Jews has led some observers to predict the disappearance of the American Jewish community within a few decades. This perceived threat to Jewish identity and culture has prompted some Jewish parents to actually arrange marriages for their children (Hartman, 1988). Moreover, some synagogues have started dating services and singles programs to discourage interfaith marriages. And since 1980 there has been a growing trend for interfaith married couples and their children to embrace Judaism and identify themselves as Jewish (Feagin and Feagin, 1996:187). Other religions as well either oppose or strongly discourage interfaith dating and marriage. As with race, many of these studies deal primarily with marriage; nonetheless, we can assume some degree of congruency between whom people date and whom they marry. Thus, religious homogamy is yet another factor that limits our pool of eligible mates.

Sex and Gender When discussing factors that limit our pool of eligible mates we cannot overlook sex. As we have indicated repeatedly, heterosexuality is the norm in mating, dating, and mate selection in the United States. Most Americans are so socialized into a heterosexual frame of reference that it is outside their scope of reality even to consider a same-sex relationship as an alternative. So important is the value of heterosexuality to many Americans that exogamous norms regulating this behavior have been encoded into law to ensure that people mate heterosexually. The stigma attached to same-sex relationships, legal constraints, and the physical abuse ("gay bashing") that such couples frequently experience can act as deterrents for some people who might otherwise choose a partner of the same sex.

Other Factors That Affect Mate Selection

As we have seen, mate selection in the United States is an individual decision, yet many social and structural barriers and limitations act to constrain our freedom to choose a partner. Besides race, class, age, religion, and sex, these barriers can also include propinquity and family and peer pressure. Let us take a brief look at these factors.

Propinquity We have already touched on the subject of propinquity and its role in mate selection, particularly as we discussed racial and ethnic homogamy. **Propinquity** is used by sociologists to denote proximity or closeness in place and space. Traditionally, Americans met, were attracted to, and married people who lived in the same community. This factor of residential proximity in mate selection was first introduced in a pioneering study of mate selection conducted by James Bossard in 1932. In his study of who married whom in the city of Philadelphia, Bossard found that more than half the couples who applied for marriage licenses lived within 20 blocks of each other. One-sixth lived only a block apart, and one-third lived within five blocks of each other. Subsequent research has reported similar results. Although we are no longer tied to our local communities in the way we were before mass transportation and the mass production of the automobile, residential propinquity continues to contribute to homogamy in mate selection.

Residential propinquity is closely tied to many of the factors we have already discussed: race, social class, sexual orientation, and to a lesser degree religion. Historically, people of the same general social characteristics have tended to live close together. For example, most U.S. cities are racially and ethnically segregated, and many are class-segregated as well. It is not unusual to go to a city and find very distinct racial or ethnic communities: the African American community, Little Italy, Chinatown, Greektown, Little Cuba. These residential patterns increase the likelihood that we will meet, date, and marry people of similar racial and social backgrounds.

Obviously propinquity is not limited to place of residence. In a mobile society such as ours, propinquity operates as much, if not more, in schools, the workplace, places of entertainment, and other institutions as we increasingly move out of our communities for a good portion of each day. Nevertheless, the probability of meeting someone and establishing an intimate relationship still depends on the likelihood of interacting with that person. And the likelihood of interacting with someone is a function of their nearness or close proximity to us.

Family and Peer Pressure Consider the following scenario:

> I am working on a doctorate; my boyfriend has never attended college. We love each other, but my family and friends insist that I should break off with him because he is not on my level. I think they might be right because sometimes even I am embarrassed by the way he speaks and carries himself. I feel so pressured by them. Can love overcome the prejudices of society?

Stated another way, this woman's question could well be: Can love overcome the pressures of family, friends, or peers? Who is or is not acceptable to parents and other relatives is of importance to most Americans. Parents in particular exercise direct and indirect influence on whom we meet and develop relationships with. Parents influence our choice of mate from the moment we are born through their teaching, their example, where they choose to live, which schools they send us to, and so forth. How, where, and when we are brought up has a profound impact on our views and decisions concerning dating, marriage, and family. Additionally, the closer we are to our parents and kin, the more likely we will consider their views.

Peers, too, can be powerful forces affecting both whom we meet and whom we decide to date or pair with. If our peer relationships are significant and close, we are far more likely to consider our friends' views and feelings about the people we date and marry. When you have completed the Writing Your Own Script exercise you will probably have a greater awareness of just how influential parents, other family members, and peers can be in choosing a mate.

Personal Qualities and Mate Selection

As we saw in Figure 5.1, social factors such as those we have just discussed act as an initial screening. Once our pool of eligibles is determined, other factors come into play, such as the personal qualities or characteristics of the people we meet and consider as potential mates. The personal qualities we consider cover a wide range that includes physical appearance, lifestyle, ability to communicate, values and attitudes, personality, and family background, to name but a few. Probably the most important, at least initially, is physical appearance, because first impressions are often based on whether or not we find a person attractive. In addition, first impressions are often lasting impressions. In the discussion that follows we take a brief look at attractiveness and companionship as classic examples of personal qualities that critically affect mate selection.

Attraction What does "Ms. Right" or "Mr. Right" look like? All of us have some image, vague though it may be, of who our ideal mate will be. Usually this image includes both physical and personality features, and we consciously or unconsciously rate or compare potential mates in accordance with these images. These ideas and images do not develop in a vacuum; rather, they are shaped in large part by the society in which we live. For most Americans, physical appearance is one of the most important ingredients in mate selection. Whether we admit it or not, how someone looks has a considerable impact on whether we choose that person as a friend or lover.

Researchers and pollsters have found a number of interesting points about physical attractiveness and its influence on mate selection. For example, Americans overwhelmingly agree that being physically attractive is a strong asset in the dating/mate selection game. In a recent Gallup poll (1999), seven out of ten Americans said that physical attractiveness was important in society today in terms of social life, happiness, and the ability to get ahead. In addition, we tend to think that we are better looking than other people think. When asked, almost no one says that they are below average in attractiveness or are downright unattractive. Furthermore, men are more likely than women to exaggerate their appearance, whereas less attractive females are more accurate in their self-evaluations. This is true, no doubt, because women get far more feedback about their appearance than men do. Likewise, younger Americans are much more likely than older Americans to ascribe above-average appearance to themselves, which suggests that older Americans may have bought into the popular notion that to be old is to be dowdy. In any event, once people meet and dating begins, personality characteristics become important considerations, although attractiveness does not decline in importance (Patzer, 1985; Newport, 1999).

Dating and marriage relationships tend to be endogamous for physical attractiveness. Various studies have documented our general tendency to look for and end up with partners whose attractiveness is roughly equivalent to our own (Stroebe et al., 1971). Attractiveness can impact the depth and duration of our relationships. For example, researcher Gary White (1980b) found that couples who are similarly attractive are more likely to progress deeper into the relationship than are couples in which one partner is relatively more attractive than the other. In the dating game, people tend to shop around for an attractive partner. The greater our level of attractiveness the greater our bargaining ability in the marriage market. Some of the physical similarities between people who become couples are probably the products of race and class endogamy. Some, however, are also probably a function of our definitions of what is physically appealing, including our assessment of where we fit in society's general definition of physical attractiveness.

Companionship Some demographers have predicted that many people who have married in recent times will likely stay married to the same person for the next 50 years or more unless death or divorce intervenes (Ramu, 1989). If they are correct, then qualities such as compatibility and companionship are critically important in mate selection. It is essential to choose a mate with whom we can communicate; enjoy sexually and socially; and depend on for friendship, support, and understanding. The presence or absence of these attributes can have a tremendous impact on the quality and longevity of the relationship. G. N. Ramu (1989) identifies communication and sexual adjustment as the two most crucial personal attributes that contribute to companionship in an intimate relationship. These attributes are complex and depend on a number of factors: the partners' intellectual compatibility, their sensitivity and empathy toward each other, each partner's ideas about the other's sexual behavior, similarity in social class and other important social characteristics, and the importance to both partners of sexual relations in marriage.

The Life Cycle and Mate Selection

The desire to date or participate generally in the mate selection process does not begin and end with youth. The fact that many people are delaying marriage until later ages, coupled with the high divorce rate, better health, and an extended life expectancy, means that an increasing number of older adults will enter or reenter into dating relationships, and some of them will look for a permanent mate. In some ways these older adults resemble their younger counterparts; they date, fall in love, and act romantically in ways that are often very similar to young people. They seek partners for companionship, for long- and short-term commitments, and to share their life with. They feel a need for emotional care and the same type of mutual aid that many younger couples share. They frequently differ, however, in terms of the ultimate goal of mate selection. Although many older adults say that they would like to remarry, few of them actually do. Many of them are independent and self-sufficient, and they want to remain that way. (See Chapter 14 for a fuller discussion of this topic.)

Given today's extended life expectancy, an increasing number of older adults will enter and reenter into dating relationships. Many middle-age couples feel a degree of freedom in personal intimate relationships that they did not experience in their youth and that allows them to explore a number of different styles of intimacy.

MEETING PARTNERS: WHERE AND HOW

"Looking for Mr. Right." "Suffering from a Man Shortage? Try Honey Hunting in the Boondocks." "Bachelors for 2001: Single Men from Coast to Coast Seek Sensible, Sensitive, Athletic and Sophisticated Mates." "A Few Good Men: Where?" "Where Are the Men?" "Where Are the Men for the Women at the Top?" "How to Meet Someone on the College Campus."

These quotes represent but a handful of the many titles that have appeared in recent popular and scientific literature. What do these titles suggest about contemporary mate selection? First, they suggest that single people in the dating market today face a great challenge, namely, finding a significant other. Moreover, they indicate that women more often than men express difficulty in finding a mate. Given what we already know about the marriage gradient and the sex ratios in some groups, this is not surprising.

Most of the literature on dating continues to focus on college students. In many ways, such studies perpetuate the myth that dating is still primarily a white, middle-class, college-aged phenomenon. The fact is, today people who date come from all walks of life, represent a wide range of ages, and are increasing in number. This fact has not gone unnoticed by an increasingly competitive service industry that has recognized and capitalized on this phenomenon. Dating is big business. One of the most significant additions to contemporary dating and mate selection is the highly developed dating technology that provides singles with increased opportunities to meet prospective partners by using a variety of new technologies. In this section we present a brief discussion of some of the traditional as well as new ways that those who want to date look for a partner.

School, Church, and Work

The high school or college campus is a traditional place where pairing and dating take place. Most high schools and colleges that used to be segregated by sex are now coeducational. Many campus dormitories are now desegregated, and even some fraternities have gone coed. These changes have increased the opportunities for heterosexual interaction and coupling. Students meet each other in the dormitories, in classes, or through friends. In addition, various groups sponsor activities such as dances, beach parties, and retreats to bring people together.

On your campus, what kinds of activities are generally conducted that seem specifically aimed at getting people of the opposite sex together? People of the same sex? If you have a significant other, did you meet her or him in high school or college? Is it difficult or easy to meet and establish relationships with people of your choosing on your campus?

Obviously, high school and college campuses are insufficient places in and of themselves for meeting possible mates. Even on campuses we find those who want to date using a variety of other methods to meet people, such as being introduced by roommates, relatives, or friends; advertising in the college or local newspaper; and using computerized dating services. In the past, the church or synagogue frequently brought people together. Today, however, as church attendance generally has declined, particularly among young adults, religious institutions and services less frequently serve this purpose.

Although the world of work at the turn of the century provided women with new and increased opportunities to meet and establish intimate relationships with the opposite sex in the sense that it got them out of the house and away from their parents' supervision, it no longer provides the same level of opportunities for pairing. As in the past, the work women do is often sex-segregated or predominantly female, for example, as elementary school teachers. Thus, it offers only limited contact with eligible males. In addition, the diversity of backgrounds that can sometimes be found in workplaces serves to limit the prospective pool of eligibles for women and men.

Singles' Bars and Gay Bars

Singles' bars reached their peak in popularity during the 1970s and early 1980s. Once symbolic of the singles' scene and a significant means of meeting potential mates, singles' bars today are rejected by many people who see them as nothing but "meat (not meet) markets." In the past and to some degree today, singles' bars provided a space where people could feel comfortable and meet other single people. Studies of why people go to singles' bars indicate that the major reason is for companionship.

Gay bars are similarly rejected by some lesbians and gays as meat markets. The motivations for attending gay bars are basically the same as those for attending heterosexual bars. Because of homophobia and discrimination against lesbians and gays, and because many lesbians and gays feel uncomfortable expressing or being themselves in a predominantly heterosexual environment, gay bars continue to serve a significant mate selection function.

Self-Advertising: Personal Ads

> Are you Italian? Petite, attrac. DIF 40+, degreed, seeking S/DIM 40+, must be finan/emot secure. No drugs/alcohol/smoking. Must like music, din out and travel.
>
> Attractive Aquarian. Gay, SWF, 33, tired of bar scenes. 5'5", 142 lbs., very romantic, honest, open-minded. Seeks honest open-minded gay SF, 30–40, nondrug user, for a long-lasting relat. Only serious need reply.
>
> Sexy and Cute. SWF, 23, wants the best and won't settle for less! If you're attra., ambitious, prof. S/D white/Hispanic, fin secure please respond. Photo please.
>
> SWM, 70, attrac., very active, outgoing & sincere, looking for a SWF who desires companionship & romance.

Although fictitious, these ads are typical of real ads found in most local newspapers around the country. Personal ads as an approach used to find mates is not a new phenomenon. For example, in the 1800s settlers in the Northwest used a mail-order system in which they advertised for a bride (Steinfirst and Moran, 1989). This type of advertising for a bride continues today in some circles. For instance, many American men use this approach to advertise for Asian brides. Some researchers and others have criticized these men, suggesting that they are looking to Asia for brides out of a stereotypical view of them as subordinate and subservient and easier to control than American women. Furthermore, there is some evidence that personal ads appeared in newspapers during colonial times. Later, men moving across the frontier also advertised for brides in newspapers (Carlier, 1972).

Not until the 1980s, however, did the use of personals become widespread and public. Since the 1980s, it seems that using personal ads has become not only acceptable but a fashionable way to meet people, especially among educated people (Steinfirst and Moran, 1989). Today, people who use the personals are no longer considered either perverted or desperate. In fact, some experts consider the use of personal ads to be a healthy and creative adaption to societal change (Bolig, Stein, and McHenry, 1984). In any case, with leisure time at a premium for many working people, with the dramatic increase in the numbers of singles, and with the sometimes difficult task of finding a partner through conventional means, an increasing number of people feel comfortable advertising themselves in the hopes of landing a mate.

Content analyses of personal ads indicate that men are twice as likely as women to place an ad seeking a partner (see, for example, Davis, 1990). Such analyses also consistently report gender differences in these ads. For example, women define or offer themselves as attractive more often than men, and men seek attractiveness and request photographs far more often than women. Men offer financial security much more than women while women seek financial security and more permanent relationships than men. Women's greater emphasis on resources and status translates into their preference for older men. In addition, personality or character is more important to women than men (Steinfirst and Moran, 1989; Smith, Waldorf, and Trembath, 1990; Fischer and Heesacker, 1995).

A recent content analysis of personal ads placed in a southeastern newspaper, a leisure magazine, a singles magazine, and a state magazine reported that the overwhelming majority of those placing ads were white, male, and heterosexual. According to the study, both females and males mentioned personality (for example, intelligent, kind, honest, warm, sense of humor) most often as a characteristic they wanted in a potential partner. For women, the second and third most frequently mentioned characteristics were nonsmoking and a professional job based on a college degree. For men, the second and third most frequently mentioned characteristics sought in a potential partner were good looks and nonsmoking. The author of the study suggests that the women's movement and changing gender roles are having an influence on the search for potential heterosexual partners. While good looks or attractiveness is still frequently mentioned in personal ads, more stress is put on personality characteristics. Women are now more educated, more professionally oriented, and more financially secure than in the past. Thus, it appears that they are beginning to place more emphasis on personality traits and somewhat less emphasis on looks. The concern with nonsmoking in a potential partner for both women and men may be a result of the increased knowledge about the health dangers of smoking (Lance, 1998). Today, it is fairly routine for single people using classified ads to dial an 800 number that puts them in contact with the person they have chosen in order to hear a more personalized message about that person's interests and attributes.

Finding dating partners through the use of personal ads has become increasingly popular and allows individuals to find partners with matching interests and specific characteristics.

Do any of these findings surprise you? Can you determine the principles of endogamy and exogamy in the sample ads presented at the beginning of this section? Check your local or school newspaper. What do personals tell us about mate selection in the United States? In your city? On your campus? About the qualities that people look for in a mate? If you were to write such an ad, what would you say?

Dating Clubs and Dating Services

Dating clubs and services advertise to and hope to attract those individuals who have difficulty meeting people through conventional routes or who are simply fed up with the commercialized nature of the singles' scene. A wide variety of dating clubs exist across the country that, for a fee, sort out compatible couples and bring them together. Rather than go the route of advertising in a newspaper or magazine, many people join or use the services of specialized dating clubs. A primary appeal of these clubs is that they provide immediate visual stimuli (which is important to those who are concerned with physical attributes and appearance). It also saves people from having to sort through pages of personals to find a person who fits what they are looking for in a mate and then, sometimes through trial and error, having to arrange to meet.

Many of these clubs are open to anyone interested in joining, but some are specialized and tailored to the interests of a particular group. Specialized dating clubs can be especially appealing because they cater to a specific clientele. A number of such clubs around the country specialize in attracting members of a specific group, for example, professionals, vegetarians, bisexuals, Catholics, Jews, African Americans, single parents, lesbians, gays, and people who

APPLYING THE SOCIOLOGICAL IMAGINATION

CHOOSING A MATE: A CONTENT ANALYSIS OF PERSONAL ADS

Read the personal ads in your local, regional, or school newspaper. Who or what types of people are typically seeking one another? List the characteristics that women and men typically seek in a romantic partner. How are these characteristics different? How are they similar? How do race, class, age, and sexual orientation intersect in these ads? That is, what do these ads tell us about these systems of experience? If you have access to a personal computer, instead of analyzing the personals in print media, go on-line to analyze dating messages and services on the Internet. Use the same set of questions listed above to guide your analysis of Internet personals. You might even do a comparative analysis of personals in each medium.

like to travel, to name but a few. There is even a dating club for the wealthy that charges its members a fee as high as $100,000 to match them with a marriage partner.

Although dating and/or singles' clubs are common in the United States, they do not exist in some cultures, and in others they are a relatively new and unique phenomenon. For example, until 1998 there was no such thing as a singles' club in the East African nation of Kenya. In that year, a Kenyan advice columnist opened the country's first singles' club. As definitions of women's and men's roles in marriages and families continue to undergo changes globally, traditional ways of mate selection in other non-Western countries may follow Kenya's lead and give way to western trends, such as singles' or dating clubs, and even the widespread use of computer technology.

Computer Dating and the Internet

The technology explosion in the late twentieth century gave rise to incredible changes in the lives of Americans. In the social arena of dating and mate selection, thousands, if not millions, of people have turned to computer technology in their search for a mate. Many unmarried people have joined computerized matching services that sell their members information on other members. Clients must complete a questionnaire covering a range of personal and demographic characteristics (sometimes as many as 200 traits) such as age, race, body build, religion, income, education, diet, tobacco use, political outlook, sense of humor, disposition, and sexual activity. This information is fed into a computer, which matches it with other clients who have similar profiles. Members of computerized matching services pay a lifetime membership fee and then a separate fee for each computer match they receive. Such services do not guarantee a match; and even if there is a match, some of the same risks one encounters in meeting potential mates in bars or other places are present such as noncompatibility or sexual aggression and violence.

Other people who want more control over the mate selection process use their personal computer to get in touch with prospective partners through dating networks called "dial-your-mate." People using these networks dial into a central computer and provide information similar to that contained in the questionnaires of the computerized matching services. Dial-your-mate services are geared toward heterosexual couples in that the information provided is compared with that of all opposite-sex participants and then ranked in terms of percentage of agreement. Subscribers can send information and messages back and forth on their computers, ignore the messages, exchange more information, or end the interaction at their discretion.

Dating in Cyberspace

Computer dating is not new. However, it has grown by leaps and bounds over the last two decades and is now estimated to be a billion-dollar social marketplace. There seems to be little doubt that the dating industry has changed dramatically as a result of new and increasing computer technology. Some observers say that a quiet revolution has overtaken the world of romance. One thing is for sure, mate selection, by way of the computer and the Internet, has become pretty routine for a variety of singles. For example, many single professionals are looking for a mate in cyberspace. Modern life for the unmarried professional today is increasingly complicated and full, making finding a partner difficult, if not impossible, for those who are interested. Today's professionals are marrying later; they travel thousands of miles each year for business reasons; they relocate frequently as they climb the corporate ladder; they run in and out of health and other exercise clubs on a tight schedule on their way to the office; they rarely date colleagues on the job; and many of them are fed up with singles' bars, blind dates, and family and friend fix-ups (rarely does what they want in a partner coincide with what family and friends think they need).

IN OTHER PLACES

INTERRACIAL DATING IN SOUTH AFRICA

Since the transition to democracy in South Africa in the 1990s, what are race relations there like today? Now, seven years after the end of apartheid, with the mingling of the races occurring at a level greater than ever before in the country's history: Are more couples forming intimate relationships across race? Is there more interracial dating in the "new" democratic postapartheid South Africa? According to a May 2001 news item on interracial dating in South Africa, such relationships, particularly public interracial relationships, are still unimaginable to some in South Africa. This is not surprising, given that the "new" South Africa is in its infancy and given the history of race, racism, and the legal bans prohibiting the intermingling of the races in South Africa. For decades, under the apartheid government, love, dating, and marriage across the color line were strictly forbidden. The first Afrikaner government came to power in 1948, and in 1949 interracial marriages were banned. Eight years later, in 1957, the apartheid government introduced a new section to the country's Immorality Act that forbade sexual relationships between whites and nonwhites.

Although the ban on interracial dating was lifted in 1985, blacks and whites were still required by law to live in separate areas. Thus, couples who dated or married across race experienced harassment as well as other negative sanctions. Interestingly, the statistics on interracial marriage under apartheid in South Africa were strikingly similar to those in the United States today, where the ban against interracial marriage was lifted almost 35 years ago. For instance, in 1987, the South African government reported that about 2 percent of all marriages that year were interracial. The latest figures on interracial marriage in the United States indicate that only about 2 percent of all marriages in 2000 were interracial and that included interracial marriages across all groups (not just blacks and whites).

True, the races are mingling more than ever before in South Africa. Black and white South Africans increasingly share public spaces, as well as office cubicles, suburban neighborhoods, and books in integrated classrooms. Indeed, some prominent blacks, including a former South African political prisoner, are married to whites, and one of South Africa's most popular soap operas, "Isidingo," features an interracial couple. However, the reality of the "new" South Africa is that most blacks and whites still live in very separate communities. Thus, not only interracial dating and marriage but also interracial friendships remain rare. And although interracial couples are no longer oddities in big cities, they are seldom visible in restaurants, shopping malls, or movie theaters. The postapartheid South African government does not collect statistics on the number of interracial marriages, but it seems that the new democracy and intimate relationships across race have not yet caught up with each other.

What do you think? *Do people in a democratic society have complete freedom to interact with, date, mate with, and marry people of a different race? If not, why not? Although there are no longer laws in South Africa that prohibit interracial dating and marriage why do you think it is still uncommon? Why do you think that the United States and South Africa have similar interracial marriage rates? Explain.*

Source: "Sunday Q & A: Interracial Dating in South Africa," *New York Times* (May 27, 2001):16.

Some experts predict that by the year 2010 just about one-half of the U.S. population will be single. It appears, therefore, that more and more singles might be using computer technology to find a mate and that there will be a service out there in cyberspace for everyone.

Recently, electronic networks, where people pay a fee and subscribe to discussion groups and chat rooms, have become the matchmaker mechanism of choice. In these cyber groups and cyber rooms, members meet hundreds of people with whom they discuss everything from the most trivial to very serious topics about love, romance, dating, marriage, children, and religion. Like dating clubs and dating services, some electronic networks cater to specific groups. For example, Jdate.com caters to Jewish singles and claims to be the largest Jewish singles network with over 300,000, or one out of every ten, Jewish singles as members. Findachristian.com is a Christian singles and pen pal network where Christians go to find each other.

Electronic networks have advantages as well as pitfalls. A major advantage of electronic networking and computer-based on-line dating services generally is that it does not require face-to-face communication, thus allowing people to portray the persona they choose while remaining anonymous through a chosen designation or code name until they are ready to get involved. This can lead to more open expression because people don't have to worry about seeing or running into each other if the on-line relationship does not work (Nichcolas and Milewski, 1999). It also saves the time and expense that might be spent on a bad blind or fix-up date, and it cuts out the need for barhopping. A pitfall is the

The Internet, via the World Wide Web, has revolutionized the dating scene. However, it has also introduced some problems. On the one hand, the Internet increases one's possibility of interacting with and dating multiple partners. On the other hand, this could be problematic for users who are seeking a monogamous relationship.

Source: Reprinted with special permission of King Features Syndicate.

potential for dishonesty and even harassment or violence if, for example, the on-line relationship does not work out. When it does work, it can lead a couple to the altar.

A number of contemporary marriages have been made in cyberspace heaven. For example, controversial talk-radio personality Rush Limbaugh reportedly met his spouse on a chat line (Nichcolas and Milewski, 1999). Unlike earlier computer introduction services, which match personal traits and introduce people who seem compatible, on-line modem-to-modem services let customers do the matchmaking, allowing them to jump into or out of any conversation with whomever they choose (Bennett, 1989). For one couple using an e-mail discussion group on the Genie on-line service, it was love at first byte. A few weeks after they met on-line they met in person and decided that their compatibility worked in person as well as on-line. Another couple, both Lebanese, with one living in Lebanon and the other in the state of Washington, went on-line and found love and happiness. Although we do not know how many of these unions take place or how long they last, the fact is that these on-line courtships are becoming increasingly popular as electronic bulletin boards are transformed into what some call "on-line pickup joints" (Baig, 1994).

A new kid on the computer technology block, so to speak, text messaging via mobile phones has recently become a popular method of flirting or asking someone out on a date, according to a survey carried out by the Finnish wireless entertainment provider Riot Entertainment. According to the survey, nine out of ten women flirt with men using short messaging service (SMS) messages rather than talking. This method of flirting and "hooking up" is particularly popular among the younger generation. For example, 82 percent of the women 18 to 25 years of age said that they believed text messaging was the best way to ensure a man responded to them. Similarly, the majority of the men surveyed said that sending a text message was much easier than physically trying to talk with a woman. Both women and men indicated that they felt more comfortable sending text messages than speaking on their mobile phones (Telecomworldwire, 2001).

Finally, another recent and unique matchmaking strategy on the dating scene is "8minuteDating," a matchmaking event popularized on such TV shows as "Frasier" and "Sex and the City." Over the course of the fall 2001 television season, a restaurant in Quincy, Massachusetts, added this latest version of the dating game to its menu. In "8minuteDating," adults 25 to 35 years of age are paired at tables and have 8 minutes to talk, which amounts to their date. The entry fee was $33.38 and included appetizers (Gale Group, 2001).

Although there are no precise figures as to how many cyberspace dating services there are today, we do know that among those that exist, many promise to find their subscribers the perfect mate (or allow the subscriber to do it her/himself). Members can swing, place ads, search thousands of classified such as personals, view photos of potential matches, engage in live on-line romance chat, flirt using a cell phone, and even order a bride through mail order. Ironically, it is the same technology that some people feel isolates us and is too invasive that is also responsible for bringing people together (Cytrynbaum, 1995).

While computer-based dating services may appeal to those concerned about AIDS, consumers of this type of technology, especially women, must be careful and alert about the risks involved. As we have pointed out, there is the risk of meeting someone who may prove to be disappointing or, worse, violent or with a violent or unsavory past. Some observers estimate that men outnumber women in cyberspace six to one, while others say that the ratio is more like two to one. Whatever the case, more and more women depend on the Internet for business and recreation. Thus, as their use of on-line dating services and discussion groups increases, we can probably expect the problem of cyberspace stalkers to increase as well.

THE FUTURE OF DATING

What is the future of dating? We cannot be sure. It is a safe bet, however, that dating will be around for some time to come, albeit in an increasingly modified form. It is also a safe bet that single people looking for that "right" partner will continue to use traditional as well as creative new ways to facilitate their search. For example, some single heterosexual women today consider the food market a good place to meet a potential partner. They believe that if a man is there doing his own shopping, chances are he is single and may also be looking for a partner. In addition, some women suggest following him around the store to see the kind of items he buys. This should give one insight into the type of person he is—what he does and does not like. And according to recent news releases, devoted fathers are a hot commodity on the twenty-first century dating scene. Some single women, it seems, find the nurturing and vulnerable tendencies exhibited by single fathers to be powerful magnets in the mate selection market; they are attracted to single fathers because they see them as trustworthy, nurturing, and compassionate. In this context, public places frequented by unattached dads and their children such as public parks and outdoor and indoor playgrounds serve as new markets for meeting potential mates. Experts attribute this trend to an increasing number of fathers awarded custody of their children, theorizing that women are attracted to the male who proves that he can be involved (with his kids). Some outspoken critics of this new trend argue that such generalizations about single fathers are unfair and even sexist. They say that we should not reserve terms like "sweet, caring and nurturing" only for men with children. Rather, we should assume that all men possess these qualities. Society should not marvel over men who are attentive to their kids, rather it should be expected behavior. It is ironic, they say, that kids are considered an asset for a single man, while they are often a liability to single women seeking a partner (Moyle, 1999).

Among some young urban professionals (sometimes referred to as "yuppies") the local launderette has become a popular meeting place for singles. In many upscale urban neighborhoods where large numbers of single professionals live, establishments with a launderette in front and a bar next door or behind it enjoy increasing popularity with some singles. Today, singles can complete a sometimes unappealing chore (washing dirty clothes) while simultaneously enjoying the company of like-minded people one of whom could potentially become a long-term partner. Along with the various methods of meeting a date that we have already discussed, today's singles also meet potential partners at singles' coffeehouses and on singles' vacations.

Whatever methods single people use to meet partners, as computer technology continues to advance people will continue to find creative ways to use the technology to meet potential partners. And whatever the future of dating, no doubt we as parents and grandparents some day will reminisce about the "good old days" when we were dating.

Although dating is often fun and can be a very positive experience in our lives, it can, and often does, involve negative experiences such as violence and abuse, and breaking up.

VIOLENCE IN DATING AND INTIMATE RELATIONSHIPS

Until the 1980s, the issues of date rape and violence received little public attention. Consequently, most people severely underestimated the extent of these problems. Since then, however, due in part to the women's movement and a more open social attitude toward sexual issues in general, the media have begun to focus on all forms of intimate violence. As a result, our society is finally realizing just how widespread abuse and violence within dating relationships are. Because of the seriousness and high incidence of violence, abuse, and rape in marriages and families, we devote a full chapter (Chapter 11) to its discussion. Here we are concerned specifically with dating violence and assault.

Physical Abuse

Dating violence, the perpetration or threat of an act of violence by at least one member of an unmarried couple on the other member within the context of dating or courtship, encompasses any form of sexual assault, physical violence, and verbal or emotional abuse (National Center for Injury Prevention and Control, 1999). Dating violence is a subject that few people like to discuss. Most people are reluctant to admit that it occurs. However, violent behavior that takes place in the context of dating or courtship is quite prevalent in U.S. society. Estimates vary because studies and surveys use different methods and definitions of dating violence. A review of dating violence research statistics, for example, shows that the rate of nonsexual, courtship violence ranges from 9 percent to 65 percent, depending on how dating violence is defined, that is, whether threats and emotional or verbal aggression are included in the definition (National Center for Injury Prevention and Control, 1999).

Some experts have suggested that violence among intimates is an epidemic whose casualties outnumber the Vietnam War in the amount of people killed (Kong, 1998). For sure, it affects all cultures, races, classes, occupations, income levels, and ages in society. Although it knows no age limit, all too often the victims and perpetrators of dating violence are teenagers and young adults. The most recent research on the prevalence of partner-inflicted violence on adolescent girls found that approximately one in five teenage girls, or about 20 percent, were victims of partner assault. They also found that health risks, such as substance use, unhealthy weight control behaviors, risky sexual behaviors, and suicide were significantly linked with lifetime prevalence of dating violence ("New Study. . . ," 2001). There are many different types of abuse, some of which are not obvious or physically harmful; however, all forms of dating abuse leave the victim with scars. According to a variety of sources, the prevalence rate for nonsexual dating violence is 32 percent among college students and 22 percent among high school students. Data on eighth- and ninth-grade students indicate that 25 percent had been victims of nonsexual dating violence and 8 percent had been victims of sexual violence (Kong, 1998; National Center for Injury Prevention and Control, 1999). A 1995 study conducted by Children Now and Kaiser Permanente found that almost half (40 percent) of teen women knew someone in an abusive relationship (California State Parent Teacher Association, 1998). Although at first the physical abuse may seem relatively mild, such as pushing or grabbing, over time the violence escalates. Physical abuse ranges from kicking, hitting, pushing, and grabbing to the use of a weapon such as a stick, gun, or knife. Every 9 seconds, a woman is battered by her partner. Every 6 hours, a woman is killed by her partner (Kong, 1998). Over 70 percent of pregnant or parenting teens are beaten by their boyfriends and, according to the Dating Violence Intervention Project, 30 percent of women aged 15–19 who are murdered in this country are killed by their boyfriend or husband (Borden, 1999).

Some studies of teenage violence suggest that both females and males inflict and receive dating violence in equal proportion, but the motivation for violence by women is most often for defensive purposes. Other studies have found that girls and women are victims of dating violence twice as often as are boys and men, and females suffer significantly more injuries than males. A recent National Crime Victimization Survey found that women are six times more likely than men to experience violence at the hands of an intimate partner (National Center for Injury Prevention and Control, 1999). This abuse typically occurs in long-term relationships, is repeated, and the victims do not terminate the relationship. Even so, most often parents are unaware of the abuse and most of the young women stay in the relationship. Hospitals report that these girls come in with facial injuries, such as a broken nose or black eyes, fractured wrists, and bruises on the neck and other parts of the body. Family therapists say that the pattern in these relationships is typically one in which male jealousy escalates into controlling and restrictive behavior, accusations, and suspicions that ultimately escalate into violence (Levy, 1992).

Control and jealousy are often confused with love by both the victims and the offenders who believe that the violence in their relationship is an indication of their love for one another and that it helps to improve the relationship. Victims who hold this "romantic" view of violence frequently blame themselves for their mistreatment, rationalizing that because their partners love them, they must have done something to "deserve" the abuse. Traditionally, females are taught to take responsibility for whatever goes wrong in a relationship. Thus, the abuser often convinces her that the abuse is her fault; that the violence used to control her is brought on by her less than perfect behavior; that she needs to be disciplined for her lack of consideration; that the discipline is for her own good; and that the abuser has a right to chastise her (Gelles and Cornell, 1990; Borden, 1999). Furthermore, it is rarely the case that violence in courtship is a one-time action. However, only about one-half of all couples in violent relationships end the relationship after the first act of violence. For female teens who remain in such relationships, if there is a child involved there is oftentimes an economic dependence toward the male. Other factors are also involved when teen victims remain in their abusive relationships:

- there might be the fear of being alone,
- there is often a feeling of loyalty or pity, in which the victim feels sorry for the perpetrator,
- there is sometimes the "savior complex," where the abused hopes that by remaining in the relationship she or he can help the abuser get better,
- denial of the situation—the victim often claims that the situation is really not that bad and is optimistic that the situation will get better,
- shame, embarrassment, and humiliation play large roles for why victims never get help and/or remain in abusive relationships,
- peer pressure—pressure to conform to the female and male gender roles. Teenage girls, for example, are often convinced that their status, indeed their femininity, depends upon their having a dating partner, and
- fear, as with adult victims of dating violence, is a major reason that teens stay in abusive relationships. In many cases, the abusive boyfriend will threaten to kill her and, all too often, he will carry through on his threat (Kong, 1998; Borden, 1999).

Various experts in the area of dating and courtship abuse have suggested that physical assault between teens is portrayed by the mass media as common and relatively harmless (see, for example, Reisman, 1998). Unfortunately, it is common, but harmless it most definitely is not. An extension of media portrayals of teen violence, as well as the romantic illusions about abuse, is indicated in the fact that most girls and women who are battered during dating hold the unreal belief that the violence will stop after the wedding (Pagelow, 1984). Unfortunately, it does not. The most recent information indicates that violence between teens who are dating or courting often precedes domestic violence or marital rape if the couple should marry. Teenage males are practicing their skills at sexual dominance and testing the boundaries of acceptable behavior. Thus, adolescent females in violent relationships before marriage or cohabitation can well expect that the violence will not disappear with the marriage vows or the moving in. Rather, the violence will likely be repeated and, in some cases, become more intensified. Most young women survive the violence they experience in their intimate relationships, but tragically many do not (Mignon, Larson, and Holmes, 2002).

In your opinion, what factors of life in the United States might account for the high incidence of dating violence? Why do you think that females are most often the victims of intimate violence? Are there battered males? What legal remedies could be enacted to deal effectively with dating violence? If you were asked to testify before the U.S. Congress on the subject of intimate violence, what would you say? How would you prepare for your testimony? What recommendations would you make?

Date and Acquaintance Rape

Sexual assault is one of the most serious and fastest growing violent crimes in the United States (American Academy of Pediatrics, Committee on Adolescence, 1994; Illinois Coalition against Sexual Assault, 1994). **Rape**—unwanted, forced, or coerced sexual intercourse—is the most extreme form of sexual abuse although sexual assault includes (but is not limited to) treating a partner like a sex object, forcing someone to go further sexually than they want to and unwanted/uncomfortable touching. U.S. Bureau of Justice statistics report that 95 percent of the reported incidents of sexual assaults in intimate relationships are committed by males, and 71 percent of these assaults are planned. According to the National Victim Center, one woman is raped every minute (Houston Area Women's Center, 1999).

Just as our consciousness has become raised about intimate battering, we are also much more aware of the widespread sexual violence suffered by females in relationships with males whom they know and, in many cases, trust enough to date. This problem received national attention in the early 1990s when William Kennedy Smith, nephew of the late president John Kennedy, and Mike Tyson, former heavyweight boxing champion, were accused of sexual assault. In widely publicized trials, Smith was acquitted, and Tyson was convicted and sentenced to prison. The public debate surrounding these cases made many people aware that the majority of rapes are not committed by strangers. Rather, current estimates are that over 85 percent of all sexual assaults involve acquaintances or friends (Houston Area Women's Center, 1999). Rape of a person who simply knows or is familiar with the rapist is called **acquaintance rape**. And rape of a victim who is actually "going out with" the rapist is known as **date rape**. Acquaintance and date rape are a violation of a person's body and her/his trust. It is an act of violence and can be with someone a person has just met, or dated a few times, or even with someone to whom the victim is engaged. The force can come from threats or tone of voice as well as from physical force or weapons. These terms are so closely interrelated that they often are used interchangeably. Although most rapes are date or acquaintance rapes, most *reported* rapes are stranger rapes. The reason for this is that most acquaintance and date rapes go unreported because many people still believe that a sexual encounter between two people who know each other cannot be rape. Researchers have found that most young people do not define violence by an acquaintance or date as a problem; like older victims, they often do not recognize that they are victims of abuse (Ferguson, 1998).

The younger the woman, the more likely that she knows the rapist. In 63 percent of reported cases of rape in which the victim was between 12 and 18 years of age and 80 percent of the cases in which the victim was younger than 12, the victim knew her attacker (Renzetti and Curran, 1992). Date rape and acquaintance rape cut across race, social class, and sexual orientation and can be found in all geographic regions. They are probably most commonplace on college campuses, however. Date and acquaintance rape occurs on virtually all campuses, public or private, urban or rural, large or small. Although most such cases go unreported (only 5 percent are reported to police), it is estimated that one in four college women (27.5 percent) have either been raped or suffered attempted rape at least once since age 14 (National Center for Injury Prevention and Control, 1999). And researchers Crystal Mills and Barbara Granoff (1992) found that one in six male college students in their sample admitted to behavior that met the legal definition of sexual assault, while almost one in three (29 percent) admitted to continuing sexual advances after a women had said no.

These findings are similar to an earlier study of sexual assault on college campuses conducted by *Ms.* magazine in 1985. In that study 1 in 12 college males admitted to having committed acts that met the legal definition of rape or attempted rape; that is, they admitted to having forced a woman to have intercourse or tried to force a woman to have intercourse through physical force or coercion. What is alarming is that almost none of these men identified themselves as rapists; 84 percent said that what they had done was *definitely* not rape. Equally alarming, of the women who were raped almost three-fourths of them did not identify their experience as rape. In a 1999 survey, 35 percent of the men surveyed indicated some likelihood that they would commit a violent rape of a woman who had fended off an advance if they were assured of getting away with it (Raoe Statistics, 1999).

Historically, fraternities have contributed to coercive and often violent sex and sexual assault. According to some researchers, fraternities are very concerned with the expression of masculinity and seek to elevate the status of men above that of women. In this context, women are treated as commodities; that is, fraternity males knowingly and intentionally use women as sexual prey, creating a climate in which rape can and does occur. Despite this fact, many institutions of higher education have only recently begun to deal with sexual assault on campus (Martin and Hummer, 1993).

Most females as well as males hold the attitude that the male use of force and aggression to have sexual intercourse is acceptable among acquaintances or dates (Koss et al., 1985), at least under certain circumstances, such as if the female arouses the male (Giarrusso et al., 1979). Other research studies provide support for the findings of the Koss and other studies cited here. They also provide support for the finding that males who rape tend to consider sexual

Date rape is commonplace on college campuses today. In response to this growing problem, some colleges such as Hobart College in Geneva, New York offer date-rape awareness workshops in an attempt to alleviate sexual assault in intimate relationships.

aggressiveness as acceptable and do not see themselves as having done anything wrong (Andersen, 1988; Lindsay, 1995).

Finally, in the last decade of the twentieth century, Rohypnol, the "date rape drug," came to public attention. It has been used on many college campuses as well as at youth parties called "raves." The drug comes in pill form and is typically slipped unnoticed into a female's drink. The combined effect of the drug and the alcohol produces such intense intoxication that upon awaking from the drug-induced sleep, the victim is unable to remember what has happened. The seriousness of Rohypnol pushed Congress to pass the Drug-Induced Rape Prevention and Punishment Act in 1996, which made it a federal crime to give someone a controlled substance without her or his knowledge with the intention of committing a violent crime (such as rape). Currently, the penalty for a person found guilty of violating this law is up to 20 years in prison and a $250,000 fine (Ray and Ksir, 1999).

Teen battering and date and acquaintance rape should not come as a surprise to us. Sociologically speaking, it is a reflection of the violence within relationships that is accepted socially and reflected in virtually every aspect of our mass culture—from movies to print and electronic advertisements to fiction as well as nonfiction to video games to MTV, BET Music Videos, and other popular music to daily talk shows to soap operas and most other forms of everyday television. In the context of a sociological analysis, rape is a behavior learned by men in the context of "masculinity." And date rape can be considered an outgrowth of a cultural socialization into masculinity (Lindsay, 1995). Male socialization sets the stage for rape in that "being aggressive is masculine; being sexually aggressive is masculine; rape is sexually aggressive behavior; therefore rape is masculine behavior" (Russel and VandeVen, 1976:261). Because American culture still supports female and male relationships that are stereotypically masculine and feminine—passive-aggressive and submissive-dominant—notions of masculinity are often associated with violence and force.

Many things can be done to reduce or eradicate courtship violence. Given that rape is learned behavior within the context of a masculine self-concept, then it can be unlearned. We can teach future generations of males new roles that do not emphasize and exaggerate domination, aggression, and sexual prowess. On college campuses, administrators must deal with sexual aggression swiftly and punitively without blaming the victim. In addition, campus security police must work cooperatively with local police officials to expedite the prosecution of offenders. Furthermore, colleges should provide counseling and other referral services for both the perpetrators and the victims of both physical and sexual assault. While some colleges and universities are responding proactively, positively, and efficiently in their attempts to prevent courtship violence or to alleviate its effects, much more remains to be done.

BREAKING UP

Although it sounds very pessimistic, some researchers claim that nearly all romances fail. Some end before they get off the ground and others sputter out early. Most serious dating relationships end after 2 or so years, and even if a relationship succeeds and the couple marry, the relationship still faces a 50–50 chance of breaking up (divorce). Couples who have the best chance of not breaking up are those who are equally matched from the start: equally committed, equally attractive, and of similar backgrounds (Manis, 2001). As with marriage, one or both dating or cohabiting partners may feel the need to get out of the relationship. Breaking up a relationship can take many forms: The partners drift apart or stop calling or coming by; they have a fight over a minor incident or something said in anger; or, in rare cases, both agree to terminate the relationship. Breaking up can be very painful, especially if the breakup is not mutually agreed upon.

As in other aspects of dating and courtship behavior, some researchers have found gender differences related to breakups before marriage. For example, most breakups are initiated by women; however, the chances of the breakup being amiable is far greater if the male initiates the breakup. As we pointed out in Chapter 4, men are more likely than women to report feeling depressed, lonely, unhappy, and less free than women after a breakup. Researchers suggest that the practicalities that women exhibit in choosing a mate may function to help them better deal with breaking up than men can do (Rubin, Peplau, and Hill, 1981). No matter the gender, however, it is easier on a person when she or he is the leaver than the person being left. Leavers feel guiltier, but otherwise much less lonely or depressed than those who are left. In fact, often the happier one person is to get out of the relationship, the worse the other person feels about the breakup (Manis, 2001).

Some social scientists claim that breaking up before marriage is less stressful than breaking up after marriage, when the couple have to deal with legally ending the relationship and possibly with custody issues. Furthermore, breaking up is viewed as a logical consequence of the courtship filtering process, whereby those who are incompatible eventually break up before they make the "ultimate" commitment: marriage. Even if this is true, breaking up is seldom easy and can have substantial consequences, no matter what the relationship or who makes the break. When people who are emotionally involved break up, they frequently experience feelings of insecurity, anxiety, low self-esteem, and guilt. "What's wrong with me?" "Will I find someone else?" "Will I be alone the rest of my life?" "What did I do to deserve this?" Unlike in marriage, there is no institutionalized means, such as divorce, to handle the breakup of a dating relationship; however, as our expert (family therapist Joan Zientek) tells us, like married couples, dating couples interested in strengthening and preserving their relationships and sorting through and dealing with anger and hurt, misunderstandings and miscommunications can avail themselves of the counseling and advice of family therapists.

WRITING YOUR OWN SCRIPT

PERSONAL BIOGRAPHY AND SOCIAL STRUCTURE: SELECTING A MATE

Think about the structure of mate selection in U.S. society generally and in the various social groups to which you belong. Write a short essay that includes an analysis of your mate selection in terms of the following framework.

First, think about what initially attracts you to another person. Consider this question within the context of some or all of the following possibilities: physical attractiveness, race, age, sexual orientation, religion, residence, occupational status, popularity, social status, personality, character. Are you attracted to people very much like you, or the opposite?

Next, ask your parents or others with whom you are close and whose opinions you value, whom among the following they would object to if you dated or married:

Race: African American, white American, Asian American, Native American, Puerto Rican, Mexican American, other Latino, other race.

Age: 15, 20, 25, 30, 35, 40, 45, 55, 65, 75, 76 or older.

Educational level: Fifth grade or below, eighth grade only, some high school, high school graduate, some college, college graduate, graduate or professional school.

Religion: Catholic, Baptist, Methodist, Muslim, Buddhist, Mormon, Lutheran, Unification Church, Orthodox Jew, Jehovah's Witness, atheist, other.

Blood relatives: First cousin, second cousin, third or more removed cousin.

Gender: Same sex.

Also think about the following questions, and incorporate your responses in the essay. How do you feel about interracial dating and marriages? Do you know anyone who is dating or married to a person of a different racial group? What problems, if any, have they encountered? Have you ever been involved in an interracial relationship? If not, would you consider such a relationship? What barriers do you think you would encounter if you were a partner in such a relationship? Are any members of your immediate family dating or married interracially? If yes, how do you feel about these relationships? To what extent do parents, relatives, and friends' attitudes about interracial dating and marriage affect your dating and marital choices?

SUMMARY

Mate selection refers loosely to the wide range of behaviors and social relationships that individuals engage in prior to marriage that lead to short- or long-term pairing. It is an institutionalized feature of social life and can be found in some form in all human societies, although the exact processes vary widely from one society to another. In the United States, the mate selection process, particularly for first marriages, is highly youth-centered and competitive.

Mate selection customs vary widely across cultures. Most researchers have divided mate selection customs along a traditional/nonindustrialized and nontraditional/industrialized society continuum. A review of mate selection cross-culturally reveals that many traditional societies now combine traditional and contemporary methods of selecting mates. Dating, an American invention that first appeared in the 1920s, is the focus of our courtship system and incorporates a wide range of social relationships prior to marriage. The history of mate selection in this country has ranged from highly visible parental involvement during the colonial and preindustrial periods to the informal, indirect involvement of parents today. Dating became a widespread phenomenon in the 1920s and 1930s; in the 1940s and 1950s it filtered down to high school students, who started to "go steady"; in the 1960s, 1970s, and 1980s it became a more casual process; and during the 1980s and 1990s dating underwent many changes that reflect contemporary social and gender roles. Today, dating is based far more on mutuality and sharing than on traditional gender roles.

The functions of dating include socialization, development of self-image, recreation, and status grading and achievement. Like all other social behavior and organization, dating is deeply rooted in the social and historical conditions of life. Race, gender, class, and sexual orientation are basic and central categories in American life and thus must be considered in any analysis of mate selection.

A wide range of theories exists that attempt to explain who selects whom and under what circumstances. These theories include explanations in terms of social exchanges and rewards, stimulus–value–role theories, and filtering theories. The process of mate selection can be viewed sociologically as a sequential or filtering process that stresses homogamy and endogamy. Mate selection in U.S. society is mediated by a range of structural and social factors: the nature of the marriage market, the marriage squeeze and marriage gradient, race, class, age, sex, religion, education, propinquity, family and peers, and cultural ideals about beauty and worth. Due to the impact of these factors we are very much like the people we meet, fall in love with, and marry—far more so than can simply be attributed to chance. Computer technology has had a dramatic impact on the nature of mate selection around the world. Increasingly, couples are using cyberspace not only for recreation but also for serious mate selection. Many of these matches are leading to matrimony.

However, not all intimate relationships lead to marriage or long-term commitment. Couples often break up under the pressure of a variety of sociopolitical factors. Moreover, a large number of dating couples are involved in physically or sexually abusive relationships. Battering and abuse among young couples as early as elementary and junior high school has reached epidemic proportions. The same can be said for date and acquaintance rape. In both cases, the victims are overwhelmingly female. Most intimate relationships, however, survive the problems of human frailty. Couples wishing to strengthen and preserve their dating and intimate relationships can and do seek family counseling.

KEY TERMS

dating
mate selection
courtship
getting together
going steady
anticipatory socialization
sex ratio
cruising
marriage market
dowries
pool of eligibles
homogamy
exogamy
endogamy
marriage squeeze
hypergamy
hypogamy
marriage gradient
propinquity
dating violence
rape
acquaintance rape
date rape

QUESTIONS FOR STUDY AND REFLECTION

1. As you have read in this chapter, dating patterns in the United States have changed dramatically over the years. What are the current norms of dating in your community? On your college campus? Are these norms different or the same for each gender? Explain. What do you consider the advantages and disadvantages of

such norms? What, if any, changes would you like to see in today's dating norms?

2. "Cupid's arrow does not strike at random." Explain this statement. Discuss the predictable factors that influence who meets, falls in love with, and marries whom in the United States.

3. Define the concepts of marriage squeeze and marriage gradient. How are the two related? How would the marriage squeeze and marriage gradient be significant in the lives of a 35-year-old female with a Ph.D. and a 35-year-old male who is a high school dropout? Why is the marriage squeeze so significant for African American women?

4. Think about the discussion in this chapter of violence in dating relationships. How prevalent is date rape and other intimate violence on your college or university campus? What are some of the attitudes, behaviors, and activities on your campus that encourage male physical and sexual aggressiveness and contribute to a climate that is conducive toward abuse? Have you ever experienced relationship violence? If yes, how did you handle it? What institutional supports and services on your campus are there for victims of dating violence? In your community, city, and state? What can be done to reduce courtship violence?

ADDITIONAL RESOURCES

SOCIOLOGICAL

BECKER, CAROL S. 1988. *Unbroken Ties: Lesbian Ex-Lovers.* Boston: Alyson. An interesting case study approach to lesbian interpersonal relations, including separation.

KAUFMAN, MICHAEL. 1995. "The Construction of Masculinity and the Triad of Men's Violence." In Michael Kimmel and Michael Messner, eds., *Men's Lives,* pp. 13–25. New York: Macmillan. Examines male violence in the social context of the construction of masculinity and the institutionalization of violence in the operation of most aspects of social, economic, and political life in the United States. Using the notion of a triad of male violence—violence by men against women, violence against other men, and violence against oneself—the article provides some interesting insights into male violence.

KIRKWOOD, CATHERINE. 1993. *Leaving Abusive Partners.* Newbury Park, CA: Sage. A compelling collection of stories by 30 formerly abused women told in their own voices.

WOOD, JULIA T., ED. 1996. *Gendered Relationships.* Mountain View, CA: Mayfield. An excellent set of readings on gendered relationships, it focuses specifically on the reciprocal influence between gender and relationships. The readings come from a wide range of well-known social scientists in the field and cover issues of communication, friendship, heterosexual love, lesbian and gay romantic relationships, sexuality and AIDS, intimate violence, sexual harassment and gender issues in the workplace.

LITERARY

FIELDING, HELEN. 1999. *Bridget Jones's Diary: A Novel.* New York: Penguin. This lively paperback is witty and full of candor. It captures very well the way modern women teeter between being independent and a pathetic girlie desire to be all things to all men. It includes Bridget's quest for the right man, her affair with her charming cad of a boss, e-mail flirtations as well as her mother's incessant attempts to arrange a date for Bridget with some guy that Bridget doesn't know. It is fun, hilarious, fresh, and an excellent novel to get students talking about many of the issues discussed in this chapter. The book was made into a movie.

MCMILLAN, TERRY. 1997. *How Stella Got her Groove Back.* New York: Signet Books. An exuberant novel that chronicles the dating and mate selection experiences of Stella Payne, a divorced superwoman who has everything—except an intimate relationship with a man, something she's convinced she can well do without. On a spur-of-the-moment Jamaican vacation she meets a man half her age, and finds, to her dismay, that he truly rocks her world. She also soon realizes that she's come to a cataclysmic juncture in her life, one that forces new and difficult questions and answers about her passions, desires, and dating, mating, and marital expectations. This novel is a good jump-off for a discussion of age differences in heterosexual intimate relationships, particularly when the woman is older than the man.

INTERNET

www.CollegeClub.com This Web site, part of the Student Advantage Network, allows students to connect with each other; it provides them with a variety of information and services from academics to love, dating and relationships, and much more. For example, through its MatchU engine it allows students to meet and match up on-line.

www.meetmeonline.com This site is advertised as the best place on the Internet to meet someone. It boasts of a membership of 3 million high-quality singles.

Chapter 6

Sexuality and Intimate Relationships

IN THE NEWS: WASHINGTON, DC

For most American teens, oral sex is not sex, so says a recent study of teenage sexuality. According to researchers at the Guttmacher Institute, a nonprofit organization that studies reproductive health (Remez, 2000), most teenagers today believe in abstinence, have never had sexual intercourse, and consider themselves virgins. Yet an increasing number of these youth—some still in middle school—are having oral sex. In a dramatic reversal from what their parents believe, it seems that today's youth do not count oral sex as *"having sex."* They have convinced themselves that oral sex is not really sex; that sex is vaginal intercourse.

The Guttmacher researchers interviewed two dozen health experts and reviewed existing research to assemble a profile of teens and oral sex. According to anecdotal data from the health experts, teenagers think that oral sex is considerably safer behavior than vaginal sex. And in some respects it is. With oral sex there is no risk of pregnancy. However, the risk of sexually transmitted diseases (STDs) is definitely there. Oral sex puts young people in jeopardy of contracting sexually transmitted diseases that can be contracted through oral sex, including the HIV/AIDS virus. In fact, a number of reports from family planning clinicians are showing evidence of dramatic increases in oral herpes and gonorrhea in the throats of teens. Part of the issue, according to one expert, is that Americans define sexual behavior in a very narrow way. We caution young people to abstain, but we are never clear as to what they should be abstaining from.

Many of these young people try to think of anything they can do so they can say they are still virgins. In one survey of teens in grades 9 through 12, of the 47 percent of those who said they were virgins, 35 percent of them indicated that they had been involved in some heterosexual genital activity in the previous year, ranging from masturbation of or by a partner to oral sex and beyond. Experts cite a number of factors that have created a generation of youth who seek oral sex:

- Early maturation. Girls are developing physically much sooner than those of 20 years ago.
- The President Clinton–Monica Lewinsky sex scandal. President Clinton indicated that he did not regard oral sex as "*having sex*."
- The media. Talk about oral sex has become commonplace in the mass media.
- The belief that oral sex is safe from pregnancy and disease. There is a widespread misconception among youth that oral sex is safe sex.
- Instant gratification. If it feels good, do it.

Many teens talk freely about what happens among their friends. A 15-year-old in Green Bay, Wisconsin, for example, reported that children from grades as early as sixth or seventh brag about having oral sex. According to this teen, the consensus at her high school is that oral sex makes girls popular, whereas intercourse would make them outcasts. The belief is that oral sex is as far as you can go without maintaining any level of emotional attachment. They say that they engage in oral sex to let out sexual tensions and that it is socially acceptable behavior for them. It's something that happens at a party, is whispered about between friends, and forgotten about the next week. Oral sex is just part of making out. Their attitude is, "What is the big deal?" Just what kind of oral sex young teens are engaging in is debatable. Most say that it is girls who perform the act on boys. But the Guttmacher study says it is about the same for girls and boys (50/50).

On the other hand, for some of these teens, intercourse is a huge leap from oral sex. Intercourse is something that is carefully thought through before acted upon. There is evidence that this behavior transcends race, income, and family structure and is much more widespread than we might think. There is not very good or consistent research on teen sexuality because most major national surveys on teen sexual activity don't ask about oral sex and most don't question the youngest teens. In general, the Guttmacher study and others on teen sexuality point up the problem inherent in classifying people as "sexually active" based on whether they have ever had vaginal intercourse (Peterson, 2000).

WHAT WOULD YOU DO? If you have teenagers or have a close relationship with teenagers would you attempt to educate them about the risk connection between oral sex and STDs generally and HIV/AIDS specifically? Would you support sex education in the schools? As early as elementary school? Regardless of their relationship to you, would you counsel them on how to use condoms and how to get them? On how to talk with a partner about either abstinence or safe-sex practices? And would you counsel them on how to get tested for HIV and other STDs?

Sex continues to be the topic "du jour" in the early years of the twenty-first century. Continuing a pattern that emerged in the late twentieth century, sex and talk of sex, images of sex, sex scandals, and media hype of sex are everywhere in the United States today. And no one is exempt from sexual scrutiny. For example, in the last decade of the twentieth century, a sitting president was involved in a highly publicized sex scandal with a young White House intern, in which he claimed, not unlike the teens in the study described in the "In the News" opening this chapter, that oral sex was not having sex.

Sex is on television (prime time, soap operas, talk shows, comedians' dialogue), in advertisements, newspapers, the films we view, the music we listen to, the books and magazines we read, and, increasingly in cyberspace. Even traditional women's magazines such as *Redbook* and *Glamour* have gotten in on the fray. These and other women's magazines as well as other forms of the media have become increasingly brazen about dealing with the subject of sex, a trend that is most assuredly tied to the fact that our entire society is loosening up about sex. The fact is, we are talking about sex today more than at any other time in our history, and this makes sex more accessible than it has ever been.

Sex sells: It is titillating; most people are intrigued by any discussion of it, particularly when it involves other people's behavior and especially when the people are well known. However, probably no topic related to issues of marriage and family life is more shrouded with mystery, curiosity, intrigue, and controversy than is sex specifically and human sexuality more generally. The concept of human sexuality often is couched in terms of morality. The purpose of this chapter, however, is not to clarify or shape your morality but rather to increase your understanding of the sociopolitical nature of human sexuality and, in the process, enhance your ability to make personal decisions concerning sexual behavior.

Because sexuality figures so prominently in marriage and family life, as well as in other intimate relationships, this chapter, in conjunction with the supplementary materials presented in Appendix A, concentrates on sexual attitudes and behaviors before, during, and after marriage or a committed relationship as well as throughout the life cycle. We begin with a brief discussion of the historical roots of Western sexuality, from the Judeo–Christian tradition to U.S. sexual codes in the early twenty-first century. We then consider the social basis of human sexuality by examining sexual learning and how sexual scripts vary across gender, as well as trends in sexual attitudes and behavior, including sexual orientation. In addition, we discuss physiological aspects of sexuality such as human sexual response and expression. We also examine various codes of sexual conduct and patterns of sexual relationships across the life cycle. Finally, we examine human sexuality within the context of sexual responsibility and protecting yourself and your partners from AIDS and other sexually transmitted diseases.

HUMAN SEXUALITY: PAST AND PRESENT

Often people use the terms *sex* and *sexuality* interchangeably. Thus, when someone talks about sexuality, we often assume that she or he is referring to sexual intercourse. On the other hand, when we speak of sex it is not always immediately clear whether we are speaking of sexual activity such as intercourse or whether we mean a person's genetic sex (that is, biologically female or male). Although neither of these uses is incorrect, for purposes of clarification we use the term *sex* in this chapter to refer to genetic or biological sex only and *sexual activity* or *sexuality* to refer to a wide range of sexual behaviors, including intercourse.

Because human sexuality is so broad, no one all-encompassing definition is appropriate. In general terms, however, **human sexuality** refers to the feelings, thoughts, and behaviors of humans, who have learned a set of cues that evoke a sexual or an erotic response. It includes behaviors well known to us, such as sexual intercourse and masturbation, as well as behaviors we do not readily identify as sexual, such as breast-feeding, giving birth, and talking affectionately with someone. In addition, human sexuality includes our feelings, thoughts, attitudes, and values (Albas and Albas, 1989b). Furthermore, human sexuality involves issues of power, authority, and emotional and physical vulnerability in relationships (Boston Women's Health Book Collective, 1992), as you shall see in the discussion of gender differences in the experience of sexuality and, particularly, of the sexual double standard.

We are sexual beings, and a large proportion of our lives consists of sexual daydreaming, fantasy, and desire; reading about sexual activities or viewing a wide range of sexual behaviors; sexual pleasure, activity, joy, and pain. Given the fact that sexuality is such an important dimension of human experience, all societies are involved, in some way, in controlling the sexual behavior of their members. Although the ways in which sexual behavior is controlled have varied over time and from culture to culture, all societies have a set of rules or codes that define appropriate sexual behavior. Throughout U.S. history, Americans have been subject to one set of sexual codes or another. The codes we adhere to today have their roots in sexual attitudes and practices that existed hundreds, if not thousands, of years ago.

Before we discuss the history of human sexuality in Western society, two points must be made:

1. Although the historical descriptions emphasize the sexual codes that were most prevalent during a given historical period, it is not our intention to imply that sexual ideas and behavior have progressed directly from very strict and repressive codes of sexual conduct to more liberal sexual norms. Rather, sexual ideas and behavior change according to cyclical patterns, with periods of extremely or moderately repressive norms followed by periods of more liberal norms. In addition, at any given time, many different sexual codes, ideas, and behaviors coexist.

2. Generalizations about human behavior are always risky. Human attitudes and behavior are so flexible that they are never the same for all people or all groups. Thus, there are many variations in sexual attitudes and behavior. The historical period in which people live; the political and economic climate; the social organization of race, class, and gender; and factors such as sexual orientation, age, and religion all affect human attitudes and behavior.

Consider, for example, the effects of gender on sexual behavior. Women historically have experienced sexuality in terms of reproduction, oppression (powerlessness), and vulnerability (victims of sexual assault). In contrast, men have experienced sexuality primarily in terms of power and control, passion and emotions, and freedom of sexual choice and behavior. Furthermore, sex and sexuality traditionally have been defined in terms of heterosexuality and monogamy, with homosexuality considered a form of deviance. Thus, for lesbians and gays, the experience of sexuality has been far more repressive and has involved a high degree of public concern and social control by outside forces such as the state.

Similarly, the sexuality of various racial groups (African Americans, Latinos, Native Americans, and Asian Americans) as well as poor people of all races has been defined primarily by outsiders. Thus, these groups have often been defined in scientific research or the popular culture as sexually promiscuous and uncontrolled. These definitions of sexuality often have been used in conjunction with other ideologies of racial inferiority to rationalize oppression and unequal treatment. These examples illustrate how human sexuality involves issues of power and authority and emotional and physical vulnerability. As you read this chapter, keep this point in mind. In addition, keep in mind that human sexuality is not static; rather, it is a dynamic, or changing, process that is continually being shaped and reshaped through the social organization of many diverse factors at any given time.

Jewish Traditions and Human Sexuality

Ancient Jewish tradition placed great emphasis on marriage and reproduction. Women and men who did not marry and have children were considered sinful. Marriage was the only appropriate context for sexual intercourse, the sole purpose of which was reproduction. Although in principle the norm of premarital chastity applied to both sexes, it was more rigidly applied to women. A woman was supposed to be a virgin at the time of marriage. If she was not, she could be put to death. Moreover, women could not own property, nor could they obtain a divorce without their husband's consent. A further restriction placed on women's sexuality can be seen in the rules surrounding menstruation. Because menstruation was considered to be unclean, menstruating women were isolated from their husbands and other family members and were forbidden to engage in sexual activities. Strongly forbidden by Jewish custom were nakedness, masturbation, and homosexuality. Although homosexuality was not mentioned in earlier Hebrew codes, it was made punishable by death in later Hebrew documents. Some scholars claim that early Judaism represented a transition from a more positive view of sexual behavior, a view prominent in ancient times, to a more restrictive view characteristic of the early Christian period (Harmatz and Novak, 1983).

The two ancient Jewish notions about human sexuality—reproduction as a married couple's obligation and male dominance over women in sexual relations—became a part of Christian as well as non-Christian doctrine and, to some degree, can still be found in contemporary U.S. sexual codes.

Christian Traditions and Human Sexuality

Although in the Gospels Jesus refers to marriage as a sacred union, values pertaining to women, marriage, and sexuality decreased as Christian ideas of chastity took hold. The early Christian sexual tradition seems to have been influenced most by St. Paul, who believed that celibacy is superior to marriage and that all humans should strive for a chaste life. A person who could not resist sexual temptation could engage in sexual intercourse, but only within marriage. In the fifth century, the Christian scholar St. Augustine continued Paul's tradition of condemning sexuality, and his influence lasted throughout the Middle Ages. Church documents of the eighth century specified that only the male-superior, or "missionary," position was to be used, because any other position might cause some enjoyment. People who engaged in other than the male-superior position faced a range of penalties (Harmatz and Novak, 1983). During the thirteenth century, the church, through the writings of St. Thomas Aquinas, renewed its position on sexuality. Sexual intercourse was seen as animalistic, an activity to be avoided. Celibacy and virginity were the ideals (Strong et al., 1978). In addition, nakedness, looking at parts of the body, dancing, singing, and touching other people were all considered sinful.

The Protestant Reformation of the sixteenth century ushered in a diversity of views and attitudes concerning human sexuality. Religious reformer Martin Luther, for example, renounced celibacy as an unnatural and unrealistic goal for human beings. Leaving the priesthood to marry, he considered sex to be a natural and appropriate act when carried out within the context of marriage. Likewise, other theologians, such as John Calvin, argued against celibacy, believing that sex was a holy act when it occurred within marriage.

Although Christianity exerted considerable influence, not everyone adhered to its teachings concerning human sexuality. For example, it has been noted that during most historical periods sexual behavior varies according to social class. Often the middle classes followed the prevailing sexual mores more closely than did the aristocrats (upper classes) or the peasants (lower classes).

Sexuality in the United States: An Overview

PURITAN SEXUALITY In the seventeenth century, Puritan immigrants from England brought their Calvinist sexual traditions to the United States. The Puritans defined marriage as a covenant of God and thus the only legitimate mechanism for sex and procreation. Inside marriage, sex was an act that brought a wife and husband together morally and physically. The Puritans also believed that a husband was obliged to satisfy his wife physically. Outside marriage, sex

In early America, sanctions against premarital and extramarital sex were strictly enforced. The novel *The Scarlet Letter* illustrated the kind of punishment women could receive for violating their marriage vows. For example, women who engaged in extramarital sex were often forced to wear an "A" on their clothing to signify that they had committed adultery.

was considered a sin and a threat to the institutions of marriage and the family. Sanctions against premarital and extramarital sex thus were very rigidly enforced. As in prior historical periods, sexual codes of conduct were especially restrictive and rigid regarding female sexuality.

Some of the Puritan views on sexuality can still be found in contemporary U.S. sexual attitudes and behavior. Writing in 1983 about the historical development of human sexuality, social scientists Morton Harmatz and Melinda Novak claimed that many of the sex laws still on the books in various states in the country are a legacy of the Puritan forefathers. For example, in some communities it is still illegal to kiss on Sundays (a law that is rarely enforced). In general, the Puritan codes of conduct continued to dominate U.S. sexual norms well into the nineteenth century, when the Victorians introduced a new and, according to some researchers, even more rigid set of sexual taboos.

VICTORIAN SEXUALITY The Victorian era was characterized by a number of sexual taboos. In general, sex, particularly premarital sex, continued to be viewed in negative terms. At the base of the Victorian view of sexuality was the notion that any kind of sexual stimulation, especially orgasm, sapped a person's "vital forces." Both women and men were fully clothed in several layers during sexual intercourse so that nudity and human flesh would not provide them with excessive stimulation (Harmatz and Novak, 1983).

According to the Victorian codes, sexuality was basically a male phenomenon. In contrast, women were idealized and considered to be morally superior to men in matters of sexuality. The prevailing belief was that decent women did not experience sexual desire. In fact, sexual desire, passion, and enjoyment in women were considered to be sinful. A woman who dared to express sexual feeling or enjoy sexual intercourse was considered to have loose morals. In contrast, males were considered sexual animals who were driven by their lust and desires whether inside or outside marriage. Because men were perceived this way, their sexuality, including premarital and extramarital affairs, was accepted (although not necessarily approved of), whereas similar behaviors by women were condemned. This differing set of norms based on gender is referred to as the **sexual double standard.**

Whereas single women were to refrain from sex altogether, married women were taught that sex with their husbands was their wifely duty; that they must tolerate and accommodate the animalistic nature of men. Given men's alleged greater sexual appetite and needs, wives were taught to look the other way when their husbands had extramarital affairs or engaged in sexual activities with prostitutes.

The degree to which people adhered to the Victorian sexual codes varied from one social group to another. As in earlier periods, the rich and ruling elites basically ignored the restrictions and enjoyed considerable freedom in their sexual behavior. At the other end of the class structure, the poor were also exempted from the prevailing codes. Sexual purity was reserved for middle-class white women. Working-class, immigrant, and nonwhite women, on the other hand, were viewed as strongly sexual; in fact, they were defined as depraved and loose. This stereotype functioned as a rationalization for the continued mistreatment of these groups, especially the repeated rapes of African American women by white men (Basow, 1992).

Sexuality and Slavery If Victorian norms regarding sexuality applied only to certain groups of whites, they did not apply at all to blacks. Whereas for middle-class whites sex was considered sacred and ideally was restricted to marriage, black female and male slaves were prohibited from legally marrying (although as we saw in Chapter 1 there were some exceptions), and they were routinely forced to mate with each other to reproduce and increase the slave population. The control and manipulation of slave sexuality, although oppressive for both sexes, was experienced differently by slave women and men. For men it took the form of being used as studs or being castrated to render them even more powerless and helpless. For women it included the experiences of concubine, mistress, and rape victim as well as the bearer of new generations of slaves. Slave women were robbed of sexual choice and had no legal protection from the rape of any white male who so chose to exploit them.

Sexual Attitudes and Behavior in the Twentieth Century and Beyond

In the twentieth century, sexual attitudes and behavior continued to change. Researcher Carol Darling and her associates (1989) have divided the century into three major eras in terms of sexual behavior. The first era lasted from 1900 to the early 1950s. Despite moral standards that defined sex as acceptable only in the context of marriage, this period witnessed an increase in the number of single women and men reporting sexual involvement prior to marriage. The sexual double standard, however, remained largely in force.

The second major era, from the 1950s to 1970, was characterized by greater sexual permissiveness. Darling refers to this period as an "era of permissiveness with affection" because sex outside marriage was acceptable as long as it occurred within a love relationship and the couple expected to marry each other. The prosperity of this era coupled with the ground-breaking work of sex researchers such as Alfred Kinsey, and William Masters and Virginia Johnson sparked an exploration of alternative lifestyles and a new openness about sex, leading into the third era.

Since 1970, technological advances leading to greater travel and increased job opportunities for women and men resulted in a decreasing emphasis on the nuclear family and an increasing view that sexuality could be recreational as well as an expression of love. Women as a group became less sexually inhibited as they became more independent in other areas of their lives. As in the previous era, many people during this era viewed sexual intercourse as natural and expected for both women and men in love relationships. The difference in this era is that the couple did not have to plan to marry to justify their sexual conduct. Sex before marriage was no longer defined as deviant; rather, it became somewhat the norm.

These changes in attitudes and behavior did not happen by chance. Not only did the mass movement of women into the labor force influence sexual attitudes and standards, but other major changes during this century such as advances in birth control technology (especially the Pill), the contemporary women's movement, the 1973 Supreme Court decision (*Roe* v. *Wade*) legalizing abortion, innovative lifestyles on college campuses, the delay in marriage and childbirth, and the lesbian and gay liberation movements all helped move U.S. society toward less rigid sexual standards. These changes exerted a tremendous impact on sexuality, the family, and heterosexual and homosexual relationships. For example, improved birth control technology enabled women to spend less time bearing and raising children. This had the effect of separating sexual intercourse from reproduction, which in turn contributed to a wider acceptance of sex outside of marriage (Lieberman, 1985).

A Sexual Revolution? Do these fundamental changes in the sexuality of Americans represent a sexual revolution? Some people say yes, given the broad scope of the changes. Others contend that there has been no revolution, just the continued evolution of sexual norms. There is little doubt that attitudes and behavior have moved toward more liberal and permissive standards, but it is also a fact that many individuals and groups still hold securely to traditional sexual norms and values.

Researcher Morton Hunt (1974) has argued that a revolution has occurred only if institutional structures have changed such that traditional attitudes and behaviors have been replaced with a radically new set of attitudes and behaviors. In the case of sexuality, for example, a revolution would include the displacement of vaginal intercourse by other sex acts or an increase in sexual activities that would alter the relationship between marriage and sex, such as mate sharing or swapping and mutually agreed-upon extramarital sex. According to Hunt, until such institutional change occurs we cannot speak of a sexual revolution. Although Hunt's statement is almost 30 years old, his linking of revolution to major institutional change is still relevant.

By the mid to late 1980s, amid the growing awareness, concerns, and fears of sexually transmitted diseases, especially AIDS, many people began to rethink the wisdom, if not the reality, of the so-called "sexual revolution," and some researchers were beginning to report either a decrease in unmarried sexual activity and a renewed emphasis on monogamous sexual relationships or a limiting of the number of sexual partners, if not both. However, for many people, the question of a sexual revolution remained open. Many Americans had come to believe that sex was rampant and that everyone (except themselves) was having lots and lots of sex, and those who were not were miserable misfits (Gorner, 1994b).

Sex surveys[1] during the 1990s indicated that, though we didn't know it, the sex lives of Americans had reached a turning point. Women and men were indeed moving away from casual sex and placing more importance on intimate relationships. Although several previous studies of sex in America helped create a popular image of casual sex, rampant experimentation, extramarital affairs, sex orgies and kinky sex, and young people gone wild with sexual activities, this new sex research paints a much more subdued picture of sexual practices in America.

These sex surveys take on added significance given that until their appearance, Kinsey's trailblazing research on sexual behavior in the United States has been, more or less, the definitive statement on America's sexual habits for almost 50 years without any serious challenge, and similar sex research has been almost nonexistent. Exceptions include the pioneering work of sex researchers William Masters and Virginia Johnson; Shere Hite's mail-in surveys on sexual behavior, including its methodological flaws; and a sprinkling of surveys using specialized groups such as college students as subjects, readers of popular magazines such as *Playboy* and *Redbook*, or focusing on sexual attitudes as opposed to actual sexual behavior. The newer studies overcome several of the flaws of Kinsey's research: For example, Kinsey's samples were not scientifically random, and the subjects were almost all white, well educated, and young. Few, if any, were poverty-level people, and the sample was geographically skewed, centering primarily on the Midwest and the Northeast, with few subjects from the South or West (Lyon, 1992).

The next section of this chapter, highlighting the sexual habits and attitudes of Americans in the 1990s, relies almost exclusively on data provided by these newer surveys. Although the methodology and expertise of the researchers are reliable and unquestioned, the findings of these surveys are likely to spur endless debates about who's doing what to whom and whether or not people answered the survey questions honestly and openly. These debates notwithstanding, when reading the next section, bear in mind that these findings simply present a snapshot of American sexuality that is neither definitive nor precise. Moreover, the relatively small sample sizes of 1049 in one study and 3432 in the other show up in the data about people of color, women, and older people. In many subgroups, such as homosexuals and various racial groups, the numbers of respondents are much too small to conclude very much with any degree of integrity and accuracy. However, by the rules of science, these survey results will be the baseline information on American sexuality until such time as other good scientific studies are implemented and reported.

Sexual Attitudes and Behaviors in the 1990s "Sex Study Shatters Kinky Assumptions." "What Is Normal?" "Generation X Is Not Generation Sex." "So, Now We Know What Americans Do in Bed, So?" "Now the Truth about Americans and Sex." "Sex in America Today." "Sex in America: Faithfulness in Marriage Thrives After All." These are but a sprinkling of the titles of articles reporting the findings of the sex surveys undertaken in the 1990s by *Parade* magazine and the NORC. Given the overwhelming attention paid to the results of these surveys it is apparent that Americans are as interested as ever in what they and their neighbors are doing sexually. Most of us, at one time or another, have had the sneaky suspicion that people across the country were having more, livelier, and better sex in traditional places such as the bedroom as well as exotic places like on the kitchen table, in a limo, in the bathtub or shower, and

[1]One of these 1990s studies is a national survey of Americans' sexual behavior and attitudes conducted in 1994 by Mark Clements for *Parade* magazine. The study, a follow-up to a similar 1984 study for *Parade*, covered a representative sample of the American population as a whole—1049 women and men, aged 18 to 65.

A second study, described as the most comprehensive and definitive study ever of Americans' sexual behavior and attitudes, is said to easily supplant the Kinsey studies of the late 1940s and early 1950s as the baseline for all comparable research because of the new study's high standards of methodology and the credentials of the researchers. This 1992 study was based at the University of Chicago's National Opinion Research Center (NORC) and was directed by a team of scholars headed by sociologists Edward Laumann, Robert Michael, John Gagnon, and Stuart Michaels. The research methodology included a voluminous questionnaire, backed by face-to-face interviews with a random national sample of 3432 Americans aged 18 to 59, representing 97.1 percent of the adult population. The findings of this study provide a wealth of data about the sex lives of ordinary people.

As social taboos have fallen away, pornographic images have become more visible and explicit in our neighborhoods. The widespread dissemination of pornography and the visibility of porn shops are believed by many to encourage male violence and dominance.

other places too scintillating to mention. At some time in our lives we have all probably eyed someone and wondered if that person has a sex life and, if so, what it must be like. As we pointed out earlier, sex is everywhere we turn in America and, by and large, what we learn from popular cultural discussions and portrayals of sex is that it is primarily the province of young, attractive hard bodies who prepare for, recover from, or engage in an endless series of copulation (Elmer-DeWitt, 1994). But just how reality-based is this view of Americans' sex life? Researchers believe that the dearth of factual information about our sexuality reinforces fear, intimidation, anxiety, and a belief in popular fictionalized depictions of sexuality.

While fantasies about sex are as old as humankind, the facts about what Americans do in bed, with whom, and how has become increasingly politicized, feeding into political skirmishes over homosexuality, abortion, sexual abuse, date and acquaintance rape, welfare reform, and even "family values" (Lewin, 1994b). Thus, given the political climate of the 1980s and 1990s, it is not surprising that those who had the power to control funding for major research such as on human sexuality were squeamish about such research, first inviting researchers to conduct the research and then refusing to fund it. So, what do recent sex studies tell us about what Americans did in bed in the 1990s?[2]

Sex by the Numbers: Sexual Partners, Practices, and Fidelity By the mid-1990s, 97 percent of the adult population had been sexually active at some time in their lives (only 2 to 3 percent were virgins); approximately 1 percent had exclusively homosexual partners, and 5 percent had both homosexual and heterosexual partners; the rest had only heterosexual partners (Laumann et al., 1994). However, contrary to popular belief, in the last decade of the twentieth century, Americans had few sex partners, a modest amount of sex, were true to their partners, and had less exotic sexual practices than reported by earlier sex surveys (especially the self-selective mail-ins for popular magazines). Although the spirit, if not overwhelming reality, of the sexual revolution was alive and well in the 1990s in some quarters—for example, approximately 17 percent of men and 3 percent of women reported having sex with 21 or more partners over their lifetime, with one man reporting having had 1016 partners and one woman reporting having had 1009 partners—overall the sex lives of most of us were not very exciting (Elmer-DeWitt, 1994).

Americans were largely monogamous, reporting having fewer sex partners in a 12-month period than in the past. More than four in five people (83 percent) had one or no sexual partner in a 12-month period, while only 3 percent admitted to having five or more sexual partners in a year. Monogamy was consistent at every age level, from 18 to 59, with an overwhelming majority (three-fourths) of people reporting that they had only one sexual partner in a year. Even over a lifetime, Americans had fewer sex partners than in the past. For example, over her lifetime, a typical woman in the 1990s had two sexual partners; a man, six. When we factor in race, the typical number of sex partners over a lifetime remains relatively small. For example, over a lifetime, a typical African American had four partners, whites and Native Americans three, Latinas/os two; and Asian Americans one (Laumann et al., 1994).

Some researchers have suggested that, given our gender role socialization, the reported number of sexual partners women and men have over a lifetime might well represent

[2]The following discussion draws heavily upon the following: Edward O. Laumann, John H. Gagnon, Robert T. Michael, and Stuart Michaels, 1994, *The Social Organization of Sexuality* (Chicago: University of Chicago Press); Tamar Lewin, 1994, "Sex in America: Faithfulness in Marriage Thrives After All," *New York Times* (October 7): A1, A11; idem, 1994, "So, Now We Know What Americans Do in Bed. So?" *New York Times* (October 9): E3; Peter Gorner, 1994, "Sex Study Shatters Kinky Assumptions," *Chicago Tribune* (October 6): 1, 28; idem, 1994, "What Is Normal?" *Chicago Tribune* (October 9): sec. 4: 1, 4; Trisha Gura, 1994, "Generation X Is Not Generation Sex," *Chicago Tribune* (October 9): sec. 4: 1; Philip Elmer-DeWitt, 1994, "Now the Truth About Americans and SEX," *Time* 144, 17 (October 17): 62–70; Mark Clements, 1994, "Sex in America," *Chicago Tribune, Parade* magazine (August 7): 4–6.

inflation of partners on the part of men and an underreporting of partners by women. Of course, another explanation might be that this pattern of sexuality is a function of Americans' growing response to the AIDS crisis. It could be that people were simply acting more responsibly and more conservatively in the 1990s than they did 10 or 20 years earlier. For example, 76 percent of the people in the NORC survey who had had five or more partners in the past year said that they had changed their sexual behavior by either slowing down, getting tested, or using condoms faithfully (Elmer-DeWitt, 1994:68).

Women and men who as children had been sexually touched by an adult were significantly less monogamous than the general population. Researchers and others have long suggested a link between child sexual abuse and adult sexuality. Data from the NORC survey give support to this thesis. For example, these women and men were more likely as adults to have 11 or more sex partners, to identify themselves as homosexual or bisexual, to express difficulties in sexuality (including anxiety, impotence, and inability to reach orgasm) and to report being unhappy. They also reported having participated in oral, anal, and group sex, as well as thinking about sex more often (Gorner, 1994a; Laumann et al., 1994; Lewin, 1994a).

When we consider people's sexual behavior by their religious affiliation, some interesting observations emerge. Roman Catholics are more likely than members of any other religious group to be virgins (4 percent). Jews have the most sex partners: 34 percent had ten or more, and over a lifetime Jews have, on average, six partners. The women who are most likely to achieve orgasm each and every time are conservative Protestants (Laumann et al., 1994).

How Often? Along with limiting the number of partners, Americans limited the number of times they had sex as well. On average, Americans reported having sex once a week, but clearly two-thirds of the population had sex less often (a few times a month, a few times a year, or not at all). Those who reported having sex only a few times a year or not at all also said that when they did have sex it made them feel happy, loved, wanted, and cared for, thus putting lie to the myth that people who do not have sex frequently are unhappy and sexually frustrated.

And, those who we believed were having the most sex were having the least, while those we thought were having the least sex were having the most. Marital status, for example, appeared to have an important impact on the frequency with which people had sex. While we tend to think of singles as sexually precocious and leading a "swinging" sexual lifestyle, the fact is that with the exception of cohabiting singles, married people have a more lively sex life than their single counterparts do and are the most likely to have orgasms. For example, two-fifths (41 percent) of all married couples in the NORC sample had sex two or more times a week compared with one-fourth (23 percent) of single people, and three-fourths of married women said they usually reached orgasm during sexual intercourse, compared with three-fifths of single women surveyed. On the other hand, 95 percent of men, either married or single, said that they usually or always had an orgasm. Cohabiting singles were the most sexually active, with 56 percent of cohabiting singles reporting that they had sex twice a week or more (Laumann et al., 1994).

How do lesbian and gay sexual practices compare? Over the years, most sex research has reported that gays are far more sexually active than are lesbians. In the *Parade* magazine sex survey (1994), gays reported having 18 partners at some time in their lives, compared with 3 reported by lesbians. According to Philip Blumstein and Pepper Schwartz (1983) (still considered to be the best study that includes data on lesbian and gay sexuality), lesbian couples have sex less frequently than any other type of couple, and they are less "sexual" as couples and as individuals than anyone else. Approximately 33 percent of the Blumstein and Schwartz sample of lesbians in relationships for two or more years had sex once or more a week, and 47 percent of lesbians in long-term relationships had sex once a month or less. Furthermore, these researchers reported that lesbians seem to be more limited in their range of sexual techniques than were other couples in their sample. A note of caution here: Until we are clear regarding the meaning of the words *sex* and *sexuality* to lesbians and whether or not the heterosexual model of these terms fits their experiences we must be somewhat skeptical of research findings that reduce their sexuality to numbers. (For a more detailed discussion of this point, see, for example, Frye, 1995.)

What about the older population? The sexual reality of the older heterosexual population is quite different from its younger counterpart. Twenty-two percent of women and 8 percent of men 50 years old report having no partnered sex in a year. And by the time Americans reach the age of 70, fully 70 percent of women and 26 percent of men report going for a year or more without partnered sex.

How do Americans compare internationally? Studies of sexual behavior conducted in England and France show, for example, that French women and men are a bit more sexually conservative than their U.S. counterparts. For example, the average French woman and man have sex about twice as often as Americans do, but they tend to have somewhat fewer sex partners over a lifetime than do Americans (Gorner, 1994b) (see Figure 6.1).

Kinky Sex? Contrary to the assumption of widespread "kinky" sex, we, as a nation, seem to prefer only a few sexual practices. Heterosexuals overwhelmingly (96 percent) prefered vaginal intercourse and included it in almost every sexual encounter. The next two most appealing sexual practices were a distant second and third: watching a partner undress (an activity that many people may not have realized is a sex act) and oral sex, which many people have experienced but which is not a regular part of most adults' lovemaking (Gorner, 1994a). In fact, many older adults, like college students and teenagers, do not consider oral sex as "having sex" at all. In any case, however, men are substantially more likely

Figure 6.1

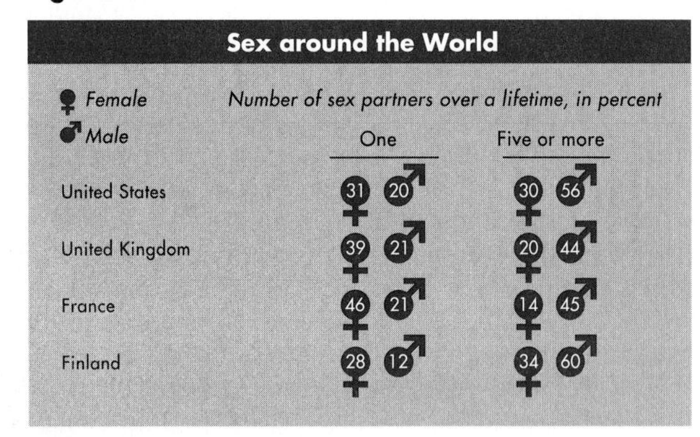

Source: Adapted from Philip Elmer-DeWitt, 1994, "Now the Truth about Americans and Sex," *Time* 144, 16 (October 17): 64. © 1994 TIME INC. Reprinted by permission.

Figure 6.2

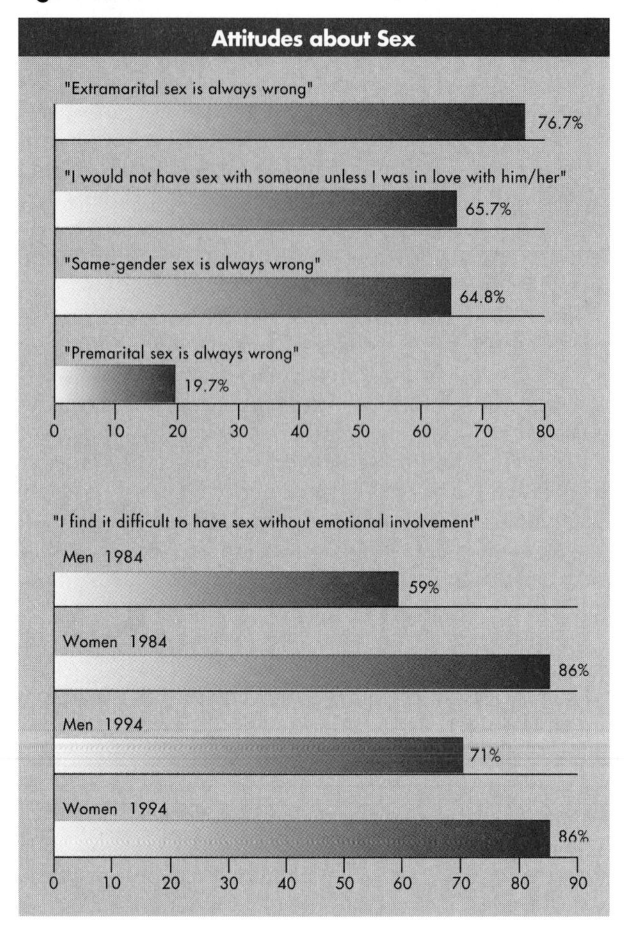

Source: Peter Gorner, 1994, "What Is Normal?" *Chicago Tribune* (October 9), sec. 4: 1; Mark Clements, 1994, "Sex in America Today," *Chicago Tribune*, *Parade* magazine: 4.

to enjoy the latter two sexual practices than are women. Sexual practices such as anal intercourse, same-sex partners, group sex, and sex with strangers are appealing to only a minute percentage of the population. Here, as elsewhere, men reported more interest in these sexual practices than did women.

Moreover, despite the alleged permissiveness and liberalization of attitudes since the 1960s, Americans held fairly conservative attitudes about marriage and sexuality at the time of these surveys and were extremely faithful to their romantic partners. A majority of people said that they would not have sex with someone unless they were in love with the person. Men, in particular, were paying more attention to the emotional aspect of sex. The 1994 *Parade* sex survey reported that 71 percent of the men in its sample reported that it was difficult for them to have sex without emotional involvement, up from 59 percent a decade earlier. The percentage of women expressing this view remained constant over both studies, at 86 percent. Furthermore, many Americans believed that sex between partners of the same gender or sex outside legal marriage was always wrong (see Figure 6.2). Finally, most Americans viewed marriage and a long-term commitment as the goal of their intimate relationships.

According to Edward Laumann (1994), marriage is alive and well in the United States, and it regulates sexual behavior with remarkable precision. While attitudes about sex outside of legal marriage may be somewhat permissive, once people marry they express a belief in fidelity as long as the relationship lasts (cited in Gorner, 1994b). In this context, Americans' sexual behavior in the 1990s was pretty consistent with their attitudes. Thus, contrary to the notion of a national wave of infidelity, adultery was the exception rather than the rule. More than seven out of ten people said that they disapproved of adultery and more important, despite seven-year itches and midlife crises, 85 percent of married women and more than 75 percent of married men said that they had never been unfaithful to their partners.

At What Age? According to responses in the NORC survey, white teens, both females and males, typically begin having sex at age 17; black males typically begin just before 16 and black females, just before 17. However, subsequent sexual encounters during teen years are sporadic. 1990s teenagers typically had sex for the first time six months earlier than their parents did. It appears that as teens reach young adulthood their sexual behavior becomes more conservative. For example, Generation X (young adults 18 to 30 years of age) told NORC researchers that they had less frequent sexual encounters and that the overwhelming majority of them practiced monogamy.

These data shatter our perceptions of young-adult sexual behavior. Most of our fantasies and ideas about delightful and delectable sex are based on what we thought were the sexual patterns of a wild and sexy Generation X. But as Trisha Gura (1994b) has stated: "Generation X is not Generation Sex." These young adults told sex researchers that they were engaging in sexual activity earlier, they were delaying getting married, and they were divorcing more frequently than their parents did. However, coming of age after AIDS, they actually are behaving far more conservatively than their predecessors. In general, they have only one sex partner at a time, they value fidelity, they tend to marry by the age of 30, and many may marry more than once. On the other hand, the survey data indicate that while Generation X is less experimental when involved in a steady, long-term relationship, they tend to have more sex partners either before or between long-term partnerships. In contrast, the parents of Generation X (the baby boomers), coming of age when they did, during a more sexually permissive and liberal period, are a much more sexually active group than their offspring. The percentage of adults, for example, who have had 21 or more sex partners over their lifetime is significantly higher among the baby boomers than among other Americans.

Choosing Partners How do Americans meet and with whom do they develop sexual relationships? From a sociological perspective, people bring to the sexual marketplace all of the characteristics of their makeup: education, occupation and earning potential, personality, looks, interests, diseases, children from prior marriages or liaisons, and so forth. As you learned in Chapter 5, the social world of mate selection—dating and sexual behavior—is constructed so that we meet, date, have sex with, and marry people very much like ourselves. According to Peter Gorner (1994a), personal ads and electronic dating services may work for short-term relationships, but they are rarely effective for long-term relationships. Sexual selection seems to rely more so on the same type of strategies that we use to buy a car, choose a college, or seek a job. In the same way that we consult with our friends, family members, and other advisors when, for example, choosing a college, we rely on our personal social networks when choosing sexual partners. It is not, therefore, surprising that Americans typically have sex with, date, and marry people of the same race, educational background, religion, and similar age. They rarely cross lines of social class and upbringing when choosing sex partners or mates.

Sexual behavior is strongly affected by friends, family, and coworkers. For example, in the NORC sex survey, more than six couples out of ten were introduced by family or mutual friends. Only 8 percent of couples met in a bar or through a personal ad. Once introduced, contrary to popular media portrayals, people do not immediately fall into bed. Rather, the pattern is typically that of getting to know one another, first as a friend, building trust and taking the relationship slowly, then finally having sex and getting married. Couples who stay together are usually those who are sexually compatible, agree on the rules, and are faithful (Gorner, 1994a).

Sexual Homogamy As we said earlier, as in dating and marriage, most people choose as sexual partners those who are very much like themselves in terms of race, religion, age, socioeconomic level, and education. Even if, as in the legendary romantic song, some enchanted evening we will meet and fall in love with a stranger across a crowded room, the odds are high that the room will be crowded with people very much like ourselves (Lewin, 1994b). Opposites may attract each other, but based on the NORC sex survey data, it is not for long. Dissimilar couples are more likely than similar ones to end up in short-term relationships (Gorner, 1994a). In the NORC study, 93 percent of people who were married were married to someone of the same race, 82 percent were of similar educational level, 78 percent were within 5 years of each other's age, and 72 percent were of the same religion. Not one woman with a graduate degree had a sexual relationship with a man who had finished only high school. Although thousands of women with high levels of education may have less educated lovers, the percentage of women who do is very small (Gorner, 1994a). According to sociologist Edward Laumann (1994), sexual homogamy among Americans has important ramifications for AIDS policy. Given that sexual choice and behavior are not random, AIDS is likely to remain concentrated within the groups that are currently most affected. Therefore, AIDS prevention should focus on those groups.

Gender Difference Not surprisingly, women and men think and behave differently in terms of sex. For example, as noted earlier, men think about sex more than women do and are drawn to a wider range of sexual practices. More than one-half of men say they think about sex every day or several times a day, compared with 19 percent of women. While a little more than two-thirds of women and men say that the actual sex act is better than foreplay, men are more likely (73 percent) to feel this way than women (58 percent). In this context, not surprisingly, more men than women say that sexual activity and orgasm are important. Furthermore, more men than women continue to rate themselves as having a high sex drive (Clements, 1994).

Perhaps the most alarming gender difference found in the NORC sex survey is the difference in female and male perception of what constitutes consensual sex. For example, 23 percent of the women reported having been forced by men to do something sexually that they did not want to do, including having vaginal intercourse, usually by someone that they knew well, were in love with, or married to. On the other hand, only about 3 percent of men said that they had ever forced a woman into a sexual act. Moreover, a little more than 4 percent of women reported being forced to have sex their very first time, compared with less than one half of 1 percent of men. Although some of the disparity in the views of women and men on the subject of forced sex might be due to underreporting, it is far more likely that the disparity is due to the fact that many men, given traditional male socialization, simply do not recognize just how coercive women find their behavior. On the other hand, many men view sexual activity as an entitlement; they feel that they are entitled to demand sex from women and, if refused, to force it on them; and some women continue to feel dependent, pressured, and/or obligated to "give in" for the sake of "keeping their man" or maintaining the relationship. Thus date and acquaintance rape are fairly common occurrences and of increasing concern among women.

In other areas of sexuality, however, women and men are converging. This is due, in large part, to the fact that over the last decade, men have shown more changes in their sexual attitudes than women have. Thus, almost 75 percent of men said it was easy to talk about sex with their partners, compared with 59 percent in 1984. Today, a similar percentage of women (70 percent) said that they found conversations about sex with a partner easy (up from 63 percent in 1984). And both women and men show a shift from seeking sex for recreation to seeking more emotional meaning in sex.

Understanding America's Changing Sexuality: Contemporary Patterns Although many of the patterns of the 1990s remain, it seems that in our increasingly sexed-up society, we are also acting upon sex—in some distinctively different ways as well. We talk more openly and publicly about sex today, and sexual acts that were once considered deviant are widely accepted now. Today people are engaging in sexual behavior at earlier ages. For example, a little more than one-half of females and two-thirds of males have engaged in sexual intercourse by the time they reach 18 years of age (Moore et al., 2000). And a recent survey of the sexual behavior of high school students indicated that 9 percent of these students had initiated sexual intercourse before they reached their thirteenth birthday. At the same time there is a noticeable increase in the number of people reporting that they are virgins. Research on high school students, for instance, shows an 11 percent increase in the incidence of virginity, driven by lower rates of intercourse for white and black male youths (Christopher and Sprecher, 2000). It seems to us that this might also be explained in terms of the increasing rate of teens that claim the status of virgin even though they have engaged in a variety of sexual activities other than vaginal intercourse (see "In the News" at the beginning of this chapter).

Although there is less insistence today that sex be tied to marriage (for example, eight of ten women and nine of ten men aged 20 to 39 are nonvirgins), premarital sex for both women and men is now more likely to occur within an affectionate, quasi-stable, if not permanent, relationship. Both women and men report feeling heightened sexual desire and pleasure when they share a mutually loving relationship with their sex partner. However, emotionally valuing a partner continues to motivate women, more than men, to engage in sexual intercourse (Christopher and Sprecher, 2000). Moreover, the shift toward more relational sex and couplehood among gays continues today, although recreational sex is still more common among gays than among lesbians and heterosexuals (Schwartz and Rutter, 1998). Although women and men continue to converge in some areas of their sexual behavior, the sexual double standard remains: Men are still more likely than women to be sexually active, have multiple partners, and be the initiator of sex (through both seduction or coercion), whereas women are still most often the one to refuse sex but are also still more likely than men to give in to sexual advances and to comply with sexual demands even when they do not want to have sex.

Clearly, today sex plays a much bigger role in some people's lives than others. Not everyone is actively engaged in sexual behavior. In fact, a growing number of people publicly and actively disengage in sex. Although there is some debate about who is a virgin and how we define virginity, the fact is, today there is a visible and growing movement to promote sexual chastity that is directed particularly at the nation's teenagers and young adults. For those in this movement, there is no debate; chastity/virginity means refraining from *all* sexual activity prior to marriage and being faithful to one's spouse after marriage (Abstinence Groups, 2000). An official tenet of fundamentalist Christian and Islamic religions, as well as most other religions, commands absolute allegiance to the authority of the church, which includes abstinence from sexual activity before marriage. In the early 1990s, True Love Waits, an international Christian organization that grew out of the Southern Baptist Convention, began asking young people in particular (teenagers and college students) to take voluntary chastity pledges committing to the following:

> Believing that true love waits, I make a commitment to God, myself, my family, my friends, my future mate and my future children to be sexually abstinent from this day until the day I enter a biblical marriage relationship. (Schemo, 2001b:1)

When conservative Republicans in Congress tacked a last-minute amendment onto the 1996 Welfare Reform bill, earmarking $250 million over 5 years to promote sexual abstinence outside of marriage, they ushered the abstinence movement from its traditional home in the religious right into the mainstream. By the end of the twentieth century, nearly one in four public school teachers said they taught about abstaining from sex until marriage as the only way to avoid pregnancy and disease, up from 1 in 50 in 1988 (Schemo, 2001b). Today, there are hundreds of groups across the country that advocate sexual abstinence until marriage, and many of them come together annually in what is advertised as a "National Week of Chastity" to promote sexual abstinence until marriage. Although there are no scientific studies that demonstrate that voluntary abstinence pledges succeed in bringing more virgins to the marriage altar, recent research does show that teenagers who take voluntary chastity pledges, under certain conditions avoid sexual intercourse substantially longer (up to 18 months) than teenagers of similar backgrounds who make no such public commitment to chastity. These chastity pledges seem more effective with 15- and 16-year-olds and least effective with 18-year-olds. Interestingly, this research found that virginity pledges did not hold when only one teenager took them or when the percentage of students signing virginity pledges increased to more than 30 percent (Schemo, 2001a, 2001b).

The movement for sexual abstinence is not limited to a focus on youth. In a contemporary culture saturated with sexual messages and innuendo, a small but growing minority of older adults live sex-free lives (practice celibacy). Calling themselves "born-again virgins" they embrace abstinence not so much on moral or religious grounds but to cleanse themselves, recharge their spirit, and reassert self-control. There are no figures for how many Americans are born-again virgins. However, the bulk of them are women, with only a tiny number of men among the ranks. This newly chaste group ranges from purists, who refrain from all sexual activity, to those who tailor their celibacy to suit their tastes, permitting a degree of kissing and fondling but drawing the line at penetration. A 1998 survey conducted by the University of Chicago for the National Science Foundation reported that 17 percent of adults over the age of 18 had no sex partner within the previous 12-month period. Many of these people were elderly or had not yet married. It is not clear, however, how many in the most sexually active years were celibate by choice (La Ferla, 2000).

Finally, although still unacceptable to the general society, sexual lifestyles different from traditional heterosexual relationships such as homosexual and bisexual relationships have become more open, and there has been a decrease in the number of people who view homosexual behavior as morally wrong—53 percent in 2001, down from 65 percent in the mid-1990s (Gallup, 2001). In general, it appears that a better understanding of one's own sexuality, rather than a simple pursuit of pleasure, is now an important sexual goal in many people's lives.

SEXUALITY AS SOCIAL LEARNING

Equally as important as the questions of what people do and with whom in the privacy of their bedrooms and whether or not a sexual revolution has occurred are questions such as, How do we become sexual beings? and what factors contribute to changes in our sexual attitudes and behaviors? Anthropologists have long shown that human sexuality is defined and learned within a particular cultural context. Thus, what constitutes sexuality will vary from one culture to another (Caulfield, 1985). In this section we consider sexual behavior as a learned social product.

Since the late nineteenth century, when Sigmund Freud first introduced his beliefs about the nature of human sexuality, the general public as well as professionals such as psychologists, social workers, and sex therapists have been influenced by his theories of human sexuality. According to Freud, the sex drive, which he viewed as a biologically determined force, is the motivator for all human behavior. In the mid–twentieth century, Alfred Kinsey's extensive sex research reflected his agreement with Freud that human sexuality is biologically determined. Both men believed that humans have innate sexual desires that require gratification. Such desires cannot go unchecked in a society, however, or they would lead to uncontrolled sexual activity, which in turn would generate social chaos. Thus, through its sexual codes, society forces the individual to repress these desires or channel them into sexually appropriate behaviors.

Even if an innate sexual drive exists in human beings, it seems clear from a variety of research across academic disciplines that this drive is given shape and direction by culture. The sexual feelings and desires that we experience may seem innate, natural, and beyond our control, but we are not born knowing how to think, feel, or behave sexually. Cultural norms *prescribe* (tell us what we should do) and *proscribe* (tell us what we should not do) our sexual behavior. They determine what is or is not sexually attractive and stimulating, why we should or should not engage in sexual behavior, and how we should or should not feel sexually.

According to social scientists John Gagnon and William Simon (1973, 1987), sexual behavior is not unlike other behavior. It does not come naturally; rather, it is socially constructed. Thus, from this point of view, what Freud commonly referred to as the *sex drive* is really something we have learned in a particular social environment. Like other behaviors, our sexual behavior is guided by cultural scripts similar to those that guide the actions of actors. These **sexual scripts** are simply our society's guidelines or blueprints for defining and engaging in sexual behaviors. We begin learning these scripts very early in life through the process of socialization. In learning our culture's sexual guidelines, we in effect create or invent our capacity for sexual behavior.

Sources of Sexual Learning

In earliest childhood, as we are learning other important norms of our culture we are also simultaneously learning about our sexuality, first from **significant others,** people such as parents, friends, relatives, and religious figures, who play an important role in our lives, and later from the point of view of **generalized others,** that is, the viewpoint of society at large. We also learn about our sexuality in school and from the mass media. Some of the cultural information about our sexuality is consciously presented and learned; much of it, however, we learn unconsciously.

Learning Sexuality in the Family Many authorities on early childhood behavior believe that the family is the first and most significant agent of socialization. Where sexuality is concerned, however, the evidence suggests that children learn very little from their parents. For example, in a 1985 report of survey data on sexuality, almost one-half of those surveyed reported that their parents did not teach them anything about sexuality (Coles and Stokes, 1985). Over a decade later, a 1998 *Time*/CNN telephone survey found that only 7 percent of teenagers reported learning about sex from their parents. Most teens report that their parents either avoid the subject of sex, miss the mark by starting the discussion long before or after the teen's sexual encounter, or just plain stonewall them (Stodghill, 1999). Mothers, on the other hand, say that they are reluctant to discuss sex and birth control with their children for fear that such discussions would embarrass their children or encourage them to become sexually active (Jaccard et al., 2000). Thus, what little most children do learn about sexuality in the family is

Historically, parents have gone to great lengths to desexualize their children's lives, including presenting themselves as asexual. However, some parents model healthy aspects of intimacy whereby they openly touch and show one another affection.

often in the form of prohibitions (for example, a negative response when a child touches her or his genitals).

Parents often go to great lengths to desexualize their children's lives. This often includes going out of their way to present themselves as asexual. They stop touching each other or showing any signs of intimacy when the children are around. They do not discuss sexuality around children except in hushed tones, and they often become embarrassed and speechless when their children ask them a frank question about some aspect of sexuality. Parents who avoid answering their children's questions concerning sexuality may teach their children that sex is something to be ashamed of.

Although research (DeLamaster, 1987; Packer, 1997) indicates that sexual play during late infancy and early childhood is positive preparation for adult sexuality and harms children only if reacted to negatively, many children are prohibited from engaging in such activities. Another way in which parents give children a negative feeling about their sexuality is through their use of euphemisms for the sexual organs (for example, kitty cat, wiener). Children often do not learn the proper name for female and male sexual organs until they are taught by others outside of the family. Researchers studying preschool-age children found that almost all of the children they studied could not give the correct name for their genitals, although they could give the correct name to the nongenital parts of their body (Wurtele, Melzer, and Kast, 1992). Using improper names for the genitals conveys the message that the genitals are embarrassing, mysterious, or taboo and significantly different from other parts of the body.

At the other end of this continuum, some experts suggest that instead of presenting themselves as asexual, sometimes parents can be negative sexual role models if they are sexually promiscuous themselves; initiate sexual activities with youth; have children outside of legal marriage; do not supervise their children's coed activities; and overemphasize the sexuality and physical appearance of their daughters such as encouraging them at ages as young as 4 to 5 years old to dress and be seductive and adultlike (Haffner, 1999; Saltzman, 1999).

Sociological studies continue to show that family and the social milieu play a significant role in the age at which teenagers will become sexually active (Brewster, Billy, and Grady, 1993). For example, teens of divorced parents are much more likely than those from families with two parents present to engage in premarital sexual intercourse; teens who feel that they can talk to their parents about sexual issues are less likely to engage in premarital sexual intercourse than those who have poor communication with their parents (Rathus, Nevid, and Fichner-Rathus, 1997). Furthermore, families who maintain relatively conservative attitudes and evoke high levels of compliance with social rules of conduct will delay the development of their adolescent's sexual behavior (Hovell, Sipan, and Blumberg, 1994). This is not to imply that all parents are uncomfortable with their own and/or their children's growing sexuality. There are many parents who actively educate their children about their sexuality and encourage them to feel positive about themselves and their bodies, embrace sexual feelings as a normal and positive part of their lives, and to develop self-control, good judgment, and responsibility in sexual matters.

What did you learn about sexuality from your parents? Did they discuss the issue with you in an open and honest manner? What information did they leave out? What happened when or if you explored your body? What euphemisms did they use for the genitals?

On an often-hidden side of the family, thousands of children are sexually abused within their families every year. Although both sexes are victims of sexual abuse, females are far more likely to be abused than are males (we examine child sexual abuse in more detail in Chapter 11). As we learned earlier in this chapter, such abuse often has a negative effect on the adult sexuality of these victims in a number of ways. In addition to those discussed earlier, a growing body of evidence indicates that childhood sexual abuse may cause sexual problems in adult life, primarily by desensitizing the individual to her or his body. This might cause the person in adulthood to be either restricted or excessive in her or his sexual behaviors (Basow, 1992). Other new and interesting research conducted over the last decade suggests a possible connection between female child sexual abuse and eating disorders in women (see, for example, Iazetto, 1989).

Gender Differences in Sexual Scripts Parents also tend to communicate the content of sexual behavior to their children differently depending on the sex of the child. Despite changes in attitudes about gender-specific behavior, certain aspects of the double standard remain, and parents continue to pass these on to their children. For example, parents tend to be more open with daughters than with sons about reproduction and its relationship to sexual activities as well as the morality of sex. In fact, because females can become pregnant, the sexual scripts they learn tie sexual activity almost exclusively to reproduction and family life. Boys, on the other hand, learn that their sexuality is connected to society's notion of masculinity and their ability to achieve in different areas of life (O'Neil, 1981). Many parents also practice a sexual double standard whereby they place more restrictions on their daughters' sexuality than on that of their sons. Thus, female movements, social activities, and friendships are far more guarded and chaperoned than are male activities. A number of researchers have identified several areas of gender difference in traditional sexual scripting:

- Interest in sex is part of the male sexual script but not part of the female sexual script.
- Males are expected to be the initiators and to take control of sexual activities; females are expected to be submissive, conform, and give pleasure.
- The sexual script for males emphasizes achievement and frequency of sexual activities; for females the emphasis is on monogamy and exclusiveness (for example, saving herself for the one right man in her life).
- Early or unmarried sexual activity carries little stigma for males. In fact, it sometimes elevates them in the eyes of their peers. Early or unmarried sexual activity for females carries a negative stigma and is subject to the criticism and moral judgment of others. Common epithets such as "whore" and "slut" are applied to their behavior.
- Exposure of the body is far more acceptable for males than females. Females are taught, early on, to keep their bodies covered by wearing restrictive clothing and to sit with their legs crossed.

Such sex role socialization, it seems, produces some definite differences in the meanings that females and males attach to sex, as well as the ways in which each gender experiences its sexuality. Despite the liberalization of sexual attitudes over the last several decades and the so-called sexual liberation of women, sexual scripts and gender socialization relative to human sexuality have changed very little. For example, women's bodies continue to be treated differently than men's in advertisements and other areas of popular culture (for example, the exploitation of women's bodies in terms of nudity to sell products). Although there is increasing emphasis and exploitation of male sexuality as well, women remain the primary objects of sexual exploitation. Virginity is still stressed for women, while prowess and scoring are stressed for males. And females are encouraged to take responsibility in sexual matters by setting limits on men's sexual behavior to make sure it doesn't get out of hand. Males, on the other hand, are encouraged to initiate, take control of, and pursue sexual activities.

Some glaring contemporary examples of the continued existence of the sexual double standard include the following: (1) the importance that insurance companies and advertisers have placed on male fertility and sexual health versus female sexual health (for example, Viagra, a male impotence pill, is widely publicized and promoted and insurance companies routinely cover the cost of such pills—around $10 per pill—but refuse to cover female contraceptions, such as birth control pills, which cost far less than Viagra); (2) the reaction of the public and public officials to the public sexual harassment and rape of women (for example, the sexual assault and rape of dozens of women in New York's Central Park following the annual Puerto Rican Day Parade a few years ago and the inaction of police in the park when some of the women reported these crimes to them); and (3) the female genital mutilation (FGM) of approximately 2 million girls and women each year worldwide (FGM is a cultural practice in at least 40 countries, most of which are in Africa and the Islamic Middle East, and involves the partial or total amputation of the external female genitalia; we do not know of any such practice

The continued existence of the sexual double standard is blatantly exposed by ads such as this Houston, Texas billboard promoting Viagra, a drug used to increase male potency. Fewer research dollars have gone into finding ways to address women's sexual needs.

against the male genitalia) (Cocco, 1998; Campo-Flores and Rosenberg, 2000; Scott and Schwartz, 2000).

The gender-based differential sexual script is rooted in the cultural belief that male sexual needs are stronger and more important than female sexual needs. This represents a classic example of the greater power and status given males in American and most other cultures of the world. These messages and scripts continue to shape our sexual behavior. Research continues to show that both women and men accept this double standard. For example, a 1991 study found that both female and male respondents rated women who engaged in premarital sex as immoral while they accepted male premarital sex (Robinson et al., 1991). Thus, as the old adage goes: The more things change the more they remain the same.

Keep in mind that these are generalizations about sexual learning. Not all females and males learn the traditional sexual scripts. The exact content of sexual scripts varies according to a number of factors including race and ethnicity, social class, and religious orientation. Thus, whatever sexual script we learn, our sexual behavior can change as our life circumstances change.

Peer Influence By the time children reach adolescence, the influence of the family diminishes, and the influence of peers increases. Peers are the most important source of sex education and are a very important influence on one's sexual values and behaviors. Various studies, for example, have found that peer pressure is probably the single most important factor, next to physiological readiness, that determines when adolescents become sexually active (Smith, Udry, and Morris, 1985; Thomsen and Chang, 2000). Peer pressure to engage in sexual activity is especially strong among young males. Male peers tend to influence each other to explore their sexuality, while female peers encourage secrecy and abstinence. Peers also serve as an important source of information concerning sexuality (see, for example, Sanders and Mullis, 1988). Up to around age 15, young people report learning about sex equally from parents, peers, and school. After this age, they learn almost twice as much about sex from peers than family; they get an increasing amount of their information about sex from the media and a decreasing amount from school (Gibbs, 1993a). Unfortunately, much of what peers think they "know" is actually inaccurate. Thus, peers frequently mislead and misinform each other. However, peers also provide positive sex socialization. For example, peers can and often do provide a forum wherein young people can openly and honestly talk about, discuss, and ask questions about human sexuality, their own developing sexuality, if they cannot get this information and discussion in the family or in formal sex education classes.

The Mass Media Popular culture and the mass media play a key role in constructing, shaping, and transforming our views and knowledge about sexuality. The media-saturated world in which we live is one in which sexual behavior is frequent and increasingly explicit. Today we can hear and see sexual talk and portrayals in every form of media. Unfortunately, much of this social construction is inaccurate, distorted, inflated, or outright false. It is most often a far cry from the ways in which average Americans experience sexuality.

As we have noted, sex has increasingly moved out of the privacy of the bedroom and into the public realm. One of the most visible manifestations of contemporary sexuality is the multibillion-dollar sex industry. Thousands of movie houses still feature X-rated movies, even though X-rated cable television stations have garnered a significant corner of the sex market. Sex magazines like *Oui*, *Playboy*, *Hustler*, and *Playgirl*, though diminishing somewhat in popularity, still enjoy a wide readership. These and other print media, such as supermarket tabloids, exploit and sensationalize sexuality to make millions of dollars from a wide variety of readers, few of whom question the validity or power of those who transmit sexual messages.

Moreover, advertisers routinely use sexuality—particularly female sexuality—in their advertising copy. Nudity or near nudity is now found in even the more established magazines today. It is now commonplace to see undressed or scantily dressed women selling a variety of products, from heavy construction equipment to designer jeans, from candy to watches. For example, an ad for Swatch watches shows a woman in her underwear, her back to the viewer and her buttocks hanging from beneath her underwear, held by a handsome young man (who is fully dressed). On her arm (when you finally notice it) are several different watches. There is little clarification that it is the watches and not the female body that is "for sale." Or take the recent ad campaign for a popular jeans label that displayed a near nude woman *without* the jeans (Lindsey, 1994).

Similarly, television, considered by some media scholars to be the most influential medium shaping our views of sexuality, routinely depicts sexual situations and behaviors. Sexual content is overt in the content of day- and nighttime soap operas and talk shows, evening shows and movies, and perhaps most overt on cable channels devoted to sexual movies and shows. They present a neverending stream of sexual liaisons between family members, friends, and strangers (anybody is fair game); explicit petting, references made to sex and actual simulations of sexual intercourse that are often so realistic that it is difficult to tell that it is just acting. Some researchers have suggested that Americans are exposed to more than 9000 scenes of suggested sexual intercourse, sexual comment, or innuendo in an average year of TV viewing (Crossen, 1991). In addition, on soap operas in particular, sex between unmarried partners, especially those with whom there is some tension or conflict, is romanticized, and few characters are sexually responsible and use condoms or seem concerned about pregnancy and sexually transmitted diseases.

The sexual lessons of the media are particularly influential in shaping the sexual views and behaviors of America's youth. Young people in the United States today spend 6 to 7 hours each day, on average, with some form of media. The majority have a television in their bedrooms; all have access to music

APPLYING THE SOCIOLOGICAL IMAGINATION

HUMAN SEXUALITY IN THE MASS MEDIA, PAST AND PRESENT

As we have seen, the mass media are a major source of information concerning sexuality. Using a sociological perspective, conduct a content analysis of television programs from each decade starting with the 1950s, focusing on the sexuality and sexual activity portrayed or implied during each decade. Compare sexuality over time but also across race, class, gender, and sexual orientation. Wherever possible, include programs that have major nonwhite, lesbian, or gay characters and that represent different social classes. Develop a list of behaviors you want to observe and tally the number of times you find them in the programs you analyze. When you are finished, analyze your results, contrasting the portrayal of sexuality during different time periods and across different groups. In addition, compare the television portrayal of sexuality with research data of sexuality in the United States throughout each corresponding historical period.

and movies. And computer and Internet use is diffusing rapidly. Soap opera portrayals of sex have been found to be particularly influential for teenaged girls, who are heavy viewers of this type of programming and who have unrealistically high estimates of the extent of extramarital sex and the frequency of intercourse in the general population. Soap operas are particularly influential because they are on everyday and viewers identify with characters. Teenaged viewers, in particular, develop their expectations of what their sex lives might or should be like from watching the soaps (Lindsey, 1994). The clash between the media's depiction of sexual relations and the real-life experiences of young people contributes to the difficulties in making healthy sexual decisions. Although we still do not know the exact influence of the media on young people's sexuality, a large body of evidence indicates that besides imparting basic information about sex, media portrayals of sex, coupled with inadequate role models from other sectors, encourage unhealthy sexual attitudes and behavior (Brown and Keller, 2000).

Despite increasing public concern about the potential health risks of early, unprotected sexual activity, only about one in eleven of the programs on television that include sexual content mentions possible risks or responsibilities. Sexually transmitted diseases other than HIV and AIDS are almost never discussed, and unintended pregnancies are rarely shown as the outcome of unprotected sex. Abortion is a taboo topic, and homosexual and transgendered youth rarely find themselves represented in the mainstream media. Although a few programs have incorporated lesbian or gay characters into their plots, what Adrienne Rich calls *compulsory heterosexuality* prevails (Brown and Keller, 2000).

Added to this mix is the influx of daytime talk shows that have deteriorated to a forum for a series of sexually dysfunctional people to air their dysfunctionalities (for example, "I had sex with my mother's husband while she fixed dinner and watched," or "I had sex with 12 bisexual midgets while waiting on the bus") publicly for hours upon hours every day on programs hosted by people such as Sally Jessy Rafael, Ricki Lake, Jerry Springer, and Jenny Jones. "The Jerry Springer Show," with the largest share of the talk show audience in the late 1990s, not only focuses entirely on the sexual dysfunctionality of guests but also mixes insults and violence with the sexual content of the show. Guests routinely fight, tear off each other's clothing, expose themselves, and use sexual language that some people refer to as *gutter language*. Like soap operas, these talk shows attract a very large and youthful audience. Many teens indicate that by the time their parents get around to talking to them about sex (if at all), they have already been indoctrinated by television programs, particularly programs such as "Dawson's Creek," the most explicit show on teen sexuality to air in the 1990s, "Jerry Springer," "Buffy the Vampire Slayer," "MTV," and "HBO after Midnight." One 14-year-old reported that he learned how to kiss at 8 years of age by watching television (Stodghill, 1999).

Critics of these programs argue that the presentation of human sexuality in a sleazy and sensational manner makes the abnormal seem normal and provides audiences with distorted notions of sexuality and perverse role models for the young (Saltzman, 1996). Pressured by critics and lobbies to present more sexually responsible media, some of the people responsible for television programming have begun to include more realistic stories about sex, its possible consequences, and sexual responsibility. They are also adding more depth and accuracy to stories involving sex, ranging from stories about teenage pregnancy to coming to terms with being lesbian or gay. For example, hit shows like "Felicity" have included sensitive portrayals of homosexual youth, have provided explicit lessons in how to put on a condom, and have portrayed teenagers postponing sexual intercourse, with little apparent decline in viewer interest (Brown and Keller, 2000). Several soap opera executives have explored ways to make "love in the afternoon" more responsible as well. This would include showing that the use of contraceptives is essential, avoiding the linkage of sex with violence, and showing that not all encounters or even relationships result in sex. And real-life television, such as MTV's "Loveline," a question-and-answer show featuring sex guru Drew Pinsky, has been hailed for its informative sexual content ("TV Soaps Focus on Role of Sex," 1994; Stodghill, 1999).

The personal ads, a feature of most major newspapers, also reflect the increasing openness of today's sexuality. In such columns, women and men publicly advertise for the type of sexual partner or experiences they want. And, increasingly since the 1970s, sex and sexual violence have become so explicit in films that a rating system is used to determine the degree of suitability for audiences under a certain age. James Bond films (regardless of who plays Bond), which are highly popular among the young, routinely depict women being raped and enjoying it, rather than as an act of criminal violence, especially if the rapist is every woman's assumed dream man—James Bond himself. The sexual double standard is as apparent in the media as it is in other cultural institutions in American society. For example, though films are full of nudity, women's and men's nude bodies are not shown in the same way. Women are often completely nude, and the view is almost always a frontal view, whereas men are generally semiclad as opposed to completely nude, or their backside is shown. Seldom, if ever, is the penis visible. Moreover, a whole genre of teenage films over the last two to three decades present sex in crude and vulgar detail for teenagers to emulate. These films typically de-emphasize sexual responsibility; as in television and other forms of the media, there is little concern about pregnancy; contraceptives are seldom, if ever, used; and sexually transmitted diseases, including AIDS, are seldom a concern. As with television and music producers, a number of groups are working with Hollywood scriptwriters to encourage more sexually responsible film content.

Celebrities have grown out of our new sexual openness. People like Dr. Ruth Westheimer have developed large followings by talking frankly and openly on radio and television talk shows about almost every conceivable aspect of human sexuality. Contemporary music, especially rock, rhythm and blues, and rap, often contains lyrics that are sexually explicit. Children as young as 3 or 4 years of age can be heard repeating lyrics such as "I want to sex you up," "Shake that bootie," "Pop that coochie," "I wanna bump and grind," and "Do it to me one more time." In addition, music videos are full of men grabbing or holding their crotch, and gyrating women and men in sexually suggestive clothing, positions, and situations. For example, in a content analysis of rock lyrics, Michael Medved (1992) counted 87 descriptions of oral sex and 117 explicit terms for female and male genitals in *one* album (*As Nasty as They Wanna Be* by 2 Live Crew).

Not much has changed since this analysis. Today sex, violence, and female victimization still go hand in hand in this medium. Sodomy or reference to it has become commonplace in these videos. Teenagers and other viewers are fed a constant diet of women asking, sometimes begging, to be raped and sodomized. Moreover, a new wave of women rappers are articulating sexual desire and activity in a manner that voices their irreverence for decorum as defined through cultural expectations of the proper behavior for "respectable" women and male expectations of female subordination (Perry, 1995). Female artists such as Lil' Kim, almost always nearly nude, prance both menacingly and sensuously through one video after another. With no respect for sexual taboos, Lil' Kim holds her crotch, grinds, gyrates, and speaks sexual language that seriously transgresses cultural boundaries of polite respectability and convention. Although some analysts have described this music as libratory, as a deconstruction of the phallocentric male rap and hip-hop lyrics, and as an inversion of the sexual gaze to make males the sexual object (Perry, 1995), the fact is, like their male counterparts, female rappers never give the slightest attention to sexual responsibility or safe sex while they are calling for every kind of sex act from cunnilingus to "buck wild" sex. The lack of a caveat concerning the sexual responsibility and protection of self that should accompany this new sexual liberation is problematic for those who emulate this behavior. There is a convincing body of research evidence that shows that many media consumers, particularly heavy television viewers, tend to uncritically accept media content as fact. Even if the content is negative, sexist, misogynistic, and/or racist, or if it distorts the reality of contemporary intimate relationships, it may nevertheless be accepted as accurate by a large segment of the viewing audience (Renzetti and Curran, 1999).

Finally, the diffusion of computer and Internet use has had a phenomenal impact, in a variety of ways, on contemporary sexuality. For example, using the selling power of female sexuality, in 2000, Victoria's Secret, a well-known lingerie company, ran half-naked models across the information superhighway while broadcasting its Cannes fashion show live on the Web (the company made history with its first such Webcast in 1999). It is estimated that more than 2 million people logged on to the Webcast to view supermodels like Tyra Banks and Stephanie Seymour strut down the catwalk in the retailer's latest and most titillating lingerie (CNNMoney, 2000). The selling of sex (in a variety of manifestations) via the Internet is particularly troublesome when it comes to today's youth, who are spending a growing amount of time surfing the Internet. Through the Internet, young people (as well as older adults) have access to almost any sexual information there is, in one place, and at any time they want it. To date, it is far easier to find sexually explicit, unhealthy sites on the Internet than it is to locate those that promote sexually responsible behavior in an equally compelling way. According to a recent survey of young (10- to 17-year-olds) Internet users, one in five said she or he had been exposed to unwanted sexual solicitations while online in the past year. One in four reported inadvertently encountering explicit sexual content. This is particularly compelling given that by the year 2010, it is estimated that most homes with children in the United States will have access to the Internet (Brown and Keller, 2000).

SEXUAL ORIENTATIONS

It is impossible to discuss human sexuality without discussing sexual orientation. Contrary to popular belief, sexual orientation, whether heterosexual or homosexual, is not synonymous with sexual behavior. **Sexual orientation** involves not only whom one chooses as a sexual partner, but, more fundamentally, the ways in which people understand and identify themselves.

Although Americans tend to think of sexual orientation in terms of clear-cut categories—for example, heterosexual versus homosexual—various sex researchers have concluded that fundamental categories of sexual desire are nonexistent for most of us. Rather, sexual desire is constructed in the context of social relationships and identities (Andersen, 1993). Cultural historian and sex researcher Shere Hite (1976) believes that we are born with a natural desire to relate to people of the same as well as the other sex. Society, however, teaches us to inhibit all of our sexual desires except those for partners with whom we can procreate. Regardless of whether we accept Hite's hypothesis, it is clear that U.S. culture historically has espoused **heterosexism,** the belief that heterosexuality is the only right, natural, and acceptable sexual orientation and that any other orientation is pathological.

Heterosexism is so strong in U.S. society that most sex research is based on the assumption of heterosexuality. This assumption overlooks the fact that many people have a homosexual orientation and even more people have engaged in homosexual behavior at least once in their life. For example, Susan Basow (1992) reported in 1992 that by age 45, somewhere between one-fifth and one-third of all men and one-sixth of all women have experienced at least one homosexual encounter. Furthermore, research suggests that sexual orientation forms a continuum with at least four recognizable levels of orientation (see, for example, Maier, 1984). According to this research, at the two extremes are exclusively heterosexual and exclusively homosexual orientations, with bisexuality and asexuality falling somewhere in the middle.

Heterosexuality

Heterosexuality refers to the preference for sexual activities with a person of the other sex. In a more sociological and political sense, heterosexuality also includes an individual's community, lifestyle, and core identity. It is difficult to know precisely how many people in the U.S. population are heterosexual. Research through the beginning of the 1990s (for example, Maugh, 1990) consistently reported that 90 percent or more of Americans identify themselves as exclusively heterosexual. More recent sex surveys (for example, Clements, 1994; Laumann, 1994) place the percentage at or near 97 percent. As the previous discussion indicates, however, some social scientists view sexual orientation, like other aspects of our identity, as an ongoing process that can vary considerably over the life course. For example, researchers have found that heterosexual and homosexual preferences do not always remain constant throughout people's lives. For any number of reasons, people sometimes change their sexual preference. Phillip Blumstein and Pepper Schwartz (1983), for example, found that people often became homosexual after satisfactory heterosexual lives or became heterosexual after many years of homosexual identity and behavior. For those who view human sexual orientation as fluid, the degree to which we identify ourselves as heterosexual reflects in part the extent to which we have internalized society's messages and definitions of what is and is not acceptable. Given the stigma associated with sexual orientations other than heterosexuality, it is not surprising that most people claim (at least publicly) to be exclusively heterosexual.

Social scientists utilizing a feminist perspective maintain that in the United States, sexuality generally and sexual activities specifically that are associated with a heterosexual orientation are *phallocentric,* male-centered, and are defined almost exclusively in terms of genital intercourse and male orgasm (which might explain why so many people do not view oral sex as having sex). According to this point of view, the ideology of heterosexuality assumes that women exist for men, that their bodies and services are men's property. If a woman rejects this definition of normal sexuality she is stigmatized no matter whom she chooses as a sexual partner (see Bunch, 1979). For men, the notion of heterosexual intercourse, with its assumptions of male power and control; male lust, passion, and aggression; and the male as the initiator of sexual activity, is the proving ground for acceptable male sexuality and identity in this society. It also provides the script that most men adopt, with some individual modification, as the foundation of both their masculinity and sexual activity.

Some feminist social scientists such as Adrienne Rich (1980) have argued that making heterosexuality compulsory stymies or restricts the sexuality of males as well as females. Rich suggests that both heterosexism and **homophobia**—an extreme and irrational fear or hatred of homosexuals—act to inhibit the possibility of some women and men finding emotional and sexual satisfaction with same-sex partners.

Homosexuality

Like heterosexuality, **homosexuality** refers to both identity and behavior. It is part of a person's core identity and includes whom she or he defines as an acceptable sexual partner, but it does not consist solely of sexual preference. Thus, to label homosexuality entirely in terms of choice of sexual partner distorts our perception of lesbians and gays. Certainly we do not define heterosexuals entirely or even primarily in terms of their choice of sexual partner. But, what if we did? If you are heterosexual, how would you feel if people defined you entirely in terms of who you slept with? What if people routinely asked you questions such as, "When or how did you first realize that you were a heterosexual?" "Do your parents know?" "What do you think caused your heterosexuality? Is it possible that it is just a phase that you are going through?" "If you choose to have children, would you want them to be heterosexual, knowing

In contrast to popular images of the casual sexual behavior of lesbians and gays, many same-sex couples share long-term monogamous relationships that often include shared parenting.

the problems they would face?" "Why do heterosexuals put so much emphasis on sex?" "If you have never slept with a person of the same sex, is it possible that all you need is a good gay lover?" (see, for example, Rochlin, 1992). Would you find such questions offensive? Can you see and understand the indignity engendered when we routinely ask such questions of lesbians and gays?

Like heterosexuality, the exact determination of homosexuality is unknown. As we have seen, some scientists explain both homosexuality and heterosexuality in terms of social learning, social experiences, and role models. However, no specific social experience or type of social relationship has been found to be significant in the development of human sexual preference (Bell, Weinberg, and Hammersmith, 1981). At the same time, there is no conclusive evidence to support the argument that sexual orientation is determined entirely by biology. Nonetheless, the debate over the relative roles of social environment and biology in determining sexual orientation continues to spark controversy among a number of groups in society, including scientists, gay activists, and religious and political leaders.

In recent years, those who take a biological stance in this debate have received a boost from research results that suggest that sexual orientation (at least in men) is determined in large part by genetic factors. If it turns out that sexual orientation is genetically determined, then can we continue to define either homosexuality or heterosexuality as sexual preference?

How Widespread Is Homosexuality? Because homosexuality is so stigmatized, it is difficult to determine with any precision how many women and men are homosexual. In the 1950s, Alfred Kinsey and his associates (1953) reported that 28 percent of their sample of almost 8000 women had experienced a homosexual activity. Almost 25 years later, Shere Hite (1976) reported that 8 percent of the women in her sample said that they actually preferred sex with another woman. A few years later, in her study of male sexuality, Hite (1981) found that 11 percent of the 7000 men in her sample preferred to have sex with a person of their same sex. Same-sex preference is clearly different from simply having a single homosexual encounter, as reported in the Kinsey study.

Agreement about the extent or prevalence of homosexuality in today's society is not unanimous. In the *Parade* magazine study of sexuality, 3 percent of the male respondents identified themselves as homosexual, and 1 percent of the women said that they were homosexual. This finding was consistent with the NORC findings in which 2.8 percent of the men and 1.4 percent of the women identified themselves as homosexual or bisexual. However, the number who reported having had same-sex experiences or same-sex attractions was considerably higher (see Figure 6.3). This disparity is evident in other, more recent national surveys in which only 0.6 of women and 1.8 percent of men identified themselves as lesbian and gays, although 1.4 percent of women and 2.6 percent of men reported that they were in exclusive same-sex relationships over the last 5 years (Black et al., 2000).

As these statistics indicate, a definition of homosexuality is complicated by the fact that sexual preference, sexual attraction, and/or actual sexual behavior are not always consistent with one's sexual self-identity. For example, in a study of men who self-identified as heterosexual, 23 percent reported that they had had sex with both women and men in the past 2 years and 6 percent said that they had had sex exclusively with men (Doll et al., 1992). Similarly, in a study of men who reported having sexual relations with both women and men, only 2 percent self-identified as homosexual and 29 percent as bisexual, whereas the overwhelming majority, 69 percent, described themselves as heterosexual.

Similarly, in the African American community, many men who have sex with other men nevertheless think of themselves as heterosexual. Whites and Latinas/os are far more likely to report being gay than are African American women and men. For example, in the NORC survey, 3 percent of white men and 3.7 percent of Latinos identified themselves as homosexual or bisexual, compared with 1.5 percent of African American men. According to some analysts, machismo has always been a strong component of African American masculinity. The concept of being gay is seen as the antithesis of manhood. Thus, many African American men who have sex with other men don't consider themselves gay. While attempting to present a heterosexual image to the outer world, these men frequently engage in compulsive, high-risk sex with men while engaged in ongoing sexual relationships with one or more women. Experts in the field have dubbed this tendency the "down low syndrome" when men have sex with other men but deny they

Figure 6.3

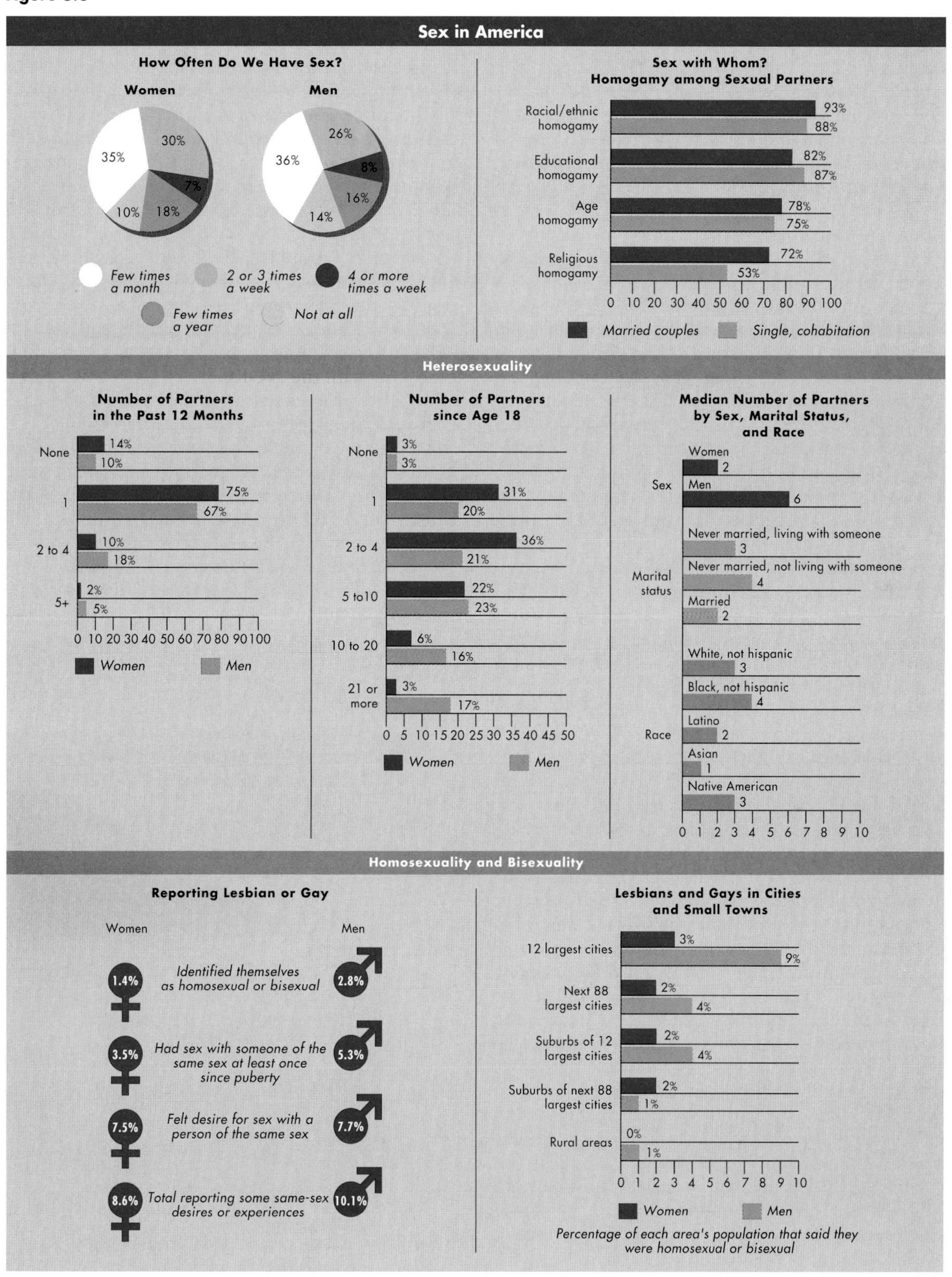

Source: Peter Gorner, "What Is Normal?" copyright © 1994 by *The Chicago Tribune*; Tamar Lewin, 1994, "Sex in America: Faithfulness in Marriage Thrives After All," *New York Times* (October 7): A11; Tamar Lewin, 1994, "So, Now We Know What Americans Do in Bed. So?" *New York Times* (October 9): 3.

are gay or even bisexual. Many believe that this "down low" behavior is a leading cause of the increasing incidence of HIV infections among African American women (Herbert, 2001a; Muwakkil, 2001).

The same discrepancy between how one self-identifies and what one actually does is also observable for women: 1.7 percent of white women and 1.1 percent of Latinas identified themselves as homosexual or bisexual, compared with less than 1 percent (0.6 percent) of the African American women in the sample.

These findings raise questions regarding the accuracy of statistics that purport to tell us the prevalence of homosexuality, heterosexuality, and bisexuality and they don't even begin to reveal the number of people who are transgendered. For example, it is estimated that somewhere around 2 percent of the American population are transgendered people. **Transgendered** refers to living life as the opposite sex. Complicating our ability to determine just how many people are transgendered is the fact that this group is not static; it includes heterosexuals, bisexuals, and homosexuals. In addition, some transgendered people are *transsexuals* (people who have undergone sex change surgery) and others are *transvestites* (people who dress in the clothing of the opposite sex).

So, given the general difficulty of defining sexual orientation, what criteria, if any, should we use to classify people in terms of their sexual orientation? Do we use their behavior? Their attitudes? Both? How many female and male partners does a person have to have in order to be classified as heterosexual, homosexual, or bisexual? Do we classify someone who has had 2 partners of the same sex and 15 of the other sex as heterosexual, homosexual, or bisexual? Or do we simply rely on self-labeling and what people feel rather than what they do? For example, how do we classify the person who feels gay, identifies as lesbian or gay, but never has same-sex sexual relations? Furthermore, given the prevalence of AIDS, the stigma associated with it, and its association to homosexuality, are people telling the truth? Although recent studies generally debunk the 10 percent figure that has been the baseline since the Kinsey studies, as Figure 6.3 shows, the NORC survey found that homosexuals are so likely to cluster in large cities (for example, New York, San Francisco, Chicago) that the 10 percent figure may well be on the mark in those cities. For example, the survey found that more than 9 percent of the men in the 12 largest cities in the United States identified themselves as homosexual, compared with less than 4 percent of the men in the suburbs of those cities and 1 percent of the men in rural areas. Lesbians also cluster in cities, but to a lesser degree than gays.

In this context, the NORC survey raises the important issue of whether or not the apparent urbanization of homosexuality is due to lesbians and gays migrating to big cities or whether the acceptance of homosexuality in the cities facilitates homosexual behavior. The study does not reach a conclusion on the issue (Lewin, 1994b).

This dichotomy of heterosexual versus homosexual, however, may be misleading. According to Kinsey and his colleagues (1948), few of us are completely and exclusively heterosexual or homosexual. Rather, although many people would prefer not to entertain the thought, there are some aspects of both orientations in all of us. Kinsey expressed this idea with a rating scale (0 to 6) of heterosexuality and homosexuality, in which each number on the scale represents the degree to which people have heterosexual or homosexual experiences (see Figure 6.4). Using this rating, Kinsey found that almost 80 percent of 25-year-old white male respondents in his study were exclusively heterosexual, and 3 percent were exclusively homosexual. The remaining respondents fell somewhere along the scale from 1 to 5. Using the same scale, he later suggested that 2 percent of women have an exclusively homosexual orientation. He suggested further that somewhere around one-third of men and one-eighth of women had at least one homosexual experience leading to orgasm.

Thus, the percentage of people who report that they are homosexual depends on how the question is asked. For example, about 9 percent of the men and 5 percent of the women in the NORC survey said that they had had at least one homosexual experience since puberty. Forty percent of the men who had had a homosexual experience sometime in their life did so before they were 18 years of age, and not since. Women, on the other hand, were 18 or older when

Figure 6.4

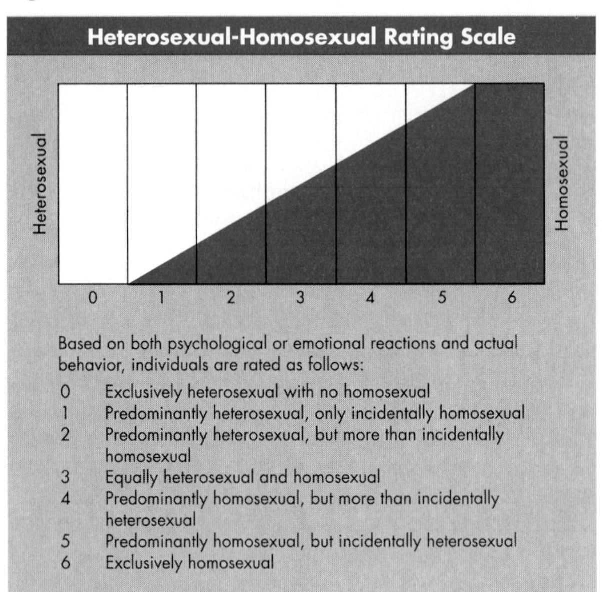

Source: From Alfred Kinsey, W. B. Pomeroy, and C. E. Martin, 1948. *Sexual Behavior in the Human Male* (Philadelphia, PA: Saunders):470. Reprinted by permission of the Kinsey Institute for Research in Sex, Gender, and Reproduction, Inc.

they had their first homosexual experience. Furthermore, when the women and men in the NORC sample were asked if having sex with someone of the same sex was appealing to them, 5.5 percent of the women said that the idea was somewhat or very appealing while 6 percent of the men said that they were "very" attracted to other men. This gives further credence to Kinsey's suggestion that sexual orientation is not a nice neat set of mutually exclusive categories, but rather is fluid.

Given Kinsey's early findings and the more contemporary work of the sex researchers cited in this chapter, as well as recent British and French studies, the 10 percent figure for exclusive homosexuality might be too high. However, while the percentage of women and men who are exclusively homosexual may be around 3 percent to 4 percent and exclusively lesbian, 1 percent to 2 percent, it seems plausible that when we broaden the concept, probably at least 10 percent of the population has had some homosexual experience. For sure, given Kinsey's findings, we cannot speak of homosexuality as if it were a monolithic behavioral and attitudinal pattern. Homosexuality varies in terms of importance, its organization, and its actualization in people's lives. It is sufficient to say here that, except for the gender of one's partner, the sexual attitudes, behaviors, and relationships of lesbians and gays do not differ significantly from those of heterosexual couples. While we provide a more in-depth discussion of lesbian and gay lifestyles in Chapter 7, lesbian and gay lifestyles, issues, and concerns can be found throughout the text.

Bisexuality

Although bisexuality is difficult to define, some researchers have suggested that it is more prevalent in American society than is homosexuality. On the one hand, **bisexuality** refers to individuals who do not have an exclusive sexual preference for one sex over the other. Rather, a bisexual has partners of both sexes, either simultaneously or at different times. On the other hand, as with other sexual orientations, bisexuality also represents an identity and a lifestyle. As we have already noted, an important aspect of sexual orientation is how one defines oneself. As with homosexuality, it is difficult to know exactly how many people are bisexual. One recent research report indicates that somewhere between 5 percent and 6 percent of Americans reported being bisexual since the onset of adulthood. In general, however, estimates range from 10 percent to 29 percent of the adult population (Maugh, 1990; Doll et al., 1992; Lever et al., 1992). One of the difficulties of attempting to estimate the bisexual population is that many researchers and laypersons alike view bisexuals exclusively as homosexuals. For example, in the NORC study, statistics on bisexuals and homosexuals are collapsed. Although some people who engage in both same-sex and heterosexual relationships categorize themselves as either heterosexual or homosexual, many bisexuals do not see themselves in this either/or dichotomy; they do not see themselves as gay or straight and their behavior does not correspond to either.

Like homosexuality, bisexuality is stigmatized in the larger society. In addition, bisexuals are often rejected by the homosexual community as well. Many people do not believe that people can really be bisexual; they have to be one thing (heterosexual) or another (homosexual) (Sapiro, 1990). As we have said, the difficulty of defining sexual orientation in clear-cut, mutually exclusive terms means we cannot place people into neat categories of sexual preference or orientation. Therefore, Hite's (1981) suggestion that the terms *homosexual* and *heterosexual* be used not as nouns but as adjectives is noteworthy. Perhaps *bisexual* should also be used as an adjective to describe people's activities and not people themselves, particularly given that few people are completely bisexual.

The complex interaction of our biology and culture is evidenced in the fact that regardless of how we choose to express our sexuality, our bodies experience a physiological response pattern when we are sexually stimulated. Next we turn to a discussion of the human sexual response cycle and some of the ways that we express our sexuality.

THE PHYSIOLOGY OF SEXUALITY

Although sex surveys tell us much about what people do, how they do it, and how often, such surveys tell us little about what goes on in our bodies when we are sexually stimulated. For example, what, if anything, happens to our pulse? Our blood pressure? What about our genitals and other areas of our bodies? How do they respond to sexual stimulation? In this section we address these and other questions concerning human sexual response.

The Sexual Response Cycle

Numerous studies of the sexuality of Americans have been conducted over the years. It was not until the pioneering work of sex researchers William Masters and Virginia Johnson (1966), however, that we began to understand with more clarity the physiological processes of sexual response in human beings. Based on over 10 years of systematic research on copulating couples (including the observation and manipulation of sexual activities in a laboratory setting), Masters and Johnson recorded and described in some detail the physiological factors associated with sexuality and **erotic arousal**—the stimulation or awakening of sexual desires that we feel ourselves or that we invoke in others. According to Masters and Johnson, all people go through the same four phases of sexual response: excitement, plateau, orgasm, and resolution.

EXCITEMENT PHASE The *excitement phase* begins the sexual response process and may last anywhere from a few minutes to several hours. In this phase the body responds to sexual stimulation such as sights, images, sounds, touches, thoughts, and smells, and it varies from one individual to another. Human beings use a variety of methods to stimulate and excite themselves and their partners, including kissing, hugging, mouth on breast or other parts of the body, rubbing, oral stimulation, and finger insertion. Most often this response is achieved through tactile stimulation of an **erogenous zone**—an area of the body that is particularly sensitive to sexual stimulation.

Plateau Phase If sexual stimulation continues, individuals move into the *plateau phase*, in which both heart rate and blood pressure intensify. This phase can last only a few minutes or for quite some time. For example, if a couple wish to prolong the plateau, they might decrease stimulation for a while and then begin it again. If the male is within a couple of years of puberty, a few drops of a clear preejaculatory fluid may be secreted during stimulation. Although the male has not ejaculated, the female can become pregnant because this preejaculatory fluid may contain some sperm cells.

Orgasmic Phase With continued stimulation both females and males enter into the *orgasmic phase*. In this phase, the sexual emotions and excitement built up in the previous phases reach a peak and are released in an **orgasm,** the involuntary release of pelvic congestion and accumulated muscular tension through rhythmic contractions in the genitals of both sexes and also through ejaculation in males. In this phase several physiological changes occur in the body: Heartbeat and blood pressure may double, the pattern of breathing may become deeper and faster, the facial muscles may contort the face, and brain wave patterns may change (Masters and Johnson, 1966). Orgasm is generally followed by a feeling of euphoria—a sense of contentment, well-being, and extreme relaxation.

According to Masters and Johnson's research, the clitoris, not the vagina, is the central organ of orgasmic response in women. This finding refutes the widely accepted Freudian notion that a vaginal orgasm is more sexually mature in women than a clitoral orgasm. For most men, orgasm usually includes **ejaculation,** the forceful release of semen through the meatus. Once ejaculation starts, a man cannot voluntarily stop it. Orgasm and ejaculation, however, are not one and the same. Although they usually happen concurrently, it is possible for one to happen without the other.

Orgasm is an intense physiological response that is not the same for all women and men, nor is it the same from one erotic experience to the next. While there are some notable differences between female and male orgasms, the most notable difference is that women are capable of achieving multiple orgasms, although only 15 percent actually do, primarily because their partners stop sexual stimulation too soon (McCary, 1978). In contrast, few men can achieve successive orgasms during a given sexual activity. A few can achieve a second orgasm shortly after the first orgasm, but this ability decreases with age.

Resolution Phase Finally, after orgasm and the cessation of stimulation, the body returns to its preexcitement physiological state. During this *resolution phase* physiological functions such as blood pressure, heart and pulse rates, breathing, and muscle tension return to their normal state. In females, the vagina decreases in size, and in males, the penis loses its erection. Masters and Johnson found that during this phase men experience a **refractory period,** a state of rest or relaxation that can last anywhere from a few minutes (in young males) to several hours (in older men). Men must remain in this period until it is completed. During this time they are physiologically incapable of rearousal (entering the excitement phase again), and some, but certainly not all, men generally lose all interest in sex during this period.

For women the resolution period generally lasts only a few minutes, although this varies with age. Unlike men, women in this phase may continue to be sexually aroused and achieve subsequent orgasms. Figure 6.5 illustrates the sexual response patterns that were identified by Masters and Johnson for females and males. As the figures reveal, considerable variation exists between female and male responses. Although males generally exhibit the same pattern, females may experience any one of three patterns: (1) a response similar to the male response except with the possibility for multiple orgasms, (2) an attainment of the plateau phase without moving on to the orgasm phase, and (3) rapid attainment of orgasm followed by a quick resolution.

Although the discussion of sexual response patterns refers to heterosexual sexuality, "Neither female nor male sexuality is limited by genital geography" (Hite, 1976:389). From the point of view of physical pleasure we can relate erotically to either sex depending on our feelings (Hite, 1976). In the next section, we examine some of the social-psychological and emotional manifestations of human sexuality; some of the ways in which people express their sexual selves.

HUMAN SEXUAL EXPRESSION

Human sexual expression covers a wide variety of behaviors. Heterosexual intercourse is simply one of many ways to express human sexuality. Sexual expression ranges from activities involving only the self—**autoeroticism**—to activities involving one or more other individuals, such as "swapping" or group sex.

Autoeroticism

In general, Americans engage in a wide variety of sexual behaviors, some of which most people recognize as sexual and others that are unique to the individuals and their situations. Some of the most common and recognizable forms of autoeroticism are masturbation, sexual fantasy, erotic dreams, and oral stimulation or sex. Until recent times, U.S. society placed particularly heavy restrictions on autoeroticism. Today, however, a range of such behaviors is considered acceptable. This fact notwithstanding, recent surveys of

Figure 6.5

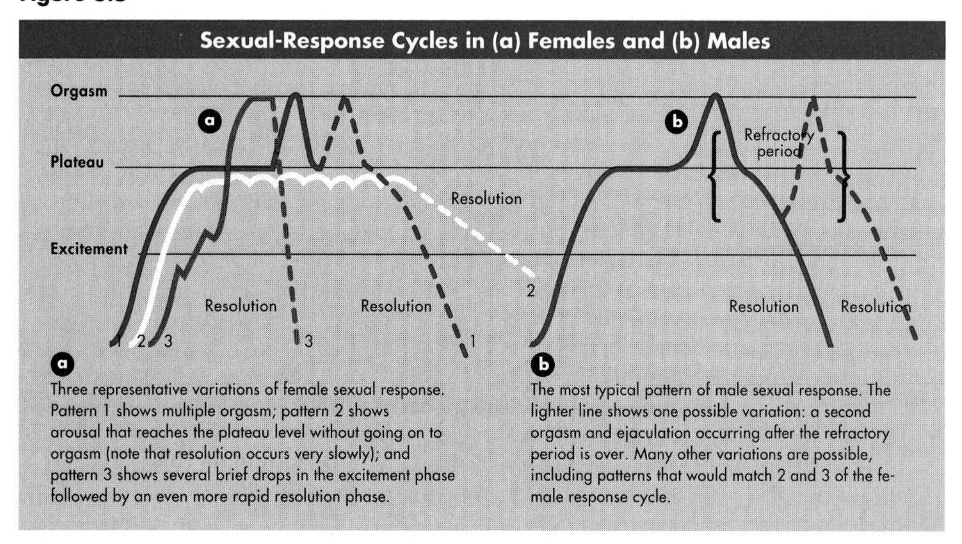

Source: William Masters, M.D., and Virginia Johnson, 1985, *Human Sexual Response* (Boston: Little, Brown).

America's sexual habits indicate that the majority of us do not engage in and enjoy a wide spectrum of exotic sexual practices with a large number of sexual partners. Rather, as our discussion of sex in the 1990s and beyond earlier in this chapter revealed, we are pretty conventional in our sexual practices, having only a small number of total partners over our lifetime and engaging most often in only three different types of sexual activity.

MASTURBATION "Don't knock masturbation. It's having sex with someone I deeply love." This now classic statement by film director Woody Allen reflects the attitudes of many people in this society, for whom masturbation is a common form of sexual expression and enjoyment. **Masturbation** involves gaining sexual pleasure from the erotic stimulation of self through caressing or otherwise stimulating the genitals. Masturbatory behavior is said to begin in infancy, when children accidentally discover the pleasure to be derived from rubbing, squeezing, caressing, or otherwise stimulating their genitals. For many people, this is the beginning of a lifelong way of expressing their sexuality.

Masturbation is not limited to the self-stimulation of the genitals; it can also include the self-stimulation of other parts of the body such as the breast, the inner thighs, and the anus. Although masturbation is becoming more common among women, boys and adult men tend to masturbate more often than girls and women do. In the 1950s, Kinsey and his colleagues found that 92 percent of males and 58 percent of females masturbated to achieve orgasm. In the 1970s, researchers reported that about 67 percent of males and 20 percent of females had masturbated by the time they were 17 years of age (Wilson, 1975). Today, sex researchers report that 42 percent of women and 63 percent of men say that they masturbate. Among those who masturbate, one man in four and one woman in ten report masturbating once or more a week (Laumann et al., 1994). Male respondents say they masturbate an average of five times a month, while women do so an average of twice a month (Clements, 1994). As women and men age they masturbate less frequently, but they do not stop altogether. One study found that as many as 43 percent of men and 33 percent of women in their 70s masturbate (Brecher, 1984).

Not only are there gender differences in masturbation rates, but women and men also differ in terms of their attitudes toward masturbation. For example, according to sex researcher Hans Hessellund (1976), masturbation functions more as a supplement to sexual life for men, whereas for women it functions more as a substitute for intercourse. Moreover, females tend to begin masturbation for orgasm at much later ages than males, sometimes for the first time in their 20s or 30s (Lindsey, 1990). Interestingly, Shere Hite (1976) found that most women have more intense and quicker orgasms with masturbation than with intercourse.

Moreover, there are also significant differences in the rate of masturbation in terms of other important categories of experience such as age, race, and class (as measured by level of educational attainment). Young people 18 to 24 years of age are less likely to masturbate than are those who are 25 to 34 years of age. Further, the higher one's level of education, generally the greater the frequency of masturbation. For example, over 33 percent of the male respondents in the NORC sex survey with a high school or college education reported that they masturbate on a regular basis, compared with 19 percent of men who did not graduate from high school. This pattern among the educated holds true for women as well: Comparable figures are 14 percent and 8 percent, respectively. And among racial and ethnic groups, African Americans report the lowest rates of masturbation.

Sixty percent of African American men and 68 percent of African American women report that they have never masturbated. Perhaps because this behavior does not conform to the stereotype of African American male sexuality, some observers have attempted to explain the low rate of masturbation among African American males by suggesting that these males shy away from such behavior because they view it as an admission of their inability to seduce a woman (Belcastro, 1985). Such interpretations should be viewed cautiously. This is clearly an underresearched area and, like other topics of human sexuality, may be an embarrassing or intimidating subject for people to respond to honestly and openly.

Although single, noncohabiting individuals report the highest rate of masturbation (41 percent for men and 12 percent for women), frequently people continue to masturbate after marriage. Husbands tend to masturbate more often than wives do. The majority of wives who masturbate rate their marriage as unsatisfactory (Petersen et al., 1983). Many married and nonmarried couples participate in mutual masturbatory activities rather than have intercourse. Others find that manual stimulation of the genitals during intercourse heightens the likelihood that both partners will reach orgasm. Furthermore, the NORC sex survey belies the myth that the majority of people who masturbate are those who are without a sex partner. According to the study, people who masturbate the most are people who have the most partnered sex.

It is interesting that so many people engage in a behavior that not long ago was thought to cause blindness, dementia (insanity), and a host of other mental and physical ills. So intense were feelings about masturbation in our early history that children's hands and feet were often tied to bedposts to prevent them from masturbating during the night. Various "experts" in the late nineteenth and early twentieth centuries as well a variety of others blamed masturbation for every kind of human malady from brain damage to blindness, deafness, heart murmurs, and destroying the genitals to acne and bad breath. So entrenched were these ideas about masturbation that there was a large and active commercial market for a variety of devices to control masturbatory activities such as metal mittens to cover the hands, rings with metal teeth or spikes to wear on the penis, vulva guards, and alarms that were activated when the bed moved (Wade and Cirese, 1991). Although many people still consider masturbation to be wrong, sex therapists have found that it serves some important positive functions, such as providing a means for people (especially women) to explore and determine in private what is most sexually stimulating for them (Gagnon and Simon, 1973). Researchers June Husted and Allan Edwards (1976) found a positive correlation between depression and frequency of masturbation; that is, the more depressed people become, the more they masturbate. They concluded that masturbation reduces tension for depressed individuals. Despite the benefits of masturbation and the more liberal attitudes toward it today, many people find that their emotional needs are not met through self-stimulation.

Sexual Fantasy and Erotic Dreams Sexual fantasy and erotic dreams, like masturbation, are common methods of autoeroticism. People use these activities to supplement or enhance a reality that is less exciting than the images they can construct in their minds. Some researchers have suggested that sexual fantasies might help prepare women for experiences that are erotically satisfying (Shope, 1975). Others suggest that they provide a harmless way for people to release pent-up sexual feelings or escape a boring sexual life (Patterson and Kim, 1991). Whatever their particular function, fantasies help maintain emotional balance in the individual (Strong et al., 1978). More males than females engage in sexual fantasy and erotic dreaming, and they do so more often. Over one-half (54 percent) of the male respondents in the NORC sex survey said that they fantasize about sex several times a day. Another 43 percent fantasize about sex several times a week. In comparison, only 19 percent of women have sexual fantasies several times a day, while over two-thirds (67 percent) do so a few times a week.

Male fantasies appear to differ from female fantasies in that males tend to fantasize situations in which they are strong and aggressive and in which the sexual activity itself is basically impersonal. Women on the other hand tend to have more romantic, passive, and submissive fantasies (Shope, 1975; Patterson and Kim, 1991). The most frequent fantasies for both women and men involve oral sex and sex with a famous person (Patterson and Kim, 1991). Beyond these two similarities between the genders, there are some interesting differences in the frequency of different types of sexual fantasies (see Table 6.1).

Table 6.1

The Most Common Sexual Fantasies among American Women and Men

	Females	Males
Oral sex	43%	75%
Sex with a famous person	39	59
Using sexual devices	29	38
Sex in a public place	26	39
Sex with someone of another race	25	52
Multiple partners	24	57
Sex with a fictional TV character	20	30
Sex with dominance or submission	19	27
Sex with a much older person	15	34
Sex with a much younger person	15	39
Swapping partners	15	42
Anal sex	14	39
Sex with a physical object	11	15

Source: Adapted from *The Day America Told the Truth* by James Patterson and Peter Kim. Copyright © 1991 by James Patterson and Peter Kim. Reprinted by permission of William Morris Agency, Inc. on behalf of the Author.

Erotic dreams, often referred to as nocturnal dreams with sexual content, frequently lead to orgasm during sleep. This phenomenon is referred to as **nocturnal emissions** or **wet dreams.** Kinsey and his colleagues found that almost all men and the majority of women have nocturnal dreams with sexual content. Men tend to have more wet dreams than women: Four-fifths of all men, as opposed to one-third of all females, had nocturnal dreams that led to orgasm. Between 2 percent and 3 percent of a woman's orgasms may be achieved during nocturnal dreaming. In contrast, for men that number may be as high as 8 percent. The content of such dreams can cover a wide variety of erotic or sexual possibilities, including any one or all of the items listed in Table 6.1. The dream need not be overtly sexual, but it is usually accompanied by sexual sensations (Strong et al., 1978).

Interpersonal Sexual Behavior

In contrast to autoerotic behavior, which involves an individual acting alone, interpersonal sexual activity involves two or more people acting in concert for the purpose of giving each other pleasure.

Pleasuring As far back as the mid–nineteenth century, women were describing what to them was sexually pleasurable. Elizabeth Blackwell, the first woman to earn a medical degree in the United States, suggested that both women and men could experience sexual pleasure from each other without penile–vaginal intercourse. This idea of giving and receiving pleasure without intercourse was described over a century later by Masters and Johnson as **pleasuring.**

Pleasuring involves a couple exploring each other's bodies. It is erotic behavior that involves one person touching, exploring, and caressing nongenital areas of her or his partner's body for the purpose of giving erotic pleasure. After a while the partners exchange roles. This exchange can continue until orgasm, or it can function as foreplay followed by genital intercourse. However pleasuring is conducted, it seems that a large number of women find touching and caressing to be a natural eroticism and the most important part of sexual activity. Hite (1976) reported that one of the most basic changes that women wished for in their sexual relationships was touching and closeness for their own sake rather than only as a prelude to intercourse. One woman respondent, for example, said that "general body touching is more important to me than orgasms." Another said: "You can't love sex without loving to touch and be touched. It is the very physical closeness of sex that is the main pleasure" (Hite, 1976:556).

Petting and Oral Sex **Petting,** which involves a variety of types of physical contact for the purpose of sexual arousal, is a common activity among adolescent girls and boys. Petting includes kissing, oral contact with the body, finger insertion, and fondling. Kinsey once said that petting was one of the most significant factors in the sexual lives of high school and college females and males. If that was true in the past, it is even more so today. The great majority of young people today have experienced some type of petting behavior before they reach adulthood (Christopher and Sprecher, 2000). Whereas in the past these behaviors were used most often as a substitute for copulation, for many couples today they are a prelude to copulation. For example, a high percentage of women and men say that they enjoy kissing, genital touching, mouth or hands on breast, body kissing, and mutual masturbation as preludes to copulation. Some couples use pornographic material, and others employ sexual devices before or during sexual activity to enhance their enjoyment (Clements, 1994).

In many parts of society oral–genital sex is an unmentionable subject and taboo behavior. As late as the 1970s, social researcher Morton Hunt (1974) reported that oral–genital sex was still classified as a punishable crime against nature in the statutes of most states. By this time, however, **cunnilingus,** the oral stimulation of the female genitals, and **fellatio,** the oral stimulation of the male genitals, had become standard practices for a majority of white people of all social classes, single or married. Such behavior has been evident to a far lesser degree among comparable samples of African Americans. For example, whereas 72 percent of single white males and 63 percent of married white males in the NORC survey reported active incidences of oral–genital activity, only 35 percent of single black males and 49 percent of married black males reported such activity. For white and black unmarried women, the rates were 67 percent and 48 percent, respectively, and for married white and black women the rates were 60 percent and 50 percent, respectively. The practice of oral sex is particularly prevalent among white, college-educated men, 80 percent, compared with only 51 percent of college-educated African American males. Post-feminist writer Camille Paglia believes that oral sex is a culturally acquired preference that a generation of white college students picked up in the 1970s when they saw oral sex performed on the wide screen (in movies such as the X-rated film *Deep Throat*) (cited by Elmer-DeWitt, 1994:68). Interestingly, as we reported earlier, today's generation does not even consider oral sex as "having sex."

As with masturbation, and all other behavior for that matter, given that the behavior of whites is taken as the norm (explicitly or implicitly), researchers have been concerned to explain racial disparities between blacks and whites. Accordingly, some observers posit that so few African Americans report that they perform or receive oral sex because of religious teaching and the legacy of slavery: According to legend, it was something that slaves were required to do for their masters (Elmer-DeWitt, 1994). Although oral–genital sex has gained acceptance over the years, it may well be on the decline among some groups given the heightened sensitivity to various sexually transmitted diseases, especially herpes and AIDS.

Coitus **Coitus** refers only to penile–vaginal intercourse. Other forms of intercourse such as anal intercourse are not included in this term. Despite all the changes in sexual behavior that occurred in the twentieth century, coitus remains the primary method through which heterosexuals seek erotic pleasure. In every sex survey that the authors reviewed, both heterosexual women and men overwhelmingly identify coitus as *the most* appealing sexual practice. Coitus can occur with the partners in any number of positions. The most common is the "missionary position," in which the female lies on her back and the male faces her, lying on top of her (D'Emilio and Freedman, 1988). Some couples also adopt a position popularly called "69," in which the couple lie down with their heads in opposite directions and simultaneously perform oral–genital sex on each other. Because sexual intercourse is personal and private, people usually employ whatever positions they find mutually satisfying.

As we said earlier, the U.S. patriarchal structure of heterosexual relations assumes that coitus is the most satisfying sexual activity for women and men. Among heterosexuals, although most men find penile–vaginal coitus most satisfying, many women find clitoral stimulation, oral–genital sexual activity, and other methods of stimulation more satisfying than coitus (Hite, 1976). In general, women have more physiologically intense and quicker orgasms from manual clitoral stimulation, especially from their own stimulation, than from heterosexual intercourse (Basow, 1992).

Sexual Expression among Lesbians and Gays

As with other aspects of behavior, there is little difference in homosexual and heterosexual sexual expression and physiological response. Like heterosexuals, lesbians and gays engage in kissing, caressing, sexual arousal, and orgasm. Lesbians are more emotionally involved with their partners and are more likely to connect sex with love than gays are (Peplau, 1981). They express affection before actual sexual activity begins, and they often reach orgasm through mutual masturbation and cunnilingus. Contrary to popular belief, lesbians seldom use dildos or other objects in an attempt to simulate heterosexual intercourse. Such a belief is rooted in the heterosexist notion that heterosexual genital intercourse is the only normal way to express sexuality. Moreover, women tend to have a higher rate of orgasm in relations with other women than with men (Hite, 1976).

Gays often kiss, caress each other's penises, and reach orgasm through anal intercourse or through fellatio (Strong et al., 1978). As indicated in Chapter 5, gays tend to have sex with more partners and in shorter-term relationships than do lesbians. Gays also tend to act on their sexuality earlier than lesbians do, just as heterosexual males act earlier than heterosexual females. Some research indicates that these behaviors have changed in recent years due to the spread of AIDS. However, many gays have been, and some continue to be, sexually active with multiple partners.

More important, as with heterosexuals, there is a diversity in sexual practice among lesbians and gays. An interesting typology of gay sexuality is presented by Alan Bell and Martin Weinberg (1978). According to these researchers, gays in the United States can be characterized in terms of five lifestyles: *dysfunctional gay lifestyle*, *functional gay lifestyle*, *open-coupled lifestyle*, *close-coupled lifestyle*, and *asexual lifestyle*. These lifestyles run the gamut from a lifestyle centered around sex and characterized by a high number of different sexual partners (the functional category); to a lack of adjustment to being homosexual and sexual problems centered around feelings of sexual inadequacy (the dysfunctional category); to coupled gays living with a special sexual partner but who are likely to seek sexual satisfaction outside the relationship (the open-couple category); to exclusivity (the closed-couple category) where two gays turn to each other, rather than outsiders, for sexual and interpersonal fulfillment; to little or no sexual activity, gays who are not coupled and have low interest in sexual activity (the asexual category).

Although interesting and valid, we should interpret the relevancy of typologies such as this with caution. Indeed, we should also consider variations across race and class. For example, as we have indicated, African American gays are significantly more likely than other gays to be bisexual in their behavior. As you learned earlier, most studies of sexuality, particularly in terms of the specific sexual practices of lesbian and gay couples, utilize a heterosexual model that homogenizes sexual practices across sexual orientations. Although there continues to be a dearth of research on the sexual practices of lesbians and gays of color, we should not assume a universality of homosexual lifestyles or that heterosexual practices are adapted or adaptable to a lesbian or gay lifestyle or preference.

SEXUALITY ACROSS THE LIFE CYCLE

As we have indicated repeatedly throughout this chapter, sexual behavior for most people begins earlier and lasts longer over the life cycle today than at any other period in U.S. history. Adolescents at increasingly younger ages report being involved in some sort of sexual behavior. At the other end of the age spectrum, many people continue to enjoy sex well into old age. The following discussion is a brief examination of sexuality in several key periods of the life cycle.

Nonmarried Sexuality and Pregnancy

Although the terms *premarital sex* and *premarital intercourse* are commonly used in research studies of human sexuality, for a number of reasons they are outdated and inadequate for discussing contemporary sexuality. First, they imply that marriage is the norm, that human life consists of two periods: before marriage and marriage. They also imply that sexual intercourse does not normally occur until after marriage. As you have learned, neither of these assumptions is true any longer of the majority of the population. The fact is, an increasing number of adults (an estimated 10 percent) will never marry, and many adults are separated, divorced, or widowed and almost one-third of them will never remarry. Thus, their sexual relationships cannot be, with any reliability and validity, categorized as "premarital." Furthermore, given that lesbians and gays are denied the legal right to marry, their sexual relationships certainly cannot be legitimately categorized as "premarital" either. Thus, whenever possible we use the term *single* or *unmarried* whenever we refer to a nonmarried status.

The incidence of intercourse among singles increased considerably over the closing decades of the twentieth century. In addition, gender was no longer a distinguishing factor in unmarried sexual behavior. The behavior of white females dramatically illustrates both of these points. Over the last three decades, intercourse among single white females increased significantly, considerably narrowing the gap between them and their male peers. Among single African American women, a significant change also occurred, although it came primarily in terms of the earlier age at which coitus begins (D'Emilio and Freedman, 1988; Smith, 1999). During the 1990s, three-fourths of unmarried women had had sexual intercourse by the age of 19 and over four-fifths by the age of 29. The median age at first sexual intercourse for women was 16.9. Among men coming to maturity, the experience of sexual intercourse was nearly universal—95 percent. The median age at first sexual intercourse for males was 16.1 (Mosher, 1990; Sonenstein et al., 1991; Smith, 1999).

This increased sexuality among the nonmarried population is fairly consistent with the sexual attitudes and morals of the general population about sex outside of a legal married relationship. For example, in answer to a 2001 Gallup poll question about whether or not it is wrong for a woman and man to have sexual relations before marriage, 64 percent of those sampled said no, it is not wrong, 32 percent answered yes, it is wrong, and 4 percent had no opinion. A slightly differently worded question on the same subject yielded a similar result: 53 percent responded that it was morally acceptable for a woman and man to have sex before marriage, and 42 percent said it was morally unacceptable. The answers to these questions varied according to age. For example, two-thirds (67 percent) of young adults think sex before marriage is morally acceptable. Similarly, 60 percent of those 30 to 49 years of age said it was morally acceptable. However, older adults were much less liberal, with 46 percent of those 50 to 64 and only 28 percent of those 65 and older saying that such behavior was morally acceptable (Gallup Poll, 2001).

Figures on the frequency of sexual intercourse give us another view (albeit limited) of who does what and how often. During the 1950s, single women under the age of 20 had, on average, sexual intercourse once every two months, and those over 20, a little more than once a month (Kinsey et al., 1953). Today, 12 percent of women and men 18 to 24 years of age have sex an average of four or more times a week (Laumann, 1994).

The sexual behavior of adolescents is of particular interest to researchers studying the sexuality of the single or unmarried population. A review of recent research indicates not only an overall increase in sexual behavior among the single population but also a steady decline in the age of first intercourse: More adolescents are having intercourse at younger ages. A Centers for Disease Control (1994) study of 14- to 17-year-olds found that almost one-half had engaged in sexual intercourse at least once. Many adolescents as young as 13 say that they have had sexual intercourse. This increasing sexual behavior among America's youth cuts across race, class, geographic region, and religious background. For example, survey data on eighth-graders (13- to 14-year-olds) from several rural counties in Maryland showed that 58 percent of the males and 47 percent of the females had experienced coitus. Even among those teens who are raised in conservative Christian families, the percentage who are sexually active is quite high (Rubin, 1990). Two decades ago, close to 33 percent of white females and Latinas and almost 50 percent of black females had experienced coitus at least once by the age of 16. In addition, by age 16, about 50 percent of white and Latino males and over 65 percent of black males had experienced sexual intercourse (Sonenstein, Pleck, and Ku, 1989). Today, more than one-half of females and three-fourths of males aged 15 to 19 have experienced sexual intercourse. For example, at age 15, 21 percent of females and 27 percent of males have had sexual intercourse. By the age of 19, almost one-half of all high school students have engaged in sexual intercourse. Although these rates differ across race, they are high for most groups. For example, the rate for white females and males is 45 percent, respectively; for African American females, it is 67 percent, for African American males it is 76 percent, for Latinas, 46 percent, and for Latinos it is 63 percent (Kann et al., 2000). A Florida survey found that 75 percent of young people had experienced sexual intercourse by the time they reached twelfth grade, with 20 percent of them having had six or more sexual partners.

Some sex researchers are suggesting that American youth are in the midst of their own sexual revolution. Children as young as 8 years of age are asking teachers and others questions such as What is oral sex? and What is anal sex? These researchers claim that television, entertainment, and even the news and children's cartoons have contributed to this sexual revolution; in addition, the pandemic openness about sex in the schoolyard, on the bus, at home when parents are not watching, and in the shopping malls has also contributed to this revolutionary sexual behavior among today's youth. Teens today seem nonchalant about sex. They know more of the mechanics of sex than do many adults. For example, a nurse at a Utah Teen Center reported recently that a 14-year-old couple came into the center for counseling because they had tried unsuccessfully to heighten their arousal during sexual intercourse. They wanted advice on the necessary steps that would lead them to a more fulfilling orgasm. In particular, the young man wanted to know how to get to his partner's G-spot. (For those who do not know, *G-spot* is a popular term for a particularly sensitive area within the vagina, about halfway between the pubic bone and the cervix at the rear of the urethra, named after gynecologist Ernst Gräfenberg (1881–1957) who first put forth a theory concerning this area.) Although this might sound unbelievable, the fact is that these young people, along with thousands of others, have clearly gone further sexually than many adults. Along with this knowledge, a growing number of young people know how to protect themselves from disease and pregnancy. Surveys suggest that as many as two-thirds of teenagers today use condoms, a proportion that is three times as high as reported in the 1970s (Stodghill, 1999).

This sexual precociousness has led to a number of problems among youth, particularly in the nation's schools. Around the country, school officials have noted an increase in mock sexual behavior on buses carrying students to school. This behavior includes young people simulating sexual intercourse and simulating masturbation. Although girls reportedly initiate some of this conduct, in most instances the aggressors are reportedly boys. In response to this increasing display of sexuality among youth, some schools have instituted a sexual-harassment policy to deal with the sharp increase in lewd language, groping, pinching, and bra-snapping incidents among sixth-, seventh-, and eighth-graders. Sex has become so pervasive among some adolescents that a private Christian junior high school in Florida began to ask students to sign cards vowing not to have sex until they marry (Stodghill, 1999). Another by-product of this youthful sexual revolution is the presumption among many adolescent boys that sex is an entitlement—an attitude that fosters a breakdown of respect for oneself and others. A Rhode Island Rape Center study of 1700 sixth- and ninth-graders reported that 65 percent of boys and 57 percent of girls believed that it was acceptable for a male to force a female to have sex if they've been dating for six months (Stodghill, 1999).

In general, although teenage sexual relationships are more unstable than adult relationships, teenagers typically have sexual intercourse within a monogamous relationship (Sonenstein et al., 1991). The major reasons teenagers give for having sex are curiosity and the desire to experiment, the desire to be more popular or impress their friends, being in love, pressure from those they were dating (Gibbs, 1993a). More recently, surveys indicate that teens identify drinking and the mass media as major factors leading to sex (Chassler, 1997).

The statistics on adolescent sexual behavior should not lead us to assume that unmarried sexual activity (adolescent or adult) is synonymous with casual sex. The majority of unmarried intercourse among adolescents as well as among adults occurs within an affectionate, serious, and steady relationship (Thornton, 1990; Hendrick and Hendrick, 1992).

Pregnancies among Unmarried Women A major practical issue associated with early coitus and declining and delayed marriage is an increase in childbirth among unmarried women. Although unmarried pregnancy is not a new phenomenon resulting from the so-called sexually liberated years of the 1960s and 1970s, births to unmarried individuals and couples have increased significantly over the decades. Approximately one-third (or three in every ten) of the births in this country in 2000 involved single women, an almost eightfold increase since 1940. The rate of birth among single women, however, decreases with age. During 2000, 44 percent of births to women in their 20s were to single women with the proportion declining to 13 percent for single women 30 years and older. The percentage of births to single women also varies across race and nativity as well as level of education (see Figure 6.6). For example, in 2000, 15 percent of all births to Asian and Pacific Islanders was to single women, compared with 62 percent for African American women, 30 percent for Latinas, 57 percent for Native Americans, Eskimos, and Aleuts, and 26 percent for white non-Hispanic women. The proportion of births among foreign-born single women was considerably lower (18 percent) than among native-born women (34 percent). And the least educated single women had the highest rate of births (54 percent) compared to college-educated women (4 percent) (U.S. Census Bureau, 2000).

A 1995 "Report to Congress" dispels several myths surrounding this kind of pregnancy. For example, the report concludes that economic factors along with significant changes in societal attitudes about marriage, sex, and childbearing have more to do with increases in unmarried childbearing than do welfare benefits. The report also concludes that "more research is needed to determine whether efforts to strengthen families; to remove barriers to adoption, abortion, and marriage; to enforce child support orders; and to remove the marriage penalty in various tax and public assistance programs would substantially reduce out-of-wedlock childbearing (quoted in "New Report Explodes Myths," 1995:1).

Teenage Pregnancy According to U.S. census data, close to 1 million teenage girls become pregnant each year. In general, the rate of pregnancy and birth for teenage girls has declined in the United States since the 1950s. The most dramatic decreases occurred during the 1990s, when in one year alone (1996–1997) the birth rate fell 4 percent, which represented a 17 percent decrease since 1990. In 2000, the teen birth rate reached a record low of 49 births per 1000 women aged 15 to 19, which was about half the peak rate recorded in 1957 and was the lowest level ever reported for the nation. Although birth rates fell for all racial and ethnic groups during the 1990s, the decline was highest for African American teenagers—down 31 percent nationwide (from 115.5 to 79.2) and showing declines of about 40 percent in seven states (the lowest rates ever recorded for this group in the 40 years that such data have been available). Overall, the birth rates are highest for Latina/o teens (94.4) and lowest for Asian and Pacific Islander teens (21.8) followed by non-Latina white and Native American teenagers with 32.8 and 67.9 percent, respectively. The birth rate for the youngest teens, 10 to 14 years old, also dropped from 1.4 births per 1000 during the early 1990s to 0.9 in 2000, the lowest level in more than 30 years. And the 1999 teenage birth rate dropped in all 50 states, although the rate varied considerably from state to state, with Vermont having the lowest rate, 24.0

Figure 6.6

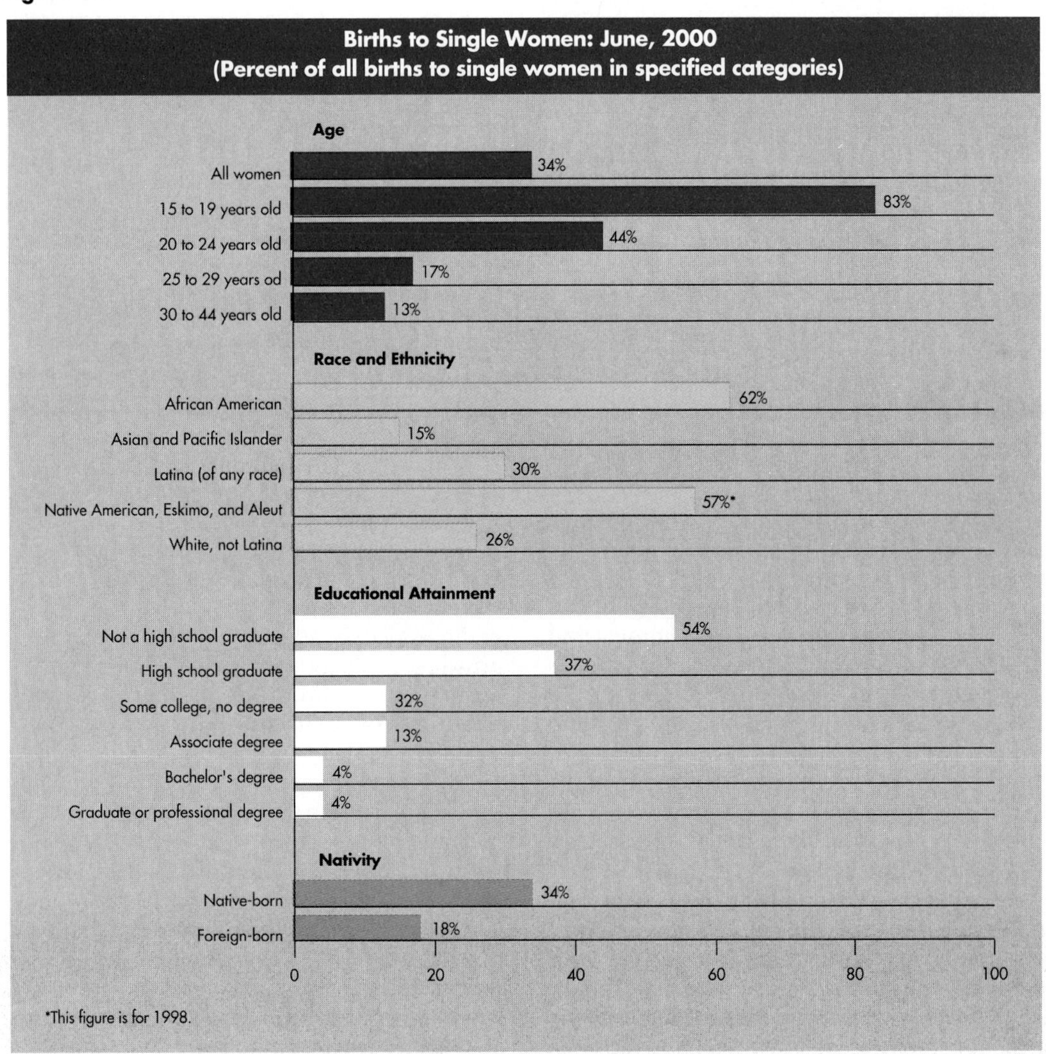

Source: U.S. Census Bureau, *Current Population Survey,* June 2000; U.S. Census Bureau, 1998.

births per 1000, and Mississippi the highest, 72.5 per 1000. The rate for the District of Columbia was 83.5 (Stolberg, 1999; U.S. Census Bureau, 2000; Ventura et al., 2001).

However, along with the decline in the teenage birth rate has been a steep rise in the proportion of births to unmarried teenagers, from 14 percent in 1957 to 67 percent in 1990 and 79 percent in 2000. According to some analysts, this might be because very few teens are marrying today and the birth rate for married teens has dropped substantially. The changing pattern in the teenage birth rate may reflect the efforts of many individuals, groups, and organizations to focus teenagers' attention on the importance of pregnancy prevention through abstinence and responsible sexual behavior.

Although most teenagers do not have sex initially to reproduce, one in ten whites and two in ten blacks say that during their first sexual intercourse they neither thought about nor cared if they got pregnant. However, the majority of teenagers who are sexually active today (over 75 percent) report using some form of birth control (most often the Pill). And, as they become more sexually active, the more consistently they use birth control methods. Some experts have suggested that approximately 20 percent of the decrease in teenage pregnancy since the late 1980s is because of decreased sexual activity and 80 percent of the decrease is because of more effective contraceptive practices. Moreover, there is some indication that the increase in AIDS awareness has led to some of the increase in the use of contraceptives, especially condoms and especially among sexually active adolescent males (Vital and Health Statistics, 1995; Kahn, Brindis, and Glei, 1999).

An instructor works with a student holding her child at the New Futures School in Albuquerque, New Mexico. The school provides education to pregnant teens and teenage mothers in a supportive environment so these young women can finish high school and participate economically in society.

The declining teenage birth rate notwithstanding, the U.S. teen birth rate remains the highest among developed countries. According to the latest statistics available, the rate is lowest in Japan at 4 births per 1000 women and is below 10 per 1000 in a number of countries including the Netherlands (Ventura et al., 2001). Perhaps we in the United States could take a lesson from the Dutch. The Dutch are so unflustered by sex, sexuality, and birth control that some groups have proposed selling contraceptive pills over the counter. The high level of openness about all aspects of sexuality has given the Netherlands the world's lowest teenage pregnancy rate (9 per 1000 females). And it is not that Dutch teenagers are less sexually active than other teenagers. Rather, the low rate of teenage pregnancy is a function of a better-informed population concerning the consequences of sexual intercourse. The Dutch use what they label a *Double Dutch* method of birth control: the Pill to prevent pregnancy combined with condoms to prevent the spread of AIDS. In addition, there is open discussion of sexuality and childbirth, in the family, schools, and the media. Teenage pregnancy cannot be traced to the liberal abortion laws in the Netherlands because they also have the lowest abortion rates in the world. Although the age of sexual consent is 16, Dutch family doctors sometimes prescribe contraceptive pills for girls aged 13 to 15 without informing their parents ("Dutch Have Lowest Teen Pregnancy," 1994:8).

Teenage pregnancy is a particularly unsettling situation in the United States, given that the majority of teen mothers live in or will live in poverty. Most teenaged parents, regardless of race, have low academic skills and high unemployment rates. They tend to come from poor families, most do not marry (at least not immediately), and they are likely to drop out of school, although black teenaged mothers are more likely than their white or Latina counterparts to continue attending school during and after pregnancy. According to sociologist Margaret Andersen (1993), regardless of their race and social class status, teenaged mothers value marriage as an ideal, but they do not see it as a viable option given both expectant parents' general lack of economic resources.

An added issue surrounding teenage pregnancy is the growing problem of teenaged girls getting pregnant by adult men. According to federal and state surveys, some two-thirds of babies born to teenaged girls are fathered by adult males. Teenage girls and adult men seek each other out for a number of complex reasons, some of which include the fact that perhaps some teenage girls perceive older as meaning more mature and more likely to offer support; and adult men, perhaps, think that there is less risk of disease and more chance of control with a teenage partner. In addition, a study out of Washington, D.C., found that a significant number of pregnant teenagers were physically or sexually abused at home. In many cases, especially among the youngest girls, the sexual encounter was with a considerably older man and was not consensual (Boyer and Washington, cited in Woodman, 1995).

In the final analysis, we should be very careful not to perpetuate myths about unmarried pregnancy or to lump single teenage and adult pregnancy together. First, the majority of unmarried births are not to teenagers, nor are they to teenagers of color. The fact is that the majority of births to unmarried women, 72 percent, occur among women who are 20 years of age or older (Ventura et al., 2001). Second, we cannot assume that unmarried pregnancies are always unwanted, nor can we assume that the custodial parent or parents are incapable of providing for the newborn simply because of age or marital status. In other words, we cannot assume that single parenting in and of itself is "problematic" and damaging. As a reviewer for this textbook so aptly pointed out, we should not "confuse unmarried pregnancy with teenage pregnancy. People married at a younger age in the past but that didn't mean that they were prepared for childbirth. Unmarried pregnancies may not be a problem for those prepared for parenting" (anonymous reviewer, 1995).

Marital Sexuality: Does Good Sex Make Good Marriages?

Because marital sex is considered the norm, scholars have not paid much attention to this subject. However, based on some of the most recent data in this regard, the changes in sexuality we have discussed in this chapter have affected married as well as unmarried people. Most marriages today have moved toward greater variety in sexual behavior, more frequent intercourse, and higher levels of sexual satisfaction. For example, a comparison of married couples in the 1970s with those studied by Kinsey in the 1940s revealed that twice as many 1970s couples departed from the missionary position. Oral sex had been routinely incorporated into the sexual behaviors of married couples, except those of African Americans. Major surveys of women's sexuality during the 1970s and 1980s pointed out major shifts among heterosexual couples from penile–vaginal intercourse and simultaneous orgasm to a variety of sexual practices directed toward the needs and desires of women. These changes have weakened what some researchers have described as the male monopoly over the nature of sex (see, for example, Ehrenreich, Hess, and Jacobs, 1986).

Married couples are not only engaging in a variety of sexual behavior more frequently, they are also enjoying it more. How often married couples have intercourse varies depending on age, social class, how long they have been married, if there are children, as well as a number of other factors. For example, factors such as job demands, household chores and demands, monetary issues and concerns, number of adults living in the household—all may conspire to limit a couple's sexual life of spontaneity and frequency. However, for the majority of married couples, the rate ranges from two to three times a week (around 40 percent) to several times a month (close to 50 percent). Frequency of marital sexual intercourse typically decreases over time with a sharp reduction after age 50 (Laumann et al., 1994; Call et al., 1995). This is not meant to imply that the frequency of sexual intercourse leads to sexual satisfaction and/or marital happiness. In fact, no such correlation has been found. Rather, it is not the quantity but the quality of their sexual lives that is important to married couples.

Sexual satisfaction is important to both wives and husbands, and over 85 percent report both emotional and physical satisfaction in their sexual relationships (Michael et al., 1994). Most research indicates that how a couple gets along sexually is an indication of how their marriage is going in general. Although most married people consider sexual activity to be important to their marriage, both wives and husbands report that the quality of the marriage relationship is more important than is sex, per se. According to the *Parade* sex survey, almost four-fifths (78 percent) of those who are married are happy with their marital status compared with 53 percent of singles. As in past surveys, men generally report being more content with their marital status than do women and singles. Likewise, husbands also report greater sexual satisfaction than wives do. Sexual intercourse is only one among many sexual activities that couples engage in. For example, the marital erotic bond might include any one or more of such sexual activities as kissing, caressing, nibbling, massaging, stroking, and romancing. In general, when couples define their sexual activities as satisfying, they also define their overall relationship as satisfying.

Extramarital Sexuality

Along with other changes in patterns of contemporary sexuality has come a change in the value attached to sexual exclusiveness in marriage. Research indicates that since the 1950s the incidence of extramarital relationships has increased substantially. Researchers estimate that by the 1980s as many as 65 percent to 70 percent of males and 45 percent to 65 percent of females had been involved in an extramarital relationship (Stayton, 1984). However, in recent surveys, the majority of females and males report fidelity in their intimate relationships. Obviously, even with the increasing tolerance of different lifestyles, an accurate assessment of the number of married people involved in extramarital relationships is difficult to determine because many of these relationships are conducted in secret. Thus, at any given time we can assume that the reported rates of extramarital relationships are significantly lower than the actual rate.

Why do people seek intimacy outside their marital relationship? There are probably as many reasons as there are individuals who engage in such relationships. In general, the lower the marital satisfaction and the lower the frequency and quality of marital intercourse, the greater the likelihood of extramarital sexual relationships. Most people indicate that they became involved in an extramarital relationship because they felt that something was missing in their marriage or that their marital sexual life was boring. Researcher Lynn Atwater (1982), however, noted some important attitudinal differences between husbands and wives who engage in extramarital relationships. Most wives indicated that they were dissatisfied with some aspect of their marriage, most often the expressive area. They also reported an improvement in their marital relationship, which they believed to be a direct result of their participation in an extramarital relationship. Husbands, on the other hand, more often participated in extramarital relationships because of the sexual excitement of such a liaison.

Discussions of extramarital relationships are complicated by the diverse number of relationships that are included in this category. Extramarital relationships can range from a one-night affair to a lifelong relationship. A husband can be involved with either a single or a married woman; likewise, a wife can be involved with either a single or a married man. A wife or husband can also have an extramarital affair with a person of the same sex. Thus, the frequency and nature of an extramarital relationship will vary not only with age, race, class, and other structural factors but also in terms of sexual orientation. Extramarital relationships are not just about sex. Nor are they always of short duration or meaningless. However, they are always about the violation of commitment, trust, and intimacy unless, of course, the couple has an *open marriage* in which they agree to have openly acknowledged and independent sexual relationships with persons other than eath other.

What is ironic about the incidence of marital infidelity is that, as a nation, we say that such behavior is improper and unacceptable. Yet, in 2001, for example, when U.S. Representative Gary Condit admitted to having an extramarital relationship with missing intern Chandra Levy, most Americans were not shocked. It was not the first time that an older, married, male political figure had admitted to having an extramarital affair with a younger female intern. Later the same year, for instance, Jesse Jackson, Sr., noted political and social activist, admitted to a long-term extramarital relationship that resulted in the birth of a daughter. In fact, it has become so routine in the lives of Americans to hear or read tabloid or other news accounts of the extramarital escapades of movie stars and other celebrities that many people no longer take notice.

Nevertheless, an overwhelming majority of Americans continue to say that extramarital affairs (no matter who the parties are) are morally wrong. That same year (2001), a Gallup poll found that 91 percent of Americans consider it to be either always or almost always wrong for married people to have sexual relations with someone other than their spouses; and in response to a separate but related question, 89 percent said that "married men and women having an affair" is morally unacceptable. Gallup polls show that more than one-half of Americans say that they know someone who has had an extramarital relationship, and two-thirds of the population believe that half or more of all married men have had an affair (Gillespie, 2001). Yet in studies such as the NORC survey, the overwhelming majority of married women and men said that they have always been faithful; and almost all of the married people (94 percent) had at least been faithful to their partner over the prior 12 months. Clearly, then, despite the stigma of marital infidelity, there is an inherent conflict between Americans' moral ideals about marriage and sexual fidelity, what they say about their sexual behavior, and what they actually do.

Atwater (1982) suggested that a primary reason for extramarital relationships is society's continued unrealistic views on love and the belief in the ability of one person to satisfy all the sexual needs of another person. How do you react to Atwater's hypothesis? Is it valid in today's society? Can one person totally satisfy another? Why do you think married people today enter into extramarital relationships? Are such relationships ever justified? Why or why not?

Postmarital Sexuality

As divorce and separation rates have increased and a growing number of widowed people—particularly women—are living into old age without a partner, a larger number of adults than in the past are confronted with the task of adjusting to a postmarital life. Popular cultural images have these individuals living either a life of great excitement, entertainment, and sexual activity, or, conversely, feeling depressed, devastated, and lonely, with no sex life. As we shall see, neither of these images is completely accurate.

Divorced People Most divorced people become sexually active within a year following their divorce, although older people are somewhat slower in this regard than people under the age of 40 (Masters, Johnson, and Kolodny, 1985). Edward Laumann and his colleagues (1994) found that among their sample of divorced, separated, or widowed respondents, 31 percent of those not living with someone had not had a sexual partner during the previous 12 months, compared with only 1 percent of those who lived with someone. Additionally, 80 percent of those living with someone had one partner in the previous year, whereas only half that percentage (41 percent) of those not living with someone had had a sexual partner during that time.

Although divorced people appear to have a fairly active sex life and find postmarital sex more pleasurable and fulfilling than married sex (Masters and Johnson, 1985), when people across marital statuses are asked whether intercourse is occurring frequently enough for their desire, divorced people are the most dissatisfied with the frequency (74 percent), compared to cohabitants and married couples (38 percent and 49 percent dissatisfied, respectively). In addition, next to single people (65 percent) over half (60 percent) of widowed people also report that they are dissatisfied with the frequency of sexual intercourse in their lives (Dunn et al., 2000). Such findings, however, should not cloud the fact that divorce often involves adjustments of many sorts, such as transition and recuperation, ending some relationships and developing new ones and adjusting to nonmarital sex and a nonmarital lifestyle generally. Loneliness and anxiety sometimes accompany this transition, as do financial strains and concerns. Some people find the world of postmarital sex to be anxiety-producing, particularly in terms of relearning the rules of dating and mate selection. Nonetheless, most divorced people manage to reintegrate their sexuality with their emotional needs. Many of them enter into intimate relationships that endure and deepen over time and very often lead to remarriage.

Widows and Widowers Widowed women and men sometimes choose to abstain from sex after their spouse's death, but almost one-half of widowers and widows eventually engage in postmarital coitus (Masters and Johnson, 1985). Because there is little or no specific research on the sexuality of separated and widowed people, much of the information on them is speculative. The prevailing view at this time is that their sexual behavior does not differ much from that of the divorced population.

Sexuality and Aging

The common stereotype of older women and men is that they are *asexual*, that is, as they age, they lose both interest in and the ability to engage in meaningful sexual activities.

A common cultural stereotype of the elderly is that they lose interest in sex along with the ability to be sexual. However, the reality is that sexuality is one of the last functions to be affected by age. Many people have healthy and active sex lives well into their advanced years.

In addition, those elderly who remain sexually active are frequently dismissed as "dirty old women" or "dirty old men." When you think about older people, how do you perceive them sexually? Can you imagine your grandparents or great-grandparents engaging in coitus or oral–genital sexual behavior? In reality, researchers have consistently found that people who are healthy and happy with their lives can continue to be sexually active well into their advanced years.

As we have emphasized throughout this chapter, sexual behavior is an integral part of human existence and it involves more than simply heterosexual vaginal intercourse. Given our views concerning aging and the elderly, many people in the United States believe that women and men must give up sex as they age. Research on sexuality and aging, however, indicates that, in fact, sexuality is one of the last functions to be affected by age. It is true that as people become older they experience biological and psychological changes that can affect their sexual functioning. For example, some older adults take longer to become aroused, are less sensitive to stimulation, and experience less intense orgasms than younger people do. However, while changes of aging affect all stages of sexual response in both women and men, the capacity to enjoy sex is not altered with age. Elderly people can be, and many often are, highly sexual beings with sexual thoughts and desires that continue into advanced age (Hodson and Skeen, 1994). These exact experiences vary from one individual to another, however.

Survey research demonstrates that while sexual activity may decline with age, a significant proportion of elderly people, including those in nursing homes, remain sexually active (Richardson and Lazar, 1995). Women and men 55 to 65 years of age report that they have sex an average of five times a month. Over 60 percent of women and men in this age category say sexual activity is important, compared with 63 percent of those aged 18 to 24. Older people may be sensual as well as sexual. As with younger people, older women and men rank hugging and kissing as top sexual pleasures. While older Americans are just as satisfied with their life in general as younger Americans are, a somewhat smaller percentage report that they are happy with their sex lives, 55 percent compared with 66 percent for 18- to 44-year-olds. In addition, a higher percentage of older people report sexual problems, the most common of which are low sex drive, impotence, and difficulty achieving orgasm. Other sexual complaints, such as self-consciousness during sex and problems with a partner, decrease with age (Clements, 1994). Nonetheless, in general, the years of middle age and beyond can be a time for exploring sex at a deeper, more confident, and more satisfying level. The need for intimacy is never outgrown, and many older adults report that their sex lives are warmer and more rewarding than ever before.

Women, Aging, and Sexuality

As women age, their reproductive ability declines gradually.[3] Somewhere around age 50, the menstrual cycle stops completely, marking the **menopause**. The onset of menopause and the symptoms that accompany it vary from woman to woman.

Although menopause does not automatically signal the end of sexual interest and desire, some menopausal women experience anxiety because they fear that they will no longer be able to enjoy sexual activity. Experts disagree on the impact of menopause on female sexuality. Some studies suggest a decline in sexual interest and possibly the loss of female orgasmic response in the immediate postmenopausal years (Masters and Johnson, 1985). Other research (Starr and Weiner, 1981), however, suggests that despite these physiological changes, menopausal women are still capable of experiencing orgasm, their sexual interest may increase, and for many of these women, the quality of their sexual experience seems to be higher than when they were younger.

Moreover, as women age many feel less inhibited and more assertive sexually; many are more frank about expressing and meeting their sexual desires. For example, according to a recent American Health Survey of baby boom women (ages 35–55), these daughters of the female sexual revolutionaries of the 1950s and 1960s are reaching midlife and changing the way that America thinks about what it means to be a middle-aged woman. These women typically reported that sex is better now than at age 25, primarily because they have become more comfortable with their bodies, their sexuality, and their partner. These women reported making healthy communication with a partner a priority and over

[3]Unless otherwise indicated, the remainder of this section relies heavily on Masters, Johnson, and Kolodny (1992).

one-half of them said that they discuss sexual issues with their partner. The result was that approximately one-third reported that they have sexual relations three to six times a week. This is in stark contrast to the three to six times a month that was typically reported in previous surveys of women in this age group.

That these women lead sexually healthy, vital, active, and imaginative lives is indicated in their reports of sexually titillating behavior—behavior that women a generation ago would probably not have acknowledged, let alone have tried. For example, more than four in ten baby boom women reported that they masturbate, 44 percent read sex self-help books, 38 percent surf into sex information Web sites or watch sex videos, 40 percent use vaginal lubricants or do Kegel exercises to strengthen vaginal muscles, and 21 percent reported that they have tried a vibrator. Not all women in this age group are this uninhibited. Among those who struggled with inhibitions in the American Health Survey, over one-half felt too fat for sex at some time in the year prior to the survey or they felt physically undesirable for some other reason (Hale, 1999).

Because of the sexual double standard, women are more likely than men to feel physically undesirable. Likewise, with society's double standard with regard to aging, we often have difficulty thinking of older people as sexually active and uninhibited, especially older women. For example, men retain their sexual eligibility as they age, whereas older women are generally considered less desirable than their younger counterparts. This perception, we should note, extends beyond sexuality to many other ways in which women and men are valued or devalued.

Men, Aging, and Sexuality Unlike women, men do not have a typical pattern of reproductive aging because there is no definite end to male fertility. Although the production of sperm abates after the age of 40, it continues into the 80s and 90s. Likewise, although the production of testosterone decreases after age 55, there is usually no major decrease in levels of sex hormones in men as there is in women. A very small percentage of men (approximately 5 percent) over the age of 60 experience what some sex researchers have labeled a *male climacteric*, which is similar in some ways to the female menopause. However, unlike women, some men father children when well into their 70s. For those who experience it, the male climacteric is generally characterized by some of the following: weakness, tiredness, decreased sexual desire, reduced or loss of potency, and irritability.

As men age, normal physical changes include a decline in the sensitivity of the penis, and some men experience an enlargement of the prostate gland. In older men, erections are also slower in developing, less precoital mucus is produced, the amount of semen is reduced, the intensity of the ejaculation is lessened, orgasmic reflex is shorter, the refractory period becomes longer, and sensitivity to distractions increases. On the other hand, they tend to experience an increased capacity to delay ejaculation, which some men (and women) find satisfying. In general, men tend to stay sexually active longer than women, although this may be explained in part by the fact that women outlive men and that the older a woman is the less access she has to a sexual partner.

Women and men who were sexually active in their younger years typically remain sexually active into their eighties and nineties, although the frequency of intercourse is limited by their physical health and social circumstances, such as having an available partner (Byer and Shainberg, 1994). Although older people generally can and do remain sexually active, the existing evidence suggests that most forms of sexual behavior decline significantly for women and men after age 75. In any event, a rising number of older adults are romantically and sexually involved in relationships, and some choose to carry out their relationships in cohabitation with their partner. (Issues related to the elderly are examined in more detail in Chapter 14.) These relationships reportedly are generally satisfying and rewarding and provide a positive example that sexuality can be pleasurable into old age.

The recognition that sex can be and often is a happy affair for older people was recently commemorated by the Finns in a summer sex fair aimed at providing people 45 years of age and older with both the inspiration to "take a roll in the hay and the hay to do it in." The goal was to attract older people who were still sexually active and who desired to find enjoyment with a sexual partner. The highlight of the one-day sex event was a marked trail through forests and meadows, with signs pointing out secluded areas that seemed especially suitable for intimate contact. For those uncomfortable with the wide open spaces, the trail also passed several barns that the organizers hoped people would use. They made sure that the barns were comfortable and romantically appealing by putting in them aromatic and comfortable hay. Lesbian and gay couples as well as heterosexuals were invited to the sex fair, but voyeurs were prohibited. It was not meant to be a sex orgy or pornographic. Rather, it was designed to be a happy affair where there was no age limit on what people could discuss and do sexually (CNN News, 1999).

SEXUAL DYSFUNCTIONS

Like other aspects of human experience, sex is not always smooth and problem-free. Most available research indicates that sexual discord or maladjustment of some sort is a widespread phenomenon in the United States. Masters, Johnson, and Kolodny (1992) contend that some kind of sexual problem can be found in at least one-half of all marriages in this country. The fact is that almost everyone who is sexually active, even couples who are very satisfied with their relationship, experiences occasional sexual problems. These problems can range anywhere from lack of interest in sexual activities to an actual **sexual dysfunction,** the inability to engage in or enjoy sexual activities. Approximately one-third of the general population (not including a geriatric subgroup) experience some type of sexual dysfunction (Hedges, 1994).

Although a few cases of sexual dysfunction can be traced to physical problems, the majority of cases are the result of social-psychological factors that interfere with or impair people's ability to respond as ordinarily expected to sexual stimuli. These factors range from anxiety about sexual performance to general life stress. Sexual dysfunctions can be distinguished along gender lines. The most common sexual dysfunctions for women are related to penetration and orgasm: inhibited sexual desire, inhibited sexual excitement, inhibited female orgasm or anorgasmia, vaginismus, rapid orgasm, and dyspareunia. The most common sexual dysfunctions for men are related to erection and ejaculation: erectile dysfunction, premature ejaculation, inhibited male orgasm, priapism, dyspareunia, and inhibited sexual desire.

In American society a great deal of emphasis is placed on performance as a measure of people's personal worth. Sexual performance, like other performance, becomes a measure of our personal adequacy and value to others. Thus, when people do not perform sexually as expected, they often feel embarrassed, guilty, frustrated, confused, and depressed. This can often cause problems in personal relationships as well as in other aspects of people's lives. We will not go into detail here regarding the specifics of these sexual dysfunctions. Rather, they are presented in some detail in Appendix A. Suffice it to say here that whenever people recognize that they have a sexual dysfunction they should seek the help of a qualified physician, psychiatrist, or marriage or sex therapist, depending on the problem (see the "Strengthening Marriages and Families" box).

We end this chapter with a discussion of sexual responsibility and protecting oneself from disease, particularly as these issues relate to AIDS.

SEXUAL RESPONSIBILITY: PROTECTING YOURSELF FROM AIDS AND OTHER STDS

Sexually transmitted diseases (STDs), diseases acquired primarily through sexual contact, are fairly common in today's society. Such diseases can be caused by viruses (AIDS, herpes, hepatitis B, and genital warts), bacteria (syphilis, gonorrhea, and chlamydia infections), and tiny insects or parasites (pubic lice). Approximately 333 million people worldwide are stricken with curable STDs each year, and in the United States an estimated 12 million new cases of STDs are reported each year to the Centers for Disease Control, a number roughly 80 times higher than new cases of TB, HIV infection, and AIDS combined. Two-thirds of those with STDs are persons under the age of 25, and another 3 million are teenagers (Centers for Disease Control, 1999b). Some experts are claiming that the United States is in the throes of an STD epidemic in poor, underserved areas of the country that rivals that of some developing countries. However, the risk is not limited to this population. Recent data show that STDs are becoming increasingly common among teenagers, including those from middle-class families (Stolberg, 1998). Because of the risks to physical and mental health, we must become more knowledgeable about STDs, and more responsible to ourselves and others in our sexual behaviors. With the exception of AIDS, which we discuss next, STDs are examined in Appendix A.

AIDS

Women and men living in the United States today are perhaps more challenged in their exploration and enjoyment of sexuality than at any other time in our history. Protracted media, public attention and information about responsible sexual behavior—abstinence, safe sex, and the use of condoms—reflect the new era of sexuality and sexual choices in America. In this new era of sexuality, HIV/AIDS continues to be a serious and deadly threat to women and men, the young and old, rich and poor, heterosexual and homosexual, and across race and ethnicity. Experts estimate that close to 1 million people in the United States are living with the human immunodeficiency virus (HIV), which is believed to be the main cause of AIDS. Identified in 1981, **acquired immune deficiency syndrome (AIDS)** is a viral syndrome, or group of diseases, that destroys the body's immune system, thereby rendering the victim susceptible to all kinds of infections and diseases. People may have HIV without knowing it, given that the incubation period can be as long as 10 years and since symptoms of AIDS usually do not appear for a year or longer. Because the body is unable to fight off HIV/AIDS infections and diseases, they eventually kill the person. In 2001, marking the twentieth anniversary of

Increasing public awareness and individual concern about sexually transmitted diseases have sparked a rise in humor about human sexuality. However, the contraction and transmission of STDs is a serious matter that should be discussed prior to having sexual relations.

Source: Reprinted with permission of V. G. Myers. © *Cosmopolitan*, 1982.

STRENGTHENING MARRIAGES AND FAMILIES

Talks with Family Therapist Joan Zientek

TALKING FRANKLY ABOUT OUR SEXUAL NEEDS

What Kinds of Sexual Issues Do People Bring to Therapy?

A couple's sexual relationship holds a very special place in the context of the total relationship. Thus, when sexual issues arise, tensions can permeate the entire relationship. These problems can arise from sexual dysfunctions, such as impotence and premature ejaculation for the male, or vaginismus or orgasmic difficulties for the female. They can also come from sexual dissatisfaction that results from boredom, from differing sexual needs and preferences, or from one partner's withholding sex as a means of retaliation for other angers sustained in the relationship. Because married couples can experience both sexual and marital problems, and because these two issues are often interwoven, a distinction needs to be made between sex therapy and marital therapy. In the 1970s, the research of William Masters and Virginia Johnson offered a new approach to sexual problems. Sex therapy consists of a repertoire of physical techniques that teaches the body new responses to enhance the couple's sex life, that lower anxiety, and that focus on the here-and-now. Marital therapy, on the other hand, treats the emotional issues that cause tension in a couple's sexual relationship, focusing on the present as well as the past. If sexual problems have preceded and triggered marital tensions, then sex therapy is recommended. However, when the sexual problems are the result of the couple's relationship issues, then marital therapy is the starting point. While the therapist makes this decision based on the initial assessment of the presenting information, the therapist needs to continually evaluate the decision by monitoring the couple's progress.

What Are Some Strategies That Therapists Use to Help People with These Issues?

The therapist generally begins by working in the here-and-now. This sometimes can be accomplished simply through education, problem-solving, and compromise. If the presenting problem is one of a difference in sexual desire, the therapist can convey that desire differences are natural and normal and may be due to chemical differences in the brain of each person. These differences are initially disguised because, according to some scientists, the euphoria of new love produces a hefty dose of PEA (phenylethylamine, a neurotransmitter), which elevates sexual desire. However, research also shows that the rapture of this infatuation burns out after 18 to 36 months, and couples then experience the natural differences in their need for sex. Understanding and accepting this natural phenomenon takes the sting out of worrying about the loss of desirability and the shame of refusal and places the couple in a better position to problem-solve and compromise in meeting their divergent sexual needs. Issues of sexual boredom or the use of sex as blackmail can often be resolved with these same techniques, along with enhancing the couple's communication skills. Couples may be shy about talking about their sexual needs, and/or may not have the vocabulary or the skills to do so. If these techniques do not work, the therapist then turns to exploring the interpsychic blocks originating from past experiences, perhaps stemming back to childhood.

What Influences How Successful People Are in Solving These Issues?

Different couples bring different strengths and resources for resolving their issues. One of the main issues is the strength of the love they have for one another. Some couples marry in a hurry and for the wrong reasons, only to wake up years later to discover they have grown apart. Other couples ignore the tensions in their relationship for years, gathering resentment and living parallel lives until a crisis such as an affair brings them to therapy. Also, if each person gets caught in blaming the other, and refuses to examine her or his own part in the problem, success can be stymied. On the other hand, if couples seek help when they first realize that their own efforts have not resolved the conflicts or when their own efforts only exacerbate the problem, there is a greater chance at success. When this is coupled with love, goodwill, and personal responsibility, most problems can be resolved.

the AIDS epidemic, experts and others expressed hope for a cure but, to date, there is still no cure for AIDS. People with HIV/AIDS are living longer, and staying healthier on new medications, but the epidemic is still spreading and people are still dying.

Of the 774,467 people in the United States diagnosed with AIDS through December 31, 2000, 448,060 (58 percent) had already died (Centers for Disease Control and Prevention, 2000). Figure 6.7 illustrates the number of AIDS cases diagnosed and the number of AIDS deaths that occurred in selective years through 2000. The AIDS epidemic is not merely a U.S. problem. Some observers have described it as a global disaster, as there are an estimated 16,000 new cases diagnosed every day worldwide (Ritter, 2001a). A person who tests positive for HIV is regarded as infected and capable of transmitting the virus to others. Major symptoms of

Figure 6.7

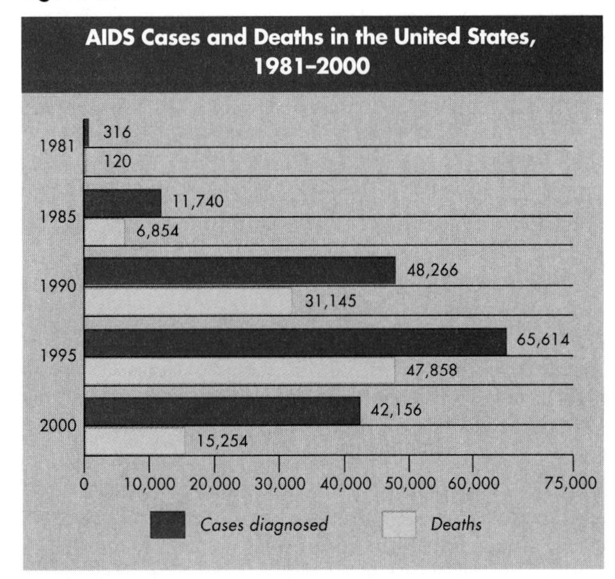

Source: Adapted from Centers for Disease Control and Prevention, 2000, *HIV/AIDS Surveillance Report, Year-end Edition,* vol. 12, no. 2, p. 29, Table 20.

AIDS include persistent fever, diarrhea, a dry or heavy cough, night sweats, chills, swollen glands, severe headaches, sore throat, excessive fatigue, dramatic weight loss, blurred vision, and unexplained bleeding from any orifice. (Some of these may be symptoms of other diseases as well.)

The Transmission of AIDS HIV/AIDS is transmitted through blood, semen, vaginal fluid, breast milk, and other body fluids containing blood. It can enter the body through a vein (such as intravenous drug use), the anus or rectum, vagina, penis, mouth, mucous membranes (such as eyes or inside of the nose), or cuts and sores. To date, the most common means of transmission is through sexual contact, as indicated in Table 6.2. For children under 13 years of age the most common means of contracting the AIDS virus is from a mother either with or at risk for HIV infection (Centers for Disease Control and Prevention, 2000).

According to current evidence, HIV cannot be transmitted by casual contact. That is, AIDS cannot be transmitted through touching, coughing, sneezing, breathing, handshakes, or socializing, nor can it be spread through toilet seats, food, eating utensils, drinking out of the same glass, water fountains, or insects. And the risk of contracting AIDS through saliva (as in kissing) is said to be extremely low. However, there is little dispute that oral and genital sex are the most risky for the transmission of AIDS. This risk can be greatly reduced, however, with the use of latex condoms. Right now, the most basic ways to control the spread of the virus are believed to be through avoiding high-risk sex (either through abstinence, exclusive relationships, latex condoms) and through careful monitoring of transfusions of blood and other body fluids.

Who Gets AIDS? High-profile stars who have contracted AIDS, like Earvin "Magic" Johnson, the late Arthur Ashe, and former national heavyweight boxer Tommy Morrison, heightened Americans' sensitivity to the problem of HIV/AIDS. However, the appearance of these people as healthy and living a well-rounded life even with the virus, coupled with increasing news about people with AIDS generally living a longer and healthier life (some people with AIDS are muscled and working out in gyms), has had the effect of dulling the sensitivity of some people to the continued crisis of HIV/AIDS—that it is still a deadly disease. Although new treatments have slowed the progression from HIV to AIDS and from AIDS to death for many people (see Figure 6.7), the virus is nonetheless spreading and taking its toll on both old and new victims.

People most frequently affected by HIV continue to be men generally and gay men more specifically; but increasingly there is a new face of AIDS: It is also an epidemic of the poor, which means it is increasingly an epidemic of some groups of color that are found disproportionately among the poor. In addition, an increasingly high percentage of new HIV infections is occurring in African American women, particularly poor rural women. And although the number of new AIDS cases among white homosexuals has declined in several major cities since 1990, the rate of infection among homosexuals of color, especially African Americans, has surged significantly. No longer confined to gay men and intravenous drug abusers, AIDS in the United States is increasingly an epidemic of the heterosexual population as well (see Table 6.2).

Table 6.2

Adult/Adolescent AIDS Cases, by Exposure Category and Sex, through December 2000*

	Females (%)	Males (%)
Homosexual and bisexual men	—	56
Intravenous drug users	41	22
Homosexual male drug users	—	8
Heterosexuals	40	5
Hemophiliacs and recipients of blood transfusions	3	2
Other/undetermined	16	7
Totals	100%	100%

*The Centers for Disease Control and Prevention tracks diagnosis of AIDS in terms of two basic age groups: adult/adolescents (13 years of age and older) and pediatric (children under 13).

Source: Adapted from Centers for Disease Control and Prevention, 2000, *HIV/AIDS Surveillance Report, Year-end Edition,* vol. 12, no. 2, p. 14, Table 5.

The Intersections of Race, Class, Gender, Age, and Sexual Orientation The intersections of race, class, gender, age, and sexual orientation are clearly revealed in various HIV/AIDS statistics (see Figure 6.8). For example, African Americans, who make up only 13 percent of the U.S. population, now account for over half of all newly reported cases of HIV infection, and they make up 38 percent of all AIDS cases ever reported in the United States. Whites make up 43 percent of persons ever reported with AIDS while Latinas/os make up 18 percent, Asian/Pacific Islanders, 1 percent, and Native American/Alaska Natives less than 1 percent. Researchers at the Centers for Disease Control and Prevention (CDC) estimate that about 1 in 50 African American men and 1 in 160 African American women are infected with HIV. By comparison, 1 in 250 white men and 1 in every 3000 white women are infected. And among young people (ages 13 to 24), 65 percent of the new HIV diagnoses are among African Americans. In addition, African Americans are ten times more likely than whites to be diagnosed with AIDS and ten times more likely to die from it. Although AIDS is no longer among the 15 leading causes of death in the United States, it is the leading cause among African Americans aged 25 to 44 (Centers for Disease Control and Prevention, 2000; Herbert, 2001; Sack, 2001). And although the incidence of new cases among Latinas/os is lower than that for African Americans it is three times the rate for whites. As among all groups, the number of Latinas/os living with AIDS has increased, with males accounting for the greatest proportion (81 percent) of cases. Latinas/os include a diverse mixture of ethnic groups and cultures, and thus the incidence of HIV/AIDS varies across groups (CDC, 2000b).

Although there is a new face to HIV/AIDS, through December 2000 the preponderance of people with AIDS were still males who have either had intimate same-sex contacts or are intravenous drug users who have shared a hypodermic needle (see Table 6.2). According to federal health officials, each year another 40,000 Americans become infected with HIV. Of those infected, 70 percent are men and about 40 percent are men who have sex with men. Although the AIDS rates are lower for women than men, women now account for roughly one-fourth of all newly diagnosed cases, more than twice the percentage from the early 1990s and a reflection of the ongoing shift in populations affected by the epidemic. Since 1985, the percentage of all AIDS cases reported among adult and adolescent women has more than tripled, from 7 percent to 23 percent. The epidemic has increased most dramatically among women of color. For example, African American and Latinas together represent less than one-fourth of all U.S. women, yet they account for 77 percent of AIDS cases reported to date among women (CDC, 2000a; Manier and Obejas, 2001).

Figure 6.8

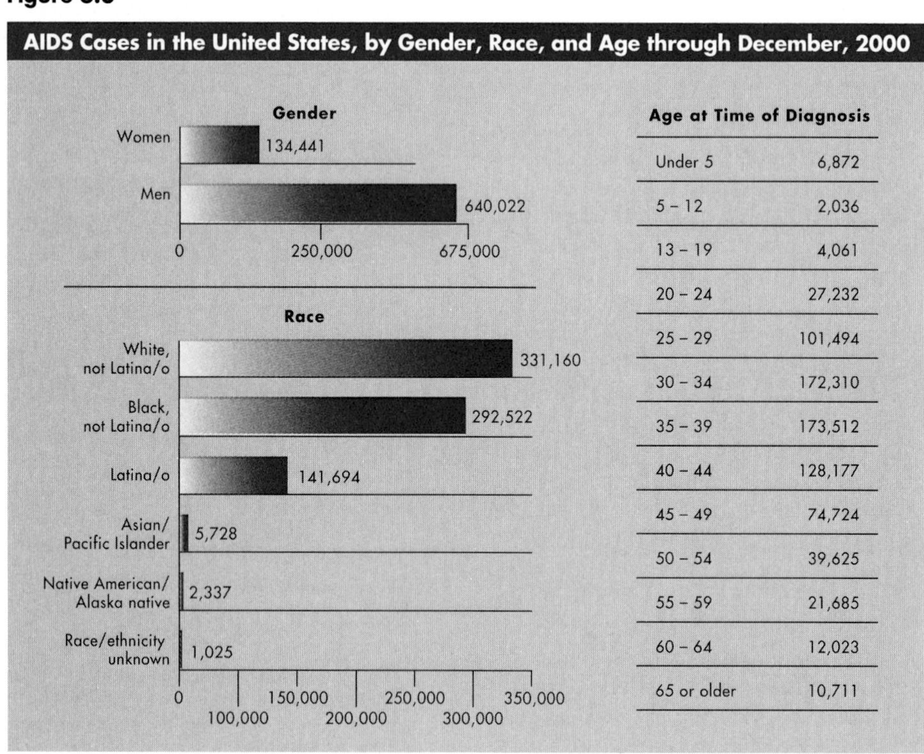

Source: Adapted from Centers for Disease Control and Prevention, 2000, *HIV/AIDS Surveillance Report, Year-end Edition*, vol. 12, no. 2, p. 16, Table 7.

African American women make up 7 percent of the nation's population but account for 16 percent of new AIDS diagnoses; they are four times more likely to carry the virus than their white counterparts. The proportion of reported HIV/AIDS cases is also rising for Latinas. Women represent 19 percent of cumulative AIDS cases among Latinas/os, but accounted for 22 percent of cases reported in 1999 alone. An increasing percentage of women are becoming infected with the HIV virus through heterosexual transmission, and many also have a history of sexually transmitted disease, intravenous drug use, or a sexual partner who is an intravenous drug abuser. Among the small number of Asian/Pacific Islander women who have AIDS, about one-half (49 percent) contracted the virus through heterosexual contact. Comparable figures for African American, Latinas, Native American, and white women are 38 percent, 47 percent, 37 percent, and 40 percent respectively (Centers for Disease Control, 2000).

The increase of HIV/AIDS among women has been driven largely by the disproportionate spread of the virus among heterosexual women, especially African American women and particularly in the rural South, where, according to U.S. health officials, the influx of crack cocaine and the sex-for-drug trade are fueling the spread of the virus. The HIV/AIDS epidemic in women initially centered on IV-drug-using women in the urban Northeast, but now it centers on women with heterosexual risk in the South. For example, HIV/AIDS has taken firm root among poor African American women in the Mississippi Delta and across the rural South. In southern states like Alabama, Mississippi, and North Carolina almost one-third (31 percent, 28.5 percent, and 27 percent, respectively) of those reporting new HIV infections in 2000 were African American women. Statistics in these states now show that more African American women than white men have contracted HIV over the course of the epidemic. According to some observers, in many ways the epidemic in the South closely resembles the situation in the developing world. Joblessness, substance abuse, teenage pregnancy, sexually transmitted diseases, inadequate schools, minimal access to health care, and entrenched poverty and racism all conspire (CDC, 2000b; Sack, 2001).

As these statistics show, with each passing year, the gap in transmission rates between women and men has narrowed (in both developing and developed countries). Women are becoming infected at a substantially younger age than men, an average of 5 to 10 years earlier, and women in their teens and early 20s are infected at a higher rate than women in older groups. On average, women tend to die sooner after the diagnosis of AIDS than do men, which might reflect the fact that AIDS in women generally continues to be diagnosed later than it is for men (Miranda-Maniquis, 1993; UNAIDS, 2001).

HIV/AIDS and Risk These statistics lead to a discussion of *risk:* Who is at risk, and why? Most observers of HIV/AIDS agree that certain kinds of behavior place people at greater risk of infection than other kinds of behavior. The highest-risk behavior is *anal sex.* Rectal bleeding, which often occurs during anal sex, allows the easy transmission of HIV from one person to another. Anal sex is often practiced by gay men (but is certainly not limited to gay men), some of whom have multiple partners, putting these men, as a category of people, at greater risk than any other group.

New research shows that young gay men are engaging in unsafe sex and contracting HIV at alarming rates. Data from the Centers for Disease Control and Prevention indicate that almost half of gay men in their teens and early 20s had

The AIDS gap between the sexes is one gap that women are not fighting to close. Unfortunately, although almost one-half of newly infected adults have been women, some health specialists warn that AIDS prevention is still too focused on men.

Source: Reprinted by permission of William Costello for *USA Today.*

unprotected sex in the 6-month period preceding the survey. Signs of the comeback of unprotected sex are easily found in gay communities across the country where ads from men seeking partners for "barebacking," or having sex without condoms, are prominent in gay magazines and on Internet sites.

The number of new infections among gays nationwide had dropped during the late 1980s and early 1990s to a record low of 2 percent. However, the epidemic has come roaring back among this population with a new infection rate today of 4.4 percent. The epidemic has hit African American gays particularly hard, 15 percent of whom are newly infected with HIV each year—a rate that is six times greater than that for white gays. More than half of all AIDS cases among African American men now occur among those who have sex with other men, up from 31 percent in 1989, when intravenous drug use was the primary mode of transmission. These statistics suggest that African American gay men are contracting HIV at rates comparable to those reported for sub-Saharan Africa (which has the highest infection rates in the world). The group hardest hit is young men 23 to 29 years of age (30 percent) (Centers for Disease Control and Prevention, 2000; Manier and Obejas, 2001).

Because the incidence of AIDS remains high among gays, there is still some feeling that the rest of the population is relatively safe from exposure to the virus. As our discussion so far has shown, this could not be farther from the truth. For example, estimates are that roughly one-fifth of gays marry heterosexually. Thus, heterosexual wives of gay men stand a high probability of being exposed to the virus. This does not include the possible exposure of women who are married to or have sexual relationships with bisexual males. In this context, of concern in African American communities is the increasing number of new HIV/AIDS cases that involve African American men who have sex with men but do not identify themselves as homosexual or bisexual. Such men are said to be "on the down-low," slang used to describe someone who has homosexual sex but hides it from friends, family, lovers, and sometimes himself. Some of these men are former prison inmates who may have been raped or started engaging in sex with men while incarcerated. As we have already indicated, this "down low" behavior may be an important source of HIV/AIDS among heterosexual African American women.

On the other hand, female-to-female transmission of HIV/AIDS appears to be a rare occurrence. Of all the women reported with AIDS to date, only a very small percentage (2 percent) were reported to have had sex with women. Of those who reported having had sex *only* with women, 98 percent also had another risk—intravenous drug use in most cases. To date, there are no studies that have confirmed female-to-female transmission, either because other risks were subsequently identified or because the women declined to be interviewed. Although these findings suggest that female-to-female transmission of HIV is uncommon, they do not negate the possibility because it could be masked by other behaviors (CDC, 1999).

Finally, a highly risky behavior for HIV infection is related to *intravenous drug use* and the *sharing of needles* among drug users. Intravenous drug users who share needles account for one-fourth of all persons with AIDS, and the sharing of needles is a major source of transmission among women (see Table 6.2). In addition, people who have multiple partners over their lifetime are at far greater risk of HIV infection than those who have few sexual partners. According to the NORC survey, no other factor predicted risk more accurately than the number of sex partners an individual had in a lifetime. Because the majority of people who are at the highest risk of contracting the virus are members of categories that this society values least (gays, poor people, people of color, women), AIDS is a deeply divisive social and political issue. However, AIDS is first and foremost a critical public health issue that, as our discussion has shown, represents not one but multiple epidemics: an inner-city epidemic; a rural epidemic; and an epidemic among women, among intravenous drug users, among gay men, among African Americans, among Latinas/os, among non-Latina/o whites, and heterosexual women.

AIDS and Children As we already know, age is an important factor in contracting AIDS. The number of children under the age of 13 with AIDS is increasing. Over the 8-year period from 1992 to 2000, the number of children under the age of 13 diagnosed with AIDS doubled from 4249 to 8908. Ninety-one percent of children with AIDS contracted the disease from their mothers before, during, or after birth (for example, during breast-feeding). Of the remaining 9 percent of children with AIDS, 7 percent contracted the disease from blood transfusions or are hemophiliacs. Today, AIDS is a leading cause of death in children under the age of 5. In addition, three-and-one-half times as many African American as white children have AIDS (Centers for Disease Control and Prevention, 2000). Seventeen percent of children with AIDS are white and 23 percent are Latino/a. Often these children, across race, have mothers who are poor, are intravenous drug abusers, or have partners who are. These women also have little or no access to drug treatment programs or health care facilities.

At the other end of the age spectrum, elderly people are seldom thought of as HIV- or AIDS-infected. Women and men over the age of 55 account for 5 percent and 6 percent of all AIDS cases, respectively. A study of AIDS patients 60 years of age and older found that most HIV-infected persons in this age group acquired their infection through sexual intercourse or intravenous drug use. The study also reported that the HIV diagnosis in the elderly was usually not considered by clinicians until late in the course of the infection, even though a high prevalence of prior sexually transmitted diseases existed (Gordon and Thompson, 1995). Findings such as these on the treatment of HIV in older adults parallel those on women. They also vividly illustrate how our misconceptions about various social and cultural groups (in this case, our misconception about older Americans, especially their sexuality) have ramifications for various other aspects of our lives, including medical diagnoses for certain diseases and illnesses.

AIDS as a National and International Issue As we have already pointed out, HIV/AIDS is a global pandemic. The Joint United Nations Programme on HIV/AIDS (UNAIDS) and the World Health Organization (WHO) estimate that as many as 36.2 million people worldwide are living with HIV/AIDS—approximately one-half under the age of 25—in more than 74 countries, with more than 95 percent in developing countries, and the number continues to rise. At the end of 2000, 5.3 million new infections had been reported, and close to 22 million (21.8 million) people around the world had died from AIDS since the beginning of the epidemic, 4.3 million of them children. In the year 2000 alone, 3 million infected people died globally, a higher global total than in any other year since the beginning of the epidemic, despite antiretroviral drugs that have helped drive down the incidence of AIDS and AIDS-related deaths in the richer countries.

Although no country is untouched by HIV infection and AIDS, 70 percent of the world's adults and 80 percent of the children infected with HIV/AIDS live in Africa and another 20 percent of people living with HIV/AIDS are in Southeast Asia. Eighty percent of AIDS deaths are in Africa, and the pandemic has left 13.3 million orphans globally, 12 million of whom are Africans. In sub-Saharan Africa HIV is now more deadly than war itself. In 1998, 200,000 Africans died in war, but more than 2 million died of AIDS (AIDS in Africa, 2001). In 16 African countries more than one in ten adults aged 15 to 49 is infected with HIV, and in 7 countries in the southern core of the continent approximately one adult in five is living with the virus. In Botswana, a staggering 35.8 percent of adults are infected with HIV, while South Africa, with a total of 4.2 million infected people, has the largest number of people living with HIV/AIDS in the world (AIDS around the World, 2001).

According to some health experts and AIDS activists, AIDS is Africa's greatest social disaster since the transatlantic slave trade (Ritter, 2001b). The social and economic consequences of AIDS in Africa have not only impacted health but also education, industry, agriculture, transportation, human resources, and the economy in general. AIDS has widened the gulf between rich and poor nations, and the United States and other wealthy nations have been criticized for completely ignoring or, at best, doing little to help fight the spread of the devastating virus in Africa. Critics say that rich countries could go a long way in helping the peoples of Africa by funding prevention programs and drug treatments. And drug companies could help by selling drugs to Africa at cost (AIDS in Africa, 2001; Ritter, 2001b).

Although more recent, the HIV infection rate in South and Southeast Asia is also at epidemic proportions. It is estimated that there are close to 6 million (5.8 million) adults and children living with HIV or AIDS in this region. The spread of HIV infection and AIDS in China, India, Thailand, and Cambodia, to name only a few, has been fueled by an extensive sex trade and the use of illicit drugs. In China, for instance, it is estimated that 1.5 million people were infected with HIV at the start of 2001, 70 percent of whom are intravenous drug abusers. According to UNAIDS, if current trends continue there could be 20 million Chinese infected with HIV or AIDS by the end of 2010 (AIDS around the World, 2001; Global Statistical Information, 2001).

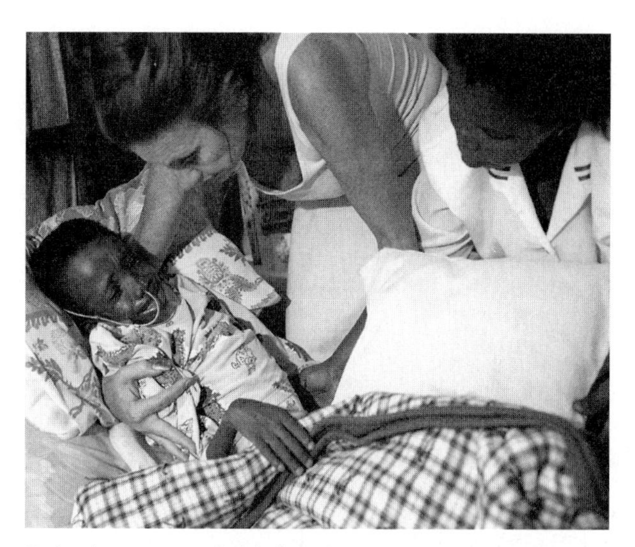

Today the majority of global HIV/AIDS cases occur in sub-Saharan Africa and Southeast Asia. Children, such as Nkosi Johnson, are increasingly vulnerable to this disease. Nkosi, who was the oldest surviving AIDS orphan in South Africa and a national icon, died in June 2001.

Globally, women represent almost half (16.4 million) of the people living with HIV/AIDS; half (2.3 million) of all people (4.7 million) newly infected with HIV, the majority of whom are believed to be between 15 and 35 years of age; and nearly half of the total number of people who have died since the onset of the HIV/AIDS epidemic (Global Statistical Information, 2001). As in the United States, the number of new cases of HIV/AIDS among women worldwide is increasing dramatically (for example, in sub-Saharan Africa, 55 percent of those with HIV or AIDS are women, and in South and Southeast Asia the figure is 35 percent). This is because in many countries women are denied equal access to information, education, training, health care, and other social services which makes it difficult to achieve effective preventive programs. In some poor countries where there are limited job opportunities, many women are forced to labor as sex workers (prostitutes), and because of their poor economic situations they are unlikely to refuse clients who don't wear condoms. In many countries (such as South Africa, China, Thailand) large numbers of prostitutes have been infected with HIV and are blamed for its spread (see the "In Other Places" box). Research indicates that in some cities in Thailand, the increase in HIV

IN OTHER PLACES

SEX WORK AND THE TRANSMISSION OF AIDS IN LADYSMITH, SOUTH AFRICA

Truckers from all over southern Africa pass through Ladysmith, South Africa, on their way to the port at Durban. An overwhelming majority of these truckers have sex with prostitutes who work the truck stops. The infrequent use of condoms by the truckers has had deadly odds for the truck-stop sex workers. In the wake of the HIV/AIDS pandemic in South Africa, sex workers in Ladysmith say they have seen small changes in the attitudes of the truckers who pass through their town. Today maybe seven men in ten will agree to use a condom versus two in ten a short while ago. Sex workers admit that they have little power to improve the odds. If they have made enough money, they will try to tell the john to wear a condom, but if they have not made enough money they will try to ask him to wear a condom. If he refuses, the sex worker will usually accommodate him, rationalizing that if she doesn't another woman at the truck stop probably will. At least one-third of the adults in the rural province of 8 million that includes Ladysmith are infected with HIV. This is the worst infection rate in a country that has more people infected with the virus than any in the world.

In 1994, health workers began coming to the truck stops, counseling women and leaving condoms. One positive consequence was that the women stopped using chemicals such as Dettol and Savlon (common antiseptics used to clean wounds) and other household products to tighten their vaginas. Some African men insist on women providing them with what they call "dry sex," and Zulu healers sell desiccating herbs for that purpose. AIDS specialists say the practice can result in vaginal tears that help transmit the virus.

In 1999, ten sex workers in Ladysmith agreed to gather data at five truck stops for a study by Gita Ramjee, a professor at the Medical Research Council (the South African version of the U.S. National Institutes of Health). For their help they earned $35 a week, in contrast to the potentially $65 a week they could earn doing sex work. The sex workers asked their clients to fill out a short questionnaire and to spit in a small jar that was kept on ice for a saliva HIV test. The ten women interviewed 320 men, some of whom requested that they be sent their test results because they did not have time to go to the doctor. The saliva test is not used very much in the United States but it is considered highly reliable by researchers in South Africa. The results were shocking. At four truck stops, 50 percent to 57 percent of the men were infected. In Newcastle, a town up the road from Ladysmith, 95 percent of the men were infected. Thirty-seven percent of the truckers who filled out questionnaires said they stopped for sex on every trip; 66 percent said that they had shown symptoms of a sexually transmitted disease in the last 6 months. Less than half (47 percent) of the truckers said that they always used condoms with prostitutes; 29 percent said they never did. Only 13 percent said they had ever used condoms with their wives. Anal sex was practiced by 42 percent; of those, only 23 percent said they used condoms. Anal sex and venereal disease sores make transmission of HIV much easier, but it is very hard for sex workers to protect themselves.

In the past, when sex workers requested that their clients use a condom, the men would typically refuse, saying that the sex worker was following the whites' rules to reduce the number of children. Sometimes, if a man used a condom, he would not pay the sex worker, or pay her only $4 instead of the usual $6. Today, more men are changing their minds because they have seen people dying from HIV/AIDS (McNeil, Jr., 2001). However, what must change is the gendered system of oppression that severely limits women's chances to live a long and healthy life.

among female sex workers is as high as 50 percent. It goes without saying that the impact of HIV/AIDS on women and their children, other family members, and their communities is devastating.

AIDS Prevention and Sexual Responsibility Like most other human choices and behavior, our sexual choices and behaviors carry with them an expectation of responsibility. Romanticized notions of sex and sexuality have sometimes caused us in the past to ignore or avoid these responsibilities. However, the AIDS pandemic has focused the spotlight on sexuality and sexual responsibility. A variety of groups have campaigned for **safe sex.** Such campaigns are geared toward informing people of how to protect themselves from AIDS and other sexually transmitted diseases through abstinence or by engaging in responsible sex. The major underlying theme is that abstinence is desirable and the only sure method of prevention, but that people who cannot or will not abstain should use protective methods, most notably condoms.

Not all people agree with the premise of the safe-sex philosophy, however. Critics contend that the premise of safe sex promotes sexual promiscuity and does little, if anything, to promote abstinence. They argue that abstinence, not safe sex, should be the official public policy. Thus, for example, many of these critics oppose such safe-sex practices as the

WRITING YOUR OWN SCRIPT

IDENTIFYING SEXUAL VALUES

Thinking about your own sexuality, write a short essay outlining your values with respect to sexuality. What have been the major sources of sexual information for you? Consider major periods in your life, for example, childhood, adolescence, young adulthood, middle age, older. Who or what has been the major influence on your sexual values? Are your sexual values the same as those of your parents? If not, how do they differ? How tolerant are you of sexual lifestyles different from your own? If you have children, what will you teach them about sexuality?

distribution of condoms in high schools and clinics because, as they see it, such practices send young people the wrong message.

The evidence on just how effective these campaigns for safe sex or complete abstinence are is mixed. Although there was some evidence in the mid-1990s that casual sex was on the decrease and sexual partners (from teenagers to the elderly) were practicing safe sex, primarily through the increased use of condoms, today there is some indication that, at least among some groups, casual sex or sex with risky partners without the use of condoms or other protective measures is on the rise again. The fact is that most people will be sexually active at some time in their lives. Sex can be healthy, wholesome, and satisfying, but there are also constraints. In the final analysis, each one of us has a responsibility to engage in sex in a manner that is protective of both our own and our partners' health and well-being. In addition, the AIDS prevention agenda today and in the future must be global and must not focus exclusively on effecting changes in individuals' sexual behavior. More broadly, it must promote improvements in the overall status and quality of life of women, poor people, people of color, children, and those living in developing countries so that they have more control over when and how sex takes place. The AIDS prevention agenda must also work toward providing individuals and families with better medical care, regardless of whether or not they are impacted by HIV/AIDS or other sexually transmitted diseases. And it must encourage continued and improved funding for research on an AIDS vaccine that would be appropriate for use in developing countries.

Sparked by the AIDS crisis, posters, advertisements, and warning signs like these amusing condoms encourage the practice of safer sex.

SUMMARY

We are all sexual beings, and we spend a large amount of our time engaged in a variety of sexual behaviors. Although some people still believe the Freudian notion that our sexuality is biologically driven, sociologists stress the social basis of human sexuality. A sociological perspective of human sexuality focuses on the tremendous role that culture plays in creating and shaping the content of our sexuality. Like other behaviors, sexual behavior is guided by cultural scripts. In learning society's sexual guidelines, we in effect create or invent our capacity for sexual behavior.

As we learn other important norms of our culture, we also simultaneously learn about our sexuality from a variety of sources including the family, peers, and mass media.

There is some debate over whether a sexual revolution has occurred. Whatever the verdict, it is clear that drastic changes occurred in the approach to sexuality in the twentieth-century United States. The most dramatic changes occurred among women, across race, class, and age cohort.

Although historically U.S. society has classified heterosexuality as the only acceptable form of human sexuality, humans actually express a range of sexual orientations or preferences. According to Alfred Kinsey, these orientations fall along a continuum, with heterosexuality and homosexuality at each extreme, and bisexuality falling somewhere in the middle. William Masters and Virginia Johnson found that a variety of physiological factors are associated with sexuality and erotic arousal, including changes in blood pressure, pulse, and breathing. According to Masters and Johnson, all people go through the same four phases of sexual response: excitement, plateau, orgasm, and resolution.

As with sexual orientation, sexual expression incorporates a wide variety of behaviors, ranging from activities involving only the self to those that involve two or more individuals. Masturbation and sexual fantasies and dreams are autoerotic activities in which the majority of people engage at some point in their lives. Petting and oral–genital sex are the most common of these sexual behaviors in which humans engage.

There have been dramatic changes in human sexuality in every phase of the life cycle. Unmarried people are engaging in sexual activities with little expectation that such relationships will lead to marriage. Teenagers in particular are increasingly sexually active. Within marriages, wives and husbands are experiencing a wider range of sexuality and are more satisfied with their sexual relationships than in the past. In addition, a growing number of married people are engaging in extramarital relationships. And although physiological changes cause changes in the sexual response of older adults, most enjoy satisfying romantic and sexual relationships well into old age.

The spread of HIV/AIDS is not just a concern in the United States. HIV/AIDS is a global pandemic affecting peoples in almost every country of the world. The hardest hit, however, are the peoples of Africa and South and Southeast Asia.

KEY TERMS

human sexuality
sexual double standard
sexual script
significant others
generalized others
sexual orientation
heterosexism
heterosexuality
homophobia
homosexuality
bisexuality
erotic arousal
erogenous zone
orgasm
ejaculation
autoeroticism
masturbation
nocturnal emissions
wet dreams
pleasuring
petting
cunnilingus
fellatio
coitus
transgendered
refractory period
menopause
sexual dysfunction
sexually transmitted diseases (STDs)
acquired immune deficiency syndrome (AIDS)
safe sex

QUESTIONS FOR STUDY AND REFLECTION

1. For the most part the media and mass advertising flaunt sexuality and define its content for all of us, including children. Consider how sexuality is presented in ads for popular products (cars, perfume, alcoholic beverages) as well as in rock videos. How have these images and definitions of sexuality affected your behavior? How closely do they resemble your everyday life? What happens when the sexual messages of the media clash with your sexual upbringing? Is it possible to ignore the sexual messages of the media? Do you think there is a relationship between media emphasis on sexuality and the high rate of unmarried pregnancies?
2. What kind of AIDS awareness, if any, takes place on your college campus? Has awareness of the disease affected sexual behavior on your campus? Do you think that people who have AIDS should be isolated from those who do not? What do you think about mandatory AIDS testing in schools and in the workplace?
3. How do your views differ from those of people you know in your own generation and those of your parents and your grandparents concerning sexual activity or pregnancy outside of legal marriage, oral–genital sexual activity, extramarital sexual behavior, homosexuality, bisexuality, and sexual behavior among older adults?
4. What were your feelings when reading this chapter? Did some subjects or topics make you feel uncomfortable? How comfortable are you discussing topics such as masturbation, wet dreams, and positions in sexual intercourse with a significant other? Parents? In a classroom? Your answers to these questions can be used as a way of getting in touch with your own orientation toward sexuality.

ADDITIONAL RESOURCES

SOCIOLOGICAL

GEER, JAMES, AND WILLIAM O'DONOHUE, EDS. 1987. *Theories of Human Sexuality*. New York: Plenum. The editors provide a wide variety of articles on human sexual behavior ranging in perspective from the theological to the feminist-political.

MICHAEL, ROBERT T., JOHN H. GAGNON, EDWARD O. LAUMANN, AND GINA KOLATA. 1994. *Sex in America: A Definitive Survey*. Boston: Little, Brown. A general-interest version of the NORC sex survey conducted by two noted sociologists, a dean of the Graduate School of Public Policy Studies at the University of Chicago, and a science reporter for the *New York Times*. The survey is said to be the most comprehensive set of data on America's sexual behavior since the Kinsey Reports in the late 1940s and early 1950s and is reputed to be more methodologically sound than any sex survey to date. This general-interest version is full of illuminating information on the sexual habits and practices of Americans. The findings are also published in a more complete volume: Edward O. Laumann, John H. Gagnon, Robert T. Michael, and Stuart Michaels. 1994. *The Social Organization of Sexuality: Sexual Practices in the United States*. Chicago: University of Chicago Press.

REINISCH, JUNE, AND RUTH BEASLEY. 1990. *The Kinsey Institute New Report on Sex: What You Must Know to Be Sexually Literate*. New York: St. Martin's Press. Over the years, the Kinsey Institute has received hundreds of questions concerning human sexuality. This book attempts to address some of the most commonly asked questions surrounding topics such as AIDS, other sexually transmitted diseases, and sexuality and aging.

RICH, ADRIENNE. 1980. "Compulsory Heterosexuality and Lesbian Existence." *Signs* 5:631–60. A classic and influential essay on the sociopolitical nature of female sexuality generally and lesbianism specifically.

LITERARY

KUDAKA, GERALDINE, ED. 1995. *On a Bed of Rice: An Asian American Erotic Feast*. New York: Anchor. An interesting anthology of contemporary erotic prose and poetry by established and up-and-coming writers of Chinese, Filipino, Japanese, Korean, Vietnamese, and Indian descent explores the themes of sexual awakening, marriage, and interracial love. This anthology is proof that sex and eroticism need not be taboo subjects for college students. The stories range from haunting to humorous; some deal with the way that race and sex are intertwined in America, others with the myths about Asian American sexuality.

LAWRENCE, D. H. 1994. *Lady Chatterley's Lover*. London: Penguin. This classic tells the tale of Constance Chatterley, a woman of warm impulses with a physically impotent husband. Constance finds refuge from her husband's demanding individualism and class snobbery by having a sexual relationship with her husband's gameskeeper. A major theme of this novel is that sex without love is a perversion. (Originally published 1928.)

INTERNET

http://www.thebody.com This site, TheBody, is a comprehensive multimedia HIV and AIDS health Internet site and information resource center. The site provides information on more than 250 topics. Its stated mission is to lower barriers between patients and clinicians, demystify HIV/AIDS and its treatment, improve patients' quality of life, and foster community through human connection.

http://www.goaskalice.columbia.edu/ This site, Go Ask Alice!, is a health question-and-answer Internet service produced by Columbia University's Health Education Program. Its mission is to increase access to, and use of, health information by providing factual, in-depth, straightforward, and nonjudgmental information to assist users' decision-making about their physical, sexual, emotional, and spiritual health.

Chapter 7

Nonmarital Lifestyles

IN THE NEWS: BERLIN, GERMANY

On August 1, 2001, in front of a gathering of family and friends, Gudrun Pannier and Angelika Baldow exchanged vows and registered their union at Berlin's town hall. Dozens of other couples across Germany held similar ceremonies on the first day that a new law allowing homosexual couples to register their unions at government offices went into effect. The law entitles same-sex couples to receive the same inheritance and health insurance rights available to married couples, and requires a court decision for divorce to dissolve the relationship. However, opponents of the law succeeded in having some tax privileges granted to heterosexual couples withheld from homosexual couples, arguing that treating their unions like marriage damages the special status of marriage. Three states—Bavaria, Mecklenburg–Western Pomerania, and Hesse—have challenged the new law and have delayed its implementation in their jurisdictions (Graham, 2001).

On July 25, 2001, Roger Phelps, a 48-year-old computer software analyst, and Elgin Hodgins, a 55-year-old lawyer, partners for 18 years, exchanged rings and formed a civil union, Vermont's legal equivalent of a heterosexual marriage. On April 25, 2000, after months of heated debate, protests, and counter-demonstrations, Vermont became the first, and to date, only state granting legal recognition to same-sex unions.

This action came in response to an order issued by the Vermont Supreme Court after its 1999 ruling in *Baker* v. *Vermont* that homosexual couples were entitled to the same legal rights and benefits of marriage as heterosexuals. Since the law was adopted in 2000, Vermont officials have recorded nearly 2500 civil unions, 502 of them between state residents and the rest between nonresidents, including couples from Israel and British Columbia (Goodman, 2000; Goldberg, 2001).

Only the Netherlands allows outright marriage for same-sex couples. However, Denmark (1989), Norway (1993), Greenland (1994), Sweden (1995), Iceland (1996), and France (1999) legally recognize and grant many of the rights and benefits of marriage to same-sex couples.

WHAT WOULD YOU DO? If your state held a referendum on legalizing same-sex relationships, how would you vote? Should unmarried couples (homosexual or heterosexual) be granted the same benefits and rights as married couples? Explain. If you were living in a committed but nonlegal relationship, would you enter a civil union if you could? Explain.

Over the course of your lifetime you will be making a number of personal decisions, perhaps none more important than whether to marry. To make an intelligent decision, it is important to understand what the alternatives are and how they came to be. Although most Americans will marry at some point in their lives, increasing numbers of people are choosing to remain single into their 30s or even permanently. Others are forming relationships that differ in significant ways from traditional family structures, such as the couples featured in the *In the News* opening to this chapter. This chapter examines the lifestyles of people who, for one reason or another, do not or cannot marry, as well as the economic and social trends that help or hinder the development of nonmarital lifestyles. As is true of marriages and families today, nonmarital lifestyles make up a diverse range of social forms. Among the most common forms are singlehood, heterosexual cohabitation, lesbian and gay relationships, communal living, and group marriages. Each of these lifestyles is examined from both a historical and a contemporary perspective.

Before we examine what it was like to be single in America's early years, we must clarify exactly what we mean by *single*. The term is frequently used to describe anyone who is not currently married—the divorced, widowed, separated, and those who have never married. Including all of these diverse groups under one heading acknowledges that their members are similar in that they do not have legal spouses. This practice, however, obscures the unique aspects of the lifestyles associated with each group. Thus, in this chapter we apply the concept of "single" to never-married people only. Those who were formerly married—the divorced, separated, or widowed—are discussed in separate chapters.

HISTORICAL PERSPECTIVES

Most of the data available on singles in colonial America refer primarily to white settlers. The marital status and lifestyles of Native Americans and African Americans, both free and enslaved, went largely unrecorded during this time. Therefore, we do not know how many individuals in these groups remained unmarried or what such a lifestyle might have been like for them.

In addition, although there is a growing body of literature on single women in the eighteenth and nineteenth centuries, particularly middle- and upper-class women, scant information exists on the role of single men during this time. It is not that single men were nonexistent; in fact, quite the opposite was true. Single men made up a large proportion of immigrants to the United States at this time. But then as now, men's economic and political roles rather than their marital status were emphasized. Thus, the conclusions we can draw about the lifestyles of singles in America's past are indeed limited and cannot be assumed to apply to all of the diverse groups living here at that time.

A survey of America's past reveals that for much of this country's history marriage was the cultural ideal and the norm. In fact, positive views concerning the permanently single were rarely articulated. Instead, a social climate evolved that tended to devalue singlehood and to discriminate against individuals who remained unmarried. Although some negative stereotypes of the never-married still persist, today more people are choosing this lifestyle for longer periods of time (some even permanently), and in the process demonstrating that singlehood can be a rewarding and satisfying experience.

Singlehood in Early America

Being single in early America was not easy; unmarried people often faced personal restrictions. For example, N. B. Shurtleff's (1853/1854) examination of public records of the Massachusetts Bay Company found that the authorities mandated "every town to dispose of all single persons and inmates within their town to service or otherwise" (quoted in Schwartz and Wolf, 1976:18). This "disposal" took the form of placing single people in the home of a responsible family, the belief being that all people need to be associated with a family to ensure that they live a proper life. The assumption that unmarried individuals could not be trusted to lead a proper life on their own gave rise to the view that the unmarried, regardless of age, were somehow not mature adults. This belief that the progression from engagement to marriage and then to parenthood represents normal growth and development still exists among some life cycle theorists today (see Chapter 2).

Like many women in her day, Susan B. Anthony (1820–1906) received several proposals of marriage. She refused them all, preferring her independence to being a wife and homemaker. She devoted her life to the pursuit of equal rights for women.

Unmarried women and men were commonly seen as defective or incomplete and were often the subject of ridicule. After studying this period, one investigator concluded that "bachelors were rare and were viewed with disapproval. They were in the class of suspected criminals" (Calhoun, 1917, 1:67). Single women were not spared derogatory labels either. Those women not married by age 20 were referred to as "stale maids." Unmarried women 5 years older became known as "ancient maids." Even today, terms such as *old maid* and *spinster* convey negative connotations.

Why were single people treated this way? The devaluation of singlehood was in large measure a result of the high value attached to marriage, a value strongly associated with religious beliefs. The Bible stressed the importance of marriage and family life. For example, in the book of Genesis (2:24), men are enjoined "to leave father and mother and cleave to a wife." There were also practical considerations. The early settlers were concerned with economic and personal survival. Hence, there was an imperative to increase the population and to share the burdens of earning a livelihood in this new land. Writer Alice Earle (1893:36) took note of this in her reflection on New England customs: "What could he do, how could he live in that new land without a wife? There were no housekeepers—and he would scarcely have been allowed to have one if there were. What could a woman do in that new settlement among unbroken forests, uncultivated lands, without a husband?"

In sum, marriage was seen as a practical necessity, and singlehood was not considered an acceptable alternative because "the man without a family was evading a civic duty . . . and the husbandless woman had no purpose in life" (Spruill, 1938:137). Despite the negative ways in which single people were viewed and treated in colonial America, their numbers in the general population gradually increased as political, social, and economic changes combined to create new opportunities for them, especially for women.

Singlehood in the Nineteenth and Early Twentieth Centuries

The percentage of single women began to increase in the last decades of the eighteenth century and continued to do so into the nineteenth. At its height, the trend represented some 11 percent of American women, those born between 1865 and 1875 (cited in Chambers-Schiller, 1984:3). This historical increase is important to recognize, because we tend to think of developments in our own period as unique rather than as a continuation of long-term trends. Sociologist Edward Kain, in his book *The Myth of Family Decline* (1990), documents the fact that, contrary to popular belief, the increase in the numbers of never-married people since the 1970s is not a new phenomenon. Rather, it represents a return to historically higher levels of singlehood that began to decline markedly only after 1940. For example, in 1890,

15 percent of women and 27 percent of men aged 30 to 34 had never married. In 1940, the comparable figures for this age group were 15 and 21 percent, respectively; by 1970, they had dropped to 6 and 9 percent (Kain, 1990:75). By 2000, however, the rates had increased to 22 percent for women and 30 percent for men (Fields and Casper, 2001).

What accounted for the increase in the single population in the nation's early years? As we saw in Chapter 5, marriage rates are related to changing demographic, economic, political, and cultural factors. So, too, are changing rates of singlehood. In the early 1800s, industrialization created new jobs for both women and men, allowing them a measure of financial independence. Furthermore, some occupations were considered incompatible with marriage. For example, it was common for communities to have rules requiring teachers to resign when they got married (Punke, 1940). Thus, the choice to continue teaching was also a choice to remain single.

The Industrial Revolution was not the only event contributing to the growth of the single population. Earlier, the American Revolution gave rise to a new cultural ethos that emphasized individualism, self-reliance, and freedom of choice in pursuing one's goals. According to historian Lee Chambers-Schiller (1984), in this climate, society's views of the unmarried woman moderated somewhat. Most Americans no longer thought of singlehood as a sin, even though to many it still seemed unnatural. An analysis of the professional and popular literature of the late nineteenth and early twentieth centuries reveals a changing attitude toward both singlehood and marriage (Freeman and Klaus, 1984). Some of that literature sounds quite modern, especially in terms of today's growing criticism of marriage and the perception that singlehood is preferable to a bad marriage. For example, in a Roper Organization survey (1990), 56 percent of single women and 59 percent of single men agreed with the statement, "I'm happier than most of my married friends."

The view that marriages should be happy rather than merely a duty evolved gradually during the early nineteenth century. The very title of Chambers-Schiller's (1984) study—*Liberty, a Better Husband*—provides insight into the decision to remain single. Marriage could now be viewed as an option, and more women chose not to marry; some even proclaimed their decision publicly. As one nineteenth-century woman explained: "I've chosen my life as deliberately as my sisters and brothers have chosen theirs. . . . I want to be a spinster, and I want to be a good one" (quoted in Freeman and Klaus, 1984:396). Other women saw their singlehood as a form of protest against the demands and restrictions of middle-class marriage and became advocates for women's rights. This criticism of marriage, the availability of employment, the opening of education to women, and the early women's movement all worked to the advantage of the unmarried, who were increasingly portrayed in a more positive light. Thus, there emerged a new ideology, called "the cult of single blessedness," which proved beneficial to families and the community at large. It became socially acceptable for unmarried women to care for aging parents, the orphaned, the sick, and the indigent members of the community. Over time such work came to be seen as appropriate vocations for women.

Singlehood Today: Current Demographic Trends

Although marriage remains the most common living arrangement for Americans today, significant numbers of people are choosing not to marry for all or for large portions of their lives. In 1999, 26.9 percent of all people 18 and over had never married, up from 15.6 percent in 1970 (Saluter, 1994:vi; U.S. Census Bureau, 2000). Most Americans who eventually marry do so by their mid-30s. Thus, as age increases, the proportion who have never married declines. This can readily be seen in Table 7.1, which compares the percentages of both sexes remaining single beyond the usual ages of marriage at two points in time.

The data in this table (the latest available) reveal two important patterns. First, the number of women and men who remain single into their late 30s has increased among all three racial and ethnic groups. Among both sexes, African Americans and Latinos have higher rates of singlehood than do their white counterparts. Some social scientists attribute these differences to the economic disadvantages and higher unemployment rates experienced by these groups, especially among men. Demographic trends play an important role in

Table 7.1

Never-Married by Age, Sex, Race, and Latina/o Origin, 1970 and 1998

	1970		March 1998	
	30–34	35–39	30–34	35–39
All Races				
Male	9.4%	7.2%	29.2%	21.6%
Female	6.2	5.4	21.6	14.3
White (non-Latina/o)				
Male	9.2	6.1	26.8	18.0
Female	5.5	4.6	16.8	10.7
Black				
Male	9.2	15.8	43.2	39.7
Female	10.8	12.1	47.2	34.3
Latina/o Origin				
Male	11.0	7.6	27.4	26.8
Female	8.4	6.9	19.5	13.2

Sources: Adapted from Arlene F. Saluter, 1994, "Marital Status and Living Arrangements: March, 1993," U.S. Census Bureau, *Current Population Reports*, Series P-20-478 (Washington, DC: U.S. Government Printing Office): p. viii, Table C; and "Marital Status and Living Arrangements: March 1998 (Update)," Series P 20-514. http//:www.census.gov/prod/99 pubs/p20-51u.pdf the lower marriage rate of African Americans, especially of African American women. As a result of the high rate of mortality among young African American men, there are more African American women than men in the United States (Staples, 1994). Furthermore, African American families often encourage their daughters to put education before marriage (Higginbotham and Weber, 1995). As we saw in Chapter 5, a greater number of black women than black men are college-educated; consequently, many of these women forgo marriage if they don't find a partner who meets their expectations. In addition, more African American men than women marry members of other racial or ethnic groups (Staples, 1994). Since fewer data are available on Latino singles, the explanations for their increasing tendency to delay marriage are mostly speculative. It may be simply that Latinas/os are adapting to the behaviors of the larger society.

Second, with the exception of African American males and females aged 30–34, the percentage of single men is higher than that of single women. This pattern holds true up until age 65, when the percentage of unmarried women surpasses that of unmarried men. This latter pattern is explained by two factors: Women have a longer life expectancy than men, and women tend to marry men older than themselves.

Comparable census data on the marital status of Asian Americans and Native Americans in these age categories are not yet available. There is evidence, however, that Asian Americans and Pacific Islanders remain single longer than other groups. For example, in 1999, only 45 percent of Asian Americans and Pacific Islanders aged 25 to 34 had never married, compared to 32 percent of non-Latina/o whites in the same age group (Humes and McKinnon, 2000). A plausible explanation for this difference is that Asian American families are more likely to give priority to getting an education than to an earlier marriage.

The United States is not the only country to experience a growth in the never-married segment of the population. In fact, Britain is predicting that if present trends continue, married people will soon be in the minority. According to the government's Actuary Department, the percentage of married adults is expected to fall from a current 55 percent to 45 percent by 2021. The proportion of women who have never married is expected to rise from 24 percent to 33 percent between 1996 and 2021. The change in the percentage of never-married men is expected to be even more dramatic, increasing from 32 percent to 41 percent during that same period ("Britain's New Minority . . . ," 1999). Similarly, in Japan women are delaying marriage or not getting married at all because they fear that marriage will mean having to give up careers, financial independence, and personal freedom. Their behavior has triggered an unintended demographic crisis, a sharp decline in the birth rate in the traditional, male-dominated Japanese culture, which has government officials alarmed (Lev, 1998).

Later in this chapter we examine the reasons people give for remaining single. Although we don't have this kind of information for all racial and ethnic groups, it is likely that part of the explanation for the different rates of singlehood is related to the availability of potential partners in their respective groups. As we saw in Chapter 5, in the United States people tend to select mates who have social characteristics much like their own.

DEMYSTIFYING SINGLEHOOD

In his analysis of the lifestyles of singles, sociologist Peter Stein (1976) observed that for many years most Americans, including social scientists, thought of single people as "those who fail to marry," believing that no one would want to remain single by choice. Stein's work has helped dispel this myth and shows that the decision of whether to marry or stay single is conditioned by psychological, social, cultural, and economic factors. He characterizes these factors as a series of **pushes,** or negative factors in a current situation, and **pulls,** or attractions to a potential situation.

Individual Decision Making

On the one hand, people are pushed toward marriage by pressures from parents, cultural expectations, loneliness, a fear of independence, and a feeling of guilt about staying single. On the other hand, parental approval, the marriages of friends, physical attraction and emotional attachment to another person, and a desire for security, social status, and children pull people toward marriage. In a similar vein, the perception of relationships as suffocating and as obstacles to self-development as well as an awareness of the high divorce rate may push people toward singlehood. Career opportunities, a sense of self-sufficiency, freedom, and the desire for psychological and social autonomy may pull people toward singlehood.

Although Stein's data represent common patterns of experiences, pressures, and desires, these are not necessarily experienced in the same way by everyone or even by the same person at different times in the life cycle. For example, some parents exert great pressure on their children to marry; others do not. Some people are self-sufficient in young adulthood but feel as they get older a greater need to be involved with someone else on a daily basis, as voiced by a 34-year-old male, "I've liked being single. It allowed me to travel to exotic places, change jobs several times, and really get to know who I am as a person, but now that I've done all that, I'm ready to share my life with someone."

The Influence of Social and Economic Forces

The decision of whether to marry is influenced by many factors. Many Americans no longer view marriage as an economic or social necessity. The stigma attached to singlehood has lessened in recent years, and there has been a corresponding reduction in the perceived benefits associated with marriage. Indeed, changes in gender role expectations (see Chapters 3 and 10) may make marriage seem more unattractive to both women and men. On the one hand, some women are putting careers before marriage, not wishing to undertake the conflict involved in balancing work and family. On the other hand, some men delay or forgo marriage because they are reluctant to share in household tasks and child care, now expected by increasing numbers of working women.

Economic factors play a critical role in the decision to stay single. A recent survey of 9100 college students found that their immediate concerns were finishing their education, establishing themselves in their chosen careers, and paying off their college loans. For now, marriage would have to wait. Nevertheless, most of those surveyed expected to marry some day (Levine and Cureton, 1998). Additionally, expanding economic opportunities have provided more women with the means to be financially independent outside of marriage. Research has shown that women in labor markets with favorable economic opportunities have lower rates of marriage than do other women (White, 1981). Researcher Judy Rollins (1986) found that most of her single respondents believe that being unmarried will help them establish their careers. Men may also delay marriage for the same reasons as women, choosing to devote their energy to finishing their education and establishing their careers. Declining economic fortunes, however, may contribute to an increase in the single population, especially for men. Women may perceive men who are unemployed or who earn low wages as less attractive candidates for marriage (Oppenheimer, 1988), or such men may not want to undertake additional responsibilities until their job situation improves. Some people face other obstacles in finding a suitable marriage partner. People who have a physical or mental disability may find that their intimacy and sexual needs go unfilled because others may perceive them as unattractive or sexless (Kelly, 1995).

Other factors that affect the decision to remain single include the liberalization of sexual norms and the availability of contraceptive devices, both of which have freed women and men to pursue an active social and sexual life outside of marriage. Today, however, as we have seen in Chapter 6, the fear of AIDS may constrain the expression of this freedom. Finally, TV programs increasingly depict attractive, stylish 30-ish singles on hit shows like "Friends," "Will and Grace," and "Ally McBeal," conveying the notion that being single is fun and exciting. And the visibility of older unmarried people leading satisfying and meaningful lives has enabled younger adults to find a greater number of role models to emulate.

Nevertheless, not everyone who remains single does so by choice. As discussed in Chapter 5, some people find their desire for marriage frustrated by a marriage squeeze. The influence of these social and economic factors is reflected in Stein's typology of singlehood.

Types of Singles

Utilizing the reasons respondents gave for being single, Stein (1981) developed a typology of singlehood that places singles, including those who have never married and those who were formerly married, into four different categories based on the likelihood of their remaining unmarried:

Many young adults no longer view marriage as an economic or social necessity. Instead, increasing numbers of women and men are creating satisfying single lifestyles for themselves.

- *Voluntary temporary singles* are currently unmarried and are not seeking mates. They remain open to the possibility of marrying someday, perhaps after completing their education or becoming established in a career.
- *Voluntary stable singles* choose to remain single and see themselves doing so on a permanent basis. Priests and nuns are included in this category.
- *Involuntary temporary singles* want to marry and are actively seeking mates.
- *Involuntary stable singles* desire marriage but have not yet found a mate. They tend to be older singles who have more or less accepted the probability of remaining single for life.

Sociologist Arthur Shostak (1987) also found four patterns corresponding to Stein's typology. However, he used more colorful terms to describe the same types of singles: ambivalents, resolveds, wishfuls, and regretfuls. Similarly, Robert Staples (1981b) developed a fivefold typology describing the variations among African American single men:

- The *free-floating single* dates a variety of people and is unattached.
- The *single in an open-couple relationship* dates others, but has a steady partner.

- The *single in a closed-couple relationship* expects her or his partner to be faithful.
- The *committed single* thinks of the relationship as permanent and may be engaged or cohabiting.
- The *accommodationist* is generally an older single who lives alone and who does not date.

Each of these typologies calls attention to the special characteristics of the single state: its heterogeneity and its fluidness. At any given time the population of singles is composed of individuals who either choose or hope to be single for only a limited period of time as well as those who plan to be or who will find themselves single for the rest of their lives. Perhaps not surprisingly research indicates that individuals who are voluntarily single tend to have a better sense of well-being than the involuntarily single (Shostak, 1987).

Regardless of which category of singlehood never-married people find themselves in, they enjoy certain advantages and cope with some disadvantages resulting from this lifestyle. Before reading the next section, reflect on your perceptions of a single lifestyle.

What do you see as the advantages of being single? What do you see as its disadvantages? How do your perceptions compare with those identified by researchers?

Advantages and Disadvantages of Singlehood

Studies have found a general agreement among single people regarding both the advantages and disadvantages of a single lifestyle. Among the most frequently cited advantages are personal freedom, financial independence, privacy, greater opportunities to pursue careers and other activities, and more time to develop a variety of friendships, including sexual relationships (Ogintz, 1991; DeMont, 2000). Consider what 34-year-old Vivian had to say about her life:

> My life is my own. I can do housework in the middle of the night, be a total vegetable all weekend, eat at ridiculous hours, or not eat at all. No one messes up my place when it's clean; no one gripes when it's dirty. I can keep fattening foods out of the house without depriving anyone. I can pig out without hiding. I see only the movies/shows/concerts I want to see. No one tells me how to spend my money. I may not be the best financial manager, but it's still my dough, and I'd rather spend it on clothes than stereo equipment. (Quoted in Lavin, 1991:3)

As we saw earlier in the case of Japan, marriage in patriarchal societies often results in a considerable loss of personal freedom and financial independence for women. Thus, in those societies, women are increasingly reluctant to give up their single status. For example, women in Thailand are even getting certificates to document their single status in order to safeguard their personal freedoms (see the "In Other Places" box.)

Given the negative view of singlehood in the past, it would be surprising if no disadvantages were associated with being single. Among the disadvantages singles report are loneliness and lack of companionship, being excluded from couple events or feeling uncomfortable in social settings involving mostly couples, not having children, and social disapproval of their lifestyle (Etaugh and Malstrom, 1981; Stein and Fingrutd, 1985). Jeffrey Ullman, president and founder of Great Expectations, a national video-dating service, summed up the view of many singles: "Nothing is wrong with being alone. However, it has a very ugly, nasty and debilitating side, and that is being lonely when you don't want to be alone" (quoted in Pauly, 1992:5). Another disadvantage of living alone is more gender-specific. Interviews with single women reveal considerable concern about issues of safety. They report that decisions about where they live, their mode of transportation, and which leisure activities they engage in are influenced by their fears of assault (Chasteen, 1994).

These advantages and disadvantages are general categories and do not necessarily apply in every individual case or at all times in the life cycle. For example, not all singles are uncomfortable in social settings involving couples; some mix easily in such situations. Economic status also affects how singlehood is experienced, as singles with low incomes or singles who lose their jobs may not be able to implement the freedoms associated with being single. According to the Census Bureau, in 2000, 56 percent (7.5 million) of men 18 to 24 years old lived at home with one or both parents. Since women typically marry earlier than men, it is not surprising to find somewhat fewer women, 5.6 million (43 percent), in that same age bracket living with their parents. Among those 25 to 34 years of age, 12 percent of men but only 5.4 percent of women live with one or both parents (Fields and Casper, 2001). For most young adults, living at home is part of an ongoing stage in their life cycle. They are either going to college or are just beginning their work life and have not yet left home to live independently. For others, however, living with their parents represents a return to an earlier pattern. They had already left home to live on their own but a change in their status, such as graduation from college, loss of a job, or a family illness, necessitated their return to their parental home. Two-thirds of these returnees are college-educated, and the average length of their stay at home is 2.5 years (Marino, 1995).

Returning home, like independent living, has its advantages and disadvantages. On the one hand, there is the benefit of economic and social support that other family members provide, whereas on the other hand, there may be some constraints on privacy and the scheduling of activities. To ensure a harmonious and workable relationship, parents and returning children must reach an understanding about finances, household rules, and the offspring's expected length of stay. Additionally, changing family circumstances may alter a lifestyle in the direction of less freedom and

IN OTHER PLACES

CERTIFICATION OF SINGLE WOMEN

In Thailand, being a single woman is often a matter of paperwork. The Thai Civil Registration Division is now issuing women single certificates as proof of their nonmarital status. This process is an outgrowth of Thailand's struggle with its patriarchal past. Under Thai law, women lose many rights when they marry. For example, a married woman must have her husband's permission to conduct business transactions, which her single counterparts can do freely on their own. If a woman marries a foreigner, she is further disadvantaged, for a foreigner is not allowed to buy land or own more than 49 percent of a business nor can he give his wife permission to conduct such transactions. In addition, Thai bureaucracies often incorrectly identify women as married. This frequently happens when doctors refer to their unmarried pregnant patients as "Mrs.," in an effort to protect them from embarrassment, and this reference is then repeated on birth certificates. As Thai women become more educated and enter well-paying occupations, they are becoming more reluctant to marry. In an effort to hold onto the rights single women enjoy, many couples are now choosing not to register their marriage with the local authorities. Although many women's groups in Thailand are fighting against the laws and attitudes that make the single certificate necessary, they welcome its introduction as a way to give women the chance to regain some of their rights.

What do you think? *Are these certificates a good idea? Explain. Are there any differences in the rights that single and married women enjoy in the United States? Should there be any differences? Explain.*

Source: Chris Gelken, 1999, "Thai Wives Can't Do a Single Thing; So Maidens Need Papers to Prove It," *Chicago Tribune* (January 11): Sec. 13, 1.

more responsibility for others, as is often the case for single adult children who find themselves caring for sick or elderly relatives.

SINGLE LIFESTYLES

The major challenge facing single people through the ages has been building a satisfying life in a society highly geared toward marriage. Until recently, the general tendency in U.S. popular culture has been to portray singles as belonging in one of two stereotypical groups. On the one side is the "swinging single"—the party goer who is carefree, uncommitted, sexually adventuresome, and the subject of envy by married friends. Poles apart from this image is the "lonely loser"—the unhappy, frustrated, depressed single who lives alone and survives on TV dinners, a fate few people would envy.

How accurate are these images? Research on the lives of single women and men contradicts these stereotypes and reveals a wide variety of patterns. For example, one in-depth study of 73 white, never-married, college-educated women and men over age 30 found significant variation in how these singles went about organizing their lives. Although there was some overlapping of activities, six different lifestyle patterns were observed, each having a central focus:

- *Supportive:* These singles spend much of their time helping and supporting others and have careers in the teaching and nursing professions.
- *Passive:* These singles spend much of their time alone, have low levels of social participation and more negative outlooks on life, and show little initiative in shaping their lives.
- *Activists:* These singles center their lives around political or community involvement. They derive a great deal of satisfaction from working for social causes.
- *Individualistic:* These singles strive for autonomy and self-growth. They see their independence, freedom, and privacy as an environment in which to grow and develop as a whole person. They enjoy reading, hobbies, and other solitary pursuits.
- *Social:* These singles have extensive personal relationships and spend little time alone. Friends and social activities have a high priority in their lives. They are deeply involved in hobbies, organizations, and family activities.
- *Professional:* These singles organize their lives around work and identify with their occupational roles. Most of their time and energy is spent on their careers (Schwartz, 1976).

A more recent study of a representative sample of never-married women and men, including both whites and blacks, also revealed a rich diversity among this population. However, this research also found that, compared with married persons, persons who never marry are overrepresented in both extremes of social interaction. Thus, singles had higher rates of never interacting with relatives, friends, and neighbors as well as higher rates of seeing these support networks several times a week. In contrast, married persons reported frequencies of interaction within these two extremes (Seccombe and Ishii-Kuntz, 1994).

More people today are delaying marriage or remaining single permanently. As their numbers have grown, so, too, has societal acceptance of nonmarital lifestyles. These single friends enjoy an afternoon bicycle trip.

Thus, the single population, like their married peers, is not a homogeneous group. Singles differ not only in lifestyle orientation but also in the type of living arrangements they select. Figure 7.1 compares the living arrangements of never-married adults in three different age groups. "Of the 25.3 million persons aged 18 to 24 in 1990, 19.6 million (77 percent) had not yet married, 66 percent of them lived with their parents, 16 percent shared a home with nonrelatives, 12 percent shared a home with relatives other than their parents, and 6 percent lived alone" (U.S. Census Bureau, 1991a:11). This pattern changes with increasing age. At each age group, more singles leave their parental home to live alone or to share living arrangements with others. Among never-married people 45 years and older, 48 percent lived alone, 27 percent lived with other relatives, 14 percent lived with nonrelatives, and only 11 percent lived with parents. Although comparable detailed data are not yet available for more recent years, preliminary analysis of new census data suggests that fewer 18–24-year-olds are living with their parents. In 2000, just half (50 percent) of this age group lived with a parent. This decline is most likely a result of an improved economy in the latter part of the decade.

A number of unmarried people live in specially designed singles areas—apartments or condominiums developed to meet the perceived needs of this population. These areas offer access to swimming pools, health facilities, restaurants, and singles bars. Although these complexes have attracted a number of singles, especially younger ones, the majority of the never-married are dispersed throughout the general population. Some singles prefer the excitement of city living; others desire the less dense suburban areas or the openness of the countryside. With the changes in credit regulations beginning in the 1970s, more singles were able to get mortgages and become homeowners. The ability to buy a house, however, is dependent on income.

Income

Earlier we noted that one of the perceived advantages of being single is financial independence. How well off are single people? Are they better off economically than married people? These questions are difficult to answer because the needs of these populations may vary significantly. On the one hand, married people with children may need a larger living space than a single person does. On the other hand, singles may find that they spend more on food and traveling, as their married counterparts benefit from buying in quantity and sharing double-occupancy rates. We can, however, gain some insight into the relative status of single people by comparing their median income with that of their married peers. As Table 7.2 reveals, female householders living alone had a median income of $18,615; the comparable figure for male householders living alone was $30,414. In contrast, married couples with both spouses present had a median income of $54,276. Furthermore, there is considerable variation in income across race and ethnicity.

What factors explain these differences between the married and single populations? One possible explanation is that singles, as a whole, are younger and less experienced than are marrieds. This argument fails to hold up, however, when age differences are controlled. At the same age levels, singles still earn less than their married peers. Two factors are particularly significant in this regard. First, many married households have more than one wage earner, thus enhancing

Figure 7.1

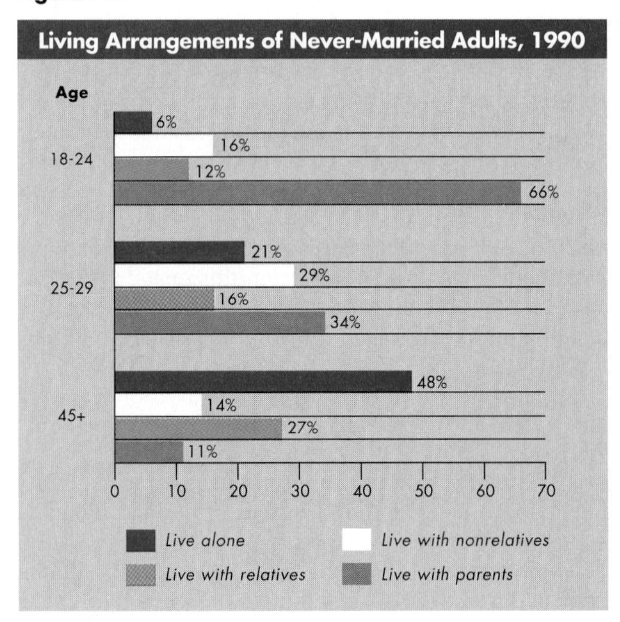

Source: Adapted from U.S. Census Bureau, 1991a, *Current Population Reports*, Series P-20-450, "Marital Status and Living Arrangements: March 1990" (Washington, DC: U.S. Government Printing Office): 11.

Table 7.2

Median Income by Household Type, 1998

	Married Couples	Single-Person Households	
		Male	Female
All Households	54,276	30,414	18,615
White	54,845	31,659	19,239
Black	47,382	20,673	13,608
Latina/o	35,207	23,427	11,699

Source: U.S. Census Bureau, 2000, *Statistical Abstract of the United States, 2000* (Washington, DC: U.S. Government Printing Office): 469, Table 741.

household earnings. Second, these earning differences may reflect a systematic bias against singles in the workplace. For example, certain data show that marital status affects men's wages. Blayne Cutler (1988:14) reports the biases single men experience in the workplace. Married white men who live with their wives earn about 12 percent more than never-married white men. The discrepancy in income is even more pronounced among black men, with married men earning about 20 percent more than never-married men. The probability of a promotion for married men is 11 percent higher than it is for single men.

What accounts for this wage difference? It may be a carryover from the past, when employers assumed that married men had greater financial needs than single men did. Some employers still believe that married men are more stable, more dedicated to their careers, better able to get along with others, and less likely to cost the company money by changing jobs. Thus, they are more eager to hire married men and reward them more. Surveys of top executives found that although half of the top-executive women were single, less than a tenth of the men were (Bradsher, 1989:3D). A 30-year-old graduate student told the authors about an experience he had looking for a job in public relations when he was 27: "When I was being interviewed, he [the personnel manager] kept referring to the social requirements of the job—entertaining, attending fundraisers and such. I could tell by his attitude that he wanted someone who was married, so I said I was engaged. The funny thing was, I didn't get the job, but I did get married a year later."

There is evidence that these attitudes are changing, at least in some professions. Executives from job search firms report that marketing and other jobs involving extensive travel now are likely to go to single men, even though administrative and supervisory positions, which often involve an after-hours social role, still go most frequently to married men (Bradsher, 1989:3D). Additionally, a recent study found that the earnings premium paid to married men compared with never-married men declined by more than 40 percent during the 1980s (Gray, 1997).

Support Networks

As we saw in Chapter 4, everyone, regardless of marital status, has intimacy needs and must work at developing intimate and supportive relationships. Singles who live alone confront a greater challenge in meeting their need for intimacy. They respond to this challenge by establishing strong friendships. A growing body of literature reveals that singles, especially women, create their own "family," a support group of friends who function in much the same way as families do—exchanging services, traveling together, giving and receiving advice, celebrating birthdays and holidays, and creating shared rituals and meanings (Cockrum and White, 1985; Simon, 1987; Inman, 1996; Johnson, 1996). Both women and men value friends, but in somewhat different ways. Women concentrate on establishing close, emotional bonds, whereas men focus more on sharing their interests and their values.

Another key intimacy need that is experienced by many people, regardless of marital status, is the bond that exists between parent and child. This need can present special problems for single people. Historically, great stigma has been attached to having children out of wedlock, and single women and men were denied the right to adopt children. However, changing attitudes as well as new reproductive technologies have made it possible for single people to bear and raise children. Consequently, more singles are doing so, a topic that will be discussed in Chapter 9.

Life Satisfaction

No examination of the single lifestyle would be complete without a discussion of life satisfaction. How satisfied with their lives are never-married people? In the past, studies consistently found that married people reported higher levels of happiness and satisfaction (Glenn and Weaver, 1988; Lee, Seccombe, and Shehan, 1991; Mastekaasa, 1992). However, these data must be interpreted with some caution. For a number of reasons, questions of happiness and life satisfaction are not always easy to answer. First, life satisfaction depends on a number of factors other than marital status, for example, good health, satisfying work, personal growth, financial security, love, family, and friends (Simenauer and Carroll, 1982; Hahn, 1993).

Second, every living arrangement contains advantages and disadvantages. Some people may experience more of the advantages, whereas others with different life circumstances may endure more disadvantages. Third, life satisfaction is not static; perceptions of satisfaction may vary over time depending on the changes occurring in an individual's life and in the society at large. For example, the percentage of married people reporting they were very happy declined between 1972 and 1988, whereas during this same time, the percentage of single people reporting they were very happy increased (Glenn and Weaver, 1988). Finally, the way society evaluates a lifestyle affects the perceived desirability of that status. Singlehood has become a more acceptable lifestyle in the United States; hence, ten years from now comparative lifestyle studies may reveal quite different patterns of happiness and life satisfaction. In one study, psychologist Janice Witzel found that this may be happening already, at least for the single women she studied. These women reported high levels of satisfaction and happiness (Ogintz, 1991).

A popular belief in the United States is that singlehood may be an exciting and satisfying lifestyle for young adults but that the opposite is true for older singles. How accurate is this belief? The next section focuses attention on a rarely studied population, the never-married elderly.

The Never-Married in Later Life

Earlier in this chapter we discussed the fact that in the past marriage was perceived as the ticket to adult status. It was also assumed that marriage was a means of achieving security and well-being in old age. Conversely, it was popularly assumed that elderly singles must be lonely and isolated individuals. Do you know any older singles? Is this view simply another version of the stereotyped images of singles, or does it reflect the lifestyles of the never-married elderly? To answer that question, let us first find out who the elderly singles are.

In 1998, approximately 1.4 million people 65 years of age or over had never married. Table 7.3 shows that the never-married represent 4.3 percent of that age group. Across all racial and ethnic groups, women are more likely than men to have never married. This is especially true for African American women and Latinas. Just as with younger singles, numerous factors account for the marital status of older people. Although some older people are unmarried by choice, for those who want to marry, gender plays a role. A longer life expectancy and a marriage gradient that favors men mean that older women find a limited pool of eligible males in their age categories, and those males that are eligible often have few resources with which to attract a prospective mate. Older women are also more likely than older men to have responsibilities for caring for elderly parents, which limit their marital prospects.

Table 7.3

Never-Married People, 65 Years of Age and over, by Age, Sex, Race, and Latina/o Origin, 1998

	Both Sexes	Male	Female
All races	4.3%	3.8%	4.7%
White (non-Latina/o)	4.1	3.7	4.5
Black	6.3	5.5	6.9
Latina/o origin	5.1	4.5	5.5

Source: Adapted from "Marital Status and Living Arrangements: March 1998 (Update)," Series P-20-514. http://www.census.gov/pubs/p20-514u.pdf

Our examination of the lifestyles of elderly singles is hampered by the fact that relatively little systematic research has been done on this population. Therefore, while instructive, the generalizations that we can make are limited and in need of further testing. Gerontologist Jaber Gubrium (1975, 1976) reviewed what research had been done on elderly singles and concluded that (1) they tend to be lifelong isolates, (2) they are not particularly lonely, (3) they evaluate everyday life in much the same way that their married peers do (both groups are more positive than the widowed or divorced), and (4) due to their single status they avoid the desolation of bereavement that follows the death of a spouse.

THE "LIFELONG ISOLATE" RECONSIDERED Later research has challenged some of these findings. For example, in his study of older men who live alone, Robert Rubinstein (1986) raises questions about the ambiguity of the meaning of "lifelong isolate." Rubinstein points out that the majority of the never-married men in his study spent many years living with other family members, particularly parents, and therefore could hardly be classified as isolates. These respondents did experience loneliness, but much less so than many of the widowers in his sample did. Although acknowledging that the married elderly may experience a unique form of desolation at the death of a spouse, Rubinstein argues that the death of a parent or sibling (and we would add friends) can be equally devastating to single people. We discuss how people cope with death and dying in Chapter 15.

Rubinstein's sample was small and exclusively male. Thus, we don't know if these patterns are typical of most older single men or to what extent these findings might apply to older women. Other research, however, indicates that there may be two distinct patterns among the older unmarried population. Some elderly people do experience a degree of isolation. Pat Keith (1986:392), in his analysis of census data, reported that about 33 percent of the elderly never see neighbors, about 30 percent never see friends, and 21 percent of the men and 14 percent of the women never see relatives. These findings must be interpreted carefully, however. Factors other than marital status may be better predictors of isolation in old age. Older singles with health problems, lower levels of education, and low-status occupations tend to be the most isolated. A second pattern appears more frequently: Many elderly singles lead active social lives. For example, Keith found that more than 50 percent of all older singles interact with family, friends, and neighbors.

Although a small sample, Katherine Allen's (1989) study of working-class women born in 1910 also shows the importance of family of origin in the lives of the elderly unmarried. Allen found that, like Rubinstein's respondents, the majority of the never-married women in her sample lived with one or both of their parents until their parents died. When this happened, however, they tended to replace the deceased parents with friends or other family members. Women appear to have an advantage over men in this regard due to early socialization experiences requiring them to concentrate more on developing interpersonal skills. Thus, single women often have a more extensive social support system than do single men. Allen also found that the majority of her respondents were pleased with their living arrangements, valued their independence, and had no regrets about not marrying.

Other researchers (for example, Kris Bulcroft and Margaret O'Connor-Roden, 1986) have examined heterosexual relationships and activities among older singles. They discovered that older singles, like their younger counterparts, enjoy movies, dances, travel, camping, plays, and romance. Further research is needed to see how race, class, and gender influence the pursuit of such activities.

Implications for Social Policy As we have seen, being single in later life presents some of the same challenges that it does in earlier years. Meeting the demands of daily living alone while building supportive networks gives the unmarried of any age a tremendous sense of accomplishment and satisfaction. Nevertheless, changes in social customs and social policy could alleviate some of the problems encountered by the never-married as they grow older. For example, we are all familiar with the rituals, showers, and gift giving that accompany the marriage ceremony. Yet rarely do we formally assist single people to establish their homes or symbolically, through a ritual celebration, recognize and give support to their lifestyle. Tax laws tend to favor homeowners (mostly marrieds), heads of households, and parents. Singles are often at a financial disadvantage, especially today when homeownership and material goods require more than one income. As single people age, they may experience other disadvantages. If they are without children of their own, they may find themselves relatively isolated due to the age-graded character of our society, or they may feel some regret at not having children to carry on their legacy (Rubinstein et al., 1991). More opportunities for intergenerational contact and perhaps even intergenerational or some form of communal living arrangements could be investigated as a means of providing support for elderly singles.

HETEROSEXUAL COHABITATION

People who are not married choose a variety of living arrangements. Some singles, like Vicki Byard (see the "Family Profile" box) are opting to share their life with an adopted child. These singles have much in common with other parents (see Chapter 9). Another arrangement that is increasingly popular among both the never-married and the formerly-married is cohabitation, popularly referred to as "living together."

Historical Perspectives

In the past, the number of cohabiting couples was difficult to determine because such relationships were not publicly sanctioned; therefore, no systematic attempt was made to collect data on them. Nevertheless, such relationships did exist under a variety of forms. The people most likely to live together outside of legal marriage were the poor or those individuals involved in unpopular relationships, for example, couples with mixed racial, religious, or ethnic backgrounds. Because of the prohibition against lesbian and gay marriages, homosexual couples have often lived together as well. As frequently occurs, however, when living together became widespread among the white middle class, researchers and other social commentators "discovered" it and gave it a new label, one not associated with poor, working-class, and nonwhite groups.

One form of living together that was visible in America's past is **common-law marriage,** "a cohabitive relationship that is based on the mutual consent of the persons involved, is not solemnized by a ceremony, and is recognized as valid by the state" (Stinnet and Birdsong, 1978:84). In sparsely populated areas of the country, clergy or judges often were not readily available to officiate at marriages. Thus, couples intending to wed established a home together without any official ceremony. Later on, if the couple wanted legal recognition of their relationship, they had to prove that they had lived as husband and wife for seven or more years and that they were legally eligible to be married. By the 1920s, most states had abandoned the concept of common-law marriage. Today, only 13 of the 50 states (Alabama, Colorado, Georgia, Idaho, Iowa, Kansas, Montana, Ohio, Oklahoma, Pennsylvania, Rhode Island, South Carolina, and Texas) continue to recognize such marriages.

The Meaning of Cohabitation Today

The U.S. Census Bureau first began to collect data on unmarried-couple households, or what the Bureau calls POSSLQS, "persons of the opposite sex sharing living quarters," in 1960. Unmarried-couple households are defined as those households containing two unrelated adults of the opposite sex (one of whom is the householder) who share a housing unit with or without children under 15 present (Saluter, 1994:vii). There are some problems with this definition—it may miss cohabiting couples in households with more than two adults, and it may include noncohabiting adults who may be boarders, roommates, or employees living in the household. Thus, although this definition is useful for measuring the number of nonrelated adults sharing living space, it does not convey the full meaning of the concept of cohabitation. The 1990 census attempted to improve the estimate of the number of cohabiting households by adding the relationship category "unmarried partner" to the 1990 census questionnaire, defining it as "a person who is not related to the householder, who shares living quarters, and who has a close personal relationship with the householder."

Cohabitation is similar to marriage in that couples create emotional and physical relationships with each other, and in some cases they also bear or rear children. It differs from marriage, however, in that it lacks formal legal, cultural, and religious support. And although attitudes are changing—over half (52 percent) of adults in a national survey said living together was a morally acceptable lifestyle, compared to 41 percent who said it was morally unacceptable for an

FAMILY PROFILE

VICKI, ALEX, AND KATE BYARD

Length of relationship: 2 years

Challenges of being a single parent: I am a single lesbian who had breast cancer at an early age, so just becoming a parent was a challenge for me. When I began to research my options, I learned that artificial insemination wouldn't be effective—or, if effective, wouldn't be safe to the fetus—because of the chemotherapy I had undergone; also, many adoption agencies won't place children with an "out" homosexual, not to mention one who has had a major illness. Eventually, I learned of an adoption agency that places only African American and biracial newborns. They accepted my application with full knowledge of my sexual orientation and cancer history. Through this agency, I adopted both my children as newborns: Alex is now 4 years old and Kate is 19 months.

The challenges I face as a single parent change as Alex and Kate grow. Both children are now in a half-day child-care program while I teach morning classes at a university. Although this arrangement is ideal for them—they get to interact with other children but still have 8 daytime hours at home with me—the strains of being the sole provider for my family and virtually a "stay-at-home" mom are tremendous. I do much of my class preparation and grading late into the night, while the kids sleep, and we have little money even for basic necessities. Another struggle this year has been that Kate has developmental delays, requiring therapy five times a week. Because I do not know a babysitter I can afford who could meet her needs, the only time I can go out without the kids is twice a year when we visit my mother and sisters, who live 700 miles away. In a few years, the struggles I face now will ease somewhat: I'll have more time to get work done when the kids are in elementary school; I can sleep more; and I won't have two day-care bills to pay. Yet even as I look forward to that time, I know I have made the right decisions in creating my family. Even at such young ages, Alex and Kate delight in each other's company, calling me to see whenever one of them has done something the other finds clever or funny so we can all applaud. To my surprise, this makes the emotional demands of parenting two children easier than parenting one. And when the practicalities of life seem unmanageable, I need only to see their faces, to hear their voices, to find fortitude. Despite our struggles, I have never been more deeply content.

Vicki, Alex, and Kate Byard

Parenting philosophy: Alex is old enough now to recognize some of the ways our family is nontraditional (he asks why he is "brown" and I am "pink"), but I know my children's identity crises will become far more complicated as they age. I strive to parent Alex and Kate so that the resiliency I see in them now will remain to serve them well into adulthood. Practically, that means bolstering their self-esteem by teaching them about their racial heritage, exposing them to other families like ours (transracial families, families formed through adoption, and/or families with homosexual parents), and giving them a wide range of experiences through which they can construct their own identities. I expect they will struggle, but I want us to be a family that can talk openly and problem-solve together. My hope is that despite whatever difficulties Alex and Kate face, their unique background will give them a deep understanding of prejudice, tolerance, pride, and compassion, lessons that people from more insular backgrounds may never be blessed to learn.

unmarried couple to live together (Saad, 2001)—it is likely that perceived parental or societal disapproval may still lead some couples to keep their relationship secret. Thus, our interpretation of past and current numbers of cohabiting couples must be somewhat tentative. In all probability the census data underestimate the total number of cases.

Current Demographic Trends Figure 7.2 traces the growth in numbers of unmarried-couple households since 1960, when they totaled only about 439,000. By 1999, this number had increased to 4.5 million. It is easy to see how dramatic this change is when we consider that in 1970, there was only one unmarried couple for every hundred married couples; in 1999, there were eight unmarried couples for every hundred married couples.

Because these census data capture living arrangements only at a given point in time, they do not reveal the full extent of the cohabitation experience in the United States. However, when we consider the cohabitation experiences of women 15–44 years of age, a much stronger pattern emerges. Over

Source: Adapted from U.S. Census Bureau, 1991a, *Current Population Reports*, Series P-20-450, "Marital Status and Living Arrangements: March 1990" (Washington, DC: U.S. Government Printing Office): 14, Table N; U.S. Census Bureau, 2000, *Statistical Abstract of the United States, 2000* (Washington, DC: U.S. Government Printing Office: 52, Table 57.

Figure 7.2

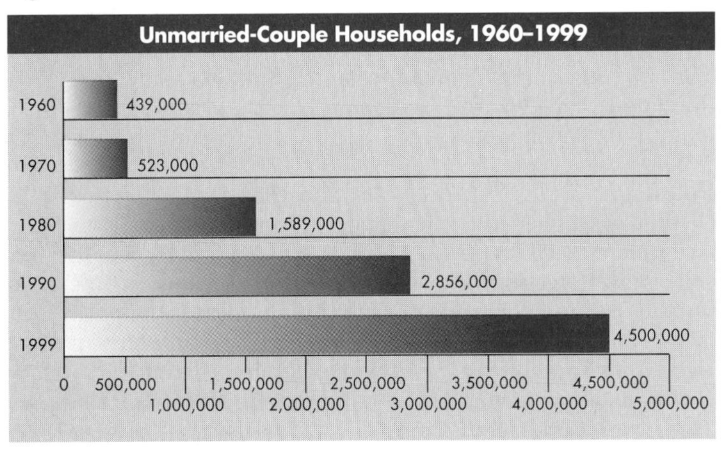

41 percent of these women have cohabited at some point in their lives. Among women 30–34 years of age, the figure is even higher; over 51 percent of these women reported having experienced cohabitation (U.S. Census Bureau, 2000). For some people today, especially among the younger population, cohabitation has become an extension of the courtship process. This pattern is reflected in the changing attitudes of high school seniors. In 1975, a minority of these students (35 percent) agreed or mostly agreed with the statement that "it is usually a good idea for a couple to live together before getting married in order to find out whether they really get along." By 1995, the corresponding figure had climbed to 59 percent (Johnston, Bachman, and O'Malley, 1997). During the 1960s, one in four remarriages was preceded by cohabitation; by the end of the 1980s, seven out of ten were (Kiernan, 1990). These data reveal the extent of cohabitation today but do not tell us who the cohabitants are. Do cohabitants differ in significant ways from the noncohabiting population?

Characteristics of Cohabitants Although it is popularly assumed that those who cohabit are young college students, the majority of cohabitants (57 percent) are between the ages of 25 and 44; 18 percent are under 25; and another 24 percent are 45 or older. Most heterosexual cohabiting relationships are childless; only 34 percent of cohabitants have children under 15 years of age living with them, either born out of their current relationship or from a previous relationship. Cohabitants may also have children from a previous marriage who live with the other biological parent (U.S. Census Bureau, 2000). Although cohabitants are found among all classes, ages, and racial and ethnic groups, cohabitation is not uniformly distributed across these groups. Cohabitants tend to be less educated, less likely to identify with an organized religion, and more likely to be politically liberal, unemployed, live in large urban areas, have divorced or remarried parents, and become sexually active at younger ages than their noncohabiting peers (Cunningham and Antill, 1995; Newport, 1996).

Race also adds an interesting dimension to cohabitation patterns. An analysis of the 1990 U.S. census data found that across all groups—black, white, Asian, and Latina/o—there is a high tendency to cohabit with people who are of a different race or ethnic group. Thus, research that does not examine cohabiting interracial couples significantly undercounts the extent of intimate interracial contact that exists in the United States today ("Love Is . . . ," 2000). It is probable that the higher rate of interracial cohabitation is due to the social pressure against interracial marriages.

Although we have comparative data on numbers and rates of cohabitation of these racial and ethnic groups, no systematic research on the cohabitive experiences of people of color has been done. Thus, we do not know if people of color attach the same meaning to this experience as do their white counterparts. We do know, however, that cohabitation is less likely to lead to legal marriage among black women than among white women (London, 1990). Additionally, black women are more likely than their white counterparts to give birth in a cohabiting relationship. Similarly, Puerto Rican women living in the United States are likely to cohabit instead of entering a legal marriage and to bear children within these cohabiting unions (Landale and Forste, 1991). These patterns may reflect the fact that rates of cohabitation are higher among educationally and economically disadvantaged groups, including relatively disadvantaged white women (Loomis and Landale, 1994; Smock and Manning, 1997). Thus, for these groups, cohabitation may serve as an alternative to marriage, or, as Judith Seltzer (2000) suggests, cohabitation is becoming more like formal marriage in that both are child-rearing institutions.

Reasons for Cohabitation

Perhaps some of you reading this book have had experience in a cohabitive relationship. Others of you may be contemplating such a relationship. Take a few minutes to reflect on why you (or others) might consider living together. The following discussion may help you illuminate thoughts you already have on the subject, as well as give you more of a sense of the variety of reasons people have for cohabiting. It is important to keep in mind that the supporting data are based on middle-class samples, frequently college students.

PUSH AND PULL FACTORS In an earlier section of this chapter we discussed Stein's model of pushes and pulls to analyze the decision to marry or to remain single. These conceptual categories are also appropriate for understanding the reasons people give for cohabiting. Among the push factors cohabitants report are loneliness, high costs of living alone, disenchantment with traditional dating and courtship, fear of marital commitment, awareness of the high divorce rate (and for the formerly-married, fear of making another mistake), sexual frustration, and education or career demands that preclude early marriage. Among the pull factors are a strong physical attraction toward someone, being in a strong emotional relationship, desire for intimacy and sex on a regular basis, desire to experiment with a new living arrangement, desire for personal growth, example of peers, desire to test compatibility for marriage (Althaus, 1991), and, today, perhaps to evaluate how likely a person is to be an egalitarian partner (Cherlin, 2000).

For many people cohabitation has become a stage in the dating process. This couple enjoys sharing tasks together.

Once again we can see the complexity of lifestyle choices. Cohabitation, like other options, is explained by a number of factors, both positive and negative. The meaning and experience of cohabitation varies considerably and reflects the different needs of individuals. For example, for some couples, living together is a new stage in a dating relationship, a "going steady" but with a live-in twist. A common pattern found among college students in the 1960s and 1970s was a gradual drifting into staying together, first spending the night, then the weekend, and then moving in (Macklin, 1972). For many, living together was a logical step in getting to know and share their lives with another person.

For other couples, cohabitation may represent a cheaper way to live (Althaus, 1991). For example, sharing expenses might enable younger cohabitants to commit more time and energy to education or career development. For older divorced or widowed people with grown children, cohabitation is sometimes chosen over marriage to avoid possible complications with social security or inheritance issues. Because there are many different motivations for cohabitation, partners should never assume agreement about where a relationship is heading. Like people entering into any relationship, the partners need to discuss and to understand each other's expectations.

TYPES OF COHABITING COUPLES Just as many reasons are given for cohabitation, the relationships established by cohabiting couples vary in terms of individual needs and degree of commitment. For some, the relationship is simply a utilitarian arrangement motivated by the desire to share expenses and household tasks or to avoid loss of financial benefits such as alimony, welfare, or pension checks. In such arrangements, intimacy may or may not be present. For others, there is intimate involvement with emotional commitment. However, they have no plans for marriage, preferring instead to take a "wait-and-see" attitude. In contrast, some cohabitors create a trial marriage to test their compatibility for a possible future marital commitment. Others go a step further. They have already decided to marry in the future and see no reason to live apart prior to that event, so for them cohabitation is a prelude to marriage. Despite this expectation, only 58 percent of cohabiting women marry their partners (National Center for Health Statistics, 1996). Marriage following cohabitation is more likely for white and Asian women (about 61 percent) than for Latinas (54 percent) or African American women (41 percent) (Abma et al., 1997). These differences are most frequently attributed to economic factors, such as low earnings and periodic unemployment, which inhibit marriage. Further, because more cohabiting couples of color have greater rates of childbearing than their white counterparts, some social scientists are coming to see them as another family form rather than a prelude to marriage (McLanahan and Casper, 1995). Another category views their living arrangement as an alternative to marriage. Included in this category are those who have had negative experiences with marriage (Tanfer, 1987). A 39-year-old cohabiting architect reflects this viewpoint:

> I am very cautious about marriage, having grown up around a not very pretty one. I am a tad cynical and a tad rebellious. I am not sure what I am rebelling against, but I really don't see a need for marriage. That isn't a statement about my feelings about the relationship, because there is no less strength of commitment. (Quoted in Steinhauer, 1995: A9)

Given these reasons for and types of cohabitation, what, then, is gained or risked by living together?

Advantages and Disadvantages of Cohabitation

Among the most commonly reported advantages of living together are better understanding of self; greater knowledge of what is involved in living with another person; increased interpersonal skills, especially communication and problem-solving skills; increased emotional maturity; better understanding of marital expectations; companionship; and the sharing of economic and domestic responsibilities. Although expenses may be shared, cohabitating couples are less likely than married couples to pool all their financial resources, preferring to maintain more independence.

Cohabitation is not without its problems, however. Among the disadvantages cohabitants report are lack of social support for their relationship, which for some contributes to a sense of guilt about their lifestyle; conflict with their partner over domestic tasks; the potential instability of the relationship; loss or curtailment of other relationships; differing expectations with partner; legal ambiguity; and the emotional trauma of breaking up (Stinnet and Birdsong, 1978; Newcomb, 1979; Steinhauer, 1995). Additionally, more recent research shows that there is often less sexual fidelity between cohabiting couples than between married couples, and cohabiting couples report less sexual fidelity and lower levels of happiness and sexual satisfaction than their married peers (Waite and Joyner, 1996; Amato and Booth, 1997).

Gender role expectations may also play a role in the degree of satisfaction with the cohabiting experience. In contrast to their married counterparts, cohabiting men are more likely to be unemployed, whereas cohabiting women are more likely to be employed (Fields and Casper, 2001). Furthermore, some women in cohabitating relationships report feeling used when their partner gives no indication of making a marital commitment (Shelton and John, 1993). This is not an uncommon response, since women are more likely to view cohabitation as a trial marriage, while men are more likely to desire sexual intimacy apart from any marital considerations.

Finally, cohabiting couples, especially younger couples, experience a higher rate of violent behavior than do married couples (Stets, 1991; Cunningham and Antill, 1995). Similarly, a study comparing 21-year-old females and males in dating and cohabiting relationships found that cohabitants were almost twice as likely as daters to be abusive toward their partners (Magdol, Moffitt, and Caspi, 1998). Although we don't have data on child abuse in cohabiting households in the United States, a study in Britain found that children living with cohabiting couples are 20 times more likely to be victims than children living with married parents. If the mother is living with a man who is not the father, the child's risk of abuse is even higher (Madigan, 1999). A variety of reasons contribute to this higher rate of violence: economic difficulties, isolation from family and friends, and differing levels of emotional involvement in the relationship.

Once again, we must not assume that each cohabiting individual experiences all of these advantages and disadvantages in the same way. The data on cohabitation, however, seem to suggest that regardless of the outcome, most individuals feel that they learned something from the experience. Furthermore, because cohabitation has become more widespread, it is likely that fewer individuals now experience a sense of guilt about their living arrangement. For some couples, however, living together may go counter to their religious upbringing or to parental values; thus, their adoption of this lifestyle may trouble them. Such feelings may be intensified if a couple hides from family or friends the fact that they are living together.

Cohabitation and the Division of Labor

How do cohabitants go about the daily tasks of living? Do they behave differently from their married peers? Research suggests that the differences are relatively minor. For example, a Canadian study of cohabiting couples found that they were only slightly more likely to have a more equitable but not equal division of household tasks (Wu, 2000). Their U.S. counterparts also divide housework a bit more equitably and enjoy more similar earnings than married couples (Brines and Joyner, 1999). However, despite the fact that many couples may start out sharing household tasks, over time traditional gender roles emerge, with women assuming a larger share of the cooking and cleaning. Numerous other studies have found more traditional patterns. Philip Blumstein and Pepper Schwartz (1983) reported that even when women worked full-time and earned as much as their partners, they did more of the housework. This is not unlike patterns found among married couples. Sociologists Beth Shelton and Daphne John (1990) analyzed data from the national survey of families and households, comparing cohabiting and married couples, and found that although cohabiting women may do less housework than their married peers, there was no difference between the amount of time married and cohabiting men devoted to housework or child care. This inequity in the household division of labor is often a source of conflict for cohabiting couples, just as it is for married couples, especially when both partners are working (see Chapter 10).

Cohabitation and Marital Stability

Earlier in this chapter we noted that one of the reasons cohabitants give for living together is that they want to test their relationship for marital compatibility. Thus, this becomes a critical research question. Is cohabitation a good predictor of marital success? To date the research in this regard has yielded some contradictory findings. Some researchers have found that cohabitants who married are more likely to remain together than are noncohabitants (White, 1987); other researchers have taken a "neutral" position, concluding that cohabitation has no clear effect on marital success or satisfaction (Watson and DeMeo, 1987). Despite these findings, the weight of the evidence seems to be that couples who engage in premarital cohabitation run a greater risk of divorce than do couples who do not cohabit prior to marriage (Axinn and Thornton, 1992; Balaguer and Markman, 1994; Hall and Zhao, 1995; Bumpass and Lu, 2000). Researchers found that premarital cohabitation was a significant risk factor for marital instability among Canadian couples as well (Wu and Penning, 1997). Obviously, more research needs to be done in this area, but there are several likely explanations for the higher divorce risk of premarital cohabitants. It may well be that some cohabitants engage in behavior that in the long run is detrimental to marriage. For example, in the cohabitive situation they may put their best foot forward and share household responsibilities on an equitable basis. After exchanging marriage vows, however, one or both partners may, without consciously realizing it, change role expectations and fall back on traditional patterns in the division of household labor. There may be outside pressure as well. Parents and friends may be tolerant of a "live-in lover" because they don't want to jeopardize the possibility of marriage. After marriage they may feel free to say or do things that could cause conflict between the now-married couple. Self-selection may also play a role. Cohabitants may hold more nontraditional views on marriage and therefore be more accepting of divorce (DeMaris and MacDonald, 1993). Finally, people who cohabit may be less concerned about homogamous factors (see Chapter 5) in partner choice (Schoen and Weinick, 1993).

Cohabitation: International Perspectives

The United States is not alone in experiencing increasing rates of cohabitation. In fact, most other industrialized countries have higher rates than the United States. One in every seven families in Canada was formed by the decision to cohabit (Wu, 2000). Approximately 25 percent of all couples in Sweden are not legally married, and almost all couples live together before getting married. Denmark follows close behind; 80 percent of its adult population has cohabited at some point in time. Austria, France, Germany, and the Netherlands all have higher rates of cohabitation than the United States. Adults in Latin American and Caribbean countries, including Ecuador, Venezuela, Panama, Cuba, and the Dominican Republic, are also likely to cohabit. China, too, has high rates of cohabitation, particularly in rural areas and among people too young to meet the legal requirements for marriage (Neft and Levine, 1997).

APPLYING THE SOCIOLOGICAL IMAGINATION

WHAT WENT WRONG?

Judy and Jim met at work. Judy, 23, worked in the personnel department, and Jim, 25, worked in the accounting office. They had many interests in common and soon started to date. After six months of dating, they fell in love. Neither felt ready for marriage, but they wanted to be together, so Judy moved in with Jim. At first, Judy's parents were upset by this arrangement and refused to go over to Judy and Jim's apartment when invited. However, after Judy told her parents that she and Jim planned to marry in the future, her parents had a change of heart, deciding that because Jim would be their son-in-law some day they should get to know him. Jim's parents divorced when he was 10. His mother is remarried and lives in another state. Jim rarely sees his father. From the start, Jim's mother approved of his living arrangement and told Jim that it was better to find out how well you get along with someone before risking marriage.

After living together successfully for two years, Judy and Jim decided to get married and start a family. After three years of marriage, however, they are experiencing problems. Judy complains that Jim has changed, that he hardly does anything around the house now. Judy feels that since they got married she is the one doing all the housework. Now she's taking care of a baby and working, too. Jim feels that all Judy does now is complain and that she's not the fun-loving girl that he married. He blames some of their problems on Judy's parents. He says that before he and Judy were married, they saw Judy's parents only occasionally. Now he claims they are over every week and that Judy's mother is always criticizing the way they take care of the baby. Judy and Jim have discussed a divorce, but because of the baby, they agreed to try counseling before making any final decision.

What do you think happened to Judy and Jim's relationship? Why were they able to have a successful cohabitive relationship and yet have a rocky marital relationship? What prediction would you make about their future? How typical do you think their problems are of couples who cohabit before marriage? What steps might they take to save their marriage?

These patterns of cohabitation are longstanding and seem to represent a substitute for marriage for many of these couples. Government policies in these countries may contribute to people's willingness to cohabit. For example, in Sweden and Norway, all parents, regardless of marital status, are eligible to receive a children's allowance from their respective governments. Further, many of these countries now provide benefits, such as insurance or pension rights, to cohabiting couples. Some have laws regulating the distribution of property in the event of a breakup. Finally, even though social acceptance of cohabitation is gaining in the United States, social approval for such relationships remains much higher in these other countries (Neft and Levine, 1997).

Cohabitation and the Law

Cohabitation, like singlehood, can be temporary and fluid. Many cohabitants are together for only short periods of time. Half break up in a year or less, after which couples either marry or go their separate ways (Bumpass and Lu, 2000). Cohabitants end their relationship for many reasons: growing apart, loss of interest, unequal commitment, value conflicts, outside pressures, or the need to relocate because of college graduation or a new job (Buunk and van Driel, 1989). Unlike the thinking underlying a legal marriage, one assumption underlying cohabitation is that you are free to leave whenever the relationship becomes unsatisfactory. However, Zheng Wu (1995) found that cohabiting couples with children in the relationship are less likely to experience union disruption than are childless couples. A possible explanation for this finding is that sharing child-rearing responsibilities may cause couples to work harder to maintain the relationship. Nevertheless, about 75 percent of children born to cohabiting parents will see their cohabiting parents break up before they reach 16, whereas only about 33 percent of the children born to married parents will experience such a breakup.

What happens, however, when cohabitants terminate a relationship? Who gets the apartment? The stereo? Can cohabitants expect compensation for their unpaid work or other contributions while living together? What are the legal aspects of cohabitation? Even though you do not need a court decree to stop living together, there may be legal ramifications to ending a cohabitive relationship. Former live-in partners may file suit for what has come to be called **palimony,** a payment similar to alimony and based on the existence of a contract (written or implied) between the partners regarding aspects of their relationship. For example, if there was a promise of future marriage, of an economic partnership, or of support for a child, courts may hold a partner responsible for legally fulfilling these obligations (Seff, 1995).

Domestic Partnerships So far we have been talking about what happens when cohabitants break up. However, a number of other areas to consider when living together could also have legal implications. For example, who is to be the beneficiary with regard to insurance and wills? Sometimes insurance companies require the beneficiary to have a conventional family tie. You cannot assume that because you live with someone you will be covered by her or his car or renter's insurance. Health benefits are problematic as well.

Some of this is changing as some communities and organizations make provisions for extending benefits generally reserved for married employees to other employees involved in what have come to be known as **domestic partnerships,** a term referring to unmarried couples who live together and share housing and financial responsibilities. Numerous cities, counties, and states have passed legislation that provides some degree of civil-rights protection for lesbians and gays. Although still relatively few in number, a growing list of nonprofit organizations and private sector employers now recognize some form of domestic partnership, although the rights and benefits involved in these arrangements vary from place to place. Generally, to gain benefits such as health insurance, family and funeral leave, family membership rates, and inheritance protection, couples are required to register their partnership. Such registration provides public recognition of the union, thereby granting it a degree of legitimacy. Some agencies, however, restrict partnership benefits to those of the same sex, arguing that heterosexual partners can marry if they wish to receive such benefits. Currently, only seven countries and the state of Vermont give recognition to homosexual marriages (in the form of "registered partnerships"). When Hawaii's Supreme Court considered the legalization of same-sex marriages in that state, some 28 states and the federal government passed laws that would block recognition of same-sex marriages should another state permit them. Recent polls indicate that the majority of adult Americans disapprove of same-sex sexual practices and oppose gay marriages ("Homosexuality," 1997). The lack of legal recognition of their union is particularly difficult for lesbians and gays who want to join a partner who has migrated to another country. Laws governing residence of a partner from another country most frequently require a blood or marital relationship, thus excluding homosexual couples (Binnie, 1997).

Further, without such recognition cohabiting partners may have little to say in the medical treatment or other affairs of their partner. In case of death, who is to inherit property? Without a properly executed will, the state makes this determination, and the decision will likely favor family members over live-in partners. You can't automatically claim ownership to any property that does not bear your name even if you helped pay for it. The status of children can be ambiguous in cohabitive relationships as well. If the biological parent dies and there is no provision for naming the live-in partner the legal guardian, again the court may decide the matter. Often it does so contrary to the wishes of the cohabitants. These are just a few of the items that cohabitants need to consider as they establish their living arrangements. Unless they have made a binding agreement, cohabitants may have no legal rights in these matters.

Over the past several decades, the struggle over lesbian and gay rights has become a recurrent issue on the political scene. Protests against homophobia such as that by members of the Irish Lesbian and Gay Organization (ILGO) along Fifth Avenue during the St. Patrick's Day Parade in New York City are common around the country.

LESBIAN AND GAY RELATIONSHIPS

Some of the legal issues we have just discussed concerning cohabitants apply to lesbian and gay relationships as well. As with our discussion of heterosexual cohabitants, our focus here is primarily on social relationships constructed by lesbian and gay couples.

Homosexual behavior has existed throughout history and in every known culture. Nevertheless, cultures have varied considerably in their attitudes toward this behavior. Certain peoples in Melanesia, Central Africa, and Egypt viewed sexual relationships between older and younger males as part of the normal socialization process. Similarly, records of classical Greece and Rome reveal acceptance of same-sex bonding for men. Historians know less about women's relationships during this period but have discovered some evidence that female same-sex bonding occurred then, too.

In U.S. society, homosexuality historically has been considered a form of deviant behavior. Medical research into this "disorder" focused on its causes, with the emphasis on discovering a "cure." Among the treatments used to effect a "cure" were castration, hysterectomy, electric shock treatment, lobotomy, and estrogen and testosterone injections (Harvey, 1992). During the twentieth century, some of these negative attitudes began to change. Lesbians and gays began to organize to challenge laws and customs discriminating against them and condemning their behaviors. Although initially these groups were predominantly white, several African American, Asian American, and Latina/o organizations have emerged since the 1970s. In 1973, an important step in the redefinition of homosexual behavior occurred when the American Psychiatric Association removed homosexuality from its list of psychiatric disorders. Current research shows that lesbians and gays are no more likely to have psychological problems than are heterosexuals, except when they experience the pressure of social rejection (Reinisch, 1990). The lesbian and gay struggle for acceptance and equal opportunity promises to be a major social movement.

Methodological Issues

Earlier in the chapter we noted the methodological problems surrounding the study of singlehood and heterosexual cohabitation. Similar problems of small, unrepresentative samples also limit the study of homosexual behavior. In addition, the long tradition of homophobia in the United States has kept many homosexual people from revealing their sexual orientation and from participating in research studies. Studies with small samples of Asian Americans (Liu and Chan, 1996), Latinas/os (Morales, 1996), and African Americans (Green and Boyd-Franklin, 1996) suggest that people of color may be even more reluctant to identify themselves as lesbian or gay because of the intense cultural disapproval of homosexuality in their respective communities.

Thus, they may find themselves caught between two communities, facing double or even triple stigmatization with the potential for losing support in both the lesbian/gay community and in their gender/ethnic/racial community. For example, an African American may feel excluded from the gay community because of racism and rejected in the African American community because of homophobia. An Asian American female who interacts in the lesbian community may have to distance herself from her cultural community in order to avoid bringing shame and humiliation to her family.

Among many of these cultures, homosexuality is widely viewed as a white, Western phenomenon. This view may be changing, however, as evidenced in a survey by state psychologists in Nanjing, China. This survey, the first by the state since the Communists took power in 1949, concluded that China has "a sizable" lesbian and gay population and classified lesbians and gays as "normal" rather than mentally ill, as was believed to be true for years (Schmetzer, 1992).

There are many variations in lesbian and gay lifestyles. Some lesbians and gays live alone; others cohabitate. Some have been involved in heterosexual marriages—one study puts the number at 33 percent for lesbians and 20 percent for gay men (Harry, 1988). Our focus here is on cohabiting same-sex couples, of which the Census Bureau counted 1.5 million in 1993 (Saluter, 1994). Additionally, many lesbians and gays are parents and grandparents. Some had their children when they were part of a heterosexual union; others elected to have children outside of a biological relationship through artificial insemination. Lesbian and gay parenting is discussed in Chapter 9.

Demystifying Lesbian and Gay Relationships

What images do you have of lesbian and gay cohabitants? No doubt you are aware of some of the many stereotypes about lesbians and gays. Among the most prevalent images are those depicting lesbians as masculine or "butch" and gay men as effeminate. The major stereotypes involving cohabiting same-sex couples assume that these couples imitate heterosexual patterns, with one partner acting as "wife" (submissive female) and the other playing the "husband" (dominant male). Research, however, shows that these stereotypes apply to only a small minority of same-sex relationships, those in which partners tend to be older, male, and from lower socioeconomic and educational levels (Bell and Weinberg, 1978; Peplau and Gordon, 1983; Harry, 1984). In fact, most lesbians and gays feel negatively about such role playing (Jay and Young, 1977).

Richard Higginbotham (1991) argues that the problem with using the marriage model in studying lesbian and gay relationships is that it brings with it a set of expectations and norms that simply do not correlate with the realities of a same-sex relationship. Some researchers suggest that a friendship model, albeit with erotic and romantic elements, provides lesbians and gays with guidelines for their intimate relationships (Harry and DeVall, 1978). The difference between the two models is that the norms for friendship assume that partners will be relatively equal in status and power, as contrasted with traditional heterosexual marriage scripts, in which the husband is assumed to be the head of the family (Peplau and Gordon, 1983). What, then, are lesbian and gay relationships like? Research comparing lesbian, gay, and heterosexual couples found no differences either in relationship satisfaction or in degree of conflict over power, personal flaws, or intimacy issues (Peplau, 1991; Kurdek, 1994).

U.S. Representative Barney Frank, a Democrat from Massachusetts, openly acknowledges his homosexuality and provides a strong voice on behalf of equality and dignity for all people.

Living Together: Domestic Tasks, Finances, and Decision Making

Because traditional gender distinctions are irrelevant to same-sex relationships, lesbian and gay couples are in a unique position to create living arrangements tailored to their needs and interests. How, then, do same-sex couples resolve the day-to-day requirements of living? Research shows that there is considerable discussion and conscious joint decision making in these areas (Harry, 1984). One study found that over half of both lesbians and gays in the sample reported sharing housework equally (Bell and Weinberg, 1978). Sociologists Philip Blumstein and Pepper Schwartz (1983) found several factors that affect the division of household tasks. Among gay couples the number of hours spent at work determines the relative contribution of each partner—the one with the fewer outside hours does more of the household tasks. There were some constraints on this pattern, however. For example, these authors found that "both heterosexual and homosexual men feel that a successful partner should not have to do housework" (1983:151). Among lesbians, preference and ability as well as the number of hours worked provide guidelines for the division of household labor. Lesbian couples work harder than either gay or heterosexual couples to create an equitable distribution of tasks.

Decision making, like housework, is often related to income; that is, the partner with the highest income tends to have the most power. In a comparative study of heterosexual and same-sex couples, Blumstein and Schwartz (1983) found this to be true for gay and heterosexual couples but not for lesbian couples. In this same study lesbian respondents reported less conflict over finances than did other couples. Among both heterosexual and gay couples, partners who feel they have equal control over how money is spent have a more tranquil relationship. Other researchers have reported equality in decision making for both lesbian and gay couples (Peplau and Cochran, 1981; Harry, 1982; Kurdek and Schmitt, 1986).

The Social and Legal Context of Lesbian and Gay Relationships

Lesbians and gays must deal with the same issues of living together that heterosexuals do: how to divide housework, decision making, and finances. "Couplehood, either as a reality or as an aspiration, is as strong among gay people as it is among heterosexuals" (quoted in Blumstein and Schwartz, 1983:45). Research comparing lesbians and gays with heterosexuals finds no significant differences regarding couple adjustment, feelings of attachment, caring, or intimacy (Cardell, Finn, and Marecek, 1981). Lesbians and gays, like their heterosexual counterparts, experience the same fears of rejection, the same relationship problems, and the same problems with sexual functioning (Reinisch, 1990). As our discussion indicates, same-sex couples experience the same disadvantages and advantages of cohabitation as heterosexual couples do. The average length of a gay cohabiting relationship is two to three years, and somewhat higher for lesbian cohabitants (Harry, 1983; Buunk and van Driel, 1989). In contrast to heterosexual couples, when lesbian and gay partners break up, they often maintain a close relationship with one another by making a transition from being lovers to being friends, and they often continue these relationships for many years (Weston, 1991). This finding is particularly significant given that these relationships exist in a society that remains largely intolerant of their lifestyle.

Many people in the United States still consider homosexuality to be abnormal or sinful. Prejudice against lesbians and gays is particularly strong among men, suburbanites, and older adults (Blum, 1997; Wolfe, 1998). Like heterosexual cohabitants, lesbians and gays in long-term relationships are generally denied legal and financial benefits such as community property rights, insurance coverage, tax breaks, leaves for the sickness or funeral of a partner, and inheritance protection.

For most lesbians and gays, coming out of the closet begins by telling a few close family members and friends. For comedian Ellen DeGeneres, coming out was a very public affair. She made television history in 2000 when she (and her television character) revealed that she was a lesbian.

A major arena in which lesbians and gays experience discriminatory treatment is in the workplace, where sexual orientation is often used to screen out applicants. For example, the U.S. government still uses sexual orientation to deny security clearance to lesbians and gays. This restriction continues to exist despite the fact that a large body of research shows that lesbians and gays are no more likely than heterosexuals to suffer from personality disorders or stress or to be psychologically unstable (Herek, 1990). Although lesbians and gays have long served in the U.S. armed forces, any open acknowledgment (or even suspicion of) one's homosexuality could result in a dishonorable discharge. In 1993 President Clinton announced he would work with Pentagon and congressional leaders to end discrimination against lesbians and gays in the military. Although the resulting "don't ask, don't tell" policy adopted by the military was intended to be less punitive than past policy, it still denies gays and lesbians equal treatment with their heterosexual counterparts. Nevertheless, in 2000 the armed forces discharged 1212 lesbians and gays, a 17 percent increase from the previous year and nearly double the number in 1993, the last year before the current policy went into effect (Marquis, 2001). Other industrialized countries have moved closer to full equality. In October 1992, Canada's Department of National Defense ended that country's practice of barring gays and lesbians from the armed forces.

Lesbians and gays also confront other problems because of their sexual orientation. They are often the victims of name-calling, ridicule, and even violence. The incidence of "gay bashing" has been increasing in U.S. society over the last several years. In 1999, 1317 such incidents were reported to the FBI, up nearly 23 percent since 1995 (FBI, 1999). Violence against homosexuals is not confined to the United States. A report by Amnesty International documents abuses in 30 countries throughout Latin America, Eastern Europe, Africa, Asia, the Caribbean, and the Middle East. Egypt recently arrested and tried 52 men for suspected homosexual behavior (MacFarquhar, 2001). In Chechnya, under the Muslim Shari'a code, men can be executed for homosexual acts (Leland, 2001). Because of the extreme prejudice and violence directed against homosexuals in their native countries, the United States grants asylum to individuals when their sexual orientation poses a serious threat to their lives. All too often, however, the asylum seekers face further rejection from their fellow countrymen who have migrated to the United States, bringing homophobic attitudes with them.

In such a climate, it is easy to understand why many lesbians and gays keep their sexual orientation hidden. Those who "come out of the closet" and acknowledge their homosexuality risk discrimination and alienating their family and friends. Given this context, lesbians and gays often create kinship structures of friends and lovers who provide the social and emotional support traditionally expected of biological kin (Weston, 1991). Even with this support, the issue of

SOCIAL POLICY ISSUES

COMING OUT

The following conversation is based on an interview with a member of Parents and Friends of Lesbians and Gays. Think about how you might react if you were in Jane's situation.

Mary: When did you learn that your son is gay?

Jane: He told us his junior year in college. I'll never forget it. He was home for Thanksgiving, and we could tell something was bothering him, but he couldn't bring himself to tell us until the night before he went back to school. I think he was afraid of how we would react.

Mary: How did you react?

Jane: Not too well, I'm afraid. My husband and I were shocked. We wanted to deny it. [*Smiling*] We tried to tell him it was just a phase he was going through and that he'd get over it. After all, he dated all through high school; he even talked about getting married. So how could he be gay? We stayed up all night talking, and he finally made us realize that he is gay. He said he had known he was gay in high school but that he tried to deny it by doing all the macho things that men were supposed to do, but it did not work.

Mary: What happened after that?

Jane: We tried to be supportive when he left, but we were devastated. Ted [Jane's husband] cried. He couldn't accept it. We started to argue. We blamed ourselves and each other. We thought we must have done something wrong, that we failed our son somehow. Our hopes for grandchildren were gone. We felt embarrassed when friends asked us how Sam was doing. Sam didn't come home again for 6 months. I think he sensed our anguish. Things got so strained between my husband and me that we decided that if our marriage was to survive we had to get help. That was the turning point for us. We started reading books that the counselor recommended, and we joined a support group. There we found we were not alone; other parents were going through the same kind of adjustments we were. We were relieved to learn that we had done nothing wrong, that being gay is not a disease that needs a cure.

Mary: How are things today?

Jane: We have a good relationship with Sam. We like his friends, especially Tom, whom he's lived with for over 3 years now. But there's still a part of me that wishes it were different. I worry about AIDS, and I'm afraid for him. Too many people don't understand.

Why do you think Sam's parents had such a hard time believing their son is gay? How do you think your family and friends would react if someone in your family "came out of the closet"? What programs, if any, could be established to help parents and children through this initial disclosure?

closeting or "coming out" has implications for the kind of personal relationships that lesbians and gays establish. For example, a study of 124 lesbians involved in a couple relationship found that closeting often has a negative impact on the couple's relationship quality. If couples can be open with family and friends, the quality of their relationship is likely to be higher. In particular, family behaviors—such as inviting a member's lesbian partner to family events and accepting demonstrations of affection between the couple—can enhance their relationship (Caron and Ulin, 1997). These findings highlight the importance of support from family members (see "Social Policy Issues" box).

Research on "coming out" suggests that patterns of disclosure and subsequent family reactions vary considerably (Merighi and Grimes, 2000). For example, mothers are more often told than fathers (D'Augelli et al., 1998). Lesbians and gays perceived more rejection and disapproval from families with high traditional values (those that emphasized religion, heterosexual marriage, having children, in addition to having a non–English language spoken at home) than those from families with low traditional values (Newman and Muzzonigo, 1993). Although some parents react negatively and distance themselves from their children, others are very supportive. A number of supportive parents formed Parents and Friends of Lesbians and Gays (PFLAG), an international organization with about 350 chapters in the United States and 28 others around the world.

Life Satisfaction: Elderly Lesbians and Gays

Given the difficulties homosexuals still face in the United States, we might expect lesbians and gays, especially those who are older, to be dissatisfied with their lives. Studies do not bear this out, however (see, for example, Friend, 1990; Dorfman et al., 1995). Older gay men are generally well adjusted, experience high levels of life satisfaction, and are not isolated (Kelly, 1977). In fact, one investigator suggested that in some ways being homosexual may actually prepare men for old age (Berger, 1982). Because many gay men cannot look to a family of procreation for support, in contrast to heterosexual men they become more independent early on. Similarly, Monika Kehoe (1989) found that the majority of elderly lesbians in her study scored in the upper percentile on the Life Satisfaction Scale and felt positive about their lifestyle.

COMMUNAL LIVING AND GROUP MARRIAGE

Thus far, this chapter has focused primarily on single people who live alone or cohabit. Not everyone, however, is content to live alone or to cohabit with just one other person. Some people join a commune to satisfy their needs for intimacy and companionship.

A **commune** refers to a group of people (single or married, with or without children) who live together, sharing many aspects of their lives. Communes have existed from earliest times. In particular, they are likely to develop or expand in periods of political and social unrest (Mead, 1970). The communal movement in the United States originated around the end of the eighteenth century (Miller, 1998). Most of the early communes were religious in origin. Some, like the Shakers, named for the way they moved during prayer and song, believed that monogamous marriage and the nuclear family were detrimental to the spiritual health of the community. Thus, they required all members, whether married or not, to live celibate lives. Today, the Shaker community, located in Sabbathday Lake, Maine, consists of seven women and two men, ranging in age from 28 to 90, and they spend their days in prayer and work, often traveling throughout the country, visiting museums and art galleries to tell the Shaker story (Brotman, 1992). Marriage and sexual relationships took other forms in other of the early communes. The Mormons, for example, practiced polygyny. Still others engaged in free love whereby members could engage in sexual relationships with any other member of the group. The political instability in the years immediately preceding and following the Civil War produced about a hundred new communes. One of them, the Hutterites, a commune with a religious origin, still has members in the United States today. The economic turmoil of the 1930s and the political activism of the 1960s also led to new waves of communal development (Zablocki, 1980). It is estimated that there are over a thousand functioning communes worldwide (Springs, 1989). Among the better-known communes surviving in the United States are Sandhill in Missouri, Twin Oaks in Virginia, and The Farm in Tennessee (see the "Searching the Internet" box).

Children share a meal on an Israeli kibbutz. Adults in this communal organization share many tasks of daily living, including child care.

Advantages and Disadvantages of the Communal Lifestyle

Have you ever considered joining a commune or wondered what motivates someone to adopt such a lifestyle? Studies of communes suggest that their members are motivated by a desire for egalitarian, personalized, cooperative, and satisfying intimate relationships—qualities they perceive are not readily available in the traditional nuclear family structure.

Among the advantages most frequently reported by members of communes are close intimate relationships with a variety of people; personal growth through group experiences; the sharing of economic resources, domestic tasks, and child care; companionship; social support; spiritual rebirth or strengthening; and a respect and reverence for nature. These advantages also create some disadvantages, including limitations on privacy, restrictions on personal freedom, limitations on parental influence and control, lack of stability, legal ambiguity, financial problems, and the possibility of sexual jealousy (Cornfield, 1983; Thies, 2000).

Most communes last for only short periods of time. Many of the problems encountered in communes center on conflicts over power, authority, and ideology. Those communes that survive the longest share certain characteristics: religious orientation, strict admission requirements, strong member commitment, controls on sexuality, adequate financing, time and space for privacy, and clearly defined authority and distribution of tasks (Mowery, 1978; Zablocki, 1980; Cornfield, 1983).

Communes, Shared Housing, and the Future

As with other lifestyles, communes are not for everyone, and we can only speculate on their future viability. Some writers believe that if the economy worsens or if new political turmoil develops, the number of communes will grow. Others predict that as populations age, some form of communal or group living will become a viable option for the elderly who otherwise might be forced to live alone (Dressel and Hess, 1983). There is some indication that this pattern is already well underway. For example, there has been a rapid growth of communes of elderly people in the Netherlands (Baars

SEARCHING THE INTERNET

THE FARM
SUMMERTOWN, TENNESSEE, USA
FREQUENTLY ASKED QUESTIONS

Q. What is The Farm?

A. The Farm community is a cooperative enterprise of families and friends living on three square miles in southern middle Tennessee. We started The Farm in the hope of establishing a strongly cohesive, outwardly-directed community, a base from which we could, by action and example, have a positive effect on the world as a whole.

The Farm is a human scale, full featured settlement founded by Stephen Gaskin, and 320 San Francisco hippies in 1971 as an experiment in sustainable, developmentally progressive human habitat.

http://www.thefarm.org/general/farmfaq.html

and Thomese, 1994). Here in the United States, one organization, the National Shared Housing Resource Center in Baltimore, a clearinghouse that helps people find ways to maintain their independence by living interdependently with others, keeps tabs on 350 shared-housing programs in 42 states. Shared housing usually takes one of two forms: group homes, in which several people share a residence, or matchups, where a homeowner and a home seeker agree to live together. Some programs are open only to the elderly; others are intergenerational.

Other experiments in cooperative living are also emerging. Two architects, Katie McCamant and Chuck Durret, intrigued by community developments in Denmark, founded the CoHousing Company in Berkeley, California, to introduce the idea in the United States. The concept of cohousing, or as some call it, "intentional neighborhood," is characterized by individuals or families living in their own private, self-sufficient units, but also sharing common spaces—a large dining room and kitchen, a garden, workshops, and a children's play area. Thus, members can share responsibilities like cooking and child care. Other benefits include ongoing support and companionship. Chicago's Natalie Salmon House is home to 38 low-income elderly, 6 low-income families, including 12 children between the ages of 5 and 18, and 7 college students ("Multigenerational Community," 1997). If forms of shared housing are to be a viable option, however, critical issues of social policy will have to be reexamined. For example, many zoning laws restrict residential occupancy to individuals who meet the traditional definition of family. Such policies exclude the possibility of "nontraditional" households developing in many areas.

Group Marriages

Group marriages represent a variation of communal living. Sociologists Larry and Joan Constantine (1973:29) define **group marriage** as "a marriage of at least four people, two female and two male, in which each partner is married to all partners of the opposite sex." The actual number of documented group marriages has been small. One of the best-known experiments with group marriage was the Oneida Community in New York, founded by the Protestant minister John Noyes. It lasted from 1849 to 1881 and had about 300 adult members. Monogamous marriage and sexual exclusivity were not permitted. Children were reared in a communal nursery by specialized caretakers, and they were taught to consider all adults in the community as parents. Thus, the entire community was to be viewed as a single family. Hostile outside pressure contributed to the demise of this experiment in group marriage (Kephart, 1988).

No one knows for sure how many group marriages currently exist in the United States. Because group marriages are neither legal nor socially acceptable to most Americans, locating them is a difficult task. The Constantines studied group marriages in the 1970s and believed that there were less than a thousand such marriages, perhaps even fewer than a hundred (Constantine and Constantine, 1972). The most commonly reported reason respondents gave for their involvement with group marriages was their dissatisfaction with traditional monogamous marriage. However, the Constantines found a high rate of breakup among the group marriages they located; the ones they studied lasted on the average only 16 months.

WRITING YOUR OWN SCRIPT

THE MARITAL DECISION

Do I want to marry? The answer to this question represents one of the most fundamental choices we will make in our lifetime. As we saw in this chapter, people are more likely today than in the past to consider alternatives to traditional marriage. Nevertheless, pressure to marry remains intense, especially for young adults. The United States is still one of the most marrying societies in the world. Although increasing numbers of individuals are not marrying at all, delaying marriage to a later age, and divorcing at high rates, demographers predict that nine out of ten people born in the United States in recent years will marry at least once in their lifetime. Thus, one must weigh the merits of alternative lifestyles.

Questions to consider *If I decide not to marry, is this a permanent decision or will I reevaluate this decision at some later time? What lifestyle will I choose? Will I cohabit with a partner or live alone? What are the advantages and disadvantages of a single or nonmarried lifestyle? If I choose not to marry will I be sexually active or remain celibate?*

SUMMARY

Over the last several decades the number of never-married people in the United States has grown. This increase is not a new phenomenon. Rather, it represents a return to historically higher levels of singlehood, which began to decline markedly only after 1940. In the past singlehood was a devalued status, and single people were often the objects of ridicule. Today there is greater acceptance of single people. Singlehood can be voluntary or involuntary, temporary or permanent. Singles engage in a variety of lifestyles. Some live alone, others live with relatives or friends, and some choose to cohabit.

In the past, cohabitation, or "living together," was more common among the poor. Today's cohabitants include people of all ages, races, and classes. Cohabitation, like living alone, can be temporary and fluid. For many, cohabitation has become an extension of the dating process. The number of unmarried-couple households has increased from 439,000 in 1960 to over 4.5 million in 1999. Cohabitation is similar to marriage in that couples create emotional and physical relationships with each other, and in some cases they also bear or rear children. It differs from marriage, however, in that it lacks formal legal, cultural, and religious support. Some couples choose to cohabit prior to marriage. The weight of research findings on the relationship of cohabitation to marital stability indicates that it increases the risk of divorce.

Some communities now allow lesbian, gay, and heterosexual cohabitants to register as domestic partners and receive some of the same benefits that married couples do. Lesbians and gays deal with the same issues of living together as heterosexuals: household division of labor, decision making, and finances. Additionally, however, they confront discrimination and social disapproval of their lifestyle.

Some individuals, seeking an alternative to traditional marriage, join a commune or participate in a group marriage. These arrangements generally meet with disapproval from the larger community, and most are relatively short-lived.

KEY TERMS

push/pull factors
common-law marriage
palimony
domestic partnership
commune
group marriage

QUESTIONS FOR STUDY AND REFLECTION

1. Identify and discuss the structural changes that have led to the increase in nonmarital lifestyles. What are some of the problems people face when they live a nontraditional lifestyle? What advice would you give to someone whose lifestyle meets with social disapproval?

2. Compare and contrast the legal status of married couples with that of cohabitants. What do you see as the advantages or disadvantages of the concept of domestic partnership? Do you favor or oppose granting domestic partnership status to heterosexual cohabitants? To homosexual cohabitants? What impact, if any, would this have on our understanding of marriages and families? Explain your position.
3. As noted earlier in this chapter, gay bashing, or attacks that are now called hate crimes, are on the increase. Has there been any such behavior on your campus, in your workplace, neighborhood, or city? What causes or triggers this behavior? What steps can be taken to minimize the likelihood of hate crimes from taking place in your immediate environments?
4. People who join communes often express dissatisfaction with traditional marriages. Can communal living provide a satisfying alternative lifestyle? What kinds of people join communes? How do they earn their living? How do they raise their children? What kind of governance structures do communes have? To find answers to these and other questions you might have about communes, search the Internet. A good starting point is the home page of The Farm, a nondenominational cooperative enterprise *http://www.thefarm.org/index.html.* Information on other intentional communities can be found by visiting *http://www.ic.org.* Now that you have discovered more about communal living, do you think you would ever want to live in a commune?

ADDITIONAL RESOURCES

SOCIOLOGICAL

GORDON, TUULA. 1994. *Single Women: On the Margins?* New York: New York University Press. Based on interviews with single women in the United States and Europe, it reveals a range of diverse lifestyles among this population.

PITZER, DONALD E., ED. 1997. *America's Communal Utopias.* Chapel Hill: University of North Carolina Press. This book, consisting of 18 essays, provides an introduction to the interesting history of American communal experiments some of which continue to thrive today.

SULLIVAN, ANDREW. 1995. *Virtually Normal: An Argument about Homosexuality.* New York: Knopf. A well-thought-out reflection on how society should deal with homosexuality.

WAITE, L. J., C. BACHRACH, M. HINDIN, E. THOMSON, AND A. THORNTON, EDS. 2000. *The Ties That Bind: Perspectives on Marriage and Cohabitation.* New York: Aldine de Gruyter. A readable volume that provides an excellent summary of recent data and current thinking on trends in marriage and cohabitation in the United States and Europe.

LITERARY

KINGSOLVER, BARBARA. 1993. *Pigs in Heaven.* New York: HarperCollins. A single woman finds and then adopts (perhaps illegally) a Cherokee child called Turtle and is faced with the possibility of losing her when a Native American lawyer enters the case.

BINCHY, MAEVE. 1992. *The Lilac Bus.* New York: Dell. Eight intriguing never-married women's and men's lives unfold as they ride the special Lilac Bus from Dublin to their families' homes for the weekend.

INTERNET

http://www.ngltf.org The National Gay and Lesbian Task Force provides data on lesbian and gay issues and links to other resources.

http://www.lifetimetv.com/shows/lifetime_live/050100_dunleavy.html This popular site examines issues that relate to personal relationships and the single life.

Chapter 8

The Marriage Experience

IN THE NEWS: **CAMBRIDGE, MASSACHUSETTS**

Detective novelist Robert B. Parker and his wife, Joan, have forged a living arrangement that many couples only dream about: his and hers apartments united by a single roof. The Parkers have been married now for almost 50 years. They have raised two children, and for the last 14 years have worked together turning his famous detective novels into television movies. He not only dedicates his books to her but she also appears in them, thinly veiled, as a major character. So how did they arrive at a divided household? Almost 20 years ago, the couple separated and considered divorce. However, after intensive psychotherapy they decided not to end their marriage. So they reunited in a loving monogamous relationship or, as they explain it, they "embarked upon their second marriage." They ended their suburban lifestyle and bought two separate condominiums. However, they soon realized that this living arrangement was not working for them. It did not afford them the intimate things they liked so much about living together. So they found a 14-room, 3-story Victorian house, big enough to let them establish their present lifestyle: two homes within one house, separated by an exterior stairway. This living arrangement allows the couple, who have different personalities (she is very outgoing and social, and he is a loner), to be together but apart.

Initially, with some renovation, Ms. Parker had a full four-room apartment on the third floor, Mr. Parker's full apartment was on the second floor, and the first floor was for entertaining guests. When the couple wanted to get together for a romantic dinner, they met at her place or his. In 1998, after Mr. Parker had knee surgery, Ms. Parker reconfigured their living arrangement once again. Three years and $1 million later, the couple has two new apartments and a new addition on the back of the house. His apartment is now on the first floor, her apartment was moved to the second floor, and the third floor is large enough that the Parkers use it not only for their frequent dinner parties but also for overnight guests. The first and second floor apartments open onto two ornately paneled atriums, one on top of the other. All three floors are brimming with family photos, as well as flea market finds and precious antiques. The Parkers also have her and his dogs; hers is a miniature English bull terrier and his is a German short-haired pointer.

According to the Parkers, their unusual living arrangement lets them avoid battles over little things, like whether to have guests for dinner and when to work, while at the same time it allows them to share their interests in the arts and their family. Mr. Parker says that he and his wife are amazingly in tune on big issues but incompatible on the creature-comfort level. The Parkers also work together, a strain on any relationship, collaborating on television screenplays. She adapts his novels, working alone in her apartment, and he edits and polishes what she does downstairs in his apartment. Then they get together to work out the details. Although they live in separate quarters they remain loving, friendly, and quite close (Diesenhouse, 2001).

WHAT WOULD YOU DO? If you were (are) married and found that you and your partner deeply loved each other but could not live together under the same roof, what would you do? Would you seek a divorce, or would you do as the Parkers did and create a her and his house divided but together under one roof? Can you think of other creative ways that you might deal with such a situation?

Deciding whether to marry is one of the most important decisions we will make in our lifetime. This decision has implications for almost every aspect of an individual's life. Although U.S. society has experienced a significant rise in the divorce rate, in the number of couples who cohabit, and in the number of people who choose either to delay marriage or not to marry at all, most people in the United States marry at least once in their lifetime. And approximately one-half of those marriages will last until one of the partners dies (Bedard, 1992). Surveys and other research continually reveal that Americans rank a good marriage at the top of their list of sources of satisfaction—above wealth, fame, good health, and a good job (Kidder, 1988; Glenn, 1999). In addition, some researchers (for example, Kain, 1990) have predicted that the rates for both marriage and remarriage will continue to remain high in the twenty-first century (see Chapter 13 for a full discussion of remarriage).

These facts notwithstanding, as pointed out in Chapter 7, people in the United States today have more options with regard to marital roles than they did in the past. The women's movement of the 1960s and 1970s has had a profound effect on social attitudes concerning the roles of women and men both inside and outside of marriages and families. Shifts in gender roles have altered not only how we view marriages and families but also how we experience them. In this chapter we examine the meaning of marriage in the United States in both traditional and contemporary terms. We pay particular attention to the legal aspects of marriage and their effect on marital relationships. In addition, we examine the nature of marriage relationships in the United States and the processes by which couples meet some of the many challenges of married life.

 WHY DO PEOPLE MARRY?

Why is it that amid much discussion and speculation about the decline in marriage and family values, millions of Americans continue to marry each year? What is so attractive about marriage? What does it offer that other lifestyles do not? Recall the discussion of love in Chapter 4, where we indicated that most people in the United States believe that romantic love and marriage naturally go together; that marriage naturally follows falling in love. Given this notion about the interrelationship of love and marriage it should not be surprising that the single most important reason that people give for getting married is that they are in love. After love comes companionship, followed by a desire to have children, happiness, money, convenience, dependence, and the fear of contracting AIDS (see Figure 8.1). For many people marriage is a formal way for a couple to express their love, devotion, and commitment to each other and share their lives with the person of their choice. In this respect, marriage represents both a private and a public statement of commitment, trust, sharing, stability, intimacy, and the expectation of a permanent relationship.

Figure 8.1

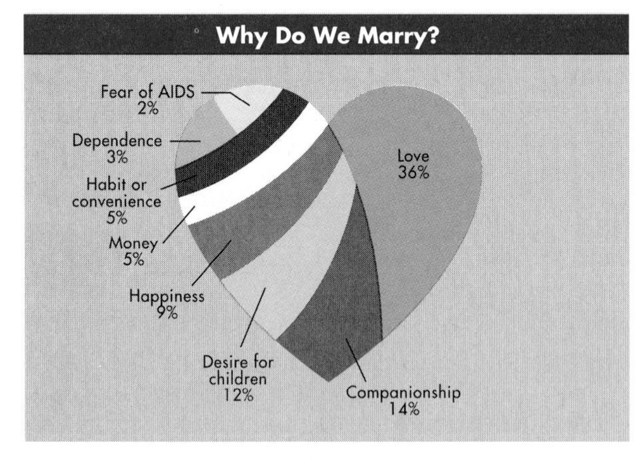

Source: Adapted from *The Day America Told the Truth* by James Patterson and Peter Kim. Copyright © 1991 by James Patterson and Peter Kim. Reprinted by permission of William Morris Agency, Inc. on behalf of the Author.

In a discussion of couples who had been married for a long time and who described their relationships as happy, *Christian Science Monitor* staff writer Rushworth Kidder (1988) reported that when asked why they married or what they thought marriage offered, these couples most frequently focused on commitment and sharing. For example, Hattie Wilkerson, a retired cook married 48 years, responded, "To share with each other." Her husband, Melvin, responded in terms of the commitment needed to sustain a marriage (1988:54). According to Kidder, these two ideas, in particular, sharing and commitment, are found throughout the responses of people who have strong marriages.

However, love and commitment are not key aspects of a durable and long-lasting marriage in all cultures. In Japan, for example, although marriages, on average, are long-lasting, many married couples live without love. In a feature article in the *New York Times,* Nicholas Kristof (1996) reported on a number of interviews with Japanese couples living in a small community 200 miles southeast of Tokyo. According to Kristof, happiness and love are not key aspects of a durable marriage in Japan. For example, when describing her 40-year marriage, a 72-year-old Japanese woman said: "There was never any love between me and my husband. But, well, we survived" (Kristof, 1996:1). According to this woman, her husband used to beat her; he has never even said he liked her, never held her hand, and has never shown her affection in any way. Japanese couples are often perplexed when asked about love in marriage. For example, when asked if he loved his wife, a Japanese man who had been married 33 years furrowed his brow and looked perplexed, then responded: "Yeah, so-so, I guess. She's like air or water. You couldn't live without it, but most of the time, you're not conscious of its existence" (Kristof, 1996:6).

This is a common theme in the narratives of the people Kristof spoke with. According to Kristof, it does not seem that Japanese marriages survive because wives and husbands love each other more than American couples, but rather because they perhaps love each other less. Many Japanese couples believe that love marriages are more fragile than arranged marriages. In love marriages, when something happens or if the couple falls out of love, they split up. Although the divorce rate in Japan is at a record high, it is still less than half that of the United States, and Japan is said to have one of the strongest marriage and family structures in the industrialized world.

While the traditional married couple household is disappearing throughout most of the world, Japan is a prominent exception. Yet couples neither marry for love nor live with it during much of their marital life. In fact, based on answers to survey questions about politics, sex, social issues, religion, and ethics, a Japanese research institute found Japanese couples to have the lowest level of compatibility than couples in 20 other countries (see Figure 8.2). The example of Japan raises the obvious questions about what love is, as defined by whom, and its relevance or relationship to marital longevity. In short, it directs our attention to the socially constructed nature of love.

In addition to love and commitment, particularly in the United States, a number of social and economic reasons motivate people to marry. For example, although marriage does not ensure companionship, most Americans perceive it to be the greatest benefit of marriage. Many people believe that being single inevitably leads to loneliness, even though there is no scientific evidence to support this view. In fact, some evidence suggests that people can be married and lonely; nonetheless, many people believe that marriage offers the best opportunity for steady companionship. In a recent survey of never-married adults, for instance, 75 percent of the women and 80 percent of the men reported that the thing they would miss most if they never married would be companionship (Coontz, 2000; Edwards, 2000).

Some people marry for personal fulfillment while some marry purely for financial reasons, although this is less true in the United States today than in the past. For some individuals, the acquisition, maintenance, or extension of wealth, power, and status are strong motivations to marry. Financial marital arrangements sometimes occur among the upper classes, who build their lives around highly selective social encounters and relationships. It is also relatively common among many recently arrived ethnic groups, whose subcultural norms may include arranged marriages, dowries, and bride prices.

Because social norms, values, and ideologies often equate adulthood with marriage, for some people, achieving adulthood means getting married. People whose religious beliefs prohibit sexual intercourse and living together outside of legal marriage marry to legitimize and sanctify their relationship. And some people marry because of peer or family pressure. Women in particular are often pressured to marry by well-meaning relatives and friends who do not want to see them end up as "lonely old maids." Finally, some people marry to give legitimacy to a sexual relationship or to cohabitation, and others marry primarily for reproductive reasons—they want to have children or heirs who are recognized as legitimate by the state. Although an increasing number of people are having children outside of legal marriage, most Americans indicate that they prefer to have children within the context of marriage.

Although in the United States we have considerable range to make a decision to marry or not, and although marriage is a personal choice and individual decision, larger sociopolitical and historical factors often shape our individual decisions of whether to marry. For example, economic factors are often key considerations. A variety of studies have indicated that during depressions and periods of high unemployment, men tend to put off getting married. However, when men have relatively good access to economic opportunities and resources they are more likely to make the decision to marry (Rodgers and Thornton, 1985; Landale and Tolnay, 1991). Women's decisions to marry, on the other hand, are impacted by economic forces in a number of ways. On the one hand, the more economically independent a woman is, the more likely she will postpone marriage until a later age. On the other hand, some researchers have suggested that when women work, they are more likely to meet eligible men, and their economic independence might be an attraction in the marriage market (Bianchi and Spain, 1986; Oropesa et al., 1994).

Figure 8.2

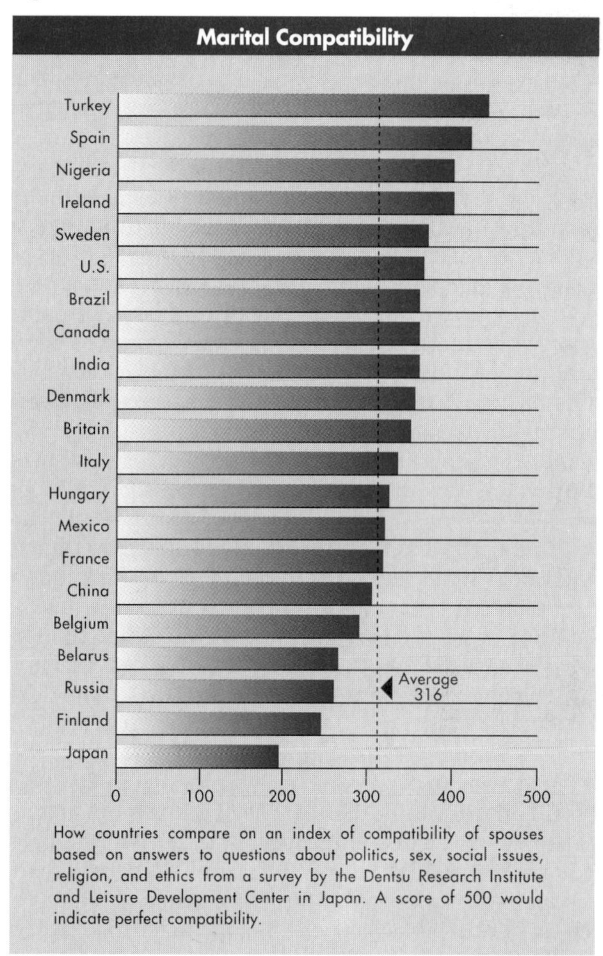

Source: Nicholas Kristof, 1996, "Who Needs Love? In Japan Many Couples Don't," *New York Times* (February 11): A6. Copyright © 1996 by The New York Times Co. Reprinted by permission.

Finally, race is an important sociopolitical construction that has a major impact on a person's decision of whether to marry. Several writers have suggested that the lack of employment opportunities, which hit poor people and people of color disproportionately, and the unlikeliness of a livable guaranteed minimum income often act as a deterrent to marriage. For example, the increasing economic marginality of many African American men has meant that marriage is often not a viable option. Given that men are still expected (consciously or unconsciously) to be the family "breadwinner," the disproportionately higher rates of African American male unemployment, sporadic or seasonal employment, and underemployment make marriage an unattractive proposition for many African American women and men (Taylor et al., 1990; Mason, 1996). In this context, it appears that among low-income African American men, many men tend to postpone marriage until they feel that they can support a family (fulfill the traditional "good provider" role).

Low income and economic marginality do not appear to affect the development and formation of intimate romantic relationships among these men, however. They become factors in the decision regarding marriage (Tucker and Taylor, 1989; DeVita, 1996). This finding is supported by research indicating that when there is economic prosperity among African Americans (for example, a high availability of jobs and/or when African American men have access to good-paying jobs), women and men are likely to marry and start a family and the chances of staying married increase dramatically (Fossett and Kiecolt, 1993; Mason, 1996). The intersection of race and family values also influences the decision to marry. For example, individuals across race who come from families that place a high value on a college education will likely delay marriage until a later age than those who do not.

Sociological Perspective

On a theoretical level, there are several ways of explaining why people marry. A dominant point of view in the field of sociology has been a structural-functional analysis that ignores individual motivation, instead explaining why people marry in terms of society's need or demand for the legitimacy of children. The **principle of legitimacy,** the notion that all children ought to have a socially and legally recognized father, was first put forth by anthropologist Bronislaw Malinowski (1929).

According to Malinowski, although many societies allow individuals the freedom to be sexually active whether or not they are married, only a very few societies allow their members the freedom to conceive children outside of marriage. Almost universally, marriage is based on the official control of childbearing. Because women give birth there is no doubt who is the mother of a child. There is, however, no visible means of identifying paternity. Thus, society must develop some means whereby men can be publicly (socially) and legally connected with their offspring. All societies, then, require that every child must have a man (a legitimately married father) who will assume the social role of father and protector and who will link the child to society. In essence, such an explanation implies that people marry solely to have children. We know, however, that this is not the case for most people. The fact that a growing number of married couples do not have children gives us cause to question the viability of this principle to explain why people marry.

In contrast, a feminist perspective challenges theories such as the principle of legitimacy, maintaining that they place far more importance on the role of social father than mother in giving children social and legal status. Instead, a feminist perspective focuses on traditional gender role socialization, in which girls are taught to consider love, marriage, and children the ultimate goals for women and the most fulfilling roles they can play in society (see Chapter 3). Thus, a woman's decision to marry can represent, in part, a response to social pressures and expectations.

Whatever reasons people have for marrying, and whatever theories we use to explain why people marry, the fact remains that an overwhelming majority of us will marry at some time in our lives. Although marriage has declined somewhat over the last three decades, more than 90 percent of Americans (down from 95 percent) still get married, and demographers predict that this trend will continue well into the future (DeVita, 1996; Smith, 1999).

THE MEANING OF MARRIAGE

As we have seen, marriage means different things to different people. Virtually everyone, however, regards marriage as a relatively permanent and committed relationship. In addition, given the fact that most marriages take place within some religious context, we can surmise that most people also view marriage as a sacrament. How many of us, however, think of marriage in terms of a legal contract?

Marriage is not an isolated event. Rather, it joins together both the couple involved and their respective families. The relationships formed by marriage sometimes become complex and can require some regulation. For example, to prevent conflict, the issue of inheritance and property rights requires a stable and consistent set of rules that prevails over time and applies fairly consistently across marriages and families. Thus, in the interest of order and stability, the state has set certain legal standards to which marriages and families must conform. These standards encompass such issues as whom we can marry, when we can marry them, who is a legitimate heir, and who has property and inheritance rights. Although the specific laws regulating marriages and families may vary from state to state, in all states marriage is a legal contract with specified rights and obligations.

In this section we take a brief look at marriage from three perspectives: as a commitment, as a sacrament, and as a legal contract.

Marriage as a Commitment

Most researchers have found that commitment is a key factor in any intimate, emotionally satisfying, and meaningful relationship. When we pledge or commit ourselves to someone we generally assume (or certainly hope) that the relationship will be long-term or permanent. According to some social scientists (Cherlin, 1981), human beings have a deep-seated need for secure, stable, and long-term relationships. Marriage is typically the type of relationship with which most people seek to fulfill this need.

In a survey of couples with long-term marriages, social researchers Jeanette Lauer and Robert Lauer (1985) found that a key factor contributing to the longevity of the relationship was the couple's belief in marriage as a long-term commitment and a sacred institution. Some of the couples viewed the marital commitment as analogous to a chain that binds the couple together whether or not they are happy. Others, however, viewed commitment as a vow to stay together and work through hard times. For example, one man in the study said: "Commitment means a willingness to be unhappy for a while. . . . You're not going to be happy with each other all the time. That's when commitment is really important" (1985:84). In a later study examining marital quality among couples who had been married 30 or more years, Linda Robinson and Priscilla Blanton (1993) found commitment to be a key factor in a long-term, enduring marriage. Couples who were highly committed to each other were usually also strongly committed to the institution of marriage. Researchers have also found that when couples are equal in terms of power in the relationship there is a high rate of exchange and commitment to each other (Lawler and Yoon, 1996).

Research (for example, Olson, 1986; Erickson, 1993) has consistently indicated that strong families are those in which marital partners and family members are committed to each other; in which there is a high degree of togetherness and support. Commitment is not a single expectation or action. There are many aspects to commitment, some of which include the personal commitment between partners to each other, commitment to the relationship itself, commitment to the overall family unit, and long-term commitment. Commitment that includes these aspects tends to create individual as well as marital and family stability.

Marriage as a Sacrament

If you have not yet married but plan to in the future, what type of wedding will you have, and who will officiate at the ceremony? From a religious perspective, marriage is regarded as a **sacrament**—a sacred union or rite. Did you know that the majority of people in this country who marry for the first time do so under the auspices of some religious figure, such as a priest, rabbi, or minister? Although for economic and other considerations many people choose to bypass a religious ceremony, three-fourths of first-time marriages and three-fifths of remarriages among divorced people take place within the context of some type of religious ceremony. Even widows and widowers frequently remarry within the context of a religious ceremony (National Center for Health Statistics, 1988; Ravo, 1991). Is your choice of wedding ceremony consistent with these data?

These statistics suggest that most people in this country regard marriage as a significant religious or holy institution based on a sacred commitment to each other and their god. In the Christian tradition, for example, the sacredness and joyfulness of marriage is often voiced in the story of Christ's first public miracle, which was said to have been the act of turning water into wine for a wedding celebration. In addition, marriage is considered to be a holy state ("holy matrimony") conducted under the direct authority of God ("What God has joined together let no man put asunder").

Marriage in the religious context is also considered to be a lifelong commitment. Recognizing that not all marriages will last a lifetime, however, some Protestant and Jewish denominations allow for the termination of marriage through divorce and sanctify remarriages based on the same principles of the sacrament. Some religions, however, most notably Catholicism, are quite literal in their interpretation of marriage as a holy union sanctioned by God. Thus, the Catholic church does not recognize divorce as a valid means of terminating a marriage. Under certain circumstances, however, the church may annul a marriage, declaring that the marriage never actually occurred.

Marriage as a Legal Contract

Some marriage and family researchers have distinguished between what they call legal and social marriage. **Legal marriage** is a legally binding agreement or contractual relationship between two people and is defined and regulated by the state. In contrast, **social marriage** is a relationship between people who cohabit and engage in behavior that is essentially the same as that within a legal marriage, but without engaging in a marriage ceremony that is validated by the state. Thus, the relationship is not, under most circumstances, legally binding. Cohabitation and common-law marriage, both of which were discussed in Chapter 7, are examples of social marriage.

Marriage in the United States is a legal and financial contractual agreement that, like most other contractual agreements, is regulated by certain legal requirements. When two people marry, they agree to abide by the terms of the marriage contract. Although the marriage contract is very similar to an ordinary private contract, there are some very important differences. Unlike an ordinary private contract, the marriage contract is either unwritten or is not written in any one place. In addition, the terms and penalties of the contract are usually unspecified, that is, they are scattered throughout marriage and family laws and court decisions handed down over the years, or they are not very well known by the parties involved. In addition, the state, and not the married couple, specifies the conditions of the marriage contract. Therefore, unlike a private contract, where the parties involved may break, modify, change, or restrict the contract by some mutual action, a married couple cannot on their own change or break the marriage contract.

Most contracts cannot be changed while they are in effect without the knowledge and consent of the parties involved. In contrast, the marriage contract, because its terms are defined by various policymakers such as judges and legislators, can be changed without the direct knowledge or consent of married couples. No other contract operates in this fashion. Because no one sends married couples a notification every time marriage laws change, most of us are unaware of these

Vermont is the first state to offer same-sex couples legal recognition of their union and many of the benefits enjoyed by married heterosexual couples. After ten years together this couple holds their recently obtained Vermont civil union license to demonstrate their love and commitment to one another.

changes unless, of course, we keep abreast of them through media reports. Thus, for example, some states have proposed legislation that would require a wife to secure the consent of her husband before she could have an abortion. Even though the couple had little or no input into the proposed legislation, if it becomes law they are legally bound by it.

The most important marriage laws are state laws. The U.S. government has both created and defined marriage, giving the individual states the responsibility for ruling marriages. Each state defines the rights and obligations of married couples through a myriad of marriage and family laws, and only representatives of the state may marry people and terminate marriages. Even when people choose to be married by a member of the clergy, only those clergy that the state has granted the right to officiate at marriages may do so. In addition, state marriage laws cover only the residents of the particular state. Thus, if a couple marry in one state and later move to another state, their marriage is covered by the laws of the new state as soon as they become residents. In a sense, then, the marriage contract is much less an expression of love for one's chosen partner and much more realistically a pact with the state. In this context, it is well worth noting that historically the states have maintained social and legal control over women and children, defined women as property, and legitimized a gender-based division of paid and unpaid labor within society—women's labor is unpaid, men's labor is paid (Brownsworth, 1996).

Most people probably do not think of marriage in this way—as a legally binding contract ruled by individual states and which disadvantages one partner to the advantage of the other. Most of us are not aware of marriage laws and the extent of the state's role in marriage until separation, divorce, or death occurs, or when inheritance or property rights are at issue.

Some Legal Aspects of the Marriage Contract

Some of the more apparent legal aspects of the marriage contract specify who can marry whom and when. Every state in this country, for example, has laws that specify who can marry whom in terms of age and sex. In addition, until 1967 some states continued to specify who could marry whom in terms of race.

Sexual Orientation Marriage is a civil right that most heterosexuals take for granted. However, lesbian and gay couples do not enjoy this same civil right. In no state in the United States can people of the same sex legally marry. This fact is not surprising given that most states define marriage as a commitment by two people to carry on their lineage by conceiving and rearing children. The topic of same-sex marriages, almost unimaginable a few decades ago, has become so potent that it is a major issue in many political campaigns and debates, public and popular discourse, and legal actions across the country. As an increasing number of lesbian and gay couples openly cohabit in long-term relationships, and are progressively more militant and litiginous in their demand for the right to express their love and commitment to one another as do heterosexual couples, they have placed greater and greater pressure on business, government, religious institutions, the workplace, and lawmakers to extend to them the rights and privileges of heterosexual married couples.

Given that most Americans view marriage as a significant religious and holy institution, it is not surprising that many lesbians and gays, like heterosexuals, want to sanctify their commitment to each other and their God. The desire to make a public commitment to one another in the church or synagogue of their choice is not only controversial but also a divisive issue within religious institutions. Increasingly today, Presbyterians, Catholics, Jews, and members of other religions have been forced to grapple with whether to sanction same-sex unions and ceremonies within the church, whether or not they are legally recognized by state and federal governments.

Some people feel that the legal prohibition of same-sex marriage prevents lesbian and gay couples from forming legal, religious, and public marital bonds that would secure their relationship rights, and it deprives them of a litany of benefits and protections, rights, and responsibilities. And this is certainly true. Although marriage has its drawbacks, some of its most striking benefits include the right of a surviving marital partner to inherit property, the right to file a joint income tax return (married couples filing jointly are taxed at a lower rate than single people and married couples who file separately), and the right to share pension and health care insurance benefits offered by many employers to their employees.

Currently, there is only one state in the country where lesbian and gay couples enjoy something close to legal marriage and the benefits and protections, rights, and responsibilities that heterosexual married couples enjoy. That state is Vermont. As we pointed out in the opening section of Chapter 7, in the spring of 2000, Vermont Governor Howard Dean signed into law the first and to-date only bill that legalizes *civil unions* for same-sex couples, giving them almost all of the rights and privileges of married couples (for example, joint property rights, inheritance rights, shared health care benefits, hospital visitation rights, and immunity from being compelled to testify against a partner) (Goldberg, 2001). A major caveat is that civil unions, unlike traditional marriage unions, are only recognized in the state of Vermont. Because marriages performed in one state are typically recognized by the other 49, in 1996, the U.S. Congress passed the Defense of Marriage Act, which stipulates that no state can be forced to recognize another state's same-sex marriage, defines marriage in all federal policies, laws, and acts of Congress as a legal union of one woman and one man, and withholds federal marriage benefits from lesbian and gay married couples (104th Congress, HR 3396).

Although some states recognize same-sex unions as domestic partnerships,[1] such recognition does not include the same legal rights that come automatically with marriage. However, for most lesbian and gay couples, unless they reside in Vermont, domestic partnerships are the closest approximation to legal marriage available to them. Over a quarter-million U.S. households consist of same-sex couples, and many of these couples would like to be married if marriage were an option. For example, in a recent survey, 85 percent of lesbians and gays said that legal marriage is "very" or "somewhat" important to them (Leland, and Miller, 1998; U.S. Census Bureau, 2000).

As homosexuality generally and gay marriage specifically have become more and more visible components of U.S. culture, domestic partners are gaining some legitimacy and protections. For instance, many states and cities, as well as many major corporations, offer medical and other benefits to the partners of lesbian and gay employees but not to unmarried heterosexual couples. According to some reports, approximately 18 percent of all U.S. employers have some form of domestic partner benefits that include health care (Swoboda, 2000). For example, in 1997, San Francisco passed the first city ordinance in the nation that extended health insurance and other benefits to its employees' domestic partners. Other cities, such as Chicago, Atlanta, New York, San Diego, and, most recently, the District of Columbia, have followed suit; and employers, such as Walt Disney Company, the Gap, Microsoft, Time Warner, Apple Computer, Lotus Development, Nynex, and Levi Strauss, have domestic partner policies (Weiser, 1996).

Same-sex marriage is not a new concept, nor is it an issue unique to the United States. Again, as we pointed out at the beginning of Chapter 7, since 1989 a number of countries have legalized same-sex unions, beginning with Denmark in 1989 and most recently with Germany in 2001. However, in the United States, most Americans view homosexual relations as immoral and oppose the legalization of same-sex marriages. For example, in a Gallup poll on morality, less than half of Americans believed that homosexual behavior was morally acceptable, whereas 53 percent believed that it was morally wrong, and most popular opinion polls consistently report that only 33 percent of Americans approve of legally sanctioned gay marriage (Gallup Poll, 1997; Associated Press, 2000; Public Opinion Polls on Same-Sex Marriages, 2001). Among those who oppose gay marriage, some believe it to be an oxymoron, an ideological invention that is designed to force societal acceptance of homosexuality. Those who hold this viewpoint believe that marriage must be the joining of a woman and man only. They believe that lesbians and gays should have the right to vote, to work, to inherit, to receive health benefits, to receive Social Security benefits from their partners, and to be free of violence—but not to marry. The most common argument against legalizing same-sex marriages is that it would subvert the stability and integrity of heterosexual marriage and family (Weiser, 1996; Associated Press, 2000).

The opposition to same-sex marriages at the state level is reflected in the fact that, through 2000, 34 states have passed "defense of marriage" legislation. All but Hawaii and Alaska have done this by statute rather than by changing their constitutions (see Figure 8.3). Moreover, in 2000, two out of three voters in California approved Proposition 22, which recognizes marriage only between a woman and man (Yuen, 1998a/b; Daniels, 2000). Essentially, then, in more than two-thirds of the United States the law sanctions heterosexual marriage and denies same-sex couples the same legal standing. As a consequence, defense of marriage laws are currently being challenged as a violation of the equal protection clause of the U.S. Constitution.

On the other hand, those who support same-sex marriage argue that rather than weakening marriages and families, gay marriage would actually strengthen them. Giving lesbians and gays the same rights to marry as heterosexuals would reinforce the commitment of many gays to live within long-term, committed relationships and encourage others who

[1]Domestic partnerships are not limited to same-sex couples but also include cohabiting heterosexual couples.

Figure 8.3

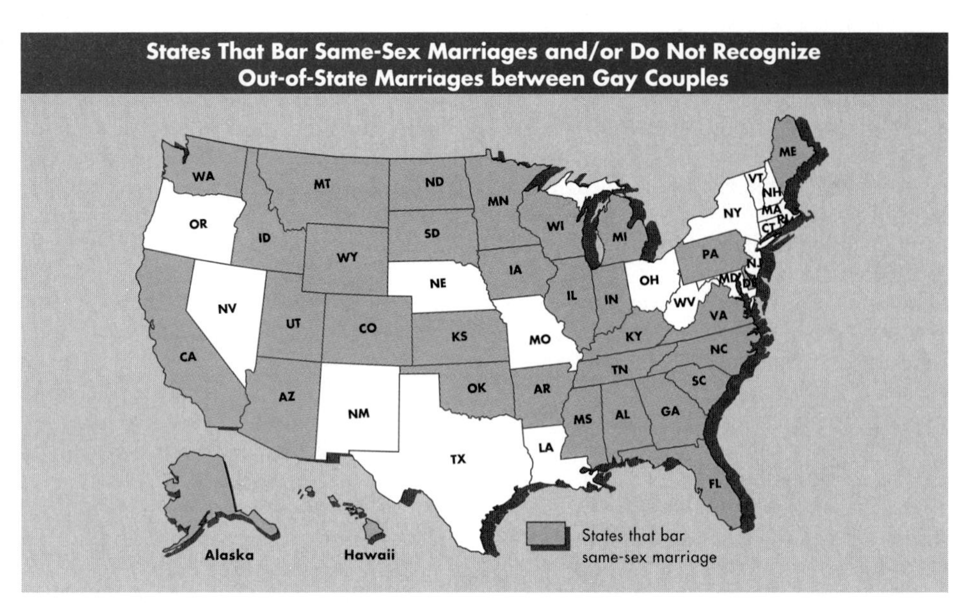

States That Bar Same-Sex Marriages and/or Do Not Recognize Out-of-State Marriages between Gay Couples

Sources: Human Rights Campaign, 1999, "States Denying Equal Marriage Rights to Lesbian and Gay Americans," **http://www.hrc.org/issues/marriage/marstate.html** (1999, April 24); M. Daniels, 2000, "United We Fall," *World Magazine* 15, 24 (June 17), **http://www.worldmag.com/world/issue/06-17-00/national_10asp.**

might not otherwise to do so. In addition, permitting such marriages would not only benefit gay couples but would also benefit society at large given that research has consistently demonstrated that marriage encourages monogamy. And in a cultural and social environment where HIV/AIDS is a pandemic that disproportionately impacts gay men, encouraging gay monogamy is a rational public health policy (Hartinger, 1994). Most importantly, however, legalizing same-sex marriages would provide lesbians and gays with the fundamental American freedom of having the right to choose whether and whom to marry (Wolfson, 1996).

? *What do you think? Do laws prohibiting same-sex marriage violate the civil rights of lesbians and gays? Should lesbians and gays have the legal right to marry with all of the benefits that come automatically with heterosexual marriage? Should they be allowed to marry in their respective churches and synagogues, even if such unions are not legal in this country? Would same-sex marriage require a redefinition of marriage? If so, how might we redefine marriage? Should American children be taught to accept same-sex marriage as a "normal" marital lifestyle?*

Whatever your position, the fact is that the issue of legal lesbian and gay marriage is not one that is likely to disappear. Rather, it will continue to be a prominent social and political issue far into the future. For what is at stake here? The debate is not just about abstract concepts such as the definition of a marriage and a family or the rights of a minority group. It is also about mundane matters such as taxes, funerals, and health benefits. As we said earlier, marriage is not just about love and companionship. Marriage is also about legal and economic/financial benefits that a couple share. Table 8.1 presents a somewhat detailed list of the kinds of benefits that are at stake for lesbians and gays seeking the rights and privileges of legal marriage.

Some proponents of same-sex marriages are optimistic that it will be a legal reality in all of the United States one day, with lesbian and gay partners sharing equally and consistently the legal and financial as well as social benefits of heterosexual marriage. Although the goal of gay marriage is not universally embraced among lesbians and gays, most gay couples feel that they deserve the same rights that nongay couples take for granted.

In addition to requiring heterosexuality in marital relationships, marriage law also requires monogamy. Under legal statutes people cannot have more than one spouse at a time. If an individual does, he or she can be prosecuted for **bigamy**—marrying one person while still being legally married to another. Although seldom enforced, many states have laws that prohibit **adultery,** extramarital sexual intercourse, and **fornication,** sexual intercourse outside legal marriage.

THE INCEST TABOO Not only does the marriage contract prohibit marriage between persons of the same sex, but it also prohibits marriage or sexual relations between a variety of relatives ranging from parents and siblings to non–

Table 8.1

The Benefits That Lesbian and Gay Partners Could Share

A marriage is not just a declaration of undying love; marriage also brings legal and financial benefits that partners share, including:

- Government benefits, such as Social Security and Medicare
- Joint insurance policies for health, home, and automobile
- Retirement benefits
- The right to make medical decisions for a partner
- Family leave to care for a sick partner or child
- Wrongful-death benefits
- Domestic violence protection orders
- Joint parental custody
- Alimony
- Tax advantages
- Inheritance rights
- Divorce rights
- Hospital visitation rights
- Confidentiality of conversations
- Right to decide what to do with a partner's corpse

Source: Carl Weiser, 1996, "Legal Gay Marriage on Hawaii's Horizon," *USA Today* (Tuesday, January 2): 6A. Copyright © 1996, *USA Today.* Reprinted by permission.

blood-related in-laws. Although the specific set of blood relatives whom we cannot legally marry or have sex with differs from state to state, no state allows us to marry a parent, a sibling, an uncle or aunt, a niece or nephew, a grandparent, or a grandchild. The majority of states prohibit marriage between half siblings and first cousins. Some states also exclude second cousins and, in a few cases, third cousins. In addition, some states go so far as to prohibit marriage between **affinal relatives,** people related by marriage, such as a brother- or sister-in-law, even though they are not related by blood.

As we discussed in Chapter 1, although the range of relatives covered by the incest taboo has varied over human history, some theorists maintain that this taboo serves an important social and political function for families and society. By forcing families to mate and reproduce outside the immediate family network, marriage helps create political and economic relationships that are vital to society's structure and survival.

Age Restrictions Marriage rules also define when we are considered mature enough to marry. In the past, the legal age at which people could marry was tied to puberty and the ages at which women and men could reproduce. If a person was old enough to reproduce, she or he was considered old enough to marry. Often the legal age for marriage was different for women and men.

Today, however, the concern is whether a person is mature enough to marry, regardless of the ability to reproduce. To ensure that a person is both old enough and mature enough, each state has set a legal age for marriage. That age varies, however, according to whether the couple has obtained their parents' consent. The marriageable age for women and men, with or without parental consent, is the same in most states. For example, in every state except one, the legal age at which marriage can be contracted without parental consent is 18 for both women and men. In Georgia, a female or male may contract a marriage without parental consent as early as 16 years of age. On the other hand, on the island of Puerto Rico, individuals cannot contract a marriage on their own until age 21. (See Appendix E for a list of marriage requirements by state.)

With parental consent the picture changes. The typical age requirement for marriage with parental consent is 16. In as many as five states (Alabama, New Hampshire, New York, Texas, and Utah), however, females and males may marry as early as 14 years of age if their parents consent. Moreover, in a few states, parental consent is not required if a minor was previously married. And two states (California and Mississippi) have no age limits. In some states minors may obtain a marriage license if the female is pregnant, if a child has already been born to the couple, or under what some states define as "special circumstances." In other states a minor wishing to marry must not only have parental consent but must also get the permission of a judge.

Blood Tests Regardless of age and whether parental consent is needed, when two people plan to marry they must file an application with the state and obtain a marriage license. In the majority of the states (approximately two-thirds), to obtain a marriage license a couple first must be tested to determine if they have a sexually transmitted disease. This procedure is commonly referred to as "getting a blood test." Usually there is a brief waiting period between the time people are tested and the time they receive the marriage license. In several states individuals are tested for other diseases in addition to sexually transmitted diseases. For example, in eight states, people (especially women) also must be tested for rubella (German measles) and their Rh blood type. In New York, certain applicants may be further required to take a test for sickle cell anemia, a condition that is far more prevalent among African Americans than among whites, before a marriage license is issued. If the sickle cell condition is present, a couple can be denied a marriage license unless it is established that procreation is not possible (*World Almanac,* 1990).

Although most states require some type of medical test for sexually transmitted diseases, there is little routine testing for AIDS prior to marriage. For example, for a short period of time in the late 1980s, Illinois law required AIDS testing before a marriage license could be obtained. In 1989, however, the law was rescinded, due in part to the fact that many people, unhappy with the law, crossed state lines and married in surrounding states. In addition, the tests proved extremely expensive and uncovered only a small number of AIDS cases (Marriage License Bureau and Cook County Clerk's Office, 1993).

One last point is that some individuals do not do any of the things discussed in the previous paragraphs, yet their relationship is recognized by the state as a legal, or common-law, marriage. As discussed in Chapter 7, although common-law marriages were once widely recognized, today only about one-fourth of the states recognize them.

Thus, in answering the question "What is marriage?" we have seen that marriage encompasses a rather wide range of behaviors and issues. It includes a complex contractual agreement among not two but three parties: the couple and the state, but can also simply be a relationship defined by two people as a marriage.

CHANGE AND CONTINUITY IN THE MEANING OF MARRIAGE

One of the most fundamental and significant premises on which U.S. marriage and family laws have been based is the historical notion that the family is the property of the husband, and therefore he is the head of the household. The other side of this argument is the belief that women are the weaker sex and need the care and protection of men. This belief reflects the common-law concept of **coverture,** the idea that a wife is under the protection and influence of her husband; that the two become one at the time of marriage, and that one is the husband. From these assumptions flow many rights, obligations, and expectations about how a married couple should behave and relate to each other. Therefore, not surprisingly, we find that over the course of time many of the rules and laws surrounding marriage have treated women and men differently based solely on their biological sex. For example, the symbolic loss of a woman's identity once she marries is still evident today in the common practice of a married woman legally taking her husband's name when she marries whereas the man's legal identity remains the same as it was before marriage. Many of the marriage traditions and rituals practiced around the world (see the "In Other Places" box on pages 238–39) are also rooted in this premise.

Historically, marriage has extended the rights of men vis-à-vis women and children. Women, in contrast, have lost many legal rights when they married, because their marital obligations and rights have been defined primarily in terms of their service to husbands and children. Under this arrangement, for example, women have suffered a long history of violence at the hands of their husbands, who, until the late 1800s, could legally beat their wives if they did not fulfill their wifely duties. (Chapter 11 contains an in-depth discussion of this issue.)

Provisions of the Modern Marriage Contract

The provisions of the modern marriage contract are similar to those based on the old principle of coverture. A quarter of a century ago, social scientist Lenore Weitzman (1977), for example, identified four basic provisions of the traditional marriage contract that have been incorporated into marriage laws in the United States: (1) the wife is responsible for caring for the home; (2) the wife is responsible for caring for any children; (3) the husband is head of the household; and (4) the husband is responsible for providing support for the family. In the language of marital rights and obligations, these provisions assert that the wife owes her husband domestic and companionship services, and in return the husband owes his wife protection and economic support. Although over the years marriage and family laws have become more equitable in the treatment of wives and husbands, these four provisions are not simply old-fashioned ideas that are no longer relevant. In many states women continue to lose legal rights when they marry, and they continue to be treated as the property of their husbands (Skolnick and Skolnick, 1987).

Although today the specific conditions of the marriage contract vary from one state to another, some common assumptions are evident. In the following discussion we examine some specific beliefs and practices from the past in terms of their impact on current marital patterns, noting both continuity and changes where they have occurred.

Residence In the past, a woman was expected to take her husband's surname and move into his domicile (place of residence). Although a wife is no longer required to take her husband's name, a husband retains the legal right to decide where the couple will live, and marriage law imposes an obligation on the wife to live in her husband's choice of residence. Therefore, when a woman marries, if her place of residence is different from her husband's, his place of residence automatically supersedes hers. If a woman lives in a different state from her husband and she does not take her husband's place of residence as her own, the legal ramifications are many. For example, she must reregister to vote; she could lose the right to attend a university in her hometown as a resident student; and she could lose the privilege of running for public office in her home state (Renzetti and Curran, 1992). Laws pertaining to the marital domicile reflect traditional gender inequalities in other ways. For example, if a husband gets a job in another city and his wife refuses to relocate with him, she is assumed by law to have abandoned him. If, on the other hand, a wife gets a job in another city and her husband refuses to relocate with her, she is still defined by law as having abandoned him.

In this sense, men are still assumed to be the head of the household and can therefore determine where the family will live (Sapiro, 1990). Over the years, however, some equalizing of marital roles and obligations has occurred. Thus, in many states today a woman can establish a separate household for a specific purpose. In addition, one state court has ruled that a wife who is the primary breadwinner can decide where the couple will live (Renzetti and Curran, 1992).

Property Rights In the past, a woman's property rights also came under the control and management of her husband once she married. Not only did a husband gain control of his wife's property on marriage, but he could also do with it as he pleased, with or without her knowledge or consent. Today, however, women have considerable property rights, although the specifics differ across states. In some states a wife and husband may own property individually, whereas in others their property may be considered community property.

Most U.S. states recognize the individual ownership of property. Whoever has proof of ownership of property owns it in the eyes of the law. If neither the wife nor husband has proof of ownership, however, most courts determine that the husband is the owner, particularly if the wife has remained in the home as a homemaker during the marriage. The court's rationale is that because the wife had no income with which to acquire the assets, they belong to the husband, who has simply allowed her use of them over the years. Thus, for example, in some cases a joint bank account has been deemed by the court to belong to the husband if the wife did not earn an income.

As this discussion makes clear, common-law property states, as they are called, give quite an advantage to husbands. It is ironic that those women who conform most closely to the patriarchal norms that surround marital roles are the ones who are hurt most by marriage laws and regulations pertaining to property ownership. Women who have spent their lives in service to their husbands (and children) end up with few assets of their own. Moreover, because of their dependency on their husbands, they are the most vulnerable during and after marriage.

In the community property system, practiced in only a few states, wives and husbands own all assets jointly and equally whether or not the wife earns an income (Sapiro, 1990). This system does not penalize women for choosing to be full-time homemakers, although it does present other problems for wives, as discussed in more detail in Chapter 12.

As disadvantaged as married women were in the past and are today under the principle of coverture, men also were and still are restricted in several important ways as well. For example, it has been argued that because marriage awarded a wife a right of inheritance, the husband's estate was reduced. In addition, marriage obligated a husband to support his wife and family, an obligation that poor and working-class men often found difficult to meet solely on their own. The continuation of this idea and the inequities it engenders for men are reflected in the fact that husbands today are still legally obliged to support their wives even if the wife works and earns a higher wage than the husband.

Given our discussion of marital rights and obligations thus far, are you wondering about the degree to which these principles are enforceable by law? We turn our attention next to an examination of this question.

The Law According to political scientist and women's studies professor Virginia Sapiro (1986), a husband's right to his wife's services is basically unenforceable by law in a direct sense. There are, however, some very important consequences of this provision of the marriage contract. As we discuss in more detail in Chapter 11, because of a husband's **conjugal rights**—rights pertaining to the marriage relationship—in about half of U.S. states a wife cannot charge her husband with rape. Furthermore, because the marriage contract obliges a wife to perform domestic labor for her husband, she cannot be directly compensated for her work, and until recent times her economic contribution to the marriage was not considered in the division of property at the time of divorce. Interestingly, although the husband has no legal obligation to compensate his wife for domestic services, if a third party injures the wife, the husband can legally sue the party for the value of the domestic services he lost.

Although a wife has a legal right to be supported by her husband, she has little control over the nature or amount of that support. Again, based on an accumulation of findings in various court cases, it seems that as long as a wife and husband live together the husband has a right to support his wife in whatever manner he chooses. If a wife feels she is not being adequately supported she has little legal recourse.

The Marriage Contract Today

Since the 1970s, marriage and family law in the United States has changed substantially, although certain traditions and legal restrictions continue to leave women at a disadvantage. As pointed out, women no longer have to take their husband's surname. In many states, however, a wife who takes her husband's surname must seek his permission to return to using her birth name. In the past the decision not to adopt the husband's surname often created legal problems and unnecessary difficulties for the couple. For example, insurance companies, banks, and other bureaucracies often had difficulty dealing with married customers with different surnames. Thus, such customers were sometimes denied services meant for married couples, or they were seriously inconvenienced. Today, however, legal and business establishments have caught up with this practice, and a woman's decision to retain her family name does not appear to cause as many difficulties.

Rather than give up their family name upon marrying, some women choose to hyphenate their name after marriage (for example, Lillian Brown-Johnson). This practice, however, is not without problems. How will the couple name their children? Will their children carry the father's surname only? Will they carry the hyphenated name? If so, when the children become adults, can they hyphenate their already-hyphenated name?

Other ways in which contemporary couples attack gender-stereotypic wedding rituals and traditions include brides having "best women" or best men, grooms having "men of honor" or women (rather than best men) stand up for them, both parents (as opposed to the father alone) giving away a daughter, one or both parents giving away the groom, or completely eliminating the ritual of someone "giving away" a human being.

IN OTHER PLACES

MARRIAGE TRADITIONS AND RITUALS IN THE UNITED STATES . . .

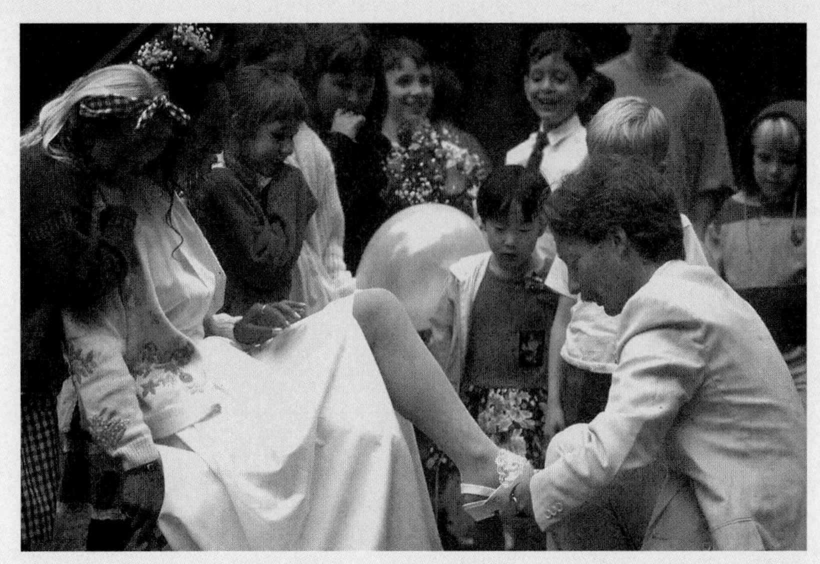

Marriage is a critical rite of passage in most cultures and includes a wide range of rituals and customs. For example, in the United States, following the bride's tossing of the bouquet, often the groom will remove and toss the bride's garter. According to tradition, the single male who catches it will be the next to marry.

As our discussion in this chapter implies, in many ways the traditional marriage contract can be viewed as a transference of property among males, that is, from father to husband. Indicative of the property status of women was the practice whereby a prospective husband had to receive the father's permission to marry his daughter. At the time of the wedding, the father gave his daughter to the groom. If you are a married male, did you carry the bride over the threshold on your wedding night? It seems that the custom of *carrying the bride over the threshold* originally symbolized the abduction of a daughter who was reluctant to leave her father's home. Further, at some earlier point in time, the *best man* was a warrior friend who helped a man capture and kidnap the woman he desired. These are only a few of many marriage traditions that reflect in some way the unequal status of women and men.

How much do you know about other rituals and traditions surrounding marriage in the United States? For example, do you know why brides today need "something old, something new, something borrowed, and something blue"? This tradition apparently dates back to ancient Hebrew society, when brides wore blue ribbons on their wedding day to signify love, purity, and fidelity. In addition, the ancient Hebrews believed that if a bride wore an item borrowed from a married woman, the married woman's wedded happiness would transfer to the bride-to-be.

The Bridal Shower

The first bridal shower is believed to have been held in Holland, when a father denied his daughter permission to marry a poor man with whom she had fallen in love. When the man's friends heard this, they gave the bride-to-be numerous gifts so that the couple could be married.

The Bachelor Party

The ritual of the bachelor party dates back to ancient Greece. The night before the wedding, a lavish dinner, called the "men's mess," was held for the groom-to-be.

The Ring

The first wedding ring might have been worn by the Romans, who believed that a small artery, or "vein of love," ran from the third finger of the left hand to the heart. Thus, wearing a ring on this finger symbolized the joining of two hearts in destiny.

Why are engagement and wedding rings typically diamond? Medieval Italians used diamonds because they believed that diamonds were created from the eternal flames of love.

The Wedding Veil

The tradition of the wedding veil cannot be traced to one single country; rather, it has its origins in many cultures. In general, to protect the bride from the evil wishes of her rivals, her face was covered on her wedding day. In ancient Rome and Greece, wedding veils were brightly colored, whereas the early Christian bride wore a white or purple veil to symbolize purity and virginity. After the marital vows were exchanged, the veil was pulled back from the bride's face to symbolize her new status as wife.

Standing Arrangements at the Wedding Ceremony

It is said that the custom that the bride stand to the left of the groom at the altar dates back to a time when men carried swords to protect themselves and their loved ones. The groom had to keep his right hand (his sword hand) free to be able to defend himself and his bride from his enemies or disgruntled in-laws.

Throwing the Bouquet

This ritual is said to have its basis in a bride's desire to save herself from an onslaught of wedding guests. In times past, it was the custom for guests to reach for the bride's garter. One bride, tiring of the practice, decided that throwing the bouquet would be safer.

According to tradition, the unmarried woman who catches the bouquet will be the next one to get married.

The Wedding Cake

The origin of the wedding cake is attributed to ancient Romans, who actually broke a specially baked cake over the head of the bride as a symbol of luck and fruitfulness. Wedding guests scrambled to catch pieces of the cake in order to share some of the couple's good luck. The wedding cake continues to be an important part of traditional weddings today because it is a symbol of oneness through sharing. The bride and groom sharing the first piece of the cake is seen as a gesture of goodwill for the happy couple. (Does this include smashing the cake in each other's face?)

The Honeymoon

Did you ever wonder why newlyweds keep their honeymoon a secret? In fact, sometimes even the bride-to-be does not know where she is going for the honeymoon. It is probably not surprising that the honeymoon originated in France, a country that is synonymous with love and romance. Several hundred years ago, to escape relatives who opposed their marriage, the newlywed couple would seclude themselves in some secret place for a month until the opposition gave up and stopped looking for them. During this time of seclusion, the couple drank a special wine made with honey while watching the moon go through all of its phases. Thus, the term honeymoon literally means "moon of honey" ("Wedding Traditions," 1988).

. . . AND AROUND THE WORLD

Sometimes we get so caught up in our own traditions we think that they are the same for all people. However, different cultures define marriage differently and have rituals and traditions that are based on their unique sociocultural and political experiences. People studying different cultures have discovered interesting marriage practices that demonstrate the uniqueness of each culture.

China

The Chinese have a perfect solution for individuals who do not marry in their lifetime: a posthumous wedding. The "spirit wedding" is an ancient custom that is being revived in the Chinese countryside today. It is supposed to ensure that people who die unmarried will have a partner in the afterlife. In this custom, an aging unmarried person buys a corpse in preparation for the "spirit wedding" when she or he dies. Upon death, the two will be "married" with a full ceremony and will be buried together (*Chicago Tribune*, 1991).

Iraq

In the 1950s, Elizabeth and Robert Fernea lived in an Iraqi peasant village and studied the women's lives in detail. In this culture, parents arranged their children's marriages, and a couple could not meet before their wedding day. For women, virginity was essential and had to be maintained at all costs until the wedding day. On the wedding day, the couple consummated their marriage while their mothers, friends, and other relatives waited outside the couple's bedroom. When they finished, the mothers inspected the wedding sheets for blood from the young bride's broken hymen (a membranous fold of tissue partly closing the external opening of the vagina) and publicly announced the proof of the bride's virginity. If there was no blood, it was assumed that the bride was not a virgin, and her family suffered great humiliation. The bride herself was often put to death as a ruined woman (Fernea, 1965).

The Tiwi of Australia

Among the Tiwi, an Aboriginal people on the islands off the coast of Australia, there is no such thing as an unmarried female. Females are betrothed by their fathers before they are born into a system of reciprocity among males. Tiwi males gain prestige through the number of marriage contracts they make. Thus, marriage contracts are highly valued, even if some are with brides who are not yet born or who are not yet old enough to join the husband's household. In this system of polygyny for males and serial marriage for females, because the husband must be an adult before an infant female can be married to him, females are likely to outlive their husbands. Thus, when a husband dies, the wife's father or next male head of family has the right and responsibility to make a new marriage contract for her. She can never be unmarried. Given the prestige for males of having many marriage contracts, all Tiwi women, including the elderly, are valuable as wives (O'Kelly and Carney, 1986).

The Islamic Custom of Muta

In the Islamic custom of *muta,* a man and unmarried woman agree to a temporary marriage, in which both the duration of the marriage and the amount of money to be exchanged are agreed upon in advance. *Muta* children are considered legitimate and are theoretically equals of half-siblings born to permanent marriages or contracts; however, Islamic law allows the father the right to deny his *muta* child's legitimacy. Government encouragement of *muta* increased with the deaths of hundreds of thousands of Islamic men in the Iran-Iraq war. Most Islamic men who enter into *muta* marriages do so as a sexual arrangement, while Islamic women's reasons vary widely (Lancaster, 1990).

What do you think? *Do you find any of the marriage traditions and rituals commonly practiced today to be demeaning to women? Do you think that following these rituals, regardless of what they symbolize, is okay for women and men today? Why, or why not? How do the roles of women and men reflected in these rituals correspond with the gendered division of labor in marriages and families? Explain.*

Marriage Traditions in the United States

Marriage is a critical rite of passage in most cultures, and, as demonstrated in the "In Other Places Box," in most cultures it is steeped with tradition and rituals. In the traditional sense, marriage in the United States is a culmination of the mate selection process: courtship, dating, engagement, parties for the bride and groom, and finally the wedding itself.

ENGAGEMENT In the United States, if during the dating period a couple decide to take their relationship to another level, deciding that they will marry at some time in the future, they will typically end the formal and private dating phase of their relationship and move it to a more public expression of their relationship and intentions toward one another—the *engagement.* The engagement formalizes the couple's commitment to marry, and, until recently, it has been a formal phase in the mate selection process whereby the man gives the woman an engagement ring, a public announcement is made in the media (newspapers, newsmagazines) either by the couple or the couple's family, and family and friends are invited to share the couple's happiness and commitment to marry (an engagement party). Ideally, at this juncture in the relationship, the couple are emotionally committed to one another, are sexually monogamous, are getting to know each other's family (if they don't already know each other), and are focused on planning the wedding.

Although the engagement functioned as a binding commitment to marry in the past, today it seems that it is more symbolic and ritualistic than a binding commitment. And given that more and more people are delaying first marriage until later ages, a growing number of people are remarrying, and an increasing number of single people are cohabiting, engagement has also become far less formal. For some groups, engagement may not even be ritualistic anymore. For example, the increasing number of couples who start their relationship by "hanging out," "getting together," or living together are less likely to become formally engaged. Rather, typically they will simply verbally announce that they plan to marry. This informal approach is less socially binding but consistent with the informality or casual nature of their relationship. The engagement phase of the mate selection process has changed in other ways as well. For example, older couples may or may not go through a formal engagement period. Rather, they might forgo public announcements in the media and simply tell family and friends their intention to marry and then quietly do so. Sometimes, particularly if both partners work, they will buy an engagement and wedding ring jointly. Likewise, couples that have cohabited prior to making the decision to marry often do not announce an engagement. For example, a couple we know cohabited for 14 years prior to making the decision to marry. Once they made the decision, they announced it to their family and close friends and within a week they flew to Las Vegas and wed.

Although engagements no longer necessarily follow traditional customs, they continue to perform several key functions. For example, the engagement helps the couple define the goal of their relationship as marriage, and it lets the rest of those in the pool of eligibles know that each person is now "spoken for," that they have entered into a commitment with someone and are no longer available. Second, it provides the couple with an opportunity to seriously and systematically examine their relationship, that is, their expectations about the reality of marriage on a day-to-day basis, including appropriate gender roles, children, money, friendships, religion, in-laws, and family traditions. Third, it gives the couple a period of time to become better acquainted with their future in-laws and to become integrated into each other's family. Fourth, it provides the couple with a reason and occasion to get information about their respective medical histories (for example, through the required blood tests; determining the Rh factor in each partner's blood, for instance, will be of major importance in any future pregnancy). Finally, an important function of engagement is premarital counseling. It can be quite useful for a couple to discuss their ideas, expectations, and plans with an objective third person such as a member of the clergy or marriage counselor (historically, the Catholic church has made premarital counseling a prerequisite for getting married in a Roman Catholic church).

An increasing number of couples today are using the engagement period not only to define what their relationship with each other will be but also to define their economic and social obligations to each other during their marriage. They are doing this by writing their own **personal marriage agreement**—a written agreement between a married couple in which issues of role responsibilities, obligations, and sharing are addressed in a manner that is tailored to their own personal preferences, desires, and expectations.

PRENUPTIAL AGREEMENTS Today, the marriage plans of many couples include the use of a personal marriage agreement in one of two ways. One is as a **prenuptial agreement,** developed and worked out in consultation with an attorney and filed as a legal document. The purpose of drawing up a prenuptial agreement in this manner is to negotiate ahead of time the settlement of property, alimony, or other financial matters in the event of death or divorce. The prenuptial agreement can also serve as a personal agreement between the partners, drafted primarily for the purpose of helping the couple clarify their expectations concerning their marriage. Formal or legal marriage agreements such as prenuptial agreements are not new. Wealthy and celebrity members of society have long used these agreements to protect family fortunes. It has been reported that prior to their marriage, the late Jacqueline Kennedy and Aristotle Onassis drew up a 170-point prenuptial agreement (Totenberg, 1985). Although most prenuptial agreements are not that elaborate, they generally go far in protecting the assets of the persons involved as well as ensuring reasonable alimony and other financial payments agreed upon by the couple. For example, after Donald Trump and Marla Maples separated in 2001, it was reported that should they divorce, Maples was entitled to between $1 million and $5 million, thanks to her prenuptial agreement (at the time, however, Trump was worth $2.5 billion).

Few topics in the modern-day marriage arena inspire more attention, headlines, discussion, and fury than the mention of the words *prenuptial agreement.* Asking your future life partner to sign a contract that limits her or his rights to your assets flies in the face of love and romance. Some people look on prenuptial agreements as cold, unromantic, businesslike, and an expression of greed. They think that such contracts are an indication of distrust on the part of the couple; that they imply that one or both partners do not have faith in the relationship and that they care more about their bank account than their soon-to-be spouse. However, most marriage advisers suggest that premarital contracting doesn't mean that a couple does not love or trust one another. Rather, according to Jacqueline Rickard, author of *Complete Premarital Contracting: Loving Communication for Today's Couples,* in many ways a prenuptial agreement can show how much two people really care about each other (cited in Edelman Financial Services, 1996). Marriage today is an economic as well as an emotional partnership. Thus, contemporary couples are advised to think with their heads and not their hearts. A prenuptial agreement is not a bad idea, even for people who do not have a lot of money. Prenuptial agreements are like insurance policies, they are good estate planning, and they force couples to agree on how they want to handle their married life, including their money and other assets.

With the number of millionaires rising steadily and new forms of wealth being developed everyday, the candidate pool for prenuptial agreements has grown significantly. It is estimated that 10 percent to 15 percent of altar-bound Americans enter into prenuptial agreements each year, mostly those who have accumulated or inherited significant wealth of a million dollars or more (CNNmoney, 2000). However, it is not just the rich and famous but an increasing number of middle-class couples, elderly couples, and divorced people who are ensuring before the wedding that in case the marriage ends their assets will go or remain where they want them. For the first time, divorced women outnumber widowed women in their 50s and 60s, and given that half of all marriages end in divorce within the first seven years, lawyers, financial planners, and others who deal with marriage and family issues strongly suggest that it is a good idea for anyone (not just the rich) who is planning to marry to consider a prenuptial agreement in order to be financially prepared should divorce or death occur. Those embarking upon a second marriage are particularly urged to consider a prenuptial agreement to protect the inheritances of children from a prior marriage (see, for example, Friedman, 1999; Hobson, 2001). Rarely do couples break engagements because of disputes over prenuptial agreements. In almost every instance, the agreement is signed and the parties are married. For example, it was widely reported in the news that prior to their well-publicized wedding, movie celebrities Catherine Zeta-Jones and Michael Douglas were squabbling over details of a prenuptial agreement and that the spat might end their marriage plans. Reportedly, she was asking for $4.5 million for every year they are married and a home for life if they split, and he was holding fast to an offer of $1.5 million a year and a house that would remain a part of his estate. Although the exact details of the agreement are not public, the couple appears to have worked out the details and are now married (ABCNEWS, 2000).

Although many people view marriage contracts as unromantic and unnecessary if a couple has little or no property, an increasing number of today's couples, especially those in remarriages, are drawing up marital agreements.

Perhaps a sign of the times, the market, including the Internet, is flooded with information and materials about prenuptial agreements. Couples planning to wed can go on the Internet where they will find an array of information from lawyers who will describe what prenuptial agreements are and their importance and offering their legal services, to what judges and courts will enforce and what they won't, to advice on how to discuss an agreement with a partner, to what topics need to be addressed in an agreement to make it valid, to books on the subject with titles such as *Prenups for Lovers: A Romantic Guide to Prenuptial Agreements.*

A law called the Uniform Pre-Marital Agreement Act provides legal guidelines for those wishing to make a prenuptial agreement. Some 20 states have adopted this act, and those that have not have similar laws. A few states have their own unique laws in this regard. For example, some states, including California, do not allow premarital agreements to modify or eliminate the right of a spouse to receive court-ordered alimony at divorce. Other states, like Maine, void all premarital agreements one and one-half years after the parties to the contract become parents, unless the agreement is renewed (Court TV's Legal Café, 1997). Although anyone can draw up a prenuptial agreement, for it to be upheld in court those involved must demonstrate that there was full, accurate, and fair disclosure of all assets at the time it was drawn up, that it was fair and reasonable when signed, and at the time of divorce or death, that it was signed voluntarily by both parties and entered into in good faith. To meet this criterion parties should secure the services of an attorney who is familiar with state laws governing marriage and community property. Even then there is no guarantee that courts will uphold all of the agreement's provisions. Although the specifications in the agreement may be morally binding, some, such as specifications concerning living arrangements, child custody, and/or the support of children, are not enforceable in court (Totenberg, 1985).

Personal Contracts The most popular version of the personal marriage agreement among couples today is the personal contract, created by the couple without advice or counsel from an attorney. Although these contracts serve primarily as guides to future behavior, they are sometimes filed as legal contracts. As with the more formal and legal prenuptial agreements, personal contracts are not new. At different times in history couples have used the personal contract to satisfy a range of personal needs. For example, in the late seventeenth century, Eleanor Veazel and John French drafted a marriage contract in which the provisions included promises by John to not take any part of the estate that Elizabeth had inherited from her former husband, to let Elizabeth sell their apples, and a promise to leave Elizabeth 4 pounds a year after his death, which could be paid in any number of ways, including in corn, malt, pork, or beef (Scott and Wishy, 1982). In the nineteenth century, suffragist and feminist Lucy Stone and her husband-to-be, Henry Blackwell, a well-known abolitionist, wrote their own personal contract in protest against the inequality of women in marriage, which they read and signed as part of their wedding ceremony. In addition, Stone refused to take her husband's surname, preferring to be known instead as "Mrs. Stone" (Schneir, 1972).

Although there is a wide range of opinions about personal marriage agreements, as we have indicated, many people find them to have several important benefits, including forcing a couple to communicate with each other their marital expectations, desires, and goals. A case in point was the 1995 premarital agreement drawn up by Rex and Teresa LeGalley of Albuquerque, New Mexico, that spelled out the rules of their life together in minute detail, including how often they would have sex (healthy sex three to five times a week), which gasoline to buy for their car (Chevron supreme), and who was responsible for doing the laundry (Ms. LeGalley). This was Rex's third marriage and Teresa's second. The premarital contract, however, was the first for each, and it was Teresa's idea. The agreement was compiled from her notes taken over their one-year courtship (she took notes on their dates). Their 16-page, single-spaced premarital contract was a legally notarized document in which the LeGalleys attempted to cover almost every possible aspect of their lives. Examples from the agreement included:

- "Lights out by 11:30 P.M. Wake up 6:30 A.M., Monday through Friday."
- "Family leadership and decision making is Mr. LeGalley's responsibility. Ms. LeGalley will make decisions only in emergencies and when Mr. LeGalley is unavailable."
- Ms. LeGalley will be in charge of "inside house chores, including laundry," while Mr. LeGalley "will be responsible for inside repairs and will maintain the outside of the house, including the garage and cars."
- "If we get angry, we will count to 10 first."
- "We will make ourselves available for discussion 15 to 30 minutes per day and we will spend time together doing things 15 to 20 hours per week."
- "Ms. LeGalley will stay on birth control for 2 years after we are married and then will try to get pregnant. When both of us are working, she can have only one child. When one parent is free, she can have another child. When both of us are free, she can have one more child. After the third pregnancy, we will both get sterilized."

The LeGalleys even built in penalties for breaking the rules. For example, there was a monetary fine for overspending at the supermarket and if one partner let the gas in her or his car fall below the one-half mark, she or he had to fill the other's tank.

In an interview a year after they were married, the LeGalleys said that the contract was working well. According to Rex, "Things couldn't be better. We worked out so many things before we married that we didn't have that transition period that most couples do in their first year of marriage." Teresa commented: "Writing the prenup was one of the best things we ever did because we discussed everything and learned a lot about each other." The document is probably not legally binding and the LeGalleys say they have no plans to enforce it. They said that it was simply "all about getting to know your partner." Although we do not have another update, Teresa was scheduled to have their first child in 1997. In their interview, Teresa said that the couple still planned to have their first child in 1997; "that's one item that's not negotiable" (Bojorquez, 1997).

Personal agreements are not always this detailed, nor are they limited to couples planning to marry. Any couple who is committed to each other or who lives together, as well as couples who are legally prohibited from marrying, can benefit from such agreements.

As the LeGalleys' agreement demonstrates, prenuptial or personal marriage agreements can include anything a couple considers appropriate, such as the general expectations a couple has for each other, the division of roles and tasks in the marriage or living arrangement, how often they will engage in sexual activities, and whether they will have children. At the end of this chapter, in the "Writing Your Own Script" box, we invite you to write your own personal marriage or relationship agreement. We present several topics for your consideration. Are other topics relevant to your relationship? Does the contract between the LeGalleys give you any ideas?

The Wedding

Today's couples tend to prefer traditional weddings, but increasingly they are infusing the wedding ceremony with a touch of personal style—from unusual or ethnic wedding attire to male bridesmaids and female groomsmen, to offbeat choices of locations for their wedding and receptions, to elaborate reception menus. For example, every Valentine's Day hundreds of couples are married in shopping malls around the country. The weddings are typically promoted by local radio stations. Other couples have gotten married as they were skydiving out of an airplane, and still others have wed via satellite with one partner in absentia. For example, every year, the Reverend Sun Myung Moon marries thousands of couples simultaneously by satellite hookups between Korea and hundreds of sites around the world. Brides and grooms who cannot be present are represented by a photo. In 2000, 20,000 couples, some long married and others newly matched, from over 100 countries, including the United States, paid a predetermined fee to take part in a marriage ceremony sponsored by the Reverend and Mrs. Sun Myung Moon and the Unification Church. Reverend Moon matches the couples, all of whom are total strangers, by age and education. The church believes that cross-cultural matchmaking will help unite the world. This belief notwithstanding, it is estimated that around three-fourths of these couples divorce (Associated Press, 1997; Baker, 2000). According to Lee Bey (1996), some weddings begin in the toilet. In January 1996, six Taiwanese couples married in a single ceremony in a custom-built one-million-dollar public bathroom.

Cultural or ethnic weddings are also rising in popularity. For example, many African Americans who marry today have what is defined as an African-centered wedding. Such a ceremony varies according to the individuals, but may include traditional African attire for the bride, groom, and other participants in the wedding made out of kente, Guinea brocade, or other expensive African fabrics; African and other cultural cuisine at the reception; African drummers and dancers; a wedding cake baked by an African or Caribbean baker; a Yoruba priest or priestess to conduct the ceremony; or "jumping the broom," a tradition carried over from slavery.

Weddings today are far more expensive than in the past. Over the last 25 to 30 years, the median age of the bride and groom has risen by 3 years to 25 and 27, respectively. Because the average couple is older, they tend to have more money to spend on an elaborate wedding. Weddings are big business in the United States. Somewhere around 2 and 2.5 million couples marry each year, spending anywhere from hundreds to tens of thousands of dollars on each ceremony. Estimates of the cost of an *average* wedding today run from a low of about $5500 to as much as $60,000. The costs of a wedding, of course, will vary depending on the quality and/or quantity of the items one chooses for the wedding, the size and type of wedding, as well as where the couple marries. For example, a wedding in Las Vegas, Nevada, can cost as little as a $35 chapel fee to several hundred dollars for a chapel wedding package that includes any assortment of or all of the following: a chapel fee, a wedding coordinator, an organist or pianist, a soloist, flowers, wedding photos, a wedding album, a professional video of the ceremony, a custom marriage certificate holder, a wedding garter, limousine service, a bottle of champagne and champagne glasses, witnesses (if needed), and a "Just Married" bumper sticker. At the other end of the continuum are the costs of the weddings of the rich and famous. For example, the November 2000 wedding of movie celebrities Catherine Zeta-Jones and Michael Douglas at New York City's swank Plaza Hotel is rumored to have cost the couple $2 million. Adding to the cost of the wedding was the meal for the 250 invited guests who feasted on an elaborate seven-course wedding meal that combined elements of American and Welsh cuisine (ABCNEWS, 2000). The more unique the wedding, the more expensive it often is.

An interesting exercise, particularly for those planning a wedding now or in the near future, is to search the Internet to find out the costs for different types, sizes, and locales for weddings. Additionally, some suggestions are: Find sources that help you budget for the wedding, as well as some that inform you as to the proper protocol in terms of who pays for what wedding items, the types of wedding planners that are available and their costs, and different unique weddings and their cost. What other resources can you find that would aid someone planning her or his own wedding? In addition, there are often costs associated with hiring a wedding consultant, buying wedding rings, and the honeymoon. Today, couples planning a honeymoon will probably spend, on average, another $3000 to $5000 depending on whether they honeymoon within or outside the country.

A growing segment of the wedding industry is a cadre of individuals and books advising couples how to keep their wedding costs down. Typical examples include making your wedding reception a lunch instead of a dinner; choosing foods that are in season; serving more vegetables and less meat (also, chicken is cheaper than beef); eliminating champagne toasts; choosing a buffet rather than a sit-down dinner. Other advice includes avoiding a Saturday wedding (Saturdays are the most expensive days to rent an event space—Sundays are always cheaper); staying away from planning a wedding on popular holidays like Mother's Day, Valentine's Day, when the cost of flowers is inflated, or New Year's Day, when band rates are inflated. In addition, hire a DJ instead of a band and hire a professional photographer to shoot only during the wedding ceremony. For the reception leave disposable cameras at each table. Instead of buying an expensive wedding gown for several thousand dollars, order one from a discount bridal store or rent one from a "rental salon" (Crawford, 1995:1).

What do you think of this kind of advice? If you are planning a wedding, will you consider some of these cost-saving devices? Why or why not? If you are already married, how much did your wedding cost? Could you have saved money by following some of the advice you have just read?

MARRIAGE VOWS As more and more people change their views of marriage, they are also changing or at least modifying many of the rituals and traditions of weddings. For example, although some people continue to recite traditional wedding vows when they marry, others have modified or rewritten those vows to accommodate their preferences and to make their wedding romantic, meaningful, and unique. Perhaps as much a sign of the times as the Internet blitz of prenuptial agreements is the fact that a wide range of resources for writing your own wedding vows, from prewritten examples to custom wedding vows, can be found on the Internet. Couples can add their own words or mix vows from different ceremonies. Even if they already have vows, they can find that one special line that adds an extra something to their wedding ceremony.

In Table 8.2 we present the traditional wedding vows, a set of vows written by a white middle-class couple (Mary and Richard) who married in the 1970s, and a set of prewritten vows found on the Internet in 2001. In 1999, we asked Richard to reread the vows that he and Mary had written and tell us what meaning, if any, those vows had for him 22 years later. Lovingly, Richard indicated that "the beautiful sentiments expressed in the vows are still very much my sentiments today. . . . My memory is fresh with my feelings of the deepest love I had for her on our wedding day. . . . I deeply love and cherish Mary and feel myself as committed as ever to share the trials and tribulations as well as all of the happiness that comes our way (Brewer, 1999). Although personalized wedding vows do not ensure a long and successful marriage, they very often serve as a guide or a set of goals that silently guides a couple's life together, as Richard's response suggests.

Table 8.2

Telling Their Love: Marriage Vows for Different Preferences

Traditional Marriage Vows[1]

I, ________, take thee, ________, to be my lawful wedded wife (husband). To have and to hold from this day forward; For better, for worse, For richer, for poorer; In sickness and in health; To love, honor, obey, and cherish; From this day forward; Till death do us part.

The Marriage Vows of Mary and Richard[2]

Mary (Richard), to manifest my deep love for you, I promise to cherish you, care for you, and to share with you the difficulties, the sorrows, and the hardships as well as the joys, the beauty, and the happiness that come our way.

I promise you a warm home and a dear and understanding heart in it, so that we may grow with and for each other.

I promise to work together with you to build and to maintain this home and this love.

Internet: Prewritten Wedding Vows[3]

I, ________, take you, ________, as my friend and love, asking that you be no other than yourself, loving what I know of you, trusting what I do not know yet, in all the ways life may find us, beside me and apart from me, in laughter and in tears, in conflict and tranquility, tending you in sickness and rejoicing with you in health, as long as we both shall live to love.

[1]Most couples, even if they recite the traditional vows, no longer vow to obey their partner.

[2]In addition to writing their own vows Mary chose to maintain her birth name.

[3]This set of vows was combined from the following two sets of Internet vows: "May This Day Shine Eternally" and "Enter Days of Togetherness" found at **http://members.aol.com/trevorb1/vows/2p.html** and **http://members.aol.com/trevorb/vow/5p.html**, respectively.

Although most women marrying today do not pledge to *obey* their husbands, the pendulum may be swinging back to vows of obedience, at least among the nation's Southern Baptists. At the close of the last decade, in response to what the leadership of the Southern Baptists viewed as a growing crisis in marriages and families, the nation's largest Protestant denomination (16 million members) issued a declaration on obedience to husbands. Those attending the Southern Baptists' 1998 national convention voted overwhelmingly to add a new article of faith, which declares that marriage is a lifelong covenant between one man and one woman, and the husband has the "God given responsibility to provide for, to protect, and to lead his family. A wife is to submit herself graciously to the servant leadership of her husband." This statement, with its emphasis on "one man and one woman," is also consistent with the Southern Baptists' campaign against homosexuality. Critics of the Baptists' declaration argue that focusing on wifely submission implies that women are inferior to men and could even offer a religious excuse for some men to abuse their wives (Kloehn, 1998; Niebuhr, 1998).

Personalizing the wedding vows, a personal marriage agreement, and the cost of weddings notwithstanding, what happens once a couple is married? What kinds of changes take place in their lives? Do women and men experience marriage in the same way? In the remaining sections of this chapter we discuss marriage as it is experienced by women and men. In this regard, we examine gender differences in the marital experience, factors related to transitions and adjustments to marriage, some common typologies of marital relationships, heterogamous marriages, and the benefits of positive and open communication in marriages and intimate relationships.

MARRIAGE AND GENDER

Marriage and family researchers across academic disciplines increasingly are acknowledging that marriage is experienced in different ways by women and men; that every marriage actually contains two marriages: hers and his. In her now-classic book *The Future of Marriage* (1972), sociologist Jessie Bernard detailed the different experiential realities of wives and husbands. When asked identical questions about their marriage, husbands and wives answered so differently that Bernard called their marriages "her marriage" and "his marriage." Even when asked basic questions like how often they had sexual relations or who made decisions, wives' and husbands' responses were so different it was as though they were talking about two different marriages. Though largely hidden, the female–male differences in the experience of marriage have a tremendous effect on the mental and physical well-being of wives and husbands.

"Her" Marriage

Does it surprise you that Bernard found that wives were much less happy in their marriages than were their husbands? Some people believe that these are just a few disgruntled wives; that couples who love each other live in a kind of identical harmony and peace. Several of Bernard's findings challenge this assumption. For example, although wives reported being happier with their lives than did single women, when compared with husbands they reported being less happy. In addition, married women reported much higher rates of anxiety, phobia, and depression than any other group in society except single men, and wives had a higher rate of suicide than did husbands.

Research continues to uncover women's and men's different perceptions and experience of marriage. Reporting on a study of married couples between the ages of 17 and 69, for example, Daniel Goleman (1987) pointed out that husbands and wives differ dramatically in terms of how they evaluate their relationship. Men tend to rate almost everything as better than do their wives. They have a much more positive perception of marital sex, family finances, ties with parents, listening to each other, tolerance of flaws, and romance. Wives, on the other hand, tend to complain more about their marriage than husbands do. Moreover, although married women experience better health than singles do, they do not benefit in terms of health from marriage as much as men do. For example, women in traditional marriages (wherein the woman assumes the traditional role of wife and homemaker) are especially prone to higher rates of illness than are husbands (Flowers, 1991; Lauer, 1992).

Perhaps something about the nature or structure of marriage itself accounts for these gender differences. The structure of traditional marriage, particularly with regard to the housewife role, is revealing in this regard. For example, the division of labor in traditional marriages leads to fewer sources of gratification for housewives than for husbands. The imbalance of power in traditional marriages further alienates the housewife from her wifely role. According to Bernard, the housewife role has a "pathogenic" effect on wives. Often when women marry they lose their legal and personal identity and become totally dependent on their husbands, which often leads to depression. Other researchers (for example, Gove, 1972) have concurred with this view, noting that the housewife role is so unstructured and devalued, restrictive and stressful that wives often have low self-esteem, are highly self-critical, and are far more vulnerable to depression and unhappiness than their husbands are.

"His" Marriage

Many of you have probably grown up on tales of men running from marriage, going to great lengths to avoid being "trapped." This folklore actually runs counter to the reality of women's and men's lives. In reality men seem to prefer marriage to being single. For example, when asked if they would marry the same person again, they respond in the affirmative twice as often as their wives do. In addition, most divorced and widowed men remarry, and at every age level the rate of marriage for these men is higher than the rate for single men. Furthermore, when compared with single men, married men live longer, have better mental and physical health, are less depressed, have a lower rate of suicide, are less likely to be incarcerated for a crime, earn higher incomes, and are more likely to define themselves as happy.

Although marriage is beneficial overall for men, it imposes certain costs. Bernard contends that a major cost of marriage for men is that they must give up their sexual freedom and take on the responsibility of supporting a wife and family. Whether or not this is a *cost* is debatable. Nonetheless, the provider role is costly in other respects, including the fact that it forces many men to work harder than they might otherwise. This, however, is changing as women and men have become more sexually free both within and outside of marriage and as more married women have begun working outside the home and contributing to the family income. According to social scientist Marie Richmond-Abbott (1983), traditional marriage reinforces stereotypical masculine roles and may actually hurt men.

TRANSITIONS AND ADJUSTMENTS TO MARRIAGES

Getting married represents a significant change in the lives of a couple. The world of married couples is in many important ways different from the world of singles. As a married couple, two people must fit their lives together and meet and satisfy each other's needs. In simple terms, **marital adjustment** is the degree to which a couple get along with each other or have a good working relationship and are able to satisfy each other's needs over the marital life course. One major adjustment that a married couple must make involves being identified with a partner and thought of by the community as one unit, as opposed to the unique individual each was before the marriage. Another marital adjustment regards seeing and relating to a partner on a daily basis, and learning to live with that person and accommodate her or his wants, needs, expectations, and desires. Still other adjustments include sharing space, money, relatives, and friends with a partner; the division of tasks in the relationship; and adjustment to the partner's sexual attitudes and behaviors. Changing from a single to a married persona does not always run smoothly. Most couples, however, manage it with a minimum of problems.

Adjustment doesn't simply happen one day in a marriage; rather, it is an ongoing process. As pointed out in Chapter 2, some family sociologists hold that marriages and families move through a series of life events over the course of the marital life cycle. Research shows that couples must continuously make adjustments in marriage as they are confronted with new and different life course events.

A Typology of Marital Relationships

What makes a happy, well-adjusted marriage? Most contemporary studies have concluded that there is no single model for a well-adjusted marriage. Helpfulness, love, mutual respect, and selflessness are but a few of the many characteristics associated with successful marital adjustment. In a now-classic study of marital adjustment and happiness, researchers John Cuber and Peggy Harroff (1966) reported on 211 couples who had been married for 10 or more years and who expressed commitment to each other. Cuber and Harroff concluded that satisfying, well-adjusted, enduring marital relationships can vary a great deal from each other and from societal ideals of a happy marriage. Although their work is over 4 decades old, and although it has been critiqued as a class-based analysis, it is still the most frequently cited research on adjustment and happiness in marriage. And until there is current and more representative research in this area, the Cuber–Harroff classification scheme continues to offer some useful insights into marriage/relationship types. Cuber and Harroff identified five distinct types of marriages, representing a wide range of communication patterns and interaction styles: conflict-habituated, devitalized, passive-congenial, vital, and total.

The Conflict-Habituated Marriage The first type, the conflict-habituated marriage is characterized by extensive tension and conflict, although for the most part the tension and conflict are managed or controlled. Channeling conflict and hostility is so important to these couples that it becomes a habitual part of their marriage. The couple engage in both verbal and physical arguments and fights, usually in private but sometimes in front of family and friends. They see their fighting as an acceptable way to solve problems and do not see it as a cause for separation or divorce. However, fighting seldom solves their problems.

The Devitalized Marriage The devitalized marriage involves very little conflict. Rather, it is characteristic of couples who were once deeply in love and had a satisfying sexual relationship but over time have lost their sense of excitement and passion. In this type of marriage the partners pay very little attention to one another. There are occasional periods of sharing and time spent together, but this is done out of a sense of "duty" not joy. Although the marriage lacks visible vitality, these couples remain together believing that their marriage is the way most marriages are.

The Passive-Congenial Marriage The passive-congenial marriage is similar in many respects to the devitalized marriage. The primary difference is that the passivity that characterizes this marriage was there from the beginning. Couples in this type of marriage began the marriage with a low emotional investment and low expectations that do not change over the course of the marriage. Although there is little conflict in this type of marriage, there is also very little excitement. Passive-congenial couples share many common interests, but their fulfillment comes from involvements and relationships outside the marriage. In fact, they feel that their type of marriage facilitates independence and security and allows them the time and freedom to pursue individual goals.

The Vital Marriage The vital marriage contrasts sharply with the previous three types. Vital couples are highly involved with each other; their sharing and togetherness provide the life force of the marriage. Despite their enjoyment of one another, the vital couple does not lose their sense of identity or monopolize each other's time; rather, they simply enjoy each other when they are together and make this time the focal point of their lives. The vital couple tries to avoid conflict; however, when it does occur, it is usually over a serious issue, and the couple makes every attempt to settle the disagreement as quickly as possible rather than let it drag on, as do the conflict-habituated couple.

The Total Marriage Finally, unlike the vital marriage in which the couple value their time together but maintain their individuality, the total marriage is characterized by constant togetherness and sharing of most if not all important life events. Couples in a total marriage often work together and share the same friends; the partners have few areas of tension or unresolved conflict primarily because tensions that do arise are dealt with as they occur. In fact, a defining characteristic of the total marriage is the fact that when faced with tension, conflict, or differences, the couple deal with the issues without losing the feeling of unity and vitality that is paramount to their relationship.

Total relationships are rare, and the total couple are often aware of their exceptionality. Such relationships do exist, however. In fact, Cuber and Harroff report that they occasionally found relationships so total that every aspect of the relationship was mutually and enthusiastically shared. In a sense, it was as if these couples did not have an individual existence.

The researchers reported that the majority of the couples they studied fell into the first three categories. They labeled these marriages as *utilitarian*, because, in their view, the marriages appeared to be based upon convenience. They labeled the remaining two types of marriages *intrinsic marriages*, because these marriages appeared to be rewarding. One of several problems with this study and the categories used to describe types of marriages is the obvious bias in the choice of terms used to describe the marriages. For example, what criteria did the researchers use to determine if a marriage is intrinsic and thus rewarding? Could not a marriage be both convenient and rewarding? More recent research on marital adjustment and happiness has built upon the Cuber and Harroff typology, adding one or more new dimensions but essentially maintaining the typology elucidated by Cuber and Harroff (see, for example, the seven-point typology put forth by Lavee and Olson, 1993; or the four-point classification scheme of Wallerstein and Blakeslee, 1995).

Given the limitations of the study and the language used to describe marriage types, do you think that you fit into one of these types of marriages or intimate relationships? Why or why not? Do you know couples who can be described in terms of one or more of these relationship types? What about your parents? Where do they fit (if at all)?

It is clear that the meaning of marriage as well as what represents marital happiness and adjustment differ among human beings. Cuber and Harroff stress the point that each of these relationship types simply represents a particular type of interaction in and adjustment to the marital relationship. Thus, people living in any one of the relationships described by Cuber and Harroff may or may not be satisfied. In addition, the categories are not mutually exclusive. Rather, some couples are on the border, and others may move from one mode of interaction to another over the course of their relationship. We should also keep in mind that the Cuber–Harroff typology represents relationships, not personality types. It is quite possible, for example, that a vital person could be living in a devitalized relationship, expressing her or his vitality through some other part of her or his life.

HETEROGAMOUS MARRIAGES

In addition to types of relationships, social scientists often classify marriages in terms of social characteristics such as race, ethnicity, and religion. Although people tend to select partners with whom they share these characteristics, some couples do come from different backgrounds or traditions. Marriages between people who vary in certain social and demographic characteristics are referred to as **heterogamous marriages.** Such marriages have become more common in recent years. The following section focuses on two major types of heterogamous marriage: interracial and interethnic marriages and interfaith marriages.

Interracial Marriages

Although many people interpret interracial marriage as referring to black–white couples, interracial marriages actually involve a wide range of combinations, including not only whites and African Americans but also Native Americans, Asian Americans, and Latinos. In fact, today, black–white marriages make up only six-tenths of 1 percent of all marriages in the United States (U.S. Census Bureau, 2000a). Interracial marriage is most common among college-educated, middle-income people of all races. Although according to some estimates there are about 600,000 interracial marriages annually in the United States, this country has a long history of intolerance of marriage across racial lines. Although down from three decades ago (38 percent), contemporary polls report anywhere from 12 to 15 percent of Americans feel that interracial marriages should be banned. This sentiment is particularly strong relative to African American–white marriages. For example, the 1994 General Social Survey conducted by the National Opinion Research Center revealed that 15 percent of the whites interviewed nationwide favored a law actually banning all marriages between African Americans and whites and, three years later, a Knight-Ridder poll reported that three in ten people opposed marriages between blacks and whites (James, 1997; Thackeray, 2000). By the end of the twentieth century, a Gallup poll reported that roughly four in ten people still disapproved of interracial marriages in general (Gallup Poll, 2000).

The paradox of white Americans' attitudes and behavior relative to interracial marriage does not go unnoticed, however. In the face of a history of forced race-mixing vis-à-vis the sexual exploitation and rape of African women under slavery, Native American women during the European conquest and colonization, and other women of oppressed and exploited racial and ethnic groups in this country, it is indeed paradoxical that, through legal prohibitions against interracial marriage, white Americans have outlawed race mixing until recent times. Some sociologists, historians, and geneticists have estimated that 75 percent of all African Americans have at least one white ancestor, and another 15 percent have predominant white ancestral lines as a result of the rape of their ancestors. Concomitantly, 95 percent of "white" Americans have widely varying degrees of black heritage. Yet miscegenation laws meant to separate the races by prohibiting interracial marriages between whites and African Americans (and whites and Native Americans) began as early as 1661 and lasted until 1999. In 1967, the U.S. Supreme Court's decision in the case of *Loving* v. *Virginia* (involving the marriage of a woman of African and Native American descent and her white husband) overturned antimiscegenation laws nationally. Prior to that, 39 states had laws that specifically prohibited miscegenation, or the interracial marriage of whites with other specific groups: Arizona, for example, prohibited marriage between whites and Native Americans; California, Utah, Wyoming, and Idaho prohibited white and Mongolian marriages; and Nebraska and Montana prohibited marriages between whites and Asian Americans (Kunerth, 1990).

Although the U.S. Supreme Court decided in 1967 that laws prohibiting interracial marriages were unconstitutional, such laws remained part of the state constitutional language of South Carolina and Alabama until the end of the twentieth century. In 1999, South Carolina removed its ban on interracial marriages, and in the November 2000 election, voters in Alabama passed Amendment 2, which erased a section of the Alabama state constitution that read: "The legislature shall never pass any law to authorize or legalize any marriage between any white person and a Negro or descendant of a Negro" (Associated Press, 1999; "Voters Remove State Interracial Marriage Ban," 2000). This fact notwithstanding, the informal restrictions—sociocultural norms—concerning these marriages remain the most inflexible of all mate selection boundaries. Even though the number of interracial couples has doubled since 1980—

1.5 million to 3 million interracial marriages today (U.S. Census Bureau, 2000a)—they still remain rare relative to marriages between people of the same race or ethnic group. As Figure 8.4 shows, racial endogamy in marriage is particularly strong for certain groups, such as African Americans. Thus, we cannot underestimate the power of informal social norms that operate in mate selection. For a better understanding of this, let us turn our attention to interracial marriages among various racial and ethnic groups in the United States.

AFRICAN AMERICANS Among various groups of color in the United States, African Americans have the highest rate of endogamous marriages and the lowest rate of exogamous marriages. Of the total number of married couples in the United States in 1999, less than 1 percent were African American–white couples. Approximately 92 percent of all African Americans who are married are married to another African American. However, as shown in Figure 8.4, when African American women and men do marry interracially, most often (seven out of ten such marriages) their mate is white.

Unlike any other race or ethnic group in the United States, African American men are more likely to marry outside the race (5.0 percent) than are African American women (2.7 percent). For example, African American men are more than twice as likely as African American women to have a white mate. Social scientists have consistently acknowledged this fact, yet there have been few empirical studies that explain why. Common theory suggests that based on the gender/race marital patterns, there are differences in the courtship processes and the amount of social support received. This theory notwithstanding, government statistics indicate that the number of African American women marrying white men is slowly increasing. For example, the number of African American women married to white men doubled from 1987 to 1999.

In most cases, African American–white couples have been raised in racially sensitive homes; are more likely to have met through their jobs than in school, in their neighborhoods, in church, or through recreational activities; begin their courtship through repeated casual conversations rather than with immediate physical attraction, friendship over a period of time, or after close association with one another; are initially attracted to one another through their shared interests; and at least one partner in the marriage has been married previously. Some scholars have suggested that some African American–white couples might also belong to religions that encourage interracial unions, such as the Baha'i religion, which teaches that God is particularly pleased with interracial unions. Moreover, the couples usually live far away from their families of orientation; mothers of daughters tend to be more supportive of the relationship than mothers of sons, and fathers of sons are more supportive of the relationship than fathers of daughters (Zebroski, 1997). These marriages also are most likely to occur among highly educated persons. This is particularly true of African American men who marry white women. These men are typically well educated, have a

Figure 8.4

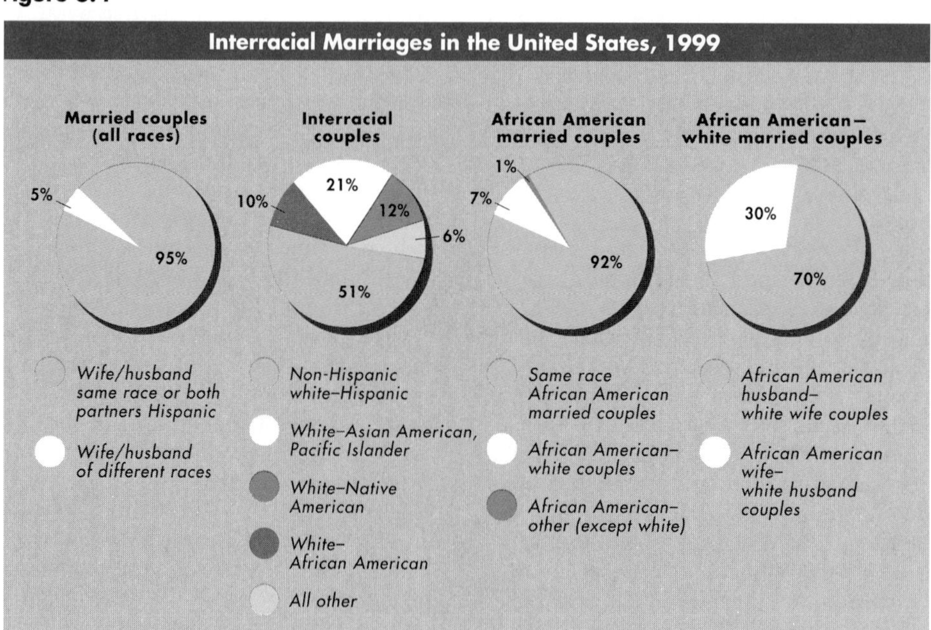

Source: U.S. Census Bureau, 2000, *Statistical Abstract of the United States, 2000* (Washington, DC: U.S. Government Printing Office): 51, Table 54.

high income, and are usually older than their mate. In fact, African American men who have attended graduate school are the most likely to marry interracially (Kalmijn, 1999). In addition, the rate of interracial marriage among young African Americans is far higher than average, with about 11 percent of the married 15- to 24-year-olds married interracially, compared to 7 percent for African Americans overall. In addition, the rate of divorce is lower for African American husband/white wife couples than for white husband/African American wife couples.

Although attitudes and behavior regarding racial intermarriages have changed somewhat, interracial couples, especially African American–white couples, are still frequently subjected to a range of societal reactions and indignities from stares to cross-burnings to physical attacks. The widely publicized and horrific murder in 1955 of 15-year-old Emmett Till, an African American teenager accused of whistling at a white woman in Mississippi, symbolized the historical deep-seated views of some whites relative to the mere suggestion of racial mixing and intimacy. Although, at least overtly, attitudes and behaviors have changed from such grotesque displays of disapproval, 66 percent of the white population still say that they would oppose a close relative's marriage to an African American person. Only 4 percent said they would favor such a marriage (Newman, 1995).

Such feelings run deep and can be found even among some of the nation's religious role models: the clergy. For example, in 2000 a pastor in Jasper, Ohio, shut the door on an interracial couple, refusing to marry them because she is white and her fiancé is African American. Although the nuptials had been scheduled in advance by the bride-to-be's brother, and although she was a member of the church, the pastor forbade the use of the building for an interracial marriage. Although the pastor refused to discuss the details of his decision, he did confirm that he prohibited the use of the church after learning that the groom-to-be was African American (Mahoney, 2000).

Reactions such as these reflect the importance that white Americans continue to attach to the preservation of racial segregation and the role of informal norms in shaping our behavior. Such statistics should not be taken to indicate that white Americans are the only group to oppose interracial marriage. There are those in almost every other racial group who also oppose such marriages. For example, many African Americans, especially women, oppose interracial marriages on the basis that it strains an already limited pool of eligible African American men. Others view such marriages as weakening cultural heritage and group solidarity. Likewise, Asian men, especially Chinese men, are opposed to interracial marriages, seeing them as a cultural and racial betrayal by Chinese women.

As indicated earlier, although interracial marriages have increased over the years, many interracial couples experience various forms of antagonism because of their relationship. According to some researchers (Rosenblatt, Karis, and Powell, 1995), interracial couples say that the most pressing problem they face, both before and after marriage, is racism. The emotional wear and tear of social and cultural attitudes toward interracial couples is often enormous. For some of these couples, their way of coping with the indignities and nonacceptance of their relationship by family, friends, and/or the larger society is to not respond to the racism; to not let others make racism their problem (see, for example, Laural and Ralph Kemp in the "Family Profile" box).

In addition to racial attitudes and beliefs that shape the informal endogamous norms surrounding mate selection in the United States, various structural features of American society also affect the rate of interracial marriages. For example, interracial marriage rates vary across geographic regions and are highest in regions where relatively large numbers of people of color live and where attitudes toward interracial relationships and race are relatively more permissive and tolerant than in other areas of the country. The rate of interracial marriages for African Americans, for instance, is highest in the West and lowest in the South (Tucker and Mitchell-Kernan, 1990).

Native Americans If African Americans represent the most racially endogamous end of the marital continuum among people of color, Native Americans are at the other end. Native Americans are more likely than any other racial group to marry outside their group. They are more likely to marry a white American than another Native American and least likely to marry an African American. Of six races studied by social scientist Richard Clayton in 1978, Native Americans were the least likely to exhibit racial endogamy in marriage patterns. In fact, Native Americans were involved in over 27 percent of all interracial marriages.

This trend of interracial marriage has increased steadily since the 1970s, so that currently approximately 74 percent (three out of four) of married Native Americans have a non–Native American spouse (Spain, 1999). As with other racial groups, the rate of interracial marriages among Native Americans varies by age, with the oldest age groups having lower rates than the youngest age groups. For example, during the 1990s, 65 percent of Native Americans under age 25 compared to 52 percent of those 65 and older were married to a person of a different race. However, unlike with some other racial groups (for example, Asian Americans) interracial marriage does not appear to be associated with gender; Native American women and men are near equally likely to marry a non–Native American.

A number of explanations for this marital pattern have been proposed. The most common is related to the size of the Native American population. Only about 2.4 million Americans today identify themselves as being of native descent (U.S. Census Bureau, 2000a). Given the already overall small size of Native Americans, geographic areas with small Native American populations have significantly higher rates of interracial marriage than do those with large populations. The high rates of Native American interracial marriages are also linked to the increased migration of Native Americans

FAMILY PROFILE

LAURAL AND RALPH KEMP

Length of relationship: 11 years

Challenges of being an interracial couple: It is difficult to address the challenges of being an interracial couple primarily because we are not aware of ourselves in the same way as others seem to be. To us we are just a woman and man who are in love with and respect one another for who we are and who are confronted with many of the same basic issues as couples of the same race. In general, we view challenges of all sorts as opportunities for growth. Our relationship itself has been a growth process and it continues to be a work in progress—one we are genuinely and strongly committed to. Without such commitment any relationship would suffer. We have learned so much from each other about ourselves, life, and human nature, and our different racial backgrounds have been a positive impetus for growth and a deeper understanding of issues of race, tolerance, love, and respect. However, we are aware that just the mere sight of our being together is a challenge for some people. Early in our relationship we decided that we would not be on the defensive about our relationship, and unless there was some overt verbal or physical attack against us we would not respond to other people's racism. To do so is to stoop to their level and that is not what our life and love is about. For those individuals who have a problem with our relationship, we see it as their challenge to deal with, not ours.

Laural and Ralph Kemp

Relationship philosophy: Our relationship philosophy is intricately tied to our practice of Nichiren Daishonin's Buddhism, which we practice through the SGI-USA. This Buddhism teaches that solutions to one's problems and life challenges lie within. To meet a challenge or change a situation, we have to first look within and change ourselves. We take full responsibility for the success of our relationship by working together to develop a more loving, compatible, satisfying, and productive life and relationship. We do not seek approval and success from outside of ourselves and our relationship.

to urban areas, expanding opportunities for education and employment in nonreservation settings, and a generally more favorable attitude about Native peoples and their cultures. In this context, interracial marriage is much higher for Native Americans living in urban areas than for those living on reservations (Mindel, Habenstein, and Wright, 1998) and is more characteristic for those Native Americans who have left the reservation to pursue educational and occupational opportunities in cities. In 1995, researcher Karl Eschbach found that approximately three-fourths of Native Americans, who lived in 23 states, were married to someone from another race. According to Eschbach, with the exception of those areas in which Native Americans live in enclaves, the Native American population is amalgamating rapidly. Other researchers, such as Yellowbird and Snipp (1994), have suggested that the extremely high rate of interracial marriage for Native Americans may accomplish what disease, Western civilization, and decades of federal policies toward Native Americans failed to achieve.

ASIAN AMERICANS Historically, social scientists have used the rates of interracial marriage with whites as an indicator of the acculturation or assimilation of various groups of color into the American mainstream. If that is the case, then Asian American families are becoming increasingly acculturated. Approximately 38 percent of Asian Americans are married exogamously, primarily with whites. This trend is particularly prevalent among younger Asian Americans. For example, 30 percent of married Asian Americans between the ages of 15 and 24 are married outside their race, and nearly one half of those under the age of 35 are interracial couples. And those Asian Americans most likely to be in an interracial marriage are those who live in relatively small immigrant communities (suro, 2001). Of course, rates of interracial marriage vary from group to group, with Japanese and Chinese Americans having the highest rates of all Asian American groups. For example, Japanese Americans have the highest rate, with over 50 percent marrying outside the group. Interracial marriages for most Asian American groups are principally among the first generation. However, for Japanese Americans, interracial marriages are primarily among the third (Sansei) generation, of whom almost 60 percent are married interracially. This younger generation of Japanese Americans, especially the college-educated, exhibits considerable differences in marital behavior from earlier generations. Whereas earlier generations were greatly constrained in marital choice by socialization and the power of the family, contemporary generations believe that parents should not interfere in the choice of a marital partner. As this belief has become more widespread, the incidence of marriage between whites and Japanese Americans has increased considerably (Kitano, 1988; Mindel, Habenstein, and Wright, 1998).

Likewise, the incidence of interracial marriage among the Chinese has dramatically increased in recent years, particularly with whites, among the younger generation. Approximately 33 percent of all marriages among Chinese are interracial. In contrast, Korean Americans have relatively low rates of interracial marriage. The trend toward interracial marriage has been most evident for Koreans living in Hawaii. For example, between 1960 and 1980, 80 percent of Koreans in Hawaii were married to non-Koreans. In addition, many of the interracial marriages among Korean Americans consist of Korean women who married American servicemen during the 1970s and 1980s. For example, according to Annual Reports by the Immigration and Naturalization Service, during this period, nearly 100,000 Korean women came to the United States as wives of American servicemen. Although no hard data are available, many of these marriages are believed to have ended in divorce (Mindel, Habenstein, and Wright, 1998).

More recent research suggests that the rate of interracial marriage may be increasing, particularly among Korean American women. It is argued that Korean American women are at a disadvantage in finding suitable Korean partners for a number of reasons: (1) the sex imbalance in the Korean American community, particularly for women aged 20–29; (2) Korean American men, far more often than women, tend to bring their marital partners from Korea; and (3) the fact that more Korean American women than men are attracted to white American partners because they expect to maintain more egalitarian conjugal relations with white partners than with Korean ones. These factors force more Korean American women than men to look for partners outside the Korean community (Mindel, Habenstein, and Wright, 1998). A study of Korean immigrants in Los Angeles and Orange counties (Min, 1993), for example, showed that 14 percent of the Korean women who got married in the previous five years married interracially compared to only 2.5 percent of their male counterparts. Like almost every other group of color in the United States, when Koreans marry interracially it is usually with whites, although Korean men prefer Japanese and Chinese partners as well. Moreover, as a result of similarities in physical and cultural characteristics, younger generations of Chinese, Japanese, and Korean Americans maintain high levels of social interaction and intermarriage (Mindel, Habenstein, and Wright, 1998).

Finally, Asian American women (especially Japanese, Filipina, Chinese) are far more likely to marry interracially than Asian American men are. For example, one-fifth of all Asian American women have a spouse of a different race or ethnicity, nearly twice the rate among Asian American men overall (suro, 2001). This pattern is believed to be causing a *marriage squeeze* for Asian American men who prefer to marry within their own race. The shrinking pool of eligible mates—the out-marriage of so many Asian American women—has caused deep resentments among some Asian American men. For example, as we have indicated, many Chinese men have strong feelings against interracial marriage and express a feeling of being betrayed and abandoned by Chinese women, whom they believe should be committed only to Chinese men (Guang, 1996). One consequence of the interracial marriage pattern among Asian Americans is the growing acculturation of Asian Americans into American society. While there may be advantages to acculturation, the costs include a loss of ethnic tradition, heritage, and a distinct sense of Asian American identity as well as intergenerational strain and conflict between some Asian American parents and their interracially married children.

Interethnic Marriages

LATINAS/OS As we have already seen, like Asian Americans, Latinas/os represent a diverse group. While inhibitions remain about marriages between African Americans and whites, Latinas/os, like Asian Americans, are increasingly marrying outside of their racial/ethnic groups. Although the rates of interracial marriage vary from one Latina/o group to another, overall the rates have increased rather dramatically in recent decades. Marriage between Latinas/os and non-Latinas/os is one of the most prevalent types of intergroup unions, as Figure 8.4 shows. At the end of the twentieth century, 41 percent of all married couples of Latina/o origin were married to a non–Latina/o (U.S. Bureau of the Census, 2000a). The majority of these marriages are between Latinas/os and whites.

As we have pointed out, most interracial/interethnic marriages occur among young, higher-income, and well-educated individuals. In this context, two-thirds of Latinas/os who have attended or graduated from college marry outside of their ethnic or racial group, as do one-third of all Latinas/os in top-income brackets. Latinas/os with a substantial income are five times as likely to marry a non–Latina/o than those who didn't finish high school or college or who live in poverty. It is reported that in the trend-setting state of California, close to 1 in 12 non–Latina/o whites who "ties the knot" marries a Latina/o or Asian American. Interracial marriage is also closely linked to youth among Latinas/os, though to a lesser extent than among Asian Americans. About one-third of all married Latinas/os under the age of 35 are involved in an interracial marriage. Although concentrated among the young, there are also significant numbers of older Latinas/os in interracial/interethnic marriages.

Gender does not seem to be a factor in these marriages, as the rates are about the same for Latinas and Latinos. As with Asian Americans, native-born Latinas/os are much more likely than immigrant Latinas/os to marry a white person, with interracial marriage rates for all native-born married couples approaching 30 percent. And the longer a

Latina/o has been in this country, the greater the prevalence of interracial/interethnic marriage. The rates of interracial marriage are far higher in states that have a large Latina/o population than in the rest of the country. For example, non–Latina/o whites and Latina/o marriages are approximately four to five times as common in California and Texas than in states that have relatively smaller Latina/o populations (suro, 2001). This pattern of interracial/interethnic marriage among various Latina/o groups suggests that there is, perhaps, less "social distance" between Latinas/os and non–Latinas/os than among people from different groups (Pollard and O'Hare, 1999).

WHITES Interethnic marriage among non–Latina/o whites is now so commonplace that most people don't pay much attention to it. Estimates are that three-fourths of U.S.–born whites are married interethnically. As with other groups, ethnic intermarriage among whites varies with age and region of residence (Alba, 1985).

Although the data indicate that the rate of interracial marriage has been increasing and seems dramatic for some groups, we must be careful in drawing conclusions from them. Keep in mind that many of these statistics represent geographic or age-specific groups and should not be generalized to a total population. We should not lose sight of the fact that, overall, interracial marriages are still an extremely low percentage of the total marriages in this country. In addition, we should remember that race is not experienced in a vacuum. As we learned in Chapter 5, race is interrelated with many other social factors that combine to have a significant effect on if and whom we marry.

Interfaith Marriages

Marrying within one's own religion was the social norm in the United States until recently. Summaries of studies of interfaith marriages (for example, Eckland, 1968; Kerckhoff, 1976) have consistently found Americans to be much like their partners in terms of religion. In the 1980s, for example, 93 percent of Protestants were married to Protestants; 88 percent of Jews were married to Jews; and 82 percent of Catholics were married to Catholics (Glenn, 1982). Most of these studies, however, simply divided religion into three categories: Protestant, Catholic, and Jewish. A problem with this classification scheme is that it overlooks the diversity within various religious categories. For example, Baptists, Presbyterians, and Methodists are all Protestant denominations. If people from these different denominations intermarry, are their marriages endogamous or exogamous? Other problems arise in trying to define an interreligious couple. For example, if a Jew marries a Protestant who then converts to Judaism, is that an interfaith marriage, or do we consider it religiously homogamous? Or what if one partner is of a religious denomination and the other is an atheist or agnostic?

With these limitations in mind, recent statistics on who marries whom suggest that Americans are much more willing to cross religious than racial boundaries in selecting a partner. For example, religious intermarriage rates are much higher today than in the past among all religious groups except Fundamentalist Christians (Kalmijn, 1998). In recent years Americans have been moving toward more religiously tolerant attitudes, which might account, at least in part, for the fact that in a recent study of attitudes toward interreligious marriage, only 27 percent of women and 15 percent of men indicated that they would not marry someone of a different religious background (Knox and Zusman, 2001). Some scholars have suggested that the increase in religious intermarriage is due to the fact that religion generally has lost some of its power and control over people's lives (Glenn, 1982).

Like interracial marriages, interfaith marriages vary according to location and population. One researcher, for example, found that cities such as New York, whose population includes a large number of Catholics and Jews, have a higher than average incidence of cross-faith (Jewish–Catholic) marriages. Likewise, Catholics and Lutherans exhibit a higher than average rate of intermarriage in states such as Pennsylvania, Iowa, and Minnesota, where the population is almost evenly split between the two religious denominations (Pace, 1986).

Most religions actively encourage same-faith marriages. One reason is the belief that cross-faith marriages have the tendency of weakening people's religious beliefs, values, and behavior, leading to a loss of faith not to mention a loss of church membership. The pattern of interfaith marriage is particularly evident today among Jews. Since 1945, the percentage of Jews in America has declined from 4 percent to 2 percent. In 1945, only one in ten Jews was married to a non-Jew, whereas one in two are today (Safire, 1995). Jewish rabbis, having long expressed a concern over the decline in the number of Jews, were so concerned about the high rate at which Jews were marrying non-Jews that in 1973 the Reform Judaism's Central Conference of American Rabbis denounced interfaith marriages, declaring that such marriages were contrary to Jewish tradition and discouraged rabbis from officiating at them. Consequently, most rabbis today will not officiate at an interfaith wedding. However, recently lay leaders of Judaism's liberal Reform Movement considered abandonment of the 1973 rabbinic statement, urging their clergy instead to rely on their individual consciences in deciding whether to officiate in interfaith unions. The lay trustees believe that rabbinic officiation at interfaith weddings could actually work in favor of Jewish continuity, since rabbis could encourage the interfaith couples they marry to keep a Jewish household and rear their children as Jews, which is, in fact, what a minority of Reform rabbis have long done anyway (Niebuhr, 1996).

Although interfaith couples are less often the victims of society's disapproval than interracial couples are, cross-faith marriages are not without difficulties. Deeply held religious beliefs are an important part of our core personality. If we believe very strongly in a particular religious ideology, to what extent will we compromise? Partners from different religions must confront a number of issues such as choosing a religion for their children and deciding which holidays to observe. These are not insurmountable barriers, of course, but they do require that a couple closely examine the ramifications of marrying across faith and find solutions that are mutually satisfying.

Some studies indicate that racially and religiously heterogamous marriages have somewhat higher divorce rates and slightly lower levels of satisfaction than do homogamous marriages (see, for example, Price-Bonham and Balswick, 1980; Glenn, 1982; Heaton and Pratt, 1990). Other researchers, however, have found no evidence that interreligious marriages are any less satisfying or successful than religiously and racially homogamous marriages (see, for example, Shehan, Bock, and Lee, 1990). As with homogamous marriages, many factors affect the success of heterogamous marriages. Lack of family, societal, and religious support; cultural hostility; and differences in background can often undermine the stability and success of these marriages. Two other critical factors in determining the success of all marriages, heterogamous and homogamous, are the ability to communicate openly and honestly and the ability to manage conflicts that arise within these relationships. The concluding section of this chapter focuses on the issues of marital satisfaction, communication, and conflict management and resolution in marriages.

MARITAL SATISFACTION, COMMUNICATION, AND CONFLICT RESOLUTION

Research has consistently found that married people, compared with unmarried people, report being happier, healthier, and generally more satisfied with their lives (Haring-Hidore et al., 1985; Glenn and Weaver, 1988; Colemen and Ganong, 1991), and new research shows that monogamous married couples enjoy greater sexual satisfaction than singles and nonmonogamous marrieds (Clements, 1994). It should be noted, however, that the "happiness gap" between married and unmarried individuals has closed considerably over the last several years. Nonetheless, what is it about the quality of married life that makes it more satisfying than a single lifestyle? Researchers exploring the quality of married life have used a variety of terms, the most notable of which are *marital success*, *marital happiness*, and *marital satisfaction*. Throughout the literature, these terms are used interchangeably as key measures of the quality of married life. Because marital success is a relative concept—it depends on who is defining it—researchers have based much of their findings on marital satisfaction as reported by married couples and on the divorce rate.

Successful Marriage How successful are American marriages? On the one hand, although the divorce rate leveled off in the 1990s, almost two-thirds of the marriages entered into in recent years are expected to end in divorce or separation. According to some researchers, these statistics are a clear indication of a decline in marital success, the causes of which are attributed to a number of factors: The motivation for marriage has become fairly selfish; individuals expect a lot from their partners in a marriage but are largely unwilling to give in order to get; the increased flexibility in marital roles has resulted in a breakdown in the consensus about what it means to be a wife or husband; the easing of moral, religious, and legal barriers to divorce has made people less willing and able to make needed commitments to and investments in marriage than they were in the past (Glenn, 1993).

On the other hand, general survey data repeatedly show that although the rate at which couples report marital happiness or satisfaction has declined in recent years, an overwhelming majority of married couples say that they are happy or very happy and describe their marriage as satisfying (Glenn and Weaver, 1988; National Opinion Research Center, 1992). Based on a variety of survey data, researchers

Conservatives and liberals alike tend to agree on the need to strengthen marriages and families. One way that some couples prepare for this goal is by participating in marriage preparation classes, which teach skills such as how to resolve conflicts.

Women and men typically use different communication styles. A lack of understanding of these differences often leads to miscommunication and conflict.
Source: © Tribune Media Services, Inc. All Rights Reserved. Reprinted by permission.

have found that well over half of married couples say that if they had it to do over again, they would marry the same person (Patterson and Kim, 1991; Family First, 1999).

What are the factors that distinguish happily married couples from unhappy or dissatisfied couples? There is a vast literature on marital satisfaction/happiness/quality/stability. Some of the more common factors elucidated in this literature are being in love; sharing aims, goals, and other important beliefs; sexual compatibility; financial security; having children; the amount of time spent together; family rituals; self-disclosure, open communication, and the ability to resolve conflict in a positive manner.[2] In fact, most research in this area has found open and effective or positive communication and successful conflict resolution to be essential to the success of marriages and other intimate relationships (for example, Gottman, 1994a/b).

Effective Communication Indeed, effective and positive communication is essential to any relationship, married or unmarried. Two key components of communication are what is said and how it is said. You have probably heard the expression: "It's not what you say, it's how you say it." For example, it is possible to say "I'm very happy in this relationship" several different ways. An individual could say it lovingly, sincerely, or sarcastically. In good communication, what we say should be consistent with how we say it. Also, communication involves not just words but gestures, actions, intonations, and sounds. Sometimes the messages couples give to each other are misinterpreted, misread, or missed all together. Missed messages and misinterpretations can build on themselves and result in conflict and hostility in a relationship. Clinical psychologist Joel Block (1981) gives this example:

> A couple have just taken a moonlight walk by the ocean. They sit down by the water's edge. The woman says, "Let's go inside, I'm sleepy." The man responds, "It's nice out here. Why don't we lie and rest here?" The woman, angry, storms into the house. The man, equally angry, gets dressed and drives off to a local bar.

What has happened here is miscommunication. When the woman suggested going inside because she was "sleepy" she was actually attempting to communicate to her partner that she wanted to make love in the house. Her partner, on the other hand, was attempting to communicate his wish to make love on the beach under the moonlight. According to Block, neither communicated her or his wishes directly; thus, the evening ended with both partners feeling rejected and angry. When this type of miscommunication becomes a pattern of interaction in a relationship, a couple could find themselves continuously upset and irritated with each other. According to family therapist Joan Zientek, situations such as this could severely strain an already precarious line of communication and hamper the couple's ability to calmly and rationally generate options and select solutions that, at least in part, will meet each partner's needs (see the "Strengthening Marriages and Families" box). Because conflict is a natural and normal part of all relationships and the inability or failure to deal with it can be destructive, the field of family therapy has become an increasingly popular method by which couples seek to resolve relationship conflicts. It is estimated that close to one-half of American households seek some sort of counseling or therapy (*Better Homes and Gardens*, 1988).

Despite our best desire to communicate, many of us fall short. Some of the most common communication problems identified by researchers and therapists include: not listening, blaming, criticizing, and/or nagging, not responding to

[2]It should be noted that the range of factors that can be used to measure marital satisfaction is immense. And the list of factors studied vary from one research study to another, thus producing different and sometimes contradictory results. Moreover, as we have pointed out, marital satisfaction is a relative concept. While the factors closely associated with marital happiness and satisfaction in the literature may apply to some marriages, it is quite possible and probable that some couples are quite satisfied with their marriages even though none or few of these factors are present.

STRENGTHENING MARRIAGES AND FAMILIES

Talks with Family Therapist Joan Zientek

COMMUNICATION, CONFLICT RESOLUTION, AND PROBLEM SOLVING IN MARRIAGES AND INTIMATE RELATIONSHIPS

How Often Is Communication a Factor in Marital Satisfaction?

The lack of effective communication is at the heart of most marital discord. The birth of a child dramatically changes the communication pattern of the marital dyad. Prior to the birth of a child, the couple only had themselves to take into account. With the birth of a child, not only does the marital dyad become a family triad, but one member of the triad is helpless and totally dependent on the other two. Very often at this point, husbands begin to feel neglected and cope by turning to their work; wives often feel overworked, overwhelmed, and alone. If the couple cannot successfully navigate this new family life stage, other issues only become compounded, and the relationship slowly settles into a comfortably distant arrangement. While each partner may accomplish the task that she or he is responsible for and needed to keep the family going, most likely the partners will lose touch with each other. If couples only talk about the tasks that are needed to get done, their marriage may end up feeling like a business arrangement, lacking the feelings of love and intimacy that only come from sharing feelings, hopes, fears, wishes, and their dreams for the future.

What Kinds of Strategies Can Couples Adopt to Improve Communication?

One of the most central communication skills is the ability to give and receive feedback from the other in a way that does not diminish either party. Speaking for yourself, giving messages that disclose the impact of the behavior of one person or the other is far more effective than messages that usually end up in name-calling and negative labeling. In addition, couples need to treat their marriage as an entity in itself that needs nurturing. They need to take time for each other on a daily, weekly, and monthly basis and not merely give halfhearted attention to their partner as they attend to the needs of children or wait for vacation time to catch up with each other. Simple things like having a cup of coffee after dinner (without interruption from the children or others) or going for a walk or sharing a hobby can be very helpful in keeping the communication lines open and the connection alive. In addition, the planning of positive exchanges, such as sending a card, notes, doing small favors, exchanging little surprise presents, all make each party feel valued and appreciated and thus more open to the needs of the other.

Is All Conflict Bad for a Relationship?

Conflict is a natural and normal part of all relationships. No two people will see a situation in the same way, have the exact same needs at the same time, or have the same priorities as they create a life together. The resolution of conflict in a positive manner can bring new life and direction to a relationship; it can prevent the storage of resentment on the part of one or both partners, thus allowing each problem its own day in court without the attachment of past unresolved issues. It can also bring a deeper understanding of the needs and vulnerabilities of each person and, many times, in the long run, it leads to better decision making than if the decision in question was to be solely based on the views of only one of the partners.

What Strategies Can Couples Use to Resolve Conflicts?

One of the main factors that impede the resolution of conflicts between partners is the lack of ability and/or skill to see a situation from another's point of view. Couples waste much time demanding, convincing, and manipulating the other to come over to their side. This often results in anger, resentment, and the stifling of their creative energies that might, under more positive circumstances, stand them in good stead in resolving their conflict. And they are not in a position to calmly and rationally generate options and select a solution that, at least in part, will meet each partner's needs. This couple conflict may be imbedded in each party's desire for control of the relationship. Nonetheless, in order to get out of this deadlock, one partner must be able to silently hold onto her or his position and begin to truly listen and discuss the other partner's view. When the listened-to partner feels understood, she or he is in a better position to listen to the other. Consequently, both partners feel respected and affirmed.

issues as they emerge, using scapegoats, using the silent treatment, and using coercion or physical threats. One of the ways that couples can learn to communicate directly with each other is by conducting what Block calls "marital checkups." This involves identifying and appraising the assets and liabilities of the relationship. If done responsibly, the marital checkup can help the couple learn more about each other's needs, desires, and expectations.

WRITING YOUR OWN SCRIPT

PREPARING YOUR RELATIONSHIP CONTRACT

The decision to marry or cohabit leads to a number of other related issues and areas of understanding that couples should consider, discuss, and resolve prior to establishing their living arrangement. Many couples have found it useful to write personal contracts that clarify their feelings and expectations for the marriage or a cohabitative relationship. To be most effective this exercise should be done with your partner. It may be easier, however, if you and your partner write separate contracts and then compare and discuss each other's contract before writing a final version that represents your collective view and consensus. Prenuptial and personal contracts include the expectations the couple bring to their relationship. In the exercise that follows we present the items commonly included in marriage and personal contracts. It is not necessary that you cover every item simply because it is here. Concern yourself only with those areas that are relevant to your particular situation. Or feel free to add topics or issues that are relevant to you and your life. (Note: If you choose to remain single, either permanently or on a temporary basis, many of these items will apply to you as well. Although you don't need to consider a partner, reflecting on these items can help you get in touch with yourself as well as build a more satisfying lifestyle.) Under each topic, we present some questions to consider. These questions are not exhaustive.

Relevant History

Couples often assume they know all they need to know about each other without really discussing their past. However, a lack of knowledge can sometimes lead to problems later on.

Questions to consider: *Will we try to share all aspects of our history that might affect our intended relationship, for example, former marriages and our own and our families' health histories?*

Division of Labor and Responsibilities

A source of difficulty for many couples is the perception of inequity in the performance of household tasks. Often partners have different assumptions about who should do these tasks. Some people believe that household tasks should be allocated on the basis of gender even when both partners are employed full-time.

Questions to consider

1. What rights do we each have as individuals, and what role expectations do we have for each other? How will we divide household responsibilities? Who will cook, clean, make the shopping lists, shop, do laundry, make house and car repairs, do yard work, wash windows, plan entertainment, take out the trash, care for children, take care of finances, pay bills, and perform all the other tasks of daily living?
2. How will decisions be made—individually or jointly? How will we resolve differences of opinion?

Sexual Exclusiveness

One of the reasons some people give for dissolving their relationship is a partner's extramarital affairs. Such behavior can lead to feelings of betrayal, jealousy, insecurity, and anger. Often couples don't discuss their views on sexual matters until after they are married or cohabiting, and sometimes they find that they have conflicting values in this area.

Questions to consider: *Will our relationship be sexually exclusive? What is our understanding about sexual access to each other? How will we communicate our personal desires? What are our feelings about outside relationships, both sexual and nonsexual? Would we feel threatened by outside relationships?*

Money Matters

Money matters are issues that all of us have to deal with regardless of our marital status. Couples may not always share the same values concerning money and the things it can buy. As a way of keeping money and money management from becoming problems, it is wise for couples to discuss their values and expectations. Agreement on financial planning, spending, and management is a key ingredient in marital or relationship satisfaction.

Questions to consider

1. How will we handle the ownership, distribution, and management of property before and after marriage? How will we decide on the contribution of each person to the total family income and support? Will it matter if one of us earns more than the other?
2. As a couple, how compatible are our spending (including the use of credit cards) and savings patterns? Are we both comfortable with these patterns, or do we need to make changes in them? What are our financial goals? What plans can we make to achieve these goals? Should we have joint or separate savings and checking accounts?

Self-Disclosure Moreover, self-disclosure is a key element in effective communication and higher levels of marital satisfaction. According to Susan Hendrick and Clyde Hendrick (1992), self-disclosure refers simply to "telling another person about oneself; to honestly offer one's thoughts and feelings for the other's perusal, hoping that truly open

What are the advantages and disadvantages of each arrangement?

3. Who will manage the family finances? How will we decide on a family budget? How will we decide how family money will be spent? Who will pay the bills and make the investments? How will we decide this? If one of us assumes this responsibility, how will that one keep the other informed about our financial matters? Will each of us be able to manage if something happens to the other?

Family Surname

Names are important symbols of identity. In some cultures a newly married couple incorporate both family names into their surname. The cultural tradition in the United States is for a wife to take her husband's surname. Many couples, however, are questioning this practice.

Questions to consider: *Will we both carry the same surname? Will we hyphenate our name or use a new one? If we have children, what surname will they have?*

Selecting a Place to Live

Where we live is an important decision that we make in adulthood. We spend a tremendous amount of time in the place we live. Thus, where and under what conditions we live is a major factor in how we perceive the quality of our lives.

Questions to consider: *What type of housing do we want? How will we decide on our place of residence? How important are each of these factors in our decision: proximity to family, schools, work; convenience to community services and public transportation; the area's tax base; the overall safety and well-being of the neighborhood? What can we afford? Which is preferable for us, to buy or to rent?*

Religion

Religion can be a source of comfort and support to couples, or it can be a source of conflict. If conflict occurs over religion, it may be because partners belong to different religions, have different values, or do not attach the same importance to religion.

Questions to consider: *What role will religion play in our relationship? Are we religiously compatible? Is this important to us? Will we attend services together? Separately? Will we raise our children in a specific religion?*

Relationships with Others

In many marriages today, couples often experience difficulty in trying to manage work, marriage, and other social responsibilities. Finding time to spend together may require making adjustments in the time devoted to other relationships.

Questions to consider: *How do we feel about each other's relatives and friends? How much interaction do we want to have with them? How will we decide where to spend our holidays and vacations? How will relationships with others be determined? How will we manage to keep time for ourselves?*

Conflict Resolution

Every couple will experience conflict in their relationship at one time or another. The critical factor in the relationship is not the experience of conflict but rather how the conflict is handled.

Questions to consider: *What will we do when things don't seem to be working out right? What mechanisms can we create for resolving disagreements? Will we be willing to get counseling if we are having problems? What are our attitudes regarding divorce?*

Renewability, Change, and Termination of Contract

People and conditions change over time. An effective contract allows for these possibilities. Couples are well advised to have periodic reviews of how the contract is working and what changes, if any, should be made.

Questions to consider: *How will we provide for a periodic reevaluation and change (if necessary) in this contract? Under what conditions will we terminate this contract?*

These are only a few of the many issues and decisions we all face in the course of our lives. For example, issues of work, jobs, or careers, or those concerning having or not having children are discussed in other chapters of this textbook. The decisions that are made will vary from one individual and family to the next. No single pattern can meet everyone's needs. Each individual and family must decide what arrangement is best for them. The most critical factor in all these areas is communication. All too frequently couples don't discuss these issues before becoming partners, with the result that they often begin a relationship with unrealistic expectations. Although communicating on these issues early in your relationship cannot by itself guarantee happiness or long-term stability, it can improve the probability of achieving these goals.

communication will follow" (1992:173). Research on self-disclosure consistently shows that reciprocal self-disclosure (when both partners self-disclose) is positively related to marital satisfaction. When couples are open and self-disclosing it creates togetherness and closeness, and thus, higher marital satisfaction. On the other hand, marital satisfaction is low when one partner is self-disclosing and the other is not, one is more self-disclosing than the other, or if neither partner is self-disclosing (Hansen and Schuldt, 1984).

Judy Pearson (1989) and others, however, have found that although marital satisfaction increases as the level of self-disclosure increases, there is a leveling off, whereby at the very highest levels of self-disclosure there is a decrease in marital satisfaction. One explanation for this phenomenon is that couples who exhibit high levels of self-disclosure tend to be more likely to express their opinions to and about each other more readily, whether positive or critical and disapproving. In turn, criticism and disapproval can become a problem in a relationship and can lead to lower relationship satisfaction (Schumm, 1986; Moss and Schwebel, 1993).

As in many other aspects of heterosexual relationships, women and men tend to differ in terms of disclosure, although the research findings are somewhat mixed. For example, some researchers have found women to be more disclosing than men (Arliss, 1991), whereas others have found no major difference between the sexes. According to Hendrick and Hendrick (1992), a major difference in female and male disclosure is in terms of the target person to whom they will disclose. Women tend to disclose more to same-sex friends, whereas men tend to disclose more to romantic partners. In contrast, research indicates that lesbians and gays are equally disclosing in their respective relationships (Nardi and Sherrod, 1994). Perhaps one of the greatest consequences of self-disclosure for marital (or intimacy) satisfaction is that when it is done well, it takes much of the guesswork out of interpersonal communication (Hendrick and Hendrick, 1992:175).

In general, successful communication includes a number of other conditions and skills. Two basic conditions are a nonthreatening, noncoercive atmosphere and mutual commitment. In addition, a couple must be willing to change as the needs and demands of the relationship change. Some of the key skills that are important for successful communication are the ability to identify, accept responsibility for, and resolve problems, as well as a willingness to listen and negotiate conflict. Based on now 25 plus years of observing couples interact in the "Marriage Lab" at his Seattle Marital and Family Institute, research psychologist John Gottman (1994a/b) argues that most marriages and similar relationships fall into one of three categories: *validating partnerships*, which are dominated by affection and compromise; *volatile partnerships*, in which conflict is intense, but so is passion; and *others*, in which a pair of conflict-avoiders agree to disagree. All of these relationships can work and all require conflict, both as fuel and as a venting mechanism. However, more importantly, to be successful they all require many more acts of positive reinforcement than of negative interaction. According to Gottman, the real reason marriages succeed or fail is really very simple: Couples who stay together are *nice* to each other more often than not. That is, Gottman claims that couples who are satisfied with their relationship maintain a five-to-one ratio of positive to negative moments in their relationship (they are five times as nice as they are nasty to each other). Couples who are unhappy and/or dissatisfied with their relationship have let the ratio slip below one-to-one. Couples can improve their relationship with some simple practices during moments of conflict, such as take a deep breath, calm down, listen and speak nondefensively, try a morning leave-taking, a chat at the end of the day, or private time together without the children or other interferences. Gottman has found that successful relationships are not those that never have conflict, rather they are those in which the couple recognizes when there is a problem and tries to fix it.

Conflict and Conflict Resolution No matter how happy or satisfying a marriage or other intimate relationship is, some conflict is inevitable. Good communication alone does not prevent conflict. Even when couples have positive and effective communication skills and high levels of self-disclosure, there are likely to be times of disagreement, conflict, and fighting. Several key areas of marriage and family life generally contribute to conflict in marriages: money, sex, children, power, loyalty, division of marital and family tasks, privacy, work, in-laws, friends, religion, and substance abuse. Gottman believes that the four most destructive behaviors to marital happiness are criticism, contempt, defensiveness, and stonewalling:

> ***Criticism*** involves attacking one's partner's personality or character rather than complaining about a specific behavior. For example, a healthy and specific complaint might be: I wish you would spend more time with me. A generalizing and blaming attack on one's personality or character might be: There's something wrong with you. You never spend time with me. The difference between these two approaches can be very significant to the listener.
>
> ***Contempt*** involves intense and intentional negative thoughts about a person and can be manifest in a number of ways, for example, subtle or not-so-subtle putdowns, hostile jokes, mocking facial expressions, or name-calling. An example might be: You're getting old and stupid. I don't know why I married you.
>
> ***Defensiveness*** is generally a response to being attacked or put down. It involves making excuses, tossing back counterattacks and insults, and denying responsibility. For example, a defensive response might be: Why is it that I'm the one who is always expected to initiate spending time together? What's wrong with you? Do you have a problem?
>
> ***Stonewalling*** means that the couple has essentially stopped communicating. They have reached a point where they refuse to respond to one another even in self-defense. According to Gottman, when a couple reaches this stage, one or both of them are thinking negative thoughts about the other most of the time, and, if their behavior is unchecked, the marriage will likely end in divorce.

When conflict arises in a relationship, as it inevitably does, it does not have to be destructive. Researchers have found that some conflict can be constructive. Conflict management is the key. When conflict is managed or resolved through negotiation and compromise, it can strengthen the

Some conflict in intimate relationships is inevitable. However, such conflict does not have to be destructive. Researchers have found that successful partners find constructive ways to manage relationship conflict that allow each partner to maintain her or his differences while negotiating a solution that is mutually agreeable.

bonds of affection between partners. When it is dealt with ineffectively it can lower satisfaction and even contribute to the dissolution of the relationship. Social researchers Don Dinkmeyer and Jon Carlson (1984) suggest some of the following strategies to resolve marital conflict: Clearly define the problem, demonstrate a mutual respect for each other, agree to cooperate with each other, and agree to make decisions together.

Some social scientists (for example, Sprey, 1979) believe that couples in lasting marriages do not really resolve most conflicts in the sense that the conflict is settled forever with a clear winner and loser. Rather, they manage most conflicts through an ongoing process of negotiation. Couples in successful marriages find ways to manage conflict so that each partner can maintain her or his differences while working collectively to find a negotiated solution that is satisfactory to both parties. According to Gottman (1994), fighting, whether rare or frequent, does not have to be destructive. The important thing in a marriage is to find a compatible fighting style, not to stop fighting altogether. In fact, in many cases fighting can be one of the healthiest things a couple can do for their relationship. More important, the key to a happy and successful marriage or other intimate relationship is relatively simple: Learn to calm down, learn to speak and listen to one another nondefensively, validate one another, and practice the former steps over and over until they become routine, even in the heat of an argument.

?

Consider the intimate relationships in which you are or have been involved. Can you distinguish particular patterns of communication in these relationships? What are or were the major barriers to communication? What strategies of conflict resolution have you and your partners employed in these relationships? Did you learn anything about conflict resolution from your parents' relationship? How can you improve communication and conflict resolution in your close relationships?

SUMMARY

Although we have witnessed some important changes in marriage and family patterns, most Americans will marry at least once in their lifetime. People marry for a number of reasons, including to have a committed relationship and to have someone to share life with. Marriage means different things to different people. For some people the key to marriage is commitment. For others, marriage is a sacrament, a sacred union or holy state under the direct authority of their god. Most people do not think of marriage as a legal contract. When two people marry, however, they are agreeing to abide by the terms of a marriage contract that they had no part in drafting. Although each individual state defines the rights and obligations of the marriage contract, all states specify who can marry whom and at what age they may do so. Marriage is a civil right that applies only to heterosexual couples in U.S. society. However, since 1991, several lesbian and gay couples have sued for the right to marry.

Historically, the marriage contract put women at a decided disadvantage. Although the process of marriage is different today, in many states women continue to lose legal rights when they marry. Marriage in the United States is imbued with rituals and traditions, many of which date back to ancient societies. Although many people continue to abide by tradition when they marry, an increasing number of people are modifying, changing, or creating their own personal marriage rituals.

Like other relationships, marriage is experienced differently depending on factors such as race, class, and gender. For example, researchers point out that women and men experience marriage differently. This has led several researchers to describe marriage as containing two marriages: hers and his. The female–male differences in the experience of marriage, though largely hidden, have a tremendous effect on the mental and physical health of wives and husbands.

Getting married represents a significant change in the lives of a couple. Marital adjustment is an important part of the marriage experience. Couples must continuously make adjustments over the life course of the marriage. The success of the relationship depends, in large part, on the degree to which both partners are able to adjust. Satisfying, well-adjusted marriages vary a great deal. A typology of marital relationships representing marital adjustment includes the conflict-habituated, the devitalized, the passive-congenial, the vital, and the total relationship.

Whenever two people live together over some period of time, some conflict is bound to occur. Conflict does not have to be destructive, however. Couples in successful marriages learn to manage or resolve conflict in such a way that is satisfactory to both parties. An essential element in managing or resolving conflict is open, honest, and direct communication. If couples are committed to the relationship, they will try to manage or resolve conflict in a constructive way. Moreover, whatever problem-solving style a couple uses, the relationship can be successful as long as positive feelings and interactions outweigh negative ones by a ratio of five to one.

KEY TERMS

principle of legitimacy
sacrament
legal marriage
social marriage
bigamy
adultery
fornication
affinal relatives
coverture
conjugal rights
personal marriage agreement
prenuptial agreement
marital adjustment
heterogamous marriage

QUESTIONS FOR STUDY AND REFLECTION

1. Why do people marry? If you are married, why did you marry? If you are not married but plan to wed, why are you going to marry? Ask three different married couples—one in their 60s, one in their 40s, and one in their 20s—why they married and what their expectations of marriage were. Do the women and men differ in their appraisals of marriage? Did you find any generational differences across couples? If so, how do you explain these differences?
2. Thinking about yourself, your parents, or some couple you are close to, do you (they) have a successful marriage? How important is communication to the success of the marriage? What communication skills does each partner possess?
3. As you have read in this chapter, important changes have taken place in marriage and family patterns. If you have computer access, locate Web sites pertaining to marriage. Classify the types of Web sites that you find on this topic. What are the most salient issues covered in these sites? What are some of the issues that concern people most about marriages today? How do these issues relate to the topics you have read in this chapter? Which of these issues seem to be Internet-specific? Gender-specific? Race/ethnicity or class-specific? Are there issues that are different depending on one's sexual orientation? Explain.
4. Jessie Bernard's typology of marriages along gender lines is a classic in the field of sociology. Do you agree that marriages are experienced differently by women and men? Can you give evidence from your own experiences or the experiences of people you know to support or refute Bernard's argument?

ADDITIONAL RESOURCES

SOCIOLOGICAL

JOHNSON, WALTON R., AND D. MICHAEL WARREN, EDS. 1993. *Inside Mixed Marriages: Accounts of Changing Attitudes, Patterns, and Perceptions of Cross-Cultural and Interracial Marriages.* Lanham, MD: University Press of America. An anthology of articles written by and from the perspective of couples in interracial or interethnic marriages.

LOUDEN, JENNIFER. 1994. *The Couple's Comfort Book: A Creative Guide for Renewing Passion, Pleasure, and Commitment.* San Francisco: Harper. A usable compendium of imaginative activities that couples can do together. It is cross-referenced so that you can skip around in the book and design your own program of relationship rebirth.

NOCK, S. L. 1998. *Marriage in Men's Lives.* New York: Oxford University Press. In this provocative book, the author uses surveys to examine how and why marriage affects men's lives so much, and marriage as a means for developing and sustaining masculinity. The author draws some interesting and far-reaching conclusions about the nature of marriage and presents an interesting and innovative model for a new marriage.

WAITE, L., AND M. GALLAGHER. 2000. *The Case for Marriage.* Cambridge, MA: Harvard University Press. The authors focus on the benefits of marriage for all concerned: women, men, and children. It has an assortment of chapters covering a variety of relevant topics, including emotional well-being, sexuality, physical health, family violence, and children's outcomes.

LITERARY

MCKINNEY-WHETSTONE, DIANE. 1996. *Tumbling.* New York: Scribner (paperback). A delightful novel and heartwarming story of a young couple in Philadelphia during the 1940s and 1950s who are unable to consummate their marriage because of a horrible secret in the wife's past. Despite their problems, the couple care deeply for one another and they struggle to keep their unconventional family whole. This novel is suspenseful, tragic, humorous, and, above all, useful for a sociological study and discussion of marriage, family, and intimacy.

NICOLSON, NIGEL. 1974. *Portrait of a Marriage.* London: Futura. A lively and interesting personal account of the author's parents, each of whom had homosexual affairs and practiced "open marriage." Despite their marital lifestyle they stayed together and loved each other in what was apparently an adjusted and satisfying relationship.

INTERNET

www.couples-place.com On-line since 1996, this site provides a learning community for solving marriage problems, improving relationship skills, celebrating marriage, and achieving happiness with your partner. The site includes practical articles about relationships, forums about marriage and couple life, bulletin boards, a relationship satisfaction quiz, and many other resources.

www.bridesandgrooms.com An interesting site that provides a free bookstore and newsletter and provides a variety of links to subjects ranging from guides and ideas for weddings and honeymoons, premarital counseling, wedding shopping, wedding attire, wedding styles, and wedding music to marriage encounters to surveys on sex and marriage.

Chapter 9

Reproduction and Parenting

IN THE NEWS: BEIJING, CHINA, AND DAFFARPUR, INDIA

Newly released Chinese census data show that in China 117 boys are born for every 100 girls, well above the international norm of 105 boys to 100 girls. The preference for boys, coupled with China's one-child policy, has led to sex-selective abortions and female infanticide. Additionally, girls have less access to medical care and other resources than their brothers. As a result, China is experiencing a skewed sex ratio, particularly in the countryside. Nationally, there are 41 million more males than females among China's 1.2 billion population. The enormous social consequences of this imbalance are already visible. "Bachelor villages," inhabited predominantly by men, have appeared in China's poorer regions. Increasing numbers of women are being kidnapped to provide husbands for lonely men ("Census shows . . . ," 2001).

A similar situation exists in India, where a strong cultural preference for sons, who will carry the family name, inherit ancestral property, care for parents in their old age, and light their fathers' funeral pyres, has led parents to embrace the use of sex-determination tests in planning their families. Although India prohibited such tests in 1994, the laws are largely ignored and rarely enforced. In fact, ultrasound testing is widely advertised, and doctors carry their compact machines from one clinic to another. The 2001 Indian census figures tell the results of this practice. Female fetuses are regularly aborted. The number of girls per 1000 boys fell to 927, from 945 in 1991 and 962 in 1981. This trend is especially acute in Punjab, India's most prosperous farming state, where over the last decade the ratio dropped from 875 to 793 girls per 1000 boys. In the leading industrial state of Gujarat during that same period the sex ratio declined from 928 to 878 (Dugger, 2001). An increasing number of groups, including the Indian Medical Association, the high priests of the Sikh religion, and nonprofit groups like the Voluntary Health Association, are concerned about the social consequences of this imbalance and are actively working to curtail sex-selective abortions.

WHAT WOULD YOU DO? If you lived in either of these countries, would you try to eliminate sex-determination tests? If so, for what reasons, and how would you go about it? Would you advocate outlawing sex-determination tests in the United States? Explain. What policies would you advocate for dealing with the social consequences of a skewed sex ratio? Explain.

Fertility—the actual number of live births in a population—is both a biological and a social phenomenon. In all societies the timing and number of births are shaped by numerous social forces: the value attached to children and parenthood, marriage patterns and gender roles, political and economic structures, and knowledge about human reproduction. Thus, fertility patterns vary greatly across cultures. For example, in some cultures children are highly valued as economic assets, and women are expected to have many children beginning at an early age. Other societies view children in terms of their emotional value. These societies promote small families and encourage women to delay childbearing until their middle or late 20s. In some societies, the birth of a first child precedes marriage; in others, a birth outside of marriage is strongly condemned. Even within a given society fertility patterns may vary considerably across racial, ethnic, and class lines. And, as the cases of China and India make clear, cultural preferences for one sex, especially when abetted by new technologies, can dramatically alter the population structure and present new and unforeseen consequences for the well-being of a society (see "In the News").

This chapter begins with a brief historical review of changing fertility patterns in the United States and then proceeds to look at the many factors that influence the decision whether to parent. The remaining sections examine some of the issues surrounding conception, pregnancy, and parenthood.

HISTORICAL OVERVIEW: FERTILITY TRENDS IN THE UNITED STATES

Demographers use the term **fertility rate** to refer to the number of births per thousand women in their childbearing years (aged 15–44 in a given year). Evidence suggests that the fertility rate in early America was quite high. For example, the **total fertility rate** (the average number of children women would have over their lifetime if current birth rates were to remain constant) in 1790, when the first census was taken, is estimated to have been 7.7 (Gill, Glazer, and Thernstrom, 1992:41), in contrast to 2.1 in 2000.

Figure 9.1 shows that by 1900 the total fertility rate had declined to half that of a century earlier. What happened to produce this dramatic decline? First, the transformation of the United States from a rural-agricultural society to an urban-industrial society lessened the economic value of children. Children are an economic asset in agricultural societies, where many hands are needed to cultivate the land. Second, the move to an urban-industrial society was accompanied by rapid advances in science and technology, leading to changes in people's views of the world. According to Robert Wells (1978), people came to adopt "modern values," which focus on planning and the future. Couples came to believe that controlling family size would have economic benefits. By having fewer children, couples could reallocate their resources from the basic costs of providing for children

Figure 9.1

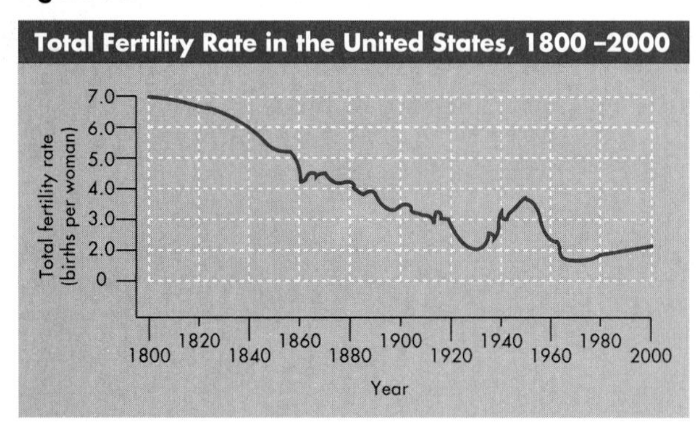

Sources: Adapted from Richard T. Gill, Nathan Glazer, and Stephan A. Thernstrom, 1992, *Our Changing Population* (Englewood Cliffs, NJ: Prentice Hall): 41. Reprinted by permission of Prentice Hall, Englewood Cliffs, NJ; J. A. Martin, B. E. Hamilton, and S. J. Ventura, 2001, "Preliminary Data for 2000," *National Vital Statistics Reports 49, 5* (Hyattsville, MD: National Center for Health Statistics): 4.

to investing more in their future. The changing technology of an urban-industrial society required a more educated labor force. Thus, not only did the economic value of children decline, but it also became more costly to raise and educate them. Over time, a general pattern has emerged—the higher the income, the lower the fertility rate.

In contrast, lower-income parents generally see larger families as more beneficial than costly. These parents are less likely to go to college, more likely to marry early, and more likely to see children as a means of attaining adult status and identity.

In the first decades of the twentieth century, the fertility rate continued to decline, particularly during the years of the Great Depression, when couples limited family size because of economic hardship. Demographers had predicted that the number of births would increase after World War II as couples put the depression and the war behind them. However, no one anticipated the dramatic rise in the total fertility rate from about 2.5 in 1945 to a high of 3.8 in 1957. Between 1946 and 1965, a period called the "baby boom," 74 million babies were born in the United States. Although demographers do not agree completely on the causes of the baby boom, two factors seem to have played a key role. First, the expanding postwar economy enabled unprecedented numbers of people to marry and have children at an early age. Second, a number of government policies were aimed at helping young families get started. The GI Bill helped veterans get an education and, hence, better-paying jobs. Federal housing loans and income tax deductions for children and interest on home mortgages encouraged people to buy houses and start families.

The baby boom was not to last, however. In 1957, the total fertility rate again began to decline, falling by more than 50 percent in less than 20 years to a low of 1.7 in 1976. This rate increased only slightly in the 1990s. This drastic decline, called the "baby bust," was not anticipated either. Among the factors thought to be responsible for this change were a slowing of the economy, the introduction of the birth control pill in the early 1960s, the legalization of abortion, the continuing increase in women's labor force participation, and increases in both the age at marriage and in the divorce rate. However, the most likely explanation is that the baby boom was simply a short-term deviation from the long-term decline begun in the nineteenth century. Whatever the reasons for the decline, another baby boom of this magnitude does not seem likely in the foreseeable future. Nevertheless, the fertility rate rose 3 percent to 67.6 per 1000 women aged 15–44 years between 1999 and 2000 (Martin, Hamilton, and Ventura, 2001). Although we don't yet know the reasons for this increase, demographers speculate that it was due to an improved economy. Given the weakening of the economy in 2001, it is questionable whether such increases will continue.

Current Fertility Patterns

Although the total fertility rate is at the population replacement level of 2.1, the rate is not uniform across all race and ethnic groups. As Figure 9.2 shows, whites have the lowest rate (1.8) and Latinos have the highest rate (3.1). However, there is great diversity even within these general categories. For example, in 1990, Mexican Americans averaged 3.2 children, whereas Cuban Americans averaged only 1.5 children. Similarly, within the Asian/Pacific Islander group, Hawaiians averaged a high of 3.2 children, whereas Japanese Americans had a low rate of 1.1 (National Center for Health Statistics, 1993). Age, cultural norms, and class combine to explain these rate variations. Asian Americans tend to marry later than other groups and, as Table 9.1 shows, are more likely than other groups to delay childbearing until their late 20s and 30s. In contrast, African Americans, Native Americans, Eskimos, and Latinas begin childbearing at early ages.

Figure 9.2

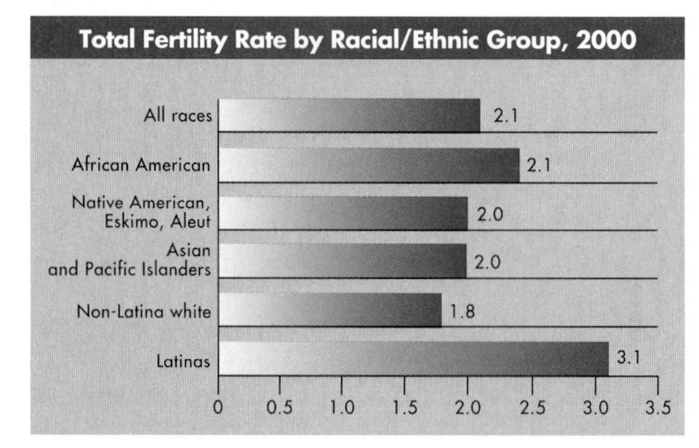

Source: J. A. Martin, B. E. Hamilton, and S. J. Ventura, 2001, "Preliminary Data for 2000," *National Vital Statistics Reports 49, 5* (Hyattsville, MD: National Center for Health Statistics).

Table 9.1

Births per 1000 Women, by Age and Race/Ethnicity, 2000									
	Total	10–14	15–19	20–24	25–29	30–34	35–39	40–44	45–49
All races	67.6	0.9	48.7	112.5	121.7	94.2	40.3	7.9	0.3
White (non-Latina)	58.7	0.3	32.8	90.1	113.4	94.2	39.0	7.2	0.4
African American	71.3	2.5	79.2	143.7	104.8	67.0	32.0	7.1	0.4
Native American Eskimo and Aleut	71.3	1.3	67.9	135.4	106.7	68.0	32.7	7.4	0.3
Asian/Pacific Islander	70.7	0.3	21.8	72.2	125.7	120.6	60.2	12.7	0.9
Latina (of any race)	105.9	1.9	94.4	184.6	170.8	109.0	48.6	11.6	0.6

Source: J. A. Martin, B. E. Hamilton, and S. J. Ventura, 2001, "Preliminary Data for 2000," *National Vital Statistics Reports* 49, 5 (Hyattsville, MD: National Center for Health Statistics): 7–8, Table1.

Although African American and Native American women also begin childbearing in the early years, between the ages of 30 and 39, they have lower fertility rates than other groups.

The U.S. birth rate has been declining over the last two centuries. Much of this decline has been attributed to the changing economic value of children, older ages at marriage, the decision of women to delay childbirth until their 30s, and the desire for smaller families than in the past. Of course, expectations are not always realized. In the next section we will explore the many factors that affect the decision to have children.

TO PARENT OR NOT

Do you want to be a parent? For what reasons? If you are already a parent, was this a conscious and planned choice? Are you satisfied with the timing and number of children that you have? Is child rearing what you expected it to be?

All too often the exposure most of us have to child rearing is of its romantic side. Advertisers surround us with images of gurgling, laughing, adorable infants and toddlers who say and do the most clever things. What we don't often see are the temper tantrums and the rebellious "no." Parenthood, like any other social activity, involves both costs and benefits that vary over the family life cycle and that people should consider before becoming parents. Even though people do sometimes change their mind after marriage, it is important to discuss the desire for children before marriage. Wives and husbands who disagree on whether to have children are likely to experience considerable marital conflict. If the issue cannot be satisfactorily resolved, the marriage may dissolve.

The Costs of Parenthood

In contrast to previous eras, when children worked at various jobs, particularly on farms and later in factories, children today are primarily consumers. According to the U.S. Department of Agriculture (2001), a family with a child born in 2000 can expect to spend about $165,630 to raise that child to the age of 17.

TIME, ENERGY, AND EMOTIONAL COSTS Raising children involves more than financial outlays; it also requires a great investment of parental time and energy. Infants and toddlers are totally dependent on parents for meeting all their physical and psychological needs. As children enter school, parents are likely to find themselves enmeshed in rounds of school activities, organized sports, religious events, Scouts, music and dance lessons, family outings, and numerous other activities compete for their time and attention. Raising children in today's environment also carries a high emotional cost in terms of parental worries over the easy accessibility of drugs, the lure of gangs, and random violence, all of which have taken a heavy toll on young people across all groups, but especially on the poor and children of color. An African American mother of two sons said, "I love my sons dearly, but if I had it all to do over again, I don't know if I would have children, especially boys. Every time my sons go out, my heart stops until they come home. Every day you read about some young African American male being shot or beaten up for being in the wrong place."

LIFESTYLE DISRUPTIONS The birth of a child can disrupt previously satisfying lifestyles. Not only do infants interrupt sleep and lovemaking and change household routines, they can alter a couple's social life and recreational pursuits. Babysitters are not always readily available, nor are babies easily compatible with work, hobbies, or leisure activities. Many parents find themselves in the position of having to forgo favorite pastimes at least until their children are much older. Although some parents find this a rather easy exchange to make, others are unprepared for the degree of change in their lives. Some parents become resentful and, as a result, both the marital relationship and the parent–child relationship may be negatively affected. Why, then, does anyone voluntarily become a parent? The answer to this question is twofold: Parenthood offers significant benefits to individuals, and society places enormous social pressure on its members to procreate.

The Benefits of Parenthood

Although all parents experience the costs of having children to some degree, most parents believe that the benefits of parenthood outweigh the costs.

Emotional Bonds Children are not only consumers and takers; they also give love and affection to parents. Furthermore, for many married couples their children are a tangible symbol of the love they share and the means for establishing "a real family life" (Neal, Groat, and Wicks, 1989). Couples who recall happy childhoods and positive family life experiences are especially likely to want to reproduce those feelings through having children of their own. Children also enlarge the social interaction network of parents by providing connecting links to other family members (grandparents, aunts, uncles, cousins) and to the larger community via schools, churches, neighbors, and places of recreation.

Adult Status Many people see raising children as a means of achieving adult status, recognition, and personal fulfillment. From early on, girls are given dolls to play with to prepare them for the day they will become mothers themselves and affirm their womanhood to the larger community. Men, too, are socialized to affirm their manhood through procreation and financial support of their families. Beyond that, however, rearing children provides parents with a sense of purpose and gives their lives meaning. By transmitting societal values to a new generation, parents feel they are making a contribution and leaving their imprint on society. Watching their children grow, and knowing they had a role to play in their children's development, gives parents a sense of pride and a feeling of immortality—that after their own deaths, part of them will live through their children and grandchildren.

Traditionally many fathers wanted sons who would someday join the family business. Today, it is not so unusual to include daughters in family enterprises.

Fun and Enjoyment Sometimes in the serious discussions of parenting another important benefit of having children is overlooked. Having children can be enormous fun. Through children adults can reexperience some of the delights of their own childhood. They can recall their own sense of wonder of the world as they observe their children's new discoveries. The presence of children legitimizes many adult desires. Many parents delight in buying trains and other toys for their children so that they, too, can enjoy them. What adult has not at times looked wistfully on as children around them swing, swim, run, jump, and play games? Parents have the advantage of being able to do all these things with their children without needing to apologize or explain.

The Social Pressures to Procreate

Although many adults acknowledge the benefits of parenthood, in isolation, they are probably not sufficient to produce a steady fertility rate. Obviously, reproduction is necessary for the continuation of a society. Without a fertility rate approaching the replacement level and in the absence of immigration, a society would, over time, become extinct. Thus, it is in society's interest to promote a **pronatalist attitude**, one that encourages childbearing. Societies vary in their strategies for accomplishing this goal. In the United States we celebrate parenthood by having special days to honor mothers and fathers. Federal and state governmental bodies show their support for childbearing by a tax structure that rewards earners with children through a system of tax deductions. Family members and friends often participate in encouraging childbearing by constantly dropping hints. "When are we going to be grandparents?" "Hurry up, our Jimmy wants a playmate (cousin)." Some religious organizations, for example the Catholic church, promote reproduction by teaching that the purpose of sex is procreation and that artificial means of birth control are contrary to that purpose.

The Child-Free Option

Throughout most of U.S. history having children was assumed to be the normal course of development for married couples. Until recently, a conscious rejection of parenthood was considered an unnatural and selfish act. About the only socially acceptable reason for not having children was biological incapacity. Those who were unable to have children were objects of pity and sympathy. Some psychoanalysts, like Sigmund Freud and Erik Erikson, believed that when couples decide not to parent, they are rejecting a major part of adult development that they may regret in later life.

However, researchers such as Marian Faux (1984) challenge this perspective. More and more couples are questioning whether to have children, and approximately 7 percent of all married couples are consciously choosing to be child-free; the rate is almost three times higher among college graduates. Among women 40 to 44 years old (who were nearing the completion of their childbearing years), 19 percent were child-free, almost twice as high (10 percent) as among their age counterparts in 1980 (Bachu and O'Connell, 2001). Just as there are numerous reasons for having children, there are many reasons for not doing so. Among them are career and marital considerations, the desire for personal fulfillment, uncertainty about parenting skills, and the influence of **antinatalist forces**—policies or practices that discourage people from having children.

Career and Marital Considerations Couples vary in their choice of priorities in their lives. Some couples prefer not to have children because they want to focus their energies on constructing satisfying careers and they want to avoid the work/family conflicts that are typical of dual-career couples with children, a topic we discuss in Chapter 10. Other couples wish to concentrate their energies on the marital relationship itself. As one 43-year-old woman said:

> My sense is that marriages are frayed, not strengthened with children. I think that one can relax in one's relationship in a way that having kids makes hard, having to make sure that somebody's doing this, that, and the other thing, and putting up with the craziness that goes on. And I don't see those marriages getting unfrayed. I see these things as permanent distances. I know it's alleged to be a cementing force, but I've only seen it go the other way. (Quoted in Morell, 1994, p. 115)

Personal Fulfillment Some couples prefer to invest the majority of their time and energy in hobbies, adult relationships, or in a variety of other activities they find personally fulfilling and satisfying. They contribute to society through working, performing volunteer activities, or interacting with and helping to support other people's children.

Qualifications for Parenthood In America's past the heavy cultural emphasis on having children rarely took into account the fact that most people can become biological parents but not all people have good parenting skills. The high incidence of child neglect and abuse, which we will discuss in Chapter 11, makes it clear that not all people are equipped to do a satisfactory job of child rearing. Some couples, remembering their own unhappiness as a child, do not want to repeat the kind of parenting they received. Others question whether they have the knowledge, patience, aptitude, stamina, communication skills, or role-model skills to be a good parent.

Antinatalist Forces Just as a society employs its institutions to encourage childbearing, it can also use them to discourage people from having children. An example of the latter approach is China's one-child policy. The Chinese government has expended much time, energy, and resources in attempting to limit its population as a means of fostering greater economic development. Some sociologists, like Joan Huber (1980) and Janet Hunt and Larry Hunt (1986), believe that antinatalist forces are at work in the United States today. They argue that current governmental and corporate policies are creating inequalities between parenting couples and child-free couples and, as a result, are influencing couples who would otherwise have children not to do so. One example of an antinatalist tendency in the United States is the failure to develop a national system of child care. Without this support, some parents, mostly women, are forced to give up their jobs or reduce their hours if they can't find alternative child care. Consequently, their standard of living is lower than that for couples without children. When both parents work, they confront many problems as they struggle to integrate work and family roles. If these conflicts remain unresolved, more dual-earner couples may decide that the costs of having children are too high.

Delayed Parenting

Delayed parenting (having a first child at 30 or after) is a relatively new trend in the United States, increasing from only 4 percent of American women in the early 1970s to over 26 percent in the late 1990s. Couples who delay parenting are more likely to be white, highly educated, to work in professional occupations, and to earn high incomes. Japan is also experiencing a growing number of older first-time mothers. However, these mothers find less acceptance due, in large part, to traditional culture values that emphasize women's mother and homemaker roles as well as concern over Japan's low birth rate. Now that Crown Princess Masako gave birth to her first child just days before her 38th birthday, delayed parenting is likely to lose its stigma in that country (French, 2001a).

Several factors have contributed to the pattern of delayed parenting. Among them are a greater cultural acceptance of singlehood as a positive lifestyle, changes in gender role expectations, apprehensions about the high divorce rate, improved contraception, and new reproductive technology that has made it possible for older women to bear children successfully. Although men can be fathers at almost any age (for example, actor Tony Randall became a father at 77), it is only recently that it became possible for menopausal women to become pregnant using donated eggs. In 1994, a 63-year-old Italian woman delivered a healthy boy, becoming the oldest woman to give birth. Cases like this have led some governments to restrict access to reproductive technologies for women over 50 and raised questions about the pros and cons of delayed parenting. Older parents may be more economically secure, more mature, and better prepared for the responsibilities of parenting than their younger counterparts, yet some older parents may lack the physical stamina needed to raise children. Children may benefit from having loving, involved older parents, yet some may find themselves caring for an ill or elderly parent while they are still in college.

It is becoming more common for parents to delay childbearing until their 30s or 40s. As this couple is discovering, parenting at a later stage in the life cycle has its advantages and disadvantages.

CONTROLLING FERTILITY

The decision whether to have children is one of the most important decisions people can make, for it affects not only their own lives but the society in which they live. Throughout history many groups and societies have attempted to control the timing and number of births to ensure an adequate supply of food and other resources for the entire community. Early efforts to control fertility took many forms. Some groups tried creating contraceptive barriers made out of animal intestines and various roots and grasses, others ingested prepared herbs and potions that were thought to have preventive power. Over time other techniques were also employed: celibacy, late marriages, abstinence from intercourse for prolonged periods of time, prolonged breastfeeding, physical actions such as jumping to dislodge the semen, and abortion. Because the process of human reproduction was not known until around the 1940s, many of these trial-and-error methods were unsuccessful. Thus, societies often resorted to other means to control their population. The most common mechanism of population control was infanticide, a practice on the increase in parts of Asia (see "In the News").

In contrast to these early methods, today efficient and safe methods of **contraception**—mechanisms for preventing fertilization—are readily available. Most of us take the availability of contraceptives for granted. However, the distribution and use of contraceptives in the United States were outlawed in the latter half of the nineteenth century and remained illegal in some states until 1965 when the Supreme Court, in *Griswold* v. *Connecticut*, invalidated laws prohibiting the use of contraceptives by married couples. Seven years later, in *Eisenstadt* v. *Baird*, the Court extended this principle to unmarried adults. In 1977, in *Carey* v. *Population Services International*, the Court extended the same constitutional right to privacy to minors, declaring that the state cannot deny them access to contraceptives.

Couples today can choose from a number of birth control methods (see Appendix D). Each method carries with it advantages and disadvantages. Some have health risks but are extremely convenient; others are safer but less convenient. Some have only a temporary effect; others are permanent. Some are costly, others are relatively inexpensive. Although a particular birth control device may prevent pregnancy, it does not necessarily provide protection against AIDS and other sexually transmitted diseases. Thus, more than one form of contraception may be advisable at any given time. Currently, among never-married women (aged 15–44) users, the birth control pill is the most popular choice (20 percent), followed by the condom (14 percent), whereas among the currently married, surgical sterilization is the most likely choice (37 percent), followed by the Pill (16 percent); 13 percent use a condom (U.S. Census Bureau, 2000a:80). African American women and Latinas are most likely to rely on female sterilization, while white women are most likely to use the Pill ("Contraceptive Use," 1998).

Finally, whichever method a couple chooses should reflect their values, needs, medical history, and desires. Decisions concerning contraception should be the responsibility of both parties and should not be left, as is frequently the case, to women simply because they are the ones who must worry about getting pregnant.

Almost half of the 6.3 million pregnancies in the United States are unintended, the result of using unreliable or defective contraceptives, misusing contraceptives, or using no contraceptives at all ("Contraceptive Use," 1998). On a worldwide level, it is estimated that about 40 percent of the 210 million pregnancies occurring each year are unplanned (Dailard, 2000). Rates of unplanned births are particularly high in Latin America, Kenya, the Philippines, and Japan. Poor women in the United States and women in developing countries often do not have access to contraceptives or family planning services. Further, their ability to control

Margaret Sanger, a public health nurse in New York City in the early 1900s, was alarmed at the high maternal and infant mortality rates associated with the large families of the working poor, who begged her for information about ways to prevent having more children. Sanger coined the term *birth control* as a positive description of family limitation and led the struggle to legalize contraceptive devices and to promote planned parenthood.

whether and when to have children is related to gender roles within the family and society, their level of educational attainment, participation in the labor force, and the likelihood of being subjected to a domineering husband and even domestic violence. In many parts of the world, women's limited participation in reproductive decision making is a reflection of their second-class status in society.

Given that there is a 2 percent to 4 percent chance of becoming pregnant after unprotected sex (which increases to 30 percent to 50 percent during ovulation), why do so many people risk the possibility of pregnancy by not using contraceptives?

Reasons for Not Using Contraceptives

As surprising as it might seem in this day and age, some young people believe they can't get pregnant the first time they have intercourse. If they were lucky and pregnancy did not occur, they are likely to be tempted to have unprotected sex again, a pattern researchers Jerry Burger and Linda Burns (1988) call the "illusion of unique invulnerability." The reasons for not using contraceptives are

- **Symbolism of sexual activity.** Being prepared with a contraceptive is a visible symbol of sexual activity, thus feelings of shame, guilt, fear, or anxiety may prohibit a person from using a contraceptive.
- **Role of peers.** Friends share information and tend to behave in similar fashion. Those whose friends aren't knowledgeable about or don't use contraceptives are also likely not to do so.
- **Role of parents.** Parents who have difficulty discussing sex with their children are more likely to have children who, if they become sexually active, will not use contraceptives.
- **Contraception is not romantic.** Some people complain that planning for and using contraceptives takes the spontaneity and romance out of a relationship.
- **The nature of the relationship.** People are more likely to use contraceptives in the context of an ongoing, steady relationship than when they begin a new relationship.

As indicated in the foregoing sections, contraceptive devices are not always used and, when used, are not always successful. Thus, many women faced with an unwanted pregnancy seek an abortion.

ABORTION

Abortion refers to the premature termination of a pregnancy before the fetus can survive on its own. This can occur either spontaneously (a miscarriage) or be induced through a variety of external methods (see Appendix C). Each year, more than half of unintended pregnancies worldwide—46 million, or 2 in 10 pregnancies—are aborted (Dailard, 2000). Similarly, in the United States approximately 50 percent of unintended pregnancies are terminated by induced abortions, 88 percent in the first trimester. In 1997, there were 1.3 million abortions, down from an estimated 1.6 million in 1990 ("Induced Abortion," 2000). The decline in the number of abortions is directly related to the lower rates of unintended pregnancy resulting from improved contraceptive use, particularly among teenagers. Throughout the world, women give similar reasons for their decision to abort: they are too young or poor to raise a child; they need or want to work; they are unemployed; they are estranged from their sexual partner; they do not want a child while in school. Abortions are most common among young, white, unmarried women. However, the abortion rate for African American women is 3 times the rate for white women and the rate for Latinas is roughly 2 times that of white women, no doubt reflecting in large part the greater economic disadvantages they face. About 52 percent of women who have abortions are younger than 25, women aged 20–24 account for 32 percent of all abortions, and teenagers are the remaining 20 percent. Induced abortion has been a method of birth control throughout human history and for a major part of U.S. history as well. However, today induced abortions are the subject of an emotionally charged and highly politicized debate involving conflicting values regarding women's reproductive rights and the question of when life begins. In recent times the struggle over the abortion issue has included violence against women's health clinics and the murder of several doctors and women who provided abortion services. Yet such polarized views of abortion were not always the case in the United States.

Historical Perspectives

Until the nineteenth century, American laws concerning abortion generally reflected the tradition in English common law that abortion is permissible until "quickening"—the time (generally between the fourth and sixth months) at which a pregnant woman could feel the fetus moving in her womb. Abortions were advertised in newspapers, and recipes for abortifacients (anything used to induce abortions) were provided in popular books of the day. Estimates are that by the middle of the nineteenth century there was one induced abortion for every four live births (cited in Tribe, 1990:28).

Connecticut was the first state to regulate abortion. It did so in 1821 not on any moral grounds but to protect women by prohibiting the inducement of abortion through the use of dangerous poisons. Over time other restrictive measures followed. By 1900 abortion was illegal in the United States except when a physician judged it necessary to save a woman's life.

Violence against abortion providers and clinics escalated in the 1990s. A sign on the door of the New York clinic of slain Dr. Bernard Slepian attests to the danger involved in protecting women's right of choice. Slepian was killed by a sniper's bullet in 1998.

Criminalizing abortion did not end abortions. Rather, it drove them underground. Abortions became expensive, difficult to get, and often dangerous. Poor women who, unlike their wealthier counterparts, were unable to travel outside the country or have a physician diagnose the need for a therapeutic abortion suffered the most. Over time, stories about botched abortions resulting in permanent injury or death began to surface. Two events in the 1960s became a catalyst for a new debate on the abortion issue. The first involved Sherri Finkbine, a mother of four, who had taken the tranquilizer thalidomide while pregnant. When she discovered that the drug was associated with major birth defects, she elected to have an abortion rather than give birth to a seriously deformed child. After unsuccessful attempts to get an abortion in the United States, she went to Sweden, where she aborted a deformed fetus. The second event was a major outbreak of rubella (German measles) during the years 1962–1965. The occurrence of rubella during pregnancy causes major birth defects. During this period, some 15,000 babies were born with such defects. The medical profession, increasingly conscious of these tragedies, changed its position from one of opposition to abortion to one advocating easing abortion restrictions. In 1973, the Supreme Court, by a seven-to-two vote in *Roe* v. *Wade*, struck down all antiabortion laws as violations of a woman's right to privacy. Women again had the right to choose an abortion. Since that time, however, there have been renewed efforts to restrict this right.

Race, Class, and Age

Although still legal, abortion has become increasingly less accessible. This is especially the case for poor women, women of color, and young women. In 1976, Congress passed the Hyde Amendment, which prohibited using federal Medicaid funds for abortions except in cases where the pregnancy threatens a woman's life. Over time, a majority of states followed the federal government's lead and prohibited state funding for abortions. Thus, although middle- and upper-class women, mostly white, are still able to choose whether to have an abortion, the rhetoric of choice is empty for poor women, regardless of race.

In the late 1970s, the first laws were passed requiring that parents be notified or give parental consent when a minor seeks an abortion. Today, well over half of the states have such laws. These laws often drive teenagers underground and can have tragic consequences, as evidenced by the Becky Bell case. This Indiana teenager died as a consequence of an illegal abortion that she had to prevent her parents from knowing about her pregnancy. These restrictions may also result in forcing women to have a child they do not want. Following the passage of a parental-consent law in Minneapolis, the birth rate for 15- to 17-year-olds increased by nearly 40 percent (Freiberg, 1991).

Other states also passed restrictive measures that were challenged by abortion rights groups all the way to the Supreme Court. In 1989 the Supreme Court in *Webster* v.

Reproductive Health Services, by a five-to-four vote, upheld Missouri's right to bar medical personnel from performing abortions in public hospitals. In 1992, in *Planned Parenthood v. Casey*, the Court narrowly upheld the right to abortion but at the same time allowed states to restrict the procedure.

The approach to abortion varies from country to country. Some countries (Austria, Greece, Hungary, Italy, Netherlands, Norway, Romania) allow abortion on demand in the first 12 weeks; other countries are more restrictive and permit abortion only under certain conditions: if the mother's health or life are in danger (Britain, Portugal, Spain, Switzerland), if the pregnancy resulted from rape (Portugal, Spain), if the fetus is malformed (Spain), or if there is substantial risk that the child will be born with physical or mental defects (Simpson, 1991). Many countries in Africa, as well as Andorra, Chile, and Malta, forbid abortions for any reason (Neft and Levine, 1997). Although women in developing countries are much more likely than women in developed countries to live under restrictive abortion laws, there is relatively little difference in abortion rates, 34 abortions per 1000 women in the developing world compared to 39 in developed countries. Thus, it seems legal access is not the determining factor in abortion rates. A much better predictor is the rate of unintended pregnancies. Research shows that abortion levels are high in countries where small families are desired but contraceptive use is low or ineffective. For example, in most of Eastern Europe and the former Soviet Union, where desired family size was small and modern contraceptives were not generally available until recently, women relied on legal abortions to control family size. In recent years, contraceptives were easier to obtain, and abortion rates fell by as much as 50 percent in some countries between 1990 and 1996. And in the Netherlands, where abortion is legal and contraceptive use is widespread, both abortion and unintended pregnancy rates are low (Dailard, 2000).

Restrictive abortion laws that prevent access to safe abortion services often lead to increased deaths and health problems. It is estimated that 20 million unsafe abortions take place every year and that at least 78,000 deaths result from unsafe abortions, mostly in developing countries. On the African continent, 58 women die each day as a result of attempts to end their pregnancies using homemade "cures" or in unsafe underground clinics (French, 1998). Deaths like these could be prevented by legalizing abortion and, thus, reducing the need for unsafe abortions. When Romania legalized abortion in 1990, its abortion-related mortality rate declined by 66 percent (Dailard, 2000). Additionally, such deaths and abortion rates in general can be cut by reducing the number of unintended pregnancies through family planning. A U.S. study found that every $1 increase per capita in public funding for family planning services was associated with a reduction of one abortion per 1000 women. Other studies have confirmed this finding, as well. For example, in Chile, between 1960 and 1990, the percentage of married women practicing family planning increased from 3 percent to 56 percent; during this same period, the abortion rate dropped from 77 abortions per 1000 married women of reproductive age to 45 (Shane, 1997:2). The abortion rates in countries in the former Soviet Union, Eastern Europe, and Latin America are also declining as a result of the introduction of effective family planning. It is perhaps here in the area of prevention that the prolife and prochoice activists can find common ground in responding to the abortion issue.

Public Attitudes toward Abortion

Attitudes toward abortion are not static. They are influenced by many factors: new information (particularly new medical knowledge), economic and political developments, media campaigns, and people's personal experiences. According to an August 2001 Gallup survey, a little over a quarter of Americans (26 percent) believe abortion should be legal in all cases, a little over half (56 percent) say it should be legal in certain cases, and only 17 percent say it should be illegal in all cases. Yet, 29 years after the landmark 1973 Supreme Court decision legalizing abortion, the issue remains controversial. Although a majority of Americans (58 percent) are either satisfied with keeping the laws as they are or want the laws made less restrictive, 39 percent want the laws to be more restrictive (Saad, 2002). People continue to support abortions for "hard reasons": danger to the mother's life, severe birth defects, and cases involving rape or incest but they are now less likely to support abortions for reasons of economics or desired family size.

The abortion debate is not likely to end soon. The United States could benefit by examining the history of abortion in other developed countries that have lowered their abortion rates by providing effective family planning services. Little of the debate on abortion in the United States focuses on strategies to prevent abortion. Until the two sides in the debate can come to some agreement about the need for this kind of action, it is likely that the United States will continue to have the highest percentage of unplanned pregnancies of any developed country in the West.

Thus far, we have treated the decision of whether to have children as one of personal choice and control. However, personal choices are not always realized. Just as some couples experience unwanted pregnancies, others want children but find they cannot have them.

INFERTILITY

The medical profession defines **infertility** as the inability to conceive after 12 months of unprotected intercourse or the inability to carry a pregnancy to live birth. Infertility affects 6.1 million American women and their partners, about 10 percent of the reproductive age population ("Fact Sheet," 2000–2001). When we examine who the infertile are and who is likely to seek and receive treatment for this problem, we find that race and class are critical factors. Reproductive impairments are more common among African Americans and couples with low incomes. Yet whites and those with higher incomes are more likely to seek treatment (Hirsch and Mosher, 1987). Infertility treatments are costly. Most insurance companies do not offer coverage for treatment, thus further limiting access to such treatment. Only 15 states have laws that require insurance carriers to cover fertility treatment ("Insurer Law . . . ," 2001).

Causes of Infertility

Because women show the visible signs of fertility—being pregnant—there is a tendency to view infertility, like birth control, as a woman's problem. This tendency is reinforced by a cultural tradition that has associated masculinity with fertility. For this reason, some men are unwilling to consider the idea that they could be infertile. However, men are as likely to experience infertility problems as are women. About 40 percent of fertility problems are traced to the male partner and an equal percentage to the female; the remaining 20 percent involve both partners. Thus, if a couple is unsuccessful in their efforts to have a child, both should be examined for any possible problems. The causes of infertility are many and varied. Some of the same factors can affect both women and men. For example, prolonged exposure to toxic chemicals can produce sterility in both women and men. So, too, can sexually transmitted diseases. Other factors are specific to each gender.

The major causes of female infertility are failure to ovulate and blockage of the fallopian tubes. The major cause of male infertility is low sperm production. Additionally, the spermatozoa may not be sufficiently active (or motile), or the sperm-carrying ducts may be blocked. Regardless of the cause, however, infertility in either sex does not impede sexual performance.

Consequences of Infertility

During the process of growing up it is common for children to imagine themselves as future parents. Few, however, ever question the possibility of being unable to have children. Thus, for couples wanting to have children, the knowledge that they can't comes as a shock. Many experience a "crisis of infertility," an emotional state characterized by a feeling of loss of control over their lives. As a result, they experience a wide range of emotions: depression, disbelief, denial, isolation, guilt, frustration, and grief (Whiteford and Gonzalez, 1995; Daly, 1999). Reactions to infertility vary by gender. Wives experience a deep sense of personal failure and often become preoccupied with the task of solving their infertility problems. Husbands are more likely to view infertility as an unfortunate circumstance. Their main concern with fertility focuses on their wives' unhappiness.

These different reactions can cause considerable strain in a couple's relationship. Some couples report an increase in conflict and a decrease in the frequency and level of satisfaction of sexual relationships after learning of their infertility. However, some of these same couples also report that the experience of confronting the crisis together improved the quality of their relationship (Greil, 1991).

In coping with their infertility, couples must ask themselves how important becoming parents is for them as individuals and as a married couple, and how much medical testing, effort, expense, and marital tension they are willing to accept in seeking to become parents. If they decide they want to rear children, they have two options: adoption or the new reproductive technologies. Historically, about the only available solution for infertile couples was adopting someone else's children. Today however, there is a scarcity of adoptable infants, especially white infants. Currently, only about 2 percent to 3 percent of babies born out of wedlock are given up for adoption compared to a high of almost 80 percent in the past (Dunkin, 2000). This scarcity has created what sociologist Barbara Katz Rothman (1989) calls a "competitive market situation." We'll discuss some of the legal and political issues surrounding adoption in Chapter 15.

Although approximately 8 percent of women who are infertile adopt (Bachrach, 1986), many others who wish to have children utilize one or more reproductive techniques.

REPRODUCTION WITHOUT SEX: THE NEW TECHNOLOGIES

Historical records show that as early as the eighteenth century women actively sought help from the developing medical profession in having a child. Outside of providing advice to relax or to adopt children, doctors had little knowledge to offer women who wanted to conceive. It was not until 1940 that researchers had developed a clear understanding of the relationship between ovulation and the menstrual cycle. This knowledge breakthrough was immediately applied to attempts to reduce unplanned pregnancies by regulating conception, pregnancy, and menopause. The result of these efforts was the mass production of an oral contraceptive.

As contraceptive technology improved, fewer unwanted children were available for the infertile to adopt. Thus, pressure grew to find ways to overcome infertility. However, these new reproductive technologies have generated considerable controversy because they have altered the relationship between sex and reproduction. In the United States the biological, rather than the sociological, aspects of parenthood have dominated thinking and social policies. Thus, as we shall see in the following section, assisted reproductive technology (ART) often challenges the traditional definitions of parenthood and family and raise numerous ethical and legal questions that are yet to be resolved.

Artificial Insemination **Artificial insemination** (AI) involves the injection of semen into the vagina or uterus of an ovulating woman. This process is one of the oldest and most successful of the reproductive technologies, initially having been developed in the animal husbandry field several centuries ago. Although conception can occur after one insemination, two to five inseminations are more common. Compared with other reproductive technologies, the cost of AI is relatively modest, averaging around $250 per insemination. Considerable secrecy still surrounds this procedure, so the true extent of AI is unknown. However, the Office of Technology Assessment (1988) estimates that AI is responsible for 65,000 births each year.

There is little controversy surrounding AI when the husband's sperm is used, because the resulting offspring is biologically related to both husband and wife. However, legal and ethical concerns are raised when donors (AID) are involved. When husbands agree to AID and willingly accept paternal responsibility for any resulting offspring, most state laws view these children as legitimate and recognize the father's obligations to support them. Similarly, the courts have held separated lesbian partners accountable for children conceived in this manner. Other problems may arise, however. If the donor's identity is known, conflicts can later develop over parental rights even when those rights were initially disavowed. Alternatively, an anonymous donor may be used for a number of different inseminations, thus creating the possibility of future inbreeding when unsuspecting couples who share the same genetic father may marry.

In Vitro Fertilization **In vitro fertilization** (IVF), sometimes called "test-tube" fertilization, involves surgically removing a woman's eggs, fertilizing them in a petri dish with the partner's or donor's sperm, and then implanting one or more of the fertilized eggs in the woman's uterus. The insertion of multiple eggs increases the chances of pregnancy, but it also increases the likelihood of multiple births and with them increased medical risks of premature birth and low birth weight (see later discussion). Two recent variations of the in vitro fertilization procedure increase the chances that the fertilized egg will implant in the uterine wall. The first variation, called *gamete intrafallopian transfer (GIFT)*, involves inserting both egg and sperm into the fallopian tube in the hope that conception will occur. In the second variation, called *zygote intrafallopian transfer (ZIFT)*, fertilized eggs are placed into the fallopian tube. In 1993 doctors began trying another technique, called *intracytoplasmic sperm injection (ICSI)*, whereby a single sperm is injected directly into an egg in a petri dish.

The first publicly acknowledged human success of IVF occurred in England in July 1978, with the birth of Louise Brown. Three years later the first IVF baby was born in the United States. When all of these IVF techniques are considered, the success rate is in the range of about 25 percent to 30 percent. In 1996, 20,659 babies were born as a result of these procedures (Centers for Disease Control and Prevention, 1999). The costs are high, though, ranging from $8000 to $15,000 per procedure, out of the range of many couples.

Several objections have been raised to IVF. Some people question the "morality" of fertilizing more than one egg, given the possibility that the other fertilized eggs may be destroyed, a situation that they see as analogous to abortion and, in their view, the destruction of human life. Sometimes the additional fertilized eggs are not destroyed but frozen with the idea that they will be implanted at a future date. This latter procedure, known as *cryopreservation*, has led to some complicated legal questions. For example, after an Australian couple died in a plane crash, the courts could not decide what to do with their frozen embryos. Who "owns" them? Do they have the right to exist, perhaps even inherit from their deceased "parents," or can someone (the doctor, a relative) decide to destroy them or implant them into an "adopting" party? These questions remain unanswered. Similarly, a divorced couple in Tennessee fought over custody of their frozen embryos. The ex-husband asked the court to prohibit any use of the embryos without his consent, arguing that he should not be forced to become a parent against his wishes. The Tennessee Court of Appeals granted joint custody of the frozen embryos to the divorced couple, avoiding questions of whether the embryos are alive and deserving of legal protection, treating them instead as property of the marriage to be equitably disposed of in the event of a divorce. In a similar case, the New Jersey Supreme Court upheld a woman's right to bar the use of frozen embryos produced by her and her ex-husband who wanted the right to implant them in another woman ("Court Upholds . . . ," 2001).

Embryo Transplant **Embryo transplant** refers to a procedure whereby a fertilized egg from a woman donor is implanted into an infertile woman. This procedure has been refined and is now available to postmenopausal women who want to become pregnant as well as to women who want to avoid passing on a known genetic defect to their children. Criticism of embryo transplants revolves around two central issues. One is the possible exploitation of women donors. Although a woman may donate ova out of a desire to assist an infertile couple, some women, especially poor women, may feel pressured to sell their ova to help support themselves or their families. Donors are paid around $2000 to $3500. However, couples have placed ads in the *Stanford Daily* student newspaper offering $50,000 and $100,000 to intelligent and athletic young women for the donation of their eggs (Enge, 2000). The second issue raises questions of what constitutes biological motherhood—the contribution of genetic material (via the ova) or pregnancy and childbirth. This question has become even more complicated with the development of surrogate motherhood.

New problems in this area have recently surfaced. Doctors at a California clinic have been accused of taking eggs or embryos from patients without authorization and giving them to other patients or researchers. Between 7 and 12 children are believed to have been born from unauthorized embryo transfers. One couple, believing their fertilized egg was given to another couple, is suing to gain custody of 6-year-old twins that were born to that couple (Brandon, 1996). In 1999, Mrs. Donna Fasano, who is white, gave birth to twin boys, one black and one white. An embryologist at the fertility clinic mistakenly implanted one of her embryos and that of another patient at the clinic (Yardley, 1999a, 1999b). To date there is relatively little regulation of fertility clinics, and these scandals are evidence of how social policy has lagged behind the new technologies.

Reproductive technology raises many questions about the meaning of parenthood.

Source: Reprinted by permission: Tribune Media Services.

SURROGACY In **surrogacy,** a woman agrees to be artificially inseminated with a man's sperm, carry the fetus to term, and relinquish all rights to the child after it is born. This is perhaps the most controversial of all the reproductive techniques, because like AID it involves a third party. Unlike AID, however, the donor is intimately involved in the reproductive process. Surrogate motherhood may develop in either of two situations. In the first, a third party is artificially inseminated with the husband's sperm (or donor sperm if he is also infertile). Here the term *surrogate* is somewhat misleading, because the woman who is inseminated is also the biological mother. In the second situation, the wife's uterus does not allow a fertilized egg to implant itself and develop. In such cases the couple uses in vitro fertilization, but the resulting embryo is then transplanted into a surrogate mother. The surrogate can be a relative or a stranger. In the latter case the woman and the couple generally sign a contract. Generally the provisions of the contract include a fee payment ($10,000 to $20,000) to the surrogate and coverage of all her medical expenses. There have been about 10,000 surrogate births in the United States in the last 20 years (Granat, 1997).

Questions inevitably arise regarding the motivations of the two parties in such an agreement. For the infertile couple there is a desire to have a child that is genetically related to at least one of them. Several motivational factors are probably involved in the decision to be a surrogate mother. Detroit psychiatrist Philip Parker conducted extensive psychological tests on over five hundred surrogate applicants and found strong altruistic aspects in their willingness to be surrogate mothers. They wanted to give the gift of a child to those who otherwise would not experience child rearing (reported in Gladwell, 1988). However, some critics of surrogate motherhood see it as reproductive exploitation whereby poor women's reproductive capacity becomes a commodity that they are forced to sell to survive (Dworkin, 1987).

The legal issues surrounding surrogate motherhood are many. What if the surrogate mother changes her mind and decides to keep the child? This has proven to be a rare occurrence—only six out of approximately four thousand surrogate mothers have not relinquished their babies; an additional ten others have expressed regrets for doing so (Curry, 1992). However, when a surrogate mother changes her mind, the results can be traumatic for all parties. One well-publicized example was the celebrated case of Baby M, whose biological mother, Mary Beth Whitehead, changed her mind after giving birth and wanted to keep the child. After a lengthy court battle, the contract was ruled invalid, but custody of the child went to the biological father and adoptive mother, who were seen as more stable and capable of parenting than the biological mother. In another contested case, the surrogate mother had no genetic relationship to the child but claimed that through pregnancy and giving birth she had bonded with the infant and was therefore the baby's mother. The judge disagreed and awarded custody to the biological parents, stating that genetics, not giving birth, constitutes parentage. The judge compared the role the surrogate provides to that of a foster parent who temporarily stands in for a parent who is unable to care for a child.

Other issues may also arise in surrogate cases. What happens if a child is born with a major physical problem? Can the contract then be rescinded? If so, does the responsibility for that child rest solely on the surrogate mother? What rights does each party have—the unborn child, the child's biological mother, the child's biological father, and the contractual parents? Do the contractual parents have a right to demand certain behaviors from the surrogate mother during her pregnancy, for example, maintaining a particular diet, refraining from drinking alcohol, or undergoing surgery to improve the life chances of the fetus? These questions have spurred considerable legislative activity in attempts to regulate surrogate parenting. However, there is as yet no consistent legal view across the country. At least 17 states have banned or restricted commercial surrogate contracts (Curry, 1992). Other states, like California, permit surrogate motherhood. Most, however, have not yet decided on what approach to take in this matter.

In sum, these new reproductive technologies have helped many infertile couples and unmarried women to realize their goal of having and rearing children. According to the American Society for Reproductive Medicine in Birmingham, Alabama, over 300,000 people worldwide have been conceived by in vitro fertilization and similar assisted reproductive technologies (cited in Engley, 1999). The use of these technologies are charting new territory and extending the boundaries of what it means to be a parent or a sibling.

THE CHOICE TO PARENT

In the previous section, we examined the issue of fertility and various factors that affect the decision to parent. Once this decision is made, individuals and couples must turn their attention to matters of conception, pregnancy, childbirth, and child rearing. All of these activities effect considerable changes in the lives of the people involved.

"It's a girl." "It's a boy." Every year millions of parents hear these words as they strain to get that first glimpse of the miraculous new life to which they have contributed. Whatever their feelings concerning pregnancy and childbirth, a majority of Americans have at least one child in their lifetime. However, as we have seen, fertility rates vary considerably among different groups, and individual cases vary greatly as well. The *Guinness Book of World Records* (1990), for example, relates that in 1981 a woman in Chile gave birth to her fifty-fifth child. We might assume that this woman made a conscious choice to have 55 children. Although most people do not choose to have 55 children, millions of people do make a conscious choice to parent. However, we should also point out that many people *do not choose* to parent, but rather they become parents as a result of unwanted pregnancies or taking on the responsibility of parenting children of family or friends. For example, as we discuss later in Chapter 14, grandparents increasingly are assuming parenting responsibilities when parents experience major life crises in order to provide a safe, stable, and secure environment for their grandchildren (Landry-Meyer and Fournier, 1997). Other people consciously choose not to parent and they take the necessary measures to ensure that they will not have children.

However many children an individual or couple does have and no matter whether the choice is conscious or not, the process always begins with the fertilization of an egg by a sperm. Between that moment and the birth of a child are many months of development.

CONCEPTION

Pregnancy and eventual childbirth begin with **conception,** the process by which a male sperm cell penetrates the female ovum (egg), creating a fertilized egg, or **zygote.** Until recently, penile–vaginal intercourse was necessary for conception to take place. As you have read in this chapter, however, today conception can take place not only inside a woman's uterus but also within a petri dish. For the purposes of this book, the term *conception* will encompass all forms of fertilization.

What makes conception possible is the process of **ovulation,** the release of a mature egg. The period of fertility in females normally begins with menstruation and ovulation and lasts until after the menopause (which occurs somewhere between 45 and 50 years of age, on average). There are always exceptions, however. In the United States girls as young as 10 years of age have conceived. The youngest female to conceive a child is recorded as a 5 1/2-year-old girl living in Peru, and the oldest on record are two 63-year-old women: Rosanna Della Corte, an Italian woman who gave birth to a healthy baby in 1994 after being implanted with a donor egg fertilized with her husband's sperm, and Arceli Keh of California in 1996 (*Guinness World Records*, 2001).

Males are capable of participating in conception when they begin to produce sperm, which occurs around puberty. According to some authorities, some men can produce viable sperm for 80 or more years. Although millions of sperm are released with a single male ejaculation, only a few reach the fallopian tube that contains the egg. These sperm emit an enzyme that dissolves the outer layer of the egg, allowing one sperm to fertilize it.

However, fertilization does not guarantee a successful birth. In fact, 18 percent of fertilized eggs are lost during the first week of pregnancy, and 32 percent are lost in the second week. Only around 37 percent of human zygotes survive to become live infants (Blank, 1988).

Multiple Conception and Births

Multiple conception, in which two or more children are conceived at one time, is relatively rare. The most common form of multiple conception and birth is twins. For reasons not clearly understood, multiple births vary across race and ethnicity. Twins are born about once in every 90 births for whites and once in every 70 births for African Americans. African American women are more likely to have twins than any other women, whereas Asian Americans tend to conceive twins less often than any other racial group in the United States. Triplets are fairly rare, occurring around once in every 9000 births, and quadruplets and larger sets of multiple conceptions and births are, at each increment, even more rare. Latinas and African American women have really low triplet (and larger multiple) birth rates (Papalia and Olds, 1989; Pike, 1999). Not surprisingly, the mortality rate for multiple births is higher than for single births. The greater the number of children born at one time, the greater the mortality rate. This fact notwithstanding, multiple births have increased dramatically over the past two decades, attributed in part to the combined effect of older mothers and fertility treatments. A report by the National Center for Health Statistics attributes about one-third of the increase in multiple births to the fact that more women are choosing to conceive and are giving birth at older ages when they are physiologically more likely to have multiple births. The remaining two-thirds of the increase is due to fertility treatments. In addition, older women are more likely to use fertility drugs (Vobejda, 1998; Pike, 1999).

In 1997 and 1998, some American mothers made history with their multiple births. For example, in May 1997, the first recorded birth of sextuplets (six babies) to an African American couple in the United States occurred in Washington, D.C. Delivered by cesarean section, one girl among the five girls and one boy was delivered stillborn. The mother had not used a fertility drug. Later, in November 1997, the first completely successful septuplet birth in the United States occurred when a 29-year-old Iowa mother gave birth to seven babies: four boys and three girls. The unusual

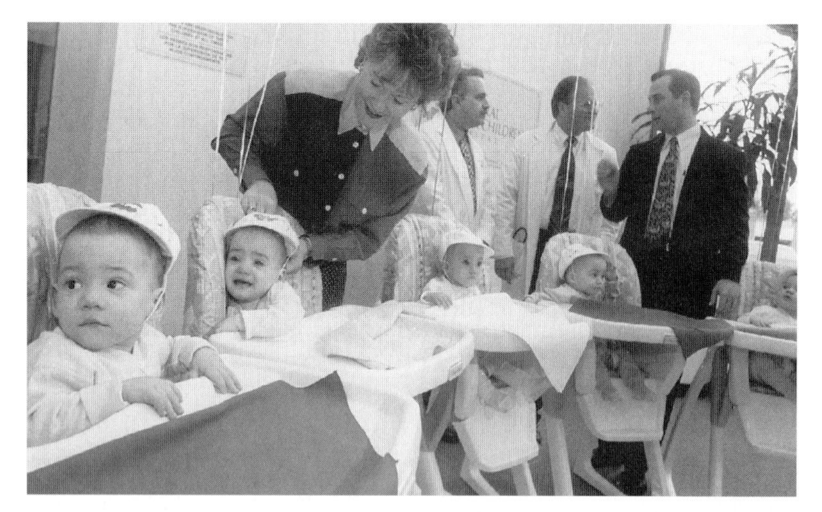

There has been a dramatic increase in multiple births due in part to women becoming pregnant later in life and to the use of fertility drugs and treatments. Since the birth of the Shier quintuplets, shown celebrating their first birthday at Long Beach Memorial Hospital in 1997, women have given birth to sextuplets, septuplets, and even octuplets.

pregnancy is believed to have been caused by the fertility drugs that the mother had been taking. There are no other known living sets of septuplets in the world; the last septuple birth in the United States was in 1985, but only three of the babies survived. A Saudi Arabian woman gave birth to septuplets in 1997, but only one remains alive (Maxwell, 1997). And in December 1998, a 27-year-old Nigerian-born mother gave birth in Texas to the only living octuplets (eight babies): six girls and two boys. Seven of the eight babies survived; one died a week after birth. The mother, who had miscarried triplets in an earlier pregnancy, had used fertility drugs. Sociologically speaking, while joyful, such births can exert a tremendous drain on the health and well-being of a woman carrying three or more babies. Multiples have an infant mortality rate that is 12 times higher than that of single births. In addition, there is a tremendous emotional strain and financial burden caused by caring for a multiple set of children.

Media-highlighted cases of multiple births, such as those cited here, have contributed much to a growing public debate about the *ethics* of trying to carry an unprecedented six, seven, or eight children into the world, as well as the *morality* of such a decision. One of the dangers of multiple births is that all of the fetuses must share the nutrients and blood supply of one mother. And they do not share the nutrients equally, thus one or more are shortchanged. Some people (including many doctors) believe that a woman should abort one or more of the fetuses to increase the chances of survival of some of the other fetuses. In London, the concern over multiple births following fertility treatments has caused fertility regulators to rule that doctors should normally transfer no more than two embryos at a time during in vitro fertilization. This action is designed to reduce the number of British women giving birth to triplets or twins after fertility treatment. According to the regulators, the aim of infertility treatment should be the delivery of a single, healthy child (Ross, 2001).

What do you think? *Should a woman who is carrying multiple fetuses abort some of them to increase the chances of survival of some of the others? Explain. Is having multiple children immoral? Given that sociologists view morality as a social construction frame your discussion within this theoretical framework.*

Sex Preference and Selection

With increasing advances in reproductive technology a couple no longer have to leave the determination of their unborn child's sex completely up to chance. For example, various Gender Clinics offer parents-to-be a chance to increase the odds of having a girl or a boy, whichever is their preference. Sex selection is a sensitive and controversial issue, however. Some experts in reproduction fear that the techniques used in sex selection might represent a health hazard to pregnant women. From a sociological perspective, such genetic engineering has important social and political implications. For example, wherever and whenever males are valued more highly than females, we can assume that such engineering will often be toward increasing the odds for a male child. This phenomenon is already dramatically evident in several Asian countries. As indicated in the "In the News" that opened this chapter, the preference for a male child has led to sex-selective abortions and female infanticide in countries such as China and India, where many women, feeling the age-old obligation to bear sons, secretly undergo abortions of female fetuses and try again to conceive a son. The preference for a male child has serious consequences for marriage, family, and community life, not to mention the girls who have escaped infanticide. As adults, sometimes these women are forced to keep having children until they have a son, and other times they are forced to abort the fetus even though they want to keep the child. Both these practices can have profound health effects on the mother and, in some ways, represent a beginning cycle of violence against these women.

Very often, the pressure to have sons comes from women themselves, particularly mothers-in-law (WuDunn, 1997). Some women feel that they have failed their husbands if they do not produce a male heir, and others fear that they will not be able to afford the exorbitant dowries their future in-laws may expect of them when their daughters get married. Still other women, knowing the reality of being female in a society that prefers males, don't want to bring a girl into the world and have to see her neglected and sometimes abused (Slovan, 1997).

There is some indication that the trend toward assuring the birth of a male is carrying over to Indian and other South Asian immigrants to the United States. For example, a family planning medical group in Chicago reports that 10 percent to 20 percent of their abortion clients are South Asian Americans, far higher than the percentage of women in the Chicago area (Patel, 2001). The cultural bias for males is not limited to Asians or Asian Americans. Research on parental sex preferences in the United States also shows an overwhelming preference for a male child over a female child. Despite the significant advances women have made over the past century and the increasing emphasis on gender equality, when it comes to having children, Americans today still prefer boys. In a recent Gallup survey conducted at the end of the year 2000, almost one-half (42 percent) of Americans said they would prefer a boy if they could have only one child. The rate of preference for boys is driven largely by the desire among men, 55 percent of whom say they would prefer to have a boy if they could have only one child. Women, on the other hand, are just as likely to prefer girls as they are to prefer boys—35 percent say they would prefer a girl and 32 percent say a boy (Simmons, 2000).

PREGNANCY

Pregnancy initiates many changes both physically and emotionally for a woman, her partner (if such a relationship exists), and the fetus. Major changes occur in the woman's hormone levels, body shape, and psychological state as the pregnancy develops. Pregnancy also brings about a variety of changes in the lives and relationship of the expectant parents. Their adjustment to the pregnancy is influenced to a large extent by whether the pregnancy was planned, their age at the time of pregnancy, their socioeconomic level, and their race and ethnicity.

Prenatal Development and Care

The attitudes and behaviors of a mother during pregnancy greatly influence the health and well-being of the fetus and later of the human infant. In addition, race, class, age, and gender experiences significantly affect maternal attitudes and behaviors during pregnancy (the prenatal period) and after (postnatal). While early confirmation and quality prenatal care are important, they are not equally available to all women or couples. Many women of color and poor women, for example, often avoid prenatal care because they do not have the resources or because of previous negative experiences involving the health care system. Often these women deliver their babies in public hospitals and teaching institutions that can be insensitive to their needs.

Pregnancy can be both a joyous occasion and one of concern. If the pregnancy is planned and/or wanted, the joy and excitement of impending parenthood can be tremendous. A pregnancy can be a rewarding experience for one or both parents. It can promote couple bonding; it can bring a couple closer together as they adapt to this new stage in their lives and as they share common hopes and dreams for their future child. Pregnancy can also be a time of challenge. For example, a pregnancy can limit opportunities or it can place considerable strain on a relationship. Pregnancy can also be a time of discomfort, self-doubt, and low self-esteem. For example, given the overwhelming emphasis we place on physical appearance in this society, it is no wonder that with the growth of a woman's body during pregnancy, some women feel ugly and unattractive. However, this is certainly not the case for all women. Some women are delighted with their appearance and believe that they are more beautiful at this time than at any other time. This attitude is particularly apparent today among female celebrities. For example, recently, supermodel Cindy Crawford posed naked and proud in prenatal splendor on the cover of *W* magazine (a fashion magazine) when she was seven months pregnant. Mimicking the famous 1991 *Vanity Fair* cover of a nude and eight-months-pregnant Demi Moore, Ms. Crawford reported that her pregnancy was all that she wanted to talk about. Although most women do not pose pregnant and nude, most feel good about themselves and their pregnancy.

Moreover, pregnancy can create anxieties and fears concerning a number of issues, some of which include the pregnancy's effect on the couple relationship, whether one or both partners will be good parents, the probability of carrying a fetus to full term versus a pregnancy loss of one kind or another, as well as concerns about the health and well-being of the unborn fetus and the probability of it being born healthy.

If there is concern about the health or well-being of the fetus, prenatal testing can provide the couple with specific information about the condition of the fetus. Two of the most commonly used prenatal tests are amniocentesis and ultrasound. **Amniocentesis** is performed when there is some concern about a hereditary disease. It can also provide information about the sex of the fetus. **Ultrasound** allows a physician and the couple to observe the developing fetus directly by viewing electronically the echoes of sound waves pulsating through the pregnant woman's body. Not only can ultrasound be used to detect various birth defects, it can also be used to determine when a child will be born (within a couple of weeks) and whether or not the mother is carrying multiple babies. For many couples, one of the rewards of the ultrasound is the **sonogram,** which allows parents to see the fetus and any movements it makes.

As the end of the pregnancy period approaches, some women feel an enormous sense of urgency for it all to be over with. For others, it is a time of increased bonding with the fetus. In any case, most often a pregnancy ends with the birth of a healthy baby. Nine out of ten babies born in the United States are healthy (Minino and Smith, 2001). Although the chances of having a healthy baby are good, most parents want to do all they can to make this a reality.

Prenatal Problems and Defects

Recent research findings are not entirely consistent concerning how many children in the United States are born with some sort of birth defect. Most estimates fall between 3 percent and 5 percent, but a few estimates are as high as 7 percent. Birth defects account for 21 percent of all infant deaths in the United States, more than from any other single cause (Minino and Smith, 2001). Birth defects include any condition that causes or leads to death or the lowering of the quality of life. Birth defects usually can be traced to one or more of the following factors: (1) the influence of the prenatal environment on the fetus, for example, exposure to toxic chemicals and the use of drugs, including alcohol and tobacco, by the mother; (2) heredity, that is, the parents' genes; and (3) injuries sustained at birth. Regardless of their causes, all defects present at birth are referred to as **congenital.** Parents who know or suspect that they might give birth to a child with a particular defect should seek some sort of counseling or professional advice.

Protecting the Prenatal Environment Only about one-fifth of birth defects can be traced to heredity. Research has shown repeatedly that experiences such as those of age, race, and class have important effects on **morbidity** (illness) and **mortality** (death). For example, although more women 40 and older are having children today than in the past, it is believed that the optimum age for pregnancy is between 20 and 35 years of age. Thus, women younger than 20 and older than 35 are at greater risk of having a miscarriage, a stillbirth (the birth of a dead fetus), a premature birth, an underweight baby, prolonged and more difficult labor, or a child with a birth defect. In addition, first-time mothers in their 40s are twice as likely to have a cesarean section performed than are women in their 20s (Kennen, 1997). Although the overall risks to maternal and fetal health for pregnant women over 35 have lessened in some areas of health and well-being, these women are still more at risk than are younger women. Women over 40, for example, have the highest rates of babies born with Down syndrome. At the other end of the spectrum, the maternal death rate from pregnancy and its complications is 60 percent higher for adolescents than for mothers in their early 20s (Ventura et al., 2001).

Race and social class further affect a woman's chances of delivering a healthy baby. Although overall rates of infant and maternal mortality in the United States have declined significantly in recent years, their incidence varies among different racial and class groups. African American women, for example, are four times as likely as white women to die in childbirth (U.S. Census Bureau, 2000a). African Americans and Puerto Ricans are more likely than whites to have premature babies or babies with low birth weights. This situation contributes to infant mortality and frequently has been associated with inadequate prenatal care and nutrition for the mother (Minino and Smith, 2001). Essentially, the fewer resources women have, such as adequate diet, financial resources and income, employment and housing facilities, and access to quality health care, the greater the likelihood of health problems or complications during pregnancy.

Moreover, the increasing cost of health care in the United States prevents many pregnant women, particularly those with limited economic resources and inadequate (if any) health insurance, from receiving proper care during pregnancy. This problem is especially acute among Native Americans, Latinas, and African Americans. This situation points up the larger and continuing problem in this country of an inadequate health care system for most individuals and families.

The health of parents, particularly mothers before and during pregnancy, and the services available to them throughout their pregnancy, especially at delivery, are important determinants of the health status of their children. Infants whose health status is compromised at birth are more vulnerable to various health problems later in life. Although we cannot control heredity, we can, to some degree, control the prenatal environment. To protect the prenatal environment properly, a woman must take care of herself during pregnancy. According to the Centers for Disease Control and Prevention, a healthy pregnancy is a major factor in reducing the risk of infant death. Timely prenatal care and the avoidance of harmful behavior like smoking are two ways pregnant mothers can protect the health of their infants (NCHS News Release, 2001). Although it is desirable to see a physician on a regular basis, primary responsibility for protecting the fetus resides with the parents. Some of the most prevalent prenatal concerns include nutrition, smoking, alcohol, drug use, and AIDS.

Nutrition Because nutrients pass from mother to fetus through the placenta, an improper diet or maternal malnutrition can have detrimental effects for the fetus—including congenital defects, small stature, and diseases such as rickets, cerebral palsy, and epilepsy; it can also cause a miscarriage or stillbirth. In addition, various research studies show that girls who are inadequately fed in childhood may have impaired intellectual capacity, delayed puberty, and possibly impaired fertility and stunted growth, leading to higher risks of complications during childbirth (World Health Report, 1998). According to most authorities, maternal malnutrition is one of the leading causes of fetal death. The probability of malnutrition during pregnancy is highest among teen mothers and poor and working-class women regardless of age.

Smoking and Alcohol Consumption Not only is smoking detrimental to the health of the smoker, it also has been shown to be detrimental to the health of the fetus.

Although the extent of damage caused by cigarette smoking during pregnancy is not fully known, since 1985 the U.S. Surgeon General has cautioned that smoking during pregnancy increases the risk of miscarriage, premature birth, low birth weight, and the probability of sickness, convulsions, or death in early infancy. As a result, fewer women today are smoking during their pregnancy. However, the smoking rate varies across race and age. For example, Native American women have the highest rate of smoking, followed by non-Latina white mothers; Latina and African American mothers have lower rates and Asian American and Pacific Islander women have the lowest rates of smoking of all groups. In addition, smoking by pregnant teens (15–19 years of age) remains high and actually increased in the mid-1990s, while the youngest and oldest mothers (under the age of 15 and 40–49, respectively) have the lowest rate of smoking during pregnancy (HHS Press Release, 1998). Smoking during pregnancy is also highly correlated with educational attainment. As the level of the mother's formal education increases, the likelihood that she will smoke during pregnancy decreases significantly (Ohio Department of Health, 1999). Pregnant women who smoke are not the only ones to put the developing fetus in jeopardy. Recent studies with human subjects suggest that smoking by fathers may have an indirect and negative effect on the fetus. Male smoking can harm or impair sperms, causing a miscarriage and passing on a slight but significant legacy of cancer, tumors, and leukemia to offspring, even if the mother doesn't smoke (Williams, 1998).

As with cigarette smoking, maternal alcohol consumption can have considerable negative effects, both for the mother and the fetus. For example, alcohol use during pregnancy is the leading cause of mental retardation in children. An alcoholic mother can give birth to a baby who is also dependent on alcohol. Heavy alcohol use during pregnancy, either alone or in conjunction with smoking, can lead to **fetal alcohol syndrome (FAS)** or *fetal alcohol effects (FAE)*, a set of birth defects characterized by abnormal features of the face and head, heart defects, growth retardation, and abnormalities of the central nervous system that are often reflected in mental retardation (Ohio Department of Health, 1999). In addition, a child with FAS or FAE may have difficulty paying attention in school, have various learning problems, have a lower IQ, and be hyperactive. FAS is one of the three leading known causes of birth defects in the United States. According to the Children's Trust Foundation, each year over 40,000 American children are born with defects because their mothers drank alcohol when pregnant. FAS birth defects have no cure, thus the effects never go away (Fetal Alcohol Fact Sheet, 1999). As with many cultural experiences, the rate of FAS varies across race and ethnicity. For example, the high prevalence of FAS among Native American/Alaska Native newborns (30 per 10,000 live births) is evidence of high rates of alcohol consumption during pregnancy and is the leading cause of disability among these newborns. FAS occurs much less frequently among other groups of women: Only 6 percent of infants born to African American women have FAS, while fewer than 1 percent of the births to Asian American, Latina, and white women have this condition (National Women's Health Information Center, 1999).

Experts have yet to agree on a safe level of alcohol consumption by pregnant women. Although many people believe that an occasional glass of wine or beer is harmless for the fetus, most physicians recommend that a pregnant woman refrain from all alcohol consumption. The fact is that when a woman drinks, her baby drinks because the alcohol passes directly through the placenta to the baby. Moreover, if a woman plans to breast-feed her child, it is advisable not to drink because alcohol can be transmitted to the nursing infant in the breast milk.

Drug and Other Substance Abuse The majority of drugs, whether street drugs, common drugs like caffeine and aspirin, or prescription and over-the-counter medications, contain chemicals that have been found to have some effect on the fetus. Almost all drugs taken or ingested during pregnancy cross the placenta. The fetus is particularly vulnerable to drugs in the first trimester, when the vital organs are forming.

An increasing number of women abuse drugs during pregnancy and thus endanger the well-being and lives of their children as well as themselves. The increasing use and abuse of cocaine, particularly in the potent form of crack, has intensified concerns about the implications of maternal drug use for unborn children. As indicated in the "Social Policy Issues" box, increasingly drug-abusing women are being legally punished for the outcome of their pregnancies. Women who use cocaine during pregnancy increase the risk of hemorrhage and miscarriages; they have significantly higher rates of premature and low-birth-weight babies, compared with those of nonusers. Babies exposed to narcotics in the womb are frequently born addicted, and the misery they suffer from withdrawal makes them difficult to care for (Drug Abuse and Pregnancy, 1999). These babies are also at greater risk of suffering strokes, seizures, brain damage, mental retardation, and congenital abnormalities. The consequences of the mother's addiction to drugs can sometimes be fatal for the offspring. The overwhelming number of severely drug-damaged children is stretching to the limits the capabilities of most major societal institutions to provide assistance. What can society do? What, if anything, is the responsibility of parents? The state? The criminal justice system?

These are questions of concern for a growing number of people in U.S. society who think that the fetus has a right to be born with the best possible chance for a healthy and long life. And, as indicated in the "Social Policy Issues" box, some of these people believe that the answer to drug and alcohol abuse by pregnant mothers is legal prosecution of the mother.

AIDS and Pregnancy Throughout this textbook we discuss the ramifications of AIDS for marriages and families. Here we limit our discussion specifically to the impact of AIDS on pregnant women and on the developing fetus.

PROTECTING FETAL RIGHTS

Increasingly, women are being singled out and subjected to a sex-specific form of criminal prosecution for their drug use. Since the mid-1980s more than half the state legislatures in the United States have considered punitive laws for women who abuse drugs or alcohol while pregnant. However, to date, no state has actually passed such a law. Nevertheless, prosecutors in several states have brought cases against these women under statutes intended for other purposes. For example, since 1990, prosecutors in at least 30 states have used a variety of criminal laws to bring charges against pregnant women who abuse drugs or alcohol. Some use drug laws, charging that women are delivering drugs to the fetus through the umbilical cord, while others, such as in South Carolina, use child-endangerment statutes, treating substance abuse during pregnancy as a crime of child abuse. State supreme courts in Florida, Kentucky, Nevada, Ohio, and Wisconsin, and many lower courts, have struck down such policies, usually ruling that a fetus is not a person under the particular criminal law. To date, only South Carolina has upheld such charges.

In 1997, the South Carolina Supreme Court upheld that "a viable fetus is a child covered by child abuse laws." That controversial ruling involved the case of a mother who, after testing positive for cocaine after her child was born healthy in 1992, was arrested and charged with violating the state's child abuse laws. Expecting to be sent to a drug treatment facility, the mother pleaded guilty. However, to most people's surprise, the judge sentenced her to prison. Her case is still on appeal. Other states are moving in a similar direction. In 2000, the Ohio Supreme Court ruled that a baby born addicted to cocaine because of its mother's addiction is legally an abused child. However, South Carolina is the leader among states in prosecuting mothers who take drugs. In 1999, more than 40 pregnant women in that state faced criminal charges stemming from their drug use. And in May 2001, in a landmark case, a 24-year-old mother of three gave birth to a stillborn infant and was charged with killing that child by smoking crack cocaine. After only 15 minutes of deliberations, jurors returned with a guilty verdict, making her the first woman in the nation to be convicted of homicide for killing an unborn child through drug abuse. Her sentence of 20 years, reduced to 12 years without the chance for parole, was the stiffest penalty yet for a woman who abused drugs while pregnant. This case has rekindled the debate about fetal rights and opens the door to future prosecutions of women for smoking, alcohol use, or other behaviors that could harm a fetus.

The tough policy against women who abuse drugs while pregnant generally and the recent South Carolina Supreme Court decision specifically are applauded by some who are frustrated by the toll that drug abuse has taken on society. Proponents argue that criminal prosecution of drug-addicted mothers is the only way to force these women to get help for their problem while simultaneously protecting the unborn infant. Others view drug addiction as a disease and thus find this policy inappropriate. In their view, punitive approaches to health problems during pregnancy are always counterproductive. In the 2001 South Carolina case critics believe that the race and class of the mother—African American and homeless—made her an easy target for prosecutors and politicians who wanted to make an example of someone. They note that South Carolina, which ranks near the bottom in money spent on drug treatment programs, will spend an estimated $300,000 to imprison this woman for 12 years. Many detractors argue further that such punitive practices single out women and hold them to an impossible standard: "If men got pregnant, the courts would take a very different view." When ranking fetal risk factors, nearly all fetal damage is due to one drug—alcohol (Sobey, 1997; Butler, 1999; Pressley, 2001).

Without a doubt, there is little consistent agreement about the value or appropriateness of these policies. Apart from the constitutional issues they raise, many feminists and health groups argue that, although prosecutors claim that such charges will encourage pregnant drug users to get treatment, in reality it frightens such women away from the medical system (Sobey, 1997). In addition, such policies fail to recognize the continuing need for drug treatment programs designed to meet the needs of women, particularly pregnant women, such as obstetric and child care, as well as special counseling (Renzetti and Curran, 1992).

What do you think of this policy? *Should women be prosecuted by a court of law and serve time in jail for using drugs while pregnant? Should this include alcohol abuse as well? What about smoking? What is the responsibility of the court? Does it have a right to prosecute a woman or take custody of her child? What are the parents' rights? Should parents have complete and total freedom to do what they want during pregnancy? If not, who should decide where to draw the line? Does a fetus have rights? If yes, what rights does it have? If no, why not? If the rights of the mother should conflict with those of the fetus, who determines which rights take precedence?*

Women who are HIV-positive face not only the probability that the infection will develop into full-blown AIDS but also face severe restrictions on their behavior, particularly their reproductive behavior. One of the biggest problems for these women, when or if they do become pregnant, is how to take care of their health and at the same time prevent transmitting the infection to their infant. It is estimated that approximately 25 percent of infants born to HIV-positive mothers contract HIV from their mothers during pregnancy or birth (vertical transmission); and, according to the Centers for Disease Control and Prevention, this problem is more acute for pregnant HIV-infected women who do not receive preventive medication. When HIV/AIDS-infected babies are born, they generally have prominent physical features that are linked directly to HIV: small heads, slanted eyes that sit far apart from each other, a square forehead, a wide and flat nose, and loosely shaped lips. This physical appearance is referred to as **embryopathy** (Marion et al., 1986).

The problem of vertical transmission of HIV infection is exacerbated by the fact that most women in the United States who are infected with HIV are not even aware that they carry the virus. This is unfortunate given that, to date, most research and clinical study trials of pregnant women with HIV/AIDS have shown conclusively that medical therapy treatments with the drug AZT reduces the likelihood that a woman will transmit HIV to her infant before, during, or after birth by two-thirds (New Mexico Governor's Task Force on HIV/AIDS, 1999), although the risk of vertical transmission is significantly increased in mothers with advanced stage AIDS (APAC, 2000). Current statistics show that pregnant women with AIDS frequently have miscarriages or, if the fetus survives, the newborn may die in early infancy.

Such research/clinical trial findings have led to recommendations from a wide range of interested parties to mandate HIV education and voluntary HIV testing of pregnant women. These data have also led some health professionals, sociologists (see, for example, Etzioni, 1997), and others to advocate the mandatory testing of newborns. This has sparked a spirited public debate concerning mandatory testing of newborns for HIV antibodies and whether the results of these tests should be disclosed to the infants' mothers. Those on each side of the debate demonize the other by accusing them of seeking to subvert fundamental rights, discriminating against gays, or causing massive deaths among infants. The primary argument for testing infants for HIV is that if mothers are properly informed and counseled, hundreds of infants would be spared severe suffering and major illness, and often death. Mothers would be spared much grief, and significant public costs could be avoided (Etzioni, 1997). For example, it is estimated that the prevention of one case of HIV infection in newborn babies could save up to $160,000 in lifetime costs (New Mexico Governor's Task Force on HIV/AIDS, 1999). On the other side of the issue, those who object to mandatory testing point out the sociological and psychological effects of having one's privacy violated by revealing a mother's HIV status without her consent. They argue that not only do such policies violate the privacy of the mother but also these mothers may be stigmatized or lose their health insurance, jobs, or housing. Those taking this position suggest that there are alternative ways of serving the same public health goals that are more effective and judicious, such as testing pregnant women after gaining their consent (voluntary testing), rather than mandatory testing of infants followed by disclosure (Etzioni, 1997).

Because of their limited access to drug treatment programs, medical information, and quality health care, poor communities and communities of color are especially at risk for HIV/AIDS babies. In fact, 82 percent of the infants that have tested positive for HIV/AIDS are nonwhite. African American children constitute only 15 percent of this country's children, but they account for 60 percent of all childhood HIV/AIDS cases. Latina/o children, who represent about 10 percent of the nation's children, account for 21 percent of these cases (Centers for Disease Control and Prevention, 2000).

We discuss other sexually transmitted diseases such as syphilis and gonorrhea in Appendix A. These diseases can also affect a fetus and can be contracted by the newborn. As with the AIDS virus, STDs in pregnant women can cause miscarriage, brain damage to the fetus, problems with eyesight, and other medical problems.

EXPECTANT FATHERS

Pregnant women are considered to be in a special condition, and we generally give them all of our attention and support. But what about the expectant father? Given that we expect men to play an increasingly active role in childbirth and child rearing, what do we know about their experiences through pregnancy and the birth of their children? Exactly what is the father's part in the process of pregnancy? Are men's experiences entirely social and psychological, or do men experience physiological symptoms as well?

Historically, pregnancy has been viewed primarily as women's work. Expectant fathers were left in the background, unnoticed until the onset of labor. Few fathers participated in pregnancy and childbirth beyond offering general support to the mother. Today, however, a growing number of fathers are participating in the pregnancy and childbirth experience. Many prospective dads are joining their pregnant partners in prenatal classes and in the delivery room, where they help their partner with breathing and other relaxation techniques. They are sometimes the first of the two to hold the newborn and a growing number of these men take some time off from work during the first few weeks after the baby is born in order to share in the caring for and bonding with the infant.

The Cultural Double Bind

In one of the few studies that examines the concerns and feelings of expectant fathers, psychologist Jerrold Lee Shapiro (1987) suggests that the pregnancy of a partner

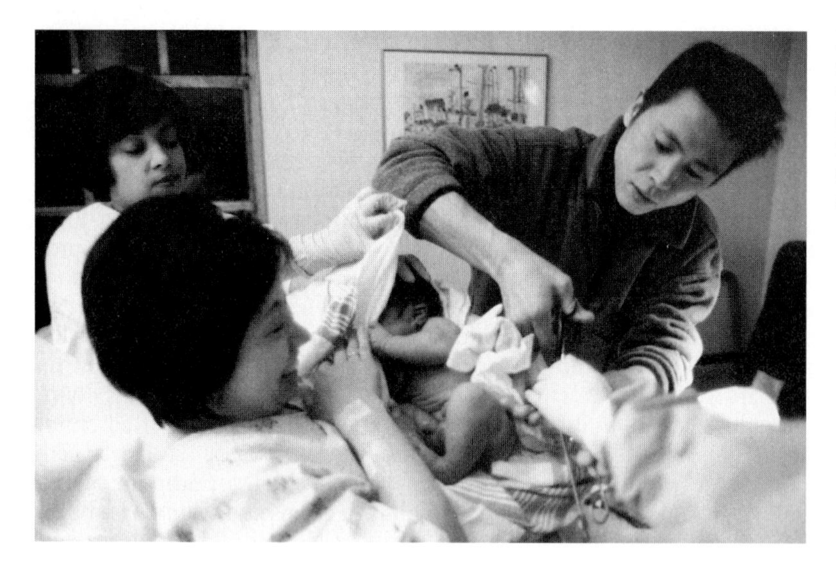

In times past, expectant fathers paced nervously in hospital waiting rooms, anxious to hear news of their child's birth. Today, fathers not only are present at the birth of their children, but many actively participate, as this father does, by cutting the umbilical cord.

thrusts a man into an alien world. He is encouraged to be part of a process about which he knows little or nothing. He doesn't have role models because his father almost certainly didn't participate actively in his mother's pregnancy. These problems are not insurmountable, however, and can be overcome with care, preparation, and education.

A more important issue here is what Shapiro calls the "cultural double bind." On the one hand, men are encouraged to participate in the pregnancy and birth of their children; but on the other hand, they are treated as outsiders by everyone concerned. They are told to be involved but at the same time they are told to keep out of the way, that they are inadequate as mothers. Although the expectant father's presence is desired, his feelings are not. At times, an expectant father might be as frightened, concerned, sad, and angry as his wife or partner. He needs to share these feelings and fears. But we allow only women to do this. The expectant father has neither the support systems nor the cultural sanctions for what he experiences.

Some men unconsciously compensate for this by developing physiological aspects of pregnancy, such as morning sickness, weight gain, or backache, but such symptoms are generally treated humorously by family and friends. When expectant fathers develop symptoms similar to those of the pregnant woman, it is sometimes referred to as a sympathetic pregnancy, or more formally as **couvade**. However humorous the pregnant-father syndrome may seem, many child psychologists believe that the more involved a man is with the pregnancy and birth of his child the more likely he is to be involved in child rearing. Sociological studies support this viewpoint. For example, one such study showed that fathers who were involved with their partner's pregnancy and were present at delivery showed more interest in looking at their infants and talking to them than did fathers who were not involved with the woman's pregnancy and were not present at the delivery (Miller and Bowen, 1982).

The exclusion of fathers-to-be (and fathers) in both the prenatal and postnatal processes reinforces the cultural notion that pregnancy, childbirth, and parenting are exclusively the domain of women. This perpetuation of sex role stereotypes does not facilitate gender equality. The good news, however, is that since Shapiro's pioneering study, the popular image of expectant fathers and fatherhood is shifting. In the past, indifference to expectant fathers' feelings was widespread and reinforced throughout popular culture, especially in the media, where expectant fathers were portrayed as bumbling idiots who couldn't even get the pregnant woman to the hospital (he often went without her). In addition, publishers produced a host of books and articles each year intended to aid new parents in the adjustment to their new roles, but they were directed almost exclusively toward mothers and motherhood, with little or no information for and about expectant fathers. Less than a generation ago, expectant dads had few places to turn to for parenting advice. A few may have traded expectant father/new dad stories with buddies or sat down with their fathers for advice, but most men navigated impending parenthood without any guidance. But much of that is changing. Since the mid-1990s, the number and variety of resources available to dads to prepare them for fatherhood and how to parent have skyrocketed. Today, expectant fathers and those who are already fathers can find hundreds of books, Web sites, newsletters, chat rooms, message boards, and organizations devoted to fatherhood advice. Resource guides and how-to books on fatherhood are more popular than ever. For example, more than 500 books on fatherhood, most published in the past few years, are listed on Amazon.com.

Today, fathers-to-be routinely witness and/or participate in the birth of their children in such roles as breathing coach or moral supporter. Even in the case of a cesarean birth, fathers often attend the surgery (Woodard, 1998). Moreover, hospitals across the country are reaching out to men by letting them play more active roles in their children's births. For example, hospitals in over 34 states now offer classes geared especially for expectant dads called "Boot Camp for New Dads," where expectant fathers can get advice and encouragement from "veteran" fathers and get to spend time with their babies. Some of these hospitals also offer expectant father classes each month providing a place where men can talk openly about issues of concern to them as expectant fathers (Marshall, 1999). When men witness their babies entering the world, they almost always become active fathers, and it gives them a sense of self-worth and feeling of inclusion in the birth and life of their child. For instance, one father remarked that he was glad to have discovered such classes when he was preparing for his daughter's birth. He said: "I was pretty clueless. It put me at ease and made me feel like dads matter. It made me feel like I was more than a sperm donor" (quoted in Marshall, 1999).

At the end of pregnancy and the birthing process, parents embark on another set of experiences that often changes their lives and their relationship with one another forever. In the last section of this chapter, we present a selective review of some of the experiences parents have after the birth of a child. In this regard, we examine the adjustment and adaptation to parenthood, the concepts of motherhood and fatherhood, and parenting strategies across social and cultural categories of experience.

PARENTAL ADJUSTMENTS, ADAPTATIONS, AND PATTERNS OF CHILD REARING

Parenting is one of the most challenging roles that individuals and couples face in their lifetime. Parents are often unprepared for the changes that this new family member will bring to their lives. Research has shown repeatedly that the addition of children to a relationship increases stress and lowers relationship satisfaction, particularly when children are still young and dependent (Glenn, 1991). Certainly, the addition of a new and dependent person requires that the couple make major lifestyle adjustments (see the "Family Profile" box). Either one or both parents or someone acting on behalf of the parents must constantly be available and responsible for the care of the child.

The ways in which people parent are significantly tied to how parenting roles and gender roles are culturally defined and the degree to which parents accept these definitions. As in other areas of social life, experiences such as age, race, class, gender, and sexual orientation interact to make the experience of parenthood different for different individuals and groups.

After the birth of a child, parents must develop a mother or father identity. Also, particularly in the early months after the baby is brought home, parents have to adjust their sleeping habits to coincide with those of the newborn. Getting up in the middle of the night can be disruptive and exhausting and can affect the parents' job performance. Financial obligations also increase with the birth of a child, as do household and child-care responsibilities. All of these changes can increase stress within the family unit.

For some women, these stresses can show up in **postnatal depression** (sometimes referred to as "the blues" or "postpartum blues"), a condition characterized by mood shifts, irritability, and fatigue. It is estimated that one in five women who give birth experience a significant level of depression in the 6 months that follow (Postnatal Depression, 2001). Until recently, postnatal depression had been considered a "woman thing." Because mothers more often than fathers are the primary infant caretaker, mothers tend to be more affected by "the blues" than fathers. However, fathers are vulnerable to similar emotions, especially if they are in primary caregiver situations. For example, a recent study of postnatal depression in fathers has found that about one in ten fathers gets serious postnatal depression. Based upon a survey of two hundred new fathers, researchers found that 9 percent of fathers suffered from depression 6 weeks after the birth of their child, and over 5 percent were still suffering after 6 months. Researchers believe that a variety of factors contribute to male postnatal depression. The most common are *fear of fatherhood* (worries related to new responsibilities and loss of freedom); *financial concerns* (stress over the added expense of a child and whether or not his salary will be sufficient); and *role anxieties* (for example, will he be a good father?). Perhaps one of the most important factors that leads to male postnatal depression might be the increasing pressure on fathers to juggle the demands of modern fatherhood, such as make money and share child-care and household responsibilities. Added to the stress that men feel during this time is the fact that men are socialized not to share their fears; rather, they are often admonished to "act like a man" and deal with it. Because we associate postnatal depression only with women and socialize men to believe that ignoring their emotions means being a *man*, when men experience such depression they seldom seek help. Recent research on men and postnatal depression raises an interesting question: Are more fathers depressed today than, say, 30 years ago? Or is it that we just hadn't raised the issue before now (Mistiaen, 1994; Kleiman, 2001)?

Additionally, a couple often have to adjust their private and intimate time together to the schedule of a child. Sexual activity often loses out to the demands of child care. Work schedules, leisure time, and outside hobbies and interests all have to be adjusted or eliminated as a result of the addition of a child in the life of parents. The sexual lifestyle of a couple may change drastically when a new child arrives. However, there is no set standard of sexual desire or behavior after childbirth. Thus, sexual activity varies greatly from couple to couple. Childbirth does not preclude the early resumption of sexual activities. However, after childbirth, sexuality often loses its spontaneity as couples must now arrange sexual activities around working hours and at times when the newborn is asleep. Such adjustments can be long-term in that as children get older couples often continue to arrange sexual activities around times when the children are at school or otherwise away from home.

FAMILY PROFILE

THE TYRPAK FAMILY

The Tyrpak family

Length of relationship: 13 years

Challenges to parenting: Ed and I were raised in two very different households, with two very different parenting philosophies. Ed generally allows me to take the lead when it comes to the basic, day-to-day aspects of parenting. And in regard to the more difficult decisions, we try and discuss the issue as a couple before discussing our decision with the kids. We find that our different styles of parenting compliment each other quite well and although this is not a perfect system, it has worked fairly well for us.

Children are exposed to so many negative influences—sex, drugs, and violence. It is difficult to know whether or not we should discuss certain issues with our kids, leave it to the school system, or let experience speak for itself. Overall, we feel it is most appropriate to touch on subjects at home before they become subjects of discussion elsewhere. If the kids need, or want, to discuss the matter further we let them know we are open to them coming to talk to us and that asking questions is okay.

Our older kids have started into a period in their lives when peer pressure will, and does, have a direct effect on decisions they make. Knowing when to let them make these decisions on their own is extremely difficult. We try to trust in their judgment, watch from a safe distance, and hope that everything that we have taught them over the years will help them to make the right choice. This is not to say that we don't stay involved in the choices that they make, only that we allow them more latitude in making their own decisions.

Education is extremely important to us and we have always made sure that our children understand the importance of doing their best when they are in school. The amount of disruptions that today's educational system tolerates concerns us, and we make sure our kids are aware of the fact that we do not tolerate them being one of those disruptions. We also try to keep our kids involved in the activities that they enjoy and that we believe will give them an opportunity to expand their interests and abilities. We believe that this can help to build their character and personal strengths.

Relationship philosophy: Our first priority has always been our kids. We have been parents for almost all of our 13 years together and we have only recently begun to feel as though we are able to take some long overdue time for ourselves. By putting our children at the forefront of our lives we are able to instill in them the morals and values that we find to be so important in today's society. We are proud of our kids, of our marriage, and of everything we have accomplished in both. We realize we have a long way to go and we take each day as it comes, but we have so much to be thankful for and we are grateful for our beautiful family.

Parental Roles

Traditionally, U.S. culture has made a clear distinction between motherhood and fatherhood. Both of these concepts reflect our ideas about gender-appropriate behavior and heterosexuality: Women are perceived as nurturant, caring, and supportive; and men as authoritative, strong, and protective. However, this idealized notion of women, men, and parenting does not fit contemporary reality. As with other aspects of social life, a social constructionist perspective would direct us to view parenting (like marriages and families) as a social construction. The roles of women and men, mothers and fathers, are not innate; women and men are not "born" to perform certain roles. Rather, what seems natural or real in terms of parenting depends on time, place, and social location. That is, the meaning of motherhood and fatherhood changes in response to different social, cultural, and historical circumstances. In this sense, parenting is socially constructed. This would help to explain why we give different meanings to the same or similar behavior depending on whether it is performed by women or men—

mothers or fathers. For example, when women are nurturant, caring, and protective of their children, it is called *mothering* and considered their duty or responsibility; it is not seen as out of the ordinary. On the other hand, when men are nurturant, caring, and protective of their children, it is not called *mothering* (for fear of de-masculinizing them). More importantly, we celebrate their actions as extraordinary and think that they are wonderful human beings. Or consider our different views of women and men who choose to remain home and raise a family. Being a housewife is acceptable behavior for a woman; being a househusband is less acceptable for a man. Furthermore, women who choose this role are viewed as "real women" or "womanly," while men who choose such a role are seen as less than "manly" (real men). The attitudes and beliefs that people hold toward appropriate gender roles have a significant influence on how they parent. Researchers have found that, for many people, the transition to parenthood means taking on more traditional gender roles.

MOTHERHOOD In Chapter 1 we discussed the general concept of the cult of true womanhood. That concept is important in our discussion here because traditional notions about motherhood are rooted in a Eurocentric (a worldview that places European culture at the center of analysis) middle-class ideology that emphasizes mothering as a woman's highest achievement and fulfillment in life. If we believe that motherhood is the only true and worthwhile role for women, then, by implication, those who consciously choose not to have children or who for various medical reasons cannot have children are less than complete women.

Some researchers (for example, Hoffnung, 1998) have referred to such traditional ideas about motherhood as the **motherhood mystique**. The motherhood mystique proposes that (1) the ultimate achievement and fulfillment of womanhood is through motherhood; (2) the body of work assigned to mothers—caring for children, home, husband—fits together in a noncontradictory manner; (3) to be a good mother, a woman has to enjoy being a mother and all the work that is defined as part of the mothering role; and (4) a woman's attitude about mothering will affect her children. The optimal situation for children is when women are devoted to mothering. According to Hoffnung, this social construction of motherhood and mothering is too narrow and limiting, and it is harmful not only to women but also to men and children. For one thing, it conflicts with other important aspects of women's lives—productive work, companionate marriage, economic independence. While traditional motherhood has benefits, it has substantial material cost for women as well.

Some benefits of motherhood include the joy of intimate contact with a growing, developing infant, the sense of importance that nurturing holds for many women, and the personal growth that comes from facing and mastering a new developmental stage. However, the pressures that push women to devote their major energies to the family and child rearing can have negative economic consequences for women individually and for their families. For example, women who work often select jobs around the scheduling needs of their families rather than according to their own career development. They are pushed to limit the careers they choose to less lucrative female occupations, to give up what they have accomplished for "mother-work," or to spread themselves very thin. The resulting part-time or intermittent employment patterns they develop contribute to the large wage differential between women and men and limit their economic contribution to their families (Hoffnung, 1998). In addition, the motherhood mystique also instills guilt in some women if they don't measure up to this ideal (Lindsey, 1990). Women who work outside the home, for instance, are often made to feel guilty for not giving their children their undivided attention. Significantly, no such expectation is made of fathers who work. The myth that children need their mother's exclusive and continuous attention also serves to make women the scapegoat for whatever happens to children and serves to support traditional gender roles that define women as subordinate to men.

In spite of the costs of mothering, most American women want to be mothers, most mothers want at least two children, and the majority of women with children are in the paid labor force. However, as Hoffnung very succinctly states: "It is not enough for women to be able to do men's work as well as *women's*, it is necessary to reconsider the value of mothering and to reorder public priorities so that caring for children counts in and adds to the lives of women and men. Until children are valued members of society and child care is considered work important enough to be done by both women and men, the special burdens and benefits of motherhood will keep women in second place" (1998:278).

Evelyn Nakano Glenn (1994) reminds us that mothering is not just gendered but is also racialized in that the concept of mothering as universally women's work disguises the fact that it is further subdivided, so that different aspects of caring are assigned to different groups of women. For example, poor women of color are often employed to care for the children of middle-class white women.

Furthermore, according to feminist sociologist Patricia Hill Collins (1991), the basic assumptions that underlie the traditional view of motherhood apply primarily to white middle-class families and most often do not reflect the realities of African American families and other families of color. As an alternative to this view, Collins has proposed a model of African American motherhood that consists of four basic themes:

- *Bloodmothers, othermothers, and women-centered networks.* Within African American communities, the boundaries distinguishing biological mothers (bloodmothers) and other women (othermothers) are nebulous. In such communities a network of bloodmothers and othermothers (mothers, grandmothers, sisters, aunts, cousins, and friends) shares responsibilities for the others' children. This responsibility includes temporary and long-term child-care arrangements that, when necessary, can turn into informal adoption.

- *Providing as part of mothering.* African American women make an essential economic contribution to the financial well-being of their families. They have long integrated economic activities into their mothering role, a combination that is looked on favorably in the African American family.
- *Community othermothers and social activism.* African American women's experiences as othermothers in their extended family networks are generalized to the larger community, where these women feel accountable for all of the community's children.
- *Motherhood as a symbol of power.* Because mothers not only raise their own children but also serve as community othermothers, motherhood is a symbol of power in the African American community.

In recent decades the demographics of motherhood have changed considerably. Thus, contemporary women's views on motherhood can be seen as falling along a continuum identified by Collins. At one end of the continuum are traditionalists who want to retain the centrality of motherhood in women's lives; at the other end are those who want to eliminate what they perceive as a cultural mandate to mother. In the middle are large numbers of women who argue for an expanded but not essentially different role for women. In their view, women can be mothers as long as they are not just mothers. Many of these women are opting for both a career and motherhood. They continue to see motherhood as fulfilling but not as the only route to personal fulfillment. The motherhood mystique notwithstanding, the reality is that women can and do find satisfaction in a variety of roles. Not all women find motherhood fulfilling. In fact, not all women desire to mother. The best circumstance is one in which a woman freely chooses this option.

FATHERHOOD The traditional notion of fatherhood emphasizes an instrumental role of father as breadwinner and authority figure: The father is expected to go out and earn money to support his family. He is expected to come home and play with the children a bit, but basically a traditional father must leave the nurturing, caring, and rearing of children to the mother. The father steps back in at later stages, disciplining, guiding, protecting, and exposing his children to the outside world (Mistiaen, 1994). According to Nancy Gibbs (1993b), American culture perpetuates this traditional definition of fatherhood in a number of ways, one of them being the many messages we transmit to men about fatherhood and fathering. Gibbs contends that fathers receive messages that say they are not up to the job; that we not only do not trust them to be parents but also we don't really need them to be. A classic example can be seen in the fact that teachers and other professionals often treat fathers as if they are incapable of parenting. For example, at parent-teacher conferences, even when a father is present, teachers will generally talk only to the mother. Likewise, when a father takes his child to the doctor's office, often the doctor will give him instructions about the child's care to pass on to his wife or partner, the assumed caretaker.

The traditional concept of fatherhood is as limiting as the traditional concept of motherhood. Attempting to adhere to this concept can deny a father an opportunity for a meaningful relationship with his children. David Blankenhorn (1998), cofounder in 1994 of the National Fatherhood Initiative, argues that fatherhood has diminished as a social role for men; it has become smaller, devalued, and decultured. This situation is problematic because all too often biological fathers are absent from the daily parenting of their children. This situation is caused by men being more devoted to their work than to their families, by women having increasing power within the home, and by high divorce rates. According to Blankenhorn, a new fatherhood has emerged, one that is increasingly estranged from mothers and removed from where children live. This rise in what Blankenhorn calls *volitional fatherhood* has contributed to most of the social problems in contemporary society.

In the past, most men—no matter how much they loved their children—were expected to work hard as breadwinners and not worry about nurturing and caring for their children. When it came to fatherhood, popular culture assumed that fathers were nincompoops who were completely inadequate as caregivers. And until recently, public policy, societal sentiment, state and federal legislation, and family law all echoed a traditional view of fatherhood. Today, however, for a growing number of people the word *"fathering,"* once a word that meant mainly to sire a child, now describes the life of a caring parent. These people contend that fatherhood is increasingly that which one does and less what one simply is. Although fathers today define their roles in many different ways, some researchers have suggested that there are five major views of fatherhood that coexist, with some degree of overlap: (1) the aloof and distant father; (2) the father as breadwinner; (3) the father as moral teacher; (4) the father as a gender role model for the couple's children; and (5) the father as an active, nurturant parent. Arlie Hochschild (1999) suggests that the older ideal of the father who commands authority and pays the bills has partly given way to the ideal of the nurturant *new father* who bonds with his child (but still pays some bills). This new ideal of fatherhood has emerged within a context of multiplying ideals and images of a "good father" and a "good family." According to this ideal, today's fathers are far more tightly bonded to their children than their fathers and grandfathers were. Although there is ample evidence that the number of fathers defining their role in terms of this "new father" ideal is growing, the traditional view of fatherhood remains the dominant view (Basow, 1992). In her research on two-job couples in the San Francisco Bay Area, for example, Hochschild (1989) found that only about one in five of the working husbands in her sample fit the "new father" model of fatherhood in the sense of fully sharing the care of children and home and fully identifying themselves as men through this sharing. Furthermore, even those fathers who actively participate in child care still see breadwinner as their primary role. They also see themselves as a helpmate assisting the main caregiver, the mother (Hochschild, 1989; Mederer, 1993).

In the past, when it came to fatherhood, much of popular culture assumed that fathers were inadequate as caregivers. Recent media images of fathers like Raymond in the program *Everybody Loves Raymond* demonstrate a changing attitude about the need and desire for men's involvement in their children's lives.

Some people are questioning the "new father," arguing that it is simply the latest adaptation of the nuclear family model. They suggest that people other than biological fathers can be/are equally beneficial to a child. For example, lesbian mothers who conceive children through artificial insemination or heterosexual mothers single by choice or necessity are legitimate alternatives to the "new father." Others, like Arlie Hochschild (1999), point out the contradictions between the ideal of the new father and the reality of what fathers actually do. According to Hochschild, these contradictions are likely to differ across class. The cultural ideal of active fathering has changed much faster, for instance, among the middle classes than the reality of new fathering. In a sense, it can be said that there is a "reality lag" for many middle-class men. That is, many of these men will want to be "new fathers." They will fall in love with and marry educated women who will probably have professional careers and who will be attracted to them because they offer to be new fathers. However, due to the demands of the male career system, many of these men will live with a contradiction between thinking new father and acting old father. On the other hand, working-class fathers may reverse this pattern. Working-class men, particularly those married to less educated wives who are more likely to prefer to stay home and who cannot afford paid help, often hold to a more traditional ideal of fatherhood but, in reality, do a great deal with home and children. In each case, fathers are living with ideals that do not match the reality of their lives.

Nonetheless, it would be erroneous to assume that fathers do not play a significant role in child rearing. As we report in the next section, a new and growing body of literature is emerging that calls into question the traditional notion of fatherhood and the popular assumption that the primary, if not only, role of fathers is that of economic support.

Gender Differences in the Experience of Parenthood

Regardless of the division of labor before the birth of a child, after a child is born mothers are typically more involved in child-care activities than fathers are. New mothers find themselves with increased housework expectations and responsibilities. Mothers of babies and young children spend more hours on their family roles than do nonmothers or mothers with older children. This is true regardless of whether or not a woman works outside the home (Adler, 1996; Bianchi, 2000).

There is little dispute that more and more fathers want to spend time with their children; they desire to have a deeper emotional connection with their children. For example, in a recent survey, 70 percent of fathers said they would take a pay cut to spend more time with their families (Newman, 2000). However, their actions often lag behind their attitudes. Fathers may be bonding more with their children but they continue to be far less involved in the day-to-day care of their children than mothers. Indeed, surveys show that the world over, fathers spend only a small fraction of the time that mothers, even employed mothers, spend on child-care activities. For example, in the United States, fathers spend as little as 45 minutes a day caring for their children by themselves compared to the more than 10 hours each day for mothers (see, for example, Adler, 1996).

Men have generally claimed that the reason they do not participate more fully in child rearing is because of their job commitments and their general exhaustion at the end of a workday. In fact, however, women who are employed manage to do both. Although mothers spend more time taking care of children than fathers do, fathers spend more time than mothers in play behavior. The net result is that mothers' energies are more divided than fathers' energies, and their lives are more frantic (Adler, 1996).

Because of this greater responsibility for child care and housework, mothers tend to experience much greater stress than fathers do. Although many women experience stress and ambivalence about motherhood, they generally feel that the rewards of parenting outweigh the negatives. Some women, however, express a resentment at their partner's general lack of involvement in parenting. Thus, motherhood is at the same time both satisfying and dissatisfying for women, and most women express contradictory feelings about it (Basow, 1992; Roper Starch Worldwide, 1996).

We should keep in mind that, until recently, fathers were all but left out when it came to collecting data on families and parenting in the United States. However, the increasing concern about child well-being, the push for fathers' rights by various groups and individuals, and the encouragement of fathers, especially divorced fathers, to become more actively involved in their children's upbringing by organizations such as the National Fatherhood Initiative have pushed some social scientists to conceptualize, reconceptualize, measure, and gather information from and about men and fathering beyond their traditional emphasis on nonmarital childbearing, child support, and child poverty. Since 1995 when President Clinton requested that every federal agency review its programs and policies and do more to support and strengthen the role of fathers in families, a new and growing body of research on fatherhood and fathering has emerged in which a primary emphasis is on the quality and quantity of father involvement and its effect on children and families. This trend toward encouraging and supporting fatherhood has carried over into the twenty-first century with governors across the country setting up special task forces on fatherhood. "Responsible fatherhood" initiatives and programs are spreading across the country and, in 2001, President George W. Bush earmarked $60 billion in his 2002 budget for grants to promote "responsible fatherhood," promote "successful parenting," and "strengthen marriage" (Page, 2001:37). The importance of fathers in the lives of their children is well documented in some South American countries where the role of the father is often shared (see the "In Other Places" box).

The importance of fathers in the lives of children has also been documented in research in the United States. For example, research shows that when fathers provide strong emotional, financial, and other support their children are more likely to be healthier. Father absence tends to have an adverse effect, particularly for sons and if the absence occurs before age 5. Boys show poor school performance and have poor relationships with peers, problems with impulse control, and a variety of adjustment issues. For girls, fathers' absence shows up later, during adolescence. For example, adolescent girls have difficulty in establishing relationships with men (Miller, 1994). According to a University of Maryland School of Medicine study (one of the first to examine the role a father plays in behavioral and mental development of his children), children who have fathers in their lives learn better, have higher self-esteem, and have fewer signs of depression than children without fathers (Rubin, 2000). In addition, research on active fatherhood indicates that children in families where fathers contribute their time and support are less likely to drop out of school, become teen parents, or abuse drugs and alcohol (Pitzer, 1992).

There are also long-range health benefits for fathers—less alcoholism, fewer strokes. However, in the short term, men are experiencing unprecedented levels of work and family conflict; they want to be good fathers and also good employees. The work-and-family juggling act—once seen as the sole burden of mothers—is now increasingly performed by men, not out of duty but out of desire. From the 1970s to the early 1990s, when women went to work in record numbers, only 15 percent of men reported difficulty reconciling work and family compared with 70 percent of all working mothers. By the early 1990s, the gap had narrowed until by the end of the twentieth century, there was no difference at all between genders (Rubin, 2000).

The political and popular interest in active and responsible fatherhood, as well as the new research on fatherhood in the United States, comes at the same time that census figures show that the fastest-growing category in American families with minor children today is the single-father family (see the discussion of single fathers later in this chapter). Does this increase in single fatherhood reflect an increased trend toward men taking a more active and equitable role in fathering? Perhaps it is still too soon to know anything definitive about gender differences and how they are played out in marriages and families with the increased focus on fatherhood. However, according to sociologist David Popenoe (1999), gender differences in parenting may be linked to hormonal changes in women during and after childbirth giving them a head start on men in caring for infants. Whereas women seem more in tune to an infant's needs from birth, men seem better able to perform the parental role after children reach the age of 18 months. By then children are more verbal and men do not have to rely on a wide range of senses. Based on his review of the literature on fathering, Michael Lamb (1987) identified three types of fathering: (1) *engagement*, which includes actions such as feeding children, playing with them, bathing them, and helping them with homework; (2) *accessibility*, which essentially involves being nearby the child but not directly engaged in child care; and (3) *responsibility*, being the one who makes sure the child gets what she or he needs. When mothers work, fathers become more engaged and accessible but not more responsible for their children.

Current research points to a number of ways in which parenting in the United States continues to be gendered even among those couples where fathers take on the "new father" role. For example, mothers clearly spend more time doing for children, including doing the emotional work of caring and worrying about them, than do fathers. In short, mothers are always on call for their children, whereas men are not. In addition, fathers across race, class, and religion tend to spend more time with sons than with daughters. Although children become just as attached to their fathers as to their mothers and fathers are just as sensitive to their infants as mothers, women and men interact with their children in different ways. For example, fathers tend to emphasize "play" over "caretaking"; they spend a larger proportion of their time together playing (40 percent versus 25 percent for mothers), and their play is more likely than mothers' to involve physical and arousing play activities (Lorber, 1994; Parents Forever, 2001). In addition, children's views of their parents typically fall along gender lines as well. For instance, children often view their fathers as stricter and more likely to use punishment than mothers.

What consequences does this unequal gendered division of labor and parenting have for children? Some scholars claim that family organization is based on very real, biological differences between women and men, and "parental androgyny" (mothers and fathers playing essentially the same social roles) is neither good for children nor marriage generally (Popenoe, 1999; Glenn, 1997). Other scholars argue that equitable social arrangements within marriages and families is a must and a definite improvement over the

IN OTHER PLACES

SHARED PATERNITY

Western social scientists historically have predicated their work on the assumption that a child can have only one biological father. However, universality of a human sexual arrangement whereby a male provides for his mate (or mates) and offspring in exchange for female fidelity and paternity certainty has now been called into question. Researchers have identified 18 widely separated and distinct cultures in South America whose members engage in the practice of "partible," or shared biological fatherhood. These South American societies are not isolated cases. Other examples of shared parenting are being discovered in indigenous societies in New Guinea, Polynesia, and India.

According to Pennsylvania State University anthropologist Stephen Beckerman, the general belief system underlying the practice of multiple fatherhood is that all of the men who have sex with a woman around the beginning of her pregnancy as well as during her pregnancy share the biological paternity of her child. The fetus is believed to grow and gain strength by repeated contributions of the men's semen. Although patterns of shared parenting vary from one society to another, anthropologists believe that this concept may function as a strategy with real benefits to the welfare of those societies that practice it. For example, studies of the Bari of Venezuela and the Ache of eastern Paraguay found that, in both societies, children with multiple fathers were more than twice as likely to survive to their adolescent years as children born to a single father. The explanation for this may be simply that the secondary fathers contribute additional food and protection to the mother and her children.

Another interesting finding of Beckerman's study is the lack of sexual jealousy among the Bari. Beckerman offers a plausible explanation for this by making an analogy to a life insurance policy: When a woman takes a lover, her husband knows that if he dies, there will be another male who has at least a residual obligation to her children, who most likely belong to the husband.

What do you think? *Does the concept of shared parenting make sense? Are there any instances of shared parenting in Western societies? What are the belief systems underlying the Western conception of sole biological fatherhood? How does it function as a strategy in modern societies? Would our society benefit from expanding our views of parental responsibilities beyond the boundaries of biological parenthood?*

Source: Kim A. McDonald, 1999. "Shared Paternity in South American Tribes Confounds Biologists and Anthropologists." *The Chronicle of Higher Education* (April): A19, A20.

traditional division of roles because such arrangements provide increased opportunities for adult self-fulfillment (Hochschild, 1989; Stacey, 1996).

Styles of Parenting

How parents rear their children and the effects of various child-rearing strategies are the subjects of a substantial literature. Professionals and the lay public alike dispense advice and analyses of what works and what doesn't. As a consequence, parents today are far better informed about child development and behavior than were parents at any other time in our history. Just as every pregnancy and child is different, so too are parenting styles. However, sociologists have identified some common patterns of parenting among families in the United States, especially within particular social classes.

Because one of the basic elements in sociological definitions of class is occupation, studies of parenting styles across class often examine the kinds of attitudes and values associated with different occupations and how these attitudes and values are related to child-rearing strategies. A classic statement using this approach is sociologist Melvin Kohn's (1977) discussion of parenting styles in terms of self-direction versus conformity parental-value orientations. According to Kohn, middle-class occupations require or allow workers much more self-direction in the ordering of activities and the selection of methods than do working-class jobs, which are more often routine and subject to strict supervision. In addition, middle-class occupations tend to call for individual action, whereas working-class occupations more often call for coordinated group or team action.

These occupational differences are reflected in general differences in values and parenting strategies among various social classes. According to Kohn, the *traditional* or *conformity value orientation* is more commonly found among working-class and lower-class parents who emphasize order, authority, obedience, and respectability. In contrast, the *developmental* or *self-direction orientation* most commonly found among middle-class parents, stresses the child's motives and the development of self-control. Emphasis is on internal qualities such as consideration, curiosity, and initiative rather than on external conformity.

Some social scientists, like Diane Baumrind (1968, 1979, 1991) have incorporated Kohn's findings into a model that divides parenting styles into three general categories:

Although a growing number of fathers are participating in child rearing today, mothers continue to be the primary providers of child care.

Source: Reprinted with special permission of King Features Syndicate.

authoritarian, permissive, and authoritative. The *authoritarian style* demands absolute obedience from children and often involves the use of physical punishment to control behavior. Although this style of parenting is commonly associated with working-class parents, variations do exist. Working-class fathers who experience autonomy at work and who have high self-esteem are more accepting of their children and less likely to try to control them psychologically than are working-class fathers whose jobs carry less autonomy and who have lower self-esteem (Grimm and Perry-Jenkins, 1994). Some parents, particularly those who live in certain environments (high poverty, high crime), believe that authoritarian measures are necessary to protect their children from danger. For example, some African American parents realize that if their children make a mistake, they are less likely than white children to be given a break by public authorities. Thus, they may feel the need to be a little more controlling in their parenting style (Hill, 1995).

The *permissive style* of parenting, more typical of middle-class parents, involves giving children autonomy and freedom to express themselves, and downplays conformity. Permissive parents generally have few rules and regulations, make few demands on their children to conform, and most often use reason instead of physical punishment to modify their children's behavior. However, permissive parents sometimes exercise too little control in conflict situations with their children and allow them to grow up with little self-control or discipline. The *authoritative style* also encourages children to be autonomous and self-reliant. Authoritative parents generally rely on positive reinforcements, while avoiding, as much as possible, punitive and repressive methods of discipline. These parents are in control of their children's behavior while at the same time they allow the children much more freedom than do authoritarian parents. Recent research on American and British youth shows that parenting style has important consequences for psychosocial development in adolescence, with an authoritative style apparently the most effective regardless of socioeconomic background or family structure (Shucksmith, Hendry, and Glendinning, 1995). Similarly, Nancy Hill (1995) found in her study of African American families that authoritative parenting was related to such positive family characteristics as cohesion, intellectual orientation, organization, and achievement. Additionally, this style was positively related to expressiveness for fathers and negatively related to family conflict. A study of African American students between the ages of 5 and 18 supported the idea that students with parents who used an authoritarian (high-control, low-nurturance) parenting style had lower grades than students whose parents practiced an authoritative style (high-control, high-nurturance). Students with permissive parents (low-control, high-nurturance) also had lower grades (Taylor, Hinton, and Wilson, 1995).

In general, these parenting styles often overlap depending on a number of factors, such as the number of children, the unique personalities of the parents and child, parents' attitudes concerning child rearing, and the structure of the family. As we saw in Chapter 1, although some of the child-rearing functions of families have been taken over by other societal institutions, parents remain the major socializers of their children. Thus, their styles of parenting have important consequences for society.

What style of parenting did you experience growing up? Is it a style you wish to replicate if you have children?

Discipline A major issue for many parents is how to change their children's behavior when it is unacceptable. In the United States it is commonly believed that physical punishment is the most effective way to control children's behavior. A recent study found that 94 percent of parents spanked their 3- and 4-year-olds, 50 percent hit their 12-year-olds, and 13 percent hit their 17-year-old children (Strauss and Stewart, 1999). Experts on child care are somewhat divided on the efficacy of spanking. On the one hand, psychologist Diana Baumrind argues that many studies do not distinguish the effects of spanking as practiced by nonabusive parents from the impact of severe physical punishment and abuse. Her analysis of data from a 12-year study of over 100 families found that mild to moderate spanking had no detrimental effects when such confounding influences were controlled (Goode, 2001a). On the other hand, Murray Strauss (1994), a nationally recognized researcher on family violence, points out the harmful consequences of spanking:

- The more frequently a child is spanked, the more aggressive the child is likely to become.
- Spanking erodes the bond of affection between parent and child.
- Spanking teaches a child what not to do, not what the right thing to do is.
- Parents who were spanked as children are more likely to spank their own children.
- Spanking can get out of hand and escalate into physical abuse. Spouses who received harsh punishment as children are more likely to be abusive to their spouses and children.

To avoid these negative effects, child experts recommend alternative methods of discipline that include removing temptations that lead to misbehavior, establishing reasonable and consistent rules, modeling appropriate behavior, praising good behavior, treating children with respect, and providing emotional support by expressing love, warmth, and acceptance (Gibson, 1991; Angermeier, 1994; Leach, 1994).

These alternative methods of discipline are viewed with skepticism by a number of immigrant groups, who perceive American parents as too lenient with their children. Many immigrant parents, among them Nigerians, West Indians, Dominicans, Mexicans, and East Europeans, are separated from their extended families, who previously helped in the socialization and control of their children. Here in the United States they must work long hours away from home. Their concern for the safety of their children often leads them to impose harsh forms of discipline for any misbehavior. As one West Indian parent said, "If I cannot beat them and they get out there, the police will shoot them when they do wrong. I love my children more than the system loves them" (quoted in Dugger, 1996).

It isn't always easy to change public attitudes that are as deeply entrenched as are attitudes toward childbearing and discipline, but it is possible, as evidenced by developments in the Scandinavian countries, where governments outlawed spanking and implemented programs to teach parents how to discipline without resorting to physical punishment (Straus, 1994).

Questions about parenting styles, including methods of discipline and control of children's behavior, loom particularly large and relevant today when so many of America's youth express feelings of conflict, anger, and alienation. There is a growing debate about the influence of parents on their children and parents' ultimate responsibility for their children's attitudes and behavior, particularly in the wake of the increasing gun violence of some of America's youth (a topic we will discuss in more detail in Chapter 15). Given the obvious troubled nature of many of today's youth, an increasing number of people have expropriated the African proverb that so often served as a guiding principle in African American communities: "It takes a village to raise a child." Using this concept, they argue that parents, regardless of parenting style, need help from "the village"—a community or network of individuals and group support—to raise a child. A number of research studies support this notion of extended parenting. For example, various research shows that when teachers and parents work collaboratively and begin intervention early in children's lives, it has a significant long-term, positive effect on children's behavior and their academic achievement (Brody, 1999).

Married and heterosexual people are not the only ones who have children or face special challenges during pregnancy, childbearing, and child rearing. As we have emphasized often, the interrelationship of the axes of social structure such as race, class, gender, sexual orientation, and age shape the experiences of *all* people in this country. Thus, it is instructive to consider some of the ways in which these structures shape the reproductive and parenting experiences of a number of groups in U.S. society. The discussion that follows is not meant to be exhaustive. Rather, it is a selective look at the intersections of race, class, gender, sexual orientation, and age. Although these general parenting styles can be found among the total population, there are some differences, modifications, and adaptations associated with race, age, and sexual orientation.

Race and Class

African Americans African American families have historically experienced issues that many other families have only recently become attentive to—combining work and family roles, single parenthood, and extended family relationships. Their experiences can be instructive for other families.

Family Structure African American families represent a variety of household types and structures. Although African American families reflect the general American culture of families and structures, African Americans have also formed some distinctive structures for surviving and getting ahead in response to a history of racism, discrimination, poverty, their own cultural heritage, and a variety of other social and political factors. In terms of family type or structure, just under half of African American family households (48 percent) are married-couple families, 44 percent are female-headed, and 8 percent are male-headed families. Like most other married-couple families, African American married-couple families are smaller than in the past; 33 percent consist of only two people, 24 percent consist of three people, and 23 percent consist of four people. Seventy-six percent of African American families have two or fewer children living at home under the age of 18. Although the poverty rate for African Americans generally fell two percentage points, from 24 percent to 22 percent, between 1999 and 2000 (the lowest rate of poverty since 1959), African American families are still more likely than white families to live below the poverty level (23 percent and 8 percent, respectively). In addition, African American children have a greater likelihood of growing up with only one parent (primarily mother-only) than children of other races/ethnicities (e.g., only 36 percent live with both parents). Such families tend to be disproportionately poor compared to two-parent African American families. However, contrary to popular myth, the majority of these families have a working head-of-household. On the other hand, at the end of the twentieth century the median household income for African Americans of $27,910 was the highest ever recorded in real terms, and census data also showed that 28 percent of African American families had an income of $50,000 or more (U.S. Census Bureau, 2000b, 2001).

As we will discuss below, it is important to keep in mind that although African Americans families share many commonalities there are also important economic and social differences among African American families. For example, African American families differ by class, region of the country they live in, age and gender of family head, and number of family members, to name but a few. However, as we discussed in Chapter 1, the one thing that African American families typically are not is the stereotypic, mythical, and/or negative images commonly applied to them in both popular culture and in some scholarly research.

Dispelling African American Family Myths Contrary to popular myth, African Americans value family life and parenthood. According to some research, African Americans believe very strongly in the institution of the family, the majority (90 percent) reporting that they are satisfied with their spouse and/or family life. This is particularly true of the middle class, who report that family life is their greatest source of life satisfaction (Thomas, 1990; Bowman, 1993; McAdoo, 1993). Other research has consistently shown that motherhood and child rearing are among the most important values in the African American community and that strong kinship bonds have had a significant impact on African American parents' ability to parent successfully in an environment that is so often negatively impacted by male sexism and white racism. Among African Americans, caring for kin is shared among female and male adults, elders and children, so that single parents, for example, are not generally left alone to raise their children. They can often rely on the assistance of family members and/or fictive kin. Both two-parent and single-parent families are more likely than white families to live in an extended family household (Fine, McKenry, Donnelly, and Voydanoff, 1992). In addition, in two-parent families African American husbands are more likely than white husbands to share in household chores and child care responsibilities (John and Shelton, 1997; Xu, Hudspeth, and Estes, 1997). Furthermore, caring is often reciprocal, whereby members may be recruited to take care of other kin who cared for them earlier. For example, children may be enlisted to take some responsibility for caring for an aunt, uncle, or grandparent (Stack and Burton, 1994).

According to Robert Staples, raising an African American child is not, and has never been, an easy task (1999:152). Given the obstacles they face, African American parents have done a tremendous job in rearing their offspring, and they have generally done so with fewer resources than most other parents. African American parents face a dual responsibility in parenting: They must teach their children the folkways of their own culture and what it means to be "black" in a racist society, while at the same time they must also socialize their children into the values of mainstream American culture to adapt successfully to mainstream group requirements and institutions. Given the poor social conditions under which many African American children are raised, it is not surprising that some of them fail in life. What is much more surprising is that so many more succeed given the adverse circumstances they encounter in the larger society (Staples, 1999).

Social Class Differences Because most African Americans have encountered racism and discrimination in some form, African American child-rearing practices and aspirations for their children tend to be similar across class boundaries. At the same time, however, they also exhibit class differences similar to those found among other groups in society. For example, African American middle-class families have a value orientation characterized by high achievement motivation, social striving, and a high regard for property ownership. In fact, slightly over one-half (53 percent) of African Americans are homeowners versus renters, and this figure increases to 71 percent for married-couple families (U.S. Census Bureau, 2000b). African American middle-class families also have high educational and occupational expectations for their offspring. Thus, they try to teach their children positive attitudes toward work and thrift. These families tend to be more egalitarian than patriarchal. Parents stress conformity, chastity, and fidelity and are more inclined to use persuasive approaches to elicit obedience and conformity than to use coercion and physical punishment. Yet they demand a high degree of respect for parental authority (Staples, 1999). In addition, researchers have found that African American fathers generally, and African American middle-class fathers particularly, are often integrally involved in parenting such as monitoring and supervising their children's behavior, teaching them life skills, stressing academic achievement, and generally being warm and loving and only moderately strict disciplinarians (McAdoo, 1993; Toth and Xu, 1999; Wagemaar and Coates, 1999).

African American working-class families hold similar attitudes concerning basic family goals, but their value orientation is much more affected by the constant struggle for survival, and they take great pride in the fact that they are self-supporting. The parenting style in working-class families includes an emphasis on respectability: Parents demand that their children behave well and not get into trouble with the police. Like their middle-class counterparts, they stress conformity and obedience (Willie, 1981; Blackwell, 1985). They typically make every attempt to buffer their children from exposure to the negative influences of drugs, gangs, and other problem behaviors by strictly monitoring their children's time and friendships (Jarrett, 1995). Like their middle-class counterparts they socialize their children to exercise self-control and succeed in school. Lower-class African American parents are often regarded as the most ineffective in their role as parents because of their reliance on physical punishment to control their children's behavior. However, what is missing from this assessment is the fact that most lower-class parents, across race, combine heavy doses of emotional nurturance with their physical measures of punishment. Some researchers suggest that this combination of child-rearing practices may be more beneficial for a child's development than the middle-class practice of withholding love if the child does not behave correctly (Staples, 1999).

Perhaps the greatest class differences in parental attitudes and parenting styles are those between the African American poor and middle class. Many poor African Americans are disenchanted, disillusioned, and alienated, and see little progress and even fewer possibilities for breaking out of their low economic status (Blackwell, 1985). As a consequence, according to sociologist Charles Willie (1981), many poor African American parents are generally limited in their ability to guide their children and often have little control over their children's behavior. Parental values and behaviors generally are those that are most expedient and offer hope of a livable or tolerable existence at the time. For example, parents are often grade school or high school dropouts, and to make their children obey and conform they sometimes hold themselves up to their children as negative images of what not to do. Although female-headed families make up a large proportion of the African American underclass, some of whom are perhaps the basis for many of the stereotypes and myths about African American families generally, it is erroneous to assume that such families are synonymous with problems, including a lack of family values. In fact, some scholars of African American families have suggested that single African American mothers may be particularly strong not only in terms of valuing and keeping their families together but also in protecting themselves and their offspring and coping in a world of chronic poverty, racism, sexism, and male violence (Sudarkasa, 1993; Edin and Lein, 1997).

African American Fathers African American fathers all too often are portrayed as uninterested and uninvolved with their children. However, as we have indicated, research that focuses on African American male roles in the family does not support such stereotypes. According to Lora Bex Lempert (1999), by accepting popular myths and cultural stereotypical images of African American families as "matriarchal," where African American men are either absent or peripheral to the family, and by focusing research attention almost exclusively on female-headed African American families, researchers have all but ignored the significant role that African American men play in supporting their families and communities.

In an interesting analysis of research data reported by African American grandparent caregivers, Lempert extends Patricia Hill Collins's work on *othermothers*—which speaks to the centrality of women in African American child rearing and extended families—to describe the role of African American men in extended family constellations. Collins cautions against assuming that the centrality of women in child rearing is predicated on the absence of husbands and fathers, noting that men may indeed be physically present and/or have well-defined and culturally significant roles in the extended family.

Lempert uses the concept of *other fathers* to present an alternative perspective on African American community caring and childrearing that highlights the central role of African American men in the lives of African American children. *Other fathers* are men who, as family members and/or as community members, actively engage themselves as providers, protectors, role models, and mentors in the lives of the children of other men: They may assume financial responsibility, in part or in whole, for these children, and serve as models of honesty, respectability, dignity, social wisdom, and race pride as they maintain a positive, interactive presence in the children's lives. Lempert's research demonstrates that while some African American children may be growing up without the care of their biological parents, they are not growing up without love and nurturing, protection, and provision from *other fathers* as well as *othermothers* (Lempert, 1999).

Family Strengths and Resiliency Historically, social science research on African American families has focused almost entirely on the so-called pathology of African American families and has almost completely ignored the diversity, strengths, and resilience of these families. Beginning in the 1970s, in response to this unbalanced depiction of African American families, a group of African American scholars across academic disciplines began to develop a corrective scholarship that debunked many of the pathology myths of traditional social science research on African American families. A pioneer in this regard, sociologist Robert Hill (1972) pointed out in his book *The Strengths of Black Families* that contrary to popular stereotypes, although some African American families experienced myriad social problems, the majority of them exhibited strong kinship bonds, a strong work orientation, a strong achievement orientation, a strong religious orientation, and flexible family roles. Twenty-five years after his pioneering work on the strengths of African American families, Hill (1997) revisited those strengths, suggesting that conventional depictions of African American families in the media and social science research continued to be unbalanced; the typical focus continued to be on the weaknesses or deficiencies of a disadvantaged minority of African American families, with little or no consideration of the majority. According to Hill, there continues to be a fixation on the nonworking poor (or underclass) that excludes an examination of the larger working class who often live in the same communities, or excessive attention is paid to the two out of ten African American families on welfare or on the one out of ten African American teenagers who had a baby outside of legal marriage. Little or no attention is paid to the majority of low-income African Americans that achieve against the odds. Despite economic adversity, the effects of continuing entrenched racism and discrimination, disproportionately high rates of unemployment, poverty and incarceration of young African American males, and the street violence, gang, and criminal activities of a minority in the community, most African American families (whether married-couple or single-parent) are family-oriented, love their partners and their children, and teach their children to have self-respect, to be self-sufficient and achievement-oriented, and to be proud of their cultural heritage (Hill, 1998; St. Jean and Feagin, 1998).

NATIVE AMERICANS Native American families are perhaps the least studied families compared to other families living in the United States. Therefore, researchers often rely on aggregate data that yield a generalized picture of Native American individuals and families. For example, as a group, as a result of a history of legal and social domination, oppression, and, at times, total neglect, Native American families have among the highest rates of poverty, unemployment, poor health, infant mortality, suicide, and alcoholism of any racial/ethnic group in the United States. The average life expectancy of Native American women is 46 and of Native American men 45. Despite some important economic gains in recent years, the majority of Native Americans still remain in the bottom tenth of the economic hierarchy and at the bottom of the class hierarchy (Scott and Schwartz, 2000).

Family Structure Currently, less than 1 percent (0.7) of all households in the United States consist of Native American peoples. Of all Native American households, 74 percent consist of families, and of these family households, 65 percent are headed by a married couple, 26 percent are headed by a female, and 9 percent are headed by a male. Native American families typically consist of two children and are among the nation's youngest households. They are also among the country's poorest, with a poverty rate of 25 percent (U.S. Census Bureau, 2000b). There has been a considerable migration of Native Americans from reservations since World War II. Thus, today, more than half of Native American families live outside tribal lands, and, although separated from their traditional tribal cultures, they typically fare better economically and socially than those who remain on reservations. Moreover, with the increasingly large numbers of Native Americans marrying non–Native Americans, a growing number of children in these families are biracial. Those who marry other Native Americans tend to marry within their respective tribal groups. As we have noted elsewhere, the high rates of intermarriage, however, have caused some Native Americans to question whether or not Native American families will maintain their ethnic identity and familial traditions (Yellowbird and Snipp, 1994).

Differences and Commonalities in Parenting Styles These generalizations about Native Americans notwithstanding, and despite their common history of racism and oppression, Native Americans are a heterogeneous people, perhaps more heterogeneous than any other group in the United States. Therefore, specific social and economic characteristics, family structure, content and behaviors vary considerably from group to group. Among the Navajo, for example, parents operate on the principle of the inviolability of the individual, which some researchers have translated as a principle of permissiveness. Navajo parents discipline their children through persuasion, ridicule, and shame rather than coercion and physical punishment. In addition, supernatural sanctions are used to control children's behavior (John, 1998). On the other hand, Native American groups such as the Hopi, Zunis, and various descendants of the ancient Anasazi continue today to be loyal to their matrilineal clan systems and religious ceremonies, and they emphasize sobriety and self-control (Coltrane and Collins, 2001).

Although there is considerable variation among different tribal groups, Native American families share a strong sense of tribalism, family identity, and pride, and parents of all backgrounds tend to stress to their children a sense of family unity, tribal identity, self-reliance, and respect for elders. Children are viewed as assets to both the family and the group. Some researchers have suggested that child rearing among Native Americans frequently is nonverbal: Parents communicate by giving stern looks or by ignoring inappropriate behavior. Furthermore, children are socialized by example and are expected to share with others, to be quiet and unassuming, to show deference to their elders, to control their emotions, to be self-reliant, and to make an economic contribution to the family from an early age (John, 1998). Interdependence and interfamily exchange are important family patterns, especially on reservations. In this context, extended families are significant. And elders typically hold a special place in Native American families. Not only are children taught to respect elders, but, also, elders expect family members to take care of them when needed. Elders, particularly grandparents, are an integral part of family life. Grandmothers, for example, are often the center of family life; they typically have primary child-care responsibilities (although responsibility for children is shared by a wide range of adults), and it is their responsibility to transmit tribal language and family customs to the younger generations (Red Horse, 1980; Yellowbird and Snipp, 1994).

Some of the recent literature on Native American families indicates that socialization practices among Native Americans have changed in recent times from "cohesive and structured" households characterized by high dominance–high support parent–child relations to "loosely structured" households with low dominance–low support parent–child relations. According to John (1998), a composite portrait of these changes is summarized as follows: In past times, when today's Native American elders were growing up, the Native American family was a much closer, more organized and protective unit where discipline and permissiveness were far better combined than is the case today; past families had the advantage of having parents (particularly the mother) around the home. Today, rigid gender roles are loosening, and more Native American women are working outside the home.

Family Strengths and Resiliency Similar to African American families, much of the popular attention and scholarly research on Native Americans focus on the social and economic problems of this group and ignore its strength and resiliency. However, like every group, Native American families exhibit important strengths. Although the problems, particularly as they are manifest on reservations, have yet to be resolved, the diversity and strengths of Native American families—extended family networks, interdependence and interfamily exchange, value of individuals and the group, group cooperation, tribal support systems, and preservation of culture and family traditions—promote a pan-Indian identity and facilitate the maintenance of strong tribal and family identities across the numerous tribes.

LATINAS/OS Like Native Americans, Latinas/os are a highly diverse people whose marriage and family behaviors vary, sometimes considerably, from group to group. Thus, the following brief description of Latina/o family structure likewise represents a generalized view of structural features that Latina/o families share.

Family Structure The structure of Latina/o families is more likely than African American families but less likely than Asian and white families to consist of two parents (70 percent). Forty-five percent of these families have one to two children, and 30 percent have three or more children. About two-thirds (68 percent) of Latina/o family households consist of married-couple families and one-fourth (24 percent) are female-headed. Like most other groups in the United States, however, a growing number of Latina/o children are living in families with only a mother present. Currently, 36 percent of Latina/o children live in single-parent families, the overwhelming majority of which are headed by a female. For some Latina/o groups such as Puerto Ricans, some of the increase in children living in single-parent households is due, as we noted earlier, to the increasing number of children born outside legal marriage. Like African and Native Americans, Latina/o families generally are more likely than others to live in poverty (23 percent). On the other hand, 31 percent of Latina/o families have an income of $50,000 or more. And almost one-half of all Latinas/os own their own home (U.S. Census Bureau, 2000b). Generally, Latina/o family households consist not only of immediate but also extended family members, an increasing number of mothers are working outside the home, and young children in these families are increasingly less likely to be under the exclusive care of their parents (del Pinal and Singer, 1997).

Parenting in Puerto Rican Families Although there is little research that focuses specifically on child-rearing patterns among Latinas/os, one can glean from existing research that some Latina/o groups, such as Puerto Ricans, exhibit an emphasis on family interdependence and unity. Among Puerto Ricans, for example, females are charged with the responsibility of creating and maintaining these values in offspring. In general, the Puerto Rican parenting style can be characterized as authoritarian. Children are rarely consulted on matters that directly affect them. They are viewed as passive people whose attitudes and behavior must be completely shaped by the parents. Good behavior is taken for granted, and reasons for punishment are seldom offered. Physical punishment is frequently used, especially by parents with the least social mobility and status. Parents born in Puerto Rico, more so than those born or raised in the United States, tend to perpetuate, although with some modifications, a double standard of conduct between the sexes. Females are trained to be modest, and overt expressions of affection are more common with girls than boys. Furthermore, mothers tend to be warmer and more playful with children than fathers are and interact more frequently with daughters than with sons.

Parenting in Mexican American Families Machismo, sex, and age grading characterize Mexican American families and child-rearing patterns. For example, female children are socialized into the roles and skills of wife and mother early on because they will carry them out both in the absence of the mother and as a future wife and mother. In contrast, after puberty the eldest male has authority over the younger children as well as his older sisters because he is expected to take on the responsibility for the family in his father's absence and for his own family as a future father (Becerra, 1998). Although Mexican American child rearing is mother-centered, some scholars have suggested that contemporary Mexican American fathers share more in child care than in the past as more Mexican American mothers enter the work force (Zavella, 1987; Mirande, 1988).

Parenting in Cuban American Families Cubans, on the other hand, particularly second-generation Cubans raised in the United States, show a lesser inclination to embrace machismo or traditional sex roles. Because Cubans value lineality, children are expected to conform and to obey their parents and elders in general. In addition, Cubans have been found to endorse a "doing" orientation that emphasizes success-oriented activities, which are usually externally measurable. As a result, they tend to judge themselves and others by what the person achieves (Suarez, 1998). This value, no doubt, is transmitted to offspring during the socialization process.

Family Strengths and Resiliency Like other families of color who have experienced racism, prejudice, and within-group social problems such as gang membership and violence, male violence, drug abuse, a high school dropout rate, teenage pregnancy, and female-headed families, Latina/o families exhibit amazing strength and resiliency. They have maintained family values and ties and adapted positively to a variety of changing social, political, and economic circumstances. This is particularly true for Latina/o immigrants who must not only learn a new language but also adjust to a new and sometime hostile environment. Some researchers have identified a number of family strengths characteristic of Latina/o families, including family unity and cohesion, extended family support networks, a strong family focus and ethnic identity, religious orientation, and flexibility of family roles (Vega, 1995).

ASIAN AND PACIFIC ISLANDER AMERICANS Perhaps more than for any other racial/ethnic group in the United States, it is difficult to talk about Asian American and Pacific Islander family type and structure, even in general terms. Although they are often lumped together, these two groups include people from a wide variety of countries (20 or more) whose cultures (representing more than 60 different ethnicities), including language (more than 100 different languages), religion, and customs, vary greatly. With this in mind, the following represents a brief discussion of Asian and Pacific Islander family structure in aggregate terms.

Family Structure Next to whites, Asian and Pacific Islanders have the highest percentage of married-couple families (80 percent) and the lowest percentage of female-headed families (13 percent) than all other major racial/ethnic groups in the United States. Asian and Pacific Islander families tend to be somewhat large; for instance, roughly one-fourth (23 percent) of married-couple families have five or more members. In most Asian and Pacific Islander families, a language other than English is spoken at home by both the younger and older generations. And in cities such as New York one out of five Asian children in the public school system has limited English proficiency. About 20 percent of Asian American family households include at least three wage-earning workers, many of whom (particularly Asian immigrants) work in industries with low wages and long hours. On the other hand, 42 percent of married-couple Asian and Pacific Islander families have incomes of over $75,000; over half (53 percent) of all Asian and Pacific Islanders (regardless of marital status) live in families with incomes of $50,000 or above; and a similar percentage (52 percent) of these families live in owner-occupied housing.

Although in the aggregate, only 11 percent of Asian and Pacific Islander families live below the poverty level, this figure masks the considerable variation among various populations of Asian and Pacific Islander Americans. Factors such as the country the family migrated from, the era in which they migrated, and the education and skill levels of adult family members contribute to whether or not an Asian or Pacific Islander family will live at, below, or above the poverty level. For example, families consisting of less advantaged migrants from Southeast Asia (e.g., Laos, Cambodia) with low education and skill levels have very high levels of poverty and welfare dependency, whereas families consisting of Japanese and Taiwanese immigrants, as well as those consisting of second and third or more generations of Asian Americans, tend to have very low levels of poverty (Half-Full or Half-Empty? 1999; NWHIC, 2000; U.S. Census Bureau, 2000b).

Asian and Pacific Islander American Parenting Styles: Commonalities and Differences Parenting styles among Asian and Pacific Islanders vary according to the degree that parents are acculturated into U.S. society. Newly immigrated or first-generation parents typically use traditional approaches based on authoritarian methods. In general, family values and child-rearing practices are similar across Asian and Pacific Islander families. Obedience and conformity, responsibility, obligation, and loyalty to the family as well as self-control and educational achievement are expected. Socialization practices are characterized by a strong parent–child bond, and in traditional families there is a rigid division of roles and tasks, and children are taught to defer to their parents' wishes and commands. Discipline is typically strict and involves physical punishment. In contrast, acculturated parents generally are more nurturing and verbal and give their children more autonomy (Kitano and Daniels, 1995; Min, 1998). Like Native American and other families in the United States, parenting styles and child-rearing practices vary among Asian and Pacific Islander families by social class as well as degree of acculturation. For example, older Korean immigrant parents whose children were born in Korea are more authoritarian and controlling of their children's behavior than their younger middle-class counterparts. The more educated Korean parents are the more liberal they are in their child-rearing practices. Although somewhat moderated from practices in Korea, Korean American parents engage in very rigid, gender-based socialization practices for their daughters and sons. For example, Korean American mothers feel that certain chores, such as setting the table, should be done only by girls (Min, 1998).

Likewise, among Chinese Americans, some of the old traditional ways of child rearing have been maintained by recent immigrants. Parental authority, for example, particularly the father's, is absolute. The extended family, if present, plays a much more significant role than typically is found in middle-class or more acculturated Chinese families. In upwardly mobile and middle-class Chinese families, the father maintains his authority and respect by means of a certain amount of emotional distance from his children. The mother does not interact with the children but commands and decides what is best for them, and the children are expected to obey. Although on the surface Chinese parents are seen as more indulgent with their young children than are parents in other racial and ethnic groups, discipline is much more strict than in the typical American home. Punishment is typically immediate and often involves removal from the social life of the family or the revocation of special privileges or objects rather than physical punishment. Moreover, Chinese parents stress independence and maturity in their children early on. Older children are expected to participate in the rearing of their younger siblings—serving as role models of adult behavior (Wong, 1998).

Acculturation shapes socialization practices in a number of ways. For example, among the Issei, or first generation of Japanese Americans born in Japan, male dominance, a stronger parent–child than husband–wife bond, a rigid division of gender roles and discipline of children, and the precedence of family over the individual characterize child rearing in these families. By the Nisei, or second generation, husband–wife relations take precedence over parent–child relations, and parents are less rigid in their child-rearing practices. The Sansei, or third-generation Japanese American families, are extremely likely to be interracial with biracial children. Because this generation marries, on average, later, parents tend to be, on average, older and increasingly less rigid in terms of gender role socialization and life expectations for their female and male children. However, for both the Nisei and Sansei generations of parents, close family ties and family loyalty, socialization for social control, including obligation and duty, continue to be part of the socialization practices of parents (Mirande, 1991; Takagi, 1994; Ferguson, 1995; Kitano and Kitano, 1998).

Myths and Facts One of the greatest stereotypes that Asian American families face is that of the "model minority." This stereotype can be harmful in that it does not acknowledge the differences within Asian and Pacific Islander families and thus masks many of the unique problems and strains that some of these families face. Some researchers have pointed out that the model minority myth also creates and fuels tensions and conflicts within and across Asian American subgroups as well as across other racial and ethnic groups; it camouflages ongoing racism and discrimination in U.S. society (though more subtle today) by suggesting that the United States is a meritocracy in which Asian and Pacific Islanders are the model of unparalleled achievement and success—the model for pulling oneself up by the bootstraps that all other groups should emulate. In this context, other groups are judged by the myth of the model minority, and if they have not been as successful it is due to factors endemic of them as a race and not U.S. policies and ongoing structural and institutional racism (Do, 1999; Aguirre and Turner, 2001). As has been amply pointed out in many other places, not all Asian and Pacific Islanders are as uniformly educated, acculturated, and financially successful as the myth of the "model minority" would have us believe. Like other communities, families, and individuals Asian Americans run the gamut in terms of achievement and success.

According to the Coalition for Asian American Children and Families (1999) some facts to contradict the model minority myth include the following:

- In the United States 17 percent of Asian American boys in fifth through twelfth grade reported physical abuse, as compared to 8 percent among white boys, and 30 percent of Asian American girls in the same grades reported depressive symptoms as compared to Latinas (27 percent), white girls (22 percent), or African American girls (17 percent) in a 1998 survey by the Commonwealth Fund.
- Asian American individuals are twice as likely to be poor as non-Hispanic whites, and they have an illiteracy rate that is five times that of non-Hispanic whites.
- Asian American women have the highest suicide mortality rate among all women between the ages of 15 and 24.
- Seventy-three percent of Asian Americans speak a language other than English.
- In New York City, one of the five urban centers where most Asian Americans live, almost one-half (48 percent) of Asian American births are paid for by Medicaid, indicating that the mothers are either poor or near poor.
- Asian Americans live in the most overcrowded housing of any broadly defined racial or ethnic group, and 46 percent of Asian American households do not have anyone over the age of 14 who can speak English well.
- Twenty-four percent of Asian Americans over age 25 do not have a high school diploma and 36 percent of Asian American students in public high schools drop out or do not graduate on time.
- The number of Asian American youths arrested for major felonies increased 38 percent between 1993 and 1996.

Family Strengths and Resiliency Although they have experienced a history of prejudice and discrimination in terms of U.S. policies and practices, resilience marks the character of Asian and Pacific Islander families. Despite adversity and cultural, political, and economic constraints, they have managed to maintain strong family values and ties that are transmitted to each new generation and, in some cases, high economic and educational success. Characteristics such as family obligation and loyalty to family and culture, respect and care for the elderly, an extended family network of support, a high value on education, close family ties across generations, a low divorce rate (which is considered to be a hallmark of family stability), and a complex system of other positive values and behaviors have helped Asian and Pacific Islander families to successfully adapt to their environments in the United States and to counter some of the deleterious effects of racism and discrimination many have experienced.

Lesbian and Gay Parents

Twenty-five years ago there were between 300,000 and 500,000 lesbian and gay parents; today it is estimated that there are between 1.5 million and 5 million lesbian mothers and between 1 million and 3 million gay fathers. Currently, between 6 million and 14 million children (about 5 percent of all children in the United States) are being raised by at least one gay parent (Kimmel, 2000). This pattern challenges traditional notions about families and parenting while at the same time pointing up the fact that many lesbians and gays, like their "straight" counterparts, view parenting as a rewarding endeavor (Macionis, 1995).

Although the body of research on lesbian and gay parenting and the outcome of their child-rearing practices is still small, the available research indicates that lesbians tend to form extended networks of support that operate like any other family except that they are not patriarchal. Lesbian households tend to be less structured around a gender-specific division of labor; thus, children in these homes tend to experience more equitable family arrangements. As mothers, lesbians tend to be more child-oriented; they tend to be more responsive to their children's needs and more actively involved in their lives than heterosexual mothers (Bozett, 1990; Andersen, 1993). In fact, some feminists have claimed that when lesbian mothers leave an unhappy heterosexual relationship where children are involved, the children may actually get more nurturing in a lesbian household where two or more women share the work of child care.

Like lesbians, many gays who raise children tend to be more nurturing and less rigid in terms of gender role socialization and the gender division of household labor than heterosexual fathers. Gay fathers also tend to be more strict disciplinarians than heterosexual fathers (Andersen, 1993). In general, lesbian and gay parents tend to have fewer problems with their children's behavior than do heterosexual parents (Bozett, 1987; Miller, 1992; Laird, 1993). When problems do arise, often it is due not to the sexual orientation of the parents but rather to outside influence and interference and the degree to which society accepts the negative stereotypes of lesbian and gay parents (Lindsey, 1994).

Many people believe that growing up in a lesbian or gay household is emotionally unhealthy for children and can cause confusion about their own sexuality. To date, however, there is no evidence of the feared consequences of lesbian and gay parenting. Rather than a negative influence on the children's development, research indicates that the outcomes for children in these families tend to be better than average. For example, lesbian mothers and their children (of both sexes) have similar patterns of gender identity development to children of heterosexual parents at comparable ages, and they display no differences in intelligence or adjustment. In addition, when fathers come out to their children, whether or not they are the custodial parent, it tends to relieve family stress and strengthen the father–child bond (Kimmel, 2000). The research consistently shows that the children of lesbians and gays are generally understanding, adaptable, and accepting of their parents' lifestyle, and they are as well adjusted as children who grow up in heterosexual households. In addition, these children experience no significant psychological damage—they are no more anxious, depressed, insecure, or prone to other emotional troubles than the children of heterosexuals—nor do they have a tendency to be homosexual themselves; in fact, they are no more likely to be homosexual than are children raised by straight parents (Gottman, 1989; Spatt, 1996). According to Charlotte Patterson (1992), there can be positive effects of being raised by lesbian or gay parents. For example, having a nontraditional adult role model gives children a greater appreciation of diversity. In addition, having a parent who is different can make it easier for a child to be different and independent. The child might be more tolerant, accepting, and less judgmental because she or he has been taught to accept social and personal differences in others. Lesbian mothers often feel that their children have strength, compassion, and maturity beyond their years.

From most studies, it seems clear that quality mothering and not sexual orientation is the critical determinant of children's development (Kimmel, 2000). However, in a recent report on their in-depth review of the research on lesbian and gay parenting, sociologists Judith Stacey and Timothy Biblarz have stirred both renewed interest and controversy on the topic by suggesting that social scientists have indeed found provocative differences between children raised by homosexual parents and those raised in more traditional homes, each with one mother and one father, but they have played down these differences for fear that the findings will be misused. According to Stacey and Biblarz, while there is no evidence that having lesbian and gay parents harms children, the idea that it has no impact on a child's life is misleading. They contend that ample evidence shows that contemporary children and young adults with lesbian or gay parents do differ in modest and interesting ways from children with heterosexual parents (cited in Goode, 2001b). These differences, however, are positive rather than negative. Stacey and Biblarz point out many of the findings we have reported here as convincing evidence of the differences between children raised by lesbian and gay parents versus those raised by heterosexual parents because these findings have remained consistent across studies carried out under a variety of conditions.

Not all lesbian and gay parenting is "out" in the open. In the past and still today, some lesbian and gay parents have remained secretive and protective of their children, and for very good reasons. Because of the threat of losing the opportunity to raise their children, some women hide the fact that they are lesbian and then live in fear that their homosexuality will be discovered and used as a weapon to take their children away from them. Other lesbians, who have gained custody of their children, often after very bitter court battles, endure continual harassment from their ex-husbands and even their own relatives and friends. Still others voluntarily give up custody of their children to spare their children a bitter and public custody fight (Lindsey, 1994). Like some lesbian mothers, some gay fathers conceal their sexual orientation to remain a part of their children's lives.

Single Parents

The number of single-parent families has increased dramatically over the past two decades as both the divorce rate and the number of children born outside of legal marriage have increased. Almost one-third of all births in the United States are now to single mothers. Although the percentage of single parents has increased most dramatically in the last 20 to 25 years, the fact is that the percentage of births to single women in this society has been steadily increasing since the 1950s (see Figure 9.3).

According to some experts, half of the children born today will live in a single-parent family before they reach adulthood. When we consider the intersection of race in family life, currently 25 percent of Latina/o children, 47 percent of African American children, and 16 percent of non-Latina/o white children live in single-parent families (Dupree and Primus, 2001). Although racial disparities in the rates of unmarried births continue, there are now more such births by white women than by any other racial or ethnic group. For example, as we pointed out in Chapter 6, the birth rate for unmarried African American women has declined significantly over the last decade. By contrast, the birth rate for unmarried non-Latina white women continued a long-term upward trend, from 7 percent in 1982 to 26 percent in 2000 (U.S. Census Bureau, 2000c).

Figure 9.3

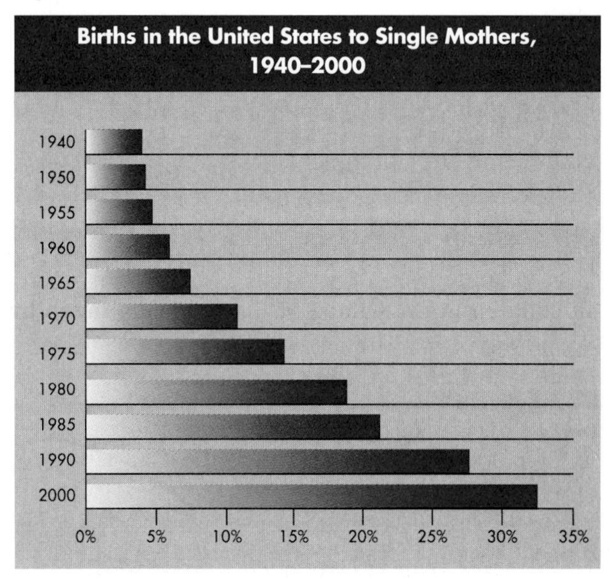

Sources: Adapted from Margaret Usdansky, 1996, "Single Motherhood: Stereotypes vs. Statistics," New York Times (February 11): 4e. Copyright © 1996 by the New York Times Co. Reprinted by permission. HSS Press Release. 1998b. "Latest Birth Statistics for the Nation Released" (June 30). http://waisgate.hhs.go...+o&WAISaction=retrieve.html, (1999, May 13); and U.S. Census Bureau, 2000, *Fertility of American Women: June 2000*" Current Population Reports, P20-543RV (Washington, DC: U.S. Department of Commerce, Economics and Statistics Administration).

The greatest increases in the rate of single childbearing has occurred among college-educated, employed white women. And although a higher percentage of such births still occur among African Americans and Latinas and among women who have dropped out of high school, these statistics illustrate that unmarried childbirth among adult women does not fit the stereotype, and it cuts across race, ethnic, and socioeconomic lines (Scott-Jones, 1996).

Single parenting is not synonymous with teenage parenting. While teenaged parents are often single (see discussion later in this section), the largest percentage of single parents are beyond the teenage years. For the past two decades, the highest birth rates for unmarried women were for women 20 to 29 years of age. However, in 2000, 83 percent of births to teenagers were outside legal marriage (U.S. Census Bureau, 2000c). Popular images of single parenthood present a dichotomous picture of these mothers as either white, affluent, college-educated professionals, near or at the end of their childbearing years, or black, poor, young (teenaged), and high school dropouts. However, the data call these assumptions into question. While the majority of single mothers are poor or working class, poorly educated, and have few marketable skills, they are also very racially and ethnically diverse: 40 percent of these mothers are non-Latina/o white, and over one-half (54 percent) are in their 20s. In fact, over the last decade or better, unmarried childbirth has risen fastest among women 20 years of age or older, who now account for 70 percent of all unmarried births (U.S. Census Bureau, 2000c; Vitagliano, 2001).

Single parents must accomplish the same parenting tasks and goals as two-parent families. These families face many of the same challenges and rewards of parenting as other types of families. However, the situation of single parents carries a unique set of challenges, not the least of which is related to their economic position. A family's resources are strongly influenced by the number of parents in the household. Women and children in single-parent homes headed by women continue to be at high risk for a life of poverty. In 2000, the rate of poverty for this group was 34 percent. Furthermore, children in lower-income families (families with income below 200 percent of the official poverty level) were more likely to live with a single mother and less likely to live with two married parents than were higher-income children (Vitagliano, 2001).

Whether the single parent is divorced or never married seems to be an important indicator of the quality of life for children in these families. For example, children living with divorced single mothers typically have an economic advantage over children living with a mother who has never married. This might be accounted for, in part, because divorced parents are typically older, have higher levels of education, and have higher incomes than parents who never married. In terms of race and ethnicity, white single-mother families are more likely to be the result of a marital disruption (50 percent were divorced) than having never married (30 percent), whereas African American single mothers are the most likely to be never married (65 percent) and the least likely to be divorced (17 percent). African American and Latinas single mothers are also more likely than white single mothers to live in an extended family household (Fields and Casper, 2001).

These trends have important implications for the well-being of children and families and the programs and policies that relate to welfare, family leave, and other areas of work and family life. Studies show that children reared in these families tend to drop out of school, to become delinquent, to have emotional problems, to get pregnant as teenagers and give birth outside of legal marriage, to be at greater risk for drug and alcohol addiction, to end up on welfare, to be poor as adults, and to get divorced more often than children from two-parent families (Whitehead, 1993; Worthington, 1994; Potok, 1995; Wallerstein and Blakeslee, 1996). Moreover, the economic challenges that single mothers face are exacerbated by race. Women of color are confronted with the same challenges as white women but added to these is the challenge of institutional racism.

Although these problems are typically attributed to the absence of a father, according to Andrew Cherlin (1981), the most detrimental aspect of the father's absence from female-headed families is not the lack of a male presence but rather the lack of a male income. Recent research confirms that poverty and inadequate income are major threats to children's well-being and development. Although child poverty is much higher in the United States than in other Western countries, it is not an unalterable fact of nature that children born to single mothers have to grow up poor. Whereas social policies in the United States express disapproval of single parents, social policies in other Western countries support the well-being of the children (Skolnick and Rosencrantz, 1994).

Single Fathers As the number of married-couple families generally as well as those with children have decreased, as marital and relationship breakups and unmarried pregnancies have increased, there has been an explosion in the number of single-father homes. For example, in about one U.S. household out of every 45, a father is raising his child or children without the mother present. This represents a 62 percent increase in such households from 1990 to 2000—to 2.2 million compared to an increase of just 25 percent in single-mother homes and a 200 percent increase since 1970 (from 0.7 percent to 2 percent). And if we add to this those fathers who are sole caregivers to their children on a part-time basis, we have a formidable population (Davis, 1998; National Center for Policy Analysis, 2001). Recent census data indicate that almost one-half (900,000) of these single fathers are divorced, nearly 700,000 have never married, 350,000 are married to an absent spouse, and 85,000 are widowed. The increase in single-father parenting has occurred across all racial groups; however, white fathers (22 percent of all white single parents) are twice as likely as African American fathers (10 percent of all African American single parents) to be the sole head of household (U.S. Census Bureau, 2000a). Some experts say that fathers' desire to be involved with their children is to the twenty-first century what women's desire to be in the workplace was to the twentieth century (Goldberg, 2001). These fathers are shattering the myth that fathers lack nurturing skills. Still, men are far less likely than women to take family leave, and despite the surge in number of stay-at-home fathers, they remain a much rarer breed than stay-at-home mothers (Rubin, 2000).

Compared with single-parent mothers, single-parent fathers tend to be older, better off financially, have a higher level of education, and hold full-time professional or higher-level jobs. They also tend to be highly motivated parents. Some experts believe, however, that an important factor contributing to the increase in single fathers is not just more men wanting to be involved with their children but rather a growing willingness on the part of mothers to cede primary custody. For example, fathers typically get custody of their children belatedly. That is, most courts in the United States are still more likely to award custody to mothers than fathers; thus, when a father does get custody it is usually with the mother's consent.

In any case, like single mothers, single fathers must balance the added demands of child care and maintain a satisfactory relationship with the noncustodial parent. Fathers who adapt well typically have higher incomes, had been involved in housework and child care during the time they were married, and actively sought custody of the children at the time of the breakup. They are also more likely to have the mother actively in the picture, sharing involvement with the children on a regular basis. This means that single fathers can often come closer to approximating an intact or nuclear family. Single mothers, on the other hand, often have to go it alone. When these factors are not present, fathers are more likely to experience difficulty in parenting. For example, one single father, after winning custody of his 2-year-old son, found that the switch to single parenting was not easy. The transition to custodial parent constituted a substantial change in his life. He had to drop out of the university where he was a doctoral student and go on welfare to make ends meet. For three months (single mothers typically get caught in this cycle a lot longer) he experienced the trap that many single mothers experience: He couldn't get a job because he didn't have child care and he couldn't get child care because he didn't have a job. According to this father, parenting alone left him drained and harried: "It is an oppressive, demanding and time consuming job, but the rewards are plentiful" (quoted in Reardon, 1992:8).

Although there is an increase in fathers parenting alone, for a significant number of families, fathers are absent. In addition, in whole neighborhoods fathers are scarce. According to statistics reported by Carol Jouzaitis (1995), about one in four children living in single-mother families were living in areas where single-mother families constituted more than one half of all families. This phenomenon is a growing trend in states around the country. In Illinois, one in eight children live in a neighborhood where fathers are scarce, compared with the national average of one in fourteen. The Illinois rate is surpassed in states such as Alabama, Maine, Massachusetts, Michigan, Mississippi, and New York. In fact, New York has the highest rate of all states, with one in six children living in communities that consist predominantly of single mothers. These data underscore the connection between poverty and family structure. One of the primary reasons that many fathers are absent from the home is unemployment and low wages. According to Jouzaitis, the median wages for young men between the ages of 25 and 34 have fallen 28 percent over the past 2 decades. Many of these young men lack the education and skills to successfully compete in today's labor force and thus be able to contribute to the support of their children.

All too often the focus on single-parent families is on the problems they face. This gives the impression that single parenting is inherently problematic and that there is absolutely nothing positive about the experience. We know, however, that this is not the case. Depending on the resources and support systems available to parents, single parents, like other parents, will determine the degree to which parenting will be more rewarding than challenging. Studies have identified many benefits of growing up in a single-parent family. One of these benefits is that there are more opportunities for the children to be androgynous—they experience less pressure to conform to rigid gender-appropriate roles and more opportunity to experience a wide range of social roles. Studies have also consistently shown that children raised by a single parent tend to be more mature and have a stronger sense of self than children in two-parent families (Lauer and Lauer, 1991).

The United States is not alone, it seems, in the spiraling rate of births to unmarried mothers and fathers. According to some sources (Ahlburg and DeVita, 1992; Russell, 1995), trends in unmarried births in the United States are very similar to those found in several other countries: 50 percent of all births in Sweden, 46 percent in Denmark, 33 percent in France, and 31 percent in the United Kingdom are to unmarried women. Although the number of births to single parents is soaring in countries around the world, Japan is a very notable exception. Only about 1 percent of births in Japan are to unmarried parents, almost unchanged for a quarter of a century (Kristof, 1996; WuDunn, 1996). Although many and complex factors account for the differential rates of unmarried births around the world, two important factors are believed to be the differential levels of contraceptive use and rates of teenage pregnancy between countries.

Teenaged Parents

As we have noted in several other discussions, the teenage birth rate has dropped steadily over the last 10 years, contributing to an overall decline in the nation's birth rate and pushing it to its lowest point since such records have been kept. Near the end of the last century, the teenage birth rate dropped in all 50 states, although there was considerable variation across states, with Vermont having the lowest and Mississippi the highest. There were also declines in all racial and ethnic groups, but the greatest declines occurred among Puerto Rican and African American teens. A change in teenage sexual behavior is cited as a major reason for the decline in birth rates. For example, some recent studies show that young people are delaying sex until they are older, having sex less frequently, and using birth control more often and more responsibly (Stolberg, 1999). The sustained declines in teenage births notwithstanding, the birth rate for American teens remains among the highest in the industrialized world, twice that of England and Canada and 10 times that of Japan and the Netherlands (Brandon, 1999).

The facts of teenage births notwithstanding, it is still popular to blame unmarried teenaged parents, especially mothers, for the majority of family and societal problems. The current trend of delayed marriage and childbearing, especially among the middle and affluent classes, is used as a measuring rod against which teenage fertility is inappropriately judged (Scott-Jones, 1996). However, researcher Cheryl Russell (1995) alerts us to the fact that the rate of teenage births today is far from being unprecedented in American history. Accordingly, Russell cites statistics from the 1950s that illustrate that the birth rate among unmarried 15- to 19-year-olds was 59 percent higher in 1957 than it is today. Today, 70 percent of Americans under the age of 20 who give birth are not married. In the past, although almost one-third of first births to women aged 15 to 34 were conceived outside of legal marriage, by the time most of these women gave birth they were married. Thus, the unmarried

Teenage fathers, especially unwed fathers, are often ignored in discussions of teenage pregnancy and childbirth. However, many young men not only want to be, but are actively involved in child rearing. Like this father trying to study and care for his son, they sometimes find they must juggle multiple roles.

WRITING YOUR OWN SCRIPT

TO PARENT OR NOT?

Another major life choice many of us will make regardless of whether we choose to marry is whether we will parent. Choosing to parent will have significant consequences for us in terms of the time, energy, and resources required to perform this critical task. The parenting decision not only affects our personal lives, but also affects the life of the society. Fertility rates and the consequent size and composition of a nation's population have enormous social implications.

In the past, it was almost a foregone conclusion that a woman would reproduce. That was defined as her proper sphere in life, and she exercised relatively little choice in or control over the matter. Deciding whether to parent is now much more a matter of choice than it was in the past.

Questions to Consider

1. Do you want children? For what reasons? What do you have to offer children? What do you expect to receive from the children you may have? How many children do you want? If you or your partner is infertile, will you consider alternatives for having children? Would you consider adoption? Any of the new reproductive technologies?
2. What advantages and disadvantages are there to being child-free? What are your options if you or your partner have an unwanted pregnancy? Are there any conditions under which you would consider abortion? Putting a child up for adoption? If you do not want children now or in the future, will you use contraception? What kind? How will you reach agreement on this with your partner?
3. What kind of parenting style did you experience in your childhood? Looking back, are you satisfied with this parenting style? What parenting style do you think you would be most comfortable enacting with your own children? Why?

birth rate was concealed to a great extent by *shotgun weddings.* Due to the steady decrease in the percentage of "shotgun weddings," the rate of births to unmarried teens has more than tripled over the last three decades, despite the fact that the teen birth rate itself is at its lowest level ever.

According to psychologist Diane Scott-Jones (1996), teenage childbearing is shrouded with myths and misconceptions, and it is oversimplified in popular culture. As in many other areas of life, teenage pregnancy is exacerbated by race and class. The typical teenaged mother in the United States today is white and in her late teens, and she is more likely to have a child outside of legal marriage than her counterparts in other industrialized countries. However, a disproportionately higher percentage of teenagers and young adults of color, particularly African Americans, Native Americans, and Latinas, are unmarried teenage mothers. In addition, a major factor impacting teenage mothers, particularly those of color, is a high unemployment rate and declining wages for both women and men. Some critics of teenage pregnancy and childbearing attribute its incidence to the availability of welfare. They suggest that welfare is a substitute for a husband's income and encourages teenage pregnancy, especially among poor teenagers. However, research studies show that the role of welfare is relatively small. There is very little evidence to support the conclusion that many unmarried teenagers deliberately allow themselves to become pregnant to collect welfare payments. Nonetheless, in the closing decade of the twentieth century, significant challenges to the traditional welfare system were well underway.

Early motherhood places tremendous demands on teenaged mothers who, like their adult counterparts, are generally raising their children without much support (financial or emotional) from the fathers. Like older mothers, teenaged mothers are responsible for managing the developmental tasks of parenting. Many young mothers manage these tasks quite well. Continued education, as well as social and financial support from family and friends, appear to be some of the predictors of the unmarried teenager's ability to successfully meet the unique challenges of childbearing. Most teenaged mothers are no less nurturant and caring than are adult mothers. However, some researchers (Miller and Moore, 1990) have found that some unmarried teenaged mothers interact less frequently and are less expressive with their children than are many older mothers. According to these researchers, teen mothers are also much more likely to have financial problems and other stresses and less likely to be able to control their emotions in the childrearing process.

As with single mothers generally, research shows that while a male role model in single-parent families may be needed to meet the challenges of parenting, their importance may be overrated. A recent national study by researchers at Ohio State University, comparing teens raised in single-parent households, found that children raised by single mothers were doing just as well as those raised by single fathers. These findings counter the notion that children in single-mother households are disadvantaged simply because there is no father present. While the sex of the single parent does not play a crucial role in raising children, time spent with children and the opportunities and stability provided them makes a significant difference. The most critical factor in a child's well-being in any form of family is a close, nurturant relationship with at least one parent. In sum, what matters in children's well-being is the parent's economic and interpersonal investment in her or his children, not her or his gender (Parenting, 1999).

Teenaged Fathers Like adult unmarried fathers, teenaged unmarried fathers are all too often left out of the parenting equation. We continue to see teenaged fathers in terms of stereotypes and myths of them being streetwise, gangbangers, or potentially so—macho males who sexually exploit a long string of women; count their offspring as notches in their belt or armor of manliness; are often illiterate, unemotional, and incapable of caring about another person; have only a passing and casual relationship with the mother; do not support the child financially by choice; and do not want to be emotionally involved in the rearing of their children.

Research on single fathers generally and teenaged fathers especially is limited. However, according to the research that does exist, contrary to popular belief, many young fathers acknowledge paternity of their children and actively seek to be involved in the rearing of their children. Many are at the hospital at the time of the birth of their children, and many sign records indicating their paternity. And, many provide some child-care support as their financial situation allows. In one study of young fathers, many of the young men studied negotiated a set of rights and responsibilities with the mothers before the birth of their children. These rights and responsibilities included not only themselves but oftentimes their own parents as well. Although these relationships were often fragile, in many cases the young father began support and care for the child during pregnancy, and he and his family, usually his mother, worked out a process of child care and support after the child was born (Lerman and Ooms, 1993).

Reporter Seth Mydans (1995), in a recent report on Latino gang members, acknowledges the strong family ties among gang members and how parenthood among some male gang members reversed their behavior during impending fatherhood, the result being that they consciously sought to be a part of the childbirth and child-rearing process. One gang member cited, for example, divested himself of gang symbols such as tattoos and a bald head and actively sought legitimate work when his 17-year-old girlfriend became pregnant with their child.

Although our knowledge of parenting styles among teenaged unmarried fathers is limited, we do know that in general fathers who are involved in the socialization of their children—who are involved in child care—have a more positive impact on their children than fathers who don't and, in turn, these fathers experience a greater degree of emotional and psychological benefit and well-being from the parent–child interaction than do traditional fathers. Research has shown consistently that children who are highly interactive with their fathers (whether teenaged or older adult) are characterized by higher levels of cognitive competence, increased empathy, and less sex-typed beliefs and behaviors.

Teenage childbirth affects many areas of social life, and as we have indicated, it is not limited to racial and ethnic groups of color. It is deeply rooted in many of our society's social problems and cannot be understood simply on an individual level. From a sociological perspective, in analyzing teenage births, we must consider structural and institutional factors such as the continuing racism, sexism, and class bias that is extant in U.S. society; the bleak economic picture for many individuals and families in the twenty-first century, especially teenagers of color; the proliferation of drugs in the United States, especially in those communities that are least able to fight them; and a mass media that continues to romanticize and popularize sexual themes and set standards about appropriate sexual behavior, often encouraging sexual intercourse and pregnancy, to name but a few. When we consider the link between individual experiences of unmarried childbirth and social structure it helps us understand the socially constructed nature of teenage childbearing as a social phenomenon and directs us to seek remedies in terms of institutional and structural change rather than focusing on alleged individual pathologies.

In sum, it is not so much who parents but how much support society gives to parents. Communities can play important roles in helping parents to succeed even in high-risk areas by providing programs for prenatal health care, parental education, job training, child abuse prevention, and other support services. It really does "take a village to raise a child."

SUMMARY

At the beginning of the nineteenth entury, the U.S. fertility rate was quite high. Since that time it has steadily declined to its current low rate, with the notable exception of the "baby boom" of the late 1940s and 1950s. Fertility rates vary across race and class; people of color and low-income groups have the highest rates.

Deciding whether to parent involves an evaluation of both the costs and benefits. Increasing numbers of people are deciding to be child-free or to delay parenting until their 30s. During the mid nineteenth century the use of contraceptives and abortion became illegal. After a long struggle, the Supreme Court invalidated laws prohibiting contraceptives, and in 1973 in *Roe* v. *Wade* it recognized a woman's right to an abortion. Since that time many efforts have been made to restrict abortion, and abortion has become a major issue in state and national politics.

The decline in the fertility rate, the legalization of abortion, and the tendency for more unmarried mothers to keep their babies have led to a scarcity of infants available for adoption. New reproductive technologies have been developed to help infertile couples achieve their desire to have children. These new reproductive techniques present many legal, ethical, and social challenges and raise questions about the nature of parenthood and the meaning of families. Social policy is only slowly emerging to deal with these questions.

Conception, pregnancy, and childbirth have a tremendous effect on the lives of individuals and couples. Conception begins with the fertilization of an egg by a sperm. From there the development of a child involves complex biological and physiological processes that culminate in birth.

Once pregnancy is confirmed, the woman should get immediate and continuous prenatal care. Research indicates that a number of factors, especially age, race, and class, affect the prenatal attitudes and behaviors of pregnant women. Poor women and women of color are at a higher risk of receiving inadequate prenatal care due to a lack of economic resources. As a consequence babies born to these women are at greater risk of birth defects, diseases, and other physical or medical problems. Some of the most common risks to the prenatal environment are poor nutrition, smoking, and drug and alcohol use. In addition, AIDS and other sexually transmitted diseases can harm the fetus.

In focusing on the pregnant woman, we often forget about the expectant father. Many expectant fathers now participate in their partner's pregnancy through a variety of actions including taking a paternity leave for the birth of their child.

Becoming a parent is a major transition in a person's life. Not all people experience parenthood in the same way. Rather, parenthood varies for individuals and groups within as well as across a number of important areas of experience: race, class, gender, age, sexual orientation, and marital status. Within all groups, however, females and males seem to experience parenting differently. Although many individuals and groups no longer adhere as strongly to the traditional gender division of labor, women nonetheless tend to spend far more time in child-rearing and housework activities than men do. In the final analysis, no matter who does the parenting, more support is needed for parenting and those who parent.

KEY TERMS

fertility
fertility rate
total fertility rate
pronatalist attitude
antinatalist forces
contraception
abortion
infertility
artificial insemination
in vitro fertilization
embryo transplant
surrogacy
conception
zygote
ovulation
amniocentesis
ultrasound
sonogram
congenital
morbidity
mortality
fetal alcohol syndrome
embryopathy
couvade
postnatal depression
motherhood mystique

QUESTIONS FOR STUDY AND REFLECTION

1. Trace and explain the changing fertility rates in the United States over the last 3 centuries. Project the patterns of fertility among various age, marital status, race, and class groupings that are most likely to develop in the first half of the twenty-first century. Explain the rationale for your projections. Discuss the implications of these changes for the society at large.
2. Discuss the legal and ethical issues surrounding assisted reproductive technology. How have these technologies affected our understanding of parenthood and families? Explain. Some countries, such as France, have banned the sale of sperm to single women on the basis that it encourages the creation of fatherless children. U.S. bioethicist Daniel Callahan sees the open market in sperm as an acceptance of the systematic downgrading of fatherhood, in that men can now produce children and have no responsibility for them. Do you agree or disagree with Callahan's view? Explain. Overall, what guidelines would you recommend be established for each of the assisted reproductive technologies? Explain.
3. Which aspects of the U.S. family system foster the gendered division of labor for mothers and fathers? It is clear that not all people support role equity for women and men in families. In fact, as we reported in this chapter, some people view gender role equity as

threatening to family life; it threatens children's development and family stability. What do you think? Develop an argument, pro or con, and cite evidence to support your position. What, if anything, should be done to reduce or eliminate gender-based inequalities in parental responsibilities?

4. What is your idea of a good mother? A good father? Based on these definitions, how do you rate yourself as a parent or prospective parent? What do you think are some of the important questions that people should ask themselves before they decide to become parents?

ADDITIONAL RESOURCES

SOCIOLOGICAL

BENKOV, LAURA. 1994. *Reinventing the Family: Lesbian and Gay Parents.* New York: Crown. Compelling personal stories provide a close-up look at the changing face of the modern family. The author examines the growing numbers of lesbian and gay parents, discussing issues such as how to raise a child in a homophobic world, child custody, foster parenting, and child development, and presents detailed advice on a number of topics including coming out.

COLTRANE, SCOTT. 1996. *Family Man: Fatherhood, Housework, and Gender Equity.* New York: Oxford University Press. An in-depth look at the role of men in the family. The author explores and refutes many of the commonly held myths about shared parenting and provides an up-close look at the changing nature of the typical American family, the reasons for this change, and their implications for family roles in the future.

MORELL, CAROLYN M. 1994. *Unwomanly Conduct: The Challenges of Intentional Childlessness.* New York: Routledge. Morell presents a highly readable account of her research based on intensive interviews with 34 married, intentionally childless women ranging in age from 40 to 78.

TONE, ANDREA. 2001. *A History of Contraceptives in America.* New York: Hill & Wang. The author provides an eye-opening look at the development of the U.S. contraceptive industry and its resilience in the face of militant attempts to suppress it.

LITERARY

ATWOOD, MARGARET. 1996. *The Handmaid's Tale.* New York: Fawcett Columbine. A scary view of a future society where women have lost their reproductive rights and no longer have control over their own bodies.

PARENT, MARC. 2001. *Believing It All: What My Children Taught Me about Trout Fishing, Jelly Toast & Life.* New York: Little, Brown. Wonderful poetic, contemplative, from-the-heart honest reflections of one man's journey of raising children through an incredible time and a unique view of life in the United States at the beginning of the twenty-first century.

INTERNET

http://www.resolve.org The RESOLVE Web site offers information on issues of infertility.

http://www.100.com/Top/Parenting A unique and interesting Web site that offers links to 100 different parenting sites. A sampling includes Movie Mom, a guide for choosing quality movies for your family; Father Magazine, an online parenting magazine for men; and At Home Mom, a site that provides resources that were compiled by stay-at-home parents.

Evolving Work and Family Structures

IN THE NEWS: **UNITED STATES, ASIA, AND AFRICA**

On February 22, 2001, a grand jury indicted one Russian and three U.S. citizens, charging them with enslaving Russian women and forcing them to work in an Anchorage, Alaska, strip club. The indictment marked the first use of the Victims of Trafficking and Violence Protection Act, legislation passed by Congress in 2000 designed to cover such cases, as well as concerns raised by a high number of reports of employers coercing illegal immigrants into years of domestic and migrant labor with little or no pay and little hope of escape (Frieden, 2001).

Contrary to popular belief, slavery did not end in the nineteenth century but continues to flourish in today's global economy. Sociologist Kevin Bales (1999) estimates that 27 million people or more, most of them women and children, are enslaved today, resulting in the disruption of millions of families worldwide. Modern slavery takes many forms such as bonded labor, child labor, forced labor, and traditional chattel slavery, all involving the ownership or control over another's life, coercion, and the restriction of movement.

In poor countries like the Sudan and Mauritania, children are kidnapped from their families and sold into domestic servitude. The Bonded Labor Liberation Front (a coalition struggling to end child labor practices) believes that as many as 1 million children in India, Nepal, and Pakistan are involved in the handmade woolen carpet industry, many of whom are as young as 5 years of age. Others are toiling in brick factories, for less than subsistence wages. Some of these children are stolen off the streets; other are entrapped in a system of debt bondage, whereby their families are forced to use them as security against a loan taken out to meet a crisis. Typically, the loan is never repaid because the lenders/employers pay low wages and subtract the cost of food, clothing, and shelter of the "workers" against their earnings, thus ensuring that the debt will pass on to the next generation and perpetuating this new form of slavery. Hundreds of thousands of Asia's and Africa's children have been taken from their homes and delivered to bordellos to work in the sex industry or sold to coffee, cocoa, or cotton plantations. Often families are given a small payment by labor contractors (as little as $14) and told their children would be educated and taught a trade. Many never see their children again. Escape is rare, and those caught attempting to escape are severely punished; sometimes they are killed.

According to Bales, three interrelated factors are instrumental in creating this new slavery: (1) the enormous population explosion in developing countries has flooded the world's labor markets with millions of impoverished, desperate people; (2) the revolution of economic globalization and modernized agriculture has dispossessed poor farmers, making them and their families ready targets for enslavement; (3) the rapid economic changes in developing countries have bred corruption and violence, destroying social norms that might once have protected the most vulnerable individuals.

WHAT WOULD YOU DO? Suppose you are an impoverished parent and someone offers you money and promises to educate one or more of your children if you will permit them to enter the person's employment. Would you agree? What are your options? If you found yourself in a situation where you were forced to work at low wages in an unhealthy atmosphere and you were punished for any sign of disobedience, what do you think you could do?

In our society we frequently think of work and family life as separate spheres, but as the cases of exploited and enslaved peoples make clear, the availability, quality, and rewards of work are major factors in the very survival of families around the world. In this chapter our focus will be on how work and families are being transformed in the United States. In Chapter 15, we will examine how globalization has affected work and families in other countries.

Research shows that the worlds of work and family affect each other in significant ways. The quality and stability of family life are dependent to a large extent on the type of work available for family members. Work provides income that determines a family's standard of living. As discussed in Chapter 1, from about the 1830s until the 1970s, the idealized image of the U.S. family consisted of an employed husband (the good provider) and a wife who stayed home and took care of the children. Although this image has never been the reality for all families in the past, it is less so today, when only a small percentage of families are supported solely by a male householder.

Because of changing economic and social conditions a single income is no longer sufficient for most families. Many husbands remain major providers, but increasingly wives are sharing this role. As we will see throughout this chapter, reactions to these changes are mixed. Although many women want to work outside the home, some feel that doing so saddles them with a double burden—besides outside employment, they still do the majority of household and family work. Some men, relieved at not having to be the sole provider, are participating more in housework and child care. Others, frustrated by the erosion in their breadwinning role, are dispirited, especially when their working spouses make demands on them to share household tasks and child care and to be more emotionally involved in family relationships. Additionally, growing numbers of families are headed by a single parent who must fulfill both the breadwinner and homemaker roles.

Work affects families in other ways as well. It can have *spillover effects*, either positive or negative, on family life. An example of positive spillover is the carryover of satisfaction and stimulation at work to a sense of satisfaction at home. Negative spillover involves bringing home the problems and stresses experienced at work, making adequate participation in family life difficult (Voydanoff, 1987). Similarly, family life can affect work in important ways. Family obligations can provide motivation for working hard, but problems at home, such as a child's illness, can hinder job performance as well.

This chapter focuses on the interconnection between the family and work, beginning with an examination of the changing composition of the labor force, notably the increasing participation of married women with small children and the impact of this change on marriage and family structures and functioning. We also examine the inequalities of wealth and resources as manifested in poverty, unemployment, and homelessness. The chapter concludes with an assessment of the kinds of changes that need to be made in the organization of work and in social policies to help individuals maintain a balance between the demands of work and family.

THE TRANSFORMATION OF WORK AND FAMILY ROLES

The idealized images of men as providers and women as homemakers continued into the second half of the twentieth century despite the fact that these roles were already being undermined. Figure 10.1 traces the changes in women's and men's labor force participation rates from 1900 to 1999. The **labor force participation rate** refers to the percentage of workers in a particular group who are employed or who are actively seeking employment. If people are not employed and are not actively seeking work, they are not counted in the labor force. As the twentieth century opened, only 20 percent of women aged 14 and older were in the labor force, compared with approximately 86 percent of men in that age category. The comparable rates 99 years later were 60 percent for women and 75 percent for men 16 years of age and over. Thus, during the

Figure 10.1

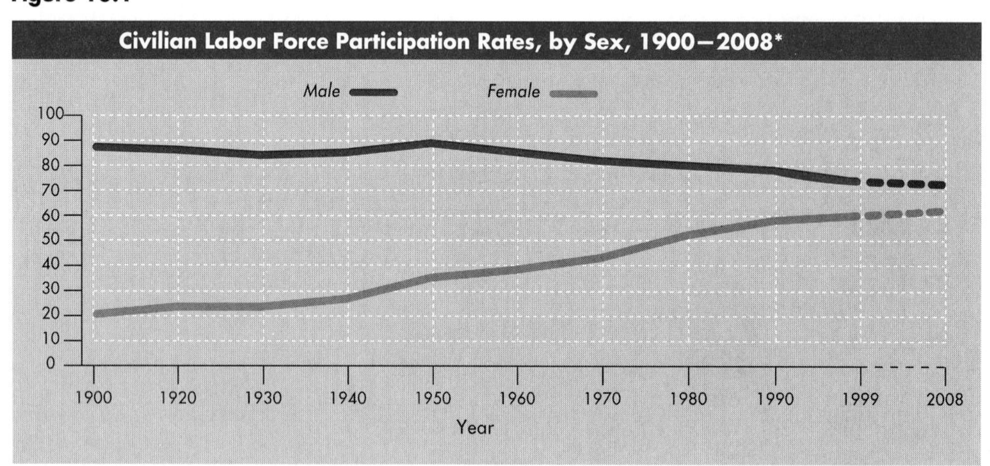

*Dotted lines represent projections for year 2008.

Sources: Adapted from U.S. Census Bureau, 1975, *Historical Statistics of the United States, Colonial Times to 1970*, bicentennial ed., part 1 (Washington, DC: U.S. Government Printing Office): 131-32; U.S. Census Bureau, 2000a, *Statistical Abstract of the United States, 2000* (Washington, DC: U.S. Government Printing Office): 403.

twentieth century the labor force participation rates for women and men have moved in opposite directions, with the result that women now constitute 46 percent of all workers, up from 18 percent in 1900. This gap between the proportion of female and male workers is expected to narrow even further in the twenty-first century, as an even higher percentage of women (61.9 percent) and a lower percentage of men (73.7 percent) are expected to be in the labor force by 2008.

The decline in the male participation rate reflects a number of changes in the U.S. economy. On the one hand, improvements in pension and other retirement benefits have allowed older men to retire early; on the other hand, the labor market demands for better-educated workers have kept younger men in school longer and led to the displacement of workers with low levels of education and marginal skills, especially men of color.

The narrowing gap between women's and men's participation rates reveals only part of the story, however. According to historian Alice Kessler-Harris (1982), a marked shift occurred in the participation patterns of women. Prior to World War II, the majority of women workers were young, single, poor, and women of color. As Figure 10.2 shows, as late as 1975 only 36.7 percent of all married mothers with children under 6 years of age were in the labor force. However, a much higher percentage of black mothers (almost 55 percent) than white mothers (about 35 percent) were working. More than two decades later, over six out of ten (62 percent) married mothers with preschool children were in the labor force. However, the gap between the percentages of working black and white mothers remains approximately the same, 80 percent to 61 percent. Even more noteworthy is the fact that 57.6 percent of white married women but 83.5 percent of black married women with children 1 year old or younger are in the labor force, compared with 29.2 percent and 50.0 percent, respectively, in 1975.

Historically, labor force participation rates varied by race as well as by gender and marital status. In the past white women were less likely than women of color to be in the labor force. As white women began to delay marriage and to divorce in greater numbers, however, their rates became similar to those of other groups of women. In 1999, the labor force participation rate for black women was 63.5 percent and for white women it was 59.6 percent. Latinas had the lowest rate of participation, 55.9 percent. These differences are expected to continue well into the new decade. White women are expected to have a slightly lower participation rate than black women—61.5 percent compared to 64.6 percent. Slightly more Latinas (57.9 percent) will be in the labor force, but they will continue to trail their white and black counterparts. For men, the differences in participation rates are more pronounced across race and ethnicity. Latinos lead with 79.8 percent, followed closely by white men with 75.6 percent. Black men have the lowest labor force participation rates, 68.7 percent (U.S. Bureau of the Census, 2000a).

Figure 10.2

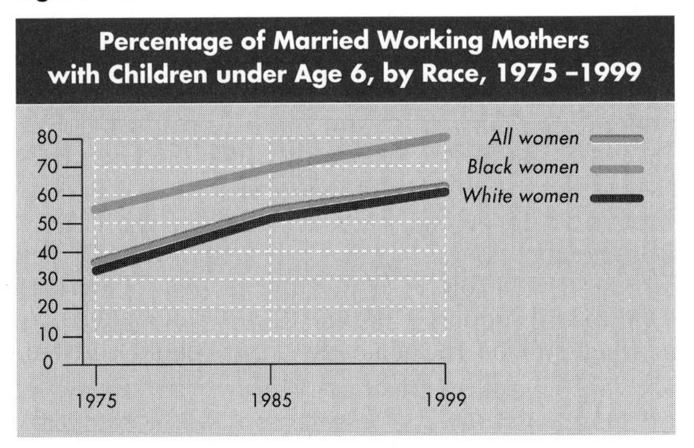

Source: Adapted from U.S. Census Bureau, 2000a, *Statistical Abstract of the United States, 2000* (Washington, DC: U.S. Government Printing Office): 654.

Reasons Women Work

Rarely do we ask men why they work; we assume they have no choice. They are expected to be family providers. But because the homemaker role was believed to be the traditional role for women, any departures from this role require explanation. According to the U.S. Department of Labor (1993), the majority of women (56 percent) work for the same reasons men do—to support themselves or their family; an additional 21 percent work to bring in extra money. Other reasons women give for working are interest and self-fulfillment.

No single factor can explain the dramatic changes in women's labor force participation rates. Rather, a complex interplay of demographic, economic, social, political, and personal factors have contributed to these changes. For example, in contrast to women in previous eras, women today are better educated, have fewer children, and live longer. Women who postpone marriage and childbearing to increase their level of education and to begin work are more likely to remain in the labor force after the birth of their children. Advanced education influences women in much the same way that it influences men. Not only does education offer better job possibilities but it also raises awareness of personal options and creates a desire for self-expression and self-fulfillment. Women today also have more time in their total life span to pursue activities other than child rearing.

In recent decades both the U.S. and world economies have experienced major changes which have had a negative impact on family budgets, thus contributing to the increase of women in the work force. For example, in the United States many high-paying jobs have disappeared: "Between 1991 and 1992, 5.5 million workers lost jobs because their plant or company closed or moved, there was insufficient work for them to do, or their positions or shifts were abolished" (Gardner, 1995:45). Although approximately 75 percent of those workers found work, slightly less than a third found full-time jobs with earnings the same as or higher than those of the lost job. For example, when American Home Products closed its plant in Elkhart, Indiana, the average hourly pay of its workers was $13.40. One year later the average pay of the workers who found new jobs was $6.00 per hour (Barlett and Steele, 1992:97). Over the last two decades, the real earnings of most male workers remained stagnant or fell. A recent study by the Economic Policy Institute found that only in 1997 was the typical American family able to match the income it enjoyed in 1989, the peak of the last business cycle. This recovery came not from an improvement in real wages but through an increase in the number of hours worked, an estimated 247 more hours per family, or approximately six additional weeks of work (Choo, 1999). Many of these extra hours came as a result of workers taking on more than one job. In 1999, 5.7 of male workers and 6.0 percent of female workers were multiple job holders. The rates were highest for black males (6.3 percent) and white females (6.2 percent).

By 1999 the United States economy had recovered and grown, resulting in one of the country's lowest unemployment rates in more than 25 years (4.2 percent). However, in 2001 another economic slowdown was under way and by September the unemployment rate had moved up to 4.9 percent. Then, on September 11, terrorists hijacked four commercial airlines, flying two of the planes into New York City's World Trade Center Towers; another flew into a section of the Pentagon and the fourth crashed in a Pennsylvania field. Thousands of lives were lost, the majority of them family breadwinners. In the immediate aftermath of the attacks, hundreds of thousands of people in the United States and across the globe lost their jobs as industry after industry coped with a lessened demand for their services by laying off employees or closing down. The full impact of this act of terrorism and the United States's response on the nation's economy is yet to be determined but the initial data show a significant effect. In December 2001 the unemployment rate had climbed to 5.8 percent (8.3 million people). Over one million jobs were lost in the last four months of 2001 (U.S. Department of Labor, 2002).

During the last half of the twentieth century, as men were experiencing changes in their work environments, there was an increased demand for women workers to fill the expanding number of jobs in the service sector, for example, teaching, health care, social services, government, and real estate. The women's movement and affirmative action legislation also enhanced employment opportunities for women and people of color. Additionally, social attitudes have become more accepting of working women. These factors, combined with the desire for a higher standard of living, led many women into the workplace.

WORK AND FAMILY STRUCTURES

The rapid entrance of married women with children into the labor force has altered family life in many ways. A variety of work and family structures have emerged as a response to these economic and social transformations, creating both opportunities and problems for family members.

Traditional Nuclear Families

The highly idealized family structure consisting of a working husband, a wife who is a full-time homemaker, and at least one child under the age of 18, currently represents only 29 percent of all families in the United States. Included within this family type are women and a small number of "househusbands"—men who stay home to care for home and family while their wives work. Estimates are that there are more than 2 million at-home dads today (Frank, 1998). Most househusbands take on this role on a temporary basis when they are unemployed, going to school, or able to do their work from home. By and large, men who take on the househusband role receive relatively little support from the larger society and often find their masculinity questioned by others. These individuals engage in activities that some authors are now calling "home production," the nonmarket production of goods and services, usually for the family but occasionally on a volunteer basis for schools, churches, or other groups. According to sociologists Randy Hodson and Teresa Sullivan (1995), what is traditionally known as "housework" is only one aspect of home production, which also includes household budgeting, grocery shopping, care of dependents, and other tasks that go beyond cleaning and laundry. They point out the enormous value to families of these activities. If these nonpaid home production "workers" were compensated for their labor, their compensation would amount to billions of dollars per year.

Like all social roles, the role of home production worker (traditionally known as "housewife") has both costs and benefits (Oakley, 1974). On the positive side it provides the possibility of scheduling activities to suit one's own priorities and the opportunity to watch children grow and develop on a daily basis. Many parents, including some women and men currently in the labor force, would prefer to stay home at least while their children are young. A 1995 study by the Families and Work Institute, "Women: The New Providers," found that 21 percent of the 460 men and 31 percent of the more than 1500 women surveyed said they would prefer this option.

Among the disadvantages of the home production role are the repetitive and sometimes boring nature of activities such as cleaning and doing laundry and the overall social devaluation of housework, often reflected in the phrase, "I'm just a housewife." Important financial costs as well become major burdens for families with only a single source of income and become particularly significant when divorce or death disrupts the family. This is particularly the case when the disruption is unexpected, as happens when accidents, natural disasters, or terrorist attacks result in the untimely death of the major breadwinner. Homemakers are economically dependent on their partners. Unlike homemakers in several European countries, U.S. homemakers are not covered by pensions, insurance, or social security. Thus, when a marriage is dissolved in the United States the displaced homemaker frequently suffers downward social mobility (see Chapter 12).

The Two-Person Career

One variation of the traditional nuclear family/work relationship is what some writers have called the "two-person career" (Papanek, 1973; Mortimer and London, 1984). This pattern, considered by Hanna Papanek to be a "structural part of the middle-class wife's role" (1973:857), incorporates the wife into her spouse's job through the expectation that she will be available to entertain his business associates, engage in volunteer activities that will enhance his organization's image, attend company parties and other events, socialize with her husband's coworkers off the job, and, at the same time, attend to the children and keep the household functioning smoothly. Much of the research on the two-person career focuses on middle- and upper-class occupations. Many business, professional, and political wives, for example, the first lady, are often viewed as typical examples of the two-person career. Thus, men in these families symbolically bring two people to their jobs (Kanter, 1977). In contrast, when women hold similar positions, husbands are rarely expected to perform these duties. One notable exception is Charles T. Hunt III, a stay-at-home dad and husband of Massachusetts Acting Governor Jane Swift, who agreed to take on some of the responsibilities usually delegated to First Ladies such as giving tours of the governor's mansion.

Charles Hunt, husband of Massachusetts Acting Governor Jane Swift, is filling the role of a political spouse usually played by women. Mr. Hunt is the primary child caregiver to their three children. Here he carries one of his newborn twins from a Boston hospital.

The two-person career marriage, like all others, has advantages and disadvantages. On the positive side, employers benefit by having additional "workers" without having to pay for their efforts. Many husbands owe much of their career advancement to the social skills of their wives. Because the husband is away from home much of the time, the wife becomes the exclusive home manager. Fulfilling this role gives wives status and a sense of accomplishment, leaving their husbands free to devote most of their energy to work. Among middle- and upper-class wives, the financial rewards for taking on this responsibility may be significant—a secure lifestyle, travel, and opportunities for cultural enrichment.

On the negative side, many wives experience unhappiness in this role. Like other nonemployed homemakers, these wives may believe that their role is not appreciated or respected by the public. Furthermore, although much is demanded of them, they may not feel a part of their husband's work. Interviews with corporate wives reveal a frequent complaint that husbands don't have time or don't want to share their work with their wives (Reeve, 1991). Wives may feel enormously limited in their behavior, constrained in their choice of friends, and restricted in their own occupational goals because of the demands of their husbands' careers (Papanek, 1973; Kanter, 1977). In addition, the husband's work often takes priority over family life, thus limiting the time spouses have to be together.

Economic shifts that require multiple family earners as well as the changing aspirations of women and men have led to a decline in the two-person career strategy. The traditional nuclear family of working husband, homemaker wife, and children is being replaced by dual-earner families, or, as some writers prefer, "two-paycheck couples."

Dual-Earner Families

Dual-earner families are not new; there have always been families where both spouses were employed outside the home. However, in the past, dual-earner families tended to be concentrated among the poor. In contrast, today's dual-earner couples constitute approximately 70 percent of all married couples and cut across all class and ethnic lines (Hayghe and Bianchi, 1994).

Nevertheless, dual-earner families do not all follow the same pattern. There is considerable variation in their commitment to work. At one end of the continuum are couples in which one of the spouses, usually the wife, works part-time. At the other end is a small (approximately 7 percent) but growing number of couples in which both spouses are highly committed to work. These are what social scientists call dual-career couples. These households differ from other dual-earner households in their approach to work. Rather than simply having a job, these couples invest in careers, which have several identifying characteristics. First, they require extensive training, usually a college or professional degree. Second, careers are more structured than jobs are, containing specific paths of upward mobility. Finally, careers involve commitment beyond a 9-to-5 workday. Sociologists Robert and Jeanette Lauer distinguish these families in the following way:

> The dual-earner family is one in which both spouses are involved in paid work, and one or both view the work only as a job. In other words, one of the spouses in the dual-earner family may be pursuing a career, while the other is merely holding down a job. In the dual-career family, on the other hand, both spouses are engaged in careers, which means that both are committed to employment that has a long-term pattern of mobility. (1991:325–26)

Later in this chapter we will see that couples in dual-earner marriages experience satisfaction as well as stress and conflict as they struggle to solve important relationship problems such as the "problem over who will do the 'family work,' the housekeeping and child care that formerly was the work of the housewife" (Lauer and Lauer, 1991:326).

Commuter Marriages

Some couples work in different geographic locations and because of distance must maintain two separate places of residence. Social scientists refer to these arrangements as **commuter marriages**. Although the exact number of commuter marriages is unknown, one estimate puts the number of such relationships at around 1 million (Maines, 1993). By contrast, estimates are that in the central region of Thailand 41 percent of all couples live apart after marriage due to economic, occupational, or educational needs (quoted in Schvaneveldt, Young, and Schvaneveldt, 2001). One form of commuter marriage has existed for a long time. Couples in which one spouse, most frequently the husband, is a politician, professional athlete, traveling salesperson, seasonal worker, prisoner, or serves in the military have had some experience with living apart while maintaining a marital relationship. Similarly, dual-residency patterns were and continue to be common among low-income families around the world, where one spouse motivated by economic necessity migrates to another country, either making occasional visits home, such as many Latina/o migrants in the United States do, or works to reunite the family in her or his new location.

Today, many commuter marriages develop because both spouses pursue careers but find that suitable jobs for each spouse are unavailable in the same location. Sometimes, too, the requirements of a job call for a transfer to a new area, and for whatever reason the other spouse can't or won't relocate. According to industrial relations expert Linda Stroh, about 7 percent of corporate relocations end up creating commuter marriages (Franklin, 1999). A recent survey found that women were more willing to relocate to another city for a spouse's or partner's career; only 14 percent of female respondents, compared to 34 percent of male respondents, said they would not move. Men's reluctance to move was related to a belief that a move would hurt their careers and/or earning power. Women were concerned that a move would disrupt strong family ties to their current community ("Men Won't Budge . . . ," 1997). When couples do commute, they are most likely to see their accommodations to their careers as a temporary lifestyle arrangement (Stewart, 1999). Generally, the geographic distance involved determines the length of separation. Some couples are able to be together on weekends; others can manage only monthly reunions. These arrangements are more stressful for younger couples, especially those with children and those who have been married for only a short time (Gross, 1980). Couples in these relationships are pioneers. Few guidelines exist to help them, and they receive little social support, because living apart is contrary to the traditional U.S. vision of married life.

In many ways being involved in a commuter marriage is like being single. On the one hand, each spouse assumes all the responsibilities of maintaining a household, which can be burdensome, especially for the spouse who provides the majority of child care in the family. On the other hand, however, each spouse enjoys a considerable amount of freedom, especially in the use of time, much of which can be devoted to work and career advancement or to favorite hobbies. Because of separate living arrangements, day-to-day conflict between work and family is not usually a problem.

Commuter couples, of necessity, have developed coping strategies for maintaining a sense of family. Many of these strategies require significant outlays of resources, particularly frequent telephone calls and travel to each other's place of residence. Many commuter couples use e-mail to keep connected on a daily basis. Research comparing commuting and noncommuting dual-career couples found that commuters are more satisfied with their work life and the time they have for themselves but are more dissatisfied with family life, their relationship with their partner, and with life as a whole (Bunker et al., 1992). This finding appears to be constant across diverse racial and ethnic groups (Jackson, Brown, and Patterson-Stewart, 2000; Schvaneveldt, Young, and Schvaneveldt, 2001).

? *Would you be comfortable as a partner in a commuter marriage? Consider some of the unique problems you would face in such a relationship. How would you handle social events? Would you attend events alone or in the company of a same-sex or an other-sex friend? How would you convey emotional support and intimacy from a distance?*

THE IMPACT OF WORK ON FAMILY RELATIONSHIPS

Much of the research conducted in the past on the impact of work on family life has been sex-segregated, that is, based on the assumption that work has a different meaning for women than for men. For women paid work was thought of as an option that had to be weighed against the disruption it would cause their families; for men it was considered a given. Men might have choices in the type of work they selected but not in whether they would work. Therefore, outside of their earning power, there is "a dearth of empirical research on the effects of fathers' employment on father–child interactions and their children's behavior" (Barling, 1991:181).

Studies of working women, in contrast, focused on different questions. Recall from Chapter 2 Talcott Parsons's functionalist view that a woman's role in the family is expressive and a man's is instrumental. According to Parsons, stepping outside these roles leads to family instability. Thus, prior to 1960 researchers assumed that the entry of mothers into the labor force would have negative consequences for the family, leading, for example, to children getting into trouble in school or with the law.

These traditional role definitions no longer (if they ever did) adequately reflect the work and family experiences of women and men, especially those in dual-earner families. A new theoretical model is required that acknowledges the labor force participation of both women and men. Thus, sociologist Joan Spade (1989) called for a sex-integrated model to understand the impact of work on the family. Such a model asks how the type of work women and men do shapes their orientations and behaviors in the home.

Given the increasing number of dual-earner families, this question takes on major significance. The attempts by dual-earner couples to integrate work and family experiences affect many aspects of family life: power relationships and decision making, marital happiness, and the household division of labor. In short, by examining dual-earner couples we can learn how gender roles in the family are changing in response to both spouses taking on paid employment.

Marital Power and Decision Making

One of the most consistent findings relating to the impact of work on family life deals with the relationship between income and power in decision making. Money frequently translates into power. When both spouses work, the traditional pattern of male dominance in the marital relationship shifts to one of greater equality in terms of more joint decision making (Godwin and Scanzoni, 1989). Spouses, most frequently wives, who do not contribute financially generally have little power in the relationship. The consequences of this may be severe. If the marriage is an unhappy one, the spouse without independent financial resources may feel compelled to stay in the relationship, whereas working may give an unhappy spouse the ability to leave the relationship. This relationship between independent resources and choice is illustrated by one of the respondents in a study of Chicana cannery workers: "It wasn't that my working hastened my divorce, in that it made my marriage worse, like Mario claims to this day. But rather it allowed me the freedom from a bad marriage" (Zavella, 1987:147).

This pattern of wives gaining more power as a result of their economic contribution holds true across most racial and ethnic groups. Researchers Jose Szapocznik and Roberto Hernandez (1988), for example, observed that Cuban women who migrated to the United States often found jobs sooner than their husbands did. Their economic contributions were then translated into gains in family decision making, thereby weakening the traditional Cuban patriarchal family structure. For the first generation of Cuban Americans these changes were often disruptive. Second-generation Cuban American couples, who grew up in the United States, are less troubled by the greater equality in decision making and have tended to construct family relationships that are less male-dominated than those of their parental generation (Boswell and Curtis, 1983; Szapocznik and Hernandez, 1988). Similar patterns have been observed among Chinese American and Korean American families (Min, 1988; Wong, 1988). Furthermore, given the consistently high level of labor force participation of African American women, it is not surprising to find that egalitarian decision making is common in African American families as well (McAdoo and McAdoo, 1995).

There are significant exceptions to these patterns. Differences in economic power and decision making are often reinforced or offset by ideological considerations. In a study of women in second marriages, Karen Pyke (1994) found that some remarried women stopped working and became full-time homemakers, yet increased their power in the marital relationship. According to Pyke, the meaning couples give to women's paid employment or unpaid household labor is key to determining the woman's power in the relationship. Thus, if unpaid household labor is valued by the working spouse, egalitarian power sharing between spouses is likely. Conversely, if couples believe that men should be the primary breadwinners and, correspondingly, have the final say in most decisions, then the man will have more power in the relationship regardless of the earnings of either spouse (Benjamin and Sullivan, 1996).

Marital Happiness

Are couples with one earner happier than those with two? The results of research on this question are inconsistent. Some studies have found homemakers to be happier than working wives (Stokes and Peyton, 1986; Saenz, Goudy, and Frederick, 1989). However, these researchers found that much of the dissatisfaction the working wives felt was attributable to the quality of the jobs they held—jobs with low pay, little status, and considerable stress. Later research also found a correlation between a stressful job and lower levels of marital adjustment (Sears and Galambos, 1992).

Other research found that working wives reported higher levels of happiness than did nonworking wives. Similarly, research has consistently found that wives in dual-earner couples are healthier, less depressed, and less frustrated than their homemaker counterparts (Coontz, 1997). This finding is probably related to the fact that a wife's income contribution gives her more power within the family as well as being a source of satisfaction and self-esteem.

More important than work per se, however, is the couple's attitude toward work. If the couple disagree about spousal employment or if the wife works only because of economic necessity, some tension and conflict are likely. Some wives who desire only a domestic role may be embittered about their need to work, whereas some husbands who adhere strongly to the good provider role might feel threatened or inadequate as a result of having a working wife. This is especially the case for some husbands whose wives earn more than they do. According to the U.S. Bureau of Labor Statistics, in 1998, in 29.2 percent of dual-earner families wives earn more than their husbands, a 22 percent increase over the past decade (Littman, 2001). This pattern is more common among black couples than white couples (Roberts, 1994). This disparity is explained by the fact that better-educated black women significantly outnumber better-educated black men and by the tendency of some employers to hire black females, but not black males. In sum, it seems that agreement on work and family roles is a key factor in marital happiness.

The experience of marital happiness is related to another constraint confronting dual-earner families: finding time to be together, especially recreational time. "Couples with less time together express less satisfaction with their marriages" (Nock and Kingston, 1990:133). This lack of time together grew more acute in the 1990s as Americans added nearly a full week to their work year, working 1979 hours (an increase of 36 hours from 1990) or nearly 49 1/2 weeks a year on the job. In comparison, Japanese workers (long the leader in working hours) worked 1842 hours, Canadian workers 1767 hours, British workers 1719, and German workers 1480 (Greenhouse, 2001). These differentials are due to variations in cultural practices and economic situations. Traditionally, European employers have granted European workers 4 to 6 weeks of vacation each year, compared to the 2 to 3 weeks most Americans receive. In the 1990s, the European economy grew much more slowly than that of the United States. European governments responded by reducing the official workweek in an attempt to pressure employers to hire more workers while U.S. employers met their needs by adding overtime work.

Time is also related to two other important aspects of family living: household tasks and the care of children. Parsons's model of the family assumes that these are the wife's responsibilities and that they complement the husband's breadwinner role. Parsons didn't anticipate the contemporary widespread need for two incomes, however. What happens to housework and child care when wives share the breadwinner function? Do husbands reciprocate and share domestic responsibilities?

Husbands and the Division of Household Labor

As more wives entered the labor force, social scientists began to investigate the degree to which husbands increased the amount of time they spent doing household work. Data collected from the 1960s to the mid-1970s show that family work remained almost exclusively the province of women, whether or not they were employed. For example, a study of 1296 New York State families found that husbands spent about 1.6 hours per day in family work compared with 8.1 hours per day for housewives and 4.8 hours per day for working wives (Walker and Woods, 1976). It is not surprising then that compared with their spouses, wives experienced more **role overload**, a situation in which a person's various roles carry more responsibilities than that person can reasonably manage. As a result of role overload women have less free time for themselves and experience a diminished sense of well-being (Robinson, 1977; Hochschild, 1997).

Although a recent study by the Families and Work Institute found that working fathers spent more time on household chores in 1997 than they did in 1977, husbands still do not make equal contributions to housework. Working fathers spent 2.1 workday hours and 4.9 non-workday hours on chores in 1997, compared to 3.3 workday hours and 5.8 non-workdays spent by working mothers (cited in Lewin, 1998a). Children's contributions to household labor are similarly gendered, with girls spending 10.2 hours per week on housework compared to boys' 2.7 hours (Waite and Goldscheider, 1992). This pattern of unequal division of household labor has been found in study after study, in the United States, Canada, and other Western countries (Nock and Kingston, 1990; Higgins, Duxbury, and Lee, 1994; Robinson and Godbey, 1997). Although a similar pattern of inequity exists in China, it represents a major change from the centuries-old tradition that placed the responsibility for housework and child care completely in women's hands. Today, the majority of Chinese women are in the labor force, and, although they still do most of the household work, an increasing number of their husbands are participating in household labor and child care (Lu, Maume, and Bellas,

When both spouses work, family roles often need to be renegotiated. As working women are seeking more equity in the division of household tasks, many men are increasing their participation in family and household labor.

2000). This observation has led some writers to describe women's dual role of worker and housewife as a "second shift" (Hochschild, 1989).

Sharing the Load: Emergent Egalitarian Relationships Inequity in family work can affect the satisfaction found in marriage. Among wives there is a clear and positive connection between a fair division of family work and marital and personal well-being (Rogers and Amato, 2000). Dutch wives, like their U.S. counterparts, are dissatisfied when their husbands' participation in household labor is only minimal (Kluwer, Heeskink, and Van De Vliert, 1996). Conversely, wives whose husbands do their share of family work are more satisfied with marriage than are other wives (Thompson and Walker, 1991). Catherine Ross and her colleagues (1983) reported that wives whose husbands share housework are less depressed than other wives. According to a 1990 national opinion poll, next to money, "how much my mate helps around the house" is the single biggest cause of resentment among women who are married or living as if married, with 52 percent of the respondents reporting this as a problem. Women cite improvement in this area as one of the most important changes that would make their lives better (Townsend and O'Neil, 1990:28). In that same survey, 70 percent of the women respondents said that more help from men could help them balance the triple role of worker/mother/wife. In addition, 64 percent of the men agreed that by doing more at home, they could help balance work and family demands.

Thus, there seems to be some consensus among both women and men for the need to alter traditional gender roles. That some of this is occurring, albeit slowly, is indicated by Audrey Smith and William Reid (1986) in their study of role-sharing marriages, by Rosanna Hertz (1986) in her study of dual-career marriages, and by Pepper Schwartz (1999) in her study of peer marriages. Hertz argues that dual-career couples generally do not start out with an ideology of equality in marital roles, but that it often emerges out of the opportunities and constraints they experience on a day-to-day basis. In contrast, the couples in Schwartz's study had strong ideas about building a marriage based on equity and equality and made conscious efforts to achieve their goal—"marital intimacy that comes from being part of a well-matched, equally empowered, equally participatory team" (1999:162). Other couples have altered traditional gender roles in the family as well. However, as Francine Deutsch (1999) discovered in a study of 150 dual-career couples with children, most couples had a work-centered family in which work and career advancement, usually the husband's, was the priority. Nevertheless, 41 couples in her study (nearly 25 percent) had child-centered families in which their children's needs were the central focus for both parents. By fully sharing all responsibilities, these parents managed to have successful work lives and also well-balanced family lives.

Other researchers have found that men in dual-earner families who see themselves as co-providers with their wives do more domestic tasks than do men who still believe in the good provider role (Perry-Jenkins and Crouter, 1990).

Social class also seems to be relevant here. Spouses with higher levels of education are more likely to share domestic tasks, especially when the wife has high earnings and a professional status (Perry-Jenkins and Folk, 1994; Spain and Bianchi, 1996). Like their U.S. counterparts, urban Chinese husbands with higher educational levels and whose wives' earnings are close to theirs have the highest rates of participation in household labor (Lu, Maume, and Bellas, 2000). The affluence of these couples, however, also allows them to hire others to do their household tasks and/or child care. Although this solution may work well for them, it often creates problems for the families of domestic workers who find themselves sacrificing time with their families to accommodate the family needs of their employers. This situation reflects the traditional racial and ethnic divisions in the United States. Historically, African American women and white ethnic immigrant women made up the core of domestic workers; today, more and more Latinas are filling these positions (Hondagneu-Sotelo and Avila, 1997).

Race and ethnicity are also factors in how family work is divided. Table 10.1 reveals the time men spent on specific household tasks. Among men who are employed full-time, blacks spent the most time in tasks such as cooking, cleaning, and caring for children, followed by Latinos and then whites. However, other researchers found that Mexican American men do less household labor than white men (Golding, 1990). Similarly, Lillian Rubin (1994) found that Latinos and Asian American men, especially those who live in ethnic neighborhoods where traditional gender roles remain strong despite women's employment, are less likely to share household work. However, other research on Mexican American couples found husbands participated more in domestic tasks

Table 10.1

Full-Time Employed Men's Time Spent on Specific Household Tasks, by Race/Ethnicity (in hours/week)

	White	Black	Latino
Preparing meals	2.3	3.3	2.2
Washing dishes	1.9	2.7	2.1
Cleaning house	1.7	3.0	2.2
Outdoor tasks	5.6	5.4	3.9
Shopping	2.3	4.0	3.1
Laundry	1.2	0.6	0.6
Paying bills	1.5	2.4	2.5
Auto maintenance	2.0	3.4	2.9
Driving	1.5	2.7	1.5

Source: Adapted from Beth Anne Shelton and Daphne John, 1993, "Ethnicity, Race, and Difference: A Comparison of White, Black, and Hispanic Men's Household Labor Time," in Jane C. Hood, ed., *Men, Work, and Family.* Newbury Park: Sage Publications, pp. 144–45. Reprinted by permission of Sage Publications, Inc.

if the wife's earnings equaled or surpassed that of her husband (Coltrane, 1996). Such findings underscore the complex nature of the work-family linkage; more research is needed to determine what may account for the different patterns of work and family role tradeoffs (Shelton and John, 1993).

Nevertheless, one dominant theme that cuts across all of these studies regards the expectations that women and men bring to their roles as partners/parents/providers. If women and men are to share equally in home production work, then women must redefine the value of their jobs or careers as providers and men must redefine the meaning of domestic work as something beneficial, not demeaning (Lorber, 1994). William Beer (1983), in a study of househusbands, redefined housework, incorporating masculine images:

> A day of cooking, cleaning, child care and household management is not unlike climbing a mountain. Some of it is sweaty, gruelling work, but the pleasures, such as sunlight through the mist on Mount Washington, or seeing a toddler learn a new game, are constant enough to make it worth it. . . . Housework may not be Everest, but it is an adventure that awaits any man who wants to forge ahead and meet the challenges of unexplored territory. (xxi)

Child Care

According to a study by the Families and Work Institute, working men are spending more time with their children than fathers did 20 years ago, (Lewin, 1998a) and, as we saw earlier, a considerable number of fathers are stay-at-home dads. Although men's parenting activities appear to be increasing, women still take the major responsibility for child care in the United States. This situation puts working women at a competitive disadvantage with male colleagues, who are freed of this responsibility by their spouses. For women, having children constrains their labor market activities. Women with small children have lower labor force participation rates, and when they are employed, they are more likely to work part-time. For example, one study found that women responded to parenthood by reducing the number of hours they worked; men did not (Grant, Simpson, and Xue, 1990). This is especially true of poor women with limited education and skills. Finding a job that pays an income sufficient to cover child-care costs is unlikely for them. In 1995, the average weekly cost of child care was $85.00 for families. In families with preschoolers and a monthly income under $1500, the costs of child care typically consume 31 percent of their income and does not ensure quality care (Smith, 2000).

Some couples respond to the difficulties of child care by split-shift employment and split-shift parenting, thereby enabling one parent to be home while the other is at work. According to a recent survey by the AFL-CIO, 51 percent of women who are married or living with a partner and have children under the age of 18 say they work different shifts than their spouse or partner ("Working Women," 2000). This arrangement has costs as well as benefits. On the one hand, parents rarely see each other. This lack of time together can cause tensions that children also experience. According to sociologist Harriet Presser, people who work nonstandard hours have higher rates of marital instability (Kleiman, 1996). On the other hand, children see their parents as co-providers. If the time each parent is at home overlaps somewhat with the children's waking hours, children are likely to experience care from both parents.

Couples who work the same shift face a different set of problems, the most serious of which is finding alternative child care. In 1977, 13 percent of employed women with a

A major concern of dual-earner families is finding adequate child care. In split-shift households one parent, like this father fixing dinner with his sons, takes primary responsibility for child-care while the other parent is at work. In some cases, the child-care dilemma is resolved when one parent, like this executive, takes her child to work.

child under 5 years of age used organized day care. Eighteen years later, 30 percent were using such facilities. Relatives remain a major provider of child care for working mothers. Figure 10.3 shows the distribution of primary-care arrangements for children in 1995. Eighteen percent of the preschool children were cared for by fathers, down from 20 percent in 1991; grandparents provided care for 30 percent of preschool children. Another 29 percent received care from a nonrelative. Another 5 percent of children under age 5 were cared for by their mothers either while working at home or on the job. These mothers were frequently employed as private household workers or were themselves child-care workers who took in other children while caring for their own at home. The type of child-care arrangements available to parents depends heavily on their resources and family systems. When families are poor or on government assistance, they must rely on relatives more so than other families. One-half of children in poor families are cared for by relatives other than the mother. African American and Latina/o children are more likely to be cared for by grandparents and other nonparental relatives and less likely to be in organized facilities than white children (Smith, 2000).

Regardless of the type of child-care arrangement in use, the majority of families who need child care confront two major problems: high cost and limited availability. Employers can help by subsidizing some of the costs of this care. Although only a small percentage of companies provide on-site child-care centers, their numbers are growing, up from 1000 in 1986 to some 8000 in 1999 (Kleiman, 1999). This arrangement allows parents to visit their children during work or lunch breaks, thus relieving parents of worry over how their children are managing without them. Yet affordable quality care is not readily accessible to all who need it, partly because many Americans still prefer mothers to be at home with their children.

For years there has been a great debate about the impact of a mother's employment (but rarely a father's) on the well-being of children. The weight of the evidence today, however, suggests that children who receive quality child care suffer little, if any, negative consequences from maternal employment (Hamburg, 1992; Harvey, 1999).

Figure 10.3

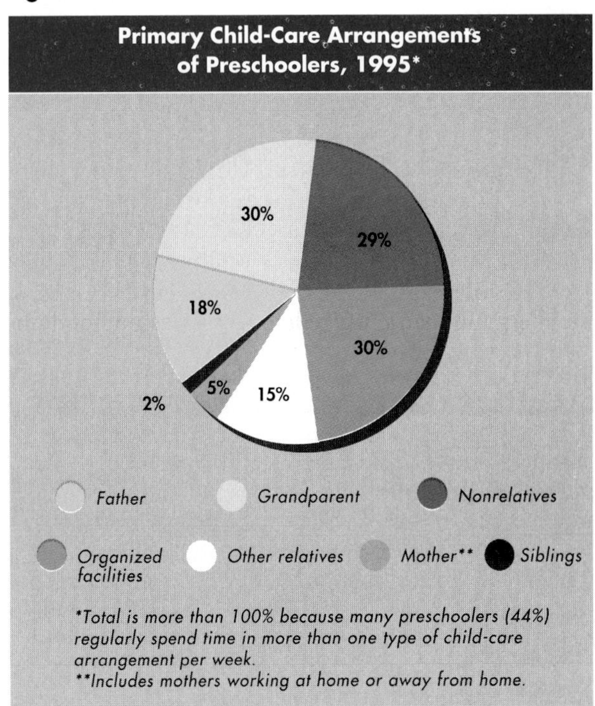

Sources: Adapted from Kristen Smith, 2000, *Who's Minding the Kids? Child Care Arrangements: Fall 1995.* Current Population Reports, P70-7. U.S. Census Bureau (Washington, DC: U.S. Government Printing Office).

THE "MOMMY TRACK" The notion that child care is still primarily a woman's problem was highlighted when corporate consultant Felice Schwartz (1989) wrote an article for the *Harvard Business Review* outlining a controversial approach to the problem of child care and working women. She suggested that employers divide women into two groups based on whether they are career-primary or career-and-family women. Schwartz described the former group as women who are willing to put their careers ahead of family needs. She advised companies to identify these women early and put them on the same career track as talented men. The other women would make good workers, but to keep them Schwartz recommended that companies provide considerations for their parental responsibilities, such as part-time employment, maternity leaves, and so on. The media labeled this position the "mommy track." A version of the "mommy track" exists in Japan as well. Although about 50 percent of Japanese companies with more than 5000 employees have a management program for women, only women are required to choose between the management program or traditional office work (called *ippanshoku*) when applying for a job (Kuriki, 1994).

Criticism was swift to Schwartz's proposal. Some writers argued that such an approach would create a two-tiered system of women workers, with working mothers receiving fewer rewards for their work efforts. Ronnie Sandroff (1989) questioned why the adjustment for having children would fall only on female workers. Rather than a "mommy track," there should be a "parent track" but without current economic penalties. In fact, some fathers want to give more priority to their families. A *Los Angeles Times* survey found 39 percent of fathers in Los Angeles and Orange counties reporting they would prefer to stay home and raise their children than work full-time outside the home. Fifty-seven percent said they felt guilty for not spending more time with their children (Cose, 1995).

Despite these claims, the reality is quite different. A Census Bureau survey found that only 2 percent of employed fathers of preschoolers adjusted work schedules due to child-rearing considerations. This pattern may not be entirely men's doing. Studies have found that when men have been offered time off or flexible work hours they have not taken advantage of them, mostly because they perceive it will hurt their future advancement. They are probably right. Research shows that work interruptions hurt both women and men, but hurt men more because, on average, they still earn more than women. Unlike Sweden, where in 1994 the Parliament passed a law requiring fathers to take a month of the government-paid 12 months of child-care leave offered to parents or lose a month of benefits, few options exist in the United States to accommodate working fathers who want to care for their children. Companies like Lotus Development, where about 100 new dads took advantage of the company's paid paternity leave in 1994, are still the exception (Moskowitz and Townsend, 1995).

The United States is about the only industrialized country that does not have a national child-care policy. This does not mean that the government does not support child-care programs; rather, it means that the existing programs, such as Head Start, were developed as isolated responses to specific problems rather than out of a consensus on the federal government's responsibility for assisting families at all economic levels. Most of the other industrialized countries are far ahead of the United States in providing quality child care. Well-established, low-cost systems of child care have existed for many years in Sweden, Denmark, Italy, and Belgium (Neft and Levine, 1997). In France, approximately 90 percent of children aged 3 to 5 attend preschools at little or no cost to their families (Hamburg, 1992).

INTEGRATING WORK AND FAMILY LIFE: RESOLVING ROLE CONFLICT

For the majority of people the transition to work, marriage, and parenthood requires taking on multiple roles. These roles frequently conflict with one another, placing a serious strain on families. **Role conflict** occurs when a person occupies two different roles that involve contradictory expectations of what should be done at a given time. Perhaps the most obvious and widespread example of role conflict in our society is the conflict between parent and worker. As more people (both married and single) find themselves occupying these roles, this form of role conflict will become even more common. Contributing to this problem are such elements as the absence of quality child care, troublesome work schedules, job-related travel, job transfers and relocations, and unanticipated emergencies.

Strategies for Conflict Resolution

Role conflict can be resolved in a variety of ways. Three common approaches are (1) establishing priorities within the home and workplace, (2) exiting one of the roles, and (3) making the role conflict public and demanding changes either within the family or within the larger society. There are benefits and costs to each of these solutions.

Establishing Priorities This process of making decisions about which activities are more important and will receive more energy and attention is often complicated by gender, class, and the organization of work itself. For example, even though the gap in the labor force participation rates of women and men is narrowing, society still assumes that men's first priority is work and that women's is the family. Hence, women who set work as their first priority and men who put their families first may confront considerable social pressure to change their priorities. Furthermore, many single-parent families as well as families requiring two earners may have limited options when selecting their priorities. Work may have to take precedence over family time. Finally, the way work is organized—starting times, days of the week, holidays, overtime requirements, and the need to bring work home—may present major obstacles to parents wishing to alter the balance of their work and family lives.

Role Exit A second method of resolving role conflicts involves exiting a role. This can occur in a variety of ways. A single parent or one of the spouses may leave the labor force or accept a less demanding job. This strategy may eliminate or minimize the immediate role conflict, but it can also be costly. Not only is family income reduced, but future employment opportunities for the affected worker may be jeopardized. Other people may choose to preserve the work role but to exit an unsatisfying marital role, either temporarily through a separation or permanently by divorce, a topic we discuss in Chapter 12.

Public Awareness A third way to deal with role conflict is to make others aware of the problem. As more women enter the labor force, women and men frequently work side by side in offices and in factories. This arrangement has the potential for allowing women and men to see that gender inequality at work and at home adversely affects everyone's family well-being. Thus, greater numbers of working parents will demand that employers implement policies to assist them in meeting their dual obligations. Through negotiations, both collective and individual, employees are seeking changes in the organization of work (optional rather than required overtime, flextime, job sharing) and in benefits such as parental leave, child care, and equal pay for women. (These issues are discussed in more detail later in the chapter.) People are also pressuring the government to introduce or modify policies to help resolve conflicts between work and family responsibilities.

INEQUITIES IN THE WORKPLACE: CONSEQUENCES FOR FAMILIES

Although the labor force participation rates of women and men are converging, women still confront issues of inequity in the labor market. These issues, in turn, can have a profound effect on women's sense of worth and their family's economic well-being. Three issues are of special significance: occupational distribution, the gender gap in earnings, and sexual harassment.

Occupational Distribution

Occupational distribution refers to the location of workers in different occupations. Although the media highlight stories of women and men who are in nontraditional occupations, for example, women construction workers and male nurses, most work is still thought of as either women's work or men's work. Table 10.2 shows the percentage of the work force in selected occupations. Women and people of color are more heavily concentrated in low-paying clerical or service jobs, whereas men are concentrated in the higher-paying jobs of craftworkers and operators. Even though slightly more women than men are working in a professional specialty, women tend to be working in the lower-paid professions such as nursing or elementary school education, whereas men are more concentrated in the higher-paid professions of law, medicine, and engineering. In 1999, only 28.8 percent of lawyers, 24.5 percent of physicians, and 10.6 percent of engineers were women. The comparable rates were 5.1, 5.7, and 4.6 for African American women and 4.0, 4.8, and 3.5 for Latinas (U.S. Census Bureau, 2000a). As Figure 10.4 clearly shows, women have fared even less well in business. Although women make up almost half of the U.S. labor force (46.5 percent), in 2000 there were only two women CEOs in the Fortune 500: Carleton S. Fiorina of Hewlett-Packard and Andrea Jung at Avon Products. And, despite gains since 1999, only 4.1 percent (93 out of 2255) of the nation's top earners are women ("Catalyst Fact Sheet," 2000). Similar patterns have been found in Canada, where women hold 12 percent of corporate officer positions ("Catalyst Census," 2000), and in Britain, where only 3 percent of corporate board members were women (Associated Press, 1997b). In all three countries, women are poorly represented in line positions, those jobs with profit-and-loss responsibilities that are the traditional route to executive promotion, and in all three countries, surveys of senior-level women identify male stereotyping and preconceptions of women's roles and abilities as obstacles to women's advancement.

The good news is that the percentages have moved upward since 1990, especially for women. Men, in contrast, have been more reluctant to enter "women's" occupations in any significant numbers. Thus, some job categories remain overwhelmingly female, for example, nursing (92.9 percent) and secretarial work (97.9 percent). To eliminate gender-segregated jobs in the United States, approximately half of all female workers would have to change jobs (Renzetti and Curran, 1995). This pattern of gender segregation in the workplace is common in other industrialized countries as well, including the country with the highest rate of women's labor force participation, Sweden. We can see that race and ethnicity also play a role in occupational distribution. Although African Americans make up 11.3 percent of all employed civilians and Latinas/os 10.3 percent, both groups are underrepresented in the higher-paying jobs and overrepresented in lower-paying jobs.

Table 10.2

Percentage of Work Force in Selected Occupations, by Sex, Race/Ethnicity, 1999

	Women	African Americans	Latinas/os
All occupations	46.5	11.3	10.3
Managerial and professional specialty (all)	49.5	8.0	5.0
Executive, administrative, and managerial	45.1	7.6	5.6
Professional specialty	53.5	8.4	4.5
Technical, sales, and administrative support (all)	63.8	11.2	8.4
Technicians and related support	51.9	10.7	6.4
Sales occupations	50.1	8.7	7.9
Service occupations (all)	60.4	18.3	15.2
Child care and household cleaning	95.2	15.1	29.3
Building janitors, maids, cleaners	45.5	21.9	23.2
Health service assistants, aides, orderlies, and attendants	89.2	31.7	9.9
Precision production, craft, and repair	9.0	8.0	12.8
Operators, fabricators, and laborers	24.1	15.7	16.6

Source: Adapted from U.S. Census Bureau, 2000a, *Statistical Abstract of the United States, 2000* (Washington, DC: U.S. Government Printing Office): 416–18, Table 669.

Occupational segregation has consequences for the well-being of workers and their families. First, it restricts the options of both women and men. Men are less likely than women to enter a sex-atypical occupation. Second, when workers enter occupations that are not traditional for their race or gender, they often encounter prejudice and hostility, resulting in high levels of stress. For women and people of color, this hostility often takes the form of exclusion from the informal work groups that are so necessary to successful job performance and advancement. In contrast, men in nontraditional occupations experience prejudice from people outside their occupation, but are less likely than women to experience discrimination at work. Sociologist Christine Williams (1992) found that while women often encounter a "glass ceiling" that limits their advancement, men in sex-atypical occupations experience a "glass escalator" that propels them to higher positions in that field. Finally, occupational segregation results in an earnings gap between women and men and between whites and people of color (Reskin and Padavic, 1994), which limits the resources families receive when women members work.

Figure 10.4

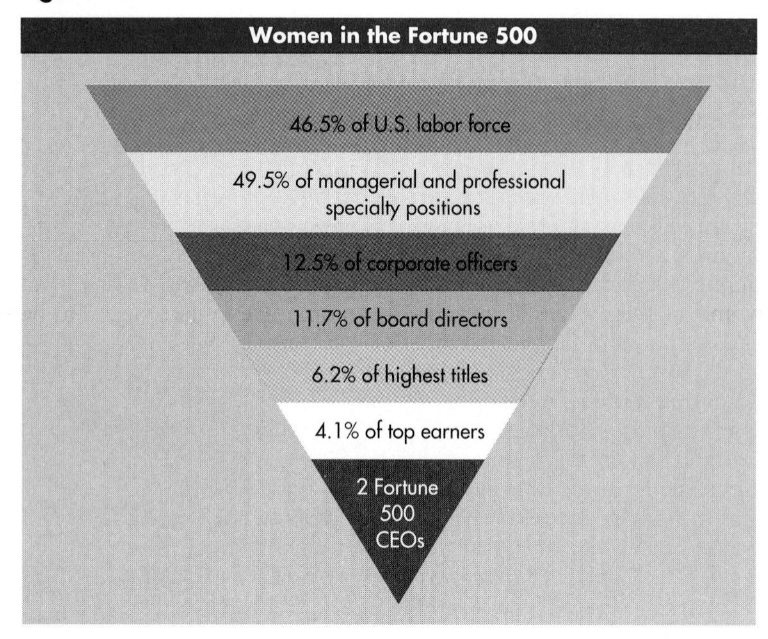

Source: Catalyst Fact Sheet: 2000 Catalyst Census of Women Corporate Officers and Top Earners of the Fortune 500, retrieved October 17, 2001. **http://www.catalystwomen.org/press/factsheets/factscote00.html.** © 2001 Catalyst, Inc.

The Race–Gender Gap in Earnings: Good News and Bad News

No matter how earnings are measured, women's wages are lower than men's, regardless of race and ethnicity. Similarly, men of color are disadvantaged in comparison with their white counterparts. In 2000, the median weekly earnings for female full-time wage and salary workers were $491, or 76 percent of the $646 median for their male counterparts. In 1979, when comparable earnings data were first available, women earned only about 63 percent as much as men did. Younger women (those 20 to 24 years old) have the greatest equity, earning almost 92 percent as much as men, while women 55 to 64 years of age experience the greatest inequity, earning only 68.5 percent of what men make. However, white workers of either gender earned more than their black or Latina/o colleagues. The differences among women were considerably smaller than those among men. White women earned $500, 16.6 percent more than black women ($429) and 37.4 percent more than Latinas ($364). In contrast, white men out-earned their black counterparts by 33 percent ($669 to $503) and their Latino counterparts by 61.6 percent ($414). The earnings gap was widest for whites, with women earning only 74.7 percent as much as men. Black women earned 85.2 percent and Latinas earned 87.7 percent as much as their male counterparts (U.S. Department of Labor, 2001).

The narrowing of the race–gender earnings gap in recent years can be attributed to a number of factors: women's increased investment in education and professional training, entry into higher-paying nontraditional occupations, fewer and shorter interruptions in their work lives, and a decline in men's wages. Between 1979 and 2000, inflation-adjusted earnings for white women grew fairly steadily, rising by 22.9 percent. Black women and Latinas did not fare quite as well; earnings for black women only grew by 14.7 percent and those for Latinas rose just 4.6 percent. However, men lost ground as the real earnings for both white and black men showed little or no net change during this same period while those for Latinos declined (U.S. Department of Labor, 2001). As we shall see later on, the gains many workers made in the 1990s as a result of low unemployment, low inflation, and the increase in the minimum wage started to erode in the economic downturn beginning in 2000. The terrorist attacks on September 11, 2001, severely exacerbated this trend as affected industries, particularly those that cater to business and tourist travel, laid off thousands of workers; the long-term impact of these actions is yet to be calculated.

Although the United States has narrowed the female/male wage gap somewhat, it is still larger than those in many other countries. For example, women in Tanzania and Vietnam earn 92 percent of what men earn, in Australia 91 percent, in Sri Lanka and Iceland 90 percent, and in Sweden 89 percent); however, women in other countries fare considerably worse when compared to their male counterparts. In China the wage gap is 59 percent, in South Korea 54 percent, Japan 41 percent, and in Russia, women earn only 40 percent of what men do (Seager, 1997).

For years researchers have struggled to explain why the wage gap persists even when workers are matched on the basis of years of experience, number of hours worked, education, occupation, and union membership. The general consensus of many of these studies is that discriminatory treatment is the major cause of the earnings gap between women and men and between whites and people of color (Cherry, 2001). Discrimination takes many forms—lack of access, denial of promotions, assignment to lower-pay jobs, violations of equal pay laws, and devaluation of women's work. Additionally, researchers have found that family responsibilities contribute to women's lower wages. For example, childbearing can lead to career interruptions that hinder women's overall advancement (Taniguchi, 1999). According to sociologist Beth Shelton, women's double workload holds down their earnings; the more time one spends on housework, the less time one has for the job. In her research, Shelton found that "8.2 percent of the gender gap in earnings was due directly to women doing more housework than men" (cited in Kleiman, 1989:5).

Gender and racial inequalities in pay deprive families of greater purchasing power. According to a joint study of the AFL-CIO and the Institute for Women's Policy Research, America's working families lose a staggering $200 billion of income annually to the wage gap—an average of more than $4000 per family, even after taking into account differences in education, age, location, and number of hours worked. The study also found that both women and men pay a steep price for unequal pay, a whopping $114 billion, when they work in jobs traditionally defined as "women's work"—nursing, library, and social work—as these jobs typically pay less than jobs where male workers are dominant ("Equal Pay . . . , 1999).

Although the earnings gap between women and men has narrowed in recent years, gender discrimination in employment still deprives women of many benefits enjoyed by their male colleagues.

Much of the race–gender gap could be eliminated by more vigorous enforcement of current equal pay laws as well as implementation of the principle of **pay equity**—equal pay for work of equal value. To put this principle into practice requires evaluating jobs in terms of education, experience, and skill requirements, as well as the job's value to the community. Employers oppose it on the grounds that it is too expensive to implement. Nevertheless, a number of unions have successfully negotiated pay equity programs for their members, albeit primarily with local and state government bodies. Strengthening protections for workers' right to organize in unions and to bargain collectively with their employers would be another potent tool for eliminating some of the current disparity in wages and thereby improving the well-being of families. Government data show that in 2000 the median weekly earnings of union members was $696, considerably higher than the $542 earned by their nonunion counterparts ("Median Weekly . . . ," 2001). Clearly, if nations are serious about improving the living conditions of their families, they must address the issue of more equitable pay for all workers.

Sexual Harassment

Another problem workers may experience is some form of **sexual harassment**, unwanted leers, comments, suggestions, or physical contact of a sexual nature that the recipient finds offensive and causes discomfort or interferes with academic or job performance. Sexual harassment occurs in all types of educational and work settings. Because of the sensitive nature of sexual harassment, accurate data on its extent are difficult to collect. However, surveys show that about 30 percent to 50 percent of female students and as many as 75 percent of female employees have been sexually harassed compared with about 15 percent to 20 percent of males (quoted in Bingham, 1996:239). Although still quite low compared with that of females, sexual harassment of males may be increasing. Men's claims now account for approximately 14 percent of all sexual harassment charges being brought to the Equal Employment Opportunity Commission, double that of a decade ago (Abelson, 2001). The perpetrators in these cases include both women and men. Men, either gay or straight, who do not conform to masculine stereotypes are frequently the target of harassment from other men (Shoop and Edwards, 1994).

Race, socioeconomic status, sexual orientation, age, and marital status affect the experience of sexual harassment. Women of color are more likely to experience sexual harassment than are white women, and the harassment is likely to include racial stereotypes (Fain and Anderson, 1987). Sexual harassment appears to be more prevalent in male-dominated occupations, where some male workers seek to maintain control over women rather than recognize them as equals. For example, women soldiers, physicians, lawyers, coal miners, and investment bankers have all reported high levels of sexual harassment (see, for example, Couric, 1989; Tallichet, 1995; Meier, 1996). One 29-year-old returning woman student provided a personal illustration of harassment at the job site: "I worked as a carpenter for 7 years. Many nights I came home and cried. I was the only woman on my first job. The men didn't want me there. They used to hide my tools and put obscene notes in my lunch bucket. My next job was easier. There was another woman at the job site, and we ate lunch together. It helped to know I wasn't alone. After the men saw we could do the job, they left us alone; a few even became my friends after a while." Single and younger women report being sexually harassed more often than married and older counterparts. Lesbians, like gays, experience physical and verbal harassment because of their sexual orientation (Shoop and Edwards, 1994).

Although sexual harassment violates equal-employment laws, enforcement is difficult. Many victims are afraid to report the harassment for fear of losing their jobs or being blamed for bringing it on themselves. These fears were crystallized for many women by the negative treatment University of Oklahoma law professor Anita Hill received when she testified before a 1991 Senate confirmation hearing that Supreme Court candidate Clarence Thomas sexually harassed her when she worked under his supervision at the Equal Employment Opportunity Commission. Fighting sexual harassment is even more difficult in countries where women's rights have yet to be recognized. Even in Japan, which possesses the world's second-largest economy, government workplace rules against sexual harassment were first put in place only in 1999. Although a recent survey of female civil servants found that 70 percent of respondents said they had been sexually harassed, only about 100 cases have been filed with the Ministry of Labor. Japan, like many other male-dominated cultures, holds women responsible for such problems. Thus, fear and shame prevent Japanese women from seeking legal redress for their grievances (French, 2001).

Workers who are sexually harassed report a number of problems both physical (chronic neck and back pain, gastrointestinal disorders, sleeplessness, and loss of appetite) and psychological (feelings of humiliation, helplessness, and fear). Harassment victims frequently bring these problems home with them, thereby adding tension to family relationships.

THE ECONOMIC WELL-BEING OF FAMILIES

All parents share a common desire to provide a decent standard of living for themselves and their families. To accomplish this goal, an increasing number of couples have made the decision to become a dual-earner family. Women's wages play an important part in the economic well-being of families. In families where both husband and wife work full-time throughout the year, the wife's wages accounted for an average of 40 percent of family earnings (U.S. Bureau of the Census, 1995). In 2000, the median income for all married couple families was $59,187; half of those families had an income higher than that and half of those families had lower incomes.

Table 10.3 reveals how important family structure has become to the economic well-being of families and the amount of money that is available to families to meet their ongoing needs. Dual-earner couples had incomes of $69,467, compared to the $39,738 of married couples where the husband was the sole breadwinner. Single householders, whether male or female, made less than their married counterparts even when the wife was not working. And, as we have seen before, female householders made considerably less than male householders. This aggregate figure, however, conceals important differences by race and ethnicity. For example, the median income for all white families in 2000 was $53,256, but only $35,050 for African American families, and $34,204 for Latinas/os families.

The median household income of Asian and Pacific Islanders was $55,521 (De Navas-Walt, Cleveland, and Roemer, 2001). Their earning power and the fact that, in general, Asians Americans have higher levels of education than other groups, has led many observers to see them as a "model minority." However, this stereotype obscures the diversity within the Asian American population and the processes involved in reaching that income level (Takagi, 1998). For example, Asian American household income generally reflects multiple wage earners, not necessarily high salaries per worker. Asian Americans, although becoming more dispersed in recent years, still tend to be concentrated in a small number of cities (San Francisco, Los Angeles, New York, Chicago, and Honolulu) where salaries, but also cost of living, are higher. And, although in 1999, 46 percent of Asian Americans aged 25 or older had a college or professional degree (compared to 31 percent of whites, 14 percent of African Americans, and 11 percent of Latinas/os (U.S. Census Bureau, 2000), in 1990 almost 67 percent of Cambodian, Hmong, and Laotian adults did not have a high school education (Lee, 1998). Like all stereotypes, the notion of a "model minority" hinders our understanding of the reality of people's lives and, thus, prevents the development of sound policies that can address their needs.

Table 10.3

Median Income of Families, by Type of Family, 2000	
Total married-couple families	$59,187
Wife in paid labor force	$69,467
Wife not in paid labor force	$39,738
Male householder, no wife present	$37,523
Female householder, no husband present	$25,787

Source: U.S. Census Bureau, 2001, Income 2000, Table 4. **http://www.census.gov/hhes/income/income00/inctab4.html**, accessed October 24, 2001.

An Uncertain Future: The Widening Income Gap

The decade of the 1990s has been characterized as one of robust economic growth and prosperity. Indeed, by some measures that assessment rings true. According to the Internal Revenue Service, the sheer number of Americans earning more than $1 million in adjusted gross income more than doubled between 1992 and 1997—jumping from 67,243 to 142,556 ("Americans . . . ," 1999). Inflation and unemployment were at their lowest levels in many years. Yet, as Figure 10.5 shows, the disparity between rich and poor families grew ever wider during the last quarter of the twentieth century. In 1976, the richest fifth of all families received 43.3 percent of all aggregate income, compared to the 4.4 percent received by the poorest fifth of all families. By 2000, the gap had widened to 49.6 percent and 3.6 percent, respectively. Families at all other income levels, with the exception of the wealthiest families (the top 5 percent), who saw their share of income jump from 16 percent to 22 percent, experienced a decrease in their share of aggregate income (De Navas-Walt, Cleveland, and Roemer, 2001).

Economists attribute this trend toward greater inequality to a number of factors: the loss of high-paid manufacturing jobs, the decline in union membership, the growth in low-paid service sector jobs, the higher salaries paid to people with higher education and technical skills, the increase in families with two high-wage earners, and the increasingly popular practice of rewarding executives with stock options and bonuses. A *Business Week* analysis found that in 1999, the average chief executive officer of a U.S. corporation earned an astonishing 475 times the average wage of a blue-collar worker, up over tenfold since 1980 (Reingold, 2000). Thus, if the average blue-collar worker earned $25,000, the average CEO brought home $11.9 million. In fact, David S. Pottruck, co-CEO of Charles Schwab Corporation, took home $127.9 million in 1999, and John T. Chambers, CEO of Cisco Systems, Inc., pocketed $121.7 million. According to a report by the Institute for Policy Studies and United for a Fair Economy, average production workers would have earned $114,035 in 1999 instead of $23,753, if their raises had grown at the same rate as average CEO pay (Stafford, 2000).

Income levels are only a partial reflection of the growing gap between rich and poor. When net worth is considered—the value of real estate, stocks and bonds, and other assets minus any outstanding debts—the chasm is even wider. Although other countries have similar patterns, income inequality in the United States is greater than in any other Western industrialized nation. Many policy analysts see this widening gap as a dangerous trend that does not bode well for the welfare of the nation as a whole. As we will see in Chapter 15, the enormous gulf between America's wealth and corresponding power and that of countries like Afghanistan is a major factor in the resentment and terrorism now being directed at the United States.

Figure 10.5

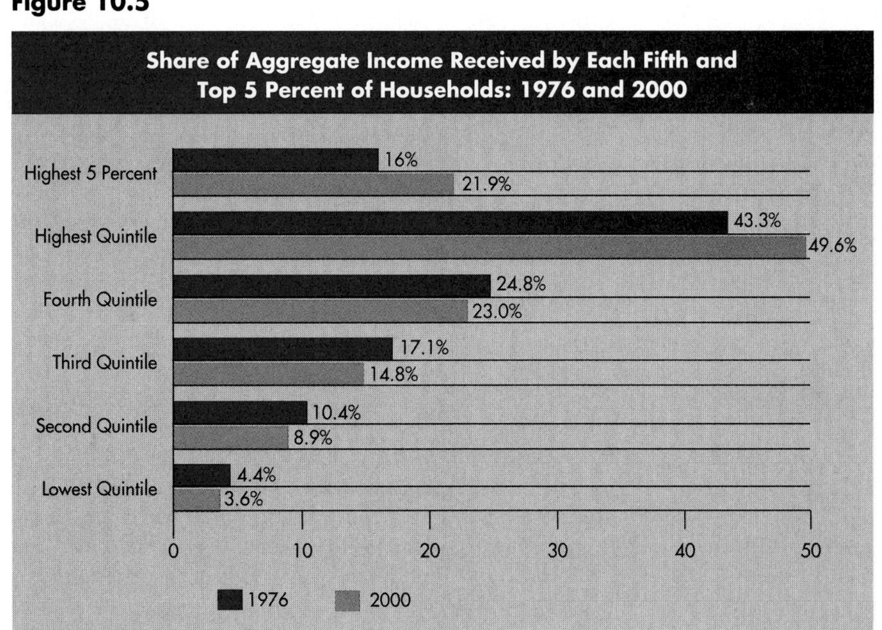

Source: Adapted from C. De Navas-Walt, R. W. Cleveland, and M. I. Roemer, 2001, *Money Income in the United States: 2000.* Current Population Reports, P60-213 (Washington, DC: U.S. Census Bureau): 21, Table A-2.

Think for a moment how your family life would be different if you had the $25,000 income or the $11.9 million. Where would you live? What changes would you make in your lifestyle? Would you support a proposal for a "living-wage" law that would lift families above the poverty level (now estimated to range from $8 to $10 per hour depending on regional economic conditions)? Would you support the proposal from groups like Responsible Wealth to set a maximum ratio between CEO and worker earnings? Explain.

Who Are the Poor?

As we have just seen, all families do not share equitably in America's wealth. In 2000, 6.2 million families (8.6 percent of all families) were poor (Dalakar, 2001), down from 7.7 million (11 percent) in 1996, but still higher than the 5.3 million families (10 percent of all families) in 1970 (U.S. Census Bureau, 2000a). Each year the federal government calculates the minimum level of income necessary to meet basic subsistence needs of families according to size and type. In 2000, the poverty level, as determined by the federal government, was $17,761 in annual income for a family of four. Many economists believe this threshold is too low because it does not take into account the variation in costs of living in different regions of the country nor the special needs some families have for elder or child care.

Poverty rates are not randomly distributed across the population. They vary by family type, race, and ethnicity. Married-couple families have a relatively low poverty rate (4.7 percent) compared to families with a female householder, no husband present (24.7 percent). Families headed by women accounted for the largest portion of the increase in poor families since 1970. As we will see in Chapter 13, over 60 percent of the children born since 1980 will spend some part of their life in a single-parent household, and, hence, are vulnerable to the risk of being poor. This increase in the numbers of women and children who are poor is referred to as the **feminization of poverty**. In 2000, the overall poverty rate among children actually declined to 16.2 percent (11.6 million children), the lowest level since 1979. Although it declined for children of color, the poverty rate remains alarmingly high for African American and Latina/o children, 30.9 percent and 28 percent, respectively. More than one in every two African American children under the age of 6 who live in female-headed families is poor, 53.9 percent (Greenstein et al., 2001). If the economy continues to slow down, poverty rates for children once again will return to higher levels.

Although in absolute numbers most of the poor are white, white families had the lowest poverty rate overall (6.9 percent) compared to other families: Asian/Pacific Islanders (8.8 percent), African Americans (19.1 percent), and Latinas/Latinos (18.5 percent) (Dalakar, 2001). The overall poverty rate for Native Americans was 27.2 percent, but varied from a low 17.3 percent for the Iroquois to a high of 47.3 percent for the Navajo (U.S. Bureau of the Census, 1998:51–54).

Although many people believe that people are poor because they are lazy and don't want to work, the reality is that the majority of people living in poverty live in households where individuals work full-time but make very low wages. They are the **working poor.** In 2000, 45 percent of the poor lived in households with one full-time worker; another 9 percent lived in families with two or more workers.

Thus, being employed is not always sufficient to avoid poverty. Many jobs pay only the minimum wage and offer few, if any, benefits. Many are part-time or temporary jobs. Although educational and skill deficiencies contribute to the employment problems of some poor workers, two-thirds of poor workers have high school diplomas. Thus, for many, it is not a lack of basic skills but a scarcity of higher-paying positions that keeps them in poverty. This is especially disturbing when we consider that in spite of the economic gains of the 1990s, child poverty increased in full-time working families. The number of poor children who live in families with a full-time year-round worker rose to 4.1 million, up from 3.8 million in 1999, and the proportion of poor children who live in families where someone worked throughout the year jumped from 33 percent in 1999 to 37 percent in 2000, double the rate (18 percent) in 1991 (Children's Defense Fund, 2001a). Given the economic uncertainty that seems to lie ahead, it is likely that poverty rates will be on the upswing once again.

Unemployment and Underemployment

To this point we have dealt with the complex connections between work and families. But what happens to families when this connection is broken or nonexistent? To date the U.S. economy has been unable to provide jobs for everyone who wants to work. In 1999 (the latest available comparative data), the U.S. unemployment rate was 4.2 percent (slightly less than 6 million people), the lowest it had been in over 25 years (U.S. Census Bureau, 2000a). This was a relatively low rate compared to those of other industrialized countries whose rates range from a low of 2.3 in Luxembourg to a high of 15.9 in Spain (see Figure 10.6). Some countries, like Japan, have traditionally low rates of unemployment. However, even in Japan, where in the past many individuals could count on lifetime employment, the unemployment rate increased from 3.4 percent in 1995 to 4.7 percent in 1999, the highest level since the government started collecting data using its present methods in 1953.

Political events and structural transformations—economic growth or slowdowns, global competition, mergers, and new technologies—all affect the size and composition of the work force and, in turn, have a major impact on family incomes. How high the unemployment rate will climb will depend not only on the U.S. government's (and its coalition allies') ability to prevent further terrorist attacks and lessen violence around the world but also on the confidence of the consuming public.

Any one set of figures, however, doesn't tell the full story of unemployment in this country. In any given year millions

Figure 10.6

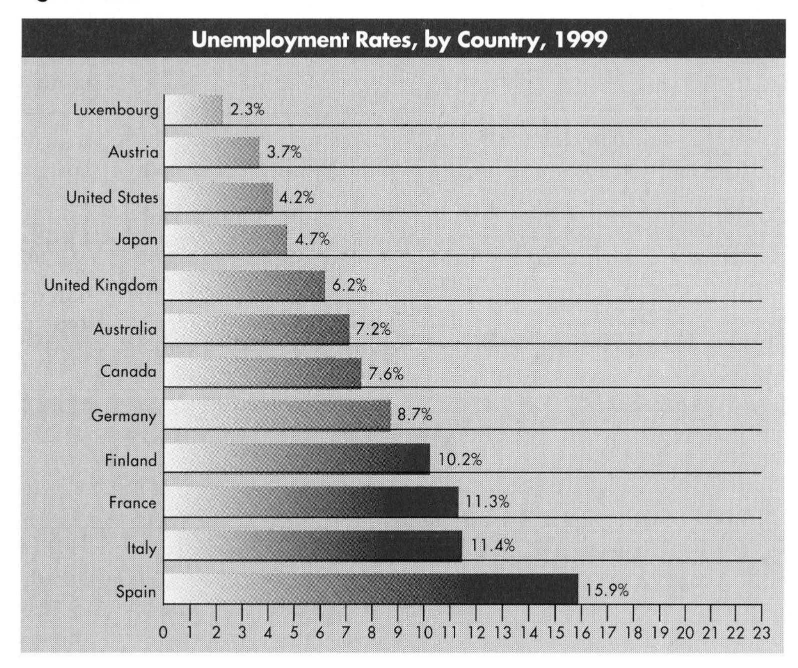

Source: U.S. Census Bureau, 2000a, *Statistical Abstract of the United States, 2000* (Washington, DC: U.S. Government Printing Office): 838, Table 1377.

of other people are not counted among the unemployed. Some cannot seek work because of family responsibilities, illness, or disability, or because they are in school. Others, unsuccessful in their job quest, give up looking for work. The federal government calls these individuals "discouraged workers." In 1999, there were approximately 300,000 such workers.

Have you ever been unemployed when you wanted to be working? Do you know anyone who is currently unemployed? How do the unemployed see themselves? How does society view them? How are family relationships changed when one or more members is unemployed?

Unemployment affects individuals and families in many ways. Clearly, the immediate result of becoming jobless is the loss of or at least a lowering of income. This loss of income puts a severe strain on family budgets and in extreme cases can lead to homelessness. Unemployment can also have a negative impact on family and social life. For example, things often taken for granted—home entertaining, going out with friends for dinner or a movie, exchanging cards and presents—may no longer be possible. Children may feel isolated and rejected when they cannot participate in the activities of their friends.

Regardless of the causes, the impact of unemployment on family members can be enormous. To understand how devastating the experience of unemployment can be requires an appreciation of the role work plays in our lives. Paid employment is a means for earning a living, for providing food, clothing, shelter, and other basic necessities for ourselves and our families. Success or failure at this task is often the yardstick by which individual self-worth is measured. The unemployed repeatedly describe themselves as "being nothing," as "being looked down on," or as "having self-doubts." Joblessness can erode a person's self-esteem, which in turn can lead to other problems. As we shall see in the next chapter, a poor self-image may be a contributing factor to family violence.

Besides giving us a sense of identity and worth, work also provides opportunities for social interactions and gives structure to our lives. Some people who lack this ordering in their lives frequently feel psychologically adrift and may seek to escape these feelings through alcohol or other drugs. Other reactions to unemployment can be deadly. One researcher has statistically correlated the increase in the aggregate unemployment rate with increases in deaths, suicides, homicides, admissions to state mental hospitals, and sentences to state prisons (Bluestone, 1987).

UNEMPLOYMENT AND MARITAL FUNCTIONING In addition to causing distress for individual family members, unemployment can affect the functioning of the family as a unit. Many researchers have found that unemployment is associated with lower levels of marital satisfaction, marital adjustment and communication, and harmony in family relations (Liem, 1985; Larson, Wilson, and Beley, 1994).

Joblessness can also lead to a disruption in previously agreed-upon family roles, resulting in dissatisfaction for one or both partners. For example, Patrick Burman (1988), in his study of unemployment in Canada, found that when wives were unemployed, the egalitarian norms they had negotiated with their spouses disappeared. Consequently, the wives were forced back into the traditional role of housekeeper. As one of his respondents reported, "When I was working, it was more of a joint effort between my husband and I to get it done. . . . But when I was off then—I don't know if it was me or just the way things went—it became more my responsibility, which I really hated. There was no escape from . . . there would always be something to do. . . . I hate it" (quoted in Burman, 1988:171).

Burman also found that when husbands were unemployed, they tended to do more housework, but not all of it. Although only a small number of househusbands were included in this sample, he found that the men most likely to accept this role were middle class, had some familiarity with feminist ideology, and felt confident that they would find another job, at which time they could abandon the househusband role.

VARIATIONS IN FAMILY RESPONSES TO UNEMPLOYMENT As in other areas of family life, families differ in their ability to respond to a member's unemployment. In some cases families can absorb the loss of income and provide emotional and physical support for their unemployed member until such time as new work is found. How family members react to unemployment depends a great deal on how the family functioned prior to the onset of unemployment as well as on the reasons for the unemployment. Patricia Voydanoff (1983) uses family stress theory to explain the conditions under which unemployment contributes to family crisis or disrupts family functioning. The model she uses is Reuben Hill's (1958) formulation of the A, B, C, X model of family crisis. A is the event (unemployment) that interacts with B (the family's crisis-meeting resources) that interacts with C (the definition the family gives to the event). This produces X (the crisis—the degree to which family functioning is affected).

Unemployment (A) hits some families harder than others. Families who receive unemployment compensation or severance pay or who anticipate new employment might experience fewer financial and psychological hardships than families lacking these benefits. Among the unemployed, women are least likely to have these benefits. Families also differ in the number and effectiveness of the resources (B) they have for coping with stressful events. Family savings, homeownership, additional sources of income, good communication, and problem-solving skills can minimize the problems associated with unemployment. Research shows that marriages based on a sharing model, in which both partners can perform economic and household labor competently, are more flexible and therefore better equipped to respond to the unemployment or loss of a partner than marriages based on strict gender specialization (Oppenheimer, 1997). Additionally, how the family defines unemployment (C) is critical to the outcome. "If the family perceives the event as a crisis-producing situation, the likelihood of crisis is increased; if the family considers the event to be normal or manageable, family vulnerability to crisis is reduced" (Voydanoff, 1983:244).

Implicit in the family stress model are mechanisms for minimizing the negative consequences of unemployment. Leaving aside the need for more jobs, adequate financial assistance in the form of unemployment compensation and health insurance would help families get through a period of unemployment with fewer difficulties. Additionally, educational or counseling programs aimed at improving family functioning would help families cope with the stresses of unemployment. Finally, knowledge about the structural causes of unemployment would help families define unemployment in a realistic way and lessen the tendency to blame individual members for the problem.

AGE, RACE, ETHNICITY, AND UNEMPLOYMENT Table 10.4 shows that like social rewards, unemployment is unevenly distributed throughout the population. In 1999, the unemployment rate for teenagers between the ages of 16 and 19 was 13.9 percent, compared with 4.2 percent for the population 16 and over. The problem was even more severe for youth of color. The unemployment rate for black teenagers was 27.9 percent, over twice that of white teenagers. Latinas/os were in the middle, with an unemployment rate of 18.6 percent. Teenaged girls had slightly lower unemployment rates than their male counterparts.

Youth unemployment is troubling for a number of reasons. First, a family may depend on income contributions from teenaged members for its economic well-being. Even when teenagers' earnings go directly toward meeting personal needs—clothing, books, and entertainment—this contribution is likely to relieve some of the pressure on

Table 10.4

Unemployment Rates by Sex, Age, Race/Ethnicity, 1999

	Age	
	16 and over	16–19
Total	4.2%	13.9%
Sex		
Males	4.1	14.7
Females	4.3	13.2
Race/Ethnicity		
Whites	3.7	12.0
Blacks	8.0	27.9
Latinas/os	6.4	18.6

Source: U.S. Census Bureau, 2000a, *Statistical Abstract of the United States, 2000* (Washington, DC: U.S. Government Printing Office): 422, Table 674.

household budgets. Second, research indicates that adolescents who have a job are less likely than their unemployed counterparts to become involved in illegal activities such as drug dealing and theft. Finally, if this high unemployment rate continues, the likelihood that these teenagers will establish stable marriages and make long-term commitments to the labor force will diminish.

Similarly, in adulthood the burden of unemployment continues to fall more heavily on people of color despite the progress in civil rights and affirmative action of the last 3 decades. Among the hardest hit by unemployment are Native Americans. According to the U.S. Department of Commerce (1993), the unemployment rate for Native Americans was 14.4 percent. However, this figure underrepresents the extent of the problem because large numbers of Native Americans live on reservations where efforts to seek employment don't make much sense since few employment opportunities exist in those areas. Thus, many Native Americans fit the profile of "discouraged workers."

Additionally, significant numbers of people experience what economists call **underemployment**. Underemployment takes several forms. Some of the underemployed are people who are employed part-time but who want to work full-time, a condition called *involuntary part-time employment*. In 1994 there were 5 million such workers (U.S. Census Bureau, 1995:409). These workers face significant problems; they are six times more likely than full-time workers to earn minimum wage and much less likely to receive health and pension benefits (Cloward and Piven, 1993). Other underemployed individuals work full-time but make very low wages. These are the working poor, discussed earlier in this chapter, and their numbers are growing. The category of underemployed also includes workers with skills higher than those required by their current job. Like the unemployed, those who are underemployed worry about family finances and may experience low levels of marital and family satisfaction as a result.

This discussion of unemployment and underemployment illustrates C. Wright Mills's distinction between personal troubles and social issues (see Chapter 1). Unemployment of this magnitude is not simply a personal trouble of affected families, it is also a social problem. Thus, solving the problem of unemployment requires action on the part of the larger society to create more jobs or to provide meaningful alternatives for those who cannot work. Two pieces of legislation—the Employment Act of 1946 and the Full Employment and Balanced Growth Act of 1978—recognize the federal government's obligation to use all practical means to secure the right to employment for all citizens. To date, however, neither the federal government nor the private sector has been able to reach this goal.

Homelessness

Unemployment can trigger many problems, one of which is homelessness. Although unemployment often leads to homelessness, employment does not always guarantee a place to live. According to the U.S. Conference of Mayors' Task Force on Hunger and Homelessness (2000), 26 percent of the homeless in the 25 cities surveyed are employed. In some cities the percentage is much higher. For example, in Chicago, 50 percent of the estimated 80,000 homeless work either part-time or full-time but cannot afford housing (*Streetwise*, 1995:2).

Homelessness is not a new phenomenon either in world history or U.S. history (Rossi, 1989). The minutes of seventeenth-century New England town meetings point to the existence of a transient homeless population composed mainly of single men and women but also including a substantial number of two-parent families. The colonial authorities responded to the problem of homelessness by making social distinctions among the homeless population. Homeless members of the community would usually be provided for in some manner. Newcomers, however, especially those without visible means of support, did not fare well. Some were subjected to a process called "binding out," in which they were indentured to local families to work as servants or common laborers.

The American Dream of owning a home is beyond the reach of many families today. In fact, increasing numbers of families have slipped into homelessness. For this San Jose family, home is a car.

Others experienced a "warning-out" process, whereby they were told to leave town. This latter process was given new meaning during the depression and in more recent years when local authorities removed the poor from their communities by providing them with bus tickets to other cities. This "Greyhound relief," as it was called, was aimed at curtailing the tax burdens of the towns by removing indigent people (Rossi, 1989; Wright, 1989).

The Homeless Today The homeless population today is diverse and encompasses every age, race, religion, and marital status. Homelessness is not confined to the United States, but is a problem in other industrialized countries as well. Even in Japan, with its high yearly per capita income of over $28,000, homelessness is on the increase. The homeless inhabit every region of the country, from inner-city neighborhoods to the rural countryside. If you spend any time in parks or public facilities, be they bus or train stations, libraries, or airports, you will encounter the homeless. What you will observe if you look closely is a population that includes the young and the old, the unmarried and family groups, veterans, the working poor, and people from all racial and ethnic groups.

How many Americans are currently homeless? No one can answer this question with certainty because there is no agreement on how to define homelessness. Sociologist Peter Rossi (1989) distinguishes two kinds of homelessness. The "literally homeless" are those who already live on the streets. The "precariously housed" are those who are in danger of losing their homes or who have lost their homes but have found temporary shelter with friends or relatives. Extended families often provide support by taking in homeless relatives, sometimes exhausting their own resources in the process. Therefore, if we use the first definition only, the number of homeless we count will be smaller than if we expand our definition to include those who are poorly or only temporarily housed. Most studies of the homeless have used the first definition, thereby understating the extent of the problem.

The fact that homeless people tend to move in and out of shelters and public view on a regular basis also makes counting them difficult. For some people homelessness is short-term—the result of a fire, an eviction, family estrangement, or temporary financial difficulties—whereas for others it is permanent. Finally, we can count people only if we can locate them. Not all homeless people are in shelters. Many live in parks, cars, cardboard boxes, doorways, or other places not readily accessible to researchers. Thus, any published figures on homelessness must be interpreted with caution. According to one study, some 12 million adult residents of the United States have been homeless at some point in their lives (Link et al., 1995). The strong economy of recent years had little positive impact on hunger and homelessness. In the 25 cities surveyed by the U.S. Conference of Mayors (2000), requests for food assistance by families with children had increased by an average of 16 percent, the highest increase since 1991. Sixty-two percent of people requesting emergency food assistance were members of families, and 32 percent of adults requesting food were employed. During the same period, requests for emergency shelter increased by an average of 15 percent, the highest one-year increase of the decade. Requests for shelter by homeless families alone increased by 17 percent, with 23 percent of those requests going unmet. Given the many factors that contribute to homelessness, these numbers are likely to continue to increase in the years ahead.

Who Are the Homeless? Officials estimate that, on average, single men constitute 44 percent of the homeless population, families with children 36 percent, single women 13 percent, and unaccompanied minors 3.7 percent. The homeless population is estimated to be 50 percent black, 35 percent white, 12 percent Latina/o, 2 percent Native American, and 1 percent Asian. Fifteen percent are veterans. Many homeless people suffer from a variety of problems, sometimes more than one. Twenty-two percent are mentally ill; 37 percent are substance abusers (U.S. Conference of Mayors, 2000).

Children account for 25 percent of the homeless population. Not only are they at risk of suffering physical and emotional problems because of their homelessness, but homelessness reduces their chances of staying in school or even remaining at their appropriate grade level. More significantly, homelessness may rob them of their parents. Twenty percent of the homeless families in one study had left minor children in someone else's care for extended periods of time (Maza and Hall, 1988). In many cities, families may have to be broken up in order to be sheltered. Some shelters deny access to older boys or fathers, and in some cases children are placed in foster care when their parents' homelessness is discovered.

Causes and Remedies Although experts disagree on the exact numbers of the homeless population, researchers, social workers, public officials, and community activists are in general agreement that homelessness occurs as a result of a number of distinct but interrelated factors:

- A rapid decline in the supply of low-income housing
- An increase in the number of families living in poverty
- Mental illness, compounded by a shortage of adequate services and government policies of deinstitutionalization
- Family violence
- Adolescent runaways
- Unemployment and low earnings
- Substance abuse
- Budget cuts in public welfare programs
- Overall increases in the cost of living
- Racism and sexism

Because homelessness has many causes, no quick and easy solutions are likely. However, reducing poverty, increasing the supply of affordable housing, and expanding employment opportunities would ameliorate a good portion of the problem. The current visibility of the homeless and the discomfort they generate in the population may become a catalyst for political action. Congress took a tentative step in this direction in 1987 with the passage of the McKinney Homeless Assistance Act, which appropriated money for shelters, medical care and services for the chronically mentally ill, and a variety of rehabilitation programs including vocational training. However, after several years of increased public support for spending more money on the homeless (Wright, 1989:34), there is evidence that the public is becoming more intolerant of the homeless population (Smolowe, 1993).

What is your reaction when you meet a homeless person on the street? Do you think your attitude reflects that of most other people? To what extent is homelessness a personal problem or a structural problem? Do you think private efforts can solve the problem of homelessness in cities like yours?

Elba Gonzalez bows her head during a moment of silence honoring those whose deaths were caused by poverty and welfare reform at a rally sponsored by the Kensington Welfare Rights Union in New York. The group, a multiracial organization of poor and homeless families, arrived at the United Nations following a 125-mile march from Philadelphia's Liberty Bell to protest federal and state welfare reform laws.

The Welfare Debate

During the 1990s, increasing attention was focused on the budget deficit and its perceived drain on the U.S. economy. A popular target of the budget cutters was the welfare system. Although many Americans across all income levels receive some government aid, for example, student loans and fellowships, farm and business subsidies, most Americans think of welfare only in terms of the poor, particularly Aid to Families with Dependent Children (AFDC). This program, originally called **Aid to Dependent Children,** was initiated in 1935 as part of the Social Security Act to provide support for children whose parents were deceased or disabled. In 1950, consistent with the then-prevailing ideology that a woman's place was in the home, Congress raised the level of benefits to allow poor mothers to stay home to care for their children. Since that time, however, much has changed. A record number of women with children across all classes are now in the paid labor force. Additionally, the composition of welfare recipients has changed. Instead of a majority of white widows and their children as historically had been the case, by the mid-1990s, the program was serving mostly divorced and unmarried mothers and their children, many of whom were people of color.

As these changes occurred, public officials and the population at large became more critical of the welfare system. Proponents of reform claimed that the existing system was unfair to hardworking taxpayers, encouraged dependency, and was the source of poverty, illegitimacy, and many other social ills. Some reformers assumed that once recipients realized that they would lose their benefits, they would come to their senses and find a job. Those lawmakers and social activists who opposed dramatic changes in the level of benefits argued that the welfare system had lifted many people out of poverty, that many welfare recipients were unable to work, and that contrary to popular belief, giving people welfare benefits did not lead to family disintegration. Rather, they argued that the decline in two-parent families stemmed primarily from a lack of economic opportunity, that a lack of jobs and poverty, not the availability of welfare, encouraged marital dissolution and nonmarriage and undermined the ability of low-income fathers to support their children. As evidence for their position, they pointed out that in other countries with more generous benefits than the United States, out-of-wedlock births, child poverty, and crime were considerably lower.

In 1996, after considerable debate, Congress passed and President Clinton signed the Personal Responsibility and Work Opportunity Reconciliation Act, popularly known as the Welfare Reform Act. Among its main provisions are a work requirement mandating 2 years of assistance with a 5-year cap on the total time a family can receive assistance (known as Temporary Assistance for Needy Families), and significant reductions in the Food Stamp Program. Under this act, states are allowed to drop unwed teenage mothers and their children from the welfare roles unless they attend school and live with an adult. Now that the policy has been in effect for a few years, we can ask the question, "Is welfare reform working?" As the "Social Policy" box indicates, the answer to that question is mixed and troubling. On the one hand, millions of people have been removed from the welfare rolls, leading public officials to claim that the reform is working. On the other hand, there is evidence that the declining welfare rolls simply indicate that fewer people are receiving benefits, not that they are doing better.

SOCIAL POLICY ISSUES

IS WELFARE REFORM WORKING?

The answer to the question, "Is welfare reform working?" depends to a large extent on how we choose to measure it. Early reports from a number of states showed a large drop in welfare rolls, that many welfare recipients, especially those with high school educations, did find jobs, and that the child poverty rate declined slightly. Additionally, the percentage of children living with a single mother declined while the percentage of those living with married parents, a single parent cohabitating with another adult, or a single father increased. However, research conducted by the Children's Defense Fund (2001a), the U.S. Conference of Mayors (2000), and the Center on Budget and Policy Priorities (2001), drawing on new national survey data, found a less optimistic picture.

- Only a small fraction of the new jobs pay above poverty wages.
- In Wisconsin's much-praised welfare experiment, nearly two out of three former recipients had lower income than during the three months before they left welfare.
- Nine state studies compiled by the National Governors' Association and other organizations found that 40 to 50 percent of families who left Temporary Assistance for Needy Families did not have a job at the time of the study.
- The number of families with children who lived in extreme poverty (with cash income below one-half of the poverty line) yet received no welfare or similar means-tested cash benefits jumped from 1.0 million in 1995 to 1.2 million in 2000—a rise of 16 percent.
- An increasing number of families leaving welfare report greater hardships than before, including struggles to get food, shelter, child and medical care. This is especially true in large urban areas.

Several factors help to explain these negative findings. First, even during the economic boom of the 1990s, there were not enough jobs, particularly in large urban areas and poor rural areas. A refrain heard frequently among job seekers is, "I see the ads in the paper. I apply. Then I wait and I wait and I wait. It's frustrating" (Garza, 1995:1). Second, many current recipients are unemployable and will remain that way without further education and training. Third, many new jobs are being created in suburban areas. Without adequate public transportation, or low-income housing matching these new entrants into the labor force with jobs will be difficult, if not impossible. Fourth, parents looking for work are handicapped by an acute shortage of safe day care for their children. Fifth, many welfare recipients are mentally, emotionally, and physically unable to work.

Unfortunately, welfare reform to date has not dealt with the structural causes of poverty or the changing nature of work (Watts, 1997). It is not enough to say, "get a job." Investments in education, job training, and job creation will be necessary to reach the goal of having all able-bodied individuals in the work force. Were such measures implemented and successful, there would still remain a cohort of people who are disabled or caring for someone who is disabled and who could not work.

What do you think? Have you ever known anyone who was a welfare recipient? What kind of experiences did they have? Were they likely to be helped or hindered by the new welfare rules? What programs would you support to help address their needs? Does the federal government have a responsibility to see that its citizens are properly fed, housed, and clothed? Explain your position. Given the reformed welfare system, what can we anticipate happening if the economy slows down or a recession hits?

RESTRUCTURING THE WORKPLACE

Throughout this chapter we have seen how the relationship between work and families has changed drastically. However, a gap exists between the current structures of families and the way other institutions continue to relate to them. For example, many businesses, medical facilities, and government offices are open from 9 A.M. to 5 P.M., when most people are at work. Such schedules may not present problems to traditional families with a single breadwinner and a full-time homemaker. Today, however, when the majority of families are composed of either dual-earner couples or single heads of households, such time conflicts have enormous consequences. This is true not only for parents with children but also for workers who are responsible for bringing an elderly parent or other relative to a doctor. One study by the Bureau of National Affairs found that such conflicts caused working parents to be absent from work about eight days per year (cited in Zedeck and Mosier, 1990:244).

This situation is slowly changing. For example, some branch offices of the U.S. Post Office and some neighborhood medical clinics have extended or altered their traditional hours. Increasingly, employers are aware that they have to make concessions in this area. Given the low birth rates of the past two decades, employers will find themselves competing for workers. The majority of new entrants into the labor force are women and people of color. Those employers who institute organizational changes to help employees balance work and family demands will probably enjoy an advantage in attracting new workers.

Some employers, like this hospital, have responded to the family needs of their employees by creating on-site day-care centers.

Workplace Changes

One of the major problems working parents face is getting children off to school in the morning and having a parent there to greet them when they come home. We are probably all familiar with stories of "latchkey children," children who return home after school to an empty house. According to one government study, approximately 7 million children between the ages of 5 and 14 (18 percent) care for themselves after school (Smith, 2000). Although some forms of unsupervised self-care may lead to the development of problem behavior such as truancy and involvement with drugs, self-care children who are monitored by parents do not seem to suffer negative consequences (Lerner, 1994). Telephone companies report an increase in calls around 3 P.M. as parents and children check in with one another. Some school districts offer afterschool programs to assist working parents, but most do not. Without outside support, families frequently find they must solve this problem by having one parent, usually the wife, work part-time rather than full-time. The economic consequences of this approach include low pay, few benefits, and little or no mobility for the affected worker.

One way companies could respond to this need is by providing permanent part-time employment with benefits for employees with young children. Another alternative is **job sharing**, in which two workers split a single full-time job. Each job sharer gets paid for half-time work, although most usually contribute more than a half-time performance. Thus far, the existing evidence suggests that companies would benefit by getting more than half-time performances for half-time wages. Despite this, however, employers have been slow to experiment with this option. Such changes, however, would help only people in higher-income brackets who could make do with reduced incomes. Other options must be developed for workers in low-paying jobs.

A third approach to meeting family scheduling needs has met with slightly more success in the United States. **Flextime** arrangements, which allow employees to choose when they arrive at and leave work—within specified time limits—can relieve some of this strain. Flextime is especially helpful when one parent can start work early and arrive home early, while the other works a later shift. To date, only about 28 percent of U.S. workers have flextime, compared with more than 50 percent of the work force in Western European countries. However, this benefit is not evenly distributed among workers. Approximately 29 percent of white workers are on flexible schedules compared to 20 percent of African American workers, and 18 percent of Latinas/os. By and large, higher-status occupations tend to provide more opportunities for flextime than lower-status occupations. Flextime often involves telecommunication. Some 30 million people worked at home at least part of the time in 1997 (Allen and Moorman, 1997). Although many people see benefits to this strategy (less travel time, reductions in cost of child care and business clothes, and more relaxed surroundings), others fear it puts more burdens on families (work stress at home, working longer hours, and more expenses in buying and maintaining equipment).

Does allowing workers to select their hours hurt a company's chances of success? To date there is no evidence that flextime diminishes worker productivity; in fact, some evidence suggests the opposite. Hence, flextime can benefit both workers and employers.

Family Leave

Much of the role conflict experienced by workers could be reduced by adequate family leave, which would include maternity and paternity leaves for the birth or adoption of a child as well as leaves to care for an elderly parent. Although more employers are attempting to meet the family needs of their workers, the majority have done little. Costs are often cited as the reason for not developing these types of programs. Some chief executives are now questioning this belief, however. In speeches to colleagues, the chair of the Evanston, Illinois–based Fel-Pro Company, which supplies

WRITING YOUR OWN SCRIPT

WORK/FAMILY DECISIONS

As we have seen in this chapter, the link between work and family is complex and constantly changing. Most families can no longer expect to survive with only the traditional male wage earner. Thus, partners in a relationship have to make considerable personal adjustments if both are working, especially if they have children.

Questions to Consider

1. Do my partner and I want jobs or careers? Will one of our jobs or careers take priority over the other? How will we make employment decisions that involve the other partner? How will we deal with career moves, including geographic relocation, especially if one of us does not want to relocate? If we both work, how will that affect our division of household labor? How will it affect our decision if and when to have children?
2. If our family does not need two wage earners, will we both work anyway? Can either of us consider staying home to take care of the children? Why or why not? If we both need to or want to work, what options do we have for quality child care? What can we do to reduce the stress of work/family conflicts? Some working parents have tried to resolve their work/family conflicts by working at home. Would one or both of us want to work at home? What would be the advantages and disadvantages of this for our personal and family relationships?

parts to the auto industry and which provides extensive family benefits to employees, argues that most businesses are shortsighted. He argues that the typical cost–benefit analyses do not include the intangible gains of improved quality of life these programs can offer workers and their families, which, over the long run, can improve worker productivity. For example, 48 percent of female employees and 25 percent of male employees have spent unproductive time at work because of child-care issues (cited in Zedeck and Mosier, 1990:244). Work disruptions from failures in child-care arrangements affected 6 percent of the 1.5 million employed women with infants in 1988 alone (U.S. Bureau of the Census, 1992:14).

Until recently, the United States was one of the few industrialized countries that did not have a national family leave policy. Finally, in 1993, after two previous failed attempts, Congress passed the **Family and Medical Leave Act**, which allows either parent to take up to 3 months of unpaid leave for births, adoptions, and family emergencies. The bill excludes workers in companies with fewer than 50 employees. Because it provides only for unpaid leave, it is of little help to low-income workers. The benefits fall far short of those in other industrialized countries. For example, in European countries, childbirth-related leave ranges from a low of 3 months in the Netherlands to a high of 3 years in Austria, Finland, Germany, and Hungary. In Sweden, both parents can share in an 18-month leave. Fathers can share in some portion of the leave in Austria, Canada, Denmark, Germany, Hungary, and Norway. Most of these leaves carry a monetary benefit as well (Kamerman, 1996).

Some U.S. business leaders oppose expanding family leave benefits, claiming that they are too expensive and that mandated benefits interfere with the free-enterprise system and should be determined by negotiations between employers and employees rather than by government policy. Proponents, on the other hand, argue that existing state laws mandating parental leave are neither costly nor difficult to implement. A study of parental-leave laws in Minnesota, Oregon, Rhode Island, and Wisconsin seems to support this argument. According to the Families and Work Institute, which conducted the study, "Only 9 percent of businesses polled said it was difficult to implement the laws; 71 percent had no increase in costs for training, and 55 percent said there were no administrative costs in implementing the policy" (Locin, 1991:3). The study also found that fathers took more leave after the laws went into effect, and, not surprisingly, women with higher household incomes took more weeks off than did women with lower household incomes.

Furthermore, unlike all other advanced industrialized countries, the United States has no statutory provision that guarantees a woman pregnancy leave, either paid or unpaid, or that guarantees that she can return to her job after childbirth. In the United States pregnancy leaves are covered by the **Pregnancy Discrimination Act of 1978**, which requires that pregnant employees be treated the same as employees with any temporary disability. One obvious limitation to this law is that employers that don't offer disability insurance to their other employees are not required to provide pregnancy leaves to their workers. Family sociologist Joseph Pleck (1988) points to an additional problem

SEARCHING THE INTERNET

THE 2001 LIST OF "100 BEST" COMPANIES FOR WORKING MOTHERS

The Top Ten:
Bristol-Meyers, Squibb, New York
Citigroup, New York
Fannie Mae, DC
IBM Corp, New York
Marriott International, DC
Morgan Stanley, New York
PricewaterhouseCoopers, New York
Procter & Gamble, Ohio
Prudential, New Jersey
Texas Instrument, Texas

http://www.workingmother.com

with using disability as the mechanism for dealing with childbirth: It excludes fathers from parental leave. Researchers found that less than 40 percent of all women employees were covered by some form of disability or sickness benefits that provided some income replacement (Zedeck and Mosier, 1990). Unfortunately, this legislation has not ended pregnancy discrimination. In 2000 alone, the EEOC received 4160 complaints from women alleging some form of pregnancy discrimination, including firing, demotion, or decreased job responsibilities (Pregnancy Discrimination Charges, 2001). This figure represents only cases reported to one federal agency. It undoubtedly underestimates the scope of the problem, as many women are unaware of this legislation and thus take no action.

Given the widespread movement of mothers into the labor force, the growing number of workers caring for elderly parents, the inability of many families to meet basic economic needs, and the lack of fit between workplace organization and other institutions, it is likely that pressure will build in the United States for improved work/family policies. That this is happening, albeit slowly, can be seen in the "Searching the Internet" box, which lists the top ten best companies for working mothers as identified by *Working Mother* magazine for 2001. When *Working Mother* began compiling a list of family-friendly companies in 1986, only 30 companies made the list; by 1992, the list included 100 companies. Each year since then, the magazine has been able to run a list of the 100 best companies for working parents.

SUMMARY

Although we frequently think of work and family life as discrete activities, research shows that the worlds of work and family affect each other in significant ways. The quality and stability of family life depend to a large extent on the type of work available to family members, and work can have spillover effects, both positive and negative, on family life.

In 1900, only 20 percent of women aged 14 and older were in the labor force, compared with approximately 86 percent of men in that age category. Today, 60 percent of women and 75 percent of men 16 and older are in the labor force. Prior to World War II, the majority of women workers were young, single, poor, and women of color. As late as 1975, only 36.7 percent of married women with children under 6 were in the labor force. By 1999, the comparable figure was approximately 62 percent.

Women work for many of the same reasons men do, particularly to support themselves and their families. The rapid entrance of married women with children into the labor force has altered family life in many ways. The traditional nuclear family consisting of a working husband and a full-time homemaker with dependent children is in the minority today. The typical family today is a dual-earner, or "two-paycheck," family. The attempts by dual-earner couples to integrate work and family experiences affect many aspects of family life: decision-making and power relationships, marital happiness, and the household division of labor. Working couples often experience role overload and role conflict as they struggle to balance the demands of work and family. Lack of affordable quality child care is particularly stressful for working parents of preschool children.

Although the labor force participation rates of women and men are converging, women still confront issues of inequity in the labor market. Among them are occupational segregation, a gender gap in earnings, and sexual harassment.

Parents differ in their ability to provide a decent standard of living for themselves and their families. An increasing number of families are living in poverty. Being employed is not always sufficient to avoid poverty. Nearly two-thirds of all people living in poor families with children live in families with a worker.

The experience of unemployment or underemployment can have severe negative impacts on marital functioning. Unemployment is unevenly distributed throughout the population. It is particularly high among teenagers and people of color. One of the problems connected with unemployment is homelessness. The homeless population today is diverse and encompasses people of every age, race, religion, and marital status.

The welfare system has come under increasing attack by taxpayers and public officials alike. Attempts to move recipients off welfare are likely to fail unless ways are found to create many new entry-level jobs.

Employers are becoming more sensitive to the family needs of their employees. Some programs that have been introduced to help workers are job sharing and flextime. Given the widespread movement of mothers into the labor force and the growing number of workers caring for elderly parents, pressure will likely build for improved work/family policies.

KEY TERMS

labor force participation rate
commuter marriage
role overload
role conflict
occupational distribution
pay equity
sexual harassment
feminization of poverty
working poor
underemployment
Aid to Dependent Children
job sharing
flextime
Family and Medical Leave Act
Pregnancy Discrimination Act of 1978

QUESTIONS FOR STUDY AND REFLECTION

1. Describe the major changes in the characteristics of the U.S. labor force during the last half of the twentieth century. How have these changes affected the quality of family life in the United States? Today, approximately 70 percent of families have two earners. For this reason many people argue that the United States needs a national family policy. To what extent do you think the federal government and employers have a responsibility for resolving some of the problems confronting working parents? Would you be willing to see tax dollars subsidize all or a portion of child care for all working families? Explain.
2. How were household tasks divided in your family of orientation? What was the basis for this division of labor? Did family members perceive this division as equitable? Do you plan to replicate this division of labor in your family of procreation? Why or why not? How is the division of household labor related to marital functioning and satisfaction? How can corporations help working couples balance work and family demands?
3. How have recent economic, social, and political trends, including acts of terrorism, impacted your lifestyle? Have they caused you to be optimistic, unenthused, or pessimistic about the future of the national economy? How has the evolution of a global economy affected the structure and functioning of families throughout the world? Discuss the pros and cons of the global economy that has developed in conjunction with the spread of capitalism. How do you feel about corporations relocating jobs to other parts of the country and to other countries to save on labor costs? Do they have an obligation to employees to pay a "living wage" regardless of their geographic location? Explain.
4. Why do you think the welfare system has become such a popular target of criticism? Why are programs that provide benefits, like deductions on home mortgages, student financial aid, and farm and business subsidies not generally perceived as welfare? What do you think of the current move to force people on welfare into the labor force? Given the increases in the number of working poor, are such efforts likely to succeed?

ADDITIONAL RESOURCES

SOCIOLOGICAL

CHERRY, ROBERT. 2001. *Who Gets the Good Jobs? Combating Race and Gender.* New Brunswick, NJ: Rutgers University Press. Cherry provides a readable and provocative synthesis of the theoretical, historical, and cultural material that sheds new light and understanding as to why discriminatory barriers faced by women and people of color persist even when they conflict with profitability measures.

COLTRANE, SCOTT. 1998. *Gender and Families.* Thousand Oaks, CA: Pine Forge Press. A thorough examination of gender's influence on family roles.

FRANK, ROBERT H., AND PHILIP J. COOK. 1996. *The Winner-Take-All Society.* New York: Free Press. The authors argue that the all-American race to the top of the financial heap has spun out of control in a way that has become too costly, too destructive, and too wasteful for society.

STRINGER, LEE. 1998. *Grand Central Winter.* New York: Seven Stories Press. A riveting chronicle of one man's homelessness and addiction to crack.

LITERARY

SINCLAIR, UPTON. 1981. *The Jungle.* New York: Bantam. Sinclair provides one of the most important and moving works in the literature of social change as he tells the story of Jurgis Rudkus, a young Lithuanian immigrant who arrives in America with dreams of wealth, freedom, and opportunity, but instead encounters injustice and "wage slavery" in the turn-of the-century meat-packing industry. This grim indictment led to government regulations of the food industry.

STEINBECK, JOHN. 1992. *The Grapes of Wrath.* Baltimore: Penguin. In his masterpiece of fiction Steinbeck traces the migration of an Oklahoma dust bowl family to California and their subsequent hardships as migrant farmworkers.

INTERNET

http://www.familiesandwork.org The Web site of the Families and Work Institute provides information on how to improve working conditions and family lives.

http://www.bls.gov The U.S. Department of Labor's Bureau of Labor Statistics provides up-to-date information on the economy, employment, and earnings.

Chapter 11

Violence and Abuse

IN THE NEWS: HOUSTON, TEXAS, AND CHICAGO, ILLINOIS

The murder trial of a Houston mother who is accused of drowning her five children in the family bathtub in June 2001 began in January 2002 with what promised to be one of the most high-profile and emotionally charged trials in recent U.S. history. According to the prosecution, 37-year-old Andrea Yates waited about an hour after her husband, a NASA engineer, went to work and then filled the bathtub in their home and set about methodically drowning her children, who ranged in age from 6 months to 7 years of age. She then called 911 and showed police to the bedroom where she had tucked four of the children into bed, as if asleep. Yates confessed to killing her children and is said to have told police that she had thought about drowning them for months and finally made the decision to act the night before she actually killed them. Yates faces two capital murder charges involving three of her children, but the trial will involve all five. Yates has pleaded not guilty by reason of insanity. Although prosecutors agree that Yates is mentally ill, it does not mean, they say, that she was insane when she killed her children. Thus, prosecutors are seeking the death penalty. Appearing on the CBS television program "60 Minutes," Yates's husband, Rusty Yates, declared his support for his wife and said: "The person that drowned those children is not Andrea. If your brain is sick, then you can think things that aren't real" (Parker, 2002).

At the other end of the age continuum of victims of family violence and abuse is the case of 73-year-old Vera Cooper, who paramedics found unresponsive in a squalid Chicago apartment that she shared with her daughter. Responding to a call a few days after Christmas 2001, police found the elderly woman severely malnourished and dehydrated. She was wearing only a light shirt, even though there were no sheets or blankets on her cockroach-infested bed. Police said they found clothes and garbage strewn around the apartment that was also heavily infested with mice and insects. The woman was taken to a local hospital where she died the next day. The daughter, Vicki Cooper, a 41-year-old airline employee, was charged with criminal neglect of an elderly person. Cooper told authorities that she had not bathed her mother for more than 4 months because she didn't want to do it and that she had "no good reason" for failing to care for her mother. Neighbors said that a stench emanated from the Coopers' apartment for more than a year; in the hallway there was a foul odor and it got stronger on the second floor where the Coopers lived. It was after a neighbor contacted the landlord about the stench coming from the apartment that the elderly Cooper was discovered (Hepp, 2001).

WHAT WOULD YOU DO? If you were called for jury duty to serve at Ms. Yates's trial, would you be sympathetic to her mentally ill defense? If yes, would you tell the judge and the lawyers of your bias so that during the screening process you could be excused from serving on the jury? If not, why not? Along another line, what would you do if you had children and began to feel really stressed and started to think about harming them in some way? What about an aging parent? How would you care for an aging parent and continue to live the lifestyle that you are committed to?

A father who wanted to avoid paying child support injected his infant son with HIV-tainted blood. Subsequently, the boy has developed full-blown AIDS. Recently, a New York mother of seven children starved her 4-year-old to death, allegedly because she neither wanted nor loved her. A 33-year-old man was charged with attempted murder after beating his girlfriend's 14-month-old son into unconsciousness. A father killed his son by repeatedly punching him in the stomach because he was making too much noise during a televised football game. Until recently, most people in the United States probably would have shaken their heads in wonderment at these stories, thinking that they were isolated and unusual acts of cruelty that only the most deranged person could commit. Families, after all, are "havens in a heartless world" (Lasch, 1977:8).

Unfortunately, this picture of families as havens of nonviolence is inaccurate. Instead of havens into which we can retreat for comfort, safety, and nurturing, for many of us, families have increasingly become places of danger. Although most family members do not inject us with HIV-tainted blood, starve us to death, or beat us into unconsciousness, every year millions of Americans intentionally injure, abuse, assault, or murder members of their own families. Domestic or intrafamily violence is interwoven into the very fabric of U.S. society. It is believed to be the most common, yet least reported, crime in this country. In no other U.S. institution or group is violence and abuse more of an everyday occurrence than it is within the family.

THE ROOTS OF FAMILY VIOLENCE: A HISTORICAL CONTEXT

Many people think of family violence as a uniquely American phenomenon that has come into being only in recent years. Records, however, show that as early as the 1640s Americans recognized the existence and seriousness of family violence and abuse and attempted to prevent or punish such behavior (Pleck, 1989). The extent of family violence in America's past is difficult to ascertain, however, because official records were not always kept. Likewise, we know very little about the history of violence across cultures because most cultures around the world have not officially recorded such data. Nonetheless, based on his examination of cultures around the world, anthropologist David Levinson (1981) concluded that family violence is not rare. Furthermore, wife beating is the most common form of family violence. Levinson's findings are consistent with those of most social science research into family violence in the United States, which finds that women are far more often the victims of violence and offenses against family members than are men. Approximately 95 percent of the adult victims of domestic violence in the United States are women. In fact, domestic violence is the single greatest cause of injury to women (Smallwood, 1995; Women against Abuse, 1996).

Violence against Women

The historical subordination of women and children is linked to their experiences of violence and assault in the family. Historical accounts by colonists and missionaries as well as anthropological studies inform us of the extent to which violence against women has been a part of the institutional structure of various societies throughout history. Consider for a moment the following historical facts about women and violence:

- Under Roman law, a husband could chastise, divorce, or kill his wife for adultery, public drunkenness, and other behaviors.
- According to the Decretum (c. 1140), the first enduring systematization of Christian church law, women were "subjects to their men" and in need of punishment to correct their supposed inferiority and susceptibility to the influence of the devil.
- Well into the seventeenth century, in many European countries, including England, a man could legally kill his wife for certain behaviors.
- English common law held that men had a legal right to beat their wives as long as the stick they used was no thicker than the husband's thumb. (This law is the basis of the contemporary saying "rule of thumb.")
- The eighteenth-century Napoleonic Civil Code, which influenced Swiss, Italian, French, and German law, gave men absolute family power. Under this code, men could legally use violence against women up to the point of attempted murder.
- In the 1800s, in both Europe and the United States, men could use "reasonable" physical force against women, which included black eyes and broken noses.
- Sexual assault, as well as severe physical beatings, was an integral part of the female slave experience in the United States.
- A nineteenth-century Mississippi court declared that husbands could use corporal punishment on their wives. Not until 1883 was wife beating banned in the United States.

The folkways and mores of various cultures show the universality of violence in women's lives. According to feminist philosopher Mary Daly (1978), such practices as the binding of young women's feet in China, the Indian suttee (the burning of Indian women on the funeral fires of their husbands), European and American witch burnings, the mutilation of African women's genitals through female circumcision,[1] and past (and some present) gynecological practices in the United States, such as unnecessary surgery and forced sterilization, are all variations of the same thing: violence against women.

As in the past, women continue to be the primary victims of violence. And violence against women continues to cross many geographic lines and borders. For example, despite the termination of military rule in Latin America, the deregulation of India's economy, and the end of apartheid in South Africa, physical and sexual assault of women is still widespread. The violence against women globally is so intense that the United Nations has described it as a "global epidemic of violence against women." Other observers call this violence "terrorism in the home." By whatever name, violence against women is global and "epidemic." For example, worldwide, one in three women have been beaten, forced to have sex, or abused in other ways during their lifetime. Violence against women crosses all borders. For instance, every 83 seconds a woman is raped in South Africa; in many Third

[1]Female circumcision takes several forms. The mildest form involves cutting the hood of the clitoris in a manner similar to the practice of male circumcision. The most severe form of female circumcision involves the removal of the clitoris, labia minora, and most of the labia majora, after which the vagina is stitched closed except for a very small opening to allow for the passage of urine and menstrual blood. Perhaps the most common form of female circumcision involves removing the clitoris and part of the labia minora. This latter type of circumcision is currently practiced in about 40 countries, including East and West Africa, Asia, the Islamic Mideast, and South America. It is not uncommon for as many as 90 to 98 percent of the female population to have undergone one or another form of circumcision without the aid of anesthetics (Renzetti and Curran, 1992; State of the World Population, 1997).

Although anyone is a potential victim of violence, historically women have been the most common victims. Violence against women is deeply rooted in human history as this painting, titled *Examination of a Witch,* shows. Although both women and men were accused of being "witches," most often the person accused was a female who was often jailed and subsequently executed. The 1692 witch trials in Salem, Massachusetts, for example, resulted in 24 executions.
T. H. Matteson, *Examination of a Witch*, 1855. Photo courtesy Peabody Essex Museum. Photo by Mark Sexton.

World countries, 500,000 or more women a year die from pregnancy-related problems, including botched abortions (Wallace, 2002). In the United States, it is estimated that a woman is physically abused every 9 seconds; 4 million women experience a serious assault by an intimate partner during an average 12-month period; 17.7 million women have been raped or been a victim of attempted rape during their lifetimes; every day in the United States four women die as a result of domestic violence, a euphemism for murders and assaults by husbands and boyfriends (Centers for Disease Control and Prevention, 1998; Clark County Prosecuting Attorney, 1999; Family Violence Prevention Fund, 1999). On and on the violence continues (see Table 11.1 for other examples of the global nature of violence against women), and one by one lives are lost, families are shattered, and communities are stunned (Pennsylvania Coalition against Domestic Violence, 2001). In the United States, domestic violence ranks as one of the nation's most expensive health problems. It is estimated that the national cost of domestic violence in medical care alone is between $3 billion and $5 billion annually. Businesses forfeit another $100 million in lost wages, sick leave, absenteeism, and nonproductivity (National Coalition against Domestic Violence, 1998).

Violence against Children

Throughout history, children also have frequently been victims of violence and abuse, including sexual assault. Violence against children is linked to cultural values and attitudes that have defined children as the property of families. In many societies, families were ruled by fathers who virtually held their children's life in their hands. Historian Samuel Radbill (1980) reports that in ancient times a father had the power to withhold the right to life from his child by abandoning the child to die. Although there are no clear records of the actual number of children who died as a result of such practice, **infanticide**—the killing of infants and young children—appears to have been widely practiced throughout much of history. In some societies infants would be killed if they cried too much or if they were sick or deformed. Infanticide has been practiced by a wide range of groups, including some early Native American cultures, where newborns were thrown into a pool of water and declared fit to live only if they rose to the surface and cried. Even adult children did not escape the power of fathers. In France, for example, fathers had the legal right to kill an adult son or daughter under certain conditions.

Historically, girls and children born to unmarried parents have been the primary victims of child violence, abuse, and murder. Like their adult counterparts, girls have been far more vulnerable to family violence and abuse than boys have. Female infanticide continues even today in some societies, such as in parts of China, where male babies are preferred. In the past, much of the violence against children was socially acceptable. Although such treatment is not generally acceptable today, some level of violence against children by parents continues to be condoned (or certainly tolerated) in the United States. Unlike in Sweden, where a parent can be imprisoned for a month for striking a child, in the United States many parents believe in and use corporal punishment when disciplining their children.

Violence against the Elderly

Another group frequently victimized by family violence is the elderly. Little is known about the historical incidence of elder abuse. We do have examples of societal violence directed against the elderly: Older women were the common targets of witchcraft trials, and older men were the most frequent murder victims. During the sixteenth, seventeenth, and eighteenth centuries, elders controlled the economic resources of the family, and independence for adult children came only with the parents' death. Elderly parents were thus frequently the targets of violence and abuse from adult children who sought to express their frustration or to take

Table 11.1

The War against Women: Domestic Violence around the World

- Approximately one-fourth of the world's women are violently abused in their own homes.
- Approximately one-fourth of Australian women who have ever been married or in a de facto relationship has experienced violence by a partner at some time during the relationship.
- In a nationally representative sample of Canadian women, almost one-third (29 percent) of those ever married reported being physically assaulted by their current or former partner.
- A study in Alexandria, Egypt, indicated that domestic violence was the leading cause of injury to women, accounting for one-fourth of all visits by women to trauma units.
- In a survey in the Kisii District of Kenya, 42 percent of women reported being "beaten regularly" by their partners.
- In South America, a study found that 70 percent of all crimes reported to police were of women beaten by their husbands.
- In India, more than 5000 women are killed each year because their dowries are inadequate according to their husbands.
- In countries of the Middle East and Latin America, husbands are often exonerated from killing an unfaithful or disobedient wife.
- Throwing acid to disfigure a woman's face is so common in Bangladesh that it warrants its own section of the penal code.

Sources: Domestic Violence Resource Centre, Brisbane, 1998, "Fact Sheet: Violence against Women Is Widespread," **http://www.dvrc.org.au/fs/stat.htm.** Accessed January 8, 2002; Charlotte Bunch, 1999, "Violence against Women and Girls: The Intolerable Status Quo," in Cheryl Albers, *Sociology of Families: Readings* (Thousand Oaks, CA: Pine Forge Press), pp. 296–98.

control of family resources. Following this period came the industrial era, during which adult children had opportunities to become independent of their parents. Parents often became financially dependent on their children rather than the other way around. This period seems to have witnessed relatively little reported elder abuse (Sigler, 1989). The situation has not changed very much today. Many elderly continue to suffer neglect and abuse in silence out of fear or embarrassment. Therefore, many of these cases go undetected, unless, of course, the victim dies, as in the case of Ms. Cooper, discussed in the section opening this chapter. (We will return to a more detailed discussion of contemporary elder abuse later in this chapter.)

Violence against Siblings

Another kind of violence that historically has occurred within families is sibling abuse. To date, however, few systematic studies of nonfatal sibling violence in the United States have been conducted. One of the problems involved in documenting sibling violence and abuse is that historically parents have considered sibling conflict to be "normal" behavior and therefore have not generally reported it. Even today, there is little information on or public awareness of sibling violence.

How much do you know about family violence? More likely than not, you probably know someone who is either a victim or perpetrator of such behavior. Moreover, it is possible that you have been or will be a victim of family violence yourself. Why is violence of all types so common among members of the most intimate of all human groups—the family? In the following pages we explore this and other questions about family violence. To begin, we look at domestic violence and assault within the context of U.S. culture.

FAMILY VIOLENCE AND U.S. CULTURE

Even a cursory look at any of the national and local media reveals that we live in an increasingly violent culture and world. Crime statistics alone do not capture the full range of violent crime in this country. Statistics from an assortment of Uniform Crime Reports indicate that one violent crime is committed in this country every 21 seconds; an aggravated assault occurs every 37 seconds; a forcible rape occurs every 6 minutes; a robbery occurs every minute; and a murder occurs every 26 minutes. Today, over one-fourth of all reported crimes are crimes of violence (U.S. Department of Justice, 1997). Despite our fears to the contrary, it is not a stranger but a so-called loved one or an acquaintance who is most likely to assault, rape, or murder us. In fact, Americans are more likely to be hit, beaten up, sexually assaulted, and killed in their own homes by other family members than anywhere else or by anyone else. Approximately one-third of all murders in U.S. society are perpetrated by one family member against another, and violent assaults within families have been estimated to account for nearly one-fourth of all serious assaults. Every 5 years the death toll of persons killed by relatives and acquaintances equals that of the entire Vietnam War (National Coalition against Domestic Violence, 1996).

These statistics notwithstanding, only in recent decades has the American public gained an informed awareness of the seriousness, magnitude, and multifaceted nature of domestic violence. This awareness is due, in part, to the efforts of the women's movement (very broadly defined), but also to a number of events that have brought family violence into our living rooms on a daily basis. Consider, for example, the infamous O. J. Simpson trial with the widely publicized 911 tapes that were interpreted as evidence of Mr. Simpson's history of stalking his wife and his verbal and physical abuse of her. Public opinion polls and surveys comparing "pre- and post–O. J. attitudes and behavior" show an increase in the number of women who identify themselves as victims of domestic violence, heightened public awareness of spousal/partner abuse, more public condemnation of domestic violence, as well as uncertainty about how to create violence-free families and communities after the Simpson trial (Family Violence Prevention Fund, 1999).

Since the Simpson trial, several local and nationally publicized cases of adult children's abuse of aging parents have reached our living rooms. For example, well before Chicagoans heard the name of Vera Cooper and how she died, an adult son in Chicago was arrested for criminal neglect and abuse when his mother was found severely emaciated, filthy, and living amidst human and animal feces, an accumulation of years of garbage, and other filth in the apartment they shared. Although we do not know the exact extent of elder abuse in cities like Chicago because of a lack of reporting and of official resources to deal with the problem, we do know that such abuse occurs in every state of the union. This pattern of older parents living in squalor and filth with an offspring who is supposed to be their caretaker is one that authorities are uncovering all too often.

Likewise, incidents of severe child abuse or murder have become almost daily news items. In a well-to-do Chicago suburb in 1999, a 41-year-old woman, despondent over her impending divorce, murdered her three children by poisoning and then smothering them in their beds, and then attempted to kill herself. Two and one-half years later, after a 3-week trial, the mother, Marilyn Lemak, was found guilty on three counts of murder. Deliberating for only 9 hours, the jury rejected the mother's guilty but mentally ill defense ("Mother Accused . . . ," 2001). Hardly before the nation had dealt with the violence of this mother toward her own children, the widely publicized case of Andrea Yates reached our living rooms (see the chapter opening discussion). This time, as we indicated earlier, a mother had killed not three but five of her children, and, again, the public heard that the mother was insane at the time of her violent acts. The jury responded to yet another case of child murder by an intimate—the mother—with a guilty verdict. According to a growing number of observers, violence is not only as American as apple pie, it is often as homemade (Wallace, 2002:5). Just how homemade it is is illustrated in Table 11.2.

Violence, abuse, and assault are deeply rooted in U.S. history and culture, beginning with the founding of this country. The early European American settlers subjected the native populations to widespread violence, abuse, and other atrocities, forcing them off their homelands and onto barren-land prisons called "reservations." Similarly, the American slave system was created and maintained through systematic violence and oppression.

Table 11.2

The Nature and Scope of Domestic Violence in the United States

- The majority of people who are murdered are not killed by a stranger during a holdup or similar crime but are killed by someone they know, 20 percent of the time by a family member.
- Twenty-five to 50 percent of homeless families headed by women left home to escape domestic violence.
- Half the murdered women in the United States are killed by a current or former partner. Women who are divorced, separated, or otherwise estranged from their partners are at highest risk of assault.
- Pregnancy is a particularly dangerous time for women. Approximately 37 percent of pregnant women are physically abused by their partners.
- A Texas survey reported that 34 percent of domestic violence calls to police were repeat calls. A similar study in Kansas found that 85 percent of calls to police were repeat offenses. Fifty percent of the time it was at least the fifth offense.
- There are an estimated 1.5 million cases of elder abuse in domestic settings each year.
- A recent study reported that almost 1 million children in this country experienced demonstrable harm as a result of abuse or neglect. 1100 died from abuse or neglect.
- Additionally, another 40,000 children were sexually abused through rape by a caretaker, and a higher number were sexually molested without rape.
- Children who are abused or witness domestic violence generally are stunted in social and emotional development.
- Physical punishment of children is one of the most effective means of teaching violence.
- Race, ethnicity, and the location of a child's home have no relationship to abuse. However, the incidence of child abuse increases with an increase in family size and an increase in the child's age.
- Sibling abuse occurs at a higher rate among children in families in which both child abuse and spousal abuse are present. While boys are more likely than girls to engage in sibling abuse, both sexes participate in this form of family violence.
- It is estimated that battering occurs in 25 to 35 percent of all same-sex relationships. Some authorities define domestic violence as the third-most severe health problem for gays.

Source: From Harvey Wallace, 1996, 2002. *Family Violence: Legal, Medical and Social Perspectives* (Needham Heights, MA: Allyn and Bacon): 5, 17, 34, 104, 218, 241, 13, 21, 38, 39.

The Media

Today, violence pervades U.S. popular culture. Violent films, for example, comprise almost two-thirds of all films released (Abelard, 2001). Among our most popular films are westerns, war movies, and crime dramas that contain (and sometimes romanticize) widespread death and destruction. The heroes of these films frequently are violent "macho" males. Crime dramas in particular often center around violence perpetrated by males against females. In these films, women are almost routinely terrorized, physically and sexually assaulted, and murdered. Many of these films are so popular they have been developed into movie series with a cultlike following. Film characters such as Jason of *Friday the Thirteenth* and Freddie Kruger from *Nightmare on Elm Street* are classic examples of film characters that have made violence a successful enterprise for movie producers (Wallace, 2002).

Television, like film, presents a constant stream of violent images. In a study of ten television channels during the course of a normal 18-hour viewing day, researchers for *TV Guide* found 1846 individual acts of violence (Zuckerman, 1993). Prime-time television has 13 acts of violence per hour, with even higher rates of violence in cartoons and other programs that are watched primarily by children. For example, some research on violence in children's television shows reports that two-thirds of the shows have violence,

Violence pervades U.S. popular culture. Among today's most popular files are those that glorify the "macho," violent male. They often romanticize and normalize widespread death and destruction through the action of fictional characters such as Gabriel Shear, portrayed by John Travolta in the movie *Swordfish*.

they contain about 20 violent acts each hour, and two-thirds of the time violence is presented in a humorous fashion. Although portraying killing less frequently than other programming, cartoons depict the highest number of violent acts and episodes of any type of television program. On any given Saturday morning, the airwaves are filled with animated violence. By the time the average American child finishes sixth grade (approximately 13 years old), she or he will have watched 100,000 acts of televised violence, including 8000 depictions of murder (Giddens, 1996; Abelard, 2001). Many television shows build their stories around violence and abuse, but ignore the consequences to the victim, perpetrator, and victim's family. They almost never show alternatives to violence. And children's programs are the least likely to depict the long-term consequences of violence ("Facts about Media Violence . . . ," 1997). Added to this are the popular trashy talkshows, like the *Jerry Springer Show*, on the television landscape that cater to sex, violence, and hostility.

Similar trends appear in contemporary music, particularly rock and rap videos. Violence is a recurrent theme, as are rape, mock rapes, the implication of rape, and the anticipation of rape and conquest by males. As sociologists Nijole Benokraitis and Joseph Feagin have concluded: "More than half of the music television videos (MTV) feature or suggest violence, present hostile sexual relations between men and women as commonplace and acceptable, and show male heroes torturing and murdering women for fun" (1986:10). In addition to the visuals, the language itself is often violent and sexually explicit. The audience for these videos includes many teenagers and young adults, who are thus exposed to these attitudes and behaviors as they are growing up. Many experts believe that children emulate what they are exposed to.

Moreover, pornographic films are big business, outnumbering other films three to one and grossing over $3.5 million a year in the United States alone. Research indicates that the major themes of pornographic films are consistent with those in other media: sex, violence, and domination of one person by another, usually women by men. In one study of X-rated films, over four-fifths of the films included scenes in which one or more men dominate and exploit one or more women; three-fourths portrayed physical aggression against women; and one-half explicitly depicted the rape of one or more women (Wood, 1994).

Although the media in general are not pornographic, they do perpetuate themes of sex, violence, and male domination of women. These same themes are pervasive elements of our everyday lives, in which men dominate in number, status, and authority. The pervasiveness of sex and violence toward women in the media acts to desensitize both women and men to the seriousness and unacceptability of violence and assault against human beings. A particularly compelling fact in this regard is the growing body of evidence that exposure to sexual violence through the media is related to greater tolerance, or even approval, of violence (Wood, 1994). For example, one study of television violence on MTV found a strong relationship between women's viewing of sexual violence on MTV and their acceptance of sexual violence as part of *normal* intimate relationships; the more they viewed such violence the more likely they were to define violence as a natural part of female/male relationships and the less likely they were to object to violence perpetrated against them or to defend themselves from violent attacks. In essence, heavy exposure to violence in the media tends to normalize it such that violence and abuse come to be viewed as natural parts of love, sex, and romance (Dieter, 1989).

Added to the traditional media methods of transmitting violence are the new and changing technologies of the Internet and video games. Violence on the Internet, or its potential for violence, has increasingly become a concern, particularly as it relates to children. However, the actual incidence of violence on the Internet is difficult to quantify because the technology has moved faster than our capability to monitor it. Currently most of the data on Internet violence are anecdotal, but its potential as a mechanism that leads to violence is evidenced in the increasing number of documented cases of cyberspace seduction by pedophiles in which children have been lured by on-line predators into traveling to locations hundreds of miles from their homes where they were then sexually assaulted. In addition, not only do a number of Internet sites market a wide variety of violent products to children including those with age restrictions due to violent content, but also anyone, child or adult, can find a variety of violent materials on the Internet that give a formula or recipe for violence and destruction. For example, the Oklahoma bomber obtained a copy of

Turner Diaries, a book that advocates the violent overthrow of government, off the Internet ("Facts about Media . . . ," 1997).

Moreover, video games, which constitute a multibillion-dollar industry in the United States, are increasingly violent, yet increasingly popular, particularly among America's youth. The violent nature of these games has been the subject of intense scrutiny in recent years, and was brought to public attention with the revelation that the young Columbine High School mass murderers, Dylan Klebold and Eric Harris, were addicted to them. Top-selling games, such as the "Mortal Kombat" series, encourage players to engage in a wide range of violent acts, including tearing off their foes' heads, ripping out their hearts, and ripping off the skin of an opponent, leaving only a bloody pile of muscle. While it is important to note that research linking media violence and the violent behavior of Americans is inconsistent, there is a consistency in the research that suggests that a constant diet of these kind of games, as well as media violence generally, desensitizes the habitual player or media observer to violence and its consequences, or at least makes it more tolerable.

Moreover, the popular depiction of the violation of women contributes to what has been called a **rape syndrome** or men's proclivity to rape—the group of factors that collectively characterize men's likelihood to rape. For example, the unwanted, unsolicited pinch on a woman's behind, the wolf whistles and lewd remarks directed at women when they walk down the street, and the unwelcome compliments about a woman's anatomy are all acceptable behaviors among various groups of men. When we tolerate these so-called minor acts, other acts of aggression and violation seem more acceptable.

Violence in popular culture has become so epidemic that in September 2000, the Federal Trade Commission addressed a U.S. Senate committee regarding the marketing of violence, particularly in the entertainment industry and particularly to young people under the age of 18. Some critics of the FTC report and others in the media industry complain that the media have become too sanitized. Whether or not this is the case, since the violence of the terrorist acts of September 11, 2001, many of those who have the power to control media content have either tacitly or overtly agreed to tone down the amount of violence they present in their respective medium.

MYTHS ABOUT VIOLENCE AND ABUSE

A number of oversimplifications, myths, and distortions block our understanding of the nature and extent of marriage, family, and intimate violence. These myths involve issues of race, class, gender, and the mental state of the abuser. Although research has shown many of these beliefs to be overstated or blatantly false, many people continue to believe them. As a consequence, much family violence and abuse goes unrecognized and unreported.

In this section, as we discuss the various forms that family and intimate violence takes, we present and debunk—that is, expose the falseness of—several common myths associated with family violence. We begin by refuting four common myths: (1) Family violence is rare, (2) only mentally ill or "sick" people abuse family members, (3) family violence is essentially a problem of the lower classes, and (4) love is absent in violent families. In following sections we then turn our attention to the many victims, targets, and perpetrators of marriage, family, and intimate violence.

***Myth 1:* Family violence is rare.**

***Fact:* Family violence occurs in epidemic proportions in the United States. Acts of family violence occur anywhere from every 9 to 12 seconds (National Council of Jewish Women, 1999).**

Until the last decade, most Americans considered family violence to be relatively rare. The fact that few reliable statistics on family violence were kept helped perpetuate this misconception. When researchers began to turn their attention to family violence, they discovered that it was far more common and severe than most of us thought.

Consider, for example, the following statistics. Approximately 11 percent of all reported criminal assaults are aggravated assaults between husbands and wives. In some states assaults between spouses constitute as many as one-half of all reported assaults (Gelles and Cornell, 1990). Violence will occur at least once in two-thirds of all marriages. Annually, compared to men, women experience ten times as many incidents of violence by an intimate. In the case of murder, 42 percent of murdered women are killed by their intimate male partners, compared to 6 percent of male homicide victims who are killed by their wives or girlfriends (Family Violence Prevention Fund, 1999). Every year more than a million women seek medical assistance for injuries caused by battering. One in four women who commit suicide was a victim of family violence at some point in her life (National Woman Abuse Action Project, 1991; Violence against Women, 1992). About 2 million U.S. women have been victims of sexual abuse by a father or stepfather. The prevalence of domestic violence among lesbian and gay couples is approximately 25 to 33 percent. Every year, 1 million to 4 million children between the ages of 3 and 17 are abused (punched, kicked, beaten, or attacked with a knife or gun) by parents, stepparents, and guardians, and each year approximately one-fifth of the violence against people 65 years old or older is committed by relatives, intimates, and other persons well known to the victim. It is projected that every year thousands of family members routinely use knives and guns against one another: Each year, approximately 50,000 parents use such weapons against their children, and 175,000 siblings use knives or guns against one another (National Coalition against Domestic Violence, 1996; U.S. Department of Justice, 2000a).

Because the majority of family life occurs in private, obtaining accurate statistics on the extent of family violence and abuse is difficult. The facts and figures presented above, however, go a long way toward indicating the pervasiveness of family violence and shattering the myth that it is a rare occurrence.

Myth 2: **Only mentally ill or "sick" people abuse family members.**

Fact: **Fewer than 10 percent of all cases of family violence and abuse are caused by mental illness or psychiatric disorders (Straus, Gelles, and Steinmetz, 1980).**

When we consider some of the atrocities that family members have committed against each other, it is easy to understand why many people accept the myth that only the mentally ill could possibly be violent toward those they love. For example, a father has sexual intercourse with his 4-month-old daughter; a mother drowns her infant twin daughters; a mother and her common-law husband batter and scald their 2-year-old daughter in boiling hot water until she dies (Straus, Gelles, and Steinmetz, 1980); a mother injects her infant son with human feces and urine ("Real People," 1996). Shrugging off these events as atypical cases in which someone has simply "gone over the edge" misrepresents the realities of family violence and serves to maintain and perpetuate a psychopathology myth of family violence.

Domestic violence is rarely caused by mental illness, but, as we have seen, it is often used as an excuse. In fact, only a small percentage of abusers are actually mentally ill. The vast majority of abusive family members possess none of the symptoms or problems normally associated with people who are mentally ill or are suffering from personality disorders. Researchers have been unable to isolate any particular mental disorder common to abusers that is distinct from those who engage in violent behavior toward the rest of the population. The fact is, domestic violence is too widespread to be caused by mental illness. Most men who assault their partners, for instance, are not violent outside the home. They don't assault or abuse their bosses, colleagues, or friends. When abusive men hit their partners, they often aim the blows at parts of the body where bruises won't show. If abusive men were truly mentally ill, they would not limit their violence in this way. In addition, most people who suffer from various forms of mental illness do not engage in violent or aggressive behavior (Wallace, 2002; Women's Health Care House, 2002). Whatever we think of their behaviors, most abusers are "normal" in the psychological sense of the word. In fact, we would probably have considerable difficulty identifying most perpetrators of violence and abuse as such if we met them at school, at work, or at a party.

It is probably less painful or emotionally easier for us to think that perpetrators of violence are "sick" or "deranged." This kind of thinking often allows us to separate ourselves from this behavior and view it as someone else's problem. However, the major difference between the mentally ill and those who abuse is that abusers use force and intimidation to control others. Abuse is a behavioral choice. The misguided tendency to locate family violence within the personal characteristics of the abuser causes us to lose sight of or ignore completely the social and structural origins of family violence and abuse. As we will see later in this chapter, sociological explanations of family violence discount the idea that violence is located solely in the personality or temperament of the perpetrator and instead focus on interactions among family members and the interplay between families and their social environment.

Myth 3: **Family violence occurs most often in heterosexual, lower-class, and ethnic families.**

Fact: **Family violence is not restricted to any one group; it cuts across all boundaries, including race, class, and sexual orientation (W.O.M.A.N., Inc., 1996; U.S. Department of Justice, 2001a).**

A review of the research on family violence reveals that such violence occurs in every type of social, racial, economic, and age group. The 1987 death of 6-year-old Lisa Steinberg and the subsequent arrest of her parents—Joel Steinberg, a New York City attorney, and Hedda Nussbaum, a former editor of children's books at Random House—may have shocked many Americans, but it also made clear that family violence can be found at every social class level.

In November 1987, New York City police, responding to a call for help, found Lisa Steinberg severely battered and abused and barely alive. Her 18-month-old brother was tied to his playpen and dressed in urine-soaked clothing. Lisa died shortly thereafter. During the trial for her murder (which ended with the conviction of her father, Joel), it was revealed that Hedda Nussbaum herself had been a constant victim of physical violence and abuse throughout her 17-year live-in relationship with her children's father. For almost 2 years this case received extensive media attention. Why do you think this particular case so captivated Americans? The answer probably is that the case did not fit the common stereotypes of family violence. Instead of being perpetrated in a run-down apartment in an inner-city neighborhood by lower-class, unemployed, "minority group" parents (as many Americans envision family violence), the abuse of Lisa, her brother, and her mother occurred within a white, middle-class, professional family environment.

Violence is the reason stated for divorce in 22 percent of middle-class marriages. Educated, successful men, such as lawyers, doctors, politicians, and business executives, beat their wives as regularly and as brutally as do men in other classes ("General Facts about Domestic Violence," 1999). The myth that family violence is confined to the lower classes is the second-most pervasive myth about family violence behind the myth of mental illness (Gelles and Cornell, 1990). The fact is, family violence is an everyday affair, and it occurs across the spectrum of class, from within families living under oppressive conditions in inner cities and the barrios to those living in penthouses and on palatial estates.

Violence against children is an all too common occurrence. This undated family photo shows four of the five children of Andrea Yates, who confessed in June 2001 to murdering all five of her children by drowning them in their home in a suburb of south Houston, Texas.

However, perhaps like many myths, this one contains a grain of truth in that researchers have repeatedly found more reported family violence and abuse among the lower and working classes than among other classes.

These data do not mean, however, that lower-class families are more violent than other families. An important bias in these data is that they are confined to reported cases. Thus, they represent only those individuals or families who get caught in the act of family violence and abuse. Members of lower-class families run a far greater risk of being labeled violent or abusers than do college graduates or highly paid professionals. This is due, in part, to the fact that the lower classes have fewer resources and lack access to and power in the institutions where such labeling takes place. Murray Straus and his colleagues, for example, report a case in which a physician declined to report a family for suspected child abuse because the suspected abuser was a fellow doctor (Gelles and Straus, 1988). In general, many middle- and upper-class abuse victims are not counted because they often have more financial means and resources to keep their abuse hidden from public view. For example, well-to-do battered women often go to a hotel, fly to another state, or see a private therapist as they work through their abuse; they see private physicians instead of going to emergency rooms; they consult lawyers instead of legal aid; and they often live in less crowded areas where people cannot easily hear what is going on behind closed doors (Boyle, 1995; Zambrano, 1995). Not all such cases remain hidden from the public, however, especially cases involving the rich and famous. Over the past 10 years, for example, a rash of male celebrities made the news for battering their wives or partners: among them, in 1993, actor Burt Reynolds; in 1994, football legend O. J. Simpson; in 1996, both Minnesota Vikings quarterback Warren Moon and actor Billie Dee Williams; in 1998, rock star Tommy Lee, husband of actress Pamela Anderson; and in 2001, 27-year-old Jason Kidd, point guard for the Phoenix Suns basketball team. Because women are overwhelmingly the victims, we sometimes find it difficult to think of them as perpetrators of violence. But, in 1998, comic Phil Hartman of "Saturday Night Live" and "NewsRadio" was shot to death in his $1.4 million mansion by his wife, who then killed herself.

To understand the relationship between social class and family violence, we must first be aware of the factors that are most closely associated with woman battering. According to researchers, violence against women is most likely when the following circumstances are present: The husband is unemployed or employed only part-time, usually in manual labor, or he is a high school dropout; the husband is under the age of 30; the wife is a full-time housewife; she has a high school diploma or less education; two or more children are present in the home, and disagreements over the children are common; family income is at or below the poverty line and both spouses are worried about economic security, or the wife is strongly dissatisfied with the family's standard of living; either or both individuals use and/or abuse alcohol and other drugs; and the husband uses alcohol or other drugs as an excuse for violence and aggression (Bachman, 1994; Gelles, 1995; Wallace, 2002). These factors tend to be more characteristic of lower-income families for a variety of reasons; therefore, rates of violence among such families may be slightly higher.

Domestic violence occurs across all sexual orientations as well as across all races and classes. According to some reports, between 50,000 and 100,000 lesbians and 500,000 gays are battered by their partners each year. Domestic violence occurs in lesbian and gay relationships without regard to age, race, class, lifestyle, and socioeconomic boundaries and with the same statistical frequency as in heterosexual relationships. However, lesbian and gay victims receive fewer protections. For example, as many as seven states define domestic violence in a way that excludes same-sex victims, and 21 states have sodomy laws that may require same-sex victims to confess to a crime in order to prove they are in a domestic relationship. In addition, although there are almost 2000 shelters or safe houses for battered women today, many of them routinely deny their services to victims of same-sex battering. Then, too, while lesbians and gays use many of the same forms of abuse that heterosexuals use, they have an additional weapon—the threat of "outing" their partner to family, friends, employees, or the community. However, many battered lesbians and gays fight back to defend themselves—it is yet another myth that same-sex battering and abuse is mutual (American Bar Association, 1999).

> ***Myth 4:* There is an absence of love in violent families.**
> ***Fact:* In spite of the horror of family violence, in most cases family members (both victims and perpetrators of violence) say that they love one another (Utech, 1994).**

This myth is closely related to the myth of family violence as confined to mentally disturbed people. It is rooted in the assumption that a person who is violent must be mentally "sick" and incapable of feelings and emotions, including love. Several researchers (for example, Gelles and Straus, 1988) of family violence have pointed to both the irony and the tragedy of such violence in that it is those who purport to "love" each other that are also the ones who most often violate one another through violence and abuse. For example, very often abused children demonstrate loyalty and love for their abusive parent even as they express fear and distrust. Likewise, wives or women whose partners are violent often indicate that in spite of the violence they experience, they still feel love for their partner. And elderly parents who have been abused by adult children often still feel love for their offspring. This should not be taken to mean that these people are masochistic; rather, according to some observers, it is indicative of the strength and power of human bonding between intimates that love can endure in spite of violence. Moreover, we must keep in mind that violent families are not violent all of the time. In fact, most violent families are characterized by relatively long periods of peace interspersed with violent episodes (Utech, 1994).

PHYSICAL ASSAULT: THE CASE OF BATTERED WOMEN

> *A spaniel, a woman, and a walnut tree*
> *The more they're beaten the better they be.*
>
> —Old English proverb

In this section we consider both the patterns of abuse and the strategies of resistance by victims of violence. Because 95 percent of all spousal or partner assaults are committed by men, we pay most attention here to woman assault or battering. Woman assault has several dimensions. Those most commonly discussed in the literature are battering and sexual assault. Battering, in fact, is the single-most common cause of injury to women—more frequent than automobile accidents, muggings, burglaries, and rapes combined (Family Violence Prevention Fund, 1999). Often, the physical assault of women is accompanied by sexual assault, and it sometimes ends in the murder of the victim. This point is nowhere more poignantly illustrated than in the anonymous letter featured in Table 11.3.

Most experts agree that woman battering is probably the most common and one of the most underreported crimes in this country. The lives, health, and well-being of 51 percent of women in the United States and their children are endangered on a daily basis due to brutal acts of violence committed by an intimate partner. Injuries that battered women receive are at least as serious as injuries suffered in 90 percent of violent felony crimes, yet under state laws, they are almost always classified as misdemeanors. As we have already indicated, a woman is battered approximately every 9 seconds. While you are reading this paragraph, four women will be severely beaten. Physical abuse by an intimate partner is the leading cause of death among women.

The person who is responsible for raising our consciousness on this subject is Erin Pizzey, whose pioneering work titled *Scream Quietly or the Neighbors Will Hear* (1974) shocked many people and made public the problem of intimate violence. Since Pizzey's book, woman battering, along with child abuse, has received a greater share of public, professional, and scientific attention than any other form of family violence.

Perhaps because the question of intimate violence was overlooked until recent times, the research that has been conducted has certain limitations. One shortcoming is the tendency to group all battering against women as "wife battering." In fact, violent treatment is not restricted to

Table 11.3

I Got Flowers Today

I got flowers today. It wasn't my birthday or any other special day. We had our first argument last night, and he said a lot of cruel things that really hurt me. I know he is sorry and didn't mean the things he said, because he sent me flowers today.

I got flowers today. It wasn't our anniversary or any other special day. Last night, he threw me into a wall and started to choke me. It seemed like a nightmare. I couldn't believe it was real. I woke up this morning sore and bruised all over. I know he must be sorry, because he sent me flowers today.

Last night, he beat me up again. And it was much worse than all the other times. If I leave him, what will I do? How will I take care of my kids? What about money? I'm afraid of him and scared to leave. But I know he must be sorry, because he sent me flowers today.

I got flowers today. Today was a very special day. It was the day of my funeral. Last night, he finally killed me. He beat me to death.

If only I had gathered enough courage and strength to leave him, I would not have gotten flowers today.

Anonymous
(Author Unknown)

married women. Rather, women in all marital categories are battered by men they date, are related to, cohabit with, or simply know.

Another limitation of the mainstream literature on woman battering is that most often it fails to represent the experiences of women of color and lesbians. Like other experiences, the experience of intimate violence is not the same for all women. How exactly it differs, however, is unclear from most research. Although some of the research indicates that race, class, and to some degree sexual orientation are important factors in the incidence and nature of intimate violence, seldom do such discussions provide clear documentation. Researchers have yet to investigate systematically, for example, whether there are any issues unique to women of color in violent relationships.

Much the same can be said about sexual orientation. Most of the research on intimate violence either fails to mention the sexual orientation of the people included in the sample or acknowledges that only heterosexuals were studied. The social pressures that contribute to family violence affect women and men of all sexual orientations and races. Due to continued prejudice against homosexuals, however, much of the violence that occurs in lesbian and gay relationships either goes unreported or is judged a "just reward" for people who pursue a "deviant" lifestyle. Moreover, many lesbians deny the very existence of lesbian battering. However, as the statistics on same-sex violence cited earlier reveal, lesbians and gays are not exempt from abusive relationships. This denial is no doubt grounded in the desire to maintain an image of lesbian relationships as violence-free and egalitarian. Unfortunately, this approach has left many lesbians vulnerable, isolated, and at high risk of being a victim of violence (Levy, 1991).

What Is Woman Battering?

In the family violence literature, the terms **woman battering** and *woman assault* are used interchangeably to refer to a range of behaviors that includes hitting, kicking, choking, and the use or threatened use of objects and weapons such as guns and knives. Because many battered women are also sexually abused, some discussions of woman battering include **sexual assault**—violence in the form of forced sexual acts, including vaginal, oral, and anal penetration; bondage, beating; torture; mutilation; bestiality; and group or gang rape. Still other discussions include emotional as well as physical assault.

In general, the pattern of the battering experienced by women is referred to as the **battered-woman syndrome** and is defined in terms of frequency, severity, intent to harm, and the ability to demonstrate injury. Following a classification scheme presented in 1979 by social scientist Murray Straus, most researchers today define and classify battering in terms of severity. Battering is said to be severe if it has a high likelihood of causing injury, causes the victim to seek medical treatment, or is grounds for arrest. Certain forms of battering like slapping, pushing, shoving, grabbing, and throwing objects at the victim do not fit this category.

Battering is generally cyclical in nature. Family violence researcher Lenore Walker (1984) proposed a *cycle of violence theory* that is still often cited today. Moreover, Walker is often called upon as an expert witness in court cases involving woman abuse. The cycle of abuse includes three stages: (1) tension building, in which tension escalates gradually, making the woman increasingly uncomfortable in anticipation of the impending abuse; as the male becomes more violent the female feels less able to defend herself; (2) acute battering, in which the woman is the victim of severe physical and verbal abuse; and (3) loving contrition, in which the man apologizes for his behavior, professes his love, and promises that he will never do it again. After a time, however, the remorse and contrition disappear, and the cycle starts all over again (Walker, 1978, 1984).

Although defining woman battering so as to include every possible type of physical violence is difficult, the limitations of current definitions should not be overlooked. Limiting battering or assault to discrete physical actions excludes a wide range of violence that women experience. Battering is often accompanied by verbal abuse, psychological abuse, and threats or actual violence toward children and other loved ones. Children whose mothers are victims of battery in the home are twice as likely to be abused themselves as those children whose mothers are not victims of abuse. In fact, as violence against women becomes more severe and more frequent in the home, children experience a 300 percent increase in physical violence by the male batterer. Moreover, ignoring "mild" or "less severe" violence overlooks the fact that any use of violence in a marriage or intimate relationship can have long-lasting detrimental effects on both the victim and the couple relationship (Wallace, 2002). In the simplest language, the bottom line is that abuse is abuse whether or not it is severe (by someone else's definition). We concur with Linda Rudnick, executive director of South Shore Women's Center in Plymouth, Rhode Island: "The dynamics are the same—someone is misusing power and controlling someone else's life. It is a pattern of coercive control" (quoted in Haddocks, 1995). According to Julia Scott, in the broadest sense, violence against women is any violation of a woman's personhood, mental or physical integrity, or freedom of movement, and includes all of the ways our society objectifies and oppresses women (1994:20). Thus, a definition of battering that takes into account a fuller range of the violence and abuse is very much needed.

How Prevalent Is Woman Battering?

Official statistics on the prevalence of woman battering rely largely on crime statistics, FBI and police reports, scattered hospital emergency room records, and records from shelters. Although many women report domestic violence only to family, friends, relatives, churches, synagogues, private physicians, and nurses, these sources of information are not included in national crime surveys. In addition, most reports do not show the number of violent incidents experienced by individual battered women and their children (National Coalition against Domestic Violence, 1998). Since 1972, a major source of information on family violence is the National Crime Survey sponsored by the Department of Justice. From a base of 60,000 to 72,000 representative U.S. households, data collection entails a rotating sample of households every 6 months in which personal interviews are used to solicit information concerning the victimization (rape, assault, robbery, and so on) of adult members of the household during the previous 6-month period. These efforts to document notwithstanding, estimating the incidence of woman battering remains difficult, primarily because it typically occurs in private and more often than not goes unreported. Added to this is the fact that women who are battered or assaulted "only once" are rarely labeled as battered. Thus, statistics do not accurately reflect the amount of violence experienced in intimate relationships and in the home. For these reasons, some researchers estimate that the true incidence of woman battering may actually be double the rates reported in most studies.

The difficulties of painting an accurate picture of the prevalence of woman battering notwithstanding, what available statistics do reveal about domestic violence is alarming. For example, at least one-third of domestic violence incidents are serious enough to require hospitalization, emergency room care, or a doctor's attention. In fact, somewhere between 22 and 35 percent of women who visit emergency rooms in the United States are there for symptoms related to ongoing abuse, and 75 percent of these women will have additional injuries requiring treatment within the year (Women against Abuse, 1996). In addition, women who are pregnant are also at great risk of abuse and injury. Almost one-half of all assaults on women by their male partners begin during the first pregnancy. Pregnant women are at twice the risk of battery than nonpregnant women. Studies reveal that 37 percent to 59 percent of pregnant women are physically abused, and the results include hemorrhaging, fetal fractures, rupture of internal organs, placental separation, miscarriages, birth defects, low-birth-weight babies, and stillbirths. Women involved with violent partners during pregnancy are in greater danger because they are less able to avoid or escape the attacker and protect the fetus. Research also indicates that because of jealousy and/or anxiety, abusers are more likely to focus their physical assault on the abdominal area. Added to these statistics is the fact that incidents of battering and abuse among women with disabilities may be as high as 85 percent. Violence defined as less severe is even more common in intimate relationships (National Coalition against Domestic Violence, 1996; Lehman College Art Gallery, 1998).

Moreover, a woman's relationship to the abuser is a key variable. Over two-thirds of violent victimizations against women were committed by someone known to them: husbands, boyfriends, acquaintances, or other relatives. In contrast, victimization by intimates and other relatives accounts for only 5 percent of all violence against men. Men are significantly more likely to be victimized by acquaintances (50 percent) or strangers (44 percent) than by intimates or other relatives. Research shows that women who are physically violated by intimates face a much higher risk of being recurring victims of violence than do women who are victims of a stranger's violence. Yet, ironically, women victimized by intimates are six times less likely than those victimized by strangers to report their violent victimization to police, because they are afraid of reprisal by the offender ("General Facts about Domestic Violence," 1999).

When woman battering is compared across marital status, married women experience battering less often than single, separated, divorced, and never-married women. Marriage also reduces the likelihood of violent crime among men. Never-married men are more likely to commit assault, and they suffer most (60 percent) assaults. They are also five times more likely to rape and commit other violent crimes than are married men (Maginnis, 1995). Women who cohabit are more likely to experience battering than are either single or married women. In fact, cohabiting women are twice as likely to suffer severe battering or violence than are married women. Experts in the field say the violence reported by cohabiting women ranges from pushing or slapping to using a knife or gun (Haddocks, 1995). How might we account for this? Possible explanations are that cohabiting women may simply report battering more often, that violence against cohabiting women is more likely to be labeled as battering than is violence directed against married women, and that cohabiting women may be less willing to accept a battering situation because they are less dependent economically and may not have children. In any case, concern about cohabiting violence is becoming significantly more important as more and more couples choose this lifestyle. Finally, women aged 16 to 24 are the most vulnerable to nonfatal intimate violence, whereas women aged 35 to 49 are the most vulnerable to murder by an intimate partner (U.S. Department of Justice, 2001). Vulnerability includes those women who have never married or are separated and have low incomes. Typically, their offenders are someone known to them, and the violence usually occurs at or near their home.

The statistics presented here notwithstanding, it is noteworthy that according to *Bureau of Justice Statistics* and the results of some recent studies, over the past several years there has been a noticeable decline in the number of reported cases of spousal abuse. There are a number of ways to understand this decline. One explanation is that shelters for abused women provide an escape valve that allows them to leave an abusive relationship. A second is that the widespread publicity in recent years (the post–O. J. Simpson years) about domestic violence might act as a deterrent. And a third possible explanation is that today there is more effective punishment and better treatment for the assaultive partner. However, even though the number of reported cases of spousal abuse may be declining, some scholars believe that its severity is increasing; it is still very prevalent and requires all professionals to be familiar with the nature and dynamics of spousal abuse (Wallace, 2002:182).

Theories of Spousal or Partner Abuse

What causes one human being to physically, emotionally, or otherwise violently abuse another human being that she or he professes to love? Perhaps if we had a definitive answer to this question we could eradicate this form of violence. Unfortunately, to date we have no such answer to this question. However, various scholars across disciplines and professions have attempted to answer this question. In this section, we present a brief and selective review of some explanations.

SOCIAL STRESS Increasingly, life in the United States is characterized by high levels of stress, both for individuals and families. Various structural and environmental forces—such as crime and violence on the streets, gangs and gang warfare, carjackings, downsizing of jobs, jobs moving to other countries, rising unemployment and underemployment, increasing intolerance and racism, fiscal mismanagement, poor social and community services, higher interest rates, decreasing credit power, and increasing personal and property taxes—converge on us, causing an untold amount of stress. The increased level of stress, in turn, finds an outlet in the family or other intimate relationships. Very often, we respond to these stresses in our lives by using violence, all too often directed at the person closest to us, a partner or spouse, and all too often in the form of physical assault. This explanation does not suggest that stress causes violence. Rather, it suggests that violence is one of many responses available to people who suffer from stress.

POWER Power and the imposition of one's will over another is at the root of family conflict and violence. A major characteristic of spousal and partner abuse is the use and abuse of power. Prominent characteristics of both the abuser and the abused are encapsulated in the concept of power. Men generally possess greater physical, social, and political power than women and have an advantage in this regard. If a man abuses power and control in intimate relationships, there is a significant potential for violence; as victims of this violence, women often feel power*less*. Research has demonstrated that couples who share power or conduct themselves as equals in their relationship have the lowest level of conflict and violence. When they do experience conflict, they are better able to resist violence. When dealing with intimate or family violence, *feminist theories* focus on this issue of power and gender inequality and encourage us to examine the influence of gender and gender-structured relations on the institution of the family and the violence and abuse within it. A key to understanding this phenomenon using one of these perspectives is understanding the historical subordination of women to men. Although women have made significant historical contributions to society, men continue to control all major aspects of society (the patriarchal tradition). Thus, feminist perspectives encourage us to examine the social structure that is designed to condone, perhaps even encourage, and perpetuate the superordination (power) of men over women as well as encourage violence toward women.

DEPENDENCY Historically, the institution of marriage has fostered women's economic dependency on a husband. Although this is changing to some degree, women often find themselves dependent on their partner not only for financial support but for emotional and other support as well. Very often, too, there are children involved, which complicates the woman's ability or willingness to leave an abusive relationship. Accordingly, this dependency makes a woman particularly vulnerable to physical abuse and increases her tolerance for it. Research on dependency and violence indicates that the more dependent a woman is, the more likely she is to suffer physical violence from her husband. Dependent wives or partners have fewer alternatives to marriage and fewer resources within the relationship with which to cope with or modify the abuser's behavior. According to Harvey Wallace, "This dependency is a pair of 'golden handcuffs' that binds the spouse to the abusive partner" (2002:186).

ALCOHOL "He had too much to drink." "He's not responsible." "He's really a nice quiet guy when he's not drinking." "When he's sober he wouldn't hurt a fly." Sound familiar? People in this society typically associate violence with alcohol consumption. Various social scientists have suggested that there is indeed a link between the two but have been unable to establish a causal relationship. *Disinhibition theorists* suggest that alcohol releases our inhibitions and alters our judgment, making us capable of behavior that we would not otherwise engage in. *Social-learning theorists* suggest that violence is a learned behavior; we learn violence by observing people who drink and become violent. We rationalize that they are not responsible for their violence because they were *drunk*. Some social-learning theorists suggest that people use alcohol as a means of increasing their power and control over others. An *integrated theoretical perspective* suggests that it is not just the consumption of alcohol but the drinking mixed with a number of other factors that leads to violence—for example, conflict in the relationship and the cultural notion of drinking as an acceptable male behavior. The fact is, although alcohol can make it easier for a man to be violent, the real cause is not alcohol but the abuser's desire for power and control over his partner. As with the claim of mental illness, abusers often use alcohol as an excuse to avoid taking responsibility for their violent behavior. While each of these explanations gives us some insight into drinking and violence, none is definitive (Wallace, 2002).

Even from this cursory and selective review of theories of spousal or partner abuse, it is clear that much more study and research are needed before we can fully understand the determinants and dynamics of spousal and partner abuse and be able to predict the risk for women who enter into intimate relationships. Until such time as we are able to do this, it is instructive for all of us to recognize and understand some of the characteristics of this kind of abuse.

Researchers have noted a number of variables that seem to be conducive to violence in intimate relationships. We have already discussed several of these factors in our discussion of the relationship of social class to abuse. Other variables include:

1. *A high level of family or intimate conflict.* Conflict is present for any number of reasons including conflicting expectations, activities, or interests; gender stereotypic role expectations; high levels of individual or family stress.

2. *A high level of societal violence.* As pointed out elsewhere, American society is characterized by a high level of violence. Violence within families and intimate relationships may simply be an extension of this external violence.

3. *Family socialization in violence.* Growing up in or living in a family that uses violence to resolve conflicts, release stress, or as a principal means of securing compliance teaches us that such behavior is acceptable.

4. *Cultural norms that legitimize family or intimate violence.* Although physical and sexual assault are illegal, various cultural norms including the historical rights of men in marriage tend to legitimize wife or woman battering and chastisement.

5. *Gender stereotypic socialization and sexual inequality.* Many families continue to socialize females and males into rigid gender-stereotypic roles that reinforce a sexual double standard and inequality between the sexes. In marriage this means that the husband is the family head and women and children are his subordinates. A husband's right to use physical force to "control" his wife and children for the most part remains unchallenged. This arrangement of roles and role expectations makes women and children particularly vulnerable to physical and emotional violence. According to J. Ross Eshleman (1991), this kind of violence is a logical extension of a patriarchal system in which the husband is defined as the ruler and head of the family with a right to use whatever means he deems necessary to extract obedience from family members.

6. *The privacy of the American family.* Because we believe that "what goes on behind closed doors" (especially if those doors are within the family residence) is not our concern, many people, including friends, relatives, and other family members, tend to ignore the signs or evidence of violence and abuse by rationalizing that it is a "private" matter between a husband and wife (or two intimate partners) and they have no right to interfere. It is curious, for example, how so many people, including close family members, knew that Nicole Brown Simpson was a battered woman yet no one spoke up until after her violent and tragic death.

Researchers have found that these variables are interrelated and do not act alone in leading to family and intimate violence. Rather they are mutually supporting and reinforcing in producing spousal or partner violence (Utech, 1994: 125–26).

Why Do Women Remain in Abusive Relationships?

If the violence and abuse are so bad, why do women stay in these relationships? This question is often raised and is indicative of our lack of information concerning battered women. Probably one of the most pervasive gender myths pertaining to woman battering is that these women somehow enjoy being beaten. In addition, battered women bear the brunt of considerable **victim blaming**—essentially, justifying the unequal treatment of an individual or group by finding defects in the victims rather than by examining the social and economic factors that contribute to their condition. Many people maintain that female victims of domestic violence are somehow responsible for their mistreatment, or are masochists who enjoy being beaten, which explains their unwillingness to leave the relationship. However, there is no empirical evidence to support this anachronistic psychological viewpoint. The fact is that women do not enjoy, provoke, or deserve battering. No one deserves to be beaten. Victim provocation is no more common in domestic violence than in any other crime. The reasons women remain in violent relationships are far more complex than a simple statement about their strength of character. Victims of domestic violence desperately want the abuse to end and engage in a variety of survival strategies, including calling the police or seeking help from family members, to protect themselves and their children. Silence may also be a survival strategy in some cases. In addition, enduring a beating to keep the batterer from attacking the children may be a coping strategy used by a victim, but it does not mean that the victim enjoys the battering. For many women, leaving is not an option. Leaving a battering situation is not as simple as just packing up and leaving. Leaving could mean living in fear and losing child custody, losing financial support, and experiencing harassment at work. But not leaving does not mean that the situation is okay or that the victim wants to be abused.

Contrary to popular myth, women in violent, abusive relationships often make repeated attempts to leave, particularly when the violence is directed at their children. While we are increasingly aware of the devastation of intimate violence, too few of us know how to help battered women and their children. Even when programs and shelters are available, unlike the shelter pictured, they often cannot accommodate children.

Battered women often make repeated attempts to leave violent relationships, but are prevented from doing so by increased violence and control tactics on the part of the abuser. Research and other scholarship in this area indicate that women remain in battering relationships for a variety of reasons (see, for example, Browne, 1993; Goode, 1994; Mignon, Larson, and Holmes, 2002; Wallace, 2002). One of the most common reasons is fear. Battered women may stay in a violent relationship because they think that the situation is inescapable. They typically feel helpless about getting out of the relationship and fear that any action on their part will contribute to more violence, perhaps even their own death. This fear is not unfounded. Battered women who make the decision to leave an abusive relationship place themselves at great risk and are often in desperate need of a safe place to stay. National statistics indicate that the danger to a victim increases 70 percent when she attempts to leave, with the abuser escalating his use of violence as he loses control. These statistics show that 75 percent of women murdered by their abusive partners are killed in the attempt to leave or after they have left (White, 1995:1). A battered woman may also be concerned for the well-being of her children and may even fear that her abuser will kill himself if she leaves.

In addition to fear, economic dependence and a lack of viable options for housing and support can keep a woman in an abusive relationship. As indicated previously, financial dependence on a man often means that a woman has no resources of her own with which to make changes. Moreover, the community may have no programs or resources to help battered women or their children. Even if there are programs or shelters in the community, most are generally full to capacity and thus cannot help prospective new clients. In addition, many such facilities cannot accommodate children. Most shelters limit the amount of time clients can stay to a brief period, usually about 30 days. Given these factors, even if a woman leaves, economic necessity may force her back to her abusive partner, who might retaliate with even more severe violence and abuse. Or she may face the risk of becoming homeless. Nationally, 50 percent of all homeless women and children are fleeing abusive and violent households. Even if a woman is financially secure, she may not perceive herself as being able to deal with economic matters outside of the relationship.

Sometimes women remain in battering relationships because of religious beliefs. They feel that their faith requires them to keep their marriage and family together at all costs and to honor and obey their husband, submitting to his will. They not only believe that it is their responsibility to make the marriage or relationship work but also that leaving the abusive situation would be an admission of failure. In addition, some women believe that they caused or deserved the battering (Wallace, 2002). Other times women remain in such relationships because they sincerely believe in the notion of the "cult of domesticity" and family harmony (Dobash and Dobash, 1979). Even though their situation does not fit this ideal, they continue to believe that they can reach the ideal. They often feel physically and emotionally trapped by society's expectation of them: Society labels them stupid if they stay in the relationship and a failure if they leave.

Table 11.4

Telltale Signs That a Woman Might Be in an Abusive Relationship

- She is withdrawn, has no close friends. She seldom if ever invites people over, especially when her partner is home. When she does invite people over, visitors get subtle clues that they must leave before her partner returns.
- Whereas she was once an active participant in social activities, she is no longer active and is seldom seen.
- She appears nervous, especially when her partner is around, and she never accepts an invitation or a responsibility without getting his approval or okay first.
- She seldom has money and often "forgets" her checkbook.
- She wears a lot of makeup or sunglasses, indoors as well as outdoors. She also wears a lot of turtlenecks, scarves, long sleeves, and slacks.
- She has many "accidents," some of which seem illogical and suspicious.
- She has unexplained bruises, marks, scratches or welts. She is often vague about how she got these injuries.
- She calls her partner frequently during the workday or whenever she is away from him.
- She seldom makes eye contact and seems aloof and detached.

Source: Adapted from *Family Violence*, M. D. Pagelow. Copyright © 1984 by Praeger Publishers. Reproduced with permission of Greenwood Publishing Group, Inc., Wesport, CT (http://www.greenwood.com).

Some women remain in battering relationships because they believe that children must be raised in a household with a father present. Thus, they endure physical and emotional abuse to keep the family together for the children's sake. Very often, it is when the violence is directed at the children that a woman will take them and leave. More than half of the children whose mothers are battered are also victims of physical abuse (see Table 11.4).

In some cases the fear of being alone keeps women in an abusive relationship. Often women in battering situations have no meaningful relationships outside their marriage or intimate relationship. The husband or lover may have systematically cut off all her ties to family, friends, and other supportive people. Having nowhere to go and no one to turn to she remains with her abuser. Although some people might not understand this, some women in abusive relationships remain because of pity—they feel sorry for their abuser. They believe that he really loves them but he simply can't control himself. In pitying the abuser they often put his needs ahead of their own. In other cases, low self-esteem keeps some women in an abusive relationship. As the battering continues, the abused loses confidence in herself, and her self-value and self-worth decline.

Finally, a common reason why women remain in violent relationships is love. Many women want the violence to end, but not the relationship. The relationship may have positive aspects that these women feel are worth saving. They love their partner and believe that he loves them as well. Additionally, many battered women believe that their abuser will change and the battering will stop. They may take many steps to try to stop the abuse; leaving home may be their last resort.

Each of the factors we have discussed acts as a barrier to a woman trying to leave an abusive relationship. However, battered women actively seek help from a variety of sources in ending the cycle of violence. Very often, however, the failure of various professionals and systems to provide adequate support keeps women in violent relationships. In spite of all the reasons why some women remain in abusive relationships, most battered women work hard to leave; most do, in fact, leave their abuser at some point, even if only temporarily. It is estimated that battered women who leave the battering situation do so, on average, eight times before they leave permanently (Boyle, 1995). Those who make it beyond the barriers and do not go back are the fortunate ones who find support for their leaving the abuser, and most of them go on to lead healthy, happy, and productive lives.

Mentally put yourself in the shoes of a battered woman. Would you leave? Where would you go? How many services are available for women who are victims of courtship or marital violence at the college or university you are now attending? Are there offices you can go to? People you can talk to? Do you know women who are in battering relationships? What reasons, if any, do they give for remaining in such relationships? Are the reasons similar to or the same as some of those found above?

Confronting Intimate Violence

Do you know someone who is in an abusive relationship? Do you know what to look for? Table 11.4 lists some of the factors that might indicate that a woman is in an abusive relationship. If you know someone who is abused have you tried to help? What have you done? Many individuals and groups are urging the public—relatives, friends, and neighbors—to get involved, to take a stand against abuse, to help stop intimate violence, to intervene to help battered women and their children. For example, in a series of powerful public service announcements depicting the plight of abused women and children, begun in 1994, the San Francisco–based Family Violence Prevention Fund (FUND), has conducted a highly successful education campaign designed to prevent and reduce family violence. Using the theme There's No Excuse for Domestic Violence, the FUND has developed public service announcements such as the one shown on page 353. Another, designed to encourage intervention with batterers, reads:

> *It's Hard to Confront a Friend Who Abuses His Wife,*
> *But Not Nearly as Hard as Being His Wife.*

Additionally, a radio announcement features a woman talking about her struggle to find the right words to say to her abused friend. The announcement concludes: "I just knew if I said the wrong thing, I'd lose her friendship. So I didn't say anything. And instead . . . I lost my friend" (New PSA's against Domestic Violence, 1996:2). These public service announcements go to the heart of the problem of society's silence about intimate violence. While we are increasingly aware of the devastation of intimate violence, too few of us know how to help battered women and children. The FUND urges the public to call a toll-free number (1-800-ABUSE) to receive a free copy of an easy-to-read booklet titled *Take Action.* The booklet provides a guide to simple, safe, and effective ways in which we can help battered women and children and includes information and tips on a range of interventions, including reaching out to women you suspect are being abused, helping children who face violence in their homes, teaching young people that violence against women is never acceptable, and approaching men you know or suspect are batterers.

THE SEXUAL ASSAULT OF WOMEN

Battering is not the only form of abuse experienced by women in intimate relationships. Millions of women in the United States and around the world have suffered or will suffer some form of sexual assault. Sexual assault is a broad term that incorporates any behaviors, either physical or verbal, intended to coerce an individual into sexual activity against her or his will. Sexual assault is extremely widespread in U.S. society, with women and children representing the majority of the victims. In fact, two decades ago, statisticians claimed that the average woman was as likely to suffer a sexual attack as she was to be diagnosed as having cancer or to be divorced (Johnson, 1980). Looking at today's statistics on rape and the sexual assault of women, it seems that this statistic has changed little.

One of the most extreme forms of sexual assault is rape. Every 2 minutes, a woman is raped somewhere in the United States (U.S. Department of Justice, 2001a). Rape is legally defined as sexual assault in which a man uses his penis to vaginally penetrate a woman against her will, by force or threat of force or when she is mentally or physically unable to give her consent. This definition overlooks the fact that men and boys are sometimes victims of rape as well. Some states have broadened the legal definition of rape by removing sex-specific language so as to include males (who are almost always victimized by other males). The U.S. Department of Justice (2001b) estimates that 1 in every 10 rape and sexual assault victims is male and that 1 in 33 (about 3 percent) men has experienced an attempted or completed rape in his lifetime, compared to 1 in 6 women. In addition, the FBI estimates that 1 woman in every 12 *will be* a victim of rape or attempted rape during her lifetime. As these figures reveal, the overwhelming majority (9 in every

Talking with a female relative or friend who we know or suspect is a victim of violence and abuse is never easy. We often remain silent for fear that we will not say the right thing in just the right way. Given that one out of every three murdered women is killed by her husband or boyfriend, our relative or friend may not have the luxury of waiting until we find the right words.

10) of rape victims are female. Contrary to what some people believe, rape is not about sexual arousal. Rather, it is about the violent abuse of power. Whether an attempted or completed sexual assault, it is an act of violence instigated by one or more persons against another human being (Doyle and Paludi, 1995). In essence, some observers have described rape as a terrorist tactic, a tangible and symbolic way for men to keep women in a subordinate position (Soroka and Bryjak, 1999). A typical female rape victim, for instance, is raped nearly three times a year, often by her husband or domestic partner. In fact, contrary to popular myth, the rapist is not typically a "masked man" or stranger. Rather, rapists are typically people known to the victim. For example, approximately two-thirds (62 percent) of female rape victims know their assailant, who is either a friend or acquaintance (43 percent), an intimate (17 percent), or some other relative (2 percent). In addition, the rapist is not typically hiding in the bushes. About 41 percent of all rapes in the United States take place in the victim's home, another 19 percent take place in the home of a friend, relative, or neighbor, and 63 percent are perpetrated by husbands or acquaintances. Of those rapes that do not occur in the victim's own home or in that of a friend or relative, more than one-half occur within one mile of where the victim lives (U.S. Department of Justice, 2001b).

Rape is the most frequently committed violent crime in the United States. It is also the least reported of all such crimes. It is estimated that as many as three-fourths of rapes and sexual assaults are not reported to law enforcement officials—three out of every four (U.S. Department of Justice, 2001c). Thus, statistics on rape are considerably understated. Estimates of rape would be even higher if they included assaults on young girls by their fathers, stepfathers, and other male relatives (usually categorized separately as incest), cases of statutory rape, and cases of male rape both within and outside of prison. Statistics on rape provided by the FBI do not include these categories, nor do they include date and marital rape.

Females of all ages have been victims of rape. That no age is immune to rape is indicated in the findings from a study of a Washington, D.C., hospital in which those treated for rape ranged from a 15-month-old baby girl to an 82-year-old woman (Benokraitis and Feagin, 1986). Approximately one-third of all juvenile victims of sexual abuse cases are children younger than 6 years of age. Adolescent and young adult women are at the highest risk, however. Risk peaks in the late teens: Girls 16 to 19 years of age are about four times more likely than the general population to be victims of rape, attempted rape, or sexual assault (U.S. Department of Justice, 2001b). Data concerning the likelihood of rape indicate a link between a woman's economic status, her race, and rape. The majority of rapists are under the age of 25, and their victims are typically white women, also under the age of 25, divorced or separated, poor, and unemployed or a student. Among people 12 years and older, 83 percent of rape victims are white, 13 percent are African American, and 4 percent are of other races (U.S. Department of Justice, 2001b). However, women of color are at greater risk, with African American, teenaged, and urban working-class girls running the greatest risk of being raped (FBI, 1999). According to some researchers, the risk of rape for African American women is so great that elderly African American women are just as likely to be raped as young white women (Gollin, 1980, cited in Doyle and Paludi, 1995:159). These statistics are all the more significant given that, in general, when violence in the African American community is discussed, its impact for African American women is usually minimized relative to the focus placed on the street violence suffered or perpetrated by African American males. While the street violence associated with African American males is significant and has a devastating impact on African American women, the most devastating form of violence in the life of African American women is sexual assault and domestic violence (Marriott, 1994). There is a significant difference among women across race in the reporting of rape and physical assault. For example, Native American and Alaska Native women are most likely to report rape and physical assault victimization, while Asian/Pacific Islander women are least likely. Nonetheless, according to the FBI arrests are made in over one-half of the forcible rapes reported to law enforcement officials in recent years (FBI, 1996; Idaho Council on Domestic Violence, 1998).

Furthermore, divorced or separated women have been found to be more vulnerable to rape than women who have never been married. Married women are much less likely to be raped than divorced, separated, or never-married women. The likelihood of being raped is also higher for female heads of households and has a direct relationship to the amount of time a woman spends in public places (Andersen, 1988). The perpetrator of rape or sexual assault is typically white (52 percent) and 25 years of age or younger. Interestingly, 22 percent of imprisoned rapists report that they are married. And in about one in three sexual assaults, the perpetrator was intoxicated either with alcohol or other drugs (National Center for Policy Analysis, 2001; U.S. Department of Justice, 2001b). Men and boys are at greatest risk of being raped under conditions of incarceration (although this is not the only environment in which the rape of males occurs). And they are even less likely than women to report that they have been raped. Gay men, like their heterosexual counterparts, seldom report this type of victimization. We will discuss male battering and rape in more detail later in this chapter.

Rape Myths

An enormous amount of myth surrounds rape. Many people, female and male alike, hold erroneous notions about rape, rape victims, and rapists. You have probably heard most of these myths, and you might even believe some of them. Two of the most persistent rape myths are that male sexual violence is caused by the attitudes and behaviors of female victims, and African American males are the primary perpetrators of rape. In the following discussion we examine these two myths more closely.

Rape and Race Because of the relentless link of African American males to violence and crime, many people mistakenly believe that the majority of rapists are African American males who are usually strangers to their victims. In fact, as we have seen, in most cases the rapist knows her/his victim. Statistics reveal that most rapes, especially those of white and young female victims, occur within the same race. Therefore, the myth that African American men commit the majority of rapes is just that—a myth.

Nevertheless, the myth of the African American male rapist, especially of white women, persists. As some scholars have pointed out, such a myth is dangerous in that it diverts the attention of white women away from the most likely sources of their sexual assault: white men. At the same time, it serves as a justification for negative attitudes toward and treatment of African American males.

Blaming the Victim Another common myth surrounding rape is that most (if not all) women secretly desire to be raped, that it is their greatest sexual fantasy. According to this belief, rape victims have generally acted in a manner that "invited" the rape; for example, they were a tease, had a sexy smile, were out too late, were too friendly, or were dressed seductively. The fact is that women actually fear rape; in fact, they fear it more than any other crime. Researcher Susan Griffin (1979), for example, expresses the view held by most women:

> I have never been free of the fear of rape. From a very early age I, like most women, have thought of rape as part of my natural environment . . . something to be feared . . . like fire or lightning. (Quoted in Doyle and Paludi, 1995:160)

Women must constantly act defensively; they must try not to be alone in public, especially at night. In one study, 40 percent of women said they avoid going out at night, while fewer than one in ten men avoid doing so (North Carolina Coalition against Domestic Violence, 2002). Such fear acts to pressure some women into accepting their oppression and subordination. See Table 11.5 for a detailed list of common rape myths. Rape myths notwithstanding, no matter how a woman dresses, walks, or talks, when she says no she means no, not yes or maybe. A man who has forced sexual intercourse with a woman who says no is exercising his power and ability to dominate her, and he is committing the violent crime of rape.

Marital Rape

The limited available information suggests that marital rape is widespread. As with other forms of intimate violence, the majority of victims are female. Victims of marital rape are often referred to as "hidden victims" because they seldom report their experiences. In their extensive research on marital rape; David Finkelhor and Kersti Yllo (1995) found a rather blasé attitude toward marital rape: respondents viewed it as simply a matter of the husband wanting it but the wife doesn't. In essence, his response is that's too bad, I'm going to do it anyway, and he does. This kind of attitude, as well as the shame and intimidation of the victim, makes it extremely hard for the wife to come forward and report her husband's assault. Marital rape is typically not a random act; it generally occurs within the context of an abusive and exploitative relationship. According to Finkelhor and Yllo, marital rape has very little to do with sex and much more to do with anger, resentment, humiliation, and degradation.

The impacts of marital rape are no less serious and are sometimes more frightening than those of rape by

Table 11.5

Common Rape Myths
• A woman who gets raped deserves it, especially if she agreed to go to the man's house or ride in his car.
• Some women enjoy rape.
• It wasn't rape, it was just "rough sex." Women like it that way.
• Women say "no" when they really mean "yes."
• Women provoke men by the way they dress, walk, talk, and behave, "leading men on." Thus, they deserve whatever happens to them.
• When men are sexually aroused they must have sex; once they are aroused, they can't control themselves.
• Rape happens only to certain kinds of women: women who are sexually active and promiscuous, women who are poor, women who take risks, women who like to party, women who previously have been abused.
• If a woman is not a virgin, she can't be raped.
• Women who don't fight back have not been raped. If they had resisted they could have prevented it.
• If the man did not have a gun or knife, then the woman has not been raped.
• If there are no bruises, she must have consented.
• Sex is the proper repayment for a man who takes a woman out to dinner or pays for a movie or drinks.
• Women are asking to be raped when they go out alone at night.
• Women generally exaggerate about rape. Most times they make up rape stories to get revenge against a man who rejected them.
• Men who rape are mentally ill and out of control.

Sources: Adapted from Robin Warshaw, 1988, *I Never Called It Rape* (New York: Harper & Row); and Liz Kelly, 1988, *Surviving Sexual Violence* (Minneapolis: University of Minnesota Press): 35–36.

strangers. Some researchers have found, for example, that the closer the association or prior association of the victim and the rapist, the more violent the rape tends to be (Russell, 1982). Consequently, wives who are raped suffer greater and longer trauma than other female rape victims do. They often feel betrayed because the person is someone they loved or cared for. As a consequence they stop trusting others. These feelings can lead to long-term anxiety and fear. Finkelhor and Yllo (1995) classified marital rape in terms of the following categories: (1) *force-only rape*, wherein the husband controls the type and frequency of sexual activity within the marriage; (2) *battering rape*, in which a husband humiliates and degrades his wife; and (3) *obsessive rape*, which involves sexual fetishes, sadism, and forcible anal intercourse.

Researchers have identified several factors associated with marital rape. Among these factors, four have been most important: (1) the historical foundations of marriage in the United States, (2) the establishment of marital exemption in rape laws, (3) the socially and economically disadvantaged position of women, and (4) the violent nature of U.S. society and its "rape culture" (Pagelow, 1988). The last two factors were discussed under family violence. Let us briefly examine the first two.

At the beginning of this chapter we pointed out the historical foundation of violence, which is firmly linked to the historical foundation of marriage. As you might recall from that discussion, husbands had absolute power over wives, including control over the wife's body. This idea, in conjunction with the British common-law notion that marriage represents a merger of husband and wife into a single identity—namely, that of the husband—provided the rationale for failing to legally recognize the concept of marital rape. Thus, historically, laws prohibiting rape contained spousal exemption clauses, which meant that a husband could not be prosecuted for sexually assaulting his wife.

Although it is perhaps difficult to conceive of today, in the past there was considerable resistance to the passage of laws that would allow a wife to charge her husband with rape. Until the mid-1970s, marital rape was not a crime in the United States. In 1977, Oregon became the first state to repeal the marital exemption clause in its rape statute. Since that time, similar clauses have been eliminated or modified in states across the country and a husband can be prosecuted for raping his wife. However, many people, the lay public and professionals alike, still have a problem with the idea that a man can be accused and convicted of raping his wife; they still believe that sex is a husband's entitlement. Thus, in some states a husband may be prosecuted for rape only if the wife can show that the assault occurred after legal papers to end the marriage had been filed in court or that the couple were not living together at the time (Russell, 1990). And at the same time, a number of states have even broadened their marital rape exemptions to prevent the prosecution of a man who rapes the woman with whom he is living. This cohabitor's rape exemption or voluntary social companion rape exemption further limits women's ability to pursue rape cases in the criminal justice system. Currently, raping one's wife is a crime in only about half of the 50 states.

THE CRIMINAL JUSTICE RESPONSE TO WOMAN ASSAULT

Every part of the criminal justice system—police, prosecutors, judges, jurors—is critical to eliminating family violence generally and woman abuse specifically. Unfortunately, the system has refused to intervene on women's behalf, except when the violence is extremely severe or death has occurred. It is often said that women are doubly victimized: first by their assailant and second by the criminal justice system. A major reason for this is that the criminal justice system, like society in general, historically has considered family violence to be a private matter, not a criminal issue. Consequently, offenders rarely have been arrested or punished, and victims have received little, if any, protection or support.

IN OTHER PLACES

GLOBAL RESPONSES TO VIOLENCE AND SEXUAL ASSAULT AGAINST WOMEN

NEPAL—Where the Consequences of Rape Result in Imprisonment of the Victim

In 1997, at age 13, Min Min Lama, a young girl from Nepal, was raped by her sister-in-law's brother and became pregnant. Scared and not knowing what else to do (given that in her society people would disapprove of her pregnant condition), she chose to have an abortion in a country where abortion is illegal. She was arrested and sentenced to 21 years in prison; her rapist went free. The International Planned Parenthood Federation (IPPF), in collaboration with other groups, worked actively for Min Min's welfare and release, including sending a mercy petition to the king of Nepal requesting him to grant Min Min amnesty for a crime she did not commit. Two years after her incarceration, at age 15, Min Min was officially released from Central Jail in Kathmandu. The Family Planning Association of Nepal, an IPPF member, along with the IPPF South Asia Region, produced a film titled *For the Sake of Our Women* on the abortion law in Nepal and its consequences on women's rights and health (IPPF, 1999; Mandate the Future, 2002).

ETHIOPIA—Where Rape Is a Marriage Proposal

In some areas of Ethiopia, abducting and raping a woman is the customary way to procure a wife. If a man wants a wife, he kidnaps her and then rapes her until she becomes pregnant. According to tribal tradition, once the abducted girl is pregnant, the man can put his claim on her. Village elders then act as mediators between families and negotiate the bride's price. Recently, 14-year-old Aberash Bekele, still a virgin, was abducted by seven men in southern Ethiopia, taken to a remote hut, and repeatedly beaten and raped by the gang's leader. On the second day of her kidnapping, taking with her a gun she found in the hut, the young girl tried to escape, but her rapist soon caught up with her. Frightened and trembling, Aberash fired three warning shots in the air, but the rapist kept advancing toward her. She lowered the gun and shot and killed him. This act broke every taboo in her village. Aberash was arrested for murder and brought to trial. The incident created a major rift between her parents and the abductor's family, who said: "Many people marry through abduction. He abducted her for marriage, not to be killed by her."

Although abduction is illegal in Ethiopia, it is a common practice and police typically turn a blind eye to it. It is almost always a matter left to the village elders to resolve. In Aberash's case, the village elders sent the young rape victim into exile in an orphanage and ordered her family to pay compensation for the abductor's death. With the assistance of the Ethiopian women's Lawyers Association, Aberash became the first woman ever to challenge and resist this kind of violence. Although the village elders were furious, after 2 years of tedious legal proceedings, the judges hearing the case were convinced that Aberash acted in self-defense and she was acquitted. Unfortunately, Aberash is not completely free. Dissatisfied by the judges' decision, the village elders decreed that Aberash remain in exile. Their ruling supersedes the power of the law. Meanwhile, the six men who participated in Aberash's abduction remain free ("Where Rape Is a Proposal of Marriage," 1999).

CAPE TOWN, SOUTH AFRICA—Where Men March against Rape

According to a number of sources, South Africa has one of the world's highest rates of rape and other crimes against women. Johannesburg, for example, has a reputation of being the world's "rape" capital. Fifty-two thousand rapes are reported each year in South Africa; many of the victims are young girls. Unreported cases would push this figure much higher. In 2000, led by the Anglican archbishop of Cape Town and other religious leaders, more than 2000 men took part in a march to condemn South Africa's high rate of violence against women. The archbishop told the marchers that real men do not rape, and he urged the men to take a stand and act as role models for boys in the fight against violence against women. The men marched to parliament where they gave the welfare minister a document stating that women were equal to men and that women and children were entitled to be safe and have their rights protected. Although there are no definitive statistics for violence against women in South Africa, organizers of the march said that, on average, three women are raped in South Africa every minute. According to some South African sources, 20 percent of intimate relationships involve violence against women (BBC News, 2000).

What do you think? *Do you think that antiabortion laws, even in the case of rape, are fair to women? Do you think that Nepali women such as Min Min should be imprisoned for making a choice about their own bodies? Who do you think should have the right to develop legislation that affects women—their bodies, their reproduction, their lives? Using sociological concepts and analysis, how would you explain how it is that Min Min is guilty of a crime but her rapist is not? How might women and other persons combat cultural practices such as those in some parts of Ethiopia that have institutionalized rape and violence against women? Do you think that men marching against violence against women is enough for men to do in the fight to eliminate violence against women?*

In this section, we briefly examine responses to woman assault in terms of the attitudes and behaviors of people involved in the criminal justice system.

Attitudes and Behaviors

The attitudes of police officers who respond to calls of family and intimate violence are critical in determining how these victims are treated. Although some progress has been made toward sensitizing police to the issues and concerns of battered and sexually assaulted women, many police still do not understand the battering cycle. They often resent having to respond again and again to the same violent household, and some simply do not want to get involved in what they believe is a "private matter."

Although for more than 2 decades now, almost all states have some sort of laws relative to domestic violence, most police calls for battering still do not result in arrest. Some police officers are reluctant to arrest an abuser, believing that his arrest would cause an economic hardship for the family. Others think that an arrest of the abuser is a waste of time, given the low probability that he will be prosecuted and given the leniency of the courts toward abusers even if they are prosecuted (Wallace, 2002). When arrests are made, the offenders are generally released after a few hours. Very often they go home and continue their violent behavior. On the other hand, it is sometimes the case that the victim does not want the police to arrest the abuser. In this circumstance, police can do little save admonish the abuser and leave him with his victim.

That the attitudes and behaviors of some police and related personnel toward victims of battering and sexual assault continue to be problematic is evidenced in a recent study of domestic violence and sexual assault in Washington, D.C., conducted by the District police department. According to the 20-page report, police officers often fail to report or follow proper investigative procedures when handling domestic violence cases. Battered women often encounter spotty investigative work and insensitive dispatchers and, at times, belligerent officers who don't take their complaints seriously. For example, one respondent in the study reported that a police officer responding to her call for help said that there were too many real crimes being committed for him to be dealing with stuff like this. Although 70 percent of the more than 300 battered and abused women in the study expressed satisfaction with police service, the study detailed a significant number of instances where police had not followed procedures. For example, despite department policy, the majority of responses to domestic violence calls were not documented. In 2000, for instance, no reports were made in two-thirds of domestic violence calls to police; officers inquired if a suspect had harmed the woman previously in only one-third of the cases; and police checked for weapons in the home in only one-fourth of the cases. Attitudes and behaviors such as these often deter victims from contacting police again. One-fourth of the women in the study said they would not call police again should another incidence of violence occur. The upside of this report is that the Washington, D.C., police department has reorganized the enforcement, training, and investigation of domestic violence cases, including requiring domestic violence training for officers. In addition, it has formed a domestic violence enforcement unit with a centralized command and oversight of domestic violence investigations (DeMillo, 2001).

Moreover, those involved throughout the criminal justice system have not been immune to the racist, sexist, and homophobic ideas prevalent in U.S. society. Thus, women have often been faced with police who believe that women provoke men into violent acts and then stay with these men because they like to be beaten. African American women have been further confronted with police and others who dismiss intimate violence as a natural part of African American culture. The reactions of police to victims of lesbian and gay violence frequently have ranged from skepticism to outright hostility and violence.

Although some studies report that today more rapes lead to jail time than just a few years ago, the overwhelming majority of rapists still remain free. Because nearly three-fourths of sexual assaults go unreported to the police, those rapists, of course, never serve a day in prison. If the rape is reported to the police, there is roughly a 50–50 chance that an arrest will be made. If an arrest is made, there is an 80 percent chance of prosecution. If there is a prosecution, there is a 58 percent chance of a felony conviction. If there is a felony conviction, there is a 69 percent chance that the convict will spend time in jail. However, these statistics add up to just 16 percent of reported rapes leading to jail time for the rapist. When we factor in the unreported rapes, only about 5 percent—1 out of 20—of all rapists will ever spend a day in jail; 19 out of 20 will walk free ("RAINN Statistics," 2002). Research continues to report that even when men who batter or rape their wives or intimate partners are arrested, prosecutors are often reluctant to prosecute these men. Prosecutors rationalize their behavior by contending that the victim would probably not show up or prosecute her assailant if the case went to trial. It is true that some women do not follow up their complaints of physical and sexual assault. This is due, however, not to some hidden masochistic trait in these women but rather to the fact that the system with which they must deal is often indifferent and insensitive and officials often actively discourage them to pursue their complaints. As a result, they lack confidence that these officials specifically or the system generally will protect them and accord them proper redress. Nonetheless, to address the problem of some women not prosecuting their abusive partner, some states such as California have adopted a zero tolerance policy toward domestic violence such that the abuser is required to stand trial for his abuse and the victim is required to testify against him whether she wants to or not. In Los Angeles County, the penalty for partner abuse is up to 6 months in jail and a fine of $1000.

If a woman's case gets to court, she often finds that she as much as her assailant is on trial. She is often questioned as if she did something wrong and "caused" the violence. Unfortunately, today there continue to be many judges who are insensitive to or uninformed about the nature of domestic violence. This helps explain why the conviction rate for male offenders is still very low. Again, rape cases are a case in point: A rape prosecution is two times as likely as a murder prosecution to be dismissed. Almost 25 percent of convicted rapists are not sentenced to jail at all but rather are released on probation, and just about 50 percent of all convicted rapists are sentenced to less than 1 year in jail (Violence against Women, 1993). Even men who kill their wives or partners and are convicted of homicide often do not get lengthy jail sentences. Moreover, men who kill their wives or partners are less severely punished than are women who kill their husbands or partners.

Have We Made Progress?

There is no clear-cut answer to the question of progress. The answer is both yes and no. One battered, violated, or sexually assaulted woman is one too many. However, there are signs of progress. On the national level, due in part to the vigorous efforts of the National Organization for Women (NOW), the NOW Legal Defense and Education Fund, and various other organizations, as well as the support of former President Bill Clinton, the Violence against Women Act was included in the Violent Crime Control and Law Enforcement Act of 1994. Under this landmark Act, administered by the Department of Health and Human Services and the Department of Justice, for the first time the federal government adopted a comprehensive approach to fighting domestic violence and violence against women, including improving official responses to violence against women by combining tough new penalties with programs to prosecute offenders and assist women victims of violence. It also offers incentives to states that arrest spouse abusers and triples the amount of federal dollars available for battered-women's shelters.

In addition, in recent years, the treatment of rape and battered victims has improved somewhat. Since the 1970s many state legislatures have changed their laws so that women no longer have to prove that they "fought back" or produce extensive evidence to corroborate their lived experience of rape or assault. Also, several states have passed "shield laws" that prevent the victim's previous sexual experiences from being used as evidence in the trial. In addition, most police officers now receive some type of training to sensitize them to the trauma of victims. Other indications of progress include the fact that some statistics show a decline in the incidence of rape, attempted rape, and sexual assault in the mid-1990s; more and more survivors are speaking out publicly, helping to lessen the stigma associated with battered women and rape victims; an increasing number of victim support and advocate services have appeared throughout the country; advocates, prosecutors, and survivors are finding ways to work together in states across the country to change laws and statutes; and more men are taking a public stand on domestic violence (U.S. Department of Justice, 1997, 2000b).

THE EFFECTS OF PHYSICAL AND SEXUAL ASSAULT ON WOMEN

A growing body of research deals with the psychological effects of physical and sexual violence against women. There is also a growing recognition of battered women as "survivors." In this section we briefly explore some of the consequences of violence and abuse for the victim, then examine some of the ways that assaulted women cope with and survive their experiences of violence.

The harm that men inflict on women takes many forms and has a wide range of effects. Research indicates that violent abuse exacts a tremendous toll on women: physically, psychologically, emotionally, and financially. The physical effects are perhaps the most obvious and can range from bruises and temporary pain to scars, permanently broken bones, disfigurement, and even death. Less visible but perhaps more damaging are the psychological and emotional scars brought on by abuse. Low self-esteem, self-hate, economic and emotional dependence on others (especially on those who perpetrate the violence), fear, self-destructive behavior such as alcohol and drug abuse, and suicide are common among abused women.

Research has found, for example, that during and after battering, women tend to think very poorly of themselves. Given their gender role socialization, many abused women attribute the violence and abuse to something they did or did not do and therefore believe that they deserve to be treated violently (Dutton, 1988). They frequently try to change themselves or the situations that they believe lead to the abuse (for example, not having dinner ready at a certain time or serving the coffee too hot or too cold). However, they usually come to realize that the abuse is unpredictable and could be triggered by almost anything they do. It is not surprising that women suffering under such conditions have a low sense of self-worth and a high sense of helplessness and hopelessness.

Women who have been victims of incestuous assault as children report feelings of severe depression throughout their lives, often to the point of suicide. Having been hurt by someone who was supposed to care for and protect them, they sometimes are unable to trust or participate in caring and intimate relationships. There is also the experience of fear, intimidation, humiliation, and degradation (Bannister, 1991). Probably the most extreme manifestation of battered women's self-blame and recrimination is their tendency toward self-destructive behavior. Self-destructiveness can be considered both an effect and a coping strategy that abused women use to deal with their violent life experience and is discussed in more detail shortly.

COPING AND SURVIVAL STRATEGIES

Millions of victimized women develop coping strategies and learn survival tactics not only through their own personal efforts but also through close ties with others, especially other women. As with any stressful situation, coping with violence and abuse requires a variety of skills and resources. Research shows that battered women have developed a wide range of strategies, both constructive (seeking help, leaving the violent situation) and destructive (substance abuse, suicide, murder). Although the ways individual women cope vary from situation to situation, their coping and survival strategies can be classified in the following ways: psychological and emotional, self-destructive, and fighting back.

Psychological and Emotional Strategies One strategy employed by battered women is avoidance or prevention of violence. Victims of abuse sometimes develop plans to avoid future attacks. Sometimes they use sex (to the degree that they still have some control over their sexuality) in an attempt to change the batterer or to avoid further beatings. Some battered women cope by trying to make the relationship work in spite of the obstacles, and others manage to cope and survive by insisting that the violence is not serious enough to end the relationship. Some women resort to dreams or fantasies that can range from being in a violence-free relationship to killing their mates. Still other women block out or repress their experiences of violence, though these experiences often resurface at some future time.

Self-Destructive Strategies For many battered women, self-destructive behavior is not only a consequence of battering and abuse; it is also a way of coping with the situation. Various addictions such as alcohol and drug abuse, overeating, and suicide are all forms of coping, although most people would consider them unhealthy, unwise, and ineffective. Battering appears to be the single-most important context for female alcoholism, suicide attempts, and a range of mental health problems. For example, battered women account for 42 percent of all attempted suicides. As previously stated, more than 25 percent of all female suicide attempts reported by hospitals are associated with battering. Of these women, 80 percent have a history of suicide attempts and have been seen in the hospital for at least one abusive injury prior to their first suicide attempt (Stark and Flicraft, 1988; Abbott et al., 1995; Frazer, 1995). For African American women, fully one-half of those who attempt suicide are abused. Indeed, the association among the experiences of violence, low self-esteem, depression, substance abuse, and suicidal tendencies is quite strong among all female victims of violence (McNeal and Amato, 1998).

Battering is also closely associated with female alcohol and drug abuse. Some researchers caution that it is unclear whether substance abuse is the context or the consequence of stress precipitated by violence (Allan and Cooke, 1985). That is, some researchers contend that alcohol abuse may contribute to a climate that makes abuse more likely. Other researchers respond that the rate of alcoholism among battered women is significantly greater than among nonbattered women. An examination of the recorded onset of alcoholism and of abusive injury among battered women reveals that three-fourths of the alcohol cases emerged only after the onset of abuse, suggesting that abuse leads to alcoholism among battered women, and not the reverse. Similarly, whereas drug abuse is no more common among battered women than nonbattered women prior to the onset of abuse, after abuse the risk of drug abuse is nine times greater than would normally be expected (Stark and Flitcraft, 1988; Brown and Anderson, 1991).

Sometimes the self-destructive coping behavior of battered women is manifested in addictive behaviors such as overeating. Although a causal relationship between abuse and addiction to food has not been established, some battered women seem to use food as a way of coping with the violence in their lives (Dutton, 1988; Iazetto, 1989).

Fighting Back Some women who cannot escape abusive relationships cope by fighting back. Most often their self-defense takes the form of hitting or shoving the batterer. Only occasionally is women's self-defense more violent, such as pushing the batterer down a flight of stairs, biting him, kicking him in the groin, cutting him, or even shooting him. Some women now take self-defense classes to protect themselves against male attackers.

A small number of women who fight back eventually kill their abuser. Although a few of these women are acquitted by the courts on the grounds of self-defense, most are convicted and jailed. The majority of those convicted serve many years in prison despite their claims of self-defense and despite a large amount of evidence indicating that they had been severely abused by the men they killed. Some people consider women who respond to male violence by fighting back and who are then imprisoned to be political prisoners (see, for example, Bannister, 1991). Whatever term we use to describe these women, the fact is that killing an abuser is more the exception than the rule. Only a small percentage of battered women use this strategy to end the abuse they suffer.

Any discussion of domestic violence is necessarily depressing, given the high rate of victimization in the United States. However, many victims of violence are also survivors. They are not passive and defeated victims. As we have indicated, some victims fight back; others seek the assistance of family, friends, professionals, and institutions. Still others find ways, sometimes after years of victimization, to leave their abusive relationships, very often at great personal risk. Through individual and collective actions, they resist, challenge, and/or change the violent forces impacting their lives. The experiences of Laura Anderson, a victim of domestic violence for over 30 years, is a case in point (see the "Family Profile" box). Many victims of domestic violence have developed interesting and self-fulfilling methods by which to celebrate their survival. A creative method in this regard is the *Clothesline Project,* which originated in Hyannis, Massachusetts, in 1990. The Clothesline Project is about direct, personal violence against women and provides an opportunity for women to bear witness to their personal experience of violence and celebrate their transformation from victim to survivor in a powerful statement of solidarity. It consists of a clothesline hung with shirts designed by survivors of assault, rape, and incest using paint, magic markers, crayons, or

FAMILY PROFILE[1]

LAURA ANDERSON

Family background: I have an extensive history with domestic violence and it is impossible to put it all into such a condensed space. However, the following is a brief history. I was born into a violent, alcoholic, very "white" and upper-middle-class family. Although our yard was always neat and clipped, there were many secrets inside our house that I learned early on to always keep to myself. As a middle child, my role in the family was to play the scapegoat. Thus, all of our family "ills" were placed on me, and I accepted this role fairly easily. After all, I thought, it was a very important role, and I played it well.

History of victimization: I was raped when I was 12 years old by a friend of the family and when I began dating at age 13, I started my first violent relationship outside of my home. This led to nine other violent relationships, each one becoming progressively more violent and dysfunctional. Over a period of 30 years, I married and divorced twice, and bore two children that I am now raising quite well by myself. As an abused and assaulted woman, I have lived through every imaginable form of domestic violence, and have spent literally years performing self-mutilations with needles, razor blades, drugs, alcohol, and sexual promiscuousness. I have been raped, gang raped, tied up with coat hangers and sodomized, beaten, drugged, taken across state lines, thrown down stairs, thrown out into the cold, homeless, friendless, and jobless. I have had my nose broken, ribs cracked, hair pulled out of my scalp, and bottles thrown at me. I still have permanent bruises. I have many times exchanged sexual favors for a warm "safe" bed to sleep in, food to eat, and a roof over my head. The first time I contemplated suicide I was 5 years old. The last time I attempted suicide I swallowed 200 sleeping pills and almost died. I spent several days in the hospital and I am very lucky to not have permanent nerve damage. In fact, after years of being a victim of domestic violence, I am lucky to be alive at all.

Laura Anderson

Agency: When I finally started to seek help, I spent years in intensive therapy. In the beginning, I always either went back or began a new and more abusive relationship. However, during much of this time I was also very politically active and feminist in my thinking and could not understand why I found it so impossible to be in a healthy relationship. I still do not fully understand how/why my life unfolded as it did. However, I do know that as a mother, my number one priority is to protect my children from violence and abuse and to raise them to be healthy functioning members of society. I am currently pursuing a degree in sociology that I began in 1985. I will graduate! I am sure of that. My slow and painstaking evolvement into the healthy, independent survivor that I am today is truly a testament to the female human spirit.

[1]This profile takes a slightly different format from the other "Family Profiles" presented in this textbook. Due to the nature of the subject matter, we present a brief history/case study of prolonged violence and human agency. Laura Anderson's courageous struggles over many years to change her life of violent victimization are noteworthy.

elaborate embroidery to create their shirt. Families and friends of women who have died as a result of violence can and do make shirts to express their deep loss (Clothesline Project, 1995).

A COMPARATIVE LOOK AT BATTERED MEN

A 30-year-old man moved out of an apartment it had taken him ages to find because of the couple who lived next door. What was it about the couple that made this young man give up his hard-won apartment? He said it was the fights: the shouting, the verbal abuse, and what sounded like physical abuse that resounded from the apartment next door. What he found most disturbing was the fact that, in his view, the woman was the abusive and violent partner (Sims, 1989).

What evidence exists for female violence and male victimization? The suggestion that men are battered by women probably sounds implausible, if not silly, to some people. For others, the image of a skinny little henpecked man chased by a large, buxom wife with a rolling pin in her hand might immediately come to mind. In fact, some research during the 1970s and 1980s suggested that the phenomenon of battered husbands was as prevalent as that of battered wives. Suzanne Steinmetz (1977) was one of the first to call attention to this issue by claiming that more women battered husbands than vice versa and that husband abuse was

Similar to the AIDS quilt, the Clothesline Project puts a human face on the statistics of violence against women. Since 1990, it has grown to include over 300 Clothesline Projects nationally and internationally, displaying an estimated 35,000 t-shirts that illustrate the personal stories of survivors, families, and friends of those who have suffered from violence against women.

the most underreported of all forms of family violence. Studies based on national survey data in the 1980s found that in homes with couple violence, approximately one-fourth of the respondents indicated that men were victims and not perpetrators of violence, an additional one-fourth reported that women were victims and not offenders, and the remaining one-half reported that both wives and husbands were violent. Some recent studies suggest that there is a higher degree of female violence and aggression than previously thought. For example, while the percentage of males arrested in California for domestic violence decreased 10 percent over the 10-year period from 1988 to 1998, the percentage of female domestic violence increased 10 percent during the same period (Wallace, 2002).

Critics of the idea of widespread husband abuse caution that statistics such as these and those of Steinmetz can be seriously misinterpreted. A major problem with claims that women use violence as often as men is that there is little or no clarification of how many of the women who use violence are actually acting in self-defense or retaliating against an abusive partner. Data from studies of violent relationships in which the police intervened clearly indicate that men are rarely the victims of battery (Gelles, 1997). Research also clearly shows that men initiate violence in the majority of cases. Moreover, men who kill their partner do so in self-defense far less frequently than do women who kill their partner. In addition, rarely do battered women report initiating violence. The most frequent motive for violence in their self-reports is "fighting back" (Saunders, 1988), and the violent acts that they report tend, most often, to be protective or self-defense actions.

Given that women are, on average, smaller and physically weaker than men, the abuse inflicted on them is far more severe and life-threatening than those instances of male or husband battering. In addition, not only are battered men less physically injured than battered women, but also they are less trapped in an abusive relationship than women because men typically have greater economic resources and can more easily leave an abusive relationship because they usually do not have responsibility for children. Although some men are injured by a wife or lover, most women are unable to defend themselves effectively against male batterers. In fact, most battered women find it far safer to submit to the battering than to fight back and risk being seriously injured or even killed. In light of this fact it seems inappropriate to generalize women's behavior in this regard as "husband abuse" or "battering." This is not meant to trivialize male battering where it exists. And it does not alter the fact that domestic violence in all forms needs to be investigated and understood.

Frequently during the last decade of the twentieth century, media-generated sensationalism drew our attention to women's abuse of men. Perhaps the most famous case in recent times of a woman accused of abusing a man is the 1993 trial of Lorena Bobbitt, who was charged with maliciously wounding her husband John Bobbitt after she cut off his penis with a kitchen knife and tossed it from her moving car window. Using a "battered woman" defense, Ms. Bobbitt claimed that she had acted impulsively after being raped by John and having endured repeated abuse during her 5-year marriage. A jury of seven women and five men acquitted her, finding her not guilty by reason of temporary insanity. However, she was not successful in her subsequent charge of marital rape in which the jury found John not guilty. One of the many unfortunate aspects of this case was the sensationalism it attracted. Rather than sensitizing us to the society-wide problem of domestic violence and woman abuse, everyone from the ordinary citizen on the street to television talkshow hosts and comedians focused instead on the fact that John Bobbitt had been "demasculinized," finding this somehow curious and amusing. Ms. Bobbitt was often dismissed as "crazy." It is noteworthy that John Bobbitt, who gained a movie career in the pornography industry after the trial, was later convicted of two domestic battery charges against a former girlfriend and served 30 days in jail.

John Bobbitt's behavior is consistent with Bureau of Justice statistics that show that domestic violence tends to be a pattern rather than a one-time occurrence. After the first blow is struck, the assaults become chronic and the violence almost always escalates, with the abuse becoming more severe, more frequent, and more dangerous. Over one-third of battered and abused women are victimized again within 6 months of an episode of domestic violence.

An interesting development in male abuse and a fact that perhaps few people know is that every year, thousands of men turn to women's rape crisis agencies because there is no other place for men who have been sexually assaulted. Unlike in the case of female rape victims, however, the perpetrators of male rape are not women. Nonetheless, this is an important form of violence that a growing number of men face. Many of the issues with male and female rape victims are the same. Both generally feel guilt, shame, and self-blame. Like women, men must also deal with "rape myths," which add to the emotional trauma of dealing with rape. Perhaps the foremost myth is that men cannot be and do not get raped. This myth prevents many men from reporting their rape. For example, during 1993 and 1994 in Chicago, a serial rapist who targeted teenaged boys and young men was never caught, partly due to the fact that most of his victims suffered in silence. According to some authorities, in cases of rape, men's emotional needs are often ignored because cultural norms do not permit men to be victims. In an early study of male rape victims, a team of Memphis gynecologists found that in one free clinic for rape victims in Memphis, Tennessee, over a 2-year period (1988–1990), 6 percent of the clients were male. More than one-half of these men had been abducted before the assault, and only two knew their attackers.

Perhaps the most common myth is that male rape occurs only within the context of prison or that it is related to a male's sexual orientation. The fact is, rape is rape. It is a crime of violence whether the victim is female or male. It goes without saying that most advocates for abused males believe that the incidence of male rape is much higher because most male rapes go unreported and because the prisoner population was not included in these figures. Men are generally silent about their rape because they think that most people won't believe them or because they think that most people will think that they are gay. Their silence about their victimization relative to rape contributes to the myth that rape affects only women and homosexuals. Research suggests that, as with women, most rapes of men are not prompted by sexual desire. Rather, it is an issue of power and control (Edelhart, 1995).

CHILD ASSAULT AND ABUSE

Although child abuse has existed throughout human history, in the United States it attracted public interest only in the early 1960s. At that time Dr. C. Henry Kempe and his associates (1962) published a national survey that described for the first time the series of behaviors known as the **battered-child syndrome.** They defined this syndrome basically as "a clinical condition in children who have received severe physical abuse, primarily from a parent or foster parent" (Kempe et al., 1962:17). Even then, however, child abuse was not widely acknowledged to be a major issue until the 1980s, when expanded media coverage brought the problem to the attention of millions of Americans. Public opinion polls conducted in the 1970s revealed that only one in ten Americans considered child abuse to be a serious problem. By the 1980s, the nation's awareness of the impact of crime and violence against children changed dramatically, as reflected in the change in that figure to nine out of ten (Gelles and Strauss, 1987).

And well we, as a nation, should not only be aware but also consciously concerned about the escalating violence in this country, especially that which is directed at children at younger and younger ages. Today, as illustrated in the discussion opening this chapter and in various other places in the chapter, hardly a day goes by without news of another child (children) who has been severely abused, neglected, starved, or murdered, usually by a parent or close relative. Consider the following statistics related to children and violence in the United States: *Every 10 seconds a child is reported to authorities as abused or neglected; every 20 seconds a child is arrested; every 44 seconds a child is born into poverty; every 4 minutes a child is arrested for drug abuse; every 8 minutes a child is arrested for a violent crime; every 2 hours a child is killed by a firearm; every 3 hours a child is a homicide victim; every 4 hours a child commits suicide; every 5 hours a child dies from abuse or neglect* (Children's Defense Fund, 2001b). The epidemic of violence against children is almost uniquely a U.S. phenomenon. Global statistics, for example, indicate that three out of four child killings in the industrialized world happen in the United States, and child suicide rates in this country are twice those of the rest of the industrialized world ("Violence Kills More U.S. Kids," 1997).

As with woman victimization, the maltreatment of children takes many forms, including physical battering and abuse, child endangerment and neglect, sexual abuse and assault, psychological or emotional abuse, exploitation, murder, children thrown away, child runaways, and child abduction by parents and by strangers. Until recently, the greatest threat to children was believed to be stranger abductions. However, today a substantial body of research has documented that, of the thousands of children each year classified as missing or abducted, parents, not strangers, are responsible for the vast majority of these abductions. In addition, the largest category of missing children today are runaway, thrownaway, and homeless youth, a substantial number of whom have been victims of prior physical or sexual abuse in their homes. Their life on the streets continues this pattern of violence (Mignon, Larson, and Holmes, 2002).

Moreover, new manifestations of child victimization have emerged over recent decades. For example, Munchausen syndrome by proxy is a rare form of abuse that is relatively new to public awareness and involves an adult, usually a white, middle-class mother with some knowledge or experience with medicine or nursing, who assumes the sick role indirectly (for example, by proxy) by feigning or inducing illness in her child (usually an infant or toddler). It can include making a child think that she or he is mentally ill, having the child committed to a mental hospital, claiming that the child suffers from depression or anxiety, inducing apnea (a cessation of breathing) by suffocating the child to the point of unconsciousness, scrubbing the child's skin with oven cleaner to produce a blistering rash, and various behavioral problems exhibited only in the presence of the perpetrator. The mother's motives range from a desire for attention from people—family, friends, and community—as the heroic caretaker of a tragically ill child, dislike or hatred for the child, to monetary returns from insurance. Many of these abusers have been found to be needy or lonely or to have psychiatric problems. Because it takes many years of illness before the secret of Munchausen by proxy is discovered, the mortality rate for this form of child abuse is 9 percent (Parnell and Day, 1998; AsherMeadow, 2001; Feldman, 2001).

Moreover, advances in technology now present serious threats and potential harm to children that we did not even imagine 10 or 20 years ago. Video cameras are increasingly used to produce homemade child pornography; personal computers with access to the Internet are used to instantly disseminate child pornography around the world and to solicit children for sexual encounters. The power of the Internet and the pervasive concern about electronic virtual sex involving unsuspecting children have led to a new generation of child protectors, including the U.S. Congress, which has repeatedly tried to impose special restrictions on Internet speech in order to protect children. Recently, a unique case of virtual rape of a child came to public attention when a 51-year-old New Jersey man acknowledged that he had made obscene phone calls to 12 girls, ranging in age from 8 to 14, and pleaded guilty to multiple counts of child endangerment. What made this case unique was the fact that the man was also charged with aggravated sexual assault because he had persuaded one of his victims, a 10-year-old girl, to insert her finger into her vagina. The man never met his victim, his only contact was by phone. Nonetheless, he was convicted of aggravated sexual assault and given a 12-year sentence, part of which will be served at the state's sex-offender treatment center. According to Wendy Kaminer (2001), this case may change the way we think about rape. The growing threat of telephone and online sexual predators notwithstanding, the overwhelming majority (93 percent) of juvenile sexual assault victims know their attacker—34 percent are family members and 59 percent are acquaintances (U.S. Department of Justice, 2000b).

Recent research has documented the adverse affect of domestic violence on the mental health and development of children, including a connection between early childhood victimization and later involvement in violent crime, whether as a victim or perpetrator. However, it is clear that more research in the area is needed in order to fully understand why some abused or neglected children become violent while the majority do not (Widom, 1992; Muller and Lemiux, 2000; Mignon, Larson, and Holmes, 2002).

Just as for most types of violence and sexual assault, trying to determine the overall incidence of child abuse is a difficult task. However, the data do indicate, as we said earlier, that child victimization in the United States is an epidemic of national scope and importance and it involves children of all ages, races, classes, sexual orientations, and both sexes. Each year in the United States, it is estimated that millions of children directly experience or witness violence in their homes, neighborhoods, and schools. It is estimated that as many as 3.3 million children are exposed to violence against their mothers or female caretakers by family members alone. In homes where partner abuse occurs, 40 to 60 percent of men who abuse women also abuse children (American Psychological Association, 2001). Considering the various forms that child abuse takes, by far the majority of reported cases of child abuse are due to child neglect (58.4 percent) or physical abuse (21.3 percent). Some children, however, suffer more than one type of maltreatment. The highest victimization rates are for infants and toddlers 3 years and younger. According to various studies and crime statistics on violent offenders and their victims, 97 percent of offenders who commit violent crimes against children are male; 25 percent are 40 years or older; 70 percent are white; only about 10 percent of these offenders of child victims receive life or death sentences; and the average prison sentence is shorter than that received by those who abuse adults (U.S. Department of Justice, 1996b; U.S. Department of Health and Human Services, 2001a).

In some ways, child abuse is even more difficult to deal with than woman abuse. Although there have been significant legislative changes relative to child victimization, children still have limited legal rights and are subject to the authority of their parents. Parents have a right and obligation to discipline their children, and few restrictions are placed on how they may do so. Perhaps more so even than woman abuse, parental violence against children historically has been considered a "family matter" with which the larger society should not interfere, except in extreme cases. The remainder of our discussion of child victimization takes a brief but closer look at the physical and sexual assault of children. This is not meant to diminish the seriousness or prevalence of other forms of child abuse, however.

The Physical Assault of Children

Because adults have great latitude in terms of the methods they may use to discipline children, violence against children must be serious before it is labeled as abuse. (How many Americans recognize spanking as a form of violence?) Of all the types of child abuse, physical abuse is probably the most likely to lead to intervention by outside forces because it most often leaves visible evidence (such as bruises, lacerations, and broken bones) that can be introduced into a court of law as evidence of maltreatment (Sigler, 1989).

PREVALENCE How prevalent is the physical assault of children? As already noted, because of a high rate of underreporting, the incidence of child assault is difficult to assess. This fact notwithstanding, the statistics we have on child assault and abuse are alarming. National surveys that ask Americans about violence in their homes have found considerable violence directed toward children. Most parents admit to using some kind of violence on their children, including beating up a child at least once, using severe forms of punishment, and threatening to use or actually using a gun or knife (Straus and Gelles, 1986; Straus and Donnelly, 2001). Newspapers across the country are replete with tragic stories about child abuse victims who die at the hands of a parent or guardian (see "In the News"). Depending on the source and the definition used to define child fatalities, the number of children who are killed each year varies significantly. According to the U.S. Department of Health and Human Services (2001a), in 1999, 1100 children died of abuse and neglect. Other sources, such as the National Center for Prosecution of Child Abuse (2000), estimate that as many as 5000 children are killed each year as a result of abuse and neglect.

Parental violence is among the five leading causes of death for children 18 years old and younger. Although, as we have said, children under the age of 3 are at greatest risk, some researchers claim that the majority of child fatalities occur within the first year of life. In 1999, 43 percent of child fatalities occurred among children younger than a year old, and 86 percent were younger than 6 years of age. Maltreatment deaths are more associated with neglect (38 percent) than any other form of abuse. Most of these victims (81 percent) were maltreated by one or more of their parents. One of the most striking differences between maltreatment fatalities and other types of maltreatment is that maltreatment fatalities are less frequently perpetrated by just one parent acting alone (U.S. Department of Health and Human Services, 2001a). From birth to 5 years of age, boys are murdered approximately one-and-a-half times more frequently than girls of the same age. And young people between the ages of 15 and 19 are the second most likely to be killed by a parent. However, their victimization rate is almost 11 times less than the rate for infants (anonymous author).

A study of child discipline conducted by the Gallup Organization and based on parents' own reports estimates that 3 million children are physically abused each year in the name of discipline. Based on the responses of a representative national sample of 1000 parents who were asked how they handle a child who misbehaves, the Gallup Organization projected that 5 percent of parents in the United States punish their children by punching, kicking, or throwing the child down, or hitting the child with a hard object on some part of the body other than the bottom (see Figure 11.1). These acts were classified as abusive in the study, while behaviors like spanking, slapping, shouting, cursing, or threatening to send a child away were not. The Gallup Organization's estimates of child mistreatment far exceed government statistics. And, according to the pollsters, their figures probably understate the problem of child abuse (cited in Lewin, 1995).

Figure 11.1

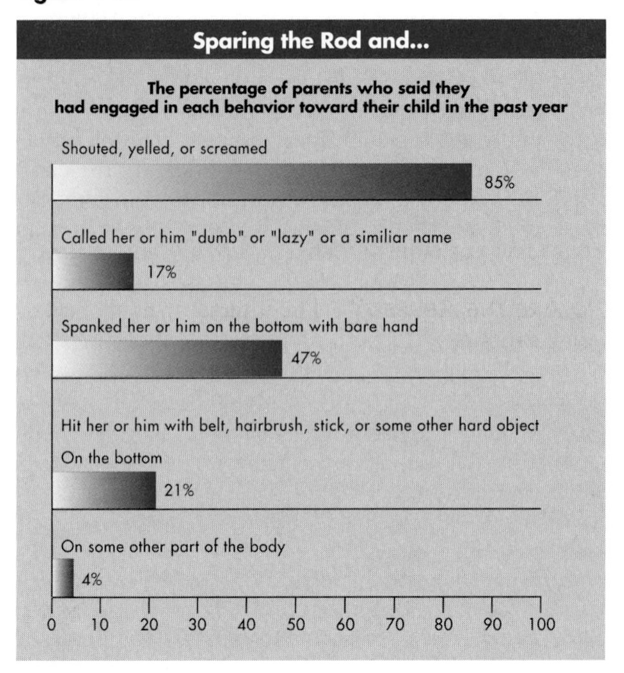

Source: Adapted from Tamar Lewin, 1995, "Parents Poll Finds Child Abuse to Be More Common," *New York Times* (December 7). Copyright © 1995 by the New York Times Co. Reprinted by permission.

Various research and statistics on the prevalence and consequences of child victimization indicate a link among children witnessing violence, drug or alcohol abuse, and their long-term mental health. In this context it is estimated that approximately 4 million children in the United States have witnessed serious violence; nearly 2 million appear to have suffered (and more than 1 million still suffer) from post-traumatic stress disorder (PTSD) a long-term mental health condition often characterized by depression, anxiety, flashbacks, nightmares, and other behavioral and physiological symptoms. And approximately 3.4 million adolescents have been drug or alcohol abusers as well (U.S. Department of Justice, 1997, 2001b).

It is estimated that as many as one-third of all abuse and neglect cases go unreported or undetected, especially if they involve middle-class or wealthy families. We can safely assume that like most family violence, child abuse is often hidden in the privacy of the home, and most people do not admit to it. Furthermore, as with most statistics on violence, child assault statistics rely heavily on self-reports and on the reports of various professionals such as doctors, nurses, social workers, teachers, child-care workers, and police. Even though the reporting of suspected child abuse has improved significantly in recent years because of increased training, awareness, and legislation, perhaps one primary reason that a significant amount of child assault continues to go unreported is that many of these professionals refuse to "get involved." Very often their biases concerning race and class affect their decision on whether to report suspected cases of child assault. For example, doctors are twice as likely to label a black child a victim of abuse as a white child. Similarly, they are twice as likely to miss abuse in two-parent families, compared with single-parent families, and they are more likely to label a case as abuse if the child is from a janitor's family than if the child is from a lawyer's family (Besharov, 1987; Jenny et al., 1999).

Who Are the Abused? The intersections of race, class, gender, and age are important considerations in any discussion of child physical assault. Current statistics indicate that the majority of victims of maltreatment are white in all categories of maltreatment except one—medical neglect. The highest percentage of medical neglect victims are African American (44 percent), with whites a close second (41 percent). However, when we look at victimization rates within the same race, such rates range from a low of 4.4 percent for Asian-Pacific Islander victims per 1000 children to 25.2 for African American victims. The victimization rate for Native American/Alaska Natives is also high, at 20.1 victims per 1000 children. The rate for Latinas/os (12.6) is slightly higher than that for whites (10.6) (U.S. Department of Health and Human Services, 2001a, 2001b, Mignon, Larson, and Holmes, 2002).

Although child maltreatment occurs in all socioeconomic groups, reported cases (and this is key) are disproportionately from among economically and socially disadvantaged families, particularly families receiving public assistance. Children in families with incomes under $15,000 a year are 22 to 25 times more likely than children in families with yearly incomes over $30,000 to be victims of some form of neglect or abuse. More specifically, they are 44 times more likely to be neglected and 16 times more likely to be a victim of physical abuse. In addition, they are also 29 times more likely to be emotionally neglected and 56 times more likely to be educationally neglected. Economic stress and poverty also appear to be related to the severity of abuse. Children whose families earn less than $15,000 per year compared with those whose family income is $30,000 or more are 14 times more likely to be harmed by some variety of abuse, 22 times more likely to be seriously injured by maltreatment or abuse, and 60 times more likely to die from some type of maltreatment or abuse. According to some studies, serious or fatal injuries to children are more prevalent among families whose annual income is below the poverty level than any other income group (U.S. Department of Health and Human Services, 1996; Barnett, Miller-Perrin, and Perrin, 1997).

Research results are mixed as to who receives more physical abuse, girls or boys. However, a recent national study of child abuse found that 52 percent of abused children are female compared to 48 percent for males (U.S. Department of Health and Human Services, 2001a).

An examination of the age of child abuse and neglect victims shows that 38 percent are under the age of 6; 45 percent are 6 to 13 years of age; 15 percent are 14 to 17 (U.S. Bureau of the Census, 2001a). Because younger children are the most frequently reported victims of child abuse, until recently little attention was paid to abused adolescents. However, along with infants and toddlers, the highest rates of physical injury occur among adolescents (Barnett, Miller-Perrin, and Perrin, 1997). Many people do not see adolescents as being particularly vulnerable because, unlike small children, they can run away, protect themselves, and get help. They are often viewed as being an accomplice in their abuse because of their size, strength, and/or behavior. In fact, however, every year an unknown number of adolescents are abused. Many run away to someone or someplace, but most end up on the streets, unprotected and vulnerable to the abuse of a variety of unscrupulous people such as pimps, pornographers, and drug dealers.

Sometimes abuse increases during adolescence as children experience independence and personality changes. Such changes sometimes cause some parents to feel a loss of power and control and they compensate for this by increasing the abuse. Sometimes adolescents fight back. Some researchers estimate that almost 2.5 million teenagers commit acts of violence against their parents each year. Approximately 2000 parents die each year at the hands of a teenage son or daughter, often in self-defense or in retaliation against abuse. **Parricide**—the killing of one's parents—is said to be most common during adolescence (Gelles and Straus, 1987; Wallace, 2002). Almost all murders of parents are committed by sons. In the few cases that involve daughters, often a male accomplice is recruited. One common scenario of parricide involves a drunken, physically abusive father who is killed by a son who sees himself as the protector of the family (Utech, 1994; Wallace, 2002). According to one source on parricide, 63 percent of boys aged 11 to 20 who commit homicide murder the man who was abusing their mother (National Coalition against Domestic Violence, 1996). Children in African American families where abuse takes place are more likely to kill their fathers (*patricide*) than their mothers (*matricide*). Sixty-one percent of African American parents killed by their children are fathers. Additionally, African American males are more likely than females to commit parent murders. On the other hand, sons are more likely to be killed by their parents in African American families than are daughters. Approximately 64 percent of African American children killed by a parent are sons. Overall, however, teenagers are more likely to employ physical violence against mothers than against fathers.

Current research indicates that certain characteristics predispose a child to being abused. Children born to unmarried parents, premature infants, children who are congenitally malformed or mentally retarded, twins, children born during a mother's depressive illness or born into large families (with four or more children), and children whose parents are substance abusers are most vulnerable to abuse. In 43 percent of the cases of child abuse examined in one study, at least one parent had a documented problem with alcohol or drugs (Murphy et al., 1991). According to the Children's Defense

Fund (2001b), an estimated 40 percent to 80 percent of the families who become child protective services cases have problems with alcohol or drugs. Usually only one child in a family is abused. That child most often is the youngest, followed, in terms of frequency, by the oldest. Prior to the age of 10 or 11, boys are more frequently abused than girls. At that point, the incidence of abuse of girls becomes greater. Research also indicates that between 30 percent and 42 percent of abused children come from single-parent homes (Tower, 2002). In addition, they are more likely to have young parents and few siblings, to have been separated from their parents during the first year of life, and to have parents who were themselves abused as children. Some research suggests that teenage mothers are more likely than older mothers to be abusive due to a number of factors, including poverty, economic strains, substance abuse, and lack of parental skills and abilities (Smith and Adler, 1991; Gaudin et al., 1996; National CASA Association, 2000; Children's Defense Fund, 2001b). And as we have already pointed out, children in families where there is woman abuse are highly likely to be maltreated as well.

The impact of child physical abuse is multifaceted. Abused children tend to have emotional scars and problems that they take into adulthood, such as low self-esteem and a tendency to abuse alcohol and other drugs. Moreover, children who grow up in abusive families, observing violence directed toward a parent, exhibit emotional problems and are likely to be "juvenile delinquents." For example, of children who witness family violence, 60 percent of the boys eventually become batterers and 50 percent of the girls become victims. Furthermore, 73 percent of male abusers were abused as children and at least 80 percent of men in prison grew up in a violent home (National Coalition against Domestic Violence, 1996; Violence against Women, 1994; Childabuse.com, 2000; National CASA Association, 2000).

Who Are the Abusers? In 90 percent of child abuse cases, the abuser is a member of the immediate family, typically a person between the ages of 20 and 39. Although half of the reported cases of parental physical violence against children involve women and half involve men, most of the literature on child abuse claims that mothers are more likely than fathers to abuse their children, although the difference between the two is small. This finding should not be taken to mean that women are, by nature, more violent than men. Rather, women's general lack of power in the family, their isolation in the home, and the emotional tensions of mothering all lead to situations in which abuse is likely to occur. In fact, if we controlled for the amount of time spent in contact with children, rates of abuse would be higher for men.

Some researchers have found that women who are abused by their husbands or lovers are most likely to use severe violence against their children, although these women account for only a small overall percentage of such cases. Other researchers have found a positive relationship between women's work and child abuse, with women in the paid labor force (compared with all mothers) exhibiting the lowest rates of overall violence toward their children. Fathers whose wives work (compared with all fathers) also have the lowest rate of violence toward children (Gelles and Hargreaves, 1987). It seems, too, that a person's occupation is significantly related to the probability of abuse. People in working-class occupations are more likely to use physical punishment and abuse their children than are their counterparts in white-collar occupations. Moreover, children in homes where the father is either unemployed or working part-time are more likely to be abused than are children in homes where the father works full-time (Wiese and Daro, 1995). Finally, like teenage parents, young adults are more likely to abuse their children than are older parents, and stepfathers and boyfriends of single mothers are frequent abusers of children, especially sexual abusers (Renzetti and Curran, 1992; Zuravin and DiBlasio, 1996).

A small number of the violently abused women who resist their abuser eventually kill the abuser. Incarcerated, they often have to develop ways to remain intimate with family members, particularly their children. This mother holds her one-and-a-half-year-old son for a few hours every week at the visitor's center inside a women's correction center.

The Sexual Assault of Children

Child sexual abuse is a major problem today, and public concern about this issue has been heightened by numerous reports by adult survivors of its impact on their lives. Increasingly, celebrities and other public figures are calling attention to child sexual assault by sharing their childhood experiences of abuse. For example, the extremely successful talk show host Oprah Winfrey revealed that she was only 9 years old when she was raped by a 19-year-old cousin, the first of three family members to sexually assault her before she reached adulthood. Approximately 35 percent of women and 20 percent of men in the United States were victims of sexual abuse as children, and almost half report that they kept the abuse to themselves (Patterson and Kim, 1991;

Mendel, 1995). More than six out of ten (67 percent) of all rape cases occurred before the victims reached age 18; 34 percent of all forcible rapes occurred when the victim was less than 12 years old; and another 32 percent occurred between the ages of 12 and 17. One of every seven victims of sexual assault reported to law enforcement agencies are under the age of 6. Convicted rape and sexual assault offenders serving time in state prisons report that two-thirds of their victims were under the age of 18, 58 percent of those—or nearly four in ten imprisoned violent sex offenders—said their victims were aged 13 or younger. Moreover, almost always the sex offender is male. For example, four different datasets used by the U.S. Department of Justice point to a profile of a sex offender as a heterosexual male who is older than other violent offenders, generally in his early 30s, and more likely to be white than other violent offenders. Despite the prevalent and popular myth, gay men are not more likely to sexually abuse children than heterosexual men are (American Psychological Association, 2001). In fact, in one study (Holmes and Slap, 1998), 98 percent of the men who raped boys identified themselves as heterosexual. In addition, the majority of child sexual offenders are family members or are otherwise known to the child. This is particularly true for juvenile victims. For example, in 93 percent of the rapes of children less than 12 years old, the child knew the offender (U.S. Department of Justice, 1998, 2000b).

There is no one single definition of child sexual abuse. In general, the term *child sexual abuse* refers to the use of a child for the sexual gratification of an adult. A central characteristic of any abuse is the dominant position of an adult that allows him or her to force or coerce a child into sexual activity. Child sexual abuse/incestuous behavior is not confined to sexual intercourse. It may include nudity, disrobing, genital exposure, kissing, fondling a child's genitals and/or other body parts, masturbation, oral-genital contact, digital penetration, sodomy, as well as vaginal and anal intercourse. Child sexual abuse is not limited to physical contact; such abuse can include noncontact abuse, such as exposure, voyeurism, child pornography (American Psychological Association, 2001:1), and as we discussed earlier in the case of "virtual rape," it can include coercion via telephone.

Such abuse can be divided into two basic categories depending on who the abuser is: familial abuse and extrafamilial abuse. Familial abuse is generally referred to as **incest**—the sexual abuse by a blood relative who is assumed to be a part of the child's family. Most definitions of incest include stepfathers and live-in boyfriends. Because most child sexual abuse is perpetrated by family members, our discussion focuses on familial rather than extrafamilial abuse.

Sexual abuse progresses over time, usually beginning with "trying-out" behavior and progressing over time in intensity of abuse. It might begin with an adult undressing in front of the child and progress to the rubbing of the perpetrator's penis on the genital or rectal area of the child. Not every case of sexual abuse progresses in the same way. No matter what the cyclic order of child sexual abuse, however, it involves an adult using her or his powers to force, coerce, or cajole compliance from a child who participates out of awe, fear, trust, respect, or love for the adult (Tower, 2002).

PREVALENCE How prevalent is child sexual abuse? Because of the extremely sensitive, embarrassing, and outrageous nature of incest, victims and perpetrators often keep it hidden. Family members and others outside the family cite personal reasons for not reporting known instances of child sexual abuse. The most common reason cited by adults is their reluctance to believe a child's claim of abuse and their hesitance to accuse an adult of such behavior. Thus, official reports of incest severely underestimate its actual occurrence.

It is estimated that between 10 percent and 20 percent of American children are victims of sexual assault by a parent or parent figure. The majority of incest cases involve stepfather and stepdaughter or father and daughter; only a small proportion of incest cases involve fathers and sons, and even more rare are cases that involve mother–son (National Coalition against Domestic Violence, 1996). Sociologist Margaret Andersen (1993) estimates that approximately 16 percent of women have been sexually abused or assaulted by a relative by the time they are 18 years of age. In the late 1990s, a survey of the health of adolescent girls and boys (Schoen et al., 1997a, 1997b) found that

- Seven percent of young girls in grades 5 to 8 and 12 percent of "older" girls in grades 9 through 12 said they had been sexually abused.
- Three percent of young boys in grades 5 through 8 and 5 percent of "older" boys in grades 9 through 12 said they had been sexually abused.
- Most of the abuse occurred at home, particularly for girls, and was recurrent. For example, girls who had been sexually abused said the abuse typically took place at home (53 percent); it occurred more than once (65 percent); and the abuser was a family member (57 percent) or family friend (13 percent). Compared to girls, 61 percent of boys reporting either physical or sexual abuse indicated that it was a recurring event. However, only 35 percent of sexually abused boys said the abuse took place in their homes and less than half (45 percent) said the abuser was a family member.
- Abused girls often didn't tell anyone about the abuse. Twenty-nine percent kept the abuse to themselves compared with 48 percent of boys who said they had not talked to anyone about the abuse. Overall, 12 percent of girls and 8 percent of boys reported feeling unsafe at home and more than one-half of the girls (58 percent) said they had wanted to leave home at some point because of the violence.

Furthermore, about one of ten pregnant adolescents reported becoming pregnant as a result of a sexual assault, primarily incest (Boyer and Fineman, 1992).

Relevant statistics on incest from various other studies include

- The median age of first encounter with sexual abuse is under 12, with the age ranging from a few months to the late teens.
- Incestuous relationships are not short-term, rather they typically endure 2 years or more.
- Incest occurs throughout the social structure, across race, class, religion, and all geographic areas.
- The majority of research suggests that a variety of negative psychological, behavioral, and interpersonal problems are more prevalent among incest victims than among individuals without such a history.
- Thirty-eight states now have laws requiring convicted child sex offenders to register with local law enforcement agencies subsequent to conviction and following any geographic move.

The Sexually Abused Child and the Abuser Can we make any generalizations concerning which children are sexually abused and who abuses them? As we have said, the typical victim of sexual abuse is female, and girls are more often sexually abused within the family and boys outside the family (for example, by the clergy or athletic coaches). Some researchers, however, dispute these conclusions saying that they are misleading because boys are less likely to report a sexual assault no matter where it occurs. Males who in early childhood are taught to be "strong" and "macho" may be unwilling or unable to admit that they have been victimized in this way. Recent research, in fact, suggests that boys are almost equally as vulnerable to incest as are girls (Tower, 2002). At the very least, these studies indicate that the incidence of abuse among male children is significantly higher than we imagined or is reported.

The underreporting of male child sexual abuse notwithstanding, we do know that in general, boys, like girls, are most likely to be victimized by men. In addition, boys are more likely than girls to be one of a number of victims of the same perpetrator; boys are more likely than girls to be victims of both sexual and physical abuse; and boys are also more likely to be subjected to anal abuse than are girls (Watkins and Bentovim, 1992). Perpetrators within the family are not limited to birth parents but also include stepfathers, mothers' boyfriends, sisters' boyfriends, siblings, grandparents, uncles, and cousins, as well as other relatives and fictive kin (see Chapter 1 for a definition of fictive kin). Children are also abused by their fathers' friends; by foster care and day-care workers; and by babysitters, the clergy, coaches, and peers. Although the majority of perpetrators are males there are cases in which women are the offenders. There are no definitive statistics on its prevalence, but it is estimated that women are perpetrators in 5 percent of cases of sexual abuse of girls and as much as 20 percent of the cases of sexual abuse of boys (Mignon, Larson, and Holmes, 2002). Furthermore, some researchers have pointed to a cycle of sexual abuse that they describe with the term **transmission of victimization**—abuse carried from one generation to the next. They suggest that over one-half of girls sexually abused by their fathers, stepfathers, or mothers' boyfriends have mothers who were also sexually abused as a child. It seems that a significant proportion of women who are abused as a child grow up and marry or live with partners who abuse them and may also abuse their daughters, thus transmitting victimization from mother to daughter. Children who live with an abused mother are 12 times more likely to be sexually abused (McCloskey, Figueredo, and Koss, 1995).

As with physical assault, white children are more likely than either black or Latino children to be sexually assaulted by a family member within the household rather than someone outside the household. Among victims of child sexual abuse, 75 percent of white children are assaulted by a member of the household, as opposed to 13 percent of black children and 9 percent of Latino children (American Humane Association, 1985). The average age of abuse victims is between 8 and 12. Some evidence suggests that boys are abused at an earlier age (8.5) than girls (12.4). In addition, the abuse of boys generally takes place for a shorter period of time. Furthermore, sexually abused boys are typically from poorer socioeconomic backgrounds than are sexually abused girls, and abused boys from families where the mother has less than a high school education are more than twice as likely as boys in families where the mother has higher education to report abuse. Moreover, Asian American boys are three times as likely as white boys to report sexual abuse (9 percent versus 3 percent). Latinos also report higher rates of sexual abuse than white boys. The sexual abuse rates among African American and white boys are very similar (Schoen et al., 1997b).

A variety of factors have been identified that place some children at greater risk than others. Many of the same characteristics cited earlier in the discussion of factors that predispose children to physical abuse apply here as well. In addition, physical or emotional handicaps, lack of supervision, a mother absent from the home, a sexually punitive or religiously fanatic mother, a mother who did not finish high school or who kept herself isolated, and a stepfather present in the home (Smith and Adler, 1991).

The Effects of Child Abuse Researchers have only recently begun to focus on the long-term consequences of child abuse. We already know that the most serious short-term effect is death. Among the findings on long-term effects are that a large percentage of sexually abused children become prostitutes or drug users and that sexually abused female runaways are more likely to be involved in deviant or criminal behavior than are nonabused females (Andersen, 1988). In addition, victims frequently suffer any one or more of a wide range of ailments, which can include (1) physical ailments, such as bruises, genital pain and bleeding, problems walking or sitting, eating disorders, headaches and stomachaches, brain injuries; infants and toddlers who have been shaken violently sometimes suffer bleeding within the brain; (2) emotional problems, such as anxiety, fear, guilt, nightmares, depression, temper tantrums, hostility, aggression, perfectionism, or phobias; (3) cognitive problems, including learning disabilities, poor attention and concentration, and declining grades in school; and (4) behavioral problems, such as social withdrawal, sexualized behavior or sexual preoccupation, regression/immaturity, hyperactivity, and family/peer conflicts (Barnett, Miller-Perrin, and Perrin, 1997).

Food, sex, alcohol, and/or drugs deaden painful memories of the abuse and expel reality, at least temporarily. Bulimia and anorexia are also forms of self-punishment, eventually leading to the ultimate self-victimization, suicide. When child victims of sexual abuse become adults, they often have problems with their sexuality; many avoid intimacy and emotional bonding; and many become abusers themselves or victims of spousal battering and abuse (Karp et al., 1995; Chandy, Blum, and Resnick, 1996; Wilsnak et al., 1997). Less is known about the gender-specific consequences of sexual abuse for male victims. According to some researchers, one of the consequences for male victims is linked to the fact that definitions of masculinity in U.S. culture can compound the consequences of male sexual victimization. For example, some studies have found that the most common reaction of boys is to try to reassert their masculinity, often inappropriately. This can take the form of disobedience, hostility, aggression, fighting, violence, and destructiveness, or they may experience some confusion about their sexual identity (Mignon, Larson, and Holmes, 2002). Finally, it should be pointed out that not all children who are sexually abused follow a deviant or self-victimization life course. With the support of parents, family members, friends, appropriate therapies, as well as individual interpersonal strength and resiliency, many of these children build healthy and constructive lives (Ambert, 2001).

ELDER ABUSE IN THE UNITED STATES

As our earlier historical account of family violence illustrates, abuse of the elderly by their adult children (and sometimes grandchildren or other relatives) is not new, nor was it always viewed as a problem. Recently, however, elder abuse has gained widespread public attention and has been defined by some people as a major social problem. For example, a recent *Chicago Sun-Times* survey on elder abuse estimated that in the city of Chicago alone, each year over 21,000 people 60 years of age or older are victims of abuse, or one such person every 24 minutes. The abuse of elders ranges from financial exploitation, property damage or theft, mental or sexual exploitation and abuse to homicide (Fornek, 2001). As we shall see in Chapter 14, a growing percentage of the U.S. population is over age 65. In fact, according to the Administration on Aging (2001), the number of elderly people living in the United States will increase dramatically over the next several decades. This is particularly true for people of color. For example, it is projected that the number of white elders will increase by approximately 97 percent compared to 265 percent for African American elders and 530 percent for Latinas/os. Given these statistics some people have suggested that, in general, older people of color might be at greater risk of abuse and neglect than white elders primarily because they are more often less able to advocate for themselves because of cultural, language, or educational barriers. Although there is little current research that examines race or ethnic specific cases of or factors involved in elder abuse, some observers have suggested that among specific racial/ethnic groups, African American elders might be at slightly higher risk than whites, because, for example, African American seniors, especially grandmothers, are more likely than whites to take in needy children, grandchildren, and even great-grandchildren. Therefore, given their increasing numbers in the population and their greater propensity to take in children, at least in theory they are thought to be at greater risk of abuse (Wallace, 2002). In any event, the greater longevity and visibility of older people have increased our awareness of and sensitivity to the many problems they experience, including violent treatment at the hands of family members. Like all other forms of family violence, elder abuse is greatly underreported. Estimates are that only one in six incidents of elder abuse is ever reported to the authorities (Wallace, 2002). Approximately 1 out of 25 elderly persons are victimized annually. This translates into about 1.4 million elderly who are abused nationally. The rates for various types of elderly maltreatment and abuse vary, with physical abuse having the highest rate, 62 percent, followed by abandonment, 56 percent; emotional or psychological abuse, 54 percent; material abuse, 45 percent; and neglect, 41 percent (Tatara, 1998). Older people in the United States are more likely to be abused by family members, intimates, or acquaintances than by strangers. Each year, for example, approximately 36,000 people 60 years of age or older are injured by a relative, intimate, or close acquaintance, and about 500 of them are killed. Relatives or intimates commit more than one in four murders and one in ten of the incidents of nonlethal violence against elders. Most of this violence and abuse occurs in or near the elder's home. Currently, the abuse of parents by their children, popularly referred to as "granny bashing" in England, is estimated to range from 500,000 to 2.5 million cases per year for acts of physical violence alone; 1 million of these parents are seriously injured (Gelles and Cornell, 1990; Wallace, 1996, 2000).

What Is Elder Abuse?

The term **elder abuse** is a broad one that includes the physical, psychological, and material maltreatment and neglect of older people. Although many older Americans are independent and in good health, the chances of poor health and dependency increase with age, as does the potential for victimization in any one or more of the following forms: physical violence, psychological abuse (such as verbal abuse, threats, intimidation, isolation, and neglect), physical and sexual maltreatment (such as physical restraint, overmedication, withholding medicine, food, or personal care, and rape or other sexual assault), material abuse (such as theft or misuse of money or other personal property), and personal violation (such as placement in a nursing home against the person's will).

Like other low-status groups in the United States, older Americans are highly vulnerable to neglect and abuse. Elder abuse takes a variety of forms. Although many older people are independent and healthy, as life expectancy increases more of the fragile elderly spend some time in a convalescent center or nursing home that may be understaffed and with inadequate resources. The result is that many of our elderly are isolated and neglected, left to try to meet their social and personal needs as best they can.

Who Are the Abused and the Abusers?

As with women and children, some older adults run a greater risk of being abused than others: women, older people with physical or mental impairments, and those dependent on a caretaker to meet their basic needs. Current research suggests that over four-fifths (84 percent) of the victims of elder abuse and neglect are white, compared to 8 percent African American, 5 percent Latina/o, 2 percent Asian American/Pacific Islander, and 0.4 percent Native American (Tatara, 1998). In addition, female elders, especially those 75 years of age and older, are the most likely victims of elder abuse. This probably reflects their lack of strength, their general lack of power, their devalued status, and the fact that they outnumber elderly men. Not everyone, however, agrees that elderly women run a greater risk of abuse than elderly men. One set of researchers, for example, found little difference in the victimization rates of older women and men, but the abuse inflicted by husbands was much more severe and serious than that inflicted by wives (Pillemer and Finkelhor, 1988; Wallace, 2002).

Although the picture is still inconclusive, family members alone are reported to be the perpetrators in nine out of ten (89.7 percent) substantiated cases of elder abuse and/or neglect (U.S. Department of Health and Human Services, 1998). Furthermore, the abuser apparently is most often an adult child (53 percent of elder abuse perpetrators) or a spouse (19 percent of elder abuse perpetrators) (Tatara, 1998). Among married elderly couples, violence and abuse are typically perpetrated by the male spouse and are often a continuation of an earlier pattern of abuse. Elderly women who abuse their husbands may be enacting revenge for previous abuse by the husband (Renzetti and Curran, 1992).

Among children who abuse their parents, sons are most likely to use physical violence whereas daughters are more likely to practice elderly neglect, and the most frequent offenders are adult daughters. This probably reflects the fact that because of gender role socialization, daughters most often have the responsibility of caring for an aging parent or other relative. Often, adult children who abuse their elderly parents were themselves abused and thus learned that violence toward intimates is acceptable behavior. In some cases, they may be acting in retaliation against an abusive parent (Wallace, 2002). In other cases, the abuser is financially dependent on the older person, and the abuse stems from this dependency and lack of power in the relationship.

Although over two-thirds of U.S. states have enacted mandatory reporting laws to deal with elder abuse, some people question the effectiveness of these laws, given that they address the problem only after the fact. Critics have suggested that a more successful strategy might be to provide adult children with greater institutional assistance and support in caring for their elderly parents. (Chapter 14 contains a fuller discussion of the elderly.) Indeed, the abuse of the elderly is part of the larger problem of structured inequality. Like other low-status groups in U.S. society, older Americans are highly vulnerable to abuse.

SIBLING ABUSE

Who most commonly abuses children? Perhaps surprisingly, the answer is not mothers or fathers or other adults, but siblings. Although the media, the public, researchers, social workers, and other relevant professionals have focused our attention on child and woman abuse, seldom have they discussed sibling violence and abuse. This fact notwithstanding, according to some authorities on the subject, it is perhaps the most common form of family violence. In fact, siblings hit, slap, kick, and beat each other so frequently that few of us pay much attention to this behavior or consider it to be a form of family violence. Indeed, such behavior is so commonplace that it is almost normative. For example, most of us have probably at one time or another during our childhood engaged in some type of altercation with a sibling: pulling hair, pushing, name-calling, biting, pinching, poking, scaring, and so on. Parents often do not take these behaviors seriously, viewing them as normal childhood behavior, labeling it sibling rivalry. In fact, critics agree with parents, arguing that much of the aggressive behavior between siblings is not really serious and thus should not be labeled as abusive. Although research confirms this argument, finding that the majority of violence between siblings could be classified as nonabusive, the fact remains that a high frequency of violence does occur between siblings that can definitely be classified as abusive

WRITING YOUR OWN SCRIPT

RECOGNIZING ABUSIVE BEHAVIOR

As you have learned from reading this chapter as well as from simply being a member of contemporary U.S. society, violence and abuse in intimate relationships are of serious concern. Because they often occur in the privacy of our intimate relationships and in the privacy of our homes, we sometimes do not know what to do or where to go if we or someone we know is a victim of intimate violence.

If you are involved in an intimate relationship, consider your relationship for a moment. Is it a violence-free relationship, or is it bad for your health? Is it heading into dangerous territory? Has your partner ever been abusive? With the high incidence of verbal, physical, emotional, and sexual abuse in intimate relationships it is very important to know as much as possible about our partners in terms of the likelihood that they could be or are abusive or violent. Although there is no specific profile of an abuser, the data presented in this chapter suggest certain characteristics or factors that are prevalent among abusers, such as poor self-esteem, rigidity, and excessive dependency. Are these characteristics familiar to you? If they are characteristic of you or your partner they should alert you to the possibility that the person with such characteristics could become abusive or violent. (This is not to say that this will happen, but you should be alert for other signs of abusive behavior and seek help before violence occurs.)

Take the following test to find out if your relationship is violent or headed toward violence.

Answer each of the following categories of questions. If you answer yes to more than two of the categories, you should seek help. Do you know or suspect that someone you know is in a violent relationship? Share these questions with that person and then help her or him get appropriate assistance.

Is your partner someone who . . .

______ 1. *Is obsessively jealous, aggressive, and possessive toward you; won't let you have friends; checks up on you; won't accept your leaving him or her?*

______ 2. *Tries to control you by being very bossy, giving you orders and demanding that you follow them; makes all of the decisions; or doesn't take your opinion seriously or doesn't allow you to have an opinion at all?*

______ 3. *Is threatening and whom you are afraid of? Do you worry about how this person will react to things you do or say? Does this person ever threaten you, or use or own weapons?*

______ 4. *Is violent? Does this person have a history of violence: losing his or her temper, bragging about mistreating others? Has the person assaulted someone within or outside of the family or has the person committed some other violent crime?*

______ 5. *Pressures you for sex, is forceful about sex? Accepts no when you say no? Thinks that women or girls are sex objects, attempts to manipulate you or make you feel guilty by saying things like: "If you really loved me, you would . . . "? Does the person get too serious about the relationship too fast for comfort?*

______ 6. *Abuses alcohol or other drugs and/or pressures you to take them? Does the person use alcohol or other drugs as an excuse for aggression?*

______ 7. *Mistreats you and then blames you for the mistreatment? Tells you that you provoked it, that you brought it on yourself?*

______ 8. *Has a history of bad relationships and blames the other person for all of the problems?*

______ 9. *Has very traditional views about women's and men's roles; believes that men should be in control and powerful and that women should be passive and submissive?*

______ 10. *Has hit, pushed, slapped, choked, kicked, had forced sex with you, or otherwise abused you?*

______ 11. *Isolates you from your family, friends, neighbors, and the community? Makes your family and friends concerned about your safety?*

Sources: Adapted from the Mount Auburn Hospital Prevention and Training Center and the Dating Violence Intervention Project.

(Barnett, Miller-Perrin, and Perrin, 1997; Perozynski and Kramer, 1999). Statistics on sibling violence suggest, however, that we reexamine our thinking about this behavior as "natural," "inevitable," and "nonabusive."

A 1980 survey that included 733 families with two or more children found that 82 percent of the children between 3 and 17 years of age reported having used some type of violence against a sibling in the previous year (Straus, Gelles, and Steinmetz, 1980). By the late 1980s, researchers suggested that every year at least 3 percent of siblings confront each other with lethal weapons, such as knives and guns (Gelles and Straus, 1988). In 1988, Mildred Pagelow reported that almost one-half of the 1025 college students whom she studied indicated that when they were adolescents, they, along with their siblings, were either the aggressors or the victims of violent acts of abuse such as kicking and punching. One in ten reported that their siblings beat them up, and 4 percent stated that their siblings had threatened them with a weapon such as a knife or gun or had actually used a knife or gun against them. Other studies estimate that upward of 29 million siblings physically abuse each other every year. These acts are not minor acts of hitting. Rather, over half of them could have resulted in legal prosecution had they been perpetrated by someone outside the family. Added to this is the fact that one in ten murders in families are committed by siblings. In addition to the physical violence between siblings, sibling sexual abuse or sibling incest is also seldom talked about but is perhaps a more common occurrence than parent–child incest. Sibling sexual assault is typically brother-to-sister initiated or coerced, but sometimes it occurs between same-sex siblings as well. Sibling victims are often much younger than the perpetrator. Sibling sexual abuse perpetrated by adolescents often occurs repeatedly and over a longer period of time than adolescent-perpetrated abuse against nonfamily members. This is due primarily to the ready availability of a sibling and the convenience of being at home (O'Brien, 1991; Smith and Israel, 1991). Even in old age, siblings often abuse one another. Some scholars suggest that it is often the case that, like elderly spouse abuse, sibling abuse in old age tends to be a continuation of earlier family violence (Mignon, Larson, and Holmes, 2002). Because of the historic acceptance of sibling violence we are unable to ascertain whether such behavior is becoming more or less common. Like the public, researchers have long ignored this pattern of violence.

Who most often initiates sibling violence? Boys of all ages are more violent than girls, but the difference is relatively small. The highest rates of sibling violence tend to occur in families with only male children. Families with all daughters have lower levels of sibling violence and, in fact, the presence of girls in the family reduces the level of sibling violence.

Sibling violence is also higher among children in families in which child and spouse assault also occur. Sibling violence is more common during the youngest ages, when siblings are home together, and decreases as children get older and spend less time at home and with each other (Straus, Gelles, and Steinmetz, 1980). Like other forms of victimization, sibling abuse involves a number of forms of maltreatment including mental, emotional, and sexual abuse. Some children both physically and sexually abuse their younger siblings. Various research studies have reported a significant amount of overlap between the various forms of sibling abuse, with emotional abuse between siblings most common, followed by sexual abuse and then physical abuse (Wieche, 1990; Worling, 1995).

Little is known about the reasons for sibling violence. Some researchers have suggested that it is a learned response. Children raised in a violent environment learn that physical punishment is an appropriate way to deal with certain situations. In contrast, children raised in an environment free of violence learn other ways to resolve conflicts with siblings and later with other intimates (Gelles and Cornell, 1990).

SUMMARY

Family and intimate relationship violence are deeply rooted in human history and widespread in contemporary society. The family is the major context within which most violence in this country occurs. A number of myths about family violence, ranging from the notion that it is a rare occurrence to the idea that women secretly desire to be raped, obscure our view of and knowledge about its pervasiveness.

Although any family member can be abused, women and children are the most common victims. Woman battering is perhaps the most common and one of the most underreported crimes in this country. Its cyclic nature has been described in terms of the battered-woman syndrome. Although we do not know a lot about battering across race and sexual orientation, we know that it can be found among all groups.

Family violence includes not only battering but also sexual assault. Here too, women and girls are the typical victims. Although information on the incidence and prevalence of marital rape is limited, there is a growing public awareness that husbands can and do rape their wives. This fact notwithstanding, the criminal justice system generally is unresponsive to battered and sexually assaulted women except in cases of severe violence or death. In fact, the attitudes of police officers, judges, prosecutors, and other personnel in the system as well as some laws and statutes often limit women's ability to find relief from a violent life situation.

Some of the most visible effects of violence against women are low self-esteem, self-hate, economic and emotional dependence on others, fear, anxiety, and self-destructive behavior. Victims also develop a number of survival strategies, some of which, such as overeating and substance abuse, are self-destructive. In addition, a growing number of women are dealing with their violent situation by fighting back. Women sometimes use violence against men, although they most often do so in self-defense against a threatened or actual physical attack.

Men are also victims of violence. However, because men often do not report their abuse we cannot be sure of the prevalence of male abuse.

Women are not the only major victims of family violence: Somewhere between 1 million and 4 million children are abused each year by parents or someone close to the family. We are only beginning to appreciate the extent of this problem today. Other, less visible victims of family violence include siblings, the elderly, and lesbians and gays.

KEY TERMS

infanticide
rape syndrome
woman battering
sexual assault
battered-woman syndrome
victim blaming
battered-child syndrome
parricide
incest
transmission of victimization
elder abuse

QUESTIONS FOR STUDY AND REFLECTION

1. Do you have siblings? Same sex or different sex? Did or do you engage in behaviors that can be defined as abusive? When does behavior between siblings become abusive? What should we do about sibling abuse? Should the abusers be subject to the same penalties as other abusers? Why or why not? What if your 7-year-old son sexually assaulted your 3-year-old daughter? What would you do?
2. Which child-rearing philosophies and economic and social factors contribute to the prevalence of child abuse in the United States today? Should children be spanked? In your opinion, is there a difference between spanking and child abuse? Have you ever hit a child with something other than your hand? Do you think your behavior constituted battering? Why or why not?
3. In your opinion, is it possible for a man to rape his wife? A woman to rape her husband? Why or why not? To what degree would you be willing to remain in a marriage if your spouse raped you or you raped your spouse?
4. What factors might explain why some societies are more likely than others to abuse their elderly members? What possible reasons do you think a person could have for battering an elderly parent? Have you ever been physically or psychologically abusive to one or both of your parents? How might we deal with the problem of elder abuse?

ADDITIONAL RESOURCES

SOCIOLOGICAL

BART, PAULINE B., AND EILEEN GEIL MORAN, EDS. 1993. *Violence against Women: The Bloody Footprints.* Newbury Park, CA: Sage. This book, by the dean of researchers on violence against women, especially sexual assault, is a compilation of articles originally published in the journal *Gender and Society.* The articles cover various types of violence as well as institutional responses to violence.

GELLES, RICHARD J., AND CLAIRE PEDRICK CORNELL. 1990. *Intimate Violence in Families.* Newbury Park, CA: Sage. This is a handy little reader aimed at undergraduate students and designed to provide a basic overview of the subject of family violence. It examines violence against children, women, siblings, adolescents, parents, and the elderly.

KIMMEL, MICHAEL S., AND MICHAEL A. MESSNER. 1995. *Men's Lives.* Boston: Allyn & Bacon. An excellent anthology focusing on the male experience. The book is organized around specific themes that define masculinity and the issues that men confront over their lifetime. Part 6 deals with men and women, including some poignant articles on the American context of male violence and the rape of women.

RENZETTI, CLAIRE, AND MILEY CHARLES, EDS. 1996. *Violence in Gay and Lesbian Domestic Partnerships.* New York: Harrington Park Press. An excellent compilation of studies and literature reviews of research on intimate violence among lesbian and gay couples.

LITERARY

GREENWOOD, TAMMY. 2000. *Nearer Than the Sky.* New York: St. Martin's Press. A haunting novel that digs into the life of a family suffering from the frightening effects of Munchausen syndrome by proxy. It is a story of a woman who wishes that her childhood had never happened. Happily married, the main character is drawn slowly backward into her past when she begins to suspect her sister of causing harm to her own newborn baby. Discovering this, she realizes that their mother is the one responsible for her sister's illness and her sister is responsible for her own daughter's mysterious sicknesses. Sociologically relevant, the novel illustrates the far-reaching effects and ultimately destructive force of this type of child abuse.

WEISS, ELAINE. 2000. *Surviving Domestic Violence: Voices of Women Who Broke Free.* Sandy, UT: Agreka Books. The book consists of the collective stories of 12 women from across the United States who are survivors of domestic violence and abuse; they left their abusers and went on to reconstruct their lives. The stories are at once painful and humorous, insightful, uplifting, and indicative of the remarkable courage of these women survivors. A domestic violence survivor herself, the author presents a clear picture of women as both victims and survivors of domestic violence. An excellent context for faculty to engage students in a discussion of human agency.

INTERNET

http://www.nomsv.org/ A Web site maintained by the National Organization on Male Sexual Victimization. This site is designed to meet the needs of adult male survivors of sexual abuse through the provision of a number of resources, including a chat room, a newsletter, books, news updates, and a directory of clinicians and therapists.

http://www.Silcom.com/~paladin/madv Sponsored by the Paladin Group Grant Mentors, this is a practical research-oriented site that offers advocacy and information as well as a variety of other resources including addresses of shelters.

The Process of Uncoupling: Divorce in the United States

IN THE NEWS: OKLAHOMA CITY

Alarm bells are ringing in the Bible Belt and both religious and political leaders are heeding the call. Although Nevada, the perennial leader in divorce, remains at the head of the list, four states with large numbers of Baptists and evangelical religious sects, known for their social conservativism and family-values orientation, round out the top five. Tennessee, Arkansas, Alabama, and Oklahoma each have divorce rates approximately 50 percent above the national average. Not only are their divorce rates higher, but over the past decade these states have also led the nation in an increase in the number of cohabitating couples (Harden, 2001). By contrast, in socially liberal states such as New York, Connecticut, and Massachusetts with high percentages of Roman Catholics, the divorce rate is half of what it is in these Bible Belt states.

Reactions to these findings were swift and sometimes emotional. Some people pointed the finger at religion, questioning the effectiveness of how its leaders minister to families. Anthony Jordan, executive director of the Baptist General Convention in Oklahoma, seemed to agree, noting that the Catholic church does not recognize divorce and that Protestant evangelists, in attempting to be compassionate, do not place the stigma on divorce that should be there. He also believes that ministers give more attention to helping young people plan a wedding than to helping them plan a marriage (Harden, 2001). Stewart Beasley, president of the Oklahoma Psychological Association, believes that the Christian teaching that there is to be no sex before marriage puts pressure on young people to marry early, thus increasing the risk of marital instability (Veith, 1999).

Other analysts view such reasoning as a logical fallacy, arguing that besides a high number of evangelicals, these states have other factors that contribute to a high divorce rate. Prime among them is the fact that these states rank at the bottom of the country for household income.

Arkansas Governor Mike Huckabee has declared a "marital emergency" and vowed to cut his state's divorce rate in half by 2010. His counterpart in Oklahoma, Frank Keating, has initiated the "Oklahoma Marriage Policy" with a goal of reducing the divorce rate in his state by a third during that same period. These governors have enlisted clergy, lawyers, psychologists, and academics in the fight to improve marriages and, thus, make divorce less likely. Critics point out, however, that as laudable as these efforts may be, they do not attack the primary structural cause of marital strife, lack of sufficient economic resources to maintain a family (Latham, 2000)

WHAT WOULD YOU DO? If you were the governor of a state with a high divorce rate, how would you react? What would you do, if anything, to lower the divorce rate? Do you advocate making it more difficult to get divorced and/or to get married? How much responsibility do you want organized religion and government to have in preparing people for marriage and/or for reducing the likelihood of divorce? Explain.

The vast majority of people who promise to love, cherish, and comfort their spouse "until death do us part" really mean it. How, then, can we account for the fact that in the 1990s approximately 1.2 million married couples in the United States divorced each year?

The fact that divorce is so common today has led many to conclude that the family is a dying or at least a critically wounded institution. This thinking reflects the myths discussed in Chapter 1, that in the past marriages were happier, families were more loving, and members treated each other with respect. People who feel this way tend to see divorce in a negative light, as a recent social problem that must be overcome. In contrast, some people see divorce as a solution to the problem of unhappy and sometimes abusive marriages. Both schools of thought find abundant evidence to support their positions.

As with so many social phenomena, however, the reality concerning divorce lies somewhere in between. Regardless of the quality of the marriage they left, few people undergo separation or divorce without experiencing some pain. In fact, some divorced people never get over the trauma they experience with the breakup of their marriage. This is especially true for the spouses who didn't want the divorce. Conversely, divorce allows people who were unhappy in their marriages to move on and build satisfying new relationships. To appreciate more fully these divergent outcomes of divorce, we need to see how the current institution of divorce came about. In this chapter we examine the historical controversies surrounding divorce, with an eye to understanding current divorce laws and social policies. We also discuss how divorce rates vary from place to place, as illustrated by the higher divorce rates in the Bible Belt (see "In the News"), who divorces and why, and the consequences of divorce for family members, as well as its implications for the larger society.

HISTORICAL PERSPECTIVES

Contrary to popular belief, divorce is not a modern phenomenon. It has been a part of U.S. history since 1639, when a Puritan court in Massachusetts granted the first divorce decree in colonial America. This does not mean, however, that divorce was socially acceptable to all the early settlers. In fact, throughout U.S. history conflict has existed between those who favor divorce and those who oppose it.

Divorce in Early America

Although early in their history the New England colonies permitted divorce, the grounds for divorce varied from one colony to another. Divorces were often adversarial in nature—one partner was required to prove that the other was at fault and had violated the marriage contract. Thus, friends, relatives, and neighbors were called as witnesses and, in effect, were forced to choose sides in what often became an acrimonious procedure. The finding of fault became the basis for harsh punishments for the "offending" party: fines, whippings, incarceration in the stocks, prohibition from remarrying, and even banishment from the colony. This faultfinding also became the basis for **alimony**, a concept originating in England in the 1650s, whereby a husband deemed to be at fault for the dissolution of the marriage was required to provide his wife with a financial allowance. Conversely, if a wife was judged to be at fault, she lost any claim to financial support. Then as today, however, the law was one thing and its implementation another in that courts did not always enforce the payment of the award. We will never know the true extent of divorce in colonial America, however, because many records are incomplete or lost. Some records were never kept.

Although the population of the time included Native Americans and African Americans, their marriages were rarely recorded in the white courts. Thus, it is likely that few Native or African Americans sought an official divorce. However, one researcher did uncover the record of a divorce granted in 1745 to a slave living in Massachusetts on the grounds of his wife's adultery. The same researcher also found that in 1768, Lucy Purnan, a free black woman, received a divorce decree on the grounds of her husband's cruelty (cited in Riley, 1991:14). Additionally, Jesuit missionaries complained about frequent divorce among the Native Americans they came to convert (Amott and Matthaei, 1991:39).

Divorce was granted more infrequently in the middle section of the colonies than in the north. Most of the middle colonies did not enact explicit statutes regarding divorce, and records show that only a few divorces were granted in the colonies of New York, New Jersey, and Pennsylvania. For the most part the southern colonies did not enact divorce legislation until after independence was achieved. The reluctance of these colonies to legalize divorce should not be interpreted to mean that marriages were happier and more tranquil there than in the rest of the country. Formal and informal separations seem to have been widespread in these colonies, including Native Americans and African Americans both free and enslaved; evidence of marital discord can be found in southern newspapers of this period, which carried disclaimers of spousal debt, stories and advertisements of runaway spouses, and other forms of marital strife.

Why did these early marriages dissolve? Historian Glenda Riley (1991) sees a variety of social and economic factors interacting to put strains on marriages and families. The growing mobility of the colonists, the movement west, and the emergence of a market economy along with new technology all combined to alter the role of the family as an economic unit, and thus to undercut to a degree a couple's sense of interdependency and common purpose. Additionally, the resistance to British rule and the ideology of the Enlightenment, with its emphasis on liberty, justice, and equality, caused people to examine their own level of personal well-being. On the individual level people sometimes made errors in their choice of spouse or married under duress of an unplanned pregnancy, only to regret their actions later on. Whatever the causes, on the eve of the American Revolution, divorce was fairly well established in the social fabric of the nation.

Divorce in Nineteenth-Century America

The period following the American Revolution was a time of rapid social, political, and economic change. Each state assumed jurisdiction for divorce. Although there were individual differences among the various states, the general trend was to liberalize divorce laws and expand the grounds for divorce. Two major exceptions to this rule were found in New York, where adultery remained the sole ground for divorce, and in South Carolina, where divorce was not permitted. These restrictive laws led to "migratory" divorce, whereby residents of one state would travel to another with more liberal laws. To discourage people from coming into their state solely to obtain a divorce, many of the more liberal states instituted minimum-residency requirements.

Data on the number of divorces were not systematically collected until the end of the nineteenth century. Newspaper accounts and scattered divorce records, however, suggest that increasing numbers of people were utilizing the liberalized divorce laws. The apparent increase in the divorce rate sent shock waves across the United States. Passionate debates were carried on in newspapers and legislative chambers and from pulpits. Those opposing divorce, like newspaper editor Horace Greeley, saw it as

IN OTHER PLACES

CROSS-CULTURAL PATTERNS IN DIVORCE

Cultures vary significantly in their degree of acceptance of divorce and the rules governing who can initiate a divorce. In some cultures, like the Hopi Native Americans of the Southwest, both women and men could initiate divorce. Among the Yoruba of West Africa, however, only women could initiate divorce; and for centuries among many Asian cultures, only men could ask for a divorce.

Researchers who studied the matrilineal Hopi 50 years ago found a high divorce rate: about one out of three marriages. The divorce process was easy. A wife could initiate divorce simply by placing her husband's belongings outside their dwelling. A divorcing husband simply moved back into his mother's house. If the couple had children, they stayed with the mother (Queen, Habenstein, and Quadagno, 1985:49–50).

According to research conducted in the 1960s, the divorce rate among the Yoruba people was also high. For the most part, women were economically independent from their husbands. Divorce was not traumatic. Remarriages were frequent, and the concept of "divorce" had little meaning (Lloyd, 1968).

In traditional Chinese societies, only men could initiate divorce. Men did so for a number of reasons: a wife's adultery, her failure to give birth to a male heir, jealousy, lecherousness, incurable disease, or not serving her parents-in-law well (Song, 1991). Today, however, as women become better educated and join the work force, they are becoming more self-confident and less willing to stay with husbands who are abusive or have affairs. In Taiwan, for example, just one in 17 marriages ended in divorce 20 years ago. Today, there is one divorce for every 4.3 marriages. It is estimated that about 40 percent of divorces are now filed by women. Twenty years ago almost all divorces were initiated by men. Wang Yu-pao, a member of the feminist group Women's Awakening, says women who seek divorce do so as a last resort. Despite women's growing independence, the courts still favor men when it comes to property and child custody. Ho Tse-suan's experience is a typical example. A 43-year-old accountant, Ho Tse-suan lost custody of her two children after divorcing her husband and only regained custody 4 years later when her former husband died in a car accident (Huang, 1999).

What do you think? *What is your reaction to these three different approaches to divorce? How do they compare with practices in the United States? Do you think there is any merit to making divorce as easy as it is for the Hopi and the Yoruba? Or as difficult as it is for Chinese women? Would similar models work in urban, technologically developed societies?*

immoral and responsible for most of the social ills of the day, and argued that restricting divorce would deter hasty or ill-advised marriages.

On the other side, social critics of the day argued that marriage, not divorce, needed reform. Women's groups spoke out against wife abuse, which had gained public visibility by the 1850s. Female divorce petitioners frequently cited cruelty, including sexual abuse, as the reason for wanting to end their marriage. Proponents of divorce, like Indiana legislator Robert Owen, saw personal happiness and fulfillment as the primary purpose of marriage; they believed that a marriage ought to end if these goals are frustrated.

In 1887, Congress responded to these public debates by authorizing Commissioner of Labor Carroll D. Wright to undertake a study of marriage and divorce in the United States. Wright found that 68,547 divorces were granted between 1872 and 1876, representing almost a 28 percent increase over the 53,574 divorces granted between 1867 and 1871 (cited in Riley, 1991:79). He noted several interesting patterns in these data: Women obtained two-thirds of the divorces (a pattern still evident today); desertion was the most common ground for divorce; and western states granted the most divorces, and southern states the fewest. Although people in all classes and occupations sought divorces, more divorces occurred among the working class than among the middle and upper classes.

Although much of the public reaction to divorce focused on its frequency and availability, other problems connected with divorce were becoming evident. After divorce many women, especially those with custody of children, became impoverished. Although alimony was often granted by the courts, enforcement was difficult. Child custody was another problem area. The traditional view in colonial America was that children belong to the father; therefore, he should automatically get custody if a marriage was dissolved by either death or divorce. Thus, some women stayed in unhappy marriages rather than risk losing their children. With industrialization and the consequent notion of separate spheres for women and men, however, judges came to adopt the "tender-years" principle that children under the age of 7 were better off with their mothers. This principle was based on the assumption that women are by nature more adept at nurturing than men are.

Men did not always agree with this interpretation. Sometimes, heated custody battles ensued, especially if the mother was seen as the spouse at fault. Judges occasionally split siblings, giving girls or younger children over to the care of mothers and boys or older children to fathers. This decision, called **split custody,** is still made by some judges. As we shall see later, the divorce reforms of the twentieth century have not been completely successful in resolving the debate over which parent should have custody of the children. In the reform efforts of the twentieth century the principle of tender years was modified, and child custody was, in principle at least, based on the best interests of the child.

Americans were also troubled by the destructive consequences that often accompanied divorce. Most of the criticism, however, focused on the divergent laws and procedures that existed in the various states. Many sought a solution to these problems by proposing a uniform divorce law that would encompass the entire country.

Twentieth-Century America: Efforts at Reform

Generally, those favoring a more restrictive and uniform approach to divorce saw it as a moral evil to be stopped. This moral-legal view was challenged by a group of scholars in the newly developing social sciences. These analysts believed that divorce originates not in legislation but rather in the social and economic environment in which marriage is located. The changing patterns of divorce seemed to support this view. The divorce rate jumped considerably after World War I, when many marriages, some hastily conceived in the midst of war, floundered under the stress of economic and political uncertainty and the strains of separation and reunion. This war-related increase in divorce was not a new phenomenon; it had been observed earlier in the United States in the period following the Civil War (and following all subsequent wars). Industrialization, the decline in economic functions of the family, employment and financial independence of women, weakening of religious beliefs, and the declining social stigma of divorce were also viewed as causes of divorce.

By the 1960s, the focus of the divorce debate began to shift once again. Although still concerned with the high rate of divorce, public attention increasingly turned to the effects of divorce on spouses and children. Numerous voices were raised against the adversarial nature of divorce, and various proposals for divorce by mutual consent were put forth, culminating in California's **no-fault divorce** bill signed into law by Governor Ronald Reagan (who was himself divorced) in 1969 (Jacob, 1988). Over the next 20 years, state after state adopted its own version of no-fault divorce, believing that the most negative consequences of divorce would be eliminated by this measure. Spouses no longer had to accuse each other of wrongdoing; instead, they could apply for a divorce on grounds of "irretrievable breakdown" or "irreconcilable differences." Indeed, no-fault divorce removed much of the acrimony of divorce while also lowering its economic cost. As we shall see later in this chapter, however, almost 30 years' experience with no-fault divorce has shown that it is not the panacea its advocates anticipated. Issues of spousal support, division of marital property, and child custody remain problematic.

What lessons are to be learned from an examination of the history of divorce in the United States? Perhaps the most important is that neither marriage nor divorce can be understood apart from its social context. As Roderick Phillips (1988:640) observed: "It is entirely futile to expect marriage to remain constant or to have a consistent social meaning while social structures, economic relationships, demographic patterns, and cultural configurations have undergone the massive changes of past centuries." The historical record also makes it abundantly clear that efforts to eliminate divorce will in all likelihood fail. Therefore, it is probably more effective to focus social efforts on strengthening marriages and creating compassionate and fair systems of helping people whose marriages have failed.

Figure 12.1 summarizes the changes in the **divorce rate**—the number of divorces occurring annually for every 1000 people over the last half century. The divorce rate reached an all-time high of 5.2 in 1980. Since then it has declined slightly, standing at 4.1 in December 2000. However, as we will see, divorce is not evenly distributed across all segments of the population.

Race, Ethnicity, and Divorce

As Table 12.1 reveals, women are more likely to be divorced than are men across all major race and ethnic groups. This pattern can be explained by the fact that men are more likely to remarry than are women, a topic we will discuss in greater detail in Chapter 13. A second pattern is also evident in this table. African Americans have the highest percentage of divorced persons; Latinas/os, the lowest; and whites are

Figure 12.1

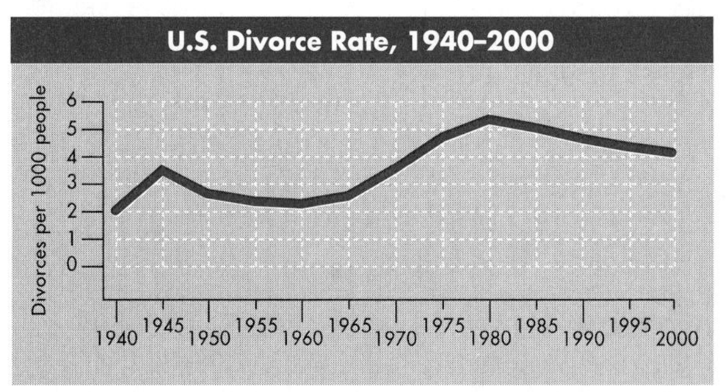

Sources: Adapted from National Center for Health Statistics, 1985, "Advance Report of Divorce Statistics, 1985," *Monthly Vital Statistics Report,* 38, 8 (Hyattsville, MD: Public Health Service [Supplement, December 7]): 2; "Births, Marriages, Divorces, and Deaths for March 1995," *Monthly Vital Statistics Report,* 44, 3 (Hyattsville, MD: Public Health Service [August 29]): 1; "Population Update," 1991, *Population Today,* 19 (July/August): 9; National Center for Health Statistics, 2000, "Births, Marriages, Divorces, and Deaths: Provisional Data for January/December 2000," *National Vital Statistics Reports* 49 (August 22): 6.

Table 12.1

Percentage of Divorced Population, by Sex, Race/Ethnicity, March 1999

	Male	Female
All races	8.9%	10.7%
White	8.9	10.6
Black	10.8	12.8
Latina/o	6.3	8.8

Source: Adapted from U.S. Census Bureau, 2000a. *Statistical Abstract of the United States, 2000* (Washington, DC: U.S. Government Printing Office): 5, Table 53, p. 51.

somewhat in the middle. A somewhat similar pattern exists in the rate of marriage dissolution. Forty-seven percent of first marriages of African American women end within 10 years compared with 34 percent for Latinas, 32 percent for white women, and 20 percent for Asian women (Bramlett and Mosher, 2001). Several factors can account for these differences.

Divorce among African Americans How do we explain the different rates of divorce among racial and ethnic groups? In the past some analysts have viewed the higher rate of divorce among African Americans as the legacy of slavery (Frazier, 1939). Subsequent scholarship, however, has found that the increase in black marital instability is a more recent development, accelerating in particular since 1960 and corresponding to a decline in the economic situation of large numbers of African Americans (Gutman, 1976; Cherlin, 1981). Numerous studies support the argument that higher divorce rates among African Americans reflect greater economic hardships (Teachman, Tedrow, and Crowder, 2000). For example, one statistical analysis showed that a significant amount of black–white differences in marital stability can be explained by differences in levels of education and income among the two groups (Jaynes and Williams, 1989). Studies in other countries have also found a strong relationship between unemployment and high divorce rates (Lester, 1996). In addition, there is a higher rate of teenage pregnancy and premarital pregnancies among African American women than in women in other groups, a factor that, in itself, increases the risk of marital dissolution across all groups (Garfinkel, McLanahan, and Robins, 1994). Finally, as we saw in Chapter 1, African Americans often rely on the extended family for social support. Thus, armed with the knowledge that there will be help for them, couples may be less reluctant to divorce than others whose communities offer less support and acceptance for divorcing couples.

Divorce among Latinas/os Because Latinas/os also experience higher rates of poverty and unemployment as a result of discrimination, we might assume that the Latina/o divorce ratio would be closer to that of blacks than to that of whites. In fact, as Table 12.1 indicates, Latinas/os had the lowest overall divorce rate of the three groups in 1999. Two factors are often cited to explain the relatively high level of marital stability among Latinas/os: a cultural tradition that emphasizes the importance of the family unit, and a religion (Catholicism) that prohibits divorce. According to a national survey, Latinas/os were less likely to see divorce as acceptable (57 percent) than the general population (66 percent) (Deane et al., 2000).

Demographers Hugh Carter and Paul Glick (1976:246) raise another issue that may be relevant here. In their analysis of 1960 census data they found that the lowest ratios of divorced to married persons for a major group were among the foreign-born white population. They speculated that lack of familiarity with the U.S. legal system and a reluctance to become involved in court actions probably led many foreign-born couples to tolerate marital problems that might have resulted in divorce among native-born groups. These conclusions might apply to those Latinas/os who have arrived in the United States most recently.

Although all these factors may contribute to the lower divorce rates found among Latinas/os, the Latina/o ratio itself presents several problems. It does not distinguish among the diverse categories of Latinas/os whose economic status and rates of marital stability might vary. Among Latinas, for example, Puerto Rican women are the most likely to be divorced and Cuban women are the least likely. The rate for Chicanas falls somewhere in between the other two groups (Sweet and Bumpass, 1987). One possible explanation for these differences is the greater economic stress experienced by Puerto Ricans; they have higher unemployment rates and less income than the other groups.

The Need for Further Research It is apparent that more research is needed if we are to understand the interactive effects of economic status, race, and ethnicity on marital stability. In particular, more data are needed on groups such as Native Americans, who have high divorce rates, and on Asian Americans, who have low rates. In 1980, 48 percent of Native American women and 43 percent of men were no longer in intact first marriages (Sweet and Bumpass, 1987:188). These high rates are probably due largely to the high rates of unemployment and poverty among Native Americans.

Like Latinas/os and Native Americans, Asian Americans include a wide spectrum of groups with different cultural traditions. Generally speaking, the number of divorces among Asian Americans is lower than the U.S. average, especially among first-generation immigrants. However, when we consider the number of households headed by women, there is considerable variation in the Asian American population. The rates are highest among some Southeast Asian groups (22 percent among Cambodians, Hmongs, and Laotians) followed by Filipinos and Vietnamese (18 percent), Koreans (13 percent), Chinese and Japanese (11 percent). Asian Indians have the lowest rate, only 7 percent (Lee, 1998:20).

Again economic factors play a role. Among Asian Americans, Cambodians, Hmongs, Laotians, and Vietnamese are the most likely to be employed in unskilled and semiskilled occupations. Asian Indians, Japanese, and Chinese workers are most likely to be employed in managerial and professional occupations (Lee, 1998:27). Many Asian American community leaders are concerned that as Asian Americans become more assimilated into mainstream U.S. culture, their traditional family patterns will change, and divorce rates will rise (O'Hare and Felt, 1991:10).

Race and ethnicity are, of course, not the only factors affecting divorce rates. The next section examines a variety of social and demographic factors that affect the likelihood of divorce.

WHO GETS DIVORCED, AND WHY?

If you are like most Americans, you are probably concerned by the high rate of divorce. Perhaps the thought has occurred to you that you or people close to you are likely to end up divorced. Although no one can say with any degree of certainty which marriages will end in divorce, based on existing patterns, researchers can predict the statistical probabilities for different groups.

Factors Affecting Marital Stability

Divorce rates vary from group to group and are associated with a wide range of factors (White, 1990; Kurdek, 1993), including age at marriage, premarital childbearing, education, income, religion, parental divorce, and the presence of children. By understanding how these factors can influence a marital relationship, people contemplating marriage can better evaluate their chances of a successful marriage. For example, knowing that the age at marriage can increase or decrease the likelihood of divorce may lead people more realistically to evaluate their readiness for marriage.

Age at First Marriage Younger brides and grooms, especially those who are still in their teens when they marry, are more likely to divorce. Forty-eight percent of marriages of women who married under age 18 dissolve within 10 years compared with 24 percent of marriages of women at least 25 years of age at marriage (Bramlett and Mosher, 2001). Social scientists also attribute the higher divorce rates found in the Bible Belt states (see "In the News") to the tendency for couples to marry at younger ages than their counterparts in other states. Similarly, marrying at a late age (35 plus) can increase the probability of divorce during the first 15 years of marriage (Booth, White, and Edwards, 1986). The reasons for marital instability among the young come easily to mind: immaturity, lack of adequate financial resources, different rates of personal growth, and often the pressures of early parenthood, particularly if it involves premarital childbearing. Numerous studies document a negative relationship between premarital childbearing and the risk of divorce after first marriage (Norton and Miller, 1992).

Compared to black and white couples, Latina/o couples have lower rates of divorce. Nevertheless, a growing number of Latinas are single parents.

By later ages, however, those problems should be resolved. Although fewer data on late marriages are available, some evidence suggests that late marriages tend to be more heterogamous and, thus, potentially more conflictual. Also, the pool of eligible marital partners becomes more restricted with increasing age. Thus, people wishing to marry may have to accept greater differences in values, ages, and educational and economic status in their partners than do younger people. It is also likely that late marriages involve a remarriage for one or both spouses; rates of divorce for remarriage are higher than those for first marriages. We examine the dynamics of remarriages in Chapter 13.

Education A complex relationship exists between divorce and levels of education for women. For example, women who drop out of high school experience the highest rates of marital disruption, whereas marriages of college graduates tend to be the most stable. This pattern reflects a number of different factors. High school dropouts are more likely to marry at an early age and to hold low-paying jobs. Thus, financial pressures on the marriage are likely to be substantial. Moreover, those who persist in school probably are better equipped to work out problems as they occur.

Interestingly, divorce rates are higher among women with 5 or more years of college education than among women with lower levels of education. This pattern, however, does not occur among comparably educated males (Glenn and Supancic, 1984). The reasons for these divergent patterns are not as yet well understood. Teresa Cooney and Peter Uhlenberg (1989) suggest that the higher level of divorce among professional women reflects the conflicts involved in balancing work and family responsibilities. In addition, professional women are less likely to be financially dependent on a spouse and thus can afford to leave an unsatisfactory relationship (Hiedemann, Suhomlinova, and O'Rand, 1998). This latter explanation is consistent with a pattern observed in earlier studies—women earning high incomes tend to have higher divorce rates than other women do (Glick and Norton, 1977; Houseknecht and Spanier, 1980).

When couples recognize that they are experiencing problems in their marriage, they sometimes seek outside help. This couple works with a marriage counselor in an effort to resolve their difficulties.

INCOME The above finding is an exception to the general relationship that exists between income and marital stability. Overall, the lower the income, the more likely a couple is to divorce (Martin and Bumpass, 1989; Kurdek, 1993). Earlier, we observed that low income and its accompanying stresses are a major factor in the higher divorce rate found among some groups. The significance of income is shown, for example, in its impact on early marriages. Young couples with sufficient financial resources had more stable marriages than similar couples with inadequate resources (Spanier and Glick, 1981).

RELIGION Historically, many religions have either prohibited or tried to discourage divorce among their members. On this basis we would predict that more religiously involved people would have lower rates of divorce, a view that is supported by a considerable body of research. Researchers Norval Glenn and Michael Supancic (1984) found that among white males, those who never attended religious services had a divorce rate over three times higher than those who did on a weekly basis. Furthermore, couples who share the same religion are less likely than interfaith couples to divorce (Lehrer and Chiswick, 1993). One explanation often given for this pattern is that religious homogamy increases the commonality spouses share in values and traditions (Wineberg, 1994). Membership in a religious organization also promotes social cohesion (Durkheim, [1897], 1951) and provides a source of support in times of difficulty. This support helps couples work through problems that otherwise might lead to divorce.

Researchers also found differences among various religious groups. Protestant couples have the highest rates of divorce, Catholics are next, and Jewish couples have the lowest rates (Glenn and Supancic, 1984; Brodbar-Nemzer, 1986). Among the Protestant denominations there is also considerable variation, with Baptists and Pentecostals having higher divorce rates than Presbyterians and Episcopalians. Some caution is required in interpreting this last finding, however. The differences in rates may be the result of an interactive effect between religious membership and other factors such as education and income. Baptists and Pentecostals tend to have lower levels of education and income than do Presbyterians and Episcopalians. Tennessee, Arkansas, and Oklahoma, each with high percentages of residents belonging to Baptist and Pentecostal denominations, also tend to be among the states with the lowest levels of household income (U.S. Census Bureau, 2000).

Although religion continues to be a factor in people's willingness to divorce, there are indications that organized religions are no longer as effective in restricting divorce as they had been. For example, in the past, Catholic countries in Europe did not permit divorce. Now virtually all do, leaving Malta as the only European country still imposing such a ban. In 1995, voters in Ireland, where 95 percent of the population is Catholic, narrowly approved a constitutional amendment to allow couples to divorce if they have lived apart for at least 4 of the previous 5 years. The previous ban on divorce did not mean that Irish couples stayed together: According to Irish officials, about 80,000 people were separated but unable to divorce at the time of the referendum. In fact, many of them were living with and had children with a new partner (Moseley, 1995).

PARENTAL DIVORCE Can the parents' divorce influence the outcome of their children's marriage? The answer apparently is yes. People whose parents divorced have higher divorce rates than do children who come from intact families (Keith and Finlay, 1988; McLanahan and Bumpass, 1988). However, this increased risk is not dramatic, on the order of only 5 to 10 percentage points higher than for children from intact families (cited in Emery, 1994). Two factors may combine to produce this outcome. First, from their parents' example, children have learned that divorce can be a solution to marital difficulties. Thus, they may be more ready than their peers from intact families to seek a divorce when problems start. Second, after a parental divorce, children often experience downward social mobility, which in turn may limit college attendance and contribute to early marriage, putting them at increased risk of a divorce themselves (Saluter, 1994). However, gender seems to play a role here. Daughters from both middle and lower socioeconomic families were at greater risks for divorce than sons from divorced parents of middle-class background. Parents are still more likely to encourage sons to go to college than daughters and, therefore, provide more resources for sons to continue their education (Feng et al., 1999).

Presence of Children A consistent research finding is that marital disruption is most likely when the marriage is child-free (Wineberg, 1988) and least likely when there is a child younger than 3 (Heaton, 1990). This finding should not be construed to mean that marriages with children are happier than those without. In fact, couples with children still at home tend to be less happy than either childless couples or those whose children have left home (Spanier, Lewis, and Cole, 1975; Nock, 1979). Rather, parents who are having marital problems often delay divorce until all the children are in school. The likelihood of divorce increases when children reach their teens (Heaton, 1990). Two plausible explanations for this behavior come readily to mind. Parents may believe that teenaged children are more capable of handling this family disruption, or it may be that coping with adolescent children puts additional strain on an already weakened relationship.

Increasingly, however, married couples are less likely to stay together because children are present in the home. Approximately half of all couples recently divorced now have children under 18 (Amato and Booth, 1996). More than 1 million children have been involved in divorce annually since 1972. Overall, parents of sons are less likely to divorce than are parents of daughters (Morgan, Lye, and Condran, 1988; Katzev, Warner, and Acock, 1994). Researchers attribute this to a greater involvement of fathers with their sons. Graham Spanier and Paul Glick (1981), who reported the same pattern, suggest that it is related to a man's desire to have a son carry on his name, a desire especially strong among traditional fathers. Additionally, they speculate that mothers of sons might resist a separation in the belief that raising sons without a father would be more difficult than raising daughters alone. We examine the effects of divorce on children later in this chapter.

Thus far, we have examined a number of risk factors associated with divorce. Take a minute to see whether any of these risk factors apply to you (see "Applying the Sociological Imagination" box). Obviously, these factors do not tell us about the process of divorce or why individuals decide to divorce. What happens to marriages that look so promising when they begin? Although every marital disruption has its unique features, social scientists have identified several common stages through which most divorcing couples pass.

APPLYING THE SOCIOLOGICAL IMAGINATION

ARE YOU AT RISK?

This exercise is designed to help you assess some of the risk factors of divorce that may be present in your life. Circle yes if the question accurately describes you or those close to you.

1.	Did you marry or do you plan to marry before your 20th birthday?	Yes	No
2.	Did you marry or do you plan to marry in your 30s or 40s?	Yes	No
3.	Are your parents divorced?	Yes	No
4.	Are any of your close friends divorced?	Yes	No
5.	For females, do you plan to have a profession?	Yes	No
	For males, do you think your wife will have a profession?	Yes	No
6.	Do you attend religious services only occasionally?	Yes	No
7.	Will both you and your spouse work?	Yes	No
8.	Do you prefer to avoid conflict rather than discuss problems?	Yes	No
9.	Do you have difficulty managing your money?	Yes	No
10.	Are you (or your spouse) reluctant to discuss problems and feelings with each other?	Yes	No

Scoring: Add up the number of times you circled yes. The higher the number of yes answers, the more risk factors you have for becoming divorced. However, this does not automatically mean you will be divorced at some point in your life. Rather, it indicates that you have some of the characteristics that researchers have found to be associated with a tendency to divorce.

What do you think? *How can knowledge of these risk factors be utilized by couples and by social institutions in attempts to develop strategies to lessen the likelihood of marital dissolution?*

THE PROCESS OF DIVORCE

Divorce doesn't just happen. It is a complex social process in which a basic unit of social organization—marriage—breaks down over time, culminating in a legal termination of the relationship.

Stages in the Divorce Process

Divorce involves more than a legal decree officially symbolizing the end of a marriage. Some researchers, like Constance Ahrons (1980) and George Levinger (1979), identify three stages in the divorce process: (1) a period of marital conflict and unhappiness, (2) the actual marital dissolution itself, and (3) a postdivorce period. James Ponzetti and Rodney Cate (1986) see divorce as a four-step process: (1) recognition by one or both spouses of serious marital problems; (2) discussion of these problems with the spouse and possibly with family, friends, or counselors; (3) initiation of legal action to dissolve the marriage; and (4) the postdissolution period, which involves adapting to a new status. Although both spouses go through the same stages, the timing may be different for each spouse, depending on who initiates the divorce.

Although these researchers propose different models, they all agree that the dissolution of a marriage occurs through a series of stages. The majority of separations and divorces follow a period of personal unhappiness, conflict, and deliberation, during which time individuals make decisions based upon three types of criteria: (1) an evaluation of the attractiveness of the relationship itself (the material, emotional, and symbolic rewards a spouse provides), (2) an evaluation of the costs and benefits of a divorce (monetary, social, and psychological), and (3) an evaluation of the attractiveness of possible alternatives, including new relationships (Levinger, 1965).

The Six Stations of Divorce

Anthropologist Paul Bohannan (1970) has identified not one but six divorces that couples experience in dissolving their marital relationship. These he calls the **stations of divorce:** emotional, legal, economic, coparental, community, and psychic divorce.

The **emotional divorce** can be present in the marriage for a long time before any legal action is taken to end the relationship. Here one spouse, or both, questions the viability or quality of the relationship and at some point shares this view with the other. There is often a period during which one or both partners withdraw emotionally from the relationship. A loss of mutual respect, trust, and affection follows. During this period both spouses may hurt or frustrate the other deliberately. Yet despite the deterioration of the relationship and talk of separation, one or both may not want a divorce for a variety of reasons: fear of living alone, concern about the children, desire to fulfill marriage vows, or the economic and social costs involved. Thus, some marriages may remain intact in form but not in substance for extended periods of time. Other spouses take action to move to the next stage. This may involve one spouse walking out or a mutual decision to begin a period of separation.

Gender plays a role in the decision-making process. Women appear to take a more active role in preparing and planning for divorce or separation. They are more likely than men to think about divorce after a spousal argument, and they are more likely to make specific plans to discuss divorce or separation with their spouse and/or with others (Crane, Soderquist, and Gardner, 1995).

The **legal divorce** officially ends the marriage and gives the former partners the right to remarry. Legal divorce generally follows a period of months or even years of deliberation. Sociologists Graham Spanier and Linda Thompson (1988:331) interviewed 50 separated and divorced people

In recent years, increasing public attention has focused on the high rate of divorce in the United States, particularly with respect to how divorce affects children. This young boy indicates his displeasure with the process by sticking out his tongue at his father during a custody hearing.

(22 women and 28 men) and found that the median length of deliberation between thinking that divorce is a possibility and the certainty of divorce was 12 months for the men and 22 months for the women. Women thought about divorce earlier than men. The divorce itself can be an adversarial process, especially when children and property are involved. In attempting to settle these issues the divorcing couple may lose control of the process itself to lawyers who advocate their client's interest generally without regard to the needs of the other party.

The **economic divorce** involves the settlement of property, a process that often involves considerable conflict. Most states now have laws specifying that both spouses are to receive an equitable share of the marital property. Equity is not always easy to determine, however. Tangible items like the house, the car, income, and bank accounts, whose values are easy to calculate, can be divided without great difficulty. But what about the current and future earning power of each individual? Should this be considered in a divorce settlement? For example, spouses with advanced degrees or special labor market skills are at a real advantage after a divorce. Considerable controversy exists over what constitutes a fair return on an investment in human capital. This question arises in cases where one spouse (most frequently the husband) earned a degree or learned a skill while the other spouse (most frequently the wife) played a major supportive role in making that possible, earning the money to pay for the spouse's education. Increasingly, courts are wrestling with issues like this.

The economic station of divorce is less often applicable than some of the other stations. It assumes that all couples have tangible assets to divide. Although this is certainly true for middle- and upper-class couples, it is not generally true for the poor and even for many working-class couples, who live in rental units and depend on public transportation. According to Judith Seltzer and Irwin Garfinkel (1990), 40 percent or more of divorcing couples don't make any property settlement because they have nothing of value to divide.

The **coparental divorce** involves decisions concerning child custody, visitation rights, and the financial and legal responsibilities of each parent. This station can also be a source of conflict, particularly when parents are engaged in a custody battle. We'll return to the topic of child custody later in this chapter.

The **community divorce** involves changing social relationships. It can involve a loss of relatives and friends who were previously shared with the spouse. In one study of 60 divorced mothers, over three-quarters reported losing former friends, usually during or immediately after the divorce (Arendell, 1986). The withdrawal of friendship may occur for several reasons. Those who were friendly with both spouses may not want to be drawn into taking sides. Others may see the divorce as a threat to their own relationships. For most of the women in the study the loss of friends was an unexpected occurrence that was painful and emotionally confusing. In this stage of divorce people may feel lonely and isolated.

The **psychic divorce** involves a redefinition of self away from the mutuality of couplehood and back to a sense of singlehood. This process takes time and involves a distancing from and an acceptance of the breakup. Many people go through a mourning process similar to that experienced by people who lose a spouse to death (see Chapter 15). The time this takes and the degree of difficulty with which this station is passed through varies considerably from individual to individual.

We examine some of the dynamics of these stations of divorce in more detail when we discuss the consequences of divorce later in this chapter.

THE CAUSES OF DIVORCE

Although we now know how couples end their marriages, we still don't have an answer to the most frequently asked questions about divorce: Why? and What went wrong? What causes people to evaluate their relationships as problematic or unsatisfactory? People who respond to a divorce by asking these questions frequently assume that some specific event or events disrupted the relationship. A key assumption here is that by eliminating the cause of the problem, the marriage could have been saved. Yet, as our historical review made clear, divorce is a complex phenomenon that needs to be understood in the context in which it occurs. Thus, changes in social structures, economic relationships, demographic patterns, and cultural configurations all play a role.

Societal Factors

Several macrolevel factors have contributed to the long-term trend of a rise in the divorce rate (Goetting, 1979; White, 1991). Perhaps the most influential factor is a change in attitudes. Although divorce is still seen as an unfortunate occurrence, it has become far more socially acceptable than in the past. All major social institutions, including religion and the family, have become more tolerant of this behavior. These attitudinal factors have been reflected in more liberal divorce laws, which many people believe have made divorce more accessible to a wider share of the population. Since the advent of no-fault divorce in all 50 states, the divorce rate increased in all but 6 states (Nakonezny, Shull, and Rodgers, 1995). As we will see later on, there is a movement under way to tighten up on divorce legislation. These changes in attitudes became possible as a result of transformations taking place in the organization and functioning of major social institutions. As we discussed in Chapter 1, the advent of industrialism weakened the family as an economic unit and placed more emphasis on the personal relationship between spouses. Under these new conditions spouses were less likely to remain in a union that was not personally fulfilling.

Similarly, as we saw in Chapter 10, changes in the economy led to major transformations in the relationship between work and family and in the gender roles of husbands and wives. Among the most striking changes in this regard is the increase in the labor participation of women in this century, especially from 1970 on. Numerous studies show that marital instability has increased along with women's labor force participation (Moore and Sawhill, 1984; Cherlin and Furstenberg, 1988; Spitze, 1988).

What is less clear, however, is why this relationship exists. One interpretation suggests that among marriages that are unsatisfactory for whatever reason, the costs of divorce are lowest for wives who are capable of self-support (Hiedemann, Suhomlinova, and O'Rand, 1998). Other explanations have been tied to changing gender role ideology. As discussed in Chapter 10, some husbands may find it difficult to adjust to a co-provider role, and some wives may feel overburdened by working outside the home while still being expected to do the bulk of the housework (Rogers and Amato, 2000). In his research, Theodore Greenstein (1995) found that nontraditional women who saw marriage as an egalitarian partnership viewed such inequalities as unjust, whereas traditional women did not perceive these inequalities as inherently unfair. Nontraditional women experienced more stress in their relationships as a result of trying to resolve the inequities.

Nevertheless, the relationship between the employment of women and divorce is not a simple cause-and-effect relationship. Other factors are at work here as well. For example, Greenstein (1990) found that the conditions under which wives work is the fundamental issue. He reported that divorce is less likely when the wife's earnings and her share of family income represent a significant part of a family's budget. Having two wage earners may relieve financial tensions that often contribute to divorce; thus, a wife's employment may contribute to greater marital stability.

Under different circumstances, however, female employment can increase marital instability. As with men, for example, women in high-stress jobs frequently find that work-related pressures carry over into domestic situations and intensify marital difficulties. In addition, employment outside the home can provide women with greater opportunities for alternative relationships, which can weaken the marital bond. Clearly, then, we must avoid simple generalizations concerning the relationship between female employment and divorce.

Like the United States, other countries are experiencing these macrolevel changes and consequently they are also experiencing higher divorce rates. For example, a cross-cultural study found that 25 out of 27 countries saw divorce rates rise between 1950 and 1985 (Lester, 1996). What is particularly noteworthy is that this trend was not confined to industrial countries. Even in some of the most traditional societies, marital dissolution has increased in recent years. For example, in China economic reforms have put pressure on marriages by giving women and men more personal freedom and life choices than they had previously. China's divorce rate now stands at 10.4 percent, low by comparison with the United States, but high for China (Faison, 1995). Although in the past there were Chinese couples who wanted to divorce, they could not break through the bureaucratic wall of refusal (Goode, 1993). With the passage of the 1980 Marriage Law and the 1989 Opinions of the Supreme People's Court, however, divorce is less difficult to obtain. Grounds for divorce now include separation, adultery, illegal cohabitation, imprisonment, disappearance, and ill treatment by one's spouse or by her or his family (Palmer, 1995). The growing divorce rate is a reflection of the rising expectations that women now bring to marriage. By the late 1980s more than two-thirds of divorce applications were brought by women.

Although a discussion of these societal factors helps us to understand the context in which divorce takes place, it does not tell us what happens on the personal level. For that we have to look to the divorcing couples themselves or to the therapists who work with them.

From the Perspective of Divorced People

Paul Rasmussen and Kathleen Ferraro (1991) interviewed 32 divorced people, in most cases both husband and wife. Their findings raise questions about how we look at the causes of divorce. The behaviors most commonly cited as leading to divorce are poor communication, extramarital sex, constant fighting, emotional abuse, drug or alcohol problems, and financial mismanagement (Colasanto and Shriver, 1989; Patterson and Kim, 1991).

Did these behaviors, however, actually "cause" the divorce? Many respondents considered these activities to be aftereffects of crises or problems that derived from other sources. Other respondents reported that these behaviors had occurred prior to dating, during dating, and during the marriage. Many of the spouses had remained committed to marriages in which such offending behaviors were present and openly acknowledged. Rasmussen and Ferraro concluded that these behaviors may exist for years without leading to divorce or even creating any serious problems. Conversely, they may be totally absent when divorce occurs. According to Rasmussen and Ferraro (1991:387):

> Husbands and wives who share strong emotional ties require . . . [a] significant crisis to break the bond. While the typically listed causes of divorce played an important role in all the divorces studied, it was in their use as tools to facilitate the divorce rather than as direct causes. The "knife of crisis" used as a means of ending a marriage was often adultery, heavy drinking, or financial ineptitude. Spouses either indulged in or complained of problem behaviors in building a case for divorce.

Thus, it appears that divorced people cannot give a single reason for their divorce. Rather, a wide variety of "causes" are cited that pertain to a spouse's behavior, to perceived difficulties in the marital relationship, or to the impact of social and economic factors existing in the larger society. This doesn't mean, however, that researchers are unable to code categories of complaints. For example, one sociologist was able to arrive at 13 "causes" reported by her respondents:

"These ranged from clear-cut justifications, such as abandonment or 'becoming gay,' to rather fuzzy references to personality differences, poor communication, or simply the need to find a happier situation" (Johnson, 1988:69). More recent studies found similar complaints (Amato and Rogers, 1997; Stewart et al., 1997; Carrere and Gottman, 1999; Rubin, 2001).

From the Perspective of Family Therapists

One survey asked members of the American Association of Marriage and Family Therapists to rate the frequency, severity, and treatment difficulty of 29 problems frequently seen among couples experiencing marital difficulties (Geiss and O'Leary, 1981:516–17). The therapists were asked to rank the areas they considered most damaging to couple relationships and those most difficult to treat.

The ten areas rated as most damaging were (1) communication, (2) unrealistic expectations of marriage or spouse, (3) power struggles, (4) serious individual problems, (5) role conflicts, (6) lack of loving feelings, (7) lack of demonstration of affection, (8) alcoholism, (9) extramarital affairs, and (10) sex.

The ten areas rated as most difficult to treat successfully were (1) alcoholism, (2) lack of loving feelings, (3) serious individual problems, (4) power struggles, (5) addictive behavior other than alcoholism, (6) value conflicts, (7) physical abuse, (8) unrealistic expectations of marriage or spouse, (9) extramarital affairs, and (10) incest. For more insight into the causes of divorce and of ways of resolving them, see the "Strengthening Marriages and Families" box.

Implications for Strengthening Marriage Understanding the causes of divorce implies that certain constructive measures can be taken to strengthen marriages. First, therapists can intervene in distressed relationships to help people improve their communication skills (see Chapter 8). Improved communication skills can help each partner understand the perspective of the other and perhaps avoid unnecessary conflict. Couples can also take certain steps to avoid entering marriage with unrealistic expectations of their relationship or each other. Discussion and negotiations (perhaps formulating a marital contract) prior to getting married as well as ongoing discussion and renegotiations are necessary if couples are to achieve satisfaction and agreement on their roles and responsibilities.

Finally, recognizing that some problems, like alcoholism, are difficult to treat effectively may encourage some people to take action sooner. For example, if a prospective spouse has a drinking problem or is abusive, perhaps marriage should be postponed until this problem has been addressed through counseling or some other means. Unfortunately, couples seeking help typically wait six years from the time marital problems surface before seeking professional advice and, by then, the anger and hurt is often too deep to allow resolution. Furthermore, studies show that 5 to 25 percent of divorcing couples did not seek any kind of counseling (reported in Barnes, 1998).

THE IMPACT OF DIVORCE ON SPOUSES

The consequences of divorce are many and varied. Although some of these are experienced by both spouses, a number of factors are gender-specific. We'll begin this section by looking at those issues that commonly affect both spouses, and then we'll isolate those features of divorce that affect women and men in distinctly different ways.

Common Consequences of Divorce

Charles Dickens could just as easily have been talking about divorce and its aftermath as about eighteenth-century London and Paris when he wrote, "It was the best of times; it was the worst of times." For most divorcing couples both statements are true. On the positive side divorce can free people from unhappy, conflict-ridden, or unsatisfactory relationships (Lund, 1990). Divorce can also be a means to achieving personal growth (Riessman, 1990). On the negative side, however, divorce can produce considerable pain, guilt, and uncertainty. This duality is clearly visible in Cheryl Buehler and Mary Langenbrunner's (1987) research. They asked 80 divorced people whose divorces had been finalized 6 to 12 months earlier to identify which of 140 items they had experienced since they separated from their spouses. The results showed that divorced people are almost equally likely to report both positive and negative outcomes. The most frequently reported items appear in Table 12.2.

Are you surprised to find that the most frequently occurring responses are positive? Many people are. However, this finding should not be interpreted to mean that the negative consequences are inconsequential. They are not. People in

Table 12.2

Most Frequently Reported Experiences of Divorced Persons	
I have felt worthwhile as a person	96%
I have experienced personal growth and maturity	94%
I have felt relieved	92%
I have felt closer to my children	89%
I have felt competent	89%
The cost of maintaining the household has been difficult	87%
I have felt angry toward my former spouse	87%
I have felt insecure	86%
My leisure activities have increased	86%
I have been depressed	86%
Household routines and daily patterns have changed	85%

Source: Cheryl Buehler and Mary Langenbrunner, 1987, "Divorce-Related Stressors: Occurrence, Disruptiveness, and Area of Life Change," © 1987, The Haworth Press, Inc., Binghamton, New York, *Journal of Divorce and Remarriage,* 11:35. Reprinted with permission of The Haworth Press.

STRENGTHENING MARRIAGES AND FAMILIES

Talks with Family Therapist Joan Zientek

RESOLVING PROBLEMS

In Your Practice, What Do You Find Are Some of the Problems That Lead to Divorce?

A good percentage of divorcing couples come from families that lacked good models of spousal interaction. Thus, as children they did not learn the skills necessary to make a relationship work. Then when they grew up and married, they often selected a partner much like one of their parents, perhaps unconsciously using their marriage to work out their family of origin issues. If their partner comes with the same level of emotional health, the marriage lacks the resources to work out the natural conflicts that come from two people blending their lives together. When offspring are added to the mix, the picture becomes even more complex, resulting in three generations of issues living in one household. Other problems can arise when people marry without allowing time to get to know their partner. They can initially be drawn by the sexual energy that exists between them but when this wears out, they realize they have selected someone with whom they have little in common. This results in a conflict of values and priorities that is difficult to compromise and, thus, resolve. Sometimes, a couple faces a trauma, such as the death of a child, where their partner's grief is too intense for them to bear as they struggle with their own grief. In situations like these, one party or the other may turn to someone outside the marriage for comfort and support; an affair may ensue, and in time the marriage may dissolve. This is especially true if, as psychologist John Gottman (1994b) suggests, they do not have an "emotional ecological balance," that is, engage in more acts of positive emotional interactions than of negative interaction. Gottman found that couples who have a five-to-one ratio of positives to negatives have the greatest chance of marital success.

Are Some Problems More Difficult to Solve than Others?

Yes. When one partner struggles with an addiction, whether it be alcoholism, gambling, or a sexual addiction, great strain is placed on the relationship. The resulting problems are often very intense and affect every aspect of family life, from lack of money to emotional withdrawal and even violence. The path to recovery is rarely smooth or easy. Even with the assistance of all the support groups that are now available, the impact is often more than the marriage can bear. An affair can also have a devastating affect on a marriage. Not only is the present condition of the relationship in question, an affair touches the meaning of the entire relationship—past, present, and future. The deception, the shattering of trust, the questioning of the relationship, and the loss of hope for a future together are all difficult issues to manage.

Can Counseling "Save" a Marriage?

When a couple enters treatment, there are no guarantees about the outcome. Much depends upon the strengths that the couple bring to the task. If, in therapy, each party is capable of observing his/her own behavior, if they speak directly to each other and not solely to the therapist, and if they refrain from placing the total blame at their partner's feet, they have a good chance to work out their problems. These behaviors act as a cushion, absorbing the pain as well as providing the energy and support needed to resolve the problem. Also, the couple needs to have realistic expectations relative to the time it may take to make the marriage more enjoyable for each party. During this time for working things through, both parties need to refrain from crying "divorce" as a way of venting their dissatisfaction and instead put their energies to constructive negotiation and problem-solving. Additionally, if the parties truly love each other, if they have a lot invested in staying in the marriage (a shared history, children, mutual friends, and financial investments), there is great motivation and hope for the resolution of their problems.

When Couples Decide to Divorce, Can Counseling or Mediation Help Make the Process Easier?

When parties divorce, they can become involved with three types of professionals: a lawyer, a mediator, and a therapist. Rather than dealing with two lawyers, couples often seek the services of a mediator, which is often more cost effective and less adversarial in nature. The mediator serves as a guide to the parties as they define the issues in dispute and negotiate an agreement that includes the division of marital property and finances and decisions regarding child custody arrangements. Therapy, on the other hand, can help a couple resolve the emotional issues that may block the efforts of the mediation process. Many mediators come from a therapy background, and the two areas may overlap. Having a third party involved in the dissolution of the marriage brings not only an objective point of view to the process, but it also provides a structure and sets limits that allow the couple a means for containing the anxiety and strong emotions that surround the situation. It also can prevent the children from becoming pawns in the process and ensure that their interests and well-being will be protected.

the process of divorce frequently encounter a number of problems. The most common problems experienced by both women and men are health problems (both physical and psychological), loneliness, the need for social and sexual readjustments, and financial changes in their lifestyles (Amato, 2000). This latter problem is more common to women than to men, so we will consider it later under gender-specific problems.

HEALTH PROBLEMS Many people experience depression and sometimes despair in the wake of a divorce. The process of divorce involves a number of major lifestyle alterations: loss of a major source of intimacy, the end of a set of daily routines, and a changed social status—going from a socially approved category (married) to a still somewhat disapproved category (divorced). Based on her research with 104 separated and divorced respondents (52 women and 52 men), sociologist Naomi Gerstel (1990) found that the stigma of divorce has not completely disappeared. Gerstel argues that although divorce is now less deviant in a statistical sense than it was in the past, and although the divorced are no longer categorized as sinful, criminal, or even wrong, the divorced still believe they are the targets of informal relational sanctions—they are excluded from social events, blamed for the marital breakup, and sometimes held in low regard. Hence, many divorced people respond to their new status with feelings of stress, guilt (especially for the initiator of divorce), and failure (especially for the partner who was asked for the divorce). Compared with their married peers, divorcees exhibit lower levels of psychological well-being, greater risk of mortality, more negative life events, greater levels of alcohol use, and lower levels of happiness and self-acceptance (Amato, 2000).

LONELINESS Although people who live alone are not inherently more lonely than people who live together, a period of loneliness often accompanies the transition from being a part of a couple to being single again. This is especially true for childless couples and older couples whose children have already left home. However, divorce can involve more than the loss of a spouse. Relationships with former in-laws can be strained or broken off completely. Ann-Marie Ambert (1988) studied 49 separated and divorced spouses and found that only 11 percent of the respondents maintained positive relationships with their former in-laws after the separation. Conversely, blood relatives might choose to retain contact with the ex-spouse even against the wishes of their own kin. The latter pattern often creates social distance among family members.

SOCIAL AND SEXUAL READJUSTMENTS Feelings of isolation and loneliness can lead to physical and psychological problems. Thus, divorced people are well advised to maintain old friends and companions or to seek new ones to offset the possible losses in their support network and to restore their self-esteem. In this regard, one of the major adjustments divorced people face is getting back into circulation. Dating is not easy at any age, but it is particularly problematic for older divorced people.

Newly dating divorced people must deal with two key issues: how to explain their unmarried status and whether to be sexually active. Divorce does not lessen social or sexual needs. Studies from Alfred Kinsey, Wardell Pomeroy, and Clyde Martin (1948) through today show that most divorced people have sex within 1 year of being separated from their partner. Besides filling a physical need, providing intimacy, and exploring a new-found freedom, sex is often used to validate a sense of self-worth that may have been seriously eroded during the divorce process. Both women and men need to know that others find them attractive and sexually desirable. Some need to test their sexual adequacy, especially if their performance was criticized by their previous spouse.

These needs are not always adequately met, however. Sexual encounters are not always satisfying. Women in particular often feel exploited by men who assume that because they are divorced, they will automatically welcome any casual sexual relationship. Although both divorced women and men are sexually active, overall men have more sexual partners than women do.

Gender Differences in Divorce

As discussed in Chapter 3, the U.S. sex/gender system structures women's and men's marital and family experiences in markedly different ways. In her study titled *The Future of Marriage*, Jessie Bernard (1972) observed that every marital relationship contains two marriages that are often widely divergent. She called these "his" and "her" marriages. The same social structures and gender expectations that create differential marriage experiences for women and men also act to create differential divorces. These can be described as "her divorce" and "his divorce."

"HER" DIVORCE The most striking, even startling, difference between women and men following a divorce is a monetary one. Media headlines about the divorce settlements of the rich and famous, like Donald Trump, suggest that women are the recipients of huge alimony payments. Volumes of research over the last 2 decades reveal a markedly different pattern, however. After divorce the standard of living of children and their custodial parents (predominantly women) drops sharply.

Downward Social Mobility According to researchers Greg Duncan and Saul Hoffman (1985), women suffer about a 30 percent decline on average in their income in the year following a separation, whereas men experience a 15 percent increase. In a pioneering study of the economic impact of California's no-fault divorce law (discussed earlier in this chapter) on divorcing spouses, sociologist Lenore Weitzman found a larger discrepancy. Weitzman analyzed 2500 California court records covering a 10-year period, some before and some after the enactment of the law. She

The economic aspects of a divorce can be quite daunting, often necessitating the sale of the family house. Having to relocate to another neighborhood can add to the trauma of divorce for family members, especially for children.

found that within a year of the final divorce decree the standard of living of women and their children declined by an average of 73 percent, whereas that of ex-husbands improved by an average of 42 percent (Weitzman, 1985:339). Other researchers have come up with somewhat different numbers, but the general pattern they found is the same: downward social mobility for women and children, often to the point of impoverishment (Smock, 1993; Peterson, 1996; Raymond, 2001). This pattern held across all racial-ethnic groups.

Women and children do not fare much better in other countries. British wives, who initiate 75 percent of divorces in their country, face similar financial difficulties. A longitudinal study over a 10-year period found that men's disposable income increased by 15 percent while women and their children experienced a 28 percent drop. Less than half of the fathers pay the full child support that was awarded and nearly one-third will pay nothing at all (Sarler, 2000). Similar patterns were also found in Scotland and Wales (Hill, 2000). In Australia, even after 12 years of improved payment of child support, 44 percent of divorced mothers and their children were below the poverty line while men were better off or just as well off as before their divorce (Horin, 2000).

The decline in living standard following a divorce may push older women into poverty as well. With so many marriages lasting only a few years, the number of women who do not meet the 10-year marriage requirement that allows them to share in their husband's pension is increasing. Thus, it is expected that the proportion of economically vulnerable aged women will increase when baby boomers retire. In 1998, 21 percent of divorced older women lived in poverty, compared to 5 percent married women and 18 percent widowed women (Butrica and Iams, 2000).

This downward mobility for women and children is explained by two key factors: the earnings gap between women and men (see Chapter 10) and the failure of courts to award, and ex-husbands to pay, alimony and child support.

The Legal System and Women's Financial Well-Being According to sociologists Frank Furstenberg and Andrew Cherlin (1991:48–49), "When marriages dissolve, the shift in family responsibilities and family resources assumes a characteristic form. Women get the children and, accordingly, assume most of the economic responsibility for their support. Men become nonresidential parents and relinquish the principal responsibility for their support." These patterns are directly related to U.S. legal practices.

Currently, the courts routinely award alimony (also called "spousal support" or "spouse maintenance") in only 15 percent of all divorce cases (Hanna, 1996). Furthermore, alimony is actually received in far fewer cases than the awards indicate. Terri Arendell interviewed 60 divorced middle-class women and found that "only 6 of the women—all of them divorced after marriages of 15 years or longer—received spousal support awards. One of them received an award for life or until she should remarry; the others were given awards of specific and short duration" (1986:33). A similar pattern has been found in child support awards, a topic examined in greater detail in the "Social Policy Issues" box.

Causes of Inequality between Divorced Women and Men What explains this economic discrepancy between divorced women and men? Weitzman (1985) attributes it to the provisions of the no-fault divorce laws, which require that husbands and wives be treated equally. In the abstract this sounds eminently fair. In reality, however, it overlooks the fact, discussed in Chapter 10, that women historically either were not in the labor force, or if they were, they received lower wages than men did. Thus, simply dividing marital property equally without regard for the resources (professional degrees, skills) or the earning power of the respective spouses puts women at a real disadvantage vis-à-vis men. Women's advocates point out that by assuming responsibility for the majority of housework and child care, women sacrifice their own employment and earning power (see Chapter 10) and enhance that of their husband. Thus, these advocates argue that an equitable divorce settlement would take into account women's contributions to a husband's present and future earnings.

SOCIAL POLICY ISSUES

WHO RECEIVES CHILD SUPPORT?

In 1995, Jeffrey A. Nichols, an investment advisor, was the first person to be charged in New York City under the 1992 Child Support Recovery Act, which makes it a federal crime to avoid paying child support by fleeing to another state. He owed $500,000 in child support to his former wife. Nichols is not alone.

In 1999, David Oakley, father of nine children by four mothers, went to trial on charges of failure to pay the $25,000 he owed in child support. In a controversial ruling, upheld by a 4–3 vote of the Wisconsin Supreme Court, Judge Fred Hazlewood gave Oakley 5 years' probation, contingent upon his not making any more children during that period without demonstrating the financial ability to care for all his progeny. If he violates these terms, he goes to jail (Pitts, 2001). Nichols and Oakley are just two of millions of parents who fail to provide financial support to their children.

In Spring 1998, there were approximately 14 million custodial parents for 23 million children under the age of 21: 12 million mothers (85 percent) and 2 million fathers (15 percent). About 56 percent of custodial mothers were white, 28 percent were black, and 14 percent were Latinas. The majority of custodial fathers (74 percent) were white, 10 percent were black, and 14 percent were Latinos. Among the 56 percent of custodial parents who were awarded child support in 1997, only 41 percent received the full amount; another 27 percent received partial payment, and the remaining 33 percent received no payments at all. Custodial parents of color were less likely to be awarded child support and, when awarded, less likely to receive it (Grall, 2000).

A total of $17.1 billion was paid in child support in 1997, $12 billion less than the amount due. Mothers received an average of $3655 compared to the $3251 fathers received. However, on average, these support payments constituted 16 percent of 1997 money income for women but only 8 percent for men. As the chart shows, parents who are awarded and receive child support have higher incomes. Nearly one-third of custodial mothers and one-tenth of custodial fathers were poor in 1997.

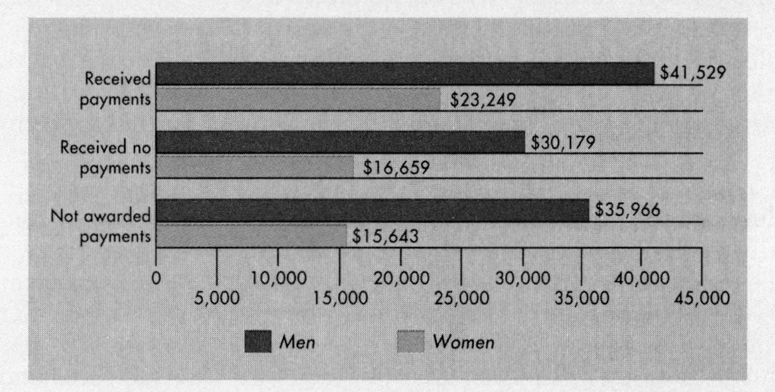

Source: T. Grall, 2000. *Child Support for Custodial Mothers and Fathers*, U.S. Census Bureau, Current Population Reports, P60-212, October (Washington, DC: U.S. Government Printing Office).

Why don't parents pay child support? Tom, a 35-year-old divorced father, offered this explanation: "I paid child support faithfully every month for 2 years after our divorce. During that time I didn't get one thank you. I was to have the kids one weekend a month. Half of the time when I went to pick them up, they weren't ready or my ex-wife said something came up and they couldn't come. I didn't like the way the kids were dressed or how they behaved. Instead of buying them nice clothes, she'd use the money for music lessons or some other thing. We'd argue. Eventually, it was easier just to let her do what she wanted. She's working and can support the kids. I hardly see the kids anymore. I've met someone else and we are getting married soon. I can't afford to pay any more child support."

Concern over the economic plight of divorced women and their children led Congress to pass federal child support legislation in an effort to give some relief to the custodial parent. A 1984 law required each state to develop guidelines for establishing minimum child support awards. Four years later legislation required judges to follow their state guidelines in decisions pertaining to child support. Any deviation from these guidelines had to be justified in the court record. This 1988 law also allowed states to withhold child support payments from the noncustodial parental paycheck when children were receiving welfare. By 1994, all new court-ordered child support awards were subject to automatic withholding, regardless of parental income or children's status. Despite these efforts, research indicates that there has been relatively little improvement in compliance with child support orders (Children's Defense Fund, 1997).

What do you think? Was Judge Hazlewood justified in restricting David Oakley's freedom to procreate? Explain. Do you think there is any validity to Tom's rationale for not paying child support? Are there any policies or programs that could deal effectively with Tom's complaints? Do you think meting out harsher penalties is the way to get more noncustodial parents to make their child support payments?

The Consequences of Divorce for Women What happens to women who experience this downward mobility? Many women, especially those in traditional marriages, suffer a loss of status, identity, and their domestic sphere—the home. Under the doctrine of equal division of property, homes are often sold so that both spouses can receive their share of the value of the house. According to Weitzman (1985) the number of cases in which there was an explicit court order to sell the home rose from one in ten in 1968 to one in three in 1977. The sale of the home often means moving out of a familiar and comfortable neighborhood into a smaller, less expensive place in a different neighborhood. Consequently, school, neighborhood, and friendship ties are often disrupted when they are most needed. Even when the house is not sold, financial strains may make maintenance and a comfortable style of living difficult.

Women with sole custody of children are often doubly burdened—they must be full-time parents as well as economic providers. In the process they must watch their children do without many things that were taken for granted in the past. As the sole parent, divorced women may find little time for themselves or for social activities with peers. All of this exacts a toll. The women Arendell (1986) interviewed spoke of recurring struggles with depression and despair. Many lost a sense of the future and felt trapped by their economic circumstances. Of the 60 women interviewed, 26 reported that they had contemplated suicide at some time after the divorce.

Despite their economic stress, evidence suggests that women fare better in terms of divorce adjustment than do men. According to Judith Wallerstein (1986), women improve the emotional and psychological quality of their lives more than men do. For example, women are more likely than men to experience a sense of growth in self-esteem after a divorce (Baruch, Barnett, and Rivers, 1983). One explanation for women's and men's differing reactions may be that as women take on more instrumental roles, for example, becoming the sole provider and family head, they feel more confident about their abilities. Such changes were expressed by a female respondent: "I'm learning how to do things. . . . There's no mystery about it now, I can get out an electric drill. . . . I got satisfaction from putting a bookcase together" (quoted in Riessman, 1990:168). Men, on the other hand, lose some of those roles. The roles they add, such as housekeeper and cook, are not highly valued in this society, and hence, adoption of these roles doesn't generally increase self-esteem (Gecas and Schwalbe, 1983).

"His" Divorce On the basis of a growing body of literature it does appear that men are better off economically after a divorce than women are. This is a result of many factors. Traditionally, society has placed greater value on male workers and therefore paid them higher wages. Even when men pay child support, these payments often represent only a relatively small amount of their take-home pay. And, as we saw in the "Social Policy Issues" box, a combination of anger, emotional pain, irresponsibility, other debts, ongoing conflict with the former spouse, and remarriage often leads to noncompliance with court-ordered child support. Legal efforts to enforce compliance are often plagued by heavy case loads, inadequate budgets, a shortage of personnel, and, until quite recently, a societal indifference to the plight of divorced women and children. Thus, a divorced husband typically has more discretionary income to support himself than his ex-wife has to support both herself and their children. Despite this finding, many divorced men feel that they have been victimized by the divorce process and the aftermath of divorce (Arendell, 1995; Lehr and MacMillan, 2001).

Although the number of single-parent fathers has increased slightly, divorced men typically do not have custody of their children. Therefore, whether men desire it or not, divorce frees them from child care. Because they have more discretionary money, they are freer than their ex-wives to pursue social and leisure activities. Men's opportunities for remarriage are also greater than women's. Unencumbered by children, they are freer to date and to begin new relationships. As we will see in the next chapter, men remarry at higher rates and more quickly than do women.

Dating for divorced men is not problem-free, however. Divorced men may feel uncomfortable in this new role and may hold back because of a fear of rejection. They confront other problems, too. One man explains these problems this way: "The relationships are shallow, let's put it that way. They're not long-range. I don't know how to put it to you. If you just get into bed with someone (names women), I suppose it satisfies your basic needs, let's put it that way. But it's not meaningful. That's the best way to explain it. So, in a sense you have your freedom. You can play the field, you're on the circuit, on the tour, as we call it. But I find that they're basically shallow. So I guess your freedom is basically shallow, as far as that goes" (quoted in Riessman, 1990:193). Many divorced men, especially those from traditional marriages, have trouble establishing a satisfying home environment and maintaining a household routine on their own. Because this was considered a wife's domain, many ex-husbands feel overwhelmed by shopping, laundry, cleaning, and cooking.

Although loneliness can be a problem for both women and men, divorced fathers without custody may feel it more intensely. Even with visitation rights, they miss out on the day-to-day contact with their children and may miss the ritual of family celebrations of special events and holidays. Dennis Meredith (1985) reports that some noncustodial fathers exhibit a child-absence syndrome, feeling depressed, anxious, and cut off from their children's lives. For some divorced fathers this triggers negative reactions. Visits with their children become more sporadic or stop completely, or the fathers become psychologically distant from their children (Amato and Booth, 1996; Weissbourd, 1994). There is, however, growing indication that the percentage of children with no contact with their fathers 2 years after divorce has decreased considerably in the last decade (Selzer, 1998). That said, however, between 8 percent and 25 percent of children still have no contact with their fathers 2 to 3 years after divorce (Maccoby and Mnookin, 1992; Braver, 1998).

Divorce also has a negative effect on men's contact with their adult children and on their perceptions of their children as potential sources of support. When men relinquish ties to their children during childhood, even when they have provided child support, rarely do they resume those ties later in life (Furstenberg, Hoffman, and Shrestha, 1995). For example, in one study, over 30 percent of middle-aged divorced fathers had lost contact with one or more of their adult children, a situation almost nonexistent for never-divorced men (Cooney and Uhlenberg, 1990). Ninety percent of the never-divorced older fathers had weekly contact with at least one of their adult children; this was true for only one-third of the divorced fathers. A similar pattern exists for fathers who divorce later in life. Over 20 percent of today's divorces involve couples married more than 15 years (Cooney, Hutchinson, and Leather, 1995). One study of adult children whose parents had recently divorced after many years of marriage found that they had less intimate and more distant relations with their fathers than their peers from nondivorced families (Cooney, 1994). Overall, the evidence suggests that divorced fathers are at greater risk for problematic relations with offspring regardless of the child's age. These studies raise questions about the degree to which family ties exist for divorced men as they age.

In sum, although men appear to benefit more than women do from divorce, particularly economically, they also experience dislocation from the breakup. Social policy must address divorced men's concerns as well as those of divorced women.

Recovering from Divorce

Given that the majority of divorcing couples face serious economic, social, and psychological problems, you may well wonder whether people ever recover from the trauma of divorce. Most do, although the process usually takes several years. For example, a study conducted over a period of 10 years by Judy Wallerstein and Sandra Blakeslee (1989) of 60 families disrupted by divorce found that women take an average of 3 to 3.5 years and men 2 to 2.5 years to reestablish a sense of external order after the separation. Not everyone recovers at the same speed, however. Wallerstein and Blakeslee found that some of their respondents had not recovered 15 years after their divorce.

Why do some people adjust more quickly than others? Do certain characteristics enable some people to cope with divorce problems more effectively than other people? An emerging body of research has begun to identify certain factors that affect people's ability to adjust to divorce. Wallerstein and Blakeslee (1989), for example, found that younger people fared better. This was especially true for women. Women under 40 fared better in terms of making life changes than did men and older women. These changes tended to cluster around two major areas: increasing competence in the management of daily life and developing a fuller sense of identity. Robert Lauer and Jeanette Lauer (1988) found that those who successfully coped with their divorce were able to redefine the divorce as an opportunity for growth. Other research suggests that women and men who are nontraditional in their gender orientation adjust better and more quickly to a marital breakdown. The explanation for this is that androgynous women and men have better coping skills with which to handle the trauma of divorce than do women and men who behave according to traditional gender role expectations (Chiriboga and Thurnher, 1980; Hansson et al., 1984). This latter point has major implications for how we socialize children to prepare them for adult roles.

THE IMPACT OF DIVORCE ON CHILDREN

With the increase in the divorce rate, more and more children have been drawn into the process. Sandra Hofferth (1985) estimated that nine out of ten black children and seven out of ten white children (and most likely growing numbers of Native American and Asian American children) will spend part of their childhood in a single-parent household, mainly because of divorce and births to unmarried mothers. In 1998, 27 percent of all children under 18 lived with only one parent, up from 12 percent in 1970. Twenty-three percent of white children, 55 percent of black children, and 31 percent of Latino children lived in one-parent families (U.S. Census Bureau, 2000a).

A child's reaction to divorce can be similar to that of divorcing parents—it often includes feelings of denial, anger, sadness, rejection, despair, grief, and loneliness.

Several social theorists have argued that the intact, two-parent family is necessary for the normal development and well-being of children. Thus, divorce is assumed to be contradictory to these ends. This view is most evident in structural-functional, social-learning, developmental, and symbolic-interaction theories (see Chapter 2), all of which see the family as one of the primary agents of socialization and role modeling for children. However, these theoretical perspectives ignore the fact that the effects of disrupted families on children might be short-lived, that the role of an absent parent might be filled by significant others (as was the case in much of human history), that the custodial parent might be warm and supportive, or that parental separation may be better for children than remaining in a conflict-ridden family (Booth and Amato, 1994; Kelly, 2000; Campbell, 2001).

Short-Term versus Long-Term Effects

There is an extensive body of literature on the effects of divorce on children. For the most part there is agreement about the short-term effects of divorce, some of which resemble those experienced by divorcing parents: rejection, anger, denial, sadness, despair, and grief. Children frequently feel guilty, blaming themselves for the divorce, especially if their parents have quarreled over them. They often entertain fantasies about reuniting their parents (Wallerstein and Kelly, 1980; Chase-Lansdale and Hetherington, 1990).

Just as with adults these stresses can result in health problems, both psychological and physical. Research shows that the physical health ratings of children from divorced families are poorer than those of children from intact families (Amato, 2000). Teresa Mauldin (1990) studied the health histories of 6000 children and found that in families where a divorce occurs, children average 13 percent more illnesses a year after their parents' divorce than before. She attributes the increase in health problems to the stresses generated from the divorce, particularly the dramatic decline in their living standard. Children living with their mothers are more likely to lack health insurance, making timely and quality health care problematic. Children with divorced parents see themselves as less competent and exhibit more depression and withdrawal than children from intact families (Peterson and Zill, 1986; Najman et al., 1997). The duration and intensity of these feelings depend in some measure on parental behavior. If parental conflict continues after the divorce, the adjustment process for children may be prolonged (Amato and Rezac, 1994).

In contrast, many of the findings of long-term effects on children are not as clear-cut or consistent. On the one hand, some researchers like Judith Wallerstein and her colleagues (2000) conclude that the effects of divorce are long-lasting and interfere with normal social-emotional development. Twenty-five years after her 1971 study of 131 children whose parents divorced, Wallerstein interviewed 93 of the original subjects, now 33 years old on average. She found that in comparison to a control group of 44 adults similar in age and socioeconomic status but whose parents had not divorced, the adult children of divorced parents experienced greater anxieties and more failures in their interpersonal relationships. On the other hand, sociologists like Andrew Cherlin (2000) have cautioned against reading too much into long-term effects without a knowledge of the state of the parental home prior to the divorce. Cherlin points out that 50 percent of the fathers and close to half of the mothers in Wallerstein's study suffered from serious mental or addiction problems. Thus, it is possible that these adults would have had the same or similar problems even if their parents had not divorced.

The fact that a number of longitudinal studies of children found that as many as half of the behavioral and academic problems of children in marriages whose parents later divorced were observed 4 to 12 years before the separation suggests that troubled families and not divorce, per se, may be more responsible for long-term negative effects (Cherlin, 2000; Kelly, 2000). Similarly, other research has found that marital conflict is a more important predictor of children's problems than is divorce itself (Buehler et al., 1998). Further, symptoms commonly found in children of divorced parents (low self-esteem, depression, and school and behavioral problems) also are more often found in children of high-conflict marriages than in children of low-conflict marriages (Vandewater and Lansford, 1998).

Stephanie Coontz (1997) reminds us that although some children of divorced parents do have problems, the majority do not experience severe or long-term problems. Andrew Cherlin (1992) believes that children, by and large, regain psychological equilibrium 1 or 2 years after the divorce and then continue on a "normal pattern of growth and development." It may be that children's age at the time of divorce has an impact on the degree to which they experience disruption in their lives. The lives of younger children may remain more stable than those of older children, who may be more aware of changes in their family's economic and social status. Cross-sectional studies limited to comparisons of differences between children from disrupted homes and those in intact families, with no control for variables of changed economic status or quality of family relationships before the divorce, are not conducive to sorting out short-term versus long-term effects. Accurate assessments of the long-term impact of divorce require more study and more precise control for the complex variables that promote or hinder growth in children's lives.

How Does Divorce Affect Children's Behavior?

Researchers report that children of divorce are absent from school more, do poorer schoolwork, are more likely to use alcohol, cigarettes, and marijuana, and have a greater risk of early pregnancy than children from intact families (Neher and Short, 1998; McLanahan, 1999; Coleman, Ganong, and Fine, 2000). Again, however, these findings must be interpreted cautiously. Factors such as race, class, and parental involvement are important here as well. Most studies of the behavioral effects of divorce involve samples of white children. The few studies of black children are dated and report mixed findings. Frank Sciara (1975) found that the absence of a father was more harmful to the academic achievement of black children than that of white children, but other researchers have found the academic achievement of black children to be unaffected by family structure (Hunt and Hunt, 1975; Shinn, 1978). Furthermore, it is estimated that the declining economic status of disrupted households accounts for as much as half of the adjustment problems found in children of divorced parents (McLanahan, 1999). Thus, unequal economic resources rather than differences in family structure may account for the observed differences in school performance. College attendance is also affected by divorce. A government study found that 71 percent of the children from intact families went to college, compared with 54 percent of those whose parents were divorced (Mathews, 1996). Only 6 percent of the custodial parents in that study expected their former spouses to help pay college bills.

Gender and Divorce While earlier studies found that within divorced families boys had more behavioral problems and had more difficulty adjusting to divorce than girls (Demo and Acock, 1988, 1991), more recent studies did not find gender differences specifically linked to divorce (Vandewater and Lansford, 1998; Hetherington, 1999). However, in the population at large, school problems, runins with the police, and aggressive behaviors have been found to be more common among boys than girls regardless of family structure. Additionally, some of the general and assumed gender-specific problems attributed to divorce may instead be a result in a decrease in parental supervision (McLanahan, 1999). For example, when divorced fathers are more involved with their children, the children do better academically and have fewer school problems than children with less involved fathers and there are no significant differences in performance and achievement between them and children in intact families (Nord, Brimhall, and West, 1997). These findings have important implications for divorcing parents: When ex-spouses provide appropriate supervision and emotional support to their children, their children are more likely to adjust better and more quickly after the parental divorce.

Not all research on the effects of divorce has found negative effects. In female-headed families both mothers and children develop more androgynous behavior as they reorganize the household after the father has left. Additionally, assuming more responsibilities leads children to greater maturity and feelings of competence (Gately and Schwebel, 1992). Finally, of course, children may feel relief to be out of a conflictual and possibly abusive family situation. Children living in a stable single-parent family are emotionally better off than if they remain in a conflict-ridden two-parent family (Hetherington, Law, and O'Connor, 1993; Kelly, 2000).

Children and Divorce in Other Countries

To date, most of the research on the effects of divorce on children has been conducted in the United States and other English-speaking countries where the findings have been fairly consistent. However, in countries like China, divorce has traditionally been condemned and those who did divorce have been stigmatized. As globalization has increased, especially in countries where women's roles are changing, divorce tends to be increasing as well. Whether children in countries with diverse cultural and economic patterns will respond to parental divorce in the same way as children in Western countries is an intriguing empirical question and one that leaders in those countries must address if they are going to be prepared to meet the needs of their newly divorced families.

Although there has been no cross-cultural study on this topic, it does seem that there is at least some initial support for the belief that findings from the United States may be generalizable to other cultures. Researchers have found that Chinese children of divorced parents, like their U.S. counterparts, are more likely to be aggressive, withdrawn, and to have more behavioral and social problems than children from intact families. Also, divorced parents report more mental and physical health problems for their children than do nondivorced parents (Liu, Guo, and Okawa, 2000). Further support that there are at least some universal factors that affect children's reactions to family conflict and divorce comes from Croatian researchers (Cudina and Obradovic, 2001). However, these two studies also suggest that there are culture-specific factors that also affect divorce outcomes. Additional research in a variety of cultures and economic settings will help to clarify our understandings of the process and effects of divorce.

Changing Patterns in Child Custody

In any marital disruption involving children, a question that must be resolved is, Who gets the children? We examine this difficult question focusing specifically on the issues of sole custody, joint custody, and visitation rights.

Sole Custody Throughout U.S. history, in divorce cases courts have almost always awarded **sole custody,** in which one parent is given legal responsibility for raising the child. Earlier we noted that in colonial America, fathers were far more likely to get custody of their children following a divorce. By the twentieth century, however, this pattern had so reversed itself that today approximately 90 percent of all divorced mothers have custody. The courts accepted the cultural bias that women are inherently better at nurturing than men are. Thus, they adopted the view that children, especially in their early years, need to be with their mothers. So entrenched did this view become by the mid–twentieth century that the only way a father could get custody was to prove his wife an unfit mother (Greif, 1985).

In the past 2 decades a small but noticeable shift has occurred in child custody cases. Although most fathers do not request custody, those who do so are often successful. It is estimated that in such cases, about one-half to two-thirds of the fathers are awarded custody (Greif, 1985; Hanson, 1988). Research shows that fathers increased their odds of receiving sole custody when they were the plaintiffs and when a friend of the court investigation was undertaken. Thus, fathers often have to exert extra legal efforts to strengthen their claims. The odds of fathers gaining custody are enhanced when they pay child support, when the children are older, and when the oldest child is male (Fox and Kelly, 1995). There are an estimated 500,000 to 1.5 million noncustodial mothers in the United States, with 75 percent voluntarily relinquishing custody (quoted in Herrerias, 1995). Given the traditional view of women as nurturers and homemakers, women who agree to give custody to the father frequently are portrayed as unloving, uncaring, selfish, and unwomanly. In her research, Catalina Herrerias (1995) found that these negative images have little to do with the woman's actual reasons for giving up custody: inadequate finances, child's preference for living with father, difficulty in controlling children, threats of legal custody fights, and physical or emotional problems experienced by the woman. Although these women did not have custody, 97 percent actively maintained a relationship with their children; 71 percent described their relationships as close and caring.

Not all women who lose custody do so voluntarily. In one study of over 500 noncustodial mothers, almost 10 percent reported losing their children in a court battle or relinquishing custody to avoid conflict (Greif and Pabst, 1988:88). Women's groups have expressed concern that some of these decisions could set precedents that would weaken women's chances for gaining custody. They point to cases in which the judge's decision was based primarily on the father's better financial position (Max, 1985). Using financial means as a criterion for child custody puts women at a real disadvantage because in the vast majority of cases fathers are better off economically.

Money is not the only issue over which custody battles are fought or decided. The sexual orientation of a parent is also an issue. In the past, lesbian and gay parents' custody of their children was often challenged and threatened solely because of their sexual orientation. A 1995 decision in a child custody case in Tallahassee, Florida, is an especially eye-opening example of the prejudice and discrimination lesbians and gays often face in child custody cases. In this case, a Florida judge took an 11-year-old girl from her mother simply because the mother was a lesbian and awarded custody to the father, a convicted murderer and accused child molester. A judge in Illinois, relying on allegations of lesbianism, denied the mother's request for custody and ordered that the mother not visit with her daughter in the presence of any woman with whom she may happen to be living.

Such judicial decisions are often based on the mistaken belief that children raised in a lesbian or gay household would "naturally" adopt a gay or lesbian lifestyle or that they would suffer some psychological harm. These beliefs, however, are contradicted by research findings that children raised by lesbian and gay parents have no significant psychological damage nor proclivity to be homosexuals themselves. Moreover, many homosexuals are forced to challenge the inherent bias of assumptions that imply that "becoming lesbian or gay" would be awful for children—worse, for example, than being molested or living with a convicted murderer.

Today only a few states (Alabama, Mississippi, Missouri, and Virginia) continue to apply categorical assumptions against lesbian and gay parents. Many other state courts now require evidence of adverse impact before a parent's sexual orientation or involvement in a nonmarital relationship can be used to limit custody or visitation rights. This adverse impact test, also referred to as the nexus test, requires a clear connection between a parent's actions and harm to the child before a parent's sexual orientation can assume any relevance in the custody determination (National Center for Lesbian Rights, 2002).

Joint Custody Spurred in part by fathers' rights advocates, who argued that the legal system discriminated against them, California passed the country's first joint-custody law in 1979. Currently 43 states allow for some form of joint custody. **Joint custody** means that both parents are involved in child rearing and decision making. Joint custody can take two forms: joint legal custody, in which

When children are involved, divorcing couples must negotiate visitation rights for the noncustodial parent. If parents can cooperate with each other in this regard, children are less likely to feel caught in the middle and can benefit from a relationship with both of their parents.

both parents are to share decision making on such issues as education and health care, and joint physical custody, which covers how much time children will spend living with each parent. However, full joint custody in this latter sense is rare. In practice, most joint custody involves shared legal custody, with physical custody remaining with one parent, usually the mother. In that sense, joint custody varies little from sole custody except for the assumption that decisions about the children's welfare will be made by both parents (Glendon, 1987).

The motives behind joint custody are to provide children with continuing contact with both parents and to relieve one parent of the total burden of child care. Some studies indicate that some of these benefits are being realized. For example, in 1997, three-quarters of parents with joint custody received either their full or partial child support awards. Of the custodial parents due support but without joint custody only 36 percent received support (Grall, 2000). Additionally, fathers with joint custody were more likely than fathers without joint custody to have at least weekly contact with their children, including overnight visits (Selzer, 1998). However, other studies have found that outside the regular child support payments, there were few differences in adjustment between children in sole versus joint physical custody (Johnston, 1995; Pruett and Hogan-bruen, 1998).

Joint custody is not for everyone. It works successfully only in cases where divorcing couples have a fairly amicable relationship and desire a pattern of shared parenting. In the absence of these two characteristics, joint custody may simply perpetuate the conflict that led to the divorce in the first place. Because joint custody is relatively new, an evaluation of its effectiveness in minimizing the adjustment problems of children is difficult. However, Mary Ann Mason (1999), a professor of law and social welfare and author of *The Custody Wars*, is critical of the joint custody trend. She argues that the push for joint custody grew more out of a concern for the rights of parents, particularly fathers, rather than out of a concern for children's rights. Based on her years of experience practicing family law and her current research, she concludes that joint custody rarely works because it requires parents to cooperate, which she believes is more than most divorced couples can manage. Although Mason concedes it would be difficult to achieve, she would like to see the court assess objectively which parent, regardless of gender, is "primary" in terms of both caregiving and emotional attachment.

All too often children have little or no voice in how custody decisions are reached. This may change, however, in light of a recent court case. Juvenile court judge Thomas Kirk granted 12-year-old Gregory Kingsley's request that the parental rights of his natural mother be terminated, thus allowing the boy's foster parents to adopt him. This ruling is believed to be the first time in which parental rights were ended based on a legal suit brought by a minor. Judge Kirk based his ruling on what he deemed the best interests of the child. Gregory's mother, an unemployed waitress, had given him up for foster care three times because of economic difficulties. Gregory testified that he had lived with his mother for only 7 months in the last 8 years and that for almost 2 years while he was in foster care his mother never visited, called, or

SEARCHING THE INTERNET

CHILDREN'S RIGHTS IN REGARD TO CUSTODY AND VISITATION

All children have the right to:

- a continuing relationship with both parents
- be treated not as a piece of property, but as a human being with unique feelings, ideas, and desires
- continuing care and proper guidance from each parent
- not be unduly influenced by either parent to view the other parent negatively
- freely express love, friendship, and respect for both parents, without feeling shame or a necessity to hide those emotions
- an explanation that the parents' divorce was in no way caused by the child's actions
- not to be the subject and/or source of any arguments.

http://www.divorcesupport.com/childcustody/info/~childsrights.html

wrote him. More recently, 17-year-old Olympic gymnast Dominique Moceanu filed suit in a Texas court to be declared a legal adult, claiming that her parents drove her to succeed and then squandered her earnings. Dominique won her case. These cases will likely set a precedent for giving children legal standing in their own right in cases where there is a clear pattern of abuse and neglect, rather than relying on adults to initiate cases for them.

Visitation Rights Regardless of the form custody takes, provisions for visitation of the other parent must be agreed upon. Noncustodial parents with visitation rights enter into a new set of interactions with their children. Often both the parent and the child are uncertain how to behave in this situation; thus, visitation itself becomes a source of stress. Logistics are a problem, too: Where to go? What to do? Whom to include? Often the spontaneity of parent–child relationships is transferred to a recreational relationship, with the time together being spent in a constant round of activities, for example, going to the movies or the zoo.

Parents and children often perceive the visits in different ways. Parents may think that by taking the children places they are being loving, whereas children may feel rejected because the relationship seems artificial. Judith Wallerstein and Sandra Blakeslee (1989) observed that what matters is not the frequency of visits but the degree to which the child feels valued in the relationship.

Thus, in the best of circumstances problems can occur with visitation. The visits can become a source of real stress, especially in the period immediately after a divorce if parents haven't worked through their own feelings. Visitation can then become a battleground through which ex-spouses carry on their conflict with each other. This takes many forms: The noncustodial parent often overindulges the children to look good in their eyes; both parents may grill the children about the other parent's new lifestyle or speak ill of the other parent; one or both parents may consistently violate the spirit of the visitation agreement by changing plans at the last minute, not having the children ready on time, or bringing them back late. Child experts agree that such behaviors have a negative impact on children. Parents are more likely to avoid these behaviors if they reflect on the rights of children caught up in divorce situations, which have been identified by the judicial system (see the "Searching the Internet" box). Colorado legislators recently passed a bill with this in mind. The legislation changed the terminology from "custody" to "parental responsibilities" to take away the psychological barrier often associated with being the noncustodial parent. The law also requires parents to file a court-approved parenting plan as a piece of the final separation agreement. Other states are considering similar legislation in an attempt to find ways to reduce conflict between the divorcing parents and to put the needs of children first (Graber, 1999).

Noncustodial parents are not the only ones concerned about visitation rights. Grandparents can play an important role in helping their grandchildren adjust to a divorce. Grandparents symbolize stability and continuity (Sanders and Trygstad, 1989). Because of the acrimony of some divorces or the geographic relocation of the custodial parent, however, grandparents may be unable to fulfill this role.

Studies have revealed certain trends in relationships between grandparents and grandchildren following divorce. In general the custodial grandparents (parents of the custodial parent) have an advantage in maintaining ties with their grandchildren. Andrew Cherlin and Frank Furstenberg (1986a) found that several years after the divorce 58 percent of noncustodial grandparents saw their grandchildren less frequently than before the divorce, compared with only 37 percent of custodial grandparents. Because women are more likely to receive custody, relationships between maternal grandparents and grandchildren tend to be maintained and even strengthened, whereas ties with paternal grandparents frequently are weakened. Increasingly, grandparents have gone to court in efforts to ensure continuing contact with their grandchildren. In 1977, only 6 states had laws that enabled a grandparent to petition a court for visitation rights to a grandchild; today, all 50 states have such laws. Not all grandparents, however, are aware of this, nor do all grandparents have the economic resources to pursue this avenue. Visitation rights are not the norm in all countries. For example, in Japan joint custody is not legal. In the past, fathers got the children most of the time. Now that most women work and can support their children, mothers routinely get custody of their children. However, the usual pattern is that the other parent does not visit or is not allowed to visit her or his children. Although some parents engage in informal visitation, according to a 1997 survey, there was no contact with the noncustodial parent in nearly 40 percent of divorces and only minimal contact in another 18 percent. When Prime Minister Junichiro Koizumi and his wife divorced over 20 years ago, Koizumi got custody of their two sons, and his wife got custody of their as yet unborn son. To date, the youngest son has not met his father, and the mother, despite her requests, has not seen her two sons since the divorce (Tolbert, 2001).

REACHING ACCORD: COUNSELING, COLLABORATIVE LAW, AND MEDIATION

Thus far, we have seen that divorce can cause a variety of problems, not only for the divorcing couple but also for their children, their extended family, and their friends. Because of the emotional content, most divorces can easily become bitter and acrimonious affairs, leaving deep emotional and psychological wounds. Therefore, a growing number of marriage counselors and other professionals have shifted some of their practice into **divorce counseling.** Their efforts are aimed at helping people conclude the psychic divorce. Essentially, their goal is to replace the adversarial and often destructive aspects that can accompany the legal divorce with a more cooperative spirit. At the same time they try to help people withdraw and distance themselves from the relationship so that acceptance of the loss and subsequent healing can take place. When these goals are accomplished, people are better able to begin new relationships. Divorcing couples or individuals may seek such counseling during the process of the divorce or at a much later stage in their life. Some states, however, require **conciliation counseling** before the courts will consider granting a divorce. The purpose behind this kind of counseling is to see whether the marital problems can be resolved and the couple reconciled.

When reconciliation is not possible, couples often find themselves caught up in an adversarial divorce proceeding. Concerned by the destructive impact this causes, Stuart Webb, a prominent Minnesota divorce lawyer, instituted a practice called **collaborative law**—where the attorneys for both parties to a family dispute agree to assist in resolving the conflict using cooperative techniques rather than adversarial strategies and litigation with the goal of reaching an efficient, fair, and comprehensive out-of-court settlement of all issues. If the process fails and either party wishes to have the matter resolved in court, both attorneys withdraw and disqualify themselves from further representation except to assist in the orderly transfer of the case to adversarial counsel. In his first two years of collaborative practice, Webb handled 99 cases, reaching full settlement in all but 4 (Florence, 2000).

Divorce mediation has a related but somewhat different emphasis. It is a procedure designed to help divorcing couples negotiate a fair and mutually agreed-upon resolution of such issues as marital property distribution, child custody, visitation rights, and financial support. Divorce mediators generally have backgrounds in law, social work, counseling, or psychology. In any given divorce one or more mediators may be involved. For example, divorce lawyers may work with counselors or therapists to help the couple reach accord. Some states actively encourage and even sponsor divorce mediation. Mediated settlements must be approved by the court to become legally binding on the parties involved.

Although divorce mediation is still relatively new, having emerged as a distinct practice only in the 1970s, evidence suggests that all parties benefit from the process. Couples can learn negotiating skills that will help them deal with each other in the future. Children do not see their parents embroiled in a constant struggle over them. Because the spouses have helped to forge the agreement based on their own needs and those of their family, they are more likely to adhere to the terms of the agreement, thereby reducing the likelihood of future conflicts (Grebe, 1986). Another key benefit appears to be that fathers stay more involved in their children's lives as a result of the experience of divorce mediation (Emery, 1995). This latter point is most likely the result of fathers feeling they have more of a say in the decisions concerning their children. Finally, mediated divorce agreements cost considerably less than adversarial divorces because less time and labor are required (Werland, 1999).

ATTEMPTS AT REFORM: COVENANT MARRIAGE

A new movement to toughen state divorce laws has emerged over the last several years in response to concerns over the impact of family breakups on children and the high incidence of poverty in single-parent households. The principal target is the no-fault divorce statutes adopted by every state over the last 25 years. Supporters of tougher divorce laws argue that the current rules encourage a casual attitude toward the dissolution of marriage. They advocate legislation that would put pressure on couples to remain together. Under the no-fault approach, a divorce is granted even if only one spouse wants it. By contrast, bills being considered in some states would deny a divorce when one spouse opposes it unless the plaintiff can show that a spouse was physically or mentally abusive, had a problem with alcohol or drugs, had committed adultery, had deserted the home, or had been incarcerated.

Another reform approach has been proposed by University of Maryland public affairs professor William Galston. He advocates that states adopt a two-tiered divorce law, keeping no-fault intact for couples without dependent children, but eliminating unilateral no-fault for couples with children. Instead, there would be a mandatory waiting period of at least a year, during which time couples would be ordered to undergo counseling (Hanna, 1996). In 1997, Louisiana (followed by Arizona in 1998) passed a law similar to this proposal. Couples can now opt for a *covenant marriage contract*, whereby they signify their commitment to their marriage, agree to forgo standard access to a quick no-fault divorce, and participate in premarital counseling. They also agree, should marital problems arise, to seek divorce only within approved fault grounds (adultery, abuse, abandonment) or after an extended waiting period of 2 years for no-fault actions. However, in either case, proceedings can go forward only after they have completed counseling aimed at saving the marriage, if possible.

Contrary to proponents' expectations, the initial research on covenant marriages found low rates of adoption, ranging from 1.6 percent to 2.7 percent of all marriages in Louisiana. Couples most likely to choose covenant marriage were white, noncohabiting, Southern Baptist or nondenominational Christians. Compared to their noncovenant peers, covenant marriage couples were more committed to traditional gender role ideology, especially the idea that men should be the unquestioned head of the family (Rosier and Feld, 2000).

Although it is too early to tell if covenant marriages will be more stable than standard marriages, opponents of these types of measures fear that they could mean a return to the anger, lies, and distortions required to obtain a divorce

WRITING YOUR OWN SCRIPT

EVALUATING RELATIONSHIPS

Although no one likes to consider the possibility that a loving relationship will come to an end, we do have to face the reality that 40 percent to 50 percent of first marriages will end in divorce. We also know that divorce is more common among certain groups and that every couple will experience problems and conflicts at one time or another. The critical factor in the relationship is not the experience of problems or conflicts in themselves but rather what resources and skills are available to help resolve them.

Questions to Consider

1. What will my partner and I do when things don't seem to be working out right? Can we create mechanisms for resolving disagreements before they occur? Will we be willing to get counseling if we are having problems?
2. Have our parents, siblings, or any of our friends been divorced? What are our attitudes regarding divorce?
3. What resources can we establish for meeting unexpected problems, such as unemployment, financial difficulties, or illness?
4. If we have children, what do we see as our responsibilities toward them should something happen to our marital relationship?

before no-fault, resulting in more pain for children as parents engage in a legal blame-game. Additionally, they believe such changes would discourage couples from getting married in the first place, thereby increasing the incidence of nonmarital births, leaving more women and children economically and socially vulnerable. They argue that rather than forcing people to stay together emphasis should be focused on reducing the economic stresses that contribute to the high rate of breakup, including requiring absent parents to meet their child support obligations. Some opponents of divorce law reform believe this effort is directed at the wrong target. Joy Feinberg, president of the Chicago chapter of the American Academy of Matrimonial Lawyers, suggests, "If you want to do something about these problems, make marriage harder. Make people go through counseling before they get married" (Hanna, 1996:6).

The United States is not the only country to reexamine its divorce laws. Proposed reforms for couples seeking a divorce in England or Wales would abolish the most common quickie divorces on the grounds of adultery and unreasonable behavior, which are granted in 3 to 6 months. Couples would be able to apply for divorce on the grounds that the marriage has irretrievably broken down, but they would be required to wait 12 months to reflect on their decision. These proposals require that the spouse initiating the divorce must attend a compulsory information session to hear about options such as counseling and mediation (Jones, 1995).

Which view do you think is most realistic? Should divorce or marriage be harder to obtain? What do you think the likely outcomes of this type of divorce reform would be?

OTHER FORMS OF MARITAL DISRUPTION

Thus far our discussion has focused on the legal concept of divorce. However, marriages can be disrupted in other ways as well, by separation, desertion, annulment, and death.

Separation refers to the termination of marital cohabitation and can take a variety of forms. Sometimes one of the partners simply moves out. This can be the result of an individual or a mutual decision. Its goal may be to give one or both partners some space and time to think about the relationship, or it may be the first step toward divorce. Because this is an informal arrangement, the courts are not involved, and the couple remains legally married.

In other cases, when the couple do not want to divorce or to continue living together, the courts order legal separation with specific regulations governing the couple's interactions, including custody, visitation rights, and economic support. Such separation orders may also provide for counseling or therapy and give a stipulated time frame for the duration of the separation. This can give the couple an opportunity to reassess and possibly learn to alter problem areas in their relationship. Couples may reconcile or divorce at the end of the legal separation. Researchers have found that close to 10 percent of currently married couples have separated and reconciled (Wineberg and McCarthy, 1993). A study of African American women found that women who were separated after age 23 were more likely to reconcile than their younger peers. Greater maturity and a greater investment in the relationship were seen as key characteristics in the pattern of reconciliation (Wineberg, 1996). The desire to have day-to-day contact with children also provides an incentive for a couple's reconciliation. For some couples, however, a legal separation may become permanent. Some people reject divorce on religious grounds and therefore agree to live apart until the death of one spouse. Although either party may begin new relationships, neither is free to remarry.

Desertion refers to the abandonment of a spouse or family. The partner simply leaves, often without a word of warning. Desertion has sometimes been called the "poor people's divorce" because it frequently occurs when the family is experiencing economic hardship. However, desertion occurs among all classes, races, and ethnic groups. Although both women and men desert, men do so in greater numbers. This is perhaps the most difficult of all marital disruptions because the family is left without the financial and domestic support of the other spouse, and the courts can't intervene unless the whereabouts of the deserting spouse are known. At the same time the deserted spouse is not legally free to remarry until a specified number of years have passed. Thus, the family's life is overshadowed by uncertainty and ambiguity.

An annulment has quite a different meaning from the other forms of disruption we have been discussing. In divorce, separation, and desertion there is agreement that a legal marriage had existed. In contrast, a civil **annulment** legally states that the marriage never existed and, thus, the parties are free to marry at will. Generally the basis for an annulment is that the couple did not meet the legal requirements for a marriage in the first place—they were underage, the degree of kinship was too close (first cousins, for example, are not legally permitted to marry in some states), the marriage was never consummated, or some form of fraud was involved. A civil annulment is distinct from the religious annulment granted by the Catholic church. The church, after investigation, may decide that a religious marriage did not take place. In the eyes of the church the individuals are free to marry, but to do so legally they must obtain a civil annulment or a divorce.

The Catholic church does not recognize divorce but it does grant annulments under certain conditions, for example, the immaturity of the partners at the time of marriage or the presence of some other impediment that prevented a valid marriage from taking place. Sheila Rauch Kennedy publicly criticized this practice when her former husband, Rep. Joseph Kennedy III, sought to have their marriage annulled.

Throughout much of U.S. history marital disruptions were generally caused by death, not divorce. This was due primarily to shorter life expectancies, harsher living conditions, and cultural patterns that discouraged divorce. Today widowhood most commonly occurs at later ages in the life cycle. We discuss the concept of widowhood in Chapter 14.

SUMMARY

Contrary to popular belief, divorce is not a modern phenomenon. It has been a part of U.S. history since 1639, when a Puritan court in Massachusetts granted the first divorce decree in colonial America. As public concern grew over the perceived consequences of divorce, reform efforts were debated.

Divorce rates vary from group to group and are associated with a wide range of factors. Among the most frequently cited factors are race and ethnicity, age at marriage, level of education and income, religion, parental divorce, and the presence of children.

Divorce doesn't just happen. It is a complex social process in which a basic unit of social organization—marriage—breaks down over time, culminating in a legal termination of the relationship. Researchers have identified several stages in this process: a period of marital conflict and unhappiness, the actual marital dissolution itself, and a period of adjustment following divorce. Both women and men in the process of divorce face some common problems: a decline in health, loneliness, and the need for social and sexual readjustment. However, there are also gender differences. Although women suffer more economic distress than men, they may fare better in terms of overall adjustment.

Increasing numbers of children are affected by divorce. Researchers generally agree that children experience some of the same short-term effects their divorcing parents do: rejection, anger, denial, sadness, despair, and grief. There is less agreement about the long-term effects. Some researchers believe that children gain equilibrium 1 or 2 years after the divorce; others feel that the effects are long-lasting and interfere with normal social-emotional development for a significant number of children.

Although the courts typically award one parent, generally the mother, sole custody of the children, more judges are awarding joint custody. It is still too early to assess the effectiveness of the latter approach for the welfare of children. Establishing fair and appropriate visitation rights for noncustodial parents (and increasingly for grandparents) is not an easy matter. Conflict over visitation rights can prolong the trauma of divorce. As a reaction to many of the problems associated with divorce, a number of legislatures across the country are debating proposals to change existing divorce laws. Divorce counseling, conciliation counseling, collaborative law, and divorce mediation increasingly are being utilized in an effort to reduce some of the conflicts in the divorce process.

KEY TERMS

alimony
split custody
no-fault divorce
divorce rate
stations of divorce
emotional divorce
legal divorce
economic divorce
coparental divorce
community divorce
psychic divorce
sole custody
joint custody
divorce counseling
conciliation counseling
collaborative law
divorce mediation
separation
desertion
annulment

QUESTIONS FOR STUDY AND REFLECTION

1. Historian Eric Sager, commenting on the growing ranks of singles, points out, "It is often said that divorce today performs the function that death did in the past. The promise to live together for better or worse, so long as you both shall live, means something very different if you anticipate a married life of 60 years, as opposed to a married life of 25 years." Do you agree or disagree with Sager? Is the goal of lifetime marriage realistic in today's society? What role, if any, does an increase in life expectancy play in marital stability? Explain.
2. Most marriages start out with many rituals. Among them are the engagement, the bridal shower, the bachelor party, the rehearsal dinner, and the wedding ceremony itself (often religious in nature). Friends and relatives offer their support by cards, gifts, and attendance at these events. Divorce, on the other hand, is often a solitary experience. In fact, the partners are not even required to be physically present when the divorce decree is issued. Yet divorce, like marriage, marks a new beginning in a person's life. Do you think society should initiate divorce rituals aimed at helping people move on with their lives? Marianne Williamson (1994) provides one example. At a ceremony, the divorcing couple can turn to each other and, in turn, say, "I bless you and release you. Please forgive me; I forgive you. Go in peace. You will remain in my heart." Other variations include readings and the return of wedding rings. What is your reaction to such rituals? Could they serve a useful purpose for the divorcing couple? Their children and other relatives? Society at large? Or do you think they would encourage more couples to divorce? Explain. Consider in your answer the benefits that rituals provide in many other aspects of our lives.
3. Consider both the positive and negative consequences of divorce. On balance, do you think restricting divorce through more stringent laws would be a wise public policy? Explain. Should couples who are experiencing marital difficulties be required to undergo counseling before being allowed to file for divorce? Should couples with children meet stricter standards for divorce than childfree couples? Conversely, should marriage licenses depend on receiving premarital counseling? Explain. Visit The Divorce Support Page on the Internet at *http://www.divorcesuport.com/ home.shtml* and examine its offerings. What role do you think Web sites like this play in a larger social context? Do they encourage more divorce or do they simply alleviate some of the problems connected with divorce? Explain.
4. As we have seen, children suffer many consequences in the aftermath of a divorce. What steps could be taken to lessen the trauma of divorce for children? How and what should children be told about their parents' divorce? Who should tell them? What reactions should parents expect from children during and after the process of divorce? Would the trauma of divorce be lessened for children if parents followed the judicial guidelines for a child's rights as outlined in the "Searching the Internet" box? Explain.

ADDITIONAL RESOURCES

SOCIOLOGICAL

FEIFER, GEORGE. 1995. *Divorce: An Oral Portrait.* New York: Free Press. In this highly readable book, 39 women and men tell the stories of their divorces.

MCGRAW, PHILLIP C. 2000. *Relationship Rescue: A Seven Step Strategy for Reconnecting with Your Partner.* New York: Hyperion. A readable, down-to-earth guide for diagnosing, repairing, and maintaining relationships.

RICCI, ISOLINA. 1997. *Mom's House, Dad's House.* New York: Simon and Schuster. Guides divorced and remarried parents through the hassles and confusions of setting up a strong working relationship with their ex-spouse in order to make two loving homes for their children.

WHITEHEAD, BARBARA DAFOE. 1997. *The Divorce Culture.* New York: Knopf. Presents a provocative argument that the growing acceptance of divorce as an individual freedom comes at the expense of children.

LITERARY

KATCH, ELISE E. 2001. *The Get: A Spiritual Memoir of Divorce.* Deerfield Beach, FL: Simcha Press. Readers of all faiths will be fascinated by the real-life experience of a modern woman who is pressured to participate in an ancient Jewish Orthodox ritual to end her 30-year marriage.

SHETTERLY, CAITLIN, ED. 2001. *Fault Lines: Stories of Divorce.* New York: Berkley Publishing Group. Stories by Ann Beattie, John Cheever, John Updike, Russell Banks, Raymond Carve, Lucia Nevai, and others take readers through the emotional terrain of separation and divorce from the viewpoints of spouses, children, and significant others who are deeply affected by the marital breakup.

INTERNET

http://www.daads.com Dads at a Distance provides suggestions and support on how to improve long-distance relationships with children.

http://www.divorcing.com This Web site provides links to resources concerning all aspects of divorce.

Chapter 13

Remarriage and Remarried Families

IN THE NEWS: NEW YORK

Beth Bruno, a mother of two and stepmother to two more, believes that there are millions of unsung heroes in our midst, women and men who deserve recognition but often get a bum rap instead. She is speaking of the growing number of stepparents in the United States today. Half of all Americans have been or will be in a stepfamily constellation at some point in their lifetime. Bruno has proposed a new national holiday: Stepparents Day. She advocates that the United States celebrate this special day on the first Sunday of August to honor the women and men who care for and nurture the children they acquire by marriage as if they were their own. She chose the month of August because the word *august* means inspiring awe and reverence, imposing and magnificent, worthy of respect because of age and dignity, venerable, and grand (Bruno, 2001).

A school psychologist who has worked in the fields of mental health and education for more than 20 years, Bruno is realistic about the special challenges stepparenting brings. Remarriages are more likely than first marriages to end in divorce. Nevertheless, Bruno also believes that stepparents and stepchildren can and do live "happily ever after." Research shows that stable, happy stepfamilies can heal the scars of divorce, because children see adults who relate well and provide a model for conflict resolution (Mitchell, 1998).

WHAT WOULD YOU DO? If you were a public official and Beth Bruno came to you with her suggestion for a national holiday honoring stepparents, would you endorse her proposal? Explain your position.

In the previous chapter, we discussed the high divorce rate in the United States. Some writers have erroneously interpreted this high rate of marital dissolution to mean that marriage is no longer a popular institution among Americans. The remarriage statistics tell another story, however. The pattern of marriage, divorce, and remarriage has become well established in the United States today. About 43 percent of recent marriages involved a second marriage for at least one of the partners (U.S. Census Bureau, 2000a). Although the United States has the highest remarriage rate in the world, stepfamilies are one of the fastest-growing family types in Great Britain and other industrialized nations as well (Simpson, 1994). Here in the United States, over half of the population is now or will be in one or more steprelationships during their lives, and by the year 2007, stepfamilies will outnumber nuclear families (Mitchell, 1998). Thus, statistically it is likely that you or a number of your classmates have lived or will live part of their life in a remarried family.

For purposes of our discussion in this chapter we will use Esther Wald's (1981:2) definition of a **remarried family:** "A two-parent, two-generation unit that comes into being on the legal remarriage of a widowed or divorced person who has biological or adopted children from a prior union with whom he or she is regularly involved. . . . The children may or may not live with the remarried couple, but, in either case, they have ongoing and significant psychological, social, and legal ties with them."

Despite the large number of remarriages, however, social and legal changes have not kept pace with this new family form. The general societal approach to these relationships is to view them in much the same way as first marriages. However, although all families share some of the same characteristics and face many of the same problems, families formed as a result of remarriage face additional problems that must be addressed if these relationships are to survive. A 1998 study by James Bray and his colleagues found that unrealistic expectations were a major factor in the divorce rate of remarried couples. To prepare themselves for the day-to-day reality of living in a remarried family, couples need to know about the structure and functioning of remarried families. Figure 13.1 illustrates some of the complexity of remarried families. William Beer (1989) identified ten fundamental ways in which the remarried family is different from the nuclear family.

1. ***Complexity.*** Remarried families take many forms: divorced individuals/single partners, divorced individuals/widowed partners, divorced individuals/divorced partners. The presence of children increases the families' complexity.

2. ***A changing cast of characters.*** Remarried families may have shifting membership. Some of the stepchildren may live together permanently, others will come and go depending on visitation arrangements, still others may appear rarely, if at all.

3. ***Unclear boundaries.*** Membership boundaries often are ambiguous in remarried families. For example, children may not include a noncustodial parent's new spouse in their definition of family. A stepparent's parents may or may not view themselves as stepgrandparents or be viewed that way by stepgrandchildren. The boundaries become further confused if there is a second divorce. Then, is the divorced stepparent still a member of the family?

4. ***Undefined rules.*** Remarried couples often find it difficult to agree on rules regarding discipline, money, and parenting responsibilities.

5. ***Unclear laws.*** Although the biological parent–child relationship is legally well defined, there still is considerable ambiguity regarding the legal rights and duties involved in stepparent–stepchild relationships.

Figure 13.1

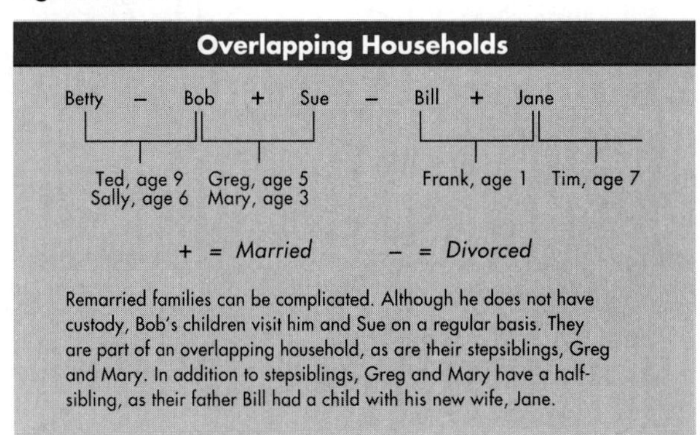

Remarried families can be complicated. Although he does not have custody, Bob's children visit him and Sue on a regular basis. They are part of an overlapping household, as are their stepsiblings, Greg and Mary. In addition to stepsiblings, Greg and Mary have a half-sibling, as their father Bill had a child with his new wife, Jane.

6. *A lack of kinship terms.* American culture has relatively few kinship terms, and in remarried families the same word is used to denote very different relationships. For example, the word *stepparent* applies to a person who has married either a custodial parent or a noncustodial parent. It also refers to a new spouse of an elderly parent, even though no parent–child relationship ever existed for this spouse. The new spouses of each biological parent may see each other frequently and join in negotiations over stepchildren. Yet there are no kinship terms for their relationship to one another.

7. *Instant families.* Remarried families come ready-made, often without appropriate time for members to establish emotional bonds with one another.

8. *Guilt.* New spouses may have unresolved feelings about their previous marriage. Children may feel guilty for showing affection to the stepparent, believing this to be disloyal to the noncustodial biological parent.

9. *Grieving.* Remarried families have undergone a loss before their formation, and some members may not have completed the grieving process. Children may be particularly affected because they must now relinquish the dream of reuniting parents.

10. *Myth of the re-created nuclear family.* Stepfamilies aren't like nuclear families. Complex stepfamilies often feel less like one family and more like two separate families than do first-married families (Banker and Gaertner, 1998, 2001). The more a remarried couple tries to make the stepfamily into a family like any other, the more likely they are to be disappointed.

These differences are only slowly being recognized. Thus, there are as yet few clearly defined role models for stepfamilies to follow. Consequently, the participants generally lack preparation for the special complexities of remarried family life (Papernow, 1998). Members of stepfamilies often find themselves questioning their feelings and experiences, uncertain of how typical or "normal" their family situation is. In this chapter we will explore the history and cultural meanings of remarried families, their special characteristics and problems, and strategies for strengthening these families.

HISTORICAL PERSPECTIVE

In the previous chapter we discussed the fact that divorce has been a feature of American family life since 1639. Remarriage has also been a part of family life from this country's beginnings. During the seventeenth and eighteenth centuries, the proportion of remarriages among all marriages was approximately 20 percent to 30 percent (Ihinger-Tallman and Pasley, 1987). The circumstances leading to remarriage were quite different then, however. Whereas in early America the overwhelming majority of remarriages followed the death of a spouse, today remarriages typically involve divorced individuals.

In the early colonies, the climate and harsh conditions as well as the lack of medical knowledge took a heavy toll on the inhabitants. For example, in Charles County, Maryland, marriages were likely to last an average of only 7 years and had only a 33 percent chance of lasting 10 years before one spouse died (Carr and Walsh, 1983). In Virginia, 25 percent of children by the age of 5 had lost one or both parents; this figure rose to 70 percent by age 21 (Fox and Quitt, 1980). No group was immune to early death. For example, the fathers of Patrick Henry, Thomas Jefferson, George Washington, and James Madison all married widows (Calhoun, 1917).

Given the value attached to marriage in colonial America, remarriage following the death of a spouse was not only common but socially expected for both women and men, especially for those with young children.

Little is known about the nature and quality of early remarried families. They were considered to be the same as first families; no special records were kept on how well they fared. However, it is likely that remarriages, then as now, faced some problems not encountered in first marriages.

What images come to mind when you hear the term stepfamily? *Are these images positive or negative? How did you learn about stepfamilies? As you read the remainder of this chapter, evaluate the accuracy of your views of stepfamilies.*

Over half of all marriages today involve a second marriage for one or both partners.
Source: © Tribune Media Services, Inc. All Rights Reserved. Reprinted by permission.

CULTURAL IMAGES OF STEPFAMILIES

One basic problem stepfamilies throughout history have had to contend with is their cultural image. The original meaning of the term *step* in *stepfamily* comes from Old German and Old English terms associated with the experiences of bereavement and deprivation. The earliest designations of *step* referred to a child who was orphaned. Later on, the term was expanded to include the replacement parent, whether a stepmother or stepfather.

The terms *stepchild*, *stepparent*, and especially *stepmother* have conveyed negative connotations from earliest times. Most of these images derive from folklore and fairy tales that through the medium of storytelling sought to provide guidelines for daily living. An analysis of children's fairy tales found that stepmothers along with bears, wolves, giants, ogres, and witches were the most frequent representations of evil (Sutton-Smith, 1971). Other analyses confirm the consistent image of the stepmother as a cruel and evil person (Dainton, 1993; Ganong and Coleman, 1997). For centuries children have been entertained and/or frightened by "Hansel and Gretel," "Snow White," and "Cinderella," with their tales of maternal loss and cruel replacement.

Professionals and laypeople alike need to be aware of the fear and anxiety such images can create, especially for young children, who today increasingly live in stepfamilies. Such images also complicate the stepmother role, making it difficult and ambiguous. Negative images also imply that "step is less," as conveyed in the metaphor that anything of lesser value is "like a stepchild" (Wald, 1981). Writer Jim Warda (2000), a stepfather, describes his pain at hearing a coworker say, "Jim, they're treating our department like a red-headed stepchild." Warda says that the comment implies that a stepchild is less than a biological child, someone whom a parent can like, and possibly love, but never to the same degree as his or her own, biological child.

Such images can affect the perceptions people have of stepfamilies. Margaret Crosbie-Burnett (1994/1995), for example, has written about the bias against stepchildren and stepparents that frequently exists in the educational system. Even today, counselors and teachers may be quick to assume that if students in remarried families are having difficulty, it is because of a faulty family structure. She recommends, therefore, that school personnel receive professional training about both the strengths and challenges associated with living in a stepfamily.

In an attempt to correct negative stereotypes, many stepparents, children's writers, and family professionals are publishing more accurate representations of today's stepfamilies. One result of this is an attempt to create more neutral terms to describe stepfamilies: *reconstituted*, *blended*, *merged*, *binuclear*, and *remarried families*. Some of these terms, however, create problems of their own. The notion of reconstituted, blended, or merged families implies that all members get along and fit comfortably into the new family structure. In fact, such a situation may never be achieved, or at least may not be achieved for a number of years. The felt pressure to measure up to such standards may add further stress to a remarriage. Thus, we prefer the term *remarried families*, agreeing with Wald (1981:33) that the use of this term is "accurately descriptive, nontechnical, and value-free, and does not imply goals achieved." Throughout this chapter we will use the term *remarried families* when referring to the family as a whole. However, since there are as yet no newly agreed-upon terms for relationships within remarried families, we will follow common practice and refer to them as steprelationships.

Throughout history many nursery rhymes and children's stories have depicted stepmothers as wicked and cruel.

THE PROCESS OF REMARRIAGE

Over time most divorced and widowed persons are able to relinquish their strong emotional ties to the past. This, of course, does not imply that they do not have warm memories of the past or that they never think about their former partner. Rather, it means that they are able to focus on the present and plan for the future. When this happens, the widowed or divorced individual confronts the issues of whether to date and perhaps whether to remarry.

Dating and Courtship Patterns

Are dating and courtship different the second time around? Older adults report many of the same anxieties about dating that adolescents do: appropriate behavior for the first date, what to talk about, who pays, whether to be sexually involved, and how to end the relationship if it is going nowhere. Adults with children may find dating even more complicated. Children often have difficulty accepting a parent's decision to date. When the parental loss was due to death, children may interpret the surviving parent's dating as an act of disloyalty to or betrayal of the deceased parent. When the loss was due to divorce, children may fantasize about their parents' getting back together again and thus react negatively to a parent's dating. Additionally, children may feel displaced by the dating partner, so they may attempt to sabotage the relationship by behaving obnoxiously. Conversely, they may pressure parents by promoting the relationship in hopes of finding a new parent.

Children are not the only ones to react to the resumption of dating. Relatives of a deceased spouse may feel hurt or betrayed if they believe that the surviving spouse is dating too soon following the death of their loved one. Ex-spouses may also be hostile to their former spouse's dating. They may be jealous themselves or fear that someone else will replace them in their children's eyes. Thus, they may withdraw cooperation over visitation rights and delay or even end financial support.

We might assume that dealing with these complications would lengthen the courtship process. The opposite pattern seems to be the case, however. Divorced and widowed individuals who remarry tend to spend only half the time in dating and courtship that they did preceding their first marriage (O'Flaherty and Eells, 1988; Ganong and Coleman, 1994).

Other researchers suggest that more than time distinguishes dating and courtship before first and second marriages. For example, Frank Furstenberg and Graham Spanier (1987) found that dating among their divorced respondents was guided more by pragmatic than by romantic considerations. The style of dating among the divorced is more informal, and courtship often involves living together before marriage. Couples often believe that the experience of cohabitation gives a marriage a better chance to succeed, but as we saw in Chapter 7, couples who cohabit first have a higher likelihood of divorce than those who do not cohabit. Yet approximately 60 percent of divorced people cohabit before remarrying (Ganong and Coleman, 1989; Bumpass, Sweet, and Castro-Martin, 1990).

The high prevalence of cohabitation after divorce has led some researchers to argue that the definition of stepfamilies should be expanded to include cohabitation with a child or children of only one partner and should recognize that stepfamilies include those formed after nonmarital childbearing as well as after marital disruption. Social demographers estimate that about 25 percent of current stepfamilies are actually cohabiting couples and a substantial number of remarriages were preceded by cohabitation (Bumpass, Raley, and Sweet, 1995).

Beyond this cohabitation strategy, however, most individuals do little to prepare themselves for living in a remarried family. Only 38 percent of the women and 25 percent of the men in the Ganong and Coleman study sought professional counseling, although many more reported getting advice from friends and self-help books. Furthermore, many couples did not use the dating or courtship period to discuss potential problems in a remarriage. For example, only 56 percent of the couples discussed the most serious problem observed by stepfamily experts, namely, children from a previous marriage. Less than 25 percent discussed the second most serious problem: finances. A full 13 percent reported that they didn't discuss any issues very seriously. As a result of this lack of preparation, many people enter remarriage with nonverbalized expectations that, if not realized, become sources of conflict and disappointment (Papernow, 1993).

Individuals who plan to marry someone with children are well advised to build a friendship with those children before assuming a stepparent role.

Doni Whitsett and Helen Land (1992) examined the interrelationships among role strain, coping, and marital satisfaction of 73 stepparents. Many of their respondents reported that prior to their remarriage they had no clear idea of what is involved in being a stepparent or what their spouse expected of them. Although couples in first marriages may be no better prepared than remarrying couples for entering a relationship, the lack of preparation may have more serious consequences for the stability of a second marriage simply because the latter is more complex, especially when children are involved.

The Decision to Remarry

Given the pain and trauma surrounding many divorces, and given the complications of resumed dating, why do so many Americans choose to remarry? First and foremost, marriage remains an important cultural value, and it is still perceived as the normal way to form an intimate connection with another person. Many of the reasons women and men give for remarriage are similar to those given for first marriages: convenience, social pressure, love, companionship, support, and for some, pregnancy. Some divorced individuals desire to alleviate the feelings of failure that accompanied the dissolution of their previous marriage (Ganong and Coleman, 1994). Furthermore, given the persistent economic inequalities between women and men and the downward mobility experienced by many divorced and widowed women, remarriage may also be a rational economic decision that results in an improved standard of living (Riessman, 1990; Folk, Graham, and Beller, 1992). Numerous studies show that women and children are almost always better off financially after remarriage (Nielsen, 1999). Finally, divorced and widowed custodial parents may be motivated to remarry so they will have help raising their children (Collins, 1991).

Patterns of Remarriage

Remarriage rates fell dramatically between 1970 and 1990. Between 1970 and 1984 there was a 16 percent drop in the proportion of people who remarried within 5 years of their divorce. This did not mean, however, that divorced people did not enter new relationships. During this same time there was a 7 percent increase in the proportion who formed a union through cohabitation (Bumpass, Sweet, and Cherlin, 1991). Data consistently show that groups remarry at different rates, with divorced men having the highest rates and widowed women the lowest.

For several reasons, remarriage after widowhood is much less frequent than remarriage after divorce. First, unlike most divorced people, the widowed may continue to hold a strong emotional attachment to the previous spouse. Thus, they may not be interested in establishing another relationship (Talbott, 1998). Second, divorce usually occurs at younger ages than widowhood. In general, the younger the age at divorce or widowhood, the greater the likelihood of remarriage, especially for women. Overall, 75 percent of divorced women remarry within 10 years. However, 81 percent of women who were under age 25 at divorce have remarried, compared with 68 percent of women age 25 years and older at divorce (Bramlett and Mosher, 2001).

Individual choice and cultural patterns help to explain these findings. Some women choose to remain unmarried, preferring their new-found independence to a second marriage. Others desire to marry again but find themselves disadvantaged by norms that encourage men to marry younger women. Rates of remarriage also vary by social class, education, race, and the presence of children.

Social Class and Education For both women and men, however, age may be less of a factor in the decision to remarry than social class. Men with higher incomes are more likely to remarry than men with lower incomes (Glick, 1980; Day and Bahr, 1986). For men with low incomes the added burden of supporting two households may be prohibitive. Conversely, inadequate income may motivate some single mothers to remarry. As we saw in the previous chapter, divorce adversely affects women's and children's economic well-being. Remarriage, by adding another (often higher) wage earner, reverses this process. Robert Emery (1994) reports that 5 years after divorce, the incomes of remarried women are 27 percent above predivorce levels.

A similar pattern emerges when we examine education and gender. A recent study in Canada found that highly educated women were less likely to remarry than their male counterparts (Wu, 1994). Studies in the United States have also found a negative correlation between level of education and remarriage for women. Women without college educations tend to remarry quickly, whereas women with higher levels of education remarry later or not at all (Glick, 1984; Folk, Graham, and Beller, 1992). Women college graduates are likely to be employed in relatively well-paying jobs; thus, they may feel less pressure to marry for economic reasons than previously married women with low incomes.

Social Class: Race and Ethnicity Rates of remarriage vary across social class, race, and ethnicity. For example, lower-income African Americans are less likely to remarry than their white counterparts. In fact, remarriage rates for African American women across all socioeconomic levels are lower than those for their white counterparts. As Figure 13.2 shows, within 6 years of divorce, 58 percent of white women, 44 percent of Latinas, and 32 percent of black women have remarried. Ten years after divorce, 79 percent of white women, 68 percent of Latinas, but only 49 percent of black women have remarried. Studies suggest that these differences are most likely related to higher rates of unemployment, incarceration, and mortality; lower levels

Figure 13.2

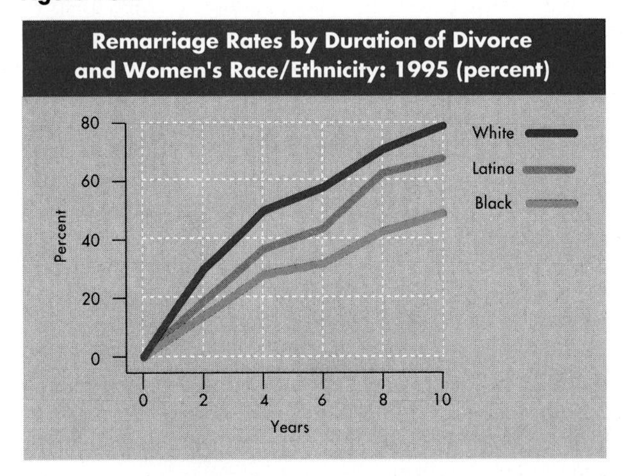

Source: Adapted from M. D. Bramlett and W. E. Mosher, 2001, *First Marriage Dissolution, Divorce, and Remarriage: United States.* Advance Data from Vital and Health Statistics, no. 323 (Hyattsville, MD: National Center for Health Statistics): 10, Table 8.

of educational attainment and earnings; previous experiences as children of unmarried or less educated parents; and higher rates of poverty and lack of job opportunities in the communities in which African Americans live (Cherlin, 1992; Tucker and Mitchell-Kerman, 1995). This overall disadvantaged economic position has led many African Americans to see the marital relationship as less effective than the larger kin network in providing support. Additionally, as we saw in Chapter 5, a sex ratio imbalance places limits on the opportunities for remarriage among African American women.

The rates of remarriage for Latinas are between those of African American and white women. However, considerable variation exists among Latina/o groups. According to the latest census data available, Puerto Rican women have the lowest rate of remarriage, and Cuban men have the highest. Similar variations in rates of remarriage have been found among Asian Americans, with Korean women and men having the highest rates and Vietnamese men the lowest. Native American women and men have fairly high rates of remarriage compared to other groups (Sweet and Bumpass, 1987). Relatively little research has been done on remarried families of color. Thus, the reasons for the varied patterns across racial and ethnic groups are not entirely clear. However, it is likely that part of the answer is to be found in the different economic positions of the various groups, the availability of support from kin members, and increased acceptability of cohabitation as an alternative to marriage.

Religion As we saw in the last chapter, religion is one of the factors affecting patterns of divorce. Within 20 years of a first marriage, 48 percent of Catholics are divorced, compared with 49 percent of Jews, 56 percent of Protestants, and 59 percent of persons with no religious affiliation (Hout, 2000). Despite the Catholic church's opposition to divorce and its ban on remarriage, except in cases involving a church annulment (see Chapter 12), at least half of all divorced Catholics will eventually remarry. This pattern is similar to that for people of other faiths (Hornike, 2001). Among the 51 million Catholic adults in the United States today, 16 percent are currently divorced or separated and another 9 percent have been divorced in the past but are now remarried, up from 7 percent in the 1980s. Divorced Catholics contemplating remarriage face the added dilemma that a decision to remarry can mean the loss of a beloved church and parish family. Seventeen percent to 20 percent of divorced Catholics leave the Catholic church as a result of their remarriage (Hout, 2000). Despite the Catholic church's official policy on remarriage, many members of the clergy have instituted a variety of programs to help remarried Catholics, including support groups, second-marriage preparation classes, and a Rainbow Program for children to help them cope with the loss and grief they experience following a parental divorce.

The Presence of Children Finally, the presence of children affects the likelihood of remarriage for women and men in different ways. Divorced men with custody of children tend to remarry sooner than their female counterparts. Perhaps because they represent such a small minority and have not been socialized to be the primary caretaker, custodial fathers often more strongly feel the need for a partner to assist them with child care. Among women, those with young children and those with fewer children are more likely to remarry than are those with large families or older children (Glick and Lin, 1986).

For all these people, the decision to remarry begins a complicated series of adjustments that must be made if the new relationship is to survive.

The Stations of Remarriage

In Chapter 12 we discussed the complex process of exiting from a marital relationship, utilizing Paul Bohannan's (1970) six stations of divorce: emotional, psychic, community, parental, economic, and legal divorces. Ann Goetting (1982) found that there is a similarity between the developmental tasks that must be mastered in the divorce process and the many personal changes and adjustments that accompany the process of remarriage. Looking at remarriage this way makes it clear that remarriage involves more than the exchange of wedding vows. It requires individuals to adopt new roles, to unlearn old expectations from previous relationships, and to cope with an ambiguous legal status.

Goetting has identified six remarriages derived from Bohannan's stations of divorce. Each station of the remarriage process presents a challenge to the formation of a new couple and a new family identity. Keep in mind that, as is the case for the stations of divorce, the six stations of remarriage do not affect all remarrying people with the same intensity, nor do they occur in exactly the same order for everyone. The presence of children, for example, can affect the intensity as well as the number of stages people experience in remarriage.

Emotional Remarriage The term **emotional remarriage** refers to the process of reestablishing a bond of attraction, love, commitment, and trust with another person. This can be a slow and difficult process for both the widowed and the divorced. The nature and quality of the previous marital experience affect the relationship with the new partner in different ways. On the one hand, people who were happily married and then widowed may idealize the deceased spouse and thus see the new partner in a less favorable light. Such people can become overly critical of the new partner's behavior if it doesn't measure up to this ideal. On the other hand, people who have been hurt and disappointed in previous relationships may be oversensitive to spousal criticism and may sense rejection by the new spouse when none is intended. For example, an intended compliment may be judged suspect because a former partner used similar comments as putdowns. Both the widowed and the divorced must be careful not to let the experiences of the first marriage unduly influence their new relationship.

PSYCHIC REMARRIAGE The process known as **psychic remarriage** requires moving back from the recently acquired identity of single person to a couple identity. This transition varies in intensity and perceived difficulty. For individuals who have accepted more traditional gender roles, regaining the status of husband or wife may be especially gratifying, and their adjustments to couple identity may be relatively minor. Other people, however, especially women who experienced a new sense of autonomy and personal independence after widowhood or divorce, may feel constrained after taking on a marital role.

COMMUNITY REMARRIAGE **Community remarriage** involves changes in social relationships. Following the dissolution of a marriage, individuals often find that the nature and frequency of contact with relatives and friends is disrupted. As we have seen in Chapter 12, relationships with other married couples often suffer following a divorce. As a result, couple friends are often replaced with new, unmarried friends. Often these friendships are deeper and more intimate because they are selected on the basis of one's personal interests and needs, not those of a couple. Reentering the couple world may result in reverting back to less intimate and more couple-oriented relationships that can be shared more easily and "fit" more readily into a couple's lifestyle. Additionally, remarriage means that new in-laws must somehow be integrated into the family network. These changes, involving both gains and losses in the social network, carry with them both joy and sadness for all affected parties.

PARENTAL REMARRIAGE Remarriage in which one or both spouses have children from a previous relationship is known as **parental remarriage.** This station of remarriage generally receives the most attention in social science literature and in the media. More than half of all remarriages involve minor stepchildren living in the household (Ganong and Coleman, 1994). Estimates are that at least 30 percent of all U.S. children under 18 are connected to a stepfamily. About 21 percent of them live with a parent and stepparent, and the remaining 9 percent live with a single parent and her or his partner (Hornike, 2001). Detailed breakdowns on the characteristics of these children are not yet available. However, according to 1990 census data, African American children are most likely to live in stepfamilies: 32.3 percent of African American children under 18 residing in married-couple families do so with a stepparent, compared with 16.1 percent of Latina/o and 14.6 percent of white children.

Establishing good working relationships with stepchildren is perhaps the most challenging and emotionally trying aspect of remarriage. Both stepparent and stepchild confront the emotional challenge of moving from the role of stranger to that of family member. This process takes time and is primarily one of trial and error. Such adjustments are often confounded by the presence of the nonresidential biological parent. The attitudes and behavior of the ex-spouse, if hostile, jealous, or uncooperative, may slow the integration of the stepparent into the family unit.

ECONOMIC REMARRIAGE **Economic remarriage** involves the establishment of a unit of economic productivity and consumption while at the same time working out mutually agreeable earning and spending habits. The presence of minor stepchildren can complicate the establishment of an economic plan for the new family unit in several ways. First, the remarried couple may be dependent, to a degree, on the economic behavior of people outside their immediate relationship. For example, when custodial parents remarry, they may be receiving alimony and child support from their ex-spouses. As we saw in the previous chapter, child support might become sporadic or stop entirely after remarriage, adding a dimension of uncertainty to the family budgeting process. Second, new spouses may themselves be noncustodial divorced parents who are paying alimony and child support to their ex-spouses, thus diminishing the financial resources available to the new family unit. Friction may develop over resource distribution: Who should get how much of what is available?

Handling issues of financial equity, need, and flexibility may prove a daunting task. The nature of the financial arrangement may have an impact on the degree and speed of family integration. Some couples choose a "common-pot" approach, putting all wages and child support together and then allocating resources according to need rather than source of income. Others choose a "two-pot" arrangement, in which each spouse contributes a fixed amount to running the household but each biological parent is responsible for her or his children's expenses. Barbara Fishman (1983) found that the "common-pot" approach is more likely to unify the stepfamily, while the "two-pot" system tends to reinforce biological loyalties and individual autonomy. Couples who have used the "one-pot" method generally reported higher family satisfaction than those who kept their money separate (Bray and Kelly, 1998).

LEGAL REMARRIAGE **Legal remarriage** also requires people to make a number of adjustments. Taking on new responsibilities as a spouse does not absolve one from responsibilities that accompanied the first marriage. Court-awarded payments of alimony and child support remain in effect. Other responsibilities to the first family are not as clear-cut, however. For example, do nonresident biological children or an ex-spouse have a right to any health or life insurance, retirement benefits, or inheritance from a noncustodial parent or former partner? Because these issues are not clearly dealt with in most states, increasing numbers of couples sign a premarital agreement, declaring which assets belong to the remarried family and which should be directed toward the ex-spouse or nonresidential children. These agreements notwithstanding, conflict may develop if circumstances change and one spouse feels that too many resources are being diverted to the other spouse's former family.

Additionally troubling is the legal ambiguity surrounding stepchild–stepparent relationships (Ramsey, 1995). Only five states have laws that obligate a stepparent to support a stepchild (Fine and Fine, 1992). This legal vacuum may create tension in several ways. On the one hand, some stepparents may resent being asked to assume responsibility for someone else's children. On the other hand, biological parents may feel guilty asking for help to support their children, or they may resent their new spouse's reluctance to help in this regard. A further complication for remarried families is stepparents' lack of legal rights concerning stepchildren. For example, in most states stepparents are not permitted to authorize medical treatment for stepchildren, nor do they have legal rights to custody and/or visitation of stepchildren who lived with them prior to the dissolution of their remarriage (Clark, 1988).

Another area in which the legal system has failed to provide adequate support and guidelines for remarried families is in the area of sexual relations. Although all 50 states prohibit marriage and sexual relations between persons closely related by blood, few make similar provisions for family members in a remarriage—for example between a stepfather and stepdaughter or between stepsiblings. Although a sexual relation between a minor stepchild and a stepparent is considered a criminal offense, and although sexual relationships between stepsiblings are not socially condoned, neither behavior is defined as incest. This differential treatment of sexual relations in first marriages and remarriages can lead to tensions and even sexual exploitation in remarried families.

STAGES IN THE DEVELOPMENT OF REMARRIED FAMILIES

These stations of remarriage take time. According to James Bray and John Kelly (1998), all stepfamilies experience up and down patterns, with the first two years being the most difficult as they attempt to master the basic tasks of stepfamily life: parenting, managing change, separating a second marriage from a first, and dealing with the nonresidential parent. This stage is followed by a leveling off of the initial difficulties and the next three or four years become more tranquil as compromises are negotiated. However, a third cycle can see the reemergence of stress and conflict, as children and parents confront issues relevant to the adolescent years.

Although stepfamilies vary considerably from one to another, Bray and Kelly (1998) found that they were able to identify three general categories of stepfamilies. The *neotraditional* family tends to be the most successful. It is a close-knit family with a strong couple relationship; these couples share compatible values, function well together, and realize that forging a stepfamily does not happen overnight. In contrast, *romantic* families are least likely to succeed because they hold unrealistic expectations, believing that feelings of love, harmony, and closeness will develop along with the wedding ceremony. *Matriarchal* families contain mothers who are highly competent and play a dominant role in the family.

REMARRIED FAMILIES: ROLES, INTERACTIONS, AND REACTIONS

The dynamic interrelationships among these stations will become clearer as we examine the roles, interactions, and reactions of various members of remarried family households beginning with stepchildren. One of the first decisions couples contemplating remarriage have to make is whether to include children from a previous marriage in the wedding ceremony.

Children and the Remarriage Service

Even though the wedding itself may take a more simple form, planning for a remarriage ceremony when children are involved can be a delicate matter. Sometimes children, especially young ones, want to take part. To meet this need, many religious bodies are modifying their wedding rituals to include the children from previous marriages. When this happens, children usually stand next to or behind the couple during the ceremony, or if old enough, serve as bridesmaids or groomsmen. Sometimes the marriage vows include a stepparent's promise to care for the spouse's children and, as in the case of a Greendale, Wisconsin, congregation, the children are given medallions signifying their membership in the new family. Family therapists stress the symbolic importance of rituals in marking the new relationships and commitments remarriage brings. For children, participation in a formal ritual can make the new family seem more "real" (Visher and Visher, 1982).

Celebrating the wedding ritual together as a family serves another key function. A remarriage ceremony can be the basis for the first collective memory that the new family will share. However, for some children the prospect of a parent's remarriage may be painful, and some older children may decline an invitation to participate in the ceremony. They may even refuse to attend the wedding. Although couples may be hurt and disappointed by this reaction, it is generally best to let children decide this matter for themselves. Often when children know the decision is really theirs and that they will be welcome if they change their minds even at the last moment, they do decide to reverse their position and attend. Forcing children to attend against their wishes may set up a power struggle that will have a long-term negative impact on the quality of family life.

Remarriages can also affect adult children who are celebrating their first marriage. Deciding whom to include in their own ceremony and wedding celebration can be difficult for these children. Have you attended any weddings where this was a problem? What problems can develop when adult children have both biological parents and stepparents? How can these problems be handled?

Children in Remarried Families

Throughout this text we have emphasized the fact that all families are influenced by persons and events outside the immediate family unit. This is particularly true for remarried

About 43 percent of all marriages today involve at least one person who has been previously married and who often has children from a first marriage. Some children feel insecure at the prospect of their parent's remarriage. However, including these children in the remarriage ceremony provides them with a sense of belonging to the newly created family.

families formed after a divorce. Although members of nuclear families generally share one household, divorce creates two separate but **overlapping households** with children having membership in both households.

This dual membership can have both positive and negative consequences for children. On the one hand, if one or both biological parents remarries, children have more adult role models to guide, love, and nurture them. Interacting in two households, each with distinct members, expectations, activities, traditions, and family culture, can provide a richness of experience not found in any one household. On the other hand, this dual membership can be a source of conflict and confusion for children. Each household has a set of rules, so children must behave differently from one household to the next. For example, one of the author's young friends who is involved in an overlapping household complained:

> When I'm at home I can go to bed anytime I want. Mom doesn't care as long as I get up right away when she calls me in the morning. When I'm at Dad's house, they make me go to bed when the other kids do, around 9 o'clock. I don't think that's fair. I'm older than they are.

Adults in both households need to understand that adjusting to two sets of rules is not easy for children; there must be time and space to allow for the transition from one to the other. Mixed emotions in these circumstances are not unique to children. Both parents and stepparents may feel insecure and jealous when children visit the other household and they may communicate these feelings to their children who, in turn, may feel that to enjoy being in the other household is somehow disloyal to the other biological parent.

Whether overlapping households are beneficial to children depends, in large measure, on the attitude and behavior of the adults involved. If all parental adults cooperate in matters of visitation, refrain from criticizing each other in front of the children, and give children permission to care about and enjoy their other family household, the positive benefits of dual household membership are likely to outweigh the negative consequences for both children and other family members. For example, a study of adolescent family life satisfaction in remarried families found that adolescents who perceived their families to be more flexible reported greater satisfaction with both overall remarried family household and the parent–stepparent subsystem. This flexibility allowed them to meet the expectations of multiple elements of the extended-family systems (Henry and Lovelace, 1995).

Nevertheless, children, too, play a role in determining the nature and quality of overlapping households. They can cooperate or be a source of friction. A major factor in their behavior is the way in which they come to define family membership.

Children's Perceptions of Family Membership

Social scientists often report on the role of children in remarried families, but usually the source of this information is adults. An interesting exception to this pattern is a study by Penny Gross (1987) of 60 Canadian children, 30 females and 30 males between the ages of 16 and 18. Each had two living divorced parents, at least one of whom had remarried. Utilizing a structured interview that focused on parent–child relationships, Gross asked the children who they considered to be family members. Four patterns emerged: retention, substitution, reduction, and augmentation.

Retention Twenty children (33 percent) defined the family in terms of its composition prior to the divorce, that is, with both biological parents but not the stepparent. Thus, some children lived with a stepparent but did not consider that person to be part of their family; nonresidential parents continued to play an important role in the lives of their children. Sons were more likely than daughters to include the nonresidential father as a family member.

Substitution Eight children (13 percent) excluded one biological parent and included at least one stepparent in their definition of family. This was most common when children lived with the remarried parent. For these children, the household membership and the family were synonymous.

Reduction Some children included fewer people than the original family. Fifteen children (25 percent) excluded their nonresidential biological parent as well as the stepparent, considering only the custodial parent as family. In most cases, the custodial parent's remarriage had occurred recently, and the children still had negative feelings about it. These children were the most dissatisfied with their lives and revealed emotional stress during the interview.

Augmentation Seventeen children (28 percent) added to their original family by including both biological parents and at least one stepparent as members. Most of these children lived with their biological fathers and their stepmothers but continued to have regular contact and a strong relationship with their biological mother. They felt free to move back and forth between the overlapping households without the fear of being disloyal to either biological parent.

A survey conducted in the United States also found variations in children's definitions of family membership. When asked, "When you think of your family, who specifically do you include?" 10 percent of the children did not list a biological parent, and 33 percent omitted a stepparent (Furstenberg and Spanier, 1987). Such research suggests that the realities for children involved in remarriages vary considerably. It also challenges definitions of the family that assume an overlap with household membership. In the eyes of both children and parents, families may include more or fewer people than current household members. Further research is needed to examine the relationships among stepsiblings and half siblings and the degree to which children incorporate these relationships into their subjective views of family.

CONSEQUENCES OF PARENTAL REMARRIAGE FOR CHILDREN How do children react to the remarriage of their parents? Do they experience more stress or behavioral problems than children in other family structures? To date, studies reveal no clear answer to these questions. On the one hand, a number of studies have found that stepchildren experience more stress, have more difficulty in school, and have higher rates of delinquency and emotional problems than children living in their original families (Peterson and Zill, 1986; Santrock and Sitterle, 1987; Dawson, 1991; Hetherington and Clingempeel, 1992). On the other hand, other studies suggest that in the long run stepchildren are only slightly more troubled than children in original families and that most stepchildren eventually adapt and emerge as reasonably competent people (Ganong and Coleman, 1994; Hetherington and Jodl, 1994). Marilyn Ihinger-Tallman and Kay Pasley (1987) found that children in stepfamilies are similar to those in intact families in self-esteem, psychological functioning, and academic achievement. How are we to reconcile these divergent findings?

The first step is to recognize the timing and complexity of divorce and subsequent remarriage. As one research team observed: "Empirical findings suggest that the age of the child at the time of parental divorce and remarriage, sex of the child, and sex of the stepparent are important factors for understanding and predicting the influence of family change on children" (Ihinger-Tallman and Pasley, 1991:461). Let's examine these factors—age and sex—more closely.

Age Studies suggest that if parental remarriage occurs early in the child's life (before age 5) it has few adverse effects. In contrast, school-aged children experience more stress after a residential parent remarries, and schoolwork and social behavior are frequently adversely affected (Wallerstein and Kelly, 1980; Arnold, 1998). In comparison with younger children, older children find it more difficult to adjust to new people and new places, and they experience a complex set of emotions regarding both. As adolescents struggle to become more autonomous, the addition of another "parenting" adult in the household may be perceived as threatening. This may be especially true for the oldest child in a single-parent family. In that position the child may have had considerable authority over younger siblings and may have acted as confidant for the custodial parent. For some children, relinquishing this responsibility may be a relief; others may resent the loss of power and status (Crosbie-Burnett, Skyles, and Becker-Haven, 1988).

Sex When sex differences are taken into account, interesting patterns emerge. Research has consistently shown that boys have more problems adjusting to divorce than do girls. In contrast, in stepfamilies girls experience more adjustment problems and report poorer relationships with parents than do boys (Clingempeel and Segal, 1986; Peterson and Zill, 1986; Ganong and Coleman, 1994). For example, after a parental divorce there is an upswing in drug use among boys but not among girls. However, the pattern is reversed following a remarriage; there is increased drug use by girls but reduced use by boys (Needle, Su, and Doherty, 1990).

Observational studies have found that compared with stepsons, stepdaughters are more sullen, withdrawn, and direct more negative problem-solving behavior toward stepfathers (Hetherington, 1989). Other researchers report similar findings, particularly in mother-custody stepfamilies (Vuchinich et al., 1991).

Part of the explanation for this pattern lies in the nature of the relationships established after divorce. The most common structure in remarried families is a biological mother, her children, and a stepfather. This pattern is a result of the fact that in the United States divorced mothers overwhelmingly get custody of their biological children. Girls often become closer to the custodial parent after a divorce and view the stepfather as an intruder or the stepmother as competition. In fact, closer mother–stepfather relationships are associated with more behavior problems in girls.

Additionally, the adolescent stepdaughter–stepfather relationship may be confusing for both parties. The emerging sexuality of adolescent girls may cause both to be uncertain about the appropriate way to express affection for each other. Girls may feel uncomfortable with a nonbiologically related adult male in the household (Hetherington, 1989). These tensions are reflected in the fact that girls in stepfamily households leave home to marry or live independently at an earlier age than those in either single- or two-parent households (Goldscheider and Goldscheider, 1993). This tendency is more pronounced in households containing stepsiblings (Aquilino, 1991). Similarly, in a British study of young adults, respondents were asked why they left their parental home. Those who had lived in stepfamily households were more likely to say they left because of "friction at home" than those in other types of households (Kiernan, 1992).

Boys, on the other hand, are initially angry that dad was "sent away," but then they become comfortable with another male presence in the household. The presence of a stepfather often eases the mother–son problems that resulted from the divorce. Boys now find themselves with a source of support and companionship. E. Mavis Hetherington (1989) found that preadolescent boys who enjoy a close supportive stepfather–stepson relationship display fewer behavior problems and increased social competence.

Although stepparent–stepchild relationships can be troublesome, most of these problems disappear by the third year into the remarriage. Perhaps the best advice, therefore, for parents in such situations is to be patient.

Stepsibling Relationships: Rivalry or Solidarity?

As is the case with the role of children in remarriages, stepsibling relationships have rarely been studied utilizing the perspective of children themselves. This is a critical omission for, as we will see later in this chapter, children can affect the stability of the remarriage. As we have just discussed, part of the difficulty lies in the relationship between stepparent and stepchild. However, a significant part of the tension in remarried families is centered on stepsibling relationships. Why is this the case? What is it like to be a stepsibling? How are stepsibling relationships different from sibling relationships in intact families?

William Beer (1988) reviewed the literature on remarried families and found only indirect references to the subject of stepsiblings. When stepsiblings were discussed, it was generally in relation to one of four themes: (1) stepsibling rivalry, (2) changes in age-order, (3) stepsibling sexuality, and (4) the role of half siblings. The following discussion relies heavily on his work.

Stepsibling Rivalry One of the main differences between siblings and stepsiblings is the origin of their relationships. In the idealized pattern children arrive after the marital relationship has been solidified. They share two biological parents and, hence, a sense of belonging to the same family unit. This does not mean, however, that their relationships are always harmonious. In fact, siblings sometimes experience intense rivalry for parental love.

Stepsiblings, however, start out in a different place than children in intact families. They were part of a family unit that was disrupted by death or divorce. Since that disruption they have formed close relationships with the custodial parent prior to a remarriage. Now they are asked to share this parent not only with another adult but with other children as well. Family therapist Emily Visher (1994) stresses the importance of maintaining one-on-one parent–child relationships. When a parent spends time alone with a child, it increases the security a child is likely to feel in the relationship. One of her clients complained:

> Before my dad got married again, I liked it. We had a lot of free time together. We played Nintendo games and we stayed up late and watched TV on Friday nights, and sometimes we went out to eat pizza. Now we have to take Kate and Shawna and Kathy with us. I liked just the two of us. (Quoted in Visher, 1994:334)

In addition, children are asked to share living space, property, and other possessions that may be in short supply. Sharing space is less of a problem when the remarried family moves into new, neutral housing, where no one has yet established territorial claims. This option, however, requires a degree of affluence that is absent for many remarried families. Thus, the more common pattern is for one part of the remarried family to move into the residence of the other. When this occurs, the former are likely to be seen as intruders and to feel like unwelcome guests. As an 8-year-old stepdaughter reported:

> We feel like guests in Jim's house. We are careful of what we do. It is like we are intruders. And I feel very bad that we took Tommy's room. They fixed up a room for him in the basement, with posters and all, but he's still mad at us for taking his room. (Cited in Fishman and Hamel, 1991:442)

Consequently, neither party is really comfortable with this arrangement, at least in the beginning, and it may give rise to stepsibling rivalry.

Imagine you were Tommy. How would you react? What can remarried families do to minimize such disruptions when households are merged?

Several other factors contribute to stepsibling rivalry. First, there is often a feeling of "them" and "us." Children see their ties to their biological parent as giving them a greater claim in the competition for love and other resources: "She's my mom, not yours." Second, when the families were separate, both units had their own rules. After remarriage, stepparents may try to impose all the rules impartially on all stepchildren, both those living in the same household and those who only visit. This attempt at impartiality, however, may not be perceived as equitable by the stepchildren, since the rules are often more familiar to one set of children than the other. Third, differential treatment by others can lead to feelings of rejection, hostility, and envy. For example, grandparents may provide generous gifts to their biological grandchildren and ignore their stepgrandchildren. Excluding some children in gift exchanges weakens the chances for establishing a sense of family integration as it reflects the image that some are "outsiders."

Changes in Age-Order In intact families the natural order of family births determines the age-order and age-interval of siblings that in turn, provide a relatively stable ranking system for children. Each position carries advantages and disadvantages for its occupant, and the children know where they fit in. However, when two sets of siblings are combined through remarriage, some siblings may find their age-order positions in the family altered. Some of these changes are easier to accept than others. For example, when an only child becomes the oldest child, a position of privilege is retained. To a degree, benefits also accompany the transition from being an only child to becoming the youngest child or "baby" of the family. The most difficult change is losing the position of being the oldest to another child, especially one of the same sex. Although these changes often cause tensions in the short run, over time children learn to adapt to the new sibling social structure.

Stepsibling Sexuality When the new sibling social structure includes adolescents of different sexes, drawing and maintaining sexual boundaries may become a critical task for remarried families. Sexual tension is usually a greater problem in remarried families than in first marriages. Several factors interact to create this atmosphere. First, the parent–stepparent union is relatively new. As a couple, they are still likely to be in a honeymoon stage, showing affection for each other, which may be sexually stimulating for adolescents. In first marriages, parents have already worked out patterns for privacy over the years. By the time their children reach adolescence, most parents no longer display sexuality overtly (Visher and Visher, 1982). Second, when a teenaged girl and boy who have not grown up together come to live in the same residence, they may become sexually attracted to each other. Parents may unintentionally contribute to this process by encouraging mutual activities as a way of bringing the children together. Third, stepsibling relationships are not covered by the same incest prohibitions as are sibling relationships. This lack of clear rules may cause confusion and uncertainty in remarried families.

Given these conditions, it is not surprising that some sort of romantic or erotic attraction sometimes develops between stepsiblings. Nevertheless, at the present time there has been no systematic attempt to measure the extent of such behavior (Ganong and Coleman, 1994). What information we have on this behavior comes primarily from clinical reports of family therapists and social workers. However, not all sexual feelings between stepsiblings are acted out. A more likely pattern is for adolescents to convert this eroticism into expressions of hostility. Parents often report that stepsiblings seem to "hate each other." This anger can be temporary or long-term; if too severe, it can threaten family stability. A more positive outcome results when children can convert their erotic feelings into warm, supportive relationships. Which outcome is more likely depends, to a large extent, on parental reaction. Open and honest discussions with the involved stepsiblings, reassuring them of the normality of such feelings and making clear that there is a difference between feelings and acting on those feelings, can reduce the possibility of a negative outcome.

The Role of Half Siblings As a result of tensions among siblings, it is often difficult for remarried family members to feel like a "real" family. One way in which remarried parents try to overcome this perception and create a cohesive family is by having a mutual child that will provide a blood tie among all members of the remarried family.

The decision to have a mutual child is quite common and occurs soon after remarriage. Half of all women who remarry will bear a child with their spouse (Wineberg, 1990). This pattern holds true for both African American and white remarried families. The rapidity with which this event takes place often causes confusion and adjustment problems for the other children. Although both adults may be biological parents in their own right, they are stepparents to each other's children, and they may or may not share responsibility for them. The birth of a mutual child adds a new role, a shared parental role.

Although this new role may help solidify the couple relationship, it is not problem-free. A pattern may emerge

Integrating members of two different families can be difficult. Remarriage can also provide emotionally satisfying relationships for stepsiblings, however.

whereby both parents exert authority over mutual children but only biological parents assert authority and take responsibility for their own children. This layering of authority and responsibility is a unique feature of remarried families and can produce problems, especially when disagreements over parenting styles arise (Giles-Sims, 1984). When this happens, there is often a tendency to form alliances—each parent siding with her or his biological offspring or criticizing the other's children, to produce what Emily Visher and John Visher (1982) have called the "two-family-under-one-roof" syndrome.

Stepchildren may see the birth of a mutual child as adding yet another competitor for parental attention. Conversely, however, stepchildren may have positive feelings about the birth of a half sibling, believing that since they are now all related by a blood tie, they finally all belong to a "real" family. Some support for the beneficial role of having a mutual child comes from the pioneering research of Lucile Duberman (1973). Forty-four percent of her parent respondents who had a mutual child reported that relationships between the siblings were excellent, compared with 19 percent of those without mutual children. More recent research supports this finding; half siblings come to see each other simply as siblings (Ganong and Coleman, 1994). These relationships are likely to be strongest when the mutual child comes at a time when the remarriage is well established and when there is only one child from each of the two prior marriages.

In sum, we have seen that stepsibling and half sibling relationships can be conflictual. However, that is only part of the story. The dynamics of living in a remarried family with stepsiblings and/or half siblings can also have positive effects. Just as in first families, stepsibling rivalry can help children distinguish themselves from others in the family, thereby giving them a strong sense of personal identity. For example, if an older stepsibling is active in sports, a younger stepsibling may turn to music to express her or his individuality. Competition among stepsiblings in some areas does not prevent them from cooperating in other areas. Just as in intact families, solidarity among stepsiblings is a likely outcome of ongoing family dynamics (Ganong and Coleman, 1994).

STEPSIBLING RELATIONSHIPS OVER TIME Sociologists Lynn White and Agnes Riedman (1992) undertook the first empirical research on adult step-/half siblings, focusing on their relationships after they grow up and leave home. In general, they found evidence of continued contact and interaction. Although contact was more frequent among full siblings (one to three times a month) compared with the several times a year that step-/half siblings were seen, less than 1 percent of the respondents in that study were so estranged that they did not even know where their step-/half sibling lived. Contact among step-/half siblings was affected by three key factors: race, gender, and proximity. As was true among full siblings, African Americans, females, and those who lived near one another had the most frequent contact.

To date we have relatively little information about the quality of these relationships. However, Marilyn Ihinger-Tallman (1987) hypothesizes that stepsibling bonding occurs most rapidly under conditions of similarity (age, sex, experience, shared values), interdependency, perceived mutual benefit of association, few perceived personal costs, and approximate equality in relinquishing aspects of a former lifestyle. Confirmation of this hypothesis awaits further research.

Children are not the only players in determining how well remarried families function. Stepparents also play key parts. Let's look first at stepmotherhood. The most typical form of stepmothering in the United States is part-time, occasioned by the weekend and holiday visits of children to their remarried biological father.

Stepmothers: A Bad Rap?

To what extent are the cultural images of the wicked stepmother valid? Although the empirical evidence does not substantiate the fairy tale image of the "wicked" stepmother, it does suggest that stepmothering can be problematic. Children who have negative images of stepmothers may not develop a positive relationship with their new stepmother. In turn, children's unpleasant behavior may cause stepmothers to be more critical of stepchildren (Berger, 1998). Deciding how to approach the new stepmother role is not easy. Margaret Draughon (1975) suggests three possibilities: (1) "other mother," or second mother; (2) primary mother, who assumes major responsibility for day-to-day caregiving; and (3) friend, who is supportive and caring but does not try to be a substitute mother. According to Draughon, the choice of role should be based on the degree of emotional comfort the stepmother feels as well as on the child's emotional state at the time. Draughon believes that if the child is still mourning the loss of the biological mother, whether through death or divorce, the role of friend works best. If, however, mourning has ended, the primary-mother role is probably more appropriate. This role, however, must be defined carefully. Generally speaking, defining it to mean primary caretaker instead of a replacement for the biological parent is likely to minimize stepparent–stepchild conflict. Draughon sees no particular advantage to the other-mother model. More recent research supports her position. Stepfamilies in which the stepmother plays the other-mother role are the most likely to experience tension and conflict (Kurdek and Fine, 1993).

STEPMOTHERS AND MOTHERING How do stepmothers fare in the mothering role? Much of the research on stepmother–stepchild relationships shows that these relationships are more tentative and difficult than are stepfather–stepchild relationships (Pasley and Ihinger-Tallman, 1987; MacDonald and DeMaris, 1996). This is due, in large part, to the greater expectations placed on women in families. Women are expected to take primary responsibility for the well-being of the family, especially in the area of child care, regardless of whose children they "mother." Such expectations can be more distressing for a woman who chooses a marital role but not necessarily a parenting role when she marries a noncustodial father. After remarriage she may find that his children visit more frequently than anticipated or that child custody has shifted unexpectedly to him. Furthermore, the expectations for women regarding nurturing are so strong that stepmothers themselves often assume that "instant love" of stepchildren should be possible. For this reason, stepmothers frequently feel guilty when they don't as yet feel a strong attachment to their spouse's children.

A stepmother's attempt to create a close-knit family structure may be misinterpreted. The biological mother may accuse her of trying to take her place. The stepchildren may also perceive her behavior as a threat to their mother's position. On the other hand, if the stepmother chooses a less involved approach toward her stepchildren, she may be accused by them and her spouse of not caring enough or not being a good mother. A common reaction to these situations is stress. Stepmothers report significantly greater role strain than do stepfathers (Whitsett and Land, 1992). Anne-Marie Ambert (1986) suggests that this greater stress stems in part from women's traditional domestic role. She found that when stepchildren visit, the stepmothers, and not the fathers, usually acquire extra work, such as housecleaning and cooking.

We should remember, however, that not all stepparenting situations are alike. In a study of 109 stepparents, Ambert found that having live-in stepchildren is less divisive than having children who live with the other parent come for visits. The former situation allows the couple more control over their lives. Wives felt more "appreciated" by their spouses because of their child-rearing contributions and felt less threatened by the biological mother. Stepmothers developed a closer and deeper relationship with their live-in stepchildren than with stepchildren living elsewhere. These research findings are significant in that they offer an explanation for why stepfathers seem to have fewer problems in their role. Most stepfathers, in contrast to most stepmothers, have live-in stepchildren. What role, then, do stepfathers play in remarried families?

Stepfathers: Polite Strangers?

In an earlier section of this chapter, we discussed the cultural images of the "wicked" stepmother. Although no comparable image or body of folktales exists for stepfathers, cases of lethal assault on children by stepfathers have focused renewed attention on this social category (Daly and Wilson, 1994). Additionally, more is known about the role of stepfathers in remarried families than about stepmothers. This is due, in large part, to their greater numbers. Stepfather families are the most common remarried family structure and, as such, they have been the focus of considerable social science research.

A fairly consistent image of stepfathers has emerged from these investigations. Overall, stepfathers tend to be more positive and responsive and less negative and directive toward children than are biological fathers (Hetherington and Henderson, 1997). Samuel Vuchinich and his colleagues (1991) characterize such behaviors as the "sociable polite stranger" role. This pattern of stepparenting might explain the finding that stepfathers in stable stepfamilies generally enjoy better relations with their stepchildren than do stepmothers (Ganong and Coleman, 1994). However, this finding should not be interpreted to mean that stepfathers don't encounter problems in this role. They do. Elizabeth Einstein (1985) identified three areas of difficulty for stepfathers: sex, money, and discipline.

Sex Stepfathers may feel uncomfortable in the presence of sexually developing adolescent stepdaughters. To prevent any misinterpretation by the stepdaughter or her mother, stepfathers often remain emotionally distant from their stepdaughter, with the result that the stepdaughter may perceive him as uncaring.

Money Money may be a source of conflict for stepfathers in a number of ways. If he is a noncustodial biological parent, he may feel guilty for not playing a more active role in his own children's lives. Thus, he may give his children money or expensive gifts to compensate for his absence, thereby creating envy among his stepchildren. This behavior may also cause friction with both his current spouse, who feels the money is needed elsewhere, and with his ex-spouse, who fears he is buying his children's love by spoiling them. In other cases, the economic demands of a second family may be so severe that he stops supporting the children from his first family.

Discipline Issues involving discipline revolve around two key questions: Who should discipline? Under what conditions? The answers to these questions may be far from clear not only on the part of the stepfather but in the minds of other family members as well. The wife/mother in the remarried family may voice a desire to share authority with her new spouse, but when he takes her up on it, she may be emotionally unprepared to relinquish any of her authority over her children. Research shows that it takes approximately 18 to 24 months for stepparents to achieve an equal "comanagement" role with the biological parent (Visher and Visher, 1982:64).

Stepchildren, too, may hold contradictory views regarding discipline by a stepfather. They may resent his efforts to make them behave. Yet if he doesn't try to discipline them, they may perceive him as indifferent and uncaring, and respond angrily, "You don't care what I do; you don't love me." Researchers have found a correlation between stepchildren's perception of being loved by a stepparent and whether the stepparent makes them behave (Bohannan, 1985). The dilemma of discipline appears to be lessened in cases where a friendship has been established first between the stepparent and the stepchild. When friendship exists, stepchildren are more likely to accept discipline from the stepparent (Wallerstein and Kelly, 1980). A study of 20 well-functioning stepfamilies confirmed this finding. These stepparents found that things work best if the stepparent does not come in as a disciplinarian right away (Kelley, 1995). Family therapist John Visher (1994) supports that viewpoint, but he also sees the need for the biological parent and the stepparent to form a parental coalition to support each other in the enforcement of household rules.

Lesbian and Gay Stepfamilies

Lesbian and gay parents who form new unions confront the same challenges facing heterosexual stepfamilies. However, because of their sexual orientation, their very existence as a family unit is often questioned. Thus, lesbian and gay stepfamilies may lack the support that is given to heterosexual stepparents and often face prejudicial and discriminatory treatment (Berger, 1998). Although no precise figures exist on the number of children being raised in lesbian and gay stepfamilies, the fact that reproductive technology and changes in adoption laws allow more lesbians and gays to become parents suggests that there are and will continue to be an increasing number of people functioning in such units. As we observed in previous chapters, studies on lesbian and gay lifestyles, particularly family lifestyle issues, are just beginning to emerge. One such study examined lesbian stepparent roles and found three distinct patterns: (1) the coparent family in which the nonbiological mother takes the role of an active parent and committed family member by being a helper and supporter of and consultant to the biological mother; (2) the stepmother family in which the lesbian stepparent fulfills many of the traditional mothering tasks while the biological mother functions as the decision maker, a pattern similar in the traditional heterosexual stepfamily model, and (3) the co-mother family where both mothers share responsibilities in the day-to-day decision-making and child-rearing tasks (Wright, 1998).

Ex-Spouses: Do They Fade Away?

Divorce ends a marriage, but it does not necessarily end the relationship between the former spouses. This is especially true for couples with children. How do couples come to view each other after divorce? One study of divorced fathers and their new wives found that most of these couples identified the children's mother as a major source of stress in their marriage. Both the ex-husband and their wives described the ex-wife in negative terms (Guisinger, Cowan, and Schuldberg, 1989). This finding seems to support the popular image of ex-spouses as warring factions. In other studies, however, researchers found that only a fraction of the sample of divorced couples fit that description. Such couples were classified as either "angry associates" whose relationships are characterized by bitterness, resentment, and ongoing conflicts over visitation and support payments or "fiery foes" whose relationships are extremely antagonistic. The lingering acrimony of their divorce made it impossible for them to cooperate with each other on any matter.

In contrast, a number of divorced couples maintained cordial relationships with each other as "cooperative colleagues" who are friendly and mutually concerned about their children's welfare. They managed to make decisions and celebrate their children's major life events together. A smaller number of ex-spouses remained "perfect pals." Their divorce was amiable; they continued to like and trust each other, and they worked cooperatively to maintain a positive environment for their children. Finally, there are the dissolved duos, ex-spouses who have little or no contact after the divorce (Ahrons and Wallisch, 1986; Ahrons, 1994).

Thus far, our discussion of remarried families has tended to focus on the numerous adjustment problems members face. This should in no way be interpreted to mean that there are few benefits to living in remarried families. Quite the opposite is true, as we will see in the next section.

THE STRENGTHS AND BENEFITS OF REMARRIED FAMILIES

The identification of strengths in remarried families is a relatively new phase in social science research. Patricia Knaub and her colleagues (1984) were among the first to undertake an empirical study of what makes remarried families strong. They asked 80 randomly selected remarried families to indicate what strengths were most important to their families. Their respondents listed love and intimacy (caring, affection, closeness, acceptance, understanding), family unity (working together; shared goals, values, and activities), and positive patterns of communication (honesty, openness, receptiveness, and a sense of humor), characteristics important to all families.

Further insight into the strengths of remarried families comes from a study of remarried couples in central Pennsylvania (Furstenberg and Spanier, 1984). These couples felt that their current marriage was stronger than their first marriage in three important ways. First, they had better

Remarried families are complex. The members of this family include a son from his first marriage, a daughter from her first marriage, and the child they had together.

communication skills. Second, they were more realistic about the existence of conflict in marriage, and perhaps as a result of having better communication skills, they reported having fewer conflicts in their second marriage. Third, the balance of power in decision making was more equal in the remarriage.

Several recent studies support the finding of equitable power sharing by spouses in stepfamilies (Crosbie-Burnett, 1994/1995; Ganong and Coleman, 1994). John Visher and Emily Visher (1993), two therapists who work with remarried families, identify six behavior patterns associated with building successful stepfamilies: (1) developing realistic expectations, (2) allowing children to mourn their losses, (3) building and maintaining a strong couple relationship, (4) proceeding slowly in constructing the stepparent roles, (5) creating their own traditions and rituals, (6) developing satisfactory rules and arrangements for children living in overlapping households.

Other researchers have also documented the critical role that a strong couple relationship plays in the success of remarried families. When children see a stable and well-functioning relationship between their parent and stepparent, it reduces their fears about the possibility of another breakup and also provides them with role models who can resolve problems in a rational and nonthreatening manner (Kheshgi-Genovese and Genovese, 1997). This primacy of the couple bond and the role it played in their 24 years of marriage is exemplified in the philosophy of the Marings (see the "Family Profile" box).

Benefits Remarriage offers a number of benefits to family members. A custodial parent gains a partner with whom to share family work as well as financial responsibility. In exchange, the new stepparent shares in the joys of family life. For the new spouses, remarriage restores the continuity of a sexual relationship and provides companionship and a sense of partnership. Additionally, although it might be viewed as a mixed blessing, the ambiguity of roles in remarried families offers family members the opportunity to create new ones that may prove to be more satisfying in the long run. For example, stepparents don't have to try to replace parents; instead, they can be friends, counselors, teachers, or companions to stepchildren. Both stepparents and stepchildren can benefit by interactions that are less encumbered by unrealistic expectations of instant family love and unity.

THE QUALITY OF THE REMARITAL RELATIONSHIP

Despite all the problems we have just discussed, most remarried couples seem to find happiness in their new relationship. In reviewing the literature on remarriage, Coleman and Ganong (1991) found that there were very few differences between spouses in first marriages and those in remarriages.

When gender is examined, however, differences in levels of happiness and satisfaction emerge. In both first marriages and remarriages men report higher levels of satisfaction than women. For stepmothers, the perception of child-care inequities were the strongest predictor of marital dissatisfaction over time (Pasley, Dollahite, and Ihinger-Tallman, 1993). The help of the biological father in child-care and household tasks was associated with better adjustment to the stepparent role (Guisinger, Cowan, and Schuldberg, 1989).

More recent research reinforces the view that successful stepfamilies require partners who not only can cope with the usual stresses of stepfamily living but who can successfully relinquish traditional gendered parenthood roles (White, 1994). In her study of well-functioning stepfamilies, Patricia Kelley (1995) found general agreement among the respondents that it works best not to define gender roles as distinctly as they are in many families. Thus, both spouses took on nurturing and provision functions. These stepparents found that discipline and primary nurturing are usually best done by the biological parent, not the stepparent, regardless of gender.

Other factors can also impact a remarried couple's relationship. Among them is the form the stepfamily takes. For example, several researchers found that marital satisfaction was higher in mother–stepfather families where the stepfather had no children from a previous marriage than in stepfamilies where the stepfather coparented children from another marriage with an ex-spouse (Giles-Sims, 1984; Clingempeel and Brand, 1985). These authors explain this qualitative difference in terms of the nature of the coparenting relationship that exists with ex-spouses. If the relationship is one of conflict over ongoing issues—for example, child support, discipline, or visitation rights—the stress created by these issues is likely to have a negative impact on the remarried couple's relationship. However, if the stepparent and ex-spouse have resolved their emotional problems and are able to relate to each other and to their children on a nonconflictual basis, then this situation should not exert stress on the remarriage.

As is true with first marriages, the presence of children in stepfamilies can affect the quality of family happiness. Studies of middle- and upper-middle-class families with adolescents reveal that the quality of the stepfather–stepchild relationship had a greater impact on family happiness than did the quality of the marital relationship (Crosbie-Burnett, 1984). Remarried couples with children from previous marriages are more likely to divorce than are remarried couples without stepchildren (Pill, 1990).

In sum, then, what can couples do to facilitate happiness in remarriage? Remarried couples who accept their children's loyalties to noncustodial parents, accept their spouse's ongoing coparenting relationship with an ex-spouse, and resolve the problems raised by their prior marriage are likely to have a happy remarriage. However, as we shall see in the next section, happiness in the remarried couple relationship may not, in and of itself, be sufficient to ensure the stability of the remarriage.

FAMILY PROFILE

THE MARING FAMILY

Jane and David Maring

Length of relationship: 24 years

Challenges of being a stepmother: My initial reaction to my stepsons was that they are beautiful and that I could easily learn to love these two little boys. However, I soon realized how difficult it is to be an "instant parent." I wasn't used to all the commotion two little boys could cause. Discipline was a problem. There were many angry outbursts on their part as well as mine. At times I felt like a wicked stepmother, and I wished that they would go live with their biological mother so I wouldn't have to put up with them. It was difficult not to resent her for leaving me to care for them during their turbulent youth. Now that they are 32 and 29, it appears to me, she seems more interested in participating in their lives. It is a challenge for me not to feel hurt and angry whenever the boys talk about her. After all these years, it is difficult to tell what makes me, their stepmother, different from any natural parent.

Relationship philosophy: Our bond as husband and wife has always come first in our relationship; we would not let the children come between us—difficult as that was at times. We also never talk negatively about the boys' biological mother. My husband and I have always felt that it was important for the boys to maintain positive contact with their mother and their mother's family. We always tried to maintain a united front when the children needed discipline, and we never put one another down in front of the boys. Another strength in our relationship is that we attend church together and pray together at home. Whenever we have arguments or disagreements, we make sure we hug, kiss, and make up before going to sleep.

Stability in Remarriage

Songwriters Sammy Cahn and James van Heusen popularized the notion that "love is lovelier the second time around." Conventional wisdom would have us believe that second marriages should be more successful than first marriages. People often assume that divorced people possess characteristics that should translate into more effective relationships. On the average, the divorced are older and seemingly more mature and experienced than those entering marriages for the first time. Thus, the argument goes, they should make more intelligent choices, have more realistic expectations, and have more negotiating skills with which to handle the stresses and strains that arise in married life.

But do they? Overall, research shows that first marriages are somewhat more stable than remarriages. A recent analysis found that the cumulative probability of first-marriage dissolution after 10 years of marriage was 33 percent, whereas the probability of second-marriage dissolution after 10 years of marriage was 39 percent (Bramlett and Mosher, 2001). However, another nationwide study that controlled for age found that slightly fewer remarriages ended in divorce compared with first marriages (Clark and Wilson, 1994). Couples who were 45 years of age or older with both partners having been married before had the most stable marriages, whereas couples who were under 25 when they married with only one spouse having been married before were the least stable. It may be that older remarried adults have more economic and social resources to help them deal with the complexities of stepfamily formation.

FACTORS AFFECTING STABILITY Several factors combine to explain divorce among remarried couples. First, as we have already observed, remarriage is a complex process, requiring a number of adjustments that are outside the scope of first marriages and for which most remarried couples are not well prepared. To cite just one example, kinship terms and interactions may be a sticky point for all those affected by remarriage. Since stepchildren already have biological parents they call "Mom" and "Dad," forms of address for stepparents must be worked out. In her study of well-functioning stepfamilies, Patricia Kelley (1995) found that most of the children called their stepparents by their first names. According to Kelley, by not having a mandate to love and obey, steprelationships could more easily flourish, and love often did develop between stepparent and stepchild.

Another potential source of divisiveness centers on how to integrate multiple sets of grandparents into holiday and family celebrations. What happens to previous family customs and traditions? Sociologist Andrew Cherlin (1978) argues that "remarriage is an incomplete institution" that

SEARCHING THE INTERNET

RELATIONSHIPS WITH EXTENDED FAMILY MEMBERS

- Flexibility is important.
- New kin should be seen as additions to, not replacements of, original family members.
- All parents need to attempt to get along so that children feel comfortable in both families.
- Biological parents and stepparents need to establish civil relationships for the good of the children.
- Children should be allowed to enjoy their households.
- Children need time to adjust to household switches.
- Special times for various household constellations should be planned.

http://www.montana.edu/wwwhd/family/comchal.html

does not provide answers to these questions. Consequently, remarried families are left adrift to find their own solutions to these problems. Without institutionalized patterns of family behavior and support, family unity is likely to be precarious.

Outside Support and Pressures In addition, the attitudes of relatives, friends, and community members can affect the stability of remarriages. Positive and supportive reactions from friends and relatives contribute to successful remarriages. Conversely, disapproval of the remarriage by significant others can put added stress on the relationship. Sometimes the announcement of a remarriage may be greeted with little enthusiasm on the part of relatives. As one stepmother said in an interview:

> My mother was thrilled for me when I told her I was going to marry, but her manner changed completely when I told her he had a child. She was wary for me, she wanted me to think about it. It was not the dream she had for my marriage. (Quoted in Smith, 1990:30)

Additionally sheer numbers can add to the challenges facing remarried couples. A stepfamily can have an unusually large extended family. For example, as Donald Duncan (2001) observes, a divorce and remarriage of a couple with three children could generate as many as 100 possible kin relationships. Duncan offers constructive guidelines for developing relationships with extended kin (see "Searching the Internet" box).

Attitudes toward Divorce Moreover, the familiarity with the divorce process itself may remove some of the social barriers to a second divorce. Having survived a first divorce, some remarried people are less likely to stay in an unhappy or deteriorating relationship. Furthermore, because they have already dealt with the reactions of family and friends to their first divorce, they are likely to be less fearful of an adverse public reaction to their course of action.

This seems to be especially true for some groups. For example, remarried white men are more likely to redivorce than remarried white women (Glick, 1984). This seems strange, given that women tend to report less happiness in second marriages than do men. Yet, the reverse pattern is found among African Americans. More African American women than men divorce a second time. The most frequently cited explanation for these opposing patterns focuses exclusively on economic motivation. According to this argument, African American women come closer to having economic equality with African American men than white women do with white men. Consequently, remarriage may not represent the same level of financial security for African American women as it does for white women. This interpretation clearly ignores many noneconomic factors. It may be that many African American women, having been socialized to be assertive and self-sufficient (Hale-Benson, 1986), simply are less willing than other women to stay in an unhappy relationship. It could also be that the African American community does not view divorce with the same stigma that the white community does.

The Presence of Children Children may play a pivotal role in the parental decision to redivorce. Indeed, several studies have found that the divorce rate is higher in remarriages with stepchildren (Pill, 1990; Booth and Edwards, 1992). Marilyn Ihinger-Tallman and Kay Pasley (1991) suggest three ways in which children can contribute to the dissolution of remarriages: personal adjustments, discipline problems, and disruptive behavior.

The presence of children makes adjustment harder for a remarried couple. Children limit a couple's privacy and their opportunities for intimacy. Couples may agree on aspects of their personal relationship but be at odds over what constitutes appropriate child behavior. This is especially likely considering the different parenting histories of each partner.

As we saw earlier, another source of conflict for remarried couples with children is discipline. Stepparents may feel that discipline was too lax in the "old" family and that new rules are in order. Stepchildren may resent such changes, and biological parents may feel caught in the middle. Consequently, all parties are likely to experience stress.

The behavior of children can be a powerful force in disrupting the marital relationship. Children can manipulate the biological parent into taking sides against the stepparent or stepsiblings. If children refuse to cooperate in matters of daily family living, they can create a tense and hostile environment. Time is often required to resolve these issues.

Time Patricia Papernow (1993) cautions stepparents to be realistic about the time involved in solidifying stepfamily relationships. She divides the process of becoming a stepfamily into three major stages, each with its own set of developmental tasks. Tasks in the early stages involve becoming aware of fantasies such as "instant love" and letting go of or grieving for unrealistic hopes as well as learning about one's own and others' needs in the new family. In the middle stage members must actively confront differences between family cultures and generate new stepfamily rituals, customs, and codes of conduct in which all members of the family participate. The later stage, generally less conflictual, finds members enjoying the family's new boundaries and relationships and functioning well.

Here, too, however, the awareness process must continue as new issues arise. According to Papernow, families differ in the length of time it takes them to complete the stepfamily cycle. Fast-paced families move through the early stages quickly, and they take about 4 years to complete the cycle; average families take about 7 years; and slow families take about 9 years. These latter families get stuck in the early stages, taking longer to resolve their fantasies and grieve their previous losses. Some families never complete the cycle.

Researchers can gain a better understanding of how stepfamilies fare over time by utilizing *longitudinal studies*, in which the same people are studied at different periods in time. Comparisons of stable remarried families with those that have dissolved should help us to identify ways to help remarried families cope with the unique aspects of remarriage. For example, the experiences of therapists show that it takes a minimum of 4 to 9 years for remarried families to begin to stabilize and develop their own customs, rituals, and history. Knowing that this is a normal pattern for

APPLYING THE SOCIOLOGICAL IMAGINATION

WHAT'S IN A CARD?

The exchange of greeting cards on special occasions has become an expected pattern of behavior in American culture. However, the greeting card industry, like many other businesses, has been slow to recognize the diversity of the American population. In the past, it was difficult to find cards representing people of color outside of ethnic specialty shops. Today, most stores stock these cards. However, it is still difficult to find cards that represent other than traditional family forms. We searched a number of stores without success before finding greeting cards for stepparents.

There was a time
when I was afraid—
afraid that once you came
into our family
there would be less love,
less understanding,
less "family" than before.
But you showed me how love can
blossom in a caring relationship,
how an understanding heart
can smooth a painful transition,
how a family can be more
than a matter of birth.

You have shown me
so much friendship,
so much caring,
so much love
that I want to thank you
for being you—
a wonderful stepparent,
a wonderful person.

Joan L. Stone

Visit your neighborhood card shop. Can you find cards for stepfamilies? What does the selection of cards in the section marked "for relatives" reveal about our culture's attitude regarding stepfamilies? Do you think there should be greeting cards specifically for stepfamilies? For other groups? Why or why not? What purposes does the exchange of cards serve?

remarried families, some remarried couples, who might otherwise contemplate divorce, may be able to stay together and wait for the "storms" to pass. Support groups for stepfamilies are increasing around the country. This should also help to stabilize this emerging family form.

In the meantime, however, existing research findings on stepfamilies suggest a number of ways in which social policy could be enlisted immediately to help support the growing number of stepfamilies in the United States.

RECOMMENDATIONS FOR SOCIAL POLICY

If any social policy is to be effective, it must first have a clear view of the targeted population it wishes to serve. As we have discussed throughout this text, most American family policies are based on a traditional nuclear family model. Yet only a small percentage of families fit this model. The processes of divorce and remarriage have created a wide variety of household forms. Thus, legal scholars and experts in family relations suggest that the conceptualization of the family change to include these households. Specifically with regard to remarried families their recommendations include clarification of legal norms, modification of the tax code, and development of educational materials about stepfamilies.

Clarification of Legal Norms

Researchers who have studied the problems of stepfamilies have identified three ways in which state laws affecting parent–child relationships could be modified to meet the needs of stepfamilies. First, they could include a form of legal guardianship that would allow stepparents to function more effectively in families. For example, stepparents should be allowed to sign school permission slips, view student records, sign emergency medical forms, and authorize driving permits. Second, lawmakers and judges need to be made aware of the probability of second or third divorces and take steps to ensure that the desires of stepparents and stepchildren regarding visitation rights be incorporated into divorce decrees (Ramsey, 1994/1995). Although all 50 states now grant some third-party visitation, the laws tend to be directed more to the rights of grandparents than to those of stepparents (Fine and Fine, 1992). Third, to reduce ambiguities and sexual tensions that often exist in stepfamilies, incest laws could be broadened to include stepparents and their children and quite possibly stepsiblings as well (Crosbie-Burnett, Skyles, and Becker-Haven, 1988).

Modification of the Tax Code

In this chapter we have referred to the financial conflicts that often affect remarried families. Yet there is little acknowledgment of the financial contribution stepparents make to the parenting process. One recommendation that has been made in this regard concerns the tax structure. Because many stepchildren are members of overlapping households, both households spend money on food, shelter, clothes, entertainment, travel, and many other items. Currently, however, dependent children can be claimed as a tax deduction for only one household. If the tax code were revised to allow stepparents to deduct their cost of shared child support, it would give them some financial assistance. Besides the monetary benefit, this change would symbolize society's recognition of the contribution stepparents make to the well-being of children and, hence, to the community at large.

Education

Schools at all levels are being encouraged to recognize the changing composition of families and to develop curricular

WRITING YOUR OWN SCRIPT

THINKING ABOUT REMARRIAGE

Consider these facts: Thirty percent of all U.S. children under the age of 18 are connected to a stepfamily; approximately 43 percent of first marriages and 60 percent of remarriages will end in divorce. Thus, it is possible that you or someone you know will spend at least part of your life in a remarried-family household.

It is important to be aware of the complexities of remarried families and not to assume that they will be like intact nuclear families.

Questions to Consider

1. What factors would you take into account in determining whether to remarry? How would you go about preparing for a remarriage?
2. What expectations do you have for how a remarried family should function? How do you think each of the following roles should be constructed in a stepfamily: (a) the biological parent, (b) the stepparent, (c) stepchildren, (d) step-in-laws, (e) biological and stepgrandparents?

materials that reflect the organization and functioning of various family structures. Proponents argue that this approach would serve several purposes. First, teachers and professional counselors would have the knowledge and understanding to work with all kinds of families. This would enable them to change any existing policies and practices that devalue or ignore remarried families. Two quick examples can illustrate this point: (1) Forms that students fill out can be changed to eliminate confusion about surnames by including all appropriate relationships, and (2) when students are asked to make cards or gifts for parents or grandparents, steprelationships could be included on a routine basis. Schools could also provide meeting space for support groups such as Stepfamily Foundation. Doing so would show stepchildren that some of their classmates experience similar problems of adjustment. This would lessen any stigma they might feel about being different.

As information on the complexity of remarried families and successful coping mechanisms for dealing with this complexity becomes more available, and as the role expectations of family members become clarified, negative cultural images of remarried families are likely to be replaced with positive ones. As a result, participants in remarried families will no longer be made to feel that they are living in a "deviant" or "lesser" family structure, and they will feel more secure and accepted by the larger society. This, in turn, is likely to be reflected in the emergence of more stable remarried families.

SUMMARY

The pattern of marriage, divorce, and remarriage has become well established in the United States. Today, however, most remarriages involve divorced individuals, whereas in previous eras most remarriages involved widowed people.

Despite the high rate of remarriage, relatively little is known about this family form, especially among different classes, races, and ethnic groups. Remarried families differ from nuclear families in fundamental ways: They are more complex; they have a changing cast of characters; their boundaries are unclear; and their rules are often undefined. Laws regarding remarried families are ambiguous, and there is a lack of kinship terms to cover all affected parties in a remarriage. Members of remarried families often feel guilty or are still grieving over previous relationships.

Divorced people who remarry tend to spend less time in dating and courtship than do people who marry for the first time. Like couples marrying for the first time, divorced people spend little time discussing issues such as finances and children.

The reasons for remarriage are similar to those for first marriage. Men remarry more frequently and sooner than do women. Men with higher incomes are more likely to remarry than men with lower incomes. College-educated women are less likely to remarry than other women. Whites have the highest rate of remarriage of any racial and ethnic group in the United States.

Children of remarried parents often find themselves living in overlapping households, having to adjust to two different sets of rules. Although stepchildren often have difficulties adjusting and may experience stepsibling rivalry, they also benefit from new extended families. A half sibling may be yet another source of competition for a parent's attention, but may also help stepchildren to feel that they are now part of a "real" family.

Both stepmothers and stepfathers face difficulty in establishing relationships with stepchildren, although stepmothers experience more stress than do stepfathers. Remarried couples report levels of marital happiness similar to those reported by those in first marriages. However, due to the greater complexity of remarriages, especially those with children, the duration of remarriages is shorter than that of first marriages.

Legal scholars and family experts recommend that social policy be directed toward clarifying the legal status of stepparents, modifying the tax code, and developing educational materials about stepfamilies.

KEY TERMS

remarried family
emotional remarriage
psychic remarriage
community remarriage
parental remarriage
economic remarriage
legal remarriage
overlapping households

QUESTIONS FOR STUDY AND REFLECTION

1. Discuss the significance of viewing remarried families as entities that are distinct from nuclear families. In a similar vein, some sociologists have argued against referring to remarried families as reconstituted or blended families. How might these latter terms cause problems for individuals living in remarried families?
2. Imagine that you are getting remarried and that both you and your spouse are custodial parents with children of the other sex who are relatively similar in age. How would you arrange your home living space? What steps would you take to create a positive remarried-family atmosphere? Explain why you think these strategies would be helpful.
3. What are some of the major tasks that confront people in stepfamilies? How are these tasks similar or different for people in intact first marriages? What can society do to assist stepfamilies? Search the Internet and evaluate the type of help and support that are available to stepfamilies. How does this information enhance your understanding of this marriage form? Two good starting points for your search are the Stepfamily Foundation *http://www.stepfam.org* and Positive Steps *http://www.positivesteps.com*.
4. To what degree do you think remarried families are seen as a legitimate family form in the United States today? Be specific. Consider their relationships to other social institutions like the schools, laws, government, and the media. What changes, if any, would you make in these institutions regarding remarried families? Explain.

ADDITIONAL RESOURCES

SOCIOLOGICAL

BRAY, JAMES H., AND JOHN KELLY. 1999. *Stepfamilies: Love, Marriage, and Parenting in the First Decade.* New York: Broadway Books. Based on findings from a comprehensive 9-year longitudinal study of 200 stepfamilies funded by the National Institutes of Health, the authors explain why over half of all stepfamilies fail, and reveal the strategies that helped the others to succeed.

LAUER, ROBERT H., AND JEANETTE C. LAUER. 1999. *Becoming Family: How to Build a Stepfamily That Really Works.* Minneapolis, MN: Augsburg Fortress, Publishers. Drawing on their own experiences and that of the stepfamilies with whom they have worked, the authors provide realistic insight into the major challenges in stepfamily life: loss, adjustment, personal and family identity, loyalty conflicts, former spouses, marital intimacy, stepparenting, and resources.

LEVIN, IRENE, AND MARVIN SUSSMAN. 1997. *Stepfamilies: History, Research, and Policy.* New York: Haworth Press. A readable compilation of studies that focus on the factors that promote family cohesiveness and integration.

STAHLMANN, R., AND W. HIEBERT. 1997. *Premarital and Remarital Counseling.* San Francisco: Jossey-Bass. The authors provide helpful guidelines to couples for what to expect from any therapist and therapy in general and examine the pluses and minuses of group counseling.

LITERARY

LOUIE, AL-LING. 1996. *Yeh-Shen: A Cinderella Story from China.* New York: Putnam Publishing Group. This Chinese version of Cinderella predates the European version by almost a thousand years and contains many familiar details—a poor overworked girl, a wicked stepmother and stepsister. But rather than being handed gifts from a fairy godmother, Yeh-Shen earns her good fortune through kindness to a magic fish.

BRUNO, BETH. 2001. *Wild Tulips.* New York: Tri-Litho. Using the metaphor of a garden, the author provides humorous yet serious perspectives about child development, parenting, and family life.

INTERNET

http://www.parentsplace.com This Web site offers advice on many aspects of parenting, particularly dealing with divorce, remarriage, and stepfamily relationships.

http://www.rainbows.org This organization offers training and curricula for establishing peer support groups in churches, synagogues, schools, and social agencies for children and adults of all ages and denominations who are grieving a death, divorce, or other painful transition in their family.

Chapter 14

Marriages and Families in Later Life

IN THE NEWS: **FREMONT, CALIFORNIA**

After three and a half years of study and research, Aegis Gardens, a for-profit assisted-living community for Asians, opened its doors. Its parent company is Aegis Assisted Living, based in Redmond, Washington. The company owns and operates 15 assisted-living communities on the West Coast, providing residents with help with daily tasks such as bathing, dressing, and taking medications. However, what makes the Fremont Aegis Gardens unique is that it is the first such institution to focus on a specific ethnic culture, offering ethnic foods and activities. That its target population is Asian underscores a relatively new trend in that community.

Traditionally, Asian elders have lived with their adult children, following a cultural norm of filial obligation to care for aging parents. Although even today 22 percent of Asians and Pacific Islanders 65 years and older live with an adult child (the highest of any group), that figure is down from earlier decades. As successive generations of Asian Americans become more integrated into the larger society, some cultural norms disappear. Increasing numbers of Asian American women are now in the labor force, and many Asian American couples pursue dual careers, leaving them less time and energy to care for elderly parents. This is upsetting to traditional parents, but others who have become more accustomed to independent living do not expect or want to live with their children. Thus, this trend away from multigenerational households in the Asian American community is likely to continue (Kong, 2002).

WHAT WOULD YOU DO? Would you invest money in assisted-living communities that have an ethnic culture focus? Explain. As you grow older, would you choose to live in an assisted-living facility composed mainly of people from your own racial/ethnic/religious groups? Explain.

The United Nations General Assembly declared 1999 as the International Year of Older Persons and chose as its theme "Towards a Society for All Ages," in an effort to highlight the challenges and opportunities presented by the world's rapidly aging population. According to UN estimates, there were some 200 million persons age 60 and over throughout the world in 1950. By the end of the century, that number had jumped to 600 million, one out of every ten persons. In another 50 years it is expected that one out of five persons will be 60 years or older (United Nations, 2000). Within the next 35 years, the elderly will approach or exceed 40 percent of the populations in Japan, Germany, and Italy ("New Problems . . . ," 1998). Like many other industrialized countries, the United States is undergoing a major demographic transition. In 1900, only 3 million people in the United States were age 65 or over, representing just 4 percent of the total population. By 2000, over 35 million people were in this age group, constituting nearly 12.4 percent of the population. By 2030, the number of elderly is expected to climb to about 70 million, 20 percent of the population (Administration on Aging, 2001). If the demographic projections are correct, 1 in 5 persons in the United States will be 65 or over in 2030, compared with 1 in 25 in 1900.

The signs of this revolution in longevity are everywhere. Television programs, movies, and commercials portray older people in active and productive roles. At the same time, public officials debate the budget implications of an aging population. Older citizens, like those in Red Cloud, Nebraska, and other farm belt communities, find themselves designing or maintaining communities that have relatively few younger residents due to an exodus of young people leaving home in search of work. Half of Red Cloud's residents are over 65; the senior class at the high school is down to 29 students, just half the size of the class 30 years ago. With a growing shortage of middle-aged and young adults, many of the older residents just keep on working. Eunice Fritz (age 89) is the county school superintendent, an elected part-time position she's had since 1974; and Worrell Reichstein (age 72) drives the county snowplow (Rimer, 1998). And for the first time in history, middle-aged adults are dealing with the benefits and the burdens of being part of a multigenerational kinship structure. According to a recent survey, 70 percent of midlife couples are part of four-generation families (Task Force on Aging Research, 1995). And in 2000 there were 3.9 million multigenerational family households, nearly 4 percent of all households in the United States (U.S. Census Bureau, 2001a). Thus, members of such families can be considered pioneers with relatively few role models to guide them. The result can be a great deal of confusion and uncertainty for all concerned. For the oldest relatives, great-grandchildren can be a source of pride and delight. They can also be a source of conflict and confusion, however, because different generations often adhere to different values and behaviors. The primary focus of this chapter is on what family expert Timothy Brubaker (1990) has called later-life families—families that are beyond the child-rearing years.

CHARACTERISTICS OF LATER-LIFE FAMILIES

Later-life families possess several characteristics that make them fascinating to study but that also have practical implications for developing meaningful social policies on aging. According to Brubaker, later-life families exhibit three characteristics: (1) They are multigenerational, (2) they have a lengthy family history, and (3) they experience a number of new life events for which they may have little preparation, for example, grandparenthood, retirement, and widowhood. As we will see throughout this chapter, these characteristics greatly influence the nature and quality of family interactions.

In this chapter we look at some of the changes in family composition over time and at the new developmental tasks that accompany these changes. In this regard, our approach utilizes the theoretical model of the family life cycle introduced in Chapter 2. Evelyn Duvall's (1977) last two stages in the life cycle incorporate "later-life families." These stages encompass middle-aged parents who must deal with the "empty nest," the period after the last child leaves home; and the aging family, whose tasks include adjusting to retirement and the death of a spouse.

People over 85 constitute the fastest growing segment of the elderly population. By the year 2050, over 1 million Americans are expected to be 100 years or older.

The Sandwich Generation

The middle-aged generation, sometimes called the **sandwich generation** because of the pressures its members experience from both ends of the age spectrum, finds itself playing many roles. Middle-aged parents must meet the challenges of their own lives—their own aging and approaching retirement from work and all the adjustments these entail. As their children reach adulthood, parents expect to be free from major family responsibilities and to have more time to spend on their own pursuits. For many parents, however, the economic realities of recent decades have put some of these expectations on hold. Many young adults find achieving financial independence difficult. Consequently, increasing numbers remain at or return to the parental home. They have been labeled the *boomerang generation* (Quinn, 1993). Historically, the number of boomerang children increases when the economy contracts. Less than 8 percent of adult children aged 25 to 34 lived with parents in 1970; the rate increased when the economy slowed in the early 1980s, then decreased as the economy prospered in the 1990s. By 2000, when the economy again started to decline, nearly 4 million (10.5 percent) of the 25- to 34-age group were living in the family home (Greider, 2001). Some psychologists believe that the September 11, 2001, terrorist attacks and the ensuing war against terrorism may motivate even more young adults to move back home. Men are almost twice as likely to live with their parents as women are. Given the cultural norm of independence in young adulthood, it would not be surprising to find both groups expressing dissatisfaction with such arrangements. This living arrangement can be stressful. Conflicts of lifestyles and values are common. Both generations complain about a lack of privacy. Marital and parental satisfaction can decline under these circumstances.

Despite some of these difficulties, however, many parents report spending enjoyable time with their co-resident adult children, especially with daughters. In a national study of parents with children age 19 to 34 living at home, researchers found a high degree of satisfaction with this arrangement. However, three factors affected the level of parental satisfaction: presence or absence of younger siblings in the home, employment status of the adult child, and the presence or absence of grandchildren in the home (Aquilino and Supple, 1991). Let's examine each of these separately.

Younger Siblings The parents who were still caring for younger children at home reported greater satisfaction with co-resident adult children than parents whose other children were living independently. There are two likely explanations for this. First, they had not expected to be free of parental responsibilities at this stage in their lives, and second, co-resident adult children are likely to assist in the care of younger siblings.

Employment Status Parents were more likely to be satisfied having adult children living with them if the child was working and, hence, on the way to becoming independent. Conversely, parents with unemployed adult children reported a considerable amount of family conflict and dissatisfaction with this relationship.

Grandchildren Divorce is often the occasion for an adult child returning home. When grandchildren are part of this new living arrangement, stress is likely to increase. Grandparents may find they have to forgo some of their own plans as they assist in the care of their grandchildren.

Do you or any of your friends still live at home? Have any of them returned home after living away? What advantages and disadvantages do you find in living at home? What can co-residential parents and adult children do to minimize conflicts in their living arrangements?

Not only do middle-aged parents frequently have adult children living at home, but they often must care for elderly parents as well. Increasing life expectancy, combined with lower birth rates, has brought about a major shift in the amount of time people spend in various roles. The middle generation, for example, will spend on average more years with parents over 65 than with children under 18. According to a recent study, 44 percent of adults between the ages of 45 and 55 find themselves still providing support for their children as well as caring for aging relatives (Dessoff, 2001). Thus, the empty-nest stage is more a myth than a reality for increasing numbers of middle-aged parents.

Although many middle-aged adults confront such changes, recent research indicates that popular images of a "midlife crisis" are largely overdrawn. A 10-year study of nearly 8000 Americans, aged 25 to 74, by the MacArthur Foundation Research Network on Successful Midlife Development, found that, for most respondents, the midlife years appear to be a time of good health, productive activity, psychic equanimity, and community involvement. Only 23 percent of the respondents reported having a "midlife crisis" and, of that group, the majority tied the crisis to a specific event in their lives, for example, a divorce. Only one-third described the crisis as a time of personal turmoil related to their realization that they were aging (Goode, 1999). According to social psychologist Orville Brim, "Normal people recognize that the lifespan, regardless of age, brings change and that a healthy response to change is to make the necessary adjustments that are required. When a change is connected to an event, and an appropriate accommodation is made, this can be called a turning point" (quoted in Kotulak, 1999).

Diversity in the Family Life Cycle

As we saw in Chapter 2, the family life cycle model has some inherent limitations that we will try to avoid. For example, our discussion of later-life families does not assume a nuclear family model. Child-free couples, single-parent families, and families that have taken in other kin or friends—a pattern common among families of color—must also make changes and confront new tasks as their members grow older. Additionally, like families at other stages of development, later-life families take diverse forms. They include couples in a first marriage, mothers who have never married, widows and divorced people who have not remarried, and people who have remarried, some more than once. Diversity is further enhanced by the fact that these households cut across all social, economic, racial, and ethnic groups. Our discussion incorporates the diversity among and within later-life families to the extent that the existing data permit. Here again, however, much of the existing research involves white, middle-class families. Thus, our ideas concerning how the poor (and for that matter the rich) and people of color experience many of these later-life stages are largely undocumented.

For much of the twentieth century, U.S. culture has emphasized youth. Consequently, many Americans have developed negative stereotypes of the elderly. Robert Butler, the former director of the National Institute of Aging and author of *Why Survive? Being Old in America* (1975), coined the term **ageism** to describe these stereotypes and the discriminatory treatment applied to the elderly. **Social gerontology**, the study of the impact of sociocultural conditions on the process and consequences of aging, shows us that the impact of aging on marriages and families is multifaceted. Some older family members are frail and in need of care, whereas others are living independent, healthy, active

APPLYING THE SOCIOLOGICAL IMAGINATION

IS AGEISM DEAD?

Imagine that when you woke up this morning you were suddenly 85 years old. How would people treat you? Would you experience ageism? Pat Moore, a 26-year-old industrial designer, decided to find out by taking on the appearance and demeanor of an 85-year-old woman. During the 3-year period of her research, she presented herself to people in two ways: as an old person and as herself. Her book *Disguised* (with C. P. Conn, 1985) provides a fascinating account of the ways in which the old Pat Moore was treated differently from the young Pat Moore. When disguised as the older woman, Moore frequently was treated with anger, disrespect, impatience, and even ridicule. For example, on two different occasions she shopped in the same store, behaved in the same way (uncertain about the product she wanted and slow to get her money out), wore the same dress, and was waited on by the same clerk. On her first visit to the store she disguised herself as the 85-year-old woman; the next day she appeared as herself. The clerk was impatient with and discourteous to the 85-year-old woman, whereas he treated the young woman with patience, respect, and good humor.

It is unlikely that you have time to replicate Moore's experiment. Nevertheless, you can imaginatively put yourself in the role of an elderly person who is experiencing some physical changes in vision, hearing, touch, and mobility as a result of the aging process. To understand better how someone like that may feel, try the following while you are in an active social setting:

- Look through a pair of glasses sprayed with hair spray.
- Turn the pages of a book or pick up a glass or finger food wearing gardening gloves.
- Wear ear plugs and try to keep up with a lively conversation with friends.
- Use a walker to get around.

Record and discuss how you felt in these social settings. How were these experiences different from your ordinary behavior in similar settings?

To a degree, being old is a matter of self-definition. Some people may feel old at age 60; others may not feel old at age 80.

Source: © Lynn Johnson Productions, Inc./Dist. by United Feature Syndicate, Inc.

lives. Some of America's elderly live in isolation in single-room occupancy hotels, but many others enjoy happy lives, interacting with family and friends and engaging in numerous new and exciting activities. Our goal throughout this chapter is to present these differing realities of America's elderly and their families. This approach requires that we balance the strengths and satisfactions of the elderly with the real problems many of the elderly confront on a daily basis.

Changing Age Norms

In general, life course development tends to follow specific **age norms**, expectations of how one is to behave at any stage in life. These age norms currently show signs of being less restrictive than in the past. For example, today it is not unusual for people to marry for the first time in their 20s, 40s, or even 60s. Similarly, women are becoming mothers at both younger and older ages. Not only are teens giving birth but, due to new reproductive technologies, so too are menopausal women (see Chapter 9). Divorced and remarried men in their 40s and 50s are starting new families. As late as the 1960s, students typically attended college for 4 years, starting at age 18 and finishing at age 22. Today, your classmates may be 20, 30, 50, or even 70 years old, and they may take 4, 5, or even 8 years to complete their degrees. Although more people are opting for early retirement at age 55, others begin new careers at age 70. As these examples indicate, there has been an ongoing shift toward a loosening of age-appropriate standards of behavior (Neugarten and Neugarten, 1992).

As a result of falling mortality rates, most of us can expect to experience many of these later-life events—launching of children and the period of the empty nest, job changes, retirement, parental care, widowhood, and, particularly for females, an extended period of solitary living. By reflecting on the experiences of the generations ahead of us, we may better prepare ourselves to deal with these events. Such a reflection also allows us to confront some of this society's popular fears of aging.

THE DEMOGRAPHICS OF AGING: DEFINING "OLD"

Who are today's elderly? When does old age begin? One easy answer is at age 65, which was arbitrarily selected by government officials in 1935 as the age at which a worker could receive full social security retirement benefits. Defining old age is more complicated than this, however. Consider, for example, the active 78-year-old friend of ours who explained why she doesn't care to go to her local senior citizen center: "The people there are all so old." By that she meant they are in their 80s and 90s and less active than she is. Her experiences confirm what many researchers have come to call **functional age**—an individual's physical, intellectual, and social capacities and accomplishments. People grow old at different rates. One person may be "old" at 60, whereas another is "young" at 75.

Although the elderly share some common experiences, we will see in the following discussions how social characteristics such as age, gender, and marital status interact in ways that lead to different experiences for different groups of elderly.

Age Categories of the Elderly

Including everyone over 65 in a single category called "the elderly" obscures significant differences in the social realities of older people. Recognizing the diversity among older people in terms of physical and social functioning, gerontologists now speak of three distinct categories: the young-old (ages 65–74), the middle-old (ages 75–84), and the old-old (ages 85 and over). The older population itself is aging at a rapid rate. Figure 14.1 shows the changes expected in these age categories by 2050. In 2000, only 12 percent of the elderly were 85 or older but in only another 50 years 23 percent of the elderly will be that old. The oldest-old make up the most rapidly growing elderly age group. In 2000, the 65–74 age group (18.4 million) was eight times larger than in 1900,

Figure 14.1

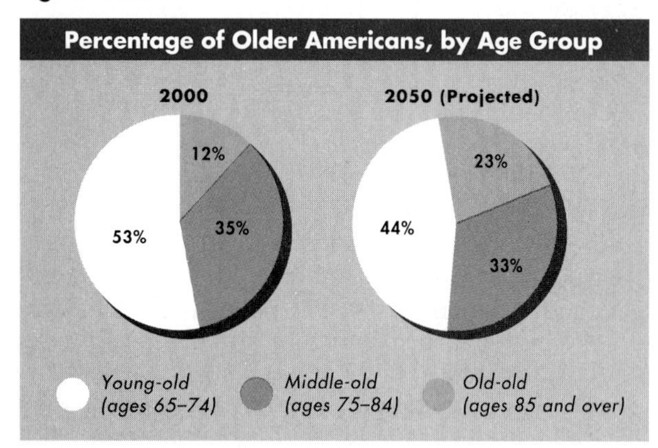

Sources: Adapted from U.S. Census Bureau, Census 2000, Table DP-1. *Profile of General Demographic Characteristics for the United States: 2000* (accessed December 28, 2001); and U.S. Census Bureau, 1998, *Statistical Abstract of the United States, 1998* (Washington, DC: U.S. Government Printing Office): 17, Table 17.

but the 75–84 group (12.4 million) was 16 times larger and the 85+ group (4.2 million) was 34 times larger. Additionally, there were over 50,000 centenarians (people 100 years of age or older) living in the United States, a 35 percent increase from the 1990 figure of 37, 306 (Administration on Aging, 2002). By 2050, that number is expected to exceed 1 million (U.S. Census Bureau, 2000a). These demographic changes present both opportunities and challenges. On the one hand, families and the society at large have much to gain by utilizing the experience and wisdom of the older population. On the other hand, families and social planners must also prepare to meet the anticipated health care requirements and other service needs of an aging population.

Gender and Marital Status

The gap between the number of women (143.7 million) and men (138.1 million) narrowed during the 1990s due to migration and declining male death rates, bringing the overall sex ratio (the number of males per 100 females) to 96.2, up from 94.5 in 1980 (Associated Press, 2001). However, among the elderly population, especially those in the oldest category, women significantly outnumber men. Six out of every ten older Americans are female. This has led some researchers to characterize old age as primarily a female experience (Longino, 1988). This, however, is a relatively recent development. Only around 1930 did women's life expectancy begin to increase more rapidly than men's as female deaths connected with pregnancy, childbirth, and infectious diseases declined dramatically. Table 14.1 shows the change in the sex ratios in the different age groups of the elderly for 1960 and 2000. Women clearly have a longevity advantage over men. Why this should be the case is not fully understood. Science has not yet unraveled all of the reasons for the gender difference in mortality rates. Gerontologist Erdman Palmore (1980) attributes half of the difference to genetics and the other half to social roles and environmental factors.

Longevity for women, however, can be a mixed blessing. On the one hand, it allows for a rich and meaningful life, and it provides an opportunity to share in the socialization of new generations. On the other hand, it often means years alone, as husbands and male relatives and friends die at earlier ages. As Figure 14.2 shows, older women were much less likely to be married than older men—43 percent compared to 74 percent. Almost half of all women were widows (45 percent). There were over four times as many widows (8.5 million) as widowers (2.0 million). Divorced and separated older persons constituted only 8 percent of all older people in 2000. However, their numbers (2.6 million) have jumped since 1990, when approximately 1.5 million of the older population were separated or divorced. By age 75 and over, the marriage rates decline for both women and men but they drop off more sharply for women with only 29 percent married while 67 percent of men were still married at this age (Fields and Casper, 2001).

These differences in marital status also vary significantly by race and ethnicity. Among males 65 and older, African Americans and Latinos were the least likely to be married with spouse present (63 percent), compared with 76 percent of whites and 74 percent of Latinos. Similarly, among elderly women, 26 percent of African Americans, 42 percent of whites, and 37 percent of Latinas were married with spouse present (cited in Treas, 1995:28). These patterns are directly related to the different rates of marriage and remarriage among the different racial and ethnic groups, as discussed in Chapters 5 and 13.

Gender differences in survivorship rates are significant because older women across all racial and ethnic groups have fewer financial resources and are more likely to experience poverty in old age than elderly men are. In Chapter 10 we noted that historically women have been disadvantaged in the labor market. They earn less money, are segregated into less prestigious jobs, and are more likely to work part-time

Table 14.1

Changing Sex Ratios in the Older Population, 1960, 1990, and 2000

	Sex Ratio		
Age Category	1960	1990	2000
Young-old (65–74)	86	77	82
Middle-old (75–84)	76	59	65
Old-old (85+)	67	38	41

Source: Adapted from Robert C. Atchley, 1991, *Social Forces and Aging*, 6th ed. (Belmont, CA: Wadsworth): 28, © 1991 Wadsworth Publishing Company. Reprinted with permission of Wadsworth Publishing Company; Lisa Hetzel and Annelta Smith, 2001, *The 65 Years and Over Population*, 2000 Census Brief (October): 3, Table 2.

Figure 14.2

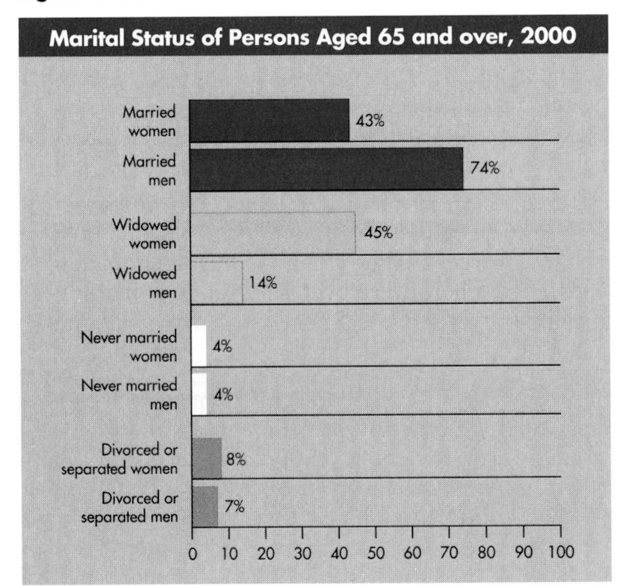

Source: Administration on Aging, 2001, "A Profile of Older Americans: 2001." **http://www.aoa.dhhs.gov/aoa/STATS/profile/2001/3.html** (accessed December 28, 2001).

and to have their work life interrupted by child rearing than are men. Consequently, women have less access than men to pension plans and receive fewer benefits when they do have access. Half of all older women receiving a private pension in 1998 got less than $3486 per year, compared with $7020 per year for older men ("It's Time for Working Women . . . ," 2001). The median income of older persons in 2000 was $10,899 for females and $19,168 for males (Administration on Aging, 2001).

Race, Ethnicity, and Class

In 2000, the overall racial composition of the population 65 and older in the United States was 83.6 percent white, 8.0 percent African American, 2.4 percent Asian/Pacific Islander, and 0.5 percent Native American/Eskimo/Aleut. Latinas/os, who may be of any race, constituted 5.6 percent of the older population (Figure 14.3). Additionally, 0.8 percent of persons 65 and over identified themselves as being of two or more races. Together, people of color make up approximately 16.4 percent of the elderly population, and their numbers are increasing at a faster rate than those of the white elderly, due primarily to higher fertility and immigration rates. This trend is likely to continue well into the twenty-first century. Projections are that by 2050 people of color will constitute almost 36 percent of the population aged 65 and over in the United States. Although all groups will experience change, the highest growth rates will be among Latinas/os and Asians/Pacific Islanders. By 2050, one in six elderly is likely to be Latina/o.

Although the gap in life expectancy rates for the white population and people of color is narrowing, these rates remain lower for people of color. For example, in 2000 life expectancy at birth was 80.0 for white females and 74.8 for white males. In contrast, it was only 75 for African

Figure 14.3

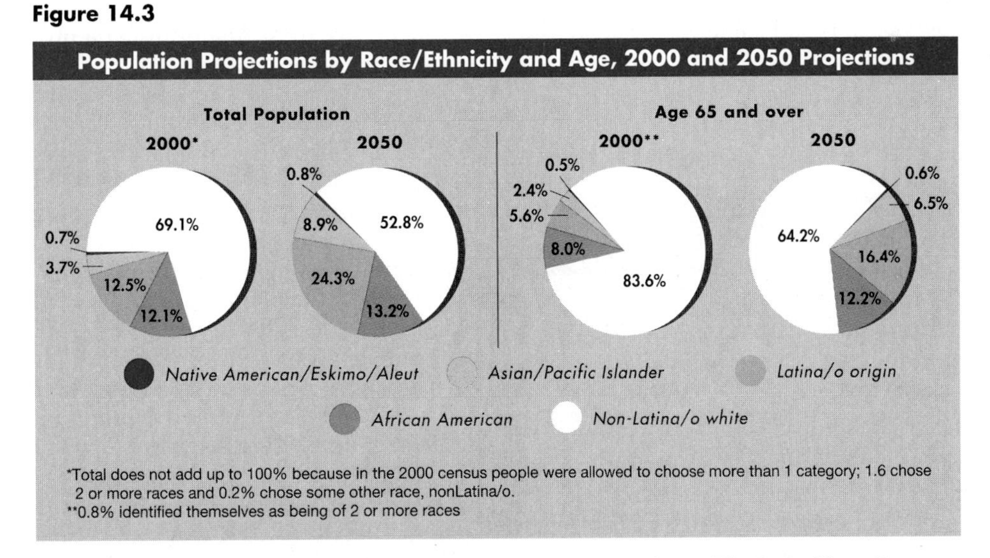

Sources: Adapted from Population Reference Bureau, 2001, "U.S. Population: The Basics." **http://www.prb.org/AmeristatTemplate.cfm?Section=2000Census1&template=ContentM...** (accessed December 29, 2001); U.S. Census Bureau, 2000, *Statistical Abstract of the United States 2000* (Washington, DC: U.S. Government Printing Office): 17, Table 16; *Older Americans 2000: Key Indicators of Well-Being, 2000*, Federal Interagency Forum on Aging-Related Statistics. http://www.agingstats.gov/chartbook2000/OlderAmericans2000.pdf (accessed January 3, 2002).

American females and 68.3 for African American males (U.S. Department of Health and Human Services, 2001). Native Americans and Latinas/os also have lower life expectancies than do whites.

What accounts for these differences? One major factor, of course, is social class. In general, families of color have fewer economic resources in old age than do their white counterparts. This is due primarily to the disadvantages they faced in the labor market in earlier years: low-paying jobs, longer and more frequent terms of unemployment, and racial discrimination. Thus, they tend to have fewer health insurance or social security benefits than do the white elderly, and they are less likely to have supplementary retirement incomes from private pensions. For example, white households containing families headed by persons 65 and older reported a median income of $33,467, compared to $27,952 for African Americans and $24,330 for Latinas/os (Administration on Aging, 2001).

Poverty among the Elderly

Although median income gives us a general picture of the economic situation of families headed by the elderly, it does not allow us to see the range of differences among elderly families. Not all elderly are poor, nor are all elderly of color poor. In 2000, for example, approximately 28 percent of households headed by an individual age 65 or older had incomes of $50,000 or more. Nevertheless, the more typical pattern was one of low income. Almost 34 percent of such households had incomes of less than $25,000. Twelve percent had incomes of less than $15,000 (Administration on Aging, 2001).

Although a smaller proportion of elderly is poor today than in the past, poverty remains a problem for millions of elderly, especially for the old-old. Table 14.2 shows the changes in the poverty rate between 1959 and 2000. In 1959, 35 percent of the elderly over 65 were poor; by 2000, only 10 percent were so identified, although many others had incomes only slightly above the poverty line. The poverty rates for people of color are significantly higher than those for whites. Additionally, women had higher poverty rates (12.2 percent) than men (7.5 percent). Older people who live alone or with nonrelatives were more likely to be poor (20.8 percent) than were older people living with families (5.1 percent). Latinas living alone or with nonrelatives had the highest poverty rate (38.3 percent). Some of the explanations for these differential rates have to do with discrimination in the workplace (see Chapter 10).

Table 14.2

Poverty Status of the Elderly by Race and Latina/o Origin, 1959–2000

Years	All Races (%)	White (%)	African American (%)	Latina/o (%)
1959	35.2	33.1	62.5	NA
1970	24.6	22.6	48.0	NA
1980	15.7	13.6	38.1	30.8
1990	12.2	10.1	33.8	22.5
2000	10.2	8.9	22.3	18.8

Sources: Adapted from the U.S. Census Bureau, 1991, *Current Population Reports*, Series P-60, no. 175, "Poverty in the United States: 1990" (Washington, DC: U.S. Government Printing Office): Table 3, pp. 18–19; Administration on Aging, 2001, "A Profile of Older Americans: 2001." http://www.aoa.gov/aoa/stats/profile/2001/8.html (accessed December 29, 2001).

The initial decline in poverty rates was due to the nation's efforts to win the "War on Poverty" in the 1960s. Many new social programs were instituted for poor people of all age groups, including the elderly. Although many social welfare programs were reduced or eliminated during the Reagan and Bush administrations, the programs that benefit the elderly remained largely in place. For example, social security benefits were improved by providing for increases in the cost of living. Many companies instituted private pension plans for workers, thus providing workers with additional retirement income. Businesses instituted discount programs for senior citizens regardless of economic need. Attempts to reduce or eliminate these programs have been resisted by effective political lobbying by groups such as the American Association of Retired Persons (AARP), which has 35 million members. Today, some public officials fear the possibility of a backlash among younger people, who complain that such programs are costly and unfair to them.

LIVING ARRANGEMENTS

If you are like most Americans, you probably share the fear that when you get old you will be sent to a nursing home. Perhaps your parents have asked you to promise never to put them in a home. Disturbing stories of the plight of elderly in nursing homes frequently appear in the pages of newspapers. Perhaps this accounts for the widely believed myth that most aged persons end up institutionalized. In fact, only a small proportion of older Americans live in an institutional setting. At any given time, only 5 percent of the elderly are in nursing homes, and they are primarily the infirm old-old (Cockerham, 1991:27). In 2000, only 1.1 percent of persons 65–74 were in nursing homes, compared to 4.7 percent of persons 75–84 and 18.2 percent of those 85 and older (Administration on Aging, 2001). Americans are entering nursing homes at a later age than in the past. Average age on admission increased from 81 years in 1985 to 83 years in 1997, and nursing home stays were shorter in 1997 than in 1987. It is likely that these changes reflect more use of home health care and/or the use of nursing homes for short-term rehabilitation (National Center for Health Statistics, 2001). Because the old-old are the fastest growing part of the elderly population, however, we can predict an increased need for quality nursing home care over the next

When independent living is no longer possible, some elderly people must move to nursing homes. Although the quality of life in nursing homes varies considerably, the elderly living in homes with programs that meet their social and intellectual needs as well as physical needs do quite well. This home provides a strong arts and crafts program for its residents.

several decades. Thus, many more families, perhaps yours included, will have to face the difficult decision of how to care for an elderly dependent relative.

As Figure 14.4 shows, the vast majority of older people maintain their independence in the community, living alone or in a household with their spouse. Living arrangements show a clear gender difference. Among the young-old (ages 65–74) men are one-and-one-half times as likely as women to live with their spouse (76.7 percent to 52.9 percent), whereas over twice as many women as men live alone (31 percent to 13.8 percent). Although both older women and men are more likely to live alone than their younger counterparts, this pattern is more pronounced for women (49.4 percent) than for men (21.4 percent). In both age categories African American women and men are more likely to be living with other relatives than are their white counterparts. Latina/o elderly are less likely than whites but more likely than African Americans to be married with their spouse present (U.S. Census Bureau, 2000a). These gender and race/ethnic differences in living arrangements are influenced by differences in life expectancies that favor women and in age-related needs and resources. For example, women are more likely than men to live with other relatives because they have lower incomes, more difficulty caring for themselves, or because they are helping to raise their grandchildren.

Housing Patterns

Of the 95 percent of elderly who live independently, the majority reside in their own homes. Homeownership offers a number of advantages: security and familiarity, lower cash outlays for shelter, a possible source of income when the home is sold, and a sense of control in one's life. The elderly are far more likely to own their own homes (77 percent) than other age groups, except householders aged 55 to 65 (80 percent). Homeownership remains high (67 percent) even among householders over the age of 85 (Naifeh, 1993). Given these rates, at first glance we may be tempted to conclude that the elderly have few housing problems. A closer look reveals this is not the case, however. First, homeownership varies from group to group. Only 64 percent of African American elderly householders and 59 percent of Latina/o elderly householders were homeowners. Married couples were more likely to own homes (91 percent) than were older persons who lived alone (64 percent).

Obviously income is a factor. Although 91 percent of householders reporting yearly incomes of $25,000 or more were homeowners, only 61 percent of elderly householders with incomes under $10,000 owned their own homes (Naifeh, 1993). Second, although overall today's elderly are less likely to be living in physically deficient housing than past generations, a significant portion of the housing occupied by the elderly is of poor quality (Grall, 1993). Many of the houses are as old as or older than their owners and require constant maintenance that is often too costly for people on fixed incomes. An estimated 20 percent of the elderly live in dwellings that are substandard. The very old (85 and older) and poor elderly of color are the most likely to live in physically deficient housing (Golant and LaGreca, 1995). Because of these housing problems the elderly are often

Figure 14.4

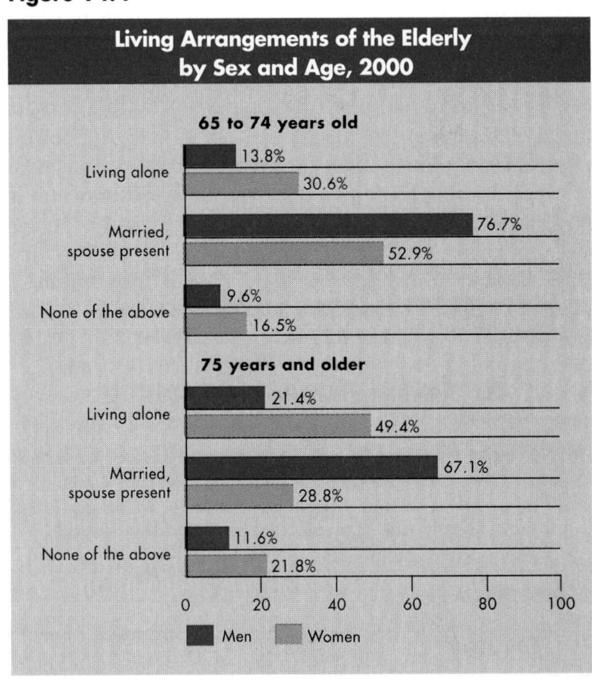

Source: J. Fields and L. M. Casper, 2001, "America's Families and Living Arrangements: March 2000," *Current Population Reports,* P20-537 (Washington, DC: U.S. Census Bureau).

exploited by unscrupulous individuals who promise to do home repairs but flee with the money without doing the work. Finally, there is concern that in the future, fewer elderly will own their homes. A study by the Harvard University Joint Center for Housing Studies (1993) found that homeownership rates for households in the 35 to 44 age group have declined since 1980.

The situation for renters can be worse (Golant and LaGreca, 1994). Renters typically live in apartments, including public housing of various quality. Some renters are boarders, and others live in residential hotels, including single-room occupancies (SROs). Increasingly, SROs, especially those that cater to low-income elderly men, have been demolished to make room for urban renewal projects. Not only does the destruction of SROs displace elderly residents, but, as we have seen in Chapter 10, it also contributes to homelessness.

Although younger Americans tend to be mobile, middle-aged and older people prefer staying in a familiar environment. Housing is more than a place to live. For many, it symbolizes continuity, independence, family history, and a sense of belonging. The majority of the elderly have lived in their current residence for 20 or more years.

As the family life cycle changes, however, so, too, do housing needs. Houses can become too big, too isolated, too expensive, or too difficult to maintain for a retired couple or the widowed after children have left home. In addition, housing that once was satisfactory may become inadequate as a result of the resident's illness or disability. The affected person may no longer be able to use stairs, reach cupboards or counters, get in or out of bathtubs alone, or maneuver a wheelchair through narrow halls or doorways. Sometimes, remodeling or the intervention of outside help can take care of these problems. In other cases, relocation to more suitable housing is the only alternative. When a change is voluntary, the personal and psychological disruption it causes is likely to be relatively minor because the perceived benefits outweigh the costs. When the elderly are forced to relocate, however, the result is often trauma, confusion, grief, and a sense of helplessness and isolation. When asked by researchers which living arrangements they prefer, the elderly consistently say they want to be independent. An 80-year-old widow said:

> My daughter feels I shouldn't be living alone. We are very close, but she and her husband have their own lives. They both work. They have a lovely home, but it is in a suburb with no sidewalks or public transportation. I'd be isolated and dependent on them for going anywhere. I like my independence. Here I can walk to the store and the bank, and I can see people every day. We keep in touch by phone, and I know they will come if I need them. That's all I want.

The elderly do not want to live with their children, and relatively few do. In a Los Angeles survey, elderly respondents were asked, "Would you prefer to live with your own children or in a separate residence?" Ninety-eight percent of the whites, 83 percent of the African Americans, and 72 percent of the Mexican Americans surveyed said that they would prefer to live independently (cited in Treas and Bengtson, 1987). When parents do live with children, however, the most common pattern is living with a daughter (Stone, Cafferata, and Sangl, 1987).

Today's families are smaller in size than in the past, resulting in fewer people to meet the needs of elderly members. Further, given that women live longer than men, increasing numbers of elderly women, like the woman above, are likely to spend their last years living alone.

Race and ethnicity also affect housing decisions. Widowed Asian American women and men were more likely than any other group to live with their adult children. Latinas/os were the second-most likely group to do so. Among the old-old, African American elderly are more likely to live with their children than are white elderly. Similarly, in Chile and Mexico, most unmarried elderly women, even those without children, lived with relatives, often nephews, nieces, or siblings (De Voss, 2000). Economic need and a cultural emphasis on the extended family are the most common explanations for these different patterns. However, as we saw at the beginning of this chapter (see "In the News"), even among Asian Americans there is a trend away from co-residence with adult children. There is concern that in the coming decades Chile and Mexico may follow the patterns now developing in the United States and other Western countries, and efforts are being made to find a balance between retaining valuable kin ties and respecting increased autonomy for all ages.

MARRIAGES IN LATER LIFE

Imagine being married to the same person for 50, 60, or even more years. Given current life expectancies, many married couples can expect to celebrate their golden wedding anniversary and beyond. What can we expect of a marital bond that endures this long? Does the quality of the relationship change over time? Is the poet Robert Browning correct in saying, "Grow old along with me/The best is yet to be"? We shall try to answer these questions by looking at two issues: marital satisfaction and adjustment to retirement.

Marital Quality and Satisfaction

Does marital quality improve with age? Linda Ade-Ridder and Timothy Brubaker (1983) reviewed more than 25 studies and found no consensus on this question. Some studies reported little or no change in marital quality in later life. Couples who are happy in earlier years are likely to be happy in later years, and early unhappiness remains in later years (Clark and Wallin, 1965). Other researchers found a gradual pattern of decline in marital love and companionship over the years (Gilford, 1984; Blood and Wolfe, 1960). A third set of studies showing improvement in marital quality revealed a pattern whereby couples start out with high levels of satisfaction, "the honeymoon phase." This period is followed by the childbearing and child-rearing years, during which stress and anxiety levels may be heightened, leading to a decline in marital satisfaction. Once the children are grown and leave home, couples can concentrate on each other again (Anderson et al., 1983). Spouses may rediscover or develop common interests and interdependence, resulting in increased feelings of affection and companionship (Dobson, 1983). More recent studies support this curvilinear relationship between family stage and the perceived marital quality of both spouses (Glenn, 1990; Vaillant and Vaillant, 1993). Negotiating such role transitions depends on a couple's prior adaptability and their degree of marital satisfaction. Studies have found that couples who are celebrating golden wedding anniversaries (3 percent of all married couples) share similar values and belief systems and are good at negotiating with each other (Roberts, 1979–80; Parron, 1982). Jean and Harry Gottlieb, who have been married for 60 years, provide a good illustration of these dynamics (see the "Family Profile" box on page 438).

What are we to make of these different findings? Some of the differences may be related to the particular methodological techniques used in the studies themselves. Much of this research involved studies of small samples of older couples taken at only one point in time. Comparisons of changes are difficult to make unless the same couples are retested at different times and unless a standardized measure of marital quality is used.

Throughout this text we have examined a number of factors that influence a couple's level of marital satisfaction. For example, in Chapter 6 we discussed sexuality among the elderly. A study by Ade-Ridder found that marital satisfaction is positively related to sexual behavior among older couples who are still sexually active. "Happier men and women report fewer changes in sexual activity and report them at a later age than do less happy people" (1990:63). This does not mean, however, that couples no longer participating in sexual intercourse had poor-quality marriages. Rather, Ade-Ridder concludes, "Sexual intercourse is not essential to a high-quality marriage in later life, but it has its rewards for those who still practice this form of intimate expression" (1990:64). Another important factor that affects later-life marriages is the way in which couples deal with retirement.

Adjustment to Retirement

Retirement, as a distinct phase in the family life cycle, is a modern phenomenon. Prior to the twentieth century, American workers typically worked until they died or were physically unable to continue working. When they stopped working, there was no pension or social security for their later years, and their welfare most frequently depended on other family members (Markides and Mindel, 1987). In the wake of the Great Depression, however, this situation changed. With the establishment of social security in 1935, the institution of retirement became part of the national culture. Nevertheless, not all elderly are retired, and those that do retire do so at different ages. In 2000, the elderly made up 3 percent of the U.S. labor force. Altogether 4.2 million

Many elderly people today continue to lead active lifestyles, participating in a variety of work and leisure activities. This couple enjoys sailing to interesting new ports.

FAMILY PROFILE

THE GOTTLIEB FAMILY

Jean and Harry Gottlieb, their children, and grandchildren

Length of relationship: 60 years

Challenges of later life: The challenge is to maintain a real and caring interest in the world around us—in our children's and friends' lives as well as the more public events of the day—even though we are less in the mainstream and more like watchers on the riverbank. We must remain convinced that we can continue to make a real contribution to the world we live in. We have the long view and should be the all-important living link between a historic past and a still-mysterious future. We have fewer constraints on our own lifestyle and can do more things on impulse.

Relationship philosophy: We never take each other for granted. Our relationship has always been based on trust, a compatible sense of humor, close family ties, and good old romantic love. After 60 years of marriage, we love and respect each other more than ever. We are confidants, best friends, co-conspirators, and last—but definitely not least—lovers. We spend more time together now, but we each have our own interests and activities as well as some mutual endeavors. When we have differences, we try not to go to bed mad. While our life remains vibrant, we are saddened by the death of dear old friends and are aware of our own mortality.

people 65 and over, including 1.8 million women (9.4 percent) and 2.4 million men (17.5 percent), were working or actively seeking work (Administration on Aging, 2001).

Like so much of social life in the United States, the experience of retirement is affected by an individual's race, class, and gender. Years ago it was common to hear housewives say, "I married him for better or worse, but not for lunch." Such a line usually produced chuckles in the listeners because they could easily envision a newly retired man who suddenly has time on his hands wandering aimlessly around the house, interfering with his wife's daily routines. (Today it can as easily be a retired wife who is disrupting the household system.) Marital satisfaction is likely to decline under these conditions. However, this pattern was more applicable in the past, when more families had a traditional household structure in which the man was in the labor force and the wife kept house. Today, retirement increasingly means more time for couples to spend together in mutually enjoyable activities, thus increasing marital satisfaction (Lee, 1988; Kotulak, 1999).

TYPES OF RETIREMENT To understand the impact of retirement today, we must ask, Whose retirement? With 60 percent of all women of working age in the labor force, couples must deal with more than one retirement. Given that men tend to be older than their wives, the timing of retirement, especially for employed wives, might be a source of friction. Brubaker (1985:31–32) has identified four patterns of retirement among older couples:

- ***Single or traditional retirement:*** Here, one spouse, usually the husband, has been employed and thus only one spouse retires from paid employment.
- ***Dissynchronized—husband initially:*** In this situation the husband retires before his wife. She continues to work because she is usually younger or started her career after his.
- ***Dissynchronized—wife initially:*** This pattern, in which the wife retires first, is rare. It may be that she has health problems or is needed to take care of an older relative.
- ***Synchronized retirement:*** In this situation both the husband and wife were employed, and they retire at the same time.

Most of the studies conducted on retirement have not taken into account these variations. It may well be that marital satisfaction is affected in different ways not by retirement itself but by the circumstances of retirement. For example, Gary Lee and Constance Shehan (1991) found that wives who continue to work after their husbands have retired have lower levels of marital satisfaction than wives in couples with any other employment status combination.

This pattern may reflect in part the fact that retired husbands only marginally increase their domestic labor, and mainly in those activities traditionally associated with male gender roles, such as yard work and car maintenance. As we saw in Chapter 10, perceived inequality in the division of household tasks is often a source of marital dissatisfaction. Researchers generally have found that retirement does not significantly alter the division of household tasks established in the earlier years of marriage (Keating and Cole, 1980). Given the consistent findings that early patterns are carried over into later years, people who desire a mutual sharing of tasks in later life are well advised to negotiate that status from the very beginning of their marriage.

Other factors also affect the quality of life after retirement. In 1986 Congress passed legislation ending mandatory retirement for most employees. Prior to that time most workers were forced to retire at age 65 whether they wanted to or not. An extensive body of research revealed that involuntary retirement is likely to produce stress and depression. In contrast, when people want to retire and make plans to do so, retirement is more likely to be a positive experience. Finally, satisfaction during the retirement years also depends on the couple's financial status and health. If retirement income is sufficient to enable couples to pursue desired activities, retirement is likely to promote satisfaction. However, if couples have been unable to save much in the earlier years of married life or if their earnings have been so low that they receive only minimal social security benefits, they may experience considerable downward mobility with retirement.

According to Judith Treas (1995), most older people see their incomes decline by one-third to one-half after retirement. Such drastic decreases can push some elderly into poverty. Although this is true to a degree for all groups, it is more likely to happen to white elderly. An analysis of data from two national longitudinal surveys showed that retirement led to a significant decline in income among white males but only a minor decline for African American males (Fillenbaum, George, and Palmore, 1985). The reason for this is that the African American workers had lower incomes than the white workers. The impact then is for African Americans already in poverty to experience greater poverty and for whites, some of whom were middle class, to sink into poverty after retirement (Markides and Mindel, 1987:184).

In general, when people control the timing of their retirement, they are more likely to feel satisfied with this stage in their lives (Floyd et al., 1992). However, the degree to which workers have this control varies considerably. African American workers are less likely to experience voluntary retirement than their white counterparts are. Although financial readiness is a major factor in the decision to retire for whites, poor health and disadvantaged labor force experiences are more likely to affect the retirement decision for African Americans. Compared with whites, African Americans are more likely to retire at earlier ages, retire because of poor health, be forced to retire, be unemployed in the 12-month period prior to retirement, and report job dissatisfaction and job search discouragement prior to retirement (R. Gibson, 1996, 1991). An earlier study by Kyriakos Markides (1978) found a similar pattern among Mexican Americans living in San Antonio, Texas. Fifty-five percent of the Mexican American respondents retired because of health problems, compared with 35 percent of the Anglo retirees. He also found that the Mexican Americans had more difficulty adjusting to the loss of the work role than did the more socioeconomically advantaged, older Anglos. Furthermore, the concept of retirement has little meaning for individuals whose jobs do not provide old-age benefits. They must keep working until they become physically incapacitated. This is particularly true for unskilled white workers and people of color, especially African American women, who often work to an advanced age. Little systematic data exist on the retirement experiences of other people of color, especially Native Americans and Asian Americans.

INTERGENERATIONAL RELATIONSHIPS

The fact that the majority of elderly live alone or with their spouse gave rise to a belief that most old people are neglected by their children. On the contrary, studies have consistently found that 50 percent to 60 percent of older people with children have at least one child within 10 minutes of their home (Shanas, 1979, 1980; Lin and Rogerson, 1995).

Retirement is well recognized in the United States as a distinct stage in the life cycle. Many employers have established rituals to mark the end of a formal work role and the beginning of a new phase in their employees' lives. As this man's colleagues in the space industry have acknowledged, he is now ready for "take off."

Many adult children talk to their parents on a regular basis. A study by the National Center for Health Statistics of 2095 Americans over age 80 substantiates earlier findings of frequent contact between the elderly and their adult children. Among the oldest segment of the population, "as many as 85 percent of them saw or spoke to their children 2 to 7 times a week" (Kolata, 1993:A16). Similar patterns were found across different racial groups (Mitchell and Register, 1984; Chan, 1988). In addition, substantial assistance in the form of financial aid, goods, and services flows in both directions (Peterson and Peterson, 1988; Bengtson and Harootyan, 1994; Soldo and Hill, 1994).

Although there is considerable diversity, both around the world (see the "In Other Places" box) and within the United States, in the way in which different generations relate to one another, family interactions are shaped to a large degree by the norm of reciprocity or complementary exchanges. Contrary to popular belief, older people are not primarily dependent recipients of aid; in many cases they are primarily donors (Bengtson, Rosenthal, and Burton, 1990; Spitze and Logan, 1992). Older parents often remain a resource for their adult children, providing financial assistance, advice, and child-care services. This is especially the case when adult children have stressful problems, for example, getting divorced or becoming widowed. In exchange, both generations expect that adult children will assist their parents in times of need (Bengtson and Harootyan, 1994; Hogan and Farkas, 1995). Social class, however, may influence the direction of tangible aid. For example, wealthier older people are likely to continue giving financial assistance to middle-aged children, whereas working-class parents are more likely to be receiving assistance.

Evidence suggests, however, that several decades of high divorce rates (see Chapter 12) are having negative effects on intergenerational exchange and contact. For example, research has found that widowed parents engage in more intergenerational transfers than divorced parents and that remarried parents are less likely to receive informal care from their children. Divorced men are particularly likely to lack intergenerational support in later life as a result of weaker ties with their children. And families containing only stepchildren have lower rates of financial and time transfers and lower rates of intergenerational co-residence than families with biological children (Pezzin and Schone, 1999). If these patterns become more pronounced, they will have widespread repercussions on the economic and social well-being of the elderly in future years.

Quality of Relationships

Although we know a great deal about the frequency of intergenerational contact, we know less about the qualitative aspects of these relationships. Frequency of contact in and of itself doesn't ensure a strong emotional bond. Nevertheless, researchers have found that most adult children and their elderly parents like one another and express satisfaction with their relationships (Blieszner and Bedford, 1995). Gender seems to play an important role in this regard. For example, mother–daughter relationships tend to be particularly close and intimate during all phases of the life span (Troll, 1988). In contrast to sons, daughters are more likely to be chosen by the aging parent as a confidant and to stay in closer contact with parents (Aldous, 1987; Aldous, Klaus, and Klein, 1985). The maxim that "a son is a son until he takes a wife, but a daughter is a daughter all of her life" seems to have some empirical support.

Patterns of Support

Do adult children really help their needy elderly parents, or do the government and taxpayers assume most of this responsibility? The weight of evidence in study after study indicates that families, not the formal system, provide the bulk of care for the elderly across all cultural groups. Nearly 80 percent of disabled elderly people who are not in health care institutions depend, in whole or in part, on family and friends for the care they receive: 70 percent rely exclusively on such helpers (Schenck-Yglesias, 1995). In addition to providing direct care, children often serve as mediators between institutional bureaucracies and elderly kin, providing older relatives with information on housing, pensions, insurance, and medical care (Sussman, 1985). Evidence also suggests that when people seek help outside the family, it is usually as a last resort. When we look more closely at the kind and degree of support the elderly receive and who is most likely to provide it, however, we find variations by gender, race, marital status, and presence of children.

Racial and Ethnic Variations Throughout this text we have presented data showing historically how race and ethnicity have functioned to provide some groups (mostly white) with access to societal resources and at the same time to restrict other groups (mostly people of color) from sharing in these resources on an equal basis. Partly as a response to the economic needs generated by this differential treatment, families of color have developed a wide range of informal support systems. For example, numerous studies have found that African Americans have a higher incidence of extended family households than do whites and that older African Americans utilized a wider variety of resources than did whites (Taylor, 1990; MacRae, 1992; Ruggles, 1994). In a similar vein, other studies concluded that although white elderly sought help from spouses and other specific family members when it was needed, African American elderly relied on a more regular basis on family, friends, neighbors, and to a significant degree, fellow church members (Coke and Twaite, 1995; Brown, 2001). In yet another study comparing African American and white families, Elizabeth Mutran (1985) found that when social class was held constant, the differences were not as pronounced, but helping patterns were still more evident among African American families. Researchers have found that Latina/o elderly also tend to be involved in extended family networks that provide mutual aid and informal support (Mindel, 1983).

IN OTHER PLACES

THE ROLE AND STATUS OF THE ELDERLY: VARIED AND CHANGING

There is a considerable amount of mythology surrounding the role of the elderly in both industrial and nonindustrial societies. In industrialized countries there is the myth that the elderly are isolated and alone. In nonindustrialized countries there is the myth that the elderly are always respected and cared for by the next generation. What we find when we examine these and other myths is that the empirical reality is a lot more varied. For example, in the United States, although a significant minority of elderly struggle to survive, there is extensive intergenerational contact. Additionally, the government provides economic security and health care for many of its elderly citizens.

How do the elderly fare in other places? Nancy Foner (1993) examined ethnographic reports for a wide range of nonindustrial cultures and found in many cases a strong ethic of intergenerational caregiving. Let's look at some examples from her review. Among the Kirghiz herders of Afghanistan, the younger son (and his family) looks after aged parents, remaining in the parental household. In exchange, he inherits the family herd, tent, and camping ground. When traditional healers and health workers of the Akamba tribe of Kenya were asked to choose between a dying old man over 60 and a dying 25-year-old man when there was only enough medicine to cure one person, many favored saving the old man, even where the young man was first in line. A man from among the Gonja of West Africa said, "When you were weak (young) your mother fed you and cleaned up your messes, and your father picked you up and comforted you when you fell. When they are weak, will you not care for them?" Similarly, among the Samia of Kenya, adult children care for parents just as the elders cared for them when they were small. Australian aborigines consider it callous and reprehensible for family members to desert an ailing elder. The Twareg pastoralists of Niger believe the elderly should be fed and served. In the 1980s, despite a severe 3-year drought and an inadequate supply of food, the Twareg daughters or granddaughters continued to feed and care for the physically weak elderly. Among the !Kung of Botswana, those who are generous to the old are likely to be honored.

Unfortunately, in many of these societies today, limited resources combined with rapid social change are undermining the reciprocal relationships that have characterized intergenerational relationships, especially for elderly without children. These elderly are often neglected, since they have not been part of an exchange relationship. Some parents take on a childless role when their children migrate to other places in search of work. According to Foner, limited resources sometimes lead to extreme behavior—gerontocide or the abandoning or killing of the elderly. In some societies, there is an understanding by both generations that when the old are no longer productive and a drain on the community, it is time to go. Among the Mardudjara hunters and gatherers of Australia, when life was too difficult, some of the elderly asked to be left behind to die. The elderly Eskimos of northern Canada would go off by themselves onto the icy tundra to die.

In sum, a cross-cultural perspective helps us to understand that kinship structures and functioning are complex phenomena and that they can be understood only by examining cultural belief systems as well as social and economic factors.

What do you think? *Which society would you prefer to live in as an elderly person? Explain. What obligations do you think the younger generation should have toward the older generation in the United States? How effective do you think this nation is at meeting the needs of all age groups?*

Source: Nancy Foner, 1993, "When the Contract Fails: Care for the Elderly in Nonindustrial Cultures." In Vern L. Bengtson and Andrew Achenbaum, eds., *The Changing Contract across Generations.* New York: Aldine de Gruyter.

Additionally, Latina/o neighborhoods serve as important sources of help and opportunities for ongoing social interaction (Becerra and Shaw, 1984).

Other research, however, suggests that family ties in the African American community are more varied than some of these findings suggest and that the differences in informal patterns of family support observed between African Americans and whites in previous studies may not be very great (Mitchell and Register, 1984; Silverstein and Waite, 1993). Some of these discrepancies in findings may be due to the fact that in today's economy the existence of a large extended family among peoples of color can be a mixed blessing. First, having a large kin network may entail multiple obligations that are increasingly difficult for members to meet, particularly for groups experiencing high unemployment or health problems. Second, the perception that these supports are in place may lead public officials to believe that elderly of color do not need assistance when, in fact, they do. Thus, policymakers and researchers should not assume that all elderly of color are embedded in a strong kin network. (See Bengtson, Rosenthal, and Burton, 1996, for a discussion of these apparent paradoxes.)

EVOLVING PATTERNS OF KINSHIP: GRANDPARENTHOOD

Changing mortality and fertility rates can have enormous consequences for the kin network. As recently as 1900, families with grandparents were rare. An analysis by Peter Uhlenberg (1980) showed that families in which three or more grandparents are alive when a child reaches age 15 increased from 17 percent in 1900 to 55 percent in 1976. Even more dramatic change is evident in the fact that today approximately 50 percent of all older adults with children are great-grandparents (Roberts and Stroes, 1992). The social role of grandparent, let alone great-grandparent, is a fairly recent one and therefore is not well defined.

Styles of Grandparenting

According to Nancy Hooyman and H. Asuman Kiyak (1993), 94 percent of older adults with children become grandparents. Nevertheless, there is great diversity in the timing of grandparenthood. Given the incidence of teenage pregnancies, some parents become grandparents as early as their 30s. Other parents who had children later in life may not become grandparents until into their 60s or 70s. This diversity in ages of grandparents contributes to the ambiguity surrounding this role. Although a great deal of folklore is connected with grandparenting, there is little agreement on how to fulfill this role. Thus, most of us will construct our grandparenting role out of our own childhood memories of our grandparents, our perceptions of the way our parents acted as grandparents, and the attitudes we pick up about grandparenting from the media and from those around us, especially our adult children.

Over the years researchers have investigated the role and meaning of grandparenthood and in the process have identified several styles of grandparenting. Bernice Neugarten and Karol Weinstein (1964:200–201) studied 70 middle-class grandparent couples and classified their interactions with their grandchildren into one of the following five categories:

- ***Formal:*** Grandparents follow what they see as a prescribed role for grandparents.
- ***Fun seeker:*** Grandparent–grandchild interaction is characterized by informality and playfulness.
- ***Distant figure:*** Interaction is limited to holidays and special occasions.
- ***Surrogate parent:*** Grandparents assume caretaking responsibilities for grandchild.
- ***Reservoir of family wisdom:*** Grandparents are the dispensers of special skills or resources.

Neugarten and Weinstein also found that age is a factor in the development of grandparenting styles. Younger grandparents were more likely to be fun seekers, whereas older grandparents were more likely to adopt the formal approach.

This study and other early descriptions of grandparent roles have been criticized for their unidimensional approach (Roberto, 1990). In Neugarten and Weinstein's study each respondent was placed exclusively into one of the five categories. No provision was made for overlapping styles of grandparenting or changes in styles over time. Two decades after the Neugarten and Weinstein study was published, Andrew Cherlin and Frank Furstenberg (1986b:52–53) analyzed telephone interviews with 510 grandparents (and personal interviews with 36 of them) and found three styles of grandparenting:

- ***Remote:*** Grandparents interacted infrequently and maintained a ritualistic or purely symbolic relationship with their grandchildren.
- ***Companionate:*** Grandparents had an easygoing, friendly style of interaction with their grandchildren.
- ***Involved:*** Grandparents took an active role in rearing their grandchildren, exerted substantial authority, and imposed definite and sometimes demanding expectations.

These three styles correspond roughly to Neugarten and Weinstein's grandparenting styles of distant figure, fun seeker, and surrogate parent. However, Cherlin and Furstenberg's analysis takes into account the dynamic quality of such relationships. They found that grandparent–grandchild relationships can change over time. For example, grandparents may have a fun-seeking relationship with young grandchildren, but when the children reach adolescence, the time spent together may decrease dramatically. Years later the relationship may change again with the arrival of great-grandchildren. Also, the same grandparent may exhibit different grandparenting styles with different grandchildren. For example, a grandparent may have a close companionate role with one grandchild and a remote relationship with another. Numerous factors influence the kind of relationship grandparents have with their grandchildren: age and employment status of grandparents, physical proximity, economic

One of the roles grandparents can fill is that of a family historian. Here Chinese grandparents share family photos with their granddaughter.

need, relationships between the grandparents and their adult children, number and ages of grandchildren, birth order, gender, and personality differences.

Benefits and Conflicts

The grandparent role has the potential to benefit all three generations. One researcher, for example, discussed several contributions that the presence of grandchildren can make in a person's life. Grandchildren contribute to a sense of immortality, that something of the grandparent will continue after death. Playing the role of teacher, family historian, and resource person enhances the self-esteem of grandparents. Grandparents can take pride in the achievements of their grandchildren and boast about them to friends. Through social contact with grandchildren, grandparents can keep up-to-date on cultural and social changes. Finally, older grandchildren can provide assistance to grandparents—shopping, lawn care, errand running, and household chores (Barranti, 1985).

In exchange, grandparents can provide grandchildren with love and guidance minus the intensity, responsibility, and tension that frequently exist in parent–child relationships. Grandparents can give children a sense of continuity, identity, belonging, and values as they share with the children stories about the family's history. In so doing they often can help younger people understand their parents, and they frequently act as mediators between the two generations. Additionally, grandparents can be role models of successful aging for both their adult children and grandchildren. Finally, the parent generation can benefit by having someone they can trust assist them in their parenting role and, if necessary, act as surrogate parents in time of need. In this latter regard grandmothers have played a key role in the lives of adolescent mothers, especially in aiding them in the care of their infants during the early months of the infant's life (Flaherty, Facteau, and Garver, 1991; Harvey, 1993). In their study of inner-city unwed adolescent mothers, Nancy Apfel and Victoria Seitz (1991) found that the presence of grandmothers often had a stabilizing effect on both the young mothers and their children.

Such benefits, however, can also produce tension and conflict. Parents and grandparents may disagree about child-rearing strategies. Parents may resent what they perceive as grandparental interference or be jealous of the child's affection for the grandparent. Older grandchildren may become preoccupied with their own lives and forget to call or visit grandparents. As a result, grandparents often feel hurt and ignored. These problems notwithstanding, much of the research on grandparenthood shows that both grandparents and grandchildren tend to be satisfied with their relationships.

The research also indicates that there was more contact with maternal grandparents and that the maternal grandmother was consistently listed as the grandparent to whom grandchildren felt closest (Matthews and Sprey, 1985). One factor that contributes to this pattern is the number of parental divorces. As we saw in Chapter 12, mothers are more likely to have sole custody of children than fathers, and many fathers lose contact with their children following a divorce. Under such conditions it is not surprising to find grandchildren losing contact with paternal grandparents. This pattern, however, may be a function of the timing of the divorce and the age of the grandchildren. Teresa Cooney and Lori Smith (1996) found that recent parental divorce was not associated with levels of affective, functional, or associational solidarity between adult grandchildren and grandparents. The issue of custody is not a factor with adult children, and they are more able than younger children to manage relations with their grandparents on their own; they no longer need the mediating role of their parents.

Not only do elderly people help in the care of their own grandchildren, but many, like this reading volunteer at the Stride Rite Intergenerational Day Care Center, play an active role in the lives of other children.

In the past and to a great extent today, helping and caring for grandchildren are more traditionally associated with grandmothers, and research suggests that grandmothers tend to be more satisfied with the grandparenting role than grandfathers are (Thomas, 1986). Sarah Cunningham-Burley (1987), however, found that some grandfathers attach great importance to the grandfather role, seeing it as an opportunity to experience the contact with babies and young children that they missed out on with their own children. Given that increasing numbers of today's fathers are more involved in child care than in the past, men might in the future become more involved in the grandparenting role.

Race and ethnicity also play a role in the degree of involvement in the grandparent role. Some research suggests that African Americans, Asian Americans, Italian Americans, and Latinas/os are more likely to be involved in the lives of their grandchildren than are other groups (Cavanaugh,

1993). The apparent greater involvement of ethnic grandparents may be a result of the greater extended kin network among these groups. For example, in a study of 48 African American and 51 white grandfathers aged 65 and older, Vira Kivitt (1991) found that the grandfather role was more central in the lives of African American men than it was for white men.

A high level of grandparent support has been found among Native Americans. Grandparents often ask their children to allow the grandchildren to live with them for a period of time so that they can teach their grandchildren about the Native American way of life (Weibel-Orlando, 1990). In particular, grandfathers are active in transmitting a knowledge of tribal history and cultural practices through storytelling (Woods, 1996). However, there is concern that the role of the elderly in Native American families is being eroded by high poverty rates and diminished social resources (Yellowbird and Snipp, 1994).

Unplanned Parenting Many grandparents routinely provide child-care services for their grandchildren, but in a growing number of cases, grandparents have assumed sole responsibility for their grandchildren. In effect, they become surrogate parents. Data from the 2000 census show more than 4.5 million children living in 2.4 million grandparent-headed households. Grandparent-headed households have grown 105 percent since 1970 (Hudnall, 2001). If informal living arrangements with grandparents were included, the figure would be considerably higher. Grandparent-headed households cut across all races and ethnic groups. In 1997, 48 percent were white, 31 percent black, and 16 percent Latina/o (Bryson and Casper, 1999). Grandparents are increasingly taking on this parental role as a direct result of the incapacity of the middle generation to care for their children because of parental unemployment, poverty, disease, substance abuse, AIDS, incarceration, or the aftermath of a divorce.

Unplanned parenting produces both positive and negative outcomes for the caregivers. In one study of 114 grandparents who provided daily care to their grandchildren, nearly two-thirds of the custodial grandparents reported that caring for their grandchildren provided more of a purpose in their lives and kept them young, active, and "in shape" (Jendrek, 1996). Nevertheless, the assumption of such responsibility is emotionally and financially exhausting for many grandparents. In some cases, the grandparents must abandon or fight their own children to provide their grandchildren with a healthy and stable environment. Keeping up with young grandchildren can be physically exhausting. Retired grandparents on a fixed income may find their household budget severely strained by the unexpected expense of children. According to an American Association of Retired Persons study, more than 50 percent of grandparents caring for their grandchildren have incomes less than $20,000 and more than 25 percent live at or below the federal poverty level (Little, 1995). In addition, the reality of unplanned parenting can be psychologically difficult to accept. The dreams these older couples have for spending time together, taking vacations, and pursuing other interests may be lost forever. Custodial grandparents may also experience profound changes in their friendship networks as their lifestyle is altered to fit the needs of children, babysitters, and finances. As one grandmother, who has been living with a grandchild for about 8 years, said:

> In our age bracket most of our friends don't have (young) children and as a result a lot of times we don't accept invitations to go because our children (the grandchildren) are not invited. . . . Most of the time it doesn't bother me. . . . Our close friends are still the same. We don't see them as often. (Quoted in Jendrek, 1996:299)

Although more communities are establishing programs to help these surrogate parents, many of these programs are underfunded, inadequately staffed, and are able to provide only minimal services. Additionally, some states deny benefits from Aid to Families with Dependent Children, the state welfare program, to any nonparent, even though grandparents should be eligible. Over the last several years support groups like Grandparents as Parents, Grandparents Raising Grandchildren, and Grandparents United for Children's Rights have been formed to assist these families.

Great-Grandparenthood

Now that four-generation families have become more common, a few researchers are beginning to examine the meaning of the great-grandparent role in later-life families. A study of great-grandparents found that the majority expressed positive feelings about the experience (Doka and Mertz, 1988; Barer, 2001). They reported a renewed zeal for life and expressed satisfaction at the continuance of their families. Despite these positive reactions, most of the respondents reported having only a remote relationship with their great-grandchildren, interacting with them on a limited and mostly ritualistic basis.

The reasons for this kind of interaction pattern are not entirely clear. A partial explanation may be that because this is a new phenomenon, few cultural norms exist to guide individual behavior in these relationships. Additionally, the geographic dispersion of family members contributes to a physical and emotional distance between the youngest and oldest generations. As some great-grandmothers reported, "I got some but I don't know the names of them." "They tell me I do have some greats, I ain't never seen them." "I got pictures but I haven't seen none of them" (quoted in Barer, 2001). There is some indication, however, that at least among women of color, the great-grandparenting role is much the same as the grandparenting role; that is, it is simply a natural progression from that role (Scott, 1991). Further research is needed to study the costs and benefits of such relationships.

THE CHILD-FREE ELDERLY

Perhaps sometime in your life someone suggested to you that you should marry and have children so that you will have someone to take care of you when you get old. Although the majority of today's elderly have surviving children, a substantial minority have none. In 1990, 25 percent of white women and 33 percent of black women aged 85 and older either never had children or had children who had already died (Himes, 1992). They have no "natural" support system of adult children to rely on in old age. Are they then without potential caregivers, as folk wisdom would have us believe?

An examination of a national sample concluded that being child-free was a predictor of social isolation in later life. Compared with elderly parents, the child-free elderly had fewer social contacts. This was particularly true for those experiencing health problems (Bachrach, 1980). When marital status was controlled, however, an interesting pattern emerged. The unmarried child-free elderly interact more frequently with friends and neighbors than do the married child-free elderly. Some researchers believe that this finding reflects the tendency of married couples to rely more on each other, thus limiting other social relationships (Johnson and Catalano, 1981).

In contrast, the unmarried elderly realize that they may need help at some point in their lives and actively create a support network for themselves. For example, Robert Rubinstein and his colleagues (1991) interviewed 31 never-married child-free women 60 years of age and older and found that they consciously developed strategies to overcome the cultural emphasis on "blood ties." Not only did these women cultivate relationships with existing kin (nieces, nephews, and siblings) but they also constructed ties, often becoming fictive kin, interacting in ways traditionally associated with those who are related by birth. Many of our families include people we call "aunt" or "uncle" who are not formally related to us. These relationships are characterized by strong affective bonds and shared activities. Rubinstein's respondents described key friendships with other women as being "sisterlike." Although research on the role of friends in later life is just beginning, some preliminary findings show that these relationships serve as important sources of support (Chappell, 1991).

Despite the fact that unmarried elderly people are resourceful and have a fairly large social network, child-free elderly women have a greater chance of becoming institutionalized than do other categories of elderly (Cantor and Little, 1985). These women are often older and in poorer health than other elderly and thus require more care. Social programs need to take account of the fact that the child-free elderly are at greater risk of being without support than are the elderly with children. In the near future, as the parents of the baby boom generation enter the ranks of the oldest age group, the percentage being child-free will be less than in 1990. However, a higher percentage of their children will be child-free. As we saw in Chapter 9, 19 percent of women aged 40 to 44 were child-free and will likely remain so. Additionally, unlike today's elderly, who preceded the period of high divorce rates, today's middle-aged population has an increasing number of stepchildren (Dortch, 1995). Whether these stepchildren will be as likely as biological children to assume care for the elderly is as yet unknown although, as we noted earlier, initial research on this population suggests that they won't (Pezzin and Schone, 1999). Since remarried men are more likely than women to live with stepchildren than with biological children, men are seen as more at risk in this regard. Hence, in the middle decades of the twenty-first century, the proportion of older people who will need to rely on institutional programs for support is likely to increase.

SIBLING RELATIONSHIPS

The social relationships of the elderly are not restricted to the younger generations. Recent research on the elderly has pointed to the importance of siblings in later-life families. Sibling relationships are particularly valuable to the elderly for two reasons. First, elderly siblings share a similar family history. Second, the relationship is potentially the longest-lasting one an individual will ever have, covering as it does the entire life course. Thus, siblings can help each other fill important needs in later life. They can reminisce about the past, be social companions, and provide emotional and other support during times of stress (Connidis, 1994). Additionally, because of their prior experiences, older siblings can serve as role models for resolving the developmental tasks of later life (Scott, 1990).

Upward of 70 percent to 80 percent of all elderly adults have at least one living sibling (Shanas, 1980; McGhee, 1985). Researchers have consistently found that contact with siblings in later life is strongly related to feelings of social and psychological well-being. This seems to be particularly true of siblings who were close during childhood. During young adulthood and middle age they may have had only limited contact because of the demands of their own families. As people age, however, they often renew or increase social contacts. Sister–sister relationships seem to be particularly important as support systems in later life (Scott, 1990). Even though much is made of sibling rivalry during childhood, researchers have found more limited conflicts in old age (Schmeeckle, Giarrusso, and Bengtson, 1994). For example, a Canadian study found five types of sibling relationships among respondents: intimate (17 percent), congenial (28 percent), loyal (35 percent), apathetic (10 percent), and hostile (10 percent). The available evidence suggests that developing positive relationships with siblings in earlier years can be a good investment for the later years.

Siblings are likely to be a good source of support for some elderly well into the twenty-first century. This may not be the case for the elderly who follow them, however. Over the last several decades life expectancy has increased and birth rates have decreased. Thus, families are becoming vertical in structure in that they cut across more generational lines but have fewer siblings and other age peers within each generation (Hagestad, 1986; Bengtson and Dannefer, 1987).

HEALTH AND ILLNESS

A common fear about growing old is the loss of health and independence. Although health problems increase with age, the health status of today's elderly is varied and not as negative as is popularly portrayed. In 1999, 74 percent of older persons assessed their health as good or excellent. Only 26 percent rated their health as fair or poor. However, older African Americans (42 percent) and older Latinas/os (35 percent) were much more likely to describe their health as fair or poor than were older whites (26 percent) (Administration on Aging, 2001). Although self-ratings of health are subjective, they have been correlated with mortality. That is, older people who describe their health as poor are more likely to die within the next 5 years than are those who report their health as good (Kaplan, Barell, and Lusky, 1988). Research on Japanese elderly confirmed that self-rated health is a powerful predictor of mortality (Sugisawa, Liang, and Liu, 1994). Thus, these self-ratings reflect with some accuracy an individual's overall health status.

Longitudinal research that followed respondents for 60 years found that younger people can exert substantial control over their eventual physical and mental health after age 65. Those subjects who developed good health habits relatively early in life, such as regular exercise, a healthy diet, flexible coping styles, and social involvement, were healthier and happier in their later years than those subjects who had not developed such habits (Bower, 2001). Today's elderly are healthier than previous generations. Nevertheless, physical changes are a natural and inevitable part of aging and may lead to chronic conditions, long-term illnesses that are rarely cured, such as diabetes, arthritis, and heart disease. Limitations on activities because of chronic conditions increase with age. In 1998, 28 percent of 65- to 74-year-olds reported a limitation caused by a chronic condition compared to almost 51 percent of people 75 years and over (Administration on Aging, 2001).

Chronic conditions, illness, and injury can impact mental health and lead to depression. In 1998, about 15 percent of persons aged 65 to 79 had severe symptoms of depression (deep feelings of sadness and worthlessness, loss of appetite and energy, difficulty in concentrating) compared with 21 percent of persons aged 80 to 84 and 23 percent of persons aged 85 or older. Although people of all ages forget words or appointments at times, forgetfulness is more common among the elderly. In 1998, the percentage of older adults with moderate or severe memory impairment ranged from about 4 percent among persons aged 65 to 69 to about 36 percent among persons aged 85 or older ("Older Americans 2000 . . . ," 2000).

A fear that many people have about growing old is the possibility that they may get Alzheimer's disease, a progressive, degenerative disease of the brain and the most common form of dementia. Approximately 10 percent of persons over 65 and nearly half of those over 85 have Alzheimer's disease; also a small percentage of people in their 30s and 40s develop the disease. A person with Alzheimer's lives an average of 8 years and as many as 20 years or more from the onset of symptoms (Alzheimer's Association, 2000). Although there is as yet no cure for this disease, research on a number of medications and treatments offers the hope that there may be a way to prevent or at least delay its onset.

FAMILY CAREGIVING

As we have seen, at any given time only a minority of elderly need assistance in their daily activities. However, the projected 88 percent increase in the number of people over age 85 within the next decade or two means that increasing numbers of families will face the challenge of providing caregiving to their oldest members (Huyck, 2001). According to a 2000 survey by the National Family Caregivers Association (NFCA), in 1999 approximately 27 percent of the adult population (54 million people) provided some care for an elderly, disabled, or chronically ill relative or friend.

Caregiving may be more prevalent among families of color, with Asian American families (42 percent) having the highest rate, followed by African American families (28 percent) and Latina/o families (34 percent); white families with 19 percent appear to have the lowest rate (American Association for Retired Persons, 2001). Cultural norms emphasizing care and respect for the elderly, as well as differences in economic resources, help explain these variations. The high rate of care among Asians is consistent with their strong sense of filial responsibility (Kao and Stuifbergern, 1999). Additionally, people of color are more likely than whites to rely on family members rather than formal agencies because of language difficulties, lack of knowledge of available services, and a distrust of these agencies because of a history of discriminatory treatment.

In the United States, as well as around the world, women have traditionally provided the overwhelming majority of informal care for elderly relatives (Stone, Cafferata, and Sangl, 1987; Cattell, 1996). Today, however, as all countries experience an increase in the number of older people, there is a growing recognition of the likelihood of a shortage of female caregivers due to demographic shifts and the increased participation of women in the labor force. Additionally, some African and Asian countries are seeing the caregiving generation being decimated by the AIDS epidemic, leaving the elderly not only to care for themselves but for the younger generation as well (Climo, 2000). Consequently as some analysts point out (see, for example, Brewer, 2001), it is imperative that nations begin to develop strategies that enhance the ability of both women and men to share the responsibility of family caregiving. There are some positive signs that this may already be happening in the United States, at least among older men. One study found that by later middle age, more men were assuming a caregiving role, narrowing the gap somewhat between themselves and women (Marks, 1996). The NFCA survey mentioned earlier provides further support that this is happening, reporting a female/male ratio involved in caregiving more evenly split than in the past, 56 percent female to 44 percent male. Spouses are the first line of defense when illness strikes, followed by adult children. Compared with spouses, however, adult children provide care over a longer period of time (Chappell, 1991).

The Spouse as Caregiver

The longer a couple live together, the more likely that one of the spouses will become ill. When this happens, the healthier spouse generally assumes the caregiver role. Because men have higher rates of morbidity and mortality, wives make up the majority of spousal caregivers. The degree to which this arrangement represents a satisfactory response to a changed living condition depends on the severity of the illness or disability and on the age and health of the spousal caregiver. Although spousal caregivers may have the greatest need for assistance in fulfilling this role, they receive less assistance from family and friends than other caregivers; they are also the least likely of any group of caregivers to use formal services, regardless of the degree of frailty (C. Cox, 1993). Without outside support, spouses can be physically overwhelmed by the demands of caregiving. If there is a need to have someone in attendance at all times, caregivers may find that they have little free time for themselves, with the result that they become isolated from friends. Alfred Fengler and Nancy Goodrich (1979) refer to such caregivers as "hidden patients."

When a spouse becomes ill, the other spouse generally assumes the caregiver role, as this husband is doing for his terminally ill wife.

Sometimes these problems can be overcome by having outside help. Nurses, physical attendants, friends, and relatives may be able to relieve the primary caregiver on a regular basis. Some senior day-care programs have been created to enable the ill spouse to participate in social activities as well as to help the primary caregiver keep going. Although by 1997 there were over 3000 such centers, experts believe that 10,000 centers are needed (Shapiro, 1997). Reactions to the caregiving role vary. Spouses who view caregiving as "reciprocity" for past affection and care experience a higher degree of gratification from their caregiving role than do spouses who view it as a matter of responsibility (Motenko, 1989). Providing care can also enhance the caregiver's sense of self-worth and well-being, especially when other family members share, at least to some degree, in caregiving tasks (Martire, Stephens, and Franks, 1997). Many elderly do not have a spouse to rely on for care, however, and they turn to their children for help.

Adult Children as Caregivers

A study of the sandwich generation (those between the ages of 45 and 55) found that 54 percent cared for children, parents, or both. Twenty-two percent focused their care exclusively on a parent or in-law (American Association for Retired Persons, 2001). Adult child caregiving is especially pronounced in families of color. Adult children comprise about 75 percent of caregivers in African American and Latina/o families, compared to 40 to 60 percent in white families (Montgomery, 1996). Among the primary forms of assistance are emotional support, financial aid, help with instrumental activities (transportation, meal preparation, shopping, housework), personal care (bathing, feeding, dressing), and mediating with agencies to obtain services. All children are not equally likely to assume this role. The degree of filial responsibility is related to proximity (the child living closest to the parent frequently assumes this responsibility) and gender.

A wide range of studies has consistently shown that across all racial and ethnic groups the role of caretaker is most frequently filled by daughters (Dwyer and Coward, 1991; Estes, Swan, and Associates, 1993). However, as we have seen earlier, the gendered nature of caregiving is beginning to change. In fact, some social scientists have questioned the true extent of previously observed gender differences (Bengtson, Rosenthal, and Burton, 1996). Several factors may render men invisible in the caregiving role. First, although studies have found gender differences, they are often quite small (Miller and Cafasso, 1992). Second, the studies of caregiving tend to focus on tasks more characteristically performed by women, such as personal care, and to discount tasks done by men, such as financial or home repair and maintenance activities (Coward, 1987). A study of adult siblings by Sarah Matthews (1995) found that brothers' actual contributions tended to be considered unimportant by both sisters and brothers. Third, demographic factors such as the longer life expectancy of women combined with a preference for personal care to be provided by a person of the same sex results in a high number of adult daughter/widowed mother caregiving relationships (Horowitz, 1992). However, a more recent study found that men were taking a more active role in performing caregiving tasks such as managing medications, changing dressings, and monitoring vital signs (National Family Caregivers Association, 2000).

Additionally, the kind of help that caregivers provide is often mediated by social class. Middle-class adult children provide more emotional support and financial aid, often assuming a "care manager" role whereby they identify needed services, help obtain them, and then supervise their delivery. Children from lower socioeconomic classes are more likely to provide the direct care themselves (Archbold, 1983; Rosenthal, 1986). Providing care is often made more difficult because of the geographic mobility of the population. Nearly 7 million Americans are long-distance caregivers for an older relative who travel a distance of one or more hours to assist in some phase of caregiving (Wagner, 1997). This factor can add stress to the process of caregiving.

The Stresses of Caregiving Although most children willingly help their parents when the need arises and express satisfaction in doing so, parental care can be stressful. Caring for an elderly relative can lead to financial hardship and can also jeopardize the caregiver's own health. The most severe consequences, however, tend to be the psychological and emotional stress that comes from seeing formerly strong and independent parents become dependent as well as from the restrictions on the caregiver's time and freedom (see the "Strengthening Marriages and Families" box).

The time demands of caring for an adult parent compete with other responsibilities and may result in conflict, particularly with regard to employment. An estimated 14.4 million full- and part-time workers are balancing caregiving and job responsibilities (Metropolitan Life Insurance Company, 1997). According to one study, providing 10 or more hours of care per week to a nonresident parent reduces a daughter's formal work by 65 hours during an 18-week period. This escalates to a reduction of 130 hours if the parent resides with her (Schenck-Yglesias, 1995). Other caregivers leave the work force entirely. Reduced employment not only diminishes current family income, but it also lowers pension benefits, which in turn contributes to the financial difficulties of many women in later life (O'Grady-LeShane, 1993). The direct caregiver is not the only one affected by the pattern of caregiving. The family's lifestyle may be disrupted. Recreational activities and vacations may have to be postponed. If the elderly person is living with the caregiver's family, lack of privacy may become a problem. If spouses and other family members are supportive, however, the intensity of these strains is lessened.

If, however, the strains become too great, caretakers or their families may resort to extreme behavior, for example, elder abuse (see Chapter 11) or abandoning the elderly relative at hospital emergency rooms. Emergency room workers refer to this phenomenon as "granny dumping." An informal survey by the American College of Emergency Physicians drew 169 responses from emergency rooms across the country, reporting an average of eight abandonments a week. The problem has been observed most often in states with larger proportions of retired people—Florida, California, and Texas ("Elderly Abandoned," 1991). Such behavior underscores the need for more outpatient and in-home services to help families cope with the demands of caring for an elderly relative. Expending public funds in this area would be a good investment. Nearly 80 percent of caregiving costs for disabled older adults at home are attributed to unpaid labor by family members (Harrow, Tennestedt, and McKinlay, 1995). For example, the value of unpaid caregiving for someone with Alzheimer's disease is about $31,000 to $35,000 per year (Max, Webber, and Fox, 1995). According to one estimate, if the work of caregivers had to be replaced by paid home care staff, it would cost between $45 billion and $94 billion per year ("Family Caregiving," 2001).

Certain situations arise, however, when regardless of the desires of the family, the ill spouse or parent can no longer be cared for at home. Institutionalization may be necessary in these circumstances. If this is to be done with a minimum of dislocation, both socially and psychologically, family, friends, and professionals must play a supportive role in the process.

THE EXPERIENCE OF WIDOWHOOD

In Chapter 15 we will discuss issues related to death and dying. In this chapter we examine the many adjustments that are required in the transition from marital to widowed status. Not only have the widowed lost their main source of support, but they often find that their entire social network is disrupted to some degree. Social life may be curtailed as in-laws and friends brought into the relationship by the deceased spouse gradually grow distant. For example, in her classic study of widowhood, Helen Lopata (1973) found that only 25 percent of the respondents saw their husbands' families on a regular basis. Additionally, both widows and widowers may feel uncomfortable in social settings dominated by couples. Widows in particular may be perceived as a potential threat to friends' marriages.

The role of the widowed itself is problematic. In the United States today there are few norms to guide the newly widowed person. In the past the role was more clearly defined. There were rules about appropriate length of time for mourning, dress, behavior, and, in some cases, guidelines for when and if remarriage could occur. Such guidelines are still available for some ethnic groups today.

Stages of Widowhood

Robert DiGiulio (1989), a widower himself, described four stages that widowed people experience. He emphasized the active processes of growing through widowhood (stages 1 and 2) and growing beyond widowhood (stages 3 and 4).

STRENGTHENING MARRIAGES AND FAMILIES

Talks with Family Therapist Joan Zientek

COPING WITH THE CAREGIVING ROLE

Why Is Caring for an Elderly Parent Such a Difficult Role?

Caring for an elderly disabled family member places great strain on the family system, whether the caregiver is the other spouse or an adult child. According to the National Family Caregivers Association, nearly one-half of all caregivers experience prolonged depression, and two-thirds feel frustrated on a regular basis. Other strong emotions emerge as well when there is a major shift in the family structure: The adult child now becomes the parent's parent and the parent slips into a childlike role of dependency. Conflict can emerge out of this role reversal, concerning whose needs will be met first. Frequently, there isn't enough time and energy to meet everyone's needs. There is often confusion about boundaries (What can Mom actually do for herself? With what tasks does she need assistance?) and struggles over difficult decisions that need to be made (Is it time for Dad to sell his house and enter an assisted-living arrangement? Who will handle Dad's finances?). As adult children struggle to sort out the answers to questions like these, the old issues rear their heads: Why do I get stuck with all the work when Mom likes him (possibly a younger sibling) better than me? Or Dad never did approve of my husband or my career; nothing I ever did was right, and now I am expected to care for him! All these feelings and confusions get buried because they are often too painful to face; yet they emerge as anger, shouting at siblings, brusqueness with parents, or fiery conversations with doctors. With all of this going on, there seem to be so precious few moments for renegotiating the bond with the most profound and influential attachments of our lives, our parents.

How Can Families Provide Care for Elderly Members without Becoming Overwhelmed?

The first thing to do is to recognize what is happening and why. Never before have so many elderly persons lived for such extended periods of time. In previous generations, before the birth of the wonders of modern medicine, the elderly did not linger as long, succumbing quickly to cancer, heart attacks, or strokes. This fact, coupled with the complexities and stresses of life today, means that caregivers of the elderly can burn out quite easily. In addition, because of the geographic mobility of some family members and the unwritten norms and expectations that family members have for one another, the caregiving all too frequently falls to just the spouse or to just one of the children, the one who is unmarried or who lives closer to the care recipient than other family members. To prevent burnout and resentment, it is essential that all family members communicate openly with one another, plan and cooperate in the caregiving, and provide periodic breaks for each caregiver, as well as set realistic expectations of what can and should be done. In many cases the family by itself cannot provide all of the care that is needed for one of its aging members. Family members need to make themselves aware of the many elder care agencies and referral services now available. Generally, when a health care crisis arises, the medical personnel of the hospital, particularly the social worker, can be most helpful in putting the family in touch with the community resources that are available. Caregiver support groups can also lessen the strains and tensions involved in ongoing caregiving.

Each stage describes in vivid terms the wide range of emotions experienced by the widowed as they first deal with their spouse's death and then gradually reconstruct a life for themselves. The stages and their characteristics are

1. ***Encounter:*** In this stage, which generally lasts from 3 months to 1 year, people may experience depression, shock, rage, loss of appetite, insomnia, and frequent crying. Initial reactions to the death include confusion, panic, and emotional numbness. Some widowed people become obsessed with the deceased spouse, seeking her or his presence by visiting places they frequented together or using her or his personal belongings.

2. ***Respondence:*** Although some of the emotional reactions of the first stage continue, there is a recognition of the reality of the spouse's death. This can be a very painful time, as the widowed now confront their unmet needs for attachment, nurturance, and reassurance. They may experience an intense loneliness that they believe can be relieved only by the deceased spouse. The widowed frequently sanctify or idealize the deceased spouse, and they frequently ask, "Why did this happen to me?" Gradually, however, the widowed begin to reach out and may join support groups or begin new relationships.

3. ***Emergence:*** Over time the widowed come to realize that death is a natural outcome of life and that although they have lost someone they loved, they can move on with their lives. This moving on requires them to acknowledge their new identity as single, unmarried people and to focus on the present and the future rather than reliving the past.

4. ***Transformation:*** This stage represents a departure from and movement beyond widowhood. The grief work is over. As a

result of having survived bereavement and grief, many widowed see themselves as changed people, as having grown from their experience. They have put their past in perspective and created a new life for themselves.

According to DiGiulio, the stages of widowhood are complex. Some people move through them quickly; others become stuck at one stage and never move to emergence or transformation; still others regress to an earlier stage. The reasons for these different reactions are varied. Those whose marital relationships were particularly close may feel the loss more keenly than those with a more distant relationship. Socioeconomic status also plays a role. Those with greater personal resources, such as income, education, hobbies, and membership in formal and informal organizations, typically make better long-term adjustments to widowhood. For those with fewer personal resources, the degree of integration within a group can be an important factor in adjustment. This can be seen in some ethnic groups, which provide a definitive role for the widowed in the kin and community network (Gelfand and Barresi, 1987). Because of strong kin support African Americans, Mexican Americans, and Asian Americans seem to adjust to widowhood more easily than their white counterparts do (Pitcher and Larson, 1989).

Finally, when death is expected, the period of adjustment may pass more quickly than when death is sudden. Anticipating widowhood and discussing key issues with a spouse before death occurs can facilitate successful adjustment. Robert Hansson and Jacqueline Remondet (1987) studied 75 widows ages 60 to 90 and found that those who were more successful in resolving their grief and getting on with their lives had discussed with their spouse finances, family reactions, their own feelings, and how their lives might change as a result of the spouse's death. Although such discussions often are initiated only at the time of a terminal illness, all couples could benefit by an annual review of family finances, wills, and contingency plans in case of illness or death.

Gender Differences in Widowhood

As Figure 14.5 shows, widowhood is largely a female experience. Among women age 65 and over, 45 percent of whites, 54 percent of African Americans, and 42 percent of Latinas are widowed. In contrast, the rates for men in the same age category are 14 percent of whites, 25 percent of African Americans, and 14 percent of Latinos. Although the probability of widowhood increases with age, among the population age 75 to 84, women are two to three times more likely to be widowed than men. Similar gender differences have been found among both Native Americans and Asian Americans. James Sweet and Larry Bumpass (1987:303) analyzed 1980 census data and found that only 28 percent of Native American men but 70 percent of Native American women aged 75 to 84 were widowed. The rates for Asian American men were 19 percent for both Japanese and Filipinos and 20 percent for Chinese. Filipino women were slightly less likely

Figure 14.5

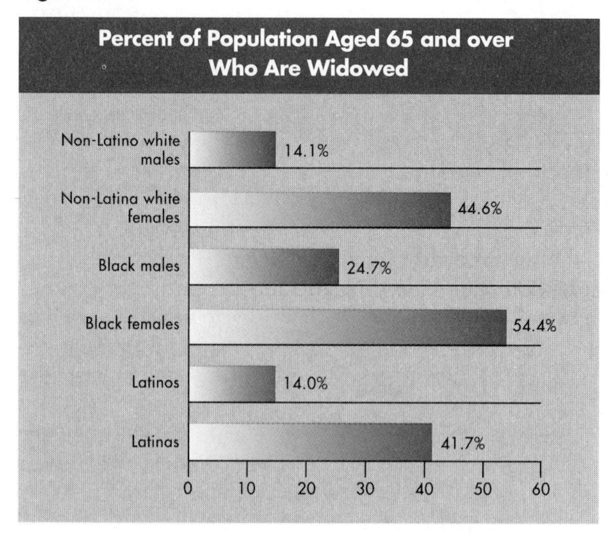

Source: Adapted from "Marital Status and Living Arrangements: March 1998," in U.S. Census Bureau, *Current Population Reports*, Series P-20-514 (Washington, DC: U.S. Government Printing Office) (update) **http://www.census.gov/prod/99pubs/p20-514u.pdf**

to be widowed (64 percent) than either Chinese women (74 percent) or Japanese women (75 percent). Although widowhood represents a major role change for both women and men, researchers have found some gender differences in how women and men experience widowhood.

Special Problems of Widows In addition to the adjustments associated with bereavement and grief, widows are likely to confront two major problems: changes in their self-identity and changes in their financial situation. For many women, especially those who are tradition-oriented, the experience of widowhood undermines the basis of their self-identity. The loss of the central role as wife may be psychologically devastating, and a widow may try to maintain her identity as "Mrs. John Smith" in her social and business interactions. Because there are few eligible men in their age category, it may be difficult for widows to recapture the wife role. Statistically, widows have less chance of remarrying than do widowers.

For other women, however, the role of wife is less central to their identity. These women place more emphasis on other roles such as mother, worker, or friend. Thus, they are less interested in preserving the wife role and more interested in being accepted in their own right. Some of these women find, however, that they must negotiate this new role with family and friends who still relate to them as "Mrs. John Smith" (Atchley, 1991).

Widows generally face a bleaker financial future than widowers do. Findings from a national sample of widows of all ages contradict the popular media portrayal of the "merry widow" grown prosperous as a result of a fat insurance policy. Instead, widowhood has a significant negative financial impact on women. The average living standard of widows dropped 18 percent following a husband's death. In addition, 10 percent of women whose income was above the poverty line prior to widowhood were pushed into poverty (Bound et al., 1991). Other researchers put the figure much higher. One study, for example, found that the average increase in poverty after widowhood was 30 percent, mostly attributable to a permanent decline in nonwage income, especially social security (cited in Logue, 1991:664). Although widowhood can cause financial distress for all women, women of color are particularly hard hit—36 percent of African American widows and 25 percent of Latinas over 65 are poor, compared with 13 percent of white widows (U.S. Census Bureau, 1987).

Inadequate income adversely affects the quality of life of the widowed. Widows with little money cannot afford to be active socially, which in turn increases their feelings of loneliness. Even widows with adequate income may experience problems related to finances. In many marriages husbands control the family finances, not wanting to bother their wives with these matters. Thus, some women have no knowledge of their family's financial status, nor do they acquire the necessary financial skills to cope with the routine tasks of handling insurance premiums and claims, balancing a checkbook, paying bills, and making a budget. Having to learn to deal with these matters during their time of mourning may heighten their levels of anxiety and frustration and lower their self-esteem.

Special Problems of Widowers Widowers, too, face several problems related to traditional roles. Earlier studies like those conducted by Felix Berado (1968, 1970) concluded that many older widowers are ill-prepared to deal with day-to-day domestic matters like cooking, cleaning, and laundry. One writer has referred to this as "the dialectical nature of gender relations," indicating that although men may benefit from women performing these tasks for them earlier in life, they may suffer from their lack of such skills when they are alone (Calasanti, 1999). As husbands come to share more of the household tasks with their wives, these problems are likely to be minimized.

In the social realm, widowers often experience a double bind. Not only do they lose their major source of intimacy but they also find it more difficult than widows to move in with their children and to find a useful place there. Researchers have found that compared with widows, widowers have fewer contacts with their families and receive less social support from them following the death of their spouse (Hooyman and Kiyak, 1993). This may be a continuation of a pattern begun years ago. In many marriages the wife is the primary initiator of family contacts; her death leaves a void in this area, lessening the interactions the widower is likely to have. Similarly, DiGiulio (1989) observed that women's support networks prior to and immediately following the death of their spouse were richer than men's. This pattern does not, however, appear to be true for African American men, who maintain contact with friends about equally as frequently as their female counterparts (Taylor, Keith, and Tucker, 1993).

Earlier research found that widowers experience higher rates of mental illness and depression than widows do (Gove, 1972) and that widowers have higher rates of death and suicide than widows during the first year following the death of their spouse (Walsh, 1980; Smith, Mercy, and Conn, 1988). More recent studies, however, suggest that there are growing similarities between the experiences of widows and widowers (Bengtson, Rosenthal, and Burton, 1990).

In sum, widowhood is a difficult stage for both women and men. There is increasing evidence, however, that a successful transition to widowhood depends on the variety of roles that make up a person's self-identity. People whose identities are multifaceted—who are involved in several activities and relationships—appear to cope better. They are less likely to become depressed or ill than are people with a more limited set of roles (DiGiulio, 1989).

Beyond Widowhood

Thus far we have discussed the traumatic aspects of widowhood. However, in the wake of widowhood there can be positive role changes as well. After the period of mourning and grief subsides, those who cared for an ill spouse may feel a sense of relief and freedom. For many people, widowhood may provide an opportunity for a reunion with friends or for making new friends. During marriage, family responsibilities often prevent people from participating in other activities. Many widowed people use their new time to return to school, take up a hobby, do volunteer work, travel, and in some cases remarry. Phyllis Silverman (1988) compared widows and widowers and found that in this phase both make changes in their lives, albeit in different directions. Women's changes tend to be more internal. The experience of coping with widowhood leads them to be more self-confident, assertive, independent, and willing to satisfy their own needs. Men, on the other hand, focus more externally, becoming more aware and appreciative of their friends and relationships. Nevertheless, both women and men are able to build satisfying new lives. For example, an Ohio State University study found that women widowed an average of 12 years were as satisfied and optimistic about their lives as were married women in the same age group (*Modern Maturity*, 1992–93).

Lesbian and Gay Elderly

As we have seen, like the general population, considerable diversity exists among elderly persons, including differences in sexual orientation. Researchers estimate that roughly 1 to 3 million Americans 65 or older are lesbian, gay, bisexual, or transgender (LGBT) and that by 2020 their numbers will grow to approximately 4 million (Roach, 2001). Until recently, their presence, especially among the oldest old, was largely invisible and, thus, their special needs ignored. Their

WRITING YOUR OWN SCRIPT

THINKING ABOUT LATER LIFE

Have you ever looked in the mirror and wondered what it would be like to be old? For most young people this is difficult to do. Old age seems such a long way off. Although most of us have a good chance of living into our 70s, 80s, and even 90s, many of us do not plan very well for this stage of our life. According to a recent Gallup poll of Americans over 30 who are not yet retired, few have drawn up a financial plan, and 31 percent saved nothing in the previous year (Moore and Saad, 1995). One way to begin thinking about the experience of aging is to examine our current intergenerational relationships. It may be useful to discuss some of the following questions with elderly family members.

Questions to Consider

1. How many generations are in your kinship structure? Are your parents, grandparents, great-grandparents still living? How healthy are they? How often do you see them? Do family members live in close proximity to one another? What kinds of services, if any, are exchanged by family members? In which generational direction do they flow? Are the patterns in your family typical of those for most later-life families? How satisfied do you think the oldest members of your family are with the quality of their lives?
2. Are your parents or grandparents retired? How well are they managing economically? Did they have a financial plan for their retirement in place before they retired? What are the sources of their income?
3. What are your later-life goals? What age do you see as a desirable age to retire? What can you begin to do now that will contribute to your reaching your goals?

invisibility is due, in large part, to generational differences. Today's LGBT elderly lived through McCarthyism and came of age before lesbian and gay rights were widely recognized. Fearing discrimination, many were reluctant to reveal their sexual orientation or to participate in LGBT organizations. Although only limited research is available on this population, what does exist suggests that older LGBT adults are satisfied with their lives and express the same kinds of concerns about aging voiced by their heterosexual peers (Cahill, South, and Spade, 2000). However, LGBT elderly confront additional problems not generally experienced by heterosexual elderly. For example, when a heterosexual spouse dies, the widow(er) receives Social Security survivor benefits, but a surviving lesbian or gay partner receives none. As noted in Chapter 7, without careful estate planning or health directives, the death or disability of an unmarried partner may leave the other partner without legal protection regarding property inheritance or other benefits or without power to make medical decisions for their loved one. Medicaid regulations protect the assets and homes of married spouses but not those of same-sex partners.

Although many older LGBT adults have close ties to their families, some have little or no contact or support because of their sexual orientation. LGBT seniors are more likely to live alone, be child-free, and may experience poverty at higher rates than heterosexual seniors. When ill, they may face what Patricia Dunn, public policy director of the San Francisco–based Gay and Lesbian Medical Association, called "homophobia in medicine." Thus, they may feel uncomfortable accessing the system or in raising health care concerns with their doctors and therefore not get the preventive medical care they need (Roach, 2001). Additionally, LGBT elderly sometimes encounter homophopic attitudes among staff and/or residents in retirement communities, assisted-living facilities, and nursing homes.

IMPLICATIONS FOR SOCIAL POLICY

Programs and policies that were successful in the past may not be adequate to meet the needs of the coming generations of elderly and their families. Many of today's elderly became poor after family illness, widowhood, or retirement. However, many of tomorrow's elderly, especially women and children and people of color, are already poor. Thus, unless we provide them with better education, job-training programs, and more extensive pension plans, the number of elderly poor will increase in the coming decades.

As the elderly population increases, greater pressure will be put on the health care system. Yet according to the U.S. Census Bureau (2001b), 14 percent of the population (39 million Americans) were without health insurance coverage in 2000. That figure has increased substantially with the 2001 economic slowdown and the additional loss of jobs following the September 11, 2001, terrorist attack on the United States. If unchanged, this trend will contribute to the creation of two very distinct groups of future elderly: those who are vital and healthy as a result of their access to high-quality health care, and those who are ill or disabled because of their history of inadequate care (Conner, 1992).

Policy analysts argue that to keep health costs down, investments should be directed to preventing illness early on.

Finally, the kinship structure for many families now and in the foreseeable future will contain more elderly than younger members. Therefore, there will likely be a greater need for support models that combine both informal caregiving (family and friends) and formal caregiving (for example, adult day care, visiting nurses, housekeeping services). Social support networks need not go in one direction only, however. The elderly represent a tremendous reservoir of skills and ability. Some public schools and universities have initiated intergenerational partners projects where the elderly serve as tutors and teachers' aides (Aday, Rice, and Evans, 1991). Other elderly serve as "foster" grandparents and as business, craft, and hobby mentors. More elderly could be encouraged to use their talents for the social good either through paid employment or volunteer work.

SUMMARY

Throughout this chapter we have seen how family relationships have been altered by increased life expectancy and changing birth rates, resulting in multigenerational kinship structures. Additionally, social and demographic changes are altering the composition of elderly cohorts. In comparison with older people today, the elderly of the twenty-first century will be more heterogeneous. Future cohorts of the elderly will include a higher proportion of people of color, and more single, divorced, widowed, remarried, and child-free elderly, many of whom will be significantly older than current and past generations of old people.

Although most Americans fear ending their life in a nursing home, only about 5 percent of the elderly are in such institutions. The majority of older people live alone or in a household with their spouse. Elderly women are more likely to live alone, whereas elderly men are more likely to live with their spouse. Elderly of color are more likely to live with their adult children than are white elderly.

Studies of marital satisfaction in later-life families have shown diverse patterns. Some older couples experience higher levels of satisfaction than in the earlier years of their marriage, some show less, and still others show no change. Marital satisfaction is related to patterns of retirement and family income. Poverty remains a serious problem for many, especially widows and people of color. Later-life families are involved in reciprocal exchanges of services across the generations. Spouses and adult children provide the vast majority of care for elderly family members who become ill.

Later-life couples must eventually deal with bereavement and grief. The experience of widowhood requires many adjustments for both women and men.

An understanding of the strengths and the needs of later-life families is critical to social planning for the future. The multigenerational structure of families and the resulting interdependence among generations can provide a model for intergenerational cooperation and interdependence at the societal level.

KEY TERMS

sandwich generation
ageism
social gerontology
age norms
functional age

QUESTIONS FOR STUDY AND REFLECTION

1. Sharon Curtin wrote in her book *Nobody Ever Died of Old Age*, "There is nothing to prepare you for the experience of growing old." Based on your attitudes toward aging and your experiences to date, do you agree or disagree with Curtin? How do your own ethnic and cultural experiences affect your attitudes toward aging? How would you advise today's families to approach the aging of their members?

2. Within the last decade, the world has experienced a number of severe political and social upheavals: terrorist attacks around the world, the growing AIDS epidemic in Africa and Asia, and economic dislocation in Argentina. Pick one of these problem areas and find demographic, economic, and social data to show how it is likely to affect the quality of life of the elderly and their families. Be specific.

3. Which style of grandparenting do you associate with your grandparents? If you become a grandparent, which style do you think you would adopt? What does this tell you about your view of grandparenthood? Should the role of grandparent be expanded? Why or why not? What kinds of problems do grandparents face when they assume the parenting role for their grandchildren? What kinds of resources and supports should society provide for such grandparents?
4. In Chapter 12, we asked whether the idea of a permanent marriage is a realistic option in today's society. In this chapter we noted that 3 percent of all married couples celebrated golden wedding anniversaries. Can you imagine yourself married for 50 or more years? What do you think it takes to stay married that long? The longer people stay married, the more likely they are to experience widowhood. Can or should married couples prepare for this eventuality? Would this make a difference in the way they experience widowhood? What advice would you give to a couple when one spouse is terminally ill? Explain your position.

ADDITIONAL RESOURCES

SOCIOLOGICAL

BURY, MICHAEL, AND ANTHEA HOLME. 1991. *Life after Ninety.* London: Routledge. The authors interviewed almost 200 people age 90 and older, living at home and in institutions. Their findings demonstrate that a good quality of life is often possible even for the oldest of the old.

MARCDANTE, MARY. 2001. *My Mother, My Friend: The Ten Most Important Things to Talk about with Your Mother.* Boston: Fireside/Simon & Schuster. Based on what she learned from over 400 personal interviews, Marcdante offers strategies for breaking down the barriers between mothers and daughters and talking more openly about such important matters as health, money, family secrets, and aging.

PIPHER, MARY. 2000. *Another Country: Navigating the Emotional Terrain of Our Elders.* New York: Riverhead Books. Using the analogy of a foreign country, Pipher provides a compassionate look at some of the generational differences between baby boomers and their parents and grandparents and suggests ways to build and maintain connections across generations.

VAILLANT, GEORGE E. 2002. *Aging Well: Surprising Guideposts to a Happier Life from the Landmark Harvard Study of Adult Development.* Boston: Little, Brown. This analysis of aging based on a Harvard Medical School study that followed 824 people from birth to old age reveals a number of factors that lead to successful physical and emotional aging.

LITERARY

SNOWDON, DAVID. 2001. *Aging with Grace: What the Nun Study Teaches Us about Leading Longer, Healthier, and More Meaningful Lives.* New York: Bantam. A deeply moving personal account of Snowdon's research on a group of elderly nuns offering insight into dementing illnesses like Alzheimer's and providing strategies to minimize the chances of getting them.

TATEMY, LALITA. 2001. *Cane River.* New York: Warner. A fascinating saga of four generations of an African American family in Louisiana.

INTERNET

http://www.nih.gov/nia The National Institute on Aging provides links to caregiving sites as well as helpful publications on topics of aging and health.

http://www.aarp.org The American Association of Retired Persons provides information and resources on a wide variety of topics and activities.

Chapter 15

Marriages and Families in the Twenty-First Century: U.S. and World Trends

IN THE NEWS: NEW YORK AND KABUL, AFGHANISTAN

In two cities, halfway around the world from each other, two families, each with a different language and culture, are united in a common experience. Each family is mourning the unexpected and tragic loss of loved ones due to a terrorist attack on the United States and the subsequent U.S. bombing of terrorist targets in Afghanistan. On the morning of September 11, 2001, Rita Lakar, a New Yorker, had her radio on. So, too, did Amin Said, who had just finished dinner in his home in Kabul, Afghanistan.

On that morning Mrs. Lasar knew that her brother, Abe Zelmanowitz, a computer programmer for Empire Blue Cross and Blue Shield, was in the north tower of the World Trade Center. Although he was on the twenty-seventh floor, and some distance below where the plane hit, he remained in the building and died with hundreds of others when the tower collapsed. Despite phone calls from his brother urging him to leave, Mr. Zelmanowitz chose to wait with his colleague Edward Beyea, a quadriplegic, who needed the help of rescue workers to get down the stairs. The building collapsed before rescue workers could reach them. Two months later, an errant U.S. bomb hit Mr. Said's house in Kabul, killing his brother Iqbal, a tailor, and his sister-in-law Zarlash, a mathematics teacher and poet, just six weeks after their marriage.

Global Exchange, a nonprofit group based in San Francisco, arranged for the members of the two grieving families to meet in Kabul to share memories of their loved ones and to try to find common ground in their sorrow. Mr. Said said he forgave the pilot who dropped the bomb that killed his brother and sister-in-law and that he understood that America was trying to destroy terrorist targets. For her part, Mrs. Lakar said she would like to see the bombing stop, recognizing that her brother, the others killed in the Pentagon and the twin towers, Mr. Said's brother and sister-in-law, and the other Afghan civilians who died in the American bombings were all collateral damage of a terrible conflict that none of them had sought (Landler, 2002).

WHAT WOULD YOU DO? How would you cope with an unexpected and violent death of a loved one precipitated, as in this case, by international terrorism? Would you participate in a program like Global Exchange? Would your attitudes be similar to or different from that of Mrs. Lakar and of Mr. Said? What recommendations would you make for helping people in the United States and in Afghanistan cope with their losses?

According to social scientist Michael J. Strada (1999), today's world is a more colorful place than the one that existed when our parents' and grandparents' generations were coming of age. Not only is today's world shrinking in time and space, but the emerging global milieu features new actors as humans around the world struggle to cope with a wide array of global issues.

Without much doubt, Strada's insights about a global age are on target. Indeed, we are living in a new historical period that some have suggested is replacing the age of modernism that has dominated over the last 500 years. Critical, profound, and sometimes rapid changes have occurred in many places around the world: In 1989, the collapse of communism in the former Soviet satellite countries of Eastern Europe; in 1990, the reunification of East Germany and West Germany; in 1994, the end of the legally sanctioned racial stratification system of apartheid in South Africa and the transfer of power from the white National Party's F. W. de Klerk to Nelson Mandela and the African National Congress, to name but a few. This new age is variously referred to by scholars as postindustrialism, postmodernism, the information age, the computer age, and the global village. However, most scholars, across academic disciplines, use the term *globalization* to capture the diverse, and sometimes conflicting, trends occurring throughout the world today (Peterson, Wunder, and Mueller, 1999).

Joan Ferrante (1992) has defined globalization in terms of the concept: **global interdependence**—a state in which the lives of people around the world are intertwined closely and in which any one nation's problems—unemployment, substance abuse, environmental pollution, disease, inequality, racism, sexism, inadequate resources, terrorism, and war—even for the noncombatants—increasingly cut across cultural and geographic boundaries. For example, as the opening story of the tragic and violent deaths of Abe Zelmanowitz and Iqbal and Zarlash Said so clearly demonstrates, the ramifications of an act of terrorism and its aftermath cut across geographic boundaries and affect both combatants and noncombatants alike. Acts of terrorism are not modern inventions; they have occurred throughout history. However, current forms of terrorism differ from earlier varieties by being more widespread, institutionalized, technologically sophisticated, and global in their reach and consequences. The September 11 attack on the Pentagon and the World Trade Center directly killed and injured people from 80 different countries who were in the United

During the decades-long armed conflicts in Afghanistan millions of families were forced to flee their homes. Husbands and fathers were often separated from their families and many were killed. In the chaos many children found themselves alone and had to join other refugees like these Afghans who sit in the sun to fight the bitter cold weather at a refugee camp in Heart, Afghanistan. According to the United Nations, at least 110 people died in just one night because of freezing conditions in refugee camps in western Afghanistan.

States on business or vacation. The U.S. response to the attack was to call on all nations to fight against international terrorism by cutting off the flow of money to groups suspected of supporting terrorist organizations, sharing their intelligence and law enforcement agencies to track down suspected terrorists, and with the direct involvement of a few countries, to launch military attacks on suspected terrorist targets inside Afghanistan. As we shall see later, millions of families were disrupted by these and other armed conflicts around the globe, and some 22 million people, or one out of every 275 persons on earth, have become refugees, forced to flee their homes and countries in search of food, shelter, safety, and their very survival (United Nations Refugee Agency, 2001).

Like terrorism, globalization is not new. It began centuries ago when explorers like Christopher Columbus left their own countries in pursuit of new sources of wealth and trade. These early international contacts produced new economic and political structures that are still evident today. What is different today, however, is the depth and breadth of this process. In the past, many families, primarily those living in the dominant countries, could live out their lives largely unaware and to a marked degree unaffected by global events. Today the opposite is true. Regardless of geographic location, today's families are feeling the effects of this deepening globalization as new technological developments provide easier, cheaper, and faster means of communication and transportation. But, as R. Dean Peterson, Delores Wunder, and Harlan Mueller (1999) inform us, the globalization process is much more than this. Not only does the globalization process restructure our socially constructed worlds, at a subjective level it also changes our self-identity.

In this final chapter we discuss some of the marriage and family trends that are immersed in a global context. Wherever possible and/or relevant, we make reference to both U.S. and global aspects of these trends. Our intent is to illuminate global trends and their consequences for marriages and families, or as C. Wright Mills (1959) encouraged us to do, to grasp history and biography and the connections between the two (see Chapter 1). By understanding the forces shaping our lives and their global significance, we can respond in ways that improve our own lives and those of the larger communities we inhabit. We begin with a brief consideration of some global economic trends and challenges.

CHALLENGES OF A WORLD ECONOMY

For the last three decades or so, global competition for new markets has intensified. Globalization was pushed forward in the aftermath of World War II as many nations increased their efforts to strengthen international relationships. The need for rebuilding the infrastructures of the countries devastated by the war also provided new opportunities for other countries seeking expanded markets for their goods and services. Additionally, advances in telecommunications, especially computers, the Internet, and cell phones, diminished the significance of national borders. At the same time, governments removed numerous protectionist barriers to the movement of capital across international boundaries, making it easier for businesses to open branches and production facilities in other countries. These *multinational corporations*, as they are called, are not under the control of any one nation. Operating decisions are made on the basis of corporate goals, often without consideration of how these decisions will affect the people in the countries in which the corporation does business. One consequence of this is a "new international division of labor," in which the process of production is broken down and the various tasks dispersed to different parts of the world (Ehrenreich and

Fuentes, 1992). Families in wealthy and poor countries alike are told that they must adapt to this increased global competition. Yet it is increasingly clear that the benefits and burdens of globalization are not shared evenly. Consider the following:

- The top fifth of countries command 82 percent of the world export markets and 68 percent of foreign direct investment; the bottom fifth have just 1 percent of each (United Nations Development Programme, 1999). Estimates are that, overall, the trade barriers maintained by the developed countries cost developing countries about $100 billion a year, twice the amount they receive in aid (Humphrys, 2001).
- Rich countries, with 15 percent of the world's population, use half of its commercial energy. In rich countries there are around 580 vehicles per 1000 people; in poor countries, there are about 10 vehicles per 1000 people. On average, a high-income country has 40 times as many computers per capita as a country in sub-Saharan Africa (World Bank, 2001). The monthly Internet access charge as a percentage of average monthly income ranges from 278 percent in Nepal to 1.2 percent in the United States (United Nations Development Programme, 2001).
- The amount of aid rich countries provide to poor countries has been declining. In 1999, only Denmark, the Netherlands, Norway, and Sweden met the United Nations targeted aid goal of 0.7 percent of the rich country's gross domestic product. In fact, net official annual development assistance per capita in donor countries has fallen from $71 in 1994 to $66 in 1999. If the 0.7 level were reached, an additional $100 billion would be available to developing countries on an annual basis (World Bank, 2001).
- One-third of the world's work force remains unemployed or underemployed (see Chapter 10 for a discussion of these concepts). Over 500 million new jobs will be needed by 2010 to accommodate new entrants to the work force and to reduce the current unemployment levels by one-half (International Labor Organization, 2001).
- Just as in the United States, in many developing countries, married women who work are still responsible for domestic labor. However, one consequence of the long work hours for married women is the shifting of a substantial share of domestic labor to young girls, who are often forced to abandon school. Consequently, they marry and bear children at an earlier age than in the developed countries.

Any one of these indicators has tremendous consequences for the well-being of the world's families. Obviously, income and wealth are related to a family's life chances. Families with a high income or substantial wealth have more control over their lives; they have greater access to the goods and services that are available in their societies. They can afford better housing, nutrition, education, and medical care. Families with limited income must devote what little resources they have to an ongoing struggle for survival.

Coalitions of environmentalists, antipoverty campaigners, trade unionists, and anticapitalist groups have demonstrated against globalization, alleging that industrialized countries, particularly the United States, have profited at the expense of developing countries. Other critics have linked the disparities that have developed along with globalization to growing resentment within impoverished nations where there are a lot of unemployed and angry people who have access to weapons and information technologies that give them the means to commit acts of terrorism at home and abroad. Increasingly, organizations like the World Bank and the United Nations are calling for what Nelson Mandela (2000) referred to as a globalization of responsibility, urgent global action to improve living conditions for people around the world by reducing the large inequities in income and wealth.

INEQUITIES IN INCOME AND WEALTH

As we saw in Chapter 10, recent studies have documented a widening income gap in the United States, although to a lesser degree, the gap between rich and poor is growing in other industrialized countries as well. For example, a study in Australia found that in the 1990s the wages of blue-collar workers dropped from 71 percent to 68 percent of their better-paid white-collar counterparts. The wages of unskilled workers shrank from 67 percent to 65 percent. Between 1980 and 1998, the earnings of the 10 percent most highly paid men jumped from 150 percent to 162 percent of middle-income workers; the income of the top 10 percent of women rose from 143 percent to 150 percent. Inequality in wealth also increased with the top earners owning a larger share of the housing market and stocks (O'Loughlin, 2000). Although there is no consensus on why inequality is increasing in developed countries, several plausible explanations have been proposed: falling wages, tax cuts favoring the rich, the decline in union membership, and global competition.

Figure 15.1 provides insight into the income disparities that exist around the globe. The average per capita gross domestic product of industrialized countries in 1999 was

Figure 15.1

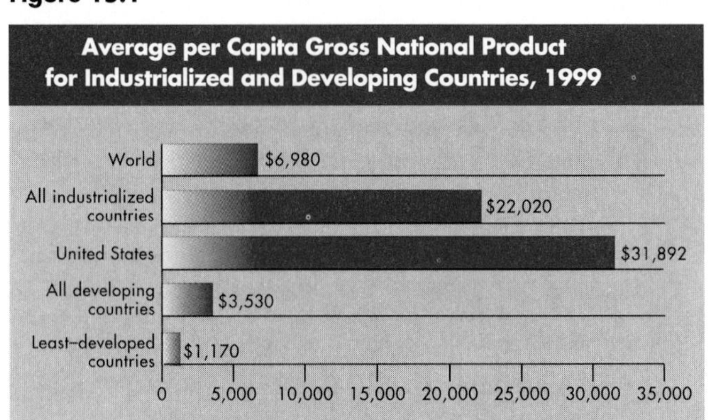

Source: From *Human Development Report 2001* by United Nations Development Programme, copyright © 2001 by the United Nations Development Programme. Used by permission of Oxford University Press, Inc.

Some form of stratification exists within and across all societies. In Brazil, the middle and upper classes live in luxurious skyscrapers and apartments while a large segment of the population barely manages to survive, without running water and electricity, in poor ramshackle hovels such as those clustered amid the trees in these *favelas* (slums) just below the opulence of Rio de Janeiro. Similar contrasts exist in the United States. Here a homeless woman seeks help from a woman in an expensive car.

$22,020, compared with only $1170 in the least developed countries. This disparity illuminates another trend. More than a quarter of the developing world's population still live in abject poverty; 2.8 billion people struggle to survive on incomes of less than $2 a day. In four years, from 1994 to 1998, the assets of the world's 200 richest people more than doubled, from $440 billion to $1042 trillion. These 200 individuals had incomes of more than the 2.36 billion people who make up the bottom 40 percent of the world's population (Brandon, 2000). The already meager share of the global income of the poorest people in the world dropped from 2.3 percent to 1.4 percent in the last decade (BBC News, 2000). Imagine trying to feed, clothe, and shelter yourself and your family on $2 a day; 1.2 billion live on less than $1 a day. Women, children, and the elderly bear the major brunt of poverty. Half a million women die each year in childbirth—10 to 100 times the mortality rate in industrial countries. Poor children are hit by malnutrition and illness just when their brains and bodies are developing. Over 160 million children are moderately or severely malnourished; 30,000 children under the age of 5 die each day from preventable diseases, and another 113 million don't go to school. Nearly a billion people are illiterate. The elderly, a growing group in all regions of the world, live out their last years in deprivation and neglect (World Bank, 2001). Approximately one-half of the world's poor live in East Asia, about a third in Africa, and a substantial proportion live on the doorstep of the United States—in Central and South America. The bulk of U.S. immigrants today are from these countries. The implications of this level of economic poverty for the future of the world's children are staggering. One example of this is in the area of health care.

HEALTH AND HEALTH CARE

According to the World Health Organization, **health** is a state of complete physical, mental, and social well-being rather than merely the absence of physical disease or infirmity. Table 15.1 examines two commonly used indicators of well-being—life expectancy and infant mortality. In 2000, a child born in Afghanistan had a one in seven chance of celebrating its first birthday. If that child managed to survive its first year, she or he could expect to live approximately 46 more years. That child's counterpart in Japan is far more fortunate; not only are the odds of surviving to the age of 1 much greater, but her or his life expectancy is almost double that of an Afghan child. Improved nutrition, sanitation, and medical care as well as economic development all combined to dramatically increase life expectancy in the developed countries

Table 15.1

Indications of Well-Being, Selected Countries, 2000

Country	Infant Mortality Rate (per 1000 births)	Life Expectancy at Birth (years)	Crude Death Rate
Afghanistan	149.3	45.9	18.0
Angola	195.8	38.3	25.0
Canada	5.1	78.4	7.4
France	4.5	78.8	9.1
Germany	4.8	77.4	10.5
India	64.9	62.5	8.9
Iraq	62.5	66.5	6.4
Japan	3.9	80.7	8.2
Malawi	122.3	37.6	22.4
Mozambique	139.9	37.5	23.3
Pakistan	82.5	61.1	9.5
United States	6.8	77.1	8.7

Source: Adapted from U.S. Census Bureau, 2000, *Statistical Abstract of the United States, 2000* (Washington, DC: U.S. Government Printing Office): Table 1355, p. 826.

during this century. If similar conditions are made available to developing countries, significant gains in life expectancy should occur. Nevertheless, despite the fact that the life expectancy of people living in developing countries increased from 55 years in 1970 to 64 years in 1999, it still trailed behind that of OECD countries, which have a life expectancy of 78 years. (The Organization for Economic Cooperation and Development is composed of 30 of the most developed countries in the world, located primarily in North America and Europe.) Thirty-eight countries, primarily in Africa, where AIDS (see Chapter 6) is rampant, saw a decline in life expectancy since 1990 (World Bank, 2001).

Similarly, between 1970 and 1999 infant mortality differences between OECD and developing countries declined in absolute terms from 86 in 1970 to 53 in 1999 but rose in relative terms: while infant mortality was around five times as high in OECD countries, it is now about ten times as high. Particularly hard hit were North Korea with an increase from 45 to 58; Kenya from 62 to 76; and Zimbabwe from 52 to 70 (World Bank, 2001). Thus, many children are growing up without parents to guide them, and many parents stand by hopelessly as their children succumb to a variety of diseases.

Without adequate controls, however, medical advances may have an opposite effect. For example, medical procedures rarely dreamed about even a decade or so ago have become commonplace in industrialized countries. Families rejoice as ill members who would have died just a few years ago now live full lives as a result of receiving organ transplants. Yet this marvelous achievement has a dark side. In India, Thailand, China, and the Philippines, the poor are selling body parts to keep themselves and their families alive, leaving themselves vulnerable to diseases and perhaps early death. Offers of up to 3 years income have induced many poor people to become commercial donors of skin patches, kidneys, and other organs (Soroka and Bryjak, 1995).

Organs are also being harvested from executed prisoners in China. Doctors in the United States are confronting ethical issues about providing after-transplant care for patients who went to China to obtain transplants they could not get at home. Since these "donors" may not have given consent to having their organs removed or may have been innocent of the crime for which they were convicted, doctors fear that providing such care would be tacitly condoning the practice and encouraging more such transplants (Smith, 2001).

Death and Disease Nowhere can we so clearly see the well-being of families than by an examination of data on death and disease. A cursory glance at Table 15.1 reveals the wide gulf between crude death rates (number of deaths during 1 year per 1000 persons based on midyear population) in the developing and developed countries. Another indication of well-being is access to primary health resources such as safe drinking water and sanitation facilities. Figure 15.2 reveals major disparities among regions on these two indexes. On one end of the scale, large numbers of families living in the least developed regions have little or no access to safe drinking water. Although access to improved water supply and sanitation increased since 1990, globally 1.1 billion people are without access to improved water supply, and a

Figure 15.2

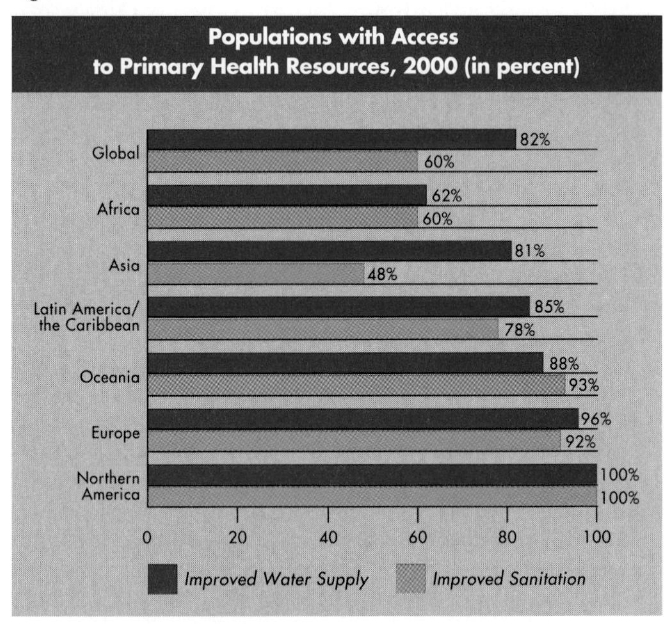

Source: World Health Organization, 2000, *Global Water Supply and Sanitation Assessment 2000 Report.* Geneva, Switzerland, Table 2. **http://www.who.int/water_sanitation_health/Global2.1htm** (accessed January 22, 2002)

Political and social unrest add to the health problems in many countries. Here a Rwanda refugee boy fills his canister with water as women wash clothes a few yards away from a decomposing body in Lake Kivu, Zaire.

staggering 2.4 billion (40 percent of the world's population) are without access to improved sanitation. For both water supply and sanitation, the vast majority of people without access live in Asia. Every year 3.4 million people die from water-related diseases (World Health Organization, 2000a).

Additionally, women and girls in many countries suffer health burdens brought on by their efforts to carry water from distant, often polluted, rivers and streams. Not surprisingly, large numbers of people living in developing regions also lack access to basic health services such as prenatal, birth, and infant care for women and their children, immunization against major diseases, an adequate supply of trained medical practitioners, and adequate public funding of health services and education. For example, in Afghanistan, which has one of the highest rates of maternal mortality in the world, less than 15 percent of deliveries are attended by trained health workers and less than 40 percent of Afghan children receive life-saving vaccinations (World Health Organization, 2002). At the other end, families in North America and Europe have nearly universal access to basic health resources. The consequences of these differences can be seen in the different causes of death in developing and developed countries. People who live in developing countries are far more likely to die from infectious and communicable diseases than people who live in the developed countries. In 1997, 42 percent of all deaths in developing countries were from infectious and parasitic diseases, compared with 1 percent in developed countries (World Health Organization, 1998). Epidemics of infectious diseases are common in some parts of the world. For example, malaria affects an estimated 300 million people and kills approximately 1 million each year, 75 percent of them children under the age of 5. The majority of cases occur in sub-Saharan Africa, followed by parts of Asia and Latin America (World Bank, 2001). This is a disease that is preventable, but because of the poverty in these regions, stocks of vaccine are too costly to maintain, and many areas are without medical services. Approximately 2 billion people still do not have access to low-cost essential medicines such as penicillin, which have been commonly available in the developed countries for decades. Fifty percent of Africa's 1-year-olds have not been immunized against diphtheria, tetanus, polio, or measles (United Nations Development Programme, 2001).

Many of the diseases in developing countries are associated with extreme poverty. In contrast, many of the diseases in developed countries are associated with affluence and unhealthful lifestyles—little physical exercise combined with a diet high in fat. Thus, diseases of the circulatory system and cancer are far more common in developed countries than in developing countries. However, as the economies of developing countries grow, many are adopting Western lifestyles and their accompanying risk factors—smoking, high-fat diets, obesity, and lack of exercise. Deaths from diseases of the circulatory system rose from 16 percent in 1985 to 24 percent in 1997 in the developing world.

The world's developed countries cannot afford to ignore infectious diseases in far-away countries. If not checked, they can easily pose a threat to the developed countries. As international travel increases, so, too, does the exposure to infectious diseases. For example, in 1996, travelers returning to the United States and Switzerland developed yellow fever, and in the United Kingdom 1000 new cases of malaria are imported each year from malaria-endemic countries (Heymann, 2000). International trade provides another means for infectious diseases to cross borders. In 1985, the tiger mosquito, which can transmit yellow fever, dengue, and other diseases, entered the United States inside a shipment of water-logged used tires from Asia. Within 2 years these mosquitoes were in 17 states (Heymann, 2000). Thus, it is in the interest of the developed countries to help eradicate infectious diseases around the world. Yet, only 10 percent of global health research focuses on the illnesses that constitute 90 percent of the global disease burden. In 1998, of the $70 billion of global spending on health research only $300 million was spent on vaccines for HIV/AIDS and about $100 million for malaria research (United Nations Development Programme, 2001). Besides more research dollars, efforts must be devoted to more rapid dissemination of new medical advances as well as to the training of more medical staff and the development of prevention programs in developing countries.

Disease is not the only health problem that individuals and families confront. Living with a long-term disability can put a strain on family resources, both economic and emotional.

Disabilities Few people realize that the experience of disability is typical rather than rare. According to some reports, there are 54 million disabled people in the United States, representing 19 percent of the total population, or one of every five Americans, making them the largest single "minority" group in the country. Disability is a normal part of life affecting people of all ages. For example, 31 percent of people aged 65 and older experience disabilities, 11 percent are 18 or younger, and the majority, 58 percent, are of working age. Increasingly, since the emergence of the disability rights movement in the United States in the 1970s, disabled persons are asserting their right to participate fully in schools, in the workplace, in businesses, in their families, and in community affairs (Abilities 2000, 2002; National Organization on Disability, 2001a). Breakthroughs in medicine and technology (such as motorized wheelchairs and computer technology that enables the hearing- and speech-impaired to communicate) have made even the most severely disabled people much more visible, while enabling them to lead the type of lives that they choose. In the United States, among its several victories, the disabled movement has been successful in making public facilities (buildings, bathrooms, elevators, classrooms) more accessible. This is significant, given that 1 out of every 250 people in the United States uses a wheelchair. Movement for disabled rights has occurred globally as well. For example, in Italy, the National League for the Right to Work of the Handicapped has been successful in eliminating architectural barriers to full participation in the labor force. Their efforts include making professional jobs accessible to the disabled (Nuebeck and Glasberg, 1996).

Disability is not easy to define. The National Organization on Disability (2001a) defines disability as a health problem that prevents a person from participating fully in work, school, or other activities; or a physical impairment of sight, hearing, or speech; an emotional or mental or learning impairment; or if one simply considers herself or himself to have a disability or says that other people would consider her or him to be a person with a disability. Sociologically speaking, Joseph Shapiro (1993) defines a **disability** as a physical or health condition that stigmatizes or causes discrimination. This definition points up the fact that disability is not purely a medical problem to be treated by nurses and doctors but, rather, is also a social phenomenon best dealt with by enabling people with disabilities to lead independent lives free of prejudice and discrimination. Unfortunately, persons with disabilities continue to be targets of prejudice and discrimination; thus the impact for their families is often similar to that experienced by families who are victims of racial and ethnic discrimination. In 1989, a U.S. Senate committee documented the extent to which disabled persons face resentment, hostility, prejudice, discrimination, and the basic denial of human rights. Some of the horror stories told to senators included: a zookeeper would not admit children with Down syndrome because he said that these children would upset the chimpanzees; a teacher said that a disabled student should be excluded from school because his appearance nauseated his classmates; a mother was fired from her job because she was caring for her son who had contracted AIDS. Other stories included incidents where persons with arthritis and cancer, and other disabled persons were denied or fired from jobs, not because they were unable to perform the work, but because of discrimination (cited in Nuebeck and Glasberg, 1996).

In the past, attitudes toward the disabled have been either negative or paternalistic. Disabled persons were viewed as *crippled*, to be distinguished from *normal*, and were often isolated, persecuted, ridiculed, and feared, even by some family members. Contemporary attitudes toward the visibly disabled still tend to regard them as persons who are to be pitied, set apart, or avoided altogether. Common reactions to them continue to be condescension, ridicule, impatience, awkwardness, embarrassment, resentment, and even anger. These attitudes are not surprising, given Americans' emphasis on independence, youth, health, and attractive appearances. Thus, persons who do not fit this image are regarded with derision and hostility (Clinard and Meier, 1995). The good news, however, is that there is some evidence of changing attitudes about disabled people, at least within some segments of the population. For example, as illustrated in the discussion of September 11 at the beginning of this chapter, there were people in the World Trade Center such as Abe Zelmanowitz who were willing to risk or give their lives to help disabled people get out of the buildings safely. Unfortunately, like Mr. Zelmanowitz, most were unsuccessful. One of the things that became very apparent in the aftermath of September 11 is that, as a country, the United States was not prepared for that kind of terrorism. And it was even less prepared to assist disabled people caught in such circumstances. In a survey conducted 3 months after the September 11 terrorist attacks, most disabled people expressed anxiety about their personal safety and said that they did not feel sufficiently prepared for future crises at work or at home. For example, 58 percent of disabled people said they did not know whom to contact about emergency plans for their community in the event of a terrorist attack or other crisis; 61 percent said that they had not made plans to quickly and safely evacuate their home; and among those employed full- or part-time, 50 percent said no plans had been made to safely evacuate their workplace. All of these percentages are higher than for those people without disabilities (National Organization on Disability, 2001a).

Approximately one-third of American families include at least one member with a disability, and most families experience having a disabled member at some time. For those persons who are severely disabled and require prolonged care and assistance, such physical or mental requirements often severely strain family relationships. Over a long period of time, even loved ones might tire of caring for a disabled family member and begin to resent the person. Finally, disabled people who date or marry often face public and family attitudes similar to those faced by interracial couples: They are expected to date and marry another disabled person. Superstitions, fear, and stigmatization of people with a disability are even more pronounced in some of the developing countries, sometimes leading parents to abandon or kill a newborn suffering from some highly visible defect.

Persons who are disabled adapt to their disabilities in a manner similar to that suggested by Elizabeth Kübler-Ross (1969) in adjusting to death and dying: denial and isolation, anger, bargaining, depression, and acceptance. During these developmental stages, the love and support of family, friends, and helping professionals are key.

The rate of poverty among the disabled is much higher than it is among the able-bodied. All over the world disabled people are among the poorest of the poor, living lives of disadvantage and deprivation. In the United States, disabled people are the poorest and least educated of all citizens. However, over the last decade, there has been a significant increase in the educational attainment of disabled people, particularly higher education. Today, for instance, nearly one-half of adults with disabilities have completed some college—a proportion nearly identical to the nondisabled population (National Organization on Disability, 2001b). Also, there are gender-related issues that make contending with disability a tougher task for women than men. For example, like their able-bodied counterparts, disabled women are found disproportionately among the poor. In addition to poverty, disabled women are vulnerable to a host of other personal and societal problems. For instance, as we pointed out in Chapter 11, women and children are more likely to be abused and suffer violence when they are disabled. This "feminization of vulnerability" is not unique to disabled women in the United States. Rather, it is a recurring pattern found in countries around the world. Women with disabilities are the poorest of poor everywhere. This is especially the reality of disabled women in the developing world, where in every single aspect of life women with disabilities experience a triple bind: they are discriminated against because they are women, because they are disabled, and because they are from the developing world. Many of these women are disabled due to violence perpetrated against them including the practice of female circumcision and infibulation. There are few educational opportunities for disabled girls. Where opportunities for education in special schools for disabled children are available, it is usually boys who receive them. In addition, the unemployment rate for disabled women in developing countries is virtually 100 percent (Disabled Women's Network Ontario, 2002).

Although disabled women are particularly vulnerable in the developing world, the quality of life for disabled women is not much better in other parts of the world. In Canada, for example, 16 percent of all women are disabled; they have an unemployment rate of 74 percent; their median income is less than half that for a disabled man ($8360 versus $19,250); and support services are often inaccessible to them and are practically nonexistent for disabled mothers. However, as we have shown repeatedly throughout this textbook, women are active agents in changing, modifying, and adapting the social worlds in which they live. Thus, like their able-bodied counterparts, disabled women globally are active agents working to tear down the barriers that prevent them from full and equal participation in society; increasingly, they are forming their own self-help groups in their countries and at the world level. For example, in Kenya, disabled women are building wheelchairs, and in Uganda, women with disabilities have started MADE—Mobility Appliances by Disabled Women Entrepreneurs—to create for themselves employment and sustainable livelihoods (Snyder, 2000; Disabled Women's Network Ontario, 2002).

A question one might ask is why are disabled people at such a distinct disadvantage in society vis-à-vis able-bodied people? One answer lies in the fact that, traditionally, disability has been viewed as a "problem" of the individual, and it has been the individual who has had to change or be changed by professionals through rehabilitation or cure. Today, however, disabled people and their organizations call attention to the fact that it is economic and social barriers that stop people with disabilities from participating fully in society and not necessarily the individual characteristics of the disabled. These barriers are so widespread that disabled people, and their families, are often prevented from enjoying a good quality of life.

This viewpoint is consistent with a sociological perspective of disability that focuses our attention on disabling social structures, institutions, and social environments that create, perpetuate, and maintain barriers to the equitable treatment of people with disabilities as opposed to focusing on the individual characteristics or disabilities of the disabled. For example, the ability to earn wages and maintain a minimum standard of living is severely limited for disabled persons. In the United States, 84.5 percent of the population with no disability is employed, compared with only 23.7 percent of those with a disability (U.S. Census Bureau, 2000a). The staggering unemployment rate of the disabled does not stem from the lack of desire to work; various national surveys show that over two-thirds of those not working wish to work. In fact, recent data show that disabled persons who work maintain above-average work attendance and productivity. Nonetheless, when persons with a disability do work, they typically are paid less than persons without a disability (National Organization on Disability, 2001c). Discrepancies in pay are even more severe for African Americans and Latinas/os with disabilities. Furthermore, many disabled persons find themselves shut out of various occupations. For example, how often have you seen a disabled salesperson in a department store? As a receptionist? Or in any public position where the public might be concerned more with personal appearance than with the ability to perform the job? On the other hand, some positive changes are occurring. Increasingly, more disabled persons, both mildly and severely disabled, are attending college and negotiating the process successfully, and they are becoming more visible in careers such as acting and television news.

Countries in the Asia-Pacific region designated 1993–2002 the Decade for the Disabled in order to sensitize the region to the problems of millions of disabled Asian women, men, and children. Although statistics are scarce, available data indicate that 1 to 3 percent of the adult population in the Asia-Pacific region are disabled. In China alone, there are an estimated 50 million disabled people, more than 8 million of them younger than 14. An estimated 80 to 90 percent of Asia's disabled live in rural areas, many of whom live in extreme poverty. Thailand, where the disabled population is estimated to be approximately 1 million, is one of the few Asian countries that is taking proactive steps to support and rehabilitate this vulnerable sector of society. Many disabled people are employed in vocational training centers but the government is also using tax and legislative incentives to encourage the private sector to train and employ disabled people (Food and Agriculture Organization of the United Nations, 1997).

According to some sources, 65 to 70 percent of the U.S. population will become disabled simply by living to their full life expectancy (Disability Rights, 1999). This will certainly have important implications for marriage and family life: For example, the range of disabilities (whether severe or mild); how and if they will be covered under health insurance; who will care for aging disabled family members; and what kinds of disability-related assistance will be available to families with disabled members are but a few of the issues.

Health Insurance Although the United States has among the highest per capita health expenditures of the industrialized countries, it ranks considerably lower than many of its counterparts in terms of the percentage of its population covered by public health insurance. In contrast to most other industrialized countries, where comprehensive government-run national health programs exist, access to the American health care system is primarily through private insurance, with two major exceptions—Medicare, which covers 99.3 percent of the elderly, and Medicaid for the poor. Yet even with this Medicaid program, 9.2 million people (29.5 percent of all poor people) had no health insurance of any kind during 2000. The insurance system in the United States has some serious flaws. Those who have private insurance generally obtain it as a fringe benefit of their employment. Sixty-four percent of the population were covered by a health plan related to their employment for some or all of 2000, up slightly from 1999. However, as insurance costs have increased, employers have shifted more of the cost to their employees, especially the cost of insuring workers' families. Workers in low-paying jobs often cannot afford insurance coverage for their families; premiums may cost several thousand dollars per year. Some employers do not provide any insurance even for employees. Additionally, when people lose their jobs, they often lose their health insurance as well. To cope with this problem, Congress passed the 1986 Consolidated Omnibus Budget Reconciliation Act (popularly known as Cobra) to bridge the insurance gap for workers who were between jobs. Although the law has been used by millions of workers (primarily middle class), it has some serious limitations. The law does not apply to people who work for businesses with fewer than 20 workers, and it requires workers to pay the full cost of their health insurance premiums plus some administrative costs, reaching as high as $400 to $600 a month for family coverage. Thus, many unemployed workers cannot exercise their right to continued insurance coverage because the cost is prohibitive.

In 2000, over 14 percent of the population (nearly 39 million Americans) did not have health insurance, down from 14.3 percent in 1999. Those most likely to be uninsured are men (14.9 percent), young adults 18 to 24 years old (27.3 percent), Latinas/os (32 percent), the foreign-born (31.6 percent), and those without a high school diploma (26.6 percent). Native Americans were the least likely of all racial groups to have health insurance. The number of uninsured children declined from 9.1 million in 1999 to 8.5 million (11.6 percent) in 2000 (U.S. Census Bureau, 2001c). It is estimated that another 20 million are underinsured; any serious illness quickly would exhaust their benefits. Lack of insurance coverage can be deadly. The uninsured generally receive little preventive care. They usually delay treatment until they are very sick, and then they most likely go to hospital emergency rooms, further straining an already overburdened system.

These problems have ignited a debate in Congress over ways to improve the health care system. Some critics have proposed establishing a national health care system modeled after the Canadian system, which guarantees all citizens equal access to health care through a national health service paid for and administered by the government. Initial attempts to reform the system during the first year of the Clinton administration failed, due in large part to the lobbying power of the insurance industry and the medical establishment. Opponents argued that such a system would be too costly and that patient–doctor relationships would be impeded by government regulation. It is unlikely that the United States will adopt the idea of a government-administered health care system any time soon. However, the economic slowdown in 2001, along with the rise in unemployment engendered by the terrorist attacks of September 11, once again exposed the vulnerability of the U.S. system of health insurance. The exact numbers of people who lost and will continue to lose jobs and their related insurance benefits as a result of these events are as yet unknown, but these events will most likely reverse the positive trend that was underway between 1999 and 2000. This factor, coupled with the steep premium increases of the past several years, is sure to reignite the health care debate in the near future.

Trends in Drug Use and Associated Health Problems

Drug use is an increasing public health issue around the world. The trend is toward an increase in the supply and the use of both legal and illegal drugs, which is accompanied by lower ages of initiation into their use, resulting in a broad spectrum of problems, including deteriorating health, social and family disruption, and economic exploitation. In both developed and developing countries, problems related to drug use have traditionally affected males. However, with the rapid social and economic changes discussed throughout this textbook, there has been a dramatic increase in use among women. Because many women drug users are of childbearing age, their use can have profound negative effects on the next generation.

Thinking about drugs is complicated by the fact that almost daily the media send out mixed messages about drugs. In the same news hour we are likely to hear about the wonders of a new drug and the devastating effects other drugs have visited on individuals or whole communities. People are often surprised to discover that they are drug users. Until relatively recently, commonly used items such as coffee, tea, and cigarettes were not viewed as drugs. There was even resistance to including alcohol on the list of commonly used drugs. Thus, it is important to clarify terms. A **drug** is any substance that alters the central nervous system and states of consciousness. Such alterations can enhance, inhibit, or distort the functioning of the body, in turn, possibly affecting patterns of behavior and social functioning.

The most commonly used and abused drugs are:

1. ***Narcotics:*** opium, morphine, codeine, and heroin.
2. ***Depressants,*** such as sedatives and hypnotics: barbiturates, benzodiazepines (such as Valium), methaqualone (Quaalude), and alcohol.
3. ***Stimulants:*** cocaine (and crack), amphetamines, and caffeine, as well as coffee, tea, and tobacco.
4. ***Hallucinogens:*** LSD (lysergic acid diethylamide), mescaline, and peyote.
5. ***Cannabis:*** marijuana and hashish.
6. ***Organic solvents:*** inhalants such as gasoline, airplane glue, and paint thinner, as well as certain foods, herbs, and vitamins (Hanson and Venturelli, 1995).

Illicit drug use is common in the United States. Nearly 40 percent of the respondents in a national household survey reported using an illicit drug at some point in their lifetime, the most common being marijuana and hashish (34 percent). In 2000, an estimated 14 million Americans (6.3 percent of the population 12 years old and older) were current illicit drug users, meaning they had used an illicit drug during the month prior to the survey (U.S. Department of Health and Human Services, 2001b). As Table 15.2 shows, rates and patterns of drug use vary considerably by age. Children as young as 12 report using illicit drugs. Rates increase with age, peaking in the age group 18 to 25 and then declining with those 26 or older. However, there is one exception to this pattern. Adults aged 40–44, who were teenagers during the 1970s when experimentation with drug use was widespread and drug use rose dramatically, had rates higher than the 35- to 39-year-old age group.

Table 15.2

Percentages Reporting Lifetime and Past Month Use of Illicit Drugs, by Age, 2000

	12–17		18–25		26 or older	
Drug	Lifetime	Past Month	Lifetime	Past Month	Lifetime	Past Month
Any illicit drug	26.9	9.7	51.2	15.9	38.5	4.2
Marijuana and hashish	18.3	7.2	45.7	13.6	34.5	3.0
Cocaine	2.4	0.6	10.9	1.4	12.4	0.4
Heroin	0.4	0.1	1.4	0.1	1.3	0.1
Hallucinogens	5.8	1.2	19.3	1.8	11.2	0.1
Inhalants	8.9	1.0	12.8	0.6	6.4	0.1
Tranquilizers	2.5	0.5	7.4	1.0	6.0	0.4
Stimulants	4.0	0.8	7.6	0.8	6.7	0.2
Sedatives	0.8	0.2	1.6	0.1	3.8	0.1
Any illicit drug other than marijuana	18.1	4.6	31.9	5.9	22.9	1.7

Source: Adapted from U.S. Department of Health and Human Services, 2001, *Summary of Findings from the 2000 National Household Survey on Drug Use* (Washington, DC: Government Printing Office), Tables F3–5.

The rates of current illicit drug use among the various racial/ethnic groups in 2000 were 6.4 percent for both whites and African Americans. Although as a category the rate was lower for Latinas/os (5.3 percent), the rate varied from group to group within that category: Cubans had the lowest rate (3.7 percent), Puerto Ricans the highest (10.1 percent), and Mexicans were in the middle (5.5 percent). The rate was highest among the Native American/Alaska Native population (12.6 percent) and among persons reporting more than one race (14.8 percent). Although Asians had the lowest rate (2.7 percent), there was considerable variation within that population, ranging from a low of 1.0 percent of Chinese to a high of 6.9 percent of Koreans. Although the rate of current illicit drug use was similar for boys 12 to 17 (9.8 percent) and their female peers (9.5 percent), adult males had a higher rate of current illicit drug use (7.7 percent) than adult females (5.0 percent).

Considering the extent of drug use, we might well ask why people use drugs and when drug use becomes drug abuse. The reasons for drug use are probably as varied as the users themselves. Nevertheless, researchers have consistently identified several themes surrounding usage: to relieve pain and illness; for fun or curiosity; for pleasure; to fit in; to escape problems; and to relieve boredom, stress, and anxiety (Robson, 1994). Illicit drug use is also correlated with educational and employment status. Although college graduates were more likely to have tried illicit drugs in their lifetime compared to adults who had not completed high school (44.6 percent versus 28.9 percent), among adults aged 18 and older in 2000, college graduates had the lowest rate of current use. The highest rate was among adults who had not completed high school. Many of these individuals were unemployed as well. An estimated 15.4 percent of unemployed adults were current illicit drug users in 2000 compared with 6.3 percent of full-time employed adults (U.S. Department of Health and Human Services, 2001b). The Food and Drug Administration defines **drug use** as the taking of a drug for its intended purpose and in an appropriate amount, frequency, strength, and manner, and **drug abuse** as the deliberate use of a substance for other than its intended purpose, in a manner that can damage health or ability to function.

Drug Use among the World's Children It is illegal for children in the United States to purchase alcohol or tobacco products. Nevertheless, according to the U.S. Department of Health and Human Services (2001b) an estimated 16.4 percent of 12- to 17-year-olds used alcohol in 2000; 10.4 percent were binge drinkers (five or more drinks on the same occasion) and 2.6 percent were heavy drinkers (five or more drinks on the same occasion at least 5 different days in the previous month). In and of themselves these patterns are cause for concern because they can lead to physical and social problems for the user. However, there is evidence that the early use of alcohol and tobacco can be a gateway to the use of illicit drugs. Indeed, the rate for illicit drug use among 12- to 17-year-olds who smoked and/or drank was considerably higher than among their peers who did not smoke or drink. As Table 15.2 makes clear, 27 percent of 12- to 17-year-olds had experimented with marijuana, inhalants, and other substances. These substances are also popular among the world's "street children," children made homeless because of family separations and conflicts associated with urbanization, economic crisis, political change, civil unrest, wars, epidemics, and natural disasters. Almost every country has some street children; various estimates put their number at between 10 million and 30 million worldwide. Studies have found that between 25 percent and 90 percent of street children use substances of one kind or another. In South Africa, 90 percent of street children are thought to be dependent on glue. In Colombia and Bolivia, 8-year-old children have been reported dealing in and smoking basuco cigarettes, a low-grade by-product of cocaine laced with kerosene and sulfuric acid (World Health Organization, 1997). The devastating consequences that follow such usage include acute and chronic health and emotional problems, disruption of interpersonal relationships, school failure, social marginalization, and criminal behavior.

One of the major factors in drug use among children is the absence of a supportive family. A study by the Partnership for a Drug Free America bears this out. Researchers found that teenagers who received strong anti-drug messages at home were 42 percent less likely to use drugs than teens whose parents ignored the issue. African American parents (57 percent) were more likely than Latina/o (45 percent) or white parents (44 percent) to say they discuss the risks of drugs regularly with their children. In that same study, 31 percent of African American children recalled having such conversations, compared with 29 percent of Latina/o and 19 percent of white children ("Talks on Drugs . . . ," 1999).

Drugs: An International Concern Drug abuse is not a problem confined within the borders of the United States. The illegal production, distribution, and use of drugs is a worldwide problem. Unofficial estimates of the United Nations Drug Control Programme put the annual global rate of illicit drug consumption in the range of 3 percent to 4 percent of the total population (180 million to 240 million, larger than the total population in many countries), with indications that the rate is increasing, particularly in developing countries and countries in transition (World Health Organization, 2000b). Nor is this a new phenomenon. Anthropologists report that the use of mood-altering agents appears to be a common characteristic among diverse human cultures. In one way or another, all societies struggle with what is appropriate use and what is abuse of these substances.

The consequences of the illegal traffic in drugs are many and varied. In the centers of production, like Colombia, it creates an economic problem, diverting money and energy that could be used for investment in legal economic activities. In the centers of consumption, like the United States, it creates a health problem, contributing annually to 3.5 percent of the total cases of diseases and millions of deaths worldwide. In both centers, where criminal organizations flourish, it is a matter that jeopardizes the very existence of the nation-state (Garcia-Pena, 1995). It is estimated that the annual revenues of the global illegal drug industry top $400 billion, equivalent to almost 8 percent of international trade, making it one of the largest commodities traded after oil and arms (Bowcott, 2001). This amount of money surpasses the gross national product of many countries and can easily be used to destabilize a country's economy.

Alcohol

Although the media pay far more attention to illegal drugs such as cocaine and heroin, alcohol abuse affects a much larger percentage of the population. The use of alcohol for recreation and social interaction has a long history. So, too, does concern with the potential for abuse. The earliest known legal code, the Hammurabi Code (circa 1758 B.C. in Babylon), contained laws regulating the operation and management of drinking establishments. The Greek philosopher Plato was concerned enough about the drinking behavior of his countrymen that he established rules for conduct at "symposia," which in reality were drinking parties (McKim, 1986, cited in Thombs, 1994). Such concerns remain with us today.

ALCOHOLISM According to the National Institute on Alcohol Abuse and Alcoholism (NIAAA), **alcoholism,** also known as alcohol dependency, is a disease that includes four symptoms: craving—a strong need or urge to drink; loss of control—not being able to stop drinking once drinking has begun; physical dependency—withdrawal symptoms, such as nausea, sweating, shakiness, and anxiety after stopping drinking; and tolerance—the need to drink greater amounts of alcohol to get high. The National Commission on Marijuana and Drug Abuse labeled alcoholism the most serious drug problem in the United States (other than tobacco use). Over 100 million Americans consume alcohol, and about 18 million have serious drinking problems. Globally, 140 million people suffer from alcohol dependence. According to the NIAAA (2000), the effects of alcohol, ranging from violence to traffic crashes to lost productivity to illnesses such as heart attacks, cancer, stroke, cirrhosis of the liver, pneumonia, mental illness, sexual dysfunctions, and premature death—all of which combined cost the nation an estimated $185 billion per year. Problem drinking in the family is also a factor in many suicides, including adolescent suicide (Fernquist, 2000).

Other costs are social. Alcohol is often implicated in antisocial behavior; it can lower inhibitions against violence, reduce a victim's resistance, and provide an excuse for behavior. For example, studies have found that when a man wants to coerce a woman into having sex, he often provides her with alcohol or other drugs to lower her ability to resist (Boeringer, Shehan, and Akers, 1991). Alcohol may also function as a cue to men for sexual access; women who drink may be perceived as "loose" or more interested in sex. Furthermore, as we saw in Chapter 11, the abuse of alcohol and other drugs is often a factor in family violence.

Addiction and the Family

Harold Doweiko (1996) identified a number of possible combinations between marriage, family, and addiction. Many people who are or who become addicted to chemicals are married. Some marry before becoming addicted; others are already addicted, but their partners may be unaware of the addiction. Sometimes addicts marry each other in a marriage of convenience that brings with it a "using partner," an additional source of chemicals and money. Finally, nonaddicts may be aware of their partner's addiction but marry anyway in the hopes of "saving" the addict.

The problem of parental chemical use and abuse is a significant one. It is estimated that 12.8 million children (18 percent of all children) under 18 years of age live with a parent who has used illicit drugs (National Institute on Drug Abuse, 1994). However, most of what we know about the role addiction plays in families is based on studies involving alcohol abuse. Hence, our focus here will be on families coping with alcohol addiction.

ALCOHOLISM: A FAMILY PROBLEM Initially, research on and treatment of alcoholism focused on the drinking alcoholic, particularly men. In the 1950s and 1960s the focus shifted to the "family disease" concept, with the recognition that all members of the family are affected by the alcoholism of a member. In particular, researchers began using systems theory to examine the alcoholism of a parent as a central organizing principle determining interactional patterns within the family (Brown and Yalom, 1995).

As we saw in Chapter 2, family systems theory explains how families function. It examines roles, rules, and communication processes that allow for predictable and consistent behavior. Whenever one part of the system is altered, all other parts are affected. This can readily be seen in the case of chronic alcoholism. When one member becomes chemically addicted, the remaining family members become enmeshed in the addiction process as they attempt to cope with the impact this behavior has on their lives. The spouse of an alcoholic is likely to deny the problem and cover up for her or his partner, taking on the role of an "enabler" who tries to help the alcoholic partner by engaging in behavior that allows the addiction to continue. For example, the nonaddicted spouse may report a partner as ill when in fact she or he is unable to go to work or attend a social function because of drunkenness.

Children as well as spouses learn how to adapt to meet the demands of the addicted parent. In attempting to avoid a family crisis and as a means of coping with family stress, family roles and responsibilities are restructured as other family members take over the addicted parent's responsibilities. Unfortunately, many of these new patterns actually encourage the alcoholic to continue drinking and to become less involved in family life. For example, the oldest child often takes on the role of *hero,* looking after younger children and attempting to prevent the alcoholic parent from drinking. Conversely, a child may misbehave and in that way deflect attention away from the problems that the alcoholism creates. As a result, the child may become a *scapegoat,* receiving the anger that would otherwise be directed toward the alcoholic. Another child may react by becoming an independent loner, staying out of everyone's way. This *lost child* role is likely to lead to low self-esteem as this child receives little nurturing or attention during childhood. Finally, a child may take on the role of *mascot,* becoming entertaining and providing comic relief in an effort to distract the family's attention from its problems.

It is important to remember that there is tremendous variation in family functioning and structures. Therefore, although some chemically dependent families have members who clearly fit one of these specific roles, other families will have members who exhibit behavior characteristics of more than one role or who will shift from one role to another over time. In some families, certain roles never emerge (Thombs, 1994). The longer these behaviors continue, the more difficult it is to change them. There is widespread agreement among family therapists that alcoholism is one of the most difficult family problems to treat, partly because many people who need treatment don't want it, at least not at first.

Just as the onset of alcoholism leads to changes in the stability of the family system, recovery may also disrupt family functioning. Individual members may resist change because it may alter the roles with which they have become comfortable. For example, the enabler may have taken control over the family finances and may feel resentful if the recovering spouse now wants to resume this behavior. Children, too, may resist change. During the period when a parent was drinking, a child may have assumed the role of confidant to the nonalcoholic parent. In recovery, this role may be lost. Furthermore, family members often believe that all problems will be over once the alcoholic member stops drinking. When they discover that problems remain and might even be exacerbated in the early stages of recovery, they may become discouraged and resentful. Further complicating the situation is the likelihood that members may be at different stages of recovery. One child described this phase in his family's recovery:

> My parents were both immersed in their recoveries. That's all they did. They didn't speak to each other for the first two years without first calling their sponsors. They barely spoke to me. I knew someone would make dinner each night, but I never knew who, or when it would appear. I spent every afternoon and evening alone in my room with my homework and my headphones. They were busy getting sober, and I felt guilty having needs. (Quoted in Brown and Yalom, 1995:300)

Recovery is a time of great stress, and some families can't cope; there is a high incidence of divorce within the first 3 to 5 years (Brown and Yalom, 1995). However, with treatment many families are able to relinquish their previously unhealthy behaviors and thinking.

Children of Alcoholics Some experts believe that one out of eight children under age 18 in the United States lives with an alcoholic parent, primarily the father (Whitehouse, 2000). For the most part these children grow up in homes where there is considerable family stress and conflict that negatively impact the parent–child relationship (Tubman, 1993). Further, children who live with an alcoholic parent are at greater risk for being physically abused and becoming abusers themselves (Widom and Hiller-Sturmhofel, 2001). Often, children of alcoholics (COAs) receive inconsistent parenting and inadequate parental support. This places these children at risk for many emotional and behavioral difficulties as they are growing up, including the probability of becoming alcoholics themselves. Another possibility is that they will marry a spouse who needs to be taken care of in the same way they took care of the addicted parent. In Chapter 3, we saw how gender identity is acquired through the process of social learning. Similarly, COAs may learn alcoholic behavior by modeling their behavior after that of an alcoholic parent, learning that drinking is an acceptable way to cope with life's problems (Lawson, Peterson, and Lawson, 1983). Researchers have established that genetic factors also play a role in the development of alcoholism, especially between fathers and sons (Perkins and Berkowitz, 1991; Jacob, 1992).

Before leaving this section, it is important to note that not all COAs become maladjusted adults. A number of recent studies comparing adult children of alcoholics and adults from nonalcoholic families found no clear differences in the grown children's emotional adjustment (Tweed and Ryff, 1991; Seilhamer, Jacob, and Dunn, 1993; Giunta and Compas, 1994). Despite the difficulties of living in an alcoholic family, many children manage to cope and develop into happy, well-adjusted adults. This seems more likely when only one parent has a drinking problem and the other parent is able to provide support and guidance for their children (Roosa et al., 1993; Schuckit and Smith, 2001), or when a parental surrogate such as an uncle, neighbor, or teacher is actively involved with the children (Werner, 1989; Parker, Barrett, and Hickie, 1992; Whitehouse, 2000).

MEETING THE NEEDS OF CHILDREN: FOSTER CARE AND ADOPTION

In recent years television coverage has brought us pictures showing how armed conflicts around the world are disrupting the lives of millions of children. Here in the United States, the home life of many children is also vulnerable to disruption (see the "Searching the Internet" box), not because of war, as in Afghanistan, but because they live in environments made dangerous by violence and crime or because their parents are unwilling or unable to care for them properly. Over 500,000 children are currently without permanent homes and living in foster care. Forty-eight percent are female and 52 percent are male, and they come from all racial and ethnic groups: African Americans (43 percent), white (36 percent), Latina/o (15 percent), Native American/Alaskan Native (1 percent), Asian/Pacific Islander (1 percent), unknown/unable to determine (4 percent) (Administration for Children and Families, 2000). Many of these children were removed from their homes as a result of being neglected or abused. Many blame the increase in drug use on escalating poverty (McKelvey and Stevens, 1994). The idea behind foster care is that substitute families will provide short-term care until the children can be adopted or returned to their biological parents. Unfortunately, the number of children needing foster care exceeds the availability of foster care homes (Chamberlain, Moreland, and Reid, 1992). Additionally, many children remain in foster care for extended periods of time; others move in and out of the system several times over. This is especially true for older children, those with behavioral or emotional problems, and children of color. The decision to provide foster care is always problematic since it involves removing children from a home generally without parental consent. Social class is often a factor in these decisions. For the most part, middle-class social workers make decisions about the children of the lower classes.

Problems within the Child Welfare System

Every day, newspapers across the country carry stories about abused and neglected children who have fallen through the cracks of the welfare system designed to protect them. The

SEARCHING THE INTERNET

KEY FACTS ABOUT AMERICAN CHILDREN

- 1 in 5 is born poor.
- 1 in 26 is born to a mother who received late or no prenatal care.
- 1 in 13 is born at low birthweight.
- 1 in 4 lives with only one parent.
- 1 in 7 has no health insurance.
- 1 in 8 lives in a family receiving food stamps.
- 2 in 5 never complete a single year of college.
- 1 in 24 lives with neither parent.
- 1 in 1056 is killed by gunfire before age 20.

http://www.childrensdefense.org/keyfacts.html

KEY FACTS ABOUT AFGHANISTAN'S CHILDREN

- 1 out of 4 children dies before her or his first birthday.
- 1 out of 2 children under age 5 is underweight.
- 2 out of 5 boys have access to education; 1 out of 33 girls has access to education.
- 4 children are injured every day by land mines.
- 50,000 children worked on the streets of Kabul before the start of hostilities with the United States.

http://www.193.129.255.931development/latest/afghan_children.pdf

situation is so bad that currently 21 states are under court supervision because they failed to take proper care of the children in their care (Pear, 1996). The problems are many and varied and their solution will require a national commitment to children not currently demonstrated. According to Carole McKelvey and JoEllen Stevens (1994:35–36):

- Welfare workers continue to turn over at a high rate, and many are underpaid, poorly trained, overworked, and demoralized.
- The pool of foster families is shrinking, especially the kind qualified to care for children with multiple problems.
- Services to prepare older youths in foster care for independent living are lacking.
- Permanent adoptive homes for older, handicapped, and healthy children of color are in short supply.
- The needs of children in care are becoming increasingly complex and specialized, and few resources are available to meet their needs.

Although foster care was designed to be a short-term arrangement ending in either the child's return to the care of a competent parent or adoption, "only half of all foster children return home but many of the rest are suspended in a legal limbo by parents who make little effort to regain their children, but refuse to relinquish them fully" (quoted in McKelvey and Stevens, 1994:39). Currently, only about 117,000 of the children in foster care (23 percent) are eligible to be adopted. Researchers have found that the prospects for many children who remain in foster care are not good. After aging out of foster care, 10 percent of females and 27 percent of males were incarcerated within 12 to 18 months; 37 percent had not finished high school; 50 percent were unemployed; and 33 percent received public assistance (National Adoption Information Clearinghouse, 2000b). And, we shall see in the next section, the adoption system has its own set of problems.

The problems of the U.S. adoption system are related to who is eligible for adoption and who is allowed to adopt. Recently, public attention focused on two cases in which unmarried biological fathers contested the biological mothers' actions in placing their children for adoption without their consent. In the past, these fathers were largely ignored by public agencies and rarely involved in adoption proceedings. After lengthy legal battles, the courts ruled in favor of the biological fathers. The media images of these two children being removed from the arms of their adoptive parents generated considerable public outrage and raised fears among many adoptive parents that such cases undermined the legitimacy of the adoption system itself. Despite these fears, adoption remains a competitive process. To get an edge, many couples advertise in newspapers and over the Internet seeking to initiate contact with birth mothers around the country.

Characteristics of Adoptive Parents

CLASS Couples who adopt are most commonly white and affluent with at least some college education (Bachrach et al., 1990; Barth, Brooks, and Iyer, 1995), whereas the children to be adopted come primarily from economically disadvantaged backgrounds. Part of this redistribution of children is the result of the requirements of adoption agencies, which set standards that many biological parents would be unable to meet, for example, that the adoptive mother not work outside the home. Due to the shortage of healthy infants, prospective parents using an adoption agency face a waiting period of 5 or more years. Thus, many couples (as well as some unmarried women and men) have sought privately arranged adoptions through an attorney or a physician rather than an agency. Lynne McTaggart (1980) exposed some of the more exploitive aspects of such arrangements in her book *The Baby Brokers.* Among some of the excesses she reported are the placement of want ads for white babies in economically depressed communities and some questionable practices involving babies from economically poor countries, including pressure to relinquish parental rights, baby selling, and even kidnapping. These practices are still occurring. In recent years, evidence of kidnapping and sale of babies was found in Paraguay and Mexico (Schemo, 1996; Thompson, 1999). In late fall of 2001, the United States interrupted the adoptions of Cambodian children (the ninth largest source of foreign babies adopted by Americans, nearly 100 a month) because of doubts that all the babies were orphans. There was suspicion that some babies were being bought and sold by a chain of corrupt officials and middlemen (Mydans, 2001). Shortly before the holidays, the U.S. Immigration and Naturalization Service allowed parents whose adoptions were put on "parole" to bring their adopted Cambodian children home. However, these parents have to report to the INS regularly, reapply to adopt within 2 years, and promise to return the children to Cambodia if it is proven that they are not orphans.

Private adoptions may be closed or open. In a **closed adoption,** the adoptive parents and the birth parents do not meet. In **open adoptions,** however, the two parties meet and together work out the process of adoption. The birth mother may even take an active role in selecting the adoptive parents. In some cases the adoptive parents will invite the birth mother to live with them during her pregnancy. Some open adoptions are characterized by ongoing contact with the birth mother. The extent of the contact may vary from periodic reports of the child's progress to the birth mother's integration into the family as a friend or **fictive kin,** in which kinship terms are attributed to nonrelatives. The costs of private adoptions can exceed $30,000. Thus, this alternative to agency adoption is limited to the wealthier classes. Even the agency fees may be out of reach for many couples. According to the National Council for Adoption, the average fee collected by agencies is $11,000 (Neikirk, 1996).

Marital Status In the past, adoption agencies considered only couples as suitable candidates to adopt children. However, around 1978 single-parent adoptions became possible. Since then there has been a steady increase in such adoptions. According to the National Adoption Center, approximately 25 percent of the adoptions of children with special needs are by single women and men; it is estimated that about 5 percent of all other adoptions are by single people (Davis, 1996). As in the case of single biological parents, concern is frequently expressed about the need for other-sex role models in single-parent adoptions. To meet this need, single adoptive parents usually create support groups involving relatives and friends. For example, one single adoptive mother described how her brother picks her children up from school, takes them home, and cooks them dinner. "I think it's really good for them to see a man cooking so they get the message that that's not just a female role" (quoted in Davis, 1996:18).

Sexual Orientation Although single heterosexuals have been accepted as adoptive parents for the past two decades, it is only recently that lesbians and gays have been allowed that same right, but not in all states. Recently, a federal judge upheld a 1977 Florida law that bars homosexuals from adopting children. Two of the plaintiffs in the case were Dough Houghton and Steven Lofton. Houghton, a nurse practitioner, became the legal guardian of a 3-year-old boy with health problems and learning disabilities. After 6 years, and with the boy's relatives amenable, he applied to adopt him (Crary, 2001). Lofton, a pediatric nurse who raised a 10-year-old boy from infancy, was recruited as a foster parent in 1988 to care for African American babies with HIV. He and his longtime partner did such a fine job as caregivers that the Children's Home Society honored them with the first Foster Parents of the Year award. When the couple moved to Oregon to be closer to Lofton's family, the court allowed Lofton to take along three children who had been placed in his long-term care, including the 10-year-old. In 2000, the Florida legislature forbade long-term foster care for children younger than 14. The state Department of Children and Families plans to put the boy up for adoption even though Lofton and his partner are the only parents he knows (Bell, 2001). Although lesbians and gays are allowed to be foster parents in Florida, they are barred from adopting children, the argument being that adoptive children belong with traditional married couples. Unlike their heterosexual counterparts, Houghton and Lofton were judged unsuitable not in terms of their ability to rear and nurture children but in terms of their sexual orientation and lifestyle. In fact, this discriminatory treatment of lesbians and gays is often applied even to biological parents.

International Adoptions

Because of a shortage of healthy babies, many couples have turned to international adoptions. The majority of international adoptions involve infants of color from economically disadvantaged countries. In 1980, there were approximately 5000 international adoptions; in 1999, 16,396 Russian, South Korean, Chinese, Romanian, and Guatemalan children were adopted by U.S. parents (National Adoption Information Clearinghouse, 2000a). In the case of China, where there is an intense preference for male heirs, it is estimated that as many as 150,000 female infants are abandoned each year. The Chinese government has allowed foreign adoptions as one means of dealing with this problem. Although not widely publicized, between 100 and 500 international adoptions involving U.S. children and Canadian and European parents occur each year ("At Least 100 Children . . . ," 1997).

International adoptions can be risky. The adoptive parents must confront numerous bureaucratic obstacles before the proceedings are finalized and the child is allowed to leave the country. These proceedings are likely to be costly, often involving legal fees in both countries as well as the payment of "contributions" or bribes to various agencies and officials. More importantly, many of the international children available for adoption have been institutionalized for extensive periods of time and, as a result, their emotional development has been stunted, making it difficult for them to bond with their new parents; others may have acute illnesses that are not disclosed to the adoptive parents. Consequently, some adoptive parents find that they are unprepared for children with so many needs, and they give up the adopted child, a process known as "disruption." Parents who make this decision do not do so lightly and they suffer pain, guilt, embarrassment, grief, and a sense of failure. Children suffer, too. They may become even more emotionally withdrawn, and, as a result, become more difficult to place with another family. Although figures are not available for disruptions involving international adoptions, social workers do report seeing an increase. They attribute this pattern to the increased number of children coming from institutionalized settings after being abused, neglected, or abandoned, as well as an increase in the number of older children placed for adoption. Domestic adoptions fail, too, often for similar reasons. Studies indicate domestic disruption rates ranging from 10 percent to 20 percent, depending on the type of adoption. Less than 1 percent of infant adoptions are disrupted compared to almost 14 percent for children aged 12 to 18 (Barth and Berry, 1988). However, adoptions of children of any age with special needs are more likely to be disrupted than children without special needs (Groza and Rosenberg, 1998). Again, the older the child and the more emotional and physical problems the child has, the higher the disruption rate. The growing public recognition of disruptions led Congress to include a provision in the 1997 Adoption and Safe Families Act that provides federal assistance for children who, their adoptions disrupted, must return to foster care.

Transracial (Interracial) Adoptions

Race is also a factor in the politics and policies of the adoption process. Approximately 64 percent of children waiting in foster care are children of color: 51 percent African American, 11 percent Latina/o, 1 percent Native American, 1 percent Asian/Pacific Islander, 32 percent white, and the remaining 5 percent unknown/unable to determine. An estimated 15 percent of the 36,000 adoptions of foster children in 1998 were transracial or transcultural adoptions (National Adoption Information Clearinghouse, 2000b, 2000c). Many children of color will remain in foster care indefinitely because prospective parents of color can't meet agency income and housing requirements and because of the curtailment of interracial adoptions (Beck, 1988). The 1960s and early 1970s witnessed a rapid growth in transracial adoptions. Between 1969 and 1974 more than 80 percent of the Native American children adopted were placed with white families. During the same time, many Native Americans were rejected as adoptive parents because they did not meet agency criteria. By 1972, approximately 10,000 African American children had been adopted by white couples (cited in McRoy, 1989).

Over the past 2 decades, people of color have become more critical of interracial adoptions, raising concerns about the possible adjustment problems these children might have and the loss of these children to their original communities. The first concern has not materialized. Research has shown that adopted children raised in interracial homes generally adjust well (Alstein and Simon, 1992). Karen Vroegh, director of research for the Chicago Child Care Society, tracked a group of transracial adoptees over a 20-year period and found that "black children adopted by white families have no more difficulties, are not more poorly adjusted and do not have lower self-esteem than black children adopted by black families, white children adopted by white families or birth children in both black and white families" (quoted in Peres, 1996).

The research findings on identity issues are mixed. Some studies have suggested that transracial adoptees do struggle with identity issues (McRoy, Grotevant, and Zurcher, 1988); part of the difficulty seems to be that transracial adoptees, now young adults, do not have the skills to cope with racism and prejudice that other African Americans acquire as children (Curtis, 1996). However, according to other research

Regina Bush hugs her two adopted daughters after Stacey's adoption became final in Flint, Michigan in 1998. Bush's adoption of 9-year-old Stacey (right) followed months of legal struggle. Stacey's adoption attracted media attention because it is one of the relatively rare cases involving the adoption of a white child by an African American parent.

this does not appear to be the case. Transracial adoptees tended to see themselves as African American or of mixed race depending on the race of their birth parents, even if they were raised in all-white neighborhoods. As a biracial young woman said, "You just have to look in the mirror." Her African American brother agreed, adding, "Or go into a store and watch how the clerk never takes his eyes off of you. I get a lesson in racial identity every time I walk through a door" (quoted in Peres, 1996).

This controversy led many agencies to revert to race matching for adoption placements; in the 1980s only about 8 percent of adoptions were interracial (Bachrach et al., 1990). Recently, however, the controversy has taken another turn. Some public officials, believing that race-matching practices deny thousands of children of color a stable and permanent home, pushed for legislation to limit the practice and to reduce the length of time children wait to be adopted or placed in foster care. In response to these pressures Congress passed the Multiethnic Placement Act of 1994. The law prohibits any agency that receives federal funds from denying a foster care or adoption placement solely on the basis of race, color, or national origin.

Until more progress is made in race relations, transracial adoptions are likely to be controversial and one-sided. With rare exception have people of color been able to adopt white children. Additionally, with an increasing number of children living in biracial or multiracial families, either as a result of adoption or birth, racial identity is fast becoming one of the most urgent and controversial issues facing marriages, families, schools, the work force, and society at large today. Given the nature of U.S. race relations and the demographic changes that ushered in the twenty-first century, it is imperative that we reexamine the manner in which people are categorized racially and ethnically and then treated on the basis of these categories. In the next section we examine some of the challenges of racism to the quality of marriage and family life.

What could be done to help adoptive parents meet the needs of children with multiple problems so as to prevent adoption disruptions? As adoptions have become more visible, so, too, have issues over privacy. Should adopted children have the right to know about their biological parents? Should biological parents have the right to privacy if they relinquish parental rights? Can these conflicting rights be resolved? Explain.

THE CHALLENGE OF RACISM AND ETHNIC AND RELIGIOUS DISCRIMINATION IN FAMILY LIFE

In the past 2 decades there has been a resurgence of racist hate groups in the United States such as the Ku Klux Klan, the Aryan Nations, the Skinheads, the White Aryan Resistance (WAR), the Posse Comitatus, and various others categorized as Christian Identity (religions that are fundamentally racist and anti-Semitic) and Black Separatists (groups whose ideologies include tenets of racially based hatred) (Farley, 1995; Southern Poverty Law Center, 2001a). According to the Southern Poverty Law Center (SPLC), which keeps track of the actions of hate groups, all hate groups have beliefs or practices that attack or denigrate an entire class of people, typically for their beliefs or immutable characteristics. The proliferation of hate-based groups in the United States was highlighted by the SPLC in a 2001 Intelligence Report that listed 602 hate groups operating in the United States. This list included only those hate groups known to be active in 2000, whether that activity included marches, rallies, speeches, meetings, leafleting, publishing literature, or criminal acts; it did not include the numerous hate groups that operate in cyberspace. The fact is that racism, prejudice, discrimination, violence, and inequality among racial and ethnic groups are deeply interwoven into the fabric of American society. However, as we will see in our discussion of racism and ethnic discrimination in a global context later in this chapter, patterns of racism and discrimination similar to those in the United States can be found in a number of countries around the world.

The increasing immigration of peoples from many of these countries into the United States has had and continues to have a significant impact on race and ethnic relations in this country; and racial and ethnic prejudice, discrimination, and violence in this country have often been influenced by international relationships. A classic example occurred during the 1940s, when 100,000 Japanese Americans, many of whom were U.S. citizens, were interned for over 2 years in concentration camps. In addition to the racially inspired imprisonment of Japanese women, men, and children, many of these individuals and families lost most or all of their possessions, property, and businesses. When the war was over, many of these families were left homeless and destitute. Another example occurred during the 1991 Persian Gulf War; hate crimes against Arab Americans tripled over the previous year. And in 2001, the September terrorist attack triggered a violent outbreak of American racism and religious intolerance against people identified as or thought to be of Middle Eastern descent and Muslim. Just 4 days after the attacks on the World Trade Center and the Pentagon, for example, shopkeepers were shot to death in California, Texas, and Arizona as a racist and anti-Muslim backlash broke out around the country. According to a spokeswoman for the American Arab Anti-Discrimination Committee (ADC), the racist and anti-Muslim incidents following September 11 ranged from hate mail to verbal threats and assaults to crimes that resulted in deaths. Exactly 1 month after the terrorist attacks, the ADC had collected more than 700 reports of hate crimes, and the Council on American-Islamic Relations had collected 785 such reports. Arab Americans and Muslims have been shot at, spat on, and physically assaulted on college campuses, on the streets, and in their workplaces. Mosques and worshipers became the targets of rocks, bullets, arson, and Molotov cocktails. In Salt Lake City, a man set fire to a Pakistani restaurant; in Palos Heights, Illinois, a man attacked a Moroccan gas station attendant with a machete, and in Reedley, California, a group of four teenagers were accused of shooting to death a Yemeni native at his convenience store. Moreover, the targets of hate were not limited to people of Middle Eastern descent. Next to natives of the Middle East, the American Sikh community was the hardest hit by hate crimes, and Native Americans, Asian Americans, Latinas/os, and natives of Israel were also targets of the racism of American "patriots," acting both individually and in groups (SPLC Intelligence Report, 2001b). According to the SPLC, a posting on abcnews.com provided a poignant view of this latest form of American racism, or **xenophobia**—a fear or hatred of strangers or foreigners or of anything foreign and/or different—that read: "We will always be at risk as long as we allow scum from other countries to live in our free society" (SPLC Intelligence Report, 2001b:2). Such attitudes and incidents of hatred and violence toward groups who are associated with "the enemy" are much more likely if people already hold significant racial or ethnic prejudice against them (Farley, 1995).

Sometimes, racial and ethnic prejudice and violence accompany surges in immigration into the United States. Most often the targets of this discrimination and violence have been non-European immigrants of color. A growing number of Americans, whose ancestors themselves were immigrants, oppose immigration and are increasingly intolerant of immigrants. For example, national polls reveal that while three-fifths of Americans believe that immigration was a good thing in the past, they think it is a bad thing today. Furthermore, among those polled, there was considerably more opposition to immigration from Latin America, Africa, Asia, and the Caribbean than to immigration from Eastern Europe. Fully one-half, or one of every two people polled believe that immigration should be limited and people immigrating illegally should be vigorously prosecuted while one in five believe that immigration should be stopped immediately (Morganthau, 1993; Zogby National Poll, 2000). Even high school students, when asked to identify their greatest concerns for the future of the United States from a list of ten issues, identified concern about immigration fourth most often. Over one-half (52 percent) of the students indicated that the solution to immigration would be to accept fewer immigrants into the country and crack down on illegal immigration (Forum on America's Future, 2000). And since September 11, 2001, a majority of Americans say they favor having Arabs, even those who are U.S. citizens, being subjected to separate, more intensive security procedures at airports, and about half favor requiring Arabs, including those who are U.S. citizens, to carry special ID (Gallup Tuesday Briefing, 2001a).

Americans' opposition and intolerance are increasingly manifest not only in violent actions and activities but also in local and national legislation. For example, the growth of the Latino population has sparked the passage of "official language" legislation; in 1993, the governor of California proposed restrictive legislation aimed at controlling so-called illegal immigration. Among the goals of the legislation was the elimination of social service benefits to which even children of illegal immigrants had previously been legally entitled (Farley, 1995); in 1996, Proposition 209—legislation that eliminated state and local government affirmative action programs in public employment, public education, and public contracting—won in the state of California by a 54 percent to 46 percent vote; and in 2001, after the September 11 attacks, the Bush administration detained for interview over 5000 young men from the Middle East who were in the United States on temporary visas. The government said the men were not suspects and the interviews were voluntary. Others, including lawyers for some of the detainees, dispute that the detention/interviews were voluntary. Rather, they charged that the government singled out these young men unfairly, solely on the basis of their national origin.

Racism in the United States

Although many forces impinge on family life in the United States, racism continues to be one of the major challenges to the well-being of many families, particularly families of color. It is commonly believed that many, if not all, of the problems that families of color experience are a function of a lack of or decline in family values. However, because of the persistent racism and discrimination in major societal institutions such as education and the work force, these families are forced, structurally, to bear a disproportionately higher percentage of poverty, unemployment and underemployment, welfare dependency, dropping out of schools, infant mortality, illness, and early death.

Racism is an ideology of domination and a set of social, economic, and political practices by which one or more groups define themselves as superior and other groups as inferior and then systematically deny the latter groups full access and participation in mainstream society. Racism can be both overt and covert. On the one hand, it can be manifested when individuals or groups considering themselves superior act against individuals whom they define as inferior. According to Stokely Carmichael and Charles Hamilton in their now classic work *Black Power: The Politics of Liberation in America* (1967), this behavior can be defined as **individual racism.** It is expressed through personal attitudes and behavior directed toward certain racial or ethnic groups by individual people. It can range from individual acts such as derogatory name-calling, biased treatment during face-to-face contact, and avoidance, to overt acts by individuals that cause death, injury, or the violent destruction of property. This type of racism can be reached by television cameras and videocassette recorders; it can often be observed while it is taking place, such as the infamous Rodney King beating by five white Los Angeles policemen; or the brutal beating of Mexican immigrants in Los Angeles; or the brutality against an African American female motorist by a highway

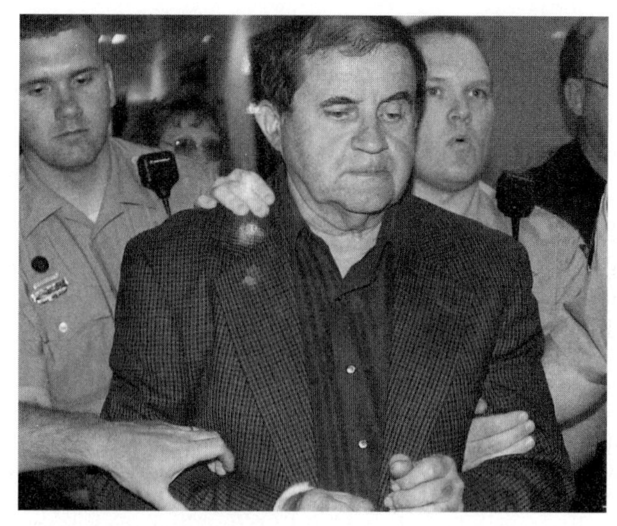

Racist acts of violence have been common throughout U.S. history. The perpetrators of such acts have often gone unpunished. However, almost 40 years after the bombing of the 16th Street Baptist Church in Birmingham, Alabama, where four young African American girls were killed, Thomas Blanton, Jr., a former Ku Klux Klansman, was finally convicted in 2001 for the murders.

patrolman, videotaped by his own police camera. This kind of racism receives the most media attention.

On the other hand, racism can be manifested when a total community acts against another entire community. This behavior can be defined as institutional racism. Institutional racism is less overt, far more subtle, and far less easy to identify in terms of specific individuals committing the acts than is individual racism. However, it is no less destructive to human life. This kind of racism has its origins in the operation of established and respected forces in the society and thus receives far less public attention, scrutiny, and condemnation than do individual acts of racism. **Institutional racism** consists of established laws, customs, and practices that systematically reflect and produce racial inequalities in a society, whether or not the individuals maintaining these practices have racist intentions (Newman, 1995).

When a group of white students at the University of Connecticut spit at and taunt a small group of Asian American students who are on their way to a dance; when white terrorists burn down African American churches; when a white female author co-opts Native American culture and artifacts for publication and profit; and when a Latino student is belittled by a teacher for not speaking "proper" English, it is an individual act of racism and condemned by many people. While the impact of these acts extends beyond the individuals involved, they are nonetheless individual actions from which "respectable" members of society can divorce themselves. However, when in cities all across this country a highly disproportionate number of African American children are born into poverty or die because of a lack of adequate food, shelter, and medical facilities; when a disproportionate percentage of Latina/o students drop out of school; when the federal government evacuates over a hundred thousand persons of Japanese ancestry into concentration camps, two-thirds of whom are American citizens; when a group of people are made wards of the government and forced to live on reservations and to assimilate and when law enforcement agencies around the country (police, state troopers, and airport immigration officials) routinely use racial profiling against minority groups—using race as a basis to stop and search an individual—it is an example of institutional racism. Although both types of racism are insidious and damaging to marriages and families, our primary concern in this section is with the impact of institutional racism for various families in the United States and globally.

Historically, various groups of color in the United States have often been routinely victimized by the powerful force of institutional racism. While the focus here is on racism, keep in mind that race does not operate in a vacuum and is intricately interwoven with class, gender, and other important social axes of experience to shape marriage and family life.

Despite the fact that life conditions for some families of color have improved, the majority of families of color remain disadvantaged by racial and ethnic inequality, on almost every measure of status and well-being in U.S. society. Numerous discriminatory processes exist that make it harder for some groups to get ahead in American society than it is for whites. For many groups of color, this means that life is a day-to-day struggle for survival. For all families of color, it means facing socially imposed disadvantages that they would not face if they were white. Poor education, concentrated poverty, and rising unemployment in the country's predominantly African American and Latino inner cities are making it increasingly difficult for the people who live there to develop the skills needed in today's high-tech economic environment.

Although discrimination is no longer legal, informal practices persist. A variety of studies (for example, ABC News, 1991; U.S. Department of Housing and Urban Development, 1991; Ahmad, 1993) show that African Americans and whites are often treated differently when they shop, apply for jobs, attempt to rent or buy housing, and apply for mortgages. In addition, increasingly, racist epithets, slurs, and actions have been perpetrated against blacks as well as Middle Easterners on college campuses, and intolerance and racism are increasingly expressed by whites on local and national talk radio and television. Likewise, the ongoing racism and hostility faced by Asian Americans such as the Chinese are said to be important factors that help explain Chinese poverty. Chicanos, whose families have lived in the United States for generations, find themselves blamed, along with new Latino immigrants, for many of the economic problems of this country. And the rights of Native American families continue to be subordinated to the rights of white Americans.

Thus, while middle-class families of color have made some gains, among most of these groups a number of their members are part of a growing underclass. This impoverished underclass, which outnumbers the middle class among all four major groups of color, is trapped in poverty and unable to move up. Moreover, the future for individuals and families who live in areas of concentrated poverty is increasingly bleak. The effects of growing up in poverty are alone enough to greatly reduce the opportunities one has in life (Farley, 1995). Various research studies provide ample evidence of a link between race and poverty. For example, institutional racism and discrimination often lock a group into a cycle of poverty, illiteracy, hopelessness, and violence. Moreover, this research shows that widespread economic inequality and marginality are perhaps the greatest threats today to the vitality and long-term survival of marriages and families of color. It has devastating effects, particularly on children of color.

Although families of color continually make serious efforts to defend the integrity of their cultures and their families and to advance their social position in the face of such persistent racism, prejudice, and discrimination from the wider society, many whites continue to think of individuals and families of color in stereotypic terms. They believe, for example, that many people of color prefer welfare to jobs, and that they are lazy, violent, less intelligent, and less patriotic than whites. In addition, many whites believe that there is little or no racial inequality present in American society today. They generally believe that the American system is a fair one and that other groups have just as many if not more opportunities for success in American society. Thus, if these groups are disadvantaged they are themselves responsible for that disadvantage (Kluegel, 1990; Duke, 1991; Polling Report, 2001).

The racial attitudes of many whites are consistent with what some researchers have labeled **symbolic racism,** the denial of the presence of racial inequality in society and the opposition to any social policy (such as affirmative action, busing) aimed at undoing the effects of racism and discrimination (Kinder and Sears, 1981; Pettigrew, 1985; McClelland and Auster, 1990). They believe that such efforts undermine the principle of achievement and reward based on merit. However, even a cursory examination of statistics descriptive of the general quality of life of families of color contradicts this point of view.

Some social scientists (for example, Wilson, 1980) have argued that race has declined as a significant factor in the discriminatory treatment and unequal socioeconomic status of some racial groups, especially African Americans. If this is the case then we would expect that middle- and upper-class members of these groups would face little, if any, discrimination. However, research shows that, in fact, middle- and upper-class members of various racial groups face discrimination and prejudice, from a lack of respect to outright exclusion. For example, in her study of the effects of race in the lives of African American elites, researcher Lois Benjamin (1991) debunked the myth that racism affects only poor people of color. Benjamin found that racism continues to shape the lives of people of color no matter how far they move up the socioeconomic ladder, that individual effort and personal achievement do not free people of color from the experience of hostility based on skin color nor the general burden of racism, and that there is a race-based "glass ceiling" that limits mobility into the highest social and political positions in this society. Other research such as that conducted by Joe Feagin (1991) is consistent with Benjamin's findings.

Not only are the quality of life and the well-being of individuals and families in the United States challenged by racism and prejudice, but so is their physical well-being. This is especially true for people of color and Jews. For example, in 1999, Benjamin Smith, a 22-year-old white youth who was a member of a midwestern-based racist hate group went on a two-state killing spree, killing an African American and an Asian American and injuring nine others, all members of minority groups, before killing himself. And, as we have noted, the health and well-being of people of Middle Eastern descent and those who embrace the Muslim religion are increasingly threatened by those who blame them for the terrorist attacks against the United States on September 11. According to Daniel Goleman (1990), two-thirds of hate crimes involve attacks made on families moving into a neighborhood where they are not welcome. Most such crimes are committed by young white males in their teens to 20s. These crimes should not be mistaken for youthful folly, however. These young perpetrators of hate and violence are acting out attitudes and values, opinions, and beliefs shared by their families, friends, and/or communities (Gelles and Levine, 1995). W.E.B. DuBois (1967) suggested at the dawn of the twentieth century that the problem of the twentieth century would be the problem of the color line. It is perhaps safe to say that the problem of the twenty-first century continues to be the problem of the color line. Unless the attitudes and institutional arrangements that serve to benefit some groups while disadvantaging others change, the well-being of families such as those described here will remain at risk.

Racism in a Global Context

Racism, prejudice, and discrimination are common throughout the world. Racial and ethnic pride and solidarity among some groups are on the rise, and racial and ethnic conflict around the world is increasing. Wherever racial and ethnic conflicts are played out, the consequences for marriages and families have been devastation and despair. In Western European countries, for example, the rise of neo-Nazism suggests that far from being a fringe activity, racism, violence, and neo-nationalism have become normal in many countries (Shah, 1998). In many of these countries, growing immigrant populations have been accompanied by high levels of prejudice and discrimination, sometimes mild and covert but increasingly overt and extremely violent. In this regard, the United Kingdom has one of the highest rates of racial violence in Western Europe. For example, in 1999, neo-Nazi groups bombed several predominantly ethnic minority areas in London within 1 week, and the summer of 2001 was characterized by a high number of race-related riots in various parts of northern England (Shah, 1998). In Germany, hatred and violent attacks against "foreigners" escalated throughout the 1990s. Members of various right-wing white supremacist groups such as the neo-Nazis and the skinheads openly sported swastikas, dressed in a manner reminiscent of Nazi storm troopers, and called for "kicking the foreigners out" of Germany. These foreigners—Africans, Turks, Gypsies, and other immigrant groups identifiable by skin color—have suffered increasing violence, including death, at the hands of these groups. Violent attacks against these groups have resulted in scores of injuries, and arson attacks on their homes have left many families homeless. In France, extremist groups push for the ouster of North African immigrants (about 8 percent of the population) and claim that France must be made "racially pure"; and in Italy, there is an increasing racist reaction to the rise in undocumented immigrants from Tunisia. Spain is also experiencing an increase in racial violence. The growing Spanish economy invites immigrants from North African countries such as Morocco. However, the poor conditions that immigrants have to endure in an already racially charged region have led to friction and racial confrontations. And in the Middle East, the most visible racism and violence occur between Palestinians and Israelis. Extreme views and religious intolerance within both groups have resulted in ongoing hostilities, racism, and violence perpetrated by people from both groups (Shah, 1998).

As nations experience increasing immigration from other countries, they often must deal with tensions arising from intolerance of racial/ethnic and religious differences. Prejudice and discrimination become more pronounced in periods of economic and political unrest, often in the form of repressive laws. Here, several hundred demonstrators in Berlin protest the new immigration law by German Interior Minister Otto Schily. The sentence on the banner reads: "Asylum rights are human rights and not privileges! Stop Schily's racist law!"

This glut of global racial and ethnic hatred and violence is perhaps nowhere more blatantly exemplified than in the case of the Yugoslavian countries of Kosovo and Bosnia-Herzegovina, where groups of people embarked on a systematic campaign of so-called **ethnic cleansing,** by which one category of people tried to rid the region of others who were different in some significant way. This policy included the massive murder of thousands of Bosnians, Serbs, Croats, and ethnic Albanians, the brutalization of a million more, and the displacement of thousands of Bosnians, Croats, and Kosovars and their families.

As in Europe, the collapse of totalitarian states in Africa and Asia has been accompanied by a resurgence of sometimes long-standing racial and ethnic hatred and conflict. The consequences of these conflicts have been devastating for individuals and families. For example, although apartheid has been dismantled in South Africa, deep racial tensions continue; in Zimbabwe, there has been increasing racism directed toward white farmers, due to poverty and a lack of landownership by Africans; and in India and other Asian nations, differences in color and culture frequently lead to prejudice, discrimination, violence, and death. In far too many instances, racial or ethnic groups have been enslaved, impoverished, disenfranchised, and even exterminated in the name of power and ethnic purity. For instance, in just 100 days in 1994, up to a million men, women, and children were slaughtered and millions more were uprooted in the African nations of Burundi and Rwanda as the result of an ethnic war between the Hutus and the Tutsi (two groups who consider themselves distinct races). The overwhelming majority of these victims were members of the Tutsi ethnic group. The genocide in Rwanda showed just how quickly racism—in this case, in the form of ethnic hatred—unchecked, can erupt into bloodshed, death, and despair, particularly when it is fueled by those with power or those seeking power (Amnesty International, 2001a). It is generally cases such as Kosovo, Bosnia-Herzegovina, Rwanda, and Burundi (some of the worst violations of human rights based on racism) that we hear about, but abuses based partially or entirely on racism take place everyday around the world. For example, have you ever heard of the Roma? Probably not. However, Roma, more commonly known as

Gypsies, have been viewed as outsiders since shortly after their arrival in Europe. During the Nazi regime, like Jews, Roma were subjected to interment, forced labor, and massacre. Thought of as "racially inferior," the Roma continue to face widespread discrimination in Europe today (Amnesty International, 2001a; U.S. Holocaust Memorial Museum, 2002). And finally, in the wake of the terrorism committed in the United States on September 11, 2001, not only has there been an outpouring of violent racial hatred against people of Middle Eastern descent in this country but also, with the American-led attacks in Afghanistan in retaliation for those terrorist attacks, from Egypt to Pakistan there have been violent street protests as well as racist acts against anyone and anything that appears to be Western, especially American (Shah, 2001). Moreover, in this contemporary age of advanced technology, a discussion of global racism would not be complete without at least mentioning the fact that ideas of racial superiority have spread to new media like the World Wide Web (Internet), fueling the prejudice and hatred of peoples around the world.

So, then, individuals and families move in and out of countries fleeing prejudice, discrimination, racism, poverty, and political oppression only to face new prejudice, discrimination, and racism. The resulting injury, humiliation, and destructiveness affect not only individual lives but also whole families and whole societies. For example, what of the mothers, fathers, siblings, and marital partners of the thousands of women, men, and children who have been slaughtered in Bosnia-Herzegovina? In Kosovo? In Burundi? What impact must the constant strife, violence, and ethnic wars have for family life and well-being? How do families cope with the reality of soldiers burning down their homes?

These are compelling and challenging questions for the future well-being of individuals and groups and of marriages and families around the world. Racism, racial discrimination, xenophobia, and related intolerance attack the most basic notion of human rights—that everyone is equal in dignity and worth (Amnesty International, 2001b). As racial discrimination and ethnic violence grow in complexity and spiral in intensity, they become more and more a challenge for the global community. Although there have been some significant advances in the global fight against racism, racial discrimination, xenophobia, and related intolerance since the 1948 adoption of the UN Universal Declaration of Human Rights, as our discussion of racism indicates, the world is nowhere near being free of racial hatred and bias. In its quest to meet the global challenge not only of making the world aware of global racism but also to create a new world vision to combat racism and other human rights violations in the twenty-first century, in 2001 the UN General Assembly held a World Conference against Racism in Durban, South Africa. Although the conference was fraught with disputes ranging from reparations for slavery to Zionism as racism against Palestinians and from castes to peoples, according to Amnesty International (2001b), it did achieve some important successes. For example, for the first time, the plight of groups such as Dalits, Roma, Tibetans, indigenous people, those who face multiple forms of racism and discrimination such as refugees, women, and gays and lesbians, and those living under political occupation was put forcefully on the world agenda. Conference attendees and the world heard from the victims of racism themselves, and despite disagreements and walk-outs, governments were still bound by their international obligations to take effective action against racism (Amnesty International, 2001b:1). A spokesperson for Amnesty International said that the level and extent of racism around the world were made clear at the conference and, if nothing else, the conference succeeded in establishing the beginnings of a global alliance against racism. How successful this alliance against racism will be remains to be seen.

Is life very different for poor, working-class, and families of color in the United States who are often caught in a web of violence, violence that is both directly and indirectly related to deep-rooted racism, bigotry, and discrimination? How do these families cope with such violence? What impact does it have on the structure and stability of family life?

SAFETY AND SECURITY: GANGS, STREET VIOLENCE, AND VIOLENCE IN AMERICA'S SCHOOLS

The term *gang* strikes fear into the hearts of some people; disgust, resentment, and hatred in others. Still others use the term as a code word to describe inner-city neighborhoods and their residents as well as to rationalize the widening gap between rich and poor, people of color and whites, and the alarming increase in police brutality and murder of people of color. Gangs are not new in the United States. Major cities across the country have long been the home of gangs, some of whom have been around consistently for 50 or more years. For example, in Chicago, the first street gangs appeared at the turn of the twentieth century, mostly in Irish communities. However, when most people think about gangs today, they picture African American and Latino/a youths. But white street gangs continue to exist (Macko, 1996). Gangs are usually composed of people of the same race or ethnicity. In Los Angeles, for example, there are street gangs representing almost every racial and ethnic group living in the city.

GANGS Gangs and gang violence is a serious problem, particularly in large urban cities. However, gangs are not limited to cities. Gangs can also be found in rural areas across the United States. Often rural areas contain chapters of major gangs found in cities. Some experts estimate that gangs account for as much as 40 percent of crime and violence in this country. Over the last 2 decades, gang violence has escalated in many cities across the country, and the attendant loss of life is staggering. According to Louis Sullivan, former secretary of the Department of Health and

Human Services, every hundred hours more young men are killed on the streets of America than were killed in a hundred hours of ground war in the Persian Gulf (cited in Soroka and Bryjak, 1995). Gang-related killings have become so common that police departments now use the term *gang homicide* to denote it as a separate and unique category of criminal behavior (Senna and Siegel, 1999).

The economic, physical, and psychological costs of gangs and their activities to individuals and their families are extremely high. Especially devastating to families and the community are the ongoing illegal activities and violence that often accompany gangs. For example, in Los Angeles County alone, it is estimated that there are over 600 gangs with a membership of 70,000. Many of these gangs are loosely organized into the two biggest gangs in the city, the Bloods and the Crips, who control a significant portion of the drug trade (Senna and Siegel, 1999). These activities can be lucrative for gang members but can have a debilitating effect on family and community life. With substantial sums of money at stake, gang members often fight over dominance and control of these illegal activities. The results of these battles are deaths and injuries that equal those of a small war. In the mid-1990s, for example, Los Angeles averaged one gang-related death a day; Los Angeles and Chicago together accounted for more than 1000 youth and adult homicides (Bryak and Soroka, 1994; Howell, 1998).

Not only do gang members kill each other, but as in contemporary war, innocent bystanders (civilians) are increasingly the victims of gang violence. A growing number of these victims are children, murdered by stray bullets from drive-by shootings or the crossfire from open gang warfare on city streets. In a Chicago community, all that is left as a reminder of the life and death of 4-year-old Robert Anderson III, who was killed by a stray bullet in the summer of 2001 while making mud pies in front of his home, is a miniature license plate with the words "You've Got a Friend in Jesus" hanging on a tree in his memory near where he was killed. All across the country today, life seems more fragile, more dangerous as a result of the September 11 attacks and subsequent threats of biological warfare. Everyday life for many people is now tinged with fear for themselves, their children, and other loved ones. However, fear for self and family was a fact of life in many communities ravaged by gangs and gang violence long before September 11 (Fountain, 2001). Most parents and family members have not had to wonder if their children would be safe playing in front of their homes, sitting on the porch, or, for that matter, sitting in their living rooms. One of the consequences of living with this kind of fear for individuals and families is the separation of family members. For example, some parents, fearing gang recruitment and other activities, send their children to live with relatives in other cities. Others who can afford it send their children to private or parochial schools or to boarding schools outside of the city. Parents worry about daughters as well as sons. Although seldom focused upon, a large number of female gangs operate around the country, and their members are sometimes equally as violent as their male counterparts. According to one study of seventh- and eighth-grade students in Rochester, New York, a significant number of girls were gang members. It is estimated that somewhere between 10 percent and 25 percent of gang members nationwide are female (Thornberry and Burch, 1997; Adler, Mueller, and Laufer, 1998).

Gangs are not only a serious problem in the United States. Canadian officials report a growing problem of gangs in cities such as Toronto, where small bands of young males attack individuals and rob stores, and in Winnipeg, where membership in gangs has exploded with police estimates as high as 800 gangs, the majority of them Aboriginal gangs (Smith, 1996). Even Japan is experiencing problems with gangs. The Japanese term *bosozoku* (translated to mean "violent running tribes") refers to Japanese street gangs whose membership includes women as well as men between the ages of 16 and the mid 20s. In Japan, bosozoku often roam the streets in packs of over one hundred members, harassing, intimidating, and physically attacking innocent victims (Yates, 1990; Sakurai, 2001).

Increasingly, we can see the global connection to gangs and gang activities in the United States. For example, once they are in the United States, many immigrant youths form or join gangs, contributing to the proliferation of gangs and gang-related problems in many major U.S. cities. The reverse is often true, as well. That is, immigrants who were gang members in the United States sometimes take their gang affiliations and criminal behavior back to their homelands. An example can be seen in the case of young El Salvadorian immigrants, many of whom became Americanized, including joining gangs. Returning home after a 12-year civil war in El Salvador, these gang members brought with them their American gang affiliations and their violent behavior. Reportedly, there are now more than 230 gangs in the capital city of San Salvador, and their members include thousands of former Los Angeles gang members who are alleged to be responsible for a significant increase in crime in that city (Wilkinson, 1994).

Moreover, many of the more powerful gangs in the United States have expanded their area of operations far beyond the local community. In many cities, affiliates or chapters of these gangs operate as a network to facilitate the drug trade and other illegal activities. For example, it is estimated that some drug-dealing Los Angeles gangs have expanded their operations into 32 states and over 100 cities; Miami-based gangs have expanded their drug trade into major cities in Georgia; and Chicago gangs have expanded into a number of midwestern cities (Soroka and Bryjak, 1999). Moreover, many of these gangs have ties to drug-producing countries around the world, from whom they secure their supplies, thus closing the circle of global connection.

STREET VIOLENCE Although the activities of street gangs constitute a high proportion of crime and violence in communities around the country, gangs are not the only source of violence. More and more, individuals worry about how to protect themselves and family members in an increasingly criminal and violent atmosphere, where crime and violence are often random and pointless. Although street violence and crimes in the United States have continuously declined over the past decade, there is still considerable violence in the U.S. (U.S. Department of Justice, 2001b). The rates of murder, robbery, rape, and aggravated assault in this country far exceed those in other industrialized countries. For example, the murder rate in the United States is 2 times that of Northern Ireland, where there is ongoing civil strife; 4 times that of Italy, 9 times higher than in England; and 11 times higher than Japan.

Any discussion of crime and violence in the United States almost always raises the issue of race, because many people link crime with certain racial or ethnic groups of color. In addition, most white Americans express fear of being victimized by African American strangers. In reality, however, two-thirds of the arrests police make for serious crimes involve white people. Furthermore, violent crime in the United States is primarily *intraracial.* That is, about 80 percent of single-offender violent crimes committed by African Americans are against African American victims. Similarly, 75 percent of such crimes committed by whites involve white victims. In addition, a little more than one-half (53 percent) of all victims know their offender (U.S. Department of Justice, 2001b). Nonetheless, the link between race and criminal victimization and its differential impact across marriages and families in the United States is clear.

Families living in big cities are especially affected by crime and random violence. Although the amount of crime varies throughout urban and rural areas, the greatest concentration of offenses occurs in poverty-stricken, inner-city communities of color. The poorest U.S. families, with incomes under $7500, are 60 percent more likely to be victimized by crime or violence than are affluent families with incomes over $75,000. The problems generated by crime are worst in overwhelmingly African American urban neighborhoods. Despite some progress in the nation's fight against violent crime over the past decade, African American youths across all age groups are more likely to be victims of violent crime than their white counterparts. Fifty-four percent of children murdered by gunfire in 1998 were African American. African American families with sons are especially at risk, particularly if they are poor and between the ages of 15 and 24. Nationwide, homicide is the leading cause of death among African American males aged 15–24, and the firearm death rate for African American males is eight times that of white males in the same age group. In eight of the country's largest urban African American communities, teenagers face probabilities of being murdered before they reach their 45th birthday that range from 1 in 53 in Brooklyn to 1 in 12 in Washington, D.C. By contrast, nationally, the average 15-year-old male faces a 1 in 185 probability of being murdered before his 45th birthday compared to 1 in 45 for a similarly aged African American male and 1in 345 probability for a white male (Davis and Mulhausen, 2000; Children's Defense Fund, 2001b). On the other hand, for females, the risk of being a homicide victim in their lifetime is 1 in 132 for African American females and 1 in 495 for white females (U.S. Department of Justice, 1996b). In 1994, African Americans killed over 5100 African Americans—almost equaling the African American death toll in the entire Vietnam War (U.S. Department of Justice, 1996a). The burden of crime and violence is not only a human tragedy for communities across the country, stifling economic and social development by scaring off businesses, particularly in the inner city, but it is also extremely tragic and disruptive of social and family life (Davis and Mulhausen, 2000).

Crime and urban violence are on the rise everywhere. For example, in Lagos, Nigeria, one of Africa's most economically and technologically advanced countries, violent crime is a constant risk, and many streets have become so dangerous that few people go out at night. Armed carjackings are common, even during daylight hours (Macionis and Parrillo, 1998). And in Japan, commuter trains, once a symbol of Japan's safety and efficiency, have become increasingly dangerous as violent crimes in Japan's trains and stations nearly doubled from 1996 to 2000, from 1306 to 2377 (Sakurai, 2001). While much of our attention to violence in the United States is directed to gangs, inner cities, black-on-black and Latina/o-on-Latina/o violence, the fact is that families, particularly those of color, must deal with a much wider range of real and potential violence. These include urban lynchings of people of color and beatings and violence perpetrated by white supremacist groups, as well as an increasing incidence of violence perpetrated by some members of the police force in cities all over the country.

YOUTH VIOLENCE The amount of violence among young people in the United States today is startling. With the proliferation of handguns, families are losing members to handgun violence at a phenomenal rate, both as victims and as offenders. Children are particularly vulnerable to handgun violence and likely to be victims. The Children's Defense Fund reports that every 2 hours a child is killed by a gun. While the rate of violent crime among adult offenders has declined some in recent years, violent crime rates among young people have been rising alarmingly, especially among 18- to 20-year-olds. Although they make up only about 4 percent of the population, 18- to 20-year-olds commit 24 percent of America's gun murders. In fact, 18-year-olds are the most violent: They commit 35 percent more gun murders than 21-year-olds; double the gun murders of 24-year-olds; triple the gun murders of 28-year-olds; and four times the murders of 30-year-olds (U.S. Newswire, 1999).

In April 1998, the cover of *Time* magazine featured a young white male toddler, smiling broadly while holding a rifle. The headline on the cover read: "Armed and Dangerous." Although this headline referred to the five schoolchildren who had been murdered in a Jonesboro, Arkansas, school that year, the words are ominous and are applicable to an increasing number of youth today and their actions on and off school grounds. Consider a few recent examples of the escalating problem of youth violence and the use/misuse of firearms.

- In 2002, a 13-year-old girl was taken into custody for shooting her 40-year-old father in the head as he slept on the couch. The two had quarreled the night before about a boy the girl was seeing and she allegedly told her father "that she was going to hurt him in some way" because he would not allow her to see the boy. The next morning, taking her father's own semiautomatic handgun and loading it, she walked up to her father, put the gun to his head, and fired one round.
- In 2001, two girls, aged 10 and 13, wearing towels on their heads and socks over their hands, attempted to rob a Pennsylvania bank. They passed a note to a teller saying they had a gun and wanted $2000. Faced with charges of attempted robbery and conspiracy, the girls told police that they did it for shopping money.
- In 2000, a 13-year-old boy shot and killed his 35-year-old teacher at a Florida middle school. After being suspended from school by a counselor earlier in the day for throwing water balloons, the boy returned to school and shot the teacher after the teacher refused to let the seventh grader talk to two girls in his class. A year later the youth was tried as an adult and convicted of second-degree murder and sentenced to 28 years in prison and 2 years of house arrest.
- In 2000, eight boys who ranged in age from 14 to 17 and lived in an upscale community in San Diego, California, attacked and robbed five aging (64–69 years of age) Latino migrant farm workers. The boys terrorized, beat, and robbed the workers as they walked along a road toward their migrant campgrounds with air-powered pellet guns and rifles, steel bars, metal pipes, and a pitchfork. They wanted to scare the men into returning to Mexico.
- In 1999, a 170-pound, 12-year-old boy battered and murdered a 6-year-old girl in the home of his mother (who was baby-sitting the girl), while imitating pro wrestlers whom he regarded as heroes. The boy said that while his mother slept in another room he played a game with the 6-year-old in which he body-slammed, kicked, and knee-dropped the girl, moves he learned from watching wrestling on television. The prosecutors in the case said that the girl's injuries—including a fractured skull, lacerated liver, fractured rib, and swollen brain—indicated that the attack was extensive and the injuries were more severe than those seen in many car crashes. Two years later, in sentencing the boy to life in prison without chance for parole, the judge described the boy's actions as cold, callous, and indescribably cruel.
- In 1998, a 15-year-old pleaded guilty to first-degree manslaughter and was sentenced to 10 years in prison for her participation in the murder of a 44-year-old man in Central Park in New York City. The 15-year-old and her boyfriend slit the throat of the victim (whom they knew and drank with), dumped his body in the lake, and continued to drink and party in the park with friends.
- In 1998, three Dallas, Texas, boys—7, 8, and 11 years of age—sexually assaulted a 3-year-old girl in their neighborhood, beat her with a brick and a shoe, and left her naked in a creek bed.

Youthful violence is not confined to the United States. In 1997, a 14-year-old Japanese boy was arrested for beheading an 11-year-old boy and placing his head on the front gate of a junior high school. Even more shocking was the fact that the 14-year-old subsequently confessed that he killed a 10-year-old girl by beating her to death with a steel pipe and that he had attacked three other teenage girls, one of whom almost bled to death. More recently, when a 43-year-old man growled at a group of Japanese youths after one of them stepped on his foot during his train commute home, the youths growled back. When the man disembarked the train, the youths followed and beat him senseless on the platform and ran away. The man, who never awakened from his coma, died a week later. Japanese sociologists suggest that the basis for the increasing youth violence in Japan may be the growing alienation among Japanese youth who are feeling increasingly disenfranchised by society. Japan, a country with one-half the population of the United States, has only approximately 700 killings a year. That compares to over 20,000 in the United States ("Japanese Teenager . . . ," 1997; Sakurai, 2001).

A large number of American families have handguns or other types of firearms in the home for self-protection or for sporting purposes, such as hunting. In fact, two of every five adults live in households where one or more guns are owned and one in every six live in households with a rifle, shotgun, and pistol present (Harris poll, 2001). Moreover, recent polls indicate that 40 percent of American households with children present have guns (Gallup Tuesday Briefing, 2001a). Put another way, 34 percent of children in the United States (representing more than 2 million children in 11 million homes) live in homes with at least one firearm, and in over two-thirds (69 percent) of these homes more than one firearm is present (RAND Corporation, 2001). It is not just the presence of firearms in these homes that is alarming; rather, it is also the fact that in at least 30 percent of handgun-owning households, the handgun(s) is stored unlocked and loaded, and in 28 percent of such households with children present guns are not always locked in a secure place (National Institute of Justice, 1997; Peter Hart Research Associates, 1999). An unfortunate byproduct of this practice is (1) the growing death rate among children living in these homes and (2) the increasing number of schoolchildren who take these weapons to school and use them against teachers and their fellow classmates. In the first instance, increasingly we read about children who have found a handgun in the home and who accidentally shoot themselves, siblings, or neighbors. In addition, handguns owned by parents are often used by children to commit suicide. According to some experts, every 7 hours a child or teenager is killed in a firearm-related accident or suicide. From 1994 to 1999, an average of 5 children died everyday in nonhomicide firearm incidents. The overall firearm-related death rate among U.S. children 14 years or younger is nearly 12 times higher than among children in 25 other industrialized countries combined. Indeed, more American children die from gunfire than from cancer, pneumonia, influenza, asthma, and HIV/AIDS combined (Centers for Disease Control and Prevention, 1997; Children's Defense Fund, 2001a; Common Sense about Kids and Guns, 2001; Hoyert et al., 2001). In the second instance, children as young as 6 years old take their parents' handguns to school, sometimes to protect themselves from gangs and other violators and other times to punish those whom they perceive to have wronged them in some way. One consequence of this has been the proliferation of violence and death in the nation's schools.

Violence in Schools Since the mid-1990s, there has been an incredible rise in the use of handguns to commit acts of violence, very often murder, in the nation's schools. Despite a drop in the percentage of students carrying weapons to school and a decrease in reports of physical fights, stolen property, and marijuana use on school property since comparable statistics in 1995, in 1997, 9 percent of students in grades 9 through 12 reported carrying a weapon to school; 7 percent reported being threatened or injured with a weapon such as a knife, gun, or club while they were at school; 15 percent reported being in a physical fight on school property; 33 percent reported violent or property victimization at school; and 32 percent reported being offered, sold, or given an illegal drug (U.S. Department of Education, 1998). Over a typical 30-day period, over 157,000 crimes occur in American schools. According to the U.S. Department of Justice (1998), 1 in 20 students claim to have seen a classmate with a gun at school. Furthermore, it is estimated that 135,000 guns are brought into schools around the country each day, and somewhere between 35 and 50 students are killed on school grounds each academic year (Cornell, 2001).

Although a link between gun ownership and violence has not been scientifically established, it is nonetheless noteworthy that, as we reported earlier, two-fifths of American households own at least one handgun. It is often these household handguns that students bring to school. Although handgun violence is most often linked in the public mind to the poor and/or African American and Latina/o inner-city communities and schools, the fact is that students in rural areas are twice as likely as their urban counterparts to bring guns to school. Indeed, the current public concern over school violence has been precipitated by the dramatic rise in small-town, middle- and upper-middle-class school shootings and violence in which the offenders almost always have been white males. Until recently, their victims were other white kids. Before white kids began killing white kids on school grounds, school violence was not an issue of national concern. However, over the 5-year period of February 1996 to March 2001, of 19 violent incidents in U.S. schools reported in the media, 16 involved white male shooters, several of which resulted in multiple deaths. Perhaps the most violent and dramatic of these incidents, certainly the one with the greatest number of casualties to date, was the 1999 mass murders at Columbine High School in Littleton, Colorado (a suburb of Denver), where two male students initiated a gun and bomb assault that killed 15 people—14 students and a teacher. The two gunmen, seniors Eric Harris and Dylan Klebold, began their attack in the parking lot and proceeded to a ground floor cafeteria, school hallways, and a second floor library before killing themselves.

A deviation from the white male shooter has become noticeable in recent incidences of school violence and threats of violence. For example, in 2001, a 14-year-old white female who was depressed and frequently teased wounded a fellow female student in the cafeteria of her Pennsylvania high school. In the same year, a 17-year-old white female was one of five students at New Bedford High School in Massachusetts who plotted to smuggle guns into the school in the folds of their black trench coats, wait for homeroom to let out, wait for the teachers to dismiss the student body into the belly of the high school and then detonate explosives and load their weapons and shoot as many people as

Despite the intense reactions to the numerous acts of violence in American schools over the past decade, efforts to quell this violence have not always succeeded. Acts of random violence continue to plague our schools. In 2001, Charles Andrew Williams, a student at Santana High School in Santee, California, opened fire on his classmates, killing 2 students and injuring 13 others. After the shooting, students comfort each other at a makeshift memorial on the school grounds.

bullets and agility permitted. Their plan was to snap photographs of the dead and grin at the living and then go to the roof of the school, smoke marijuana, maybe drop acid, and then shoot each other. In addition, unlike the affluent and/or rural/suburban schools where most shootings have occurred since 1996, New Bedford is an industrial port city in perpetual economic crisis, where unemployment is consistently 50 percent higher than the state average, the annual average income is below $30,000, and more than half of the residents have not gone beyond eighth grade (Ferdinand, 2001).

Although as we indicated in Chapter 11, children are far more likely to be killed at home or by someone they know and love, notwithstanding the fact that violent crime in schools is down since it peaked in the mid-1990s, violence, threats, and bullying at or around schools continue to be of national concern. While there are no official statistics on student threats, schools across the country have had to deal with threats ranging from bomb threats, hit lists, and angry remarks to detailed plots of murder and revenge (as in the case of New Bedford High School). In addition, bullying is so pervasive in American schools that it is often regarded as a normal part of the school experience. One national survey found that 6 percent of high school students and 12 percent of middle school students are bullied on a regular basis. Another study of bullying, in a Virginia middle school, found that 10 percent of boys and 5 percent of girls report being bullied several times per week. Thus, with approximately 50 million children in schools throughout the United States, literally millions of them are affected by bullying on an ongoing basis. Bullying is not a trivial matter. As the evidence shows, although most victims of bullying suffer in silence, many of the recent school shooters were victims of bullying and decided to strike back. Besides the violence and death that can be the consequence of bullying, some research shows that victims of chronic bullying are more likely than other students to suffer long-term problems with depression and anxiety and to be academic underachievers. In addition, by the time they reach adulthood, they are six times more likely to commit violent crimes than their peers (Cornell, 2001).

Responses to violence in U.S. schools have come from almost everyone, including then-president of the United States Bill Clinton, who held a town hall meeting on school violence in 1999 and, that same year, pushed for stiffer gun legislation. Since 1996, the U.S. Congress has proposed a number of bills aimed at violence prevention, including the Children's Gun Violence Prevention Act, the Internet Trafficking Act, and the Child Safety Lock Act. Some people have even talked about legislating morality. For example, in Louisiana the state legislature proposed an act that would require all schoolchildren to use titles of respect when addressing adults (e.g., Miss, Mrs., Mr., Sir, Madam). Other people are calling for stiffer gun laws, while still others are calling for parental responsibility legislation.

It has long been argued that America is characterized by a subculture of violence that is learned and embraced by many people in society. This subculture of violence is perpetrated and expressed throughout the mass media, where children and adults alike entertain themselves on a steady diet of violence and murder. In addition, as we have indicated, the whole genre of video games is built around a model of hunt and kill, violence, and the total annihilation of one's opponents. Research that was once mixed now seems to suggest strongly that there is a positive relationship between media violence and aggressive behavior, crime, and violence in the larger society. In this context, particularly since the terrorist acts of September 11, 2001, local and national leaders have called on the entertainment industry and the expanding Internet and video industries to take responsibility and reduce the violence in their medium.

Parental Sports Rage Finally, although we have framed our discussion of violence and its impact on individuals and families primarily around the issues of gang, street, youth, and school violence, we do not want to leave the reader with the impression that only those segments of U.S. society perpetrate and experience violence, that violence is simply a phenomenon of young, poor, urban dwellers of color. The fact is, as we pointed out in Chapter 11, violence cuts across social boundaries such as race, class, gender, age, and geographic location and is almost an everyday occurrence in nearly every aspect of American life. Road rage, sky (airplane) rage, cell phone rage, violence via the Internet, workplace violence, domestic violence, the increasing violence of women—these are just a few of the examples of the incidence and distribution of violence throughout American society.

Of growing concern today, for example, is the increasing rage and violence of middle-class parents in the arenas where their children play team sports. An estimated 30 million children play on youth league teams and 6.5 million teenagers compete in high school sports. According to the American Academy of Pediatrics, the benefits of such participation include improved health, fitness, and social skills. However, the downside is the increasing violence of parents who take these games too seriously (Mann, 2000). Some observers have described such parental rage as an epidemic sweeping through youth sports. By whatever label, in hockey arenas in Maine to soccer fields in New Mexico and baseball and T-ball fields in Florida, parents, coaches, and other adults are jeering, yelling, spitting, brawling, punching, and, in the most extreme cases, poisoning and killing as a result of what some experts call "sideline rage." For example, in Las Vegas, during practice for a championship game, eight members of a football team suddenly ran off the field holding their stomachs and vomiting violently on the sideline. When parents and coaches took the boys, aged 12 to 14, to the hospital they found that the boys had been poisoned. They later learned that a parent poisoned the boys in an attempt to get back at a player on the team who had picked on his 12-year-old son (Dahlberg, 2002). Although most of the assaults and acts of violence on youth sports fields are nonfatal, in 2000, a Boston father beat another father to death after the two argued over their sons' hockey game (while both sons watched).

As a result of these and other incidents, sports psychologists and others are trying to find ways to stop parental violence at youth sporting events. For instance, leagues are banning rowdy parents from the stands, holding silent games, and trying to teach coaches and parents how to behave. When these efforts fail, the worst offenders are jailed. For example, the father who poisoned members of the Las Vegas football team was given 6 months house arrest and ordered to perform 1 year of community service; in San Fernando, California, a father was sentenced to 45 days in jail for beating and berating a coach who took his 11-year-old son out of a baseball game; and a Pennsylvania police officer was sentenced to 23 months in jail for giving a pitcher $2 to hit another 10-year-old Little Leaguer with a fast ball during a game. In Illinois, the state legislature recently passed a bill mandating a minimum penalty of $1000 for people who assault sports officials, and 15 other states have similar laws. And in El Paso, Texas, city officials have initiated mandatory sportsmanship training for parents; in Jupiter, Florida, parents have to sign a pledge of good conduct before their children can play; and in some cities, booing, taunts, and other verbal attacks at games have been banned (Young, 2001; Dahlberg, 2002).

While we can come up with crude estimates of the economic costs of gangs, street and random violence, school violence, crime, and sports violence to families, the physical pain and mental anguish suffered by families are incalculable. Victimization often results in expenditures that many families cannot afford, such as for medical treatment, prolonged illness, and the need for a caretaker. The victims of violence and their families are not the only victims or losers. The perpetrators of violence and their families are also victims. For example, if the victim or the perpetrator of violence is a major economic provider for the family, that person's loss can be an added strain on family members and resources; a decreased ability or inability to work and earn a living and/or contribute to family income; a dependency on the tax-subsidized welfare system; and vulnerability to further victimization. Because of violence and crime, families across America, especially those in poor and inner-city neighborhoods, are faced with communities where economic and community resources and services are few to nonexistent. Certain kinds of crimes and violence such as gang and street crime violence discourage economic development, leaving these families stigmatized as violence prone and vulnerable to price gouging for inferior products and services that are sold to community residents by outsiders who are often hostile to community residents and who take over poor communities by day and abandon them by night.

TERRORISM AND WAR

Gangs, crime, violence, terrorism, and war are different faces of the same coin. In the past, when Americans have thought of terrorism, they have generally thought about faraway lands where governments have practiced terrorism to sustain their power and individuals and groups within these countries have practiced it in retaliation for oppressive governmental rule. However, today we are far more aware of terrorism in this country and recognize that it does not just occur in "foreign" or developing countries. Increasingly, since the early 1990s and culminating with the September 11, 2001, terrorist attacks on New York's World Trade Center and the Pentagon, Americans are not only more aware of terrorism but also have experienced firsthand its consequences for individuals, marriages, and families, as well as the terror that people in other countries around the world have, in the past and continue today, to experience on a daily basis. Terrorists around the world have been able to intimidate and blackmail powerful governments; technology (for example, jet travel, satellite communications, plastic bombs, compact automatic weapons) has enabled terrorists to invade political arenas around the world and to make known their ideological view and goals; and the end of colonial rule has been accelerated by terrorist actions carried out in the name of various oppressed racial and ethnic groups seeking self-rule (Demaris, 1991).

Terrorism can be defined as the calculated use of unlawful violence or the threat of unlawful violence by individuals or groups intended to inculcate fear or to intimidate and/or coerce governments or societies as a political or revolutionary strategy to achieve political, religious, or ideological goals (Center for Defense Information, 2001a). According to Michael Soroka and George Bryjak (1999), political terrorism is a form of warfare without any humanitarian constraints or rules. In general, the goal of such actions is to initiate a significant change in or outright overthrow of existing governments. Often the goal is simply to intimidate. The Palestine Liberation Organization (PLO), the Irish Republican Army (IRA), the Red Brigades in Italy, and the Basque separatists in Spain have all come to be household names in the vocabulary of political terrorism. Regional or domestic terrorism has existed throughout human history. However, terrorism as an international concern only emerged during the 1960s after a series of airplane hijackings became international news. And when the 1972 Munich Olympic Games were disrupted by a Palestinian group's attempt to take Israeli athletes hostage, terrorism as an international concern was put on the UN General Assembly's agenda under the long and tedious title "Measures to prevent terrorism and other forms of violence which endanger or take innocent lives or jeopardize fundamental freedoms and study of the underlying causes of the forms of terrorism and acts of violence which lie in misery, frustration, grievance and despair and which cause some people to sacrifice human lives, including their own, in an attempt to effect radical changes" (United Nations Office of Drug Control and Crime Prevention, 2001:3).

In the past, the majority of terrorist attacks fell under the heading of state-sponsored terrorism—governments that support international terrorism either by engaging in terrorist activity themselves or by providing arms, training, safe haven, diplomatic facilities, financial backing, and material, logistic, or other support to terrorists. Increasingly, each year, almost one-half of the terrorist attacks worldwide have been labeled anti-United States. Although there has been a slight increase in the number of terrorist attacks worldwide (for example, 423 attacks in 2000 versus 392 in 1999), state-sponsored terrorism has declined. This decline is attributed, at least in part, to the declining willingness of national governments to take part directly in terrorist attacks and the United States' vigorous campaign of sanctions and other punitive measures against terrorist-supporting countries (Snowden and Hayes, 2001).

However, the September 11 terrorist attacks against the United States dramatically brought into focus the new trends in international terrorism. The most significant of these trends has been the emergence of smaller militant organizations such as Aum Shrinrikyo, a Japanese cult that carried out a nerve gas attack on the Tokyo subway in 1995, killing 12 people and injuring thousands of other subway passengers, and the al-Qaeda (Arabic for "the Base"), led by Osama bin Laden, responsible for embassy bombings in Nairobi, Kenya, and in Dar es Salaam, Tanzania, killing hundreds and injuring thousands of people, and believed to be the mastermind behind the September 11 attack. Groups such as these, with their nebulous membership and widely diverse agendas, are difficult to localize and it is almost impossible to predict their actions (Center for Defense and International Security Studies, 1999; Snowden and Hayes, 2001). One thing that is crystal clear, however, is that such groups will use any method available to achieve their goals, including killing themselves in suicide missions, and inflicting indiscriminate violence and terror on innocent civilians, including children.

To date, terrorists have been overwhelmingly male. However, some women have joined their ranks. Some observers (for example, Laquer, 1987) claim that women terrorists are actually more effective because they are tougher, more fanatical, more loyal, and have a greater capacity for suffering than their male counterparts. Regardless of gender, however, terrorists and their leaders always profess that they seek to redress some political, social, or religious injustice and are fueled by a hatred that knows no bounds. For example, according to the Center for Defense Information (2001a), at the heart of Osama bin Laden's al-Qaeda terrorism is a fierce duel hatred of the present rulers of his native Saudi Arabia, whom he considers to be apostates to Islam (secularists) and thus unworthy to rule, and of the United States, whose presence in Saudi Arabia he believes defiles the holy land of Mecca and Medina. As the various terrorist acts, including the September 11 attacks on New York and Washington, D.C., perpetrated by Osama bin Laden and his followers indicate, their hatred is so deep that they rationalize and justify the use of unlimited violence, unencumbered by pity or compassion, in the name of religious rage.

Terrorism in the United States

As we have indicated, in the past, American citizens were most vulnerable to terrorism and violence when traveling in foreign lands, particularly those openly hostile toward the American government. Although American citizens continue to be prime targets of terrorism worldwide (targets in one in four terrorist acts), over the last decade, not only individual citizens but also entire families have become increasingly vulnerable to and victims of terrorist actions at home. For example, in 1993, terrorists planted truck bombs in the parking garage under the World Trade Center in New York City, killing six people, injuring hundreds of others, and requiring more than $20 million to repair the physical damage to the World Trade Center. In the same year, police broke up a terrorist plot to kill thousands of people and reduce New York City to chaos by bombing the United Nations buildings as well as the city's major traffic tunnels (Macionis, 1995; Center for Defense Information, 2001b). Barely a year has passed since the early 1990s, without some such actions, many of which have been both successful and deadly for Americans and their families and which have culminated, to date, with the September 11, 2001 attacks on the World Trade Center and the Pentagon and a loss of life of an estimated 3000 to 5000 American and foreign-born women, men, and children. Most people still cannot fathom the full extent of the carnage, horror, grieving, and loss of this act: three of four hijacked airplanes smashed into the World Trade Center and the Pentagon, and a fourth plane crashed in Pennsylvania before it could reach its target (although it is not clear what the intended target was). The outpouring of grief and the federal government's response to this terrorism have surpassed that of any other response to acts of terrorism against the United States and its people, including the Oklahoma City bombing. Almost overnight, the president of the United States embarked on a war of retaliation that he labeled a "war on terrorism." Targeting terrorist organizations with a global reach, he launched a military assault on Afghanistan whose ruling Taliban Party had harbored Osama bin Laden, who is not only suspected of masterminding the September 11 attacks but also many other successful terrorist acts and operations against the United States since 1993 (see a more detailed discussion of the war on terrorism in the next section) (Center for Defense Information, 2001b; Public Agenda, 2002). For example:

- February 23, 1993: The truck bombing of the World Trade Center.
- October 3 and 4, 1993: Al-Qaeda–trained fighters claimed responsibility for bringing down two U.S. helicopters in Somalia and killing 18 U.S. rangers.
- June 25, 1996: A truck bomb kills 19 U.S. servicemen in the air force's Khobar Towers housing complex in Dhahran, Saudi Arabia, wounding over 500 people.
- August 7, 1998: Truck bombs destroy U.S. embassies in Nairobi, Kenya, and Dar es Salaam, Tanzania, killing 234, including 12 Americans, and injuring more than 5000.
- October 12, 2000: Two suicide bombers in a boat detonated explosives that blew a 40-foot hole in the side of the USS *Cole* (a 505-foot U.S. Navy guided missile destroyer) as the ship took on fuel in Aden, Yemen, killing 17 crew members and wounding 39.

- September 11, 2001: Al-Qaeda operatives hijacked U.S. aircrafts using them as bombs to destroy the twin towers and other buildings in the World Trade Center complex, and severely damaged the Pentagon with an estimated loss of life between 3000 and 5000 people (Center for Defense Information, 2001b; CNN.com, 2001).

Terrorists in the United States are not always imported from other countries. Many are homegrown. For example, U.S. citizen Timothy McVeigh was convicted of perpetrating perhaps the single-most destructive terrorist act ever committed on U.S. soil: the bombing of a federal building in 1995, in Oklahoma. One hundred sixty-eight people died and another 467 were injured as a result of the blast. The loss of life and the devastation of this terrorist act for individuals and families will last a lifetime and beyond. This fact notwithstanding, however, the September 11 attacks struck at the very heart and soul of the American people and have been described as the worst acts of terrorism in modern history, leaving Americans feeling stunned and extremely vulnerable. For example, in a December 2001 Fox News poll, 37 percent of those polled said that they were either somewhat or very worried that terrorist attacks might take place where they live or work. And in a January 2002 Gallup poll, 47 percent of those polled said they were somewhat or very dissatisfied with the nation's security from terrorism; only 10 percent said that they were very satisfied (Polling Report, 2002). For more facts and figures about terrorism, see the "Searching the Internet" box.

War

Most experts on war agree that the intensity and frequency of wars increased in the twentieth century. Since the mid-1940s alone, more than 23 million people have died as a result of war and another 20 million have died as a result of war-related factors. A major characteristic of contemporary war is that civilians are the primary victims. For example, in the 1980s, 74 percent of wartime casualties were civilians. By 1990, civilians constituted 90 percent of such casualties (Sivard, 1991). Today, wars are fought not on some distant battlefield but deep within the homeland of the warring factions. Even when civilians are not purposefully targeted, they end up the major casualties. For example, as horrific as the terrorist attacks on the United States were their consequences for individuals, marriages, and families extend far beyond the American borders. For instance, the United States' intense campaign of aerial bombardment of various targets in Afghanistan immediately after September 11 has killed an untold number of Afghan civilians (see chapter opener) and has prompted a humanitarian disaster with 20,000 civilians pushed up against closed borders and hundreds of thousands more on the move (see the later discussion of refugees). Although there are no official statistics available on the civilian death toll in Afghanistan as a result of the U.S. "war on terrorism," there have been increasing reports of civilian casualties arising from U.S.-led attacks on civilian objectives, including an air attack on the village of Khorum, where a number of civilians were reportedly killed; an attack on an International Red Cross warehouse in Kabul, killing at least one civilian; and an air attack on an Afghan radio station. And eyewitnesses have described seeing bodies of Afghan civilians buried in the rubble of houses or those of people killed while riding in civilian vehicles. U.S. officials have admitted that a number of civilian targets have been hit as a result of error (Amnesty International, 2001c, 2001d). Most often, the majority of civilian casualties of war are women and children. For instance, in the 1991 Persian Gulf War, one estimate of the loss of life among Iraqi soldiers was 40,000 while twice this number (83,000) of civilians, primarily women and children, were killed as a result of the war. Approximately 16 percent of these civilians died during air strikes and bombings; the remaining 84 percent died as a result of the collapse of the public health system, which was destroyed during bombings. Water purification and sewage systems were destroyed, creating the conditions for the development of water-transported diseases that are especially fatal for children and older people (Soroka and Bryjak, 1999).

The September 11 terrorist acts against the United States ushered in a new era and new type of war: "the war on terrorism." This new type of war is unlike any other that America has engaged in—one where the enemy is not easily defined. Although many in the Arab world view it as a war against Islam, President Bush has said that the war is not aimed at Islam but at terrorist organizations and governments that provide them safe haven. In any event, the United States has responded to the terrorist actions of September 11 in an unprecedented way. For example, for the first time in U.S. history, there is now a cabinet-level Homeland Security Office to coordinate the country's antiterrorism efforts. In addition, new and tightened security measures have been initiated at airports, including the takeover of airport security by the federal government; law enforcement has been given broader authority to wiretap and detain terrorism suspects; and steps have been taken to tighten up immigration provisions in an effort to keep terrorists out of the country.

Terrorism as a weapon of war is not new. It has been used historically in domestic, regional, and international disputes. It sometimes has been linked to specific conflicts such as in Northern Ireland and the Basque separatist movement in Spain. And, as we have indicated, the United States has dealt with the different manifestations of terrorism for years. However, as Americans have found since September 11, the weapons of war are no longer just the traditional bombs and warheads of the past but increasingly include chemical and biological weapons as well. After September 11, for example, Americans faced the threat of bioterrorism. The American postal system was targeted for germ warfare, as well as government offices, including Congress, and major news organizations. Postal employees, as well as others in the population, were victimized. Thus far, only a few people have actually developed anthrax and four have died, but thousands more have been forced to take antibiotics as a precaution, and the anthrax threat continues. Although the anthrax terrorism followed right after the September 11 terrorism, it is not clear what, if any, connection it has to the September 11 attack. In any event, bioterrorism is uncharted territory. Many believe that the United States is not well prepared to handle a major domestic incident of bioterrorism. Nonetheless, Americans' confidence that their country will win the war on terrorism is high (Public Agenda, 2002).

The weapons of war often have an impact on individuals and families well after the war is officially over. For example, land mines victimize more civilians than soldiers, and their impact on life and limbs extends well beyond the war. Even after the war is over, land mines are left behind, rendering those returning home after the war at high risk of losing a limb or even their lives. As a result of conflict and war, an estimated 110 million land mines lie across 64 countries worldwide, killing or severely maiming thousands of people every year. For example, Afghanistan is littered with an estimated 10 million land mines, making it one of the most heavily mined countries in the world (Amnesty International, 1999). It is estimated that 500 people are killed and wounded every week from land mines. In Cambodia, for example, approximately 30 percent of the population has lost a limb (usually a leg) as a result of stepping on land mines. And America's use of cluster bombs in Afghanistan has a similar consequence as land mines. According to experts on the subject, at least 5 percent of such bombs do not explode upon impact, becoming de facto land mines and remaining a threat to people, including civilians, who come into contact with them (Amnesty International, 2001c). Moreover, during the Persian Gulf War, U.S. soldiers (women and men) were exposed to chemical warfare that has affected not only their own health but also that of their partners and children. Testifying before a Senate committee about the symptoms they suffer as a result of chemical attacks in the Persian Gulf, hundreds of soldiers reported that their spouses and children displayed the same symptoms as they, raising the possibility that exposure to debilitating chemicals can be passed on (Soroka and Bryjak, 1999).

Perhaps the most heinous war-related behavior, to date, is the mass rape of women and girls. For example, the Serbs not only brutalized and murdered thousands of Muslim men but they conducted mass rapes of Muslim women and girls. Some eyewitness accounts of these atrocities as well as first-person accounts by survivors tell how women and girls were often assaulted in their own homes, in front of their families, while others were taken to hotels or camps where they were locked up and raped repeatedly by soldiers. Sometimes girls as young as 6 years of age were raped in front of their parents and other family members. Entire villages became "rape camps," where women were raped and sodomized by as many as 20 men per night, every night. The attacks were so violent and vicious that many of the victims died. Added to this horror is the fact that many of the women and girls who survived this assault to their humanity were held captive until impregnated by their rapists (*Ms.* magazine, 1993; Post, 1993; Bryjak and Soroka, 1994; Gelles and Levine, 1995).

Mass rape as a tool of men's wars is not unique to Bosnia. Women fleeing Kosovo also reported stories of systematic rape by Serb forces. The pattern was the same and echoed the rape horror stories that emerged from the Bosnian war: Young Albanian girls and women were separated from their families and brutally sexually assaulted (ABC News, 1999). Historically, the sexual assault of women has been an integral part of war and conquest. What better way to conquer an enemy than to destroy families, and what better way to destroy families than to attack its most vulnerable members—women and girls. When a girl or woman is raped, she, her family, and her community are all victims (Peterson, Wunder, and Mueller, 1999). Table 15.3 presents a brief snapshot of some of the documented cases of war and mass rape in recent human history. The damage done to families as a result of the rape and impregnation of thousands of women is manifold. Women and girls who survive the physical assault of rape often are so psychologically traumatized that they never completely recover. Many of these women never marry or reproduce, because of the lingering psychological damage or because they are considered damaged goods (no matter that they were raped) and are ostracized when the war is over.

Children, Terrorism, and War Children around the world are bearing a disproportionately high cost of war; they are displaced, disabled, and psychologically traumatized by war. In the last decade alone, wars in countries such

Table 15.3

War and Mass Rape
• From 1937 to 1938, during the infamous "Rape of Nanking," Japanese soldiers slaughtered more than a quarter of a million people and raped 20,000 or more Chinese women, many of whom died after repeated sexual assaults.
• During World War I, German soldiers raped thousands of Belgian women.
• During World War II, 3 million Polish Jews and an untold number of Russian women were raped and murdered by Nazi soldiers.
• During World War II, as many as 250,000 Korean, Chinese, Manchurian, and Filipino girls and women (age 13 and up) were forcibly abducted and raped for extended periods of time by Japanese soldiers.
• In the waning days of World War II, Soviet soldiers brutalized and raped 2 million German women.
• During the 1971 civil war between Bangladesh and Pakistan, Pakistani soldiers raped more than 280,000 Bangali girls and women.
• During the U.S. and Vietnamese War, American soldiers gang-raped Vietnamese women and girls.

Source: George J. Bryjak and Michael P. Soroka, 1994, *Sociology: Cultural Diversity in a Changing World* (Needham Heights, MA: Allyn and Bacon): 300–301; Michael P. Soroka and George J. Bryjak, 1999, *Social Problems: A World at Risk* (Needham Heights, MA: Allyn and Bacon).

as Rwanda, Bosnia-Herzegovina, Kosovo, Mozambique, Angola, Somalia, Sudan, Afghanistan, Cambodia, and Haiti claimed the lives of and injured far more children than soldiers. For example, more than 2 million children died in wars, 4 million to 5 million were physically disabled, another 1 million were orphaned, 12 million were left homeless, and some 10 million suffer psychological trauma (OneWorld, 2002; UNICEF, 2002). Children are the victims of war in many ways. Thousands are killed in the indiscriminate bombing and shelling of their homes, schools, or playing fields; thousands are or have been subject to deliberate and arbitrary killings at the hands of armed political groups. And many children have been killed or maimed by the millions of land mines (1 for every 20 children around the world) that litter their countries. Decades of war, for example, have devastated the lives of millions of Afghan children. Families have been torn apart; many of these children have been separated from or have lost parents or siblings and are psychologically scarred from their exposure to violence, death, and illness. Others have been forced to flee their homes, and all have suffered from disrupted schooling and economic hardship. Land mines pose a particular threat to children who often have the responsibility for gathering firewood, hauling water, or tending cattle; just simple natural curiosity puts them at risk. It is estimated, for instance, that every day, approximately seven Afghan children are killed by land mines. Of those who survive, many later die due to a lack of medical facilities. Others are left blind or deaf or without limbs (Amnesty International, 1999; UNICEF, 2002). Afghan children face daily danger as well from the continuing bombing, shelling, and other military activities in their country since the September 11 terrorist attacks against the United States. The physical, emotional, and mental development of Afghan children continues to be severely affected by past and ongoing conflicts and wars in their country. The psychological trauma experienced by Afghan and other children under conditions of war is unprecedented. For example, a UNICEF survey of 3000 Rwandan children in 1995 found that during the genocidal massacres in their country in 1994, 95 percent of these children had witnessed massacres, over one-third had seen the murders of family members, almost all of the children believed they would die, almost two-thirds were threatened with death, and over 80 percent of them said they had had to hide to protect themselves, sometimes up to 8 weeks or longer (UNICEF, 2002). In the United States, the terrorist attacks of September 11 have left many children with questions about things that many small children in this country typically have not had to face in the past. Buildings on fire, buildings falling down, daddy or mommy or both suddenly yanked from their lives—missing or dead.

Children are also the most vulnerable to bioterrorism. Unlike Afghan children and those in other countries, however, American children have not been left to find their own means of coping with the horrors of terrorism and war. Even before September 11, 2001, the American Academy of Pediatrics released a report that cautioned about the disproportionately and potentially devastating effect of a terrorist attack with chemical or biological weapons on children. Thus, as the federal government has moved to tighten defenses against a repeat of September 11, responses at the macro and micro levels of society include special attention to the vulnerability and needs of children. For example, nerve gases like the one used in a Tokyo subway in 1995 are very dense, which causes them to settle close to the ground—the breathing zone of children. Children have more rapid respiratory rates than adults, which means that children are more easily affected by agents entering their bodies through the respiratory system or the skin. Furthermore, many of the chemical and biological agents that might be used by terrorists cause severe vomiting and diarrhea. And children are much more susceptible than adults to dehydration and going into shock and cardiovascular collapse. In this context, in October 2001, Senator Hillary Rodham Clinton introduced legislation to create a National Task Force on Children and Terrorism to determine what needs to be done to ensure the safety of American children in the event of a bioterrorist attack (Herbert, 2001). In addition, parents around the country have found ways to talk to their children about the terror, horror, and fear of September 11 and to help them understand what happened; and teachers, family therapists, and a host of other professionals and laypersons have developed curricula and methods by which adults can work collectively to ease the trauma of September 11 for American children (see the "Strengthening Marriages and Families" box).

Sometimes children are deliberately used or targeted in war. In many conflict situations children are used as soldiers to supplement adult armies and militias. Those who do not die, but live to see peace, are usually left with the legacy of a violent past. In recent years, in more than 40 countries, including in Latin America, the Middle East, Asia, and Africa, thousands of children under the age of 18, some as young as 7 years old, have been routinely used in this way. According to a published report on child soldiers produced by a coalition of groups against the use of children as soldiers, more than 500,000 children, girls and boys, under the age of 18 are in government armies or guerrilla groups around the world, and, at any one time, more than one-half (300,000) of them are in actual combat. These children—small, agile, and relatively powerless—are recruited, captured, demobilized, wounded, or even killed everyday. Children are considered to be a cheap and expendable commodity, and the lighter weight of today's weapons makes it easier to arm them. The dangers these children face are not only on the frontlines of war but also in myriad other situations. For example, children are routinely used as spies, messengers, sentries, porters, servants, and sexual slaves; they are often used to lay and clear land mines or are conditioned to commit atrocities even against their own families and communities. Moreover, most child soldiers suffer physical and other abuses within the armed forces and in extreme cases, they commit suicide or murder when the mistreatment becomes unbearable (Coalition to Stop the Use of Child Soldiers, 2001).

STRENGTHENING MARRIAGES AND FAMILIES

Talks with Family Therapist Joan Zientek

TALKING ABOUT TERRORISM AND THE WAR

Why is it important to talk about the events of 9/11 and their aftermath?

Since September 11, 2001, our world has changed. The security that we took for granted is gone. We lost our sense of personal safety and we lost the image of America as untouchable. The trauma of the events of that day was unexpected, sudden, and overwhelming. We thought something like this could never happen. Now, as adults, we are struggling to meet the challenges of picking up the pieces and of trying to make some sense and meaning out of the devastation. We are now living in an era of "New Normalcy" that requires that we return to our routine while keeping a vigilant eye on our surroundings.

Do adults and children react the same way to disasters?

Common responses to any disaster include disbelief and shock, fear and anxiety about the future, disorientation (difficulty making decisions or concentrating), emotional numbing, irritable and angry behavior, somatic complaints, difficulty sleeping, nightmares, sadness, and depression. Children may develop regressive behaviors: bed wetting, thumb sucking, and separation anxiety. Adolescents may cover their fears with an attitude of false bravado or by engaging in reckless behaviors. However, most of these reactions will diminish with time and with the resumption of a normal routine. Each person will have her or his own time line of recovery, so it is important not to compare oneself to others or to judge others' reactions and responses.

How can parents help themselves and their children cope with these events?

There are several things we all can do to cope:

- **Talk about it.** Sharing feelings, worries, and fears keeps us connected to others and gives us support. We realize that what we are experiencing is normal and that we are not alone.
- **Take care of ourselves.** Get extra rest and exercise. Eat healthy foods. Do things that we enjoy and that are soothing and relaxing.
- **Maintain a sense of balance.** Keep up to date about the facts of the war; however, limit our exposure. Pay attention to our feelings so we will know when to take a break and focus on other aspects of our lives.
- **Stay connected to family and friends.** Plan family nights and family outings. Do fun things together. Play games and plan family meals. Keep in touch with those out of town by phone or e-mail. Send care packages to college students.
- **Take some action.** Get involved in war-related activities that your church or community sponsors. Donate food or clothing. Write letters of appreciation.
- **Gain a sense of control.** Do something that gives a sense of completion like baking cookies, cleaning closets, doing a hobby, or painting a room.

As we adults struggle with a multitude of feelings and fears, our children are looking to us to provide the guidance and reassurance they need as well as a hope of better days to come. Young children do not have the experience or the verbal or cognitive ability to understand what is happening, let alone to put these events into perspective. Children take their cues from the adults around them and pattern their own reactions on the behavior they observe. Children's reactions will vary according to their age. Young children worry most about the safety of their parents and fear that they will be separated from them. School-age children worry that the events of 9/11 will be repeated or that something worse may happen. They focus on how the war and terrorism will affect and change their lives. Because young children confuse fact with fantasy and mix reality with movie scripts, they may come to mistakable conclusions. While adolescents may mask their feelings, the trauma they have experienced prompts them to reflect on the meaning of life and moves them to desire to take some action. Letting our children, regardless of age, know that we will protect and keep them safe and that we love them is the number one reassurance that we can provide. We need to give our children a signal that we are available to talk by talking about the war and terrorism in a calm, loving manner. By admitting our fears and worries and showing that we can handle them, we teach our children how to cope and give them the confidence that intense emotions can be managed. Because younger children are not as able to express themselves, they work out their feelings through play and creative outlets. They may draw pictures about the war or reenact scenes that they have seen on TV. Some children, as well as adults, may need help in their efforts to cope with their fears and worries. If a person is preoccupied with the traumatic events and is unable to get involved in the daily tasks of life, the need for professional help may be indicated. Persons who have been subjected to past traumas or experience current traumas in their lives may be most affected.

In spite of the turmoil of the era of the "New Normalcy," people are able to make changes to improve the quality of their lives. Many have come to a new appreciation of friends and family, recommitted to relationships with a willingness to work out problems, pursued interests otherwise neglected, and rekindled their love of and loyalty to America.

The good news (if there can be good news about children in armed conflict) is that, in part, due to the work of UNICEF and human rights organizations and groups around the world, 73 countries to date have adopted legislation that prohibits the recruitment of children under the age of 18. In addition, 80 countries, including the United States, have signed an international agreement barring children in armed conflict, although only five of these countries—Andorra, Bangladesh, Canada, Congo, and Sri Lanka—have ratified the treaty. On the other side of this coin, however, thousands of children are still being recruited or forced to fight in armies in various African countries. In Colombia, at least 14,000 children are fighting with both guerrilla groups and anti-rebel paramilitaries, and in Sri Lanka, a guerrilla army is still recruiting or drafting girls and boys into the army, some of whom are drafted specifically to undertake suicide missions (Crossette, 2001).

Although this discussion of the well-being of children has focused on the impact of war, violence, and terrorism, we do not mean to give the impression that these are the only threats to the well-being of children globally or that they are the most important. Rather, given the continuing, and in some cases, escalating, pattern of global violence, terrorism, and war, and given the fact that many of the factors that impact children's well-being (such as malnutrition, starvation, homelessness, lack of medical facilities, sexual assault and abuse, human rights violations, and so on) are often a consequence of war and terrorism, we have thus chosen to focus our discussion here on the impact of war, violence, terrorism, and human rights abuses on the well-being of children worldwide. Although abbreviated, it is meant to illuminate not only the perils of terrorism and war but also the burden of armed conflict on the stability of individuals, marriages, and families and the ability of the youngest members of a society to become part of future solutions rather than future problems. Even when they are not the direct targets of war and human rights abuses, the majority of children in war-torn countries witness acts of violence and destruction that have destroyed their families, communities, and country, and many are left psychologically damaged for life.

A World of Refugees

One of the most significant global demographic trends of the twentieth century was the massive immigration of people from one country to another all over the world. Exacerbated by ongoing and new wars and conflicts and international and domestic terrorism at the end of the twentieth century and the beginning of the twenty-first, this trend continues today. Sometimes this immigration is voluntary, in that people leave their homelands seeking economic opportunities in other lands. All too often, however, the massive movement of people from one land to another has been and continues to be the result of communal violence and war. According to some sources, 22 million, or 1 out of every 275 persons on earth, has been forced into flight. These **refugees**—people who leave their country because of a "well-founded fear" of persecution for reasons of race, religion, nationality, social group, or political opinion (United Nations High Commissioner for Refugees, 2001)—are sometimes welcomed in the host countries; at other times they are met with resentment, hostility, and violence.

The mass movement of millions of refugees has transformed or is currently transforming the way of life in many countries throughout the world, the majority of which are in developing nations that are often already struggling to meet the needs of their own citizens. For example, as a result of the civil war in Afghanistan in the late 1970s and early 1980s, more than 5 million people left that country for neighboring Pakistan, an extremely poor country with over 142 million people and enormous problems of its own. Although many of these people returned home, the United Nations estimated prior to September 11, 2001, that 1 million refugees remained in Pakistan and another 1.6 million remained in Iran. However, the terrorism of September 11 again catapulted Afghanistan into the epicenter of fear and war and millions of Afghan civilians, half a world away, became unintentional victims in the fallout, following history's worst single act of terrorism in the United States. Today, more than 1.5 million refugees are expected to amass in new camps in and around Afghanistan, in addition to the more than 3.6 million Afghan refugees who have left Afghanistan for Pakistan and Iran since September 11. In a 10-day period in February 2002 alone, more than 20,000 Afghan refugees crossed the border into Pakistan. According to the United Nations High Commissioner for Refugees (UNHCR, 2001), Afghans constitute the largest single refugee population in the world (30 percent of the global refugee population). Civilians from the Central African state of Burundi constitute the second largest group with 568,000 refugees living mainly in Tanzania, and Iraqis comprise the third largest population, with 512,800 refugees living mainly in Iran.

Civil war and revolutions in Central American countries such as Nicaragua, El Salvador, and Guatemala have contributed significantly to the migrant population of the United States. As many as 300,000 El Salvadorans currently live in Los Angeles County alone. To escape ethnic cleansing carried out by Serb forces, over 1 million people from the former Yugoslavia have fled to other European countries, most notably Germany. And some 2.4 million Rwandans have left their central African homeland primarily for Zaire and Tanzania in an effort to escape the genocidal war that pitted Hutus and Tutsis against each other (Alliance for a Global Community, 1996; Soroka and Bryjak, 1999).

As we have already indicated, gender and age are important factors in communal war and violence. Women and children, for example, make up more than 80 percent of the world's refugees. An estimated 45 percent of refugees are below the age of 18, and 14 percent are below the age of 5. Ten percent of refugees are 60 years or older, over one-half of whom are females. The massive number of displaced children is of immense concern. In Kigali, the capital city of Rwanda, thousands of abandoned or displaced children

SEARCHING THE INTERNET

FACTS AND FIGURES ABOUT TERRORISM

- From 1981 to 2000, there were a total of 9179 international terrorist attacks (excluding intra-Palestinian violence), averaging about 459 attacks a year.
- Terrorism was at its lowest in 1998, with only 274 recorded attacks. It increased in 1999 to 392 attacks, and 423 attacks in 2000.
- Businesses are the primary target of international terrorists. From 1995 to 2000, 1842 businesses were attacked abroad by international terrorists.
- From 1995 to 2000, 77 Americans died and 651 were wounded as a result of international terrorist attacks. By comparison, 9713 Asians, 5762 Africans, 2190 Middle Easterners, and 1212 people in Western Europe died as a result of international terrorist attacks.
- In 2000, 86 percent of anti-American attacks occurred in Latin America. Only 1 percent came from the Middle East. This includes attacks against U.S. facilities and attacks in which American citizens suffered casualties.

http://www.heritage.org/shorts/20010914terror.htm

roam the streets. Small boys, some illegitimate, all of them alone and destitute, struggle to survive in the aftermath of the civil war. Girls are not seen or talked about much because they are used for sex or housework; the fate of these girls is a taboo subject. Another 100,000 "unaccompanied" Rwandan children (refugee children without an accompanying parent or other family) can be found in Zaire; many are seriously injured. In Sudan, approximately 20,000 Sudanese children, mostly boys between 7 and 17 years of age, referred to as the "lost boys of the Sudan," have been separated from their families and have sought refuge in Ethiopia, Kenya, and Uganda (UNICEF, 1996; UNHCR, 2001).

Although the majority of refugees prefer to and do return home as soon as circumstances permit (generally, when a war or conflict has ended and a degree of stability has been restored), at any given time only about 6 percent of refugees return home. In any event, the magnitude of the mass movement of people can be fraught with challenges—both for the refugees and for the host country. There must be an adjustment on the part of the host society as well as at the individual level. For example, on a societal level, large numbers of refugees into a society can impact the stability of the society, particularly if the society is poor and already overcrowded. Newcomers to societies often intensify the competition for scarce resources; for jobs, education, housing, recreational activities, and sources of supplemental financial assistance. Because of diverse cultural practices, language barriers, and few or no personal resources, they also create a need for increasing numbers of professionals and service providers, such as social workers, lawyers, judges, child and family therapists and workers, to name but a few.

On an individual and familial level, the first order of business for refugees is often the task of trying to piece together their families, who were shattered and separated by war, violence, and the exodus from their homelands. In addition, not only do refugees have to deal with the trauma of war and being separated from their cultural base, but they must also adjust to and adapt to a new way of life. As we have indicated, their existence in foreign lands is sometimes complicated by racism, discrimination, and/or intolerance. For example, as new immigrants are added to the demographic mix in the United States, Canada, and Europe, balancing cultural variety with the mainstream values is often a tricky business. Some people believe that some of the cultural practices that refugees bring with them test the limits of tolerance on the part of the host society. People within host societies are often willing to accept cultural practices that seem to reinforce their own cultural values. However, those that differ are often met with intolerance, rejection, ridicule, and sometimes legal ramifications. For example, in Maine, a refugee from Afghanistan was observed kissing the penis of his baby son, a traditional expression of love by this father. However, to his American neighbors, social service agencies, and the police, this behavior was seen as child abuse and the man's son was taken away from him (the child was later returned to the father by a state Supreme Court ruling). Some sociologists and other social scientists argue that American laws and welfare services have often left immigrants terrified of the intrusive power of the government (Crossette, 1999).

Does being tolerant mean accepting cultural practices such as "female genital mutilation," "immolation of widows," and "coining"?[1] Many Americans confront the issue of whether the government should have the power to intervene in the most intimate details of family life (Crossette, 1999) and/or if being nonethnocentric or tolerant means accepting cultural practices that are harmful to the health and well-being of fellow human beings. Does it mean accepting cultural practices that repel Western ideals, such as the disciplinary techniques of shaming and physical punishment, parent/child co-sleeping arrangements, rituals of group identity and ceremonies of initiation involving scarification and body piercing, arranged marriage and child marriage, polygamy, the segregation of gender roles, and bilingualism? As this discussion should make clear, war, terrorism, violence, and the often resulting mass migration of people seeking asylum in a host country have an impact on all of us. Refugees have to adapt to the cultural and legal norms of a host society, and the host society must confront large-scale economic and political issues as well as the social issues of tolerance and *cultural relativism.*

FAMILIES COPING WITH LOSS: DYING AND DEATH

Someone once wrote that in all of life there are only two certainties: death and taxes. We have located the topic of death in this chapter because death is a universal experience for families everywhere. Although death comes at different times and under very diverse conditions around the world, when death occurs all families must cope with the loss of a loved one and each culture must construct its own rules for mourning that loss. However, space constraints limit our focus to dying and death in the United States.

The Process of Dying

Dying is a complex process. For our purposes we will utilize Robert Atchley's (1991) definition of a dying person, one identified as having a condition from which no recovery can be expected. Much has been written about how people react to the news that they are terminally ill. Psychiatrist Elizabeth Kübler-Ross (1969) invited dying patients to express their thoughts, fears, and anxieties about this last phase in their lives. On the basis of two hundred interviews with dying patients of different ages, she identified five stages through which she believed the dying patient moves:

- ***Denial:*** "No, not me. It must be a mistake" is a common reaction.
- ***Anger:*** "Why me?" becomes the question.
- ***Bargaining:*** "Please let me live to see my daughter get married." "Please let me live to make amends for what I did." The appeal may be made to God or to one's doctors.
- ***Depression:*** This stage is characterized by generalized feelings of loss.
- ***Acceptance:*** The denial, anger, bargaining, and depression are replaced by contemplation of the approaching death with a quiet readiness.

In a later work Kübler-Ross (1974) pointed out that patients may skip a stage, experience some or all of the stages simultaneously, or move through the stages in any order. Kübler-Ross's stages of dying have not received any empirical support; nevertheless, many practitioners as well as family members continue to use them in an effort to understand and respond appropriately to the behaviors of dying people. Critics of Kübler-Ross reject the notion of a progression through stages. They see the dying person as experiencing a variety of feelings and emotions and engaging in psychological defenses and maneuvers (Shneideman, 1980; Baugher et al., 1989–90). For example, Richard Kalish (1985) argues that what Kübler-Ross calls stages are simply common reactions to one's impending death. He believes that dying people also experience other reactions such as hope, relief, curiosity, and apathy. Despite such criticism, Kübler-Ross's work remains noteworthy for providing insights into the needs and tasks of the terminally ill and for initiating a much-needed discussion of these issues.

The Needs and Tasks of the Dying

One of the needs that most dying people have is to know that they are dying, yet access to this information is not always available. Although in recent years the tendency in the medical community has been to tell the patient, some doctors are still reluctant to do so. This need is strongly related to the tasks that the dying person must attend to—getting insurance and financial paperwork in order, making decisions about medical treatment, arranging for distribution of personal property, making a will, letting people know her or his wishes regarding funeral arrangements, and saying goodbye. Too often these preparations are not made until the last minute, if ever, thus leaving the grief-stricken spouse or family to cope with them during a period of enormous stress. No one likes to anticipate the loss of a loved one or to think of her or his own demise, yet doing so before the inevitable happens can make the necessary adjustments easier.

Do you remember your first wake or funeral? How did you feel? Were you uncomfortable in that setting? Were you uncertain about the proper way to behave?

In the nineteenth century the overwhelming majority of Americans died at home, in the presence of family and friends. Information and skills for preparing the dead body

[1]As we indicated in Chapter 11, female genital mutilation, at minimum, usually involves removing the clitoris; immolation of widows involves sacrificing women's lives upon the death of their husbands; and coining involves pressing hot objects on a child's forehead or back as cures for various maladies.

were part of the common domestic knowledge of the day. The wake was held in the front parlor, and family and friends came there to pay their respects. In contrast, by the twentieth century death had become culturally invisible (Aries, 1981). Physicians, hospitals, and nursing homes took control of the process. Today, few people ever see an untreated dead body. Instead, professional funeral directors quickly remove the body and prepare it out of sight of family members in an effort to make it appear "natural" or "sleeplike." Rather than say that someone died, we use a variety of euphemisms like *passed away*, *departed*, and *left us* (DeSpelder and Strickland, 1988). In the process, dying has become more depersonalized, and the rituals surrounding death have been shortened.

One of the consequences of these changes is that survivors experience greater difficulties in receiving support throughout their period of bereavement and in expressing their grief openly. **Bereavement** refers to the state of being deprived of a loved one by death; **grief** is the emotional response to this loss. Coping with a loved one's death involves a series of responses and adjustments. First is the painful process of bereavement. This typically involves a period of confusion; difficulty in concentrating; and intense feelings of loss, depression, and loneliness. There may also be physical manifestations of grief, for example, a loss of appetite, an inability to sleep, and deteriorating health. In her classic study of widows, sociologist Helen Lopata (1973) pointed out the necessity of doing "grief work," confronting and acknowledging the emotions brought about by death. Successful grief resolution involves four tasks: accepting the reality of the loss, experiencing the pain of grief, adjusting to an environment in which the deceased is missing, and withdrawing emotional energy and reinvesting it in another relationship (Worden, 1982).

Mourning refers to the outward expressions of grief, including a society's customs, rituals, and rules for coping with loss. Whatever the loss, be it an individual child, sibling, parent, spouse, or partner, or a national collective loss stemming from natural disasters like earthquakes or floods or from armed conflicts, people don't just get over it and move on with their lives. Rather, people reorganize their lives by finding ways to readjust to living in a world without the person or persons who died (Silverman, 2000). Mourning may be private or public, involving a few people or a whole country.

National Mourning

Following the September 11 terrorist attacks that killed over 3000 people, President Bush declared Friday, September 14, 2001, as a day of national mourning. All schools, government departments and offices, and most businesses either closed or took time off from routine matters to pause and recall the tragic events of that day. Heads of major religious denominations and public officials at all levels arranged for memorial services around the country. At noon on that day, bells were rung, and in the evening candlelight ceremonies were held in people's homes, places of worship, and public buildings to remember and honor those who died. Similar activities took place in other countries to show their sympathy for the United States. Such public expressions of grief occur whenever a nation or group of people experience a common loss, be it a political leader such as the assassination of President John F. Kennedy, or a celebrity figure who has touched the hearts of the people, for example, Princess Diana, or when many innocent people are suddenly and violently killed, sending shock waves through their communities. The rituals associated with national mourning help people make sense out of the loss, allow them to share their fears and insecurities, and create or reinforce people's feelings of collective solidarity.

How a person dies, the age of the person, and the relationship to the survivors all affect the nature of the grieving experience.

Death of a Child In contrast to some of the developing countries with high infant mortality rates, here in the United States, parents generally expect to live longer than their children. Since a child represents the past as well as future hopes and dreams, the death of a child is particularly devastating. Parents who have lost a child have consistently told researchers that they have never completely resolved their grief. The two main causes of death of children are accidents and malignant disease. The sudden, unexpected nature of an accidental death intensifies the grief experience, especially if one or the other parent was in any way involved, for example, driving the car in which a child was killed or giving permission to go to the beach where the drowning occurred. The involved parent is likely to feel guilty. Blame from the other parent can compound such feelings. If parents are unable to forgive each other and to help each other mourn the death in appropriate ways, over time the marriage itself may dissolve. When death follows a lengthy illness, there is the added physical, emotional, and financial stress of caregiving. However, there may also be a process of gradual adaptation to the reality of the child's impending death.

Death of a Sibling The well sibling of terminally ill children faces many problems. The signs of sorrow, illness, and death are everywhere. A child sees the signs on a parent's face and recognizes them in the disruptions to household routines even when parents try to shield the child from what is going on. When a child is dying, the parents may be preoccupied with his or her care and the well sibling may feel excluded or deprived of parental attention. The well child may be struggling with conflicting emotions. She or he may love the ill sibling, but resent the attention the sibling is getting. When death occurs, the well child may feel guilt for the death, especially if there was any sibling rivalry in the past. Many of these feelings are kept inside because the child does not want to upset the parents any further.

A child takes its cues for coping with a sibling's death from parents. If the parents' response is dysfunctional, it can impede the surviving child's ability to cope. For example, sometimes parents resent a surviving child because she or he can be a painful reminder of the deceased child. This may compound the child's feeling of guilt. If, however, the parents listen to the surviving child, answer any questions the child has, and share their feelings of loss, giving the bereaved child opportunities to acknowledge and express grief, too, chances are good that the child will cope successfully with this loss.

Death of a Parent Reactions to the death of a parent vary depending on the age of the child. If the death occurs in childhood, the child's sense of loss may be accompanied by feelings of insecurity. The child may fear abandonment by the other parent as well. Just as we saw in the case of siblings, a child may assume responsibility for the parent's death and, hence, guilt: "If I had been better, Dad wouldn't have died." Often people assume that young children don't experience the depth of grief that adults do, or they assume that children will get over the death quickly. Yet children and adults grieve in similar ways. Both cry, get angry, blame themselves, and have problems eating and sleeping. The surviving parent or other close relatives or friends need to be sensitive to the feelings of bereaved children, providing reassurance and helping them to work through their grief.

Even for adults, the death of parents can be very traumatic. No longer do they have the people in their lives that they could always turn to for guidance and acceptance. They have, in fact, become the older generation and thus much more aware of their own mortality.

Death of a Spouse or Partner The death of a spouse has been identified as the most stressful event that can occur in a person's life (Holmes and Rahe, 1967). Spouses and partners provide an individual with a specific role, security, and many kinds of support—physical, emotional, financial, and social. All of these losses must be dealt with and a new role must be constructed. The intensity of the grief reaction depends on a number of factors. If the spouse was ill for a long time, the grief may be coupled with relief. If the death was untimely, acceptance may be more difficult.

Suicide According to the American Association of Suicidology (2001), suicide is the eleventh leading cause of death in the United States. In 1999, over 29,000 people took their own lives. The United States has a moderate rate of suicide (10.7 per 100,000 population) compared with other countries, for example, Hungary (33.5), Finland (26.4), Japan (15.1), and Italy (7.1) (U.S. Census Bureau, 1998). With the exception of some parts of China, the suicide rate for males is considerably higher than for their female counterparts. The groups most at risk for suicide in the United States include the unmarried, males, whites, adolescents, the elderly, and Native Americans. Although there are no official statistics compiled on attempted suicides, estimates are that 730,000 attempts are made each year. There are three female attempts for each male attempt. Firearms are the most common method of suicide, accounting for about 57 percent of all suicides (American Association of Suicidology, 2001). An extensive body of research from the United States, Finland, Sweden, and the United Kingdom point to mental disorders, especially depression, and substance abuse disorders as the leading risks for suicide (Hyman, 2000).

Suicide is not new; it has been documented throughout recorded history. Nevertheless, it is perhaps the least understood of all human behaviors (Stillion, 1995). Cultural attitudes toward suicide vary widely. In some societies suicide was obligatory under certain conditions. Among the Japanese samurai warriors ritual suicide called *hara-kiri* often followed

Although September 14 was an official day of mourning for all those who died in the terrorist attacks on the United States, the families and friends of those who died held their own mourning rituals. Here the family and friends of fireman Lt. Dennis Mojica remember him at his funeral at New York's St. Patrick's Cathedral. Lt. Mojica was one of nearly 300 firefighters who died in the World Trade Center Towers.

disgrace in battle. In premodern India the wife of a nobleman was expected to throw herself upon her husband's cremation pyre, a practice known as *suttee.* Other societies condemned suicide, viewing it as a crime or a sin. Acceptance or condemnation depends on many factors, for example, religious beliefs, level of education, and the circumstances surrounding the suicide (Ingram and Ellis, 1992). Since the 1980s one particular form of suicide has been especially devastating and the source of much political and religious debate. Suicide bombings have become a staple of the ongoing conflict in the Middle East and elsewhere, including the September 11 attacks on the United States. Although suicide is prohibited in Islam as it is in Judaism and Christianity, some Islamic fundamentalist religious leaders approve and even encourage the practice, preferring to use the term *martyrdom,* or *shahid,* instead of suicide, arguing that one who blows himself up among enemies in order to defend his land (until quite recently suicide bombers were almost exclusively male) is a martyr. Although the families and friends of these suicide bombers often see them as heroic figures, most cases of suicide are still met with dismay and disapproval.

All grief work is difficult, but suicide is particularly stressful for survivors. They constantly ask why and often blame themselves for not preventing the death. That someone they love has intentionally taken his or her life is difficult to accept. There is often anger and frustration. To many, a suicide conveys the ultimate rejection. Because others may also "blame" the survivors for the suicide, especially when the suicide involves children or young adults, they may not be able to provide the support needed in this situation. Suicide, like accidental death, is unexpected. The shock of sudden death may compound the grief by adding to it the burdensome feeling that the death was premature (DeSpelder and Strickland, 1996).

AIDS Although we discussed AIDS in some detail in Chapter 6, we mention it here because the AIDS epidemic has played a leading role in heightening awareness of dying and death around the world. Although there has been considerable medical progress in treating this disease, the death rate from AIDS remains high. Just as in the case of suicide, grief work following the AIDS-related death of a loved one can be especially difficult, and survivors may not receive the support from others that is natural in times of bereavement. Several factors account for this. First of all, there is the issue of social disapproval. Some people may blame the victim for hastening her or his own death. For many, AIDS is viewed as a "dirty disease" brought on by illicit sexual behavior or intravenous drug use. Their compassion may be limited to people who are seen as "blameless," such as infants and transfusion recipients (Friedland, 1995). Second, people who die from AIDS tend to be relatively young. This makes their deaths seem untimely and out of the natural order of life. Third, despite a heavy campaign of public education, many people still worry about the possibility of contracting the disease through any kind of contact with a person with AIDS. Finally, family members may be burdened by feelings of guilt if the relationship with the deceased had been estranged because of conflicts over lifestyle.

Suicide and AIDS are not the only situation where grief work is likely to be compounded by external factors. There are a number of situations where grief is, to a large extent, disenfranchised.

Disenfranchised Grief Gerontologists such as Kenneth Doka (1989) have called attention to **disenfranchised grief**—circumstances in which a person experiences a sense of loss but does not have a socially recognized right, role, or capacity to grieve. Societies construct norms, or "grieving rules," that tell us who can grieve, when, where, and how, and for how long and for whom. Employers reinforce those rules by establishing personnel policies that specify how much time, if any, we can take for the death of a loved one. Only some relationships, primarily familial, are socially recognized and sanctioned. When the relationship between the bereaved and deceased is not based on recognizable kin ties, the depth of the relationship may not be understood, appreciated, or acknowledged by others. Yet the roles of friends, roommates, neighbors, colleagues, in-laws, and foster parents can be intense and long-lasting. Other relationships may not be socially sanctioned, for example, homosexual relationships, cohabitation, and extramarital affairs. In still other cases the loss itself may not be defined as significant by others. Examples may include losses due to miscarriages or abortions and even the death of a pet. In other situations a person may not be thought of as being capable of grief, for example, a child or a person with a mental disability. In these cases the bereaved persons lack the supports that facilitate mourning. Although they have experienced a deep loss, they usually are not given time off from work. They may not have the opportunity to talk about their loss or to receive the expressions of sympathy and support that help people through this difficult time. Thus, their grief may be prolonged and intensified.

The Right-to-Die Movement

The discussion of death and dying would be incomplete without consideration of a major debate taking place in the United States and many other countries. With the advent of modern medical technology, it is possible to sustain life (from premature babies to the very old) under conditions that would have led to certain death in the past. People increasingly question such actions when any meaningful gain in the quality of life is unlikely. This issue is not new. For centuries people have debated the ethical issues surrounding euthanasia, or as it is popularly called, "mercy killing." The term *euthanasia* derives from Greek words meaning "good death," or dying without pain or suffering.

The 1976 landmark case involving Karen Ann Quinlan gave public impetus to the debate over the right to die with dignity. Karen, then 21, was admitted to a New Jersey hospital in a comatose state. Doctors held out no hope for her recovery. Karen's parents asked that the respirator artificially sustaining her life be disconnected. The hospital refused, and Karen's parents sued. After a lengthy legal battle, the respirator was disconnected. Karen continued in a vegetative state until her death in 1985. The Quinlan case resulted in public discussion of euthanasia.

Euthanasia can take two forms. In passive euthanasia, medical treatment is terminated, and nothing is done to prolong the patient's life artificially. Forty states and the District of Columbia have passed some form of natural death legislation that allows patients or their families to refuse treatment in the final stages of a terminal illness (Hooyman and Kiyak, 1993). This is usually done through what is called a living will, a legal document that stipulates a person's wishes in this regard. However, there is no guarantee that families, physicians, or hospitals will follow them. A more controversial form of euthanasia is active euthanasia, which refers to actions deliberately taken to end a person's life. The most recent debate on this issue relates to physician-assisted suicide (see the "Social Policy Issues" box).

SOCIAL POLICY ISSUES

THE DEBATE OVER PHYSICIAN-ASSISTED SUICIDE

On April 13, 1999, Dr. Jack Kevorkian was convicted of second-degree murder and sentenced to 10 to 25 years in prison following the nationally televised death of a terminally ill Michigan man. He was also found guilty on a separate charge of "delivering a controlled substance" and was sentenced to an additional 3 to 7 years in the same case. Both charges stemmed from Kevorkian's having administered a lethal injection the previous September to Thomas Youk, who had suffered from the degenerative neuromuscular illness known as Lou Gehrig's disease and had requested Kevorkian's help in ending his life. By his own admission, Kevorkian, dubbed "Dr. Death" by the media, has assisted more than 130 people in dying. Although his medical license was suspended, until Youk's death all attempts to try him had ended in mistrials or acquittals.

Kevorkian and other proponents of physician-assisted suicide argue that it is cruel to prolong a terminally ill patient's suffering when she or he desires to die, that people are capable of making rational decisions about the quality of life they want and, therefore, should have the right to die with dignity with the help of a medically trained person. Opponents of physician-assisted suicide counter that this practice would cheapen human life and put society on a "slippery slope" that could lead to the killing of people who are considered a burden. They also argue that doctors are not always right and that "hopeless cases" have sometimes been reversed and that to assist someone in dying is contrary to the role of healer.

Several public opinion polls have indicated popular support for physician-assisted suicide for terminally ill patients who request it (H. Cox, 1993; Hooyman and Kiyak, 1993). However, it may be that after the public airing of Mr. Youk's death on CBS's "60 Minutes," some of that support eroded.

In 1994, Oregon passed a law permitting physician-assisted suicide, but its implementation was held up by legal challenges. Voters were given the opportunity to repeal the measure in 1997, but instead they voted 60 to 40 to retain the practice. According to Oregon officials, in the third year the program was in place, 27 terminally ill people ended their lives with legal medication. The median age of the 12 men and 15 women who took their lives was 69 (Oregon Department of Human Services, 2002). On November 6, 2001, U.S. Attorney General John Ashcroft reinterpreted the Controlled Substance Act so as to nullify Oregon's Death with Dignity Act. Ashcroft's directive made using a controlled substance to "assist suicide," per se, "illegitimate" and put physicians prescribing a controlled substance in jeopardy of having their prescribing license revoked. Two days later the attorney general of Oregon, a physician, a pharmacist, and four terminally ill patients went to court to seek judicial relief. U.S. District Judge Robert Jones granted a permanent injunction against the Justice Department that prevents it from enforcing Ashcroft's directive. Initiatives on physician-assisted suicide have been blocked or rejected in at least 20 states.

Other countries are also struggling with this issue. Physician-assisted suicide was briefly legalized in the Northern Territory of Australia from July 1996 to March 1997. In the Netherlands, assisted suicide has been decriminalized. Thus, in effect under stringent conditions, physicians are permitted to take steps to end the lives of patients who request a "dignified death." The terminal diagnosis must be confirmed with a second opinion, the patient must demonstrate unwavering desire to die and confirm her or his wish in writing, and unbearable and incurable physical suffering must be present. There are approximately 2700 cases of euthanasia and assisted suicide annually in the Netherlands (DeSpelder and Strickland, 1996). A recent study in the *Journal of Medical Ethics* found evidence of a "slippery slope" in the Netherlands in that cases of physician-assisted suicide are not being checked to see that all those conditions are being met (Verhovek, 1999).

What do you think? Should physician-assisted suicide be legal? If so, under what conditions? Do you support or oppose this practice? Explain. How do you think you would react if you discovered today that you had a terminal illness? How would you want those around you to react?

STRENGTHENING MARRIAGES AND FAMILIES: THE ONGOING CHALLENGES OF LIVING IN A GLOBAL WORLD

Finally, as we have seen, families everywhere are experiencing the challenges of living in a global world. After reading this chapter you may be tempted to think that the world is out of control, that the challenges humans face are so complex and overwhelming that positive change is not only improbable but next to impossible. This kind of thinking can give rise to feelings of depression and hopelessness. However, history teaches us that problems can be solved; that concerned people can and do meet a wide variety of human challenges. An example from the past comes quickly to mind. Legalized discrimination, for example the apartheid system in South Africa or the "Jim Crow" system of racial segregation in the southern United States, has been abolished. Clearly this has not eliminated racism, but it is a major step forward and an example of people working individually and collectively to find solutions. Although we have pointed out some horrific problems that exist locally, nationally, and globally, there are movements to alleviate many of these conditions. For example, at the United Nations Millennium Summit in the fall of 2000, the world's leaders put forth their vision for the world, adopting the United Nations Millennium Declaration and recognizing their "collective responsibility to uphold the principles of human dignity, equality and equity at the global level." Among the many objectives set out by the declaration are specific, quantified, and monitorable goals for development and poverty eradication by 2015:

- To halve the proportion of the world's people living on less than $1 a day.
- To halve the proportion of the world's people suffering from hunger.
- To halve the proportion of the world's people without access to safe water.
- To achieve universal completion of primary schooling.
- To achieve gender equality in access to education.
- To reduce maternal mortality ratios by three-quarters.

WRITING YOUR OWN SCRIPT

THINKING GLOBALLY

At the beginning of the chapter we asked you to reflect on how globalization affected you and your family. We invite you to continue that reflection here. At the end of one century and into the beginning of a new one, we find ourselves living in a world that is filled with contradictions. On the one hand, there are deep conflicts, tensions, and forms of extreme inequality. On the other hand, technological innovations provide us with amazing power to improve our lives for the better. One thing is certain, however. Human beings everywhere are, for better or worse, part of a common future. The choices we make as individuals and in groups will shape the quality of life we all experience.

Questions to Consider

1. Given the rate of change taking place around the world, what are you doing and can you do in the future to prepare yourself for living in a global society? Do you think any new political structures are warranted in terms of global interdependence? If so, what kind of structures can you envision?
2. What do you think the advantages and disadvantages of the worldwide migration currently taking place are? Would you consider migrating to another country? Why or why not? If you did migrate to another country, what problems do you think you and your family would encounter as "outsiders"? How do you think you would feel in such a situation?
3. Have you or any one in your family ever been discriminated against? What do you think the basis of that discrimination was? What was your reaction? Did you ever, consciously or unconsciously, discriminate against someone else? Why or why not? Can you as an individual or can your family do anything to eliminate discrimination here in the United States or in the larger society? If yes, what can you do? If no, why can't you? Do societies have a moral responsibility to end all forms of discrimination?
4. What do you think of the movement to allow transracial adoptions? Would you consider adopting a child from another racial or ethnic group? If so, why or why not? Do you think transracial adoptions are good for the adopted child? If you were raising a child from another race or ethnic group, how would you prepare her or him to live in a society that frequently undervalues her or his group?
5. If you could change anything about the society (or world) in which we live today, what would it be? How would you want things changed? Why? Do you think any other people share your view? What could you begin to do now to help bring this change about?

- To reduce under-5-years-of-age mortality rates by two-thirds.
- To halt and begin to reverse the spread of HIV/AIDS, malaria, and other major diseases (United Nations Development Programme, 2001:21, 23).

Imagine for a moment what the achievement of any one of these goals would have on millions of families around the world.

There are many reasons to assume that some of the marriage and family trends and challenges that we have observed since the 1950s will continue well into the twenty-first century. Families will continue to play a central, if somewhat altered, role in people's lives. Currently, the vast majority of people report satisfaction with their family life, and there is every reason to believe that this trend will continue. Nevertheless, families require a supportive social environment if they are to remain strong and vital. The United States faces several serious family-related problems: the declining economic welfare of families; increasing hostility toward welfare assistance programs, poor people, people of color, and immigrants; the declining welfare of children; violence and abuse within the family, on the streets, and in the nation's schools; crime, particularly involving children both as victims and offenders; controversial adoption policies; the rapid growth in the numbers of the elderly; concern about the rights of terminally ill members of society; and the unequal valuation of women's contributions to the global economy.

These trends and challenges are complex and multifaceted; thus, resolutions will not be easy or quick. Many of the factors contributing to these problems are structural in nature and therefore will require structural changes to solve them. However, we should not be overwhelmed by them either. As we have indicated throughout this textbook, earlier generations confronted numerous family-related problems. Despite repeated fears that the family is a dying institution, it has survived by adapting to changing economic and political circumstances. Therefore, rather than worry about any specific changes in families or engage in nostalgia for a particular family form, we need to enact social policies that focus on the concrete realities within which families exist. Social policies that are truly "profamily" will recognize the diversity of the world's families and our connections to one another.

SUMMARY

Increasingly, the lives of people around the world are intertwined. Any one nation's problems—unemployment, substance abuse, disease, inequality, racism, sexism, inadequate resources, terrorism, war, and displacement—cut across cultural and geographic boundaries. The process of globalization is not new. What is different today is the depth and breadth of the process. For the past three decades or so, global competition for new markets has intensified. Families in wealthy and poor countries alike are hearing that they must adapt to this increased competition, yet the benefits and the burdens of adapting are not shared evenly.

These inequities are apparent in the health of a population as well as in its access to health care. For example, although one part of the world benefits from the most recent major medical advances, the other part is reduced to selling body parts to keep themselves and their families alive, leaving themselves vulnerable to diseases and perhaps early death. Even in the United States, where per capita health expenditures are the highest of any of the industrialized countries, over 14 percent of the population, nearly 39 million people, do not have health insurance.

Another challenge that many families face is coping with members who are addicted to alcohol or other drugs. The abuse of alcohol and other drugs creates numerous economic and health problems and often causes major restructuring of family roles, in some cases leading to the death of a family member or to the dissolution of the family.

Over 500,000 children are currently without permanent homes in this country alone. Many of these children were removed from their homes as a result of being neglected or abused as a result of parental addiction and escalating poverty. Only a small percentage of children currently in foster care are eligible for adoption. There are many controversies surrounding adoption today. Adoption costs are high, thus prohibiting many poor and working-class families, especially those of color, from being able to adopt.

Although many forces impinge on family life in the United States, racism continues to be one of the major challenges to the well-being of many families, particularly families of color. In the past two decades there has been a resurgence of racist hate groups in the United States. Because of the persistence of racism and discrimination in major U.S. institutions such as education and the work force, families of color are forced to bear a disproportionately higher amount of poverty, unemployment and underemployment, welfare dependency, dropping out of school, infant mortality, illness, and death. Despite improvements in the life conditions of some families of color, the majority remain disadvantaged by racism and discrimination. And since the September 11, 2001, terrorist attacks on the United States, there has been an alarming rise in xenophobia among Americans from all walks of life. However, racism, ethnic discrimination, xenophobia, hate, and violence are not limited to the United States but can be found in a number of countries around the world.

In addition to the challenge of racism and discrimination, families around the world are confronted with gangs and gang violence. Although street violence and crime decreased in the United States in the mid-1990s, the rate of juvenile or youth violence and criminal behavior has increased at an alarming rate. In addition, young people are increasingly playing out their violent behavior inside the nation's schools. Over the 5-year period from 1996 to 2001, there were at least 19 violent incidents in U.S. schools, 80 percent (16) of which involved white male student shooters, many of which resulted in multiple deaths.

Terrorism, war, and displacement also take a tremendous toll on family life. Although American citizens continue to be prime targets of terrorism worldwide, the terrorist events of September 11, 2001, dramatically demonstrated Americans' increasing vulnerability to terrorist acts at home. One of the most significant global demographic trends of the twentieth century and continuing today is the massive immigration of people from one country to another all over the world, particularly that which emerged as a result of communal conflict, terrorism, and war. Refugees have to adapt to the cultural and legal norms of a host society, and the host society must confront large-scale economic and political issues, as well as social issues such as tolerance and *cultural relativism*.

Finally, all families must cope with the loss of loved ones. People need to be able to express their sorrow and to receive social support as they do their grief work. Because some social relationships are either unrecognized or socially disapproved, many individuals experience disenfranchised grief.

Although these challenges sometimes seem insurmountable, history teaches us that problems can be solved and that concerned people can and do meet a variety of challenges.

KEY TERMS

global interdependence
health
disability
drug
drug use
drug abuse
alcoholism
closed adoption
open adoption
fictive kin
xenophobia
racism
individual racism
institutional racism
symbolic racism
ethnic cleansing
terrorism
refugee
bereavement
grief
mourning
disenfranchised grief

QUESTIONS FOR STUDY AND REFLECTION

1. Throughout this chapter we have examined a number of international issues (globalization, worldwide inequalities, health issues, substance abuse, foster care and adoption, racism, street violence, terrorism, war, and death and dying). How appropriate is it to consider these issues in a Marriages and Families text? Would you add to this list or eliminate any issues? Explain. Does the United States, and by extension its citizens, have a responsibility to be involved in what happens to families in other parts of the world? Explain.
2. Describe some of the patterns of drug use and abuse in the United States. How does drug abuse affect families? Is the "war on drugs" being won? Can it be? What still needs to be done? Explain. Given the social and economic costs of alcohol abuse in this country, do you think it should be made illegal like other drugs? Why or why not?
3. Search the Internet for sites pertaining to either disabilities or the status and welfare of children. What do these sites tell us about disabilities? The status of children? Compare the data/information of different countries around the globe. Write an essay on either topic that includes a comparative analysis of data you find and that ends with a policy statement on the subject.
4. It is often said that the United States is a death-denying society, that we remove the dying to hospitals and nursing homes and use euphemisms for death—she has "passed on," he has "gone to a better place," and that, consequently, Americans are not well prepared for this last stage of life. Do you agree or disagree? Explain. How much experience have you had with death or dying? Should there be death education in the schools? What should people do to prepare for their own death or that of a loved one? Explain.

ADDITIONAL RESOURCES

SOCIOLOGICAL

MICKELSON, ROSLYN, ED. 2000. *Children on the Streets of the Americas: Globalization, Homelessness and Education in the United States, Brazil, and Cuba.* New York: Routledge. The contributors to this volume provide insight into why the number of street children is increasing in the midst of prosperity, give glimpses into the devastating lives they lead, and suggest the kinds of programs most likely to serve their needs.

QUADANGO, JILL. 1994. *The Color of Welfare: How Racism Undermined the War on Poverty.* New York: Oxford University Press. A thought-provoking examination of how racism perpetuates poverty and impedes solutions to social problems.

ROSENBLUM, KAREN E., AND TONI-MICHELLE C. TRAVIS. 1996. *The Meaning of Difference.* New York: McGraw-Hill. An anthology of readings that examine the contemporary American constructions of race, class, sexual orientation, and gender. It includes both classic and new articles on the subject.

STEINBERG, GAIL, AND BETH HALL. 2000. *Inside Transracial Adoption.* Indianapolis, IN: Perspective Press. The authors, both adoptive moms, tackle the challenges, emotions, responsibilities, and joys of transracial adoptions and insist that adoptive parents face the realities of racism in the United States.

LITERARY

HOLTHE, TESS URIZA. 2002. *When the Elephants Dance.* New York: Crown. An interesting war story about the experience of the Japanese occupation of the Philippines during World War II from a variety of civilian perspectives. The novel centers on a small, mismatched group of families and neighbors who huddle in a cellar while Japanese occupiers terrorize and pillage above. Grounded in Philippine myth and culture, the novel conveys the terrifying experience of war, including the torture of civilians, especially children, and the equally horrendous experience of waiting for loved ones to return from war.

TERKEL, STUDS. 2001. *Will the Circle Be Unbroken? Reflections on Death, Rebirth and Hunger for a Faith.* New York: New Press. In the latest oral history by a Pulitzer Prize–winner, 63 people share their feelings about faith and death in a readable and moving way.

INTERNET

http://www.who.int The World Health Organization site contains excellent information on environmental, health, and human rights issues around the world and offers links to many governmental and nongovernmental sites that also deal with these issues.

http://www.globalissues.org/ This Web site looks into global issues that affect everyone and attempts to show how most of them are interrelated. It provides links to news articles and Web sites on a variety of social issues, such as human rights, geopolitics, poverty and globalization, the economy, and the environment.

Appendix A

Sexual Dysfunctions and Sexually Transmitted Diseases

SEXUAL DYSFUNCTIONS

Sexual dysfunction is a broad term that includes a number of specific problems. We describe the most common sexual dysfunctions found among women and men, distinguishing them as much as possible along gender lines.

Sexual Dysfunctions in Women

The most common sexual dysfunctions found among women are related to penetration and orgasm.

Inhibited sexual excitement refers to a lack of erotic response or feeling during sexual activity. A woman who experiences inhibited sexual excitement does not show any of the physiological manifestations of arousal such as expansion of the vagina, nipple erection, or vaginal lubrication. Consequently, sexual intercourse might be uncomfortable or even painful. In some cases a woman may never have experienced arousal (a *primary* dysfunction). In other cases a woman may have experienced arousal in the past but is not currently experiencing it (a *secondary* dysfunction).

Anorgasmia refers to the inability of a woman to reach orgasm. Prior to 1970, this dysfunction along with several others was lumped under the term *frigidity*. There are many forms of anorgasmia. In *primary anorgasmia*, no matter what type of stimulation has been tried, a woman has never experienced orgasm. In *secondary anorgasmia*, a woman has been regularly orgasmic in the past but is not currently orgasmic. A third category, *situational anorgasmia*, describes a woman who experiences orgasm only under certain specific circumstances, such as in a hotel room but not in her own bedroom. Finally, *random anorgasmia* refers to a woman who has experienced orgasm in a variety of sexual activities but only on an infrequent basis.

The immediate cause of anorgasmia is an involuntary inhibition of the natural orgasmic reflex, but other factors can contribute to this condition, such as severe chronic illness, drug and alcohol abuse, hormonal deficiencies, diabetes, and various medications such as tranquilizers and blood pressure medications. In addition, social factors such as the double standard regarding the acceptability of sexual feelings in women and men can also contribute to anorgasmia. Some anorgasmic women find sexual activities pleasurable and satisfying even though they do not experience orgasm; others experience depression, a lack of self-esteem, or a sense of futility.

About 2 to 3 percent of adult women experience pain during penetration. *Vaginismus* is a condition in which the muscles around the outer part of the vagina contract involuntarily during penetration, closing the vagina almost totally. In most cases, vaginismus is specific to vaginal penetration and does not necessarily affect other aspects of a woman's sexual responsiveness. In some women, however, the same involuntary muscle spasms may occur in response to any attempt to enter the vagina. Therefore, foreplay, such as the insertion of a finger, or even gynecological exams will produce the involuntary spasms and vaginal closure.

Vaginismus may be caused by factors such as poor vaginal lubrication, the use of various drugs, some illnesses, vaginal infections, and pelvic disorders. Most often, however, it seems to be a result of psychological factors, for example, a strict religious upbringing, having been taught that sex is unpleasant and painful, fear of or hostility toward men, and psychological reactions to rape. Reactions by partners of a woman with vaginismus range from self-blame or passivity about sex to impatience, resentment, and open hostility. Sometimes vaginismus can be treated with simple relaxation exercises.

Another sexual dysfunction of women is *dyspareunia*, or painful intercourse, which can occur at any point during or immediately following intercourse. The pain of dyspareunia can range from burning sensations to sharp, searing pain or cramps and can occur in the vagina or in the pelvic region or abdomen. Although the exact incidence of dyspareunia is not known, it is estimated that approximately 15 percent of adult women experience painful intercourse a few times each year, and 1 to 2 percent experience it on a regular basis. The anxiety about the pain associated with intercourse can make a woman tense and decrease her sexual enjoyment or cause her to abstain altogether either from sexual intercourse or from all forms of sexual activity.

Finally, a very small number of women experience *rapid orgasm*, a condition in which a woman reaches orgasm too quickly. A minority of women who experience rapid orgasm lose interest in further sexual activity and may even find further activity to be physically uncomfortable. Most of these women, however, remain sexually aroused and interested, sometimes going on to have multiple orgasms. These women frequently view this condition as an asset rather than a liability. Sometimes the woman's partner will view this condition in personal terms, taking it to be symbolic of her or his unique lovemaking ability.

Sexual Dysfunctions in Men

The most common sexual dysfunctions among males are related to erection and ejaculation.

Erectile dysfunction refers to the condition in which a male cannot have or maintain an erection that is firm enough for coitus. Erectile dysfunction is sometimes referred to as *impotence* and can be classified as either *primary*, in which case a male has never experienced an erection that has been adequate enough to have sexual intercourse, or *secondary*, in which case a male has previously experienced one or more erections. Of the two, secondary erectile dysfunction is more common. Erectile dysfunction can occur at any age, and it takes many forms. In only a few cases is the man totally unable to have an erection. Usually the man has partial erections, but they are not firm enough for vaginal or anal insertion. In some cases, a man may be able to have an erection but only under certain conditions, such as during masturbation. Because losing or not having erections is so common among men, isolated incidents do *not* constitute a sexual dysfunction. Only when such incidents occur in at least 25 percent of a man's sexual activities is the man said to be experiencing secondary impotence.

Although some physical conditions can cause primary erectile dysfunction, most cases are caused by psychological conditions such as a high level of anxiety or stress, a highly religious upbringing, early homosexual experiences that led to feelings of guilt and confusion, or a single traumatic sexual intercourse experience. Secondary erectile dysfunction is also caused by a number of factors. In most cases it is brought on by some precipitating event such as fatigue, work pressure, financial problems, drug or alcohol abuse, depression, or arguments. Men react to erectile dysfunction in a number of ways, the most common of which is a feeling of dismay. The partner of a male with erectile dysfunction may blame herself or himself, thinking that she or he is not skilled enough to arouse the man's passion.

Premature ejaculation, or *rapid ejaculation*, is a common dysfunction in which a male reaches orgasm too quickly. In most cases, the male ejaculates just before or immediately after entering his partner. Because ejaculation is so rapid, stimulation of his partner does not occur. As a result, both partners are often dissatisfied. Some men are not bothered by ejaculating quickly, whereas others become embarrassed or frustrated, develop low self-esteem, or question their masculinity.

Premature ejaculation is believed to be the most common male sexual dysfunction, affecting an estimated 15 to 20 percent of men on a regular basis. Less than 20 percent of these men consider this condition to be problematic enough to seek therapy. The primary causes of premature ejaculation are psychological factors such as anxiety or early experiences with rushing through intercourse or other sexual activity for fear of being caught (for example, having sex in the backseat of a car).

Another sexual dysfunction for men is *inhibited male orgasm*, sometimes referred to as *retarded ejaculation*, in which a man is unable to ejaculate during sexual intercourse despite a firm erection. Although the muscle contractions of orgasm do not occur, fluid containing sperm may leave the penis and enter the vagina; thus, pregnancy is possible. As with erectile dysfunction, inhibited orgasm can be *primary*, in which a man has never ejaculated during coitus, or *secondary*, in which a man who has experienced ejaculation and orgasm in the past suddenly develops a problem. In both instances, ejaculation is often possible by masturbation or some other noncoital stimulation. Drug and alcohol use accounts for about 10 percent of cases of inhibited male orgasm. Inhibited male orgasm should be distinguished from *retrograde ejaculation*, a condition in which the bladder neck does not close off properly during orgasm, causing the semen to spurt backward into the bladder.

Another male dysfunction, *priapism*, is a condition in which the penis remains erect for prolonged periods of time. Priapism results from damage to valves that are supposed to regulate penile blood flow. Under this condition, erection can last for days, but it is generally not accompanied by a desire for sex. Prolonged erection can be painful as well as embarrassing for most men.

Finally, men, like women, can suffer from *painful intercourse*, or *dyspareunia*. Typically, the pain is felt in the penis. Some men, however, experience the pain in the testes or even internally, where it might be related to a problem with the prostate or seminal vesicles. Both physical and psychological factors can contribute to dyspareunia. Physical factors include inflammation or infection of the penis, testes, urethra, foreskin, or prostate. A few men experience pain if the tip of the penis is irritated by vaginal contraceptive foams or creams.

Sexually Transmitted Diseases

Sexually transmitted diseases (STDs) is a broad term used to describe a variety of bacterial, viral, yeast, and protozoan infections that are almost always transmitted by sexual contact and to refer to various other infections that are sometimes transmitted in nonsexual ways. In the past, many of these diseases were referred to as *venereal diseases.* Most STDs are transmitted through genital–genital, oral–genital, and anal–genital contact. Some STDs, such as AIDS and hepatitis B, however, can be transmitted through blood transfusions or the use of infected needles. In addition, as we pointed out in Chapter 9, some STDs can also be passed from the mother to the fetus through the placenta and from the mother to the newborn as it passes through the birth canal.

STDs vary greatly in terms of their symptoms, progressions, treatments, seriousness, and outcomes. Most STDs can be prevented with proper care and can be cured with drugs. Being cured does not mean that a person cannot contract the same STD again at a later time. In addition, it is possible for a person to contract more than one STD at a time. In this appendix we present some of the most common

STDs: chlamydia, gonorrhea, syphilis, genital herpes, papilloma, hepatitis B, trichomoniasis, moniliasis, lymphogranuloma venereum, and chancroid. A full discussion of AIDS appears in Chapter 6.

Chlamydia is probably the most common sexually transmitted disease in this country. It affects between 3 million and 4 million people every year. Chlamydial infections are caused by a bacterium (*Chlamydia trachomatis*) that attacks the reproductive system. The majority of infected females and about one-third of infected males experience no symptoms. In the other two-thirds of males, symptoms include a whitish discharge from the penis. Sometimes infected females or males experience a mild irritation of the genitals and an itching or burning sensation during urination. Because chlamydia has symptoms similar to gonorrhea, it sometimes goes undetected. Untreated, it can result in sterility in both females and males, pelvic inflammatory disease (PID), infection of the uterus and tubes, infections in newborns, miscarriages, and stillbirths (Allgeier and Allgeier, 1988). Chlamydia can be cured with antibiotics such as tetracycline.

Gonorrhea is a highly infectious disease that can affect the genitourinary tract, tissues of the genitals, fallopian tubes, rectum, and cervix. It can also occur in other areas of the body such as the mouth, throat, and eyes. Gonorrhea is caused by the bacterium *Neisseria gonorrhoeae.* It can be transmitted by any form of sexual contact ranging from sexual intercourse to fellatio, anal intercourse, and, in rare cases, cunnilingus and kissing. It is almost always transmitted through sexual intercourse, however, because the bacterium cannot live more than a few seconds outside the human body. It generally takes from 2 to 7 days after contact with an infected person for symptoms to appear. A woman who has intercourse once with an infected male runs a 50 percent risk of contracting gonorrhea, whereas a man who has intercourse once with an infected female runs only about a 20 to 25 percent risk of contracting the disease.

Symptoms in women include a yellowish green vaginal discharge, pain in the abdominal area, burning during urination, fever, abnormal menstrual bleeding, and pain in the stomach. In males, symptoms include a thick yellowish green discharge from the penis, inflammation of the tip of the penis, burning during urination, and the appearance of pus or blood in the urine. As with chlamydia, many males and the majority of females show no symptoms during the early stages of the disease. When left untreated, gonorrhea can cause considerable damage to a person's reproductive capabilities, possibly causing sterility. It can also cause PID, heart disease, arthritis, and blindness. Gonorrhea can be cured with antibiotics, the most effective of which is penicillin G.

Syphilis is a chronic infectious disease caused by a type of bacterium known as a spirochete. Because the bacterium generally dies within seconds outside the body, it is usually transmitted through sexual intercourse, but it can also be contracted from a blood transfusion, or it can be transmitted from a mother to the fetus. Syphilis progresses through three stages of increasing severity: the primary, secondary, and tertiary stages. If allowed to run its full course, syphilis can cause paralysis, blindness, heart disease, nervous disorders, insanity, and even death. The incubation period for syphilis is 10 to 90 days.

Primary stage. Between 2 and 4 weeks after infection a hard, crusty, painless oval sore called a *chancre* appears on the vaginal wall, cervix, penis, scrotum, anus, tongue, lips, or throat. It begins as a dull red spot that develops first into a pimple and then into the chancre. If immediate attention is not given to these symptoms they may disappear, but this does not mean that the syphilis has cured itself. The syphilis remains, and after several months the symptoms of the secondary stage appear.

Secondary stage. The secondary stage begins anywhere from 1 week to 6 months after the chancre heals if it has been untreated. In this phase, a person may experience reddish patches in the mouth and around the genitals that emit a clear liquid and are highly infectious. Other symptoms include a nonitching rash, sore throat, fever, headaches, and weight and hair loss. These symptoms can last from 3 to 6 months, but, as in the primary stage, they may disappear if they are not treated. For some people, these symptoms will appear and disappear many times if untreated. Between 50 and 70 percent of people with untreated syphilis remain in this stage for the rest of their lives. In the remaining cases, syphilis resurfaces after a latency period that can last for many years.

Tertiary stage. In this stage a number of more serious symptoms appear. Some people develop ulcers in the eyes, liver, lungs, or digestive tract. A few people suffer damage to the brain and spinal cord, which can result in paralysis, dementia, or fatal heart damage. Pregnant women with syphilis almost always pass it on to their offspring, who may be born blind, deaf, or deformed, or may die soon after birth.

Penicillin is the best treatment for syphilis and is effective at all stages of the disease. Although existing damage cannot be reversed, penicillin can prevent further damage.

The term *herpes* refers to any one of several viral diseases characterized by the eruption of blisters of the skin or mucous membrane. One type, *genital herpes,* received widespread attention in the 1980s as a result of its epidemic spread. Genital herpes is caused by the herpes simplex virus types 1 and 2. Genital herpes is usually transmitted by sexual contact but can also be transmitted by kissing or by touching your genitals after putting your fingers in your mouth. The incubation period for genital herpes is 2 to 6 days after being infected. Symptoms of the infection are similar for women and men. The first signs are itching, irritation, and a rash at the site of the infection. Other fairly common symptoms include pain or burning during urination, discharge from the urethra or vagina, soreness and swelling of lymph nodes in the groin, fever, weakness, and fatigue. Symptomatic blisters usually occur on the penis, scrotum, anus, vulva, clitoris, cervix, or mouth. These blisters are extremely painful and, over time, will rupture and eventually heal themselves even without treatment.

As with syphilis, the disappearance of the blisters does not mean that the virus is no longer in the body. Instead, the virus is still present, and blistering can recur at any time. Untreated, genital herpes can increase the risk of cervical cancer in women and can spread to women's and men's eyes from the hands. Women, more often than men, also develop aseptic meningitis, an inflammation of the covering of the brain. Pregnant women with herpes are likely to pass it on to their offspring, who might suffer blindness, brain damage, or even death. There is no cure for genital herpes, nor is there a single effective treatment. A drug called acyclovir is useful in lessening the severity of the symptoms. People with herpes should avoid having sexual contact during periods when the blisters are apparent.

Papilloma, or venereal warts, is one of the fastest-growing STDs. Venereal warts are dry, often painless, grayish white warts with a cauliflowerlike surface that grow on, inside, or near the genitals or anus. These warts are caused by a sexually transmitted virus and are not always visible. There may be one or a cluster of warts, and they may coexist with other STDs. Venereal warts may cause pain during sex and may multiply during pregnancy. If untreated, venereal warts increase the risk of cervical cancer in women and penile cancer in men. There is no known cure for venereal warts. They can, however, be treated with liquid nitrogen or podophyllin ointment, or they can be burned off surgically.

Hepatitis B is one of three main types of viral hepatitis (the other two are hepatitis A, and non-A, non-B hepatitis). It is a viral infection of the liver and varies in terms of seriousness from mild symptoms such as poor appetite or indigestion, to diarrhea, vomiting, fever, and fatigue; to more serious medical problems such as jaundiced skin and eyes. Although hepatitis B is generally transmitted through blood or blood products, many Americans contract the disease through sexual contact. Hepatitis B can also be spread by saliva, vaginal secretions, seminal fluid, and other body fluids. Many people with hepatitis B remain in a carrier state for years or even a lifetime. Hepatitis B increases the risk of liver cancer and other liver diseases.

Trichomoniasis is caused by a one-celled protozoan, *Trichomonas vaginalis*, that thrives and grows rapidly in moist, warm tissues such as the vagina and the urethra. The disease is most common among women. As many as 25 percent of women will probably contract trichomoniasis at some point. Trichomoniasis has probably received the least attention of all STDs. In fact, because it can be transmitted in many different ways besides sexual contact, some experts in the field do not consider it an STD.

Among women symptoms are generally a foul-smelling, foamy, yellowish green vaginal discharge accompanied by vaginal itching and irritation. In addition, sexual intercourse may be painful. Men experience itching, pain in the urethra, and a slight discharge similar to that caused by gonorrhea. Most infected people do not exhibit symptoms, however. Although lack of treatment does not carry any serious consequences, it does make control of the spread of trichomoniasis difficult. Trichomoniasis is commonly treated with the drug metronidazole, which is about 80 percent effective in both women and men.

Moniliasis, like trichomoniasis, is an infection that can be contracted through both sexual and nonsexual contact. Sometimes referred to as a *yeast infection*, moniliasis is caused by the fungus *Candida albicans*. Women and men seldom exhibit symptoms of this infection. When it invades the vaginal area of women, however, it sometimes produces a lumpy, white discharge that resembles cottage cheese. There is also itching and inflammation of the vaginal area, and intercourse becomes extremely painful. If untreated, moniliasis does not produce any serious complications, but it is extremely uncomfortable and severely limits sexual activity. It is generally treated with vaginal creams or suppositories that contain the drug nyastatin, but the infection can and does recur repeatedly with some women.

Lymphogranuloma venereum (LGV) is a bacterial infection caused by *Chlamydia trachomatis*, which invades the lymph system, a network of vessels in close contact with blood vessels. Of Asian origin, this disease was almost nonexistent in the United States before the Vietnam War. The first symptom of LGV is a small blister that usually appears on the external genitals between 5 and 21 days after contact. Sometimes, however, the blister appears inside the vagina or the urethra. The blister usually heals itself within a few days, but the disease moves on and settles in the lymph glands nearest the infected site. The glands swell and form a painful sausage-shaped mass that settles within the fold of the groin. Other symptoms are similar to those of the flu, including chills, fever, headache, pain in the joints, and upset stomach. If untreated, LGV can produce serious effects, including swelling of the inguinal (groin) lymph nodes, penis, labia or clitoris, and closure of the rectum. Although the disease is curable, treatment is often difficult because the infection responds very slowly to antibiotics. The most effective forms of treatment seem to be tetracycline and sulfa drugs.

Chancroid, like LGV, is a tropical bacterial infection that is usually transmitted by sexual intercourse, although it also can be contracted through less intimate contact. Chancroid is caused by the bacterium *Haemophilus ducreyi* and is particularly contagious if there are breaks or cuts in the skin. The primary symptom of chancroid is one or more ulcerated sores that appear on the genitals 3 to 7 days after exposure. In the beginning the sores appear as pimplelike bumps, that eventually burst into very painful and open sores that bleed easily. The lymph glands in the groin area may also become swollen, and in some cases the sores may spread over the entire genital area. If the disease is left untreated, chancroid gangrene can occur. Chancroid can be cured within a short period of time with tetracycline or sulfa drugs.

Appendix B

Human Anatomy and Reproduction

FEMALE INTERNAL ANATOMY AND PHYSIOLOGY

The parts of a woman's anatomy that are critical to reproduction are internal and include the vagina, ovaries, paired fallopian tubes, uterus, and cervix. Figure B.1 shows the female reproductive system and the major structures of the uterus.

Leading from the vaginal opening to inside the woman's body is the *vagina*, a thin-walled elastic structure 3 to 4 inches long. The vagina functions in a number of ways: It receives the penis during heterosexual intercourse and serves as a depository for sperm during intercourse, as a passageway for menstrual flow, and as the birth canal.

The female body contains two *ovaries*, almond-shaped structures that lie on each side of the uterus. The ovaries produce ova (eggs) and the hormones estrogen and progesterone. Ova are embedded in follicles near the surfaces of ovaries; each follicle contains one ovum. A female is born with about 400,000 immature eggs. Only about 400 of these eggs mature and are released over the course of a woman's fertile years, however. More specifically, each month during a woman's reproductive years one or the other ovary releases one (or infrequently more than one) egg on a day approximately midway between the menstrual periods into the abdominal cavity, a process known as *ovulation*.

Following ovulation the egg begins to migrate toward the *fallopian tubes*, small structures extending 4 inches laterally from each side of the uterus to the ovaries. Hairlike projections called *fimbria* at the end of the fallopian tubes create currents with lashing movements that draw eggs into and down through the tube. Fertilization generally occurs inside the fallopian tubes at the end closest to the ovaries.

Once fertilized, the egg continues its journey through the fallopian tube and into the *uterus*, or *womb*. The uterus is a hollow, pear-shaped organ, approximately 3 inches long and 3 inches wide, composed of three alternating layers of muscle: endometrium, myometrium, and perimetrium. The endometrium—the innermost layer—is rich in blood vessels after ovulation. If fertilization does not occur, the endometrium sloughs off and is discharged from the body during menstruation. If the egg is fertilized, it implants in the endometrium, where it develops, is nourished, and grows for approximately 9 months.

At the lower end of the uterus is the *cervix*, a narrow opening leading into the vagina. At birth, the baby forces itself through the cervix and the vagina to the outside world.

MALE INTERNAL ANATOMY AND PHYSIOLOGY

Male reproductive organs can be found both within and outside the body (see Figure B.2). The external organs (testes, scrotum, penis) are important in both sexual arousal and gratification as well as reproduction. The internal reproductive system includes the seminal vesicles, prostate gland, vas deferens, seminiferous tubules, Cowper's glands, urethra, epididymis, and interstitial cells.

The *testes* (*testicles*), the primary reproductive organs in males, produce both the spermatozoa necessary for reproduction and male hormones, primarily testosterone. Each testicle consists of three sets of tissue that come together to form a tube: seminiferous tubules, where sperm are produced; epididymis, where sperm are stored; and interstitial cells, where the male sex hormones are produced. From the testes the sperm travel through a duct system (epididymis, vas deferens, ejaculatory duct, and urethra) until they are expelled from the penis during ejaculation.

If ejaculation occurs, sperm leave the testes through the second part of the duct, two small tubes called the *vas deferens*, which lead from the testes to the prostate gland, where they form the urethra. Contractions during ejaculation send the sperm into the two *ejaculatory ducts* that run through the prostate gland. After mixing with seminal fluid to form semen, sperm are propelled through the *urethra*, the tube through which males urinate and through which sperm leave the body.

Three male organs play key roles in helping the sperm move through the reproductive system to the penis and outside the body: the seminal vesicles, the prostate gland, and the Cowper's glands. The *seminal vesicles*, two small organs located behind the bladder, secrete fluids, many of which come from the prostate gland. These fluids add volume to the semen. The *prostate gland*, located under the bladder, where the vas deferens meet, adds an alkaline fluid to semen that protects the sperm. During orgasm it contracts, helping the semen to move out of the urethra. Located just below

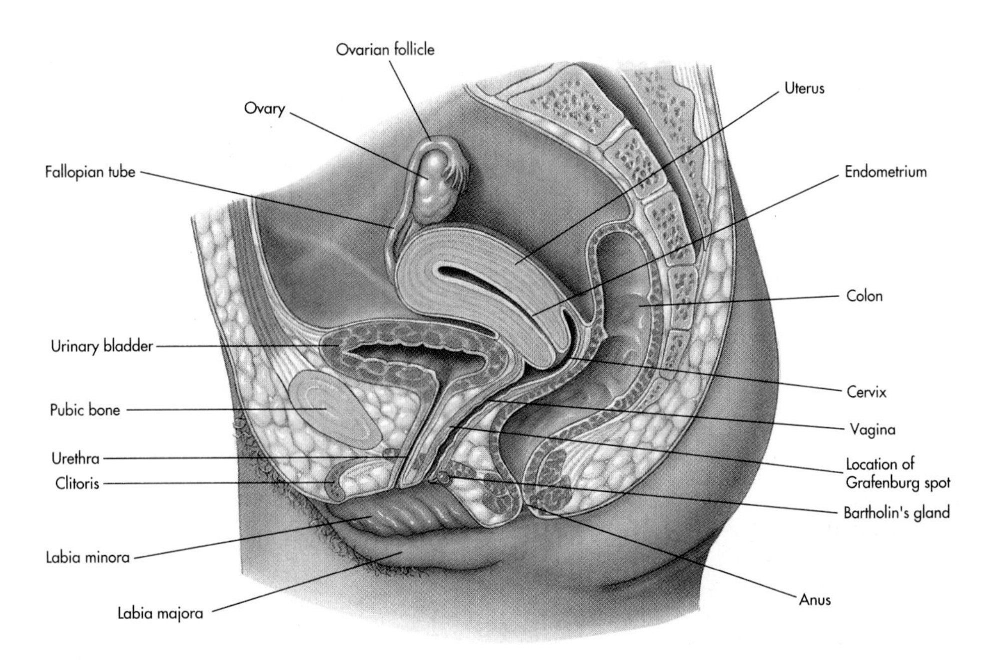

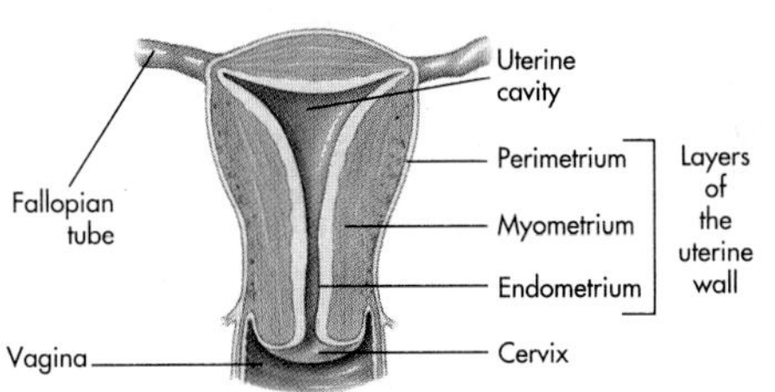

Figure B.1

Female Reproductive System (above) and Major Structures of the Uterus (right)

Source: Adapted from Frederic Martini, *Fundamentals of Anatomy and Physiology*, 2nd ed. Englewood Cliffs, NJ: Prentice Hall, 1992. Drawings by William C. Ober, M.D., and Claire W. Garrison, R.N.

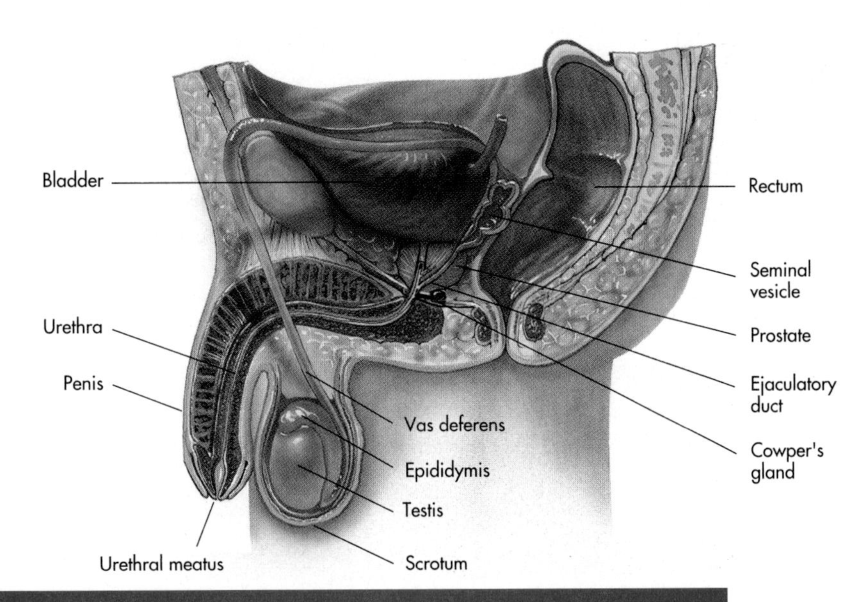

Figure B.2

Male Reproductive System and Structures of the Scrotum

Source: Adapted from Frederic Martini, *Fundamentals of Anatomy and Physiology*, 2nd ed. Englewood Cliffs, NJ: Prentice Hall, 1992. Drawing by Craig Luce.

the prostate gland are two glands called *Cowper's glands*, or *bulbourethral glands*. These tiny glands produce an alkaline fluid that prolongs the life of sperm.

CONCEPTION, PREGNANCY, AND CHILDBIRTH

Conception, pregnancy, and childbirth are profound events. When female ovum and male sperm unite, conception occurs, marking the beginning of pregnancy. During the course of a pregnancy a woman's body experiences a number of internal and external changes as she carries a developing embryo and later fetus within her uterus. By the end of the fourth month of pregnancy, most women begin to "show" (their stomach swells as the fetus develops and grows) and can feel the fetus moving. Once the fetus is ready for birth it will turn its body so that its head is downward toward the cervix. Figure B.3 illustrates the various stages of labor and delivery. In most cases, the fetus is expelled from the uterus without complications.

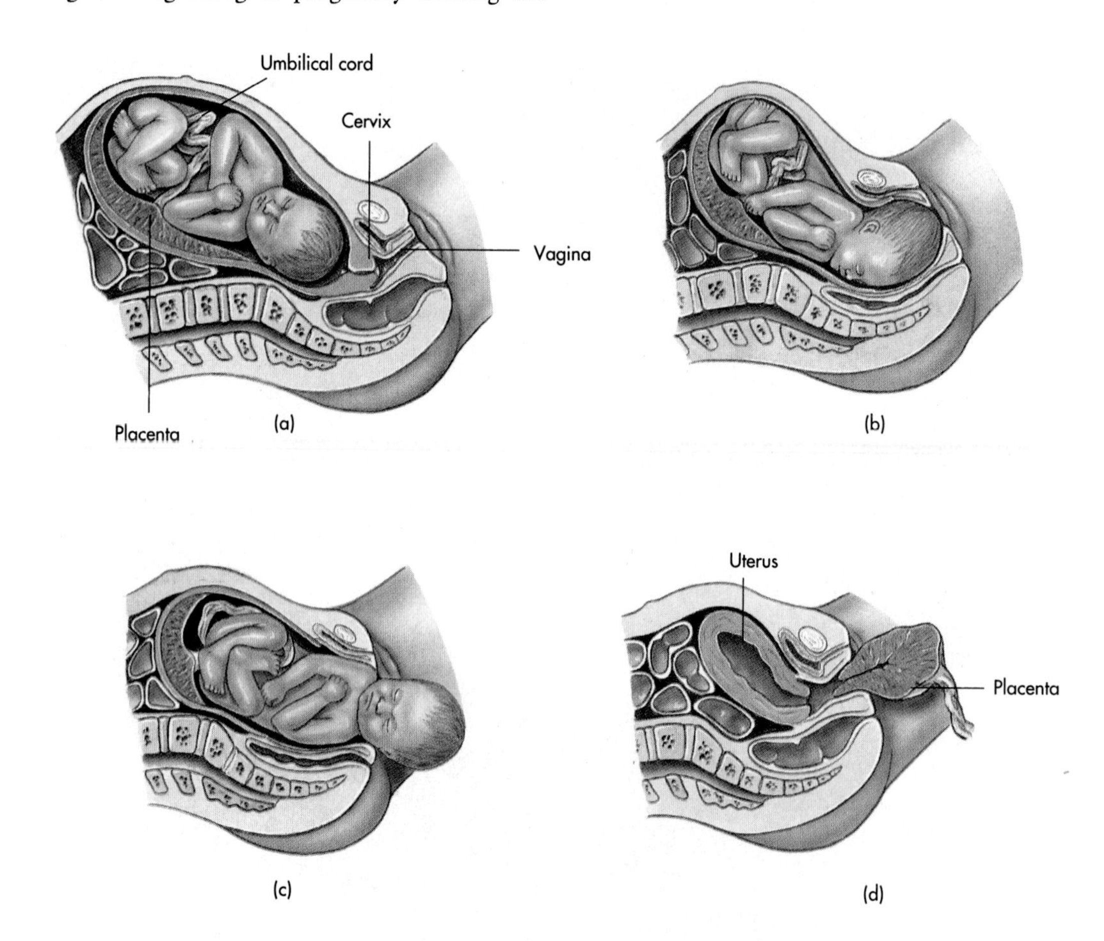

Figure B.3

Labor and Delivery

Source: Adapted from Frederic Martini, *Fundamentals of Anatomy and Physiology*, 2nd ed. Englewood Cliffs, NJ: Prentice Hall, 1992, p. 977, Figure 29–14.

Appendix C

Methods of Abortion

Approximately one-third of all reported abortions are spontaneous (miscarriages). In these cases the developing embryo, or fetus, is expelled from the uterus naturally. A number of factors can trigger a spontaneous abortion. Emotional shock, abnormal development of the fetus, wearing an IUD while pregnant, and any problems of the uterus that would prevent further development of the fetus are among the most common sources of miscarriages. Abortions can also be induced either medically or surgically.

MEDICALLY INDUCED ABORTIONS

Medically induced abortions are sometimes used during the second trimester. Abortifacients are either injected into the amniotic sac or are used as vaginal suppositories. Prostaglandins (a type of fatty acid), saline solutions, and other toxic solutions are among the most common abortifacients. These substances bring on uterine contractions that cause the cervix to open. As a result, the fetus and placenta are expelled, as in a normal delivery. The process takes anywhere from 12 to 36 hours. This procedure is riskier than surgical methods due to the possibility of complications such as infection, hemorrhaging, and embolism. Possible side effects include gastrointestinal cramping and fever.

Mifepristone (formerly known as RU 486) is a safe, effective, nonsurgical form of early abortion. The drug, developed in France, blocks the action of progesterone, a hormone necessary to sustain pregnancy. Mifepristone is used in combination with a prostaglandin called misoprostol and has been successfully used by over 200,000 women worldwide. For years protests against the drug by antiabortion groups delayed its testing in the United States until 1993. It wasn't until September 2000 that the Food and Drug Administration approved its use in the United States. Mifepristone has also shown promise in treating fibroid tumors, ovarian cancer, endometriosis, meningloma, and some types of breast cancer. The drug, however, remains controversial in the United States, and its use has been greatly restricted.

SURGICALLY INDUCED ABORTIONS

Abortion in the early stages of pregnancy is a relatively simple and safe procedure, although any surgical procedure runs some risk and can have varying degrees of discomfort. The most common surgical methods of abortion in the first trimester are dilation and curettage (D&C) and vacuum aspiration. Dilation and evacuation (D&E) and hysterotomy are the methods used in second-trimester abortions.

Dilation and Curettage (D&C) In this surgical procedure the cervix is dilated (made larger), after which a curette (a spoon-shaped surgical instrument) is used to scrape the uterine wall. This procedure is usually done in a hospital, with the woman under local or general anesthesia. Although some women experience pain and bleeding after this procedure, full recovery occurs within 10 to 14 days. After a D&C women are advised to abstain from sexual intercourse for several weeks.

Vacuum Aspiration Most abortions today utilize the vacuum aspiration method (also called vacuum curettage) because it is quicker, involves less blood loss, and has a shorter recovery time than a D&C. The procedure is performed under local anesthesia and takes less than 10 minutes. It can be done in a doctor's office. The cervix is dilated by a speculum (an expanding instrument), after which a small tube attached to a vacuum is inserted into the uterus. The fetus, placenta, and endometrial tissue are gently suctioned out. Over the next few days the woman may experience some cramping and bleeding. She is advised not to use tampons or have sexual intercourse for a week or two after the procedure.

Dilation and Evacuation (D&E) Dilation and evacuation is similar to a D&C but is performed later in the pregnancy, usually between the thirteenth and sixteenth weeks. Local or general anesthesia is used. Because the pregnancy is more advanced and the fetus is larger, the cervix requires more dilation, and the uterine contents are removed through a combination of suction equipment, special forceps, and scraping with a curette. Because this procedure is performed later in the pregnancy, it carries a higher risk. Women may experience cramping and blood loss after undergoing a D&E.

Hysterotomy Hysterotomy carries the most risk and therefore is rarely used. It is performed in the second trimester and involves removing the fetus through an incision made in the woman's abdomen. It is equivalent to a Cesarean section. Because it involves major surgery, hospitalization is required.

Appendix D

Methods of Birth Control

Avoiding sexual intercourse is the surest, safest, and most cost-effective way to prevent pregnancy. Many sex education programs aimed at adolescents stress abstinence as a way to avoid both pregnancy and sexually transmitted diseases, including AIDS. However, abstinence is not a popular choice with people who desire a mutually satisfying sexual relationship but do not want children. The following section examines the birth control techniques that are legally available to couples living in the United States.

Sterilization

Surgical sterilization runs a close second to abstinence in both reliability and, if a long-term view is taken, cost-effectiveness. This is now the most popular form of birth control among married couples in the United States. In the past, female sterilization, called tubal ligation, involved a major operation done under general anesthesia, requiring a hospital stay of 3 or 4 days. In this procedure an incision is made in the abdominal cavity so that each of the fallopian tubes (the ducts between the ovaries and the uterus) can be cut and tied, thus preventing sperm and ova from reaching each other. As with any major surgery, there is some risk of infection (around 7 percent) and some amount of discomfort. In addition, the procedure is costly.

In recent years two new procedures have been introduced that reduce all three of these problems. The first of these procedures is laparoscopy. Here the surgeon inserts a laparoscope (a thin instrument with a viewing lens) into a small incision in the abdomen. The incision requires only a stitch or two to close; thus, the procedure has been dubbed the "band-aid" approach. Using this incision or a tiny second one, the surgeon inserts another small instrument that cauterizes the interior of the fallopian tubes. This procedure leads to the formation of scar tissue, which seals the tubes. The second method is minilaparotomy. As with laparoscopy, general anesthesia is used, and a small incision is made in the lower abdomen, bringing the fallopian tubes into view. The tubes are then tied off or sealed with clips, rings, or electric current. Compared with tubal ligation, these two procedures are less painful, quicker (about 15 minutes), less likely to cause infection (1 percent), require less recovery time, and, because hospitalization is generally not required, less expensive (several hundreds as compared with several thousands of dollars). Many insurance policies cover both female and male sterilization.

Male sterilization is called a vasectomy. It costs about $400, takes about 30 minutes, and is usually done on an out-patient basis. During the procedure small incisions are made on each side of the scrotum, and then the vasa deferentia (sperm-carrying ducts) are cut and tied. This procedure does not prevent sperm production. Rather, when sperm are produced, instead of being ejaculated they are absorbed in the man's body. Discomfort is minimal. Although men should refrain from lifting heavy objects for a few days after surgery, most miss little or no work after the procedure, and they can resume sex within a week of the surgery. However, live sperm remain in parts of the reproductive system for several weeks after the vasectomy, so to be safe a couple should use an additional form of contraception. This other form of contraception can be eliminated once the semen is examined and found to be sperm-free. Overall, vasectomies are successful. In only about 1 percent of cases has a severed vas deferens rejoined itself, allowing sperm to be ejaculated again. Periodic semen examinations can detect any possible changes.

Sterilization has several clear advantages. Once it is done, no further thought need be given to the task of prevention. It is 100 percent effective, except in rare instances when the procedures haven't been performed properly. Most women and men who have undergone sterilization report little or no decrease in sexual desire or sexual pleasure. Some even report more enjoyment after the fear of pregnancy is removed. Sterilization has the added advantage of not interfering with sexual spontaneity.

Sterilization has certain drawbacks, however. A small percentage of women and men experience some psychological problems after sterilization, equating their loss of fertility with diminished feelings of femininity and masculinity. The biggest drawback is that sterilization is permanent, so couples should use this method only if they are certain that they don't want any children. Problems arise when couples change their mind about wanting children or when they remarry and their new spouse wants children.

If a reversal is sought, women can undergo surgery or men can have a vasovasostomy (reconnecting the vas). Neither procedure is generally covered by insurance or is guaranteed to be successful. Today, affluent couples can now avoid concern over permanency by freezing and storing sperm and ova before sterilization (see Chapter 9).

Hormonal Methods: Implants

Among the newest contraceptives on the market, approved by the Food and Drug Administration (FDA) in late 1990, is a thin, matchstick-sized, soft capsule containing the hormone progestin. Doctors implant six silicone rubber capsules under the skin of a woman's upper arm; they are not visible but can be felt by touch. The procedure is simple, done in a doctor's office under local anesthesia. The capsules slowly release the hormone and are effective for up to 5 years. Preliminary studies show a failure rate of less than 1 percent. Another major advantage of implants is that they are easy to remove and when removed their contraceptive effects are immediately reversed. There are some disadvantages. The initial cost is high. The implants called Norplant cost $200 to $300, not including the fee for the procedure. Thereafter, though, there is no expense until they are removed. Some women with implants experience menstrual irregularities, including prolonged periods and spotting between periods. At this time the FDA considers this method as safe and effective as any other contraceptive currently available.

Depo-Provera Injections

Although Depo-Provera has been widely used as a contraceptive outside the United States, the FDA first approved its use for that purpose in 1992. Depo-Provera contains a synthetic progesterone that blocks ovulation. It is injected into the buttocks every 3 months, and effectiveness is 99 percent. Although some women experience irregular bleeding during the first year of use, most women stop menstruating entirely after a year. Depo-Provera has a number of beneficial effects: It relieves the breast tenderness, headaches, and cramping associated with premenstrual syndrome; it decreases the risk of inflammatory disease and yeast infections; and preliminary studies suggest that it may decrease the risk of ovarian cancer. On the negative side, women who use Depo-Provera may gain weight, experience mood swings or depression, and initially were thought to be at greater risk for developing breast cancer. The World Health Organization has given its approval to this drug.

Oral Contraceptives ("The Pill")

The birth control pill, available since the early 1960s, contains synthetically produced hormones estrogen and progesterone, which would be present during pregnancy. The hormones work to prevent ovulation, and they thicken cervical mucus, which prevents the entry of sperm. In the event that fertilization occurs, these hormones inhibit implantation. Birth control pills are available only with a doctor's prescription. A woman's medical history may rule out use of the Pill. Women suffering from hypertension, poor blood circulation, and other risk factors should not take the Pill because of the danger of blood clots and high blood pressure.

Pills come in packages of 20, 21, or 28 and cost $15 to $20 per package. For the pills to be effective, a woman must take them according to a monthly cycle. The woman takes the first pill on the fifth day after the start of menstruation. Thereafter, she takes one pill each day at about the same time for 20 or 21 consecutive days. Her next menstrual period follows 2 to 5 days later, and she repeats the pattern. Some women prefer taking the 28-day pills (7 of which contain no hormones) because they find it easier to remember to take a pill every day. If a woman misses one pill, she must take it as soon as she remembers, taking the next pill right on schedule. If she misses two pills, she can't rely on the method, and she must use an additional method of contraception to protect herself.

The advantages of the Pill are its convenience, its noninterference with spontaneity during intercourse, and its high rate of effectiveness; when used correctly about 95 to 98 percent. Use of the Pill may also reduce the risk of ovarian and endometrial cancers, although this is not certain. Additionally, many women report reduced premenstrual tension and cramps and lighter blood flows during menstruation. However, the Pill causes side effects in about 25 percent of users. Some of these side effects are slight and only temporary and can sometimes be eliminated by adjusting the dosage of hormones in the Pill. Others are so adverse as to warrant discontinuance of the Pill. Among the more serious side effects are nausea, breast tenderness, weight gains due to water retention, migraine headaches, mood changes, and an increased tendency to develop yeast infections. More serious are visual disorders and the risk of cardiovascular disease. A yet unresolved controversy is a hypothesized link between long-term Pill use and cervical cancer. Women who have used the Pill for more than 5 years, who smoke, and who are over 35 are more prone to develop cardiovascular disease.

Intrauterine Device (IUD)

The intrauterine device (IUD) is a small metal or plastic loop, ring, or spiral that is inserted into the uterus through the cervical opening. If inserted improperly, it can pierce the uterine wall and cause serious injury. For this reason an IUD should be inserted only by a medical practitioner. It can remain there for short or extended periods of time. Small strings are left in the vagina to allow women to check to see if the IUD is still in place. Spontaneous expulsions occur in about 10 percent of users, primarily during menstruation, so periodic checking is important. Expulsion is more common among younger women who have not yet given birth, so these women may be advised to use an alternative method. Although the IUD is quite effective (90 to 96 percent), requires little care, is reversible, is relatively inexpensive over the long term ($50 to $100 for insertion), and does not interfere with sexual spontaneity, it has been the subject of much controversy, resulting in decreased use in this country. Only a few types of IUDs remain on the market.

Part of the controversy stems from the fact that technically an IUD does not prevent conception; rather, it prevents the fertilized egg from implanting itself in the uterine wall. Some people equate this with abortion, which they find morally objectionable. However, the more publicized part of the controversy swirled around lawsuits brought in the 1970s against A. H. Robbins, the maker of the Dalkon Shield. This IUD was taken off the market after reports of high rates of uterine infections and an unusually high pregnancy rate among its users. Despite the problems with the Dalkon Shield, most users of other IUDs have few, if any, serious problems with these products. Nonetheless, some women experience cramping during and even after insertion, longer and heavier menstrual periods, and infections, in particular pelvic inflammatory disease.

Male Condom

This contraceptive device has been around for a long time. In ancient Rome men used a condom made of animal intestine and bladder. A latex rubber condom became available in the United States in 1876. The condoms used today consist of a thin cover of rubber or processed sheep's intestine that is placed over the erect penis by either partner to prevent the sperm from entering the vagina. Condoms come in different sizes and colors. They are convenient (can be carried in a wallet or purse) and inexpensive (around 70 cents) and can be purchased over the counter in drugstores and supermarkets.

Condoms are about 90 percent effective. In addition, latex condoms protect against various sexually transmitted diseases, including AIDS. Increasing numbers of women who use other forms of contraception are buying condoms for the added protection they afford. The drawback to the condom is that it is put on after the man is aroused but before he enters his partner. Because sexual activity must be interrupted to do this, some couples neglect or forget to put it on. Some men complain that condoms interfere with sensation and spontaneity. Also, condoms can tear or slip off when in use and must be carefully removed after intercourse to avoid spilling the ejaculate.

Female Condom

In 1992, a female condom became available in Switzerland and France and is now being tested in the United States. The female condom is a large, lubricated, thin polyurethane pouch with an inner and outer ring. The inner ring is inserted into the vagina and the outer ring is spread over the front of the vaginal area. The female condom has several advantages over the male condom. It tears less, and there is less chance of exposure to semen. Like the latex male condom, it can prevent the spread of sexually transmitted diseases, including AIDS. The female condom is more expensive ($2.25) and more cumbersome than the male condom. Some couples find the pouch less spontaneous and somewhat comical.

Diaphragm

The forerunners of the diaphragm, scooped-out halves of lemons and pomegranates, were used in Western Europe as early as 1600. The modern diaphragm is a flexible, dome-shaped rubber cup that is inserted into the vagina to cover the mouth of the cervix. It is used with contraceptive creams and jellies, and it functions as a barrier to sperm. A diaphragm is obtained by prescription after an internal pelvic examination. To be effective it must be properly fitted to conform to a woman's vaginal opening, and to ensure proper fit it should be checked every 2 years or after childbirth, an abortion, or

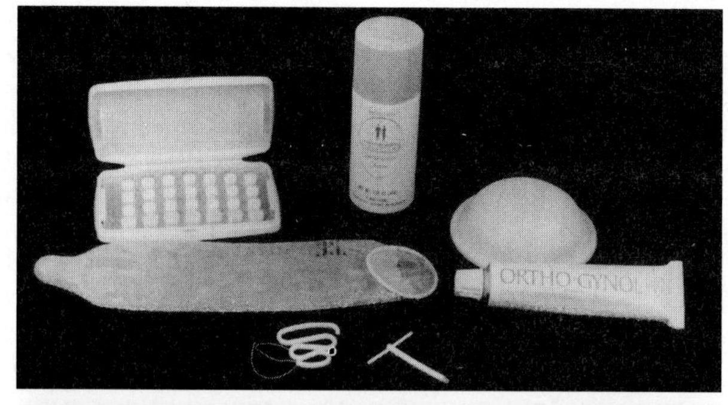

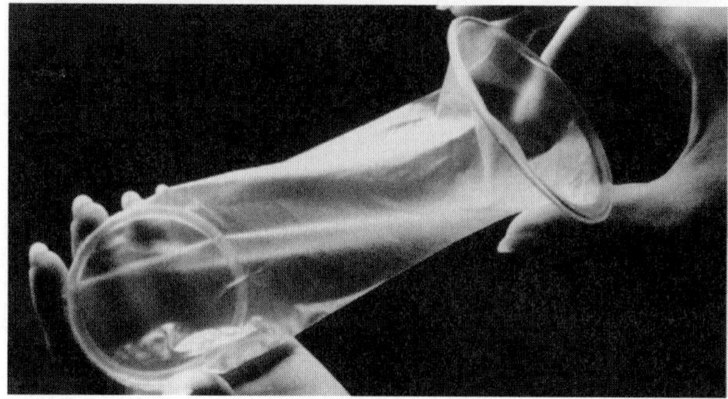

Birth control devices include IUDs, male and female condoms, oral contraceptives, and diaphragms

significant weight changes. A woman (or her partner) inserts the diaphragm before having sex, and it must stay in place for 6 hours after intercourse so that the spermicide has sufficient time to kill all sperm. The diaphragm is about 85 to 90 percent effective. It can be inserted up to 2 hours before intercourse and left in place for up to 24 hours. Its main advantage is that it is reversible and does not interfere with a woman's hormonal system. Although there are few side effects, some women develop bladder infections or experience a mild allergic reaction to the rubber, cream, or jelly. Some women see it as messy, and some feel that the preparation takes away from spontaneity. Initial cost is $50 to $75 for the fitting.

Cervical Cap

A cervical cap is a thimble-shaped device, similar to a diaphragm in appearance and function but considerably smaller. It is designed to fit snugly over the cervix and must be fitted by a trained practitioner. The cap is partially filled with spermicidal cream or jelly and placed inside the vagina. It must be left in place 6 hours after intercourse. The FDA approved the cervical cap in 1988; it is not yet widely used in the United States. Effectiveness ranges from 73 to 92 percent. Some women find the cervical cap more comfortable than the diaphragm. Like the diaphragm it does not interfere with body hormones, but it can become dislodged during intercourse.

Contraceptive Sponge

Approved for over-the-counter sales in 1983, the contraceptive sponge is a small polyurethane sponge containing spermicide. The sponge fits over the cervix, blocking and killing sperm. It can be inserted hours before intercourse and left in place for up to 24 hours. It is 75 to 90 percent effective, easily available, and convenient. However, there are as yet no long-term studies of its safety, and there have been some reports of users developing toxic shock syndrome, a systemic infection that can result in death, and vaginitis, an inflammation of the vagina.

Chemical Barriers

A variety of chemical sperm-killing agents called spermicides (foams, creams, jellies, suppositories, tablets, and contraceptive film) can be purchased over the counter. They are more effective when used with a barrier method, but they can be used alone. They are inserted into the vagina and have a range of effectiveness from 83 to 90 percent. A month's supply averages around $10, depending on frequency of intercourse. They are safe, simple to use, and reversible. However, some users complain of irritation and burning sensations, and some find them messy. Because they must be used shortly before intercourse, couples sometimes feel they interrupt the sexual mood.

Fertility Awareness

Fertility awareness, also called natural family planning because it uses no mechanical or hormonal barriers to conception, makes use of the recurring pattern of fertile and infertile phases of a woman's body during the menstrual cycle. The goal of fertility awareness methods is to predict these phases so that couples can abstain from sexual activity during the fertile period. To determine the "safe" days, it is necessary to determine the time of ovulation. This can be done in several ways:

1. The rhythm method uses a calendar calculation of unsafe days based on the length of a woman's menstrual cycle.
2. The basal body temperature (BBT) method calculates temperature change. A woman's temperature dips slightly just before ovulation and increases after ovulation.
3. The cervical mucus method, also called the Billings or ovulation method, examines the change in appearance and consistency of cervical mucus. The general pattern moves from no visible mucus for several days after menstruation to whitish, sticky mucus then to clear and slippery mucus during ovulation and then back to a cloudy discharge when ovulation ends.
4. The symptothermal method is a combination of the BBT and mucus methods. This method is the most successful because it uses two indicators of fertility rather than one.

All of these methods are designed to help women check changing body signs so that they will know when ovulation occurs. Thus, the effectiveness of these methods depends on a woman's knowledge of her reproductive cycle as well as the couple's self-control (abstinence) during fertile periods. Although it is difficult to ascertain exactly when ovulation occurs, when these methods are used diligently they have a high effectiveness rate. However, risk taking during the fertile phase contributes to a fairly high failure rate. These methods are acceptable to most religious groups. They are also free, except for the purchase of a calendar, chart, and thermometer, and perhaps the expense of taking a class to learn to use the methods properly. There are no side effects. However, couples may experience frustration during periods of abstinence, which can last from 7 to 14 days.

Withdrawal (Coitus Interruptus)

The withdrawal of the penis from the vagina prior to ejaculation can be an attractive form of contraception because it is simple, it doesn't require any devices, and it is free. Unfortunately, it also doesn't work very well. Withdrawal requires great control by the man, and it may limit sexual gratification for one or both partners. In addition, leakage of semen can occur prior to ejaculation.

Douching

Douching, or washing out the vagina, is another old but unreliable method of birth control. Douching after intercourse may actually push some sperm toward the cervix. In addition, douching can lead to pelvic inflammatory disease.

Morning-After Pills

In 1997, the Food and Drug Administration, responding to the request of women's advocacy groups, issued a statement saying that high doses of ordinary birth control pills taken soon after unprotected sex were a good way to prevent pregnancy. European women have long been prescribed regular contraceptive pills for this purpose, and they can get the pills in special packages to have on hand. Drug manufacturers in the United States had been reluctant to sell birth control pills for "morning after" use because of the politics surrounding the abortion issue. However, at the urging of the Food and Drug Administration, some companies are now marketing ordinary birth control pills that, taken at a high dose, can prevent pregnancy if taken within 72 hours of unprotected intercourse. They work by keeping a fertilized egg from implanting into the uterus where it could grow into an embryo. The pills are about 98 percent effective in preventing pregnancy. However, if a woman is already pregnant, the pills will have no effect. The most common side effects are nausea and vomiting, which are expected to affect 10 percent to 40 percent of those taking the Pill. The cost is about $20 a prescription.

Future Contraceptive Strategies

Research to find safer, more effective, and less expensive methods of birth control is under way in many countries. For example, doctors in India are developing a birth control vaccine for women that would be effective for a year. Preliminary testing is encouraging, but the vaccine will not be available for several years. Most contraceptive research remains centered on the woman's reproductive system. However, some researchers are now investigating a male contraceptive pill that would inhibit sperm production. It is unlikely that such a pill will be available in the near future.

Glossary

ABORTION The termination of a pregnancy before the fetus can survive on its own. This can occur either spontaneously (miscarriage) or be induced through a variety of external methods.

ACHIEVED STATUS A position we hold in society by virtue of our own efforts, for example, that of teacher or mother.

ACQUAINTANCE RAPE Sexual assault by a person with whom the victim is familiar.

ACQUIRED IMMUNE DEFICIENCY SYNDROME (AIDS) A viral syndrome that destroys the body's immune system.

ADULTERY Extramarital sexual intercourse.

AFFINAL RELATIVES People related by marriage and not by blood, for example, a brother- or sister-in-law.

AGEISM The application of negative stereotypes and discriminatory treatment to elderly people.

AGE NORMS The expectations of how one is to behave at specific ages in the life cycle.

AGENTS OF SOCIALIZATION Individuals, groups, and institutions that help form an individual's attitudes, behaviors, and self-concepts.

AID TO DEPENDENT CHILDREN A program initiated in 1935 as part of the Social Security Act, it provides support for children whose parents are deceased or disabled.

ALCOHOLISM A chronic behavioral disorder manifested by repeated drinking of alcoholic beverages in excess of dietary and social uses of the community and to the extent that it interferes with the drinker's health or social and economic functioning.

ALIMONY Court-ordered financial support paid to a former spouse following a divorce.

AMNIOCENTESIS A prenatal test in which a needle is inserted into the mother's uterus to collect cells cast off by the fetus for the purpose of testing for genetic diseases or defects in the fetus.

ANDROGYNOUS Expressing a wide range of attitudes and behaviors with no gender role differentiation. Androgyny is the combination of both culturally defined feminine and masculine traits in an individual.

ANNULMENT A legal declaration that a marriage never existed, leaving both parties free to marry.

ANTICIPATORY SOCIALIZATION Socialization directed toward learning future roles.

ANTINATALIST FORCES Policies or practices that discourage people from having children.

ARTIFICIAL INSEMINATION The injection of sperm into the vagina or uterus of an ovulating woman.

ASCRIBED STATUS A position we hold in society because we were born into it, for example, that of being female or male.

AUTOEROTICISM Sexual activities involving only the self, for example, masturbation, sexual fantasy, and erotic dreams.

BATTERED-CHILD SYNDROME A group of symptoms that collectively describe a clinical condition in children who have received severe physical abuse.

BATTERED-WOMAN SYNDROME A group of symptoms that collectively describe a general pattern of physical battering experienced by women. It is defined in terms of frequency, severity, deliberateness, and ability to demonstrate injury.

BEREAVEMENT The state of being deprived of a loved one by death.

BIGAMY The act of marrying one person while still being legally married to another person.

BISEXUALITY A person who has partners of both sexes either simultaneously or at different times.

CASE STUDY A detailed and in-depth examination of a single unit or instance of some phenomenon.

CENOGAMY (GROUP MARRIAGE) A situation in which the women and men in a group are simultaneously married to one another.

CLOSED ADOPTION A form of adoption in which the adoptive parents and the birth parents do not meet.

COGNITIVE-DEVELOPMENT THEORY A theory that asserts that children take an active role in organizing their world, including learning gender identity.

COITUS Penile–vaginal intercourse.

COLLABORATIVE LAW A way of practicing law in which the attorneys for both parties to a family dispute agree to assist in resolving the conflict using cooperative techniques rather than adversarial strategies and litigation, with the goal of reaching an efficient, fair, and comprehensive out-of-court settlement of all issues.

COMMON-LAW MARRIAGE A cohabitive relationship that is based on the mutual consent of the persons involved, is not solemnized by a ceremony, and is recognized as valid by the state.

COMMUNE A group of people (single or married, with or without children) who live together, sharing many aspects of their lives.

COMMUNITY DIVORCE The changes in social relationships that often accompany a divorce—the loss of relatives and friends who were previously shared with a spouse and their replacement with new friends.

COMMUNITY REMARRIAGE The changes in social relationships that often accompany a remarriage—the integration of new in-laws and "couple-oriented" relationships, and sometimes the loss of unmarried friends.

COMMUTER MARRIAGE A marriage in which each partner works in a different geographic location and therefore maintains a separate place of residence.

CONCEPTION The process by which a female ovum (egg) is penetrated by a male sperm cell, creating a fertilized egg.

CONCILIATION COUNSELING Counseling intended to determine whether marital problems can be resolved and the couple reconciled. Some states require conciliation counseling before the courts will consider granting a divorce.

CONFLICT THEORY A theoretical perspective that focuses on conflicting interests among various groups and institutions in society.

CONGENITAL Existing at birth but not hereditary.

CONJUGAL RIGHTS A set of rights pertaining to the marriage relationship.

CONTENT ANALYSIS A research technique used to examine the content of books, documents, and programs.

CONTRACEPTION Mechanisms for preventing fertilization.

COPARENTAL DIVORCE The arrangements divorcing couples work out concerning child custody, visitation rights, and the financial and legal responsibilities of each parent.

COURTSHIP The process of selecting a mate and developing an intimate relationship.

COUVADE Sympathetic pregnancy; a condition in which some men experience many of the symptoms of pregnancy.

COVERTURE The traditional belief that a wife is under the protection and influence of her husband.

CRUISING An activity in which several teenagers (usually male) pack into a car and drive around the neighborhood looking for females to pick up.

CUNNILINGUS Oral stimulation of the female genitals.

DATE RAPE Sexual assault by a person with whom the victim had gone on a date.

DATING A process of pairing off that involves the open choice of mates and engagement in activities that allow people to get to know one another and progress toward mate selection.

DATING VIOLENCE The perpetration or threat of an act of violence by at least one member of an unmarried couple on the other member within the context of dating or courtship, encompassing any form of sexual assault, physical violence, and verbal or emotional abuse.

DESERTION The abandonment of a spouse or family.

DEVELOPMENTAL FAMILY LIFE CYCLE THEORY A theory that explains family life in terms of a process that unfolds over the life course of families.

DISABILITY A physical or mental condition that often stigmatizes or causes discrimination.

DISENFRANCHISED GRIEF Circumstances in which a person experiences a sense of loss but does not have a socially recognized right, role, or capacity to grieve.

DIVORCE COUNSELING Counseling intended to help couples replace the adversarial and often destructive aspects that frequently accompany divorce with a more cooperative spirit and to help them distance themselves from the relationship so that acceptance of the loss and subsequent healing can take place.

DIVORCE MEDIATION A procedure in which trained professionals help divorcing couples negotiate a fair and mutually agreed-upon resolution of such issues as marital property distribution, child custody, visitation rights, and financial support.

DIVORCE RATE The number of divorces occurring annually for every 1000 people over the age of 15.

DOMESTIC PARTNERSHIP A category of relationships consisting of unmarried couples who live together and share housing and financial responsibilities. Some communities and businesses allow unmarried couples who register as domestic partners to receive certain legal rights similar to those of married couples.

DOWRY A sum of money or property brought by the female to a marriage.

DRUG Any substance that alters the central nervous system and states of consciousness.

DRUG ABUSE The deliberate use of a substance for other than its intended purpose, in a manner that can damage health or ability to function.

DRUG USE The taking of a drug for its intended purpose and in an appropriate amount, frequency, strength, and manner.

DYSFUNCTIONAL Having a negative consequence or performing a negative service by hampering the achievement of group goals or disrupting the balance of the system.

ECONOMIC DIVORCE The division of marital property and assets between the two former partners.

ECONOMIC REMARRIAGE The establishment of a new marital household as an economically productive unit.

EJACULATION Expulsion of semen from the penis.

ELDER ABUSE Physical, psychological, or material maltreatment and neglect of older people.

EMBRYOPATHY Prominent physical features in babies born with HIV, for example, slanted eyes that sit far apart from each other, a small head, a flat forehead and nose, and loosely shaped lips.

EMBRYO TRANSPLANT A procedure whereby a fertilized egg from a donor is implanted into an infertile woman.

EMOTIONAL DIVORCE A period during which one or both partners withdraw emotionally from a marriage.

EMOTIONAL REMARRIAGE The process of reestablishing a bond of attraction, love, commitment, and trust with another person.

EMPIRICAL EVIDENCE Data or evidence that can be confirmed by the use of one or more of the human senses.

ENCULTURATED LENS THEORY A theory of gender role acquisition that argues that hidden cultural assumptions about how societal members should look, behave, and feel are so deeply embedded in social institutions and cultural discourse, and hence individual psyches, that these behaviors and ways of thinking are systematically reproduced from one generation to the next.

ENDOGAMY The practice of requiring people to marry within a particular social group.

ENVY Unhappiness or discontent that arises from the belief that something about oneself does not measure up to the level of someone else.

EROGENOUS ZONE An area of the body that is particularly sensitive to sexual stimulation.

EROTIC AROUSAL The stimulation or awakening of sexual feelings and desires in human beings.

ETHNIC CLEANSING A term euphemistically applied to the process whereby one group of people tries to rid the region of others who are different in some significant way.

ETHNOGRAPHY A research technique of describing a social group from the group's point of view.

EXOGAMY The practice of requiring people to marry outside particular groups.

EXPRESSIVE TRAITS Personality traits that encourage nurturing, emotionality, sensitivity, and warmth.

EXTENDED OR MULTIGENERATIONAL FAMILY A family consisting of one or both parents, siblings, if any, and other relatives, such as grandparents, aunts, uncles, or cousins.

FAMILY Any relatively stable group of people who are related to one another through blood, marriage, or adoption or who simply live together, and who provide one another with economic and emotional support.

FAMILY AND MEDICAL LEAVE ACT A law that allows either parent to take up to 3 months of unpaid leave for births, adoptions, and family emergencies.

FAMILY OF ORIENTATION The family into which a person is born and raised.

FAMILY OF PROCREATION A family that is created when two people marry or enter into an intimate relationship and have or adopt children of their own.

FELLATIO Oral stimulation of the male genitals.

FEMINIZATION OF POVERTY The increase in the proportion of poor people who are women or children.

FERTILITY The actual number of live births in a population.

FERTILITY RATE The number of births per 1000 women in their childbearing years (ages 15 to 44).

FETAL ALCOHOL SYNDROME A condition caused by a mother's consumption of alcohol during pregnancy and characterized by physical deformities in the fetus.

FICTIVE KIN The attribution of kinship terms to nonrelatives.

FLEXTIME An arrangement that allows employees to choose within specified time limits when they arrive at and leave work.

FORNICATION Sexual intercourse outside legal marriage.

FUNCTIONAL Having a positive consequence or performing a positive service by promoting the achievement of group goals or helping maintain a system in a balanced state.

FUNCTIONAL AGE The use of an individual's physical, intellectual, and social capacities and accomplishments as a measurement of age rather than the number of years lived.

GENDER The socially learned behaviors, attitudes, and expectations that are associated with being female or male; what we call femininity and masculinity.

GENDER IDENTITY A person's awareness of being female or male.

GENDER ROLE SOCIALIZATION The process whereby people learn and adopt the gender roles that their culture deems appropriate for them.

GENDER ROLE STEREOTYPES The oversimplified expectations of what it means to be a woman or a man.

GENERALIZED OTHERS The viewpoints of society at large—widespread cultural norms and values that individuals use as a reference when evaluating themselves.

GETTING TOGETHER A pattern of dating that involves women and men meeting in groups, playing similar roles in initiating dates, and sharing equally in the cost of activities.

GLOBAL INTERDEPENDENCE A state in which the lives of people around the world are intertwined closely and in which any one nation's problems increasingly cut across cultural and geographic boundaries.

GOING STEADY An exclusive dating relationship with one partner.

GRIEF The emotional response to the loss of a loved one.

GROUP MARRIAGE A marriage of at least four people, two female and two male, in which each partner is married to all partners of the opposite sex.

HAWTHORNE EFFECT The distortion of research results that occurs when people modify their behaviors, either deliberately or subconsciously, because they are aware they are being studied.

HEALTH A state of complete physical, mental, and social well-being, not merely the absence of physical disease or infirmity.

HETEROGAMOUS MARRIAGE Marriage in which the partners are unlike each other in terms of various social and demographic characteristics, such as race, age, religious background, social class, and education.

HETEROSEXISM The notion that heterosexuality is the only right, natural, and acceptable sexual orientation.

HETEROSEXUALITY Both identity and behavior; includes a preference for sexual activities with a person of the other sex.

HOMOGAMY The attraction of people who are alike in terms of various social and demographic characteristics such as race, age, religious background, social class, and education.

HOMOPHOBIA An extreme and irrational fear or hatred of homosexuals.

HOMOSEXUALITY Both identity and behavior; includes preference for sexual activities with a person of the same sex.

HOUSEHOLDS All persons who occupy a housing unit, such as a house, apartment, single room, or other space intended to be living quarters.

HUMAN SEXUALITY The feelings, thoughts, and behaviors of humans who have learned a set of cues that evoke a sexual or an erotic response.

HYPERGAMY Marrying upward in social status.

HYPOGAMY Marrying downward in social status.

HYPOTHESIS Statement of a relationship between two or more variables.

IDEOLOGY A set of ideas and beliefs that support the interests of a group in society.

INCEST Sexual abuse by a blood relative or someone who is thought of as a part of a person's family.

INDIVIDUAL RACISM Behavior by individuals or groups who define themselves as superior toward individuals whom they define as inferior.

INFANTICIDE Killing of infants and young children.

INFATUATION A strong attraction to another person based on an idealized picture of that person.

INFERTILITY The inability to conceive after 12 months of unprotected intercourse or the inability to carry a pregnancy to live birth.

INSTITUTION Patterns of ideas, beliefs, values, and behavior that are built around the basic needs of individuals and society and that persist over time.

INSTITUTIONAL RACISM Established laws, customs, and practices that systematically reflect and produce racial inequalities in a society, whether or not the individuals maintaining these practices have racist intentions.

INSTRUMENTAL TRAITS Personality traits that encourage self-confidence, rationality, competition, and coolness; for example, an orientation to action, achievement, and leadership.

INTERSEXUALITY Condition where an infant's genitalia are ambiguous in appearance and whose sexual anatomy cannot clearly be differentiated at birth.

INTERVIEW A method of collecting data in which a researcher asks subjects a series of questions and records the answers.

IN VITRO FERTILIZATION A reproductive technique that involves surgically removing a woman's eggs, fertilizing them in a petri dish with the partner's or donor's sperm, and then implanting one or more of the fertilized eggs in the woman's uterus.

JEALOUSY Thoughts and feelings of envy, resentment, and insecurity directed toward someone a person is fearful of losing.

JOB SHARING An employment pattern in which two workers split a single full-time job.

JOINT CUSTODY A situation in which both divorced parents are given legal responsibility for raising their children.

KINSHIP Relationships resulting from blood, marriage, or adoption, or among people who consider one another family.

LABOR FORCE PARTICIPATION RATE The percentage of workers in a particular group who are employed or who are actively seeking employment.

LATENT FUNCTIONS Unintended, unrecognized consequences or effects of any part of a social system or the system as a whole for the maintenance and stability of that system.

LEGAL DIVORCE The official dissolution of a marriage by the state, leaving both former partners legally free to remarry.

LEGAL MARRIAGE A legally binding agreement or contractual relationship between two people that is defined and regulated by the state.

LEGAL REMARRIAGE The establishment of a new legally recognized relationship.

LIKING A positive feeling toward someone that is less intense than love—a feeling typical of friendship in its most simple terms.

LIMERENCE A style of love characterized by a complete absorption or obsessive preoccupation with and attachment to another person. It is accompanied by extreme emotional highs when the love is reciprocated and lows when it is not.

LOVE MAP A group of physical, psychological, and behavioral traits that one finds attractive in a mate.

MANIFEST FUNCTIONS Intended, overt consequences or effects of any part of a social system or the system as a whole for the maintenance and stability of that system.

MARITAL ADJUSTMENT The process by which marital partners change or adapt their behavior, attitudes, and interactions to develop a good working relationship and to satisfy each other's needs over the marital life course.

MARRIAGE A union between people that unites them sexually, socially, and economically; that is relatively consistent over time; and that accords each person certain agreed-upon rights.

MARRIAGE GRADIENT Phenomenon by which women marry upward in social status and men marry downward in social status. As a result, women at the top and men at the bottom of the social class ladder have a smaller pool of eligible mates to choose from than do members of the other classes.

MARRIAGE MARKET Analogy of the commercial marketplace to explain how individuals choose the people they date, mate, live with, and marry by "comparison shopping" and "bargaining for" the mate with the most desirable characteristics.

MARRIAGE SQUEEZE A condition in which one sex has a more limited pool of eligibles from which to choose than the other does. Sociologists use the concept to describe the phenomenon of an excess of baby boom women who had reached marriageable age during the 1960s compared with marriage-aged men.

MASTER (KEY) STATUS A position we hold that affects all aspects of our lives, for example, being female or male.

MASTURBATION Erotic stimulation of self through caressing or otherwise stimulating the genitals for the purpose of sexual pleasure.

MATE SELECTION The wide range of behaviors and social relationships individuals engage in prior to marriage and that lead to long- or short-term pairing or coupling.

MATRILINEAL Kinship or family lineage (descent) and inheritance come through the mother and her blood relatives.

MENOPAUSE A period in the female life cycle (typically between ages 45 and 50) characterized by the cessation of ovulation, the menstrual cycle, and fertility.

MIDWIFE Most often a woman who is trained either to deliver a baby or to assist a woman in childbirth. Most midwives today are professionals who practice in birth centers or who deliver babies at home.

MODELING A process of learning through imitation of others.

MODIFIED EXTENDED FAMILY Family in which a variety of relatives live, not necessarily in the same household, but in very close proximity to one another, interact on a frequent basis, and provide emotional and economic support to each other.

MONOGAMY Exclusivity in an intimate relationship. In marriage, it means marriage to only one person at a time.

MORBIDITY The rate of occurrence of illness or disease in a population.

MORTALITY The rate of occurrence of death in a population.

MOTHERHOOD MYSTIQUE The traditional belief that the ultimate achievement and fulfillment of womanhood is through motherhood.

MOURNING The outward expression of grief, including a society's customs, rituals, and rules for coping with loss.

MYTH A false, fictitious, imaginary, or exaggerated belief about someone or something.

NOCTURNAL EMISSIONS (WET DREAMS) Erotic dreams that lead to orgasm during sleep.

NO-FAULT DIVORCE The dissolution of a marriage on the basis of irreconcilable differences; neither party is judged at fault for the divorce.

NORMS Cultural guidelines or rules of conduct that direct people to behave in particular ways.

NUCLEAR FAMILY A family consisting of a mother and father and their natural or adopted offspring.

OCCUPATIONAL DISTRIBUTION The location of workers in different occupations; for example, women are more heavily concentrated in lower-paying clerical or service jobs, whereas men are concentrated in the higher-paying jobs of craft workers and operators.

OPEN ADOPTION A form of adoption in which the adoptive parents and the birth parents meet and together work out the process of adoption.

ORGASM A human sexual response that occurs at the height of sexual arousal. It is characterized by the involuntary release of sexual tension through rhythmic contractions in the genitals and is accompanied in most males by ejaculation.

OVERLAPPING HOUSEHOLDS The dual membership of children in the separate households of their divorced (and frequently remarried) parents.

OVULATION The release of the mature egg.

PALIMONY A payment similar to alimony made to a former unmarried live-in partner and based on the existence of a contract (written or implied) between the partners regarding aspects of their relationship.

PARENTAL REMARRIAGE A process that involves the establishment of relationships with the children of the new spouse.

PATRIARCHAL FAMILY A family organized around the principle of male dominance, wherein the male (husband or father) is head of the family and exercises authority and decision-making power over other family members, especially his wife and children.

PATRILINEAL Kinship or family lineage (descent) and inheritance come through the father and his blood relatives.

PAY EQUITY Equal pay for work of equal value.

PERSONAL MARRIAGE AGREEMENT A written agreement between a married couple in which issues of role responsibility, obligation, and sharing are addressed in a manner tailored to their own personal preferences, desires, and expectations.

PETTING A variety of types of physical contact and activities for the purpose of sexual arousal and pleasure without engaging in penile–vaginal intercourse. It is common among adolescent girls and boys.

PLEASURING Engaging in activities during a sexual encounter that feel good; giving and receiving pleasurable feelings without the necessity of intercourse.

POLYANDRY A form of marriage in which one female is married to two or more males.

POLYGAMY A broad category applied to forms of marriage that involve multiple partners. In heterosexual marriage, polygamy involves a person of one sex being married to two or more people of the other sex (either polyandry or polygyny).

POLYGYNY A form of marriage in which one male is married to two or more females.

POOL OF ELIGIBLES People who are potential mates by virtue of birth and societal definition as appropriate or acceptable partners.

POSTNATAL DEPRESSION A condition experienced after the birth of a child and characterized by mood shifts, irritability, and fatigue.

PREGNANCY DISCRIMINATION ACT OF 1978 Requires that pregnant employees be treated the same as employees with any temporary disability.

PRENUPTIAL AGREEMENT An agreement developed and worked out in consultation with an attorney and filed as a legal document prior to marriage.

PRINCIPLE OF LEGITIMACY The notion that all children ought to have a socially and legally recognized father.

PRONATALIST ATTITUDE A cultural attitude that encourages childbearing.

PROPINQUITY Proximity, or closeness in time, place, and space; an important factor in mate selection.

PSYCHIC DIVORCE A redefinition of self away from the mutuality of couplehood and back to a sense of singularity and autonomy.

PSYCHIC REMARRIAGE A process in which a remarried individual moves from the recently acquired identity of a single person to a couple identity.

PSYCHOANALYTIC/IDENTIFICATION THEORY A theory developed by Sigmund Freud that asserts that children learn gender-appropriate behaviors by unconsciously identifying with their same-sex parent and that they pass through a series of stages in their psychosexual development.

PUSH/PULL FACTORS Negative and positive factors in a current situation that influence our decision making.

QUALITATIVE METHOD Research method used to study conditions or processes that are difficult to measure numerically; relies heavily on subjective interpretation.

QUANTITATIVE METHOD Research method used to study variables or processes that can be measured numerically.

QUESTIONNAIRE A research method of collecting data in which research subjects read and respond to a set of printed questions.

RACISM An ideology of domination and a set of social, economic, and political practices by which one or more groups define themselves as superior and other groups as inferior and then systematically deny these groups full access to and participation in mainstream society.

RAPE Sexual intercourse forced by one person upon another against the person's will; usually perpetrated by a male against a female.

RAPE SYNDROME Men's proclivity to rape—the group of factors that collectively characterize men's likelihood to rape.

REFRACTORY PERIOD A stage in the sexual response cycle occurring after orgasm. During this period a male experiences a state of rest or relaxation, during which he cannot become sexually aroused.

REFUGEE A person who leaves his country because of a fear of persecution for reason of race, religion, nationality, social group, or political opinion.

RELIABILITY The degree to which scientific research measures or instruments yield the same results when repeated by the same researcher or other researchers, or when applied to the same individuals over time or different individuals at one time; consistency in measurement.

REMARRIED FAMILY A two-parent, two-generation unit that comes into being on the legal remarriage of a widowed or divorced person who is regularly involved with biological or adopted children from a prior union. The children may or may not live with the remarried couple, but in either case, they have ongoing and significant psychological, social, and legal ties with them.

ROLE A set of socially prescribed behaviors associated with a particular status or position in society.

ROLE CONFLICT A situation in which a person occupies two different roles that involve contradictory expectations of what should be done at a given time.

ROLE OVERLOAD A situation in which a person's various roles carry more responsibilities than that person can reasonably manage.

ROMANTIC LOVE A deeply tender or highly intense set of feelings, emotions, and thoughts coupled with sexual passion and erotic expression directed by one person toward another.

SACRAMENT A sacred union or rite.

SAFE SEX Protection from AIDS and other sexually transmitted diseases through abstinence or use of protective methods such as condoms.

SANDWICH GENERATION The middle-aged adults who find themselves pressured by responsibilities for both their children and their elderly parents.

SCIENTIFIC METHOD A set of procedures intended to ensure accuracy and honesty throughout the research process.

SCIENTIFIC RESEARCH Research that provides empirical evidence as a basis for knowledge or theories.

SELF-ESTEEM The overall feelings, positive and negative, that a person has about her- or himself.

SEPARATION The termination of marital cohabitation; the couple remains legally married, and neither party is free to remarry.

SERIAL MONOGAMY A system in which an individual marries several times but only after each prior marriage is ended by death or divorce.

SEX The physiological characteristics that differentiate females from males. These include external genitalia (vulva and penis), gonads (ovaries and testes), sex chromosomes, and hormones.

SEXISM An ideology or set of beliefs about the inferiority of women and the superiority of men that is used to justify prejudice and discrimination against women.

SEX RATIO The number of men to every 100 women in a society or group.

SEXUAL ASSAULT Violence in the form of forced sexual acts that include vaginal, oral, or anal penetration; bondage; beating; mutilation; beastiality; and group or gang rape.

SEXUAL DOUBLE STANDARD Differing sets of norms based on gender.

SEXUAL DYSFUNCTION A psychological or physical condition in which a person is unable to engage in or enjoy sexual activities.

SEXUAL HARASSMENT Unwanted leers, comments, suggestions, or physical contact of a sexual nature, as well as unwelcome requests for sexual favors.

SEXUAL ORIENTATION The ways in which people understand and identify themselves sexually.

SEXUAL SCRIPT Societal or cultural guidelines for defining and engaging in sexual behaviors.

SEXUALLY TRANSMITTED DISEASES (STDs) Contagious diseases transmitted or acquired primarily through sexual contact or that can be, but are not always, spread through sexual contact.

SIGNIFICANT OTHERS People who play an important role in a person's life, such as parents, friends, relatives, and religious figures.

SOCIAL CONSTRUCTIONISM A perspective that focuses on the processes by which human beings give meaning to their own behavior and the behavior of others.

SOCIAL CONSTRUCTION OF REALITY The process by which individuals shape or determine reality as they interact with other human beings.

SOCIAL-EXCHANGE THEORY A theoretical perspective that adopts an economic model of human behavior based on cost, benefit, and the expectation of reciprocity and that focuses on how people bargain and exchange one thing for another in social relationships.

SOCIAL GERONTOLOGY The study of the impact of sociocultural conditions on the process and consequences of aging.

SOCIALIZATION The lifelong process of social interaction through which people learn knowledge, skills, patterns of thinking and behaving, and other elements of a culture that are essential for effective participation in social life.

SOCIAL-LEARNING THEORY A theory that asserts that gender roles and gender identity are learned directly through a system of positive reinforcement (rewards) and negative reinforcement (punishments).

SOCIAL MARRIAGE A relationship between people who cohabit and engage in behavior that is essentially the same as that within legal marriages except that the couple has not engaged in a marriage ceremony that is validated or defined as legally binding by the state.

SOCIAL STRUCTURE Recurrent, stable, and patterned ways that people relate to one another in a society or group.

SOCIOLOGICAL IMAGINATION A way of looking at the world whereby one sees the relations between history and biography within society.

SOLE CUSTODY A situation in which one divorced parent is given legal responsibility for raising children.

SONOGRAM A visual image made of a fetus and generated and printed out on a screen during ultrasound.

SPLIT CUSTODY A situation whereby siblings are split up between their two biological parents following a divorce. A typical pattern is for mothers to have custody of daughters and fathers to have custody of sons.

STATIONS OF DIVORCE The multiple types of divorces that couples experience in dissolving their marital relationship: emotional, legal, economic, coparental, community, and psychic.

STATUS A social position that a person occupies within a group or society.

STRUCTURAL FUNCTIONALISM A theoretical perspective that views society as an organized system, analogous to the human system, that is made up of a variety of interrelated parts or structures that work together to generate social stability and maintain society.

SURROGACY The process whereby a woman agrees to be artificially inseminated with a man's sperm, carry the fetus to term, and relinquish all rights to the child after it is born.

SURVEY A research method in which researchers collect data by asking people questions, for example, using questionnaires or face-to-face interviews.

SYMBOLIC INTERACTIONISM A theoretical perspective that focuses on micro patterns (small-scale) of face-to-face interactions among people in specific settings, such as in marriages and families.

SYMBOLIC RACISM The denial of the presence of racial inequality in society and the opposition to any social policy that would enable disadvantaged groups, such as those of color, to escape their disadvantaged position in society.

SYMBOLS Objects, words, sounds, or events that are given particular meaning and are recognized by members of a culture.

TERRORISM The employment or threat of violence, fear, or intimidation by individuals or groups as a political or revolutionary strategy to achieve political goals.

THEORY A set of interrelated statements or propositions constructed to explain some phenomenon.

THEORY MODEL A minitheory; a set of propositions that are intended to account for a limited set of facts.

TOTAL FERTILITY RATE The average number of children women have over their lifetime if current birth rates were to remain constant.

TRANSSEXUALS Persons who believe that they were born with the body of the wrong sex.

TRUST Feelings of confidence and belief in another person; reliance upon another person to provide for or meet one's needs.

ULTRASOUND A prenatal test that allows a physician to observe the developing fetus directly by viewing electronically the echoes of sound waves pulsating through the pregnant woman's body.

UNDEREMPLOYMENT A concept that refers to several patterns of employment: part-time workers who want to work full-time, full-time workers who make very low wages, and workers with skills higher than those required by their current job.

VALIDITY The degree to which scientific research or instruments measure exactly what they are supposed to measure.

VARIABLE A factor or concept whose value changes from one case or observation to another.

VICTIM BLAMING Justifying the unequal or negative treatment of individuals or groups by finding defects in the victims rather than examining the social and economic factors or conditions that create and contribute to their condition.

WET DREAMS Erotic dreams that lead to orgasm during sleep.

WHEEL THEORY OF LOVE A perspective of love developed by social scientist Ira Reiss in which love is viewed in terms of a four-stage, circular progression from rapport through self-revelation, mutual dependence, and personality need-fulfillment as a couple interacts over time.

WOMAN BATTERING A range of behaviors that includes hitting, kicking, choking, and the use or threatened use of weapons, such as guns and knives.

WORKING POOR Underemployed individuals who work full time but make very low wages.

XENOPHOBIA A fear or hatred of strangers or foreigners or of anything foreign or different.

ZYGOTE A single-celled fertilized ovum (egg) that contains the complete genetic code for a human being.

References

Abbott, J., R. Johnson, J. Koziol-McLain, and S. Lowenstein. 1995. "Domestic Violence against Women: Incidence and Prevalence in an Emergency Department Population." *JAMA, The Journal of the American Medical Association* 273:1763–68.

ABC News. 1991. "True Colors." *Prime Time Live* (September 26).

———. 1999. "Accusations of Rape: Women Say They Were Attacked by Serb Forces" (April 13). http://abcnews.go.com/sections/world/DailyNews/Kosovo990413-refugees.html (June 10).

———. 2000. "Pre-Nup Woes: Douglas, Zeta-Jones Deny Pre-Nup Spat." http://more.abcnews.go.com/sections/entertainment/DailyNews/zetadouglas000627.html (2001, November 10).

abelard. 2001. "Children and Television Violence." http://www.abelard.org/tv/tv.htm (2002, January 8).

Abelson, R. 2001. "Men, Increasingly, Are the Ones Claiming Sex Harassment by Men." *New York Times* (June 10):1, 29.

Abilities 2000. 2002. "Myths and Facts about People with Disabilities." http://www.abilities2000.com/myths.html (2002, January 30).

Abma, J., A. Chandra, W. Mosher, L. Peterson, and L. Piccino. 1997. *Fertility, Family Planning, and Women's Health: New Data from the 1995 National Survey of Family Growth.* Washington, DC: National Center for Health Statistics, Vital Health Stat 23, 19.

"Abstinence Groups Sponsor 'National Week of Chasity'." 2000. *Maranatha Christian Journal.* http://www.mcjonline.com/news/00/20000214e.htm (2001, February 4).

Adams, S., J. Kuebli, P.A. Boyle, and R. Fivush. 1995. "Gender Differences in Parent-Child Conversations about Past Emotions: A Longitudinal Investigation." *Sex Roles* 33:309–23.

Adams, V. 1982. "Getting at the Heart of Jealous Love." *Psychology Today* (May):38–47.

Aday, R. H., C. Rice, and E. Evans. 1991. "Intergenerational Partners Project: A Model Linking Elementary Students with Senior Center Volunteers." *Gerontologist* 31, 2:263–66.

Ade-Ridder, L. 1990. "Sexuality and Marital Quality among Older Married Couples." In T. H. Brubaker, ed., *Family Relationships in Later Life*, 48–67. Newbury Park, CA: Sage.

———, and T. H. Brubaker. 1983. "The Quality of Long-Term Marriages." In T. H. Brubaker, ed., *Family Relationships in Later Life*, 19–30. Beverly Hills, CA: Sage.

Adler, F., G. Mueller, and W. Laufer. 1998. *Criminology*. Boston: McGraw-Hill.

Adler, J. 1996. "Building a Better Dad." *Newsweek* (June 17): 58–64.

Adler, N. L., S. S. Hendrick, and C. Hendrick. 1987. "Male Sexual Preference and Attitudes toward Love and Sexuality." *Journal of Sex Education and Therapy* 12, 2:27–30.

Administration on Aging. 2001. "A Profile of Older Americans." http://www.aoa.dhhs.gov/aoa/STATS/profile/2001/highlights.html (2001, December 28).

Administration for Children and Families. 2000. "How Many Children Were in Foster Care on March 31, 1999?" Washington, DC: U.S. Department of Health and Human Services. http://www.aacf.dhhs.gov/programs/cb/publications/afcars/rpt0100/ar0100c.htm (2002, January 15).

Aguirre, A., and J. Turner. 2001. *American Ethnicity: The Dynamics and Consequences of Discrimination.* Boston: McGraw-Hill.

Ahlburg, D. A., and C. J. DeVita. 1992. "New Realities of the American Family." *Population Bulletin* 47, 2 (August):1–44. Washington, DC: Population Reference Bureau.

Ahmad, I. L. 1993. "Redliners Better Beware: Discrimination in Housing Hits Pocketbooks." *St. Louis American* (July 1–7):1A, 7A.

Ahrons, C. 1980. "Crises in Family Transitions." *Family Relations* 29:533–40.

———. 1994. *The Good Divorce: Keeping Your Family Together When Your Marriage Comes Apart.* New York: HarperCollins.

———, and L. Wallish. 1986. "The Close Relationships between Former Spouses." In S. Duck and D. Perlman, eds., *Close Relationships: Development, Dynamics, and Deterioration*, 269–96. Beverly Hills, CA: Sage.

"AIDS around the World." 2001. http://www.unaids.org (2001, December 13).

"AIDS in Africa." 2001. *Avert.* http://www.avert.org/aafrica.htm (2001, December 14).

Alba, R. D. 1985. "Marriage across Ethnic Lines." *Marriage and Divorce Today* 10:3.

Albas, D., and C. M. Albas. 1989a. "Love and Marriage." In K. Ishwaran, ed., *Family and Marriage: Cross-Cultural Perspectives*, 125–42. Toronto: Wall and Thompson.

———. 1989b. "Sexuality and Marriage." In K. Ishwaran, ed., *Family and Marriage: Cross-Cultural Perspectives*, 145–62. Toronto: Wall and Thompson.

———. 1987. "The Pulley Alternative for the Wheel Theory of the Development of Love." *International Journal of Comparative Sociology* 28 (3–4):223–27.

Aldous, J. 1987. "New Views of the Family Life of the Elderly." *Journal of Marriage and the Family* 49:227–34.

———, E. Klaus, and D. Klein. 1985. "The Understanding Heart: Aging Parents and Their Favorite Children." *Child Development* 56:303–16.

Allan, C. A., and D. J. Cooke. 1985. "Stressful Life Events and Alcohol Misuse in Women: A Critical Review." *Journal of Studies on Alcohol* 46:147–52.

Allan, G. 1989. *Friendship: Developing a Sociological Perspective.* Boulder, CO: Westview Press.

Allen, K. 1989. *Single Women/Family Ties.* Newbury Park, CA: Sage.

Allen, K. S., and G. F. Moorman. 1997. "Leaving Home: The Emigration of Home-Office Workers." *American Demographics* 19 (October):57–61.

Allgeier, E., and Wiederman, M. 1991. "Love and Mate Selection in the 1990s." *Free Inquiry* 11, 25–27.

Alliance for a Global Community. 1996. "Flight: Global Refugee Protection." *Connections* 2, 5 (Summer).

Alpert-Gillis, L. J., and J. P. Connell. 1989. "Gender and Sex-Role Influences on Children's Self-Esteem." *Journal of Personality* 57:97–114.

Alstein, H., and R. J. Simon. 1992. *Adoption, Race, and Identity: From Infancy through Adolescence.* New York: Praeger.

Althaus, F. 1991. "Young Adults Choose Alternatives to Marriage, Remain Single Longer." *Family Planning Perspectives* 23:45–46.

Altschuler, C. L. 2000. "Help from Afar: How to Care for a Parent When You Can't Be There." *Chicago Tribune* (May 31):sec. 8, 1.

Alzheimer's Association. 2000. "General Statistics/Demographics." http://www.alz.org/research/current/stats.htm (2002, January 7).

Amato, P. R. 2000. "The Consequences of Divorce for Adults and Children." *Journal of Marriage and the Family* 62, 4:1269–87.

———, and A. Booth. 1996. "A Prospective Study of Divorce and Parent-Child Relationships." *Journal of Marriage and the Family* 58 (May):356–65.

———. 1997. *A Generation at Risk.* Cambridge, MA: Harvard University Press.

Amato, P. R., and S. J. Rezac. 1994. "Contact with Nonresident Parents, Interparental Conflict, and Children's Behavior." *Journal of Family Issues* 15 (June):191–207.

Amato, P. R., and S. J. Rogers. 1997. "A Longitudinal Study of Marital Problems and Subsequent Divorce." *Journal of Marriage and the Family* 59 (August):612–24.

Ambert, A. 1986. "Being a Stepparent: Live-in and Visiting Children." *Journal of Marriage and the Family* 48:795–804.

———. 1988. "Relationships with Former In-Laws after Divorce: A Research Note." *Journal of Marriage and the Family* 50:679–86.

———. 2001. *Families in the New Millennium.* Boston: Allyn & Bacon.

American Academy of Pediatrics. Committee on Adolescence. 1994. "Sexual Assault and the Adolescent." 94, 5 (November):761–65.

American Association for Retired Persons. 2001. "In the Middle: A Report on Multicultural Boomers Coping with Family and Aging Issues." http://research.aarp.org/il/in_the_middle_1.html (2002, January 7).

American Association of Suicidology. 2001. "U.S.A. Suicide: 1999 Official Final Data." Washington, DC. http://www.suicidology.org (2002, January 27).

American Association of University Women (AAUW). 1991. *Shortchanging Girls, Shortchanging America.* Washington, DC: Greenberg-Lake Analysis Group.

———. 1995. *How Schools Shortchange Girls.* New York: Marlowe.

American Bar Association. 1999. "The Commission on Domestic Violence: Statistics." Chicago. http://www.abanet.org/somviol/stats.html (1999, June 4).

American Psychological Association. 1996. "Violence and the Family: Report of the American Psychological Association Presidential Task Force on Violence and the Family," 11, 80.

American Psychological Association. 2001. "Understanding Child Sexual Abuse: Education, Prevention, and Recovery." Office of Public Communications, Washington, DC. PsycNET. http://www.apa.org/releases/sexabuse/homepage.html (2002, January 19).

"Americans and the Wealth Gap."1999. *Chicago Tribune* (September 27):14.

Amnesty International. 1999. "Children Devastated by War" (January 11). http://web.amnest.org/ai.nsf/Index/ASA110131999?OpenDocument& of=THEMES\CHIL... (2002, February 3).

———. 2001a. "Racism and the Administration of Justice." http://www.Amnesty.org/ai.nsf/Index/ACT400202001?OpenDocument&of=THEMES\RACIS...(2002, February 3).

———. 2001b. "World Conference against Racism Ends: Successes Must Not Be Overshadowed by Disputes." http://www.amnesty.org (2002, February 5).

———. 2001c. "Afghanistan: Accountability for Civilian Deaths" (October 26). http://web.amnesty.org/ai.nsf/Index/ASA110222001?OpenDocument&of=COUNTRIES\A... (2002, February 3).

———. 2001d. "Afghanistan: The Hidden Human Face of the War" (December 20). http://web.amnesty.org/ai.nsf/Index/ASA110502001?OpenDocument&of=COUNTRIES\A... (2002, February 3).

Amott, T. 1993. *Caught in the Crisis: Women and the U.S. Economy Today.* New York: Monthly Review Press.

———, and J. A. Matthaei. 1991. *Race, Gender, and Work: A Multicultural History of Women in the United States.* Boston: South End Press.

Anders, G. 1994. "The Search for Love Goes On." *Washington Post* (September 19):D5.

Andersen, M. 1988. *Thinking about Women: Sociological Perspectives on Sex and Gender,* 2d ed. New York: Macmillan.

———. 1993. *Thinking about Women: Sociological Perspectives on Sex and Gender,* 3d ed. New York: Macmillan.

———. 2000. *Thinking about Women: Sociological Perspectives on Sex and Gender,* 5th ed. Boston: Allyn & Bacon.

———, and P. H. Collins. 1992. *Race, Class, and Gender: An Anthology.* Belmont, CA: Wadsworth.

Anderson, S. A., C. S. Russell, and W. R. Schumm. 1983. "Perceived Marital Quality and Family Life-Cycle Categories: A Further Analysis." *Journal of Marriage and the Family* 45:127–39.

Angermeier, W. F. 1994. "Operant Learning." In V. S. Ramachandran, ed., *Encyclopedia of Human Behavior:* 23, 351–66. New York: Academic Press.

Apfel, N. H., and V. Seitz. 1991. "Four Models of Adolescent Mother-Grandmother Relationships in Black Inner-City Families." *Family Relations* 40:421–29.

Aquilino, W. S. 1991. "Predicting Parents' Experiences with Coresident Adult Children." *Journal of Family Issues* 12:323–42.

———, and K. R. Supple. 1991. "Parent-Child Relations and Parental Satisfaction with Living Arrangements When Adult Children Live at Home." *Journal of Marriage and the Family* 53:13–27.

Archbold, P. G. 1983. "The Impact of Parent-Caring on Women." *Family Relations* 32:39–45.

Arendell, T. 1986. *Mothers and Divorce: Legal, Economic, and Social Dilemmas.* Berkeley: University of California Press.

———. 1995. *Fathers and Divorce.* Thousand Oaks, CA: Sage.

Aries, P. 1981. *The Hour of Our Death.* New York: Knopf.

Arkes, H. 1991. "Principled Playfulness: Case Study 1." *National Review* 43 (June 24):26–27.

Arliss, L. 1991. *Gender Communication.* Upper Saddle River, NJ: Prentice Hall.

Arndt, B. 1985. "The Great Male Shortage." *World Press Review* 32 (July):58.

Arnold, Chandler. 1998. "Children and Stepfamilies: A Snapshot." http://www.clasp.org/pubs/familyformation/stepfamiliesfinal.BK!.htm.

AsherMeadow. 2001. "The Many Faces of MSP." *MSP Magazine.* http://www.ashermeadow.com/amm/notes2.htm (2002, January 24).

Associated Press. 1997a. "28,000 Couples at Moon's Marriage Pledge." *Chicago Tribune* (November 30):15.

———. 1997b. "UN: Women Still Hold Few Top Jobs; Pay Also Lagging." *Chicago Tribune* (December 11):8.

———. 1999. "Alabama Moves to End Biracial Marriage Ban." *Chicago Tribune* (April 18):14.

———. 2000. "Americans Vote No to Gay Marriage, Yes to Partner Rights." *Daily Reflector* (June 1):A3.

———. 2001. "U.S. Male Population Nears That of Women." *Chicago Tribune* (September 10):6.

Atchley, R. 1991. *Social Forces and Aging,* 6th ed. Belmont, CA: Wadsworth.

"At Least 100 Children a Year Leave U.S. to Be Adopted." 1997. *Baltimore Sun* (August 28):10A.

Atwater, L. 1982. *The Extramarital Connection: Sex, Intimacy, Identity.* New York: Irvington.

Axinn, W. G., and A. Thornton. 1992. "The Relationship between Cohabitation and Divorce: Selectivity or Causal Influence?" *Demography* 29:357–74.

Baars, J., and F. Thomese. 1994. "Communes of Elderly People: Between Independence and Colonization." *Journal of Aging Studies* 8 (Winter):341–56.

Baca Zinn, M. 1994. "Adaptation and Continuity in Mexican-Origin Families." In R. L. Taylor, ed., *Minority Families in the United States: A Multicultural Perspective,* 64–71. Englewood Cliffs, NJ: Prentice Hall.

Bachman, R. 1994. *Violence against Women: A National Crime Victimization Survey Report.* U.S. Department of Justice, Office of Justice Programs, Bureau of Justice Statistics (Fall).

Bachrach, C. A. 1980. "Childlessness and Social Isolation among the Elderly." *Journal of Marriage and the Family* 42:627–37.

———. 1986. "Adoption Plans, Adopted Children, and Adoptive Mothers." *Journal of Marriage and the Family* 48:243–53.

———, P. F. Adams, S. Sambrano, and K. A. London. 1990. *Adoption in the 1980s.* U.S. National Center for Health Statistics, Advance Data no. 181 (January 5).

Bachu, A., and M. O'Connell. 2001. *Fertility of American Women: June 2000.* Current Population Reports, P20–543RV. Washington, DC: U.S. Census Bureau.

Baig, E. C. 1994. "Love at First Byte." *Business Week* (May 18):128.

Bailey, R. H. 1978. *The Home Front: U.S.A.* Alexandria, VA: Time-Life Books.

Baker, M. 2000. "Adolphus Gets Married; Soon He'll Meet his Wife." *Christian Science Monitor.* (February):15, 7.

Balaguer, A., and H. Markman. 1994. "Mate Selection." In V. S. Ramachandran, ed., *Encyclopedia of Human Behavior,* vol. 3, 127–35. New York: Academic Press.

Bales, K. 1999. *Disposable People: New Slavery in the Global Economy.* Berkeley: University of California Press.

Ball, E. 1998/1999. *Slaves in the Family.* New York: Ballantine.

Banker, B. S., and S. L. Gaertner. 1998. "Achieving Stepfamily Harmony: An Intergroup-Relations Approach." *Journal of Family Psychology* 12, 3 (September):310–25.

———. 2001. *Intergroup Relations in Stepfamilies: In Search of Processes Involved in the Attainment of Stepfamily Harmony.* Paper presented at the annual meeting of the Society for the Study of Social Problems, Anaheim, CA.

Bannister, S. A. 1991. "The Criminalization of Women Fighting Back against Male Abuse: Imprisoned Battered Women as Political Prisoners." *Humanity and Society* 15, 4:400–16.

Barcus, E. F. 1983. *Images of Life on Children's Television: Sex Roles, Minorities and Families.* New York: Praeger.

Barer, B. M. 2001. "The 'Grands and Greats' of Very Old Black Grandmothers." *Journal of Aging Studies* 15, 1 (March):1–11.

Barlett, D. L., and J. B. Steele. 1992. *America: What Went Wrong?* Kansas City, MO: Andrews and McMeel.

Barling, J. 1991. "Father's Employment: A Neglected Influence on Children." In J. V. Lerner and N. L. Galambos, eds., *Employed Mothers and Their Children,* 181–209. New York: Garland.

Barnes, S. 1998. "Keeping It Together." *Chicago Tribune* (August 2):sec. 13, 1.

Barnett, O. W., C. L. Miller-Perrin, and R. D. Perrin. 1997. *Family Violence across the Lifespan.* Thousand Oaks, CA: Sage.

Barranti, C. R. 1985. "The Grandparent-Grandchild Relationship: Family Resources in an Era of Voluntary Bonds." *Family Relations* 34:343–52.

Barth, R. P., and M. Berry. 1988. *Adoption and Disruption Rates, Risks, and Responses.* Hawthorne, NY: Aldine de Gruyter.

Barth, R. P., D. Brooks, and S. Iyer. 1995. *Adoptions in California: Current Demographic Profiles and Projections through the End of the Century.* Berkeley: Child Welfare Research Center.

Bartkowski, J. 1999. "One Step Forward, One Step Back: Progressive Traditionalism and the Negotiation of Domestic Labor in Evangelical Families." *Gender Issues* 17, 4 (Fall):37–61.

Baruch, G., R. Barnett, and C. Rivers. 1983. *Lifeprints: New Patterns of Love and Work for Today's Women.* New York: McGraw-Hill.

Basow, S. 1986. *Gender Stereotypes: Traditions and Alternatives.* Monterey, CA: Brooks/Cole.

———. 1992. *Gender: Stereotypes and Roles,* 3d ed. Belmont, CA: Brooks/Cole.

Baugher, R. J., C. Burger, R. Smith, and K. Wallstron. 1989–90. "A Comparison of Terminally Ill Persons at Various Time Periods to Death." *Omega* 20:103–15.

Baumrind, D. 1968. "Authoritarian versus Authoritative Parental Control." Adolescence 3:255–72.

———. 1979. "Current Patterns of Parental Authority." *Developmental Psychology Monographs* 41:255.

———. 1991. "Effective Parenting during the Early Adolescent Transition." In P. Cowan and E. M. Hetherington, eds., *Advances in Family Research:* vol. 2, Family Transition, 111–63. Hillsdale, NJ: Erlbaum.

BBC News. 2000. "Globalisation: What on Earth Is It All About?" (September 14). http://news.bbc.co.uk/hi/english/special_report/1999/02/99/e-cyclopedia/newsid_711000/71... (2002, January 18).

Bean, F., R. Curtis, Jr., and J. Marcum. 1977. "Familism and Marital Satisfaction among Mexican Americans: The Effects of Family Size, Wife's Labor Force Participation, and Conjugal Power." *Journal of Marriage and the Family* 39 (November):759–67.

Becerra, R. M. 1998. "The Mexican-American Family." In Charles H. Mindel, R. W. Habenstein, and R. Wright, Jr. *Ethnic Families in America: Patterns and Variations,* 153–71. Upper Saddle River, NJ: Prentice Hall.

———, and D. Shaw. 1984. *The Hispanic Elderly.* Lanham, MD: University Press of America.

Beck, M. 1988. "Willing Families, Waiting Kids." *Newsweek* (September 12):64.

Becker, H. 1977 . "Whose Side Are We On?"

Bedard, J. 1992. *Breaking with Tradition: Diversity, Conflict, and Change in Contemporary American Families.* Dix Hills, NY: General Hall.

Beer, W. R., 1983. *Househusbands: Men and Housework in American Families.* South Hadley, MA: Bergen and Garvey.

———. 1989. *Strangers in the House: The World of Stepsiblings and Half-Siblings.* New Brunswick, NJ: Transaction.

Behrens, L. 1990. "Study Shows Men's Capacity for Care." *Chicago Tribune* (October 28):sec. 6, 2.

Belcastro, P. A. 1985. "Sexual Behavior Differences between Black and White Students." *Journal of Sex Research* 21:56–57.

Bell, A. P., and M. Weinberg. 1978. *Homosexualities: A Study of Diversities among Men.* New York: Simon & Schuster.

———, and S. Hammersmith. 1981. *Sexual Preference: Its Development in Men and Women.* Bloomington: Indiana University Press.

Bell, M. 2001. "Gay Adoption Ban Upheld by U.S. Judge." *Chicago Tribune* (August 31):1, 2.

Bell, R. 1971. *Marriage and Family Interaction,* 3d ed. Homewood, IL: Dorsey.

Bem, S. L. 1983. "Gender Schema Theory and Its Implications for Child Development: Raising Gender-Schematic Children in a Gender-Schematic Society." *Signs* 8:598–616.

———. 1993. *The Lenses of Gender: Transforming the Debate on Social Inequality.* New Haven, CT: Yale University Press.

Bengtson, V., and D. Dannefer. 1987. "Families, Work and Aging: Implications of Disordered Cohort Flow for the 21st Century." In R. Ward and S. Tobin, eds., *Health in Aging: Sociological Issues and Policy Directions,* 256–89. New York: Springer.

Bengtson, V., and R. Harootyan, eds. 1994. Hidden Connections: Intergenerational Linkages in American Society. New York: Springer.

Bengtson, V., C. Rosenthal, and L. Burton. 1990. "Families and Aging: Diversity and Heterogeneity." In R. H. Binstock and L. K. George, eds., *Handbook of Aging and the Social Sciences,* 3d ed., 263–87. New York: Academic Press.

———. 1996. "Paradoxes of Families and Aging." In R. H. Binstock and L. K. George, eds., *Handbook of Aging and the Social Sciences,* 3d ed., 253–82. New York: Academic Press.

Benjamin, L. 1991. *The Black Elite: Facing the Color Line in the Twilight of the Twentieth Century.* Chicago: Nelson-Hall.

Benjamin, O., and O. Sullivan. 1996. "The Importance of Difference." *Sociological Review* 44, 2:225–51.

Bennett, J. 1989. "The Data Game." *New Republic* 200 (February 13):20–22.

Benokraitis, N. V., and J. R. Feagin. 1986. *Modern Sexism.* Englewood Cliffs, NJ: Prentice Hall.

Berado, F. M. 1968. "Widowhood Status in the U.S.: Perspectives on a Neglected Aspect of the Family Life Cycle." *Family Coordinator* 17:191–203.

———. 1970. "Survivorship and Social Isolation: The Case of the Aged Widower." *Family Coordinator* 19:11–15.

Berger, R. 1982. *Gay and Gray: The Older Homosexual Man.* Chicago: University of Illinois Press.

———. 1998. *Stepfamilies: A Multi-Dimensional Perspective.* New York: Haworth Press.

Berlin, I. 1974. *Slaves without Masters: The Free Negro in the Antebellum South.* New York: Pantheon.

Bernard, J. 1972. *The Future of Marriage.* New York: World.

———. 1982. *The Future of Marriage,* 2d ed. New Haven, CT: Yale University Press.

———. 1984. "The Good-Provider Role: Its Rise and Fall." In P. Voydanoff, ed., *Work and Family: Changing Roles of Men and Women,* 43–60. Palo Alto, CA: Mayfield.

Besharov, D. J. 1987. "Suffer the Little Children: How Child Abuse Programs Hurt Poor Families." *Policy Review* 39 (Winter):52–55.

Best, J., ed. 1995. *Images of Issues: Typifying Contemporary Social Problems.* New York: Aldine de Gruyter.

Better Homes and Gardens. 1988. "What's Happening to American Families? Report from the Editors." Meredith Corporation.

Bianchi, S. 2000. "Maternal Employment and Time with Children: Dramatic Change or Surprising Continuity?" Presidential address to the Population Association of America, Los Angeles, March 24.

———, and D. Spain. 1986. *American Women in Transition.* New York. Russell Sage Foundation.

Billingsley, A. 1968. *Black Families in White America.* Englewood Cliffs, NJ: Prentice Hall.

Bingham, S. G. 1996. "Sexual Harassment on the Job, on the Campus." In J. T. Wood, ed., *Gendered Relationships,* 233–51. Belmont, CA: Wadsworth.

Binnie, J. 1997. "Invisible Europeans: Sexual Citizenship in the New Europe." *Environment and Planning* A. 29 (February):237–48.

Black, D., G. Gates, S. Sanders, and L. Taylor. 2000. "Demographics of the Gay and Lesbian Population in the United States: Evidence from Available Systematic Data Sources." *Demography* 37:139–54.

Blackwell, J. E. 1985. *The Black Community: Diversity and Unity.* New York: Harper & Row.

Blanchard, R., B. W. Steiner, and L. H. Clemmensen. 1985. "Gender, Dysphoria, Gender Reorientation, and the Management of Transsexualism." *Journal of Consulting and Clinical Psychology* 53, 3:295–304.

Blank, R. 1988. "Making Babies: The State of the Art." In J. Gipson Wells, ed., *Current Issues in Marriage and the Family,* 171–77. New York: Macmillan.

Blankenhorn, D. 1998. "The Diminishment of American Fatherhood." In S. J. Ferguson, ed., *Shifting the Center: Understanding Contemporary Families,* 337–35. Mountain View, CA: Mayfield.

Blassingame, J. 1979. *The Slave Community,* 2d ed. New York: Oxford University Press.

Blau, P. 1964. *Exchange and Power in Social Life.* New York: Wiley.

———, and O. Duncan. 1967. *The American Occupational Structure.* New York: Wiley.

Blieszner, R., and R. C. Adams. 1992. *Adult Friendships.* Newbury Park, CA: Sage.

Blieszner, R., and V. H. Bedford, eds. 1995. *Handbook of Aging and the Family.* Westport, CT: Greenwood.

Block, J. 1981. "Your Marriage Survival Kit." *Parents* (April):61+.

Blood, R. O., Jr., and D. M. Wolfe. 1960. *Husbands and Wives.* New York: Macmillan.

Bluestone, B. 1987. "Deindustrialization and Unemployment in America." In P. D. Staudohar and H. E. Brown, eds., *Deindustrialization and Plant Closure,* 6–7. Lexington, MA: D. C. Heath.

Blum, D. 1997. *Sex on the Brain.* New York: Viking.

Blumstein, P., and P. Schwartz. 1983. *American Couples: Money, Work, Sex.* New York: Morrow.

Boeringer, S. B., C. L. Shehan, and R. L. Akers. 1991. "Social Contests and Social Learning in Sexual Coercion and Aggression: Assessing the Contribution of Fraternity Membership." *Family Relations* 40:58–64.

Bohannan, P. 1970. *Divorce and After.* New York: Doubleday.

———. 1985. *All the Happy Families.* New York: McGraw-Hill.

Bojorquez, J. 1997. "Line by Line, Their Marriage Is Working." *Sacramento Bee* (February 10). http://www.sacbee.com/static/archive/news/projects/lessons/linebyline.html (2001, November 11).

Bolig, R., P. J. Stein, and P. C. McHenry. 1984. "The Self-Advertisement Approach to Dating: Male-Female Differences." *Family Relations* 33:587–92.

Booth, A., and P. R. Amato. 1994. "Parental Marital Quality, Parental Divorce, and Relations with Parents." *Journal of Marriage and the Family* 56:21–34.

Booth, A., and J. N. Edwards. 1992. "Starting Over: Why Remarriages Are More Unstable." *Journal of Family Issues* 13, 2 (June):179–94.

Booth, A., D. Johnson, L. K. White, and J. N. Edwards. 1986. "Divorce and Marital Instability over the Life Course." *Journal of Family Issues* 7:421–42.

Borden, S. 1999. "Teen Dating Violence." http://www.infolane.com/save/teen.html.

Borland, D. M. 1975. "An Alternative Model of the Wheel Theory." *Family Coordinator* 24 (July):289–92.

Bossard, J. 1932. "Residential Propinquity as a Factor in Mate Selection." *American Journal of Sociology* 38:219–24.

Boston Women's Health Book Collective. 1992. *The New Our Bodies, Ourselves,* rev. ed. New York: Simon & Schuster.

Boswell, T. D., and J. R. Curtis. 1983. *The Cuban-American Experience: Culture, Images and Perspectives.* Totowa, NJ: Rowman and Allanheld.

Botta, R. A. 1999. "Television Images and Adolescent Girls' Body Image Disturbance." *Journal of Communication* 49, 2 (Spring):22–41.

Bound, J., G. Duncan, D. Laren, and L. Oleinick. 1991. "Poverty Dynamics in Widowhood." *Journal of Gerontology* 46, 3 (May):S115–24.

Bowcott, O. 2001. "Counting Costs of Illegal Drug Trade." *The Guardian* (July 4). http://www.guardian.co.uk/drugs/Story/o,2763,516481,00.html (2002, January 23).

Bower, B. 2001. "Healthy Aging May Depend on Past Habits." *Science News* 159, 24 (June 16):373.

Bowman, P. J. 1993. "The Impact of Economic Marginality among African American Husbands and Fathers. In H. P. McAdoo, ed., *Family Ethnicity: Strength in Diversity,* 120–37, Thousand Oaks, CA: Sage.

Boyer, D., and Fineman, F. "Sexual Abuse as a Factor in Adolescent Pregnancy and Child Maltreatment." *Family Planning Perspectives* 14, 1 (January/February):4–12.

Boyle, M. 1995. "Abuse Victims Trapped in Violent Cycle." Standard-Times [online].

Bozett, F. W. 1987. *Gay and Lesbian Parents.* New York: Praeger.

———. 1990. *Homosexuality and Family Relations.* New York: Haworth Press.

Bradsher, K. 1989. "Employers Urge Men to Wed for Success." *News and Observer* (December 23):3D.

Bramlett, M. D., and W. D. Mosher. 2001. *First Marriage Dissolution, Divorce, and Remarriage: United States.* Advance Data from Vital and Health Statistics, no. 323 (May 31). Hyattsville, MD: National Center for Health Statistics, 2001.

Brandon, J. 2000. "Raising the World's Standard of Living." *Christian Science Monitor* (January 3). http://www.igc.org/globalpolicy/socecon/global/livstand.htm (2002, January 18).

Brandon, K. 1996. "Emerging Fertility Clinic Scandal Has Californians Rapt." *Chicago Tribune* (March 24):6.

———. 1999. "Teen Girls Wising up on Having Children: Peers, Parents and Contraception Bring Drop in Pregnancies." *Chicago Tribune* (May 3):1.

Braver, S. L. 1998. *Divorced Dads: Shattering the Myths.* New York: Tarcher/Putnam.

Bray, J., and J. Kelly. 1998. *Stepfamilies: Love, Marriage and Parenting in the First Decade.* New York: Broadway Books.

Brecher, E. 1984. *Love, Sex, and Aging.* Boston: Little, Brown.

Brehm, S. S. 1992. *Intimate Relationships.* New York: McGraw-Hill.

Brewer, L. 2001. "Gender Socialization and the Cultural Construction of Elder Caregivers." *Journal of Aging Studies* 15, 3 (September):217–35.

Brewer, R. 1999. "Marriage Vows Revisited." Interview, Chicago.

Brewster, K., J. Billy, and W. R. Grady. 1993. "Social Context and Adolescent Behavior: The Impact of Community on the Transition to Sexual Activity." *Social Forces* 71:713–40.

Brines, J., and K. Joyner. 1999. "The Ties That Bind: Principles of Cohesion in Cohabitation and Marriage." *American Sociological Review* 64 (June):333–55.

"Britain's New Minority." 1999. *Chicago Tribune* (January 31):sec. 13, 3.

Brod, H., ed. 1987. *The Making of Masculinities: The New Men's Studies.* Boston: Allen & Unwin.

Brodbar-Nemzer, J. Y. 1986. "Divorce and Group Commitment: The Case of Jews." *Journal of Marriage and the Family* 48:329–40.

Brody, J. E. 1999. "Earlier Work with Children Steers Them from Crime." *New York Times* (March 15):A16.

Bronstein, P. 1988. "Father-Child Interaction: Implications for Gender Role Socialization." In P. Bronstein and C. P. Cowan, eds., *Fatherhood Today: Men's Changing Role in the Family,* 107–24. New York: Wiley.

Brotman, B. 1992. "A Shaker Cares." *Chicago Tribune* (February 19):sec. 5, 1, 5.

Broverman, I., D. M. Broverman, F. E. Clarkson, P. S. Rosenkrantz, and S. R. Vogel. 1970. "Sex-Role Stereotypes and Clinical Judgments of Mental Health." *Journal of Consulting and Clinical Psychology* 34:1–7.

Brown, G., and B. Anderson. 1991. "Psychiatric Morbidity in Adult Inpatients with Childhood Histories of Sexual and Physical Abuse." *American Journal of Psychiatry* 148:55–61.

Brown, J., and S. Keller. 2000. "Can the Mass Media Be Healthy Sex Educators?" *Family Planning Perspectives.* 32, 5 (September/October): 255–56.

Brown, M. R. 2001. "African Americans in the Middle." *Black Enterprise* 32, 2 (September):26.

Brown, S., and I. D. Yalom. *Treating Alcoholism.* San Francisco: Jossey-Bass.

Browne, A. 1993. "Family Violence and Homelessness: The Relevance of Trauma Histories in the Lives of Homeless Women." *American Journal of Orthopsychiatry* 63, 3 (July):370–84.

Brownsworth, V. 1996. "Tying the Knot or the Hangman's Noose: The Case against Marriage." *Journal of Gay, Lesbian, and Bisexual Identity* 1 (January):91–98.

Brubaker, T. H. 1985. *Later Life Families.* Beverly Hills, CA: Sage.

———. 1990. *Family Relationships in Later Life,* 2d ed. Newbury Park, CA: Sage.

Bruno, B. 2001. "A New National Holiday: Stepparents Day." http://www/selfgrowth.com/articles/Bruno.html (2001, December 3).

Bryjak, G. J., and M. P. Soroka. 1994. *Sociology: Cultural Diversity in a Changing World.* Needham Heights, MA: Allyn & Bacon.

Bryson, K., and L. M. Casper. 1999. "Coresident Grandparents and Grandchildren." *Current Population Reports,* P23–198. Washington, DC: U.S. Census Bureau.

Buehler, C., A. Krishnakuman, G. Stone, C. Anthony, S. Pemerton, and J. Gerard. 1998. "Interparental Conflict Styles and Youth Problem Behaviors: A Two-Sample Replication Study." *Journal of Marriage and the Family* 60:119–32.

Buehler, C., and M. Langenbrunner. 1987. "Divorce-Related Stressors: Occurrence, Disruptiveness, and Area of Life Change." *Journal of Divorce* 11:25–50.

Bulcroft, K., and M. O'Connor-Roden. 1986. "Never Too Late." *Psychology Today* (June): 66–69.

Bulcroft, R. A., and K. A. Bulcroft. 1993. "Race Differences in Attitudinal and Motivational Factors in the Decision to Marry." *Journal of Marriage and the Family* (May):55:338–55.

Bumiller, E. 1996. "Enter Smiling, the Stylish Carolyn Bessette." *New York Times* (September 29):sec. 1, 39.

Bumpass, L. L., and H. Lu. 2000. "Trends in Cohabitation and Implications for Children's Family Contexts in the United States." *Population Studies* 54:29–41.

Bumpass, L. L., R. K. Raley, and J. A. Sweet. 1995. "The Changing Character of Stepfamilies: Implications of Cohabitation and Nonmarital Childbearing." *Demography* 32, 3 (August):425–35.

Bumpass, L. L., J. A. Sweet, and A. Cherlin. 1991. "The Role of Cohabitation in Declining Rates of Marriage." *Journal of Marriage and the Family* 53:913–27.

Bumpass, L. L., J. A. Sweet, and T. Castro-Martin. 1990. "Changing Patterns of Remarriage." *Journal of Marriage and the Family* 52:747–56.

Bunch, C. 1979. "Learning from Lesbian Separatism." In Sheila Ruth, ed., *Issues in Feminism,* 551–56. Boston: Houghton Mifflin.

Bunker, B. B., J. M. Zubek, V. J. Vanderslice, and R. W. Rice. 1992. "Quality of Life in Dual-Career Families: Commuting versus Single-Residence Couples." *Journal of Marriage and the Family* 54:399–407.

Burger, J. M., and L. Burns. 1988. "The Illusion of Unique Invulnerability and the Use of Effective Contraception." *Personality and Social Psychology Bulletin* 14:264–70.

Burgess, E. W. 1926. "The Family as a Unity of Interacting Personalities." *Family* 7:3–9.

Burman, P. 1988. *Killing Time, Losing Ground: Experiences of Unemployment.* Toronto: Wall and Thompson.

Burns, A. L., G. Mitchell, and S. Obradovich. 1989. "Of Sex Roles and Strollers: Female and Male Attention to Toddlers at the Zoo." *Sex Roles* 20:309–15.

Burns, J. F. 1998. "Though Illegal, Child Marriage Is Popular in Part of India." *New York Times* (May 11):A1.

Bussey, K., and A. Bandura. 1984. "Influence of Gender Constancy and Social Power on Sex-Linked Modeling." *Journal of Personality and Social Psychology* 47:1292–1302.

Butler, D. 1999. "Healthy Ideas: Pregnant and Prosecuted." http://healthyideas.com/poll/980825/html (1999, May 19).

Butler, R. 1975. *Why Survive? Being Old in America.* New York: Harper & Row.

Butrica, B. A., and H. M. Iams. 2000. "Divorced Women at Retirement: Projections of Economic Well-Being in the Near Future." *Social Security Bulletin* 63, 3:3–12.

Buunk, B. B., and B. van Driel. 1989. *Variant Lifestyles and Relationships.* Newbury Park, CA: Sage.

Byer, C., and L. Shainberg. 1994. *Dimensions of Human Sexuality.* Madison, WI: Brown and Benchmark.

Cahill, S., K. South, and J. Spade. 2000. *Outing Age: Public Policy Issues Affecting Gay, Lesbian, Bisexual and Transgender Elders.* Washington, DC: National Gay and Lesbian Task Force.

Calasanti, T. 1999. "Feminism and Gerontology: Not Just for Women." *Hallym International Journal of Aging* 1, 1:44–55.

Calhoun, A. W. 1917. *A Social History of the American Family: from Colonial Times to the Present,* vol. 1. Cleveland: Arthur H. Clark.

California State Parent Teacher Association. 1998. "Teen Dating Violence." *Newsletter* 60, 3 (Winter). http://www.capta.org/I...o.3winter/7dating.html (1999, March 19).

Call, V., S. Sprecher, and P. Schwartz. 1995. "The Incidence and Frequency of Marital Sex in a National Sample." *Journal of Marriage and the Family* 57:639–52.

Campbell, S. 2001. "Moving On: Parental Breakups May Not Always Be Bad for Kids." *Psychology Today* 34, 4 (July/August):16.

Campo-Flores, B., and Y. Rosenberg. 2000. "A Return to Wilding." *Newsweek* (June 26):28.

Canada, G. 1998. *Reaching Up for Manhood: Transforming the Lives of Boys in America.* Boston: Beacon Press.

Cancian, F. M. 1991. "The Feminization of Love." In M. Hutter, ed., *The Family Experience*, 367–82. New York: Macmillan.

———. 1993. "Gender Politics: Love and Power in the Private and Public Spheres." In B. J. Fox, ed., *Family Patterns, Gender Relations*, 204–12. Toronto: Oxford University Press.

Cantor, M. H., and V. Little. 1985. "Aging and Social Care." In R. H. Binstock and E. Shanas, eds., *Handbook of Aging*, 745–81. New York: Van Nostrand Reinhold.

Cardell, M., S. Finn, and J. Marecek. 1981. "Sex-Role Identity, Sex-Role Behavior, and Satisfaction in Heterosexual, Lesbian, and Gay Male Couples." *Psychology of Women Quarterly* 5:488–94.

Carlier, A. 1972. *Marriage in the United States.* New York: Arno Press.

Carlson, D. 2001. "Over Half of Americans Believe in Love at First Sight." *Gallup News Service* (February 14). http://www.gallup.com/poll/releases/pr010214d.asp (2001, September 28).

Carmichael, S., and C. V. Hamilton. 1967. *Black Power: The Politics of Liberation in America.* New York: Vintage Books/Random House.

Caron, S. L., and M. Ulin. 1997. "Closeting and the Quality of Lesbian Relationships." *Families in Society* 78 (July/August):413–19.

Carr, L. G., and L. S. Walsh. 1983. "The Planter's Wife: The Experience of White Women in 17th Century Maryland." In M. Gordon, ed., *The American Family in Social-Historical Perspective*, 263–88. New York: St. Martin's Press.

Carrere, S., and J. Gottman. 1999. "Predicting Divorce among Newlyweds from the First Three Minutes of a Marital Conflict Discussion." *Family Process* 38 (Fall):293–302.

Carrigan, T., B. Connell, and J. Lee. 1987. "Toward a New Sociology of Masculinity." In H. Brod, ed., *The Making of Masculinities*, 63–100. Boston: Allen & Unwin.

Carter, B. 1991. "Children's TV, Where Boys Are King." *New York Times* (May 1):A1, C18.

Carter, H., and P. Glick. 1976. *Marriage and Divorce: A Social and Economic Study*, 2d ed. Cambridge, MA: Harvard University Press.

"Catalyst Census Finds Few Women Corporate Officers." 2000. Catalyst (February 8). http://www.catalystwomen.org/press/releases/release020800. html (2001, October 17).

"Catalyst Fact Sheet: 2000 Catalyst Census of Women Corporate Officers and Top Earners of the Fortune 500." 2000. *Catalyst.* http://www.catalystwomen.org/press/factsheets/factscote00.html (2001, October 17).

Cattell, M. 1996. "Gender, Aging, and Health: A Comparative Approach." In E. Sargent and C. Bretell, eds., *Gender and Health: An International Perspective*, 87–111. Upper Saddle River, NJ: Prentice Hall.

Caulfield, M. D. 1985. "Sexuality in Human Evolution: What Is Natural in Sex?" *Feminist Studies* 11 (Summer):343–64.

Cavanaugh, J. 1993. *Adult Development and Aging*, 2d ed. Pacific Grove, CA: Brooks/Cole.

CDC. 2000a. "HIV/AIDS among U.S. Women: Minority and Young Women at Continuing Risk." Centers for Disease Control and Prevention. (September).

———. 2000b. "HIV/AIDS among Hispanics in the United States." Centers for Disease Control and Prevention (September).

Center on Budget and Policies Priorities. 2001. "Poverty Trends for Families Headed by Working Single Mothers, 1993 to 1999." http://www.cbpp.org/8-16-01.wel.htm (2001, October 24).

Center for Defense Information. 2001a. "On Terror and Terrorism." Terrorism Project (December 3). http://www.cdi.org/terrorism/onterror-pr/cfm (2002, January 18).

———. 2001b. "The International Islamic Terrorist Network." Terrorism Project (September 14). http://www.cdi.org/terrorism/terrorist-network-pr.cfm (2002, January 18).

Center for Defense and International Security Studies. 1999. "Terrorism." http://www.cdiss.org/terror.htm (2002, February 16).

Centers for Disease Control and Prevention. 1994. "1992 National Health Interview Survey [NHIS]," *Morbidity and Mortality Weekly Report* 43, 13 (April 8):231–33.

———. 1997. "Rates of Homicide, Suicide, and Firearm-Related Death among Children—26 Industrialized Countries." *Morbidity and Mortality Weekly Report* 46(05):101–5 (February 7).

———. 1998. "Joint HHS and DOJ Survey Shows Extent of Violence against Women." CDC, National Center for Injury Prevention and Control. http://waisgate.hhs.go...+O&WAISaction+retrieve (1999, June 2).

———. 1999. *Assisted Reproductive Technology Success Rates: National Summary and Fertility Clinic Reports.* Atlanta: Division of Reproductive Health. http://www.cdc.gov/nccdphp/drh/art.htm.

———. 2000. *HIV/AIDS Surveillance Report, Year-End Edition*, vol. 12, no. 2.

"Census Shows Trend to Bachelor Villages." 2001. *Chicago Tribune* (May 30):6.

Chafetz, J. S. 1988. *Feminist Sociology: An Overview of Contemporary Theories.* Itasca, IL: Peacock.

Chamberlain, P., S. Moreland, and K. Reid. 1992. "Enhanced Services and Stipends for Foster Parents: Effects on Retention Rates and Outcomes for Children." *Child Welfare* 71, 5 (September/October):387–402.

Chambers-Schiller, L. V. 1984. *Liberty, a Better Husband: Single Women in America, the Generations of 1780–1840.* New Haven, CT: Yale University Press.

Chan, F. 1988. "To Be Old and Asian: An Unsettling Life in America." *Aging* 358:14–15.

Chandy, J., R. Blum, and M. Resnick. 1996. "History of Sexual Abuse and Parental Alcohol Misuse: Risk, Outcomes and Protective Factors in Adolescents." *Child and Adolescent Social Work Journal* 13:411–34.

Chappell, N. 1991. "Living Arrangements and Sources of Caring." *Journal of Gerontology* 46, 1 (January):51–58.

Chase-Lansdale, P. L., and E. M. Hetherington. 1990. "The Impact of Divorce on Life-Span Development: Short and Long Term Effects." In P. B. Bates, D. L. Featherman, and R. M. Lerner, eds., *Life-Span Development and Behavior*, vol. 10, 105–50. Hillsdale, NJ: Erlbaum.

Chassler, S. 1997. "Teenage Girls Talk about Pregnancy." *Parade* magazine (February 2).

Chasteen, A. L. 1994. "The World around Me: The Environment and Single Women." *Sex Roles* 31, 5/6:309–28.

Cheal, D. 1989. "The Meanings of Family Life: Theoretical Approaches and Theory Models." In K. Ishwaran, ed., *Family and Marriage: Cross-Cultural Perspectives*, 33–42. Toronto: Wall and Thompson.

Cherlin, A. 1978. "Remarriage as an Incomplete Institution." *American Journal of Sociology* 84, 3:634–50.

———. 1981. *Marriage, Divorce, Remarriage.* Cambridge, MA: Harvard University Press.

———. 1992. *Marriage, Divorce, Remarriage*, rev. ed. Cambridge, MA: Harvard University Press.

———, and F. F. Furstenberg, Jr. 1983. "The American Family in the Year 2000." *Futurist* (June):7–14.

———. 1986a. "Styles and Strategies of Grandparenting." In Vern L. Bengston and Joan Robertson, eds., *Grandparenthood*, 97–116. Beverly Hills, CA: Sage.

———. 1986b. *The New American Grandparent: A Place in the Family, a Life Apart.* New York: Basic Books.

———. 1988. "The Changing European Family." *Journal of Family Issues* 9:291–97.

———. 2000a. "Toward a New Home Socioeconomics of Union Formation." In L. J. Waite, C. Bachrach, M. Hindin, E. Thomson, and A. Thornton, eds., *Ties That Bind: Perspectives on Marriage and Cohabitation,* 126–44. Hawthorne, NY: Aldine de Gruyter.

———. 2000b. "The Unexpected Legacy of Divorce" (book review). *The Nation* 271, 19 (December 11):62–68.

Cherry, K. 1987. *Womansword: What Japanese Words Say about Women.* Tokyo/New York: Kodansha International.

Cherry, R. 2001. *Who Gets the Good Jobs? Combating Race and Gender Disparities.* New Brunswick, NJ: Rutgers University Press.

Chicago Tribune. 1991. "Chinese Find Perfect Solution for Those Who Put Off Marriage." (May 14):sec. 1, 8.

Childabuse.com. 2000. "The Relationship between Domestic Violence and Child Abuse." Study Number: 20. http://www.childabuse.com/fs20.htm (2002, January 6).

"Child Marriages and the Impact on Girls." 2001. http://3rdworld.about.com/library/weekly/aa031501.htm?PM=59_0103_T (2001, July 13).

Children's Defense Fund. 1997. *The State of America's Children Yearbook: 1997.* Washington, DC.

———. 2001a. "Overall Child Poverty Rate Dropped in 2000 but Poverty Rose for Children in Full-Time Working Families." http://www.childrensdefense.org/release010925.htm (2001, October 24).

———. 2001b. "Moments in America for Children." http://www.childrensdefense.org/factsfiguresmoments.htm (2002, January 5).

———. 2001c. "Protect Children Instead of Guns." (December). http://www.childrensdefense.org/gunsfacts,htm (2002, February 10).

———. 2001d. "In America…Facts on Black Youth, Violence, & Crime." http://www.childrensdefense.org/ssviolence_youthdev_factsbl.htm (2002, February 9).

Chiriboga, D. A., and M. Thurnher. 1980. "Marital Lifestyles and Adjustments to Separation." *Journal of Divorce* 3:379–90.

Chodorow, N. 1978. *The Reproduction of Mothering: Psychoanalysis and the Sociology of Gender.* Berkeley: University of California Press.

———. 1990. *Feminism and Psychoanalytic Theory.* New Haven, CT: Yale University Press.

Choo, K. 1999. "Mothers Are Paying Children's Expenses at the Expense of the Children." *Chicago Tribune* (January 10):sec. 13, 1.

Christopher, S., and S. Sprecher. 2000. "Sexuality in Marriage, Dating, and Other Relationships: A Decade Review." *Journal of Marriage and the Family* 62, 4 (November):999–1018.

Clanton, G., and L. G. Smith, eds. 1986. *Jealousy.* Lanham, MD: University Press of America.

Clark, A. L., and P. Wallin. 1965. "Women's Sexual Responsiveness and the Duration and Quality of Their Marriage." *American Journal of Sociology* 71:187–96.

Clark, H. 1988. *The Law of Domestic Relations in the United States,* 2d ed. Minneapolis: West.

Clark, R. A. 1994. "Children's and Adolescents' Gender Preferences." *Journal of Social and Personal Relationships* 11:313–19.

Clark, S. C., and B. F. Wilson. 1994. "The Relative Stability of Remarriages: A Cohort Approach Using Vital Statistics." *Family Relations* 43, 3 (July):305–10.

Clark County Prosecuting Attorney. 1999. "Myths and Facts about Domestic Violence." http://www.clarkprosec...html/domviol/myths.htm (1999, June 1).

Clements, M. 1994. "Sex in America Today." *Chicago Tribune Parade* magazine (August 7):4–7.

Climo, J. 2000. "Eldercare as Woman's Work in Poor Countries." In N. Johnson and J. Climo, eds., *Special Issue: Aging and Elder Care in Lesser Developed Countries,* 692–713. Thousand Oaks, CA: Sage.

Clinard, M. B., and R. F. Meier. 1995. *Sociology of Deviant Behavior,* 9th ed. New York: Harcourt Brace.

Clingempeel, W. G., and E. Brand. 1985. "Quasi-Kin Relationships, Structural Complexity, and Marital Quality in Stepfamilies: A Replication, Extension, and Clinical Implications." *Family Relations* 34:401–9.

Clingempeel, W. G., and S. Segal. 1986. "Stepparent-Stepchild Relationships and the Psychological Adjustment of Children in Stepmother and Stepfather Families." *Child Development* 57:474–84.

Clothesline Project, The. 1995. "Bearing Witness to Violence against Women" (August 26). http://home.cybergrrl.com/dv/orgs/cp.html (1999, June 4).

Cloward, R., and F. F. Piven. 1993. "The Fraud of Workfare." *Nation* (May 24):693–96.

CNN. 2000. "Bob Jones University Ends Ban on Interracial Dating" (March 4, 2000). http://www/cnn.com/2000/US/03/04/bob.jones/index.html (2001, September 3).

CNN.com. 2001. "USS Cole Relaunched with Little Fanfare" (September 16). http://www.cnn.com/2001/US/09/16/gen.cole.repairs/ (2001, February 16).

CNN.com/World. 2001. "Wife Accepts Archbishop's Decision." http://www.cnn.com/2001/WORLD/europe/08/30/bishop,wife/index.html (2001, September 8).

CNNmoney. 2000. "Pragmatism and Prenups." http://money.cnn.com/2000/05/06/home_auto/sat_prenup/ (2001, November 9).

Coalition for Asian American Children and Families." 1999. http://www.cacf.org/ (2002, January 5).

Coalition to Stop the Use of Child Soldiers. 2001. "Child Soldiers: Global Report." http://www.child-soldiers.org/report2001/global_report_contents.html (2002, February 23).

CNN News. 1999. "The 'Fishing' Promises to be Good at Lake Lovemaking." http://cnn.com/WORLD/e...OlderSex.ap/index.html (January 16), (1999, March 24).

Coates, J. 1986. *Women, Men and Language.* New York: Longman.

Coats, P. P., and S. J. Overman. 1992. "Childhood Play Experiences of Women in Traditional and Nontraditional Professions." *Sex Roles* 26:261–71.

Cocco, M. 1998. "Viagra Is Sign of Double Standard." *Baltimore Sun* (May 24):41.

Cockerham, W. C. 1991. *This Aging Society.* Englewood Cliffs, NJ: Prentice Hall.

Cockrum, J., and P. White. 1985. "Influences on the Life Satisfaction of Never-Married Men and Women." *Family Relations* 34:551–56.

Coke, M. M., and J. A. Twaite. 1995. *The Black Elderly: Satisfaction and Quality of Later Life.* New York: Haworth Press.

Coker, D. R. 1984. "The Relationship among Concepts and Cognitive Maturity in Preschool Children." *Sex Roles* 10:19–31.

Colapinto, John. 2000. *As Nature Made Him: The Boy Who Was Raised as a Girl.* New York: HarperCollins.

Colasanto, D., and J. Shriver. 1989. "Middle-Aged Face Marital Crises." *Gallup Report* 284 (May):34–38.

Coleman, M., and L. H. Ganong. 1991. "Remarriage and Stepfamily Research in the 1980s." In A. Booth, ed., *Contemporary Families: Looking Forward, Looking Back,* 192–207. Minneapolis: National Council on Family Relations.

———, and M. Fine. 2000. "Reinvestigating Remarriage: Another Decade of Progress." *Journal of Marriage and the Family* 62, 4:1288–1307.

Coles, R., and G. Stokes. 1985. *Sex and the American Teenager.* New York: Harper & Row, Colophon Books.

Collins, P. H. 1989. "The Social Construction of Black Feminist Thought," *Signs: Journal of Women in Culture and Society* 14, 4:745–73.

———. 1991. "The Meaning of Motherhood in Black Culture." In R. Staples, ed., *The Black Family: Essays and Studies*, 4th ed., 169–78. Belmont, CA: Wadsworth.

Collins, R. 1986. "Courtly Politics and the Status of Women." In R. Collins, ed., *Weberian Sociological Theory*. New York: Cambridge University Press.

Collins, S. 1991. "The Transition from Lone Parent Family to Stepfamily." In M. Hardey and G. Crow, eds., *Lone Parenthood: Coping with Constraints and Making Opportunities in Single-Parent Families*, 156–74. Toronto: University of Toronto Press.

Coltrane, S. 1996. *Family Man: Fatherhood, Housework, and Gender Equality*. New York: Oxford University Press.

———. 1998. *Gender and Families*. Thousands Oaks, CA: Pine Forge Press.

———, and R. Collins. 2001. *Sociology of Marriage and the Family*. Belmont, CA: Wadsworth/Thompson Learning.

Coltrane, S., and M. Messineo. 2000. "The Perpetuation of Subtle Prejudice: Race and Gender Imagery in 1990s Television Advertising." *Sex Roles* 42, 5/6 (March):363–80.

Common Sense about Kids and Guns. 2001. Centers for Disease Control and Prevention's National Center for Health Statistics, 1994–1999. http://www.kidsandguns.org/study/fact_file.asp (2002, February 10).

Condry, J. 1989. *The Psychology of Television*. Hillsdale, NJ: Erlbaum.

Conner, K. 1992. *Aging America: Issues Facing an Aging Society*. Englewood Cliffs, NJ: Prentice Hall.

Connidis, I. A. 1994. "Sibling Support in Older Age." *Journal of Gerontology* 49, 6 (November):309–17.

Constantine, L., and J. Constantine. 1972. "The Group Marriage." In M. Gordon, ed., *The Nuclear Family in Crisis: The Search for an Alternative*, 204–22. New York: Harper & Row.

———. 1973. *Group Marriage*. New York: Collier.

"Contraceptive Use." 1998. New York: The Alan Guttmacher Institute. http://www.agi-usa.org (2001, December 17).

Cooney, T. 1994. "Young Adults' Relations with Parents: The Influence of Recent Parental Divorce." *Journal of Marriage and the Family* 56:45–56.

Cooney, T., M. K. Hutchinson, and D. M. Leather. 1995. "Surviving the Breakup: Predictors of Parent-Adult Child Relations after Parental Divorce." *Family Relations* 44:153–61.

Cooney, T., and L. A. Smith. 1996. "Young Adults' Relations with Grandparents Following Recent Parental Divorce." *Journal of Gerontology: Social Sciences* 51B, 2:591–95.

Cooney, T., and P. Uhlenberg. 1989. "Family-Building Patterns of Professional Women: A Comparison of Lawyers, Physicians, and Postsecondary Teachers." *Journal of Marriage and the Family* 51:749–58.

———. 1990. "The Role of Divorce in Men's Relations with Their Adult Children after Mid-Life." *Journal of Marriage and the Family* 52:677–88.

Coontz, S. 1988. *The Social Origins of Private Life*. New York: Verso.

———. 1992. *The Way We Never Were: American Families and the Nostalgia Trap*. New York: Basic Books.

———. 1997. *The Way We Really Are: Coming to Terms with America's Changing Families*. New York: Basic Books.

———. 2000. "Marriage: Then and Now." *Phi Kappa Phi Journal* 80:16–20.

Cornell, D. 2001. "School Violence Fear versus Facts." Charlottesville: University of Virginia, Youth Violence Project. http://cox.house.gov/scott/youth_violence_briefing_cornell_remarks.htm (2002, February 10).

Cornfield, N. 1983. "The Success of Urban Communes." *Journal of Marriage and the Family* 45, 1:115–26.

Cose, E. 1995. *A Man's World*. New York: HarperCollins.

Couric, E. 1989. "An NLJ/West Survey, Women in the Law: Awaiting Their Turn." *National Law Journal* 11 (December):S1, S12.

Court TV's Legal Café. 1997. "Frequently Asked Questions about Prenuptial Agreements." http://www.courttv.com/legalcafé/family/prenup/prenup_background.html. (2001, November 10).

"Court Upholds Right to Bar Embryo Use." 2001. *New York Times* (August 15):A21.

Coward, R. T. 1987. "Factors Associated with the Configuration of the Helping Networks of Noninstitutionalized Elders." *Gerontological Social Work* 10:113–32.

Cox, C. 1993. *The Frail Elderly: Problems, Needs, and Community Responses*. Westport, CT: Auburn House.

Cox, H. 1993. *Later Life: The Realities of Aging*, 3d ed. Englewood Cliffs, NJ: Prentice Hall.

Crane, D. R., J. N. Soderquist, and M. D. Gardner. 1995. "Gender Differences in Cognitive and Behavioral Steps toward Divorce." *American Journal of Family Therapy* 23, 2:99–105.

Crary, D. 2001. "Florida Gay-Adoption Ban to Face Federal Challenge." *Chicago Tribune* (June 4):13.

Crawford, L. 1995. "Whittling Down Your Wedding Cost." *San Francisco Examiner* (June 25) [online].

Creager, E. 1995. "So Old So Soon." *Chicago Tribune* (November 12):sec. 13, 10.

Crosbie-Burnett, M. 1984. "The Centrality of the Step Relationship: A Challenge to Family Theory and Practice." *Family Relations* 33:459–64.

———. 1994/1995. "The Interface between Stepparent Families and Schools: Research Theory, Policy and Practice." In K. Pasley and M. Ihinger-Tallman, eds., *Stepparenting: Issues in Theory, Research, and Practice*, 199–216. Westport, CT: Greenwood.

Crosbie-Burnett, M., Ada Skyles, and June Becker-Haven. 1988. "Exploring Stepfamilies from a Feminist Perspective." In Sanford M. Dornbush and Myra H. Strober, eds., *Feminism, Children, and the New Families*, 297–326. New York: Guilford Press.

Crossen, C. 1991. "Is TV Too Sexy?" *McCalls* 119 (October):100.

Crossette, B. 1999. "Testing the Limits of Tolerance as Cultures Mix." *New York Times* (March 6):A15,17.

———. 2001. "War Endangers Legions of World's Young, U.N. Report Says." *New York Times* (June 14):A10.

Cuber, J. F., and P. B. Harroff. 1966. *The Significant Americans*. New York: Random House. (Published also as "Five Types of Marriage." In A. S. Skolnick and J. H. Skolnick, eds., *Family in Transition*, 7th ed., 177–88. New York: HarperCollins, 1992.)

Cudina, M., and J. Obradovic. 2001. "A Child's Emotional Well-Being and Parental Marriage Stability in Croatia." *Journal of Comparative Family Studies* 32, 2 (Spring):247–61.

Cunningham, J. D., and J. K. Antill. 1995. "Current Trends in Nonmarital Cohabitation: In Search of the POSSLQ." In J. T. Wood and S. Duck, eds., *Under-Studied Relationships: Off the Beaten Track*, 148–72. Thousand Oaks, CA: Sage.

Cunningham-Burley, S. 1987. "The Experience of Grandfatherhood." In C. Lewis and M. O'Brien, eds., *Reassessing Fatherhood: New Observations on Fathers and the Modern Family*, 91–105. Beverly Hills, CA: Sage.

Curry, G. E. 1992. "New York State May Bar Mothers for Hire." *Chicago Tribune* (May 31):17, 22.

Curtis, C. M. 1996. "The Adoption of African American Children by Whites: A Renewed Conflict." *Families in Society: The Journal of Contemporary Human Services* (March):156–64.

Cutler, B. 1988. "Band of Gold: The Earnings of Married versus Unmarried Males." *American Demographics* 10 (November):14.

Cyranowski, J. M., E. Frank, E. Young, and M. K. Shear. 2000. "Adolescent Onset of the Gender Difference in Lifetime Rates of Major Depression." *Archives General Psychiatry* 57:21–27.

Cytrynbaum, P. 1995. "Today's Singles Are Looking for Match Made in Cyberspace." *Chicago Tribune* (October 25):sec. 1, 1,15.

Dahir, M. 1998. "Gay Marriage Looking Up." http:/www.suba.com/~outlines/dahir1298.html (1999, April 23).

Dahlberg, T. 2002. "Violence Plagues Youth Sports." http://www.davie.net/ayflmain/pages/violence.htm (2002, February 10).

Dailard, C. 2000. "Abortion in Context: United States and Worldwide." New York: The Alan Guttmacher Institute. http://www. guttmacher.org/pubs/ib_0599.html (2001, December 17).

Dainton, M. 1993. "The Myth and Misconceptions of the Stepmother Identity." *Family Relations* 42:93–98.

Dalakar, J. 2001. *Poverty in the United States: 2000.* Current Population Reports, P60–214. Washington, DC: U.S. Census Bureau.

Daly, K. J. 1999. "Crisis of Genealogy: Facing the Challenges of Infertility." In H. I. McCubbin et al., eds., *The Dynamics of Resilient Families,* 1–40. Thousand Oaks, CA: Sage.

Daly, M., 1978. *Gyn/Ecology: The Metaethics of Radical Feminism.* Boston: Beacon Press.

Daly, M., and M. Wilson. 1994. "Some Differential Attributes of Lethal Assaults on Small Children by Stepfathers vs. Genetic Fathers." *Ethology and Sociobiology* 15:207–17.

Daniels, R. 1990. *Coming to America: A History of Immigration and Ethnicity in American Life.* New York: HarperCollins.

Darling, C., D. J. Kallen, and J. E. VanDusen. 1989. "Sex in Transition: 1900–1980." In A. S. Skolnick and J. H. Skolnick, eds., *Family in Transition,* 6th ed., 236–78. New York: Scott, Foresman.

Darrett, B., and A. H. Rutman. 1979. "New Wives and Sons-in-Law: Parental Death in Seventeenth-Century Virginia Country." In T. W. Tote and D. L. Ammerman, eds., *The Chesapeake in the Seventeenth Century.* Chapel Hill: University of North Carolina Press.

D'Augelli, A. R., S. L. Hershberger, and N. W. Pilkington. 1998. "Lesbian, Gay, and Bisexual Youth and Their Families: Disclosure of Sexual Orientation and Its Consequences." *American Journal of Orthopsychiatry* 68, 3:361–71.

Davis, G., and Mulhausen, D. 2000. "Young African American Males: Continuing Victims of High Homicide Rates in Urban Communities." http://www.heritage.org/library/cda/cda00-05.html (2001, February 9).

Davis, K. E. 1985. "Near and Dear: Friendship and Love Compared." *Psychology Today* (February 24):22–28, 30.

———, and M. Todd. 1985. "Assessing Friendship: Prototypes, Paradigm Cases and Relationship Description." In S. Duck and D. Perlman, eds., *Understanding Personal Relationships: An Interdisciplinary Approach,* 17–38. London: Sage.

Davis, K. 1940. "Extreme Social Isolation of a Child." *American Journal of Sociology* 45, 4 (January):554–65.

———. 1947. "Final Note on a Case of Extreme Isolation." *American Journal of Sociology* 52, 5 (March):432–37.

Davis, R. F. 1998. "Life with Father: A Solo Dad Documents the Ties That Thrive." *Chicago Tribune* (November 29):sec. 2, 5.

———. 1996. "Adoptive Parents Not Going It Alone." *Chicago Tribune* (April 15):1.

Davis, S. 1990. "Men as Success Objects and Women as Sex Objects: A Study of Personal Advertisements." *Sex Roles* 23, 1/2:43–50.

Dawson, D. 1991. "Family Structure and Children's Health and Well-Being: Data from the 1988 National Health Survey on Child Health." *Journal of Marriage and the Family* 53:573–84.

Day, R. D., and S. J. Bahr. 1986. "Income Changes Following Divorce and Remarriage." *Journal of Divorce* 9:75–88.

Deane, C., et al. 2000. "Leaving Tradition Behind: Latinos in the Great American Melting Pot." *Public Perspective* 11 (May/June):5–7, 10.

Degler, C. 1980. *At Odds: Women and the Family in America from the Revolution to the Present.* New York: Oxford University Press.

DeLamaster, J. 1987. "Gender Differences in Sexual Scenarios." In K. Kelly, ed., *Females, Males, and Sexuality,* 127–39. Albany: State University of New York Press.

DeLisi, R., and L. Soundranayagam. 1990. "The Conceptual Structure of Sex-Role Stereotypes in College Students." *Sex Roles* 23, 11/12:593–611.

del Pinal, J., and A. Singer. 1997. "Generations of Diversity: Latinos in the United States." *Population Bulletin* 52 (October). Washington, DC: Population Reference Bureau.

DeMaris, A., and W. MacDonald. 1993. "Premarital Cohabitation and Marital Instability: A Test of the Unconventionality Hypothesis." *Journal of Marriage and the Family* 50 (August):619–48.

Demaris, O. 1991. "Political Terrorism." In J. Stimson, A. Stimson, and V. N. Parrillo, eds., *Social Problems: Contemporary Readings,* 2d ed., 123–31. Itasca, IL: Peacock.

De Mente, B. 1989. *Everything Japanese.* Lincolnwood, IL: Passport Books.

D'Emilio, J., and E. B. Freedman. 1988. *Intimate Matters: A History of Sexuality in America.* New York: Harper & Row.

DeMillo, A. 2001. "Home Violence Study Reveals Police Findings." *Washington Post* (August 25):B01.

Demo, D. H., and A. C. Acock. 1988. "The Impact of Divorce on Children." *Journal of Marriage and the Family* 50:619–48.

DeMont, J. 2000. "I Am Single." *Maclean's* 113, 9 (May 8):36–40.

Demos, J. 1970. *A Little Commonwealth: Family Life in Plymouth Colony.* New York: Oxford University Press.

———. 1974. "The American Family in Past Time." *American Scholar* 43:422–46.

De Navas-Walt, C., R. W. Cleveland, and M. I. Roemer. 2001. *Money Income in the United States: 2000.* Current Population Reports, P60–213, Washington, DC: U. S. Census Bureau.

Dermer, M., and T. A. Pyszczynski. 1978. "Effects of Erotica upon Men's Loving and Liking Responses for Women They Love." *Journal of Personality and Social Psychology* 24:1–10.

DeSpelder, L. A., and A. L. Strickland. 1988. *The Last Dance.* Mountain View, CA: Mayfield.

———. 1996. *The Last Dance: Encountering Death and Dying,* 4th ed. Mountain View, CA: Mayfield.

Dessoff, A. 2001. "Caregiving Burdens Hit Low-Income and Minority Boomers the Hardest." *AARP Bulletin* (September):6.

Deutsch, F. M. 1999. *Halving It All: How Equally Shared Parenting Works.* Cambridge, MA: Harvard University Press.

DeVault, M. L. 1990. "What Counts as Feminist Ethnography?" Paper presented at Exploring New Frontiers: Qualitative Research Conference, York University, Toronto.

DeVita, C. 1996. "The United States at Mid-Decade." *Population Bulletin* 50:4. Washington, DC: Population Reference Bureau.

De Voss, S. 2000. "Kinship Ties and Solitary Living among Unmarried Elderly Women in Chile and Mexico." *Research on Aging* 22, 3 (May):262–90. http://www.aoa.gov/may2001/factsheets/family-caregiving.html (2001, December 29).

DHHS. 2000. "Domestic Violence." U.S. Department of Health and Human Services, Administration for Children and Families. http://www.acf.dhhs.gov/programs/opa/facts/domsvio.htm (2002, January 8).

Diamond, M., and H. K. Sigmundson. 1997. "Sex Reassignment at Birth: Long-Term Review and Clinical Implication." *Archives of Pediatric and Adolescent Medicine* 151:298–304.

Diesenhouse, S. 2001. "His and Hers: A House Divided, Lovingly." *New York Times* (August 23):B1, B9.

Dieter, P. 1989. "Shooting Her with Video, Drugs, Bullets, and Promises." Paper presented at the meeting of the Association of Women in Psychology, Newport, RI.

DiGiulio, R. C. 1989. *Beyond Widowhood: From Bereavement to Emergence and Hope.* New York: Free Press.

Dinkmeyer, D., and J. Carlson. 1984. *Time for a Better Marriage.* Circle Pines, MN: American Guidance Service.

Dion, K. K., and K. L. Dion. 1998. "Individualistic and Collectivistic Perspectives on Gender and the Cultural Context of Love and Intimacy." In D. L. Anselmi and A. L. Law, eds., *Questions of Gender: Perspectives and Paradoxes*, 520–31. New York: McGraw-Hill.

Dionne, E. J. Jr. 2001. "Day Care Culture War." *Washington Post* (April 26).

Disability Rights. 1999. "Statistics Page." http://www.comsource.net/~awiggins/statistics.html (June 11).

Disabled Women's Network Ontario. 2002. "Fact Sheet." http://www.servl.thot.net/~dawn/fact.html (2002, February 2).

Do, D. 1999. *The Vietnamese Americans.* Westport, CT: Greenwood.

Dobash, R. E., and R. P. Dobash. 1979. *Violence against Wives: A Case against Patriarchy.* New York: Free Press.

Dobson, C. 1983. "Sex-Role and Marital-Role Expectations." In T. H. Brubaker, ed., *Family Relationships in Later Life*, 109–26. Beverly Hills, CA: Sage.

Doka, K., ed. 1989. *Disenfranchised Grief: Recognizing Hidden Sorrow.* Lexington, MA: Lexington Books.

Doll, L., L. Petersen, C. White, E. Johnson, J. Ward, and the Blood Donor Study Group. 1992. "Homosexual and Nonhomosexual Identified Men: A Behavioral Comparison." *Journal of Sex Research* 29:1–14.

Dorfman, R., K. Walters, P. Burke, L. Hardin, T. Karanki, and E. Silverstein. 1995. "Old, Sad, and Alone: The Myth of the Aging Homosexual." *Journal of Gerontological Social Work* 24 (1/2):29–44.

Dover, K. 1978. *Greek Homosexuality.* Cambridge, MA: Harvard University Press.

Dortch, S. 1995. "The Future of Kinship." *American Demographics* (September):4, 6.

Dow, B. J. 1996. *Prime-Time Feminism.* Philadelphia: University of Pennsylvania Press.

Doweiko, H. E. 1996. *Concepts of Chemical Dependency.* Boston: Brooks/Cole.

Downs, A. C. 1983. "Letters to Santa Claus: Elementary School-Age Children's Sex-Typed Toy Preferences in a Natural Setting." *Sex Roles* 9:159–63.

Doyle, J. A., and M. A. Paludi. 1995. *Sex and Gender: The Human Experience.* Dubuque, IA: William C. Brown.

Draughon, M. 1975. "Stepmother's Model of Identification in Relation to Mourning in the Child." *Psychological Reports* 36:183–89.

Dreger, A. D. 1998. "'Ambiguous Sex'—Or Ambivalent Medicine? Ethical Issues in the Treatment of Intersexuality." *The Hastings Center Report* 28, 3:23–36.

Drell, A. 1999. "Parents of Teenage Killer in Contempt." *Chicago Sun-Times* (May 7):24.

Dressel, P. L., and B. B. Hess. 1983. "Alternatives for the Elderly." In E. D. Macklin and R. Rubin, eds., *Contemporary Families and Alternative Lifestyles: Handbook on Research and Theory.* Beverly Hills, CA: Sage.

"Drug Abuse and Pregnancy." 1999. http://medceu.com/test...buse_and_pregnancy.html (May 19).

Duberman, L. 1973. "Stepkin Relationships." *Journal of Marriage and the Family* 35:283–92.

DuBois, W. E. B. 1967. *The Philadelphia Negro: A Social Study.* New York: Schocken. (Originally published 1899.)

Dugger, C. W. 1996. "Immigrant Cultures Raising Issues of Child Punishment." *New York Times* (February 29):A1.

———. 2001. "Abortions in India Spurred by Sex Test Skew the Ratio against Girls." *New York Times International* (April 22):10.

Duke, I. 1991. "Whites' Racial Stereotypes Persist: Most Retain Negative Beliefs about Minorities, Survey Finds." *Washington Post* (January 1): A1, A4.

Duncan, G., and S. Hoffman. 1985. "A Reconsideration of the Economic Consequences of Marital Dissolution." *Demography* 22:485–97.

Duncan, S. F. 2001. "Relationships with Extended Family Members." http://www.montana.edu/wwwhd/family/comchal.html (2001, December 3).

Dunkin, A. 2000. "Adopting? You Deserve Benefits, Too." *Business Week* (February 21):160.

Dunn, K., P. Croft, and G. Hackett. 2000. "Satisfaction in the Sex Life of a General Population Sample." *Journal of Sex and Marital Therapy* 26:141–51.

Dupree, A., and W. Primus. 2001. "Declining Share of Children Lived with Single Mothers in the Late 1990s." Washington, D C: Center on Budget and Policy Priorities. http://www.cbpp.org (2002, January 5).

Durkheim, E. 1951/1897. *Suicide, A Study in Sociology.* New York: Free Press.

"Dutch Have Lowest Teen Pregnancy." 1994. *Chicago Tribune* (February 28):1.

Dutton, D. G. 1988. *The Domestic Assault of Women.* Boston: Allyn & Bacon.

Duvall, E. M. 1977. *Marriage and Family Development*, 5th ed. Philadelphia: Lippincott.

Dworkin, A. 1987. *Intercourse.* New York: Free Press.

Dwyer, J., and R. T. Coward. 1991. "A Multivariate Comparison of the Involvement of Adult Sons versus Daughters in the Care of Impaired Parents." *Journal of Gerontology* 46, 5 (September):5259–69.

Earle, A. M. 1893. *Customs and Fashions in Old New England.* New York: Scribner's.

Eckland, B. 1968. "Theories of Mate Selection." *Eugenics Quarterly* 15:79.

Edelhart, C. 1995. "Male Rape Survivors Also Deal with Myths." *Chicago Tribune* (June 1):4.

Edelman, R. 1996. "Prenuptial Agreements—True Love or True Greed?" http://www.ricedelman.com/planning/weddingtips/prenuptial.asp (2001, November 10).

Edin, K., and L. Lein. 1997. *Making Ends Meet: How Single Mothers Survive Welfare and Low-Wage Work.* New York: Russell Sage Foundation.

Edwards, T. M. 2000. "Flying Solo." *Time* (28 August):47–53.

Edwards, J. N. 1969. "Familial Behavior as Social Exchange." *Journal of Marriage and the Family* 31:518–26.

Ehrenreich, B., and A. Fuentes. 1992. "Life on the Global Assembly Line." In H. F. Lena, W. B. Helmreich, and W. McCord, eds. *Contemporary Issues in Society*, 104–11. New York: McGraw-Hill.

Ehrenreich, B., E. Hess, and G. Jacobs. 1986. *Re-Making Love: The Feminization of Sex.* Garden City, NY: Anchor Press.

Einstein, E. 1985. *The Stepfamily: Living, Loving, and Learning.* Boston: Shambhala.

"Elderly Abandoned at Hospitals: Granny Dumping Is a Variation of Baby-on-Doorstep." 1991. *Chicago Tribune* (November 29):sec. 1, 27.

Elles, L. 1993. *Social Stratification and Socioeconomic Inequality.* Westport, CT: Praeger.

Elmer-Dewitt, P. 1994. "Now for the Truth about Americans and SEX." *Time* (October 17):62–70.

Emery, R. E. 1994. *Renegotiating Family Relationships: Divorce, Child Custody, and Mediation.* New York: Guilford Press.

———. 1995. "Divorce Mediation: Negotiating Agreements and Renegotiating Relationships." *Family Relations* 44:377–83.

Enge, M. 2000. "Ad Seeks Donor Eggs for $100,000, Possible New High." *Chicago Tribune* (February 10):3.

Engley, H. L. 1999. "A Nuclear Family Reaction." *Chicago Sun-Times* (March 21):35A.

"Equal Pay for Working Families: National and State Data." 1999. AFL-CIO. http://www/aflcio.org/women/exec99.htm (2001, October 20).

Erickson, R. J. 1993. "Reconceptualizing Family Work: The Effect of Emotion Work on Perceptions of Marital Quality." *Journal of Marriage and the Family* 55 (November):888–900.

Erikson, E. 1968. *Identity: Youth and Crisis.* New York: W. W. Norton.

Eschbach, K. 1995."Enduring and Vanishing American Indian: American Indian Population Growth and Intermarriage in 1990." *Ethnic and Racial Studies*, 18 (1):89–108.

Eshleman, J. R. 1991. *The Family: An Introduction.* Boston: Allyn & Bacon.

Estes, C. L., J. H. Swan, and Associates. 1993. *The Long-Term Care Crisis: Elderly Trapped in the No-Care Zone.* Newbury Park, CA: Sage.

Estioko-Griffin, A. 1986. "Daughters of the Forest." *Natural History* 95 (May):5.

Etaugh, C., and J. Malstrom. 1981. "The Effect of Marital Status on Person Perception." *Journal of Marriage and the Family* 43:801–5.

Etzioni, A. 1997. "HIV Testing for Infants and Pregnant Women: A Case Study in Privacy and Public Health." *The Communication Network.* http://www.gwu.edu/~ccps/hivtest.html (2001, December 21).

Evans, L. 2000. "No Sissy Boys Here: A Content Analysis of the Representation of Masculinity in Elementary School Reading Textbooks." *Sex Roles* 42, 3/4:255–70.

"Fact Sheet: In Vitro Fertilization (IVF)." 2000–2001. American Society for Reproductive Medicine. http://www.asrm.com/Patients/ Fact Sheets/invitro.html (2001, December 17).

"Facts about Media Violence and Effects on the American Family." 1997. Baby Bag Online. http://www.babybag.com/articles/amaviol.htm. (2002, January 8).

Faderman, L. 1989. "A History of Romantic Friendship and Lesbian Love." In B. Risman and P. Schwartz, eds., *Gender and Intimate Relationships,* 26–31. Belmont, CA: Wadsworth.

Fain, T. C., and D. L. Anderson. 1987. "Sexual Harassment: Organizational Context and Diffuse Status." *Sex Roles* 5/6:291–311.

Faison, S. 1995. "In China, Rapid Social Changes Bring a Surge in the Divorce Rate." *New York Times* (August 22):A1.

Falk, C. 1984. *Love, Anarchy, and Emma Goldman.* New York: Holt, Rinehart & Winston.

"Family Caregiving-Fact Sheet." 2001. Administration on Aging. http://www.aoa.dhhs.gov/may2001/factsheets/family%2Dcaregiving.html (2001, December 29).

Family First. 1999. "Marriage Survey Summary." http://flfamily.org/marrig.html (1999, April 17).

Family Violence Prevention Fund. 1999. "General Statistics." http://www.fvpf.org/the_facts/stats.html (1999, June 2).

Farley, J. E. 1995. *Majority-Minority Relations,* 3d ed. Englewood Cliffs, NJ: Prentice Hall.

Fausto-Sterling, A. 1985. *Myths of Gender.* New York: Basic Books.

———. 2000. "The Five Sexes, Revisited." *Sciences* 40, 4 (July/August). http://ehostvgw19.epnet.com/get_xml.asp?booleanTerm=The+Five+Sexes&fuzzyTerm=&l…(2001, July, 25).

Faux, M. 1984. *Childless by Choice: Choosing Childlessness in the 80s.* Garden City, NY: Anchor Press/Doubleday.

FBI Uniform Crime Report, 1999. http://www.fbi.gov/ucr/99hate.pdf (2001, September 20).

Feagin, J. R. 1991. "The Continuing Significance of Race: Antiblack Discrimination in Public Places." *American Sociological Review* 56:101–16.

———, and C. B. Feagin. 1996. *Racial and Ethnic Relations,* 5th ed. Upper Saddle River, NJ: Prentice Hall.

Federal Bureau of Investigation (FBI). 1996. *Crime in the United States, 1995.* Washington, DC: U.S. Government Printing Office.

Feldman, M. 2001. "Parenthood Betrayed: The Dilemma of Munchausen Syndrome by Proxy." http://www.shpm.com/articles/parenting/hsmun.html (2002, January 24).

Feng, D., R. Giarruso, V. L. Bengston, and N. Frye. 1999. "Intergenerational Transmission of Marital Quality and Marital Instability." *Journal of Marriage and the Family* 61 (May):451–63.

Fengler, A., and N. Goodrich. 1979. "Wives of Elderly Men: The Hidden Patients." *Gerontologist* 19 (April):175–83.

Ferber, M. A. 1982. "Women and Work: A Review Essay." *Signs* 8 (Winter):273–95.

Ferdinand, P. 2001. "Shaken but Unharmed, Mass. School Says, 'The System Worked.'" *Washington Post* (December 27):A03.

Ferguson, C. 1998. "Dating Violence as a Social Phenomenon." In N. A. Jackson and G. C. Oates, eds., *Violence in Intimate Relationships: Examining Sociological and Psychological Issues,* 83–118. Boston, MA: Butterworth-Heinemann.

Ferguson, S. 1995. "Marriage Timing of Chinese American and Japanese American Women." *Journal of Family Issues* 16:314–43.

———, ed. 2001. *Shifting the Center: Understanding Contemporary Families,* 2d ed., 129–39. Mountain View, CA: Mayfield.

Fernea, E. 1965. *Guests of the Sheik.* Garden City, NY: Doubleday.

Fernquist, R. M. 2000. "Problem Drinking in the Family and Youth Suicide." *Adolescence* 35, 139 (Fall):551–58.

Ferrante, J. 1992. *Sociology: A Global Perspective.* Belmont, CA: Wadsworth.

Fetal Alcohol Fact Sheet. 1999. http://weber.u.washing...oMoreLabels/fetal.html (1999, May 13).

Field, A. E., et al. 1999. "Exposure to the Mass Media and Weight Concerns among Girls." *Pediatrics* 103, 3 (March):36. http://www.pediatrics.org/cgi/content/full/103/3/e36 (2001, August 3, 2001).

Fields, J., and L. M. Casper. 2001. *America's Families and Living Arrangements: March 2000.* Current Population Reports, P20–537. Washington, DC: U.S. Census Bureau.

Fillenbaum, G. G., L. K. George, and E. B. Palmore. 1985. "Determinants and Consequences of Retirement among Men of Different Races and Economic Levels." *Journal of Gerontology* 40:85–94.

Fine, M., and D. Fine. 1992. "Recent Changes in Laws Affecting Stepfamilies: Suggestions for Legal Reform." *Family Relations* 41:334–40.

Fine, M. A., P.C. McKenry, B.W. Donnelly, and P. Voydanoff. 1992. "Perceived Adjustment of Parents and Children: Variations by Family Structure, Race, and Gender." *Journal of Marriage and the Family* 54:118–127.

Finkelhor, D., G. Hotaling, and A. Sedlak. 1990. "Abducted, Runaway, and Throwaway Children in America." *First Report: Numbers and Characteristics, National Incidence Studies, Executive Summary.* Washington, DC: U.S. Department of Justice, Office of Juvenile Justice and Delinquency Prevention.

Finkelhor, D., and K. Yllo. 1995. "Types of Marital Rape." In Patricia Searles and Ronald Berger, eds., *Rape and Society: Readings on the Problem of Sexual Assault,* 152–59. Boulder, CO: Westview Press.

Finkelman, P., ed. 1989. *Women and the Family in a Slave Society.* New York: Garland.

Fischer, J., and M. Heesacker. 1995. "Men's and Women's Preferences Regarding Sex-Related and Nurturing Traits in Dating Partners." *Journal of College Student Development* 36, 3:258–68.

Fisher, H. 1999. "The Origin of Romantic Love and Human Family Life." In L. H. Stone, ed., *Selected Readings in Marriage and Family,* 65–68. San Diego, CA: Greenhaven Press.

Fishman, B. 1983. "The Economic Behavior of Stepfamilies." *Family Relations* 32:359–66.

———, and B. Hamel. 1991. "From Nuclear to Stepfamily Ideology: A Stressful Change." In J. N. Edwards and D. H. Demo, eds., *Marriage and Families in Transition,* 436–52. Boston: Allyn & Bacon.

Flaherty, Sr., M. J., L. Facteau, and P. Garver. 1991. "Grandmother Functions in Multigenerational Families: An Exploratory Study of Black Adolescent Mothers and Their Infants." In R. Staples, ed., *The Black Family: Essays and Studies,* 4th ed., 192–200. Belmont, CA: Wadsworth.

Florence, B. 2000. "A Different Divorce—Collaborative Lawyering." *Utah Bar Journal* 13, 10 (December):18–19.

Flowers, B. J. 1991. "His and Her Marriage: A Multivariate Study of Gender and Marital Satisfaction." *Sex Roles* 24:209–21.

Floyd, F. J., S. N. Hanes, E. R. Doll, D. Winemiller, C. Lemsky, T. M. Burgy, M. Werle, and N. Heilman. 1992. "Assessing Retirement

Satisfaction and Perceptions of Retirement Experiences." *Psychology and Aging* 7:609–21.

Folk, K. F., J. W. Graham, and A. H. Beller. 1992. "Child Support and Remarriage: Implications for the Economic Well-Being of Children." *Journal of Family Issues* 13:142–47.

Foner, N. 1993. "When the Contract Fails: Care for the Elderly in Nonindustrial Cultures." In V. L. Bengtson and A. Achenbaum, eds., *The Changing Contract across Generations.* New York: Aldine de Gruyter.

Food and Agriculture Organization of the United Nations. 1997. "Pioneer Project on Mushroom-Growing for Disabled People in Thailand—A First for FAO" (July 4). http://www.fao.org/News/1997/970701-e.html (1997, June 11).

Fornek, S. 2001. "Elder Abuse Ranges from Scams to Murder." *Chicago Sun-Times,* News Special Edition (December 16):16.

Forum on America's Future. 2000. *Chicago Tribune* (July 23).

Fossett, M. A., and K. J. Kiecolt. 1993. "Mate Availability and Family Structure among African Americans in U.S. Metropolitan Areas." *Journal of Marriage and the Family* 55 (May):288–302.

Fountain, J. 2001. "Fear Is No Stranger in Chicago Ghetto." *New York Times* (October 21), Premium Archive. http://nytimes.qpass.com (2002, January 10).

Fox, G. L. 1980. "Love Match and Arranged Marriage in a Modernizing Nation: Mate Selection in Ankara, Turkey." *Journal of Marriage and the Family* 42, 4 (November):180–93.

———, and R. F. Kelly. 1995. "Determinants of Child Custody Arrangements at Divorce." *Journal of Marriage and the Family* 57 (August):693–708.

Fox, V. C., and M. H. Quitt. 1980. "Stage VI: Spouse Loss." In V. C. Fox and M. H. Quitt, eds., *Loving, Parenting and Dying: The Family Cycle in England and America, Past and Present,* 49–61. New York: Psychohistory Press.

Frank, R. 1998. "Dads Find Contentment Tending to Home Alone." *Chicago Tribune* (March 15):sec. 13, 9.

Franklin, C. W. 1988. *Men and Society.* Chicago: Nelson-Hall.

———. 1992. "Friendship among Black Men." In P. Nardi, ed., *Men's Friendships,* 201–14. Newbury Park, CA: Sage.

Franklin, M. 1999. "Till a Long-Distance Job Do Us Part." *Kiplinger's* 56, 1 (January):56.

Frazer, J. 1995. "Community Justice Course." http://www.tafe.lib.rmit.edu.au/judy/overview.html (1995, December 12).

Frazier, E. F. 1939. *The Negro Family in the United States.* Chicago: University of Chicago Press.

Freeman, R., and P. Klaus. 1984. "Blessed or Not: The New Spinster in England and the United States in the Late Nineteenth and Early Twentieth Centuries." *Journal of Family History* 9:394–414.

Freiberg, P. 1991. "Parental-Notification Laws Termed Harmful." *APA Monitor* (March):28.

French, H. W. 1998. "In Africa's Back-Street Clinics, Illicit Abortions Take Heavy Toll." *New York Times* (June 3):A1.

———. 2001a. "Royal Path: Late Births Lose Stigma in Japan." *New York Times* (December 9):A25.

———. 2001b. "Fighting Sex Harassment, and Stigma, in Japan." *New York Times* (July 15):1, 10.

Frieden, T. 2001. "Four Charged with Enslaving Russian Women" (February 22). http://www5.cnn.com/2001/LAW/02/22/slavery.indictment/ (2001, September 26).

Friedland, G. H. 1995. "Clinical Care in the AIDS Epidemic." In J. B. Williamson and E. S. Shneidman, eds., *Death: Current Perspectives,* 4th ed., 105–17. Mountain View, CA: Mayfield.

Friedman, B. 1999. "Prenuptial Agreements: Not Just for the Rich and Famous." http://www.barnsl.org/stlawyer/archive/99/Oct99/bruce_friedman.htm. (2001, November 8).

Friend, R. A. 1990. "Older Lesbian and Gay People: A Theory of Successful Aging." *Journal of Homosexuality* 20 (3/4):99–118.

Fromm, E. 1956. *The Art of Loving.* New York: Bantam.

Frye, M. 1995. "Lesbian Sex." In A. Kesselman, L. D. McNair, and N. Schniedewind. eds., *Women: Images and Reality,* 122–24. Mountain View, CA: Mayfield.

Furnham, A. 1999. "Sex-Role Stereotyping in Television Commercials: A Review and Comparison of Fourteen Studies Done on Five Continents over 25 Years." *Sex Roles* 41, 5/6 (September):413–38.

Furstenberg, F., Jr., and A. Cherlin. 1991. *Divided Families: What Happens to Children When Parents Part?* Cambridge, MA: Harvard University Press.

Furstenberg, F., Jr., S. D. Hoffman, and L. Shrestha. 1995. "The Effect of Divorce on Intergenerational Transfers: New Evidence." *Demography* 32, 3 (August):319–33.

Furstenberg, F., Jr., and G. B. Spanier. 1984. *Recycling the Family: Remarriage after Divorce.* Beverly Hills, CA: Sage.

———. 1987. *Recycling the Family: Remarriage after Divorce.* Newbury Park, CA: Sage.

Furukawa, S. 1994. "The Diverse Living Arrangements of Children: Summer 1991." U.S. Census Bureau, Current Population Reports, Series P–70, no. 38. Washington, DC: U.S. Government Printing Office.

Gagnon, J. H., and W. Simon. 1973. *Sexual Conduct: The Social Sources of Human Sexuality.* Chicago: Aldine.

———. 1987. "Sexual Scripting of Oral Genital Contacts." *Archives of Sexual Behavior* 16(1):1–25.

Gale Group. 2001. "Restaurant Adds Latest Version of 'Dating Game' to Menu." *Restaurant News,* 1.

Gallup Poll. 1996. *Gender and Society: Status and Stereotypes.* Princeton, NJ: Gallup Organization.

———. 1997. "Global Study of Family Values." http://www.gallup.com/poll/reports/family.asp (2001, November 6).

Gallup Tuesday Briefing. 2001a. Special Edition. "Attack on America: Public Opinion" (September 18). http://www.gallup.com/tuesdaybriefing.asp (2001, September 18).

———. 2001b. *Gallup Poll Vault* (December 4). http://www.gallup.com/tuesdaybriefing.asp (2001, December 4).

Ganong, L. H., and M. Coleman. 1987. "Sex, Sex Roles, and Familial Love." *Journal of Genetic Psychology* 148:45–52.

———. 1989. "Preparing for Remarriage: Anticipating the Issues, Seeking Solutions." *Family Relations* 38:28–33.

———. 1994. *Remarried Family Relationships.* Thousand Oaks, CA: Sage.

———. 1997. "How Society Views Stepfamilies." *Marriage & Family Review* 26, 1/2:85–106.

Garcia-Pena, R. P. 1995. "The Issue of Drug Traffic in Colombian–U.S. Relations: Cooperation as an Imperative." *Journal of Interamerican Studies and World Affairs* 37, 1 (Spring):101–11.

Gardner, J. 1995. "Worker Displacement: A Decade of Change." *Monthly Labor Review* (April):45–57.

Garfinkel, I., S. S. McLanahan, and P. K. Robins, eds. 1994. *Child Support and Child Well-Being.* Washington, DC: Urban Institute Press.

Garza, M. M. 1995. "Unemployed Find the Pressure's On." *Chicago Tribune* (December 19):sec. 3, 1.

Gately, S., and A. I. Schwebel. 1992. "Favorable Outcomes in Children after Parental Divorce." In E. Everett, ed., *Effects on Young Adults' Patterns of Intimacy and Expectations for Marriage,* 57–78. New York: Haworth Press.

Gaudin, J., N. Polansky, A. Kilpatrick, and P. Shilton. 1996. "Family Functioning in Neglectful Families." *Child Abuse and Neglect* 20 (April):363–77.

Gecas, V., and M. L. Schwalbe. 1983. "Beyond the Looking-Glass Self: Social Structure and Efficacy-Based Self-Esteem." *Social Psychology Quarterly* 46:77–88.

Geiss, S. K., and K. D. O'Leary. 1981. "Therapists' Ratings of Frequency and Severity of Marital Problems: Implications for Research." *Journal of Marital and Family Therapy* 7:515–20.

Gelfand, D. E., and C. M. Barresi, eds. 1987. *Ethnic Dimensions of Aging.* New York: Springer.

Gelles, R. J. 1995. *Contemporary Families: A Sociological View.* Thousand Oaks, CA: Sage.

———. 1997. *Intimate Violence in Families,* 3d ed. Thousand Oaks, CA: Sage.

———, and C. P. Cornell. 1990. *Intimate Violence in Families,* 2d ed. Newbury Park, CA: Sage.

Gelles, R. J., and E. F. Hargreaves. 1987. "Maternal Employment and Violence toward Children." In R. J. Gelles, ed., *Family Violence,* 108–25. Newbury Park, CA: Sage.

Gelles, R. J., and A. Levine. 1995. *Sociology,* 5th ed. New York: McGraw-Hill.

Gelles, R. J., and M. Straus. 1987. "Is Violence toward Children Increasing? A Comparison of 1975 and 1985 National Survey Rates." *Journal of Interpersonal Violence* 2:212–22.

———. 1988. *Intimate Violence: The Definitive Study of Cases and Consequences of Abuse in the American Family.* New York: Simon & Schuster.

"General Facts about Domestic Violence." 1999. http://www.newcountryc... n/statistics/facts.html (1999, June 4).

Genovese, E. D. 1974. *Roll, Jordan, Roll.* New York: Pantheon.

Gerstel, N. 1990. "Divorce and Stigma." In Christopher Carlson, ed., *Perspectives on the Family: History, Class, and Feminism,* 460–78. Belmont, CA: Wadsworth.

Giarrusso, R., P. Johnson, J. Goodchilds, and G. Zellman. 1979. "Adolescents' Cues and Signals: Sex and Assault." Paper presented at the annual meeting of the Western Psychological Association, San Diego, CA, April.

Gibbs, N. 1993a. "How Should We Teach Our Children about SEX?" *Time* (May 24):60–66.

———. 1993b. "Bringing Up Father." *Time* (June 28):53–56.

Gibson, J. T. 1991. "Disciplining Toddlers." *Parents* (May):190.

Gibson, R. 1986. "Blacks in an Aging Society." *Daedalus* 115:349–71.

———. 1991. "Retirement in Black America." In J. S. Jackson, ed., *Life in Black America,* 179–98. Newbury Park, CA: Sage.

———. 1996. "The Black American Retirement Experience." In J. Quadagno and D. Street, eds., *Aging for the Twenty-First Century: Readings in Social Gerontology,* 309–26. New York: St. Martin's Press.

Giddens, A. 1996. *Introduction to Sociology.* New York: W. W. Norton.

Gilbert, E. 1994. "Pregnancy Discrimination Alert." *Working Mother* (June):34–35.

Gilbert, L. A., and M. Scher. 1999. *Gender and Sex in Counseling and Psychotherapy.* Boston: Allyn & Bacon.

Giles-Sims, J. 1984. "The Stepparent Role: Expectations, Behavior, and Sanctions." *Journal of Family Issues* 5, 1:116–30.

Gilford, R. 1984. "Contrasts in Marital Satisfaction throughout Old Age: An Exchange Theory Analysis." *Journal of Gerontology* 39:325–33.

Gill, R. T., N. Glazer, and S. A. Thernstrom. 1992. *Our Changing Population.* Englewood Cliffs, NJ: Prentice Hall.

Gillespie, M. 2001. "Americans Consider Infidelity Wrong, but Acknowledge Its Prevalence in Society." *The Gallup Organization.* http://www.gallup.com/poll/releases/pr010709b.asp (2001, November 4).

Gilligan, C. 1990. "Teaching Shakespeare's Sister: Notes from the Underground of Female Adolescence." In C. Gilligan, N. P. Lyons, and T. J. Hammer, eds., *Making Connections,* 6–29. Cambridge, MA: Harvard University Press.

Gillis, J. 1999. "Myths of Family Past." In A. Skolnick and J. Skolnick, eds., *Family in Transition,* 10th ed., 21–34. New York: Longman.

Gilmore, D. 1990. *Masculinity in the Making: Cultural Concepts of Masculinity.* New Haven, CT: Yale University Press.

Giuliano, T. A., and K. E. Popp. 2000. "Footballs versus Barbies: Childhood Play Activities as Predictors of Sports Participation by Women." *Sex Roles* 42, 3 (February):159–82.

Giunta, C. T., and B. E. Compas. 1994. "Adult Daughters of Alcoholics: Are They Unique?" *Journal of Studies on Alcohol* 55:600–606.

Glaberson, W. 1999."What Did Parents Know, and Are They to Blame?" *New York Times* (April 27):A20.

Gladwell, M. 1988. "Surrogate Parenting: Legal Labor Pains." In J. G. Wells, ed., *Current Issues in Marriage and the Family,* 179–84. New York: Macmillan.

Glendon, M. A. 1987. *Abortion and Divorce in Western Law.* Cambridge, MA: Harvard University Press.

Glenn, E. N. 1983. "Split Household, Small Producer and Dual Wage Earner: An Analysis of Chinese American Family Strategies." *Journal of Marriage and the Family* 45 (February):35–46.

———. 1994. "Social Constructions of Mothering: A Thematic Overview." In E. N. Glenn, G. Chang, and L. R. Forcey, eds., *Mothering: Ideology, Experience, and Agency,* 1–29. New York: Routledge.

Glenn, N. D. 1982. "Interreligious Marriage in the United States: Patterns and Recent Trends." *Journal of Marriage and the Family* 44 (August):555–66.

———. 1990. "Quantitative Research on Marital Quality in the 1980s: A Critical Review." *Journal of Marriage and the Family* 52:818–31.

———. 1991. "Quantitative Research on Marital Quality in the 1980s." In A. Booth, ed., *Contemporary Families: Looking Forward, Looking Back,* 28–41. Minneapolis: National Council on Family Relations.

———. 1997a. *Closed Hearts, Closed Minds, A Report from the Council on Families.* New York: Institute for American Values.

———. 1997b. "A Critique of Twenty Family and Marriage Textbooks." *Family Relations* 46 (July):197–208.

———. 1999. "Values, Attitudes, and the State of American Marriage." In C. Albers, ed., *Sociology of Families Reader,* 58–67. Thousand Oaks, CA: Pine Forge Press.

———, and M. Supancic. 1984. "The Social and Demographic Correlates of Divorce and Separation in the United States: An Update and Reconsideration." *Journal of Marriage and the Family* 46:563–75.

———, and C. N. Weaver. 1988. "The Changing Relationship of Marital Status to Reported Happiness." *Journal of Marriage and the Family* 50:317–24.

Glick, P. 1980. "Remarriage: Some Recent Changes and Variations." *Journal of Family Issues* 1, 4:455–78.

———. 1984. "Marriage, Divorce, and Living Arrangements: Prospective Changes." *Journal of Family Issues* 5:7–26.

———, and S. Lin. 1986. "Recent Changes in Divorce and Remarriage." *Journal of Marriage and the Family* 48:737–47.

———, and A. Norton. 1977. "Marrying, Divorcing, and Living Together in the U.S. Today." *Population Bulletin* 32:2–39.

Glick, P., and R. Parke. 1965. "New Approaches in Studying the Life Cycle of the Family." *Demography* 2:187–202.

"Global Statistical Information." 2001. http://www.unaids.org (2001, December 13).

Godwin, D. D., and J. Scanzoni. 1989. "Couple Consensus during Marital Joint Decision-Making: A Context, Process, Outcome Model." *Journal of Marriage and the Family* 51:943–56.

Goetting, A. 1979. "Some Societal-Level Explanations for the Rising Divorce Rate." *Family Therapy* 6, 2:83–87.

———. 1982. "The Six Stations of Remarriage: Developmental Task of Remarriage after Divorce." *Family Relations* 31:213–22.

Golant, S. M., and A. J. LaGreca. 1994. "Differences in the Housing Quality of White, Black, and Hispanic U.S. Elderly Households." *Journal of Applied Gerontology* 13:413–37.

———. 1995. "The Relative Deprivation of U.S. Elderly Households as Judged by Their Housing Problems." *Journal of Gerontology*, Series B, 50B:513–23.

Goldberg, C. 2001. "Quiet Anniversary for Civil Unions." *New York Times* (July 31):A14.

———, with J. Elder. 1998. "Public Backs Abortion, but Wants Limits, Poll Says." *New York Times* (January 16):A1.

Golding, J. M. 1990. "Division of Household Labor, Strain, and Depressive Symptoms among Mexican American and Non-Hispanic Whites." *Psychology of Women Quarterly* 14:103–17.

Goldscheider, F. K., and C. Goldscheider. 1993. *Leaving Home before Marriage: Ethnicity, Familism, and Generational Relationships.* Madison: University of Wisconsin Press.

Goleman, D. 1987. "Two Views of Marriage Explored: His and Hers." In O. Pocs, ed., *Marriage and Family 87/88: Annual Editions*, 58–59. Sluice Dock, Guilford, CT: Dushkin.

———. 1990. "As Bias Crimes Seem to Rise, Scientists Study Roots of Racism." *New York Times* (March 29):C1.

———. 1995. "Eating Disorder Rates Surprise the Experts." *New York Times* (October 4):B7.

———. 1996. *Emotional Intelligence.* New York: Bantam Books.

Goode, E. 1994. "Till Death Do Them Part?" *U.S. News and World Report* (July 4):24–28.

———. 1999. "New Study Finds Middle Age Is Prime of Life." *New York Times* (February 16):D6.

———. 2001. "Findings Give Some Support to Advocates of Spanking." *New York Times* (August 25):A6.

———. 2001b. "A Rainbow of Differences in Gays' Children." *New York Times* (July 17):F1.

Goode, W. 1959. "The Theoretical Importance of Love." *American Sociological Review* 24, 1 (February):38–47.

———. 1993. *World Changes in Divorce Patterns.* New Haven, CT: Yale University Press.

Goodman, D. 2000. "A More Civil Union." *Mother Jones* (July/August):48–53, 78.

Gordon, S. M., and S. Thompson. 1995. "The Changing Epidemiology of Human Immunodeficiency Virus Infection in Older Persons." *Journal of the American Geriatrics Society* 43 (January):7–9.

Gorner, P. 1994a. "Sex Study Shatters Kinky Assumptions." *Chicago Tribune* (October 6):1, 28.

———. 1994b. "What Is Normal?" *Chicago Tribune* (October 9):1, 4.

Gottman, J. 1990. "Children of Gay and Lesbian Parents." In F. W. Bozett and M. B. Sussman, eds., *Homosexuality and Family Relations.* New York: Harrington Park Press.

———. 1994a. "What Makes Marriage Work?" *Psychology Today* (March/April):38–43, 68.

———. 1994b. *What Predicts Divorce? The Relationship between Marital Processes and Marital Outcomes.* Hillsdale, NJ: Erlbaum.

Gove, W. 1972. "The Relationship between Sex Roles, Marital Status, and Mental Illness." *Social Forces* 51:34–44.

Graber, J. L. 1999. "Words Can Hurt Divorced Parents' Best Intentions." *Chicago Tribune* (March 14):sec. 13, 1.

Graham, S. 2001. "German Gays Embrace Union Law." *Chicago Tribune* (August 2):8.

Grall, T. S. 1993. "Our Nation's Housing in 1991." In U.S. Census Bureau, Current Housing Reports, Series H121/93–2. Washington, DC: U.S. Government Printing Office.

———. 2000. *Child Support for Custodial Mothers and Fathers.* Current Population Reports, P60–212 (October). U.S. Census Bureau. Washington, DC: U.S. Government Printing Office.

Granat, D. 1997. "She's Having Our Baby." *Washingtonian* 32 (July):54–57.

Grant, L., L. Simpson, and L. R. Xue. 1990. "Gender, Parenthood, and Work Hours of Physicians." *Journal of Marriage and the Family* 52:39–49.

Gray, J. S. 1997. "The Fall in Men's Return to Marriage: Declining Productivity Effects or Changing Selection?" *Journal of Human Resources* 32 (Summer):481–504.

Grebe, S. C. 1986. "Mediation in Separation and Divorce." *Journal of Counseling and Development* 64:377–82.

Green, B., and N. Boyd-Franklin. 1996. "African American Lesbians: Issues in Couple Therapy." In J. Laird and R. Green, eds., *Lesbians and Gays in Couples and Families*, 251–71. San Francisco: Jossey-Bass.

Greenhouse, S. 2001. "Americans' International Lead In Hours Worked Grew in 90's, Report Shows." *New York Times* (September 1):A6.

Greenstein, B., K. Porter, W. Primus, and I. Shapiro. 2001. "Poverty Rates Fell in 2000 as Unemployment Reached 31-Year Low." Center on Budget and Policy Priorities. http://www/cbpp.org/9-25-01pov.htm (2001, October 24).

Greenstein, T. N. 1990. "Marital Disruption and the Employment of Married Women." *Journal of Marriage and the Family* 52:657–76.

———. 1995. "Gender Ideology, Marital Disruption and the Employment of Married Women." *Journal of Marriage and the Family* 57 (February):31–32.

Greider, L. 2001. "Hard Times Drive Adult Kids Home." *AARP Bulletin* (December):3, 14.

Greif, G. L. 1985. *Single Fathers.* Lexington, MA: Lexington Books.

———, and M. S. Pabst. 1988. *Mothers without Custody.* Lexington, MA: D. C. Heath.

Greil, A. L. 1991. *Not Yet Pregnant: Infertile Couples in Contemporary America.* New Brunswick, NJ: Rutgers University Press.

Greven, P. 1970. *Four Generations: Population, Land and Family in Colonial Andover, Mass.* Ithaca, NY: Cornell University Press.

Griffin, J. L. 1992. "Most Take Middle Ground on Abortion." *Chicago Tribune* (July 2):1.

Griffin, S. 1979. *Rape: The Power of Consciousness.* San Francisco: Harper & Row.

Grimm, T. K., and M. Perry-Jenkins. 1994. "All in a Day's Work: Job Experience, Self-Esteem, and Fathering in Working-Class Families." *Family Relations* 43, 2 (April):174–81.

Griswold del Castillo, R. 1984. *La Familia.* Notre Dame, IN: University of Notre Dame Press.

Gross, H. E. 1980. "Dual Career Couples Who Live Apart: Two Types." *Journal of Marriage and the Family* 42:567–76.

Gross, P. 1987. "Defining Post-divorce Remarriage Families: A Typology Based on the Subjective Perceptions of Children." *Journal of Divorce* 10, 1/2:205–17.

Grossman, H., and S. H. Grossman. 1994. *Gender Issues in Education.* Boston: Allyn & Bacon.

Groza, V., and K. Rosenberg. 1998. *Clinical and Practice Issues in Adoption: Bridging the Gap between Adoptees Placed as Infants and as Older Children.* Westport, CT: Praeger.

Guang, X. 1996. "A Comment on Interracial Marriage" (March 18):1 [online].

Gubrium, J. F. 1975. "Being Single in Old Age." *Aging and Human Development* 6:29–41.

———. 1976. *Time, Roles, and Self in Old Age.* New York: Human Science Press.

Guinness Book of World Records. 1990. New York: Sterling.

Guinness World Records 2001. 2001. Tim Footman, ed. New York: Bantam.

Guisinger, S., P. A. Cowan, and D. Schuldberg. 1989. "Changing Parent and Spouse Relations in the First Years of Remarriage of Divorced Fathers." *Journal of Marriage and the Family* 51:445–56.

Gura, T. 1994a. "New Factor Found in Fixing Sex." *Chicago Tribune* (August 1):4.

———. 1994b. "Generation X Is Not Generation Sex." *Chicago Tribune* (October 9):1, 6.

Gutman, H. G. 1976. *The Black Family in Slavery and Freedom: 1750–1925.* New York: Vintage Books.

Gwartney-Gibbs, P. A. 1986. "The Institutionalization of Premarital Cohabitation: Estimates from Marriage License Applications, 1970 and 1980." *Journal of Marriage and the Family* 48:423–34.

Haddocks, R. 1995. "Live-in Relationships More Prone to Violence." *Standard-Times* [online], 3.

Haffner, D. 1999. "Facing Facts: Sexual Healing for American Adolescents." *Human Development and Family Life Bulletin* 4 (Winter):1–3.

Hagestad, G. 1986. "The Family: Women and Grandparents as Kinkeepers." In A. Pifer and L. Bronte, eds., *Our Aging Society,* 141–60. New York: W. W. Norton.

Hahn, B. A. 1993. "Marital Status in Women's Health: The Effect of Economic and Marital Acquisitions." *Journal of Marriage and the Family* 55:495–504.

Halberstadt, A. G., and M. B. Saitta. 1987. "Gender, Nonverbal Behavior, and Perceived Dominance: A Test of the Theory." *Journal of Personality and Social Psychology* 53:257–72.

Hale, D. 1999. "The Joy of Midlife SEX." In S. J. Bunting, ed., *Human Sexuality 99/00,* 164–67. Sluice Dock, Guilford, CT: Dushkin/McGraw-Hill.

Hale-Benson, J. 1986. *Black Children: Their Roots, Culture, and Learning Styles,* rev. ed. Provo, UT: Brigham Young University Press.

"Half-Full or Half-Empty? Health Care, Child Care, and Youth Programs for Asian American Children in New York City." 1999. *Executive Summary* (April). New York: Coalition for Asian American Children and Families.

Hall, D. R., and J. Zhao. 1995. "Cohabitation and Divorce in Canada: Testing the Selectivity Hypothesis." *Journal of Marriage and the Family* 57 (May):421–27.

Hall, R. M., and B. R. Sandler. 1985. "A Chilly Climate in the Classroom." In A. Sargent, ed., *Beyond Sex Roles,* 503–10. New York: West.

Hamburg, D. A. 1992. *Today's Children: Creating a Future for a Generation in Crisis.* New York: Time Books.

Hanna, J. 1996. "Divorce Law: A Debate about to Happen, Again." *Chicago Tribune* (January 7):sec. 2, 1.

Hansen, K. 1992. "Our Eyes Behold Each Other: Masculinity and Intimate Friendship in Antebellum New England." In P. Nardi, ed., *Men's Friendships,* 35–58. Newbury Park, CA: Sage.

Hansen, G. L. 1985. "Perceived Threats and Marital Jealousy." *Social Psychology Quarterly* 48:262–68.

Hansen, J. E., and W. J. Schuldt. 1984. "Marital Self-Disclosure and Marital Satisfaction." *Journal of Marriage and the Family* 46:923–32.

Hanson, G., and P. Venturelli. 1995. *Drugs and Society.* Boston: Jones and Bartlett.

Hanson, S. M. 1988. "Divorced Fathers with Custody." In P. Bronstein and C. P. Cowan, eds., *Fatherhood Today: Men's Changing Role in the Family,* 166–94. New York: Wiley.

Hansson, R. O., M. F. Knopf, E. A. Downs, P. R. Monroe, S. E. Stegman, and D. S. Wadley. 1984. "Femininity, Masculinity, and Adjustment of Divorce among Women." *Psychology of Women Quarterly* 8, 3:248–49.

Hansson, R. O., and J. H. Remondet. 1987. "Relationships and Aging Family: A Social Psychological Analysis." In S. Oskamp, ed., *Family Processes and Problems: Social Psychological Aspects.* Beverly Hills, CA: Sage.

Harden, B. 2001. "Bible Belt Couples 'Put Assunder' More, Despite New Efforts." *New York Times* (May 21):A1, A14.

Haring-Hidore, M., W. A. Stock, M. A. Okum, and R. A. Witter. 1985. "Marital Status and Subjective Well-Being: A Research Synthesis." *Journal of Marriage and the Family* 47 (November):947–53.

Harmatz, M. G., and M. A. Novak. 1983. *Human Sexuality.* New York: Harper & Row.

Harris Poll. 2001. "Gun Ownership: Two in Five Americans Live in Gun-Owning Households." Harris Poll #25 (May 30).

Harrow, B. S., S. L. Tennestedt, and J. B. McKinlay. 1995. "How Costly Is It to Care for Disabled Elders in a Community Setting?" *The Gerontologist* 35, 6:803–13.

Harry, J. 1982. "Decision Making and Age Differences among Gay Couples." *Journal of Homosexuality* 2:9–21.

———. 1983. "Gay Male and Lesbian Relationships." In E. D. Macklin and R. H. Rubin, eds., *Contemporary Families and Alternative Lifestyles: Handbook on Research and Theory,* 216–54. Newbury Park, CA: Sage.

———. 1984. *Gay Couples.* New York: Praeger.

———. 1988. "Some Problems of Gay/Lesbian Families." In C. Chilman, E. W. Nunally, and F. M. Cox, eds., *Variant Family Forms,* 96–113. Newbury Park, CA: Sage.

———, and W. DeVall. 1978. *The Social Organization of Gay Males.* New York: Praeger.

Hartinger, B. 1994. "A Case for Gay Marriage: In Support of Loving and Monogamous Relationships." In Robert T. Francoeur, ed., *Taking Sides: Clashing Views on Controversial Issue in Human Sexuality,* 236–41. Guilford, CN: Dushkin.

Hartman, S. 1988. "Arranged Marriages Live On." *New York Times* (August 10): C12.

Harvard Law Review. 1993. "Notes." *Harvard Law Review* 106:1905–25.

Harvard University, Joint Center for Housing Studies. 1993. *The State of the Nation's Housing* 1993. Cambridge, MA.

Harvey, D. 1992. "The Psychologists Who Changed Our Minds." *San Francisco Chronicle,* Datebook (June 14):31–32.

Harvey, D. L. 1993. *Potter Addition: Poverty, Family, and Kinship in a Heartland Community.* New York: Aldine de Gruyter.

Harvey, E. 1999. "Short-Term and Long-Term Effects of Early Parental Employment on Children of the National Longitudinal Survey of Youth." *Developmental Psychology* 35, 21:445–59.

Hatfield, E. 1983. "What Do Women and Men Want from Love and Sex?" In E. R. Allgeier and N. B. McCormick, eds., *Changing Boundaries: Gender Roles and Sexual Behavior,* 106–34. Mountain View, CA: Mayfield.

———, and G. W. Walster. 1978. *A New Look at Love.* Reading, MA: Addison-Wesley.

Hayghe, H. V., and S. M. Bianchi. 1994. "Married Mother's Work Patterns: The Job-Family Compromise." *Monthly Labor Review* (June):24–30.

Hazan, C., and P. Shaver. 1987. "Conceptualizing Romantic Love as an Attachment Process." *Journal of Personality and Social Psychology* 52:511–24.

Heaton, T. B. 1990. "Marital Stability throughout the Childrearing Years." *Demography* 27, 1 (February):55–63.

Heaton, T. B., and E. L. Pratt. 1990. "The Effects of Religious Homogamy on Marital Satisfaction and Stability." *Journal of Family Issues* 11:191–207.

Hedges, W. 1994. "Sexual Dysfunction." http://h-devil-www.mc.... h-devil/sex/dysfun.html (1999, April 4).

Hendrick, C., and S. Hendrick. 1989. "Research on Love: Does It Measure Up?" *Journal of Personality and Social Psychology* 56:784–94.

Hendrick, S., and C. Hendrick. 1983. *Liking, Loving, and Relating.* Monterey, CA: Brooks Cole.

———. 1987. "Love and Sexual Attitudes, Self-Disclosure and Sensation Seeking." *Journal of Social and Personal Relationships* 4:281–97.

———. 1992. *Liking, Loving, and Relating.* Pacific Grove, CA: Brooks/Cole.

———. 1993. "Lovers as Friends." *Journal of Social and Personal Relationships* 10:459–66.

———. 1995. "Gender Differences and Similarities in Sex and Love." *Personal Relationships* 2:55–65.

———. 1996. "Gender and the Experience of Heterosexual Love." In Julia T. Wood, ed., *Gendered Relationships*, 131–48. Mountain View, CA: Mayfield.

———, and N. L. Adler. 1988. "Romantic Relationships: Love, Satisfaction, and Staying Together." *Journal of Personality and Social Psychology* 34, 6:980–88.

Henry, C. S., and S. G. Lovelace. 1995. "Family Resources and Adolescent Family Life Satisfaction in Remarried Family Households." *Journal of Family Issues* 16, 6 (November):765–86.

Hepp, R. 2001. "Mom Dies, Daughter Accused of Neglect." *Chicago Tribune* (December 31).

Herbert, B. 2001a. "A Black AIDS Epidemic." *New York Times* (June 4):A21.

———. 2001b. "In America: Protecting Children." *New York Times* (October 11):A23.

Herek, G. 1990. "Gay People in Government Security Clearances: A Social Science Perspective." *American Psychologist* 45, 9:1035–40.

Herman, D. F. 1989. "The Rape Culture." In J. Freeman, ed., *Women: A Feminist Perspective*, 4th ed., 20–44. Mountain View, CA: Mayfield.

Herrerias, C. 1995. "Noncustodial Mothers Following Divorce." *Marriage and Family Review* 20, 1/2:233–55.

Hertz, R. 1986. *More Equal Than Others: Women and Men in Dual-Couples.* Berkeley: University of California Press.

Hessellund, H. 1976. "Masturbation and Sexual Fantasy in Married Couples." *Archives of Sexual Behavior* 5:133–47.

Hetherington, E. M. 1989. "Coping with Family Transitions: Winners, Losers, and Survivors." *Child Development* 60:1–18.

———, ed. 1999. *Coping with Divorce, Single Parenting, and Remarriage: A Risk and Resiliency Perspective.* Mahwah, NJ: Erlbaum.

———, and W. C. Clingempeel. 1992. "Coping with Marital Transitions: A Family Systems Perspective." *Monographs of the Society for Research in Child Development* 57, 2/3, serial no. 227.

Hetherington, E. M., and S. H. Henderson. 1997. "Fathers in Stepfamilies.: In M. E. Lamb, ed., *The Role of the Father in Child Development*, 212–26. New York: Wiley.

Hetherington, E. M., and K. M. Jodl. 1994. "Stepfamilies as Settings for Child Development." In A. Booth and J. Dunn, eds., *Stepfamilies: Who Benefits? Who Does Not?* 55–79. Hillsdale, NJ: Erlbaum.

Hetherington, E. M., T. C. Law, and T. G. O'Connor. 1993. "Divorce: Challenges, Changes, and New Chances." In F. Walsh, ed., *Normal Family Processes*, 2d ed., 208–34. New York: Guilford Press.

Heymann, D. L. 2000. "The Urgency of a Massive Effort against Infectious Diseases." Statement presented to the Committee on International Relations of the U.S. House of Representatives, June 29. Washington, DC.

HHS Press Release. 1998. "Smoking among Teen Mothers Is on the Rise: Overall Smoking during Pregnancy Drops Steadily" (November 19). http://www.hhs.gov/new...s/1998pres/981119.html.

Hiedemann, B., O. Suholinova, and A. M. O'Rand. 1998. "Economic Independence, Economic Status, and Empty Nest in Midlife Marital Disruption." *Journal of Marriage and the Family* 60 (February):219–31.

Higginbotham, E., and L. Weber. 1995. "Moving Up with Kin and Community: Upward Social Mobility for Black and White Women." In M. L. Andersen and P. H. Collins, eds., *Race, Class and Gender: An Anthology*, 2d ed., 134–47. Belmont, CA: Wadsworth.

Higginbotham, R. 1991. "Friendship as an Ethical Paradigm for Same-Sex Couples." Unpublished paper, Seabury-Western Theological Seminary, Evanston, IL.

Higgins, C., L. Duxbury, and C. Lee. 1994. "Impact of Life-Cycle Stage and Gender on the Ability to Balance Work and Family Responsibilities." *Family Relations* 43, 2 (April):144–50.

Hill, A. 2000. "Divorce: He's Richer, She's Poorer." *The Observer* (October 22). http://www.observer.co.uk/Print/ 0,3858,4079957,00. html (2001, November 8).

Hill, C.T. 1989. "Attitudes to Love." In A. Campbell, ed., *The Opposite Sex*, 152–57. Topsfield, MA: Salem House.

Hill, C., Z. Rubin, and L. Peplau. 1976. "Breakups before Marriage: The End of 103 Affairs." *Journal of Social Issues* 32, 1 (Winter): 147–68.

Hill, N. 1995. "The Relationship between Family Environment and Parenting Style: A Preliminary Study of African American Families." *Journal of Black Psychology* 31, 4 (November):408–23.

Hill, R. 1958. "Generic Features of Families under Stress." *Social Casework* 39 (February/March):139–50.

———. 1972. *The Strengths of Black Families.* New York: Emerson Hall.

———. 1997. *The Strengths of African American Families: Twenty-Five Years Later.* Washington, DC: R & B Publishers.

———. 1998. "Understanding Black Family Functioning: A Holistic Perspective." *Journal of Comparative Family Studies* 29 (Spring):15–25.

Himes, C. L. 1992. "Future Caregivers: Projected Family Structures of Older People." *Journals of Gerontology* 47, 1:23.

Hirsch, M. B., and W. D. Mosher. 1987. "Characteristics of Infertile Women in the United States and Their Use of Fertility Services." *Fertility and Sterility* 47:618–25.

Hite, S. 1976. *The Hite Report: A Nationwide Study of Female Sexuality.* New York: Macmillan.

———. 1981. *The Hite Report on Male Sexuality.* New York: Knopf.

Hobson, M. 2001. "Divorce's Financial Toll." New York: ABCNews.com (June 28) (2001, November 10).

Hochschild, A. R. 1989. *The Second Shift: Working Parents and the Revolution at Home.* New York: Viking.

———. 1997. *The Time Bind: When Work Becomes Home and Home Becomes Work.* New York: Metropolitan Books.

———. 1999. "Understanding the Future of Fatherhood: The 'Daddy Hierarchy' and Beyond." In C. C. Albers, ed., *Sociology of Families: Readings*, 195–207. Thousand Oaks, CA: Pine Forge.

Hodson, D. S., and P. Skeen. 1994. "Sexuality and Aging: The Hammerlock of Myths." *Journal of Applied Gerontology* 13 (September):219–35.

Hodson, R., and T. Sullivan. 1995. *The Social Organization of Work.* Belmont, CA: Wadsworth.

Hoff, L. A. 1990. *Battered Women as Survivors.* New York: Routledge.

Hofferth, S. L. 1985. "Updating Children's Life Course." *Journal of Marriage and the Family* 47:93–115.

Hoffnung, M. 1998. "Motherhood: Contemporary Conflict for Women." In S. J. Ferguson, ed., *Shifting the Center: Understanding Contemporary Families*, 277–91. Mountain View, CA: Mayfield.

Hogan, D. P., and J. I. Farkas. 1995. "The Demography of Changing Intergenerational Relationships." In V. L. Bengtson and K. W. Schaie, eds., *Adult Intergenerational Relations: Effects of Societal Change*, 1–18. New York: Springer.

Holland, D. C., and M. A. Eisenhart. 1990. *Educated in Romance: Women, Achievement, and College Culture.* Chicago: University of Chicago Press.

Holmes, T., and R. Rahe. 1967. "The Social Readjustment Rating Scale." *Journal of Psychosomatic Research* 11:213–18.

Holmes, W., and G. Slap. 1998. "Sexual Abuse of Boys: Definition, Prevalence, Correlates, Sequelae, and Management." *JAMA.* 280:1855–62.

Homans, G. 1961. *Social Behavior in Elementary Forms.* New York: Harcourt, Brace and World.

"Homosexuality." 1997. *The Public Perspective* 8 (October/November):22.

Hondagneu-Sotelo, P., and E. Avila. 1997. "I'm Here, but I'm There: The Meanings of Latina Transnational Motherhood." *Gender and Society* 11 (October):548–71.

"Hooking Up, Hanging Out, and Hoping for Mr. Right: College Women on Dating and Mating Today." 2001. Independent Women's Forum. http://www.iwf.org/news/010727.shtml (2001, October 20).

hooks, b. 1984. *Feminist Theory: From Margin to Center.* Boston: South End Press.

Hooyman, N., and H. A. Kiyak. 1993. *Social Gerontology: A Multi-disciplinary Perspective*, 3d ed. Boston: Allyn & Bacon.

Horin, A. "Why Mothers Need Work Insurance against Divorce. 2000." *News Review* (May 27). http://www.smh.com.au/news/0005/27/review/review13.html (2000, November 8).

Horney, K. 1967. *Feminine Psychology.* New York: W. W. Norton.

Hornike, D. 2001. "Can the Church Get in Step with Stepfamilies?" *U.S. Catholic* 66, 7 (July):33–34.

Horowitz, A. 1992. "Methodological Issues in the Study of Gender within Family Caregiving Relationships." In J. Dwyer and R. Coward, eds., *Gender, Families, and Elder Care*, 132–50. Newbury Park, CA: Sage.

Hort, B. E., B. I. Fagot, and M. D. Leinbach. 1990. "Are People's Notions of Maleness More Stereotypically Framed Than Their Notions of Femaleness?" *Sex Roles* 23, 3/4:197–212.

Houseknecht, S. K., and G. B. Spanier. 1980. "Marital Disruption and Higher Education among Women in the United States." *Sociological Quarterly* 21:375–89.

Houston Area Women's Center. 1999. "The Facts." http://www.hawc.org/teen/facts.html (1999, March 19).

Hout, M. 2000. "Angry and Alienated: Divorced and Remarried Catholics in the United States." *America* 183, 20 (December 16):10–12.

Hovell, M. F., C. Sipan, and E. Blumberg. 1994. *Journal of Marriage and the Family* 56 (November):73–86.

Howell, J. 1998. "Youth Gangs: An Overview." *Juvenile Justice Bulletin.* U.S. Department of Justice, Office of Juvenile Justice and Delinquency Prevention (August).

Hoyenga, K. B., and K. T. Hoyenga. 1993. *Gender-Related Differences.* Boston: Allyn & Bacon.

Hoyert, D., E. Arias, B. Smith, S. Murphy, and K. Kochanek. 2001. "Deaths: Final Data for 1999." Centers for Disease Control and Prevention, National Center for Health Statistics. NVSR 49(8) (September 21).

Huang, A. 1999. "More Women in Taiwan Choose Divorce." *Chicago Tribune* (January 10):sec. 13, 8.

Hubbard, R. 1990. *The Politics of Women's Biology.* New Brunswick, NJ: Rutgers University Press.

Huber, J. 1980. "Will U.S. Fertility Decline toward Zero?" *Sociological Quarterly* 21:481–92.

Hudnall, C. E. 2001. "Grandparents Get Help." *AARP Bulletin* (November):9, 12.

Hughes, Z. 2001. "How to Get What You Want from the Man in Your Life." *Ebony* (March):124–28.

Humes, K., and J. McKinnon. 2000. *The Asian and Pacific Islander Population in the United States: March 1999.* U.S. Census Bureau, Current Population Reports, Series P20–529. Washington, DC: U.S. Government Printing Office.

Humphrys, J. 2001. "We're Tricking the Poorer Nations Out of Their Money." *Sunday Times* (November 4). http://www.igc.apc.org/globalpolicy/socecon/inequal/2001/1/1104trade.htm (2002, January 18).

Hunt, J. G., and L. L. Hunt. 1986. "The Dualities of Careers and Families: New Integrations or New Polarizations?" In A. S. Skolnick and J. H. Skolnick, eds., *Family in Transition: Rethinking Marriage, Sexuality, Child Rearing and Family Organization*, 275–89. Boston: Little, Brown.

Hunt, L. L., and J. G. Hunt. 1975. "Race and the Father–Son Connection: The Conditional Relevance of Father Absence for the Orientations and Identities of Adolescent Boys." *Social Problems* 23:35–52.

Hunt, M. 1959. *The Natural History of Love.* New York: Knopf.

———. 1974. *Sexual Behavior in the 1970s.* Chicago: Playboy Press.

Hupka, R. 1981. "Cultural Determinants of Jealousy." *Alternative Lifestyles* 4:310–56.

———. 1985. "Romantic Jealousy and Romantic Envy: A Seven-Nation Study." *Journal of Cross-Cultural Psychology*, 16:423–46.

Husted, J., and A. Edwards. 1976. "Personality Correlates of Male Sexual Arousal and Behavior." *Archives of Sexual Behavior* (March).

Huston, M., and P. Schwartz. 1996. "Gendered Dynamics in the Romantic Relationships of Lesbians and Gay Men." In J. T. Wood, ed., *Gendered Relationships*, 163–76. Mountain View, CA: Mayfield.

Huyck, M. H. 2001. "Returning a Mother's Kindness." *Chicago Tribune* (May 13):sec. 2, 1.

Hyde, J. S. 1984. "Children's Understanding of Sexist Language." *Developmental Psychology* 20, 4:697–706.

Hyman, S. E. 2000. Statement before the Senate Appropriations Committee, Hearing on Suicide Awareness and Prevention, Washington, DC (February 8). http://www.nimh.nih.gov/about/000208.cfm (2002, January 26).

Iazetto, D. 1989. "When the Body Is Not an Easy Place to Be." Ph.D. diss., Union Institute, Cincinnati, OH.

Idaho Council on Domestic Violence. 1998. "Rape Is a Crime Principally Committed against Young People." National Institute of Justice "Fax" Sheet.

Ihinger-Tallman, M. 1987. "Sibling and Stepfamily Bonding in Stepfamilies." In K. Pasley and M. Ihinger-Tallman, eds., *Remarriage and Stepparenting: Current Research and Theory*, 164–82. New York: Guilford Press.

———, and K. Pasley. 1987. "Divorce and Remarriage in the American Family: A Historical Review." In K. Pasley and M. Ihinger-Tallman, eds., *Remarriage and Stepparenting: Current Research and Theory*, 3–18. New York: Guilford Press.

———. 1991. "Children in Stepfamilies." In J. N. Edwards and D. H. Demo, eds., *Marriage and Family in Transition*, 453–69. Boston: Allyn & Bacon.

Illinois Coalition against Sexual Assault. 1994. "Sexual Violence: Facts and Statistics."

"Induced Abortion." 2000. New York: Alan Guttmacher Institute. http://www.guttmacher.org/pubs/fb_induced_abortion.html (2001, December 17).

Ingram, E., and J. B. Ellis. 1992. "Attitudes toward Suicidal Behavior: A Review of the Literature." *Death Studies* 16:31–43.

Inman, C. 1996. "Friendships among Men: Closeness in the Doing." In J. T. Wood, ed., *Gendered Relationships*, 95–110. Mountain View, CA: Mayfield.

"Insurer Law for Fertility Treatments." 2001. *New York Times* (September 1):A10.

International Labor Organization. 2001. *World Employment Report* 2001. Geneva, Switzerland.

IPPF. 1999. "15-Year-Old Girl Jailed for Abortion in Nepal Released from Prison This Week" (October 4). http://www.ippf.org/newsinfo/pressreleases/nepal9910.htm (2002, January 21).

"It's Time for Working Women to Earn Equal Pay." 2001. American Federation of Labor-Congress of Industrial Organizations. http://www.aflcio.org/women/equalpay.htm (2001, October 20).

Jaccard, J., P. Dittus, and V. Gordon. 2000. "Parent-Teen Communication about Premarital Sex: Factors Associated with the Extent of Communication." *Journal of Adolescent Research* 15:187–208.

Jackson, A. P., R. P. Brown, and K. E. Patterson-Stewart. 2000. "African Americans in Dual-Career Commuter Marriages: An Investigation of Their Experiences." *Family Journal: Counseling and Therapy for Couples and Families* 8:22–36.

Jacob, H. 1988. *Silent Revolution: The Transformation of Divorce Law in the United States.* Chicago: University of Chicago Press.

Jacob, T. 1992. "Family Studies of Alcoholism." *Journal of Psychology* 5:319–38.

James, R. 1997. "Campus Interracial Couple." *Eclipse* (October 14). http://www.inform.umd.edu/News/Eclipse/eclipse/10-14-97/10-14-97-campusinterracial.html (2001, November 12).

Jankowiak, W. R., and E. F. Fischer. 1992. "A Cross-Cultural Perspective on Romantic Love." *Ethnology* 31, 2 (April):149–55.

Janofsky, M. 2001. "Polygamy Case Raises Thorny Issues." *Chicago Tribune* (May 15):sec. 1, 9.

"Japanese Teenager Charged in Second Murder." *New York Times* (July 16):7.

Jarrett, R. L. 1992. "A Family Case Study: An Examination of the Underclass Debate." In J. F. Gilgun, K. Daly, and G. Handel, eds., *Qualitative Methods in Family Research*, 173–96. Newbury Park, CA: Sage.

———. 1995. "Growing up Poor: The Family Experiences of Socially Mobile Youth in Low-Income African American Neighborhoods." *Journal of Adolescent Research* 10 (January):111–35.

Jay, K., and A. Young. 1977. *The Gay Report.* New York: Summit.

Jaynes, G. D., and R. M. Williams, Jr., eds. 1989. *A Common Destiny: Blacks and American Society.* Washington, DC: National Academy Press.

Jendrek, M. P. 1996. "Grandparents Who Parent Their Grandchildren: Effects on Lifestyle." In J. Quadagno and D. Street, eds., *Aging for the Twenty-First Century*, 286–305. New York: St. Martin's Press.

Jenny, C., K. Hymel, A. Ritzen, S. Reinert, and T. Hay. 1999. "Analysis of Missed Cases of Abusive Head Trauma," *JAMA* 281 (February):621–26.

John, D., and B. Shelton. 1997. "The Production of Gender among Black and White Women and Men: The Case of Household Labor." *Sex Roles* 36 (February):171–93.

John, R. 1998. "Native American Families." In C. H. Mindel, R. W. Habenstein, and R. Wright, Jr., eds., *Ethnic Families in America: Patterns and Variations*, 382–421. Upper Saddle River, NJ: Prentice Hall.

Johnson, A. G. 1980. "On the Prevalence of Rape in the United States." *Signs* 6:136–46.

Johnson, C. L. 1988. *Exfamilia.* New Brunswick, NJ: Rutgers University Press.

———, and D. J. Catalano. 1981. "Childless Elderly and Their Family Supports." *Gerontologist* 21:610–18.

Johnson, F. L. 1996. "Friendships among Women: Closeness in Dialogue." In J. T. Wood, ed., *Gendered Relationships*, 79–93. Mountain View, CA: Mayfield.

Johnston, J. R. 1995. "Research Update: Children's Adjustment in Sole Custody Compared to Joint Custody Families and Principles for Custody Decision Making." *Family Conciliation Courts Review* 33:415–25.

Johnston, L. D., J. G. Bachman, and P. M. O'Malley. 1997. *Monitoring the Future: Questionnaire Responses from the Nation's High School Seniors, 1995.* Ann Arbor, MI: Institute for Social Research.

Jones, A. 1995. "For Better or Worse for a Little While Longer." *Chicago Tribune* (September 21):1.

Kahle, J. 1990. "Why Girls Don't Know." In M. Rowe, ed., *What Research Says to the Science Teacher: The Process of Knowing*, 655–67. Washington, DC: National Science Teachers Association.

Kahn, J., C. Brindis, and D. Glei. 1999. "Pregnancies Averted among U.S. Teenagers by the Use of Contraceptives." *Family Planning Perspectives* (January/February): 31, 1.

Kain, E. 1990. *The Myth of Family Decline: Understanding Families in a World of Rapid Social Change.* Lexington, MA: D. C. Heath.

Kalish, R. A. 1985. *Death, Grief, and Caring Relationships*, 2d ed. Monterey, CA: Brooks/Cole.

Kalmijn, M. 1998. "Intermarriage and Homogamy: Causes, Patterns, Trends." *Annual Review of Sociology* 24:395–421.

———. 1999. "Father Involvement in Childrearing and the Perceived Stability of Marriage." *Journal of Marriage and the Family* 61 (May):409–21.

Kamerman, S. B. 1996. "Child and Family Policies: An International Overview." In E. F. Zigler, S. L. Kagan, and N. W. Hall, eds., *Children, Families, and Government: Preparing for the Twenty-First Century*, 31–48. New York: Cambridge University Press.

Kaminer, W. 2001. "Virtual Rape." *The New York Times Magazine.* (November 25):70–73.

Kanin, E. J., K. B. Davidson, and S. R. Scheck. 1970. "A Research Note on Male-Female Differentials in the Experience of Heterosexual Love." *Journal of Sex Research* 6, 1 (February):64–72.

Kann, L., S. Kinchen, B. Williams, J. Ross, R. Lowry, J. Grunbaum, and L. Kolbe. 2000. "Youth Risk Behavior Surveillance—United States, 1999." CDC Surveillance Summaries, June. *Morbidity and Mortality Weekly Report.* 49:1–96.

Kanter, R. M. 1977. *Work and Family in the United States.* New York: Russell Sage Foundation.

Kao, H., and A. Stuifbergen. 1999. "Family Experiences Related to the Decision to Institutionalize an Elderly Member in Taiwan: An Exploratory Study." *Social Science and Medicine* 49:1115–23.

Kaplan, G., V. Barell, and A. Lusky. 1988. "Subjective State of Health and Survival among Elderly Adults." *Journal of Gerontology* 43:S114–120.

Karen, R. 1987. "Giving and Getting in Love and Marriage." *Cosmopolitan* (March):228–31, 236–37, 293.

Karp, D. A., and W. Yoels. 1993. *Sociology in Everyday Life.* Itasca, IL: Peacock.

Karp, S., D. Silber, R. Holmstrom, and L. Stock. 1995. "Personality of Rape Survivors as a Group and by Relation of Survivor to Perpetrator." *Journal of Clinical Psychology* 51:587–92.

Katzev, A. R., R. L. Warner, and A. C. Acock. 1994. "Girls or Boys? Relationship of Child Gender to Marital Instability." *Journal of Marriage and the Family* 56 (February):89–100.

Kauffold, M. P. 1990. "Seeds of Doubt: Bill Takes Aim at 'Test Tube' Baby Industry." *Chicago Tribune* (October 14):4.

Keating, N. C., and P. Cole. 1980. "What Do I Do with Him 24 Hours a Day? Changes in the Housewife Role after Retirement." *Gerontologist* 20:84–89.

Kehoe, M. 1989. *Lesbians over 60 Speak for Themselves.* New York: Haworth Press.

Keith, P. 1986. "Isolation of the Unmarried in Later Life." *Family Relations* 35:389–96.

Keith, V. M., and B. Finlay. 1988. "The Impact of Parental Divorce on Children's Educational Attainment, Marital Timing, and Likelihood of Divorce." *Journal of Marriage and the Family* 50:797–809.

Kelley, P. 1995. *Developing Healthy Stepfamilies: Twenty Families Tell Their Stories.* New York: Haworth Press.

Kelly, G. F. 1995. *Sexuality Today.* Dubuque, IA: Brown and Benchmark.

Kelly, J. 1977. "The Aging Male Homosexual: Myth and Reality?" *Gerontologist* 17:328–32.

Kelly, J. B. 2000. "Children's Adjustment in Conflicted Marriage and Divorce: A Decade Review of Research." *Journal of the American Academy of Child and Adolescent Psychiatry* 39, 8 (August):963–73.

Kempe, C. H., F. N. Silverman, B. Steele, W. Droegemueller, and H. K. Silver. 1962. "The Battered Child Syndrome." *Journal of the American Medical Association* 181:17–24.

Kennen, R. 1997. "Midlife Pregnancy." http://www.midlifemomm.../midlifepregnancy.htm l (May 13).

Kephart, W. 1967. "Some Correlates of Romantic Love." *Journal of Marriage and the Family* 29:470–74.

Kephart, W. M. 1988. "The Oneida Community." In N. D. Glenn and M. Tolbert, eds., *Family Relations: A Reader*, 17–24. Belmont, CA: Wadsworth.

Kerckhoff, A. C. 1976. "Patterns of Marriage and Family Formation and Dissolution." *Journal of Consumer Research* 2:262.

Kessler, S. J. 1996. "The Medical Construction of Gender: Case Management of Intersexed Infants." In B. Laslett, S. G. Kohlstedt, H.

Longino, and E. Hammonds, eds., *Gender and Scientific Authority*, 340–63. Chicago: University of Chicago Press.

Kessler-Harris, A. 1981. *Women Have Always Worked: A Historical Overview*. New York: Feminist Press.

———. 1982. *Out to Work: A History of Wage-Earning Women in the United States*. New York: Oxford University Press.

Kheshgi-Genovese, S., and T. A. Genovese. 1997. "Developing the Spousal Relationship within Stepfamilies." *Families in Society: The Journal of Contemporary Human Services* 78 (May–June):255–64.

Kidder, R. M. 1988. "Marriage in America: Why Marry?" In O. Pocs, ed., *Marriage and Family. 88/89: Annual Editions*, 44–47. Sluice Dock, Guilford, CT: Dushkin.

Kiernan, K. 1990. "Ringing Changes." *New Statesman and Society* 3 (February 16):25.

———. 1992. "The Impact of Family Disruption in Childhood on Transitions Made in Young Adult Life." *Population Studies* 46:213–34.

Kimmel, M. 2000. *The Gendered Society*. New York: Oxford University Press.

———, and M. Messner. 2001. Men's Lives, 5th ed. Needham Heights, MA: Allyn & Bacon.

Kinder, D. R., and D. O. Sears. 1981. "Symbolic Racism versus Racial Threats to the Good Life." *Journal of Personality and Social Psychology* 40:414–31.

King, D. K. 1990. "Multiple Jeopardy, Multiple Consciousness." In M. R. Malson, E. Mudimbe-Boyi, J. F. O'Barr, and M. Wyer, eds., *Black Women in America*, 265–95. Chicago: University of Chicago Press.

Kinsey, A., W. B. Pomeroy, and C. E. Martin. 1948. *Sexual Behavior in the Human Male*. Philadelphia: Saunders.

———, and P. H. Gebhard. 1953. *Sexual Behavior in the Human Female*. Philadelphia: Saunders.

Kitano, H. L. 1988. "The Japanese American Family." In C. H. Mindel, R. W. Habenstein, and R. Wright, Jr., eds., *Ethnic Families in America: Patterns and Variations*, 258–75. New York: Elsevier.

Kitano, K., and H. Kitano. 1998. "The Japanese American Family." In C. Mindel, R. Habenstein, and R. Wright, Jr., eds. *Ethnic Families in America: Patterns and Variations*, 311–30. Upper Saddle River, NJ: Prentice Hall.

Kivett, V. R. 1991. "Centrality of the Grandfather Role among Older Rural Black and White Men." *Journal of Gerontology* 46, 5 (September):250–58.

Kleiman, C. 1989. "Men Clean Up in Wages as Women Keep House." *Chicago Tribune* (September 18):4, 5.

———. 1996. "Odd Hours: Moving to and around the Clock Economy." *Chicago Tribune* (January 28):sec. 6.

———. 1999. "Corporations Find On-site Day Care a Two-Way Perk." *Chicago Tribune* (February 2):sec. 3, 1.

Kleiman, K. 2001. "Can Men Get the Postpartum Blues?" http://www.babycenter.com/expert/3870.html (2001, December 21).

Klerman, G. L., and M. M. Weissman. 1980. "Depressions among Women: Their Nature and Causes." In M. Guttentak, S. Salasin, and D. Belle, eds., *The Mental Health of Women*, 57–92. New York: Academic Press.

Klimek, D. 1979. *Beneath Mate Selection in Marriage: The Unconscious Motives in Human Pairing*. New York: Van Nostrand Reinhold.

Kloehn, S. 1998. "Southern Baptists Approve Submissive Wives Doctrine." *Chicago Tribune* (June 10):1, 11.

Kluegel, J. R. 1990. "Trends in Whites' Explanation of the Black-White Gap in Socioeconomic Status, 1977–1989." *American Sociological Review* 55:512–25.

Kluwer, E. S., J. A. M. Heesink, and E. Van De Vliert. 1996. "Marital Conflict about the Division of Household Labor and Paid Work." *Journal of Marriage and the Family* 58 (November):958–69.

Knaub, P., S. L. Hanna, and N. Stinnett. 1984. "Strengths of Remarried Families." *Journal of Divorce* 7, 3:41–55.

Knox, D., C. Schacht, and M. Zusman. 1999. "Love Relationships among College Students." *College Student Journal* 33, 1 (March):149–51.

Knox, D., and M. Zusman. 2001. "Marrying a Man with 'Baggage': Implications for Second Wives." *Journal of Divorce and Remarriage* 35, 3/4:67–79.

———, M. Kaluzny, and C. Cooper. 2000. "College Student Recovery from a Broken Heart" 34, 3 (September):322–324.

Kohlberg, L. 1966. "A Cognitive-Developmental Analysis of Children's Sex-Role Concepts and Attitudes." In E. Maccoby, ed., *The Development of Sex Differences*, 82–173. Stanford, CA: Stanford University Press.

Kohn, M. 1977. *Class and Conformity*. Chicago: University of Chicago Press.

Koivula, N. 1999. "Gender Stereotyping in Televised Media Sport Coverage." *Sex Roles* 41, 7/8 (October):589–605.

Kong, C. 1998. "Sometimes Love Hurts: When Romance Turns Rocky." *Summer Romance:* special issue. http://enterprise.sjme...talhigh/love/abuse.html (March 19).

Kong, D. 2002. "Home for Asian Elderly Defies Past." *Chicago Tribune* (January 2):9.

Koss, M. P., K. E. Leonard, D. A. Beezley, and C. J. Oros. 1985. "Non-Stranger Sexual Aggression: A Discriminant Analysis of the Psychological Characteristics of Undetected Offenders." *Sex Roles* 12:981–92.

Kotulak, R. 1999. "Study Finds Midlife 'Best Time, Best Place to Be'." *Chicago Tribune* (February 16):1.

Kristof, N. 1996. "Who Needs Love? In Japan Many Couples Don't." *New York Times* (February 11):A6.

Kübler-Ross, E. 1969. *On Death and Dying*. New York: Macmillan.

———. 1974. *Questions and Answers on Death and Dying*. New York: Macmillan.

Kuebli, J., S. A. Butler, and R. Fivush. 1995. "Mother-Child Talk about Past Emotions: Relations of Maternal Language and Child Gender over Time." *Cognition and Emotion* 9:265–83.

Kurdek, L. A. 1993. "Predicting Marital Dissolution: A 5-Year Prospective Longitudinal Study of Newlywed Couples." *Journal of Personality and Social Psychology* 64, 2:221–42.

———. 1994. "Areas of Conflict for Gay, Lesbian, and Heterosexual Couples: What Couples Argue about Influences Relationship Satisfaction." *Journal of Marriage and the Family* 56, 4 (November):923–24.

———, and M. A. Fine. 1993. "The Relation between Family Structure and Young Adolescents' Appraisals of Family Climate and Parenting Behavior." *Journal of Family Issues* 14:279–90.

Kurdek, L. A., and J. P. Schmitt. 1986. "Relationship Quality of Partners in Heterosexual Married, Heterosexual Cohabiting, and Gay and Lesbian Relationships." Journal of Personality and Social Psychology 51 (October):711–20.

Kuriki, C. 1994. "Japanese Law Does Little to Reach Workplace Equality." *Chicago Tribune* (October 9):sec. 6, 9.

Lacey, N. A. 1999. "Love + Loving + Better Health." *Conscious Choice: The Journal of Ecology and Natural Living* (February). http://www.consciouschoice.com/issues/cc1202.healthoflove.html (2001, September 8).

La Ferla, R. 2000. "The Once and Future Virgins." *New York Times* (July 23). http://www.nytimes.qpass.com/qpass-archives (2001, December 4).

Lai, T. 1992. "Asian American Women: Not for Sale." In M. Anderson and P. H. Collins, eds., *Race, Class, and Gender*, 163–71. Belmont, CA: Wadsworth.

Laird, J. 1993. "Lesbian and Gay Families." In F. Walsh, ed., *Normal Family Process*, 2d ed., 282–330. New York: Guilford Press.

Lakoff, R. 1975. *Language and Woman's Place*. New York: Colophon.

Lamb, M. 1987. *The Father's Role: Cross-Cultural Perspectives*. Hillsdale, NJ: Erlbaum.

Lance, L. M. 1998. "Gender Differences in Heterosexual Dating: A Content Analysis of Personal Ads." *Journal of Men's Studies* 6, 3 (Spring):297–305.

Landale, N. S., and R. Forste. 1991. "Pattern of Entry into Cohabitation and Marriage among Mainland Puerto Rican Women." *Demography* 28:587–607.

Landale, N. S., and S. E. Tolnay. 1991. "Group Differences in Economic Opportunity and the Timing of Marriage." *American Sociological Review* 56, 1 (February):33–45.

Landler, M. 2002. "Sharing Grief to Find Understanding." *New York Times* (January 17):A14.

Landrine, H. 1985. "Race and Class Stereotypes of Women." *Sex Roles* 13:65–75.

———, and E.A. Klonoff. 1997. *Discrimination against Women: Prevalence, Consequences, Remedies.* Thousand Oaks, CA: Sage.

Landry-Meyer, L., and K. Fournier. 1997. "Grandparents Raising Grandchildren." Columbus: The Ohio State University, Cooperative Extension Service.

Laquer, W. 1987. *The Age of Terrorism.* Boston: Little, Brown.

Larson, J. H., S. M. Wilson, and R. Beley. 1994. "The Impact of Job Insecurity on Marital and Family Relationships." *Family Relations* 43, 2 (April):138–43.

Lasch, C. 1977. *Haven in a Heartless World: The Family Besieged.* New York: Basic Books.

———. 1978. *The Culture of Narcissism.* New York: W. W. Norton.

Laslett, P. 1971. *The World We Have Lost,* 2d ed. New York: Scribner's.

Lasswell, M. E., and N. M. Lobsenz. 1981. *Styles of Loving: Why You Love the Way You Do.* New York: Ballantine.

Latham, L. M. 2000. "Southern Governors Declare War on Divorce." *Salon* (January 24). www.salon.com/mwt/featire/2000/01/24/divorce/ (2001, October 30).

Lauer, J., and R. Lauer. 1985. "Marriages Made to Last." *Psychology Today* (June):22–26.

Lauer, R., and J. Lauer. 1988. *Watersheds: Mastering Life's Unpredictable Crises.* New York: Little, Brown.

———. 1991. *The Quest for Intimacy.* Dubuque, IA: Brown.

Lauer, R. H. 1992. *Social Problems and the Quality of Life,* 5th ed. Dubuque, IA: William C. Brown.

Laumann, E. O., J. H. Gagnon, R. T. Michael, and S. Michaels. 1994. *The Social Organization of Sexuality: Sexual Practices in the United States.* Chicago: University of Chicago Press.

LaVee, Y., and D. H. Olson. 1993. "Seven Types of Marriage: Empirical Typology Based on Research." *Journal of Marital and Family Therapy* 19 (October):325–40.

Lavin, C. 1991. "What's Best, and Worst, about Being Single." *Chicago Tribune* (July 21):sec. 5, 3.

Lawler, E., and J. Yoon. 1996. "Commitment in Exchange Relations: Test of a Theory of Relational Cohesion. *American Sociological Review* 61:89–108.

Lawson, G., S. Peterson, and A. Lawson. 1983. *Alcoholism and the Family: A Guide to Treatment and Prevention.* Rockville, MD: Aspen.

Leach, P. 1994. *Children First: What Society Must Do (and Is Not Doing) for Our Children Today.* New York: Knopf.

Lee, G. R. 1988. "Marital Intimacy among Older Persons." *Journal of Family Issues* 9:273–84.

———, K. Seccombe, and C. L. Shehan. 1991. "Marital Status and Personal Happiness: An Analysis of Trends and Data." *Journal of Marriage and the Family* 53:839–44.

Lee, G. R., and C. L. Shehan. 1991. "Retirement and Marital Satisfaction." *Journal of Gerontology* 44, 6:226–30.

Lee, G. R., and L. H. Stone. 1980. "Mate-Selection Systems and Criteria: Variation According to Family Structure." *Journal of Marriage and the Family* 42:319–26.

Lee, J. A. 1974. "The Styles of Loving." *Psychology Today* 8, 5 (October): 46–51.

Lee, S. M. 1998. "Asian Americans: Diverse and Growing." *Population Bulletin* 53, 2 (June). Washington, DC: Population Reference Bureau.

Lehman College Art Gallery. 1998. "Myths vs. Reality." http://math240.lehman...rt/Hernandez/myths.html (1999, June 4).

Lehr, R., and P. MacMillan. 2001. "The Psychological and Emotional Impact of Divorce: The Noncustodial Fathers' Perspective." *Families in Society* 82, 4 (July/August):273–382.

Lehrer, E. L., and C. U. Chiswick. 1993. "Religion as a Determinant of Marital Stability." *Demography* 30, 3 (August):385–404.

Leland, J. "Gays Seeking Asylum Find Familiar Prejudices in U.S." *New York Times* (August 1):A10.

———, and M. Miller. 1998. "Can Gays Convert?" *Newsweek* (August 17):47.

LeMasters, E. 1957. *Modern Courtship and Marriage.* New York: Macmillan.

Lempert, L. B. 1999. "Other Fathers: An Alternative Perspective on African American Community Caring." In R. Staples, ed., *The Black Family: Essays and Studies,* 6th ed., 189–201. Belmont, CA: Wadsworth.

Lengermann, P. M., and J. N. Brantley. 1988. "Feminist Theory." In G. Ritzer, ed., *Sociological Theory,* 400–443. New York: Knopf.

Lepowsky, M. 1993. *Fruit of the Motherland: Gender in an Egalitarian Society.* New York: Columbia University Press.

Lerman, R. I., and T. J. Ooms, eds. 1993. *Young Unwed Fathers: Changing Roles and Emerging Policies.* Philadelphia: Temple University Press.

Lerner, J. V. 1994. *Working Women and Their Families.* Thousand Oaks, CA: Sage.

Lessinger, J. 2002. "Asian Indian Marriages—Arranged, Semi-Arranged, or Based on Love?" In Nijole Benokraitis, ed., *Contemporary Ethnic Families in the United States,* 101–4, Upper Saddle River, NJ: Prentice Hall.

Lester, D. 1996. "The Impact of Unemployment on Marriage and Divorce." *Journal of Divorce and Remarriage* 25, 3/4:151–53.

Lev, M. A. 1998. "Japan Worries as Women Turn from Marriage." *Chicago Tribune* (March 30):1.

Lever, J. 1978. "Sex Differences in the Complexity of Children's Play and Games." *American Sociological Review* 43:471–83.

———, D. Kanouse, W. Rogers, S. Carson, and R. Hertz. 1992. "Behavior Patterns and Sexual Identity of Bisexual Males." *Journal of Sex Research* 29:141–67.

Levine, A., and J. Cureton, eds. 1998. *When Hope and Fear Collide: A Portrait of Today's College Students.* San Francisco: Jossey-Bass.

Levinger, G. 1965. "Marital Cohesiveness and Dissolution: An Integrative Review." *Journal of Marriage and the Family* 27:19–28.

———. 1979. "A Social Psychological Perspective on Marital Dissolution." In G. Levinger and O. Moles, eds., *Divorce and Separation,* 37–60. New York: Basic Books.

Levinson, D. 1981. "Physical Punishment of Children and Wife Beating in Cross-Cultural Perspective." *Child Abuse and Neglect* 5, 4:193–96.

Levy, B., ed. 1991. *Dating Violence: Young Women in Danger.* Seattle, WA: Seal Press.

———. 1992. "A Closer Look." NBC.

Lewin, T. 1994a. "Sex in America: Faithfulness in Marriage Thrives after All." *New York Times* (October 7):A1, A11.

———. 1994b. "So, Now We Know What Americans Do in Bed. So?" *New York Times* (October 9):E3.

———. 1995. "Parents Poll Finds Child Abuse to Be More Common." *New York Times* (December 7).

———. 1998a. "Men Assuming Bigger Share at Home, New Study Shows." *New York Times* (April 15):A16.

———. 1998b. "New Families Redraw Racial Boundaries." *New York Times* (October 27):A1.

———. 1999. "Father Awarded $375,000 in a Parental Leave Case." (February 3):A11.

Lieberman, B. 1985. "Extra-Premarital Intercourse." Unpublished manuscript, University of Pittsburgh, Department of Sociology, Pittsburgh.

Liem, R. 1985. "Unemployment: A Family as Well as a Personal Crisis." In J. Boulet, A. M. Debritto, and S. A. Ray, eds., *Understanding the Economic Crisis,* 112–18. Ann Arbor: University of Michigan Press.

Light, D., S. Keller, and C. Calhoun. 1989. *Sociology,* 5th ed. New York: Knopf.

Lin, G., and P. A. Rogerson. 1995. "Elderly Parents and the Geographic Availability of Their Adult Children." *Research on Aging* 17, 3:303–31.

Lindsay, J. W. 1995. *Teen-Age Couples: Caring, Commitment, and Change.* Buena Park, CA: Morning Glory Press.

Lindsey, L. 1990. *Gender Roles: A Sociological Perspective.* Englewood Cliffs, NJ: Prentice Hall.

———. 1994. *Gender Roles: A Sociological Perspective,* 2d ed. Englewood Cliffs, NJ: Prentice Hall.

Link, B., et al. 1995. "Life-Time and Five-Year Prevalence of Homelessness in the United States: New Evidence on an Old Debate." *American Journal of Orthopsychiatry* 65, 3 (July):347–54.

Lips, H. 1993. *Sex and Gender: An Introduction.* Mountain View, CA: Mayfield.

Liss, M. B. 1992. "Home, School, and Playroom: Training Grounds for Adult Gender Roles." *Sex Roles* 26, 3/4:129–47.

Little, H. 1995. "Out of Retirement: Parenting the Second Time Around Isn't Always So Grand." *Chicago Tribune* (September 10):1.

Littman, M. 2001. "She Can Bring Home the Bacon. . . ." *Chicago Tribune* (March 7):sec. 8, 1, 7.

Liu, P., and C. S. Chan. 1996. "Bisexual Asian Americans and Their Families." In J. Laird and R. Green, eds., *Lesbians and Gays in Couples and Families,* 137–52. San Francisco: Jossey-Bass.

Liu, X., C. Guo, and M. Okawa. 2000. "Behavioral and Emotional Problems in Chinese Children of Divorced Parents." *Journal of the American Academy of Child Adolescent Psychiatry* 39, 7:896–903.

Lloyd, P. C. 1968. "Divorce among the Yoruba." *American Anthropologist* 70:67–81.

Lloyd, S. A., and R. M. Cote. 1984. "Predicting Premarital Relationship Stability: A Methodological Refinement." *Journal of Marriage and the Family* 46:71–76.

Locin, M. 1991. "Study: Parental-Leave Laws Work Well." *Chicago Tribune* (May 22):sec. 1, 3.

Logue, B. J. 1991. "Women at Risk: Predictions of Financial Stress for Retired Women Workers." *Gerontologist* 31, 5:657–65.

London, K. A. 1990. *Cohabitation, Marriage, Marital Dissolution, and Remarriage: United States, 1988.* Vital and Health Statistics, Advance Data no. 194. Hyattsville, MD: National Center for Health Statistics.

Long, B. C. 1989. "Sex-Role Orientation, Coping Strategies, and Self-Efficacy of Women in Traditional and Nontraditional Occupations." *Psychology of Women Quarterly* 13:307–24.

Longino, C. F., Jr. 1988. "A Population Profile of Very Old Men and Women in the United States." *Sociological Quarterly* 29:559–64.

Loomis, L. S., and N. Landale. 1994. "Nonmarital Cohabitation and Childbearing among Black and White American Women." *Journal of Marriage and the Family* 56 (November):949–62.

Lopata, H. Z. 1973. *Widowhood in an American City.* Cambridge, MA: Schenkman.

Lorber, J. 1994. *Paradoxes of Gender.* New Haven, CT: Yale University Press.

Lott, B. 1994. *Women's Lives: Themes and Variations in Gender Learning,* 2d ed. Pacific Grove, CA: Brooks/Cole.

"Love Is Colorblind . . . Or Is It?" 2000. *American Demographics* 22, 6 (June):11.

Lowenstein, S. F. 1985. "On the Diversity of Love Object Orientations among Women." *Journal of Social Work and Human Sexuality* 3, 2/3 (Winter/Spring, 1984/85):7–24.

Lu, Z., D. J. Maume, and M. L. Bellas. 2000. "Chinese Husbands' Participation in Household Labor." *Journal of Comparative Family Studies* 31, 2 (Spring):191–215.

Luhman, R. 1996. *The Sociological Outlook: A Text with Readings.* San Diego, CA: Collegiate Press.

Lund, K. 1990. "A Feminist Perspective and Divorce Therapy for Women." *Journal of Divorce* 13, 3:57–67.

Lynn, D. 1966. "The Process of Learning Parental and Sex-Role Identification." *Journal of Marriage and the Family* 28:466–70.

Lyon, J. 1992. "Keeping Score." *Chicago Tribune* magazine (November 29):14–16, 28–32, 34–35.

Maccoby, E., and C. Jacklin. 1987. "Gender Segregation in Childhood." *Advances in Child Development and Behavior* 20:239–87.

Maccoby, E., and R. Mnookin. 1992. *Dividing the Child: Social and Legal Dilemmas of Custody.* Cambridge, MA: Harvard University Press.

MacDonald, K., and R. D. Parke. 1986. "Parent-Child Physical Play: The Effects of Sex and Age on Children and Parents." *Sex Roles* 15:367–78.

MacDonald, W. L., and A. DeMaris. 1996. "Parenting Stepchildren and Biological Children: The Effects of Stepparent's Gender and New Biological Children." *Journal of Family Issues* 17, 1 (January):5–25.

MacFarquhar, N. 2001. "Egypt Tries 52 Men Suspected of Being Gay." *New York Times* (July 19):A10.

Macionis, J. 1991. *Sociology,* 3rd ed. Englewood Cliffs, NJ: Prentice Hall.

———. 1995. *Sociology,* 5th ed. Englewood Cliffs, NJ: Prentice Hall.

———, and V. Parrillo. 1998. *Cities and Urban Life.* Upper Saddle River, NJ: Prentice Hall.

Macklin, E. D. 1972. "Heterosexual Cohabitation among Unmarried Students." *Family Coordinator* 21:463–72.

Macko, S. 1996. "Street Gangs Come to a Quiet Chicago Neighborhood." *EmergencyNet News Service,* vol. 2, no. 30. http://www.emergency.com/swcjgng.htm (2002, February 5),

MacRae, H. 1992. "Fictive Kin as a Component of the Social Networks of Older People." *Research on Aging* 14:226–47.

Madigan, C. M. 1999. "Marriage 101: Skip the Trial Run." *Chicago Tribune* (January 31):sec. 2, 1.

Madsen, W. 1964. *The Mexican American of South Texas.* New York: Holt, Rinehart & Winston.

Magdol, L., T. E. Moffitt, and A. Caspi. 1998. "Hitting without a License: Testing Explanations for Differences in Partner Abuse between Young Adult Daters and Cohabitants." *Journal of Marriage and the Family* 60, 1 (February):41–55.

Maginnis, R.L. 1995. "Marriage Protects Women from Violence." *Insight.* Washington, DC: Family Research Council, 1–3.

Mahoney, D. 2000. "Pastor Shuts Door on Interracial Couple." *Columbus Dispatch* (July 8). http://www.dispatch.com/news/newsfea00/jul00/341709.html (2001, November 15).

Maier, R. 1984. *Sexuality in Perspective.* Chicago: Nelson-Hall.

Maines, J. 1993. "Long-Distance Romances." *American Demographics* (May):47.

Majors, R. 1995. "Cool Pose: The Proud Signature of Black Survival." In M. S. Kimmel and M. A. Messner, eds., *Men's Lives,* 82–85. Boston: Allyn & Bacon.

Malinowski, B. 1929. *The Sexual Life of Savages in North Western Melanesia.* New York: Harcourt Brace.

Mandate the Future. 2002. "13-Year-Old Rape Victim Sentenced to 21 Years in Prison!!" (February 5). http://www.ctrkaktesc,irg/abortion/01/02/02/0656200.shtml (2002, January 21).

Mandela, N. 2000. "Globalizing Responsibility." *Boston Globe* (January 4). http://www.igc.apc.org/globalpolicy/socecon/inequal/nelson.htm (2002, January 18).

Manier, J., and O. Obejas. 2001. "AIDS Roars Back; Blacks Hit Hardest." *Chicago Tribune* (June 1):1, 24.

Manis, R., ed. 2001. *The Marriage and Family Workbook: An Interactive Reader, Text, and Workbook.* Boston: Allyn & Bacon.

Mann, D. 2000. "Fatal Beating Calls Attention to Problem at Youth Sporting Events." WebMD Medical News. http://webmd.lycos.com/content/article/1728.59319 (2002, February 10).

Mann, J. 1995. "Girls and TV: A Dearth of Role Models." *Washington Post* (September 29):E3.

Marino, V. 1995. "When Children Flock Back to the Family Roost." *Chicago Tribune* (November 7):sec. 6.

Marion, R., A. A. Wiznia, G. Hutcheon, and A. Rubinstein. 1986. "Human T-Cell Lymphotrophic Virus Type III (Htlv–III) Embryopathy." *American Journal of Diseases of Children* 140:638–40.

Markides, K. S. 1978. "Reasons for Retirement and Adaptation to Retirement by Elderly Mexican Americans." In E. P. Stanford, ed., *Retirement: Concepts and Realities of Minority Elders*, 83–90. San Diego, CA: San Diego State University.

———, and C. H. Mindel. 1987. *Aging and Ethnicity.* Newbury Park, CA: Sage.

Marks, N. F. 1996. "Caregiving across the Lifespan: National Prevalence and Predictors." *Family Relations* 45:27–36.

Marquis, C. 2001. "Military's Ouster of Gays Rose 17 Percent Last Year." *New York Times* (June 2):A9.

Marriage License Bureau and Cook County Clerk's Office. 1993. "Marriage License Requirements for the State of Illinois." Telephone interview, Chicago.

Marriott, N. 2001. "What's Love Got to Do with It?" In Robert Manis, ed., *Marriage and Family: An Interactive Reader, Text, and Workbook*, 79–81. Boston: Allyn & Bacon.

Marriott, S. S. 1994. "Violence and Its Impact on Women." *Vital Sign* 10, 2:6.

Marshall, J. 1999. "A Wealth of Information Tells Dads How to Parent." *Chicago Tribune* (November 7):sec. 13, 8.

Martin, C. L. 1990. "Attitudes and Expectations about Children with Nontraditional and Traditional Gender Roles." *Sex Roles* 22:151–65.

Martin, J., B. Hamilton, and S. Ventura. 2001. *Preliminary Data for 2000.* National Vital Statistics Reports 49, 5:4. Hyattsville, MD: National Center for Health Statistics: 4.

Martin, P., and R. Hummer. 1993. "Fraternities and Rape on Campus." In P. Bart and E. Moran, eds., *Violence against Women*, 114–31. Thousand Oaks, CA: Sage.

Martin, T. C., and L. L. Bumpass. 1989. "Recent Trends in Marital Disruption." *Demography* 26:37–52.

Martire, L. M., M. P. Stephens, and M. M. Franks. 1997. "Multiple Roles of Women Caregivers: Feelings of Mastery and Self-Esteem as Predictors of Psychosocial Well-Being." *Journal of Women & Aging* 9, 1/2:117–31.

Mason, M. A. 1999. *The Custody Wars.* New York: Basic Books.

Mason, P. 1996. *Joblessness and Unemployment: A Review of the Literature* (LR-JU-96–03). Philadelphia: National Center on Fathers and Families.

Mastekaasa, A. 1992. "Marriage and Psychological Well-Being: Some Evidence on Selection into Marriage." *Journal of Marriage and the Family* 54:901–11.

Masters, W., and V. Johnson. 1966. *Human Sexual Response.* Boston: Little, Brown.

———, and R. C. Kolodny. 1985. *Human Sexual Response*, 2d ed. Boston: Little, Brown.

———. 1986. *On Sex and Human Loving.* Boston: Little, Brown.

———. 1992. *Human Sexual Response*, 4th ed. Boston: Little, Brown.

Mathews, L. 1996. "Who Pays?" *Chicago Tribune* (January 21):sec. 3.

Matthews, S. H. 1995. "Gender and the Division of Filial Responsibility between Lone Sisters and Their Brothers." *Journal of Gerontology: Social Sciences* 50B:S312–S320.

———, and J. Sprey. 1985. "Adolescents' Relationships with Grandparents: An Empirical Contribution to Conceptual Clarification." *Journal of Gerontology* 40:621–26.

Maugh, T. H. H. 1990. "Sex: American Style Trend to the Traditional." *Los Angeles Times* (February 18):sec. A1, A22.

Mauldin, T. A. 1990. "Women Who Remain above the Poverty Level in Divorce: Implications for Family Policy." *Family Relations* 39:141–46.

———, and C. B. Meeks. 1990. "Sex Differences in Children's Time Use." *Sex Roles* 22, 9/10:537–54.

Max, E. 1985. "Custody Criteria, Visitation and Child Support." *Women's Advocate* (September):1–4.

Max, W., P. Webber., and P. Fox. 1995. "Alzheimer's Disease: The Unpaid Burden of Caring." *Journal of Aging of Health* 7, 2:179–99.

Maxwell, J. 1997. "Oh Baby, Mom Delivers 7." Channel 4000. http://www.wcco.com/news/stories/news971119–130925.html (1999, May 6).

Mays, V. M., and S. D. Cochran. 1991. "The Black Women's Relationships Project: A National Survey of Black Lesbians." In R. Staples, ed., *The Black Family: Essays and Studies*, 4th ed., 92–100. Belmont, CA: Wadsworth.

Maza, P., and J. A. Hall. 1988. *Homeless Children and Their Families: A Preliminary Study.* Washington, DC: Child Welfare League of America.

Mazur, E. 1989. "Predicting Gender Differences in Same-Sex Friendships from Affiliation Motive and Value." *Psychology of Women Quarterly* 13:277–91.

———. 1993. "Decision Making and Marital Satisfaction in African American Families." In H. P. McAdoo, ed., *Family Ethnicity: Strength in Diversity*, 109–19. Thousand Oaks, CA: Sage.

McAdoo, J. L., and J. B. McAdoo. 1995. "The African-American Father's Roles within the Family." In M. S. Kimmel and M. A. Messner, eds., *Men's Lives*, 3d ed. Boston: Allyn & Bacon.

McCary, J. L. 1978. *Human Sexuality: Instructor's Guide.* New York: Van Nostrand.

McClelland, K., and C. Auster. 1990. "Public Platitudes and Hidden Tensions: Racial Climates at Predominantly White Liberal Arts Colleges." *Journal of Higher Education* 61:607–42.

McCloskey, L., A. Figueredo, and M. Koss. 1995. "The Effects of Systemic Family Violence on Children's Mental Health." *Child Development* 66:1239–61.

McGhee, J. L. 1985. "The Effects of Siblings on the Life Satisfaction of the Rural Elderly." *Journal of Marriage and the Family* 47:85–91.

McGrath, E., G. B. Keita, B. R. Strickland, and N. F. Russo, eds. 1990. *Women and Depression: Risk Factors and Treatment Issues.* Hyattsville, MD: American Psychological Association.

McKelvey, C. A., and J. Stevens. 1994. *Adoption Crisis: The Truth behind Adoption and Foster Care.* Golden, CO: Fulcrum.

McKeough, K. 2001. "A Date or Not a Date?" *Chicago Tribune* (May 2):sec 8, 2.

McKim, W. A. 1986. *Drugs and Behavior: An Introduction to Behavioral Pharmacology.* Englewood Cliffs, NJ: Prentice Hall.

McLanahan, S. S. 1999. "Father Absence and Children's Welfare." In E. M. Hetherington, ed., *Coping with Divorce, Single Parenting, and Remarriage: A Risk and Resiliency Perspective.* Mahwah, NJ: Erlbaum.

———, and L. Bumpass. 1988. "Intergenerational Consequences of Family Disruption." *American Journal of Sociology* 94:130–52.

McLanahan, S., and L. Casper, 1995. "Growing Diversity and Inequality in the American Family." In R. Farley, ed., *State of the Union: America in the 1990s*, vol. 2, 1–46. New York: Russell Sage Foundation.

McNeal, C., and P. Amato. 1998. "Parents' Marital Violence: Long-Term Consequences for Children." *Journal of Family Issues* 19:123–40.

McNeil, D., Jr. 2001. "Rare Condoms, Deadly Odds for Truck-Stop Prostitutes." *New York Times* (November 29):A14.

McRoy, R. G. 1989. "An Organizational Dilemma: The Case of Transracial Adoptions." *Journal of Applied Behavioral Science* 25, 2:145–60.

———, H. Grotevant, and L. A. Zurcher, Jr. 1988. *Emotional Disturbances in Adopted Adolescents: Origins and Development.* New York: Praeger.

McTaggart L. 1980. *The Baby Brokers: The Marketing of White Babies in America.* New York: Dial Press.

Mead, M. 1935. *Sex and Temperament in Three Primitive Societies.* New York: Morrow.

———. 1970. "Communes: A Challenge to All of Us." *Redbook* 35 (August):51–52.

Mederer, H. J. 1993. "Division of Labor in Two-Earner Homes: Task Accomplishment versus Household Management as Critical Variables in Perceptions about Family Work." *Journal of Marriage and the Family* 55:133–45.

"Median Weekly Earnings of Full-Time Wage and Salary Workers by Union Affiliation and Selected Characteristics." 2001. U.S. Department of Labor. http://www.bls.gov/news.release/union2.t02.htm (2001, October 25).

Medved, M. 1992. *Hollywood vs. America: Popular Culture and the War on Traditional Values.* New York: HarperCollins.

Meier, B. 1996. "Bias Complaints against Wall St. Firms." *New York Times* (November 21):D4.

Melton, W., and L. Lindsey. 1987. "Instrumental and Expressive Values in Mate Selection among College Students Revisited: Feminism, Love and Economic Necessity." Paper presented at the annual meeting of the Midwest Sociological Society, Chicago.

Mendel, M. 1995. *The Male Survivor: The Impact of Sexual Abuse.* Thousand Oaks, CA: Sage.

"Men Won't Budge for Wives' Careers." 1997. *Chicago Tribune* (July 13):sec. 13, 3.

Meredith, D. 1985. "Mom, Dad, and the Kids." *Psychology Today* (June): 62–67.

Merighi, J. R., and M. D. Grimes. 2000. "Coming Out to Families in a Multicultural Context." *Families in Society* 81, 1 (January/February): 32–41.

Metropolitan Life Insurance Company. 1997. *The Met Life Study of Employer Costs for Working Caregivers.* Westport, CT: MetLife Mature Market Group.

Michael, R., J. Gagnon, E. O. Laumann, and G. Kolata. 1994. *Sex in America: The Definitive Survey.* Boston: Little, Brown.

Middlebrook, P. N. 1974. *Social Psychology and Modern Life.* New York: Knopf.

Mignon, S., C. Larson, and W. Holmes. 2002. *Family Abuse: Consequences, Theories, and Responses.* Boston: Allyn & Bacon.

Miller, B. 2001. "Life-Styles of Gay Husbands and Fathers." In M. Kimmel and M. Messner,, eds., *Men's Lives*, 443–50. Needham Heights, MA: Allyn & Bacon.

Miller, B. C., and S. L. Bowen. 1982. "Father-to-Newborn Attachment Behavior in Relation to Prenatal Classes and Presence at Delivery." *Family Relations* 31:71–78.

Miller, B., and L. Cafasso. 1992. "Gender Differences in Caregiving: Fact or Artifact?" *Gerontologist* 32, 4:498–507.

Miller, B. C., and K. A. Moore. 1990. "Adolescent Sexual Behavior, Pregnancy, and Parenting: Research through the 1980s." *Journal of Marriage and the Family* 52 (November):1025–44.

Miller, L. 1993. "Spurning Isolation to Forge a New Generation of Communities." *USA Today* (December 14):8D.

Miller, N. 1992. *Out in the World.* New York: Random House.

Miller, S. 1994. "Conference Proceedings: The Role of Men in Children's Lives." Nashville, TN (July 10–11). St. Paul: Minnesota Children, Youth and Families Consortium Electronic Clearinghouse.

Miller, T. 1998. *The Quest for Utopia in Twentieth Century America, Vol. 1:1900–1960.* Syracuse, NY: Syracuse University Press.

Mills, C., and B. Granoff. 1992. "Date and Acquaintance Rape among a Sample of College Students." *Social Work* 37:504–9.

Mills, C. W. 1959. *The Sociological Imagination.* New York: Oxford University Press.

Min, P. G. 1988. "The Korean American Family." In C. H. Mindel, R. W. Habenstein, and R. Wright, Jr., eds., *Ethnic Families in America*, 199–229. New York: Elsevier.

———. 1993. "Korean Immigrants in Los Angeles." In Ivan Light and Parminder Bhachu, eds., *Immigration and Entrepreneurship*, 185–204. New York: Transaction.

———. 1998. "The Korean-American Family." In C. H. Mindel, R. W. Habenstein, and R. Wright, Jr., eds., *Ethnic Families in America: Patterns and Variations*, 223–53. Upper Saddle River, NJ: Prentice Hall.

Mindel, C. H. 1983. "The Elderly in Minority Families." In T. H. Brubaker, ed., *Family Relationships in Later Life*, 193–208. Beverly Hills, CA: Sage.

———, R. W. Habenstein, and R. Wright. 1998. *Ethnic Families in America: Patterns and Variations.* Upper Saddle River, NJ: Prentice Hall.

Minino, A., and B. Smith. 2001. "Deaths: Preliminary Data for 2000." *National Vital Statistics Report.* Department of Health and Human Services, Centers for Disease Control and Prevention, National Center for Health Statistics (October 9), vol. 49, no. 12.

Mintz, S., and S. Kellog. 1988. *Domestic Revolution: A Social History of American Family Life.* New York: Free Press.

Miranda-Maniquis, E. 1993. "The Silence about Women." *World Press Review* 40 (February):26.

Mirande, A. 1985. *The Chicano Experience: An Alternative Perspective.* Notre Dame, IN: University of Notre Dame Press.

———. 1988. "Chicano Fathers: Traditional Perceptions and Current Realities." In P. Bronstein and C. Cowan, eds., *Fatherhood Today*, 93–106. New York: Wiley.

———. 1991. "Ethnicity and Fatherhood." In F. W. Bozett and S. M. H. Hanson, eds., *Fatherhood and Families in Cultural Context*, 33–82. New York: Springer.

Mirchandi, V. K. 1973. "Attitudes toward Love among Blacks." Master's thesis, East Carolina University, Greenville, NC.

Mistiaen, V. 1994. "New-Baby Blues? Here's the News: Dad's Got 'Em Too." *Chicago Tribune* (October 2):1.

Mitchell, J. 1998. "Happy Stepfamilies Don't Happen Overnight." http://seattletimes.com/news/lifestyles/html98/altstep081398.html.

Mitchell, J., and J. C. Register. 1984. "An Exploration of Family Interaction with the Elderly by Race, Socioeconomic Status and Residence." *Gerontologist* 24:48–54.

Modern Maturity. 1992/1993. "Time Improves Lives of Older Widows" (December/January):8.

Money, J., and A. Ehrhardt. 1972. *Man and Woman, Boy and Girl.* Baltimore, MD: Johns Hopkins University Press.

Montgomery, P. 1996. "The Influence of Social Context on the Caregiving Experience." In Z. S. Khachaturian and T. S. Radenbaugh, eds., *Alzheimer's Disease: Causes, Diagnosis, Treatment and Care*, 313–21. New York: CRC Press.

Moore, D. W., and L. Saad. 1995. "Most Americans Worried about Retirement." *Gallup Poll Monthly* (May):17–21.

Moore, F. 1995. "Girls Shortchanged by TV, Seek More Diverse Shows." *Chicago Tribune* (October 1):sec. 13.

Moore, J., and H. Pachon. 1985. *Hispanics in the United States*. Englewood Cliffs, NJ: Prentice Hall.

Moore, K. A., and I. V. Sawhill. 1984. "Implication of Women's Employment for Home and Family Life." In P. Voydanoff, ed., *Work and Family: Changing Roles of Men and Women*, 153–71. Palo Alto, CA: Mayfield.

Moore, P., with C. P. Conn. 1985. *Disguised.* Waco, TX: Word Books.

Moore, W. E. 1978. "Functionalism." In T. Bottommore and R. Nisbet, eds., *A History of Sociological Analyses*, 321–61. New York: Basic Books.

Morales, E. 1996. "Gender Roles among Latino Gay and Bisexual Men: Implications for Family and Couple Relationships." In J. Laird and R. Green, eds., *Lesbians and Gays in Couples and Families*, 272–97. San Francisco: Jossey-Bass.

Morell, C. 1994. *Unwomanly Conduct: The Challenges of Intentional Childlessness.* New York: Routledge.

Morgan, S. P., D. Lye, and G. Condran. 1988. "Sons, Daughters, and the Risk of Marital Disruption." *American Journal of Sociology* 94:110–29.

Morganthau, T. 1993. "America: Still a Melting Pot?" *Newsweek* (August 9):16–23.

Morin, R., and M. Rosenfeld. 1998. "With More Equity, More Sweat." *Washington Post* (March 22):A1.

Morris, J. 1974. *Conundrum.* New York: Harcourt Brace Jovanovich.

Mortimer, J. T., and J. London. 1984. "The Varying Linkages of Work and Family." In P. Voydanoff, ed., *Work and Family: Changing Roles of Men and Women*, 20–35. Palo Alto, CA: Mayfield.

Moseley, R. 1995. "Ireland Narrowly Lifts Divorce Ban." *Chicago Tribune* (November 26):1.

Mosher, W. D. 1990. "Contraceptive Practice in the United States, 1982–1988." *Family Planning Perspectives* 22:198–205.

Moskowitz, M., and C. Townsend. 1995. "100 Best Companies for Working Mothers." *Working Mother* (October):18+.

Moss, B. F., and A. I. Schwebel. 1993. "Marriage and Romantic Relationships, Defining Intimacy in Romantic Relationships." *Family Relations* 42:31–37.

Motenko, A. K. 1989. "The Frustrations, Gratifications and Well-Being of Dementia Caregivers." *Gerontologist* 29, 2:166–72.

"Mother Accused of Killing Her 3 Children Found Guilty." 2001. *USATODAY.com.* http://www.usatoday.com/news/nation/2001/12/19/killer-mom.htm (2002, January 13).

Mowery, J. 1978. "Systemic Requisites of Communal Groups." *Alternative Lifestyles* 2:235–61.

Moyle, E. 1999. "Catch of Day: Single Dads" (March 18). http://www.canoe.com:8...3/19_singlefather.html.

Moynihan, D. P. 1965. *The Negro Family: The Case for National Action.* U.S. Department of Labor, Office of Policy Planning and Research. Washington, DC: U.S. Government Printing Office.

Ms. magazine. 1993. "Action Alert: International News." (January/February):12–13.

Muller, R., and K. Lemieux. 2000. "Social Support, Attachment, and Psychopathology in High Risk Formerly Maltreated Adults." *Child Abuse and Neglect* 24:883–900.

Mullis, I., and L. Jenkins. 1988. *The Science Report Card*, Report no. 17–S–01. Princeton, NJ: Educational Testing Service.

"Multigenerational Community Recreates Family." 1997. *Journal of Property Management* 62 (July/August):30.

Murphy, M., et al. 1991. "Substance Abuse and Serious Child Mistreatment, Child Abuse and Neglect." *International Journal* 15, 3:197–211.

Murray, B., and B. Duffy. 1998. "Jefferson's Secret Life." *U.S. News & World Report* (November 9).

Murstein, B. I. 1971. "A Theory of Marital Choice." In B. I. Murstein, ed., *Theories of Attraction and Love*, 100–51. New York: Springer.

———. 1974. *Love, Sex, and Marriage through the Ages.* New York: Springer.

———. 1980. "Mate Selection in the 1970's." *Journal of Marriage and the Family* 42:777–92.

———. 1986. *Paths to Marriage.* Beverly Hills, CA: Sage.

———. 1987. "A Classification and Extension of the SVR Theory of Dyadic Pairing." *Journal of Marriage and the Family* 42:777–92.

Mutran, E. 1985. "Intergenerational Family Support among Blacks and Whites." *Journal of Gerontology* 40 (May):382–89.

Muwakkil, S. 2001. "AIDS and the State of Denial." *Chicago Tribune* (June18):11.

Mydans, S. 1995. "Hispanic Gang Members Keep Strong Family Ties." *New York Times* (September 11):1.

———. 2001. "U.S. Interrupts Cambodian Adoptions." *New York Times* (November 5):A7.

Myers, D. J., and K. B. Dugan. 1996. "Sexism in Graduate School Classrooms: Consequences for Students and Faculty." *Gender & Society* 10:330–50.

Naifeh, M. L. 1993. "Housing of the Elderly: 1991." *Current Housing Reports*, Series H123/93–1. Washington, DC: U.S. Government Printing Office.

Najman, J. M., B. C. Behrens, M. Anderson, W. Bor, M. O'Callaghan, and G. M. Williams. 1997. "Impact of Family Type and Family Quality on Child Behavior Problems: A Longitudinal Study." *Journal of the American Academy of Child and Adolescent Psychiatry* 36:1357–65.

Nakonezny, P. A., R. D. Shull, and J. L. Rodgers. 1995. "The Effect of No-Fault Divorce Laws on the Divorce Rate across the 50 States and Its Relation to Income, Education and Religiosity." *Journal of Marriage and the Family* (May):477–88.

Nardi, P. 2001. "The Politics of Gay Men's Friendships." In M. Kimmel and M. Messner. *Men's Lives*, 5th ed., 380–83. Needham Heights, MA: Allyn & Bacon.

Nardi, P., and Sherrod, D. 1994. "Friendship in the Lives of Gay Men and Lesbians." *Journal of Social and Personal Relationships* 11 (May):185–99.

National Adoption Information Clearinghouse, 2000a. "Intercountry Adoption." http://www;calib.com/naic/pubs/s_inter.htm (2002, January 15).

———. 2000b. "Adoptions from Foster Care." http://calib.com/naic/pubs/s_foster.htm (2002, January 15).

———. 2000c. "Transracial Adoptions." http://www.calib.com/naic/pubs/s_trans.htm (2002, January 15).

National Association of Anorexia Nervosa and Associated Disorders. 2001. "Facts about Eating Disorders." http://www.anad.org/facts.htm (2001, August 26).

National CASA Association. 2000. "Statistics on Child Abuse and Neglect, Foster Care, Adoption and CASA Programs." http://www.casanet.org/library/abuse/abuse-stats98.htm (2002, January 26).

National Center for Health Statistics. 1993. Morbidity and Mortality Weekly Report 23, 20. Washington, DC: U.S. Government Printing Office.

———. 1996. "Advance Report of Mortality Statistics." Monthly Vital Statistic Report 45, 3 (supplement):63.

———. 2001. "New Series of Reports to Monitor Health of Older Americans." http://www.cdc.gov/nchs/releases/01/olderame.htm (2001, December 4).

National Center for Injury Prevention and Control Division of Violence. 1999. Centers for Disease Control and Prevention, Atlanta, GA. http://www.cdc.gov/ncipc/dvp/datviol.html (March 19).

National Center for Lesbian Rights. 2002. "Fact Sheet: Custody Cases." http://www.nclrights.org/publications/pubs_custody.html (2002, January 31).

National Center for Policy Analysis. 2001. "Single Father Households on the Rise." http://www.ncpa.org/pd/social/pd051801d.html (2001, December 19).

National Center for Prosecution of Child Abuse. 2000. *Child Fatalities Fact Sheet.* Washington, DC: National Clearinghouse on Child Abuse and Neglect Information (June).

National Coalition against Domestic Violence. 1996. (April 22) [online].

———. 1998. "Research & Statistics on Domestic Violence." http://www.healthtouch.com (1999, June 2).

National Council of Jewish Women. 1999. "Myths and Facts about Domestic Violence." http://www.ncjw.org/programs/myths.htm (1999, June 4).

National Family Caregivers Association. 2000. *Caregiver Survey—2000.* Kensington, MD.

National Institute on Alcohol Abuse and Alcoholism. 2000. *10th Special Report to the U.S. Congress on Alcohol and Health.* Bethesda, MD.

National Institute on Drug Abuse. 1994. "Substance Abuse among Women and Parents" (July) [onlinc].

National Institute of Justice. 1997. "Guns in America: National Survey on Private Ownership and Use of Firearms." U.S. Department of Justice, Office of Justice Programs (May).

National Opinion Research Center (NORC). 1992. "The National Health and Social Life Survey." http://www.norc.uchicago.edu/split/fags/sex.htm.

National Organization on Disability. 2001a. "People with Disabilities Unprepared for Terrorist, Other Crises at Home or at Work, New Poll Finds" (December 11). http://www.nod.org/cont/dsp_cont_item_view.cfm?viewTypeitemView&contentld (2002, January 30).

———. 2001b. "Education Levels of People with Disabilities" (July 25). http://www.nod.org/cont/dsp_cont_item_view.cfm?viewType-itemView&contentld (2002, January 30).

———. 2001c. "Employment Rates of People with Disabilities" (July 24). http://www.nod.org/cont/dsp_cont_item_view.cfm?viewType-itemView&contentld (2002, January 30).

National Woman Abuse Action Project. 1991. *Understanding Domestic Violence.* Washington, DC: National Woman Abuse Action Project.

National Women's Health Information Center. 1999. "Substance Use during Pregnancy." http://www.4woman.gov/x/owh/Pub/woc/figure24.html (May 19).

Nature. 1998. "Scientific Correspondence." 36, 5 (November):27–28.

NCHS (National Center for Health Statistics). 2001. "Life Expectancy Hits New High in 2000; Mortality Declines for Several Leading Causes of Death" (news release). Hyattsville, MD: U.S. Department of Health and Human Services, Centers for Disease Control and Prevention.

Neal, A. G., H. T. Groat, and J. W. Wicks. 1989. "Attitudes about Having Children: A Study of 600 Couples in the Early Years of Marriage." *Journal of Marriage and the Family* 59:313–28.

Needle, R. H., S. S. Su, and W. J. Doherty. 1990. "Divorce, Remarriage and Adolescent Substance Use." *Journal of Marriage and the Family* 52:157–70.

Neft, N., and A. D. Levine. 1997. *Where Women Stand: An International Report on the Status of Women in over 140 Countries,* 1997–1998. New York: Random House.

Neher, L. S., and J. L. Short. 1998. "Risk and Protective Factors for Children's Substance Use and Antisocial Behavior Following Parental Divorce." *American Journal of Orthopsychiatry* 68:154–61.

Neikirk, W. 1996. "Clinton Adds Endorsement to Tax Break for Adoption." *Chicago Tribune* (May 7):1.

Nelson, N. 1999. "The Crime of Rape, Statistics." http://www.nancynelson.com/makedif/crime2.htm (2002, January 18).

Nelson, S. 1992. "It's Not Black and White." *Seventeen* 51(January):80–83.

Neugarten, B., and D. Neugarten. 1992. "Age in the Aging Society." In H. Lena, W. Helmreich, and W. McCord, eds., *Contemporary Issues in Society,* 208–19. New York: McGraw-Hill.

Neugarten, B., and K. Weinstein. 1964. "The Changing American Grandparent." *Journal of Marriage and the Family* 26:199–204.

Neumark-Sztainer, and P. J. Hannan. 2000. "Weight-Related Behaviors among Adolescent Girls and Boys." *Archives Pediatrics & Adolescent Medicine* 154:569–77.

Newcomb, P. R. 1979. "Cohabitation in America: An Assessment of Consequences." *Journal of Marriage and the Family* 41:597–602.

Newman, B. S., and P. G. Muzzonigro. 1993. "The Effects of Traditional Family Values on the Coming Out Process of Gay Male Adolescents." *Adolescence* 28,109:213–26.

Newman, D. M. 1995. *Sociology: Exploring the Architecture of Everyday Life.* Thousand Oaks, CA: Pine Forge Press.

Newman, J. 2000. "Dad Has His Day: Fathers' Growing Involvement with the Family Makes Them Increasingly a Media Target." *Ladies Home Journal.*

New Mexico Governor's Task Force on HIV/AIDS. 1999. "Position Statement: HIV Counseling and Testing of Pregnant Women." *Infonet.* http://www.aidsinfonet.org/gatf/gatf-[regmamt-women.html (2001, December 21).

Newport, F. 1996. "Americans Generally Happy with Their Marriages." Gallup Poll Monthly (September):18–22.

———. 1999. "Americans Agree That Being Attractive Is a Plus in American Society." *Gallup News Service, Poll Analyses* (September 15):1-5. http://www.gallup.com/poll/releases/pr990915.asp (2001, September 8).

———. 2001. "Americans See Women as Emotional and Affectionate, Men as More Aggressive." http://www.gallup.com/poll/release/pr010221.asp (2001, July 12).

"New Problems Seen as World's Young and Old Increase Rapidly." 1998. *Chicago Tribune* (September 2):9.

"New Report Explodes Myths on Nonmarital Pregnancy." 1995. *Footnotes* 23, 8 (November):1.

"New Study Finds One in Five Girls Suffer Dating Violence." 2001. Brown University Child and Adolescent Behavior Letter. http://www.findarticles.com/cf_0/m0537/9_17/77841748/print.jhtml (2001, October 24).

"New Survey Shows Attitudes More Open toward Interracial Relationships." 1995. *Jet* 88 (October 2):22.

Nezu, A. M., and C. M. Nezu. 1987. "Psychological Distress, Problem-Solving, and Coping Reactions: Sex Role Differences." *Sex Roles* 16:205–14.

Nicholas, M., and K. Milewski. 1999. "Downloading Love: A Content Analysis of Internet Personal Advertisements Placed by College Students." *College Student Journal.* (March). http://www.findarticles.com/cf_0/mOFCR/1_33/62894065/p1/article.jhtml?term=Research (2001, October 26).

Niebuhr, G. 1996. "An Interfaith-Marriage Vote Has Reform Judaism Divided." *New York Times* (December 14):11.

———. 1998. "Southern Baptists Declare Wife Should 'Submit' to Her Husband." *New York Times* (June 10):A1, A20.

Nielsen, L. 1999. "College Aged Students with Divorced Parents: Facts and Fiction." *College Student Journal* 33, 4 (December):543–72.

———. 2000. "Black Undergraduate and White Undergraduate Eating Disorders and Related Attitudes." *College Student Journal* 34, 3 (September):353–70.

Nock, S. L. 1979. "The Family Life Cycle." *Journal of Marriage and the Family* 41 (February):15–26.

———, and P. W. Kingston. 1990. *The Sociology of Public Issues.* Belmont, CA: Wadsworth.

Nord, C. W., D. Brimhall, and J. West. 1997. *Fathers' Involvement in Their Children's Schools.* Washington, DC: National Center for Education Statistics.

Norment, L. 1994. "Black Men/White Women: What's Behind the Furor?" *Ebony* 50 (November):44–47.

North Carolina Coalition against Domestic Violence. 2002. "A Fact Sheet on Sexual Assault." http://www.nccadv.org/Handouts/Sexual_Assault.htm (2002, January 8).

Norton, A. J., and L. F. Miller. 1992. "Marriage, Divorce, and Remarriage in the 1990's." In U.S. Census Bureau, Current Population Reports, P23–180. Washington, DC: U.S. Government Printing Office.

Nowinski, J. 1980. *Becoming Satisfied: A Man's Guide to Sexual Fulfillment.* Englewood Cliffs, NJ: Prentice Hall.

Nuebeck, K. J., and D. S. Glasberg. 1996. *Sociology: A Critical Approach.* New York: McGraw-Hill.

NWHIC. 2000. "Factors Affecting the Health of Women of Color: Asian Americans." *The National Women's Health Information Center.* Washington, DC: Department of Health and Human Services. http://www.4woman.gov/owh/pub/woc/asian.htm (2002, January 2).

Oakley, A. 1974. *The Sociology of Housework.* New York: Pantheon.

O'Brien, M. 1991. "Taking Sibling Incest Seriously." In M. Q. Patton, ed., *Family Sexual Abuse,* 75–92. Newbury Park, CA: Sage.

Office of Technology Assessment. 1988. *Infertility: Medical and Social Choices.* Washington, DC: U.S. Government Printing Office.

O'Flaherty, K. M., and L. W. Eells. 1988. "Courtship Behavior of the Remarried." *Journal of Marriage and the Family* 50:499–506.

Ogintz, E. 1991. "Goodbye to the Myth of Unmarried Women." *Chicago Tribune* (October 22):sec. 5, 1, 2.

Ogletree, S., S. Williams, P. Raffeld, B. Mason, and K. Fricke. 1990. "Female Attractiveness and Eating Disorders: Do Children's Television Commercials Play a Role?" *Sex Roles* 22, 11/12:791–97.

O'Grady-LeShane, R. 1993. "Changes in the Lives of Women and Their Families: Have Old Age Pensions Kept Pace?" *Generations* 17, 4 (Winter):27–33.

O'Hare, W. P., and J. C. Felt. 1991. "Asian Americans: America's Fastest-Growing Minority Group." *Population Trends and Public Policy* 19 (February). Washington, DC: Population Reference Bureau.

Ohio Department of Health. 1999. "Alcohol and Tobacco Use during Pregnancy." http://www.odh.state.o.../book2/statssmoke.html (1999, May 13).

O'Kelly, C. G., and L. Carney. 1986. Women and Men in Society: *Cross-Cultural Perspectives on Gender Stratification.* Belmont, CA: Wadsworth.

"Older Americans 2000: Key Indicators of Well-Being." 2000. Federal Interagency Forum on Aging-Related Statistics. http://www.agingstats.gov/chartbook2000/OlderAmericans2000.pdf (2002, January 7).

O'Loughlin, T. 2000. "Gap between Rich and Poor Grows" (November 15). http://www.smh.com.au/news/0011/15/pageone/pageone14.html (2001, October 19).

Olson, D. H. 1986. "What Makes Families Work?" In S. VanZandt, *Family Strengths Seven: Vital Connections,* 1–12. Lincoln: University of Nebraska Press.

O'Neil, J. M. 1981. "Patterns of Gender-Role Conflict and Strain: The Fear of Femininity in Men's Lives." *Personnel and Guidance Journal* 60:203–10.

OneWorld. 2002. "Children and War." http://www.oneworld.org/childrights/chwar.htm (2002, February 18).

Oppenheimer, V. K. 1988. "A Theory of Marriage Timing." *Journal of Marriage and the Family* 42:777–92.

———. 1997. "Women's Employment and the Gain to Marriage: The Specialization and Trading Model." *Annual Review of Sociology* 23:431–53.

Oregon Department of Human Services. 2002. *Oregon's Death with Dignity Act, Annual Report,* Table 1. Portland. http://www.Ohd.hr.state.or.us/chs/pas/ar-tbl-1.htm (2002, January 29).

Orenstein, P. 1994. *School Girls: Young Women, Self-Esteem, and the Confidence Gap.* New York: Anchor Press.

Ornish, D. 1998. *Love and Survival, The Scientific Basis for the Healing Power of Intimacy.* New York: HarperCollins.

Oropesa, R. S., D. T. Lichter, and R. N. Anderson. 1994. "Marriage Markets and the Paradox of Mexican American Nuptiality." *Journal of Marriage and the Family* 56 (November):889–907.

Pace, L. 1986. "Interfaith Marriage Barrier Proves Not Insurmountable." *Norwich Bulletin* (February 12).

Packer, A. J. 1997. "Everything Your Kids Want to Know about Sex and Aren't Afraid to Ask." In S. J. Bunting, ed., *Human Sexuality: Annual Editions,* 163–65. Sluice Dock, Guilford, CT: Dushkin/McGraw-Hill.

Page, C. 2001. "2-Parent Homes Are Disappearing." *Chicago Tribune* (June 3):37.

Pagelow, M. D. 1984. *Family Violence.* New York: Praeger.

———. 1988. "Marital Rape." In V. B. Van Hasselt, R. L. Morrison, A. S. Bellack, and M. Hersen, eds., *Handbook of Family Violence,* 207–32. New York: Plenum.

Palmer, M. 1995. "The Re-Emergence of Family Law in Post-Mao China: Marriage, Divorce, and Reproduction." *China Quarterly* (March): 110–34.

Palmore, E. 1980. "The Facts on Aging Quiz: A Review of Findings." *Gerontologist* 20:669–72.

Papalia, D., and S. Olds. 1989. *Human Development.* New York: McGraw-Hill.

Papanek, H. 1973. "Men, Women, and Work: Reflections on the Two-Person Career." *American Journal of Sociology* 78, 4 (January):852–72.

Papernow, P. L. 1993. *Becoming a Stepfamily: Patterns of Development in Remarried Families.* San Francisco: Jossey-Bass.

———. 1998. *Becoming a Stepfamily: Patterns of Development in Remarried Families.* Hillsdale, NJ: Analytic Press.

Parenting. 1999. "Single Mothers as Good as Dads." *Chicago Tribune* (January 17):sec. 13, 3.

Parents Forever. 2001. "Gender Differences in Parenting." The University of Minnesota Extension Service. http://www.extension.umn.edu/parentsforever/unit1/unit1=3a.asp (2001, December 30).

Parker, G. B., E. A. Barrett, and I. B. Hickie. 1992. "From Nurture to Network: Examining Links between Perceptions of Parenting Received in Childhood and Social Bonds in Adulthood." *American Journal of Psychiatry* 149:877–85.

Parker, L. 2002. "Mom's Sanity Focus of Drowning Trial; Texas Woman Faces Death in 5 Kids' Slayings." *USA Today* (January 4).

Parnell, T., and D. Day, eds. 1998. *Munchausen by Proxy Syndrome.* Thousand Oaks, CA: Sage.

Parron, E. M. 1982. "Golden Wedding Couples: Lessons in Marital Longevity." *Generations* 7, 2:14–16.

Parrot, A., and M. J. Ellis. 1985. "Homosexuals Should Be Allowed to Marry and Adopt and Rear Children." In H. Feldman and M. Feldman, eds., *Current Controversies in Marriage and Family.* Beverly Hills, CA: Sage.

Parrot, W. G., and R. H. Smith. 1987. "Differentiating the Experiences of Envy and Jealousy." Paper presented at the annual meeting of the American Psychological Association, New York, August.

Parsons, T. 1955. "The American Family." In T. Parsons and R. Bales, eds., *Family, Socialization and Interaction Process*, 3–34. Glencoe, IL: Free Press.

———. 1964. *The Social System*. New York: Free Press.

Pasley, K., D. C. Dollahite, and M. Ihinger-Tallman. 1993. "Clinical Applications of Research Findings on the Spouse and Stepparent Roles in Remarriage." *Family Relations* 42:315–22.

Pasley, K., and M. Ihinger-Tallman. 1987. "The Evolution of a Field of Investigation: Issues and Concerns." In K. Pasley and M. Ihinger-Tallman, eds., *Remarriage and Stepparenting: Current Research and Theory*, 303–13. New York: Guilford Press.

Patel, P. 2000. "Pakistan: Killing in the Name of Honor." *The Asia Pacific Advocate* (Summer). http://www,apcjp.org/pakistan.htm (2001, May 15).

———. 2001. "Immigrants Bring Gender Bias to U.S." *Chicago Sun-Times* (September 3):7.

Patterson, C. J. 1992. "Children of Lesbian and Gay Parents." *Child Development* 63 (October):1025–42.

Patterson, J., and P. Kim. 1991. *The Day America Told the Truth: What People Really Believe about Everything That Really Matters*. Englewood Cliffs, NJ: Prentice Hall.

Patzer, G. L. 1985. *The Physical Attractiveness Phenomenon*. New York: Plenum.

Paul, A. M. 1998. "Not Married—And Not Interested." *Psychology Today* 31 (March/April):19.

Pauly, B. 1992. "The Number of Happily Never-Marrieds Is on the Rise." *Chicago Tribune* (October 4):sec. 6, 5.

Pear, R. 1996. "Many States Fail to Meet Mandates on Child Welfare." *New York Times* (March 17):A1.

Pearson, J. 1989. *Communication in the Family*. New York: Harper & Row.

Pennsylvania Coalition against Domestic Violence. 2001. "Are You as Outraged as We Are?" Harrisburg. www.pcadv.org. (2002, January 7).

Peplau, L. A. 1981. "What Do Homosexuals Want?" *Psychology Today* (March):28–38.

———. 1986. "What Homosexuals Want." In L. Simkins, ed., *Alternative Sexual Lifestyles*, 118–23. Acton, MA: Copley Publishing Group.

———. 1991. "Lesbian and Gay Relationships." In J. C. Gonsiorek and J. D. Weinrich, eds., *Homosexuality: Research Implications for Public Policy*. Newbury Park, CA: Sage.

———. 1994. "Men and Women in Love." In D. L. Sollie and L. A. Leslie, eds. *Gender, Families, and Close Relationships: Feminist Research Journeys.*" Thousand Oaks, CA: Sage.

———, and S. D. Cochran. 1981. "Value Orientations in the Intimate Relationships of Gay Men." *Journal of Homosexuality* 6:1–29.

Peplau, L. A., and S. L. Gordon. 1983. "The Intimate Relationships of Lesbians and Gay Men." In E. R. Allgeier and N. McCormick, eds., *Changing Boundaries: Gender Roles and Sexual Behavior*, 1–14. Mountain View, CA: Mayfield.

Peres, J. 1996. "Adoptees Say Love, Not Race, Matters." *Chicago Tribune* (May 12):21.

Perkins, H. W., and A. D. Berkowitz. 1991. "Collegiate COAs and Alcohol Abuse: Problem Drinking in Relation to Assessments of Parent and Grandparent Alcoholism." *Journal of Counseling and Development* 69:237–40.

Perkins, K. P. 2000. "Cultural Victims Die in 'Crimes of Honor.'" *Seattle Post-Intelligencer* (February 28). http://seatlep-i.nwsource.com/printer/ (2001, May 15).

Perozynski, L., and L. Kramer. 1999. "Parental Beliefs about Managing Sibling Conflict." *Developmental Psychology* 35:489–99.

Perry, I. 1995. "It's My Thang and I'll Swing It the Way That I Feel." In Gail Dines and Jean Humez, eds., *Gender, Race and Class in Media*, 524–30. Thousand Oaks, CA: Sage.

Perry-Jenkins, M., and A. C. Crouter. 1990. "Men's Provider Role Attitudes: Implications for Household Work and Marital Satisfaction." *Journal of Family Issues* 11:136–56.

Perry-Jenkins, M., and K. Folk. 1994. "Class, Couples, and Conflict: Effects of the Division of Labor on Assessments of Marriage in Dual-Earner Families." *Journal of Marriage and the Family* 56 (February):165–80.

Pert, C. 1997. *Molecules of Emotion, Why You Feel the Way You Do*. New York: Scribner's.

Peter Hart Research Associates. 1999. "Americans' Attitudes on Children's Access to Guns: A National Poll for Common Sense about Kids and Guns" (June 16).

Petersen, J., A. Kretchner, B. Nellis, J. Lever, and R. Hertz. 1983. "The Playboy Reader's Sex Survey, Parts I and II." *Playboy* (February/March):108, 241–50.

Peterson, C., and J. Peterson. 1988. "Old Men's and Women's Relationships with Adult Kin: How Equitable Are They?" *International Journal of Aging and Human Development* 27, 3:221–31.

Peterson, J. L., and N. Zill. 1986. "Marital Disruption, Parent-Child Relationships, and Behavior Problems in Children." *Journal of Marriage and the Family* 48:295–307.

Peterson, K. 2000. "Younger Kids Trying It Now, Often Ignorant of Disease Risks." *USA Today* (November 16). http://pqasb.pqarchiver.com/USAToday/main/doc (2001, November 29).

———. 1997. "Teen-age Dating Shows Racial Barriers Falling" (November 3). http://www.detnews.com...n/9711/03/11030094.html (March 5).

———. 2001. "College Women Can't Find Mr. Right." *Chicago Sun-Times* (July 27):1, 2.

Peterson, R. D., D. F. Wunder, and H. L. Mueller. 1999. *Social Problems: Globalization in the Twenty-First Century*. Upper Saddle River, NJ: Prentice Hall.

Peterson, R. R. 1996. "A Re-Evaluation of the Economic Consequences of Divorce." *American Sociological Review* 61:528–36.

Pettigrew, T. F. 1985. "New Black-White Patterns: How Best to Conceptualize Them." In R. H. Turner and J. F. Short, eds., *Annual Review of Sociology* 2:329–46. Palo Alto, CA: Annual Reviews.

Pezzin, L. E., and B. S. Schone. 1999. "Parental Marital Disruption and Intergenerational Transfers: An Analysis of Lone Elderly Parents and Their Children." *Demography* 36, 3 (August):287–97.

Phillips, R. 1988. *Putting Asunder: A History of Divorce in Western Society*. Cambridge, MA: Cambridge University Press.

Pike, R. 1999. "Multiple Births Add Up." ABCNews Health and Living. http://more.abcnews.go.com/sections/living/septuplets_numbers/index.html (May 6).

Pill, C. J. 1990. "Stepfamilies: Redefining the Family." *Family Relations* 39:186–93.

Pillemer, K. A., and David Finkelhor. 1988. "The Prevalence of Elder Abuse: A Random-Sample Survey." *Gerontologist* 28, 1:51–57.

Pines, A., and E. Aronson. 1983. "Antecedents, Correlates, Consequences of Secret Jealousy." *Journal of Personality* 51:108–9.

Pipher, M. 1994. *Reviving Ophelia: Saving the Selves of Adolescent Girls*. New York: Ballantine.

Pitcher, B. L., and D. C. Larson. 1989. "Early Widowhood." In S. J. Bahr and E. T. Peterson, eds., *Aging and the Family*, 59–81. Lexington, MA: Lexington Books.

Pitts, L. 2001. "Deadbeat Dad's Punishment Is Troubling." *Chicago Tribune* (July 17):17.

Pitzer, R. 1992. "Research on Father Involvement." Specialist Research Report. Minnesota Extension Service. St. Paul: Minnesota Children, Youth and Families Consortium Electronic Clearinghouse (March).

Pizzey, E. 1974. *Scream Quietly or the Neighbors Will Hear*. Harmondsworth, England: Penguin.

Pleck, E. 1989. "Criminal Approaches to Family Violence." In L. Ohlin and M. Tonry, eds., *Family Violence*, 19–58. Chicago: University of Chicago Press.

Pleck, J. H. 1988. "Fathers and Infant Care Leave." In E. F. Zigler and M. Franks, eds., *The Parental Leave Crisis*, 177–94. New Haven, CT: Yale University Press.

Pollack, W.S. 1998. *Real Boys: Rescuing Our Sons from the Myths of Boyhood.* New York: Random House.

Pollard, K., and W. O'Hare. 1999. "America's Racial and Ethnic Minorities." *Population Bulletin*, 54, 3 (September):50.

Polling Report. 2001. "Race and Ethnicity." http://www.pollingreport.com/race.htm (2002, February 3).

———. 2002. "War on Terrorism." http://www.pollingreport.com/terror.htm (2002, February 3).

Pomerleau, A., D. Bolduc, G. Makuit, and L. Cossette. 1990. "Pink or Blue: Environmental Stereotypes in the First Two Years of Life." *Sex Roles* 22, 5/6:359–67.

Pomeroy, S. 1975. *Goddesses, Whores, Wives, and Slaves: Women in Classical Antiquity.* New York: Schocken.

Ponzetti, J., Jr., and R. M. Cate. 1986. "The Development Course of Conflict in the Marital Dissolution Process." *Journal of Divorce* 10:1–15.

Popenoe, D. 1999. "Parental Androgyny." In C. Albers, ed., *Sociology of Families: Readings*, 187–94. Thousand Oaks, CA: Pine Forge.

Post, T. 1993. "A Pattern of Rape." *Newsweek* (January 4):32–36.

"Postnatal Depression." 2001. http://health.iafrica.com/psychonline/articles/postnatal.htm (2001, December 21).

Potok, M. 1995. "Out-of-Wedlock Childbirth Rising." *USA Today* (November 8):2.

Pound, P., C. Sabin, and S. Ebrahim. 1999. "Observing the Process of Care: A Stroke Unit, Elderly Care Unit and General Medical Ward Compared." *Age and Ageing* 28, 5 (September):433–40.

Poussaint, A. F., and J. P. Comer. 1993. *Raising Black Children.* New York: Plume.

Powers, E. 1966. *Crime and Punishment in Early Massachusetts, 1620–1692: A Documentary History.* Boston: Beacon Press.

Pregnancy Discrimination Charges. 2001. U.S. Equal Opportunity Commission. www/eepc/gpv/stats/pregnanc.html (2001, October 26).

President's Council on Physical Fitness and Sports. 1997. *Physical Activity and Sport in the Lives of Girls.* Minneapolis: Center for Research on Girls and Women in Sport, University of Minnesota.

Pressley, S. 2001. "S.C. Verdict Fuels Debate Over Rights of the Unborn: Jury Finds Mother Guilty of Homicide in Stillbirth." *Washington Post* (May 27):A03.

Price-Bonham, S., and J. O. Balswick. 1980. "The Noninstitutions: Divorce, Desertion, and Remarriage." *Journal of Marriage and the Family* 42, 4:959–72.

"Probe Interracial Dating Policy at Bible College." 1987. *Jet* 71 (February 23):21.

Pruett, M. K., and K. Hoganbruen. 1998. "Joint Custody and Shared Parenting: Research and Interventions." *Child Adolescent Psychiatric Clinic North America* 7:273–94.

Public Agenda. 2002. "Terrorism. Overview: The Issue at a Glance." http://www.publicagenda.org/specials/terrorism/terror_overview.htm (2002, February 3).

Public Opinion Polls on Same-Sex Marriages. 2001. http://www.religioustolerance.org/hom_marp.html (2001, November 8).

Punke, H. H. 1940. "Marriage Rate among Women Teachers." *American Sociological Review* 5, 4:505–11.

Purcell, P., and L. Stewart. 1990. "Dick and Jane in 1989." *Sex Roles* 22:177–85.

Pyke, K. D. 1994. "Women's Employment as Gift or Burden?" *Gender and Society* 8:73–91.

Queen, S. A., R. W. Habenstein, and J. S. Quadagno. 1985. *The Family in Various Cultures.* New York: Harper & Row.

RAINN Statistics. 2002. http://www.rainn.org/statistics.html (2002, January 20).

Ramsey, S. 1995. "Stepparents and the Law: a Nebulous Status and a Need for Reform." In K. Pasley and M. Ihinger-Tallman, eds., *Stepparenting: Issues in Theory, Research, and Practice*, 217–37. Westport, CT: Praeger.

Ramu, G. N. 1989. "Patterns of Mate Selection." In K. Ishwaran, ed., *Family and Marriage: Cross-Cultural Perspectives*, 165–78. Toronto: Wall and Thompson.

RAND Corporation. 2001. "Guns in the Family: Firearm Storage Patterns in U.S. Homes with Children" (March). http://www.rand.org/publications/RB/RB4535/.

Rank, M. R. 1989. "Fertility among Women on Welfare: Incidence and Determinants." *American Sociological Review* 54:296–304.

Rape Statistics. 1999. http://www.cs.utk.edu/~bartley/sa/stats.html (1999, March 19).

Rasmussen, P. K., and K. J. Ferraro. 1991. "The Divorce Process." In J. N. Edwards and D. H. Demo, eds., *Marriage and Family in Transition*, 376–88. Boston: Allyn & Bacon.

Rathus, S. A., J. S. Nevid, and L. Fichner-Rathus. 1997. *Human Sexuality in a World of Diversity*, 3d ed. Boston: Allyn & Bacon.

Ravo, N. 1991. "Forget the Dress, the Flowers, Mendelssohn. Just Run Away." *New York Times* (October 2):C1.

Rawlings, S. 1978. "Perspectives on American Husbands and Wives." *Current Population Reports*, Series P–23, no. 77. Washington, DC: U.S. Census Bureau.

Rawlins, W. K. 1993. "Communication in Cross-Sex Friendships." In L. Arliss and D. Borisoff, eds., *Women and Men Communicating.* Fort Worth, TX: Harcourt Brace Jovanovich.

Ray, O., and C. Ksir. 1999. *Drugs, Society and Human Behavior*, 8th ed. Boston: WCB/McGraw-Hill.

Raymond, J. 2001. "The Ex-Files." *American Demographics* 23, 2 (February):60–64.

"Real People." 1996. NBC (April 25).

Real, T. 1997. *I Don't Want to Talk about It.* New York: Scribner's.

Reardon, P. T. 1992. "More Dads Trying Single-Parenting." *Chicago Tribune* (August 9):1, 8.

Red Horse, J. 1980. "Family Structure and Value Orientation in American Indians." *Social Casework* 61(8):462–67.

Reeve, C. 1991. "Corporate Wives." *Chicago Tribune* (March 17):sec. 6, 1, 7.

Reid, G.M. 1994. "Maternal Stereotyping of Newborns." *Psychological Reports* 75:1443–50.

Reik, T. A. 1946. *A Psychologist Looks at Love.* New York: Lancer.

Reingold, J. 2000. "Executive Pay." *Business Week.* http://www.businessweek.com:/2000/00_16/b3677014.htm?scriptFramed (2001, October 24).

Reinisch, J. M. 1990. *The Kinsey Institute New Report on Sex.* New York: St. Martin's Press.

Reisman, J. 1998. "Images of Children, Crime and Violence in Playboy, Penthouse, and Hustler." Abstract of final report for OJJDP Grant 84–JN–AX–K007. http://www.iglou.com/first-principles/abstract.html (2001, January 27).

Reisman, J. M. 1990. "Intimacy in Same-Sex Friendships." *Sex Roles* 23:65–82.

Reiss, I. L. 1960. "Toward a Sociology of Heterosexual Love Relationship." *Marriage and Family Living* 22, 2 (May):139–45.

———. 1971. *The Family System in America.* New York: Holt, Rinehart & Winston.

———. 1980. *Family Systems in America*, 3d ed. New York: Holt, Rinehart & Winston.

"Remarriage Can Strain Family Ties." 1998. *Chicago Tribune* (July 12):sec. 13, 3.

Remez, L. 2000. "Oral Sex among Adolescents: Is It Sex or Is It Abstinence?" *Family Planning Perspectives* 32 (November/December):6.

Rempel, J., and J. Holmes. 1986. "How Do I Love Thee?" *Psychology Today* (February):30–31.

Renzetti, C. M., and D. J. Curran. 1992. *Women, Men, and Society: The Sociology of Gender,* 2d ed. Boston: Allyn & Bacon.

———. 1995. *Women, Men, and Society,* 3d ed. Boston: Allyn & Bacon.

———. 1999. *Women, Men, and Society,* 4th ed. Boston: Allyn & Bacon.

Report from the Urban Institute. 1999. "A General Profile of the Welfare Population." http://www.doleta.gov/ohrw2w/recruit/urban.html (February 2).

Reskin, B. F., and I. Padavic. 1994. *Women and Men at Work.* Thousand Oaks, CA: Pine Forge Press.

Rheingold, H. L., and K. V. Cook. 1975. "The Content of Boys' and Girls' Rooms as an Index of Parents' Behavior." *Child Development* 46:459–63.

Rich, A. 1980. "Compulsory Heterosexuality and Lesbian Existence." *Signs* 5:631–60.

Richardson, J. P., and A. Lazar. 1995. "Sexuality in the Nursing Home Patient." *American Family Physician* 51 (January):121–24.

Richmond-Abbott, M. 1983. *Masculine and Feminine.* New York: Random House.

Riessman, C. K. 1990. *Divorce Talk: Women and Men Make Sense of Personal Relationships.* New Brunswick, NJ: Rutgers University Press.

Riley, G. 1987. *Investing the American Woman: A Perspective on Women's History.* Arlington Heights, IL: Harlan Davidson.

———. 1991. *Divorce: An American Tradition.* New York: Oxford University Press.

Rimer, S. 1998. "Rural Elderly Create Vital Communities as Young Leave Void." *New York Times* (February 1):A18.

Ritter, J. 2001a. "AIDS 20 Years Later: Hope, but No Cure." *Chicago Sun-Times* (June 1):6–7.

———. 2001b. "AIDS Experts Say U.S. Ignores Africa." *Chicago Sun-Times* (February 5):8.

Roach, M. 2001. "New Challenges Ahead as Gay Population Ages." *Chicago Tribune* (October 24):7.

Robbins, R. H. 1993. *Cultural Anthropology: A Problem-Based Approach.* Itasca, IL: Peacock.

Roberto, K. A., 1990. "Grandparent and Grandchild Relationships." In T. H. Brubaker, ed., *Family Relationships in Later Life,* 100–12. Newbury Park, CA: Sage.

Roberts, K. A., and J. Stroes. 1992. "Grandchildren and Grandparents: Roles, Influences, and Relationships." *Journal of Aging and Human Development* 34:227–39.

Roberts, S. 1994. "Black Women Graduates Outpace Male Counterparts." *New York Times* (October 31):A8.

Roberts, W. L. 1979/1980. "Significant Elements in the Relationship of Long-Married Couples." *International Journal of Aging and Human Development* 10:265–72.

Robertson, J., and L. F. Fitzgerald. 1990. "The (Mis)treatment of Men: Effects of Client Gender Role and Life-Style on Diagnosis and Attribution of Pathology." *Journal of Counseling Psychology* 37:3–9.

Robinson, I., K. Ziss, B. Ganza, and S. Katz. 1991. "Twenty Years of the Sexual Revolution, 1965–1985: An Update." *Journal of Marriage and the Family* 53 (February):216–20.

Robinson, J. P. 1977. *How Americans Use Time.* New York: Praeger.

———, and G. Bodbey. 1997. *Time for Life: The Surprising Ways Americans Use Their Time.* University Park: Pennsylvania State University Press.

Robinson, L. G., and P. W. Blanton. 1993. "Marital Strengths in Enduring Marriages." *Family Relations* 42:38–45.

Robson, P. 1994. *Forbidden Drugs: Understanding Drugs and Why People Take Them.* New York: Oxford University Press.

Rochlin, M. 1992. "The Heterosexual Questionnaire." In M. Kimmel and M. A. Messner, *Men's Lives,* 2d ed., 482–83. New York: Macmillan.

Rodgers, W. L., and A. Thornton. 1985. "Changing Patterns of First Marriage in the United States." *Demography* 22:265–79.

Rogers, S. J., and P. R. Amato. 2000. "Have Changes in Gender Relations Affected Marital Quality?" *Social Forces* 79, 2:731–53.

Rollins, J. 1986. "Single Men and Women: Differences and Similarities." *Family Perspectives* 20:117–25.

Roosa, M. W., J. Tein, N. Croppenbacher, N. Michaels, and L. Dumea. 1993. "Mother's Parenting Behavior and Child Mental Health in Families with a Problem-Drinking Parent." *Journal of Marriage and the Family* 55:107–18.

Roper Organization. 1990. *The Virginia Slims Opinion Poll: A 20-Year Perspective of Women's Issues.* Storrs: University of Connecticut.

Rosenblatt, P., Karis, T., and Powell, R. 1995. *Multiracial Couples.* Thousand Oaks, CA: Sage.

Rosenblum, K. E., and T. C. Travis. 1996. *The Meaning of Difference.* New York: McGraw-Hill.

Rosenfeld, M. 1998. "Little Boys Blue: Reexamining the Plight of Young Males." *Washington Post* (March 26):A1.

Rosenthal, C. J. 1986. "Family Supports in Later Life: Does Ethnicity Make a Difference?" *Gerontologist* 26:19–24.

Rosier, K. B., and L. S. Feld. 2000. "Covenant Marriage: A New Alternative for Traditional Families." *Journal of Comparative Family Studies* 31, 3 (Summer):385–94.

Ross, C. E., J. Mirowsky, and J. Huber. 1983. "Dividing Work, Sharing Work and In Between: Marriage Patterns and Depression." *American Sociological Review* 48:809–23.

Ross, E. 2001. "British Put Limits on Embryo Transfers." *Chicago Tribune* (August 15):sec. 8, 5.

Ross, L. E., and A. C. Davis. 1996. "Black-White College Student Attitudes and Expectations in Paying for Dates." *Sex Roles: A Journal of Research* (July) 35, 1–2:43–56.

Rossi, P. H. 1989. *Down and Out in America.* Chicago: University of Chicago Press.

Rothman, B. K. 1989. *Recreating Motherhood: Ideology and Technology in a Patriarchal Society.* New York: W. W. Norton.

Ruane, J. M., and K. A. Cerulo. 1997. *Second Thoughts: Seeing Conventional Wisdom through the Sociological Eye.* Thousand Oaks, CA: Pine Forge Press.

Rubin, B. 2000. "More Dads Are Earning the Title of Father." *Chicago Tribune* (June18):1, 8.

———. 2001. "The Thirty-Year Itch." *Chicago Tribune Magazine* (April 15): 4–20, 32.

Rubin, B. M., and J. Anderson. 1997. "What Is an Exec's Wife Worth? Plenty, If You Ask Court." *Chicago Tribune* (December 14):sec. 4, 1.

Rubin, J. Z., F. J. Provenzano, and Z. Luria. 1974. "The Eye of the Beholder: Parents' Views on Sex of Newborns." *American Journal of Orthopsychiatry* 44:512–19.

Rubin, L. B. 1985. *Just Friends: The Role of Friendship in Our Lives.* New York: Harper & Row.

———. 1990. *Erotic Wars: What Happened to the Sexual Revolution?* New York: HarperCollins.

———. 1994. *Families on the Fault Line: America's Working Class Speaks about the Family, the Economy, Race, and Ethnicity.* New York: HarperCollins.

Rubin, Z. 1973. *Liking and Loving: An Invitation to Social Psychology.* New York: Holt, Rinehart & Winston.

———. 1974. "Lovers and Other Strangers: The Development of Intimacy in Encounters and Relationships." *American Scientist* 62:182–90.

Rubin, Z., L. A. Peplau, and C. T. Hill. 1981. "Loving and Learning: Sex Differences in Romantic Attachments. *Sex Roles* 7:821–35.

Rubinstein, R. L. 1986. *Singular Paths: Old Men Living Alone.* New York: Columbia University Press.

———, B. B. Alexander, M. Goodman, and M. Luborsky. 1991. "Key Relationships of Never-Married Childless Older Women: A Cultural Analysis." *Journal of Gerontology* 46, 5 (September):270–77.

Ruggles, S. 1994. "The Origins of African-American Family Structure." *American Sociological Review* 59:136–51.

Rusbult, C. E. 1983. "A Longitudinal Test of the Investment Model: The Development (and Deterioration) of Satisfaction and Commitment in Heterosexual Involvements." *Journal of Personality and Social Psychology* 45:101–17.

Russel, D., and N. VandeVen. 1976. *International Crimes against Women.* Conference publication. Proceedings les Femmes.

Russell, C. 1995. "Why Teen Births Boom." *American Demographics* (September):8.

Russell, D. 1982. *Rape in Marriage.* New York: Macmillan.

———. 1990. *Rape in Marriage,* 2d ed. Bloomington: Indiana University Press.

Saad, L. 2001. "Majority Considers Sex before Marriage Morally Okay." *Gallup News Service* (May 24). http://www.gallup.com/poll/releases/pr010524.asp (2000, July 24).

Sack, K. 2001. "Epidemic Takes Toll on Black Women." *New York Times* (July 3):A1, A12.

Sadker, M., and D. Sadker. 1994. *Failing at Fairness: How America's Schools Cheat Girls.* New York: Scribner's.

Saenz, R., W. J. Goudy, and L. Frederick. 1989. "The Effects of Employment and Marital Relations on Depression among Mexican American Women." *Journal of Marriage and the Family* 51:239–51.

Safire, W. 1995. "News about Jews." *New York Times* (July 17).

Sakurai, J. 2001. "Train Violence Shocks Japan." *Chicago Sun-Times* (October 22):26.

Saline, C. 1984. "Bleeding in the Suburbs." *Philadelphia* magazine (August): 81–85, 144–51.

Salovey, P., and J. Rodin. 1989. "Envy and Jealousy in Close Relationships." In C. Hendrick, ed., *Close Relationships,* 221–46. Newbury Park, CA: Sage.

Saluter, A. F. 1994. "Marital Status and Living Arrangements: March 1993." U.S. Census Bureau, Current Population Reports, Series P20–478. Washington, DC: U.S. Government Printing Office.

Saltzman, A. 1999. "From Diapers to High Heels." *U.S. News & World Report.* (July 26):57–58.

Salzman, J. 1996. "Why Ordinary Americans Like Daytime Talk Shows." *USA Today* (November):63.

Sanders, G. F., and R. L. Mullis. 1988. "Family Influences on Sexual Attitudes and Knowledge as Reported by College Students." *Adolescence* 92 (Winter):837–46.

Sanders, G. F., and D. W. Trygstad. 1989. "Stepgrandparents and Grandparents: The View from Young Adults." *Family Relations* 38:71–75.

Sandnabba, N. K., and C. Ahlberg. 1999. "Parents' Attitudes and Expectations about Children's Cross-Gender Behavior." *Sex Roles* 40, 3/4 (February):249–64.

Sandroff, R. 1989. "Why Pro-Family Policies Are Good for Business and America." *Working Women* (November):126.

Santrock, J . W., and K. A. Sitterle. 1987. "Parent-Child Relationships in Stepmother Families." In K. Pasley and M. Ihinger-Tallman, eds., *Remarriage and Stepparenting: Current Research and Theory,* 273–299. New York: Guilford Press.

Sapiro, V. 1986. *Women in American Society.* Mountain View, CA: Mayfield.

———. 1990. *Women in American Society,* 2d ed. Mountain View, CA: Mayfield.

———. 1999. *Women in American Society: An Introduction to Women's Studies,* 4th ed. Mountain View, CA: Mayfield.

Sarler, C. 2000. "Divorce Your Husband and Watch Him Get Rich." *New Statesman* 129 (October 30):8–9.

St. Jean, Y., and Feagin, J. 1998. *Double Burden: Black Women and Everyday Racism.* New York: M. E. Sharpe.

Saunders, D. G. 1988. "What Do You Know about Abuser Recidivism? A Critique of Recidivism in Abuser Programs." *Victimology: An International Journal.*

Scanzoni, J. 1980. "Contemporary Marriage Types." *Journal of Family Issues* 1:125–40.

Schemo, D. J. 1996. "Adoptions in Paraguay: Mothers Cry Theft." *New York Times* (March 19):A1.

———. 2001a. "Virginity Pledges by Teenagers Can Be Highly Effective, Federal Study Finds." *New York Times* (January 4). http://www.nytimes.qpass.com/qpass-archives (2001, December 4).

———. 2001b. "Word for Word/Saving Themselves: What Teenagers Talk about When They Talk about Chastity." *New York Times* (January 28). http://www.nytimes.qpass.com/qpass-archives (2001, December 4).

Schenck-Yglesias, C. G. 1995. "A Frail Mom Is a Full-Time Job." *American Demographics* (September):14–15.

Schmeeckle, M., R. Giarrusso, and V. L. Bengtson. 1994. "Siblings: The Role of a Lifetime." Paper presented at the annual meeting of the Gerontological Society of America, Atlanta, GA.

Schmetzer, U. 1992. "Puritan China Faces Gay Question." *Chicago Tribune* (September 27):sec. 1.

———. 1999a. "In Bangladesh, Acid Ruins Women's Faces and Their Dreams." *Chicago Tribune* (January 31):15.

———. 1999b. "Thinking Small." *Chicago Tribune* (February 3):6.

Schneir, M., ed. 1972. *Feminism: The Essential Historical Writing,* 104–5. New York: Vintage Books/Random House.

Schoen, R., and R. M. Weinick. 1993. "Partner Choice in Marriages and Cohabitation." *Journal of Marriage and the Family* 55:408–14.

Schoen, C., K. Davis, K. Collins, L. Greenberg, C. DesRoches and M. Abrams. 1997. "The Commonwealth Fund Survey of the Health of Adolescent Girls." http://www.cmwf.org/programs/women/adoleshl.asp (2002, January 19).

Schoen, C., K. Davis, C. DesRoches, and A. Shekhdar. 1997. "The Health of Adolescent Boys: Commonwealth Fund Survey Findings. http://www.cmwf.org/programs/women/boysv27.asp (2002, January 19).

Schuckit, M. A., and T. L. Smith. 2001. "Correlates of Unpredicted Outcomes in Sons of Alcoholics and Controls." *Journal of Studies on Alcohol* 62, 4 (July):477–85.

Schuman, H., and C. Steeh. 1992. "Young White Adults: Did Racial Attitudes Change in the 1980s?" *American Journal of Sociology* 98 (September):340–67.

Schumm, W. R. 1986. "Marital Quality over the Marital Career: Alternative Explanations." *Journal of Marriage and the Family* 48:165–68.

Schvaneveldt, P. L., M. H. Young, and J. D. Schvaneveldt. 2001. "Dual-Resident Marriages in Thailand: A Comparison of Two Cultural Groups of Women." *Journal of Comparative Family Studies* 32, 3 (Summer):347–60.

Schwartz, F. N. 1989. "Management Women and the New Facts of Life." *Harvard Business Review* (January/February):65–76.

Schwartz, M. A. 1976. "Career Strategies of the Never-Married." Paper presented at the 71st annual meeting of the American Sociological Association, New York, August.

———, and P. Wolf. 1976. "Singlehood and the American Experience: Prospectives for a Changing Status." *Humboldt Journal of Social Relations* 4, 1 (Fall/Winter):17–24.

Schwartz, P. 1999. "Peer Marriage: What Does It Take to Create a Truly Egalitarian Relationship?" In A. S. Skolnick and J. H. Skolnick, *Family in Transition,* 154–63. New York: Addison Wesley Longman.

———, and V. Rutter. 1998. *The Gender of Sexuality.* Thousand Oaks, CA: Pine Forge Press.

Sciara, F. J. 1975. "Effects of Fathers' Absence on the Educational Achievement of Urban Black Children." *Child Study Journal* 5:45–55.

Scott, B. M. 1988. "The Making of a Middle-Class Black Woman: A Socialization for Success." Ph.D. diss., Northwestern University, Evanston, IL.

———. 1991. Unpublished interviews with African American women.

———, and M. A. Schwartz. 2000. *Sociology: Making Sense of the Social World.* Boston: Allyn & Bacon.

Scott, D., and B. Wishy, eds., 1982. *America's Families: A Documentary History.* New York: Harper & Row.

Scott, J. 1980. "Black Polygamous Family Formulation." *Alternative Lifestyles* 3:41–64.

Scott, J. P. 1990. "Sibling Interaction in Later Life." In T. H. Brubaker, ed., *Family Relationships in Later Life,* 86–99. Newbury Park, CA: Sage.

Scott, J. 1994. "Social and Cultural Issues Related to Violence." *Vital Signs* 10, 2 (April/May/June):8.

Seager, J. 1997. *The State of Women in the World Atlas,* 2d ed. London: Penguin Reference.

Sears, H. A., and N. L. Galambos. 1992. "Women's Work Condition and Marital Adjustment in Two-Career Couples: A Structural Model." *Journal of Marriage and the Family* 54:789–97.

Seccombe, K., and M. Ishir-Kuntz. 1994. "Gender and Social Relationships among the Never-Married." *Sex Roles* 30, 7/8:585–603.

Seff, M. A. 1995. "Cohabitation and the Law." *Marriage and Family Review* 21, 3/4:141–65.

Segura, D. A. 1994. "Working at Motherhood: Chicana and Mexicana Immigrant Mothers and Employment," In Evelyn Nakano Glenn, Grace Chang, and Linda Rennie Forcey, eds., *Mothering: Ideology, Experience, and Agency.* New York: Routledge.

———, and J. L. Pierce. 1993. "Chicana/o Family Structure and Gender Personality: Chodorow, Familism and Psychoanalytic Sociology Revisited." *Sign* 19:62–91.

Seidman, S. 1992. *Embattled Eros.* New York: Routledge, Chapman and Hall.

Seilhamer, R. A., T. Jacob, and N. J. Dunn. 1993. "The Impact of Alcohol Consumption on Parent-Child Relationships in Families of Alcoholics." *Journal of Studies of Alcohol* 54, 2:189–98.

Seltzer, J. 1998. "Father by Law: Effects of Joint Legal Custody on Nonresident Fathers' Involvement with Children." *Demography* 35:135–46.

———. 2000. "Families Formed Outside of Marriage." *Journal of Marriage and the Family* 62, 4:1247–69.

———, and I. Garfinkel. 1990. "Inequality in Divorce Settlements: An Investigation of Property Settlements and Child Support Awards." *Social Science Research* 19:82–111.

Senna, J., and L. Siegel. 1999. *Introduction to Criminal Justice.* Belmont, CA: West/Wadsworth.

Shah, A. 2001. "Global Issues: Racism" (July 20). http://www.globalissues.org/HumanRights/Racism.asp (2002, February 1).

Shanas, E. 1979. "The Family as a Social Support System in Old Age." *Gerontologist* 19:169–74.

———. 1980. "Older People and Their Families: The New Pioneers." *Journal of Marriage and the Family* 42, l:9–15.

Shane, B. 1997. "Family Planning Saves Lives, Prevents Abortion." *Population Today* 25, 3 (March):1–2.

Shapiro, J. 1993. *No Pity: People with Disabilities Forging a New Civil Rights Movement.* New York: Time Books.

Shapiro, J. L. 1987. "The Expectant Father." *Psychology Today* (January): 36–9, 42.

Shapiro, J. P. 1997. "The Un-Nursing Home." *U. S. News & World Report* (June 2):72.

Sharma, A. R., M. K. McGue, and P. I. Benson. 1996. "The Emotional and Behavioral Adjustment of United States Adopted Adolescents: Part I. An Overview." *Children & Youth Services Review* 18:83–100.

Shaver, P., and C. Hazan. 1988. "A Biased Overview of the Study of Love." *Journal of Social and Personal Relationships* 5:473–501.

———, and D. Bradshaw. 1988. "Love as Attachment: The Integration of Three Behavioral Systems." In R. J. Sternberg and M. L. Barnes, eds., *The Psychology of Love,* 68–99. New Haven, CT: Yale University Press.

Sheehy, S. 2000. *Connecting the Enduring Power of Female Friendship.* New York: HarperCollins.

Shehan, C. L., E. W. Bock, and G. R. Lee. 1990. "Religious Heterogamy, Religiosity, and Marital Happiness: The Case of Catholicism." *Journal of Marriage and the Family* 52:73–79.

Shelton, B. A., and D. John. 1990. "The Division of Household Labor: A Comparison of Cohabiting and Married Couples." Paper presented at the 85th annual meeting of the American Sociological Association, Washington, DC, August.

———. 1993. "Does Marital Status Make a Difference? Housework among Married and Cohabiting Men and Women." *Journal of Family Issues* 14:401–20.

Shenon, P. 1994. "Wanted: A Wife." *Chicago Tribune* (September 11):sec. 6, 5.

Shettel-Neuber, J., J. Bryson, and I. E. Young. 1978. "Physical Attractiveness of the 'Other' Person." *Personality and Social Psychology Bulletin* 4:612–15.

Shinn, M. 1978. "Father Absence and Children's Cognitive Development." *Psychological Bulletin* 85:295–324.

Shneidman, E. 1980. *Voices of Death.* New York: Harper & Row.

Shoop, R. J., and D. L. Edwards. 1994. *How to Stop Sexual Harassment in Our Schools.* Boston: Allyn & Bacon.

Shope, D. F. 1975. *Interpersonal Sexuality.* Philadelphia: Saunders.

Shostak, A. 1987. "Singlehood." In M. Sussman and S. Steinmetz, eds., *Handbook of Marriage and the Family,* 355–66. New York: Plenum.

Shucksmith, J. L., B. Hendry, and A. Glendinning. 1995. "Models of Parenting: Implications for Adolescent Well-Being within Different Types of Family Contexts." *Journal of Adolescence* 18:253–70.

Sigler, R. T. 1989. *Domestic Violence in Context.* Lexington, MA: D. C. Heath.

Signorielli, N. 1997. *A Content Analysis: Reflections of Girls in the Media.* Menlo Park, CA: Children Now and the Kaiser Family Foundation.

———, and A. Bacue. 1999. "Recognition and Respect: A Content Analysis of Prime-Time Television Characters across Three Decades." *Sex Roles* 40, 7/8 (April):527–45.

Silverman, P. 1988. "Research as a Process: Exploring the Meaning of Widowhood." In S. Reinharz and G. Rowles, eds., *Qualitative Gerontology,* 217–40. New York: Springer.

———. 2000. *Never Too Young to Know: Death in Children's Lives.* New York: Oxford University Press.

Silverstein, M., and L. J. Waite. 1993. "Are Blacks More Likely Than Whites to Receive and Provide Social Support in Middle and Old Age? Yes, No, and Maybe So." *Journal of Gerontology: Social Sciences* 48:S212–22.

Simenauer, J., and D. Carroll. 1982. *Singles: The New Americans.* New York: Simon & Schuster.

Simmons, W. 2000. "When It Comes to Having Children, Americans Still Prefer Boys." *Gallup News Service* (December 26).

Simon, B. L. 1987. *Never-Married Women.* Philadelphia: Temple University Press.

Simpson, B. 1994. "Bringing the Unclear Family into Focus: Divorce and Remarriage in Contemporary Britain." *Man* 29 (December):831–51.

Simpson, V. 1991. "Europe's Liberal Laws Debated." *Milwaukee Journal* (May 12):J3.

Sims, S. 1989. "Violent." *Chicago Tribune* (June 11):sec. 6, 1, 6.

Sivard, R. L. 1991. *World Military and Social Expenditures: 1991.* Washington, DC: World Priorities.

Skipper, J. K., Jr., and G. Nass. 1966. “Dating Behavior: A Framework for Analysis and an Illustration.” *Journal of Marriage and the Family* 28:412–20.

Skolnick, A. S., and J. H. Skolnick, eds. 1987. *The Family in Transition*, 6th ed. Glenview, IL: Scott, Foresman.

———. 1999. *Family in Transition*, 10th ed. New York: Longman.

Skolnick, A.S., and S. Rosencrantz. 1994. “The New Crusade for the Old Family.” *The American Prospect* (Summer):59–65.

Slovan, M. 1997. “Some Go to Great Lengths to Avoid Having a Baby Girl.” *Chicago Tribune* (August 3):sec. 13, 1.

Smallwood, D. 1995. “Domestic Violence: How to Get Help.” *N'DIGO* 86 (June 15–28):6–9.

Smith, A. D., and W. J. Reid. 1986. *Role-Sharing Marriage*. New York: Columbia University Press.

Smith, C. 2001. “Quandary in U.S. over Use of Organs of Chinese Inmates.” *New York Times* (November 11):A1, A10.

Smith, D. 1990. *Stepmothering*. New York: St. Martin's Press.

———, and M. Hindus. 1975. “Premarital Pregnancy in America: 1640–1971.” *Journal of Interdisciplinary History* 4 (Spring):537–70.

Smith, E. A., J. R. Udry, and N. M. Morris. 1985. “Pubertal Development and Friends: A Biosocial Explanation of Adolescent Sexual Behavior.” *Journal of Health and Social Behavior* 26:183–92.

Smith, H., and E. Israel. 1997. “Sibling Incest: A Study of the Dynamics of 25 Cases.” *Child Abuse and Neglect* 11:101–8.

Smith, H. W. 1981. *Strategies of Social Research: The Methodological Imagination*. Englewood Cliffs, NJ: Prentice Hall.

Smith, J., J. Mercy, and J. Conn. 1988. “Marital Status and the Risk of Suicide.” *American Journal of Public Health* 78, 1:78–80.

Smith, J., V. Waldorf, and D. Trembath. 1990. “Single White Male Looking for Thin, Very Attractive. . . .” *Sex Roles* 23:675–85.

Smith, K. 2000. *Who's Minding the Kids? Child Care Arrangements, Fall 1995*. Current Population Reports, P70–7. Washington, DC: U.S. Census Bureau..

Smith, J. A., and R. G. Adler. 1991. “Children Hospitalized with Child Abuse and Neglect: A Case-Control Study.” *International Journal* 5, 4:437–45.

Smith, L. G., and G. Clanton. 1977. *Jealousy*. Englewood Cliffs, NJ: Prentice Hall.

Smith, M. 1996. “Aboriginal Street Gangs in Winnipeg.” Canada's National Aboriginal News Service. http://www.ayn.ca/[ages/gangs.htm (2002, February 5).

Smith, S. 1996. “Dating-Partner Preferences among a Group of Inner-City African American High School Students.” *Adolescence* 31 (Spring): 79–90.

Smith, T. W. 1999. “Teenage Sexuality and Contraceptive Use: An Update.” http://www.welfareref.../papers/smith_talk.html (April 4).

———. 1999. “The Emerging 21st Century American Family.” *GSS Social Change Report Number 42*. Chicago: National Opinion Research Center, University of Chicago.

Smock, P. J. 1993. “The Economic Costs of Marital Disruption for Young Women over the Past Two Decades.” *Demography* 30 (August): 353–71.

———, and W. Manning. 1997. “Cohabiting Partners' Economic Circumstances and Marriage.” *Demography* 34, 3:331–41.

Smolowe, J. 1993. “Giving the Cold Shoulder.” *Time* (December 6):28–31.

Snowden, B., and L. Hayes. 2001. “International Terrorism Trends.” Learning Network. http://www.infoplease.com/spot/terrorism1.html (2002, January 17).

Snyder, M. 2000. “Issues in Gender-Sensitive and Disability-Responsive Policy Research, Training and Action.” http://www.un.org/esa/socdev/enable/disrppeg.htm (2002, January 30).

Sobey, A. R. 1997. “Alert: All Pregnant Women Avoid South Carolina.” http://kubby.com/pr/971031.html (1999, October 31).

Soldo, B. J., and M. C. Hill. 1994. *Intergenerational Transfers and Family Structure in the Health and Retirement Survey*. Health and Retirement Working Paper no. 94–1004. Ann Arbor, MI: University of Michigan, Institute for Social Research.

Solomon, R. C. 1981. *Love, Emotion, Myth, and Metaphor*. Garden City, NY: Anchor/Doubleday.

Some Statistics on Bi-Racial Families. 1999. http://www.geocities.com/Athens/Oracle/1103/stats.htm.

Sonenstein, F., J. Pleck, and L. Ku. 1989. “Sexual Activity, Condom Use and AIDS Awareness among Adolescent Males.” *Family Planning Perspective* 21, 4:152–58.

———. 1991. “Levels of Sexual Activity among Adolescent Males in the United States.” *Family Planning Perspectives* 23:162–67.

Song, I. Y. 1991. “Single Asian American Women as a Result of Divorce: Depressive Affect and Changes in Social Support.” In S. S. Volgy, ed., *Women, Men, and Divorce: Gender Differences in Separation, Divorce, and Remarriage*, 219–30. New York: Haworth Press.

Soroka, M. P., and G. J. Bryjak. 1995. *Social Problems: A World at Risk*. Boston: Allyn & Bacon.

———. 1999. *Social Problems: A World at Risk*, 2d ed. Boston: Allyn & Bacon.

Southern Poverty Law Center. 2001a. “Active Hate Groups in the U.S. in 2000.” http://www.splcenter.org/intelligenceproject/ip-2.html (2002, February 2).

———. 2001b. Intelligence Report. “Raging against the Other.” http://www.splcenter.org/intelligenceproject/ip-4t6.html (2002, February 2).

Spade, J. 1989. “Bringing Home the Bacon: A Sex-Integrated Approach to the Impact of Work on the Family.” In B. Risman and P. Schwartz, eds., *Gender in Intimate Relationships*, 184–92. Belmont, CA: Wadsworth.

Spain, D. 1999. *America's Diversity: On the Edge of Two Centuries*. Washington, DC: Population Reference Bureau.

———, and S. M. Bianchi. 1996. *Balancing Act*. New York: Russell Sage Foundation.

Spanier, G. B., and P. C. Glick. 1981. “Marital Instability in the United States: Some Correlates and Recent Changes.” *Family Relations* 31 (July):329–38.

Spanier, G. B., R. A. Lewis, and C. L. Cole. 1975. “Marital Adjustment over the Family Life Cycle: The Issue of Curvilinearity.” *Journal of Marriage and the Family* 37 (May):263–75.

Spanier, G. B., and L. Thompson. 1988. “Moving toward Separation.” In N. D. Glenn and M. T. Coleman, eds., *Family Relations: A Reader*, 326–41. Belmont, CA: Wadsworth.

Spitze, G. 1988. “Women's Employment and Family Relations: A Review.” *Journal of Marriage and the Family* 50:585–618.

———, and J. Logan. 1992. “Helping as a Component of Parent-Adult Child Relations.” *Research on Aging* 14, 3:291–312.

Sprecher, S. 1989. “Pre-Marital Sexual Standards for Different Categories of Individuals.” *Journal of Sex Research* 26, 2 (May):232–48.

———, and S. Metts. 1989. “Development of the ‘Romantic Beliefs Scale’ and Examination of the Effects of Gender and Gender-Role Orientation.” *Journal of Social and Personal Relationships* 6:387–411.

Sprey, J. 1979. “Conflict Theory and the Study of Marriage and the Family.” In W. Burr, R. Hill, F. I. Nye, and I. L. Reiss, eds., *Contemporary Theories about the Family*, 20–22. New York: Free Press.

Springs, H. H. 1989. *New Age Community Guidebook*. Available from Community Bookshelf, Rte. 1, Box 155–F, Rutledge, MO 63563.

Spruill, J. C. 1938. *Women's Life and Work in the Southern Colonies*. New York: Russell and Russell.

Stacey, J. 1996. *In the Name of the Family: Rethinking Family Values in the Postmodern Age*. Boston: Beacon Press.

Stack, C., and L. Burton. 1994. “Kinscripts: Reflections on Family, Generation and Culture.” In E. N. Glenn, G. Chang, and L. R. Forcey, eds., *Mothering: Ideology, Experience, and Agency*, 33–44. New York: Routledge.

Stafford, D. 2000. "Disparity between Pay for Average Worker, CEO Draws Fire." *Kansas City Star* (September 15). http://www/lcstar/cp,/item/pages/business.pat,business/3774c332.915,.html (2001, October 24).

Stainton, M. C. 1985. "The Fetus: A Growing Member of the Family." *Family Relations* 34:321–26.

Staples, R. 1981b. *The World of Black Singles: Changing Patterns of Male/Female Relations.* Westport, CT: Greenwood Press.

———. 1988. "The Black American Family." In C. H. Mindel, R. Habenstein, and R. Wright, Jr., eds., *Ethnic Families in America: Patterns and Variations,* 303–24. New York: Elsevier.

———, ed. 1991. *The Black Family: Essays and Studies,* 4th ed. Belmont, CA: Wadsworth.

———, ed. 1994. *The Black Family: Essays and Studies,* 5th ed. Belmont, CA: Wadsworth.

———. 1999. *The Black Family: Essays and Studies,* 6th ed. Belmont, CA: Wadsworth.

———, and T. Jones. 1985. "Culture, Ideology, and Black Television Images." *Black Scholar* 16:10–20.

Stark, E., and A. Flitcraft. 1988. "Violence among Intimates: An Epidemiological Review." In V. Van Hasselt, R. Morrison, A. Bellack, and M. Hersen, eds., *Handbook of Family Violence,* 293–318. New York: Plenum.

Starr, B. D., and M. B. Weiner. 1981. *Sex and Sexuality in the Mature Years.* New York: Stein and Day.

State of the World Population 1997 Report. 1997. "Rights for Sexual Reproductive Health." In *The Right to Choose: Reproductive Rights and Reproductive Health.* Online (November 11):1–17.

Stayton, W. R. 1984. "Lifestyle Spectrum 1984." Sex Information and Educational Council of the U.S. Reports (SIECUS) 12, 3:1–4.

Steck, L., D. Levitan, D. McLane, and H. H. Kelley. 1982. "Care, Need, and Conceptions of Love." *Journal of Personality and Social Psychology* 43:481–91.

Stein, P. 1976. *Single.* Englewood Cliffs, NJ: Prentice Hall.

———, ed. 1981. *Single Life: Unmarried Adults in Social Context.* New York: St. Martin's Press.

———, and M. Fingrutd. 1985. "The Single Life Has More Potential for Happiness Than Marriage and Parenthood for Both Men and Women." In H. Feldman and M. Feldman, eds., *Current Controversies in Marriage and the Family,* 81–89. Beverly Hills, CA: Sage.

Steinfirst, S., and B. B. Moran. 1989. "The New Mating Game: Matchmaking via the Personal Columns in the 1980's." *Journal of Popular Culture* 22, 4:129–40.

Steinhauer, J. 1995. "Living Together without Marriage or Apologies." *New York Times* (July 6):A9.

Steinmetz, S. 1977. "The Battered Husband Syndrome." *Victimology: An International Journal* 2, 3/4:499–509.

Sternberg, R. J. 1986. "A Triangular Theory of Love." *Psychological Review* 93, 2:119–35.

———. 1988. *The Triangle of Love: Intimacy, Passion, and Commitment.* New York: Basic Books.

——— 1998. *Love Is a Story.* London: Oxford University Press.

———. 2001. *What's Your Love Story?* In Kathleen R. Gilbert, ed., Annual Editions: *The Family.* Guilford, CT: McGraw-Hill/Duskin.

Stets, J. E. 1991. "Cohabiting and Marital Aggression in Marriage: The Role of Social Isolation." *Journal of Marriage and Family* 53:669–80.

Stewart, A. J., A. P. Copeland, N. L. Chester, J. E. Malley, and N. B. Barenbaum. 1997. *Separating Together: How Divorce Transforms Families.* New York: Guilford Press.

Stewart, J. K. 1999. "Long-Distance Marriages Not Such a Long Shot." *Chicago Tribune* (October 6):sec. 8, 1, 8.

Stillion, J. M. 1995. "Premature Exits: Understanding Suicide." In L. A. DeSpelder and A. L. Strickland, eds., *The Paths Ahead: Readings in Death and Dying,* 182–97. Mountain View, CA: Mayfield.

Stinnet, N., and C. Birdsong. 1978. *The Family and Alternative Life Styles.* Chicago: Nelson-Hall.

Stodghill, R. 1999. "Where'd You Learn That?" In S. J. Bunting, ed., *Human Sexuality 99/00,* 140–44. Sluice Dock, Guilford, CT: Dushkin/McGraw-Hill.

Stokes, J. P., and J. S. Peyton. 1986. "Attitudinal Differences between Full-Time Homemakers and Women Who Work Outside the Home." *Sex Roles* 15:299–310.

Stolberg, S. 1998. "U.S. Awakes to Epidemic of Sexual Diseases." *New York Times* (March 9):A1, A14.

———. 1999. "U.S. Birth Rate at New Low as Teen-Age Pregnancy Falls." *New York Times* (April 29):A22.

———. 2001. "Study Paints Daycare as Hothouse for Aggression." *National Post* (April 20).

Stone, L. H., ed. 1999. *Selected Readings in Marriage and Family.* San Diego, CA: Greenhaven Press.

Stone, R., G. L. Cafferata, and J. Sangl. 1987. "Caregivers of the Frail Elderly: A National Profile." *Gerontologist* 27:616–26.

Stoneman, Z., G.H. Brody, and C.E. MacKinnon. 1986. "Same-Sex and Cross-Sex Siblings: Activity Choices, Roles, Behavior, and Gender Stereotypes." *Sex Roles* 15:495–511.

Strada, M. J. 1999. *Through the Global Lens: An Introduction to the Social Sciences.* Upper Saddle River, NJ: Prentice Hall.

Straus, M. 1994. *Beating the Devil Out of Them: Corporal Punishment in American Families and Its Effect on Children.* New York: Lexington Books.

———, and D. Donnelly. 2001. *Beating the Devil Out of Them: Corporal Punishment in American Families and Its Effects on Children.* New Brunswick, NJ: Transaction.

Straus, M., R. Gelles, and S. Steinmetz. 1980. *Behind Closed Doors.* Garden City, NY: Anchor Books.

Straus, M. A., and J. H. Stewart. 1999. "Corporal Punishment by American Parents: National Data on Prevalence, Chronicity, Severity, and Duration, in Relation to Child and Family Characteristics." *Clinical Child and Family Psychology Review* 2 (June):55–70.

Streetwise. 1995. "Special Report: Life in the Streets." 4, 1 (September 16–30):2–14.

Stroebe, W., C. A. Insko, V. D. Thompson, and B. D. Layton. 1971. "Effects of Physical Attractiveness, Attitude Similarity, and Sex on Various Aspects of Interpersonal Attraction." *Journal of Personality and Social Psychology* 18:79–91.

Strong, B., S. Wilson, L. M. Clarke, and T. Johns. 1978. *Human Sexuality.* New York: West.

"Study." 1998. *Chicago Tribune* (July 12):sec. 13, 3.

Suarez, Z. E. 1998. "Cuban-American Families." In C H. Mindel, R. W. Habenstein, and R. Wright, Jr. *Ethnic Families in America: Patterns and Variations,* 172–98. Upper Saddle River, NJ: Prentice Hall.

Sudarkasa, N. 1993. "Female-Headed African American Households: Some Neglected Dimensions." In H. P. McAdoo, ed., *Family Ethnicity: Strength in Diversity.* Newbury Park, CA: Sage.

Sugisawa, H., J. Liang, and X. Liu. 1994. "Social Networks, Social Support, and Mortality among Older People in Japan." *Journal of Gerontology* 49:S3–S13.

suro, roberto. 2001. "Mixed Doubles." *American Demographics.* http://www.inside.com/product/product_print.asp?pf_id (2001, November 14).

Surra, C. A. 1991. "Research and Theory on Mate Selection and Premarital Relationships in the 1980s." In A. Booth, ed., *Contemporary Families: Looking Forward, Looking Back.* Minneapolis: National Council on Family Relations.

Sussman, M. 1985. "The Family Life of Old People." In R. Binstock and E. Shanas, eds., *Handbook of Aging and the Social Sciences*, 415–49. New York: Van Nostrand Reinhold.

Sutton-Smith, B. 1971. "The Expressive Profile." In A. Paredes and R. Bauman, eds., *Toward New Perspectives in Folklore*, 80–92. Austin: University of Texas Press.

Swanbrow, D. 1989. "The Paradox of Happiness." *Psychology Today* (July/August):37–39.

Sweeney, J. F. 2001. "Jay Belsky Doesn't Play Well with Others." http://www.salon.com/mwt/feature/2001/04/26/belsky/index.html (2001, July 20).

Sweet, J. A., and L. L. Bumpass. 1987. *American Families and Households.* New York: Russell Sage Foundation.

Swoboda, F. 2000. "Big 3 Extend Benefits to Domestic Partners." *Washington Post* (June 6):A1, A22.

Szapocznik, J., and R. Hernandez. 1988. "The Cuban American Family." In C. H. Mindel, R. W. Habenstein, and R. H. Wright, Jr., eds., *Ethnic Families in America: Patterns and Variations*, 160–72. New York: Elsevier.

Takagi, D. Y. 1998. "Japanese American Families." In R. L. Taylor, ed., *Minority Families in the United States: A Multicultural Perspective*, 2d ed., 159–75. Upper Saddle River, NJ: Prentice Hall.

———. 1994. "Japanese American Families." In R. L. Taylor, ed., *Minority Families in the United States: A Multicultural Perspective*, 146–63. Upper Saddle River, NJ: Prentice Hall.

Talbott, M. M. 1998. "Older Widows' Attitudes toward Men and Remarriage." *Journal of Aging Studies* 12, 4 (Winter):429–49.

"Talks on Drugs Linked to Use." 1999. *Chicago Tribune* (April 26):4.

Tallichet, S. E. 1995. "Gendered Relations in the Mines and the Division of Labor Underground." *Gender & Society* 9:697–711.

Tanfer, K. 1987. "Patterns of Premarital Cohabitation among Never-Married Women in the United States." *Journal of Marriage and the Family* 49:483–97.

Taniguchi, H. 1999. "The Timing of Childbearing and Women's Wages." *Journal of Marriage and the Family* 61 (November):1008–19.

Tannen, D. 1990. *You Just Don't Understand: Women and Men in Conversation.* New York: Ballantine.

———. 1994. *Talking from 9 to 5. Women and Men in the Workplace: Language, Sex and Power.* New York: Avon Books.

Task Force on Aging Research. 1995. *The Threshold of Discovery: Future Directions for Research on Aging.* Washington, DC: U.S. Government Printing Office.

Tatara, T. 1998. "The National Elder Abuse Incidence Study." The National Center on Elder Abuse and the American Public Humane Services Association. http://www.aoa.gov/abuse/report/main-pdf.htm (2001, December 18).

Tavris, C. 2000. "Women as Love's Experts and Love's Victims." In N. Benokraitis, ed., *Feuds about Families*, 123–30. Upper Saddle River, NJ: Prentice Hall.

Taylor, L. C., I. D. Hinton, and M. Wilson. 1995. "Parental Influences on Academic Performance in African-American Students." *Journal of Child and Family Studies* 4:293–302.

Taylor, R. J. 1990. "Need for Support and Family Involvement among Black Americans." *Journal of Marriage and the Family* 52:114–25.

———, M. B. Tucker, and E. Lewis. 1990. "Development in Research on Black Families: A Decade Review." *Journal of Marriage and the Family* 52 (November):993–1014.

Taylor, R. J., V. M. Keith, and M. B. Tucker. 1993. "Gender, Marital, Familial, and Friendship Roles." In J. S. Jackson, L. M. Chatters, and R. J. Taylor, eds., *Aging in Black America*, 49–68. Newbury Park, CA: Sage.

Taylor, R. L. 1998. *Minority Families in the United States: A Multicultural Perspective.* Upper Saddle River, NJ: Prentice Hall.

Teachman, J. D., L. M. Tedrow, and K. D. Crowder. 2000. "The Changing Demography of America's Families." *Journal of Marriage and the Family* 62, 4:1234–46.

Telecomworldwire. 2001. "Both Men and Women Turn to SMS to Find New Partners—Study" (September 19). http://www.findarticles.com/cf_0/m0ECZ/2001_Sept_19/78408573/pl/article.jhtml?term=... (2001, October 24).

Temple, A. 1998. "Dating Rituals May Be a Matter of Keeping the Faith." *Chicago Tribune* (August 9):sec. 13, 1, 8.

Tennov, D. 1979. *Love and Limerence: The Experience of Being in Love.* Briarcliff Manor, NY: Stein and Day.

Thackeray, A. 2000. "Interracial Acceptance: Is America Ready?" *One Magazine* (Spring). http://www.onemagazine.net/race.htm (2001, November 12).

Thies. C. F. 2000. "The Success of American Communes." *Southern Economic Journal* 67, 1 (July):186–99.

Thomas, J. L. 1986. "Gender Differences in Satisfaction with Grandparenting." *Psychology and Aging* 1:215–19.

Thomas, V. G. 1990. "Determinants of Global Life Happiness and Marital Happiness in Dual-Career Black Couples." *Family Relations* 39:174–78.

Thombs, D. 1994. *Introduction to Addictive Behaviors.* New York: Guilford Press.

Thompson, B. W. 1994. *A Hunger So Wide and So Deep: American Women Speak Out on Eating Problems.* Minneapolis: University of Minnesota Press.

Thompson, G. 1999. "Smugglers Made False Promises to Poor Mexican Mothers." *Chicago Tribune* (October 20).

Thompson, L., and A. J. Walker. 1991. "Gender in Families." In A. Booth, ed., *Contemporary Families: Looking Forward, Looking Back*, 76–102. Minneapolis: National Council on Family Relations.

Thomsen, D., and I. Chang. 2000. "Predictors of Satisfaction with First Intercourse: A New Perspective for Sexuality Education." Poster Presentation at 62nd Annual Conference of the National Council on Family Relations, Minneapolis (November).

Thornberry, T., and J. Burch. 1997. "Gang Members and Delinquent Behavior." Washington, DC: Office of Juvenile Justice and Delinquency Prevention.

Thornton, A. 1990. "The Courtship Process and Adolescent Sexuality." *Journal of Family Issues* 11, 3:239–73.

Thornton, E. 1994. "Video Dating in Japan." *Fortune* (January 24):12.

Tilly, L., and J. W. Scott. 1978. *Women, Work and Family.* New York: Holt.

Tolbert, K. 2001. "Premier's Family Reflects Japan's Painful Divorce Custom." *Chicago Tribune* (May 20):4.

Totenberg, N. 1985. "How to Write a Marriage Contract." In O. Pocs and R. Walsh, eds., *Marriage and Family: Annual Editions*, 46–47. Sluice Dock, Guilford, CT: Dushkin.

Toth, J., and X. Xu. 1999. "Ethnic and Cultural Diversity in Fathers' Involvement: A Racial/Ethnic Comparison of African American, Hispanic, and White Fathers." *Youth and Society* 31 (September):76–99.

Tower, C. 2002. *Understanding Child Abuse and Neglect*, 5th ed. Boston: Allyn & Bacon.

Townsend, B., and K. O'Neil. 1990. "American Women Get Mad." *American Demographics* (August):26–29, 32.

Tracy, L. 1990. "The Television Image in Children's Lives." *New York Times* (May 13):sec. M.

"Transgendered Economist Publishes First Book as a Woman." 1997. *Chronicle of Higher Education* (May 2):A15.

Treas, J. 1995. "Older Americans in the 1990s and Beyond." *Population Bulletin* 50:2. Washington, DC: Population Reference Bureau.

———, and V. L. Bengtson. 1987. "The Family in Later Years." In M. B. Sussman and S. K. Steinmetz, eds., *Handbook of Marriage and the Family*, 625–48. New York: Plenum.

Tribe, L. H. 1990. *Abortion: The Clash of Absolutes.* New York: W. W. Norton.

Troll, L. 1988. "New Thoughts on Old Families." *Gerontologist* 28, 5:586–91.

Tubman, J. G. 1993. "Family Risk Factors, Parental Alcohol Use, and Problem Behaviors among School-Age Children." *Family Relations* 42:81–86.

Tucker, M., and C. Mitchell-Kernan. 1990. "New Trends in Black American Interracial Marriage: The Social Structural Context." *Journal of Marriage and the Family*, 26:279–90.

———, eds. 1995. *The Decline in Marriage among African Americans.* New York: Russell Sage Foundation.

———. 1999. "Marital Behavior and Expectations: Ethnic Comparisons of Attitudinal and Structural Correlates." In Cheryl Albers, *Sociology of Families Readings*, 90–100. Thousand Oaks, CA: Pine Forge Press.

Tucker, M. B., and R. J. Taylor. 1989. "Demographic Correlates of Relationship Status among Black Americans." *Journal of Marriage and the Family* 51:655–66.

Turner, J., and A. Z. Maryanski. 1979. *Functionalism.* Menlo Park, CA: Benjamin/Cummings.

"TV Soaps Focus on Role of Sex." 1994. *Chicago Tribune* (October 23):8.

Tweed, S. H., and C. D. Ryff. 1991. "Profiles of Wellness amidst Distress." *Journal of Studies on Alcohol* 52:133–41.

Tyson, A. S. 1997. "Young Love Bridges Race Divide" (December 3). http://www.csmonitor.c...997/12/03/us/us.4.html (1999, March 5).

Uhlenberg, P. 1980. "Death and the Family." *Journal of Family History* (Fall):313–21.

UNAIDS. 2001. "Report on the Global HIV/AIDS Epidemic: Global Summary of the HIV/AIDS Epidemic, End 1999." http://www.unaids.org/epidemic_update/report/Epi_report_chap_glo_estim.htm (2001, December 13).

UNICEF. 1996. "The State of the World's Children." http://www.unicef.org/sowc96/16relief.html (1998, April 8).

———. 2002. "Children and War." Voices of Youth. http://www/imocef/prg/voy/meeting/war-exp2.hmtl (2002, February 18).

United Nations. 2000. "The Aging of the World's Population." http://www.un.org/esa/socdev/ageing/agewpop.htm (2001, December 28).

United Nations Development Programme. 1999. *Human Development Report, 1999.* New York: Oxford University Press.

———. 2001. *Human Development Report, 2001.* New York: Oxford University Press.

United Nations High Commissioner for Refugees. 2001. "Refugees by Numbers 2001 Edition (July 1). http://www.unhcr.ch/cgi-bin/texis/vtx/[romt?tbl=VISITORS&id=3b028097c (2002, January 14).

United Nations Office of Drug Control and Crime Prevention. 2001. "Terrorism." The Terrorism Prevention Branch. http://www.undcp.org/terrorism.html (2002, February 16).

United Press International. 1990. "Men Love Looks, Women Love Money: U.M. Study." *Chicago Tribune.*

U.S. Census Bureau. 1987. "Money Income and Poverty Status of Families and Persons in the United States: 1986 (Advance Data from the March 1987 Current Population Survey)." *Current Population Reports*, Series P–60, no. 157. Washington, DC: U.S. Government Printing Office.

———. 1991. "Marital Status and Living Arrangements: March 1990." *Current Population Reports*, Series P–20, no. 450. Washington, DC: U.S. Government Printing Office.

———. 1992. "Who's Minding the Kids?" *Current Population Reports*, Series P–70, no. 30. Washington, DC: U.S. Government Printing Office.

———. 1993. *Statistical Abstract of the United States*, 113th ed. Washington, DC: U.S. Government Printing Office.

———. 1995. *Statistical Abstract of the United States*, 115th ed. Washington, DC: U.S. Government Printing Office.

———. 1997. *Statistical Abstract of the United States, 1997*, 117th ed. Washington, DC: U.S. Government Printing Office.

———. 1998. *Statistical Abstract of the United States, 1998*, 118th ed. Washington, DC: U.S. Government Printing Office.

———. 1999. "Poverty Rate Down, Household Income Up." Press Release. http://www.census.gov/Press-Release/cb98-175.html.

———. 2000a. *Statistical Abstract of the United States, 2000*, 120th ed. Washington, DC: U.S. Government Printing Office.

———. 2000b. "Current Population Survey, March 2000. Racial Statistics Population Division. Washington, DC: U.S. Department of Commerce (2001, February 22).

———. 2000c. "Fertility of American Women: June 2000." Current Population Reports, P20–543RV. Washington, DC: U.S. Department of Commerce, Economics and Statistics Administration.

———. 2001a. "Multigenerational Households Number 4 Million." http://www.census.gov/Press-Release/www/2001/cb01cn182.html (2001, December 3).

———. 2001b. "More People Have Health Insurance, Census Bureau Reports." http://www.census.gov/ftp/pub/Press-Release/www/2001/cb01-162.html (2001, September 28).

———. 2001c. "Health Insurance Coverage: 2000." Table A (September 28). http://www.census.gov/ftp/pub/hhes/hlthins/hlthin00/hi00ta.html (2001, September 28).

U.S. Conference of Mayors. 2000. *A Status Report on Hunger and Homelessness in America's Cities, 2000.* Washington, DC.

U.S. Department of Agriculture. 2001. "USDA Estimates Child Rearing Costs." News Release (June 11). http://www.usda.gov/news/releases/2001/06/0097.htm (2001, December 17).

U.S. Department of Commerce. 1993. *Social and Economic Characteristics: United States.* Washington, DC: U.S. Government Printing Office.

U.S. Department of Education. 1997. *1994 Elementary and Secondary School Civil Rights Compliance Report.* Washington, DC.

———. 1998. *Digest of Education Statistics.* Washington, DC: National Center for Education Statistics.

U.S. Department of Health and Human Services, National Center on Child Abuse and Neglect. 1996. *Third National Incidence Study of Child Abuse and Neglect: Final Report* (NIS–3). Washington, DC: U.S. Government Printing Office.

———. 1998. *The National Elder Abuse Incidence Study* (September). Washington, DC.

———. 2001a. *Child Maltreatment 1999: Reports from the States to the National Child Abuse and Neglect Data System.* Washington, DC: U.S. Government Printing Office.

———. 2001b. "Closing the Health Gap: Reducing Health Disparities Affecting African Americans." http://www.aoa.dhhs.gov/pressroom/Pr2001/healthgap-FS.html (2001, December 26).

———. 2001c. *Summary of Findings from the 2000 National Household Survey on Drug Use.* Washington, DC: U.S. Government Printing Office.

U.S. Department of Housing and Urban Development. 1991. *1989 Housing Discrimination Study.* Washington, DC: U.S. Government Printing Office.

U.S. Department of Justice. 1996a. Bureau of Justice Statistics. *Sourcebook of Criminal Justice Statistics, 1996.* Washington, DC.

———. 1996b. Bureau of Justice Statistics. *Statistics about Crime and Victims.* Bureau of Justice Crime and Victims Publication. BJS Home Page (April 22) [online].

———. 1997. Bureau of Justice Statistics. *Criminal Offenders Statistics.* http://www.ojp.usdoj.gov/bjs/crimoff/htm#summary (1999, May 29).

———. 1998. "Joint Justice Department/Education Department Study Shows Little Increase in School Crime between 1989 and 1995" (April 12). http://www.ojp.usdoj.gov/bjs/pub/press/srsc.pr (1999, June 15).

———. 1998. "Sex Offenses and Offenders." Bureau of Justice Statistics. http://www.ojp.usdoj.gov/bjs (2002, January 19).

———. 2000a. "People 65 Years Old and Older Are Less Likely to Be Victims of Violent Crime Than Younger U.S. Residents." Bureau of Justice Statistics. http://www.ojp.usdoj.gov/bjs/ (2002, January 7).

———. 2000b. "Sexual Assault of Young Children as Reported to Law

Enforcement: Victim, Incident, and Offender Characteristics." Bureau of Justice Statistics. http://www.ojp.usdoj.gov/bjs/abstract/saycrle.htm (2002, January 7).

———. 2001a. "Victim Characteristics." Bureau of Justice Statistics. http://www.ojp.usdoj.gov/bjs/cvict_v.html (2002, January 7).

———. 2001b. "Criminal Victimization 2000: Changes 1999–2000 with Trends 1993–2000." Bureau of Justice Statistics. http://www.ojp.usdoj.gov/bjs/cvict_v.html (2002, January 18).

———. 2001c. "Criminal Victimization in United States, 1999 Statistical Tables." National Crime Victimization Survery. Washington, DC: Office of Justice Programs, Bureau of Justice Statistics.

U.S. Department of Labor. 2001. *Highlights of Women's Earnings in 2000.* Washington, DC: U.S. Government Printing Office.

———. 2002. "The Employment Situation: December 2001" (January 4). Washington, DC: Bureau of Labor Statistics. ftp://ftp.bls.gov/pub/news.release/empsit.txt (2002, January 11).

U.S. Holocaust Memorial Museum. 2002. "Genocide of European Roma." http://www.ushmm.org/wle/article.jsp?Moduleld=10005219 (2002, March 21).

U.S. Newswire. 1999. "Gore Releases New Study Showing High Rate of Gun Violence among Teenagers" (June 14). http://www.usnewswire..._Releases/0614–136.html (1999, June 15).

Utech, M. R. 1994. *Violence, Abuse, and Neglect: The American Home.* Dix Hills, NY: General Hall.

Vaillant, C. O., and G. E. Vaillant. 1993. "Is the V-Curve of Marital Satisfaction an Illusion? A 40-Year Study of Marriage." *Journal of Marriage and the Family* 55, 1:230–39.

Vandewater, E., and J. Lansford. 1998. "Influences of Family Structure and Parental Conflict on Children's Well-Being." *Family Relations* 47: 323–30.

Vazquez-Nuttall, E., I. Romero-Garcia, and B. DeLeon. 1987. "Sex Roles and Perceptions of Femininity and Masculinity of Hispanic Women: A Review of the Literature." *Psychology of Women Quarterly* 11:409–25.

Vedantam, S. 2001. "Child Aggressiveness Study Cites Day Care." *Washington Post* (April 19).

Vega, W. 1995. "The Study of Latino Families." In R. Zambrana, ed., *Understanding Latino Families.* Thousand Oaks, CA: Sage.

Veith, G. E. 1999. "Bible Belt Breakups." *World* (November 27). www.worldmag.com/world/issue/11-27-99/cultural_2.asp (2001, October 30).

Ventura, S., T. Matthews, and B. Hamilton. 2001. "Births to Teenagers in the United States, 1940–2000." *Centers for Disease Control and Prevention, National Vital Statistics Reports* (September 25):49, 10.

Verhovek, S. H. 1999. "Oregon Reporting 15 Deaths in Year under Suicide Law." *New York Times* (February 18):A1.

Violence against Women. 1992. *The National Women's Health Report.* The National Women's Health Resource Center (September/October) [online].

———. 1994. *A National Crime Victimization Survey Report.* U.S. Department of Justice, Washington, DC (January) [online].

"Violence Kills More U.S. Kids." 1997. *San Francisco Chronicle* (February 7):A1.

Visher, E. 1994. "Lessons from Remarried Families." *American Journal of Family Therapy* 22, 4:327–36.

———, and J. Visher. 1982. *How to Win as a Stepfamily.* New York: Dembner Books.

———. 1993. "Remarriage, Families, and Stepparenting." In F. Walsh, ed., *Normal Family Processes,* 2d ed., 235–53. New York: Guilford Press.

Vitagliano, E. 2001. "Majority of Unwed Moms Are Not Teens." http://www.thruthcast.com/agape/010625unwedmoms.htm (2002, January 5).

Vital and Health Statistics from the Centers for Disease Control and Prevention. 1995. "Fertility, Family Planning, and Women's Health: New Data from the 1995 National Survey of Family Growth." Washington, DC: National Center for Health Statistics, Series 23, No. 19.

Vobejda, B. 1998. "Multiple Births in Dramatic Increase." *Seattle Times.* http://kyle.seattletimes.com/news/nation-world/html98/altbirt_070198.html (1999, May 6).

"Voters Remove State Interracial Marriage Ban." 2000. *Birmingham News* (November 8):1.

Voydanoff, P. 1983. "Unemployment and Family Stress." In H. Z. Lopata and J. H. Pleck, eds., *Research in the Interweave of Social Roles: Families and Jobs,* 239–50. Greenwich, CT: JAI Press.

———. 1987. *Work and Family.* Beverly Hills, CA: Sage.

Vuchinich, S., E. M. Hetherington, R. Vuchinich, and W. G. Clingempeel. 1991. "Parent-Child Interaction and Gender Differences in Early Adolescents' Adaptation to Stepfamilies." *Developmental Psychology* 27, 4:618–26.

Wade, C., and S. Cirese. 1991. *Human Sexuality,* 2d ed. New York: Harcourt Brace Jovanovich.

Wagner, D. L. 1997. *Healthcare and Aging.* Washington, DC: National Council on the Aging.

Waite, L., and F. K. Goldscheider. 1992. "Work in the Home: The Productive Context of Family Relationships." In S. J. South and S. E. Tolnay, eds., *The Changing American Family,* 267–69. Boulder, CO: Westview Press.

Waite, L. J., and K. Joyner. 1996. "Men's and Women's General Happiness and Sexual Satisfaction in Marriage, Cohabitation and Single Living." Unpublished manuscript. Chicago: Population Research Center, University of Chicago.

Wald, E. 1981. *The Remarried Family: Challenge and Promise.* New York: Family Service Association of America.

Walker, K. 1994. "Men, Women, and Friendship: What They Say, What They Do." *Gender and Society* 8:246–65.

———. 1995. "Always There for Me: Friendship Patterns and Expectations among Middle and Working Class Men and Women." *Sociological Forum* 10 (2):273–96.

———. 2001. "I'm Not Friends the Way She's Friends: Ideological and Behavioral Constructions of Masculinity in Men's Friendships." In M. Kimmel and M. Messner, *Men's Lives,* 5th ed., 367–79. Needham Heights, MA: Allyn & Bacon.

Walker, K. E., and M. Woods. 1976. *Time Use: A Measure of Household Production of Goods and Services.* Washington, DC: American Home Economics Association.

Walker, L. 1978. "Treatment Alternatives for Battered Women." In J. R. Chapman and M. Gates, eds., *The Victimization of Women,* 143–74. Beverly Hills, CA: Sage.

———. 1984. *The Battered Woman Syndrome.* New York: Springer.

Wallace, C. P. 1992. "For Sale: The Poor's Body Parts." *Los Angeles Times* (April 27):A1.

Wallace, H. 1996. *Family Violence: Legal, Medical, and Social Perspectives.* Needham Heights, MA: Allyn & Bacon.

———, 2002. *Family Violence: Legal, Medical, and Social Perspective,* 3d ed. Boston: Allyn & Bacon.

Wallace, R. A., and A. Wolf. 1991. *Contemporary Sociological Theory.* Englewood Cliffs, NJ: Prentice Hall.

Waller, W. 1937. "The Rating and Dating Complex." *American Sociological Review* 2:727–35.

———, and R. Hill. 1951. *The Family: A Dynamic Interpretation.* New York: Dryden Press.

Wallerstein, J. S. 1986. "Women after Divorce: Preliminary Report from a Ten-Year Follow-Up." *American Journal of Orthopsychiatry* 56:65–77.

———, and S. Blakeslee. 1989. *Second Chances: Men, Women, and Children a Decade after Divorce.* New York: Ticknor and Fields.

———. 1992. *Second Chances: Men, Women, and Children a Decade after Divorce,* 3d ed. Boston: Houghton Mifflin.

———. 1995. *The Good Marriage: How and Why Love Lasts.* Boston: Houghton Mifflin.

———. 1996. *Second Chances: Men, Women, and Children a Decade After Divorce*, 4th ed. Boston: Houghton Mifflin.

Wallerstein, J. S., and J. Kelly. 1980. *Surviving the Break-up. How Children Actually Cope with Divorce*. New York: Basic Books.

Wallerstein, J. S., J. M. Lewis, and S. Blakeslee. 2000. *The Unexpected Legacy of Divorce: A 25 Year Landmark Study*. New York: Hyperion.

Walsh, A. 1991. *The Science of Love: Understanding Love and Its Effects on Mind and Body*. Buffalo, NY: Prometheus Books.

Walsh, F. 1980. "The Family in Later Life." In E. A. Carter and M. McGoldrick, eds., *The Family Life Cycle: A Framework for Family Therapy*. New York: Gardner Press.

Walster, E., W. Walster, and J. Traupmann. 1978. "Equity and Premarital Sex." *Journal of Personality and Social Psychology* 36:82–92.

Ward, M. C. 1999. *A World Full of Women*, 2d ed. Boston: Allyn & Bacon.

Warda, J. 2000. "Stepping Up to Protect a Son's Feelings." *Chicago Tribune* (July 30):sec. 13, 2.

Wade, C., and S. Cirese. 1991. *Human Sexuality*, 2d ed.. New York: Harcourt Brace Jovanovich.

Wagemaar, T., and R. Coates. 1999. "Race and Children: The Dynamics of Early Socialization." *Education* 120 (Winter):220–36.

Watkins, B., and A. Bentovim. 1992. "Male Children and Adolescents as Victims: A Review of Current Knowledge." In . G. Mezey and M. King, eds., *Male Victims of Sexual Assault*, 27–66. Oxford: Oxford University Press.

Watson, R., and P. DeMeo. 1987. "Premarital Cohabitation vs. Traditional Courtship: Their Effects on Subsequent Marital Adjustment: A Replication and Follow Up." *Family Relations* 36:193–97.

Watts, J. 1977. "The End of Work and the End of Welfare." *Contemporary Sociology* 26 (July):409–12.

"Wedding Traditions Date Back for Centuries." 1988. *Chicago Sun-Times* (January 17):special advertising sec., 2.

Weerth, C., and A. Kalma. 1995. "Gender Differences in Awareness of Courtship Initiation Tactics." *Sex Roles* (June):32, 717–34.

Weibel-Orlando, J. 1990. "Grandparenting Styles: Native American Perspectives." In J. Sokolovsky, ed., *The Cultural Context of Aging*, 109–25. New York: Bergin and Garvey.

Weiser, C. 1996. "Legal Gay Marriage on Hawaii's Horizon." *USA Today* (January 2):6A.

Weissbourd, R. 1994. "Divided Families, Whole Children." *The American Prospect* 18 (Summer):66–72.

Weitzman, L. 1977. "To Love, Honor, and Obey: Traditional Legal Marriage and Alternative Family Forms." In A. S. Skolnick and J. H. Skolnick, eds., *Family in Transition*, 2d ed., 288–313. Boston: Little, Brown.

———. 1985. *The Divorce Revolution: The Unexpected Social and Economic Consequences for Women and Children in America*. New York: Free Press.

Weitzman, N., B. Birns, and R. Friend. 1985. "Traditional and Nontraditional Mothers' Communication with Their Daughters and Sons." *Child Development* 56:894–96.

Wellman, B. 1992. "Men in Networks: Private Communities, Domestic Friendships." In P. Nardi, ed., *Men's Friendships*, 74–114. Newbury Park, CA: Sage.

Wells, R. 1978. "Family History and Demographic Transition." In M. Gordon, ed., *The American Family in Social-Historical Perspective*, 516–32. New York: St. Martin's Press.

Welter, B. 1978. "The Cult of True Womanhood: 1820–1860." In M. Gordon, ed., *The American Family in Social-Historical Perspective*, 313–33. New York: St. Martin's Press.

Werking, K. J. 1994. "Hidden Assumptions: A Critique of Cross-Sex Friendship." *Research Issues* 2:8–11.

Werland, R. 1999. "A Kinder, Gentler Divorce." *Chicago Tribune* (September 26):sec. 13, 1, 5.

Werner, E. E. 1989. "Children of the Garden Island." *Scientific American* 260, 4:106–11.

Westoff, C. F., and N. Goldman. 1988. "Figuring the Odds in the Marriage Market." In J. G. Wells, ed., *Current Issues in Marriage and the Family*, 39–46. New York: Macmillan.

Weston, K. 1991. *Families We Choose: Lesbians, Gays, Kinship*. New York: Columbia University Press.

"Where Rape Is a Proposal of Marriage." 1999 (June 18). http://www.sn.apc.org/wmail/issues/990618/NEWS47.HTML (2002, January 21).

Whisman, M. A., and N. S. Jacobson. 1988. "Depression, Marital Satisfaction, and Marital and Personality Measures of Sex Roles." *Journal of Marital and Family Therapy* 15:177–86.

White, G. L. 1980a. "Including Jealousy: A Power Perspective." *Personality and Social Psychology Bulletin* 6:222–27.

———. 1980b. "Physical Attractiveness and Courtship Progress." *Journal of Personality and Social Psychology* 39:660–68.

White, J. 1987. "Premarital Cohabitation and Marital Stability in Canada." *Journal of Marriage and the Family* 49:641–47.

White, L. K. 1981. "A Note on Racial Differences in the Effect of Female Opportunity on Marriage Rates." *Demography* 18:349–54.

———. 1990. "Determinants of Divorce: A Review of Research in the Eighties." *Journal of Marriage and the Family* 52:904–12.

———. 1991. "Determinants of Divorce." In A. Booth, ed., *Contemporary Families: Looking Forward, Looking Back*, 150–61. Minneapolis: National Council on Family Relations.

———. 1994. "Growing Up with Single Parents and Stepparents: Long-Term Effects on Family Solidarity." *Journal of Marriage and the Family* 56 (November):935–48.

———, and A. Riedman. 1992. "When the Brady Bunch Grows Up: Step-/Half- and Full-Sibling Relationships in Adulthood." *Journal of Marriage and the Family* 54:197–208.

White, N. 1995. "Batterers Seldom Stop after the First Time." *New Standard*, pp. 1–7 [online].

Whiteford, L. M., and L. Gonzalez. 1995. "Stigma: The Hidden Burden of Infertility." *Social Science and Medicine* 40 (January):27–36.

Whitehead, B. 1993. "Dan Quayle Was Right." *Atlantic Monthly* 271 (April):47–84.

Whitehouse, B. 2000. "Alcohol and the Family." *Parenting* 14, 5 (June/July):154–62.

Whiting, B., and C. P. Edwards. 1988. *Children of Different Worlds: The Formation of Social Behavior*. Cambridge, MA: Harvard University Press.

Whitsett, D., and H. Land. 1992. "The Development of a Role Strain Index for Stepparents." *Families in Society: The Journal of Contemporary Human Services* 73, 1:14–22.

Whyte, M. K. 1990. *Dating, Mating, and Marriage*. New York: Aldine de Gruyter.

———. 2001. "Choosing Mates—The American Way." In S. Ferguson, ed., *Shifting the Center: Understanding Contemporary Families*, 2d ed., 129–39. Mountain View, CA: Mayfield.

Widom, C. S. 1992. *The Cycle of Violence, Research in Brief*. Washington, DC: U.S. Department of Justice, National Institute of Justice (September), NCJ 136607.

———, and S. Hiller-Sturmhofel. 2001. "Alcohol Abuse as a Risk Factor for and Consequence of Child Abuse." *Alcohol Research and Health* 25, 1:52–57.

Wieche, V. R. 1990. *Sibling Abuse: Hidden Physical, Emotional, and Sexual Trauma*. Lexington, MA: Lexington Books.

Wiese, D., and D. Daro. 1995. *Current Trends in Child Abuse Reporting and Fatalities: The Results of the 1994 Annual Fifty States Survey*. Chicago: National Committee to Prevent Child Abuse.

Wiggins, G. 1994. "Children's TV Needs Fine-Tuning Says APA." *APA Monitor* (September):6.

Wilkinson, T. 1994. "Gangs Find Fresh Turf in Salvador." *Los Angeles Times* (June 16):A1.

Williams, C. 1992. "The Glass Escalator: Hidden Advantages for Men in the 'Female' Professions." *Social Problems* 39, 3 (August):253–67.

Williams, G. 1998. "Toxic Dads." *Parental Magazine.* Online Collection: parenting.com. (October).

Williams, J. 1993. "Sexuality in Marriage." In B. Wolman and J. Money, eds., *Handbook of Human Sexuality*, 93–122. Northvale, NJ: Jason Aronson.

Williams, J. E., and D. L. Best. 1990. *Measuring Sex Stereotypes: A Multinational Study*, rev. ed. Newbury Park, CA: Sage.

Williamson, M. 1994. *Thoughts, Prayer, Rites of Passage.* New York: Random House.

Willie, C. V. 1981. *A New Look at the Black Family.* Bayside, NY: General Hall.

Wilsnak, S., N. Vogeltanz, A. Klassen, and T. Harris. 1997. "Childhood Sexual Abuse and Women's Substance Abuse: National Survey Findings." *Journal of Studies on Alcohol* 58:264–72.

Wilson, E., and S. H. Ng. 1988. "Sex Bias in Visual Images Evoked by Generics: A New Zealand Study." *Sex Roles* 18:159–68.

Wilson, E. D. 1975. *Sociology: The New Synthesis.* Cambridge, MA: Harvard University Press.

Wilson, W. J. 1980. *The Declining Significance of Race.* Chicago: University of Chicago Press.

———. 1987. *The Truly Disadvantaged: The Inner City, the Underclass, and Public Policy.* Chicago: University of Chicago Press.

Winch, R. R., T. Ktsanes, and V. Ktsanes. 1954. "The Theory of Complementary Needs in Mate Selection: An Analytic and Descriptive Study." *American Sociological Review* 19:241–49.

Wineberg, H. 1988. "Duration between Marriage and First Birth and Marital Stability." *Social Biology* 35:91–102.

———. 1990. "Childbearing in Remarriage." *Journal of Marriage and the Family* 52:31–38.

———. 1994. "Marital Reconciliation in the United States: Which Couples Are Successful?" *Journal of Marriage and the Family* 56 (February):80–88.

———. 1996. "The Prevalence and Characteristics of Blacks Having a Successful Marital Reconciliation." *Journal of Divorce and Remarriage* 25, 1/2:75–86.

———, and J. McCarthy. 1993. "Separation and Reconciliation in American Marriages." *Journal of Divorce and Remarriage* 20:21–42.

Wolfe, A. 1998. *One Nation, After All.* New York: Viking.

Wolfson, E. 1996. "Why We Should Fight for the Freedom to Marry: The Challenges and Opportunities That Will Follow a Win in Hawaii." *Journal of Gay, Lesbian, and Bisexual Identity* 1 (1):79–89.

W.O.M.A.N., Inc. 1996. "Myths and Facts about Violence." http://www.norcov.com/womaninc/myths.html (1999, June 4).

Women against Abuse. 1996. "Statistics on Domestic Violence." Philadelphia: Women against Abuse.

Wong, M. G. 1988. "The Chinese American Family." In C. Mindel, R. W. Habenstein, and R. Wright, Jr., eds., *Ethnic Families in America: Patterns and Variations*, 230–57. New York: Elsevier.

Women's Health Care House. 2002. "Fact Sheet: Domestic Violence." http://www.members.iinet.net.au/~wwwhch/womanhealth/dvl.html (2002, January 8).

Women's Sports Foundation. 1998. *Women's Sports Facts.* East Meadow, NY: Women's Sports Foundation.

Wong, M. G. 1998. "The Chinese-American Family." In C. H. Mindel, R. W. Habenstein, and R. Wright, Jr. *Ethnic Families in America: Patterns and Variations*, 284–310. Upper Saddle River, NJ: Prentice Hall.

Wood, J. T. 1994. *Gendered Lives: Communication, Gender, and Culture.* Belmont, CA: Wadsworth.

———, ed. 1996. *Gendered Relationships.* Mountain View, CA: Mayfield.

Woodard, A. 1998. "Father-Child Relationships." *Gale Encyclopedia of Childhood and Adolescence.* Detroit: Gale.

Woodman, S. 1995. "How Teen Pregnancy Has Become a Political Football." *Ms.* (January/February):90–91.

Woods, R. D. 1996. "Grandmother Roles: A Cross Cultural View." *Journal of Instructional Psychology* 23 (December):286–92.

Worden, J. W. 1982. *Grief Counseling and Grief Therapy: A Handbook for the Mental Health Practitioner.* New York: Springer.

"Working Women Say . . . 2000. AFL-CIO. http://www.aflcio.org/women/survey1.htm (2001, October 17).

World Almanac Book of Facts, 1991. 1990. New York: Pharos Books.

World Bank. 2001. *World Development Indicators, 2001.* Washington, DC.

World Health Organization. 1997. "Substance Use among Street Children and Other Children and Youth in Especially Difficult Circumstances" (March):Fact Sheet N151. http://www.who.org/inf-fs/en/fact151.html.

———. 1998. "Fifty Facts from the World Health Report 1998." http://www.who.int/whr/1998/factse.htm.

———. 2000a. *Global Water Supply and Sanitation Assessment 2000 Report.* Geneva, Switzerland. http://www.who.int/water_sanitation_health/Globassesment/Global2.1.htm (2002, January 22).

———. 2000b. "Substance Dependence." http://www.who.int/substance_abuse/More.html (2002, January 22).

———. 2002. "Special Report: Health in Afghanistan Situation Analysis" (January 21). http://www.who.int/disasters/emergency.cfm?emergencyID=2&doctypeID=2 (2002, January 22).

World Health Report. 1998. "Executive Summary: Life in the 21st Century—A Vision for All" (March 5). http://www.who.int/whr/1998/exsum98e.html.

Worling, J. R. 1995. "Adolescent Sibling-Incest Offenders: Differences in Family and Individual Functioning When Compared to Adolescent Nonsibling Sex Offenders." *Child Abuse & Neglect* 19:633–643.

Worthington, R. 1994. "Adding Father to Family: Paternity Law Takes Aim at Poor." *Chicago Tribune* (February 14):1, 8.

Wright, J. D. 1989. *Address Unknown: The Homeless in America.* New York: Aldine de Gruyter.

Wright, J. M. 1998. *Lesbian Step Families: An Ethnography of Love.* New York: Haworth Press.

Wu, Z. 1994. "Remarriage in Canada: Exchange Perspective." *Journal of Divorce and Remarriage* 21, 3/4:191–224.

———. 1995. "The Stability of Cohabitation Relationships: The Role of Children." *Journal of Marriage and the Family* 57 (February):231–36.

———. 2000. *Cohabitation: An Alternative Form of Family Living.* Toronto: Oxford University Press.

Wu, Z., and M. J. Penning. 1997. "Marital Instability after Midlife." *Journal of Family Issues* 18 (September):459–78.

WuDunn, S. 1996. "In Single Motherhood, Japan Trails the World." *New York Times* (March 13):sec. A.

———. 1997. "Korean Women Still Feel Demands to Bear a Son." *New York Times* (January 14):3.

Wurtele, S., A. Melzer, and L. Kast. 1992. "Preschoolers Knowledge of and Ability to Learn Genital Terminology." *Journal of Sex Education and Therapy* 18, 2:115–22.

Xu, X., C. Hudspeth, and S. Estes. 1997. "The Effects of Husbands' Involvement in Child Rearing Activities and Participation in Household Labor on Marital Quality: A Racial Comparison." *Journal of Gender, Culture, and Health* 2 (3):171–93.

Yardley, J. 1999a. "Investigators Say Embryologist Knew He Erred in Egg Mix-Up." *New York Times* (April 17):A13.

———. 1999b. "After Embryo Mix-Up, Couple Say They Will Give Up One Baby." *New York Times* (March 30).

Yates, R. E. 1990. "Japan's Violent Young Rebels Fight Back." *San Diego Union* (April 8).

Yednak, C. 2001. "Wilmette Principal Has Gender Changed." *Chicago Tribune* (August 22):5.

Yellowbird, M., and C. M. Snipp. 1994. "American Indian Families." In R. L. Taylor, ed., *Minority Families in the United States: A Multicultural Perspective*, 179–201. Upper Saddle River, NJ: Prentice Hall.

Yuen, M. 1998a. "Same-Sex Marriage Strongly Rejected" (November 4). http://starbulletin.co...11/04/news/story3.html.

Yuen, M. 1998b. "Same-Sex Marriage Debate Rages On, Now over Domestic Partnership Bill" (November 6). http://starbulletin.co... 11/06/news/story9.html.

Zablocki, B. 1980. *Alienation and Charisma: A Study of Contemporary Communes.* New York: Free Press.

Zambrano, M. 1995. "Social and Cultural Reasons for Abuse." In A. Kesselman, L. McNair, and N. Schniedewind, eds., *Women: Images and Realities,* 316–18. Mountain View, CA: Mayfield.

Zavella, P. 1987. *Women's Work and Chicano Families: Cannery Workers of the Santa Clara Valley.* Ithaca, NY: Cornell University Press.

Zebroski, S. 1997. "Findings for Research on Interracial Marriages." Interrace: SoftLine Information, Inc. http://www.sistahspace.com/nommo/ir13.html (2001, November 14).

Zedeck, S., and K. Mosier. 1990. "Work in the Family and Employing Organizations." *American Psychologist* 45, 2:240–51.

Zernike, K. 1998. "Feminism Has Created Progress, but Man, oh, Man, Look What Else." *Chicago Tribune* (June 21):1, 8.

Zimmerman, J., and G. Reavill. 1998. *Raising Our Athletic Daughters: How Sports Can Build Self-Esteem and Save Girls' Lives.* New York: Doubleday.

Zogby National Poll. 2000. *Zogby International* (February). http://www.zogby.com (2002, February 3).

Zuckerman, D. M., and D. H. Sayre. 1982. "Cultural Sex-Role Expectations and Children's Sex-Role Concepts." *Sex Roles* 8:853–62.

Zuckerman, M. B. 1993. "The Victims of Violence." *U.S. News & World Report* (August 2):64.

Zuger, A. 1998. "Girls and Women Are as Aggressive as Males, Studies Show." *Chicago Tribune* (December 27):sec. 13, 2.

Zuravin, S., and F. DiBlasio. 1996. "The Correlates of Child Physical Abuse and Neglect by Adolescent Mothers." *Journal of Family Violence*, 11 (June):149–66.

Photo Credits

CHAPTER 1: Ariel Skelley/Corbis/Stock Market, *5;* AP/Wide World Photos, *7;* Joan Zientek, *10;* Fox/Getty Images, Inc., *13* (*left*); Anthony Neste/Getty Images, Inc., *13* (*right*); AP/Wide World Photos, *16;* Fotopic/Omni-Photo Communications, Inc., *18;* CORBIS, *21;* AP/Wide World Photos, *23.*

CHAPTER 2: Elizabeth Crews/Stock Boston, *33;* SuperStock, Inc., *40;* Wamucii Zjogu, *42;* The Granger Collection, New York, *45* (*top left*); The Granger Collection, New York, *45* (*top center*); CORBIS, *45* (*top right*); The Granger Collection, New York, *45* (*middle left*); Culver Pictures, Inc., *45* (*middle center*); The Granger Collection, New York, *45* (*middle right*); Patricia Hill Collins, McMicken College of Arts and Sciences, *45* (*bottom left*); Randall Collins, *45* (*bottom center*); Center for Working Families, *45* (*bottom right*); Paul White/AP/Wide World Photos, *53.*

CHAPTER 3: The Boston Public Library, Rare Book Department, Courtesy of the Trustees, *64* (*left and right*); David Burges/Getty Images, Inc., *67* (*left and right*); Ken Karp/Pearson Education/PH College, *70;* Photofest, *76;* Greg Smith/Corbis/SABA Press Photos, Inc., *79;* Tony Freeman/PhotoEdit, *80;* Ariel Skelley/Corbis/Stock Market, *81.*

CHAPTER 4: AP/Wide World Photos, *94;* Ursula Markus/Photo Researchers, Inc., *95;* Tony Neste/Anthony Neste, *98;* Getty Images, Inc., *103;* Photofest, *109.*

CHAPTER 5: Chris Brown/Stock Boston, *120;* Jeff Greenberg/Photo Researchers, Inc., *124*; Douglas Mason/Woodfin Camp & Associates, *125* (*top left*); Jim Whitmer/Stock Boston, *125* (*top right*); Carolyn A. McKeone/Photo Researchers, Inc., *125* (*lower left*); Myrleen Ferguson/PhotoEdit, *140;* Spencer Grant/PhotoEdit, *142;* B. Mahoney/The Image Works, *149.*

CHAPTER 6: CORBIS, *157;* Barbara Rios/Photo Researchers, Inc., *160;* Jeff Maloney/Getty Images, Inc./PhotoDisc, Inc., *166;* Bob Daemmrich/Stock Boston, *167;* Shelley Gazin/CORBIS, *172;* Stephen Ferry/Getty Images, Inc., *184;* Blair Seitz/Photo Researchers, Inc., *187;* Per-Anders Pettersson/Getty Images, Inc., *195;* Vecto Verso/eStock Photography LLC, *197.*

CHAPTER 7: CORBIS, *202;* Reporters Press Agency/eStock Photography LLC, *205;* Bachman/Lonely Planet Images/Photo 20-20, *208;* Darlene Queen, *212;* Frank Siteman, *214;* Monika Graff/The Image Works, *218;* Luke Frazza/AFP/CORBIS, *219;* AP/Wide World Photos, *220;* ASAP/Sarit Uzieli/Photo Researchers, Inc., *222.*

CHAPTER 8: Joel Gordon Photography, *232;* The Terry Wild Studio, Inc., *238;* David Young-Wolff/PhotoEdit, *241;* Laural E. Kemp, *250;* Michael Newman/PhotoEdit, *253;* Robert Brenner/PhotoEdit, *259.*

CHAPTER 9: Antman/The Image Works, *266;* E. Crews/The Image Works, *268;* AP/Wide World Photos, *269;* Wayne Scarberry/Getty Images, Inc., *270;* Sam Mircovich/Reuters/Getty Images, Inc., *276;* Joel Gordon Photography, *282;* Michele Tyrpak, *284;* Photofest, *287;* Tony Freeman/PhotoEdit, *301.*

CHAPTER 10: AP/Wide World Photos, *311;* Bob Daemmrich/The Image Works, *314;* Myrleen Ferguson/PhotoEdit, *316* (*left and right*); Jennifer K. Berman, *321;* Rick Browne/Stock Boston, *327;* AP/Wide World Photos, *329;* Jonathan Nourok/PhotoEdit, *331.*

CHAPTER 11: Warner Bros. and Village Roadshow Films/Getty Images, Inc., *342;* Yates Family/Getty Images, Inc., *345;* A. Ramey/PhotoEdit, *350;* Family Violence Prevention Fund/Ad Council, © 1994, *353;* Laura Anderson, *360;* Summer Productions, *361;* Sean Cayton/The Image Works, *366;* Pauline Lubens/Detroit Free Press, Inc., *370.*

CHAPTER 12: Gale Zucker/Stock Boston, *381;* Michael Newman/PhotoEdit, *382;* David Schreiber/copyright, The Daily Breeze/David Schreiber, Oct. 7, 1990, All rights reserved, *384;* Steve Mason/Getty Images, Inc./PhotoDisc, Inc., *390;* Elizabeth Zuckerman/PhotoEdit, *393;* Bob Daemmrich/Stock Boston, *396;* Reuters/Jim Bourg/Getty Images, Inc., *401.*

CHAPTER 13: CORBIS, *407;* Getty Images, Inc./PhotoDisc, Inc., *408;* Michael Newman/PhotoEdit, *413;* Topham/OB/The Image Works, *416;* Mimi Forsyth, *419;* Jane Maring, *421.*

CHAPTER 14: Carolyn Wendt/Actuality, Inc., *429;* Lawrence Migdale/Lawrence Migdale/Pix, *435;* Joseph Nettis/Photo Researchers, Inc., *436;* Michael Philip Manheim/International Stock Photography Ltd., *437;* Mr. And Mrs. Harry Gottlieb, *438;* David M. Barron/Oxygen Group Photography, *439;* Ken Huang/Getty Images, Inc., *442;* © Rick Friedman Photography, *443;* Janice Fullman/Index Stock Imagery, Inc., *447.*

CHAPTER 15: AP/Wide World Photos, *457;* David R. Frazier Photolibrary, Inc., *459;* Phyllis Picardi/Stock Boston, *459;* Michel Ulli/Reuters/CORBIS, *461;* AP/Wide World Photos, *471;* AP/Wide World Photos, *474* (*left and right*); AP/Wide World Photos, *476;* AP/Wide World Photos, *481;* Joe Raedle/Getty Images, Inc., *493.*

APPENDIXES: Materials courtesy Planned Parenthood, NYC/Teri Stratford/S&S PH College, *510* (*top*); The Female Health Company, *510* (*bottom*).

Name Index

A

Abelard, 341–42
Abelson, R., 321
Abilities, 462
Abma, J., 214
Abrams, M., 367–68
Achenbaum, A., 441
Acock, A. C., 383, 395
Adams, P. F., 469, 472
Adams, R. C., 98
Adams, S., 71
Adams, V., 110
Aday, R. H., 453
Ade-Ridder, L., 437
Adler, F., 478
Adler, J., 287
Adler, N. L., 94, 96
Adler, R. G., 366
Ahlberg, C., 69
Ahlburg, D. A., 24, 301
Ahmad, I. L., 475
Ahrons, C., 384, 419
Akers, R. L., 467
Alba, R. D., 252
Albas, C., 91, 101, 156
Albas, D., 91, 101, 156
Albers, C., 340
Aldous, J., 440
Alexander, B. B., 211
Allan, C. A., 359
Allan, G., 98
Allen, K., 210
Allen, K. S., 331
Allgeier, E., 106
Alpert-Gillis, L. J., 77
Alstein, H., 471
Althaus, F., 214
Amato, P. R., 215, 315, 383, 386–87, 389, 392, 394
Ambert, A., 369, 389, 418
Amott, T., 136, 377
Anders, G., 136
Andersen, M., 4, 39, 110, 149, 171, 184, 298, 354, 367–68
Andersen, M. L., 52, 54
Anderson, D. L., 321
Anderson, M., 394
Anderson, R. N., 229
Anderson, S. A., 437
Angermeier, W. F., 291
Anthony, C., 394
Antill, J. K., 213, 215
Apfel, N. H., 443
Aquilino, W. S., 415, 429
Archbold, P. G., 448
Arendell, T., 385, 390, 392
Arias, E., 480
Aries, P., 492
Arkes, H., 137
Arliss, L., 258
Arndt, B., 136
Arnold, C., 414
Aronson, E., 111–12
Atchley, R. C., 432, 450, 491
Atwater, L., 185–86
Auster, C., 475
Avila, E., 315
Axinn, W. G., 216

B

Baars, J., 223
Baca Zinn, M., 40
Bachman, J. G., 213
Bachman, R., 345
Bachrach, C. A., 272, 445, 469, 472
Bachu, A., 267
Bacue, A., 75
Bahr, S. J., 409
Baig, E. C., 145
Bailey, R. H., 23
Baker, M., 243
Balaguer, A., 216
Bales, K., 306
Ball, E., 17
Balswick, J. O., 253
Bandura, A., 70
Banker, B. S., 406
Bannister, S. A., 358–59
Barcus, E. F., 74
Barell, V., 446
Barenbaum, N. B., 387
Barer, B. M., 444
Barlett, D. L., 310
Barling, J., 313
Barnes, S., 387
Barnett, O. W., 365, 369, 371
Barnett, R., 392
Barranti, C. R., 443
Barresi, C. M., 450
Barrett, E. A., 468
Barth, R. P., 469, 471
Bartkowski, J., 36–37
Baruch, G., 392
Basow, S., 65, 70, 74, 80, 128, 158, 166, 171, 180, 286–87
Baugher, R. J., 491
Bean, F., 21
Becerra, R. M., 295, 441
Beck, M., 471
Becker, H., 38
Becker-Haven, J., 414, 424
Bedard, J., 227
Bedford, V. H., 440
Beer, W. R., 316, 405, 415
Beezley, D. A., 148
Behrens, B. C., 394
Behrens, L., 67
Belcastro, P. A., 178
Beley, R., 325
Bell, A. P., 172, 180, 219
Bell, M., 470
Bell, R., 91
Bellas, M. L., 314–15
Beller, A. H., 409
Bem, S. L., 70–71, 83
Bengtson, V. L., 383, 436, 440–41, 445–47, 451
Benjamin, L., 475
Benjamin, O., 313
Bennett, J., 145
Benokraitis, N. V., 342, 353
Berado, F. M., 451
Berger, R., 221, 417, 419
Berkowitz, A. D., 468
Berlin, I., 17
Bernard, J., 19, 48, 244–45, 389
Berry, M., 471
Besharov, D. J., 365
Bessell, H., 99
Best, D. L., 64
Best, J., 49
Bianchi, S. M., 229, 287, 311, 315
Biblarz, T., 298
Billingsley, A., 11, 15
Billy, J., 166
Bingham, S. G., 321
Binnie, J., 217
Birdsong, C., 211, 215
Birns, B., 71
Black, D., 172
Blackwell, J. E., 293
Blakeslee, S., 246, 300, 393, 398
Blanchard, R., 63
Blank, R., 275
Blankenhorn, D., 286
Blanton, P. W., 231
Blassingame, J., 15
Blau, P., 39, 50
Blieszner, R., 98, 440
Block, J., 254
Blood, R. O., Jr., 437
Bluestone, B., 325
Blum, D., 220
Blum, R., 369
Blumberg, E., 166
Blumstein, P., 35, 107, 109, 161, 171, 215, 219
Bock, E. W., 138, 243
Boeringer, S. B., 467
Bohannan, P., 384, 410, 418
Bojorquez, J., 242
Bolduc, D., 72
Bolig, R., 142
Booth, A., 215, 381, 383, 392, 394, 422
Bor, W., 394
Borden, S., 147
Borland, D. M., 101
Boswell, T. D., 313
Botta, R. A., 76
Bound, J., 451
Bowcott, O., 466
Bowen, S. L., 282
Bower, B., 446
Bowman, P. J., 292
Boyd-Franklin, N., 218
Boyer, D., 367
Boyle, M., 345, 352
Boyle, P. A., 71
Bozett, F. W., 298
Bradshaw., D., 94
Bradsher, K., 209
Bramlett, M. D., 380–81, 409, 421
Brand, E., 420
Brandon, K., 273, 301
Brantley, J. N., 51
Braver, S. L., 392
Bray, J., 405, 411–12
Brecher, E., 177
Brehm, S. S., 104–5
Brewer, L., 446
Brewerton, T. D., 75
Brewster, K., 166
Brimhall, D., 395
Brindis, C., 183
Brines, J., 215
Brod, H., 65
Brodbar-Nemzer, J. Y., 382
Brody, G. H., 72
Brody, J. E., 291
Bronstein, P., 71
Brooks, D., 469
Brotman, B., 222
Broverman, D. M., 80
Broverman, I., 80
Brown, J., 169–70
Brown, M. R., 440
Brown, R. P., 312
Brown, S., 467–68
Browne, A., 351
Brownsworth, V., 232
Brubaker, T. H., 428, 437–38
Bruno, B., 404
Bryjak, G. J., 353, 460, 478, 483, 485–86, 489
Bryson, J., 112

Bryson, K., 444
Buehler, C., 387, 394
Bulcroft, K., 211
Bulcroft, K. A., 138
Bulcroft, R. A., 138
Bumiller, E., 129
Bumpass, L. L., 216–17, 380, 382, 408–10, 450
Bunch, C., 171, 340
Bunker, B. B., 312
Burch, J., 478
Burger, C., 491
Burger, J. M., 269
Burgess, E. W., 48
Burgy, T. M., 439
Burke, P., 221
Burman, P., 326
Burns, A. L., 71
Burns, J. F., 7
Burns, L., 269
Burton, L., 292, 440–41, 447, 451
Bussey, K., 70
Butler, D., 280
Butler, R., 430
Butler, S. A., 71
Butrica, B. A., 390
Buunk, B. B., 220
Byer, C., 188
Byrd, J. C., 135

C

Cafasso, L., 447
Cafferata, G. L., 436, 446
Cahill, S., 452
Calasanti, T., 451
Calhoun, A. W., 202, 406
Calhoun, C., 46
Call, V., 185
Campbell, S., 394
Campo-Flores, B., 168
Canada, G., 78
Cancian, F. M., 91, 106–7
Cantor, M. H., 445
Cardell, M., 219
Carlier, A., 141
Carlson, D., 89
Carlson, J., 259
Carmichael, S., 473
Carney, L., 239
Caron, S. L., 221
Carr, L. G., 406
Carrere, S., 387
Carrigan, T., 55
Carroll, D., 209
Carter, B., 75
Carter, H., 380
Casper, L. M., 12, 24, 203, 206, 214–15, 300, 432, 435, 444
Caspi, A., 215
Castro-Martin, T., 408
Catalano, D. J., 445
Cate, R. M., 384
Cattell, M., 446
Caulfield, M. D., 165
Cavanaugh, J., 443
Cerulo, K. A., 99
Chafetz, J. S., 51
Chamberlain, P., 468
Chambers-Schiller, L. V., 202–3
Chan, C. S., 218
Chan, F., 440
Chandra, A., 214
Chandy, J., 369
Chang, I., 168
Chappell, N., 445, 447
Chase-Lansdale, P. L., 394
Chassler, S., 182
Chasteen, A. L., 206
Cheal, D., 42, 44
Cherlin, A., 123, 214, 230, 300, 380, 386, 390, 394, 398, 409–10, 421, 442
Cherry, K., 112
Cherry, R., 321
Chester, N. L., 387
Childress, A. C., 75
Chiriboga, D. A., 393
Chiswick, C. U., 382
Chodorow, N., 53, 69
Choo, K., 310
Cirese, S., 178
Clanton, G., 110, 113
Clark, A. L., 437
Clark, H., 412
Clark, R. A., 82
Clark, S. C., 421
Clarke, L. M., 157, 178–80
Clarkson, F. E., 80
Clements, M., 160, 162–63, 171, 177, 179, 187, 253
Clemmensen, L. H., 63
Cleveland, R. W., 322–23
Climo, J., 446
Clinard, M. B., 462
Clingempeel, W. G., 414, 418, 420
Cloward, R., 327
Coates, J., 83
Coates, R., 293
Coats, P. P., 73
Cocco, M., 168
Cochran, S. D., 107, 131, 219
Cockerham, W. C., 434
Cockrum, J., 209
Coke, M. M., 440
Coker, D. R., 70
Colapinto, J., 62
Colasanto, D., 386
Cole, C. L., 383
Cole, P., 439
Coleman, M., 253, 394, 407–9, 411, 414, 416–18, 420
Coles, R., 165
Collins, K., 367–68
Collins, P. H., 4, 53, 72, 285–86, 293
Collins, R., 91
Collins, S., 409
Coltrane, S., 77, 89, 91–92, 316
Compas, B. E., 468
Condran, G., 383
Condry, J., 76
Conn, C. P., 430
Conn, J., 451
Connell, B., 55
Connell, J. P., 77
Conner, K., 452
Connidis, I. A., 445
Constantine, J., 223
Constantine, L., 223
Cook, K. V., 72
Cooke, D. J., 359
Cooney, T., 393, 443
Coontz, S., 3, 9, 12, 14, 20, 229, 313, 394
Copeland, A. P., 387
Cornell, C. P., 147, 343–45, 369, 372
Cornell, D., 481–82
Cornfield, N., 222
Cose, E., 317
Cossette, L., 72
Cote, R. M., 126
Couric, E., 321
Courtney, M., 469
Cowan, P. A., 419–20
Coward, R. T., 447
Cox, C., 447
Cox, H., 495
Crane, D. R., 384
Crary, D., 470
Crawford, L., 243
Creager, E., 79
Croft, P., 186
Croppenbacher, N., 468
Crosbie-Burnett, M., 407, 414, 420, 424
Crossen, C., 168
Crossette, B., 489–90
Crouter, A. C., 315
Crowder, K. D., 380
Cuber, J. F., 246–47
Cudina, M., 395
Cunningham, J. D., 213, 215
Cunningham-Burley, S., 443
Cureton, J., 205
Curran, D. J., 63, 78, 107, 148, 170, 236, 280, 319, 338, 366, 370
Curry, G. E., 274
Curtis, C. M., 471
Curtis, J. R., 313
Curtis, R., 21
Cutler, B., 209
Cyranowski, J. M., 80
Cytrynbaum, P., 145

D

Dahlberg, T., 482–83
Dailard, C., 268–69, 271
Dainton, M., 407
Dalakar, J., 324
Daly, K. J., 272
Daly, M., 338, 418
Daniels, M., 234
Daniels, R., 20, 233
Dannefer, D., 446
Darling, C., 158
Daro, D., 366
Darrett, B., 15
D'Augelli, A. R., 221
Davidson, K. B., 106
Davis, A. C., 127
Davis, G., 479
Davis, K., 92, 94–97, 103, 112, 367–68
Davis, R. F., 300, 470
Davis, S., 142
Dawson, D., 414
Day, R. D., 409
Deane, C., 380
Degler, C., 15
DeLamaster, J., 166
DeLeon, B., 65
DeLisi, R., 64
del Pinal, J., 295
DeMaris, A., 216, 417
Demaris, O., 483
De Mente, B., 93
DeMeo, P., 216
D'Emilio, J., 180–81
DeMillo, A., 357
Demo, D. H., 395
DeMont, J., 206
Demos, J., 14, 19
De Navas-Walt, C., 322–23
Dermer, M., 99
DeSpelder, L. A., 492, 495
DesRoches, C., 367–68
Dessoff, A., 430
Deutsch, F. M., 315
DeVall, W., 219
DeVault, M. L., 38
DeVita, C. J., 24, 230, 301
De Voss, S., 426
de Weerth, C., 128
Diamond, M., 62
DiBlasio, F., 366
Diesenhouse, S., 227
Dieter, P., 342
DiGiulio, R. C., 448, 451
Dinkmeyer, D., 259
Dion, K. K., 93, 128
Dion, K. L., 93, 128
Dionne, E. J., Jr., 31
Dittus, P., 165
Do, D., 297
Dobash, R. E., 351
Dobash, R. P., 351

Dobson, C., 437
Doherty, W. J., 414
Doka, K., 444, 494
Doll, E. R., 439
Doll, L., 172, 175
Dollahite, D. C., 420
Donnelly, B. W., 292
Donnelly, D., 364
Dorfman, R., 221
Dortch, S., 445
Dover, K., 90
Dow, B. J., 75
Doweiko, H. E., 467
Downs, A. C., 70
Downs, E. A., 393
Doyle, J. A., 353–54
Draughon, M., 417
Dreger, A. D., 63
Dressel, P. L., 222
Droegemueller, W., 362
Duberman, L., 417
DuBois, W. E. B., 475
Duffy, B., 17
Dugan, K. B., 74
Dugger, C. W., 263, 291
Duke, I., 475
Dumea, L., 468
Duncan, D., 422
Duncan, G., 389, 451
Duncan, O., 39
Dunkin, A., 272
Dunn, K., 186
Dunn, N. J., 468
Dupree, A., 299
Durkheim, E., 382
Dutton, D. G., 358–59
Duvall, E. M., 50–51, 428
Duxbury, L., 314
Dworkin, A., 274
Dwyer, J., 447

E

Earle, A. M., 202
Ebrahim, S., 36
Eckland, B., 252
Edelhart, C., 362
Edin, K., 293
Edwards, A., 178
Edwards, C. P., 72
Edwards, D. L., 321–22
Edwards, J. N., 132, 381, 422
Edwards, T. M., 229
Eells, L. W., 409
Ehrenreich, B., 185, 457–58
Ehrhardt, A., 70
Einstein, E., 418
Eisenhart, M. A., 130
Elles, L., 98
Ellis, J. B., 494
Ellis, M. J., 130
Elmer-Dewitt, P., 160–62, 179
Emery, R. E., 382, 399, 409
Enge, M., 273
Engley, H. L., 274
Erickson, R. J., 231
Erikson, E., 69, 266
Eschbach, K., 250
Eshleman, J. R., 350
Estes, C. L., 447
Estes, S., 292
Estioko-Griffin, A., 65
Etaugh, C., 206
Etzioni, A., 281
Evans, E., 453
Evans, L., 74

F

Facteau, L., 443
Faderman, L., 109
Fain, T. C., 321
Faison, S., 386
Falk, C., 112
Farkas, J. I., 440
Farley, J. E., 472–73, 475
Fausto-Sterling, A., 62–63
Faux, M., 266
Feagin, C. B., 138
Feagin, J. R., 138, 294, 342, 353, 475
Feld, L. S., 399
Felt, J. C., 381
Feng, D., 383
Fengler, A., 447
Ferber, M. A., 41
Ferdinand, P., 482
Ferguson, C., 148
Ferguson, S., 121–22
Fernquist, R. M., 467
Ferrante, J., 26, 48, 456
Ferraro, K. J., 386
Fichner-Rathus, L., 166
Field, A. E., 76
Fields, J., 12, 24, 203, 206, 215, 300, 432, 435
Fillenbaum, G. G., 439
Fine, D., 412, 424
Fine, F., 367
Fine, M. A., 292, 394, 412, 417, 424
Fingrutd, M., 206
Finkelhor, D., 354–55, 370
Finkelman, P., 16
Finlay, B., 382
Finn, S., 219
Fischer, E. F., 88
Fisher, H., 88–89, 105
Fishman, B., 411, 415
Fitzgerald, L. F., 80
Fivush, R., 71
Flaherty, Sr. M. J., 443
Flitcraft, A., 359
Florence, B., 399
Flowers, B. J., 245
Floyd, F. J., 439
Folk, K. F., 315, 409
Foner, N., 441
Fornek, S., 369
Forrest, C., 31
Forste, R., 213
Fossett, M. A., 230
Fountain, J., 478
Fournier, K., 275
Fox, G. L., 121, 396
Fox, P., 448
Fox, V. C., 406
Frank, E., 80
Frank, R., 310
Franklin, C. W., 54, 98
Franklin, M., 312
Franks, M. M., 447
Frazier, E. F., 380
Frederick, L., 313
Freedman, E. B., 180–81
Freeman, R., 203
Freiberg, P., 270
French, H. W., 267, 271, 322
Freud, S., 68–69, 165, 266
Fricke, K., 76
Frieden, T., 306
Friedland, G. H., 494
Friedman, B., 241
Friend, R. A., 71, 221
Fromm, E., 94–95
Frye, M., 161
Frye, N., 383
Fuentes, A., 457–58
Furnham, A., 76
Furstenberg, F. F., Jr., 386, 390, 393, 398, 408, 414, 419, 442
Furukawa, S., 424

G

Gaertner, S. L., 406
Gagnon, J. H., 159–61, 165, 177–78, 185–86
Galambos, N. L., 313
Ganong, L., 394
Ganong, L. H., 253, 407–9, 411, 414, 416–18, 420
Ganza, B., 168
Garcia-Pena, R. P., 466
Gardner, J., 309
Gardner, M. D., 384
Garfinkel, I., 380, 385
Garver, P., 443
Garza, M. M., 330
Gately, S., 395
Gates, G., 172
Gebhard, P. H., 172
Gecas, V., 392
Geiss, S. K., 387
Gelfand, D. E., 450
Gelken, C., 207
Gelles, R. J., 147, 343–46, 361–62, 364–66, 369, 371–72, 475, 486
Genovese, E. D., 16
Genovese, T. A., 420
George, L. K., 439
Gerard, J., 394
Gerstel, N., 389
Giarruso, R., 383
Giarrusso, R., 148, 445
Gibbs, N., 168, 182, 286
Gibson, J. T., 291
Gibson, R., 439
Giddens, A., 342
Gilbert, L. A., 80
Giles-Sims, J., 417, 420
Gilford, R., 437
Gill, R. T., 263–64
Gillespie, M., 186
Gilligan, C., 78
Gillis, J., 11–12
Gilmore, D., 65
Giuliano, T. A., 73
Giunta, C. T., 468
Gladwell, M., 274
Glasberg, D. S., 462
Glazer, N., 263–64
Glei, D., 183
Glendinning, A., 290
Glendon, M. A., 397
Glenn, E. N., 20, 285
Glenn, N. D., 209, 227, 252–53, 283, 288, 382, 437
Glick, P., 50, 380, 382, 409–10, 422
Glick, P. C., 382–83
Godbey, G., 314
Godwin, D. D., 313
Goetting, A., 385, 410
Golant, S. M., 435–36
Goldberg, C., 201, 233, 300
Golding, J. M., 315
Goldman, N., 136
Goldscheider, C., 415
Goldscheider, F. K., 415
Goleman, D., 71, 76, 245, 475
Gonzalez, L., 272
Goodchilds, J., 148
Goode, E., 291, 298, 430
Goode, W., 88, 386
Goodman, D., 201
Goodman, M., 211
Goodrich, N., 447
Gordon, S. L., 219
Gordon, S. M., 194
Gordon, V., 165
Gorner, P., 13, 159–63, 173–74
Gottman, J., 254, 258–59, 298, 387–88
Goudy, W. J., 313
Gove, W., 245, 451
Graber, J. L., 398
Grady, W. R., 166
Graham, J. W., 409
Graham, S., 200
Grall, T., 391, 397
Grall, T. S., 435

Granat, D., 274
Granoff, B., 148
Grant, L., 316
Gray, J. S., 209
Grebe, S. C., 399
Green, B., 218
Greenberg, L., 367–68
Greenhouse, S., 314
Greenstein, B., 324
Greenstein, T. N., 386
Greider, L., 429
Greif, G. L., 395–96
Greil, A. L., 272
Greven, P., 14
Griffin, S., 354
Grimes, M. D., 221
Grimm, T. K., 290
Griswold del Castillo, R., 21
Groat, H. T., 266
Gross, H. E., 312
Gross, P., 413
Grossman, H., 74
Grossman, S. H., 74
Grotevant, H., 471
Grotstein, J., 97
Groza, V., 471
Grunbaum, J., 181
Guang, X., 251
Gubrium, J. F., 210
Guisinger, S., 419–20
Guo, C., 395
Gura, T., 61, 160–61
Gutman, H. G., 16–17, 380
Gwartney-Gibbs, P. A., 123

H

Habenstein, R. W., 91, 93, 250–51, 378
Hackett, G., 186
Haddocks, R., 347–48
Haffner, D., 166
Hagestad, G., 446
Hahn, B. A., 209
Halberstadt, A. G., 65
Hale, D., 188
Hale-Benson, J., 72, 422
Hall, D. R., 216
Hall, J. A., 328
Hall, R. M., 74
Hamburg, D. A., 317–18
Hamel, B., 415
Hamilton, B., 183–84, 264–65, 278
Hamilton, C. V., 473
Hammersmith, S., 172
Hanes, S. N., 439
Hanna, J., 390, 399–400
Hanna, S. L., 419
Hannan, P. J., 75
Hansen, G. L., 111
Hansen, J. E., 258
Hansen, K., 98
Hanson, G., 465
Hanson, S. M., 396
Hansson, R. O., 393, 450
Harden, B., 375–76
Hardin, L., 221
Hare, J., 136
Hargreaves, E. F., 366
Haring-Hidore, M., 253
Harmatz, M. G., 62, 156–58
Harootyan, R., 440
Harris, T., 369
Harris Poll, 480
Harroff, P. B., 246–47
Harrow, B. S., 448
Harry, J., 130–31, 218–20
Hartinger, B., 234
Hartman, S., 138
Harvey, D. L., 218, 443
Harvey, E., 317
Hatfield, E., 99, 105–6
Hay, T., 365
Hayes, L., 484
Hayghe, H. V., 311
Hazan, C., 94
Heaton, T. B., 253, 383
Hedges, W., 189
Heesink, J. A. M., 315
Heilman, N., 439
Henderson, S. H., 418
Hendrick, C., 92, 94, 96, 106, 182, 256, 258
Hendrick, S., 92, 94, 96, 106, 182, 256, 258
Hendry, B., 290
Henry, C. S., 413
Herbert, B., 174, 192, 487
Herek, G., 220
Herman, D. F., 106
Hernandez, R., 313
Herrerias, C., 396
Hershberger, S. L., 221
Hertz, R., 178, 315
Hess, B. B., 222
Hess, E., 185
Hessellund, H., 177
Hetherington, E. M., 394–95, 414–15, 418
Hetzel, L., 432
Heymann, D. L., 461
Hickie, I. B., 468
Hiedemann, B., 382, 386
Higginbotham, E., 204
Higginbotham, R., 219
Higgins, C., 314
Hill, A., 390
Hill, C. T., 105–6, 150
Hill, M. C., 440
Hill, N., 290
Hill, R., 132, 293–94, 326
Hiller-Sturmhofel, S., 468
Himes, C. L., 445
Hindus, M., 122
Hinton, I. D., 290
Hirsch, M. B., 271–72
Hite, S., 159, 171–72, 175–77, 179–80
Hobson, M., 241
Hochschild, A. R., 47, 286–87, 314–15
Hodges, E. L., 75
Hodson, D. S., 187
Hodson, R., 310
Hoff, L. A., 112
Hofferth, S. L., 393
Hoffman, S. D., 389, 393
Hoffnung, M., 285
Hogan, D. P., 440
Hoganbruen, K., 397
Holland, D. C., 130
Holmes, J., 110
Holmes, T., 493
Holmes, W., 147, 351, 362–63, 365, 367–69, 372
Holmstrom, R., 369
Homans, G., 50
Hondagneu-Sotelo, P., 315
Hood, J. C., 315
hooks, b., 52
Hooyman, N., 442, 451, 495
Horin, A., 390
Horney, K., 69
Hornike, D., 410–11
Horowitz, A., 448
Houseknecht, S. K., 382
Hout, M., 410
Hovell, M. F., 166
Howell, J., 478
Hoyenga, K. B., 61
Hoyenga, K. T., 61
Hoyert, D., 480
Hsu, G., 76
Huang, A., 378
Hubbard, R., 62
Huber, J., 267, 315
Hudspeth, C., 292
Hughes, Z., 108
Humes, K., 204
Hummer, R., 148
Humphrys, J., 458
Hunt, J. G., 267, 395
Hunt, L. L., 267, 395
Hunt, M., 91, 159, 179
Hupka, R., 111
Husted, J., 178
Huston, M., 108, 130–31
Hutcheon, G., 281
Hutchinson, M. K., 393
Huyck, M. H., 446
Hyde, J. S., 62, 72
Hyman, S. E., 493
Hymel, K., 365

I

Iams, H. M., 390
Iazetto, D., 166, 359
Ihinger-Tallman, M., 406, 414, 417, 420, 422
Ingram, E., 494
Inman, C., 81, 209
Insko, C. A., 140
Ishir-Kuntz, M., 207
Iyer, S., 469

J

Jaccard, J., 165
Jacklin, C., 72
Jackson, A. P., 312
Jacob, H., 379
Jacob, T., 468
Jacobs, G., 185
Jacobson, N. S., 80
James, R., 247
Jankowiak, W. R., 88
Janofsky, M., 3
Jarrell, M. P., 75
Jarrett, R., 37–38, 293
Jay, K., 219
Jaynes, G. D., 380
Jendrek, M. P., 444
Jenkins, L., 79
Jenny, C., 365
Jodl, K. M., 414
John, D., 215, 292, 315–16
John, R., 294–95
Johns, T., 157, 178–80
Johnson, A. G., 352
Johnson, C. L., 387, 445
Johnson, D., 381
Johnson, E., 172, 175
Johnson, F. L., 81, 209
Johnson, P., 148
Johnson, V., 158–59, 175–77, 179, 186–88
Johnston, J. R., 397
Johnston, L. D., 213
Jones, A., 400
Jones, T., 74
Jouzaitis, C., 300
Joyner, K., 215

K

Kahle, J., 79
Kahn, J., 183
Kain, E., 79, 202–3, 227
Kalish, R. A., 491
Kallen, D. J., 158
Kalma, A., 128
Kalmijn, M., 249, 252
Kamerman, S. B., 332
Kaminer, W., 363
Kanin, E. J., 106
Kann, L., 181
Kanter, R. M., 311
Kao, H., 446
Kaplan, G., 446
Karanki, T., 221

Karen, R., 109
Karis, T., 249
Karp, D. A., 88, 94
Karp, S., 369
Kast, L., 166
Katz, S., 168
Katzev, A. R., 383
Keating, N. C., 439
Kehoe, M., 221
Keita, G. B., 80
Keith, P., 210
Keith, V. M., 382, 451
Keller, S., 46, 169–70
Kelley, H. H., 99
Kelley, P., 419–21
Kellog, S., 12–18, 22–23
Kelly, G. F., 107, 205
Kelly, J., 221, 394, 405, 411–12, 414, 419
Kelly, J. B., 394–95
Kelly, R. F., 396
Kempe, C. H., 362
Kennen, R., 278
Kephart, W. M., 106, 223
Kerckhoff, A. C., 138, 252
Kessler, S. J., 63
Kessler-Harris, A., 20, 309
Kheshgi-Genovese, S., 420
Kidder, R. M., 227–28
Kiecolt, K. J., 230
Kiernan, K., 415
Kim, P., 178, 228, 254, 366, 386
Kimmel, M., 54
Kinchen, S., 181
Kinder, D. R., 475
King, D. K., 4
Kingston, P. W., 314
Kinsey, A., 158–59, 165, 172, 174–75, 179, 181, 185, 389
Kitano, H. L., 251, 297
Kitano, K., 297
Kivett, V. R., 444
Kiyak, H. A., 442, 451, 495
Klassen, A., 369
Klaus, E., 440
Klaus, P., 203
Kleiman, C., 321
Kleiman, K., 283, 316–17
Klein, D., 440
Klerman, G. L., 80
Klimek, D., 133
Kloehn, S., 244
Klonoff, E. A., 80
Kluegel, J. R., 475
Kluwer, E. S., 315
Knaub, P., 419
Knopf, M. F., 393
Kochanek, K., 480
Kohlberg, L., 70
Koivula, N., 76
Kolata, G., 440
Kolbe, L., 181
Kolodny, R. C., 186–88
Kong, C., 146–47
Kong, D., 428
Koss, M. P., 148
Kotulak, R., 430, 438
Kretchner, A., 178
Krishnakuman, A., 394
Kristof, N., 228–29, 301
Ksir, C., 149
Ktsanes, T., 100
Ktsanes, V., 100
Ku, L., 181–82
Kübler-Ross, E., 463, 491
Kuebli, J., 71
Kurdek, L. A., 219, 381–82, 417
Kuriki, C., 317

L

Lacey, N. A., 92
La Ferla, R., 165
LaGreca, A. J., 435–36
Lai, T., 65
Lakoff, R., 82
Lamb, M., 288
Lance, L. M., 142
Land, H., 408, 418
Landale, N. S., 213, 229
Landler, M., 456
Landrine, H., 65, 80
Landry-Meyer, L., 275
Langenbrunner, M., 387
Lansford, J., 394–95
Laquer, W., 484
Laren, D., 451
Larson, C., 147, 351, 362–63, 365, 368–69, 372
Larson, D. C., 391
Larson, J. H., 325
Lasch, C., 6, 19, 337
Laslett, P., 14
Lasswell, M. E., 95
Latham, L. M., 376
Lauer, J., 231, 301, 311, 393
Lauer, R., 231, 245, 301, 311, 393
Laufer, W., 478
Laumann, E. O., 159–63, 171, 177, 185–86
LaVee, Y., 246
Lavin, C., 206
Law, T. C., 395
Lawler, E., 231
Lawson, A., 468
Lawson, G., 468
Layton, B. D., 140
Lazar, A., 187
Leach, P., 291
Leather, D. M., 393
Lee, C., 314
Lee, G. R., 120, 138, 209, 243, 380–81, 438
Lee, J., 55
Lee, J. A., 95–96
Lee, S. M., 438
Lehr, R., 392
Lehrer, E. L., 382
Lein, L., 293
Leland, J., 220, 233
LeMasters, E., 123
Lempert, L. B., 293
Lemsky, C., 439
Lengermann, P. M., 51
Leonard, K. E., 148
Lepowsky, M., 66
Lerman, R. I., 303
Lerner, J. V., 331
Lessinger, J., 120–21
Lester, D., 380, 386
Lev, M. A., 204
Lever, J., 73, 175, 178
Levine, A. D., 205, 216–17, 271, 318, 475, 486
Levinger, G., 384
Levinson, D., 338
Levitan, D., 99
Levy, B., 147, 347
Lewin, T., 60, 160–61, 163, 173–74, 314, 316, 364
Lewis, E., 230
Lewis, R. A., 383
Liang, J., 446
Lichter, D. T., 229
Lieberman, B., 158
Liem, R., 325
Light, D., 46
Lin, G., 439
Lin, S., 410
Lindsay, J. W., 149, 168–69, 177
Lindsey, L., 101, 128, 136, 285, 298–99
Link, B., 328
Lips, H., 72, 83
Liss, M. B., 72
Little, H., 444
Little, V., 445
Littman, M., 314
Liu, P., 218
Liu, X., 395, 446
Lloyd, S. A., 126
Lobsenz, N. M., 95
Locin, M., 332
Logan, J., 440
Logue, B. J., 451
London, K. A., 213, 469, 472
Long, B. C., 80
Longino, C. F., Jr., 432
Loomis, L. S., 213
Lopata, H. Z., 448, 492
Lorber, J., 288, 316
Lott, B., 72
Lovelace, S. G., 413
Lowry, R., 181
Lu, H., 216–17
Lu, Z., 314–15
Luborsky, M., 211
Luhman, R., 93
Lund, K., 387
Luria, Z., 71
Lusky, A., 446
Lye, D., 383
Lynn, D., 69
Lyon, J., 159

M

McAdoo, J., 292–93
McAdoo, J. B., 313
McAdoo, J. L., 313
McCarthy, J., 400
McCary, J. L., 176
McClelland, K., 475
Maccoby, E., 72, 392
MacDonald, K., 71
MacDonald, W. L., 216, 417
MacFarquhar, N., 220
McGhee, J. L., 445
McGrath, E., 80
McHenry, P. C., 142
Macionis, J., 26, 298, 479, 484
McKelvey, C. A., 468–69
McKenry, P. C., 292
McKeough, K., 125
McKim, W. A., 466
McKinlay, J. B., 448
MacKinnon, C. E., 72
McKinnon, J., 204
Macklin, E. D., 214
Macko, S., 477
McLanahan, S. S., 214, 380, 382, 394–95
McLane, D., 99
MacMillan, P., 392
McNeil, D., Jr., 196
MacRae, H., 440
McRoy, R. G., 471
McTaggart, L., 470
Madigan, C. M., 215
Madsen, W., 21
Magdol, L., 215
Maginnis, R. L., 348
Mahoney, D., 249
Maier, R., 171
Maines, J., 311
Majors, R., 72–73
Makuit, G., 72
Malinowski, B., 230
Malley, J. E., 387
Malstrom, J., 206
Mandate the Future, 356
Mandela, N., 458
Manier, J., 192, 194
Mann, D., 482
Manning, W., 213
Marcum, J., 21
Marecek, J., 219
Marino, V., 206
Marion, R., 281
Markides, K. S., 437, 439

Markman, H., 216
Marks, N. F., 447
Marquis, C., 220
Marriott, N., 88
Marriott, S. S., 354
Marshall, J., 283
Martin, C. E., 174, 181, 389
Martin, C. L., 69, 72
Martin, J., 264–65
Martin, P., 148
Martin, T. C., 382
Martire, L. M., 447
Marx, K., 46
Maryanski, A. Z., 46
Mason, B., 76
Mason, M. A., 397
Mason, P., 230
Mastekaasa, A., 209
Masters, W., 159, 175–77, 179, 186–88
Mathews, L., 395
Matthaei, J. A., 377
Matthews, S. H., 443, 447
Matthews, T., 183–84, 278
Maugh, T. H. H., 171, 175
Mauldin, T. A., 72, 394
Maume, J. D., 314–15
Max, E., 396
Max, W., 448
Maxwell, J., 276
Mays, V. M., 131
Maza, P., 328
Mazur, E., 81
Mead, M., 65, 126, 222
Mederer, H. J., 286
Medved, M., 170
Meeks, C. B., 72
Meier, B., 321
Meier, R. F., 462
Melton, W., 128
Melzer, A., 166
Mercy, J., 451
Meredith, D., 392
Merighi, J. R., 221
Mertz, M. E., 444
Messner, M., 54
Metts, S., 105
Michael, R. T., 159–61, 177, 185–86
Michaels, N., 468
Michaels, S., 159–61, 177, 185–86
Middlebrook, P. N., 94
Mignon, S., 147, 351, 362–63, 365, 368–69, 372
Milewski, K., 144–45
Mill, C., 148
Miller, B., 55, 447
Miller, B. C., 282, 302
Miller, L. F., 381
Miller, N., 298
Miller, S., 288
Miller, T., 222, 233
Miller-Perrin, C. L., 365, 369, 371
Mills, C. W., 25–26, 327, 457
Min, P. G., 251, 296, 313
Mindel, C. H., 250–51, 437, 439–40
Minino, A., 277–78
Mintz, S., 12–18, 22–23
Miranda-Maniquis, E., 193
Mirande, A., 21, 295, 297
Mirchandi, V. K., 108
Mirowsky, J., 315
Mistiaen, V., 283, 286
Mitchell, G., 71
Mitchell, J., 405, 440–41
Mitchell-Kerman, C., 127, 249, 410
Mnookin, R., 392
Moffitt, T. E., 215
Money, J., 70
Monroe, P. R., 393
Montgomery, P., 447
Moore, D. W., 452
Moore, F., 75–76
Moore, K. A., 302, 386
Moore, P., 430
Moore, W. E., 46
Moorman, G. F., 331
Morales, E., 218
Moran, B. B., 141–42
Moreland, S., 468
Morell, C., 267
Morgan, S. P., 383
Morganthau, T., 473
Morin, R., 66
Morris, J., 63
Morris, N. M., 168
Moseley, R., 382
Mosher, W., 214
Mosher, W. D., 181, 271–72
Mosher, W. E., 380–81, 409, 421
Mosier, K., 330, 332
Moskowitz, M., 318
Moss, B. F., 258
Mowery, J., 222
Moyle, E., 146
Moynihan, D. P., 39–40
Mueller, G., 478
Mueller, H. L., 456–57, 486
Mulhausen, D., 479
Mullis, I., 79
Mullis, R. L., 168
Murphy, M., 365
Murphy, S., 480
Murray, B., 17
Murstein, B. I., 90, 100, 106, 132, 138
Mutran, E., 440
Muwakkil, S., 174
Muzzonigro, P. G., 221
Mydans, S., 303, 470
Myers, D. J., 74

N

Naifeh, M. L., 435
Najman, J. M., 394
Nakonezny, P. A., 385
Nardi, P., 98, 258
Nass, G., 125
Neal, A. G., 266
Needle, R. H., 414
Neft, N., 216–17, 271, 318
Neher, L. S., 394
Neikirk, W., 470
Nellis, B., 178
Nelson, S., 137
Neugarten, B., 431, 442
Neugarten, D., 431
Neumark-Sztainer, 75
Nevid, J. S., 166
Newcomb, P. R., 215
Newman, B. S., 221
Newman, D. M., 100, 249, 474
Newman, J., 287
Newport, F., 64, 77, 140, 213
Nezu, A. M., 80
Nezu, C. M., 80
Ng, S. H., 72
Nicholas, M., 144–45
Niebuhr, G., 244, 252
Nielsen, L., 76, 409
Njogu, W., 41–43
Nock, S. L., 314, 383
Nord, C. W., 395
Norment, L., 136
Norton, A. J., 381–82
Novak, M. A., 62, 156–58
Nowinski, J., 92
Nuebeck, K. J., 462

O

Oakley, A., 310
Obejas, O., 192, 194
Obradovic, J., 395
Obradovich, S., 71
O'Callaghan, M., 394
O'Connell, M., 267
O'Connor, T. G., 395
O'Connor-Roden, M., 211
O'Flaherty, K. M., 409
Ogintz, E., 206, 210
Ogletree, S., 76
O'Grady-LeShane, R., 448
O'Hare, W., 252
O'Hare, W. P., 381
Okawa, M., 395
O'Kelly, C. G., 239
Okum, M. A., 253
Olds, S., 275
O'Leary, K. D., 387
Oleinick, L., 451
O'Loughlin, T., 458
Olson, D. H., 231, 246
O'Malley, P. M., 213
O'Neil, J. M., 167
O'Neil, K., 315
OneWorld, 487
Ooms, T. J., 303
Oppenheimer, V. K., 205, 326
O'Rand, A. M., 382, 386
Orenstein, P., 74
Ornish, D., 92
Oropesa, R. S., 229
Oros, C. J., 148
Overman, S. J., 73

P

Pabst, M. S., 396
Pace, L., 252
Packer, A. J., 166
Padavic, I., 319
Pagelow, M. D., 147, 351, 355, 371
Paglia, C., 179
Palmer, M., 386
Palmore, E. B., 432, 439
Paludi, M. A., 353–54
Papalia, D., 275
Papanek, H., 311
Papernow, P. L., 406, 408, 423
Parke, R., 50
Parke, R. D., 71
Parker, G. B., 468
Parker, P., 274
Parrillo, V., 479
Parron, E. M., 437
Parrot, A., 130
Parrot, W. G., 111
Parsons, T., 44
Pasley, K., 406, 414, 417, 420, 422
Patel, J., 277
Patel, P., 2
Patterson, C., 298
Patterson, J., 178, 228, 254, 366, 386
Patterson-Stewart, K. E., 312
Patzer, G. L., 140
Pauly, B., 206
Pear, R., 469
Pearson, J., 258
Pemerton, S., 394
Penning, M. J., 216
Peplau, L., 105
Peplau, L. A., 105, 107, 150, 180, 219
Peres, J., 471–72
Perkins, H. W., 468
Perkins, K. P., 2
Perrin, R. D., 365, 369, 371
Perry, I., 170
Perry-Jenkins, M., 290, 315
Pert, C., 92
Petersen, J., 178
Petersen, L., 172, 175
Peterson, C., 440
Peterson, J., 440
Peterson, J. L., 394, 414

Peterson, K., 118, 155
Peterson, K. S., 137
Peterson, L., 214
Peterson, R. D., 456–57, 486
Peterson, R. R., 390
Peterson, S., 468
Pettigrew, T. F., 475
Peyton, J. S., 313
Pezzin, L. E., 440, 445
Phillips, R., 379
Piccino, L., 214
Pierce, J. L., 69
Pike, R., 275
Pilavin, I., 469
Pilkington, N. W., 221
Pill, C. J., 420, 422
Pillemer, K. A., 370
Pines, A., 111–12
Pipher, M., 73
Pitcher, B. L., 450
Pitts, L., 391
Pitzer, R., 288
Piven, F. F., 327
Pleck, J. H., 181–82, 332, 338
Pollard, K., 252
Polling Report, 475, 485
Pomerleau, A., 72
Pomeroy, S., 90
Pomeroy, W. B., 174, 181, 389
Ponzetti, J., Jr., 384
Popenoe, D., 288
Popp, K. E., 73
Porter, K., 324
Post, T., 486
Potok, M., 300
Pound, P., 36
Powell, R., 249
Powers, E., 15
Pratt, E. L., 253
Price-Bonham, S., 253
Primus, W., 299, 324
Provenzano, F. J., 71
Pruett, M. K., 397
Punke, H. H., 203
Purcell, P., 74
Pyke, K. D., 313
Pyszczynski, T. A., 99

Q

Quadagno, J. S., 91, 93, 378
Queen, S. A., 91, 93, 378
Quinn, J. B., 429
Quitt, M. H., 406

R

Radbill, S., 339
Raffeld, P., 76
Rahe, R., 493
Raley, R. K., 408
Ramsey, S., 411, 424
Ramu, G. N., 120, 122–23, 125–26, 138, 140
Rank, M. R., 34
Rape Statistics, 148
Rasmussen, P. K., 386
Rathus, S. A., 166
Rawlings, S., 138
Rawlins, W. K., 82
Ray, O., 149
Raymond, J., 390
Real, T., 80
Reardon, P. T., 300
Reavill, G., 73
Red Horse, J., 295
Reeve, C., 311
Register, J. C., 440–41
Reid, G. M., 71
Reid, K., 468
Reid, W. J., 315
Reik, T. A., 112
Reinert, S., 365
Reingold, J., 323
Reinisch, J. M., 218, 220
Reisman, J. M., 82, 147
Reiss, I. L., 100, 114, 119
Remondet, J. H., 450
Rempel, J., 110
Renzetti, C. M., 63, 78, 107, 148, 170, 236, 280, 319, 338, 366, 370
Reskin, B. F., 319
Resnick, M., 369
Rezac, S. J., 394
Rheingold, H. L., 72
Rice, C., 453
Rice, R. W., 312
Rich, A., 52, 169, 171
Richardson, J. P., 187
Richmond-Abbott, M., 245
Riedman, A., 417
Riessman, C. K., 387, 392, 409
Riley, G., 15, 377–78
Rimer, S., 428
Ritter, J., 190, 195
Ritzen, A., 365
Rivers, C., 392
Roach, M., 451–52
Robbins, R. H., 93
Roberto, K. A., 442
Roberts, S., 314
Roberts, W. L., 437
Robertson, J., 80
Robins, P. K., 380
Robinson, I., 168
Robinson, J. P., 314
Robinson, L. G., 231
Robson, P., 466
Rochlin, M., 172
Rodgers, J. L., 385
Rodgers, W. L., 229
Rodin, J., 111
Roemer, M. I., 322–23
Rogers, S. J., 315, 386–87
Rogerson, P. A., 439
Rollins, J., 205
Romero–Garcia, I., 65
Roosa, M. W., 468
Rosenberg, K., 471
Rosenberg, Y., 168
Rosenblatt, P., 249
Rosenblum, K. E., 49
Rosencrantz, S., 300
Rosenfeld, M., 66, 78
Rosenkrantz, P. S., 80
Rosenthal, C., 440–41, 447–48, 451
Rosier, K. B., 399
Ross, C. E., 315
Ross, E., 276
Ross, J., 181
Ross, L. E., 127
Rossi, P. H., 327–28
Rothman, B. K., 272
Ruane, J. M., 99
Rubin, B., 288, 300, 387
Rubin, J. Z., 71
Rubin, L., 98, 315
Rubin, L. B., 81–82, 181
Rubin, Z., 99, 105, 150
Rubinstein, A., 281
Rubinstein, R. L., 210–11
Ruggles, S., 440
Rusbult, C. E., 103
Russell, C., 301
Russell, C. S., 437
Russell, D., 149, 355
Russo, N. F., 80
Rutman, A. H., 15
Ryff, C. D., 468

S

Saad, L., 92, 212, 271, 452
Sabin, C., 36
Sack, K., 192–93
Sadker, D., 74
Sadker, M., 74
Saenz, R., 313
Safire, W., 252
St. Jean, Y., 294
Saitta, M. B., 65
Sakurai, J., 478–80
Salovey, P., 111
Saltzman, A., 166
Saluter, A. F., 12, 203, 211, 218, 383
Salzman, J., 169
Sambrano, S., 469, 472
Sanders, G. F., 168, 398
Sanders, S., 172
Sandler, B. R., 74
Sandnabba, N. K., 69
Sandroff, R., 317
Sangl, J., 436, 446
Santrock, J. W., 414
Sapiro, V., 74, 175, 236–37
Sarler, C., 390
Saunders, D. G., 361
Sawhill, I. V., 386
Sayre, D. H., 70
Scanzoni, J., 103, 313
Scheck, S. R., 106
Schemo, D., 164
Schemo, D. J., 470
Schenck-Yglesias, C. G., 440, 448
Scher, M., 80
Schmeeckle, M., 445
Schmetzer, U., 66, 218
Schmitt, J. P., 219
Schneir, M., 21, 242
Schoen, C., 367–68
Schoen, R., 216
Schone, B. S., 440, 445
Schuckit, M. A., 468
Schuldberg, D., 419–20
Schuldt, W. J., 258
Schuman, H., 137
Schumm, W. R., 258, 437
Schvaneveldt, J. D., 311–12
Schvaneveldt, P. L., 311–12
Schwalbe, M. L., 392
Schwartz, F. N., 317
Schwartz, M. A., 168, 202, 207, 294
Schwartz, P., 35, 107–9, 130–31, 161, 171, 185, 215, 219, 315
Schwebel, A. I., 258, 395
Sciara, F. J., 395
Scott, B. M., 38, 127, 129, 168, 294, 444
Scott, D., 242
Scott, J., 127
Scott, J. P., 445
Scott, J. W., 14
Scott-Jones, D., 299–300, 302
Seager, J., 320
Sears, D. O., 475
Sears, H. A., 313
Seccombe, K., 207, 209
Seff, M. A., 217
Segal, S., 414
Segura, D. A., 52, 69
Seidman, S., 92
Seilhamer, R. A., 468
Seitz, V., 443
Seltzer, J. A., 213, 385
Selzer, J., 392, 397
Senna, J., 478
Shah, A., 476–77
Shainberg, L., 188
Shanas, E., 439, 445
Shane, B., 271
Shapiro, I., 324
Shapiro, J., 462
Shapiro, J. L., 281–82
Shapiro, J. P., 447
Shaver, P., 94
Shaw, D., 441
Shear, M. K., 80
Sheehy, S., 97–98

Shehan, C. L., 138, 209, 243, 438, 467
Shelton, B., 292
Shelton, B. A., 215, 315–16
Shenon, P., 121
Sherrod, D., 258
Shettel-Neuber, J., 112
Shinn, M., 395
Shneidman, E., 491
Shoop, R. J., 321–22
Shope, D. F., 178
Short, J. L., 394
Shostak, A., 205–6
Shrestha, L., 393
Shriver, J., 386
Shucksmith, J. L., 290
Shull, R. D., 385
Siegel, L., 478
Sigler, R. T., 340, 363
Sigmundson, H. K., 62
Signorielli, N., 75–76
Silber, D., 369
Silver, H. K., 362
Silverman, F. N., 362
Silverman, P. R., 451, 492
Silverstein, E., 221
Silverstein, M., 441
Simenauer, J., 209
Simmons, W., 113, 277
Simon, B. L., 209
Simon, R. J., 471
Simon, W., 165, 178
Simpson, B., 405
Simpson, L., 316
Simpson, V., 271
Sims, S., 360
Singer, A., 295
Sipan, C., 166
Sitterle, K. A., 414
Sivard, R. L., 485
Skeen, P., 187
Skipper, J. K., Jr., 125
Skolnick, A. S., 12, 236, 300
Skolnick, J. H., 12, 236
Skyles, A., 414, 424
Slap, G., 367
Smallwood, D., 338
Smith, A., 432
Smith, A. D., 315
Smith, B., 277–78, 480
Smith, C., 460
Smith, D., 122
Smith, E. A., 168
Smith, H. W., 34
Smith, J., 142, 451
Smith, J. A., 366
Smith, K., 316–17, 331
Smith, L. A., 443
Smith, L. G., 110, 113
Smith, M., 478
Smith, R., 491
Smith, R. H., 111
Smith, S., 128
Smith, T. L., 468
Smith, T. W., 181, 230
Smock, P., 213
Smock, P. J., 390
Smolowe, J., 329
Snipp, C. M., 250, 294–95, 444
Snowden, B., 484
Snyder, M., 463
Sobey, A. R., 280
Soderquist, J. N., 384
Soldo, B. J., 440
Solomon, R. C., 90, 97
Sonenstein, F., 181–82
Song, I. Y., 378
Soroka, M. P., 353, 460, 478, 483, 485–86, 489
Soundranayagam, L., 64
South, K., 452
Spade, J., 313, 452
Spain, D., 229, 249, 315
Spanier, G. B., 382–84, 408, 414, 419
Spitze, G., 386, 440
Sprecher, S., 92, 105, 185
Sprey, J., 259, 443
Springs, H. H., 222
Spruill, J. C., 202
Stacey, J., 298
Stack, C., 292
Stafford, D., 323
Stainton, M. C., 71
Staples, R., 21, 74, 127, 136, 204–5, 292–93
Stark, E., 359
Starr, B. D., 187
Steck, L., 99
Steeh, C., 137
Steele, B., 362
Steele, J. B., 310
Stegman, S. E., 393
Stein, P., 204–6
Stein, P. J., 142
Steiner, B. W., 63
Steinfirst, S., 141–42
Steinhauer, J., 215
Steinmetz, S., 344, 360, 371–72
Stephens, M. P., 447
Sternberg, R. J., 101–2, 104–5, 114
Stets, J. E., 215
Stevens, J., 468–69
Stewart, A. J., 387
Stewart, J. H., 291
Stewart, J. K., 312
Stewart, L., 74
Stillion, J. M., 491
Stinnet, N., 211, 215
Stinnett, N., 419
Stock, L., 369
Stock, W. A., 253
Stodghill, R., 165, 169–70, 182
Stokes, G., 165
Stokes, J. P., 313
Stolberg, S., 189, 301
Stolberg, S. G., 32, 183
Stone, G., 394
Stone, L. H., 120
Stone, R., 436, 446
Stoneman, Z., 72
Strada, M. J., 456
Straus, M., 291, 344–47, 362, 364–65, 371–72
Strauss, M. A., 291
Strickland, A. L., 492, 495
Strickland, B. R., 80
Stroebe, W., 140
Stroes, J., 442
Strong, B., 157, 178–80
Stuifbergen, A., 446
Su, S. S., 414
Suarez, Z. E., 296
Sugisawa, H., 446
Suholinova, O., 382, 386
Sullivan, O., 313
Sullivan, T., 310
Supancic, M., 382
Supple, K. R., 429
suro, r., 250–52
Surra, C. A., 132
Sussman, M., 440
Sutton-Smith, B., 407
Swan, J. A., 447
Swanbrow, D., 94
Sweeney, J. F., 31
Sweet, J. A., 380, 408–10, 450
Szapocznik, J., 313

T

Takagi, D., 297
Takagi, D. Y., 322
Talbott, M. M., 409
Tallichet, S. E., 321
Tanfer, K., 214
Taniguchi, H., 321
Tannen, D., 82
Tatara, T., 369–70
Tavris, C., 106
Taylor, L., 172
Taylor, L. C., 290
Taylor, R. J., 230, 440, 451
Taylor, R. L., 11
Teachman, J. D., 380
Tedrow, L. M., 380
Tein, J., 468
Temple, A., 120
Tennestedt, S. L., 448
Tennov, D., 92, 97, 103–4, 114
Thackeray, A., 247
Thernstrom, S. A., 263–64
Thies, C. F., 222
Thomas, J. L., 443
Thomas, V. G., 292
Thombs, D., 466–67
Thomese, F., 223
Thompson, B. W., 76
Thompson, G., 470
Thompson, L., 315, 384
Thompson, S., 194
Thompson, V. D., 140
Thomsen, D., 168
Thornberry, T., 478
Thornton, A., 182, 216, 229
Thornton, E., 121
Thurnher, M., 393
Tilly, L., 14
Todd, M., 96–97, 103
Tolbert, K., 398
Tolnay, S. E., 229
Totenberg, N., 240, 242
Toth, J., 293
Tower, C., 366–68
Townsend, B., 315
Townsend, C., 318
Tracy, L., 74
Traupmann, J., 132
Travis, T. C., 49
Treas, J., 432, 436, 439
Trembath, D., 142
Tribe, L. H., 270
Troll, L., 440
Trygstad, D. W., 398
Tubman, J. G., 468
Tucker, M., 249, 410
Tucker, M. B., 127, 230, 451
Turner, J., 46
Twaite, J. A., 440
Tweed, S. H., 468
Tyson, A. S., 137

U

Udry, J. R., 168
Uhlenberg, P., 393, 442
Ulin, M., 221
Usdansky, M., 299
Utech, M. R., 346, 349–50, 365

V

Vaillant, C. O., 437
Vaillant, G. E., 437
Vanderslice, V. J., 312
VandeVen, N., 149
Van De Vliert, E., 315
Vandewater, E., 394–95
van Driel, B., 220
VanDusen, J. E., 158
Vazquez-Nuttall, E., 65
Vedantam, S., 32
Vega, W., 296
Veith, G. E., 376
Ventura, S., 183–84, 264–65, 278
Venturelli, P., 465
Verhovek, S. H., 495
Visher, E., 412, 415–18, 420
Visher, J., 412, 416–20
Vitagliano, E., 299

Vobejda, B., 275
Vogel, S. R., 80
Vogeltanz, N., 369
Voydanoff, P., 292, 308, 326
Vuchinich, R., 414, 418
Vuchinich, S., 414, 418

W

Wade, C., 178
Wadley, D. S., 393
Wagemaar, T., 293
Wagner, D. L., 448
Waite, L. J., 215, 441
Wald, E., 405, 407
Waldorf, V., 142
Walker, A. J., 315
Walker, K., 81, 98–99
Walker, K. E., 314
Walker, L., 347
Wallace, H., 339, 341, 344–45, 347–49, 351, 357, 361, 365, 369–70
Wallace, R. A., 47
Waller, W., 121, 123, 132
Wallerstein, J. S., 246, 300, 392–94, 398, 414, 419
Wallin, P., 437
Wallish, L., 419
Wallstron, K., 491
Walsh, A., 106
Walsh, F., 451
Walsh, L. S., 406
Walster, E., 132
Walster, G. W., 99
Walster, W., 132
Walters, K., 221
Ward, J., 172, 175
Ward, M. C., 62
Warda, J., 407
Warner, R. L., 383
Warshaw, R., 355
Watson, R., 216
Watts, J., 330
Weaver, C. N., 209, 253
Webber, P., 448
Weber, L., 204
Weibel-Orlando, J., 444
Weinberg, M., 172, 180, 219
Weiner, M. B., 187
Weinick, R. M., 216
Weinstein, K., 442
Weiser, C., 233, 235
Weissbourd, R., 392
Weissman, M. M., 80
Weitzman, L., 236, 389–91
Weitzman, N., 71
Wellman, B., 98
Wells, R., 263
Welter, B., 19
Werking, K. J., 82
Werland, R., 399
Werle, M., 439
Werner, E. E., 468
West, J., 395
Westoff, C. F., 136
Weston, K., 107, 220
Whisman, M. A., 80
White, C., 172, 175
White, G. L., 112, 140
White, J., 216
White, L. K., 205, 381, 385, 417, 420
White, N., 351
White, P., 209
Whiteford, L. M., 272
Whitehead, B., 300
Whitehouse, B., 468
Whiting, B., 72
Whitsett, D., 408, 418
Whyte, M., 121–22, 124
Whyte, M. K., 129
Wicks, J. W., 266
Widom, C. S., 363, 468
Wieche, V. R., 372
Wiederman, M., 106
Wiese, D., 366
Wiggins, G., 32
Wilder-Smith, B., 78
Wilkinson, T., 478
Williams, B., 181
Williams, C., 319
Williams, G., 279
Williams, G. M., 394
Williams, J., 91
Williams, J. E., 64
Williams, R. M., 380
Williams, S., 76
Willie, C. V., 293
Wilsnak, S., 369
Wilson, B. F., 421
Wilson, E., 72
Wilson, E. D., 62, 177
Wilson, M., 290, 418
Wilson, S., 157, 178–80
Wilson, S. M., 325
Wilson, W. J., 37, 475
Winch, R. R., 100
Wineberg, H., 382–83, 400, 416
Winemiller, D., 439
Wishy, B., 242
Witter, R. A., 253
Witzel, J., 210
Wiznia, A. A., 281
Wolf, A., 47
Wolf, P., 202
Wolfe, A., 220
Wolfe, D. M., 437
Wolfson, E., 234
Wong, M. G., 20, 297, 313
Wood, J. T., 65, 76, 89, 94, 106, 342
Woodard, A., 282
Woodman, S., 184
Woods, M., 314
Woods, R. D., 61, 444
Worden, J. W., 492
Worling, J. R., 372
Worthington, R., 300
Wright, J. D., 328–29
Wright, J. M., 419
Wright, R., 250–51
Wu, Z., 215–17, 409
WuDunn, S., 301
Wunder, D. F., 456–57, 486
Wurtele, S., 166

X

Xu, X., 292–93
Xue, L. R., 316

Y

Yalom, I. D., 467–68
Yardley, J., 273
Yates, R. E., 478
Yednak, C., 63
Yellowbird, M., 250, 294–95, 444
Yllo, K., 354–55
Yoels, W., 88, 94
Yoon, J., 231
Young, A., 219
Young, E., 80
Young, I. E., 112
Young, M. H., 311–12
Yuen, M., 233

Z

Zablocki, B., 222
Zavella, P., 295, 313
Zebroski, S., 248
Zedeck, S., 330, 332
Zellman, G., 148
Zernike, K., 54
Zhao, J., 216
Zientek, J., 10, 67–68, 150, 190, 254, 488
Zill, N., 394, 414
Zimmerman, J., 73
Ziss, K., 168
Zogby National Poll, 473
Zubek, J. M., 312
Zuckerman, D. M., 70
Zuckerman, M. B., 341
Zuger, A., 62
Zuravin, S., 366
Zurcher, L. A., 471

Subject Index

A

Aboriginal peoples:
  elderly, 441
  marriage ritual, 239
Abortifacients, 270
Abortion, 269–71
  cross-cultural view, 271
  defined, 269
  historical view, 270
  induced abortion, 270
  legalization of, 158, 270
  public opinion on, 271
  reasons for, 269
  for sex selection, 276–77
Abuse. *See* Family violence; Violence
Achieved status, 61
Acquaintance rape. *See* Date and acquaintance rape
Acquired immune deficiency syndrome (AIDS). *See* HIV/AIDS
Adjustment:
  of children to divorce, 394–95
  to divorce, 393
  to marriage, 245
  to parenthood, 283
  to retirement, 438–39
Adolescents. *See also* Teenage pregnancy; Teenaged parents
  and dating violence, 146–47
  and interracial dating, 137
  parenthood of, 301–3
  parent murder, 365
  stepsibling relationships, 415–17
  and unemployment, 326–27
  and violence and crime, 477–81
Adolescent sexuality, 181–82
  age and sexual initiation, 162, 164, 181
  birth control, use of, 183
  motivations for sex, 182
  racial and ethnic minorities, 181
  sexual knowledge of teens, 181–82
  and sexually transmitted disease (STDs), 189
  teenage pregnancy, 182–84
Adoption, 469–72
  adoptive parents, characteristics of, 469–70
  baby brokers, 470
  international adoption, 470–71
  interracial adoption, 471
  open and closed, 470
Adult children:
  as caregivers for elderly, 447–48
  living with parents, 429
  parental relationship, 439–41
Adultery, 234. *See also* Extramarital sex
Advertising:
  personal ads, 141–42, 163
  sexual content, 168
Affinal relatives, defined, 235
Affirmative action, elimination in California, 473
Afghanistan:
  American occupation of, 455–56
  children of, 469
  elderly in, 441
  gender inequality, 66
  land mines, 486, 487
  maternal mortality rate, 461
  refugees from, 489
  war against terrorism in, 485
Africa. *See also* Kenya; South Africa
  elderly in, 441
  ethnic wars, 476
  and HIV/AIDS, 195
  kidnapping and slavery, 306–7
  U.S. embassy bombings, 484
African American family, 291–94
  divorce and children, 395
  divorce rate, 380
  extended family, 16–17, 440–41
  fathers, role of, 293
  free slaves, 17, 20–21
  historical view (*see* Slavery)
  interracial marriage, 247–49
  myths related to, 11–12, 292
  nineteenth century, 20–21
  parenting styles, 290, 292–93
  single-parent family, 11, 17, 292, 299
  social class differences, 292–93
  strength and resiliency of, 293–94
  structure of, 291–92
  well-functioning families study, 37–38
African Americans. *See also* Racial and ethnic minorities
  black church, 127
  crime and crime victims, 479
  dating, 127–28, 131–32
  decision to marry, 229–30
  elder abuse, 369
  exclusion from research studies, 39–41
  fertility rate for, 264–65
  hate crimes against, 473–75
  HIV/AIDS, 191–94
  income, median household, 292
  interracial dating, 128
  lesbians and gays, 131, 172
  love relationships, 108–9
  male rapist myth, 354
  and masturbation, 178
  and oral sex, 179
  parent murders, 365
  peer group and socialization, 72–73
  and poverty, 292, 293, 324
  racism and discrimination, 474–75
  and remarriage, 409–10
  retirement, 439
  sex ratio imbalance, 127–28, 136
  sexual behavior, 162
  singlehood, 203–4, 205–6
  social classes of, 11, 130
  twin births occurrence, 275
  unique experiences of, 15
  wedding, African-centered, 243
African American women:
  and abortion, 269
  black matriarchy myth, 39–40, 293
  cotillions, 130
  educational level and marriage probability, 136, 204
  and female beauty ideal, 76
  lesbians, 131
  and marriage gradient, 136
  motherhood, 285–86
  as rape victims, 353–54
  self-esteem and girls, 78
  as single parents, 11, 17, 292, 299
  slaves and white men, 17–18
  teenage pregnancy, 182
  working women, 21, 309
Agape, 89, 91, 96
Age:
  and abortion, 269–70
  of abused children, 365, 366
  and battered women, 348
  and cohabitation, 213
  and dating, 128, 138, 140
  delaying parenting, 267
  and divorce risk, 381
  and HIV/AIDS, 194
  legal age for marriage, 235
  marriage squeeze, 134–36
  and masturbation, 177
  maternal, and pregnancy complications, 278
  and mate selection, 140
  older adults (*see* Aging)
  and rape victim, 353
  and remarriage of parents, 414, 416
  and self-esteem, 77–78
  of sexual initiation, 162, 164, 181
  and sexually transmitted disease (STDs), 189
Ageism, defined, 430
Age norms, 431
Aggression, and day care, 30–32
Aging. *See also* Elderly
  age norms, changing of, 431
  and communal lifestyle, 222–23
  families (*see* Later-life family)
  functional age, 431
  male climateric, 188
  menopause, 187
  and sexual double standard, 188

of U.S. population, 431–32
of world population, 428
Aid to Families with Dependent Children (AFDC), 329
AIDS (acquired immune deficiency syndrome). *See* HIV/AIDS
Alcohol abuse:
child abusers, 365–66
child abuse survivors, 364, 369
and fetal alcohol syndrome (FAS), 279
historical view, 466
personal and social costs of, 467
rape survivors, 359
and violent behavior, theories of, 349
and woman battering, 349
Alcoholism:
children of alcoholics, 467–68
defined, 467
and family functioning, 467–68
Alimony, 377, 390
Al-Qaeda, 484
Alyha, 63
American Men's Studies Association (AMSA), 54
Amniocentesis, 277
Anal intercourse, 162
Anal sex, and HIV transmission, 193
Anal stage, 68
Ancient times. *See* Greece, ancient; Rome, ancient
Androcentrism, defined, 71
Androgyny:
children of single parents, 301, 395
and love relationships, 107
and self-esteem, 79
Annulment, 401
Anorexia nervosa, behaviors of, 76
Anthrax terrorism, 485–86
Anticipatory socialization, 126
Arranged marriage:
ancient Rome, 90
bride price, 121
cross-cultural view, 119–20
semiarranged marriage, 121
Artificial insemination, 272–73
Ascribed status, 61
Asexual, meaning of, 186
Asian American family, 296–98
divorce, 380–81
elders in, 427–28, 446
parenting styles, 296–97
structure of, 296
Asian Americans. *See also* Racial and ethnic minorities
fertility rate for, 264–65
income, median household, 296, 322
interracial marriage, 250–51
marriage squeeze, 251
model minority myth, 40, 297, 322
and remarriage, 410
singlehood, 203
Assault, sexual. *See* Rape
Attachment, pattern and later relationships, 94
Aum Shrinrikyo, 484
Australia, sex ratio imbalance, 136
Authoritarian parenting, 290
Authoritative parenting, 290
Autoeroticism, 176–79
defined, 176
erotic dreams, 179
masturbation, 177–78
sexual fantasy, 178

B

Baby boom, time period of birth, 264
Baby bust, time period of, 264
Baker v. Vermont, 201
Bangladesh, acid mutilations, 66
Basuco cigarettes, 466
Battered-child syndrome, 362. *See also* Child abuse
Battered men, 360–62
prevalence of, 360–61
relationship to abuser, 348
theories of, 361
Battered women. *See also* Family violence
battered-woman syndrome, 347
children of, 347, 363
cyclical nature of, 347
fighting back, 359
historical view, 338–39
indications of battering, 351
marital rape, 354–55
prevalence of, 346, 347–48
public recognition of, 346–47
relationship to abuser, 343, 348
remaining in abusive relationship, 349, 350–52
self-test, 371
theories of, 349–50
woman battering, definitions, 347
Behavior problems, gender differences, 78
Berdache, 63
Bereavement, defined, 492
Bias. *See* Discrimination; Gender inequality; Racism and discrimination; Workplace inequality
Bigamy, meaning of, 234
Bin Laden, Osama, 484
Biological processes:
nature-nurture issue, 61–62
sex differentiation, 61
Bioterrorism, 485–86, 487
Birth control. *See also* Contraception
pill, and sexual revolution, 158
Bisexuality, defined, 175
Black church, 127
Black feminist theory, basic concepts, 52–53
Blacks. *See* African American family; African American women; African Americans
Bloods, 478
Blood tests, pre-marriage testing, 235–36
Boomerang generation, 429
Bosnia, ethnic war, 476, 486
Botillion, 130
Bride price, 121
Bulimia, behaviors of, 76
Bullying, 482
Buppy (black urban professional), 127

C

California, affirmative action elimination, 473
Canada, gang violence, 478
Cannabis, 465
Capitalism, in Marxist theory, 46
Careers. *See* Work and women; Work-family structures
Caregivers for elderly, 446–48
adult children as, 447–48
and racial and ethnic minorities, 446, 447
spouse as, 447
stress of, 448, 449
Carey v. Population Services International, 268
Case study, 36–37
Catholics:
annulment, 401
divorce rate, 382
interfaith marriage, 252
and remarriage, 410
Celibacy. *See also* Sexual abstinence
Christian view of, 157
Cenogamy, 223
defined, 3
Central America, refugees from, 489
Chemical warfare, 486
Chicanos. *See* Mexican American family
Child abuse, 362–69. *See also* Child sexual abuse
abuser profile, 363, 366
and cohabiting couples, 215
and death of child, 364
emotional consequences of, 364, 366
forms of, 362–63
historical view, 339
Munchausen syndrome, 362–63
prevalence of, 343, 362, 364–65
victim profile, 365–66
Childbearing, 5. *See also* Pregnancy
Childbirth, father's participation, 282–83
Child care, 316–18
cost of, 316
day care and aggression, 30–32
by fathers, 316, 317–18
federal programs, 318
by grandparents, 317, 443, 444
workplace support of, 331
Child custody, 395–98
historical view, 378–79
joint custody, 396–98
lesbian and gay parents, 396
sole custody, 395–96
split custody, 379
visitation rights, 398
Child-free option, 266–67
Child-rearing:
colonial era, 15
Native Americans, 18
Children. *See also* Parenting styles
abuse of (*see* Child abuse; Child sexual abuse)

of abused mothers, 347, 363
adoption, 469–72
as adults (*see* Adult children)
of alcoholics, 467–68
child labor, 20
child marriage, 7
child pornography, 363
costs of parenting, 265
custody arrangements, 395–98
death of, 492
and decision to remarry, 410
discipline methods, 291
divorce, effects of, 394–98
divorce risk and presence of, 383
and drug abuse, 465, 466
foster care, 468–69
gun violence, 479–81
and handgun crimes, 479–80
historical view of, 15–16, 19–20
and HIV/AIDS, 194
homeless, 328
housework of, 314
kidnapping and enslavement of, 306–7
outcome in single-parent family, 300, 301
parenting styles, 289–91
parricide, 365
in poverty, 324
as refugees, 489–90
and remarriage, 412–15, 422–23
of remarried couple, 416–17
street children, 466
of teenaged mothers, 302–3
and terrorism and war, 486–89
violence against, historical view, 339
Children's Gun Violence Prevention Act, 482
Children's TV programs, gender role stereotyping, 74–75
Child Safety Lock Act, 482
Child sexual abuse, 366–69
abuser profile, 368
child pornography, 363
definition of, 367
emotional consequences of, 368–69
forms of, 367
incest, 367
and later sexuality, 161, 166
prevalence of, 367–68
sibling abuse, 372
transmission of victimization, 368
victim profile, 368
Child support, 391
Child Support Recovery Act of 1992, 391
Child-welfare system:
adoption, 469–72
foster care, 468–69
problems of, 469
China:
adoption of children from, 470–71
division of household labor, 314–15
divorce, 378, 386
divorce and children, 395
female infanticide, 121, 262, 276, 339
and HIV/AIDS, 195
love, concept of, 93
marriage ritual, 239
one-child policy, 262, 267
people with disabilities, 464
sex ratio imbalance, 121, 262
violence against women, 338
Chinese Americans. *See also* Asian American family; Asian Americans
interracial marriage, 251
parenting styles, 296–97
Chinese Exclusion Act of 1882, 20
Chinese immigrants, nineteenth-century workers, 20
Chlamydia infection, 189
Chores. *See also* Division of labor
assignment and gender, 72
Christianity:
on family violence, 338
fundamentalist (*see* Fundamentalism)
love, concept of, 90–91
on virginity, 157, 161, 375–76
Chromosomes, and sex differentiation, 61
Church:
meeting potential mate, 127, 141
organized (*see* Religion)
Cigarette smoking, and pregnancy complications, 278–79
Circumcision, female genital mutilation (FGM), 167, 338, 490–91
Class system. *See* Social Class
Closed adoption, 470
Clothing, and gender role socialization, 71
Cognitive-developmental theory, 70
Cohabitation:
battered women, 348
cohabitant characteristics, 213
cross-cultural view, 216–17
defined, 123
demographic trends, 212–13
division of labor, 215
of divorced individuals, 408
domestic partnerships, 217
and future marriage, 215
gender role expectations, 215
historical view, 211
lesbians and gays, 211, 220
and marital success, 216
palimony, 217
pros and cons of, 215–16
public opinion of, 211–12
reasons for, 213–14
and sexual activity, 161
as social marriage, 231
types of couples, 214
Coining, 491
Coitus, 179–80
Collaborative law, 399
Collective societies, 93
College:
date and acquaintance rape, 148
dating patterns, 124
and mate selection, 123, 133
teacher gender bias, 74
Colonial era, 13–15
children in, 15, 406
courting and mate selection, 122
divorce, 377
economic well-being, 14
homelessness, 327–28
household composition, 14
human sexuality in, 14, 157
marital roles, 14–15
remarriage, 406
singlehood, 202
Columbine school shootings, 481
Coming out, 220–21
Coming-out parties, 130
Commitment:
and love relationships, 101
and marriage, 228, 230–31
Common-law marriage. *See also* Cohabitation
meaning of, 211
Communal lifestyle, 222–23
Commune, defined, 222
Communication:
barriers to, 254–55, 258
improvement of, 255
in marriage, 254–55
self-disclosure, 256–58
style, gender differences, 82–83
Community divorce, 385
Community remarriage, 411
Commuter marriages, 312
Compadrazgo, 21
Compadres, 21
Companionship:
and mate selection, 140
motive for marriage, 228
Computer dating, 143
Conception, 275–77
biological conditions for, 275
multiple conception, 275–76
Conciliation counseling, 399
Condoms, safe sex, 196–97
Conflict-habituated marriage, 246
Conflict resolution, in marriage, 255, 258–59
Conflict theory, 46–47
Conflict views, family, 46–47
Congenital defects. *See* Pregnancy complications
Conjugal rights, meaning of, 237
Consolidated Omnibus Budget Reconciliation Act of 1986, 464
Content analysis:
defined, 74
television shows, 74–75
Contraception, 268–69
adolescent use, 183
defined, 268
legal restrictions, 268
unprotected sex, reasons for, 269
Cooperative living, 222–23
Coparental divorce, 385
Corporal punishment, negative effects, 291

Corporate wives, 311
Corporations, multinational, 457–58
Cotillions, 130
Counseling. *See* Family therapy
Courtly love, 91
Courtship. *See also* Dating; Mate selection
defined, 119
historical view, 122
Couvade, meaning of, 282
Covenant marriage, 399–400
Coverture, meaning of, 14, 236
Crime. *See also* Violence
and racial and ethnic minorities, 479
Criminal justice system:
racial profiling, 474
and rape victim, 355, 357–58
Crips, 478
Cross-cultural research, 42–43
Cross-cultural view:
abortion, 271
arranged marriage, 2, 119–20
child care, 318
child and teen marriage, 7
cohabitation, 216–17
death rate, 460
disease, 461
divorce, 378, 382, 386, 390, 395, 398
divorce and children, 395
drug abuse and children, 466
elderly, status of, 441
family leave, 318, 332
family violence, 338–40
gang violence, 478
gender role variations, 65–66
HIV/AIDS, 195–96
honor killings, 2
household labor, 314–15, 318
incest taboo, 5
income inequality, 320, 458–59
infant mortality rate, 459–60
jealousy, 111–12
kidnapping and slavery, 306–7
life expectancy, 459–60
love, 93, 228
marriage, 228–29
marriage rituals, 239
mate selection, 119–21
multiple genders, 63
persons with disabilities, 463–64
racism as, 476–77
rape, 356
same-sex marriage, 200–201, 233
sex ratio imbalance, 121, 136, 262–63
sex selection, 121, 262, 276–77
sexual frequency, 161
shared paternity, 289
single-parent family, 301
suicide, 493–94
teenage pregnancy, 184
unemployment, 325
Cruising, 129
Cryopreservation, 273
Cuban American family, parenting style, 295–96
Cult of domesticity, 19
Cultural differences. *See* Cross-cultural view
Cultural relativism, 491
Cunnilingus, 179
Custody. *See* Child custody
Cyber-dating, 143–45
Cycle of violence theory, violence and abuse, 347, 368

D

Date and acquaintance rape, 148–49
date rape drug, 149
defined, 148
prevalence of, 163
reduction of, 149
Dating. *See also* Courtship; Mate selection
among African Americans, 127–28
breaking-up, 149–50
defined, 119
after divorce, 389, 392, 407–8
functions of, 125–26
future view, 146
gender differences, 128
historical view, 121–25
hookup partners, 117–18, 124
lesbians and gays, 130–31
and social class, 128–30
social-learning theory, 128
Dating market, 140–45
for African Americans, 127–28
computer dating, 143
cyber-dating, 143–45
dating services/dating clubs, 142–43
personal ads, 141–42
singles bars, 127, 141
traditional meeting places, 141
Dating scripts, 128
Dating services/dating clubs, 142–43
Dating violence, 146–49
and adolescents, 146–47
date and acquaintance rape, 148–49
and jealousy, 113, 147
physical abuse, forms of, 147
prevalence of, 146–47
remaining in relationship, 147
Day care. *See* Child care
Death and dying, 491–95
and AIDS, 494
of child, 492
grief and bereavement, 492, 494
needs of dying, 491–92
of parent, 493
right-to-die movement, 494–95
of sibling, 492–93
of spouse/partner, 493
stages of dying, 491
suicide, 493–94
Death rate:
colonial era family, 15
cross-cultural view, 460
slave children, 16
Decision making:
lesbian and gay families, 219
and marital power, 313
and marriage, 229–30
and parenthood, 265–67
and remarriage, 408–9
Defense of Marriage Act of 1996, 233
Demographics:
of aging population, 428, 431–32
fertility measures, 263
HIV/AIDS incidence, 190, 195
Dengue fever, 461
Dependability, and love relationships, 110
Dependence, mutual, in love relationships, 100–101
Dependent variables, 33
Depressant drugs, types of, 465
Depression:
of dying persons, 491
gender differences, 80
postnatal depression, 283
rape and incest survivors, 358, 359
Descent patterns, 18
Desertion, marital, 401
Developmental family life cycle model, 50–51
evaluation of, 51
stages of family life, 50–52
Devitalized marriage, 246
Disability. *See also* Persons with disabilities
defined, 462
Discipline methods. *See also* Parenting styles
positive methods, 291
spanking, negative effects, 291
of stepchildren, 418–19
Discrimination. *See also* Racism and discrimination
of persons with disabilities, 462
in workplace, 318–22
Disease. *See also* Health status
as global problem, 461–62
global transmission, 461–62
sexually-transmitted, 189–98
Disenfranchised grief, 494
Disinhibition theory, of alcohol and violence, 349
Dissynchronized retirement, 438
Division of labor:
chores and gender, 72
and cohabitation, 215
colonial era family, 14–15
and gendered roles, 288–89
lesbian and gay families, 219
Mexican American family, 21
and working women, 314–16
Divorce, 377–400
adjustment factors, 393
alimony, 377, 390
child adjustment, 394–95
child custody, 395–98
child support, 391
counseling and mediation, 387, 388, 398–99
covenant marriage for prevention of, 399–400

cross-cultural view, 378, 382, 386, 390, 395, 398
dating after divorce, 389, 392, 407–8
economic decline and women, 389–92
economic independence and women, 382, 386
gender differences in experience of, 389–93
historical view, 377–79
and intergenerational relationships, 440
no-fault divorce, 379, 385, 389, 399
and overlapping families, 413
personal factors related to, 381–83, 387
post-divorce problems, 389
racial and ethnic minorities, 379–81
and religion, 231
sexual behavior after, 186
societal factors related to, 385–86
stages in process, 384
stations of divorce, 384–85
Divorce mediation, 399
Divorce rate, defined, 379
DNA testing, 17–18
Domestic partnerships. *See also* Cohabitation; Same-sex marriage
legal factors, 217
Domestic work. *See* Division of Labor
Domicile, marriage, legal aspects, 236
Double standard:
and aging, 188
sexual, 158, 167–68
Down syndrome, 278
Dowries, defined, 134
Dreams, erotic, 179
Drug abuse, alcohol. *See* Alcohol abuse
and children, 465, 466
defined, 466
as global problem, 466
IV drug use and HIV/AIDS, 191, 194
maternal, and fetal rights, 280
and pregnancy complications, 279
prevalence of, 465–66
Drug use, defined, 466
Dual-earner families, 311–12, 315. *See also* Work and women
Dying. *See* Death and dying
Dysfunctions:
defined, 44
sexual (*see* Sexual dysfunctions)

E

Earnings gap. *See* Income inequality
Eastern Europe, ethnic cleansing, 476–77
Eating disorders:
child sexual abuse survivors, 369
and dieting, 76
and rape survivors, 359
television influences on, 76
Economic dependency, and battered women, 349, 351
Economic divorce, 385
Economic relationships, in Marxist theory, 46
Economic remarriage, 411
Economic status. *See also* Poverty; Social class
in decision to marry, 229–30
divorce and economic decline, 389–92
and divorce risk, 381–82, 386
dual-earner family, 322
elderly, 432–35, 439
as family function, 6
and family size, 263–64
homelessness, 22, 327–29
and income gap, 323
of later-life family, 433
of lesbian and gay partners, 219
and male role, 19
median income of families by type, 322
poverty, 323–27
and prenuptial agreement, 240–42
racial and ethnic minorities, 322
single-parent family, 299, 300, 322, 324
of singles, 205, 208–9
underemployment, 327
unemployment, 324–27
welfare reform, 329–30
of widows, 450–51
working women, 313
Economic well-being, 322–29
historical view, 14, 19
Educational level:
African American women marriage probability, 136, 204
and cohabitation, 213
and divorce risk, 381–82
and husband household participation, 315
and interracial marriage, 248–49
and masturbation, 177
and remarriage, 409
singlehood as lifestyle choice, 205
and working women, 309, 312
Education Amendment Act of 1972, Title IX, 73
Egalitarian relationships. *See also* Gender equality
lesbian and gay families, 298
lesbian and gay relationships, 107–8
and low conflict level, 349
and working women, 313–16
Eighteenth century:
family violence, 338
mate selection, 122
singlehood, 202
Eisenstadt v. Baird, 268
Ejaculation:
dysfunctions of, 189
and orgasm, 176
Elder abuse, 369–70
abandonment of elderly, 448
abuser profile, 370
defined, 369
forms of, 369
historical view, 339–40
prevalence of, 369
and racial and ethnic minorities, 369–70
Elderly. *See also* Aging; Elder abuse; Grandparents; Later-life family
categories of, 431–32
child-free/unmarried elderly, 445
cross-cultural view, 427–28, 441
economic status, 432–35, 439
health status, 446
HIV/AIDS and older adults, 194
housing, 222–23, 435–36
lesbians and gays, 221, 451–52
life expectancy and gender, 432–33
in Native American family, 294–95, 444
retirement, 437–39
and sexual behavior, 161, 186–88
and singlehood, 210–11
social policy issues, 452–53
widows and widowers, 448–51
Electra complex, 68–69
El Salvador:
gang violence, 478
refugees from, 489
Embryopathy, AIDS babies, 281
Embryo transplant, 273
Emotional bonds, and parenthood, 266
Emotional divorce, 384
Emotional remarriage, 410
Emotions, as symbolic states, 88
Empirical evidence, defined, 33
Employment. *See* Work and women; Work-family structures; Workplace inequality
Employment Act of 1946, 327
Employment inequality. *See* Income inequality; Workplace inequality
Empty nest, 51, 429
Enculturated-lens theory:
evaluation of, 71
gender role socialization, 70–71
Enculturation, and gender role socialization, 71
Endogamy:
defined, 2, 134
and mate selection, 134, 140
Engagement, 240
England, sexual frequency in, 161
Envy, 111
Epidemics, as global problem, 461–62
Equality. *See* Egalitarian relationships; Gender equality; Workplace equality
Equity theory, mate selection, 132
Erikson's theory, gender role socialization, 69
Erogenous zone, meaning of, 175
Eros, 89–90
Erotic arousal, defined, 175
Erotic dreams, 179
Erotic love, 95
Eskimos, elderly, 441
Ethiopia, abduction and rape in, 356
Ethnic cleansing, 476–77
Ethnic minorities. *See* Racial and ethnic minorities
Ethnocentrism, 19
Ethnography, 37–38
Eurocentrism:
meaning of, 285
and motherhood, 285

Euthanasia. *See* Right-to-die movement
Evangelical households, gender roles, 36–37
Exchange theory. *See* Social-exchange theory
Excitement state, sexual response, 175–76
Exogamy:
  defined, 2, 134
  and mate selection, 134
Expectations, role, 61
Expressive traits, 44
Extended family:
  African Americans, 16–17
  child care in, 317
  defined, 3–4
  elderly in, 436
  Mexican Americans, 21
  modified, 4
  Native Americans, 18
Extramarital sex, 185–86
  prevalence of, 162, 185
  public opinion on, 186
  reasons for, 185
  types of relationships, 185–86

F

Family. *See also* Marriage; Parents; Remarriage; Stepfamily
  African American family, 291–94
  and aging (*see* Later-life family)
  in American history (*see* Historical perspectives)
  Asian American family, 296–98
  contrasting views of, 6–8
  defined, 3
  economic well-being, 322–29
  extended family, 3–4
  family of orientation, 3
  family of procreation, 3
  foster family, 4, 468–69
  gay and lesbian families, 4, 219–20
  Latina and Latino family, 295–96
  and maternal employment (*see* Work and women)
  Mexican American family, 21–22
  modified extended family, 4
  Native American family, 294–95
  Pacific Islander American family, 296–98
  parental influence (*see* Parents)
  patriarchal family, 4
  and singlehood, 204
  single-parent family, 299–300
  social functions of, 5–6
  stepfamily, 4, 412, 415–20
  types of, 3–4
  work-family structures, 310–12
Family leave, 331–33
  cross-cultural view, 318, 332
  legislation related to, 332–33
  opponents of, 332
Family and Medical Leave Act of 1993, requirements of, 59, 332
Family of orientation, defined, 3
Family of procreation, defined, 3
Family therapy:
  and divorce, 387, 388
  divorce counseling and mediation, 387, 388, 398–99
  gender behavior issues, 68
  purpose and benefits of, 10
  sexual issues, 190
  trauma of terrorism, 488
Family values, 22, 77, 160
Family violence. *See also* Battered men; Battered women; Child abuse; Elder abuse; Sibling abuse
  battered men, 360–62
  battered women, 347–52
  child abuse, 362–69
  costs of, 339
  cross-cultural view, 338–40
  cycle of violence theory, 347
  elder abuse, 369–70
  examples from news, 336–37, 340–41, 344, 345
  family conditions related to, 345, 350
  feminist theory of, 349
  forms of, 338–40
  historical view, 338–40
  and lesbian and gay relationships, 343, 345–46
  and loving family, 346, 351–52
  and mental illness, 344
  myths related to, 343–46
  prevalence in U.S., 340–41, 343
  prevention and reduction of, 352
  sibling abuse, 340, 370–72
  and social class, 344–45
Family Violence Prevention Fund (FUND), 352
Fatherhood, 286–87
  adjustments to newborn, 283
  benefits and costs of, 288
  national initiatives/programs, 287–88
  "new father," 286–87
  traditional role, 286
  views of, 286
Fathers:
  absence, effects of, 288
  African Americans, 293
  childbirth participation, 282–83
  and child care, 316, 317–18
  child custody, 396, 397
  child support, 391
  expectant fathers, 281–82
  play and gender role, 71
  shared paternity, 289
  single-father family, 288, 300–301
  stepfathers, 418–19
  teenaged fathers, 303
  time/involvement of, 287
Fellatio, 179
Female athletes, and earlier socialization, 73
Female genital mutilation (FGM), 167, 338, 490–91
Female infanticide, China, 121, 262, 276, 339
Female role:
  colonial era, 14–15
  cult of domesticity, 19
  motherhood, 285–86
  traditional role, 64–65
Femininity. *See also* Female role
  traits associated with, 64, 79
Feminist theory, 51–54
  on decision to marry, 230
  evaluation of, 53–54
  family, view of, 53
  of family violence, 349
  female-centered basis of, 51
  goals of, 38, 51–52
  on heterosexism, 171
  life history research method, 38
  theoretical perspectives of, 52–53
Feminization of love, 106–7
Feminization of poverty, 324
Fertility:
  defined, 263
  U.S. pattern, 263–65
Fertility control:
  abortion, 269–71
  contraception, 268–69
Fertility rated, defined, 263
Fetal alcohol effects (FAE), 279
Fetal alcohol syndrome (FAS), 279
Fetal rights, and maternal drug abuse, 280
Fictive kin, defined, 470
Films:
  pornographic, 342
  sexual content, 168, 170
  violent, 341
Filter theories, mate selection, 133
Flextime, 331
Food Stamp Program, 329
Fornication, defined, 234
Foster care, 468–69
Foster family, composition of, 4
France:
  child care in, 318
  racism in, 476
  sexual frequency in, 161
Free slave families, 17, 19–21
Freud's theory. *See* Psychoanalytic theory
Friendships:
  characteristics of, 97
  cross-sex friendships, 81–82
  development of, 97–98
  gender differences, 81, 98
  versus love, 96–99
Full Employment and Balanced Growth Act of 1978, 327
Functional, defined, 44
Functional age, defined, 431
Functions:
  defined, 43
  of family, 5–6
  manifest and latent functions, 44
Fundamentalism:
  divorce rates, 375, 382
  gender roles and family, 36–37

on interracial dating, 137
on virginity, 164–65

G

Games, video, 343, 482
Gamete intrafallopian transfer (GIFT), 273
Gang violence, 477–78
Gay bars, 130, 141
Gay bashing, 220
Gay men. *See* Homosexuality; Lesbian and gay families; Lesbians and gays
Gays and lesbians, death of partner, 493
Gender:
in context of family, 4
defined, 61
exclusion from research studies, 39, 41
Gender ambiguity:
intersexed individuals, 62–63
multiple genders, 63
sex reassignment, 62–63
transexuals, 63
transgendered individuals, 174
transvestites, 174
Gender differences:
behavior problems, 78
communication style, 82–83
dating, 128
divorce and children, 395
divorcing couple, 389–93
friendships, 80, 81, 98
jealousy, 112
life expectancy, 432–33
lifestyle choices, 77
love relationships, 96, 104–7
marriage experience, 244–45
masturbation, 177
math and science, 79
mental health, 80
nature-nurture issue, 61–62
orgasm, 176
parenthood, 287–88
personal ads, 142
and remarriage of parents, 414–15
self-confidence, 79
self-esteem, 77–79
sexual behavior, 163–65
sexual fantasy, 178
sexual scripts, 167–68
widows and widowers, 450–51
Gender equality. *See also* Egalitarian relationships
and mental health, 80
movement toward, 66–67
pay equity, 321
slave family, 16
Vanatinai peoples, 66
working-class family, 20
workplace measures, 330–33
Gender gap:
labor force participation, 309
wage gap, 320–21
Gender identity, defined, 61
Gender inequality:
cross-cultural view, 66
and family violence, 350
gender biased language, 72
income inequality, 320–21
occupational discrimination, 319
and research studies, 39–41
Gender reproduction, 69
Gender role socialization:
cognitive-developmental theory, 70
defined, 63
enculturated-lens theory, 70–71
gender reproduction concept, 69
and language, 72
and lesbian and gay parents, 298
and love relationships, 109
and mass media, 74–77
and parents, 71–72, 83
and peers, 72–73
and play, 73
psychoanalytic theory, 68–69
in single-parent family, 301
social-learning theory, 69–70
and teachers, 73–74
Gender roles. *See also* Female role; Gender role socialization; Gender role stereotypes; Male role
and cohabitation, 215
Evangelical households, 36–37
and family functioning, 68
in Marxist theory, 46
Mead's study, 65
Mexican American families, 21
traditional roles, 64–65
transition from traditional roles, 66–67
variations, cross-cultural view, 65–66
Gender role stereotypes:
consequences of, 77–83
and dating, 128
defined, 61
television programs, 74–77
Generalized others, defined, 165
Generation X, sexual behavior of, 162–63
Genitals, euphemisms used for, 166
Genocide, ethnic cleansing, global view, 476–77
Germany, racism in, 476
Gerontology, social, study of, 430
Getting together, defined, 122
Glass ceiling, 319, 475
Global interdependence, defined, 465
Globalization:
benefits and costs of, 458
and income inequality, 458–59
multinational corporations, 457–58
Global problems:
disease, 461–62
drug production/distribution/abuse, 466
and economic globalization, 458
infectious disease transmission, 461–62
racism and discrimination, 476–77
refugees, 489–90
terrorism and war, 483–91
water supply/sanitation, 460–61
Godmothers, 21
Going steady, defined, 123
Gonorrhea, 189
Good provider role, 19
Grandparents, 442–44. *See also* Later-life family
child care by, 317, 443, 444
grandchildren residing with, 429–30
grandparent-headed households, 444
grandparenting styles, 442
involvement, factors related to, 443–44
visitation rights, 398, 443
Granny dumping, 448
Great Depression, family problems, 22
Great-grandparents, 444
Greece, ancient:
alcohol abuse in, 466
love in, 89–90
Grief:
death of loved one, 492, 494
disenfranchised grief, 494
of dying persons, 491
Griswold v. Connecticut, 268
Group marriage, 223
G-spot, 181–82
Guns, ownership in U.S., 480
Gun violence, 479–81
handgun crimes by youth, 479–80
Gypsies, massacre of, 476–77

H

Hallucinogenic drugs, types of, 465
Hammurabi Code, 466
Harassment, sexual. *See* Sexual harassment
Hate crimes:
and homosexuals, 220
and racial and ethnic minorities, 472–73, 475
Hate groups, 472
Hawthorne effect, 36
Head Start program, 318
Health:
defined, 459
global problems, 460–62
persons with disabilities, 463–64
Health insurance:
for domestic partners, 233
national system issue, 464
problems in system, 464
uninsured, 464
Health status:
caregivers for elderly, 446–48
and divorce, 389, 394
of elderly, 446
and love, 92
Hemings, Sally, -Jefferson relationship, 17–18
Hepatitis B, 189
Hermaphrodites, 62
Hero role, child of alcoholic, 467
Heterogamous marriage:
interethnic marriage, 251–52
interfaith marriage, 252–53

interracial marriage, 247–51
meaning of, 247
Heterosexism, meaning of, 171
Heterosexuality:
defined, 171
and life cycle, 171
and patriarchal system, 109–10
power element, 171
Hispanic Americans. *See* Latina and Latino family; Latinas and Latinos; Mexican American family
Historical perspectives, 158–70
abortion, 270
alcohol abuse, 466
cohabitation, 211
communal lifestyle, 222
divorce, 377–79
eighteenth century, 122
family, 13–25
family violence, 338–40
female employment, 20–23, 309
group marriage, 223
homelessness, 327–28
homosexuality, 90, 156, 218
human sexuality, 156–65
immigration, 20–21, 23–24
interracial marriage, 247, 249
love, 89–92
masturbation, 178
mate selection, 121–25
remarriage, 406
singlehood, 201–4
slavery, 15–17, 158
Historical view, 377–79
HIV/AIDS, 189–98
and children, 194
and conservative sexual behavior, 161, 163
cross-cultural view, 195–96
death, coping with, 494
as global pandemic, 195
high-risk groups, 191–94
incidence of, 190, 195
maternal transmission to newborn, 279, 281
and older adults, 194
premarital blood testing, 235
prevention of, 196–97
and racial and ethnic minorities, 192–93
symptoms of, 191
transmission of, 191
Homeland Security Office, 485
Homelessness, 22, 327–29
causes of, 328
historical view, 327–28
prevalence of, 328
profile of homeless, 328
remedies, 328–29
Homicide. *See also* Violence
by abused women, 359
and child abuse, 364
gang homicide, 478
by male partner, 343, 348, 361
of parents by children, 365
Homogamy:
defined, 134
and mate selection, 134
sexual homogamy, 163
Homophobia, 218
meaning of, 171
Home production, 310
Homosexuality, 171–75. *See also* Lesbian and gay families; Lesbians and gays
defined, 171
historical view, 90, 156, 218
and HIV/AIDS, 191, 192, 193–94
prevalence of, 172–75
safe sex, decline in, 193–94
study of, limitations, 218
theories of cause, 172
Honeymoon, 239
Honor killings (Pakistan), 2
Hookup partners, 117–18, 124
Household, defined, 24
Household work, 310–11
cross-cultural view, 314–15, 318
husband participation, 310, 314–15, 326
scope of activities, 310
Househusbands, 310, 326
Housing, for elderly, 222–23, 435–36
Human sexuality. *See* Sexual behavior
Hutterites, 222
Hutus, 476
Hwame, 63
Hyde Amendment, 270
Hypergamy, defined, 136
Hypogamy, defined, 136
Hypotheses, defined, 33

I

Idealization, of nuclear family, 12–13
Identification, and gender role behavior, 68–69
Ideology, defined, 38
Immigrant families:
cultural practices, U.S. acceptance of, 490–91
nineteenth century, 20–21
twentieth century, 23–24
Immigration:
public opinion on, 473
and racism/discrimination, 472–73
refugees, 489–90
Incest. *See also* Child sexual abuse
defined, 367
emotional consequences of, 358
siblings, 372
Incest taboo, marriage as regulation of, 5, 234–35
Income. *See* Economic status; Income inequality; Poverty; Social class
Income inequality:
cross-cultural view, 320
family losses from, 321
glass ceiling, 319
global view, 458–59
income gap, 323
occupational discrimination, 319
race-gender gap, 320–21
racial and ethnic minorities, 475
Independent variables, 33
India:
arranged marriage, 120
child and teen marriage, 7
female fetus, abortion of, 263, 276–77
immolation of widows, 490–91, 494
as low-jealousy culture, 111–12
multiple gendered persons, 63
sex ratio imbalance, 121, 263
violence against women, 338
Individualistic societies, 93
Inequality. *See* Discrimination; Gender inequality; Income inequality; Racism and discrimination; Workplace inequality
Infanticide:
defined, 339
female, 121, 262, 276, 339
Infant mortality rate, cross-cultural view, 459–60
Infants, love and attachment needs, 93–94
Infatuation, versus love, 99, 103
Infectious disease transmission, as global problem, 461–62
Infertility:
causes of, 272
defined, 271
reactions to, 272
treatment (*see* Reproductive technologies)
Institution, defined, 3
Institutionalization:
of marital love, 91–92
of marriage, 3
Institutional racism, 11–12, 474–75
Instrumental traits, 44
Intentional neighborhoods, 223
Interethnic marriage, 251–52
Latinas and Latinos, 251–52
white Americans, 252
Interfaith marriage, 252–53
International adoption, 470–71
Internet:
child pornography, 363
cyber-dating, 143–45
sexual content, 170
violence on, 342
Internet Trafficking Act, 482
Interracial adoption, 471
Interracial marriage, 247–51
African Americans, 247–49
Asian Americans, 250–51
historical view, 247, 249
Native Americans, 249–50, 294
Interracial relationships, 128
adolescent attitudes toward, 137
dating, 128, 137
fundamentalism on, 137
slavery era, 17–18
South Africa, 144
Intersexed individuals, 62–63

Interviews, survey research, 35
Intimacy, and love relationships, 101, 105–6
Intracytoplasmic sperm injection (ICSI), 273
Intrinsic marriage, 246
In vitro fertilization (IVF), 273
Iraq, marriage ritual, 239
Irish Republican Army (IRA), 483

J

Japan:
 hara-kiri, 493–94
 love in marriage, 228
 as low-jealousy culture, 112
 mommy track in, 317
 sex ratio imbalance, 121
 sexual harassment, 322
 singlehood, 203
 terrorism in, 484
 visitation and divorce, 398
 youth crime, 480
Japanese Americans. *See also* Asian American family; Asian Americans
 internment of, 23, 474
 interracial marriage, 250–51
 parenting styles, 297
Jealousy, 110–13
 cross-cultural view, 111–12
 defined, 110
 destructive jealousy, 113
 and envy, 111
 gender differences, 112
 personality traits associated with, 111
 psychoanalytic view, 68–69
 and violent behavior, 113, 147
Jefferson, Thomas, -Hemings relationship, 17–18
Jewish Americans:
 divorce rate, 382
 hate crimes against, 475
 interfaith marriage, 252
 mate selection, 138
 and remarriage, 410
Job sharing, 331
Joint custody, 396–98
Journal of Men's Studies, The, 54
Judaism:
 on interfaith marriage, 252
 on sexual behavior, 156

K

Kama Sutra, 89
Keeping company, 122
Kenya:
 child and teen marriage, 7
 dating service, 143
 elderly in, 441
 HIV/AIDS knowledge, 43
Key status, 61
Kidnapping:
 baby brokers, 470
 potential brides, 121
Kinship:
 defined, 13
 descent patterns, 18
 fictive kin, 470
 Mexican American families, 21
 slave families, 16–17
Kohlberg's theory, gender identity, 70
Korean Americans. *See also* Asian American family; Asian Americans
 interracial marriage, 251
 parenting styles, 296
Kosovo, ethnic war, 476, 486
Ku Klux Klan, 472, 473
!Kung, love, concept of, 93

L

Labor force participation, 308–10
 gender gap, 309
 women, 309–10
Labor force participation rate, defined, 308
Land mines, 486, 487
Language, gender biased words, 72
Latchkey children, 23
Latent functions, 44
Later-life family. *See also* Elderly; Grandparents
 and adult children, 429, 439–41
 caregivers for elderly, 446–48
 diversity of, 430–31
 extended family, 440–41
 grandparents, 442–44
 great-grandparents, 444
 marital satisfaction, 437, 438
 retirement, 437–39
 sandwich generation, 429–30
 sibling relationships, 445–46
 social characteristics of, 432–33
 widowhood, 448–51
Latina and Latino family, 295–96. *See also* Mexican American family
 and divorce, 380
 extended family, 440–41
 men and housework, 315
 parenting styles, 295–96
 single-parent family, 295, 299
 strengths and resiliency of, 296
 structure of, 295
Latinas and Latinos. *See also* Racial and ethnic minorities
 and abortion, 269
 fertility rate for, 264–65
 HIV/AIDS, 192–93
 interethnic marriage, 251–52
 and poverty, 324
 and remarriage, 409–10
 self-esteem of girls, 78
 singlehood, 203–4
 working women, 309
Laws:
 abortion, 270–71
 child support, 391
 contraception prohibitions, 268
 divorce, 390
 domestic partnerships, 217, 233
 fetal rights, 280
 interracial adoption, 472
 interracial marriage, 247
 marriage as contract, 231–37
 parental leave, 59, 332
 pregnancy discrimination, 332–33
 prenuptial agreements, 240–41
Learning theory. *See* Social-learning theory
Legal divorce, 384–85
Legal remarriage, 411–12
Lesbian feminist theory, basic concepts, 52
Lesbian and gay families:
 adoptive parents, 470
 child custody, 396
 composition of, 4
 decision making, 219
 division of labor, 219
 fatherhood and gays, 55, 298
 compared to heterosexuals, 219–20
 legal restrictions, 217, 232–34
 motherhood and lesbians, 298
 parenthood, 212, 218
 parenting styles, 298–99
 same-sex marriage, 232–34
 stepfamilies, 419
Lesbians and gays:
 African Americans, 131, 172
 cohabitation, 211, 220
 coming out, 220–21, 298
 dating patterns, 130–31
 discrimination against, 220
 elderly, 221, 451–52
 exclusion from research studies, 41
 friendship, 98
 homophobia, 171, 218
 lifestyle typology, 180
 love relationships, 107–8
 in military, 220
 patriarchy as obstacle to love, 109–10
 sexual behavior, 161, 164
 sexual expression, 180
 singles bars, 130, 141
 social constraints on, 138, 219
 stereotypes of, 219
 in U.S. population, 41
 violence against, 220
 violence among couples, 343, 345–46
Liberal feminist theory, basic concepts, 52
Life cycle:
 and mate selection, 140
 sexual preference, change in, 171
Life expectancy:
 cross-cultural view, 459–60
 gender differences, 432–33
Life history research method, 38
Lifestyle choices. *See also* Lesbians and gays; Parenthood; Singlehood
 and gender expectations, 77
Liking, versus loving, 99, 105
Limerence theory, of love, 103–4

Living arrangements:
of elderly, 222–23, 435–36
of singles, 208
Living will, 495
Loneliness, and divorce, 389, 392
Longhouse, 18
Longitudinal studies, 423
Lost child, child of alcoholic, 467
Love. *See also* Love relationships
contemporary view of, 113
cross-cultural view, 93, 228
development, modern view, 89
and family violence, 346, 351–52
feminization of, 106–7
historical view, 89–92
institutionalization of, 91–92
limerence theory, 103–4
love story theory, 102–5
and marriage, 228
physical and emotional importance of, 92–94
romantic love, 88
self-love, 94
social constructionist view, 88–89, 114
social-exchange theory, 103
styles of love, 95–96
triangular theory of, 100–101
versus infatuation, 99, 103
versus liking, 99, 105
wheel theory of, 100
Love map, 88
Love relationships:
among African Americans, 108–9
and androgyny, 107
and attachment patterns, 94
gender differences, 96, 104–7
and gender role socialization, 109
jealousy, 110–13
lesbians and gays, 107–8
patriarchy as obstacle to, 109–10
and trust, 110
versus friendship, 96–99
Loving v. Virginia, 247
Lower class, dating patterns, 130
Ludus love, 95

M

Machismo, 21, 295
Madrinas, 21
Magazines, sexually oriented, 168
Malaria, 461
Male climateric, 188
Male rape, 352, 354, 362
Male role:
colonial era, 14–15
fatherhood, 286–87
good provider role, 19
machismo, 21
new fatherhood, 55
patriarchal family, 14–15
traditional role, 64–65
and violent behavior, 149
Malnutrition, maternal, and fetal death/defects, 278
Manic love, 95–96
Manifest functions, 44
Marital rape, 237, 354–55
Marital satisfaction:
factors in, 253–54
later-life couples, 437, 438
and remarriage, 420–24
sexual, 161, 185
and working wives, 313–14
Marriage. *See also* Divorce; Family; Remarriage
adjustment to, 245
and commitment, 228, 230–31
communication in, 254–55
conflict resolution, 255, 258–59
conjugal rights, 237
contemporary practices, 237
coverture concept, 14, 236
cross-cultural view, 228–29
death of spouse, 448–51, 493
decision to marry, 228–30
defined, 3
destructive behaviors, 258
engagement, 240
gender differences in experience of, 244–45
group marriage, 3, 223
heterogamous, 247–53
as institution, 3
interethnic marriage, 251–52
interfaith marriage, 252–53
interracial marriage, 247–51
in later life, 437
as legal contract, 231–37
marital rape, 237, 354–55
marital satisfaction, 161, 185, 313–14
masturbation as sexual activity, 178
monogamy, 3
myths associated with, 8–13
naming traditions, 237
personal marriage contracts, 240, 242, 256–57
polyandry, 3
polygamy, 3
polygyny, 3
postponement of, 25
prenuptial agreements, 240–41
principle of legitimacy, 230
property rights, 236–37
religious context, 231
residence laws, 236
same-sex marriage, 232–34
self-disclosure in, 256–58
sexual behaviors in, 185
sexual frequency in, 185
sexual satisfaction in, 161, 185
spousal caregivers, 447
successful, survey results, 253–54
types of, 3
typology of relationships, 246–47, 258
vows, 243–44
wedding, 238–39, 242–44
Marriage brokers, 120
Marriage disruption:
annulment, 401
desertion, 401
divorce, 377–400
separation, 400–401
Marriage gradient, meaning of, 136
Marriage market, 133–38
defined, 134
marriage squeeze, 134–36
pool of eligibles, 134
and sexual behavior, 163
Marriage rituals, 238–44
cross-cultural view, 239
wedding, 238–39, 242–44
Marriage squeeze, 134–36, 251
Marxist feminist theory, basic concepts, 52
Marxist theory, basic concepts in, 46
Masai, 5
Mascot role, child of alcoholic, 467
Masculinity. *See also* Male role
and mental health, 80
traits associated with, 64, 79
Mass media:
and gender role socialization, 74–77
and sexual learning, 168–71
and violence, 341–43
Master status, 61
Masturbation, 177–78
gender differences, 177
positive functions of, 178
Matchmakers, 120–21
Maternal employment. *See* Women and work
Mate selection. *See also* Courtship; Dating
in American history, 121–25
cross-cultural view, 119–21
defined, 119
and endogamy, 134
equity theory, 132
and exogamy, 134
factors related to selection, 136–39
filter theories, 133
finding partner (*see* Marriage market)
homogamy, 134
and life cycle, 140
and marriage gradient, 136
and physical attraction, 139–40
and propinquity, 138–39
and racial and ethnic minorities, 136–37
sex ratio imbalances, 121
and sexual behavior, 163
social-exchange theory, 131–32
stimulus-value-role theory, 132
Math achievement, gender differences, 79
Matriarchy, black matriarchy myth, 39–40, 293
Matrilineal descent, defined, 18
Mediation, divorce, 399
Medieval era, courtly love, 91
Men. *See also* Fatherhood; Fathers; Gender differences; Male role
battered men, 360–62
child sexual abuse of, 368
housework participation, 310, 315, 326

male climateric, 188
male preference at birth, 276–77
rape of, 352, 354, 362
rapist profile, 354
sexual dysfunctions, 189
sexual harassment of, 321
and sibling abuse, 372
as terrorists, 484
violent, married versus single, 348
Menarche, 78
Menopause, 187
Men's movement, 54
Men's studies, 54–55
evaluation of, 55
focus of, 55–56
Menstruation:
first, menarche, 78–79
Judaism on, 156
and menopause, 187
Mental health, gender differences, 80
Mental illness. *See also* Depression
and family violence, 344
Metamessages, and gender role socialization, 71
Mexican American family, 21–22
extended family, 21
familism, 21
gender roles, 21–22
parenting style, 295
Mexican Americans, retirement, 439
Mexico, arranged marriage, 120
Middle age, sandwich generation, 429–30
Middle class:
dating patterns, 129–30
parenting style, 290
Midlife crisis, 430
Military, lesbians and gays in, 220
Miscegenation laws, 247
Modeling:
defined, 69
gender role socialization, 69
and grandparents, 443
versus discipline, 291
Model minority myth, Asian Americans, 40, 297, 322
Modified extended family, defined, 4
Mommy track, 317–18
Monogamy:
defined, 3
serial monogamy, 3
sexual studies on, 160–61
Morbidity, defined, 278
Mormons, 3, 222
Mortality, defined, 278
Motherhood, 285–86
adjustments to newborn, 283
African Americans, 285–86
benefits and costs of, 285
motherhood mystique, 285
stepmothers, 417–18
and stress, 287
unmarried mothers, 182, 184
working mothers, 285
Mourning:
defined, 492
national mourning, 492
Moynihan Report, 39
Multiethnic Placement Act of 1994, 472
Multigenerational family. *See* Extended family
Multinational corporations, 457–58
Multiple births, 275–76
and fertility drugs, 276
Multiple genders, 63
Munchausen syndrome, 362–63
Mundugumor, gender roles, 65
Murder. *See* Homicide
Music videos:
sexual content, 170
violence in, 342
Muslim Americans, hate crimes against, 472–73
Muslims, marriage ritual, 239
Muta, 239
Mutual dependence, 100–101
Myths, about marriage and family, 8–13

N

Naming practices:
in marriage, 237
slaves, 17
Narcotics, types of, 465
National Fatherhood Initiative, 287
National mourning, 492
Native American family, 18–19, 294–95
descent patterns, 18
divorce, 377, 378, 380
dwellings of, 18
elderly in, 294–95, 444
European genocide/segregation of, 18–19
parenting styles, 294–95
population in U.S., 249
strengths and resiliency of, 295
structure of, 294
Native Americans. *See also* Racial and ethnic minorities
and dating, 127
exclusion from research studies, 40
fertility rate for, 264–65
and fetal alcohol syndrome (FAS), 279
as high-jealousy culture, 111
infanticide, 339
interracial marriage, 249–50, 294
multiple genders, 63
and poverty, 294, 324
problems related to, 294
and suicide, 493
unemployment, 327
Nature-nurture issue, gender differences, 61–62
Needle sharing, and HIV/AIDS, 191, 194
Negotiation, conflict resolution, 255, 258–59
Neo-Nazis, 476
Nepal:
gender roles, 65
rape victims in, 356
Netherlands:
same-sex marriage, 201
teenage pregnancy, 184
New Deal, 22
Nineteenth century:
American family in, 19–22
divorce, 377–78
economic well-being, 19
family violence, 338
love, concept of, 92
mate selection, 122
sexual behavior, 157–58
singlehood, 202–3
Nocturnal emission, 179
No-fault divorce, 379, 385, 389, 399
Nonmarital lifestyles. *See* Cohabitation; Lesbians and gays; Singlehood
Norms:
age norms, 431
defined, 5
proscriptive and prescriptive, 165
Nuclear family:
colonial era, 14
defined, 3
and maternal employment, 310–11
myths related to, 9, 12–13
structural functionalist view, 44

O

Observational study, 36
Obsessive love, limerence theory, 103–4
Occupational distribution, gender and racial inequality, 319
Oedipus complex, 68–69
Oklahoma City, federal building bombing, 484, 485
Older adults. *See* Aging; Elderly; Later-life family
Oneida Community, 223
Open adoption, 470
Oral sex, 161–62, 179
adolescent view of, 153–54
cultural influences, 179
in marital sex, 185
Oral stage, 68
Organ harvesting, cross-cultural view, 460
Organic solvents, 465
Organization for Economic Cooperation and Development (OECD), 460
Orgasm:
dysfunctions related to, 189
and erotic dreams, 179
gender differences, 176
Orgasmic phase, sexual response, 176
Overlapping families, defined, 413
Ovulation, and conception, 275

P

Pacific Islander American family, 296–98
income, median income, 296, 322
parenting styles, 296–97
strengths and resiliency of, 297–98
Padrinos, 21

Pakistan, honor killings, 2
Palestine Liberation Organization (PLO), 483
Palimony, 217
Parental remarriage, 411
Parenthood. *See also* Fatherhood; Motherhood
adjustments to newborn, 283
child discipline, 291
child-free option, 266–67
costs and benefits of, 265–66
delaying parenting, 267
fatherhood, 286–87
gender differences in experience of, 287–88
motherhood, 285–86
parental roles, social construction of, 284–85
parenting styles, 289–91
pregnancy, 277–81
procreation, social pressures, 266
reproduction, 275–81
single-parent family, 299–300
social constructionist view, 284–85
teenaged parents, 301–3
Parenting styles, 289–91
African American family, 290, 292–93
Asian American family, 296–97
authoritarian style, 290
authoritative style, 290
Latina and Latino family, 295–96
lesbian and gay parents, 298–99
Native American family, 294–95
Pacific Islander American family, 296–97
permissive style, 290
and social class, 289–90
Parents. *See also* Parenthood; Parenting styles
and child drug abuse, 466
death of, 493
and divorce risk of children, 382–83
gendered roles, 288–89
and gender role socialization, 71–72, 83
lesbian and gay parents, 212, 218, 298–99
and mate selection, 129, 139
murder by children, 365
and sexual learning, 165–68
sports rage, 482–83
Parricide, defined, 365
Part-time employment, involuntary, 327
Passion, and love relationships, 89–90, 95, 101
Passive-congenial marriage, 246
Patriarchal family, defined, 4
Patriarchy:
colonial era, 14–15
obstacle to same-sex love, 109–10
Patrilineal descent, defined, 18
Peers:
and gender role socialization, 72–73
and sexual learning, 168
Penis envy, 69
Pentagon attack. *See* Terrorist attacks (September 11)
Permissive parenting, 290
Persian Gulf War, 485, 486
Personal ads:
to find mate, 141–42, 163
gender differences, 142
sexual content, 170
Personal marriage contracts, 240, 242
issues to consider, 256–57
Personal Responsibility and Work Opportunity Reconciliation Act of 1996, 329
Persons with disabilities, 463–64
cross-cultural view, 463–64
and discrimination, 462
and poverty, 463
racial and ethnic minorities, 463–64
women, 463
Petting, 179
Phallic stage, 68
Phallocentric, meaning of, 171
Philos, 89
Physical assault. *See* Battered men; Battered women; Child abuse; Violence
Physical attraction:
and gay mate selection, 131
and mate selection, 139–40
Physician-assisted suicide, 495
Planned Parenthood v. Casey, 271
Plateau phase, sexual response, 176
Plato, on love, 89–90
Platonic love, 90
Play:
and gender role socialization, 73, 79
parent-child and gender, 71
Pleasuring, 179
Police. *See* Criminal justice system
Polyandry, defined, 3
Polygamy:
defined, 3
polygamous groups, 3, 222
Polygyny:
Aboriginal peoples, 239
defined, 3
Pool of eligibles, 134
Pornography:
child pornography, 363
violence in, 342
Postmarital sex, 186
Postnatal depression, 283
Post-traumatic stress disorder (PTSD), abused children, 364
Poverty, 323–27
and African Americans, 292, 293, 324
feminization of, 324
homelessness, 22, 327–29
income gap, 323
of later-life family, 433
perpetuation of, 324
and persons with disabilities, 463
and racial and ethnic minorities, 292, 294, 324
rates in U.S., 324
and single-parent family, 299, 300, 324
underclass, 475
of widows, 450–51
working poor, 324
Power:
and heterosexuality, 171
and male rapist, 353
in Marxist theory, 46
and research studies, 41
and sexual behavior, 156
violence against women, 338
and woman battering, 349
and working women, 313
Pragma, pragmatic lover, 96
Pregnancy, 277–81
battered women, 348
conception, 275–77
expectant fathers during, 281–83
fetal rights issue, 280
multiple births, 275–76
postnatal depression, 283
prenatal development, 277
prenatal testing, 277
sex selection, 276–77
teenage pregnancy, 182–84
unmarried pregnancy, 182
workplace leave for, 332–33
Pregnancy complications:
AIDS transmission, 279, 281
and cigarette smoking, 278–79
fetal alcohol syndrome (FAS), 279
and maternal age, 278
and maternal malnutrition, 278
racial and ethnic minorities, 278
and substance abuse, 279
Pregnancy Discrimination Act of 1978, 332–33
Premarital sex. *See* Single sexuality
Prenatal tests, types of, 277
Prenuptial agreements, 240–41
Prescriptive norms, 165
Principle of legitimacy, and marriage, 230
Process theories, mate selection, 133
Pronatalist attitude:
meaning of, 266
versus antinatalist forces, 267
Property rights, and marriage, 236–37
Propinquity:
defined, 138–39
and mate selection, 138–39
Proposition 209, 473
Proscriptive norms, 165
Prostitution:
ancient Greece, 90
and Chinese men, 121
and Japanese men, 112
Protection, as family function, 6
Protestant Reformation, on sexual behavior, 157
Protestants:
divorce rate, 382
interfaith marriage, 252
and remarriage, 410
Psychic divorce, 385
Psychic remarriage, 411
Psychoanalytic theory:
feminist challenges to, 69
gender role socialization, 68–69
on sex drive, 165
Puberty, and female self-esteem, 78–79

Pubic lice, 189
Puerto Rican family, parenting style, 295
Puritans, and sexual behavior, 157
Pushes and pulls:
  and cohabitation, 215–16
  meaning of, 204
  and singlehood, 204–5

Q

Qualitative research, 37
Quantitative research, 37
Questionnaires, survey research, 35
Quickening, 270
Quinceañera, 130

R

Race, in context of family, 4
Racial and ethnic minorities. *See also* specific ethnic and racial groups
  abused drugs, types of, 465
  adolescent sexuality, 181
  caregivers for elderly, 446, 447
  cohabitation, 213
  drug abuse, 465
  economic status, 322
  and elder abuse, 369–70
  ethnic communities, 139
  exclusion from research studies, 39–41
  fertility pattern in U.S., 264–65
  and friendships, 98
  hate crimes against, 472–73, 475
  and HIV/AIDS, 192–93
  homelessness, 328
  income inequality, 320–21, 475
  interethnic marriage, 251–52
  interracial adoptions, 471–72
  interracial dating, 137
  interracial marriage, 247–51
  later-life family, 433–34
  and mate selection, 136–37
  persons with disabilities, 463–64
  and poverty, 292, 294, 324
  pregnancy complications, 278
  racism and discrimination, 472–75
  singlehood, 203–4
  survival strategies, 359–60
  teenaged parents, 302
  teenage pregnancy, 182
  unmarried pregnancy, 182
Racial profiling, 474
Racism, defined, 473
Racism and discrimination, 472–75
  as global problem, 476–77
  hate groups, 472
  and immigrants to U.S., 472–73
  individual racism, 473–74
  institutional racism, 11–12, 474–75
  symbolic racism, 475
  xenophobia, 473
Radical feminist theory, basic concepts, 52
Rape, 352–60
  African American women, 353–54
  criminal justice response to, 355, 357–58
  cross-cultural view, 356
  date and acquaintance rape, 148–49
  defined, 148
  emotional consequences of, 358
  male rape, 352, 354, 362
  marital rape, 237, 354–55
  mass rape in wartime, 486
  myths related to, 354
  prevalence of, 352–53
  rapist profile, 354
  victim profile, 353–54
Rape syndrome, 343
Rapport, in love relationships, 100
Reality, social construction of, 48
Recreation:
  dating as, 126
  and parenthood, 266
Refractory period, sexual response, 176
Refugees, 489–90
Reliability, research study, 35
Religion:
  and dating services, 144
  and divorce rate, 231, 381–82
  interfaith marriage, 252–53
  marriage as sacrament, 231
  and mate selection, 138
  and remarriage, 410
  and sexual behavior, 156–57, 161, 375–76
Remarriage. *See also* Stepfamily
  and children, 412–15
  cultural patterns, 409–10
  dating, 407–8
  decision making about, 408–9
  and ex-spouse, 419
  historical view, 406
  quality relationship, factors in, 420–24
  social policy issues, 424–25
  stations of, 410–12
Remarried family, defined, 405
Reproduction. *See also* Pregnancy
  as marital function, 5
Reproductive technologies, 272–74
  artificial insemination, 272–73
  embryo transplant, 273
  multiple births from, 275–76
  surrogacy, 274
  in vitro fertilization (IVF), 273
Research methods:
  case study, 36–37
  cross-cultural research, 42–43
  ethnography, 37–38
  in feminist research, 38
  longitudinal studies, 423
  observational study, 36
  qualitative and quantitative methods, 37
  scientific method, 33–34
  sex/race/class/gender exclusions from, 39–41
  shortcomings of, 39–41
  surveys, 35–36
  validity and reliability of, 35
Reservations, 19
Residence, marriage, legal aspects, 236
Resolution phase, sexual response, 176
Retirement, 437–39
  patterns of, 438
  and quality of life, 438–39
Right-to-die movement, 494–95
Rites of passage, 130
Roe v. Wade, 158, 270
Rohypnol, date rape drug, 149
Role conflict, 318
Role models. *See* Modeling
Role overload, working women, 314–15, 386
Roles. *See also* Gender roles
  defined, 5
  role expectations, elements of, 61
Romantic love, 88. *See also* Love
Rome, ancient:
  family violence, 338
  love in, 90
Rubella, 270

S

Sacrament, marriage as, 231
Safe sex:
  AIDS prevention campaigns, 196 97
  decline and gay men, 193–94
Same-sex marriage, 232–34
  benefits and health care, companies offering, 233
  cross-cultural view, 200–201, 233
  domestic partnerships, 217, 233
  legalization in Vermont, 217, 233
  legal restrictions, 217, 232–34
  proponent views, 233–34
  rationale for, 232
Sandwich generation, 429–30
Scapegoat, child of alcoholic, 467
Schools:
  bullying, 482
  mate selection, 123, 141
  new family structures, recognition of, 424–25
  violence in, 481–82
Science achievement, gender differences, 79
Scientific method, 33–34
Scientific research, defined, 33
Scripts:
  dating scripts, 128
  sexual scripts, 165
Self-assessment, gender differences, 79
Self-confidence, gender differences, 79
Self-disclosure:
  defined, 256
  in marriage, 256–58
Self-esteem:
  children and divorce, 394
  and dating, 126
  defined, 77
  divorced women, 392
  gender differences, 77–79

and self-love, 94
and unemployment, 325
Self-fulfillment, and love relationships, 101
Self-revelation, in love relationships, 100
Separation:
dating break-up, 149–50
marital, 400–401
September 11. *See* Terrorist attacks (September 11)
Serial monogamy, defined, 3
Sex, defined, 61
Sex differentiation, process of, 61
Sex drive, 165
Sexism, defined, 52
Sex ratio, defined, 127
Sex ratio imbalance:
and African Americans, 127–28, 136
cross-cultural view, 121, 262
marriage squeeze, 134–36
Sex ratios, in older population, 431–32
Sex reassignment, 62–63
Sex therapy, 190
Sex typing:
feminine traits, 64
masculine traits, 64
and self-esteem, 79
Sexual abstinence:
Christianity on celibacy, 157
fundamentalist teachings, 164–65
sex-free adults, 165
virginity, 157, 164
Sexual assault. *See* Child sexual abuse; Rape
Sexual behavior:
age of initiation, 164
and aging, 186–88
in American history, 14, 157–65
defined, 156
of divorced individuals, 389, 392
extramarital sex, 185–86
learning about (*see* Sexual learning)
marital sexuality, 185
postmarital sex, 186
power and authority issues, 156
regulation and marriage/family, 5, 162
and religion, 157–58, 161
sexual acts (*see* Sexual expression)
sexual research, 158, 159
single sexuality, 181–85
and stepsiblings, 416
studies on (*see* Sexual studies)
Sexual double standard:
and aging, 188
defined, 158
examples of, 167–68
Sexual dysfunctions:
common types of, 189
defined, 188
sex therapy, 190
Sexual experts, and media, 170
Sexual expression:
autoeroticism, 176–79
coitus, 179–80
lesbians and gays, 180
oral sex, 179
petting, 179
pleasuring, 179
Sexual fantasy, 178
Sexual habits. *See* Sexual expression
Sexual harassment, 321–22
legal remedies, difficulty of, 322
prevalence of, 321
and rape syndrome, 343
Sexual learning:
and family, 165–68
and mass media, 168–71
and peers, 168
Sexually transmitted disease (STDs):
and age, 189
HIV/AIDS, 189–98
incidence of, 189
premarital blood testing, 235
Sexual orientation:
bisexuality, 175
changing over life cycle, 171
defined, 171
heterosexuality, 171
homosexuality, 171–75
Kinsey rating scale, 174
Sexual response cycle, stages of, 175–76
Sexual revolution, 158–59
Sexual scripts:
defined, 165
gender differences, 167–68
Sexual studies:
on age of sexual initiation, 162, 164
on frequency of sexual activity, 161
and heterosexism, 171
on kinky sex, 161–63
on mate selection, 163
on number of sex partners, 160–61
pioneers, 158, 159
on sex and gender, 163–65
on sexual homogamy, 163
sexual surveys, 159
Sex workers, children as, 307
Shakers, 222
Shield laws, rape victim, 358
Shotgun weddings, 302
Sibling abuse, 370–72
historical view, 340
prevalence of, 371–72
sexual assault, 372
Siblings:
death of, 492–93
elderly siblings, 445–46
stepsibling relationships, 415–17
Significant others, defined, 165
Single, use of term, 201
Singlehood:
economic factors, 205, 206
of elderly, 210–11, 445
and family, 204
historical view, 201–4
and income, 208–9
and life satisfaction, 209–10
lifestyle patterns, 207–8
living arrangements, 208
living with parents, 206, 208
in mass media, 205
pros and cons of, 206–7
pushes and pulls in, 204–5
racial and ethnic minorities, 203–4
sexual behavior, 181–85
and social networks, 209
types of singles, 205–6
unmarried pregnancy, 182, 184
Single-parent family, 299–300
adoptive parents, 470
African Americans, 11, 17, 292, 299
children, future outcome, 300, 301
colonial era, 15
composition of, 4
cross-cultural view, 301
divorced mother versus single mother, 299–300
and economic well-being, 299, 300, 322, 324
gender-role flexibility, 301, 395
homosexual parents, 212
Latina and Latino family, 295, 299
parental profile, 299
single-father family, 288, 300–301
women as rape victims, 354
Singles bars:
gay and lesbian bars, 130, 141
meeting potential mate, 127, 141
Single sexuality, 181–85
adolescent sexuality, 181–82
frequency of sex, 181
unmarried pregnancy, 182, 184
Slavery, 15–17
children, 16
extended kinship, 16–17
modern, 306–7
naming patterns, 17
and oral-genital sex, 179
racial mixing, 17–18
and sexual oppression, 158
slave marriages, 15–16
Social class:
and abortion, 270–71
of adoptive parents, 469–70
and child abuse, 365, 366
in context of family, 4
dating patterns, 128–30
exclusion from research studies, 39–41
and family violence, 344–45
and friendship, 98
historical perspective, 19–20
and marriage gradient, 136
in Marxist theory, 46
and mate selection, 137–38
and parenting styles, 289–90
and remarriage, 409–10
and sexual behavior, 158
similarities within class, 137–38
and teenage pregnancy, 184

Social constructionism, 48–49
basic concepts in, 48
evaluation of, 49
Social constructionist view:
family, 48–49
love, 88–89, 114
motherhood, 285
parenting, 284–85
Social construction of reality, defined, 48
Social-exchange theory, 49–50
basic concepts in, 49–50
evaluation of, 50
family, view of, 50
of love, 103
mate selection, 131–32
Social gerontology, study of, 430
Socialist feminist theory, basic concepts, 52
Socialization:
anticipatory socialization, 126
and dating, 125–26
as family function, 6
and gender (*see* Gender role socialization)
Social-learning theory:
of alcohol abuse, 468
of alcohol use and violence, 349
dating scripts, 128
evaluation of, 69–70
gender role socialization, 69–70
sex drive, 165
Social marriage, cohabitation as, 231
Social networks, and singlehood, 209
Social policy issues:
elderly, 452–53
stepfamilies, 424–25
Social Security Act of 1935, 329
Social status, as family function, 5–6
Social structure, defined, 5
Social support:
and remarriage, 422
and singles, 209
Sociobiological view, gender roles, 62
Sociological imagination, 25–26
Sociological perspective:
Mill's sociological imagination, 25–26
research methods, 33–41
theories (*see* Theoretical perspectives)
Sole custody, 395–96
Sonogram, 277
South Africa:
and HIV/AIDS, 195, 196
interracial dating, 144
as rape capital, 356
violence against women, 338
Southeast Asia, and HIV/AIDS, 195
Spanking, negative effects, 291
Sperm, and conception, 275
Spillover effect, meaning of, 308
Spirit wedding, 239
Split custody, 379
Sports participation:
benefits for girls, 73
parental sports rage, 482–83
State laws, and marriage contract, 232, 233, 235
Stations of divorce, 384–85
Stations of remarriage, 410–12
Status:
ascribed and achieved statuses, 61
and dating, 126
defined, 5
and marriage gradient, 136
master status, 61
and parenthood, 266
Stepfamily. *See also* Remarriage
benefits and strengths of, 419–20
categories of, 412
composition of, 4
lesbian and gay stepfamilies, 419
mutual child in, 416–17
compared to nuclear family, 405–6
stepfathers, 418–19
stepmothers, 417–18
stepsibling relationships, 415–17
stereotype of, 407
Stereotyping:
gender role (*see* Gender role stereotypes)
of lesbians and gays, 219
of stepfamilies, 407
Stimulant drugs, types of, 465
Stimulus-value-role theory, mate selection, 132
Storage love, 95, 96
Street children, 466
Street violence, 478–79
Stress:
of caregivers for elderly, 448, 449
of mothers, 287, 318
of teenaged parents, 302
trigger for family violence, 349
Structural functionalism, 43–46
basic concepts of, 43–44
evaluation of theory, 44, 46
Structural functionalist view:
family, 43–44
nuclear family, 44
working women, 313
Substance abuse. *See* Alcohol abuse; Drug abuse
Suicide, 493–94
at-risk groups, 493
cross-cultural view, 493–94
physician-assisted suicide, 495
of rape/incest survivors, 358, 359, 369
suicide bombings, 484, 494
of victims of violence, 343
and widowers, 451
Support networks. *See* Social support
Surrogacy, 274
Surrogate family, composition of, 4
Survey research, 35–36
Surveys, sexual surveys, 159
Suttee, 494
Sweden:
child protection, 339
parental leave and fathers, 318, 332
Symbolic-interactionism, 47–48
basic concepts in, 47–48
and social constructionism, 48
Symbolic-interactionist view, family, 48
Symbolic racism, 475
Symbols, defined, 48
Synchronized retirement, 438
Syphilis, 189

T

Taboos, incest taboo, 5, 234–35
Talk shows, sexual content, 169
Taxation, and stepfamilies, 424
Tchambuli, gender roles, 65
Teachers, and gender role socialization, 73–74
Teenaged parents, 301–3
as child abusers, 366
children of, 302–3
fathers, 303
racial and ethnic minorities, 302
stress of motherhood, 302
Teenage pregnancy, 182–84
cross-cultural view, 184
decline in rate, 301
fathering by adult men, 184
and social class, 184
Television:
content analysis of shows, 74–75
gender-role stereotyping, 74–77
and sexual learning, 168–71
sexual topics ignored by, 169
shows about singles, 205
violence on, 341–42
Temporary Assistance for Needy Families, 329
Terrorism and war, 483–91
bioterrorism, 485–86, 487
chemical warfare, 486
and children, 486–89
defined, 483
ethnic cleansing, 476–77
land mines, 486, 487
mass rape, 486
by militant groups, 484
and refugees, 489–90
state-sponsored, 483–84
suicide bombings, 484, 494
in U.S., incidents of, 484–85
U.S. war on terrorism, 485–86
Terrorist attacks (September 11):
and Afghanistan, 485–87, 489
casualties, 484, 485
children's trauma, 487–88
as international event, 456–57
national mourning, 492
perpetrators of, 484
survivors of victims, 455–56
and unemployment, 310, 320
and violence against Muslim Americans, 472–73
Thailand:
people with disabilities, 464
single women status, 207
Theoretical perspectives:
conflict theory, 46–47

developmental family life cycle model, 50–51
feminist theory, 51–54
men's studies, 54–55
social constructionism, 48–49
social-exchange theory, 49–50
structural functionalism, 43–46
symbolic-interactionism, 47–48
Theory, defined, 33
Theory model, defined, 42
Total fertility rate, defined, 263
Total marriage, 246
Toys, and gender stereotyping, 71–72
Traits:
instrumental and expressive, 44
masculine and feminine, 64, 79
Transexuals, 63, 174
Transgendered, 174
Transmission of victimization, 368
Transvestites, 174
Triangular theory of love, 100–101
Truly Disadvantaged, The (Wilson), 37
Trust:
defined, 110
and love relationships, 110
and self-disclosure, 256–58
Turkey, arranged marriage, 121
Tutsi, 476
Twentieth century:
American family in, 22–24
divorce, 379
love, concept of, 92
mate selection, 122–24
sexual behavior, 158–65
singlehood, 203
and youth culture, 430
Twenty-first century:
family in, 24–25
love, concept of, 92
mate selection, 124–25
sexual behavior, 164–65
singlehood, 203–4
Twin births, 275
Two-person career, 311

U

Ultrasound, 277
Underclass, 475
Underemployment, 327
Unemployment, 324–27
and adolescents, 326–27
of adult children, 429
conditions related to, 324
consequences for family, 325
cross-cultural view, 325
family responses to, 326
marital effects, 325–26
post-terrorist attacks, 310, 320
and self-esteem, 325
Unification Church, mass weddings, 243
Uniform Pre-Marital Agreement Act, 241
United Nations Declaration of Human Rights, 477
United Nations Millennium Declaration, 496–97
Unmarried pregnancy, 182, 184, 299. *See also* Single-parent family; Teenage pregnancy; Teenaged parents
Upper class, dating patterns, 129
Utilitarian marriage, 246

V

Validity, research study, 35
Variables, 33
Vermont, domestic partnership law, 217, 233
Viagra, 167
Victim blaming:
of battered women, 350
of rape victim, 354
Victims of Trafficking and Violence Protection Act, 306
Victorian era, sexual behavior in, 157–58
Video games, violent games, 343, 482
Violence. *See also* Family violence; Terrorism and war
against lesbians and gays, 220
and alcohol abuse, 349
and cohabitation, 215
dating violence, 146–49
gang violence, 477–78
and guns, 479–81
and mass media, 341–43
men, married versus single, 348
prevention legislation, 482
racism-based crimes, 472–76
rape, 352–60
school violence, 481–82
sports rage and parents, 482–83
street violence, 478–79
terrorism, 483–89
youth violence, 479–81
Violence Against Women Act, 358
Violent Crime Control and Law Enforcement Act of 1994, 358
Virginity:
and Christianity, 157, 161
contemporary acceptance of, 164
and religious orientation, 161
Visitation rights, 392, 398, 424, 443
Vital marriage, 246
Vows, marital, 243–44

W

Wage gap, 320–21
Warfare. *See* Terrorism and war
War on Poverty, 434
Water supply, as global problem, 460
Wealth:
income gap, 323
support for adult children, 440
Webster v. Reproductive Health Services, 270–71
Weddings, 242–44
of remarriage, 412
as ritual, 238–39
types of, 243
Welfare reform, 329–30
negative findings, 330
proponent/opponent views, 329
Wet dreams, 179
Wheel theory of love, 100
White Americans:
fertility rate for, 264–65
interethnic marriage, 252
White supremacy groups, 472, 473, 476
Widows and widowers, 448–51
gender differences and experience, 450–51
grief reaction, 493
immolation of widows, 490–91, 494
Native Americans, 18
positive role changes, 451
sexuality of, 186
stages of widowhood, 448–50
Wife beating. *See* Battered women
Wigwam, 18
Witch burnings, 338, 339
Woman battering. *See* Battered women
Womb envy, 69
Women. *See also* African American women; Female role; Gender differences; Gender equality; Gender inequality; Lesbians and gays; Motherhood; Pregnancy; Work and women
caregivers for elderly, 446–48
cult of domesticity, 19
divorce and economic decline, 229–30
feminization of poverty, 324
and HIV/AIDS, 192–94
household work, 310–11
menopause, 187
pressure to marry, 229
sexual double standard, 158, 167
sexual dysfunctions, 189
support network of singles, 209
as terrorists, 484
violence and abuse of (*see* Battered women; Family violence; Rape)
women with disabilities, 463
Women-of-color feminist theory, basic concepts, 52
Work, labor force participation, 308–10
Work and women:
best companies, 333
child care, 316–18
commuter marriages, 312
and division of labor, 314–16
divorce and economic independence, 382, 386
dual-earner families, 311–12, 315
and educational level, 309, 312
equality measures (*see* Workplace equality)
and family (*see* Work-family structures)
historical view, 20–23, 309
increase in, reasons for, 309–10
inequality and discrimination (*see* Income inequality; Workplace inequality)
and marital power/decision making, 313
and marital satisfaction, 313–14

mommy track, 317–18
racial and ethnic minorities, 21–22, 309
role conflict, 318
role overload, 314–15, 386
sexual harassment, 321–22
structural-functionalist view, 313
work force participation rates, 308–9
World War II era, 23
Work-family structures:
commuter marriages, 312
dual-earner families, 311–12, 315
of traditional family, 310–11
two-person career, 311
Working-class family:
gender equality, 20
parenting style, 289–90
Working poor, 324
Workplace equality, 330–33
child care support, 331
family leave, 331–33
flextime, 331
job sharing, 331
Workplace inequality, 318–22
income inequality, 320–21
occupational distribution, 319
World economy. *See* Globalization
World problems. *See* Global problems
World Trade Center attack. *See* Terrorist attacks (September 11)
World War II era, families of, 22–23

X

Xenophobia, defined, 473

Y

Yellow fever, 461
Yuppies (young urban professionals), meeting places for, 146

Z

Zygote, 275
Zygote intrafallopian transfer (ZIFT), 273